HANDBOOK

OF

STATISTICAL TABLES

This book is in the

ADDISON-WESLEY SERIES IN STATISTICS

Z. W. BIRNBAUM
Consulting Editor

HANDBOOK
OF
STATISTICAL TABLES

---

by

D. B. OWEN

Sandia Corporation

ADDISON-WESLEY PUBLISHING COMPANY, INC.

READING, MASSACHUSETTS

PALO ALTO · LONDON

PREFACE

This book of tables is intended for three audiences: the student in statistics who needs some readily accessible tables to be used in conjunction with his courses in statistics; the practicing statistician, quality control man, or industrial engineer who wants a set of tables from which he can obtain answers with a minimum of interpolation and other calculation; and the research worker who will find in this collection many functions more extensively tabulated than ever before.

In writing the description of the tables, the temptation was strong to write too much. It was decided that the best procedure was to keep the examples to a minimum and, wherever possible, to try to pick unusual examples, unusual in the sense that the particular applications are not widely shown in textbooks of today. However, some examples were included merely to define certain parameters in terms of the quantities tabulated, and not to expound on the examples *per se*. Unless stated otherwise, when a sample is considered, it is to be assumed that the sample has been taken at random from the population, and that the observations are statistically independent of each other.

Concerning the selection of tables for this book, the choice has been dictated largely by two considerations: (a) amount of space taken by the table *vs.* its usefulness, and (b) a desire to make this compilation all-inclusive enough so that it can be used as a supplementary handbook for most courses in statistics, and so that at the same time it would contain as many as possible of the unusual tables of merit which are not given in other compilations now on the market. For example, short tables of the binomial and Poisson distributions have been included. The reader should not infer, however, that the Wilcoxon (Mann-Whitney) two-sample distribution (Sections 11.2 through 11.5), which covers many pages here, is more important than the Poisson distribution, which is represented by very few pages (Sections 9.3 and 9.4). The Poisson distribution has tables which are widely distributed, while the Wilcoxon (Mann-Whitney) distribution tables are not nearly as well distributed as they should be, considering their usefulness.

The references have been chosen either on the basis of special usefulness or, more often, on the basis that they appeared in the more recent literature, and referred back to the older literature. Hence, the research worker could, if he so desired, start with these current references and work back through the bibliographies to the older papers. In other words, a current paper was often chosen over an older paper, even though the older paper

v

may have been more pertinent to the example under discussion. The descriptions of the tables generally follow the tone and style set in the work from which the table was taken.

The tables have been reproduced directly from the output of digital computers wherever possible. This, of course, did not allow the flexibility in set-up of the tables that is possible with typescript, but it undoubtedly eliminated many transcription errors. The tables were checked against as many different sources as possible, and discrepancies were resolved wherever possible. In some cases, this was an agonizing process when tables which we thought were accurate were found to contain errors, and each error had to be resolved. Some tables were taken from journals and other sources. These are indicated by a number in square brackets following the table on the first page of each table. The number corresponds to an entry in the bibliography. We wish to express our appreciation to the authors, editors, and publishers who gave their permission to copy tables.

Many individuals helped with suggestions on this set of tables. If we tried to account for all of them, we would surely inadvertently leave someone out. Nevertheless, we will mention a few individuals whose suggestions have been most helpful: Dr. P. Olmstead, Professor Harold Ruben, Dr. L. H. Koopmans, Professor J. Rosenblatt, Professor W. Kruskal, Professor Z. W. Birnbaum, Dr. G. P. Steck, Dr. J. R. Blum, Dr. Marvin Zelen, and Dr. Churchill Eisenhart. Most of these people saw only a table of contents or a particular section of the book, and made their suggestions based on these. Any omissions or errors are clearly the author's responsibility. In addition, we wish to mention Mrs. Marjorie E. Endres who, over a two-year period, carried out many of the computations and checks, and supervised the work of a group of data reduction workers who prepared the tables. She has remained helpful and cheerful throughout the long periods of checking and rechecking that were applied to these tables.

The author, however, acknowledges the responsibility for the accuracy and extent of the tables. The author made the decisions, always, about what should be done and how it should be done.

Albuquerque, New Mexico   D. B. O.

January, 1962

CONTENTS

CONTENTS

CONTENTS

SECTION 10. NONPARAMETRIC TOLERANCE LIMITS

SECTION 11. WILCOXON (MANN-WHITNEY) TESTS

SECTION 12. SIGN, RUNS, AND QUADRANT TESTS

CONTENTS

1. NORMAL DISTRIBUTION

1.1 The Normal Distribution and Related Functions

The various quantities given in this table are defined as follows:

$P(X)$ = the cumulative distribution function of a standardized normal random variable (a standardized normal random variable will be abbreviated as a random variable with an $N(0, 1)$ distribution)

= Pr {a normal random variable with mean zero and standard deviation one is less than or equal to X}

$$= \frac{1}{\sqrt{2\pi}} \int_{-\infty}^{X} \exp\left(-t^2/2\right) dt.$$

$Z(X)$ = the probability density of a standardized normal random variable

= the derivative of $P(X)$ with respect to X

$$= \frac{1}{\sqrt{2\pi}} \exp\left(-X^2/2\right).$$

$Q(X) = 1 - P(X).$

Q/Z = Mill's ratio.

$Z^{(1)}(X)$ = the first derivative of $Z(X)$ with respect to X

$$= \frac{-X}{\sqrt{2\pi}} \exp\left(-X^2/2\right).$$

$Z^{(2)}(X)$ = the second derivative of $Z(X)$ with respect to X

$$= \frac{(X^2 - 1)}{\sqrt{2\pi}} \exp\left(-X^2/2\right).$$

$Z^{(3)}(X)$ = the third derivative of $Z(X)$ with respect to X

$$= \frac{-X}{\sqrt{2\pi}} (X^2 - 3) \exp\left(-X^2/2\right).$$

Mill's ratio, Q/Z, and P/Z have applications in many places. Among them is the solution of the maximum likelihood equations for estimating

1

the biserial correlation coefficient [218].* Among the uses of $Z(X), Z^{(1)}(X),$ $Z^{(2)}(X),$ and $Z^{(3)}(X)$ is the expansion of an arbitrary continuous probability density function $f(X)$ into a series of the form

$$f(X) = \sum_{j=0}^{\infty} c_j Z^{(j)}(X),$$

where

$$c_0 = 1, \quad c_1 = 0, \quad c_2 = \tfrac{1}{2}(\sigma^2 - 1), \quad c_3 = \frac{-1}{6}\,\mu_3, \quad \text{etc.},$$

where σ^2 is the variance of X, and μ_3 is the third moment about the mean of X. This is a Gram-Charlier Series of Type A. See Reference [104], pp. 147–154, for some of the conditions under which an expansion of this type may be made. Haight [83] gives an index of probability distribution functions.

The value of $P(X)$ was computed on an IBM 704 using a Taylor's Series expansion about the nearest $X = 0(0.25)3.5$. The other functions are straightforward computations, given $P(X)$, and were done simultaneously with $P(X)$ on a digital computer. The results were checked against the tables given by Sheppard [172], pp. 104–110.

---

*Numbers in brackets refer to the Bibliography.

The Normal Distribution and Related Functions

$P(X) = \Pr\{N(0, 1)\text{r.v.} \leq X\}; Q = 1 - P; Z(X) = $ density of $N(0, 1)$r.v.; $Z^{(i)} = $ ith derivative of Z

X	P(X)	Z(X)	Q/Z	P/Z	$Z^{(1)}(X)$	$Z^{(2)}(X)$	$Z^{(3)}(X)$
0.00	0.500000	0.398942	1.25331	1.2533	-0.00000	-0.39894	0.00000
0.01	0.503989	0.398922	1.24338	1.2634	-0.00399	-0.39888	0.01197
0.02	0.507978	0.398862	1.23356	1.2736	-0.00798	-0.39870	0.02393
0.03	0.511966	0.398763	1.22387	1.2839	-0.01196	-0.39840	0.03588
0.04	0.515953	0.398623	1.21430	1.2943	-0.01594	-0.39799	0.04781
0.05	0.519939	0.398444	1.20484	1.3049	-0.01992	-0.39745	0.05972
0.06	0.523922	0.398225	1.19550	1.3156	-0.02389	-0.39679	0.07159
0.07	0.527903	0.397966	1.18627	1.3265	-0.02786	-0.39602	0.08344
0.08	0.531881	0.397668	1.17716	1.3375	-0.03181	-0.39512	0.09524
0.09	0.535856	0.397330	1.16816	1.3486	-0.03576	-0.39411	0.10699
0.10	0.539828	0.396953	1.15926	1.3599	-0.03970	-0.39298	0.11869
0.11	0.543795	0.396536	1.15047	1.3714	-0.04362	-0.39174	0.13033
0.12	0.547758	0.396080	1.14179	1.3830	-0.04753	-0.39038	0.14190
0.13	0.551717	0.395585	1.13321	1.3947	-0.05143	-0.38890	0.15341
0.14	0.555670	0.395052	1.12474	1.4066	-0.05531	-0.38731	0.16484
0.15	0.559618	0.394479	1.11636	1.4186	-0.05917	-0.38560	0.17618
0.16	0.563559	0.393868	1.10809	1.4308	-0.06302	-0.38379	0.18744
0.17	0.567495	0.393219	1.09991	1.4432	-0.06685	-0.38185	0.19861
0.18	0.571424	0.392531	1.09183	1.4557	-0.07066	-0.37981	0.20968
0.19	0.575345	0.391806	1.08384	1.4684	-0.07444	-0.37766	0.22064
0.20	0.579260	0.391043	1.07594	1.4813	-0.07821	-0.37540	0.23150
0.21	0.583166	0.390242	1.06814	1.4944	-0.08195	-0.37303	0.24224
0.22	0.587064	0.389404	1.06043	1.5076	-0.08567	-0.37056	0.25286
0.23	0.590954	0.388529	1.05281	1.5210	-0.08936	-0.36798	0.26336
0.24	0.594835	0.387617	1.04527	1.5346	-0.09303	-0.36529	0.27373
0.25	0.598706	0.386668	1.03782	1.5484	-0.09667	-0.36250	0.28396
0.26	0.602568	0.385683	1.03046	1.5623	-0.10028	-0.35961	0.29405
0.27	0.606420	0.384663	1.02318	1.5765	-0.10386	-0.35662	0.30401
0.28	0.610261	0.383606	1.01599	1.5909	-0.10741	-0.35353	0.31381
0.29	0.614092	0.382515	1.00887	1.6054	-0.11093	-0.35035	0.32346
0.30	0.617911	0.381388	1.00184	1.6202	-0.11442	-0.34706	0.33295
0.31	0.621720	0.380226	0.99488	1.6351	-0.11787	-0.34369	0.34228
0.32	0.625516	0.379031	0.98801	1.6503	-0.12129	-0.34022	0.35145
0.33	0.629300	0.377801	0.98121	1.6657	-0.12467	-0.33666	0.36045
0.34	0.633072	0.376537	0.97448	1.6813	-0.12802	-0.33301	0.36927
0.35	0.636831	0.375240	0.96783	1.6971	-0.13133	-0.32927	0.37791
0.36	0.640576	0.373911	0.96126	1.7132	-0.13461	-0.32545	0.38638
0.37	0.644309	0.372548	0.95475	1.7295	-0.13784	-0.32155	0.39466
0.38	0.648027	0.371154	0.94832	1.7460	-0.14104	-0.31756	0.40275
0.39	0.651732	0.369728	0.94196	1.7627	-0.14419	-0.31349	0.41065
0.40	0.655422	0.368270	0.93567	1.7797	-0.14731	-0.30935	0.41835
0.41	0.659097	0.366782	0.92944	1.7970	-0.15038	-0.30513	0.42586
0.42	0.662757	0.365263	0.92329	1.8145	-0.15341	-0.30083	0.43317
0.43	0.666402	0.363714	0.91720	1.8322	-0.15640	-0.29646	0.44027
0.44	0.670031	0.362135	0.91118	1.8502	-0.15934	-0.29203	0.44717
0.45	0.673645	0.360527	0.90522	1.8685	-0.16224	-0.28752	0.45386
0.46	0.677242	0.358890	0.89932	1.8870	-0.16509	-0.28295	0.46034
0.47	0.680822	0.357225	0.89349	1.9059	-0.16790	-0.27831	0.46660
0.48	0.684386	0.355533	0.88772	1.9250	-0.17066	-0.27362	0.47265
0.49	0.687933	0.353812	0.88201	1.9443	-0.17337	-0.26886	0.47848

The Normal Distribution and Related Functions (cont.)

X	P(X)	Z(X)	Q/Z	P/Z	$Z^{(1)}(X)$	$Z^{(2)}(X)$	$Z^{(3)}(X)$
0.50	0.691462	0.352065	0.87636	1.9640	-0.17603	-0.26405	0.48409
0.51	0.694974	0.350292	0.87078	1.9840	-0.17865	-0.25918	0.48948
0.52	0.698468	0.348493	0.86525	2.0043	-0.18122	-0.25426	0.49465
0.53	0.701944	0.346668	0.85977	2.0248	-0.18373	-0.24929	0.49959
0.54	0.705401	0.344818	0.85436	2.0457	-0.18620	-0.24427	0.50431
0.55	0.708840	0.342944	0.84900	2.0669	-0.18862	-0.23920	0.50880
0.56	0.712260	0.341046	0.84370	2.0885	-0.19099	-0.23409	0.51306
0.57	0.715661	0.339124	0.83845	2.1103	-0.19330	-0.22894	0.51710
0.58	0.719043	0.337180	0.83326	2.1325	-0.19556	-0.22375	0.52091
0.59	0.722405	0.335213	0.82812	2.1551	-0.19778	-0.21853	0.52448
0.60	0.725747	0.333225	0.82303	2.1780	-0.19993	-0.21326	0.52783
0.61	0.729069	0.331215	0.81799	2.2012	-0.20204	-0.20797	0.53094
0.62	0.732371	0.329184	0.81301	2.2248	-0.20409	-0.20265	0.53383
0.63	0.735653	0.327133	0.80807	2.2488	-0.20609	-0.19729	0.53648
0.64	0.738914	0.325062	0.80319	2.2731	-0.20804	-0.19192	0.53891
0.65	0.742154	0.322972	0.79835	2.2979	-0.20993	-0.18652	0.54110
0.66	0.745373	0.320864	0.79357	2.3230	-0.21177	-0.18110	0.54306
0.67	0.748571	0.318737	0.78883	2.3486	-0.21355	-0.17566	0.54480
0.68	0.751748	0.316593	0.78414	2.3745	-0.21528	-0.17020	0.54630
0.69	0.754903	0.314432	0.77949	2.4009	-0.21696	-0.16473	0.54758
0.70	0.758036	0.312254	0.77489	2.4276	-0.21858	-0.15925	0.54863
0.71	0.761148	0.310060	0.77034	2.4548	-0.22014	-0.15376	0.54945
0.72	0.764238	0.307851	0.76583	2.4825	-0.22165	-0.14826	0.55005
0.73	0.767305	0.305627	0.76137	2.5106	-0.22311	-0.14276	0.55043
0.74	0.770350	0.303389	0.75695	2.5392	-0.22451	-0.13725	0.55058
0.75	0.773373	0.301137	0.75257	2.5682	-0.22585	-0.13175	0.55052
0.76	0.776373	0.298872	0.74824	2.5977	-0.22714	-0.12624	0.55023
0.77	0.779350	0.296595	0.74394	2.6277	-0.22838	-0.12074	0.54973
0.78	0.782305	0.294305	0.73969	2.6581	-0.22956	-0.11525	0.54901
0.79	0.785236	0.292004	0.73548	2.6891	-0.23068	-0.10976	0.54808
0.80	0.788145	0.289692	0.73131	2.7206	-0.23175	-0.10429	0.54694
0.81	0.791030	0.287369	0.72718	2.7527	-0.23277	-0.09883	0.54559
0.82	0.793892	0.285036	0.72309	2.7852	-0.23373	-0.09338	0.54403
0.83	0.796731	0.282694	0.71904	2.8184	-0.23464	-0.08795	0.54227
0.84	0.799546	0.280344	0.71503	2.8520	-0.23549	-0.08253	0.54031
0.85	0.802337	0.277985	0.71106	2.8863	-0.23629	-0.07714	0.53814
0.86	0.805105	0.275618	0.70712	2.9211	-0.23703	-0.07177	0.53579
0.87	0.807850	0.273244	0.70322	2.9565	-0.23772	-0.06643	0.53324
0.88	0.810570	0.270864	0.69935	2.9925	-0.23836	-0.06111	0.53049
0.89	0.813267	0.268477	0.69553	3.0292	-0.23894	-0.05582	0.52757
0.90	0.815940	0.266085	0.69173	3.0665	-0.23948	-0.05056	0.52445
0.91	0.818589	0.263688	0.68798	3.1044	-0.23996	-0.04533	0.52116
0.92	0.821214	0.261286	0.68425	3.1430	-0.24038	-0.04013	0.51769
0.93	0.823814	0.258881	0.68057	3.1822	-0.24076	-0.03497	0.51404
0.94	0.826391	0.256471	0.67691	3.2222	-0.24108	-0.02985	0.51023
0.95	0.828944	0.254059	0.67329	3.2628	-0.24136	-0.02477	0.50624
0.96	0.831472	0.251644	0.66971	3.3042	-0.24158	-0.01973	0.50210
0.97	0.833977	0.249228	0.66615	3.3462	-0.24175	-0.01473	0.49779
0.98	0.836457	0.246809	0.66263	3.3891	-0.24187	-0.00977	0.49332
0.99	0.838913	0.244390	0.65914	3.4327	-0.24195	-0.00486	0.48871

The Normal Distribution and Related Functions

X	P(X)	Z(X)	Q/Z.	P/Z	$Z^{(1)}(X)$	$Z^{(2)}(X)$	$Z^{(3)}(X)$
1.00	0.841345	0.241971	0.65568	3.4771	-0.24197	0.00000	0.48394
1.01	0.843752	0.239551	0.65225	3.5222	-0.24195	0.00481	0.47903
1.02	0.846136	0.237132	0.64885	3.5682	-0.24187	0.00958	0.47398
1.03	0.848495	0.234714	0.64549	3.6150	-0.24176	0.01429	0.46879
1.04	0.850830	0.232297	0.64215	3.6627	-0.24159	0.01896	0.46346
1.05	0.853141	0.229882	0.63885	3.7112	-0.24138	0.02356	0.45801
1.06	0.855428	0.227470	0.63557	3.7606	-0.24112	0.02812	0.45243
1.07	0.857690	0.225060	0.63232	3.8109	-0.24081	0.03261	0.44673
1.08	0.859929	0.222653	0.62910	3.8622	-0.24047	0.03705	0.44092
1.09	0.862143	0.220251	0.62591	3.9144	-0.24007	0.04143	0.43499
1.10	0.864334	0.217852	0.62274	3.9675	-0.23964	0.04575	0.42895
1.11	0.866500	0.215458	0.61961	4.0217	-0.23916	0.05001	0.42281
1.12	0.868643	0.213069	0.61650	4.0768	-0.23864	0.05420	0.41657
1.13	0.870762	0.210686	0.61342	4.1330	-0.23807	0.05834	0.41023
1.14	0.872857	0.208308	0.61036	4.1902	-0.23747	0.06241	0.40380
1.15	0.874928	0.205936	0.60733	4.2485	-0.23683	0.06641	0.39728
1.16	0.876976	0.203571	0.60433	4.3080	-0.23614	0.07035	0.39067
1.17	0.879000	0.201214	0.60135	4.3685	-0.23542	0.07423	0.38399
1.18	0.881000	0.198863	0.59840	4.4302	-0.23466	0.07803	0.37724
1.19	0.882977	0.196520	0.59548	4.4931	-0.23386	0.08177	0.37041
1.20	0.884930	0.194186	0.59257	4.5571	-0.23302	0.08544	0.36352
1.21	0.886861	0.191860	0.58970	4.6224	-0.23215	0.08904	0.35656
1.22	0.888768	0.189543	0.58684	4.6890	-0.23124	0.09257	0.34955
1.23	0.890651	0.187235	0.58402	4.7569	-0.23030	0.09603	0.34248
1.24	0.892512	0.184937	0.58121	4.8260	-0.22932	0.09942	0.33536
1.25	0.894350	0.182649	0.57843	4.8966	-0.22831	0.10274	0.32820
1.26	0.896165	0.180371	0.57567	4.9685	-0.22727	0.10599	0.32099
1.27	0.897958	0.178104	0.57294	5.0418	-0.22619	0.10916	0.31375
1.28	0.899727	0.175847	0.57022	5.1165	-0.22508	0.11226	0.30648
1.29	0.901475	0.173602	0.56754	5.1928	-0.22395	0.11529	0.29917
1.30	0.903200	0.171369	0.56487	5.2705	-0.22278	0.11824	0.29184
1.31	0.904902	0.169147	0.56222	5.3498	-0.22158	0.12113	0.28449
1.32	0.906582	0.166937	0.55960	5.4307	-0.22036	0.12393	0.27712
1.33	0.908241	0.164740	0.55699	5.5132	-0.21910	0.12667	0.26974
1.34	0.909877	0.162555	0.55441	5.5973	-0.21782	0.12933	0.26235
1.35	0.911492	0.160383	0.55185	5.6832	-0.21652	0.13192	0.25495
1.36	0.913085	0.158225	0.54931	5.7708	-0.21519	0.13443	0.24755
1.37	0.914657	0.156080	0.54679	5.8602	-0.21383	0.13687	0.24015
1.38	0.916207	0.153948	0.54430	5.9514	-0.21245	0.13923	0.23276
1.39	0.917736	0.151831	0.54182	6.0445	-0.21104	0.14152	0.22537
1.40	0.919243	0.149727	0.53936	6.1394	-0.20962	0.14374	0.21800
1.41	0.920730	0.147639	0.53692	6.2364	-0.20817	0.14588	0.21065
1.42	0.922196	0.145564	0.53450	6.3353	-0.20670	0.14795	0.20331
1.43	0.923641	0.143505	0.53210	6.4363	-0.20521	0.14995	0.19600
1.44	0.925066	0.141460	0.52972	6.5394	-0.20370	0.15187	0.18871
1.45	0.926471	0.139431	0.52735	6.6447	-0.20217	0.15372	0.18145
1.46	0.927855	0.137417	0.52501	6.7521	-0.20063	0.15550	0.17423
1.47	0.929219	0.135418	0.52268	6.8619	-0.19906	0.15721	0.16704
1.48	0.930563	0.133435	0.52038	6.9739	-0.19748	0.15884	0.15988
1.49	0.931888	0.131468	0.51809	7.0883	-0.19589	0.16040	0.15277

The Normal Distribution and Related Functions (cont.)

X	P(X)	Z(X)	Q/Z	P/Z	$Z^{(1)}(X)$	$Z^{(2)}(X)$	$Z^{(3)}(X)$
1.50	0.933193	0.129518	0.51582	7.2051	-0.19428	0.16190	0.14571
1.51	0.934478	0.127583	0.51356	7.3245	-0.19265	0.16332	0.13869
1.52	0.935745	0.125665	0.51133	7.4464	-0.19101	0.16467	0.13172
1.53	0.936992	0.123763	0.50911	7.5709	-0.18936	0.16595	0.12481
1.54	0.938220	0.121878	0.50690	7.6981	-0.18769	0.16717	0.11795
1.55	0.939429	0.120009	0.50472	7.8280	-0.18601	0.16831	0.11114
1.56	0.940620	0.118157	0.50255	7.9607	-0.18433	0.16939	0.10440
1.57	0.941792	0.116323	0.50040	8.0964	-0.18263	0.17040	0.09772
1.58	0.942947	0.114505	0.49826	8.2350	-0.18092	0.17134	0.09111
1.59	0.944083	0.112704	0.49614	8.3766	-0.17920	0.17222	0.08456
1.60	0.945201	0.110921	0.49404	8.5214	-0.17747	0.17304	0.07809
1.61	0.946301	0.109155	0.49195	8.6694	-0.17574	0.17379	0.07168
1.62	0.947384	0.107406	0.48988	8.8206	-0.17400	0.17447	0.06535
1.63	0.948449	0.105675	0.48782	8.9752	-0.17225	0.17509	0.05910
1.64	0.949497	0.103961	0.48578	9.1332	-0.17050	0.17565	0.05292
1.65	0.950529	0.102265	0.48376	9.2948	-0.16874	0.17615	0.04682
1.66	0.951543	0.100586	0.48175	9.4600	-0.16697	0.17659	0.04081
1.67	0.952540	0.098925	0.47975	9.6289	-0.16521	0.17697	0.03487
1.68	0.953521	0.097282	0.47777	9.8016	-0.16343	0.17729	0.02903
1.69	0.954486	0.095657	0.47580	9.9782	-0.16166	0.17755	0.02326
1.70	0.955435	0.094049	0.47385	10.159	-0.15988	0.17775	0.01759
1.71	0.956367	0.092459	0.47192	10.344	-0.15811	0.17790	0.01200
1.72	0.957284	0.090887	0.46999	10.533	-0.15633	0.17799	0.00650
1.73	0.958185	0.089333	0.46808	10.726	-0.15455	0.17803	0.00110
1.74	0.959070	0.087796	0.46619	10.924	-0.15277	0.17802	-0.00422
1.75	0.959941	0.086277	0.46431	11.126	-0.15099	0.17795	-0.00944
1.76	0.960796	0.084776	0.46244	11.333	-0.14921	0.17783	-0.01456
1.77	0.961636	0.083293	0.46058	11.545	-0.14743	0.17766	-0.01959
1.78	0.962462	0.081828	0.45874	11.762	-0.14565	0.17744	-0.02453
1.79	0.963273	0.080380	0.45692	11.984	-0.14388	0.17717	-0.02937
1.80	0.964070	0.078950	0.45510	12.211	-0.14211	0.17685	-0.03411
1.81	0.964852	0.077538	0.45330	12.444	-0.14034	0.17648	-0.03875
1.82	0.965620	0.076143	0.45151	12.682	-0.13858	0.17607	-0.04329
1.83	0.966375	0.074766	0.44973	12.925	-0.13682	0.17562	-0.04774
1.84	0.967116	0.073407	0.44797	13.175	-0.13507	0.17512	-0.05208
1.85	0.967843	0.072065	0.44622	13.430	-0.13332	0.17458	-0.05633
1.86	0.968557	0.070740	0.44448	13.692	-0.13158	0.17399	-0.06047
1.87	0.969258	0.069433	0.44275	13.960	-0.12984	0.17337	-0.06452
1.88	0.969946	0.068144	0.44104	14.234	-0.12811	0.17270	-0.06846
1.89	0.970621	0.066871	0.43934	14.515	-0.12639	0.17200	-0.07231
1.90	0.971283	0.065616	0.43765	14.803	-0.12467	0.17126	-0.07605
1.91	0.971933	0.064378	0.43597	15.097	-0.12296	0.17048	-0.07969
1.92	0.972571	0.063157	0.43430	15.399	-0.12126	0.16966	-0.08323
1.93	0.973197	0.061952	0.43265	15.709	-0.11957	0.16881	-0.08667
1.94	0.973810	0.060765	0.43100	16.026	-0.11788	0.16793	-0.09002
1.95	0.974412	0.059595	0.42937	16.351	-0.11621	0.16701	-0.09326
1.96	0.975002	0.058441	0.42775	16.684	-0.11454	0.16607	-0.09640
1.97	0.975581	0.057304	0.42614	17.025	-0.11289	0.16509	-0.09944
1.98	0.976148	0.056183	0.42454	17.374	-0.11124	0.16408	-0.10239
1.99	0.976705	0.055079	0.42295	17.733	-0.10961	0.16304	-0.10523

The Normal Distribution and Related Functions (cont.)

X	P(X)	Z(X)	Q/Z	P/Z	$Z^{(1)}(X)$	$Z^{(2)}(X)$	$Z^{(3)}(X)$
2.00	0.977250	0.053991	0.42137	18.100	-0.10798	0.16197	-0.10798
2.01	0.977784	0.052919	0.41980	18.477	-0.10637	0.16088	-0.11063
2.02	0.978308	0.051864	0.41825	18.863	-0.10476	0.15976	-0.11319
2.03	0.978822	0.050824	0.41670	19.259	-0.10317	0.15862	-0.11565
2.04	0.979325	0.049800	0.41516	19.665	-0.10159	0.15745	-0.11801
2.05	0.979818	0.048792	0.41364	20.082	-0.10002	0.15626	-0.12028
2.06	0.980301	0.047800	0.41212	20.509	-0.09847	0.15504	-0.12245
2.07	0.980774	0.046823	0.41062	20.947	-0.09692	0.15381	-0.12454
2.08	0.981237	0.045861	0.40912	21.396	-0.09539	0.15255	-0.12653
2.09	0.981691	0.044915	0.40764	21.857	-0.09387	0.15128	-0.12843
2.10	0.982136	0.043984	0.40616	22.330	-0.09237	0.14998	-0.13024
2.11	0.982571	0.043067	0.40470	22.815	-0.09087	0.14867	-0.13196
2.12	0.982997	0.042166	0.40324	23.312	-0.08939	0.14735	-0.13359
2.13	0.983414	0.041280	0.40179	23.823	-0.08793	0.14600	-0.13513
2.14	0.983823	0.040408	0.40036	24.347	-0.08647	0.14464	-0.13659
2.15	0.984222	0.039550	0.39893	24.886	-0.08503	0.14327	-0.13797
2.16	0.984614	0.038707	0.39751	25.438	-0.08361	0.14188	-0.13926
2.17	0.984997	0.037878	0.39610	26.005	-0.08220	0.14049	-0.14046
2.18	0.985371	0.037063	0.39470	26.586	-0.08080	0.13907	-0.14159
2.19	0.985738	0.036262	0.39331	27.184	-0.07941	0.13765	-0.14263
2.20	0.986097	0.035475	0.39193	27.797	-0.07804	0.13622	-0.14360
2.21	0.986447	0.034701	0.39055	28.427	-0.07669	0.13478	-0.14449
2.22	0.986791	0.033941	0.38919	29.074	-0.07535	0.13333	-0.14530
2.23	0.987126	0.033194	0.38783	29.738	-0.07402	0.13188	-0.14604
2.24	0.987455	0.032460	0.38649	30.420	-0.07271	0.13041	-0.14670
2.25	0.987776	0.031740	0.38515	31.121	-0.07141	0.12894	-0.14729
2.26	0.988089	0.031032	0.38382	31.841	-0.07013	0.12747	-0.14781
2.27	0.988396	0.030337	0.38250	32.581	-0.06886	0.12599	-0.14826
2.28	0.988696	0.029655	0.38118	33.340	-0.06761	0.12450	-0.14864
2.29	0.988989	0.028985	0.37988	34.121	-0.06638	0.12301	-0.14895
2.30	0.989276	0.028327	0.37858	34.923	-0.06515	0.12152	-0.14920
2.31	0.989556	0.027682	0.37729	35.748	-0.06394	0.12003	-0.14938
2.32	0.989830	0.027048	0.37601	36.595	-0.06275	0.11854	-0.14950
2.33	0.990097	0.026426	0.37474	37.466	-0.06157	0.11704	-0.14956
2.34	0.990358	0.025817	0.37348	38.361	-0.06041	0.11554	-0.14955
2.35	0.990613	0.025218	0.37222	39.282	-0.05926	0.11405	-0.14949
2.36	0.990863	0.024631	0.37097	40.228	-0.05813	0.11256	-0.14937
2.37	0.991106	0.024056	0.36973	41.201	-0.05701	0.11106	-0.14919
2.38	0.991344	0.023491	0.36850	42.201	-0.05591	0.10957	-0.14896
2.39	0.991576	0.022937	0.36727	43.230	-0.05482	0.10808	-0.14868
2.40	0.991802	0.022395	0.36605	44.288	-0.05375	0.10660	-0.14834
2.41	0.992024	0.021862	0.36484	45.376	-0.05269	0.10512	-0.14795
2.42	0.992240	0.021341	0.36364	46.495	-0.05164	0.10364	-0.14752
2.43	0.992451	0.020829	0.36244	47.647	-0.05062	0.10217	-0.14703
2.44	0.992656	0.020328	0.36125	48.831	-0.04960	0.10070	-0.14650
2.45	0.992857	0.019837	0.36007	50.050	-0.04860	0.09924	-0.14593
2.46	0.993053	0.019356	0.35889	51.304	-0.04762	0.09778	-0.14531
2.47	0.993244	0.018885	0.35773	52.594	-0.04665	0.09633	-0.14464
2.48	0.993431	0.018423	0.35657	53.923	-0.04569	0.09489	-0.14394
2.49	0.993613	0.017971	0.35541	55.289	-0.04475	0.09345	-0.14320

8

The Normal Distribution and Related Functions (cont.)

X	P(X)	Z(X)	Q/Z	P/Z	$Z^{(1)}(X)$	$Z^{(2)}(X)$	$Z^{(3)}(X)$
2.50	0.993790	0.017528	0.35427	56.696	-0.04382	0.09202	-0.14242
2.51	0.993963	0.017095	0.35313	58.145	-0.04291	0.09060	-0.14160
2.52	0.994132	0.016670	0.35199	59.636	-0.04201	0.08919	-0.14075
2.53	0.994297	0.016254	0.35087	61.171	-0.04112	0.08779	-0.13986
2.54	0.994457	0.015848	0.34975	62.751	-0.04025	0.08639	-0.13894
2.55	0.994614	0.015449	0.34863	64.379	-0.03940	0.08501	-0.13798
2.56	0.994766	0.015060	0.34753	66.055	-0.03855	0.08364	-0.13700
2.57	0.994915	0.014678	0.34643	67.782	-0.03772	0.08227	-0.13599
2.58	0.995060	0.014305	0.34533	69.560	-0.03691	0.08092	-0.13495
2.59	0.995201	0.013940	0.34425	71.391	-0.03610	0.07957	-0.13388
2.60	0.995339	0.013583	0.34316	73.278	-0.03532	0.07824	-0.13279
2.61	0.995473	0.013234	0.34209	75.223	-0.03454	0.07692	-0.13167
2.62	0.995604	0.012892	0.34102	77.226	-0.03378	0.07560	-0.13053
2.63	0.995731	0.012558	0.33996	79.290	-0.03303	0.07431	-0.12937
2.64	0.995855	0.012232	0.33890	81.417	-0.03229	0.07302	-0.12818
2.65	0.995975	0.011912	0.33785	83.609	-0.03157	0.07174	-0.12698
2.66	0.996093	0.011600	0.33681	85.869	-0.03086	0.07048	-0.12576
2.67	0.996207	0.011295	0.33577	88.198	-0.03016	0.06923	-0.12452
2.68	0.996319	0.010997	0.33474	90.600	-0.02947	0.06799	-0.12326
2.69	0.996427	0.010706	0.33371	93.075	-0.02880	0.06676	-0.12199
2.70	0.996533	0.010421	0.33269	95.628	-0.02814	0.06555	-0.12071
2.71	0.996636	0.010143	0.33168	98.260	-0.02749	0.06435	-0.11941
2.72	0.996736	0.009871	0.33067	100.98	-0.02685	0.06316	-0.11810
2.73	0.996833	0.009606	0.32967	103.77	-0.02622	0.06199	-0.11677
2.74	0.996928	0.009347	0.32867	106.66	-0.02561	0.06082	-0.11544
2.75	0.997020	0.009094	0.32768	109.64	-0.02501	0.05968	-0.11410
2.76	0.997110	0.008846	0.32669	112.71	-0.02442	0.05854	-0.11274
2.77	0.997197	0.008605	0.32571	115.88	-0.02384	0.05742	-0.11139
2.78	0.997282	0.008370	0.32474	119.15	-0.02327	0.05631	-0.11002
2.79	0.997365	0.008140	0.32377	122.53	-0.02271	0.05522	-0.10865
2.80	0.997445	0.007915	0.32280	126.01	-0.02216	0.05414	-0.10727
2.81	0.997523	0.007697	0.32184	129.61	-0.02163	0.05308	-0.10589
2.82	0.997599	0.007483	0.32089	133.32	-0.02110	0.05202	-0.10450
2.83	0.997673	0.007274	0.31994	137.15	-0.02059	0.05099	-0.10312
2.84	0.997744	0.007071	0.31900	141.10	-0.02008	0.04996	-0.10173
2.85	0.997814	0.006873	0.31806	145.18	-0.01959	0.04895	-0.10034
2.86	0.997882	0.006679	0.31713	149.40	-0.01910	0.04795	-0.09895
2.87	0.997948	0.006491	0.31620	153.75	-0.01863	0.04697	-0.09755
2.88	0.998012	0.006307	0.31528	158.25	-0.01816	0.04600	-0.09616
2.89	0.998074	0.006127	0.31436	162.89	-0.01771	0.04505	-0.09478
2.90	0.998134	0.005953	0.31345	167.68	-0.01726	0.04411	-0.09339
2.91	0.998193	0.005782	0.31254	172.64	-0.01683	0.04318	-0.09201
2.92	0.998250	0.005616	0.31164	177.75	-0.01640	0.04227	-0.09063
2.93	0.998305	0.005454	0.31074	183.04	-0.01598	0.04137	-0.08925
2.94	0.998359	0.005296	0.30985	188.50	-0.01557	0.04048	-0.08788
2.95	0.998411	0.005143	0.30896	194.14	-0.01517	0.03961	-0.08651
2.96	0.998462	0.004993	0.30808	199.98	-0.01478	0.03875	-0.08515
2.97	0.998511	0.004847	0.30720	206.00	-0.01440	0.03791	-0.08380
2.98	0.998559	0.004705	0.30633	212.24	-0.01402	0.03708	-0.08245
2.99	0.998605	0.004567	0.30546	218.68	-0.01365	0.03626	-0.08111

The Normal Distribution and Related Functions (cont.)

X	P(X)	Z(X)	Q/Z	P/Z	$Z^{(1)}(X)$	$Z^{(2)}(X)$	$Z^{(3)}(X)$
3.00	0.998650	0.004432	0.30459	225.33	-0.01330	0.03545	-0.07977
3.01	0.998694	0.004301	0.30373	232.22	-0.01295	0.03466	-0.07845
3.02	0.998736	0.004173	0.30287	239.34	-0.01260	0.03389	-0.07713
3.03	0.998777	0.004049	0.30202	246.70	-0.01227	0.03312	-0.07582
3.04	0.998817	0.003928	0.30118	254.31	-0.01194	0.03237	-0.07452
3.05	0.998856	0.003810	0.30034	262.18	-0.01162	0.03163	-0.07323
3.06	0.998893	0.003695	0.29950	270.32	-0.01131	0.03090	-0.07195
3.07	0.998930	0.003584	0.29866	278.75	-0.01100	0.03019	-0.07068
3.08	0.998965	0.003475	0.29784	287.47	-0.01070	0.02949	-0.06943
3.09	0.998999	0.003370	0.29701	296.48	-0.01041	0.02880	-0.06818
3.10	0.999032	0.003267	0.29619	305.81	-0.01013	0.02813	-0.06694
3.11	0.999065	0.003167	0.29538	315.47	-0.00985	0.02746	-0.06571
3.12	0.999096	0.003070	0.29456	325.46	-0.00958	0.02681	-0.06450
3.13	0.999126	0.002975	0.29376	335.80	-0.00931	0.02617	-0.06330
3.14	0.999155	0.002884	0.29295	346.50	-0.00905	0.02555	-0.06211
3.15	0.999184	0.002794	0.29215	357.58	-0.00880	0.02493	-0.06093
3.16	0.999211	0.002707	0.29136	369.06	-0.00856	0.02433	-0.05977
3.17	0.999238	0.002623	0.29057	380.93	-0.00832	0.02374	-0.05861
3.18	0.999264	0.002541	0.28978	393.23	-0.00808	0.02316	-0.05747
3.19	0.999289	0.002461	0.28900	405.97	-0.00785	0.02259	-0.05635
3.20	0.999313	0.002384	0.28822	419.16	-0.00763	0.02203	-0.05523
3.21	0.999336	0.002309	0.28744	432.82	-0.00741	0.02148	-0.05413
3.22	0.999359	0.002236	0.28667	446.97	-0.00720	0.02095	-0.05305
3.23	0.999381	0.002165	0.28590	461.63	-0.00699	0.02042	-0.05198
3.24	0.999402	0.002096	0.28514	476.82	-0.00679	0.01991	-0.05092
3.25	0.999423	0.002029	0.28438	492.56	-0.00659	0.01940	-0.04987
3.26	0.999443	0.001964	0.28363	508.86	-0.00640	0.01891	-0.04884
3.27	0.999462	0.001901	0.28287	525.76	-0.00622	0.01843	-0.04782
3.28	0.999481	0.001840	0.28213	543.28	-0.00603	0.01795	-0.04682
3.29	0.999499	0.001780	0.28138	561.43	-0.00586	0.01749	-0.04583
3.30	0.999517	0.001723	0.28064	580.25	-0.00568	0.01704	-0.04485
3.31	0.999534	0.001667	0.27990	599.75	-0.00552	0.01659	-0.04389
3.32	0.999550	0.001612	0.27917	619.98	-0.00535	0.01616	-0.04294
3.33	0.999566	0.001560	0.27844	640.95	-0.00519	0.01573	-0.04201
3.34	0.999581	0.001508	0.27772	662.70	-0.00504	0.01532	-0.04109
3.35	0.999596	0.001459	0.27699	685.25	-0.00489	0.01491	-0.04018
3.36	0.999610	0.001411	0.27627	708.64	-0.00474	0.01451	-0.03929
3.37	0.999624	0.001364	0.27556	732.90	-0.00460	0.01413	-0.03841
3.38	0.999638	0.001319	0.27485	758.07	-0.00446	0.01375	-0.03755
3.39	0.999651	0.001275	0.27414	784.18	-0.00432	0.01338	-0.03670
3.40	0.999663	0.001232	0.27343	811.27	-0.00419	0.01301	-0.03586
3.41	0.999675	0.001191	0.27273	839.38	-0.00406	0.01266	-0.03504
3.42	0.999687	0.001151	0.27203	868.55	-0.00394	0.01231	-0.03423
3.43	0.999698	0.001112	0.27134	898.82	-0.00381	0.01197	-0.03344
3.44	0.999709	0.001075	0.27065	930.24	-0.00370	0.01164	-0.03266
3.45	0.999720	0.001038	0.26996	962.86	-0.00358	0.01132	-0.03189
3.46	0.999730	0.001003	0.26928	996.72	-0.00347	0.01100	-0.03114
3.47	0.999740	0.000969	0.26859	1031.9	-0.00336	0.01070	-0.03040
3.48	0.999749	0.000936	0.26791	1068.4	-0.00326	0.01040	-0.02967
3.49	0.999758	0.000904	0.26724	1106.3	-0.00315	0.01010	-0.02895

The Normal Distribution and Related Functions (cont.)

X	P(X)	Z(X)	Q/Z	P/Z	$Z^{(1)}(X)$	$Z^{(2)}(X)$	$Z^{(3)}(X)$
3.50	0.999767	0.000873	0.26657	1145.6	-0.00305	0.00982	-0.02825
3.51	0.999776	0.000843	0.26590	1186.5	-0.00296	0.00954	-0.02757
3.52	0.999784	0.000814	0.26523	1229.0	-0.00286	0.00927	-0.02689
3.53	0.999792	0.000785	0.26457	1273.1	-0.00277	0.00900	-0.02623
3.54	0.999800	0.000758	0.26391	1318.9	-0.00268	0.00874	-0.02558
3.55	0.999807	0.000732	0.26326	1366.5	-0.00260	0.00849	-0.02494
3.56	0.999815	0.000706	0.26260	1415.9	-0.00251	0.00824	-0.02432
3.57	0.999822	0.000681	0.26195	1467.3	-0.00243	0.00800	-0.02370
3.58	0.999828	0.000657	0.26131	1520.8	-0.00235	0.00777	-0.02310
3.59	0.999835	0.000634	0.26066	1576.3	-0.00228	0.00754	-0.02252
3.60	0.999841	0.000612	0.26002	1634.0	-0.00220	0.00732	-0.02194
3.61	0.999847	0.000590	0.25939	1694.0	-0.00213	0.00710	-0.02138
3.62	0.999853	0.000569	0.25875	1756.3	-0.00206	0.00689	-0.02082
3.63	0.999858	0.000549	0.25812	1821.2	-0.00199	0.00669	-0.02028
3.64	0.999864	0.000529	0.25749	1888.6	-0.00193	0.00649	-0.01975
3.65	0.999869	0.000510	0.25686	1958.7	-0.00186	0.00629	-0.01923
3.66	0.999874	0.000492	0.25624	2031.7	-0.00180	0.00610	-0.01873
3.67	0.999879	0.000474	0.25562	2107.5	-0.00174	0.00592	-0.01823
3.68	0.999883	0.000457	0.25500	2186.4	-0.00168	0.00574	-0.01774
3.69	0.999888	0.000441	0.25439	2268.5	-0.00163	0.00556	-0.01727
3.70	0.999892	0.000425	0.25378	2353.9	-0.00157	0.00539	-0.01680
3.71	0.999896	0.000409	0.25317	2442.8	-0.00152	0.00522	-0.01635
3.72	0.999900	0.000394	0.25256	2535.2	-0.00147	0.00506	-0.01590
3.73	0.999904	0.000380	0.25196	2631.5	-0.00142	0.00491	-0.01547
3.74	0.999908	0.000366	0.25136	2731.6	-0.00137	0.00475	-0.01504
3.75	0.999912	0.000353	0.25076	2835.9	-0.00132	0.00461	-0.01463
3.76	0.999915	0.000340	0.25017	2944.3	-0.00128	0.00446	-0.01422
3.77	0.999918	0.000327	0.24957	3057.4	-0.00123	0.00432	-0.01383
3.78	0.999922	0.000315	0.24898	3175.0	-0.00119	0.00419	-0.01344
3.79	0.999925	0.000303	0.24840	3297.5	-0.00115	0.00405	-0.01306
3.80	0.999928	0.000292	0.24781	3425.0	-0.00111	0.00392	-0.01269
3.81	0.999931	0.000281	0.24723	3557.9	-0.00107	0.00380	-0.01233
3.82	0.999933	0.000271	0.24665	3696.2	-0.00103	0.00368	-0.01198
3.83	0.999936	0.000260	0.24607	3840.4	-0.00100	0.00356	-0.01164
3.84	0.999938	0.000251	0.24550	3990.5	-0.00096	0.00344	-0.01130
3.85	0.999941	0.000241	0.24493	4147.0	-0.00093	0.00333	-0.01098
3.86	0.999943	0.000232	0.24436	4310.0	-0.00090	0.00322	-0.01066
3.87	0.999946	0.000223	0.24379	4479.8	-0.00086	0.00312	-0.01035
3.88	0.999948	0.000215	0.24323	4656.8	-0.00083	0.00302	-0.01004
3.89	0.999950	0.000207	0.24267	4841.3	-0.00080	0.00292	-0.00975
3.90	0.999952	0.000199	0.24211	5033.6	-0.00077	0.00282	-0.00946
3.91	0.999954	0.000191	0.24155	5234.1	-0.00075	0.00273	-0.00918
3.92	0.999956	0.000184	0.24100	5443.0	-0.00072	0.00264	-0.00891
3.93	0.999958	0.000177	0.24045	5660.9	-0.00069	0.00255	-0.00864
3.94	0.999959	0.000170	0.23990	5888.2	-0.00067	0.00247	-0.00838
3.95	0.999961	0.000163	0.23935	6125.1	-0.00064	0.00238	-0.00813
3.96	0.999963	0.000157	0.23881	6372.2	-0.00062	0.00230	-0.00788
3.97	0.999964	0.000151	0.23826	6630.0	-0.00060	0.00223	-0.00764
3.98	0.999966	0.000145	0.23772	6898.8	-0.00058	0.00215	-0.00741
3.99	0.999967	0.000139	0.23719	7179.3	-0.00056	0.00208	-0.00718

1.2 Inverse of the Normal Probability Distribution

This table was computed using Newton's method to find that value of X which gives $P(X)$ equal to the values in the column headed P. For $X \le$ 3.5, the values of $P(X)$ were obtained from the program used for Section 1.1. For $X > 3.5$, the values of $P(X)$ were obtained using the continued fraction given by

$$R(t) = \cfrac{1}{t + \cfrac{1}{t + \cfrac{2}{t + \cfrac{3}{t + \cdots}}}}$$

and then $Q(X) = Z(X)R(X)$.

Inverse of the Normal Probability Distribution

$$P(X) = \Pr\{N(0, 1)\text{r.v.} \leq X\}; \quad Q = 1 - P; \quad Z(X) = \text{density of } N(0, 1)\text{r.v.}$$

P	X	Z	Q	P	X	Z	Q
0.50	0.00000	0.39894	0.50	0.925	1.43953	0.14156	0.075
0.51	0.02507	0.39882	0.49	0.930	1.47579	0.13427	0.070
0.52	0.05015	0.39844	0.48	0.935	1.51410	0.12679	0.065
0.53	0.07527	0.39781	0.47	0.940	1.55477	0.11912	0.060
0.54	0.10043	0.39694	0.46	0.945	1.59819	0.11124	0.055
0.55	0.12566	0.39580	0.45	0.950	1.64485	0.10314	0.050
0.56	0.15097	0.39442	0.44	0.955	1.69540	0.09479	0.045
0.57	0.17637	0.39279	0.43	0.960	1.75069	0.08617	0.040
0.58	0.20189	0.39089	0.42	0.965	1.81191	0.07727	0.035
0.59	0.22754	0.38875	0.41	0.970	1.88079	0.06804	0.030
0.60	0.25335	0.38634	0.40	0.975	1.95996	0.05845	0.025
0.61	0.27932	0.38368	0.39	0.980	2.05375	0.04842	0.020
0.62	0.30548	0.38076	0.38	0.985	2.17009	0.03787	0.015
0.63	0.33185	0.37757	0.37	0.990	2.32635	0.02665	0.010
0.64	0.35846	0.37412	0.36				
0.65	0.38532	0.37040	0.35	0.991	2.36562	0.02431	0.009
0.66	0.41246	0.36641	0.34	0.992	2.40892	0.02192	0.008
0.67	0.43991	0.36215	0.33	0.993	2.45726	0.01949	0.007
0.68	0.46770	0.35761	0.32	0.994	2.51214	0.01700	0.006
0.69	0.49585	0.35279	0.31	0.995	2.57583	0.01446	0.005
0.70	0.52440	0.34769	0.30	0.996	2.65207	0.01185	0.004
0.71	0.55338	0.34230	0.29	0.997	2.74778	0.00915	0.003
0.72	0.58284	0.33662	0.28	0.998	2.87816	0.00634	0.002
0.73	0.61281	0.33065	0.27	0.999	3.09023	0.00337	0.001
0.74	0.64335	0.32437	0.26				
0.75	0.67449	0.31778	0.25	0.9991	3.12139	0.00306	0.0009
0.76	0.70630	0.31087	0.24	0.9992	3.15591	0.00274	0.0008
0.77	0.73885	0.30365	0.23	0.9993	3.19465	0.00243	0.0007
0.78	0.77219	0.29609	0.22	0.9994	3.23888	0.00210	0.0006
0.79	0.80642	0.28820	0.21	0.9995	3.29053	0.00178	0.0005
0.80	0.84162	0.27996	0.20	0.9996	3.35279	0.00145	0.0004
0.81	0.87790	0.27137	0.19	0.9997	3.43161	0.00111	0.0003
0.82	0.91537	0.26240	0.18	0.9998	3.54008	0.00076	0.0002
0.83	0.95417	0.25305	0.17	0.9999	3.71902	0.00040	0.0001
0.84	0.99446	0.24331	0.16				
0.85	1.03643	0.23316	0.15	0.9999 5	3.89059	0.00021	0.0000 5
0.86	1.08032	0.22258	0.14	0.9999 9	4.26489	0.00004	0.0000 1
0.87	1.12639	0.21155	0.13	0.9999 95	4.41717	0.00002	0.0000 05
0.88	1.17499	0.20004	0.12	0.9999 99	4.75342	0.00000	0.0000 01
0.89	1.22653	0.18804	0.11	0.9999 995	4.89164	0.00000	0.0000 005
0.900	1.28155	0.17550	0.10	0.9999 999	5.19934	0.00000	0.0000 001
0.905	1.31058	0.16902	0.095	0.9999 9995	5.32672	0.00000	0.0000 0005
0.910	1.34076	0.16239	0.090	0.9999 9999	5.61200	0.00000	0.0000 0001
0.915	1.37220	0.15561	0.085	0.9999 9999 5	5.73073	0.00000	0.0000 0000 5
0.920	1.40507	0.14867	0.080	0.9999 9999 9	5.99781	0.00000	0.0000 0000 1

1.3 Extreme Values of the Normal Distribution and Mill's Ratio

This table was computed using the continued fraction noted in Section 1.2. When X is large, $Q/Z \cong 1/X$, and hence $Q(X) \cong Z(X)/X$.

Extreme Values of the Normal Distribution and Mill's Ratio

$Q(X) = \Pr\{N(0, 1)\text{r.v.} \geq X\}$; $Z(X) =$ density of $N(0, 1)$r.v.

X	$Q(X) = b \times 10^{-a}$ a	$Q(X) = b \times 10^{-a}$ b	Mill's Ratio Q/Z	X	$Q(X) = b \times 10^{-a}$ a	$Q(X) = b \times 10^{-a}$ b	Mill's Ratio Q/Z
3.0	3	1.3499	0.30459	8.0	16	6.2210	0.12313
3.1	4	9.6760	0.29619	8.2	16	1.2019	0.12021
3.2	4	6.8714	0.28822	8.4	17	2.2324	0.11743
3.3	4	4.8342	0.28064	8.6	18	3.9858	0.11477
3.4	4	3.3693	0.27343	8.8	19	6.8408	0.11222
3.5	4	2.3263	0.26657	9.0	19	1.1286	0.10979
3.6	4	1.5911	0.26002	9.2	20	1.7897	0.10745
3.7	4	1.0780	0.25378	9.4	21	2.7282	0.10522
3.8	5	7.2348	0.24781	9.6	22	3.9972	0.10307
3.9	5	4.8096	0.24211	9.8	23	5.6293	0.10101
4.0	5	3.1671	0.23665	10	24	7.6199	0.099029
4.1	5	2.0658	0.23143	11	28	1.9106	0.090173
4.2	5	1.3346	0.22642	12	33	1.7765	0.082767
4.3	6	8.5399	0.22161	13	39	6.1172	0.076476
4.4	6	5.4125	0.21700	14	45	7.7935	0.071069.
4.5	6	3.3977	0.21257	15	51	3.6710	0.066375
4.6	6	2.1125	0.20831	16	58	6.3888	0.062259
4.7	6	1.3008	0.20421	17	65	4.1060	0.058622
4.8	7	7.9333	0.20027	18	73	9.7409	0.055385
4.9	7	4.7918	0.19647	19	81	8.5273	0.052487
5.0	7	2.8665	0.19281	20	89	2.7536	0.049875
5.1	7	1.6983	0.18928	25	138	3.0567	0.039936
5.2	8	9.9644	0.18587	30	198	4.9067	0.033296
5.3	8	5.7901	0.18258	40	350	3.6559	0.024984
5.4	8	3.3320	0.17940	50	545	1.0806	0.019992
5.5	8	1.8990	0.17632	60	784	1.2376	0.016662
5.6	8	1.0718	0.17335	70	1067	5.4230	0.014283
5.7	9	5.9904	0.17047	80	1393	9.0242	0.012498
5.8	9	3.3157	0.16769	90	1762	5.6750	0.011110
5.9	9	1.8175	0.16499	100	2174	1.3442	0.0099990
6.0	10	9.8659	0.16238	125	3396	3.7873	0.0079995
6.2	10	2.8232	0.15739	150	4889	4.0915	0.0066664
6.4	11	7.7689	0.15269	175	6653	1.6734	0.0057141
6.6	11	2.0558	0.14825	200	8689	2.5718	0.0049999
6.8	12	5.2310	0.14407	250	13575	3.1652	0.0039999
7.0	12	1.2798	0.14010	300	19547	7.4490	0.0033333
7.2	13	3.0106	0.13635	350	26604	3.3100	0.0028571
7.4	14	6.8092	0.13279	400	34747	2.7561	0.0025000
7.6	14	1.4807	0.12941	450	43976	4.2796	0.0022222
7.8	15	3.0954	0.12619	500	54290	1.2351	0.0020000

1.4 Inverse of the Normal Probability Distribution with Probability in Multiples of One-Half

This table was computed using the same method described in Section 1.2.

Consider a normal distribution with zero mean and unit variance divided, say, into 8 parts such that the probability of the normal variable being in any one of these parts is $\frac{1}{8}$. Then the boundaries, medians, and means for these parts are given in the following table:

Boundaries			Median	Mean
$X = -\infty$	to	$X = -1.1503494$	-1.5341205	-1.646828
$X = -1.1503494$	to	$X = -0.6744898$	-0.8871466	-0.895385
$X = -0.6744894$	to	$X = -0.3186394$	-0.4887764	-0.491349
$X = -0.3186394$	to	$X = 0$	-0.1573107	-0.157977
$X = 0$	to	$X = +0.3186394$	$+0.1573107$	$+0.157977$
$X = +0.3186394$	to	$X = +0.6744898$	$+0.4887764$	$+0.491349$
$X = +0.6744898$	to	$X = +1.1503494$	$+0.8871466$	$+0.895385$
$X = +1.1503494$	to	$X = +\infty$	$+1.5341205$	$+1.646828$

The upper boundary for the first entry is found by looking up $P = 1 - \frac{1}{8} = \frac{7}{8} = \frac{224}{256}$, and then taking X from the table. The next boundary is found by looking up $\frac{224}{256} - \frac{1}{8} = \frac{192}{256}$, etc. The median value for the first cell is found by looking up $P = 1 - (\frac{1}{2})(\frac{1}{8}) = \frac{15}{16} = \frac{240}{256}$, and then stepping back $\frac{1}{8}$ from this value for each succeeding cell. The mean value of each cell is given by $[Z \text{ (lower limit)} - Z \text{ (upper limit)}]8$. For example, the first cell in the above example has mean $[0 - 0.2058535]8 = -1.646828$. If the distribution is divided into 2^k cells, then the 8 in the formula for mean value of a cell is replaced by 2^k.

Inverse of the Normal Probability Distribution
with Probability in Multiples of One-Half

$$P(X) = \Pr\{N(0, 1)\text{r.v.} \leq X\}; \ Q = 1 - P; \ Z(X) = \text{density of } N(0, 1)\text{r.v.}$$

P	X	Z	Q	P	X	Z	Q
128/256	0.00000 00	0.39894 23	128/256	160/256	0.31863 94	0.37919 52	96/256
129/256	0.00979 17	0.39892 32	127/256	161/256	0.32895 79	0.37793 04	95/256
130/256	0.01958 43	0.39886 58	126/256	162/256	0.33931 16	0.37662 52	94/256
131/256	0.02937 88	0.39877 02	125/256	163/256	0.34970 18	0.37527 95	93/256
132/256	0.03917 61	0.39863 63	124/256	164/256	0.36012 99	0.37389 31	92/256
133/256	0.04897 72	0.39846 41	123/256	165/256	0.37059 73	0.37246 59	91/256
134/256	0.05878 29	0.39825 36	122/256	166/256	0.38110 55	0.37099 78	90/256
135/256	0.06859 44	0.39800 48	121/256	167/256	0.39165 59	0.36948 85	89/256
136/256	0.07841 24	0.39771 77	120/256	168/256	0.40225 01	0.36793 79	88/256
137/256	0.08823 80	0.39739 22	119/256	169/256	0.41288 96	0.36634 59	87/256
138/256	0.09807 22	0.39702 83	118/256	170/256	0.42357 61	0.36471 21	86/256
139/256	0.10791 58	0.39662 60	117/256	171/256	0.43431 12	0.36303 66	85/256
140/256	0.11776 99	0.39618 52	116/256	172/256	0.44509 65	0.36131 90	84/256
141/256	0.12763 54	0.39570 59	115/256	173/256	0.45593 39	0.35955 92	83/256
142/256	0.13751 34	0.39518 81	114/256	174/256	0.46682 51	0.35775 70	82/256
143/256	0.14740 48	0.39463 16	113/256	175/256	0.47777 20	0.35591 21	81/256
144/256	0.15731 07	0.39403 65	112/256	176/256	0.48877 64	0.35402 43	80/256
145/256	0.16723 20	0.39340 26	111/256	177/256	0.49984 03	0.35209 34	79/256
146/256	0.17716 98	0.39272 99	110/256	178/256	0.51096 58	0.35011 92	78/256
147/256	0.18712 52	0.39201 84	109/256	179/256	0.52215 49	0.34810 14	77/256
148/256	0.19709 91	0.39126 80	108/256	180/256	0.53340 97	0.34603 98	76/256
149/256	0.20709 27	0.39047 86	107/256	181/256	0.54473 25	0.34393 41	75/256
150/256	0.21710 69	0.38965 01	106/256	182/256	0.55612 56	0.34178 40	74/256
151/256	0.22714 31	0.38878 24	105/256	183/256	0.56759 13	0.33958 92	73/256
152/256	0.23720 21	0.38787 55	104/256	184/256	0.57913 22	0.33734 96	72/256
153/256	0.24728 52	0.38692 92	103/256	185/256	0.59075 07	0.33506 47	71/256
154/256	0.25739 35	0.38594 35	102/256	186/256	0.60244 95	0.33273 42	70/256
155/256	0.26752 82	0.38491 83	101/256	187/256	0.61423 13	0.33035 79	69/256
156/256	0.27769 04	0.38385 34	100/256	188/256	0.62609 90	0.32793 54	68/256
157/256	0.28788 14	0.38274 88	99/256	189/256	0.63805 56	0.32546 64	67/256
158/256	0.29810 24	0.38160 43	98/256	190/256	0.65010 41	0.32295 05	66/256
159/256	0.30835 46	0.38041 98	97/256	191/256	0.66224 77	0.32038 74	65/256

Inverse of the Normal Probability Distribution
with Probability in Multiples of One-Half (cont.)

P	X	Z	Q	P	X	Z	Q
192/256	0.67448 98	0.31777 66	64/256	228/256	1.22985 88	0.18726 79	28/256
193/256	0.68683 37	0.31511 78	63/256	229/256	1.25099 17	0.18242 27	27/256
194/256	0.69928 33	0.31241 05	62/256	230/256	1.27269 86	0.17749 38	26/256
195/256	0.71184 22	0.30965 45	61/256	231/256	1.29502 24	0.17247 90	25/256
196/256	0.72451 44	0.30684 91	60/256	232/256	1.31801 09	0.16737 56	24/256
197/256	0.73730 40	0.30399 41	59/256	233/256	1.34171 78	0.16218 11	23/256
198/256	0.75021 54	0.30108 88	58/256	234/256	1.36620 38	0.15689 24	22/256
199/256	0.76325 30	0.29813 28	57/256	235/256	1.39153 75	0.15150 65	21/256
200/256	0.77642 18	0.29512 57	56/256	236/256	1.41779 71	0.14601 98	20/256
201/256	0.78972 65	0.29206 69	55/256	237/256	1.44507 26	0.14042 86	19/256
202/256	0.80317 26	0.28895 58	54/256	238/256	1.47346 76	0.13472 87	18/256
203/256	0.81676 54	0.28579 19	53/256	239/256	1.50310 29	0.12891 55	17/256
204/256	0.83051 09	0.28257 46	52/256	240/256	1.53412 05	0.12298 39	16/256
205/256	0.84441 51	0.27930 33	51/256	241/256	1.56668 86	0.11692 82	15/256
206/256	0.85848 45	0.27597 74	50/256	242/256	1.60100 87	0.11074 19	14/256
207/256	0.87272 59	0.27259 62	49/256	243/256	1.63732 54	0.10441 77	13/256
208/256	0.88714 66	0.26915 90	48/256	244/256	1.67593 97	0.09794 73	12/256
209/256	0.90175 41	0.26566 51	47/256	245/256	1.71722 81	0.09132 10	11/256
210/256	0.91655 67	0.26211 38	46/256	246/256	1.76167 04	0.08452 74	10/256
211/256	0.93156 28	0.25850 42	45/256	247/256	1.80989 22	0.07755 30	9/256
212/256	0.94678 18	0.25483 57	44/256	248/256	1.86273 19	0.07038 16	8/256
213/256	0.96222 32	0.25110 72	43/256	249/256	1.92135 08	0.06299 29	7/256
214/256	0.97789 75	0.24731 80	42/256	250/256	1.98742 79	0.05536 14	6/256
215/256	0.99381 59	0.24346 71	41/256	251/256	2.06352 79	0.04745 32	5/256
216/256	1.00999 02	0.23955 35	40/256	252/256	2.15387 47	0.03922 16	4/256
217/256	1.02643 31	0.23557 62	39/256	253/256	2.26622 68	0.03059 77	3/256
218/256	1.04315 83	0.23153 41	38/256	254/256	2.41755 90	0.02146 71	2/256
219/256	1.06018 05	0.22742 61	37/256	255/256	2.66006 75	0.01159 81	1/256
220/256	1.07751 56	0.22325 10	36/256	511/512	2.88563 49	0.00620 51	1/512
221/256	1.09518 07	0.21900 76	35/256	1023/1024	3.09726 91	0.00329 46	1/1024
222/256	1.11319 43	0.21469 45	34/256	2047/2048	3.29719 34	0.00173 86	1/2048
223/256	1.13157 66	0.21031 03	33/256	4095/4096	3.48710 41	0.00091 29	1/4096
224/256	1.15034 94	0.20585 35	32/256				
225/256	1.16953 66	0.20132 26	31/256				
226/256	1.18916 44	0.19671 60	30/256				
227/256	1.20926 12	0.19203 17	29/256				

1.5 Operating Characteristics for the Test of a Mean for a Normal Distribution with Standard Deviation Known

The quantity tabulated is λ, where for one-sided tests

$$\frac{1}{\sqrt{2\pi}} \int_{-\infty}^{z_\alpha - \lambda} \exp\left(-t^2/2\right) dt = 1 - \beta$$

and where z_α is defined by

$$\frac{1}{\sqrt{2\pi}} \int_{-\infty}^{z_\alpha} \exp\left(-t^2/2\right) dt = \alpha.$$

For two-sided tests, λ is defined by

$$\frac{1}{\sqrt{2\pi}} \int_{-z_\alpha - \lambda}^{z_\alpha - \lambda} \exp\left(-t^2/2\right) dt = 1 - \beta,$$

where z_α is a critical value of the normal distribution chosen so that

$$\frac{1}{\sqrt{2\pi}} \int_{-z_\alpha}^{z_\alpha} \exp\left(-t^2/2\right) dt = \alpha.$$

For example, to test the hypothesis $H\colon \mu \leq \mu_0$ against the alternative $\mu > \mu_0$ where the standard deviation σ is known and the random variable is assumed to be normally distributed, one rejects H if

$$\frac{\bar{x} - \mu_0}{\sigma} \sqrt{n} \geq z_\alpha, \qquad \text{where } \bar{x} = \sum \frac{x_i}{n},$$

and the probability of accepting the hypothesis H if indeed $\mu = \mu_1$ is given by $1 - \beta$, where

$$\lambda = \frac{\mu_1 - \mu_0}{\sigma} \sqrt{n}.$$

Note also that the quantities tabulated here correspond to $f = \infty$ if $\delta = \lambda$ in the graphs of the operating characteristic of Student's t-test (Section 2.2). The tables given here may be used to determine n, the sample size needed for tests where σ is known. However, special graphs for determining sample size are given in Sections 1.6 and 1.7 for two special cases.

1.5

Operating Characteristics for the Test of a Mean for a Normal Distribution with Standard Deviation Known

$$\lambda = (\mu_1 - \mu_0)\sqrt{n}/\sigma; \text{ oc} = \text{operating characteristic}$$

5% oc	One-sided λ	5% oc	Two-Sided λ
0.95	0.000	0.95	0.000
0.90	0.363	0.90	0.652
0.80	0.803	0.80	1.114
0.75	0.970	0.75	1.283
0.70	1.120	0.70	1.435
0.60	1.392	0.60	1.706
0.50	1.645	0.50	1.960
0.40	1.898	0.40	2.213
0.30	2.169	0.30	2.484
0.25	2.319	0.25	2.634
0.15	2.681	0.15	2.996
0.10	2.926	0.10	3.242
0.05	3.290	0.05	3.605
0.01	3.971	0.01	4.286
0.001	4.735	0.001	5.050

1% oc	One-Sided λ	1% oc	Two-Sided λ
0.99	0.000	0.99	0.000
0.90	1.045	0.90	1.294
0.80	1.485	0.80	1.734
0.75	1.652	0.75	1.901
0.70	1.802	0.70	2.052
0.60	2.073	0.60	2.323
0.50	2.326	0.50	2.576
0.40	2.580	0.40	2.829
0.30	2.851	0.30	3.100
0.25	3.001	0.25	3.250
0.15	3.363	0.15	3.612
0.10	3.608	0.10	3.857
0.05	3.971	0.05	4.221
0.01	4.653	0.01	4.902
0.001	5.417	0.001	5.666

1.5

1.6 Graphs of Sample Sizes Needed for a Test on the Mean of a Normal Distribution with Known Standard Deviation

The graphs given here show the relationship of $\Delta = (\mu_1 - \mu_0)/\sigma$ to n for various values of α and β where $\Delta = \lambda/\sqrt{n}$, and the other quantities are all defined as in Section 1.5. That is, these graphs are set up to enable one to read the sample size needed to achieve given values of α and β when testing hypotheses about a single mean.

Graphs of Sample Sizes Needed for a Test on the Mean of a Normal Distribution with Known Standard Deviation

$$\alpha = 0.05 \text{ (one-sided)}$$

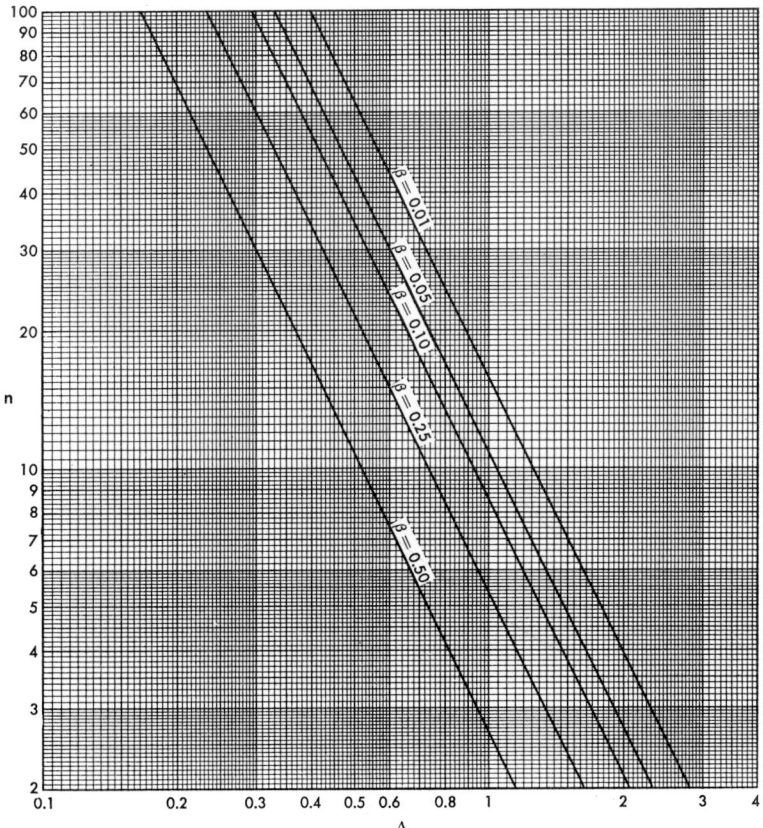

Graphs of Sample Sizes Needed for a Test on the Mean of a Normal Distribution with Known Standard Deviation

$$\alpha = 0.01 \text{ (one-sided)}$$

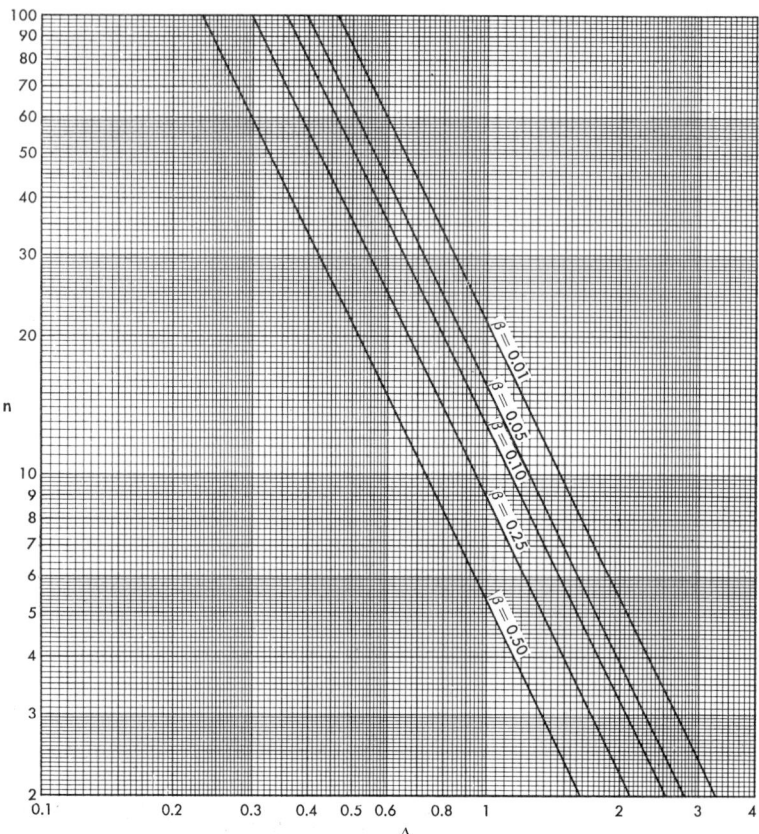

Graphs of Sample Sizes Needed for a Test on the Mean of a Normal Distribution with Known Standard Deviation

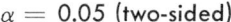

$$\alpha = 0.05 \ (\text{two-sided})$$

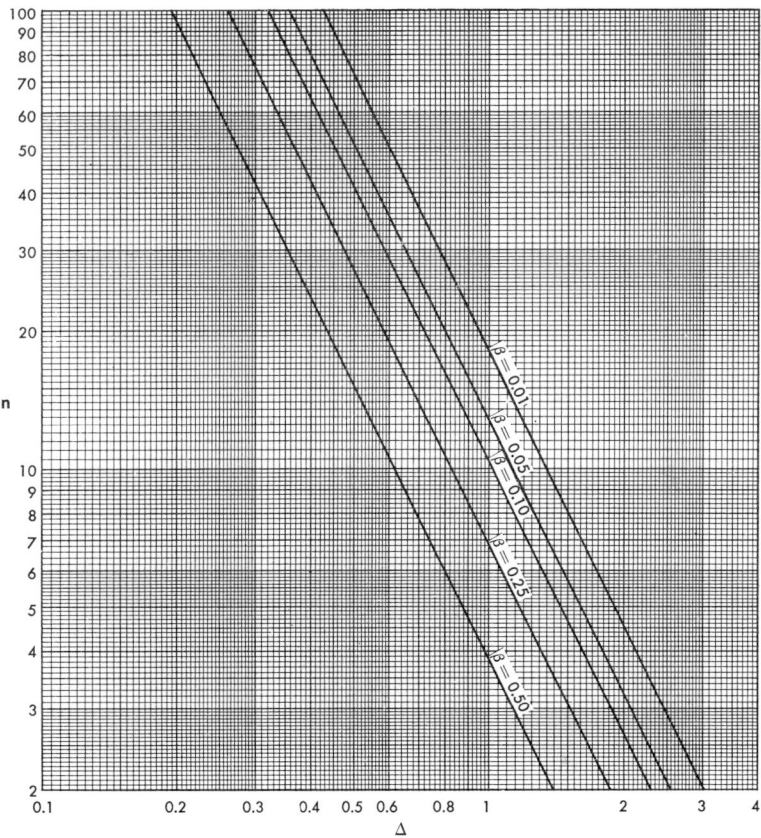

Graphs of Sample Sizes Needed for a Test on the Mean of a Normal Distribution with Known Standard Deviation

$$\alpha = 0.01 \text{ (two-sided)}$$

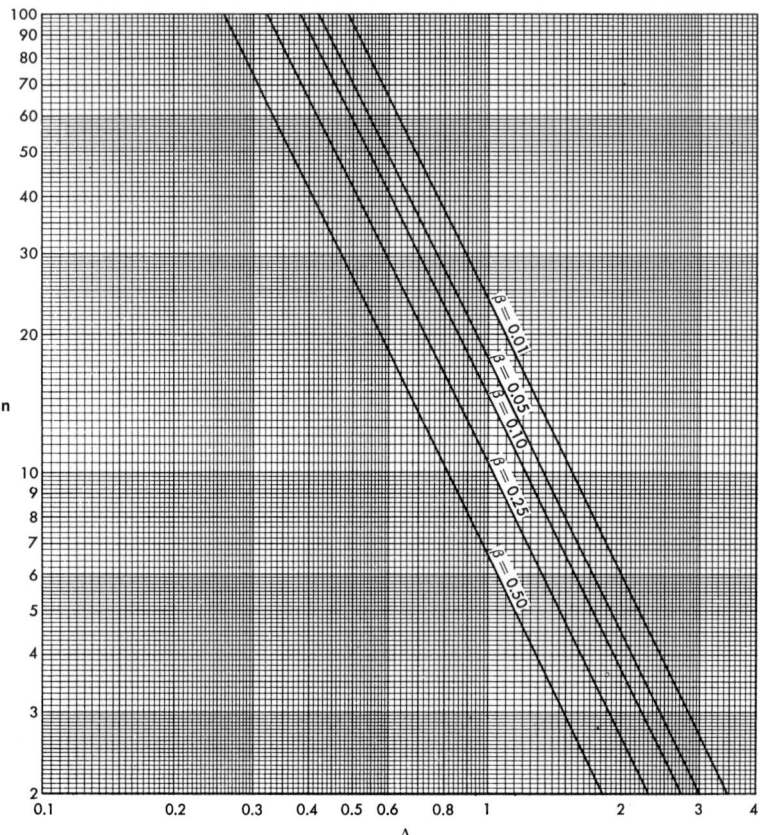

1.7 Graphs of Sample Sizes Needed for a Test Comparing the Means of Two Normal Distributions with Known and Equal Standard Deviations

The graphs given here show the relationship of $\Delta = (\mu_1 - \mu_2)/\sigma$ to n for various values of α and β. These are useful for determining the number of observations required to achieve given values of α and β when testing the hypothesis $H: \mu_1 = \mu_2$ against $\mu_1 > \mu_2$ for one-sided tests, and against $\mu_1 \neq \mu_2$ for two-sided tests. The probability of rejecting H if $(\mu_1 - \mu_2)/\sigma = \Delta$ is equal to β, provided samples of n observations are taken on each of the two populations, and the population standard deviations are known and are equal. The test statistic is

$$z = \frac{(\bar{x}_1 - \bar{x}_2)\sqrt{n}}{\sigma\sqrt{2}}.$$

The values for the graphs were computed from the tables in Section 1.5 by putting $\Delta = \lambda\sqrt{2}/\sqrt{n}$.

Graphs of Sample Sizes Needed for a Test Comparing the Means of Two Normal Distributions with Known and Equal Standard Deviations

$$\alpha = 0.05 \text{ (one-sided)}$$

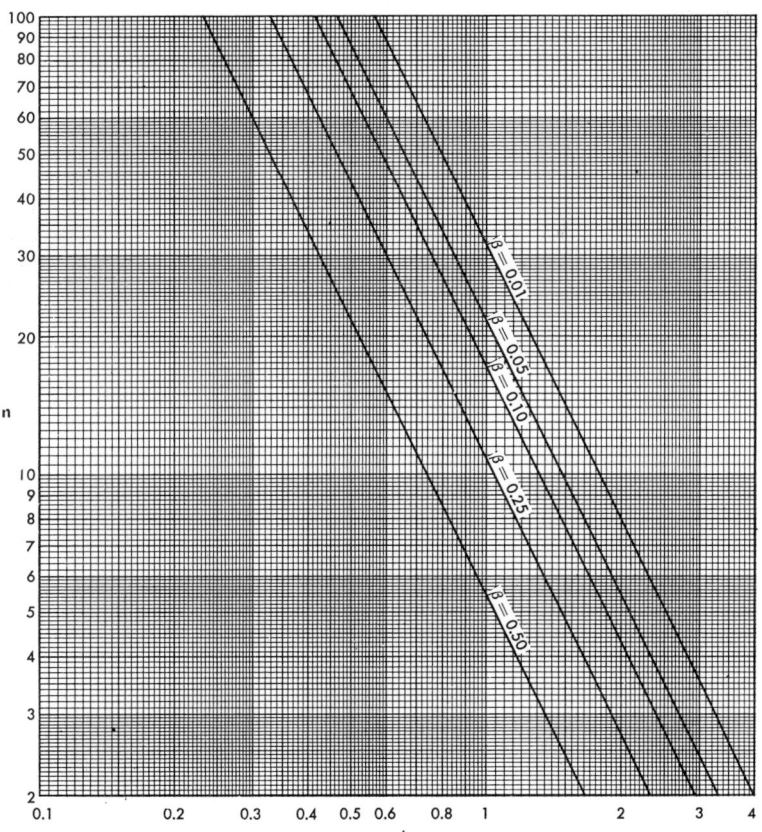

Graphs of Sample Sizes Needed for a Test Comparing the Means of Two Normal Distributions with Known and Equal Standard Deviations

$\alpha = 0.01$ (one-sided)

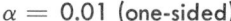

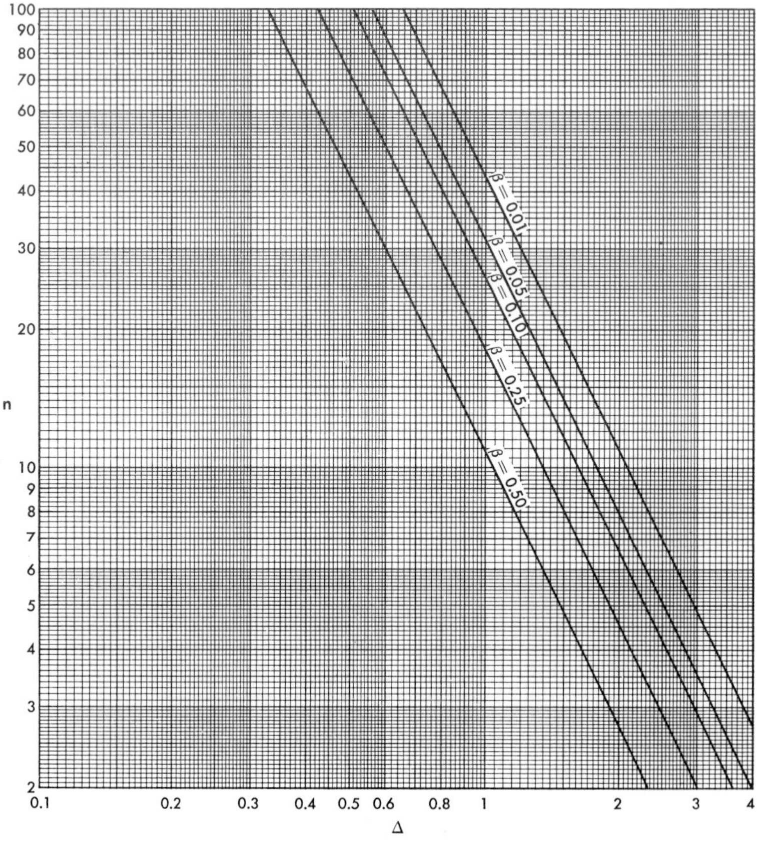

Graphs of Sample Sizes Needed for a Test Comparing the Means of Two Normal Distributions with Known and Equal Standard Deviations

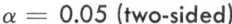

$\alpha = 0.05$ (two-sided)

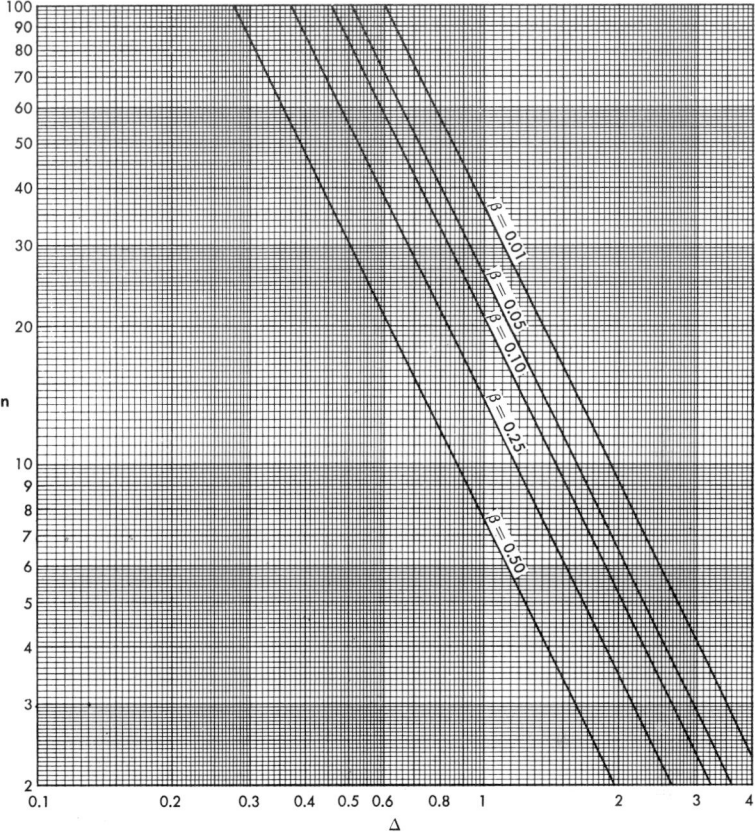

Graphs of Sample Sizes Needed for a Test Comparing the Means of Two Normal Distributions with Known and Equal Standard Deviations

$$\alpha = 0.01 \text{ (two-sided)}$$

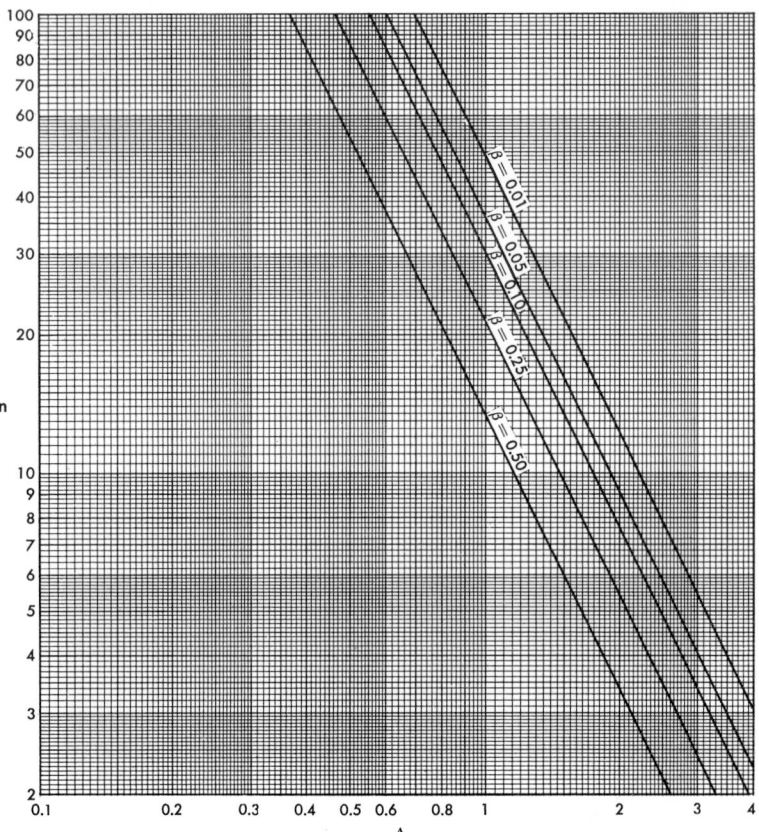

2. STUDENT'S t-DISTRIBUTION

2.1 Critical Values for Student's t-Distribution

The values given in the table are the solutions of the following equation for t:

$$\frac{\Gamma\left(\frac{f+1}{2}\right)}{\sqrt{\pi f}\,\Gamma(f/2)} \int_{-\infty}^{t} \left(1 + \frac{x^2}{f}\right)^{-(f+1)/2} dx = \gamma,$$

where $\gamma = 0.75, 0.90, 0.95, 0.975, 0.99,$ and 0.995. The values for $f = 1(1)30$ were obtained by putting $\delta = 0$ in the formulas given for the non-central t-distribution for Table 5.1. For the other values of f, the Cornish-Fisher formulas were used as given in [65], p. 216.

Federighi [63] gives a table for $\gamma = 0.75, 0.90, 0.95, 0.975, 0.99, 0.995,$ 0.9975, 0.999, 0.9995, 0.99975, 0.9999, 0.99995, 0.999975, 0.99999, 0.999995, 0.9999975, 0.999999, 0.9999995, 0.99999975, and 0.9999999 to three decimal places by $f = 1(1)30(5)60(10)100, 200, 500, 1000, 2000,$ and 10000. See [93] for a direct tabulation of the distribution function of Student's t. Wallace [235] gives bounds on normal approximations to Student's t-distribution.

Critical Values for Student's *t*-Distribution

Pr{Student's $t \leq$ tabled value} $= \gamma$

f	0.75	0.90	0.95	0.975	0.99	0.995
1	1.0000	3.0777	6.3138	12.7062	31.8207	63.6574
2	0.8165	1.8856	2.9200	4.3027	6.9646	9.9248
3	0.7649	1.6377	2.3534	3.1824	4.5407	5.8409
4	0.7407	1.5332	2.1318	2.7764	3.7469	4.6041
5	0.7267	1.4759	2.0150	2.5706	3.3649	4.0322
6	0.7176	1.4398	1.9432	2.4469	3.1427	3.7074
7	0.7111	1.4149	1.8946	2.3646	2.9980	3.4995
8	0.7064	1.3968	1.8595	2.3060	2.8965	3.3554
9	0.7027	1.3830	1.8331	2.2622	2.8214	3.2498
10	0.6998	1.3722	1.8125	2.2281	2.7638	3.1693
11	0.6974	1.3634	1.7959	2.2010	2.7181	3.1058
12	0.6955	1.3562	1.7823	2.1788	2.6810	3.0545
13	0.6938	1.3502	1.7709	2.1604	2.6503	3.0123
14	0.6924	1.3450	1.7613	2.1448	2.6245	2.9768
15	0.6912	1.3406	1.7531	2.1315	2.6025	2.9467
16	0.6901	1.3368	1.7459	2.1199	2.5835	2.9208
17	0.6892	1.3334	1.7396	2.1098	2.5669	2.8982
18	0.6884	1.3304	1.7341	2.1009	2.5524	2.8784
19	0.6876	1.3277	1.7291	2.0930	2.5395	2.8609
20	0.6870	1.3253	1.7247	2.0860	2.5280	2.8453
21	0.6864	1.3232	1.7207	2.0796	2.5177	2.8314
22	0.6858	1.3212	1.7171	2.0739	2.5083	2.8188
23	0.6853	1.3195	1.7139	2.0687	2.4999	2.8073
24	0.6848	1.3178	1.7109	2.0639	2.4922	2.7969
25	0.6844	1.3163	1.7081	2.0595	2.4851	2.7874
26	0.6840	1.3150	1.7056	2.0555	2.4786	2.7787
27	0.6837	1.3137	1.7033	2.0518	2.4727	2.7707
28	0.6834	1.3125	1.7011	2.0484	2.4671	2.7633
29	0.6830	1.3114	1.6991	2.0452	2.4620	2.7564
30	0.6828	1.3104	1.6973	2.0423	2.4573	2.7500
31	0.6825	1.3095	1.6955	2.0395	2.4528	2.7440
32	0.6822	1.3086	1.6939	2.0369	2.4487	2.7385
33	0.6820	1.3077	1.6924	2.0345	2.4448	2.7333
34	0.6818	1.3070	1.6909	2.0322	2.4411	2.7284
35	0.6816	1.3062	1.6896	2.0301	2.4377	2.7238
36	0.6814	1.3055	1.6883	2.0281	2.4345	2.7195
37	0.6812	1.3049	1.6871	2.0262	2.4314	2.7154
38	0.6810	1.3042	1.6860	2.0244	2.4286	2.7116
39	0.6808	1.3036	1.6849	2.0227	2.4258	2.7079
40	0.6807	1.3031	1.6839	2.0211	2.4233	2.7045
41	0.6805	1.3025	1.6829	2.0195	2.4208	2.7012
42	0.6804	1.3020	1.6820	2.0181	2.4185	2.6981
43	0.6802	1.3016	1.6811	2.0167	2.4163	2.6951
44	0.6801	1.3011	1.6802	2.0154	2.4141	2.6923
45	0.6800	1.3006	1.6794	2.0141	2.4121	2.6896

Critical Values for Student's *t*-Distribution (*cont.*)

f	0.75	0.90	0.95	0.975	0.99	0.995
46	0.6799	1.3002	1.6787	2.0129	2.4102	2.6870
47	0.6797	1.2998	1.6779	2.0117	2.4083	2.6846
48	0.6796	1.2994	1.6772	2.0106	2.4066	2.6822
49	0.6795	1.2991	1.6766	2.0096	2.4049	2.6800
50	0.6794	1.2987	1.6759	2.0086	2.4033	2.6778
51	0.6793	1.2984	1.6753	2.0076	2.4017	2.6757
52	0.6792	1.2980	1.6747	2.0066	2.4002	2.6737
53	0.6791	1.2977	1.6741	2.0057	2.3988	2.6718
54	0.6791	1.2974	1.6736	2.0049	2.3974	2.6700
55	0.6790	1.2971	1.6730	2.0040	2.3961	2.6682
56	0.6789	1.2969	1.6725	2.0032	2.3948	2.6665
57	0.6788	1.2966	1.6720	2.0025	2.3936	2.6649
58	0.6787	1.2963	1.6716	2.0017	2.3924	2.6633
59	0.6787	1.2961	1.6711	2.0010	2.3912	2.6618
60	0.6786	1.2958	1.6706	2.0003	2.3901	2.6603
61	0.6785	1.2956	1.6702	1.9996	2.3890	2.6589
62	0.6785	1.2954	1.6698	1.9990	2.3880	2.6575
63	0.6784	1.2951	1.6694	1.9983	2.3870	2.6561
64	0.6783	1.2949	1.6690	1.9977	2.3860	2.6549
65	0.6783	1.2947	1.6686	1.9971	2.3851	2.6536
66	0.6782	1.2945	1.6683	1.9966	2.3842	2.6524
67	0.6782	1.2943	1.6679	1.9960	2.3833	2.6512
68	0.6781	1.2941	1.6676	1.9955	2.3824	2.6501
69	0.6781	1.2939	1.6672	1.9949	2.3816	2.6490
70	0.6780	1.2938	1.6669	1.9944	2.3808	2.6479
71	0.6780	1.2936	1.6666	1.9939	2.3800	2.6469
72	0.6779	1.2934	1.6663	1.9935	2.3793	2.6459
73	0.6779	1.2933	1.6660	1.9930	2.3785	2.6449
74	0.6778	1.2931	1.6657	1.9925	2.3778	2.6439
75	0.6778	1.2929	1.6654	1.9921	2.3771	2.6430
76	0.6777	1.2928	1.6652	1.9917	2.3764	2.6421
77	0.6777	1.2926	1.6649	1.9913	2.3758	2.6412
78	0.6776	1.2925	1.6646	1.9908	2.3751	2.6403
79	0.6776	1.2924	1.6644	1.9905	2.3745	2.6395
80	0.6776	1.2922	1.6641	1.9901	2.3739	2.6387
81	0.6775	1.2921	1.6639	1.9897	2.3733	2.6379
82	0.6775	1.2920	1.6636	1.9893	2.3727	2.6371
83	0.6775	1.2918	1.6634	1.9890	2.3721	2.6364
84	0.6774	1.2917	1.6632	1.9886	2.3716	2.6356
85	0.6774	1.2916	1.6630	1.9883	2.3710	2.6349
86	0.6774	1.2915	1.6628	1.9879	2.3705	2.6342
87	0.6773	1.2914	1.6626	1.9876	2.3700	2.6335
88	0.6773	1.2912	1.6624	1.9873	2.3695	2.6329
89	0.6773	1.2911	1.6622	1.9870	2.3690	2.6322
90	0.6772	1.2910	1.6620	1.9867	2.3685	2.6316

2.1.

Critical Values for Student's *t*-Distribution (*cont.*)

f	0.75	0.90	0.95	0.975	0.99	0.995
91	0.6772	1.2909	1.6618	1.9864	2.3680	2.6309
92	0.6772	1.2908	1.6616	1.9861	2.3676	2.6303
93	0.6771	1.2907	1.6614	1.9858	2.3671	2.6297
94	0.6771	1.2906	1.6612	1.9855	2.3667	2.6291
95	0.6771	1.2905	1.6611	1.9853	2.3662	2.6286
96	0.6771	1.2904	1.6609	1.9850	2.3658	2.6280
97	0.6770	1.2903	1.6607	1.9847	2.3654	2.6275
98	0.6770	1.2902	1.6606	1.9845	2.3650	2.6269
99	0.6770	1.2902	1.6604	1.9842	2.3646	2.6264
100	0.6770	1.2901	1.6602	1.9840	2.3642	2.6259
102	0.6769	1.2899	1.6599	1.9835	2.3635	2.6249
104	0.6769	1.2897	1.6596	1.9830	2.3627	2.6239
106	0.6768	1.2896	1.6594	1.9826	2.3620	2.6230
108	0.6768	1.2894	1.6591	1.9822	2.3614	2.6221
110	0.6767	1.2893	1.6588	1.9818	2.3607	2.6213
112	0.6767	1.2892	1.6586	1.9814	2.3601	2.6204
114	0.6766	1.2890	1.6583	1.9810	2.3595	2.6196
116	0.6766	1.2889	1.6581	1.9806	2.3589	2.6189
118	0.6766	1.2888	1.6579	1.9803	2.3584	2.6181
120	0.6765	1.2886	1.6577	1.9799	2.3578	2.6174
122	0.6765	1.2885	1.6574	1.9796	2.3573	2.6167
124	0.6765	1.2884	1.6572	1.9793	2.3568	2.6161
126	0.6764	1.2883	1.6570	1.9790	2.3563	2.6154
128	0.6764	1.2882	1.6568	1.9787	2.3558	2.6148
130	0.6764	1.2881	1.6567	1.9784	2.3554	2.6142
132	0.6764	1.2880	1.6565	1.9781	2.3549	2.6136
134	0.6763	1.2879	1.6563	1.9778	2.3545	2.6130
136	0.6763	1.2878	1.6561	1.9776	2.3541	2.6125
138	0.6763	1.2877	1.6560	1.9773	2.3537	2.6119
140	0.6762	1.2876	1.6558	1.9771	2.3533	2.6114
142	0.6762	1.2875	1.6557	1.9768	2.3529	2.6109
144	0.6762	1.2875	1.6555	1.9766	2.3525	2.6104
146	0.6762	1.2874	1.6554	1.9763	2.3522	2.6099
148	0.6762	1.2873	1.6552	1.9761	2.3518	2.6095
150	0.6761	1.2872	1.6551	1.9759	2.3515	2.6090
200	0.6757	1.2858	1.6525	1.9719	2.3451	2.6006
300	0.6753	1.2844	1.6499	1.9679	2.3388	2.5923
400	0.6751	1.2837	1.6487	1.9659	2.3357	2.5882
500	0.6750	1.2832	1.6479	1.9647	2.3338	2.5857
600	0.6749	1.2830	1.6474	1.9639	2.3326	2.5840
700	0.6748	1.2828	1.6470	1.9634	2.3317	2.5829
800	0.6748	1.2826	1.6468	1.9629	2.3310	2.5820
900	0.6748	1.2825	1.6465	1.9626	2.3305	2.5813
1000	0.6747	1.2824	1.6464	1.9623	2.3301	2.5808
∞	0.6745	1.2816	1.6449	1.9600	2.3263	2.5758

2.2 Graphs of the Operating Characteristic of Student's t-Test

Given a sample $x_1, x_2, \ldots, x_n$ of n observations from a normal distribution with mean μ and standard deviation σ, the distribution of

$$t = \frac{\sqrt{n}\,(\bar{x} - \mu)}{s},$$

where

$$\bar{x} = \sum_{i=1}^{n} \frac{x_i}{n} \quad \text{and} \quad s^2 = \sum_{i=1}^{n} \frac{(x_i - \bar{x})^2}{n - 1},$$

is Student's t-distribution with $(n - 1)$ degrees of freedom. The distribution of $t(\delta) = [\sqrt{n}(\bar{x} - \mu) + \delta\sigma]/s$ is noncentral t with $(n - 1)$ degrees of freedom and noncentrality parameter δ.

The graphs given in this section give values of the probability Pr {noncentral t with f degrees of freedom $\leq \alpha$th critical value of Student's t-distribution with f degrees of freedom} $= \beta$. If $\delta = 0$, then $\beta = 1 - \alpha$. These graphs may be used for many different problems (see also Sections 5.1, 5.2, and 5.3), but they are especially designed to yield the operating characteristic of various tests based on Student's t-distribution.

There are also many other applications of these graphs to operating characteristics of t-tests [151]. Various approximations to the noncentral t-distribution have been given in [101], [230], and [138].

Graphs of the Operating Characteristic of Student's *t*-Test for $\alpha = 0.005$

$$\delta = (\mu - \mu_0)\sqrt{n}/\sigma; \; f = \text{degrees of freedom}$$

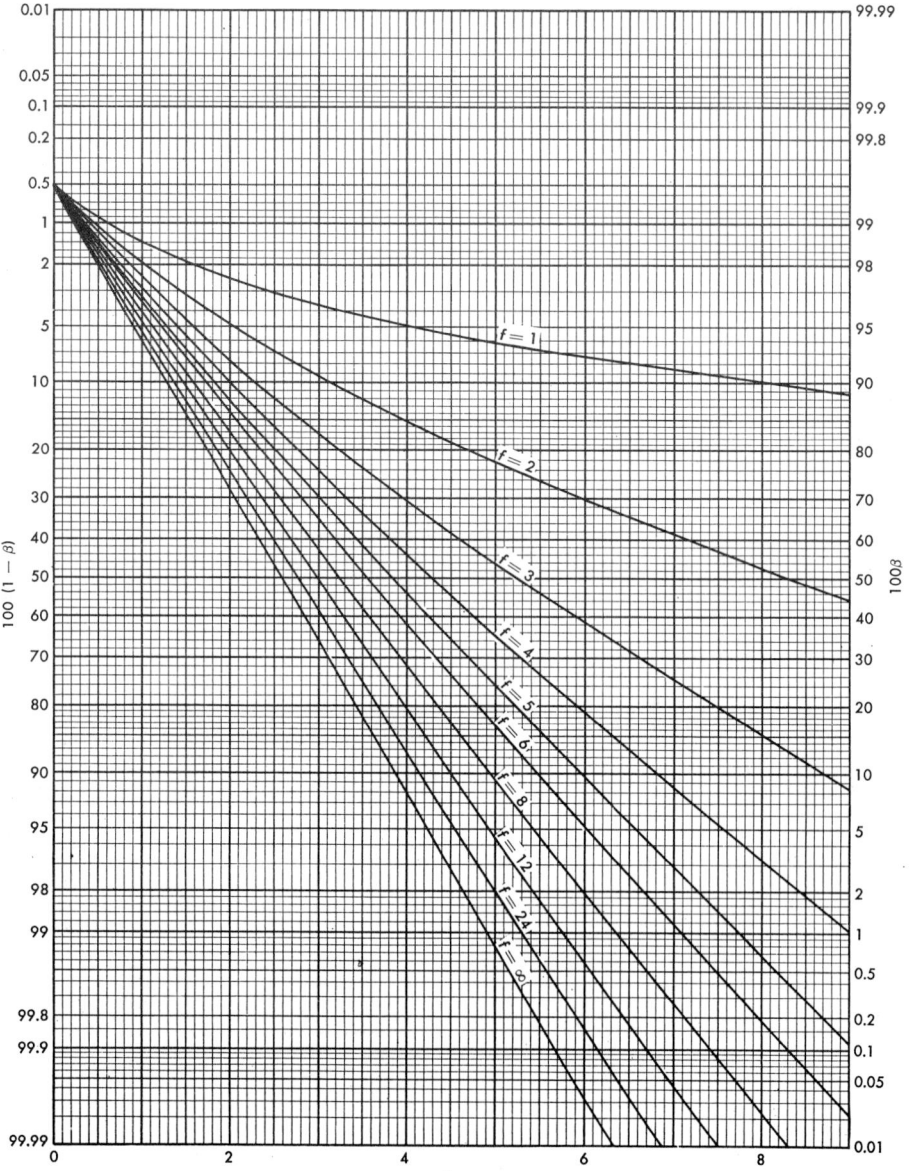

Graphs of the Operating Characteristic of Student's *t*-Test for $\alpha = 0.01$

$$\delta = (\mu - \mu_0)\sqrt{n}/\sigma; \quad f = \text{degrees of freedom}$$

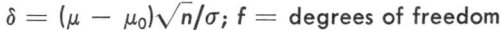

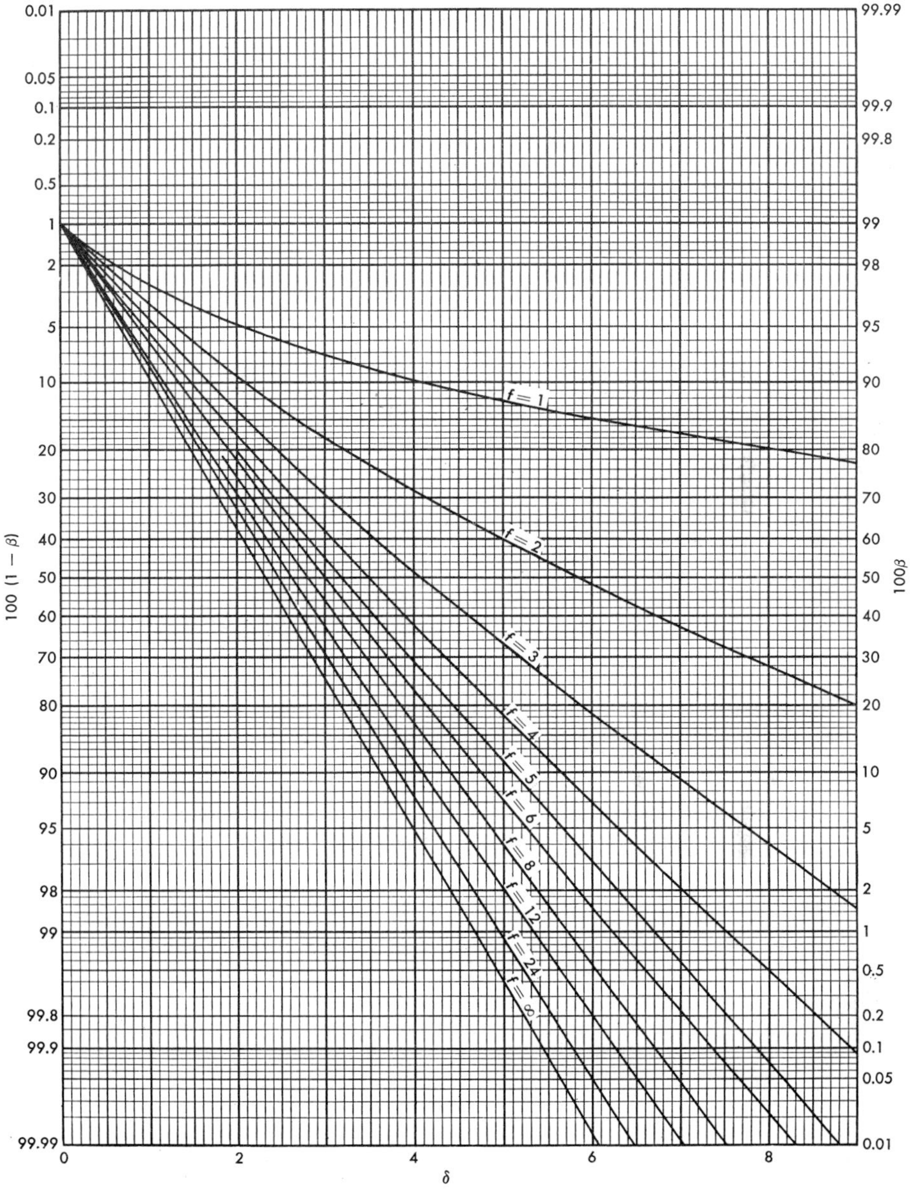

Graphs of the Operating Characteristic of Student's *t*-Test for $\alpha = 0.025$

$$\delta = (\mu - \mu_0)\sqrt{n}/\sigma; \; f = \text{degrees of freedom}$$

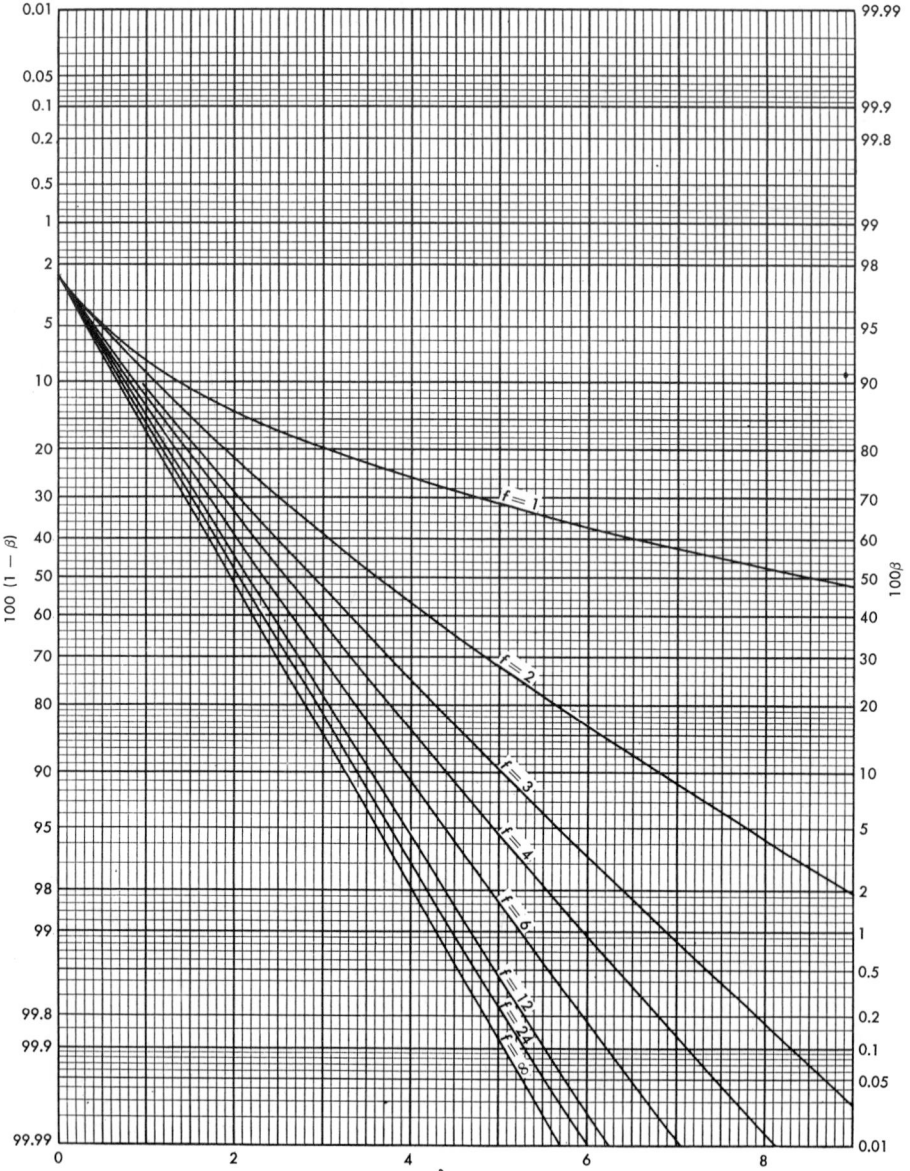

Graphs of the Operating Characteristic of Student's *t*-Test for $\alpha = 0.05$

$$\delta = (\mu - \mu_0)\sqrt{n}/\sigma; \ f = \text{degrees of freedom}$$

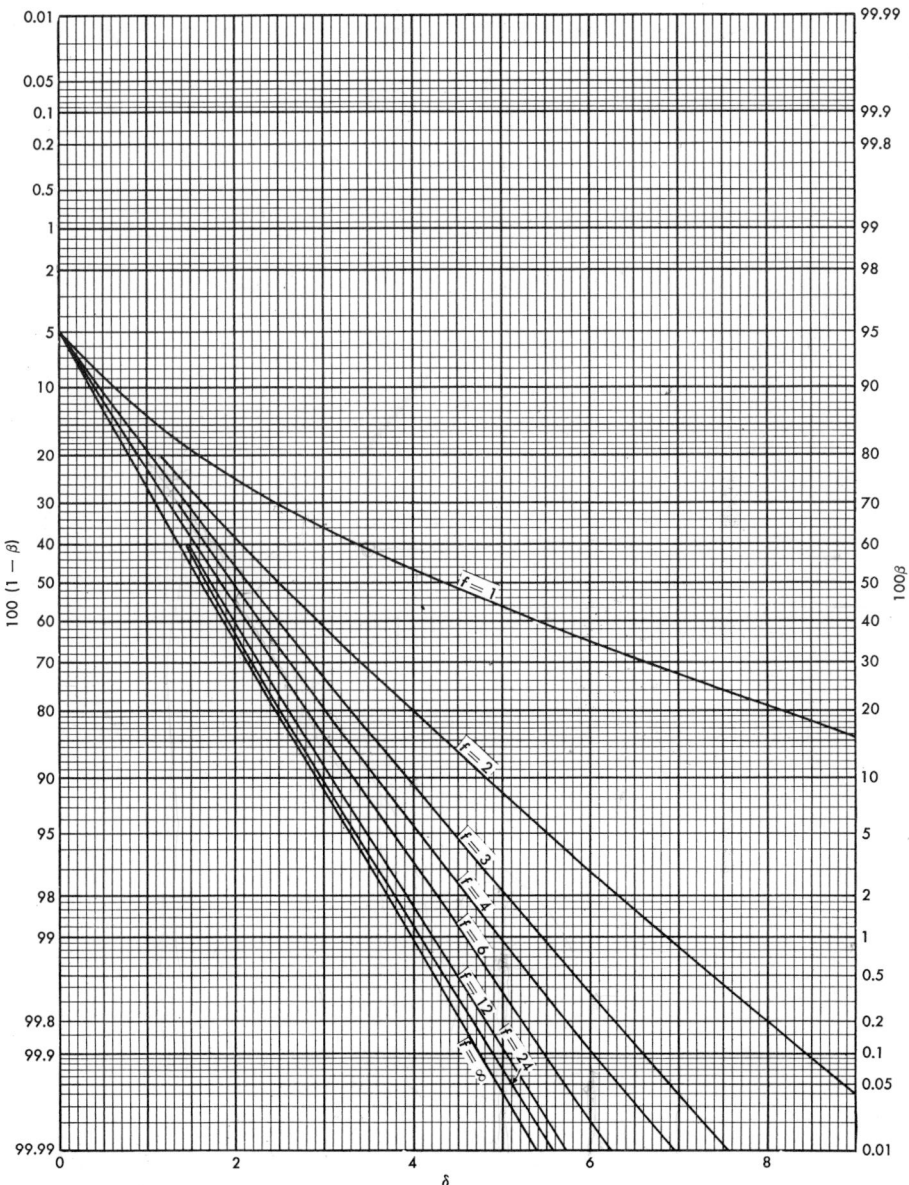

2.3 Graphs of Sample Sizes Needed for a Test on the Mean of a Normal Distribution with Unknown Standard Deviation

The graphs given here are derived from the graphs of Section 2.2 for the special problem of finding the sample size needed to achieve given values of α and β for a test on a single mean with unknown standard deviation.

To test the hypothesis $H: \mu = \mu_0$ against the alternative $\mu < \mu_0$, assuming that a sample of n observations from a normal distribution is at hand, first choose $\alpha = \Pr\{\text{rejecting the hypothesis when true}\}$. Next compute $t = \sqrt{n}(\bar{x} - \mu_0)/s$. Reject the hypothesis H if $t \le t_{\alpha,f}$, where $t_{\alpha,f}$ is the αth critical value of Student's t-distribution based on f degrees of freedom, where in this case $f = n - 1$. The probability of accepting the hypothesis H is given by the operating characteristic curve of Section 2.2, where $\delta = \sqrt{n}(\mu - \mu_0)/\sigma$. The graphs of this section are used to obtain sample sizes needed to control the values of α and β, and to expedite this, $\Delta = (\mu - \mu_0)/\sigma$ is plotted against n.

Suppose $\alpha = 0.01$ (one-sided test) and $\beta = 0.05$ for $\Delta = 1.0$. Entering the graph for a one-sided $\alpha = 0.01$ test, one finds that the necessary sample size to achieve $\beta = 0.05$ is $n = 19$. Davies [48], pp. 606–607, gives a table of values of n; for this problem he gives $n = 19$.

The charts given here have been computed separately for one-sided and two-sided tests. The two-sided test charts may be used to approximate one-sided test results, however, by halving α. The one-sided test charts may be used for approximating two-sided test results by doubling α.

Graphs of Sample Sizes Needed for a Test on the Mean of a Normal Distribution with Unknown Standard Deviation

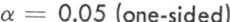

$\alpha = 0.05$ (one-sided)

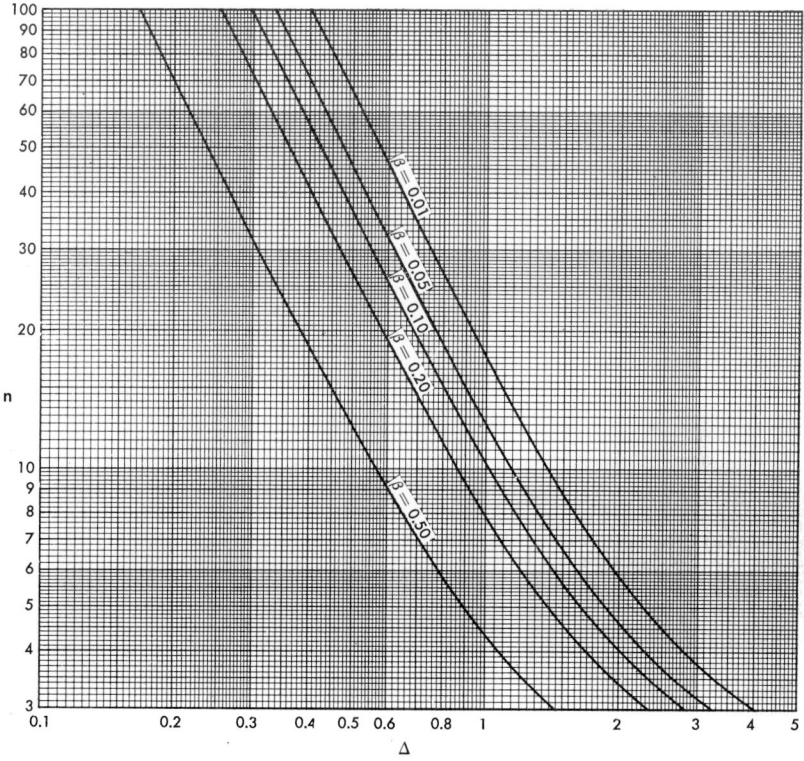

Graphs of Sample Sizes Needed for a Test on the Mean of a Normal Distribution with Unknown Standard Deviation

$\alpha = 0.01$ (one-sided)

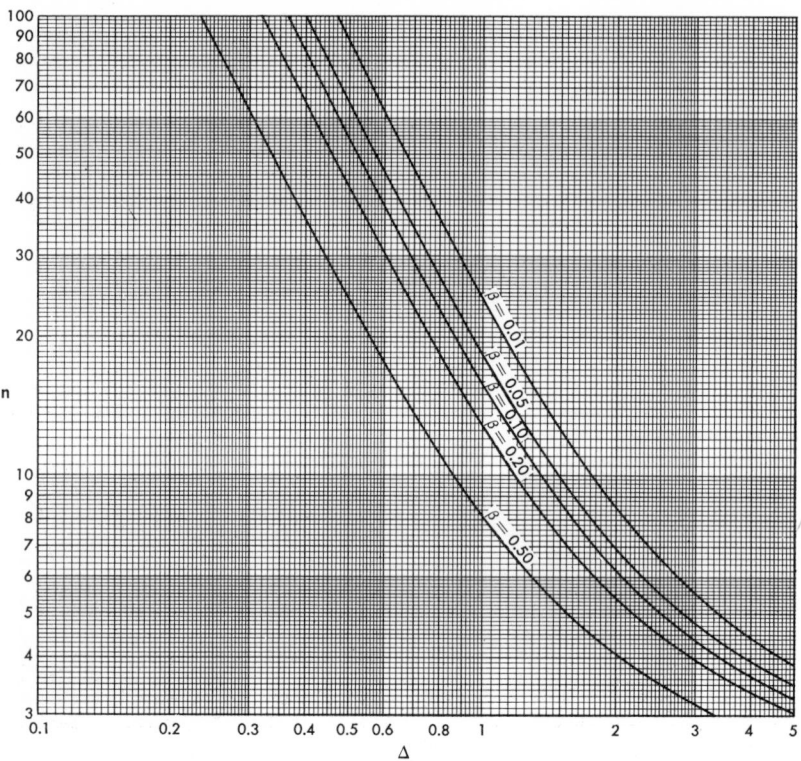

Graphs of Sample Sizes Needed for a Test on the Mean of a Normal Distribution with Unknown Standard Deviation

$$\alpha = 0.05 \text{ (two-sided)}$$

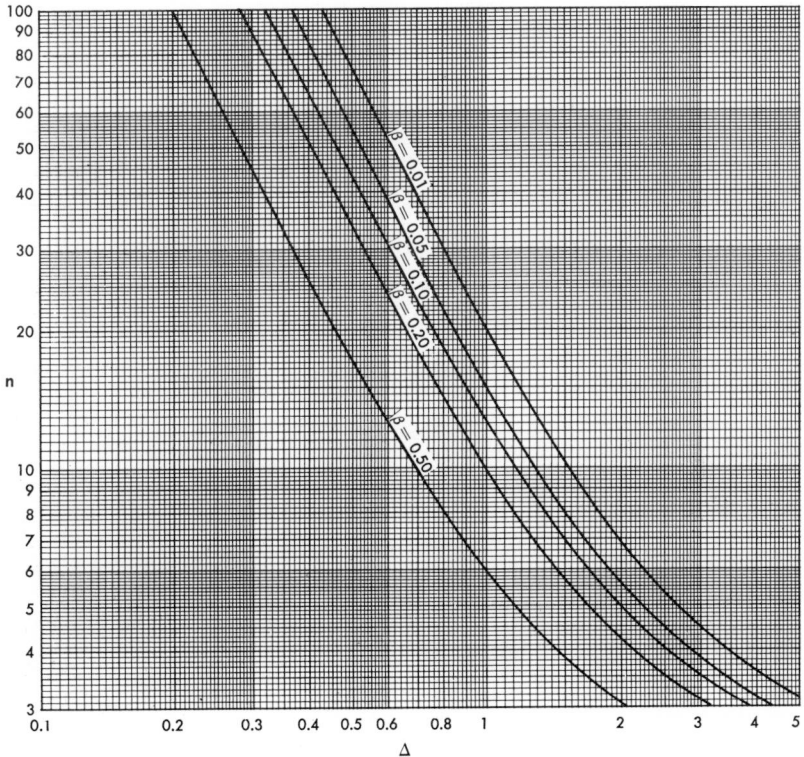

Graphs of Sample Sizes Needed for a Test on the Mean of a Normal Distribution with Unknown Standard Deviation

$\alpha = 0.01$ (two-sided)

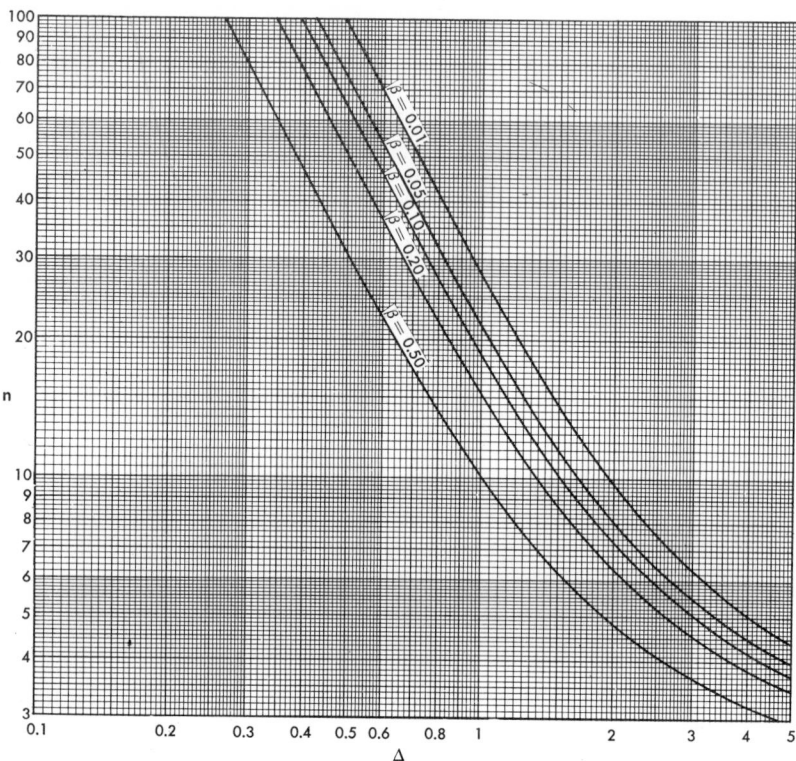

2.4 Graphs of Sample Sizes Needed for a Test Comparing the Means of Two Normal Distributions with Unknown, but Equal, Standard Deviations

The graphs given here are derived from the graphs of Section 2.2 for the special problem of finding the sample size needed to achieve given values of α and β for a test of the hypothesis which states the equality of two means $H: \mu_1 = \mu_2$, where there is a common but unknown variance. The statistic

$$t = \frac{\bar{x}_1 - \bar{x}_2}{s_p\sqrt{(1/n_1) + (1/n_2)}}$$

is used, where t has Student's t-distribution with $f = n_1 + n_2 - 2$ degrees of freedom and

$$s_p^2 = \frac{(n_1 - 1)s_1^2 + (n_2 - 1)s_2^2}{n_1 + n_2 - 2}.$$

In this case take

$$\delta = \frac{\mu_1 - \mu_2}{\sigma\sqrt{(1/n_1) + (1/n_2)}}$$

and then the Pr {accepting the hypothesis H} $= \beta$, which may be read from the graphs of Section 2.2.

Suppose now $n_1 = n_2$ and it is necessary to find n_1 such that $\Delta = (\mu_1 - \mu_2)/\sigma = 0.50$ when $\alpha = 0.05$ and $\beta = 0.10$. Note that the Δ given here is related to the δ of Section 2.2 as follows: $\Delta = \delta\sqrt{2}/\sqrt{n}$ where $n = n_1 = n_2$. Enter the graph with $\alpha = 0.05$ (one-sided test), $\Delta = 0.5$, and $\beta = 0.10$. The value of sample size needed is $n = 72$. Davies [48], pp. 609–610, gives a table of these n. For the example just considered he gives $n = 70$.

The charts given here have been separately computed for one-sided and two-sided tests. The two-sided test charts may be used to approximate one-sided test results, however, by halving α. The one-sided test charts may be used for approximating two-sided test results by doubling α.

Graphs of Sample Sizes Needed for a Test Comparing the Means of Two Normal Distributions with Unknown, but Equal, Standard Deviations

$$\alpha = 0.05 \text{ (one-sided)}$$

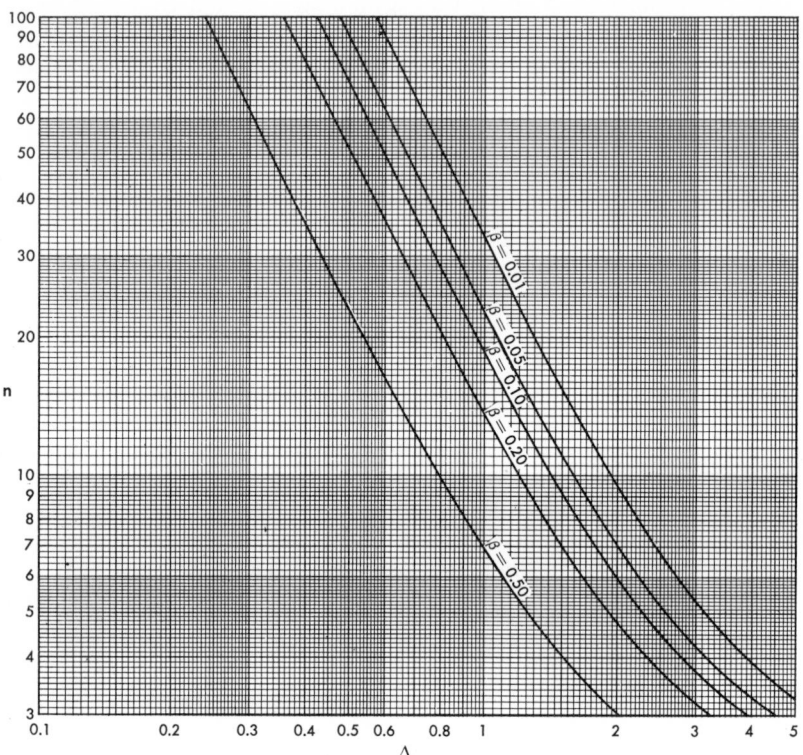

Graphs of Sample Sizes Needed for a Test Comparing the Means of Two Normal Distributions with Unknown, but Equal, Standard Deviations

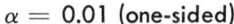

$\alpha = 0.01$ (one-sided)

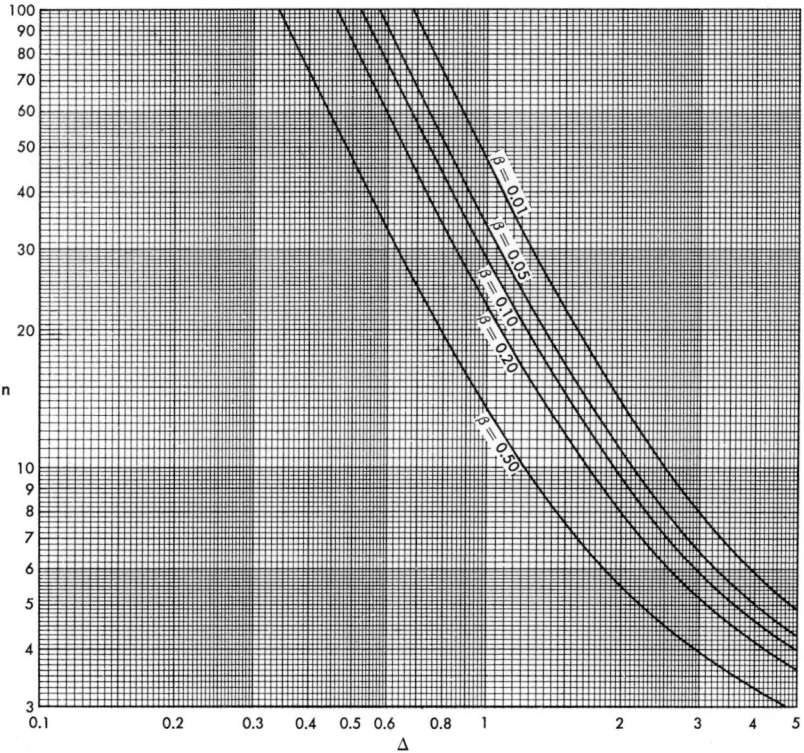

Graphs of Sample Sizes Needed for a Test Comparing the Means of Two Normal Distributions with Unknown, but Equal, Standard Deviations

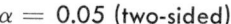

$\alpha = 0.05$ (two-sided)

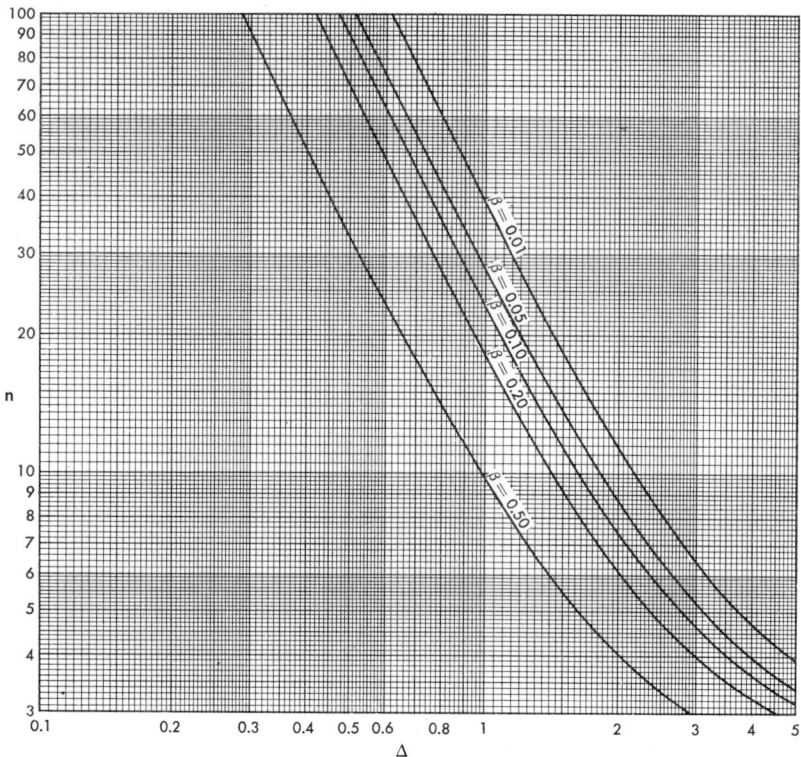

Graphs of Sample Sizes Needed for a Test Comparing the Means of Two Normal Distributions with Unknown, but Equal, Standard Deviations

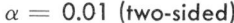

$\alpha = 0.01$ (two-sided)

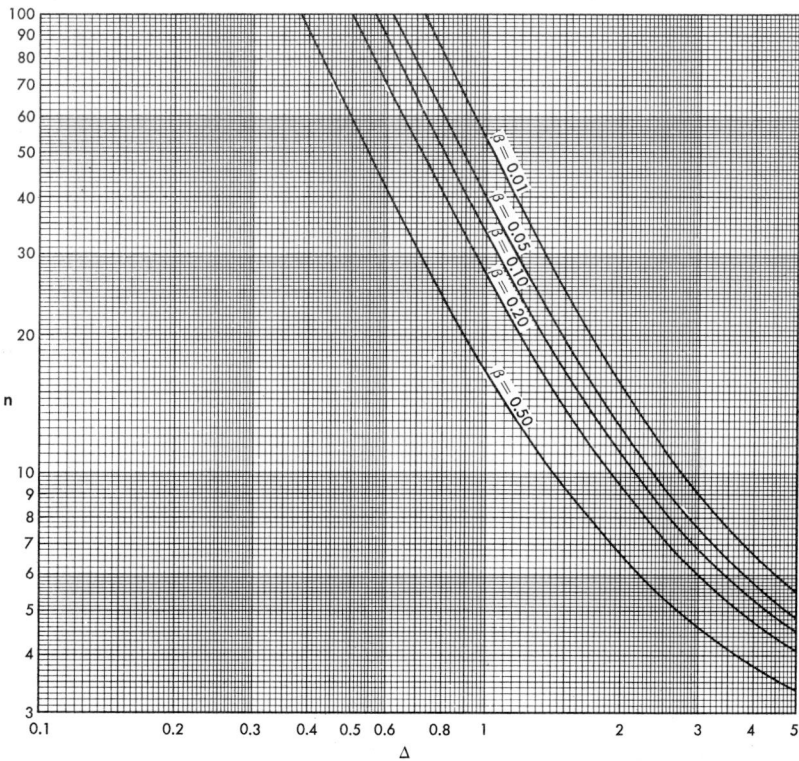

2.4

2.5 Approximate Sample Size for Design of Experiments

The table given here is based on two assumptions: (1) the population is normal, and (2) an estimate s_f^2 of the variance is known based on f degrees of freedom. A sample of size $n + 1$ is to be drawn so that the probability will be β of rejecting the hypothesis H_0: $\mu = 0$ against $\mu = a > 0$ where H_0 is tested at the $\alpha = 0.05$ level for one-tailed tests. If a two-tailed test is needed, $\alpha = 0.10$. The quantity given in the table is $k = a/s_f$ for $\beta = 0.80$ (first line) and $\beta = 0.95$ (second line). The table is only approximate since an error [142] was made in the derivation of the underlying distribution function. The quantity listed under $f = \infty$ was computed from Neyman and Tokarska's table [151] which gives the power of the Student t-test (see Section 2.2). Examples using this table are given in [86] and [160].

Approximate Sample Size for Design of Experiments [86]

$\beta = 0.80$ (first line); $\beta = 0.95$ (second line)

Values of $k = a/s_f$ are given such that

$$\Pr\{(x - a)\sqrt{n}/s_{n-1} \leq t_{n-1}, 0.10\} = \beta$$

n	1	2	3	4	5	6
1	13.8	8.52	7.39	6.93	6.68	6.51
	57.1	19.5	14.4	12.6	11.6	11.0
2	5.88	3.51	3.02	2.81	2.70	2.62
	24.2	7.74	5.60	4.77	4.39	4.15
3	4.30	2.55	2.20	2.03	1.96	1.91
	17.6	5.58	4.03	3.39	3.13	2.94
4	3.55	2.10	1.80	1.67	1.60	1.56
	14.5	4.58	3.28	2.79	2.56	2.40
5	3.12	1.85	1.58	1.47	1.41	1.37
	12.6	3.97	2.88	2.41	2.23	2.09
6	2.81	1.66	1.43	1.32	1.27	1.23
	11.2	3.55	2.57	2.17	2.00	1.88
7	2.56	1.52	1.30	1.21	1.16	1.12
	10.3	3.26	2.36	1.99	1.83	1.72
8	2.37	1.41	1.21	1.12	1.07	1.04
	9.70	3.05	2.19	1.86	1.70	1.60
9	2.23	1.32	1.14	1.05	1.01	0.978
	9.12	2.87	2.06	1.75	1.60	1.50
10	2.11	1.25	1.07	0.993	0.952	0.925
	8.62	2.72	1.95	1.65	1.51	1.42
12	1.92	1.14	0.975	0.902	0.865	0.840
	7.83	2.47	1.77	1.50	1.37	1.29
14	1.77	1.05	0.899	0.831	0.797	0.775
	7.22	2.28	1.63	1.38	1.26	1.19
16	1.65	0.976	0.838	0.775	0.743	0.722
	6.73	2.13	1.52	1.29	1.18	1.11
18	1.56	0.921	0.790	0.731	0.701	0.681
	6.35	2.01	1.44	1.22	1.11	1.04
20	1.48	0.873	0.750	0.693	0.665	0.646
	6.02	1.90	1.36	1.15	1.05	0.991
25	1.32	0.779	0.669	0.619	0.593	0.577
	5.37	1.70	1.22	1.03	0.940	0.884
30	1.20	0.708	0.608	0.563	0.540	0.525
	4.89	1.54	1.11	0.935	0.855	0.804
40	1.04	0.613	0.526	0.486	0.467	0.454
	4.23	1.33	0.962	0.809	0.739	0.696
50	0.925	0.548	0.471	0.435	0.417	0.405
	3.78	1.19	0.854	0.722	0.661	0.622
60	0.844	0.499	0.429	0.396	0.380	0.369
	3.45	1.09	0.778	0.658	0.602	0.567
80	0.730	0.432	0.371	0.342	0.328	0.319
	2.98	0.940	0.672	0.569	0.520	0.490
100	0.652	0.385	0.331	0.306	0.293	0.285
	2.67	0.840	0.600	0.508	0.465	0.438

Approximate Sample Size for Design of Experiments (cont.)

n	f 8	12	16	24	32	∞
1	6.31	6.13	6.04	5.96	5.92	5.79
	10.4	9.85	9.58	9.33	9.21	8.86
2	2.53	2.45	2.41	2.37	2.35	2.30
	3.86	3.61	3.49	3.38	3.33	3.19
3	1.85	1.78	1.75	1.72	1.70	1.65
	2.74	2.55	2.46	2.39	2.35	2.23
4	1.50	1.45	1.43	1.40	1.39	1.36
	2.23	2.08	2.01	1.94	1.91	1.82
5	1.32	1.28	1.25	1.23	1.22	1.18
	1.93	1.82	1.76	1.69	1.66	1.58
6	1.19	1.15	1.13	1.11	1.10	1.07
	1.73	1.62	1.57	1.52	1.49	1.42
7	1.08	1.05	1.03	1.02	1.01	0.979
	1.58	1.48	1.43	1.38	1.36	1.30
8	1.00	0.972	0.956	0.940	0.932	0.910
	1.48	1.39	1.34	1.29	1.27	1.21
9	0.944	0.913	0.898	0.883	0.875	0.854
	1.39	1.30	1.26	1.21	1.19	1.13
10	0.893	0.863	0.849	0.835	0.828	0.805
	1.32	1.23	1.19	1.15	1.13	1.07
12	0.811	0.784	0.771	0.758	0.752	0.732
	1.20	1.12	1.08	1.04	1.02	0.971
14	0.748	0.723	0.710	0.699	0.693	0.676
	1.11	1.03	0.993	0.959	0.942	0.893
16	0.697	0.673	0.662	0.651	0.646	0.631
	1.03	0.959	0.924	0.893	0.878	0.834
18	0.658	0.635	0.624	0.614	0.609	0.594
	0.972	0.904	0.872	0.842	0.828	0.785
20	0.624	0.602	0.592	0.583	0.578	0.563
	0.921	0.858	0.827	0.798	0.785	0.744
25	0.557	0.538	0.529	0.520	0.515	0.502
	0.822	0.765	0.738	0.712	0.700	0.663
30	0.507	0.489	0.481	0.473	0.469	0.456
	0.748	0.695	0.671	0.647	0.636	0.605
40	0.438	0.423	0.416	0.409	0.405	0.395
	0.646	0.601	0.580	0.560	0.550	0.525
50	0.391	0.378	0.371	0.365	0.362	0.353
	0.577	0.537	0.518	0.500	0.492	0.469
60	0.356	0.344	0.338	0.333	0.330	0.322
	0.525	0.490	0.472	0.456	0.448	0.428
80	0.308	0.298	0.292	0.288	0.285	0.278
	0.454	0.423	0.408	0.395	0.388	0.369
100	0.275	0.266	0.261	0.257	0.255	0.249
	0.405	0.378	0.365	0.353	0.347	0.329

2.5

3. CHI-SQUARE DISTRIBUTION

3.1 Critical Values for the Chi-Square Distribution

The quantity tabulated is that value of u such that

$$\frac{1}{2^{f/2}\Gamma(f/2)} \int_0^u x^{(f-2)/2} \exp(-x/2)\, dx = \gamma \quad \text{for } 0 \leq u < \infty,$$

where $\gamma = 0.005, 0.01, 0.025, 0.05, 0.10, 0.25, 0.75, 0.90, 0.95, 0.975,$ 0.99, 0.995. For $f \geq 30$, the values given in the table were computed by the methods given in [65]. For $f < 30$, direct calculation using the results of integration by parts was carried out. See [196] and [235] for normal approximations to the chi-square distribution. Also note the relationship between the Poisson distribution and the chi-square distribution given in Section 9.3. Lindley *et al.* [121] and Pachares [165] give tables of critical values based on chi-square for the two-sided uniformly most powerful test of the hypothesis that a variance is equal to a fixed value. Critical values for the chi-square distribution with $\gamma = 0.001$ and 0.999 are given by Lewis [119].

3.1

Critical Values for the Chi-Square Distribution

Pr$\{\chi^2$ r.v. with f degrees of freedom $\leq$ tabled value$\} = \gamma$

f	\(\gamma\)					
	0.005	0.01	0.025	0.05	0.10	0.25
1	-	-	0.001	0.004	0.016	0.102
2	0.010	0.020	0.051	0.103	0.211	0.575
3	0.072	0.115	0.216	0.352	0.584	1.213
4	0.207	0.297	0.484	0.711	1.064	1.923
5	0.412	0.554	0.831	1.145	1.610	2.675
6	0.676	0.872	1.237	1.635	2.204	3.455
7	0.989	1.239	1.690	2.167	2.833	4.255
8	1.344	1.646	2.180	2.733	3.490	5.071
9	1.735	2.088	2.700	3.325	4.168	5.899
10	2.156	2.558	3.247	3.940	4.865	6.737
11	2.603	3.053	3.816	4.575	5.578	7.584
12	3.074	3.571	4.404	5.226	6.304	8.438
13	3.565	4.107	5.009	5.892	7.042	9.299
14	4.075	4.660	5.629	6.571	7.790	10.165
15	4.601	5.229	6.262	7.261	8.547	11.037
16	5.142	5.812	6.908	7.962	9.312	11.912
17	5.697	6.408	7.564	8.672	10.085	12.792
18	6.265	7.015	8.231	9.390	10.865	13.675
19	6.844	7.633	8.907	10.117	11.651	14.562
20	7.434	8.260	9.591	10.851	12.443	15.452
21	8.034	8.897	10.283	11.591	13.240	16.344
22	8.643	9.542	10.982	12.338	14.042	17.240
23	9.260	10.196	11.689	13.091	14.848	18.137
24	9.886	10.856	12.401	13.848	15.659	19.037
25	10.520	11.524	13.120	14.611	16.473	19.939
26	11.160	12.198	13.844	15.379	17.292	20.843
27	11.808	12.879	14.573	16.151	18.114	21.749
28	12.461	13.565	15.308	16.928	18.939	22.657
29	13.121	14.257	16.047	17.708	19.768	23.567
30	13.787	14.954	16.791	18.493	20.599	24.478
31	14.458	15.655	17.539	19.281	21.434	25.390
32	15.134	16.362	18.291	20.072	22.271	26.304
33	15.815	17.074	19.047	20.867	23.110	27.219
34	16.501	17.789	19.806	21.664	23.952	28.136
35	17.192	18.509	20.569	22.465	24.797	29.054
36	17.887	19.233	21.336	23.269	25.643	29.973
37	18.586	19.960	22.106	24.075	26.492	30.893
38	19.289	20.691	22.878	24.884	27.343	31.815
39	19.996	21.426	23.654	25.695	28.196	32.737
40	20.707	22.164	24.433	26.509	29.051	33.660
41	21.421	22.906	25.215	27.326	29.907	34.585
42	22.138	23.650	25.999	28.144	30.765	35.510
43	22.859	24.398	26.785	28.965	31.625	36.436
44	23.584	25.148	27.575	29.787	32.487	37.363
45	24.311	25.901	28.366	30.612	33.350	38.291

Critical Values for the Chi-Square Distribution (cont.)

f	γ 0.75	0.90	0.95	0.975	0.99	0.995
1	1.323	2.706	3.841	5.024	6.635	7.879
2	2.773	4.605	5.991	7.378	9.210	10.597
3	4.108	6.251	7.815	9.348	11.345	12.838
4	5.385	7.779	9.488	11.143	13.277	14.860
5	6.626	9.236	11.071	12.833	15.086	16.750
6	7.841	10.645	12.592	14.449	16.812	18.548
7	9.037	12.017	14.067	16.013	18.475	20.278
8	10.219	13.362	15.507	17.535	20.090	21.955
9	11.389	14.684	16.919	19.023	21.666	23.589
10	12.549	15.987	18.307	20.483	23.209	25.188
11	13.701	17.275	19.675	21.920	24.725	26.757
12	14.845	18.549	21.026	23.337	26.217	28.299
13	15.984	19.812	22.362	24.736	27.688	29.819
14	17.117	21.064	23.685	26.119	29.141	31.319
15	18.245	22.307	24.996	27.488	30.578	32.801
16	19.369	23.542	26.296	28.845	32.000	34.267
17	20.489	24.769	27.587	30.191	33.409	35.718
18	21.605	25.989	28.869	31.526	34.805	37.156
19	22.718	27.204	30.144	32.852	36.191	38.582
20	23.828	28.412	31.410	34.170	37.566	39.997
21	24.935	29.615	32.671	35.479	38.932	41.401
22	26.039	30.813	33.924	36.781	40.289	42.796
23	27.141	32.007	35.172	38.076	41.638	44.181
24	28.241	33.196	36.415	39.364	42.980	45.559
25	29.339	34.382	37.652	40.646	44.314	46.928
26	30.435	35.563	38.885	41.923	45.642	48.290
27	31.528	36.741	40.113	43.194	46.963	49.645
28	32.620	37.916	41.337	44.461	48.278	50.993
29	33.711	39.087	42.557	45.722	49.588	52.336
30	34.800	40.256	43.773	46.979	50.892	53.672
31	35.887	41.422	44.985	48.232	52.191	55.003
32	36.973	42.585	46.194	49.480	53.486	56.328
33	38.058	43.745	47.400	50.725	54.776	57.648
34	39.141	44.903	48.602	51.966	56.061	58.964
35	40.223	46.059	49.802	53.203	57.342	60.275
36	41.304	47.212	50.998	54.437	58.619	61.581
37	42.383	48.363	52.192	55.668	59.892	62.883
38	43.462	49.513	53.384	56.896	61.162	64.181
39	44.539	50.660	54.572	58.120	62.428	65.476
40	45.616	51.805	55.758	59.342	63.691	66.766
41	46.692	52.949	56.942	60.561	64.950	68.053
42	47.766	54.090	58.124	61.777	66.206	69.336
43	48.840	55.230	59.304	62.990	67.459	70.616
44	49.913	56.369	60.481	64.201	68.710	71.893
45	50.985	57.505	61.656	65.410	69.957	73.166

Critical Values for the Chi-Square Distribution (cont.)

f	0.005	0.01	0.025	γ 0.05	0.10	0.25
46	25.041	26.657	29.160	31.439	34.215	39.220
47	25.775	27.416	29.956	32.268	35.081	40.149
48	26.511	28.177	30.755	33.098	35.949	41.079
49	27.249	28.941	31.555	33.930	36.818	42.010
50	27.991	29.707	32.357	34.764	37.689	42.942
51	28.735	30.475	33.162	35.600	38.560	43.874
52	29.481	31.246	33.968	36.437	39.433	44.808
53	30.230	32.018	34.776	37.276	40.308	45.741
54	30.981	32.793	35.586	38.116	41.183	46.676
55	31.735	33.570	36.398	38.958	42.060	47.610
56	32.490	34.350	37.212	39.801	42.937	48.546
57	33.248	35.131	38.027	40.646	43.816	49.482
58	34.008	35.913	38.844	41.492	44.696	50.419
59	34.770	36.698	39.662	42.339	45.577	51.356
60	35.534	37.485	40.482	43.188	46.459	52.294
61	36.300	38.273	41.303	44.038	47.342	53.232
62	37.068	39.063	42.126	44.889	48.226	54.171
63	37.838	39.855	42.950	45.741	49.111	55.110
64	38.610	40.649	43.776	46.595	49.996	56.050
65	39.383	41.444	44.603	47.450	50.883	56.990
66	40.158	42.240	45.431	48.305	51.770	57.931
67	40.935	43.038	46.261	49.162	52.659	58.872
68	41.713	43.838	47.092	50.020	53.548	59.814
69	42.494	44.639	47.924	50.879	54.438	60.756
70	43.275	45.442	48.758	51.739	55.329	61.698
71	44.058	46.246	49.592	52.600	56.221	62.641
72	44.843	47.051	50.428	53.462	57.113	63.585
73	45.629	47.858	51.265	54.325	58.006	64.528
74	46.417	48.666	52.103	55.189	58.900	65.472
75	47.206	49.475	52.942	56.054	59.795	66.417
76	47.997	50.286	53.782	56.920	60.690	67.362
77	48.788	51.097	54.623	57.786	61.586	68.307
78	49.582	51.910	55.466	58.654	62.483	69.252
79	50.376	52.725	56.309	59.522	63.380	70.198
80	51.172	53.540	57.153	60.391	64.278	71.145
81	51.969	54.357	57.998	61.261	65.176	72.091
82	52.767	55.174	58.845	62.132	66.076	73.038
83	53.567	55.993	59.692	63.004	66.976	73.985
84	54.368	56.813	60.540	63.876	67.876	74.933
85	55.170	57.634	61.389	64.749	68.777	75.881
86	55.973	58.456	62.239	65.623	69.679	76.829
87	56.777	59.279	63.089	66.498	70.581	77.777
88	57.582	60.103	63.941	67.373	71.484	78.726
89	58.389	60.928	64.793	68.249	72.387	79.675
90	59.196	61.754	65.647	69.126	73.291	80.625

Critical Values for the Chi-Square Distribution (*cont.*)

f	0.75	0.90	0.95	0.975	0.99	0.995
46	52.056	58.641	62.830	66.617	71.201	74.437
47	53.127	59.774	64.001	67.821	72.443	75.704
48	54.196	60.907	65.171	69.023	73.683	76.969
49	55.265	62.038	66.339	70.222	74.919	78.231
50	56.334	63.167	67.505	71.420	76.154	79.490
51	57.401	64.295	68.669	72.616	77.386	80.747
52	58.468	65.422	69.832	73.810	78.616	82.001
53	59.534	66.548	70.993	75.002	79.843	83.253
54	60.600	67.673	72.153	76.192	81.069	84.502
55	61.665	68.796	73.311	77.380	82.292	85.749
56	62.729	69.919	74.468	78.567	83.513	86.994
57	63.793	71.040	75.624	79.752	84.733	88.236
58	64.857	72.160	76.778	80.936	85.950	89.477
59	65.919	73.279	77.931	82.117	87.166	90.715
60	66.981	74.397	79.082	83.298	88.379	91.952
61	68.043	75.514	80.232	84.476	89.591	93.186
62	69.104	76.630	81.381	85.654	90.802	94.419
63	70.165	77.745	82.529	86.830	92.010	95.649
64	71.225	78.860	83.675	88.004	93.217	96.878
65	72.285	79.973	84.821	89.177	94.422	98.105
66	73.344	81.085	85.965	90.349	95.626	99.330
67	74.403	82.197	87.108	91.519	96.828	100.554
68	75.461	83.308	88.250	92.689	98.028	101.776
69	76.519	84.418	89.391	93.856	99.228	102.996
70	77.577	85.527	90.531	95.023	100.425	104.215
71	78.634	86.635	91.670	96.189	101.621	105.432
72	79.690	87.743	92.808	97.353	102.816	106.648
73	80.747	88.850	93.945	98.516	104.010	107.862
74	81.803	89.956	95.081	99.678	105.202	109.074
75	82.858	91.061	96.217	100.839	106.393	110.286
76	83.913	92.166	97.351	101.999	107.583	111.495
77	84.968	93.270	98.484	103.158	108.771	112.704
78	86.022	94.374	99.617	104.316	109.958	113.911
79	87.077	95.476	100.749	105.473	111.144	115.117
80	88.130	96.578	101.879	106.629	112.329	116.321
81	89.184	97.680	103.010	107.783	113.512	117.524
82	90.237	98.780	104.139	108.937	114.695	118.726
83	91.289	99.880	105.267	110.090	115.876	119.927
84	92.342	100.980	106.395	111.242	117.057	121.126
85	93.394	102.079	107.522	112.393	118.236	122.325
86	94.446	103.177	108.648	113.544	119.414	123.522
87	95.497	104.275	109.773	114.693	120.591	124.718
88	96.548	105.372	110.898	115.841	121.767	125.913
89	97.599	106.469	112.022	116.989	122.942	127.106
90	98.650	107.565	113.145	118.136	124.116	128.299

3.1

Critical Values for the Chi-Square Distribution (*cont.*)

f	0.005	0.01	0.025	0.05	0.10	0.25
91	60.005	62.581	66.501	70.003	74.196	81.574
92	60.815	63.409	67.356	70.882	75.100	82.524
93	61.625	64.238	68.211	71.760	76.006	83.474
94	62.437	65.068	69.068	72.640	76.912	84.425
95	63.250	65.898	69.925	73.520	77.818	85.376
96	64.063	66.730	70.783	74.401	78.725	86.327
97	64.878	67.562	71.642	75.282	79.633	87.278
98	65.694	68.396	72.501	76.164	80.541	88.229
99	66.510	69.230	73.361	77.046	81.449	89.181
100	67.328	70.065	74.222	77.929	82.358	90.133
102	68.965	71.737	75.946	79.697	84.177	92.038
104	70.606	73.413	77.672	81.468	85.998	93.944
106	72.251	75.092	79.401	83.240	87.821	95.850
108	73.899	76.774	81.133	85.015	89.645	97.758
110	75.550	78.458	82.867	86.792	91.471	99.666
112	77.204	80.146	84.604	88.570	93.299	101.575
114	78.862	81.836	86.342	90.351	95.128	103.485
116	80.522	83.529	88.084	92.134	96.958	105.396
118	82.185	85.225	89.827	93.918	98.790	107.307
120	83.852	86.923	91.573	95.705	100.624	109.220
122	85.520	88.624	93.320	97.493	102.458	111.133
124	87.192	90.327	95.070	99.283	104.295	113.046
126	88.866	92.033	96.822	101.074	106.132	114.961
128	90.543	93.741	98.576	102.867	107.971	116.876
130	92.222	95.451	100.331	104.662	109.811	118.792
132	93.904	97.163	102.089	106.459	111.652	120.708
134	95.588	98.878	103.848	108.257	113.495	122.625
136	97.275	100.595	105.609	110.056	115.338	124.543
138	98.964	102.314	107.372	111.857	117.183	126.461
140	100.655	104.034	109.137	113.659	119.029	128.380
142	102.348	105.757	110.903	115.463	120.876	130.299
144	104.044	107.482	112.671	117.268	122.724	132.219
146	105.741	109.209	114.441	119.075	124.574	134.140
148	107.441	110.937	116.212	120.883	126.424	136.061
150	109.142	112.668	117.985	122.692	128.275	137.983
200	152.241	156.432	162.728	168.279	174.835	186.172
250	196.161	200.939	208.098	214.392	221.806	234.577
300	240.663	245.972	253.912	260.878	269.068	283.135
400	330.903	337.155	346.482	354.641	364.207	380.577
500	422.303	429.388	439.936	449.147	459.926	478.323
600	514.529	522.365	534.019	544.180	556.056	576.286
700	607.380	615.907	628.577	639.613	652.497	674.413
800	700.725	709.897	723.513	735.362	749.185	772.669
900	794.475	804.252	818.756	831.370	846.075	871.032
1000	888.564	898.912	914.257	927.594	943.133	969.484

Critical Values for the Chi-Square Distribution (cont.)

f	γ 0.75	0.90	0.95	0.975	0.99	0.995
91	99.700	108.661	114.268	119.282	125.289	129.491
92	100.750	109.756	115.390	120.427	126.462	130.681
93	101.800	110.850	116.511	121.571	127.633	131.871
94	102.850	111.944	117.632	122.715	128.803	133.059
95	103.899	113.038	118.752	123.858	129.973	134.247
96	104.948	114.131	119.871	125.000	131.141	135.433
97	105.997	115.223	120.990	126.141	132.309	136.619
98	107.045	116.315	122.108	127.282	133.476	137.803
99	108.093	117.407	123.225	128.422	134.642	138.987
100	109.141	118.498	124.342	129.561	135.807	140.169
102	111.236	120.679	126.574	131.838	138.134	142.532
104	113.331	122.858	128.804	134.111	140.459	144.891
106	115.424	125.035	131.031	136.382	142.780	147.247
108	117.517	127.211	133.257	138.651	145.099	149.599
110	119.608	129.385	135.480	140.917	147.414	151.948
112	121.699	131.558	137.701	143.180	149.727	154.294
114	123.789	133.729	139.921	145.441	152.037	156.637
116	125.878	135.898	142.138	147.700	154.344	158.977
118	127.967	138.066	144.354	149.957	156.648	161.314
120	130.055	140.233	146.567	152.211	158.950	163.648
122	132.142	142.398	148.779	154.464	161.250	165.980
124	134.228	144.562	150.989	156.714	163.546	168.308
126	136.313	146.724	153.198	158.962	165.841	170.634
128	138.398	148.885	155.405	161.209	168.133	172.957
130	140.482	151.045	157.610	163.453	170.423	175.278
132	142.566	153.204	159.814	165.696	172.711	177.597
134	144.649	155.361	162.016	167.936	174.996	179.913
136	146.731	157.518	164.216	170.175	177.280	182.226
138	148.813	159.673	166.415	172.412	179.561	184.538
140	150.894	161.827	168.613	174.648	181.840	186.847
142	152.975	163.980	170.809	176.882	184.118	189.154
144	155.055	166.132	173.004	179.114	186.393	191.458
146	157.134	168.283	175.198	181.344	188.666	193.761
148	159.213	170.432	177.390	183.573	190.938	196.062
150	161.291	172.581	179.581	185.800	193.208	198.360
200	213.102	226.021	233.994	241.058	249.445	255.264
250	264.697	279.050	287.882	295.689	304.940	311.346
300	316.138	331.789	341.395	349.874	359.906	366.844
400	418.697	436.649	447.632	457.305	468.724	476.606
500	520.950	540.930	553.127	563.852	576.493	585.207
600	622.988	644.800	658.094	669.769	683.516	692.982
700	724.861	748.359	762.661	775.211	789.974	800.131
800	826.604	851.671	866.911	880.275	895.984	906.786
900	928.241	954.782	970.904	985.032	1001.630	1013.036
1000	1029.790	1057.724	1074.679	1089.531	1106.969	1118.948

3.2 Operating Characteristics for the Tests on a Standard Deviation σ against a Standard Value σ_0 Based on a 5-Percent Significance Level

For the table at the top of the page, the quantity tabulated is the square root of the ratio of the 0.95 critical value of chi-square to the critical value of chi-square, which is indicated by the column headings. For the table on the bottom half of the page, the quantity tabulated is the square root of the ratio of the 0.05 critical value of chi-square to the critical value of chi-square, which is indicated by one minus the column headings.

As indicated by the title, this table gives the operating characteristics for one-sided tests on the standard deviation where an underlying normal distribution is assumed. It may be used to obtain an estimate of sample size as follows: Suppose we want to test the hypothesis $H: \sigma = \sigma_0$ against $\sigma > \sigma_0$ at the 5-percent level, and we want to be 90 percent sure of rejecting H if the true $\sigma/\sigma_0 \geq 2$. Following down the 0.10 column of the table at the top of the page, we find $\lambda = \sigma/\sigma_0 = 2.015$ for $f = 9$, and $\lambda = 1.940$ for $f = 10$. Hence the needed sample size is $n = f + 1 = 11$.

A more extensive table similar to the one at the top of the page is given on p. 272 of [62] and on p. 276 of [62] for the 0.01 significance level. Professor John W. Tukey has suggested that a warning be given to the effect that slight departures from normality for the underlying distribution can have a very marked effect on these operating characteristics.

3.2

Operating Characteristics for the Tests on a Standard Deviation σ
against a Standard Value σ_0 **Based on a 5-Percent Significance Level**

$$\Pr\{\text{accepting } \sigma = \sigma_0 \text{ if } \sigma = \lambda\sigma_0\} = \gamma$$

Values of $\lambda = \sigma/\sigma_0$ for the test for $\sigma = \sigma_0$ against $\sigma > \sigma_0$

f	0.95	0.90	0.50	0.10	0.05	0.01
1	1.000	1.192	2.906	15.597	31.256	156.378
2	1.000	1.141	2.079	5.332	7.642	17.265
3	1.000	1.118	1.817	3.657	4.713	8.249
4	1.000	1.104	1.681	2.987	3.654	5.651
5	1.000	1.095	1.595	2.622	3.109	4.469
6	1.000	1.088	1.534	2.390	2.775	3.800
7	1.000	1.082	1.489	2.228	2.548	3.369
8	1.000	1.077	1.453	2.108	2.382	3.069
9	1.000	1.073	1.424	2.015	2.256	2.847
10	1.000	1.070	1.400	1.940	2.155	2.675
15	1.000	1.059	1.320	1.710	1.855	2.186
20	1.000	1.051	1.274	1.589	1.701	1.950
25	1.000	1.046	1.244	1.512	1.605	1.808
30	1.000	1.043	1.222	1.458	1.539	1.711
35	1.000	1.040	1.204	1.417	1.489	1.640
40	1.000	1.037	1.191	1.385	1.450	1.586
60	1.000	1.031	1.154	1.305	1.353	1.452
80	1.000	1.027	1.133	1.259	1.299	1.379
100	1.000	1.024	1.119	1.229	1.263	1.332

Values of $\lambda = \sigma/\sigma_0$ for the test for $\sigma = \sigma_0$ against $\sigma < \sigma_0$

f	0.95	0.90	0.50	0.10	0.05	0.01
1	1.000	0.499	0.093	0.038	0.032	0.024
2	1.000	0.698	0.272	0.149	0.131	0.106
3	1.000	0.776	0.386	0.237	0.212	0.176
4	1.000	0.817	0.460	0.302	0.274	0.231
5	1.000	0.843	0.513	0.352	0.322	0.276
6	1.000	0.861	0.553	0.392	0.360	0.312
7	1.000	0.875	0.584	0.425	0.393	0.343
8	1.000	0.885	0.610	0.452	0.420	0.369
9	1.000	0.893	0.631	0.476	0.443	0.392
10	1.000	0.900	0.649	0.496	0.464	0.412
15	1.000	0.922	0.712	0.571	0.539	0.487
20	1.000	0.934	0.749	0.618	0.588	0.537
25	1.000	0.942	0.775	0.652	0.623	0.574
30	1.000	0.947	0.794	0.678	0.650	0.603
35	1.000	0.952	0.809	0.698	0.672	0.626
40	1.000	0.955	0.821	0.715	0.690	0.645
60	1.000	0.964	0.853	0.762	0.739	0.699
80	1.000	0.969	0.872	0.791	0.770	0.733
100	1.000	0.973	0.886	0.811	0.792	0.758

3.2

3.3 Factors λ for Determining Sample Size for Bounds on the Endpoints of Confidence Intervals on a Standard Deviation from a Normal Distribution

The quantity tabulated here is the square root of the ratio of the $(1 + \gamma)/2$ critical value of chi-square to the $(1 - \gamma)/2$ critical value of chi-square. Hence, the column headed $\gamma = 0.90$ is the same as the 0.05 column in Table 3.2.

If a confidence interval on σ is based on s (Section 2.2) with f degrees of freedom computed from a sample from a normal distribution, one can be 100γ percent sure that *the endpoints* of the confidence interval on s will be between σ/λ and $\lambda\sigma$. In References [36] and [78] the quantity u given in their tables is related to λ by $\lambda = (1 + u)/(1 - u)$. The difference between the tables given here and those in [36] and [78] is that here the endpoints of the confidence interval on s are between σ/λ and $\lambda\sigma$, whereas [36] and [78] require that s be between only $(1 - u)\sigma$ and $(1 + u)\sigma$.

As an example of the use of the table, consider the problem of finding the sample size needed in order that the following probability statement may be made:

$$\Pr\left\{\frac{\sigma}{\lambda} \leq \sqrt{\frac{fs^2}{X_f^2\left(\frac{1 + \gamma}{2}\right)}} \leq \sigma \leq \sqrt{\frac{fs^2}{X_f^2\left(\frac{1 - \gamma}{2}\right)}} \leq \lambda\sigma\right\} = \gamma.$$

That is, the confidence interval

$$\sqrt{\frac{fs^2}{X_f^2\left(\frac{1 + \gamma}{2}\right)}}, \quad \sqrt{\frac{fs^2}{X_f^2\left(\frac{1 - \gamma}{2}\right)}}$$

simultaneously covers σ and is contained in the interval $(\sigma/\lambda, \lambda\sigma)$ with confidence γ. Now suppose it is desired to be 90 percent sure that the endpoints of our confidence interval are within 20 percent of σ. What sample size is needed if a single sample is taken from a normal distribution? Look in the table under $\gamma = 0.90$ for $\lambda = 1.20$. For $f = 160$ read 1.202, and for $f = 180$ read $\gamma = 1.190$. By linear interpolation, then, $f = 163+$, which to be on the safe side one should take to be 164. Thus $n = f + 1 = 165$ is the required sample size. Then the lower endpoint of the confidence interval on σ is never less than $[1 - (1/\lambda)]\sigma = [1 - (1/1.2)]\sigma = 0.167\sigma < 0.2\sigma$ units below σ, and the upper endpoint of the confidence interval on σ is never more than $(\lambda - 1)\sigma = (1.2 - 1)\sigma = 0.2\sigma$ units above σ with confidence γ. It is in this sense that the confidence interval estimates σ to within ± 20 percent of σ.

Factors λ for Determining Sample Size for Bounds on the Endpoints of Confidence Intervals on a Standard Deviation from a Normal Distribution

The upper endpoint of a $100\gamma\%$ two-sided confidence interval on the standard deviation σ based on f degrees of freedom is less than $100(\lambda - 1)\%$ of σ above σ and the lower endpoint is more than $100[1 - (1/\lambda)]\%$ of σ below σ with confidence γ.

f	γ 0.50	0.90	0.95	0.99	f	γ 0.50	0.90	0.95	0.99
1	3.61	31.26	71.52	447.94	40	1.164	1.450	1.558	1.796
2	2.20	7.64	12.07	32.51	50	1.145	1.393	1.486	1.685
3	1.84	4.71	6.58	13.38	60	1.132	1.353	1.434	1.609
4	1.67	3.65	4.80	8.47	70	1.121	1.323	1.396	1.552
5	1.57	3.11	3.93	6.38	80	1.113	1.299	1.366	1.508
6	1.51	2.77	3.42	5.24	90	1.106	1.279	1.341	1.472
7	1.46	2.55	3.08	4.53	100	1.100	1.263	1.321	1.443
8	1.42	2.38	2.84	4.04	120	1.091	1.238	1.289	1.397
9	1.39	2.26	2.65	3.69	140	1.084	1.218	1.265	1.362
10	1.36	2.16	2.51	3.42	160	1.078	1.202	1.246	1.335
11	1.34	2.07	2.40	3.21	180	1.074	1.190	1.230	1.313
12	1.33	2.01	2.30	3.03	200	1.070	1.179	1.217	1.295
13	1.31	1.95	2.22	2.89	220	1.067	1.170	1.206	1.279
14	1.30	1.90	2.15	2.77	240	1.064	1.162	1.196	1.266
15	1.29	1.86	2.10	2.67	260	1.061	1.155	1.188	1.254
16	1.28	1.82	2.04	2.58	280	1.059	1.149	1.181	1.244
17	1.27	1.78	2.00	2.50	300	1.057	1.144	1.174	1.235
18	1.26	1.75	1.96	2.44	400	1.049	1.123	1.149	1.200
19	1.25	1.73	1.92	2.37	500	1.044	1.110	1.132	1.177
20	1.24	1.70	1.89	2.32	600	1.040	1.100	1.120	1.161
21	1.24	1.68	1.86	2.27	700	1.037	1.092	1.110	1.148
22	1.23	1.66	1.83	2.23	800	1.034	1.086	1.103	1.138
23	1.22	1.64	1.80	2.18	900	1.032	1.081	1.097	1.129
24	1.22	1.62	1.78	2.15	1000	1.031	1.076	1.092	1.122
25	1.21	1.61	1.76	2.11	2000	1.022	1.053	1.064	1.085
26	1.21	1.59	1.74	2.08	3000	1.018	1.043	1.052	1.069
27	1.20	1.58	1.72	2.05	4000	1.015	1.037	1.045	1.059
28	1.20	1.56	1.70	2.02	5000	1.014	1.033	1.040	1.053
29	1.20	1.55	1.69	2.00	10000	1.010	1.024	1.028	1.037
30	1.19	1.54	1.67	1.97					

Along with [36] and [78], Reference [209] discusses two other approaches to the problem in addition to the one given here. Reference [77] discusses the problem when a preliminary estimate of σ is known. The sample sizes required vary widely according to the conditions assumed. Professor John W. Tukey has suggested that a warning be given to the effect that the table given here can be used safely for determining sample size only when the underlying distribution is normal, and slight departures from normality can lead to erroneous statements when this table is used.

3.4 Critical Values of the Noncentral Chi-Square Distribution

The quantity tabled is that value of λ such that

$$\exp\left(-\frac{\lambda}{2}\right) \sum_{j=0}^{\infty} \frac{\lambda^j}{j! 2^{(f/2)+2j} \Gamma[(f/2)+j]} \int_u^{\infty} x^{(f/2)+j-1} \exp\left(-x/2\right) dx = \beta,$$

where u is a critical value of the central chi-square distribution (see Section 3.1), i.e.,

$$\frac{1}{2^{f/2}\Gamma(f/2)} \int_0^u x^{(f/2)-1} \exp\left(-x/2\right) dx = 1 - \alpha.$$

Fix [66] gives an application to the power of a test of the hypothesis that a system of independent normal variables have specified means. Fix, Hodges, and Lehmann [68] describe another test whose power is non-central chi-square. Johnson [99] shows a connection between the non-central chi-square distribution and the distribution of the difference between two independent Poisson variables. Various approximations [1], [189], [170], and [168] also have been considered.

Critical Values of the Noncentral Chi-Square Distribution [66]

$$\alpha = 0.01$$

Values of λ are given such that $\Pr\{$noncentral χ^2 r.v. with parameters $f, \lambda \leq \alpha$th critical value of central $\chi^2\} = \beta$

f	0.1	0.2	0.3	0.4	0.5	0.6	0.7	0.8	0.9
1	1.67	3.01	4.21	5.39	6.64	8.00	9.61	11.68	14.88
2	2.30	3.94	5.37	6.76	8.19	9.75	11.57	13.88	17.43
3	2.76	4.62	6.22	7.75	9.31	11.01	12.97	15.46	19.25
4	3.15	5.19	6.91	8.56	10.23	12.04	14.12	16.75	20.74
5	3.49	5.68	7.52	9.27	11.03	12.94	15.12	17.87	22.03
6	3.79	6.13	8.07	9.90	11.75	13.74	16.01	18.87	23.19
7	4.08	6.53	8.57	10.48	12.41	14.47	16.83	19.79	24.24
8	4.34	6.91	9.03	11.02	13.02	15.15	17.59	20.64	25.21
9	4.58	7.27	9.47	11.52	13.59	15.79	18.30	21.43	26.12
10	4.82	7.60	9.88	12.00	14.13	16.39	18.97	22.18	26.98
11	5.04	7.92	10.27	12.45	14.64	16.96	19.60	22.89	27.80
12	5.25	8.23	10.64	12.89	15.13	17.51	20.20	23.56	28.58
13	5.45	8.52	11.00	13.30	15.59	18.03	20.78	24.21	29.32
14	5.65	8.80	11.35	13.70	16.04	18.53	21.34	24.83	30.03
15	5.84	9.07	11.68	14.08	16.48	19.01	21.88	25.43	30.72
16	6.02	9.34	12.00	14.45	16.90	19.48	22.40	26.01	31.39
17	6.20	9.59	12.31	14.81	17.30	19.93	22.90	26.57	32.03
18	6.37	9.84	12.61	15.16	17.70	20.37	23.39	27.12	32.66
19	6.54	10.08	12.91	15.50	18.08	20.80	23.86	27.65	33.26
20	6.70	10.31	13.19	15.83	18.45	21.21	24.32	28.16	33.85
22	7.02	10.76	13.74	16.47	19.17	22.01	25.21	29.15	34.99
24	7.32	11.20	14.27	17.08	19.86	22.78	26.06	30.10	36.07
26	7.61	11.61	14.78	17.66	20.51	23.51	26.87	31.01	37.11
28	7.89	12.01	15.26	18.23	21.15	24.21	27.65	31.88	38.11
30	8.16	12.40	15.73	18.77	21.76	24.89	28.40	32.72	39.07
32	8.42	12.77	16.19	19.29	22.35	25.55	29.13	33.53	40.01
34	8.67	13.13	16.63	19.80	22.92	26.18	29.84	34.32	40.91
36	8.92	13.48	17.05	20.29	23.48	26.80	30.52	35.08	41.78
38	9.16	13.82	17.47	20.77	24.02	27.40	31.19	35.83	42.63
40	9.39	14.15	17.88	21.24	24.54	27.99	31.84	36.55	43.46
45	9.95	14.95	18.85	22.36	25.80	29.39	33.39	38.28	45.44
50	10.48	15.71	19.77	23.42	26.99	30.72	34.86	39.92	47.31
55	10.98	16.43	20.64	24.43	28.13	31.98	36.25	41.47	49.09
60	11.46	17.11	21.47	25.39	29.21	33.18	37.59	42.96	50.79
70	12.37	18.40	23.05	27.20	31.25	35.44	40.10	45.76	53.99
80	13.22	19.61	24.51	28.90	33.15	37.55	42.43	48.37	56.95
90	14.01	20.74	25.89	30.48	34.93	39.53	44.62	50.80	59.74
100	14.76	21.81	27.19	31.98	36.61	41.40	46.69	53.16	62.39

3.4

62

Critical Values of the Noncentral Chi-Square Distribution (*cont.*)

$$\alpha = 0.05$$

f	0.1	0.2	0.3	0.4	0.5	0.6	0.7	0.8	0.9
1	0.43	1.24	2.06	2.91	3.84	4.90	6.17	7.85	10.51
2	0.62	1.73	2.78	3.83	4.96	6.21	7.70	9.64	12.66
3	0.78	2.10	3.30	4.50	5.76	7.15	8.79	10.90	14.17
4	0.91	2.40	3.74	5.05	6.42	7.92	9.68	11.94	15.41
5	1.03	2.67	4.12	5.53	6.99	8.59	10.45	12.83	16.47
6	1.13	2.91	4.46	5.96	7.50	9.19	11.14	13.62	17.42
7	1.23	3.13	4.77	6.35	7.97	9.73	11.77	14.35	18.28
8	1.32	3.33	5.06	6.71	8.41	10.24	12.35	15.02	19.08
9	1.40	3.53	5.33	7.05	8.81	10.71	12.89	15.65	19.83
10	1.49	3.71	5.59	7.38	9.19	11.15	13.40	16.24	20.53
11	1.56	3.88	5.83	7.68	9.56	11.58	13.89	16.80	21.20
12	1.64	4.05	6.06	7.97	9.90	11.98	14.35	17.34	21.83
13	1.71	4.20	6.29	8.25	10.24	12.36	14.80	17.85	22.44
14	1.78	4.36	6.50	8.52	10.55	12.73	15.22	18.34	23.02
15	1.84	4.50	6.71	8.78	10.86	13.09	15.63	18.81	23.58
16	1.90	4.65	6.91	9.03	11.16	13.44	16.03	19.27	24.13
17	1.97	4.78	7.10	9.27	11.45	13.77	16.41	19.71	24.65
18	2.03	4.92	7.29	9.51	11.73	14.09	16.78	20.14	25.16
19	2.09	5.05	7.47	9.73	12.00	14.41	17.14	20.56	25.65
20	2.14	5.18	7.65	9.96	12.26	14.71	17.50	20.96	26.13
22	2.25	5.42	8.00	10.39	12.77	15.30	18.17	21.74	27.06
24	2.36	5.66	8.33	10.80	13.26	15.87	18.82	22.49	27.94
26	2.46	5.88	8.64	11.19	13.72	16.41	19.44	23.20	28.79
28	2.56	6.10	8.94	11.57	14.17	16.93	20.04	23.89	29.60
30	2.65	6.31	9.24	11.93	14.60	17.43	20.61	24.55	30.38
32	2.74	6.51	9.52	12.28	15.02	17.91	21.17	25.19	31.14
34	2.83	6.70	9.79	12.62	15.43	18.38	21.70	25.81	31.87
36	2.91	6.89	10.06	12.96	15.82	18.84	22.23	26.41	32.58
38	3.00	7.08	10.32	13.28	16.20	19.28	22.73	26.99	33.27
40	3.08	7.26	10.57	13.59	16.58	19.71	23.23	27.56	33.94
45	3.27	7.69	11.18	14.35	17.47	20.74	24.41	28.92	35.55
50	3.46	8.10	11.75	15.06	18.31	21.72	25.53	30.20	37.07
55	3.63	8.49	12.29	15.74	19.12	22.65	26.59	31.43	38.51
60	3.80	8.86	12.81	16.38	19.88	23.53	27.61	32.59	39.89
70	4.11	9.56	13.79	17.60	21.32	25.20	29.52	34.79	42.48
80	4.41	10.21	14.70	18.73	22.67	26.75	31.29	36.83	44.89
90	4.69	10.83	15.56	19.80	23.93	28.21	32.96	38.74	47.15
100	4.95	11.41	16.37	20.81	25.12	29.59	34.54	40.56	49.29

3.4

4. F-DISTRIBUTION AND MULTIPLE COMPARISON

4.1 Critical Values of the F-Distribution

The quantity tabulated here is that value of F such that

$$K \int_0^F \frac{y^{(f_1/2)-1}}{(f_2 + f_1 y)^{(f_1+f_2)/2}} \, dy = \gamma, \qquad 0 \le F \le \infty,$$

where

$$K = \frac{\Gamma\left(\dfrac{f_1 + f_2}{2}\right)}{\Gamma(f_1/2)\Gamma(f_2/2)} f_1^{f_1/2} f_2^{f_2/2}$$

and where f_1 is referred to as the number of degrees of freedom of the numerator and f_2 is referred to as the number of degrees of freedom for the denominator. The numerator and denominator terminology arises in that this probability distribution is the distribution of the ratio of two independent chi-square divided by degrees of freedom statistics, with the one occurring in the numerator having f_1 degrees of freedom and the one occurring in the denominator having f_2 degrees of freedom.

The table given here was taken from Merrington-Thompson [139], but it has had certain corrections made in it. Those given by Norton [153] were used. These all occur at $\gamma = 0.99$ as follows:

f_1	f_2	M-T table	Corrected value
3	120	3.9493	3.9491
8	1	5981.6	5981.1
∞	2	99.501	99.499

In addition some checks were made of $f_1 = 2$, and five round-off errors were found as follows:

f_1	f_2	γ	M-T table	Corrected value
2	14	0.995	7.9217	7.9216
2	24	0.995	6.6610	6.6609
2	28	0.75	1.4572	1.4573
2	30	0.99	5.3904	5.3903
2	60	0.90	2.3932	2.3933

There are numerous applications of the F-tables. A use not widely mentioned in texts is given in [86]. Critical values for $\gamma < \frac{1}{2}$ can be read from the table by interchanging f_1 and f_2 and taking the reciprocal of the number tabulated. The entries in the table for $f_1 = 11, 13, 14, 18,$ and 48 and for $f_2 = 48$ and 80 were obtained by linear interpolation according to the reciprocal of f. The critical values given for these f may be correct to only two decimal places.

4.1

Critical Values of the *F*-Distribution [139]

Pr{r.v. with *F*-distribution $\leq$ tabled value} $= \gamma$

Degrees of Freedom for Numerator

	γ	1	2	3	4	5	6	γ	
	.500	1.0000	1.5000	1.7092	1.8227	1.8937	1.9422	.500	
	.750	5.8285	7.5000	8.1999	8.5810	8.8198	8.9833	.750	
	.900	39.864	49.500	53.593	55.833	57.241	58.204	.900	
1	.950	161.45	199.50	215.71	224.58	230.16	233.99	.950	1
	.975	647.79	799.50	864.16	899.58	921.85	937.11	.975	
	.990	4052.2	4999.5	5403.3	5624.6	5763.7	5859.0	.990	
	.995	16211	20000	21615	22500	23056	23437	.995	
	.500	.66667	1.0000	1.1349	1.2071	1.2519	1.2824	.500	
	.750	2.5714	3.0000	3.1534	3.2320	3.2799	3.3121	.750	
	.900	8.5263	9.0000	9.1618	9.2434	9.2926	9.3255	.900	
2	.950	18.513	19.000	19.164	19.247	19.296	19.330	.950	2
	.975	38.506	39.000	39.165	39.248	39.298	39.331	.975	
	.990	98.503	99.000	99.166	99.249	99.299	99.332	.990	
	.995	198.50	199.00	199.17	199.25	199.30	199.33	.995	
	.500	.58506	.88110	1.0000	1.0632	1.1024	1.1289	.500	
	.750	2.0239	2.2798	2.3555	2.3901	2.4095	2.4218	.750	
	.900	5.5383	5.4624	5.3908	5.3427	5.3092	5.2847	.900	
3	.950	10.128	9.5521	9.2766	9.1172	9.0135	8.9406	.950	3
	.975	17.443	16.044	15.439	15.101	14.885	14.735	.975	
	.990	34.116	30.817	29.457	28.710	28.237	27.911	.990	
	.995	55.552	49.799	47.467	46.195	45.392	44.838	.995	
	.500	.54863	.82843	.94054	1.0000	1.0367	1.0617	.500	
	.750	1.8074	2.0000	2.0467	2.0642	2.0723	2.0766	.750	
	.900	4.5448	4.3246	4.1908	4.1073	4.0506	4.0098	.900	
4	.950	7.7086	6.9443	6.5914	6.3883	6.2560	6.1631	.950	4
	.975	12.218	10.649	9.9792	9.6045	9.3645	9.1973	.975	
	.990	21.198	18.000	16.694	15.977	15.522	15.207	.990	
	.995	31.333	26.284	24.259	23.155	22.456	21.975	.995	
	.500	.52807	.79877	.90715	.96456	1.0000	1.0240	.500	
	.750	1.6925	1.8528	1.8843	1.8927	1.8947	1.8945	.750	
	.900	4.0604	3.7797	3.6195	3.5202	3.4530	3.4045	.900	
5	.950	6.6079	5.7861	5.4095	5.1922	5.0503	4.9503	.950	5
	.975	10.007	8.4336	7.7636	7.3879	7.1464	6.9777	.975	
	.990	16.258	13.274	12.060	11.392	10.967	10.672	.990	
	.995	22.785	18.314	16.530	15.556	14.940	14.513	.995	
	.500	.51489	.77976	.88578	.94191	.97654	1.0000	.500	
	.750	1.6214	1.7622	1.7844	1.7872	1.7852	1.7821	.750	
	.900	3.7760	3.4633	3.2888	3.1808	3.1075	3.0546	.900	
6	.950	5.9874	5.1433	4.7571	4.5337	4.3874	4.2839	.950	6
	.975	8.8131	7.2598	6.5988	6.2272	5.9876	5.8197	.975	
	.990	13.745	10.925	9.7795	9.1483	8.7459	8.4661	.990	
	.995	18.635	14.544	12.917	12.028	11.464	11.073	.995	

Degrees of Freedom for Denominator

Degrees of Freedom for Denominator

Critical Values of the F-Distribution (cont.)

	γ	Degrees of Freedom for Numerator						γ	
		7	8	9	10	11	12		
	.500	1.9774	2.0041	2.0250	2.0419	2.0558	2.0674	.500	
	.750	9.1021	9.1922	9.2631	9.3202	9.3672	9.4064	.750	
	.900	58.906	59.439	59.858	60.195	60.473	60.705	.900	
1	.950	236.77	238.88	240.54	241.88	242.99	243.91	.950	1
	.975	948.22	956.66	963.28	968.63	973.04	976.71	.975	
	.990	5928.3	5981.1	6022.5	6055.8	6083.3	6106.3	.990	
	.995	23715	23925	24091	24224	24334	24426	.995	
	.500	1.3045	1.3213	1.3344	1.3450	1.3537	1.3610	.500	
	.750	3.3352	3.3526	3.3661	3.3770	3.3859	3.3934	.750	
	.900	9.3491	9.3668	9.3805	9.3916	9.4006	9.4081	.900	
2	.950	19.353	19.371	19.385	19.396	19.405	19.413	.950	2
	.975	39.355	39.373	39.387	39.398	39.407	39.415	.975	
	.990	99.356	99.374	99.388	99.399	99.408	99.416	.990	
	.995	199.36	199.37	199.39	199.40	199.41	199.42	.995	
	.500	1.1482	1.1627	1.1741	1.1833	1.1909	1.1972	.500	
	.750	2.4302	2.4364	2.4410	2.4447	2.4476	2.4500	.750	
	.900	5.2662	5.2517	5.2400	5.2304	5.2223	5.2156	.900	
3	.950	8.8868	8.8452	8.8123	8.7855	8.7632	8.7446	.950	3
	.975	14.624	14.540	14.473	14.419	14.374	14.337	.975	
	.990	27.672	27.489	27.345	27.229	27.132	27.052	.990	
	.995	44.434	44.126	43.882	43.686	43.523	43.387	.995	
	.500	1.0797	1.0933	1.1040	1.1126	1.1196	1.1255	.500	
	.750	2.0790	2.0805	2.0814	2.0820	2.0823	2.0826	.750	
	.900	3.9790	3.9549	3.9357	3.9199	3.9066	3.8955	.900	
4	.950	6.0942	6.0410	5.9988	5.9644	5.9357	5.9117	.950	4
	.975	9.0741	8.9796	8.9047	8.8439	8.7933	8.7512	.975	
	.990	14.976	14.799	14.659	14.546	14.452	14.374	.990	
	.995	21.622	21.352	21.139	20.967	20.824	20.705	.995	
	.500	1.0414	1.0545	1.0648	1.0730	1.0798	1.0855	.500	
	.750	1.8935	1.8923	1.8911	1.8899	1.8887	1.8877	.750	
	.900	3.3679	3.3393	3.3163	3.2974	3.2815	3.2682	.900	
5	.950	4.8759	4.8183	4.7725	4.7351	4.7038	4.6777	.950	5
	.975	6.8531	6.7572	6.6810	6.6192	6.5676	6.5246	.975	
	.990	10.456	10.289	10.158	10.051	9.9623	9.8883	.990	
	.995	14.200	13.961	13.772	13.618	13.490	13.384	.995	
	.500	1.0169	1.0298	1.0398	1.0478	1.0545	1.0600	.500	
	.750	1.7789	1.7760	1.7733	1.7708	1.7686	1.7668	.750	
	.900	3.0145	2.9830	2.9577	2.9369	2.9193	2.9047	.900	
6	.950	4.2066	4.1468	4.0990	4.0600	4.0272	3.9999	.950	6
	.975	5.6955	5.5996	5.5234	5.4613	5.4094	5.3662	.975	
	.990	8.2600	8.1016	7.9761	7.8741	7.7891	7.7183	.990	
	.995	10.786	10.566	10.391	10.250	10.132	10.034	.995	

Degrees of Freedom for Denominator

Degrees of Freedom for Denominator

4.1

Critical Values of the F-Distribution (cont.)

	γ	13	14	15	18	20	24	γ	
			Degrees of Freedom for Numerator						
	.500	2.0773	2.0858	2.0931	2.1104	2.1190	2.1321	.500	
	.750	9.4399	9.4685	9.4934	9.5520	9.5813	9.6255	.750	
	.900	60.903	61.073	61.220	61.567	61.740	62.002	.900	
1	.950	244.69	245.37	245.95	247.32	248.01	249.05	.950	1
	.975	979.85	982.54	984.87	990.36	993.10	997.25	.975	
	.990	6125.9	6142.7	6157.3	6191.6	6208.7	6234.6	.990	
	.995	24504	24572	24630	24767	24836	24940	.995	
	.500	1.3672	1.3725	1.3771	1.3879	1.3933	1.4014	.500	
	.750	3.3997	3.4051	3.4098	3.4208	3.4263	3.4345	.750	
	.900	9.4145	9.4200	9.4247	9.4358	9.4413	9.4496	.900	
2	.950	19.419	19.424	19.429	19.440	19.446	19.454	.950	2
	.975	39.421	39.426	39.431	39.442	39.448	39.456	.975	
	.990	99.422	99.427	99.432	99.443	99.449	99.458	.990	
	.995	199.42	199.43	199.43	199.44	199.45	199.46	.995	
	.500	1.2025	1.2071	1.2111	1.2205	1.2252	1.2322	.500	
	.750	2.4520	2.4537	2.4552	2.4585	2.4602	2.4626	.750	
	.900	5.2097	5.2047	5.2003	5.1898	5.1845	5.1764	.900	
3	.950	8.7286	8.7148	8.7029	8.6744	8.6602	8.6385	.950	3
	.975	14.305	14.277	14.253	14.196	14.167	14.124	.975	
	.990	26.983	26.923	26.872	26.751	26.690	26.598	.990	
	.995	43.271	43.171	43.085	42.880	42.778	42.622	.995	
	.500	1.1305	1.1349	1.1386	1.1473	1.1517	1.1583	.500	
	.750	2.0827	2.0828	2.0829	2.0828	2.0828	2.0827	.750	
	.900	3.8853	3.8765	3.8689	3.8525	3.8443	3.8310	.900	
4	.950	5.8910	5.8732	5.8578	5.8209	5.8025	5.7744	.950	4
	.975	8.7148	8.6836	8.6565	8.5921	8.5599	8.5109	.975	
	.990	14.306	14.248	14.198	14.079	14.020	13.929	.990	
	.995	20.602	20.514	20.438	20.257	20.167	20.030	.995	
	.500	1.0903	1.0944	1.0980	1.1064	1.1106	1.1170	.500	
	.750	1.8867	1.8858	1.8851	1.8830	1.8820	1.8802	.750	
	.900	3.2566	3.2466	3.2380	3.2171	3.2067	3.1905	.900	
5	.950	4.6550	4.6356	4.6188	4.5783	4.5581	4.5272	.950	5
	.975	6.4873	6.4554	6.4277	6.3616	6.3285	6.2780	.975	
	.990	9.8244	9.7697	9.7222	9.6092	9.5527	9.4665	.990	
	.995	13.292	13.214	13.146	12.984	12.903	12.780	.995	
	.500	1.0647	1.0687	1.0722	1.0804	1.0845	1.0907	.500	
	.750	1.7650	1.7634	1.7621	1.7586	1.7569	1.7540	.750	
	.900	2.8918	2.8808	2.8712	2.8479	2.8363	2.8183	.900	
6	.950	3.9761	3.9558	3.9381	3.8955	3.8742	3.8415	.950	6
	.975	5.3287	5.2966	5.2687	5.2018	5.1684	5.1172	.975	
	.990	7.6570	7.6045	7.5590	7.4502	7.3958	7.3127	.990	
	.995	9.9494	9.8769	9.8140	9.6639	9.5888	9.4741	.995	

Degrees of Freedom for Denominator

Degrees of Freedom for Denominator

Critical Values of the F-Distribution (cont.)

Degrees of Freedom for Denominator (left side, vertical)

Degrees of Freedom for Denominator (right side, vertical)

	γ	30	40	48	60	120	∞	γ	
	.500	2.1452	2.1584	2.1650	2.1716	2.1848	2.1981	.500	
	.750	9.6698	9.7144	9.7368	9.7591	9.8041	9.8492	.750	
	.900	62.265	62.529	62.662	62.794	63.061	63.328	.900	
1	.950	250.09	251.14	251.67	252.20	253.25	254.32	.950	1
	.975	1001.4	1005.6	1007.7	1009.8	1014.0	1018.3	.975	
	.990	6260.7	6286.8	6299.9	6313.0	6339.4	6366.0	.990	
	.995	25044	25148	25201	25253	25359	25465	.995	
	.500	1.4096	1.4178	1.4220	1.4261	1.4344	1.4427	.500	
	.750	3.4428	3.4511	3.4553	3.4594	3.4677	3.4761	.750	
	.900	9.4579	9.4663	9.4705	9.4746	9.4829	9.4913	.900	
2	.950	19.462	19.471	19.475	19.479	19.487	19.496	.950	2
	.975	39.465	39.473	39.477	39.481	39.490	39.498	.975	
	.990	99.466	99.474	99.478	99.483	99.491	99.499	.990	
	.995	199.47	199.47	199.47	199.48	199.49	199.51	.995	
	.500	1.2393	1.2464	1.2500	1.2536	1.2608	1.2680	.500	
	.750	2.4650	2.4674	2.4686	2.4697	2.4720	2.4742	.750	
	.900	5.1681	5.1597	5.1555	5.1512	5.1425	5.1337	.900	
3	.950	8.6166	8.5944	8.5832	8.5720	8.5494	8.5265	.950	3
	.975	14.081	14.037	14.015	13.992	13.947	13.902	.975	
	.990	26.505	26.411	26.364	26.316	26.221	26.125	.990	
	.995	42.466	42.308	42.229	42.149	41.989	41.829	.995	
	.500	1.1649	1.1716	1.1749	1.1782	1.1849	1.1916	.500	
	.750	2.0825	2.0821	2.0819	2.0817	2.0812	2.0806	.750	
	.900	3.8174	3.8036	3.7966	3.7896	3.7753	3.7607	.900	
4	.950	5.7459	5.7170	5.7024	5.6878	5.6581	5.6281	.950	4
	.975	8.4613	8.4111	8.3858	8.3604	8.3092	8.2573	.975	
	.990	13.838	13.745	13.699	13.652	13.558	13.463	.990	
	.995	19.892	19.752	19.682	19.611	19.468	19.325	.995	
	.500	1.1234	1.1297	1.1329	1.1361	1.1426	1.1490	.500	
	.750	1.8784	1.8763	1.8753	1.8742	1.8719	1.8694	.750	
	.900	3.1741	3.1573	3.1488	3.1402	3.1228	3.1050	.900	
5	.950	4.4957	4.4638	4.4476	4.4314	4.3984	4.3650	.950	5
	.975	6.2269	6.1751	6.1488	6.1225	6.0693	6.0153	.975	
	.990	9.3793	9.2912	9.2466	9.2020	9.1118	9.0204	.990	
	.995	12.656	12.530	12.466	12.402	12.274	12.144	.995	
	.500	1.0969	1.1031	1.1062	1.1093	1.1156	1.1219	.500	
	.750	1.7510	1.7477	1.7460	1.7443	1.7407	1.7368	.750	
	.900	2.8000	2.7812	2.7716	2.7620	2.7423	2.7222	.900	
6	.950	3.8082	3.7743	3.7571	3.7398	3.7047	3.6688	.950	6
	.975	5.0652	5.0125	4.9857	4.9589	4.9045	4.8491	.975	
	.990	7.2285	7.1432	7.1000	7.0568	6.9690	6.8801	.990	
	.995	9.3583	9.2408	9.1814	9.1219	9.0015	8.8793	.995	

4.1

Critical Values of the F-Distribution (cont.)

	γ	Degrees of Freedom for Numerator						γ	
		1	2	3	4	5	6		
	.500	.50572	.76655	.87095	.92619	.96026	.98334	.500	
	.750	1.5732	1.7010	1.7169	1.7157	1.7111	1.7059	.750	
	.900	3.5894	3.2574	3.0741	2.9605	2.8833	2.8274	.900	
7	.950	5.5914	4.7374	4.3468	4.1203	3.9715	3.8660	.950	7
	.975	8.0727	6.5415	5.8898	5.5226	5.2852	5.1186	.975	
	.990	12.246	9.5466	8.4513	7.8467	7.4604	7.1914	.990	
	.995	16.236	12.404	10.882	10.050	9.5221	9.1554	.995	
	.500	.49898	.75683	.86004	.91464	.94831	.97111	.500	
	.750	1.5384	1.6569	1.6683	1.6642	1.6575	1.6508	.750	
	.900	3.4579	3.1131	2.9238	2.8064	2.7265	2.6683	.900	
8	.950	5.3177	4.4590	4.0662	3.8378	3.6875	3.5806	.950	8
	.975	7.5709	6.0595	5.4160	5.0526	4.8173	4.6517	.975	
	.990	11.259	8.6491	7.5910	7.0060	6.6318	6.3707	.990	
	.995	14.688	11.042	9.5965	8.8051	8.3018	7.9520	.995	
	.500	.49382	.74938	.85168	.90580	.93916	.96175	.500	
	.750	1.5121	1.6236	1.6315	1.6253	1.6170	1.6091	.750	
	.900	3.3603	3.0065	2.8129	2.6927	2.6106	2.5509	.900	
9	.950	5.1174	4.2565	3.8626	3.6331	3.4817	3.3738	.950	9
	.975	7.2093	5.7147	5.0781	4.7181	4.4844	4.3197	.975	
	.990	10.561	8.0215	6.9919	6.4221	6.0569	5.8018	.990	
	.995	13.614	10.107	8.7171	7.9559	7.4711	7.1338	.995	
	.500	.48973	.74349	.84508	.89882	.93193	.95436	.500	
	.750	1.4915	1.5975	1.6028	1.5949	1.5853	1.5765	.750	
	.900	3.2850	2.9245	2.7277	2.6053	2.5216	2.4606	.900	
10	.950	4.9646	4.1028	3.7083	3.4780	3.3258	3.2172	.950	10
	.975	6.9367	5.4564	4.8256	4.4683	4.2361	4.0721	.975	
	.990	10.044	7.5594	6.5523	5.9943	5.6363	5.3858	.990	
	.995	12.826	9.4270	8.0807	7.3428	6.8723	6.5446	.995	
	.500	.48644	.73872	.83973	.89316	.92608	.94837	.500	
	.750	1.4749	1.5767	1.5798	1.5704	1.5598	1.5502	.750	
	.900	3.2252	2.8595	2.6602	2.5362	2.4512	2.3891	.900	
11	.950	4.8443	3.9823	3.5874	3.3567	3.2039	3.0946	.950	11
	.975	6.7241	5.2559	4.6300	4.2751	4.0440	3.8807	.975	
	.990	9.6460	7.2057	6.2167	5.6683	5.3160	5.0692	.990	
	.995	12.226	8.9122	7.6004	6.8809	6.4217	6.1015	.995	
	.500	.48369	.73477	.83530	.88848	.92124	.94342	.500	
	.750	1.4613	1.5595	1.5609	1.5503	1.5389	1.5286	.750	
	.900	3.1765	2.8068	2.6055	2.4801	2.3940	2.3310	.900	
12	.950	4.7472	3.8853	3.4903	3.2592	3.1059	2.9961	.950	12
	.975	6.5538	5.0959	4.4742	4.1212	3.8911	3.7283	.975	
	.990	9.3302	6.9266	5.9526	5.4119	5.0643	4.8206	.990	
	.995	11.754	8.5096	7.2258	6.5211	6.0711	5.7570	.995	

Degrees of Freedom for Denominator

Degrees of Freedom for Denominator

Critical Values of the *F*-Distribution (cont.)

			Degrees of Freedom for Numerator				
γ	7	8	9	10	11	12	γ

	γ	7	8	9	10	11	12	γ	
	.500	1.0000	1.0126	1.0224	1.0304	1.0369	1.0423	.500	
	.750	1.7011	1.6969	1.6931	1.6898	1.6868	1.6843	.750	
	.900	2.7849	2.7516	2.7247	2.7025	2.6837	2.6681	.900	
7	.950	3.7870	3.7257	3.6767	3.6365	3.6028	3.5747	.950	7
	.975	4.9949	4.8994	4.8232	4.7611	4.7091	4.6658	.975	
	.990	6.9928	6.8401	6.7188	6.6201	6.5377	6.4691	.990	
	.995	8.8854	8.6781	8.5138	8.3803	8.2691	8.1764	.995	
	.500	.98757	1.0000	1.0097	1.0175	1.0239	1.0293	.500	
	.750	1.6448	1.6396	1.6350	1.6310	1.6274	1.6244	.750	
	.900	2.6241	2.5893	2.5612	2.5380	2.5184	2.5020	.900	
8	.950	3.5005	3.4381	3.3881	3.3472	3.3127	3.2840	.950	8
	.975	4.5286	4.4332	4.3572	4.2951	4.2431	4.1997	.975	
	.990	6.1776	6.0289	5.9106	5.8143	5.7338	5.6668	.990	
	.995	7.6942	7.4960	7.3386	7.2107	7.1039	7.0149	.995	
	.500	.97805	.99037	1.0000	1.0077	1.0141	1.0194	.500	
	.750	1.6022	1.5961	1.5909	1.5863	1.5822	1.5788	.750	
	.900	2.5053	2.4694	2.4403	2.4163	2.3959	2.3789	.900	
9	.950	3.2927	3.2296	3.1789	3.1373	3.1022	3.0729	.950	9
	.975	4.1971	4.1020	4.0260	3.9639	3.9117	3.8682	.975	
	.990	5.6129	5.4671	5.3511	5.2565	5.1774	5.1114	.990	
	.995	6.8849	6.6933	6.5411	6.4171	6.3136	6.2274	.995	
	.500	.97054	.98276	.99232	1.0000	1.0063	1.0116	.500	
	.750	1.5688	1.5621	1.5563	1.5513	1.5468	1.5430	.750	
	.900	2.4140	2.3772	2.3473	2.3226	2.3016	2.2841	.900	
10	.950	3.1355	3.0717	3.0204	2.9782	2.9426	2.9130	.950	10
	.975	3.9498	3.8549	3.7790	3.7168	3.6645	3.6209	.975	
	.990	5.2001	5.0567	4.9424	4.8492	4.7710	4.7059	.990	
	.995	6.3025	6.1159	5.9676	5.8467	5.7456	5.6613	.995	
	.500	.96445	.97661	.98610	.99373	.99999	1.0052	.500	
	.750	1.5418	1.5346	1.5284	1.5230	1.5181	1.5140	.750	
	.900	2.3416	2.3040	2.2735	2.2482	2.2267	2.2087	.900	
11	.950	3.0123	2.9480	2.8962	2.8536	2.8176	2.7876	.950	11
	.975	3.7586	3.6638	3.5879	3.5257	3.4733	3.4296	.975	
	.990	4.8861	4.7445	4.6315	4.5393	4.4619	4.3974	.990	
	.995	5.8648	5.6821	5.5368	5.4182	5.3190	5.2363	.995	
	.500	.95943	.97152	.98097	.98856	.99480	1.0000	.500	
	.750	1.5197	1.5120	1.5054	1.4996	1.4945	1.4902	.750	
	.900	2.2828	2.2446	2.2135	2.1878	2.1658	2.1474	.900	
12	.950	2.9134	2.8486	2.7964	2.7534	2.7170	2.6866	.950	12
	.975	3.6065	3.5118	3.4358	3.3736	3.3211	3.2773	.975	
	.990	4.6395	4.4994	4.3875	4.2961	4.2193	4.1553	.990	
	.995	5.5245	5.3451	5.2021	5.0855	4.9878	4.9063	.995	

Degrees of Freedom for Denominator

Degrees of Freedom for Denominator

4.1

Critical Values of the *F*-Distribution (*cont.*)

Degrees of Freedom for Denominator

	γ	13	14	15	18	20	24	γ	
				Degrees of Freedom for Numerator					
7	.500	1.0469	1.0509	1.0543	1.0624	1.0664	1.0724	.500	7
	.750	1.6819	1.6799	1.6781	1.6735	1.6712	1.6675	.750	
	.900	2.6543	2.6425	2.6322	2.6072	2.5947	2.5753	.900	
	.950	3.5501	3.5291	3.5108	3.4666	3.4445	3.4105	.950	
	.975	4.6281	4.5958	4.5678	4.5004	4.4667	4.4150	.975	
	.990	6.4096	6.3585	6.3143	6.2084	6.1554	6.0743	.990	
	.995	8.0962	8.0274	7.9678	7.8253	7.7540	7.6450	.995	
8	.500	1.0339	1.0378	1.0412	1.0491	1.0531	1.0591	.500	8
	.750	1.6216	1.6191	1.6170	1.6115	1.6088	1.6043	.750	
	.900	2.4875	2.4750	2.4642	2.4378	2.4246	2.4041	.900	
	.950	3.2588	3.2371	3.2184	3.1730	3.1503	3.1152	.950	
	.975	4.1618	4.1293	4.1012	4.0334	3.9995	3.9472	.975	
	.990	5.6085	5.5584	5.5151	5.4111	5.3591	5.2793	.990	
	.995	6.9377	6.8716	6.8143	6.6769	6.6082	6.5029	.995	
9	.500	1.0239	1.0278	1.0311	1.0390	1.0429	1.0489	.500	9
	.750	1.5756	1.5729	1.5705	1.5642	1.5611	1.5560	.750	
	.900	2.3638	2.3508	2.3396	2.3121	2.2983	2.2768	.900	
	.950	3.0472	3.0252	3.0061	2.9597	2.9365	2.9005	.950	
	.975	3.8302	3.7976	3.7694	3.7011	3.6669	3.6142	.975	
	.990	5.0540	5.0048	4.9621	4.8594	4.8080	4.7290	.990	
	.995	6.1524	6.0882	6.0325	5.8987	5.8318	5.7292	.995	
10	.500	1.0161	1.0199	1.0232	1.0310	1.0349	1.0408	.500	10
	.750	1.5395	1.5364	1.5338	1.5269	1.5235	1.5179	.750	
	.900	2.2685	2.2551	2.2435	2.2150	2.2007	2.1784	.900	
	.950	2.8868	2.8644	2.8450	2.7977	2.7740	2.7372	.950	
	.975	3.5827	3.5500	3.5217	3.4530	3.4186	3.3654	.975	
	.990	4.6491	4.6004	4.5582	4.4563	4.4054	4.3269	.990	
	.995	5.5880	5.5252	5.4707	5.3396	5.2740	5.1732	.995	
11	.500	1.0097	1.0135	1.0168	1.0245	1.0284	1.0343	.500	11
	.750	1.5102	1.5069	1.5041	1.4967	1.4930	1.4869	.750	
	.900	2.1927	2.1790	2.1671	2.1377	2.1230	2.1000	.900	
	.950	2.7611	2.7383	2.7186	2.6705	2.6464	2.6090	.950	
	.975	3.3913	3.3584	3.3299	3.2607	3.2261	3.1725	.975	
	.990	4.3411	4.2928	4.2509	4.1496	4.0990	4.0209	.990	
	.995	5.1642	5.1024	5.0489	4.9198	4.8552	4.7557	.995	
12	.500	1.0044	1.0082	1.0115	1.0192	1.0231	1.0289	.500	12
	.750	1.4861	1.4826	1.4796	1.4717	1.4678	1.4613	.750	
	.900	2.1311	2.1170	2.1049	2.0748	2.0597	2.0360	.900	
	.950	2.6598	2.6368	2.6169	2.5680	2.5436	2.5055	.950	
	.975	3.2388	3.2058	3.1772	3.1076	3.0728	3.0187	.975	
	.990	4.0993	4.0512	4.0096	3.9088	3.8584	3.7805	.990	
	.995	4.8352	4.7742	4.7214	4.5937	4.5299	4.4315	.995	

Degrees of Freedom for Denominator

Critical Values of the F-Distribution (cont.)

	Υ	Degrees of Freedom for Numerator						Υ
		30	40	48	60	120	∞	
	.500	1.0785	1.0846	1.0877	1.0908	1.0969	1.1031	.500
	.750	1.6635	1.6593	1.6571	1.6548	1.6502	1.6452	.750
	.900	2.5555	2.5351	2.5247	2.5142	2.4928	2.4708	.900
7	.950	3.3758	3.3404	3.3224	3.3043	3.2674	3.2298	.950	7
	.975	4.3624	4.3089	4.2817	4.2544	4.1989	4.1423	.975
	.990	5.9921	5.9084	5.8660	5.8236	5.7372	5.6495	.990
	.995	7.5345	7.4225	7.3657	7.3088	7.1933	7.0760	.995
	.500	1.0651	1.0711	1.0741	1.0771	1.0832	1.0893	.500
	.750	1.5996	1.5945	1.5919	1.5892	1.5836	1.5777	.750
	.900	2.3830	2.3614	2.3503	2.3391	2.3162	2.2926	.900
8	.950	3.0794	3.0428	3.0241	3.0053	2.9669	2.9276	.950	8
	.975	3.8940	3.8398	3.8121	3.7844	3.7279	3.6702	.975
	.990	5.1981	5.1156	5.0736	5.0316	4.9460	4.8588	.990
	.995	6.3961	6.2875	6.2324	6.1772	6.0649	5.9505	.995
	.500	1.0548	1.0608	1.0638	1.0667	1.0727	1.0788	.500
	.750	1.5506	1.5450	1.5420	1.5389	1.5325	1.5257	.750
	.900	2.2547	2.2320	2.2203	2.2085	2.1843	2.1592	.900
9	.950	2.8637	2.8259	2.8066	2.7872	2.7475	2.7067	.950	9
	.975	3.5604	3.5055	3.4774	3.4493	3.3918	3.3329	.975
	.990	4.6486	4.5667	4.5249	4.4831	4.3978	4.3105	.990
	.995	5.6248	5.5186	5.4645	5.4104	5.3001	5.1875	.995
	.500	1.0467	1.0526	1.0556	1.0585	1.0645	1.0705	.500
	.750	1.5119	1.5056	1.5023	1.4990	1.4919	1.4843	.750
	.900	2.1554	2.1317	2.1195	2.1072	2.0818	2.0554	.900
10	.950	2.6996	2.6609	2.6410	2.6211	2.5801	2.5379	.950	10
	.975	3.3110	3.2554	3.2269	3.1984	3.1399	3.0798	.975
	.990	4.2469	4.1653	4.1236	4.0819	3.9965	3.9090	.990
	.995	5.0705	4.9659	4.9126	4.8592	4.7501	4.6385	.995
	.500	1.0401	1.0460	1.0490	1.0519	1.0578	1.0637	.500
	.750	1.4805	1.4737	1.4701	1.4664	1.4587	1.4504	.750
	.900	2.0762	2.0516	2.0389	2.0261	1.9997	1.9721	.900
11	.950	2.5705	2.5309	2.5105	2.4901	2.4480	2.4045	.950	11
	.975	3.1176	3.0613	3.0324	3.0035	2.9441	2.8828	.975
	.990	3.9411	3.8596	3.8179	3.7761	3.6904	3.6025	.990
	.995	4.6543	4.5508	4.4979	4.4450	4.3367	4.2256	.995
	.500	1.0347	1.0405	1.0435	1.0464	1.0523	1.0582	.500
	.750	1.4544	1.4471	1.4432	1.4393	1.4310	1.4221	.750
	.900	2.0115	1.9861	1.9729	1.9597	1.9323	1.9036	.900
12	.950	2.4663	2.4259	2.4051	2.3842	2.3410	2.2962	.950	12
	.975	2.9633	2.9063	2.8771	2.8478	2.7874	2.7249	.975
	.990	3.7008	3.6192	3.5774	3.5355	3.4494	3.3608	.990
	.995	4.3309	4.2282	4.1756	4.1229	4.0149	3.9039	.995

Degrees of Freedom for Denominator

Degrees of Freedom for Denominator

Critical Values of the F-Distribution (cont.)

	γ	Degrees of Freedom for Numerator						γ	
		1	2	3	4	5	6		
	.500	.48141	.73145	.83159	.88454	.91718	.93926	.500	
	.750	1.4500	1.5452	1.5451	1.5336	1.5214	1.5105	.750	
	.900	3.1362	2.7632	2.5603	2.4337	2.3467	2.2830	.900	
13	.950	4.6672	3.8056	3.4105	3.1791	3.0254	2.9153	.950	13
	.975	6.4143	4.9653	4.3472	3.9959	3.7667	3.6043	.975	
	.990	9.0738	6.7010	5.7394	5.2053	4.8616	4.6204	.990	
	.995	11.374	8.1865	6.9257	6.2335	5.7910	5.4819	.995	
	.500	.47944	.72862	.82842	.88119	.91371	.93573	.500	
	.750	1.4403	1.5331	1.5317	1.5194	1.5066	1.4952	.750	
	.900	3.1022	2.7265	2.5222	2.3947	2.3069	2.2426	.900	
14	.950	4.6001	3.7389	3.3439	3.1122	2.9582	2.8477	.950	14
	.975	6.2979	4.8567	4.2417	3.8919	3.6634	3.5014	.975	
	.990	8.8616	6.5149	5.5639	5.0354	4.6950	4.4558	.990	
	.995	11.060	7.9216	6.6803	5.9984	5.5623	5.2574	.995	
	.500	.47775	.72619	.82569	.87830	.91073	.93267	.500	
	.750	1.4321	1.5227	1.5202	1.5071	1.4938	1.4820	.750	
	.900	3.0732	2.6952	2.4898	2.3614	2.2730	2.2081	.900	
15	.950	4.5431	3.6823	3.2874	3.0556	2.9013	2.7905	.950	15
	.975	6.1995	4.7650	4.1528	3.8043	3.5764	3.4147	.975	
	.990	8.6831	6.3589	5.4170	4.8932	4.5556	4.3183	.990	
	.995	10.798	7.7008	6.4760	5.8029	5.3721	5.0708	.995	
	.500	.47628	.72406	.82330	.87578	.90812	.93001	.500	
	.750	1.4249	1.5137	1.5103	1.4965	1.4827	1.4705	.750	
	.900	3.0481	2.6682	2.4618	2.3327	2.2438	2.1783	.900	
16	.950	4.4940	3.6337	3.2389	3.0069	2.8524	2.7413	.950	16
	.975	6.1151	4.6867	4.0768	3.7294	3.5021	3.3406	.975	
	.990	8.5310	6.2262	5.2922	4.7726	4.4374	4.2016	.990	
	.995	10.575	7.5138	6.3034	5.6378	5.2117	4.9134	.995	
	.500	.47499	.72219	.82121	.87357	.90584	.92767	.500	
	.750	1.4186	1.5057	1.5015	1.4873	1.4730	1.4605	.750	
	.900	3.0262	2.6446	2.4374	2.3077	2.2183	2.1524	.900	
17	.950	4.4513	3.5915	3.1968	2.9647	2.8100	2.6987	.950	17
	.975	6.0420	4.6189	4.0112	3.6648	3.4379	3.2767	.975	
	.990	8.3997	6.1121	5.1850	4.6690	4.3359	4.1015	.990	
	.995	10.384	7.3536	6.1556	5.4967	5.0746	4.7789	.995	
	.500	.47385	.72053	.81936	.87161	.90381	.92560	.500	
	.750	1.4130	1.4988	1.4938	1.4790	1.4644	1.4516	.750	
	.900	3.0070	2.6239	2.4160	2.2858	2.1958	2.1296	.900	
18	.950	4.4139	3.5546	3.1599	2.9277	2.7729	2.6613	.950	18
	.975	5.9781	4.5597	3.9539	3.6083	3.3820	3.2209	.975	
	.990	8.2854	6.0129	5.0919	4.5790	4.2479	4.0146	.990	
	.995	10.218	7.2148	6.0277	5.3746	4.9560	4.6627	.995	

Degrees of Freedom for Denominator

Degrees of Freedom for Denominator

Critical Values of the F-Distribution (cont.)

	γ	7	8	Degrees of Freedom for Numerator 9	10	11	12	γ	
	.500	.95520	.96724	.97665	.98421	.99042	.99560	.500	
	.750	1.5011	1.4931	1.4861	1.4801	1.4746	1.4701	.750	
	.900	2.2341	2.1953	2.1638	2.1376	2.1152	2.0966	.900	
13	.950	2.8321	2.7669	2.7144	2.6710	2.6343	2.6037	.950	13
	.975	3.4827	3.3880	3.3120	3.2497	3.1971	3.1532	.975	
	.990	4.4410	4.3021	4.1911	4.1003	4.0239	3.9603	.990	
	.995	5.2529	5.0761	4.9351	4.8199	4.7234	4.6429	.995	
	.500	.95161	.96360	.97298	.98051	.98670	.99186	.500	
	.750	1.4854	1.4770	1.4697	1.4634	1.4577	1.4530	.750	
	.900	2.1931	2.1539	2.1220	2.0954	2.0727	2.0537	.900	
14	.950	2.7642	2.6987	2.6458	2.6021	2.5651	2.5342	.950	14
	.975	3.3799	3.2853	3.2093	3.1469	3.0941	3.0501	.975	
	.990	4.2779	4.1399	4.0297	3.9394	3.8634	3.8001	.990	
	.995	5.0313	4.8566	4.7173	4.6034	4.5078	4.4281	.995	
	.500	.94850	.96046	.96981	.97732	.98349	.98863	.500	
	.750	1.4718	1.4631	1.4556	1.4491	1.4432	1.4383	.750	
	.900	2.1582	2.1185	2.0862	2.0593	2.0363	2.0171	.900	
15	.950	2.7066	2.6408	2.5876	2.5437	2.5064	2.4753	.950	15
	.975	3.2934	3.1987	3.1227	3.0602	3.0073	2.9633	.975	
	.990	4.1415	4.0045	3.8948	3.8049	3.7292	3.6662	.990	
	.995	4.8473	4.6743	4.5364	4.4236	4.3288	4.2498	.995	
	.500	.94580	.95773	.96705	.97454	.98069	.98582	.500	
	.750	1.4601	1.4511	1.4433	1.4366	1.4305	1.4255	.750	
	.900	2.1280	2.0880	2.0553	2.0281	2.0048	1.9854	.900	
16	.950	2.6572	2.5911	2.5377	2.4935	2.4560	2.4247	.950	16
	.975	3.2194	3.1248	3.0488	2.9862	2.9332	2.8890	.975	
	.990	4.0259	3.8896	3.7804	3.6909	3.6155	3.5527	.990	
	.995	4.6920	4.5207	4.3838	4.2719	4.1778	4.0994	.995	
	.500	.94342	.95532	.96462	.97209	.97823	.98334	.500	
	.750	1.4497	1.4405	1.4325	1.4256	1.4194	1.4142	.750	
	.900	2.1017	2.0613	2.0284	2.0009	1.9773	1.9577	.900	
17	.950	2.6143	2.5480	2.4943	2.4499	2.4122	2.3807	.950	17
	.975	3.1556	3.0610	2.9849	2.9222	2.8691	2.8249	.975	
	.990	3.9267	3.7910	3.6822	3.5931	3.5179	3.4552	.990	
	.995	4.5594	4.3893	4.2535	4.1423	4.0488	3.9709	.995	
	.500	.94132	.95319	.96247	.96993	.97606	.98116	.500	
	.750	1.4406	1.4312	1.4230	1.4159	1.4095	1.4042	.750	
	.900	2.0785	2.0379	2.0047	1.9770	1.9532	1.9333	.900	
18	.950	2.5767	2.5102	2.4563	2.4117	2.3737	2.3421	.950	18
	.975	3.0999	3.0053	2.9291	2.8664	2.8132	2.7689	.975	
	.990	3.8406	3.7054	3.5971	3.5082	3.4331	3.3706	.990	
	.995	4.4448	4.2759	4.1410	4.0305	3.9374	3.8599	.995	

Degrees of Freedom for Denominator

Degrees of Freedom for Denominator

4.1

Critical Values of the F-Distribution (cont.)

	γ	13	14	15	18	20	24	γ	
		Degrees of Freedom for Numerator							
13	.500	1.0000	1.0038	1.0071	1.0148	1.0186	1.0243	.500	
	.750	1.4658	1.4622	1.4590	1.4507	1.4465	1.4397	.750	
	.900	2.0799	2.0656	2.0532	2.0224	2.0070	1.9827	.900	
	.950	2.5765	2.5533	2.5331	2.4836	2.4589	2.4202	.950	13
	.975	3.1145	3.0814	3.0527	2.9827	2.9477	2.8932	.975	
	.990	3.9046	3.8568	3.8154	3.7149	3.6646	3.5868	.990	
	.995	4.5726	4.5123	4.4600	4.3335	4.2703	4.1726	.995	
14	.500	.99626	1.0000	1.0033	1.0109	1.0147	1.0205	.500	
	.750	1.4485	1.4447	1.4414	1.4327	1.4284	1.4212	.750	
	.900	2.0367	2.0221	2.0095	1.9782	1.9625	1.9377	.900	
	.950	2.5068	2.4833	2.4630	2.4129	2.3879	2.3487	.950	14
	.975	3.0113	2.9781	2.9493	2.8789	2.8437	2.7888	.975	
	.990	3.7446	3.6970	3.6557	3.5554	3.5052	3.4274	.990	
	.995	4.3584	4.2986	4.2468	4.1213	4.0585	3.9614	.995	
15	.500	.99300	.99675	1.0000	1.0076	1.0114	.01720	.500	
	.750	1.4337	1.4297	1.4263	1.4172	1.4127	1.4052	.750	
	.900	1.9998	1.9850	1.9722	1.9403	1.9243	1.8990	.900	
	.950	2.4477	2.4240	2.4035	2.3528	2.3275	2.2878	.950	15
	.975	2.9244	2.8910	2.8621	2.7913	2.7559	2.7006	.975	
	.990	3.6108	3.5633	3.5222	3.4220	3.3719	3.2940	.990	
	.995	4.1806	4.1212	4.0698	3.9450	3.8826	3.7859	.995	
16	.500	.99018	.99392	.99716	1.0048	1.0086	1.0143	.500	
	.750	1.4207	1.4166	1.4130	1.4037	1.3990	1.3913	.750	
	.900	1.9679	1.9529	1.9399	1.9075	1.8913	1.8656	.900	
	.950	2.3968	2.3729	2.3522	2.3011	2.2756	2.2354	.950	16
	.975	2.8500	2.8165	2.7875	2.7164	2.6808	2.6252	.975	
	.990	3.4974	3.4500	3.4089	3.3088	3.2588	3.1808	.990	
	.995	4.0306	3.9716	3.9205	3.7963	3.7342	3.6378	.995	
17	.500	.98769	.99143	.99466	1.0022	1.0060	1.0117	.500	
	.750	1.4093	1.4051	1.4014	1.3917	1.3869	1.3790	.750	
	.900	1.9400	1.9248	1.9117	1.8788	1.8624	1.8362	.900	
	.950	2.3526	2.3286	2.3077	2.2562	2.2304	2.1898	.950	17
	.975	2.7857	2.7521	2.7230	2.6515	2.6158	2.5598	.975	
	.990	3.4000	3.3527	3.3117	3.2116	3.1615	3.0835	.990	
	.995	3.9024	3.8438	3.7929	3.6692	3.6073	3.5112	.995	
18	.500	.98550	.98922	.99245	1.0000	1.0038	1.0095	.500	
	.750	1.3992	1.3948	1.3911	1.3812	1.3762	1.3680	.750	
	.900	1.9154	1.9001	1.8868	1.8535	1.8368	1.8103	.900	
	.950	2.3138	2.2896	2.2686	2.2166	2.1906	2.1497	.950	18
	.975	2.7296	2.6959	2.6667	2.5949	2.5590	2.5027	.975	
	.990	3.3155	3.2682	3.2273	3.1272	3.0771	2.9990	.990	
	.995	3.7917	3.7333	3.6827	3.5594	3.4977	3.4017	.995	

Degrees of Freedom for Denominator

Critical Values of the F-Distribution (cont.)

	γ	30	40	48	60	120	∞	γ	
				Degrees of Freedom for Numerator					
	.500	1.0301	1.0360	1.0389	1.0418	1.0476	1.0535	.500	
	.750	1.4324	1.4247	1.4206	1.4164	1.4075	1.3980	.750	
	.900	1.9576	1.9315	1.9179	1.9043	1.8759	1.8462	.900	
13	.950	2.3803	2.3392	2.3179	2.2966	2.2524	2.2064	.950	13
	.975	2.8373	2.7797	2.7501	2.7204	2.6590	2.5955	.975	
	.990	3.5070	3.4253	3.3833	3.3413	3.2548	3.1654	.990	
	.995	4.0727	3.9704	3.9180	3.8655	3.7577	3.6465	.995	
	.500	1.0263	1.0321	1.0350	1.0379	1.0437	1.0495	.500	
	.750	1.4136	1.4055	1.4011	1.3967	1.3874	1.3772	.750	
	.900	1.9119	1.8852	1.8712	1.8572	1.8280	1.7973	.900	
14	.950	2.3082	2.2664	2.2447	2.2230	2.1778	2.1307	.950	14
	.975	2.7324	2.6742	2.6442	2.6142	2.5519	2.4872	.975	
	.990	3.3476	3.2656	3.2235	3.1813	3.0942	3.0040	.990	
	.995	3.8619	3.7600	3.7077	3.6553	3.5473	3.4359	.995	
	.500	1.0229	1.0287	1.0316	1.0345	1.0403	1.0461	.500	
	.750	1.3973	1.3888	1.3842	1.3796	1.3698	1.3591	.750	
	.900	1.8728	1.8454	1.8311	1.8168	1.7867	1.7551	.900	
15	.950	2.2468	2.2043	2.1822	2.1601	2.1141	2.0658	.950	15
	.975	2.6437	2.5850	2.5546	2.5242	2.4611	2.3953	.975	
	.990	3.2141	3.1319	3.0895	3.0471	2.9595	2.8684	.990	
	.995	3.6867	3.5850	3.5327	3.4803	3.3722	3.2602	.995	
	.500	1.0200	1.0258	1.0287	1.0315	1.0373	1.0431	.500	
	.750	1.3830	1.3742	1.3694	1.3646	1.3543	1.3432	.750	
	.900	1.8388	1.8108	1.7962	1.7816	1.7507	1.7182	.900	
16	.950	2.1938	2.1507	2.1283	2.1058	2.0589	2.0096	.950	16
	.975	2.5678	2.5085	2.4778	2.4471	2.3831	2.3163	.975	
	.990	3.1007	3.0182	2.9756	2.9330	2.8447	2.7528	.990	
	.995	3.5388	3.4372	3.3848	3.3324	3.2240	3.1115	.995	
	.500	1.0174	1.0232	1.0261	1.0289	1.0347	1.0405	.500	
	.750	1.3704	1.3613	1.3564	1.3514	1.3406	1.3290	.750	
	.900	1.8090	1.7805	1.7656	1.7506	1.7191	1.6856	.900	
17	.950	2.1477	2.1040	2.0812	2.0584	2.0107	1.9604	.950	17
	.975	2.5021	2.4422	2.4112	2.3801	2.3153	2.2474	.975	
	.990	3.0032	2.9205	2.8777	2.8348	2.7459	2.6530	.990	
	.995	3.4124	3.3107	3.2583	3.2058	3.0971	2.9839	.995	
	.500	1.0152	1.0209	1.0238	1.0267	1.0324	1.0382	.500	
	.750	1.3592	1.3497	1.3446	1.3395	1.3284	1.3162	.750	
	.900	1.7827	1.7537	1.7385	1.7232	1.6910	1.6567	.900	
18	.950	2.1071	2.0629	2.0398	2.0166	1.9681	1.9168	.950	18
	.975	2.4445	2.3842	2.3528	2.3214	2.2558	2.1869	.975	
	.990	2.9185	2.8354	2.7924	2.7493	2.6597	2.5660	.990	
	.995	3.3030	3.2014	3.1488	3.0962	2.9871	2.8732	.995	

Degrees of Freedom for Denominator

Degrees of Freedom for Denominator

Critical Values of the *F*-Distribution (*cont.*)

Degrees of Freedom for Numerator

	γ	1	2	3	4	5	6	γ	
	.500	.47284	.71906	.81771	.86987	.90200	.92375	.500	
	.750	1.4081	1.4925	1.4870	1.4717	1.4568	1.4437	.750	
	.900	2.9899	2.6056	2.3970	2.2663	2.1760	2.1094	.900	
19	.950	4.3808	3.5219	3.1274	2.8951	2.7401	2.6283	.950	19
	.975	5.9216	4.5075	3.9034	3.5587	3.3327	3.1718	.975	
	.990	8.1850	5.9259	5.0103	4.5003	4.1708	3.9386	.990	
	.995	10.073	7.0935	5.9161	5.2681	4.8526	4.5614	.995	
	.500	.47192	.71773	.81621	.86830	.90038	.92210	.500	
	.750	1.4037	1.4870	1.4808	1.4652	1.4500	1.4366	.750	
	.900	2.9747	2.5893	2.3801	2.2489	2.1582	2.0913	.900	
20	.950	4.3513	3.4928	3.0984	2.8661	2.7109	2.5990	.950	20
	.975	5.8715	4.4613	3.8587	3.5147	3.2891	3.1283	.975	
	.990	8.0960	5.8489	4.9382	4.4307	4.1027	3.8714	.990	
	.995	9.9439	6.9865	5.8177	5.1743	4.7616	4.4721	.995	
	.500	.47108	.71653	.81487	.86688	.89891	.92060	.500	
	.750	1.3997	1.4820	1.4753	1.4593	1.4438	1.4302	.750	
	.900	2.9609	2.5746	2.3649	2.2333	2.1423	2.0751	.900	
21	.950	4.3248	3.4668	3.0725	2.8401	2.6848	2.5727	.950	21
	.975	5.8266	4.4199	3.8188	3.4754	3.2501	3.0895	.975	
	.990	8.0166	5.7804	4.8740	4.3688	4.0421	3.8117	.990	
	.995	9.8295	6.8914	5.7304	5.0911	4.6808	4.3931	.995	
	.500	.47033	.71545	.81365	.86559	.89759	.91924	.500	
	.750	1.3961	1.4774	1.4703	1.4540	1.4382	1.4244	.750	
	.900	2.9486	2.5613	2.3512	2.2193	2.1279	2.0605	.900	
22	.950	4.3009	3.4434	3.0491	2.8167	2.6613	2.5491	.950	22
	.975	5.7863	4.3828	3.7829	3.4401	3.2151	3.0546	.975	
	.990	7.9454	5.7190	4.8166	4.3134	3.9880	3.7583	.990	
	.995	9.7271	6.8064	5.6524	5.0168	4.6088	4.3225	.995	
	.500	.46965	.71446	.81255	.86442	.89638	.91800	.500	
	.750	1.3928	1.4733	1.4657	1.4491	1.4331	1.4191	.750	
	.900	2.9374	2.5493	2.3387	2.2065	2.1149	2.0472	.900	
23	.950	4.2793	3.4221	3.0280	2.7955	2.6400	2.5277	.950	23
	.975	5.7498	4.3492	3.7505	3.4083	3.1835	3.0232	.975	
	.990	7.8811	5.6637	4.7649	4.2635	3.9392	3.7102	.990	
	.995	9.6348	6.7300	5.5823	4.9500	4.5441	4.2591	.995	
	.500	.46902	.71356	.81153	.86335	.89527	.91687	.500	
	.750	1.3898	1.4695	1.4615	1.4447	1.4285	1.4143	.750	
	.900	2.9271	2.5383	2.3274	2.1949	2.1030	2.0351	.900	
24	.950	4.2597	3.4028	3.0088	2.7763	2.6207	2.5082	.950	24
	.975	5.7167	4.3187	3.7211	3.3794	3.1548	2.9946	.975	
	.990	7.8229	5.6136	4.7181	4.2184	3.8951	3.6667	.990	
	.995	9.5513	6.6609	5.5190	4.8898	4.4857	4.2019	.995	

Degrees of Freedom for Denominator

Degrees of Freedom for Denominator

Critical Values of the F-Distribution (cont.)

Degrees of Freedom for Denominator

	γ	7	8	9	10	11	12	γ	
	.500	.93944	.95129	.96056	.96800	.97411	.97920	.500	
	.750	1.4325	1.4228	1.4145	1.4073	1.4008	1.3953	.750	
	.900	2.0580	2.0171	1.9836	1.9557	1.9317	1.9117	.900	
19	.950	2.5435	2.4768	2.4227	2.3779	2.3398	2.3080	.950	19
	.975	3.0509	2.9563	2.8800	2.8173	2.7640	2.7196	.975	
	.990	3.7653	3.6305	3.5225	3.4338	3.3589	3.2965	.990	
	.995	4.3448	4.1770	4.0428	3.9329	3.8403	3.7631	.995	
	.500	.93776	.94959	.95884	.96626	.97237	.97746	.500	
	.750	1.4252	1.4153	1.4069	1.3995	1.3928	1.3873	.750	
	.900	2.0397	1.9985	1.9649	1.9367	1.9125	1.8924	.900	
20	.950	2.5140	2.4471	2.3928	2.3479	2.3096	2.2776	.950	20
	.975	3.0074	2.9128	2.8365	2.7737	2.7203	2.6758	.975	
	.990	3.6987	3.5644	3.4567	3.3682	3.2934	3.2311	.990	
	.995	4.2569	4.0900	3.9564	3.8470	3.7548	3.6779	.995	
	.500	.93624	.94805	.95728	.96470	.97079	.97587	.500	
	.750	1.4186	1.4086	1.4000	1.3925	1.3857	1.3801	.750	
	.900	2.0232	1.9819	1.9480	1.9197	1.8953	1.8750	.900	
21	.950	2.4876	2.4205	2.3661	2.3210	2.2825	2.2504	.950	21
	.975	2.9686	2.8740	2.7977	2.7348	2.6813	2.6368	.975	
	.990	3.6396	3.5056	3.3981	3.3098	3.2351	3.1729	.990	
	.995	4.1789	4.0128	3.8799	3.7709	3.6790	3.6024	.995	
	.500	.93486	.94665	.95588	.96328	.96937	.97444	.500	
	.750	1.4126	1.4025	1.3937	1.3861	1.3792	1.3735	.750	
	.900	2.0084	1.9668	1.9327	1.9043	1.8798	1.8593	.900	
22	.950	2.4638	2.3965	2.3419	2.2967	2.2580	2.2258	.950	22
	.975	2.9338	2.8392	2.7628	2.6998	2.6463	2.6017	.975	
	.990	3.5867	3.4530	3.3458	3.2576	3.1830	3.1209	.990	
	.995	4.1094	3.9440	3.8116	3.7030	3.6114	3.5350	.995	
	.500	.93360	.94538	.95459	.96199	.96807	.97313	.500	
	.750	1.4072	1.3969	1.3880	1.3803	1.3733	1.3675	.750	
	.900	1.9949	1.9531	1.9189	1.8903	1.8656	1.8450	.900	
23	.950	2.4422	2.3748	2.3201	2.2747	2.2359	2.2036	.950	23
	.975	2.9024	2.8077	2.7313	2.6682	2.6146	2.5699	.975	
	.990	3.5390	3.4057	3.2986	3.2106	3.1361	3.0740	.990	
	.995	4.0469	3.8822	3.7502	3.6420	3.5506	3.4745	.995	
	.500	.93245	.94422	.95342	.96081	.96688	.97194	.500	
	.750	1.4022	1.3918	1.3828	1.3750	1.3680	1.3621	.750	
	.900	1.9826	1.9407	1.9063	1.8775	1.8526	1.8319	.900	
24	.950	2.4226	2.3551	2.3002	2.2547	2.2158	2.1834	.950	24
	.975	2.8738	2.7791	2.7027	2.6396	2.5859	2.5412	.975	
	.990	3.4959	3.3629	3.2560	3.1681	3.0936	3.0316	.990	
	.995	3.9905	3.8264	3.6949	3.5870	3.4959	3.4199	.995	

Degrees of Freedom for Denominator

Degrees of Freedom for Denominator

4.1

Critical Values of the F-Distribution (cont.)

	γ	13	14	15	18	20	24	γ	
	.500	.98354	.98725	.99047	.99802	1.0018	1.0075	.500	
	.750	1.3901	1.3857	1.3819	1.3717	1.3666	1.3582	.750	
	.900	1.8936	1.8781	1.8647	1.8310	1.8142	1.7873	.900	
19	.950	2.2796	2.2552	2.2341	2.1817	2.1555	2.1141	.950	19
	.975	2.6802	2.6464	2.6171	2.5450	2.5089	2.4523	.975	
	.990	3.2414	3.1942	3.1533	3.0532	3.0031	2.9249	.990	
	.995	3.6952	3.6370	3.5866	3.4635	3.4020	3.3062	.995	
	.500	.98178	.98549	.98870	.99623	1.0000	1.0057	.500	
	.750	1.3820	1.3775	1.3736	1.3632	1.3580	1.3494	.750	
	.900	1.8741	1.8585	1.8449	1.8108	1.7938	1.7667	.900	
20	.950	2.2490	2.2245	2.2033	2.1506	2.1242	2.0825	.950	20
	.975	2.6363	2.6024	2.5731	2.5007	2.4645	2.4076	.975	
	.990	3.1761	3.1289	3.0880	2.9878	2.9377	2.8594	.990	
	.995	3.6102	3.5523	3.5020	3.3792	3.3178	3.2220	.995	
	.500	.98019	.98389	.98710	.99462	.99838	1.0040	.500	
	.750	1.3747	1.3701	1.3661	1.3555	1.3502	1.3414	.750	
	.900	1.8566	1.8409	1.8272	1.7928	1.7756	1.7481	.900	
21	.950	2.2217	2.1970	2.1757	2.1226	2.0960	2.0540	.950	21
	.975	2.5972	2.5632	2.5338	2.4611	2.4247	2.3675	.975	
	.990	3.1179	3.0708	3.0299	2.9297	2.8796	2.8011	.990	
	.995	3.5349	3.4771	3.4270	3.3044	3.2431	3.1474	.995	
	.500	.97875	.98245	.98565	.99316	.99692	1.0026	.500	
	.750	1.3680	1.3634	1.3593	1.3485	1.3431	1.3341	.750	
	.900	1.8408	1.8249	1.8111	1.7764	1.7590	1.7312	.900	
22	.950	2.1970	2.1722	2.1508	2.0974	2.0707	2.0283	.950	22
	.975	2.5620	2.5279	2.4984	2.4255	2.3890	2.3315	.975	
	.990	3.0659	3.0188	2.9780	2.8776	2.8274	2.7488	.990	
	.995	3.4677	3.4100	3.3600	3.2376	3.1764	3.0807	.995	
	.500	.97744	.98113	.98433	.99183	.99558	1.0012	.500	
	.750	1.3620	1.3572	1.3531	1.3421	1.3366	1.3275	.750	
	.900	1.8263	1.8103	1.7964	1.7614	1.7439	1.7159	.900	
23	.950	2.1746	2.1497	2.1282	2.0745	2.0476	2.0050	.950	23
	.975	2.5301	2.4960	2.4665	2.3933	2.3567	2.2989	.975	
	.990	3.0190	2.9719	2.9311	2.8307	2.7805	2.7017	.990	
	.995	3.4073	3.3498	3.2999	3.1776	3.1165	3.0208	.995	
	.500	.97624	.97993	.98312	.99061	.99436	1.0000	.500	
	.750	1.3564	1.3516	1.3474	1.3363	1.3307	1.3214	.750	
	.900	1.8131	1.7970	1.7831	1.7478	1.7302	1.7019	.900	
24	.950	2.1543	2.1293	2.1077	2.0537	2.0267	1.9838	.950	24
	.975	2.5013	2.4671	2.4374	2.3640	2.3273	2.2693	.975	
	.990	2.9766	2.9295	2.8887	2.7882	2.7380	2.6591	.990	
	.995	3.3529	3.2954	3.2456	3.1235	3.0624	2.9667	.995	

Degrees of Freedom for Numerator

Degrees of Freedom for Denominator

4.1

Critical Values of the F-Distribution (cont.)

	γ	30	40	48	60	120	∞	γ	
				Degrees of Freedom for Numerator					
	.500	1.0132	1.0189	1.0218	1.0246	1.0304	1.0361	.500	
	.750	1.3492	1.3394	1.3342	1.3289	1.3174	1.3048	.750	
	.900	1.7592	1.7298	1.7143	1.6988	1.6659	1.6308	.900	
19	.950	2.0712	2.0264	2.0030	1.9796	1.9302	1.8780	.950	19
	.975	2.3937	2.3329	2.3012	2.2695	2.2032	2.1333	.975	
	.990	2.8442	2.7608	2.7175	2.6742	2.5839	2.4893	.990	
	.995	3.2075	3.1058	3.0531	3.0004	2.8908	2.7762	.995	
	.500	1.0114	1.0171	1.0200	1.0228	1.0285	1.0343	.500	
	.750	1.3401	1.3301	1.3247	1.3193	1.3074	1.2943	.750	
	.900	1.7382	1.7083	1.6926	1.6768	1.6433	1.6074	.900	
20	.950	2.0391	1.9938	1.9701	1.9464	1.8963	1.8432	.950	20
	.975	2.3486	2.2873	2.2554	2.2234	2.1562	2.0853	.975	
	.990	2.7785	2.6947	2.6512	2.6077	2.5168	2.4212	.990	
	.995	3.1234	3.0215	2.9687	2.9159	2.8058	2.6904	.995	
	.500	1.0097	1.0154	1.0183	1.0211	1.0268	1.0326	.500	
	.750	1.3319	1.3217	1.3161	1.3105	1.2983	1.2848	.750	
	.900	1.7193	1.6890	1.6730	1.6569	1.6228	1.5862	.900	
21	.950	2.0102	1.9645	1.9405	1.9165	1.8657	1.8117	.950	21
	.975	2.3082	2.2465	2.2142	2.1819	2.1141	2.0422	.975	
	.990	2.7200	2.6359	2.5922	2.5484	2.4568	2.3603	.990	
	.995	3.0488	2.9467	2.8938	2.8408	2.7302	2.6140	.995	
	.500	1.0082	1.0139	1.0168	1.0196	1.0253	1.0311	.500	
	.750	1.3245	1.3140	1.3083	1.3025	1.2900	1.2761	.750	
	.900	1.7021	1.6714	1.6552	1.6389	1.6042	1.5668	.900	
22	.950	1.9842	1.9380	1.9138	1.8895	1.8380	1.7831	.950	22
	.975	2.2718	2.2097	2.1772	2.1446	2.0760	2.0032	.975	
	.990	2.6675	2.5831	2.5391	2.4951	2.4029	2.3055	.990	
	.995	2.9821	2.8799	2.8268	2.7736	2.6625	2.5455	.995	
	.500	1.0069	1.0126	1.0155	1.0183	1.0240	1.0297	.500	
	.750	1.3176	1.3069	1.3011	1.2952	1.2824	1.2681	.750	
	.900	1.6864	1.6554	1.6389	1.6224	1.5871	1.5490	.900	
23	.950	1.9605	1.9139	1.8894	1.8649	1.8128	1.7570	.950	23
	.975	2.2389	2.1763	2.1435	2.1107	2.0415	1.9677	.975	
	.990	2.6202	2.5355	2.4913	2.4471	2.3542	2.2559	.990	
	.995	2.9221	2.8198	2.7665	2.7132	2.6016	2.4837	.995	
	.500	1.0057	1.0113	1.0142	1.0170	1.0227	1.0284	.500	
	.750	1.3113	1.3004	1.2945	1.2885	1.2754	1.2607	.750	
	.900	1.6721	1.6407	1.6240	1.6073	1.5715	1.5327	.900	
24	.950	1.9390	1.8920	1.8672	1.8424	1.7897	1.7331	.950	24
	.975	2.2090	2.1460	2.1130	2.0799	2.0099	1.9353	.975	
	.990	2.5773	2.4923	2.4479	2.4035	2.3099	2.2107	.990	
	.995	2.8679	2.7654	2.7120	2.6585	2.5463	2.4276	.995	

Degrees of Freedom for Denominator (left margin)

Degrees of Freedom for Denominator (right margin)

4.1

Critical Values of the F-Distribution (cont.)

	γ	Degrees of Freedom for Numerator						γ	
		1	2	3	4	5	6		
	.500	.46844	.71272	.81061	.86236	.89425	.91583	.500	
	.750	1.3870	1.4661	1.4577	1.4406	1.4242	1.4099	.750	
	.900	2.9177	2.5283	2.3170	2.1843	2.0922	2.0241	.900	
25	.950	4.2417	3.3852	2.9912	2.7587	2.6030	2.4904	.950	25
	.975	5.6864	4.2909	3.6943	3.3530	3.1287	2.9685	.975	
	.990	7.7698	5.5680	4.6755	4.1774	3.8550	3.6272	.990	
	.995	9.4753	6.5982	5.4615	4.8351	4.4327	4.1500	.995	
	.500	.46793	.71195	.80975	.86145	.89331	.91487	.500	
	.750	1.3845	1.4629	1.4542	1.4368	1.4203	1.4058	.750	
	.900	2.9091	2.5191	2.3075	2.1745	2.0822	2.0139	.900	
26	.950	4.2252	3.3690	2.9751	2.7426	2.5868	2.4741	.950	26
	.975	5.6586	4.2655	3.6697	3.3289	3.1048	2.9447	.975	
	.990	7.7213	5.5263	4.6366	4.1400	3.8183	3.5911	.990	
	.995	9.4059	6.5409	5.4091	4.7852	4.3844	4.1027	.995	
	.500	.46744	.71124	.80894	.86061	.89244	.91399	.500	
	.750	1.3822	1.4600	1.4510	1.4334	1.4166	1.4021	.750	
	.900	2.9012	2.5106	2.2987	2.1655	2.0730	2.0045	.900	
27	.950	4.2100	3.3541	2.9604	2.7278	2.5719	2.4591	.950	27
	.975	5.6331	4.2421	3.6472	3.3067	3.0828	2.9228	.975	
	.990	7.6767	5.4881	4.6009	4.1056	3.7848	3.5580	.990	
	.995	9.3423	6.4885	5.3611	4.7396	4.3402	4.0594	.995	
	.500	.46697	.71059	.80820	.85983	.89164	.91317	.500	
	.750	1.3800	1.4573	1.4480	1.4302	1.4133	1.3986	.750	
	.900	2.8939	2.5028	2.2906	2.1571	2.0645	1.9959	.900	
28	.950	4.1960	3.3404	2.9467	2.7141	2.5581	2.4453	.950	28
	.975	5.6096	4.2205	3.6264	3.2863	3.0625	2.9027	.975	
	.990	7.6356	5.4529	4.5681	4.0740	3.7539	3.5276	.990	
	.995	9.2838	6.4403	5.3170	4.6977	4.2996	4.0197	.995	
	.500	.46654	.70999	.80753	.85911	.89089	.91241	.500	
	.750	1.3780	1.4547	1.4452	1.4272	1.4102	1.3953	.750	
	.900	2.8871	2.4955	2.2831	2.1494	2.0566	1.9878	.900	
29	.950	4.1830	3.3277	2.9340	2.7014	2.5454	2.4324	.950	29
	.975	5.5878	4.2006	3.6072	3.2674	3.0438	2.8840	.975	
	.990	7.5976	5.4205	4.5378	4.0449	3.7254	3.4995	.990	
	.995	9.2297	6.3958	5.2764	4.6591	4.2622	3.9830	.995	
	.500	.46616	.70941	.80689	.85844	.89019	.91169	.500	
	.750	1.3761	1.4524	1.4426	1.4244	1.4073	1.3923	.750	
	.900	2.8807	2.4887	2.2761	2.1422	2.0492	1.9803	.900	
30	.950	4.1709	3.3158	2.9223	2.6896	2.5336	2.4205	.950	30
	.975	5.5675	4.1821	3.5894	3.2499	3.0265	2.8667	.975	
	.990	7.5625	5.3903	4.5097	4.0179	3.6990	3.4735	.990	
	.995	9.1797	6.3547	5.2388	4.6233	4.2276	3.9492	.995	

Degrees of Freedom for Denominator

Degrees of Freedom for Denominator

Critical Values of the F-Distribution (cont.)

	γ	Degrees of Freedom for Numerator						γ	
		7	8	9	10	11	12		
	.500	.93140	.94315	.95234	.95972	.96579	.97084	.500	
	.750	1.3976	1.3871	1.3780	1.3701	1.3630	1.3570	.750	
	.900	1.9714	1.9292	1.8947	1.8658	1.8408	1.8200	.900	
25	.950	2.4047	2.3371	2.2821	2.2365	2.1974	2.1649	.950	25
	.975	2.8478	2.7531	2.6766	2.6135	2.5597	2.5149	.975	
	.990	3.4568	3.3239	3.2172	3.1294	3.0551	2.9931	.990	
	.995	3.9394	3.7758	3.6447	3.5370	3.4461	3.3704	.995	
	.500	.93042	.94217	.95135	.95872	.96478	.96983	.500	
	.750	1.3935	1.3828	1.3737	1.3656	1.3584	1.3524	.750	
	.900	1.9610	1.9188	1.8841	1.8550	1.8299	1.8090	.900	
26	.950	2.3883	2.3205	2.2655	2.2197	2.1805	2.1479	.950	26
	.975	2.8240	2.7293	2.6528	2.5895	2.5357	2.4909	.975	
	.990	3.4210	3.2884	3.1818	3.0941	3.0198	2.9579	.990	
	.995	3.8928	3.7297	3.5989	3.4916	3.4008	3.3252	.995	
	.500	.92952	.94126	.95044	.95779	.96385	.96889	.500	
	.750	1.3896	1.3788	1.3696	1.3615	1.3542	1.3481	.750	
	.900	1.9515	1.9091	1.8743	1.8451	1.8199	1.7989	.900	
27	.950	2.3732	2.3053	2.2501	2.2043	2.1650	2.1323	.950	27
	.975	2.8021	2.7074	2.6309	2.5676	2.5137	2.4688	.975	
	.990	3.3882	3.2558	3.1494	3.0618	2.9875	2.9256	.990	
	.995	3.8501	3.6875	3.5571	3.4499	3.3594	3.2839	.995	
	.500	.92869	.94041	.94958	.95694	.96298	.96802	.500	
	.750	1.3860	1.3752	1.3658	1.3576	1.3502	1.3441	.750	
	.900	1.9427	1.9001	1.8652	1.8359	1.8106	1.7895	.900	
28	.950	2.3593	2.2913	2.2360	2.1900	2.1507	2.1179	.950	28
	.975	2.7820	2.6872	2.6106	2.5473	2.4934	2.4484	.975	
	.990	3.3581	3.2259	3.1195	3.0320	2.9578	2.8959	.990	
	.995	3.8110	3.6487	3.5186	3.4117	3.3213	3.2460	.995	
	.500	.92791	.93963	.94879	.95614	.96218	.96722	.500	
	.750	1.3826	1.3717	1.3623	1.3541	1.3466	1.3404	.750	
	.900	1.9345	1.8918	1.8568	1.8274	1.8020	1.7808	.900	
29	.950	2.3463	2.2782	2.2229	2.1768	2.1374	2.1045	.950	29
	.975	2.7633	2.6686	2.5919	2.5286	2.4745	2.4295	.975	
	.990	3.3302	3.1982	3.0920	3.0045	2.9303	2.8685	.990	
	.995	3.7749	3.6130	3.4832	3.3765	3.2863	3.2111	.995	
	.500	.92719	.93889	.94805	.95540	.96144	.96647	.500	
	.750	1.3795	1.3685	1.3590	1.3507	1.3432	1.3369	.750	
	.900	1.9269	1.8841	1.8490	1.8195	1.7940	1.7727	.900	
30	.950	2.3343	2.2662	2.2107	2.1646	2.1251	2.0921	.950	30
	.975	2.7460	2.6513	2.5746	2.5112	2.4571	2.4120	.975	
	.990	3.3045	3.1726	3.0665	2.9791	2.9049	2.8431	.990	
	.995	3.7416	3.5801	3.4505	3.3440	3.2538	3.1787	.995	

Degrees of Freedom for Denominator

4.1

Critical Values of the F-Distribution (cont.)

	γ	13	14	15	18	20	24	γ	
			Degrees of Freedom for Numerator						
	.500	.97514	.97882	.98201	.98950	.99324	.99887	.500	
	.750	1.3513	1.3464	1.3422	1.3309	1.3252	1.3158	.750	
	.900	1.8011	1.7849	1.7708	1.7353	1.7175	1.6890	.900	
25	.950	2.1357	2.1106	2.0889	2.0346	2.0075	1.9643	.950	25
	.975	2.4749	2.4407	2.4110	2.3373	2.3005	2.2422	.975	
	.990	2.9381	2.8910	2.8502	2.7496	2.6993	2.6203	.990	
	.995	3.3034	3.2460	3.1963	3.0743	3.0133	2.9176	.995	
	.500	.97412	.97780	.98099	.98846	.99220	.99783	.500	
	.750	1.3466	1.3417	1.3374	1.3259	1.3202	1.3106	.750	
	.900	1.7900	1.7737	1.7596	1.7238	1.7059	1.6771	.900	
26	.950	2.1186	2.0934	2.0716	2.0171	1.9898	1.9464	.950	26
	.975	2.4508	2.4165	2.3867	2.3128	2.2759	2.2174	.975	
	.990	2.9029	2.8558	2.8150	2.7143	2.6640	2.5848	.990	
	.995	3.2584	3.2011	3.1515	3.0295	2.9685	2.8728	.995	
	.500	.97318	.97685	.98004	.98751	.99125	.99687	.500	
	.750	1.3423	1.3372	1.3329	1.3213	1.3155	1.3058	.750	
	.900	1.7798	1.7634	1.7492	1.7131	1.6951	1.6662	.900	
27	.950	2.1029	2.0777	2.0558	2.0010	1.9736	1.9299	.950	27
	.975	2.4286	2.3942	2.3644	2.2903	2.2533	2.1946	.975	
	.990	2.8706	2.8235	2.7827	2.6820	2.6316	2.5522	.990	
	.995	3.2172	3.1600	3.1104	2.9885	2.9275	2.8318	.995	
	.500	.97231	.97598	.97917	.98663	.99036	.99598	.500	
	.750	1.3382	1.3332	1.3288	1.3171	1.3112	1.3013	.750	
	.900	1.7703	1.7538	1.7395	1.7033	1.6852	1.6560	.900	
28	.950	2.0884	2.0630	2.0411	1.9861	1.9586	1.9147	.950	28
	.975	2.4082	2.3737	2.3438	2.2695	2.2324	2.1735	.975	
	.990	2.8409	2.7938	2.7530	2.6521	2.6017	2.5223	.990	
	.995	3.1793	3.1222	3.0727	2.9508	2.8899	2.7941	.995	
	.500	.97150	.97517	.97835	.98581	.98954	.99515	.500	
	.750	1.3344	1.3293	1.3249	1.3130	1.3071	1.2971	.750	
	.900	1.7615	1.7449	1.7306	1.6941	1.6759	1.6465	.900	
29	.950	2.0749	2.0495	2.0275	1.9722	1.9446	1.9005	.950	29
	.975	2.3892	2.3547	2.3248	2.2503	2.2131	2.1540	.975	
	.990	2.8135	2.7664	2.7256	2.6247	2.5742	2.4946	.990	
	.995	3.1445	3.0874	3.0379	2.9160	2.8551	2.7594	.995	
	.500	.97075	.97441	.97759	.98504	.98877	.99438	.500	
	.750	1.3309	1.3258	1.3213	1.3093	1.3033	1.2933	.750	
	.900	1.7533	1.7367	1.7223	1.6856	1.6673	1.6377	.900	
30	.950	2.0624	2.0369	2.0148	1.9594	1.9317	1.8874	.950	30
	.975	2.3717	2.3371	2.3072	2.2325	2.1952	2.1359	.975	
	.990	2.7881	2.7410	2.7002	2.5992	2.5487	2.4689	.990	
	.995	3.1122	3.0551	3.0057	2.8839	2.8230	2.7272	.995	

Degrees of Freedom for Denominator

Degrees of Freedom for Denominator

Critical Values of the F-Distribution (cont.)

	γ	30	40	48	60	120	∞	γ	
				Degrees of Freedom for Numerator					
	.500	1.0045	1.0102	1.0131	1.0159	1.0215	1.0273	.500	
	.750	1.3056	1.2945	1.2884	1.2823	1.2689	1.2538	.750	
	.900	1.6589	1.6272	1.6103	1.5934	1.5570	1.5176	.900	
25	.950	1.9192	1.8718	1.8468	1.8217	1.7684	1.7110	.950	25
	.975	2.1816	2.1183	2.0850	2.0517	1.9811	1.9055	.975	
	.990	2.5383	2.4530	2.4084	2.3637	2.2695	2.1694	.990	
	.995	2.8187	2.7160	2.6624	2.6088	2.4960	2.3765	.995	
	.500	1.0035	1.0091	1.0120	1.0148	1.0205	1.0262	.500	
	.750	1.3002	1.2889	1.2827	1.2765	1.2628	1.2474	.750	
	.900	1.6468	1.6147	1.5976	1.5805	1.5437	1.5036	.900	
26	.950	1.9010	1.8533	1.8280	1.8027	1.7488	1.6906	.950	26
	.975	2.1565	2.0928	2.0593	2.0257	1.9545	1.8781	.975	
	.990	2.5026	2.4170	2.3722	2.3273	2.2325	2.1315	.990	
	.995	2.7738	2.6709	2.6171	2.5633	2.4501	2.3297	.995	
	.500	1.0025	1.0082	1.0110	1.0138	1.0195	1.0252	.500	
	.750	1.2953	1.2838	1.2775	1.2712	1.2572	1.2414	.750	
	.900	1.6356	1.6032	1.5859	1.5686	1.5313	1.4906	.900	
27	.950	1.8842	1.8361	1.8106	1.7851	1.7307	1.6717	.950	27
	.975	2.1334	2.0693	2.0356	2.0018	1.9299	1.8527	.975	
	.990	2.4699	2.3840	2.3389	2.2938	2.1984	2.0965	.990	
	.995	2.7327	2.6296	2.5757	2.5217	2.4078	2.2867	.995	
	.500	1.0016	1.0073	1.0101	1.0129	1.0186	1.0243	.500	
	.750	1.2906	1.2790	1.2726	1.2662	1.2519	1.2358	.750	
	.900	1.6252	1.5925	1.5750	1.5575	1.5198	1.4784	.900	
28	.950	1.8687	1.8203	1.7946	1.7689	1.7138	1.6541	.950	28
	.975	2.1121	2.0477	2.0137	1.9796	1.9072	1.8291	.975	
	.990	2.4397	2.3535	2.3082	2.2629	2.1670	2.0642	.990	
	.995	2.6949	2.5916	2.5375	2.4834	2.3689	2.2469	.995	
	.500	1.0008	1.0064	1.0093	1.0121	1.0177	1.0234	.500	
	.750	1.2863	1.2745	1.2680	1.2615	1.2470	1.2306	.750	
	.900	1.6155	1.5825	1.5649	1.5472	1.5090	1.4670	.900	
29	.950	1.8543	1.8055	1.7796	1.7537	1.6981	1.6377	.950	29
	.975	2.0923	2.0276	1.9934	1.9591	1.8861	1.8072	.975	
	.990	2.4118	2.3253	2.2799	2.2344	2.1378	2.0342	.990	
	.995	2.6601	2.5565	2.5022	2.4479	2.3330	2.2102	.995	
	.500	1.0000	1.0056	1.0085	1.0113	1.0170	1.0226	.500	
	.750	1.2823	1.2703	1.2637	1.2571	1.2424	1.2256	.750	
	.900	1.6065	1.5732	1.5554	1.5376	1.4989	1.4564	.900	
30	.950	1.8409	1.7918	1.7657	1.7396	1.6835	1.6223	.950	30
	.975	2.0739	2.0089	1.9745	1.9400	1.8664	1.7867	.975	
	.990	2.3860	2.2992	2.2536	2.2079	2.1107	2.0062	.990	
	.995	2.6278	2.5241	2.4696	2.4151	2.2997	2.1760	.995	

Degrees of Freedom for Denominator

Degrees of Freedom for Denominator

4.1

Critical Values of the F-Distribution (cont.)

	γ	Degrees of Freedom for Numerator						γ	
		1	2	3	4	5	6		
40	.500	.46330	.70531	.80228	.85357	.88516	.90654	.500	40
	.750	1.3626	1.4355	1.4239	1.4045	1.3863	1.3706	.750	
	.900	2.8354	2.4404	2.2261	2.0909	1.9968	1.9269	.900	
	.950	4.0848	3.2317	2.8387	2.6060	2.4495	2.3359	.950	
	.975	5.4239	4.0510	3.4633	3.1261	2.9037	2.7444	.975	
	.990	7.3141	5.1785	4.3126	3.8283	3.5138	3.2910	.990	
	.995	8.8278	6.0664	4.9759	4.3738	3.9860	3.7129	.995	
48	.500	.46192	.70327	.79999	.85115	.88267	.90399	.500	48
	.750	1.3560	1.4272	1.4147	1.3947	1.3760	1.3599	.750	
	.900	2.8134	2.4168	2.2018	2.0660	1.9713	1.9008	.900	
	.950	4.0430	3.1911	2.7984	2.5656	2.4089	2.2950	.950	
	.975	5.3548	3.9882	3.4029	3.0669	2.8450	2.6859	.975	
	.990	7.1956	5.0780	4.2193	3.7387	3.4264	3.2049	.990	
	.995	8.6612	5.9307	4.8525	4.2569	3.8730	3.6024	.995	
60	.500	.46053	.70122	.79770	.84873	.88017	.90144	.500	60
	.750	1.3493	1.4188	1.4055	1.3848	1.3657	1.3491	.750	
	.900	2.7914	2.3933	2.1774	2.0410	1.9457	1.8747	.900	
	.950	4.0012	3.1504	2.7581	2.5252	2.3683	2.2540	.950	
	.975	5.2857	3.9253	3.3425	3.0077	2.7863	2.6274	.975	
	.990	7.0771	4.9774	4.1259	3.6491	3.3389	3.1187	.990	
	.995	8.4946	5.7950	4.7290	4.1399	3.7600	3.4918	.995	
80	.500	.45914	.69920	.79542	.84633	.87769	.89891	.500	80
	.750	1.3428	1.4106	1.3964	1.3751	1.3555	1.3385	.750	
	.900	2.7696	2.3703	2.1537	2.0167	1.9208	1.8493	.900	
	.950	3.9607	3.1111	2.7192	2.4862	2.3292	2.2145	.950	
	.975	5.2191	3.8650	3.2848	2.9510	2.7302	2.5714	.975	
	.990	6.9641	4.8820	4.0375	3.5644	3.2562	3.0373	.990	
	.995	8.3368	5.6672	4.6132	4.0303	3.6541	3.3884	.995	
120	.500	.45774	.69717	.79314	.84392	.87521	.89637	.500	120
	.750	1.3362	1.4024	1.3873	1.3654	1.3453	1.3278	.750	
	.900	2.7478	2.3473	2.1300	1.9923	1.8959	1.8238	.900	
	.950	3.9201	3.0718	2.6802	2.4472	2.2900	2.1750	.950	
	.975	5.1524	3.8046	3.2270	2.8943	2.6740	2.5154	.975	
	.990	6.8510	4.7865	3.9491	3.4796	3.1735	2.9559	.990	
	.995	8.1790	5.5393	4.4973	3.9207	3.5482	3.2849	.995	
∞	.500	.45494	.69315	.78866	.83918	.87029	.89135	.500	∞
	.750	1.3233	1.3863	1.3694	1.3463	1.3251	1.3068	.750	
	.900	2.7055	2.3026	2.0838	1.9449	1.8473	1.7741	.900	
	.950	3.8415	2.9957	2.6049	2.3719	2.2141	2.0986	.950	
	.975	5.0239	3.6889	3.1161	2.7858	2.5665	2.4082	.975	
	.990	6.6349	4.6052	3.7816	3.3192	3.0173	2.8020	.990	
	.995	7.8794	5.2983	4.2794	3.7151	3.3499	3.0913	.995	

Degrees of Freedom for Denominator

4.1

Critical Values of the F-Distribution (cont.)

Degrees of Freedom for Numerator

	γ	7	8	9	10	11	12	γ	
40	.500	.92197	.93361	.94272	.95003	.95604	.96104	.500	**40**
	.750	1.3571	1.3455	1.3354	1.3266	1.3186	1.3119	.750	
	.900	1.8725	1.8289	1.7929	1.7627	1.7365	1.7146	.900	
	.950	2.2490	2.1802	2.1240	2.0772	2.0370	2.0035	.950	
	.975	2.6238	2.5289	2.4519	2.3882	2.3337	2.2882	.975	
	.990	3.1238	2.9930	2.8876	2.8005	2.7265	2.6648	.990	
	.995	3.5088	3.3498	3.2220	3.1167	3.0275	2.9531	.995	
48	.500	.91938	.93100	.94008	.94737	.95336	.95835	.500	**48**
	.750	1.3460	1.3341	1.3237	1.3146	1.3063	1.2995	.750	
	.900	1.8460	1.8019	1.7655	1.7349	1.7082	1.6860	.900	
	.950	2.2078	2.1386	2.0821	2.0349	1.9943	1.9605	.950	
	.975	2.5653	2.4703	2.3932	2.3292	2.2744	2.2287	.975	
	.990	3.0384	2.9082	2.8031	2.7162	2.6421	2.5805	.990	
	.995	3.4000	3.2421	3.1152	3.0105	2.9216	2.8475	.995	
60	.500	.91679	.92838	.93743	.94471	.95068	.95566	.500	**60**
	.750	1.3349	1.3226	1.3119	1.3026	1.2941	1.2870	.750	
	.900	1.8194	1.7748	1.7380	1.7070	1.6799	1.6574	.900	
	.950	2.1665	2.0970	2.0401	1.9926	1.9516	1.9174	.950	
	.975	2.5068	2.4117	2.3344	2.2702	2.2151	2.1692	.975	
	.990	2.9530	2.8233	2.7185	2.6318	2.5578	2.4961	.990	
	.995	3.2911	3.1344	3.0083	2.9042	2.8157	2.7419	.995	
80	.500	.91422	.92578	.93481	.94207	.94803	.95299	.500	**80**
	.750	1.3239	1.3113	1.3003	1.2907	1.2819	1.2746	.750	
	.900	1.7935	1.7484	1.7112	1.6797	1.6522	1.6293	.900	
	.950	2.1266	2.0567	1.9995	1.9516	1.9101	1.8756	.950	
	.975	2.4508	2.3556	2.2781	2.2136	2.1582	2.1120	.975	
	.990	2.8724	2.7431	2.6386	2.5520	2.4779	2.4162	.990	
	.995	3.1893	3.0337	2.9083	2.8047	2.7164	2.6429	.995	
120	.500	.91164	.92318	.93218	.93943	.94537	.95032	.500	**120**
	.750	1.3128	1.2999	1.2886	1.2787	1.2696	1.2621	.750	
	.900	1.7675	1.7220	1.6843	1.6524	1.6245	1.6012	.900	
	.950	2.0867	2.0164	1.9588	1.9105	1.8686	1.8337	.950	
	.975	2.3948	2.2994	2.2217	2.1570	2.1013	2.0548	.975	
	.990	2.7918	2.6629	2.5586	2.4721	2.3980	2.3363	.990	
	.995	3.0874	2.9330	2.8083	2.7052	2.6172	2.5439	.995	
∞	.500	.90654	.91802	.92698	.93418	.94010	.94503	.500	**∞**
	.750	1.2910	1.2774	1.2654	1.2549	1.2452	1.2371	.750	
	.900	1.7167	1.6702	1.6315	1.5987	1.5698	1.5458	.900	
	.950	2.0096	1.9384	1.8799	1.8307	1.7879	1.7522	.950	
	.975	2.2875	2.1918	2.1136	2.0483	1.9918	1.9447	.975	
	.990	2.6393	2.5113	2.4073	2.3209	2.2467	2.1848	.990	
	.995	2.8968	2.7444	2.6210	2.5188	2.4313	2.3583	.995	

Degrees of Freedom for Denominator

4.1

Critical Values of the F-Distribution (cont.)

Degrees of Freedom for Denominator

	Υ	13	14	15	18	20	24	Υ	
		Degrees of Freedom for Numerator							
40	.500	.96530	.96895	.97211	.97952	.98323	.98880	.500	40
	.750	1.3055	1.3000	1.2952	1.2823	1.2758	1.2649	.750	
	.900	1.6945	1.6773	1.6624	1.6243	1.6052	1.5741	.900	
	.950	1.9731	1.9471	1.9245	1.8674	1.8389	1.7929	.950	
	.975	2.2473	2.2123	2.1819	2.1058	2.0677	2.0069	.975	
	.990	2.6097	2.5625	2.5216	2.4198	2.3689	2.2880	.990	
	.995	2.8869	2.8302	2.7811	2.6593	2.5984	2.5020	.995	
48	.500	.96260	.96624	.96939	.97678	.98048	.98604	.500	48
	.750	1.2928	1.2871	1.2822	1.2687	1.2620	1.2505	.750	
	.900	1.6656	1.6481	1.6329	1.5939	1.5744	1.5424	.900	
	.950	1.9297	1.9033	1.8805	1.8225	1.7935	1.7465	.950	
	.975	2.1875	2.1522	2.1216	2.0446	2.0061	1.9443	.975	
	.990	2.5253	2.4780	2.4370	2.3346	2.2834	2.2017	.990	
	.995	2.7815	2.7249	2.6758	2.5538	2.4928	2.3959	.995	
60	.500	.95990	.96352	.96667	.97404	.97773	.98328	.500	60
	.750	1.2801	1.2742	1.2691	1.2551	1.2481	1.2361	.750	
	.900	1.6366	1.6188	1.6034	1.5635	1.5435	1.5107	.900	
	.950	1.8862	1.8595	1.8364	1.7775	1.7480	1.7001	.950	
	.975	2.1277	2.0921	2.0613	1.9834	1.9445	1.8817	.975	
	.990	2.4408	2.3934	2.3523	2.2493	2.1978	2.1154	.990	
	.995	2.6760	2.6195	2.5705	2.4483	2.3872	2.2898	.995	
80	.500	.95722	.96084	.96398	.97133	.97501	.98054	.500	80
	.750	1.2674	1.2613	1.2560	1.2414	1.2341	1.2215	.750	
	.900	1.6081	1.5899	1.5742	1.5333	1.5128	1.4790	.900	
	.950	1.8440	1.8169	1.7935	1.7334	1.7034	1.6543	.950	
	.975	2.0701	2.0343	2.0032	1.9242	1.8847	1.8207	.975	
	.990	2.3607	2.3131	2.2719	2.1681	2.1162	2.0327	.990	
	.995	2.5770	2.5205	2.4716	2.3490	2.2877	2.1894	.995	
120	.500	.95454	.95815	.96128	.96861	.97228	.97780	.500	120
	.750	1.2547	1.2483	1.2428	1.2276	1.2200	1.2068	.750	
	.900	1.5796	1.5611	1.5450	1.5031	1.4821	1.4472	.900	
	.950	1.8017	1.7743	1.7505	1.6893	1.6587	1.6084	.950	
	.975	2.0126	1.9764	1.9450	1.8649	1.8249	1.7597	.975	
	.990	2.2806	2.2329	2.1915	2.0869	2.0346	1.9500	.990	
	.995	2.4781	2.4216	2.3727	2.2496	2.1881	2.0890	.995	
∞	.500	.94922	.95282	.95593	.96322	.96687	.97236	.500	∞
	.750	1.2291	1.2222	1.2163	1.1997	1.1914	1.1767	.750	
	.900	1.5232	1.5039	1.4871	1.4428	1.4206	1.3832	.900	
	.950	1.7192	1.6909	1.6664	1.6025	1.5705	1.5173	.950	
	.975	1.9016	1.8646	1.8326	1.7499	1.7085	1.6402	.975	
	.990	2.1285	2.0803	2.0385	1.9317	1.8783	1.7908	.990	
	.995	2.2923	2.2358	2.1868	2.0621	1.9998	1.8983	.995	

Degrees of Freedom for Denominator

Critical Values of the F-Distribution (cont.)

	Υ	Degrees of Freedom for Numerator						Υ	
		30	40	48	60	120	∞		
	.500	.99440	1.0000	1.0028	1.0056	1.0113	1.0169	.500	
	.750	1.2529	1.2397	1.2323	1.2249	1.2080	1.1883	.750	
	.900	1.5411	1.5056	1.4864	1.4672	1.4248	1.3769	.900	
40	.950	1.7444	1.6928	1.6651	1.6373	1.5766	1.5089	.950	40
	.975	1.9429	1.8752	1.8390	1.8028	1.7242	1.6371	.975	
	.990	2.2034	2.1142	2.0668	2.0194	1.9172	1.8047	.990	
	.995	2.4015	2.2958	2.2398	2.1838	2.0635	1.9318	.995	
	.500	.99162	.99721	1.0000	1.0028	1.0085	1.0141	.500	
	.750	1.2379	1.2239	1.2160	1.2081	1.1898	1.1679	.750	
	.900	1.5083	1.4715	1.4513	1.4312	1.3862	1.3342	.900	
48	.950	1.6968	1.6436	1.6147	1.5858	1.5220	1.4491	.950	48
	.975	1.8791	1.8096	1.7722	1.7348	1.6526	1.5597	.975	
	.990	2.1160	2.0251	1.9765	1.9279	1.8218	1.7027	.990	
	.995	2.2945	2.1874	2.1302	2.0730	1.9488	1.8102	.995	
	.500	.98884	.99441	.99721	1.0000	1.0056	1.0112	.500	
	.750	1.2229	1.2081	1.1997	1.1912	1.1715	1.1474	.750	
	.900	1.4755	1.4373	1.4163	1.3952	1.3476	1.2915	.900	
60	.950	1.6491	1.5943	1.5643	1.5343	1.4673	1.3893	.950	60
	.975	1.8152	1.7440	1.7054	1.6668	1.5810	1.4822	.975	
	.990	2.0285	1.9360	1.8862	1.8363	1.7263	1.6006	.990	
	.995	2.1874	2.0789	2.0206	1.9622	1.8341	1.6885	.995	
	.500	.98609	.99164	.99443	.99722	1.0028	1.0084	.500	
	.750	1.2075	1.1917	1.1825	1.1734	1.1515	1.1231	.750	
	.900	1.4425	1.4025	1.3801	1.3578	1.3061	1.2421	.900	
80	.950	1.6017	1.5448	1.5132	1.4817	1.4096	1.3216	.950	80
	.975	1.7526	1.6791	1.6387	1.5984	1.5069	1.3963	.975	
	.990	1.9443	1.8494	1.7977	1.7460	1.6297	1.4906	.990	
	.995	2.0857	1.9749	1.9147	1.8546	1.7198	1.5598	.995	
	.500	.98333	.98887	.99165	.99443	1.0000	1.0056	.500	
	.750	1.1921	1.1752	1.1654	1.1555	1.1314	1.0987	.750	
	.900	1.4094	1.3676	1.3440	1.3203	1.2646	1.1926	.900	
120	.950	1.5543	1.4952	1.4621	1.4290	1.3519	1.2539	.950	120
	.975	1.6899	1.6141	1.5720	1.5299	1.4327	1.3104	.975	
	.990	1.8600	1.7628	1.7093	1.6557	1.5330	1.3805	.990	
	.995	1.9839	1.8709	1.8089	1.7469	1.6055	1.4311	.995	
	.500	.97787	.98339	.98615	.98891	.99445	1.0000	.500	
	.750	1.1600	1.1404	1.1284	1.1164	1.0838	1.0000	.750	
	.900	1.3419	1.2951	1.2676	1.2400	1.1686	1.0000	.900	
∞	.950	1.4591	1.3940	1.3560	1.3180	1.2214	1.0000	.950	∞
	.975	1.5660	1.4835	1.4359	1.3883	1.2684	1.0000	.975	
	.990	1.6964	1.5923	1.5327	1.4730	1.3246	1.0000	.990	
	.995	1.7891	1.6691	1.6008	1.5325	1.3637	1.0000	.995	

Degrees of Freedom for Denominator

Degrees of Freedom for Denominator

4.1

4.2 Graphs of the Power of the F-Test

The graphs and nomograms given here are of the noncentral F-distribution. The noncentral F arises as the distribution of the ratio of a noncentral chi-square with f_1 degrees of freedom and noncentrality parameter δ to an independent central chi-square with f_2 degrees of freedom. The relationship plotted is

$$\Pr\{(\text{noncentral } F \text{ with parameters } f_1, f_2, \delta) > [(1 - \alpha)\text{th}$$
$$\text{critical value of the central } F \text{ with parameters } f_1, f_2]\} = \beta,$$

where in the graphs $\phi = \delta(f_1 + 1)^{-1/2}$.

The two nomograms are intended to simplify interpolation to values of β different from 0.5, 0.7, 0.8, and 0.9. For a given pair of values (β, ϕ) the points corresponding are located in each of the two grids, and then the straight line through these two points is the approximate contour of ϕ.

P. C. Tang [217] tabulated the values of $1 - \beta$ for $\alpha = 0.01$ and $\alpha = 0.05$ and fixed values of ϕ. These tables have been reproduced in many books, especially those dealing with the analysis of variance.

An example will make clear how the graphs of the power of the F-tests are used. It will be taken from Fox's paper [72]: "We consider the design of an experiment to test for possible effects of geographic locality on electrodermal resistance in 10-year-old children. We shall test children from $k = 6$ cities. Let the hypothesis to be tested at the 5-percent significance level be that the locality effects are zero. Suppose we want a reasonable chance β of detecting that the locality effects are not zero when they are really δ_i, $i = 1, \ldots, k$, where $\sum_{i=1}^{k} \delta_i = 0$. In particular suppose that when $\sum \delta_i^2/\sigma^2 = 2$, that is, when the sum of squares of locality effects in units of the standard deviation σ of a single measurement is 2, we want the probability that we conclude that the locality effects are not zero to be at least $\beta = 0.8$. What number n of children must be tested in each city to achieve this power?

"In this case, $f_1 = k - 1 = 5$ and $f_2 = k(n - 1) = 6(n - 1)$. Furthermore,

$$\phi = \delta/\sqrt{f_1 + 1} = \sqrt{n\sum \delta_i^2/(k\sigma^2)}.$$

A procedure for determining n is the following:

"(a) We assume a trial value of n. When one of the graphs is to be used, we may obtain this trial value by reading the value of ϕ for the curve meeting $f_2 = \infty$ at our value of f_1 and then solving for n in the relation $\phi = \sqrt{n\sum \delta_i^2/(k\sigma^2)}$ using the next larger integer. (In this case we read $\phi = 1.46$. Solving for n we obtain $n = \phi^2 k\sigma^2/\sum \delta_i^2 = 6(1.46)^2/2 = 6.39$. Thus, we use $n = 7$ as our first trial value.)

"(b) We fix $\sum \delta_i^2/\sigma^2$ at the value for which it is desired that the power be β. (In this case $\sum \delta_i^2/\sigma^2 = 2$.)

"(c) We compute ϕ and f_2. (In this case $\phi = \sqrt{7(2)/6} = 1.527$ and $f_2 = 6(6) = 36$.)

"(d) Turning to the chart appropriate to our α and β, we find the intersection of the curve for the value of ϕ in (c) with the line for the value of f_1. (In this case we find the intersection of the curve for $\phi = 1.527$ with the line $f_1 = 5$. This is at $f_2 = 60$.)

"(e) We repeat steps (a) through (d) until we have two consecutive values of n such that for one, the value of f_2 obtained in (e) is larger than that obtained in (d), and for the other it is smaller. The larger of these two consecutive values of n is the required value.

"The following table summarizes the results of this procedure for our example:

Trial n	$\phi = \sqrt{n(2)/6}$	$f_2 = 6(n-1)$	f_2 from chart
7	1.527	36	60
8	1.633	42	23

Thus, we require $n = 8$.

"Suppose we require a more stringent design. For example, suppose that with α, k, and $\sum \delta_i^2/\sigma^2$ as before, we wish $\beta \geq 0.85$. Since interpolation in β is necessary, a nomogram must be used. Otherwise the procedure is the same. In this case the above table becomes:

Trial n	$\phi = \sqrt{n(2)/6}$	$f_2 = 6(n-1)$	f_2 from chart
10	1.825	54	17
9	1.732	48	25
8	1.633	42	55

"Here we obtained the line for trial value $n = 10$ by connecting with a ruler the interpolated point for $\beta = 0.85$, $\phi = 0.825$ on the left grid with the interpolated point on the right grid. Reading horizontally from the intersection of this line extended to the line $f_1 = 5$, we found $f_2 = 17$.

"Since for trial value $n = 9$ the computed f_2 is larger than f_2 from the chart, while for trial value $n = 8$ the computed f_2 is smaller than f_2 from the chart, we require $n = 9$."

See [196] and [115] regarding normalization of the noncentral F-distribution. See also [168] for an approximation and applications. Anscombe [7] and Daniel [38] consider various procedures for rejecting outlying observations.

Graphs of the Power of the F-Test [72]

Pr{noncentral F with parameters f_1, f_2, $\delta > [(1 - \alpha)$th critical value of F with parameters f_1, $f_2]\} = \beta$

$$\phi = \delta/\sqrt{f_1 + 1}$$

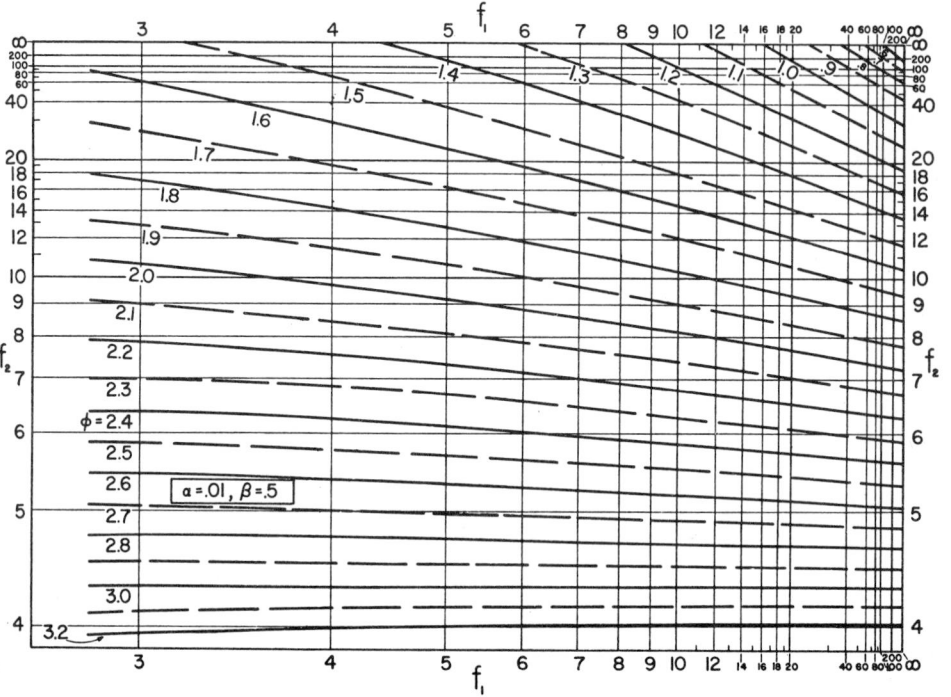

Curves of constant ϕ for the case $\alpha = 0.01$, $\beta = 0.5$

Graphs of the Power of the F-Test (cont.)

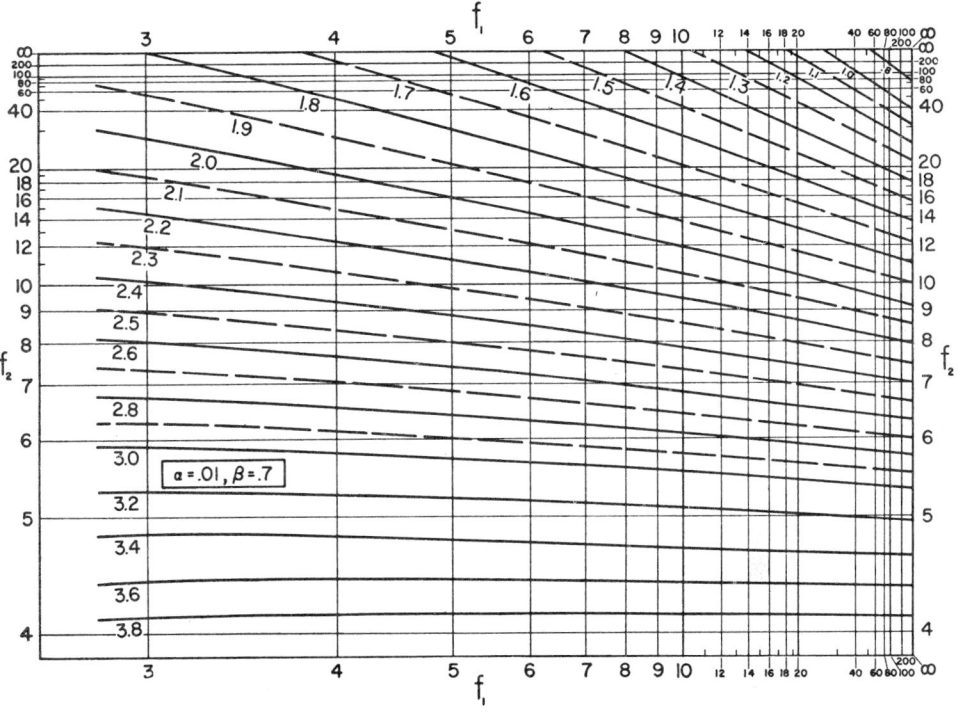

Curves of constant ϕ for the case $\alpha = 0.01$, $\beta = 0.7$

Graphs of the Power of the F-Test (cont.)

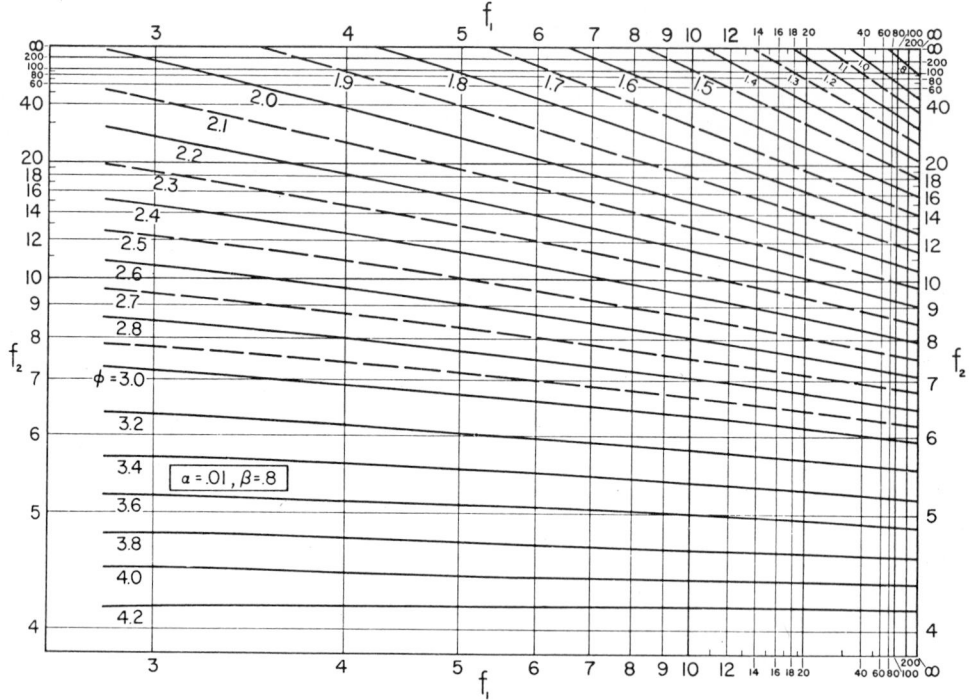

Curves of constant ϕ for the case $\alpha = 0.01$, $\beta = 0.8$

4.2

Graphs of the Power of the F-Test (cont.)

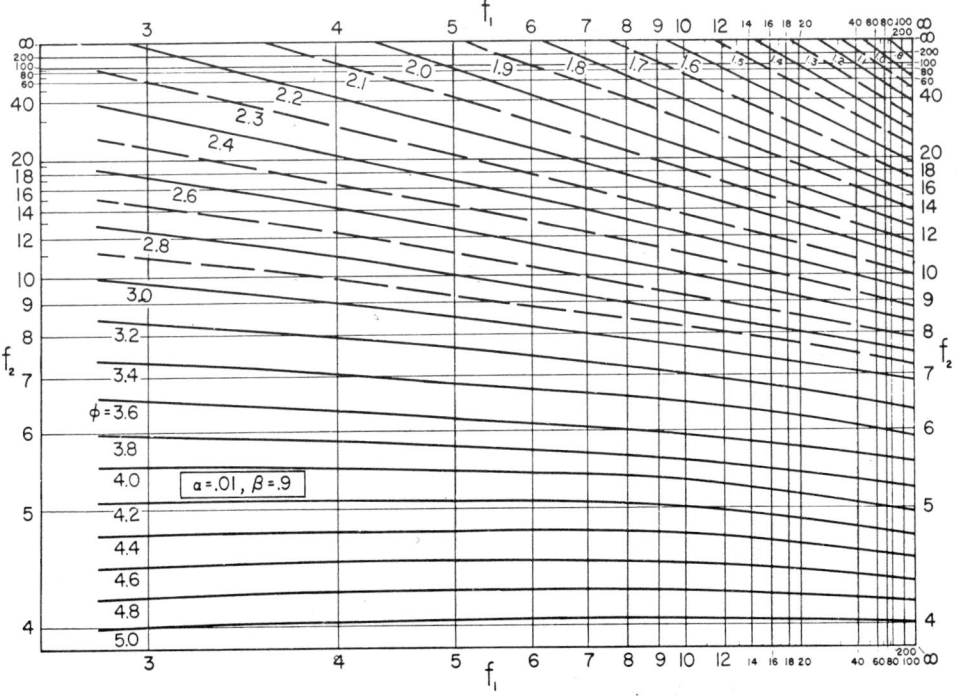

Curves of constant ϕ for the case $\alpha = 0.01$, $\beta = 0.9$

4.2

94

Graphs of the Power of the F-Test *(cont.)*

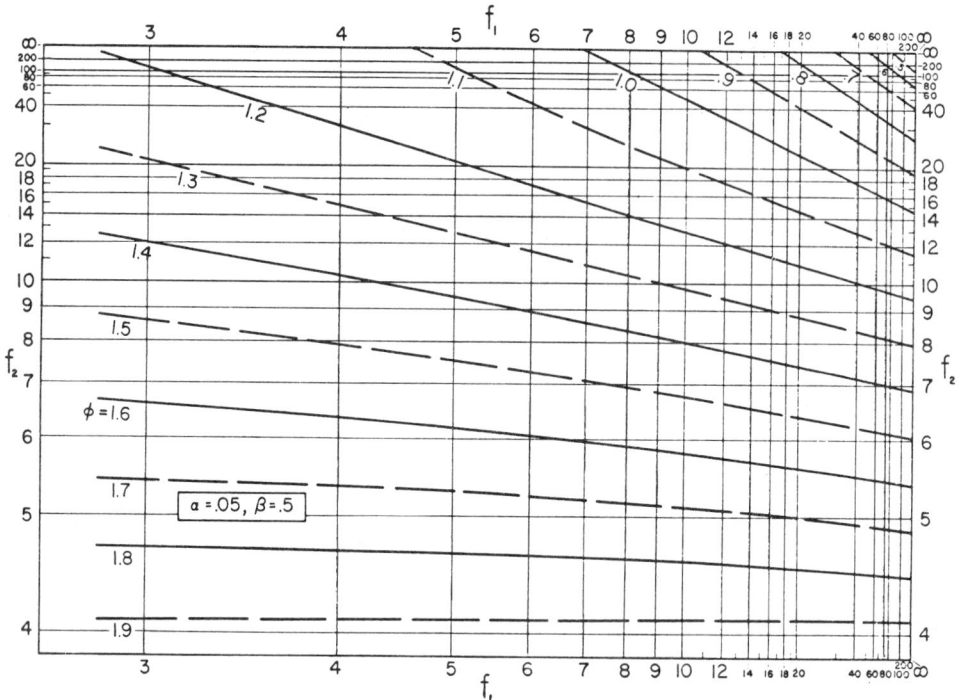

Curves of constant ϕ for the case $\alpha = 0.05$, $\beta = 0.5$

4.2

Graphs of the Power of the F-Test (cont.)

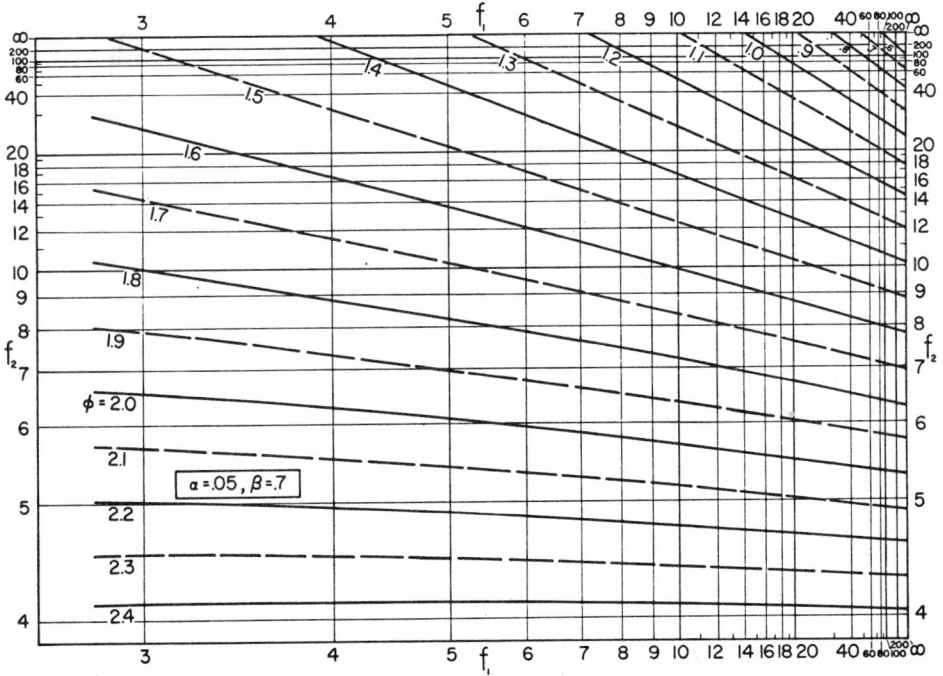

Curves of constant ϕ for the case $\alpha = 0.05$, $\beta = 0.7$

4.2

Graphs of the Power of the F-Test (cont.)

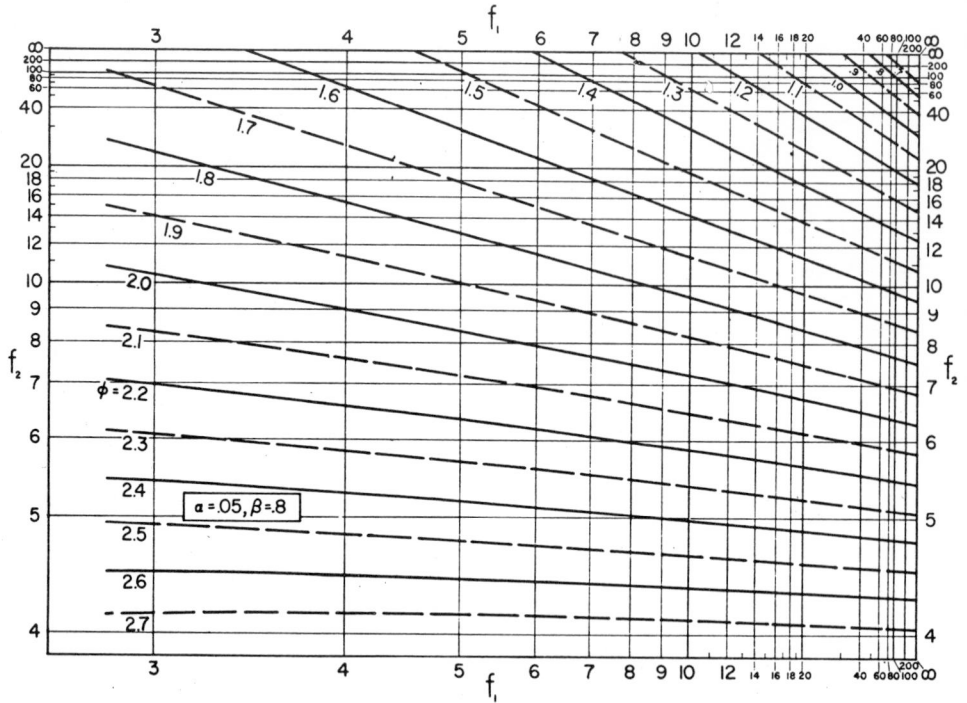

Curves of constant ϕ for the case $\alpha = 0.05$, $\beta = 0.8$

Graphs of the Power of the F-Test (cont.)

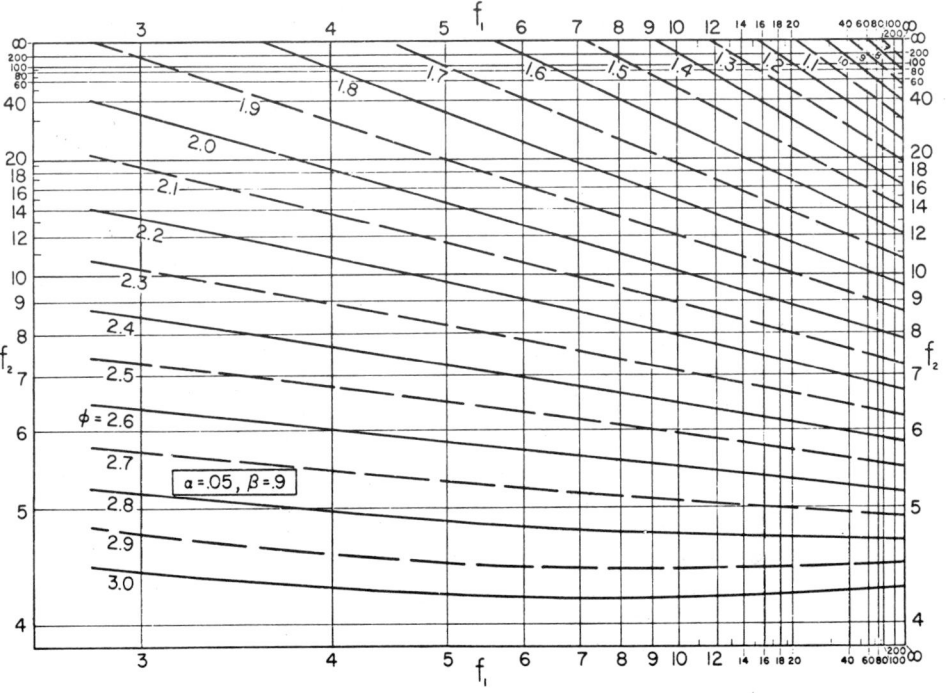

Curves of constant ϕ for the case $\alpha = 0.05$, $\beta = 0.9$

Graphs of the Power of the *F*-Test (*cont.*)

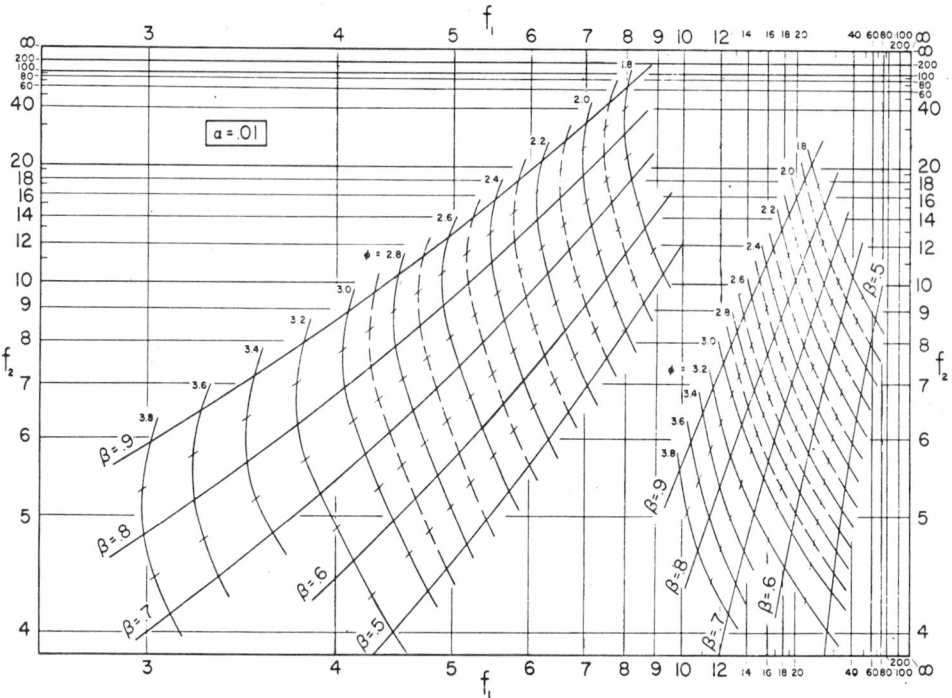

Nomogram for the case $\alpha = 0.01$

4.2

Graphs of the Power of the F-Test (cont.)

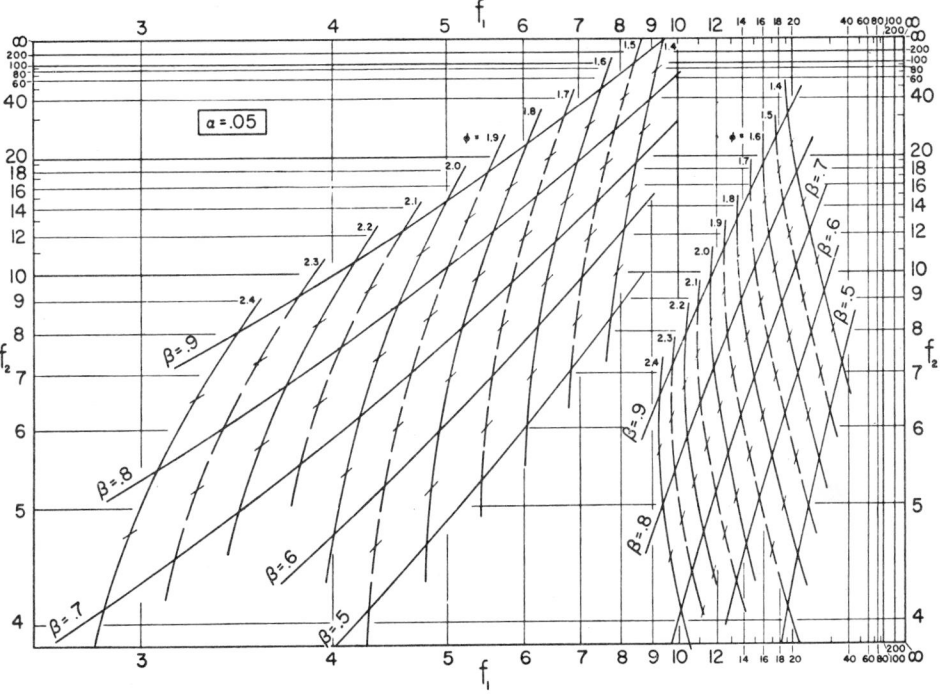

Nomogram for the case $\alpha = 0.05$

4.3 Critical Values for the Maximum F-Ratio

The ratio of the largest to the smallest in a set of k independent random variables, each having the chi-square distribution with f degrees of freedom, is considered. The quantity tabulated is F_{max}, where

$$k \int_0^\infty h(x) |H(xF_{max}) - H(x)|^{k-1} dx = 0.95 \text{ or } 0.99,$$

where $h(x)$ is the density of the chi-square distribution,

$$h(x) = \frac{1}{2^{f/2}\Gamma(f/2)} x^{(f/2)-1} \exp(-x/2), \qquad x \geq 0$$

and

$$H(xF_{max}) = \int_0^{xF_{max}} h(x) \, dx.$$

This distribution is useful in testing the hypothesis of homogeneity of variance in a sample from a normal distribution, that is, s^2_{max}/s^2_{min} is computed, and if F_{max} is exceeded, the variance is assumed to be heterogenous.

Critical Values for the Maximum *F*-Ratio [46]

95% points (first line), 99% points (second line)

k	2	3	4	5	6	7	8	9
2	39.0	15.4	9.60	7.15	5.82	4.99	4.43	4.03
	199	47.5	23.2	14.9	11.1	8.89	7.50	6.54
3	87.5	27.8	15.5	10.8	8.38	6.94	6.00	5.34
	448	85	37	22	15.5	12.1	9.9	8.5
4	142	39.2	20.6	13.7	10.4	8.44	7.18	6.31
	729	120	49	28	19.1	14.5	11.7	9.9
5	202	50.7	25.2	16.3	12.1	9.70	8.12	7.11
	1036	151	59	33	22	16.5	13.2	11.1
6	266	62.0	29.5	18.7	13.7	10.8	9.03	7.80
	1362	184	69	38	25	18.4	14.5	12.1
7	333	72.9	33.6	20.8	15.0	11.8	9.78	8.41
	1705	216	79	42	27	20	15.8	13.1
8	403	83.5	37.5	22.9	16.3	12.7	10.5	8.95
	2063	249	89	46	30	22	16.9	13.9
9	475	93.9	41.1	24.7	17.5	13.5	11.1	9.45
	2432	281	97	50	32	23	17.9	14.7
10	550	104	44.6	26.5	18.6	14.3	11.7	9.91
	2813	310	106	54	34	24	18.9	15.3
11	626	114	48.0	28.2	19.7	15.1	12.2	10.3
	3204	337	113	57	36	26	19.8	16.0
12	704	124	51.4	29.9	20.7	15.8	12.7	10.7
	3605	361	120	60	37	27	21	16.6

k	10	12	15	20	30	60	∞
2	3.72	3.28	2.86	2.46	2.07	1.67	1.00
	5.85	4.91	4.07	3.32	2.63	1.96	1.00
3	4.85	4.16	3.54	2.95	2.40	1.85	1.00
	7.4	6.1	4.9	3.8	3.0	2.2	1.0
4	5.67	4.79	4.01	3.29	2.61	1.96	1.00
	8.6	6.9	5.5	4.3	3.3	2.3	1.0
5	6.34	5.30	4.37	3.54	2.78	2.04	1.00
	9.6	7.6	6.0	4.6	3.4	2.4	1.0
6	6.92	5.72	4.68	3.76	2.91	2.11	1.00
	10.4	8.2	6.4	4.9	3.6	2.4	1.0
7	7.42	6.09	4.95	3.94	3.02	2.17	1.00
	11.1	8.7	6.7	5.1	3.7	2.5	1.0
8	7.87	6.42	5.19	4.10	3.12	2.22	1.00
	11.8	9.1	7.1	5.3	3.8	2.5	1.0
9	8.28	6.72	5.40	4.24	3.21	2.26	1.00
	12.4	9.5	7.3	5.5	3.9	2.6	1.0
10	8.66	7.00	5.59	4.37	3.29	2.30	1.00
	12.9	9.9	7.5	5.6	4.0	2.6	1.0
11	9.01	7.25	5.77	4.49	3.36	2.33	1.00
	13.4	10.2	7.8	5.8	4.1	2.7	1.0
12	9.34	7.48	5.93	4.59	3.39	2.36	1.00
	13.9	10.6	8.0	5.9	4.2	2.7	1.0

4.4 Critical Values for a Multiple Comparison Test Between p Treatment Means and a Control

These tables may be used in setting confidence limits on the difference between any one of p treatment means and the mean of a control. In order to use the tables, the same number of observations on each of the means and on the control must be at hand. The confidence limit is then set in the same manner as the confidence limit on the difference of two means is set where the random variables are assumed to be normally distributed with a common variance σ^2. In the two-variables (one treatment, one control) case, a critical value from Student's t-distribution is used. This value will be replaced by a critical value from these tables for the p-variate (and control) case. See [57] for more information on this application. If there is no control, then Tukey's [225] use of the Studentized range or Scheffé's [195] use of the F-distribution or Duncan's use of the Studentized range (Section 4.5) may apply.

Mathematically, the quantity tabulated may be described as follows: There are p variates $t_{if} = z_i/s$ $(i = 1, 2, \ldots p)$, where the z_i have a nonsingular multivariate normal distribution with means 0, common unknown variance σ^2, and known correlation matrix $\{\rho_{ij}\}$, and fs^2/σ^2 has a chi-square distribution with f degrees of freedom, independent of the z_i. The joint density function of the t_{if} is given by

$$f(t_{1f}, \ldots, t_{pf}) = \frac{A^{1/2}\Gamma\{\frac{1}{2}(f+p)\}}{(f\pi)^{1/2}\Gamma(f/2)}\left[1 + \frac{1}{f}\sum_{i,j} a_{ij}t_{if}t_{jf}\right]^{-(f+p)/2},$$

where A is the determinant of the positive definite matrix

$$\{a_{ij}\} = \{\rho_{ij}\}^{-1}.$$

The quantity in the table for one-sided multiple comparisons gives a value of t such that

$$\int_{-\infty}^{t}\int_{-\infty}^{t}\cdots\int_{-\infty}^{t} f(t_{1f}, \ldots, t_{pf})\, dt_{1f}\ldots dt_{pf} = 0.95 \text{ or } 0.99,$$

where $\rho_{ij} = \frac{1}{2}$, and for the two-sided case

$$\left[\int_{-t}^{t}\int_{-t}^{t} f(t_{1f}, t_{2f})\, dt_{1f}\, dt_{2f}\right]^{p/2} = 0.95 \text{ or } 0.99.$$

The two-sided case is actually given by integrals from $-t$ to $+t$ of the type used for the one-sided case. However, the $(p/2)$th power of the two-variate case may be considered an upper bound and an approximation to this integral [57]. See also [58] on approximations. See Section 8.14 for a tabulation of additional critical values of the bivariate t-distribution with $\rho = \frac{1}{2}$ and $\rho = -\frac{1}{2}$.

Critical Values for One-Sided Multiple Comparisons between
p Treatment Means and a Control [57]

For joint confidence coefficients of 0.95 (first line) and of 0.99 (second line)

f	1	2	3	4	5	6	7	8	9
5	2.02	2.44	2.68	2.85	2.98	3.08	3.16	3.24	3.30
	3.37	3.90	4.21	4.43	4.60	4.73	4.85	4.94	5.03
6	1.94	2.34	2.56	2.71	2.83	2.92	3.00	3.07	3.12
	3.14	3.61	3.88	4.07	4.21	4.33	4.43	4.51	4.59
7	1.89	2.27	2.48	2.62	2.73	2.82	2.89	2.95	3.01
	3.00	3.42	3.66	3.83	3.96	4.07	4.15	4.23	4.30
8	1.86	2.22	2.42	2.55	2.66	2.74	2.81	2.87	2.92
	2.90	3.29	3.51	3.67	3.79	3.88	3.96	4.03	4.09
9	1.83	2.18	2.37	2.50	2.60	2.68	2.75	2.81	2.86
	2.82	3.19	3.40	3.55	3.66	3.75	3.82	3.89	3.94
10	1.81	2.15	2.34	2.47	2.56	2.64	2.70	2.76	2.81
	2.76	3.11	3.31	3.45	3.56	3.64	3.71	3.78	3.83
11	1.80	2.13	2.31	2.44	2.53	2.60	2.67	2.72	2.77
	2.72	3.06	3.25	3.38	3.48	3.56	3.63	3.69	3.74
12	1.78	2.11	2.29	2.41	2.50	2.58	2.64	2.69	2.74
	2.68	3.01	3.19	3.32	3.42	3.50	3.56	3.62	3.67
13	1.77	2.09	2.27	2.39	2.48	2.55	2.61	2.66	2.71
	2.65	2.97	3.15	3.27	3.37	3.44	3.51	3.56	3.61
14	1.76	2.08	2.25	2.37	2.46	2.53	2.59	2.64	2.69
	2.62	2.94	3.11	3.23	3.32	3.40	3.46	3.51	3.56
15	1.75	2.07	2.24	2.36	2.44	2.51	2.57	2.62	2.67
	2.60	2.91	3.08	3.20	3.29	3.36	3.42	3.47	3.52
16	1.75	2.06	2.23	2.34	2.43	2.50	2.56	2.61	2.65
	2.58	2.88	3.05	3.17	3.26	3.33	3.39	3.44	3.48
17	1.74	2.05	2.22	2.33	2.42	2.49	2.54	2.59	2.64
	2.57	2.86	3.03	3.14	3.23	3.30	3.36	3.41	3.45
18	1.73	2.04	2.21	2.32	2.41	2.48	2.53	2.58	2.62
	2.55	2.84	3.01	3.12	3.21	3.27	3.33	3.38	3.42
19	1.73	2.03	2.20	2.31	2.40	2.47	2.52	2.57	2.61
	2.54	2.83	2.99	3.10	3.18	3.25	3.31	3.36	3.40
20	1.72	2.03	2.19	2.30	2.39	2.46	2.51	2.56	2.60
	2.53	2.81	2.97	3.08	3.17	3.23	3.29	3.34	3.38
24	1.71	2.01	2.17	2.28	2.36	2.43	2.48	2.53	2.57
	2.49	2.77	2.92	3.03	3.11	3.17	3.22	3.27	3.31
30	1.70	1.99	2.15	2.25	2.33	2.40	2.45	2.50	2.54
	2.46	2.72	2.87	2.97	3.05	3.11	3.16	3.21	3.24
40	1.68	1.97	2.13	2.23	2.31	2.37	2.42	2.47	2.51
	2.42	2.68	2.82	2.92	2.99	3.05	3.10	3.14	3.18
60	1.67	1.95	2.10	2.21	2.28	2.35	2.39	2.44	2.48
	2.39	2.64	2.78	2.87	2.94	3.00	3.04	3.08	3.12
120	1.66	1.93	2.08	2.18	2.26	2.32	2.37	2.41	2.45
	2.36	2.60	2.73	2.82	2.89	2.94	2.99	3.03	3.06
∞	1.64	1.92	2.06	2.16	2.23	2.29	2.34	2.38	2.42
	2.33	2.56	2.68	2.77	2.84	2.89	2.93	2.97	3.00

4.4

Critical Values for Two-Sided Multiple Comparisons between
p Treatment Means and a Control

For joint confidence coefficients of 0.95 (first line) and of 0.99 (second line)

f	1	2	3	4	5	6	7	8	9
5	2.57	3.03	3.39	3.66	3.88	4.06	4.22	4.36	4.49
	4.03	4.63	5.09	5.44	5.73	5.97	6.18	6.36	6.53
6	2.45	2.86	3.18	3.41	3.60	3.75	3.88	4.00	4.11
	3.71	4.22	4.60	4.88	5.11	5.30	5.47	5.61	5.74
7	2.36	2.75	3.04	3.24	3.41	3.54	3.66	3.76	3.86
	3.50	3.95	4.28	4.52	4.71	4.87	5.01	5.13	5.24
8	2.31	2.67	2.94	3.13	3.28	3.40	3.51	3.60	3.68
	3.36	3.77	4.06	4.27	4.44	4.58	4.70	4.81	4.90
9	2.26	2.61	2.86	3.04	3.18	3.29	3.39	3.48	3.55
	3.25	3.63	3.90	4.09	4.24	4.37	4.48	4.57	4.65
10	2.23	2.57	2.81	2.97	3.11	3.21	3.31	3.39	3.46
	3.17	3.53	3.78	3.95	4.10	4.21	4.31	4.40	4.47
11	2.20	2.53	2.76	2.92	3.05	3.15	3.24	3.31	3.38
	3.11	3.45	3.68	3.85	3.98	4.09	4.18	4.26	4.33
12	2.18	2.50	2.72	2.88	3.00	3.10	3.18	3.25	3.32
	3.05	3.39	3.61	3.76	3.89	3.99	4.08	4.15	4.22
13	2.16	2.48	2.69	2.84	2.96	3.06	3.14	3.21	3.27
	3.01	3.33	3.54	3.69	3.81	3.91	3.99	4.06	4.13
14	2.14	2.46	2.67	2.81	2.93	3.02	3.10	3.17	3.23
	2.98	3.29	3.49	3.64	3.75	3.84	3.92	3.99	4.05
15	2.13	2.44	2.64	2.79	2.90	2.99	3.07	3.13	3.19
	2.95	3.25	3.45	3.59	3.70	3.79	3.86	3.93	3.99
16	2.12	2.42	2.63	2.77	2.88	2.96	3.04	3.10	3.16
	2.92	3.22	3.41	3.55	3.65	3.74	3.82	3.88	3.93
17	2.11	2.41	2.61	2.75	2.85	2.94	3.01	3.08	3.13
	2.90	3.19	3.38	3.51	3.62	3.70	3.77	3.83	3.89
18	2.10	2.40	2.59	2.73	2.84	2.92	2.99	3.05	3.11
	2.88	3.17	3.35	3.48	3.58	3.67	3.74	3.80	3.85
19	2.09	2.39	2.58	2.72	2.82	2.90	2.97	3.04	3.09
	2.86	3.15	3.33	3.46	3.55	3.64	3.70	3.76	3.81
20	2.09	2.38	2.57	2.70	2.81	2.89	2.96	3.02	3.07
	2.85	3.13	3.31	3.43	3.53	3.61	3.67	3.73	3.78
24	2.06	2.35	2.53	2.66	2.76	2.84	2.91	2.96	3.01
	2.80	3.07	3.24	3.36	3.45	3.52	3.58	3.64	3.69
30	2.04	2.32	2.50	2.62	2.72	2.79	2.86	2.91	2.96
	2.75	3.01	3.17	3.28	3.37	3.44	3.50	3.55	3.59
40	2.02	2.29	2.47	2.58	2.67	2.75	2.81	2.86	2.90
	2.70	2.95	3.10	3.21	3.29	3.36	3.41	3.46	3.50
60	2.00	2.27	2.43	2.55	2.63	2.70	2.76	2.81	2.85
	2.66	2.90	3.04	3.14	3.22	3.28	3.33	3.38	3.42
120	1.98	2.24	2.40	2.51	2.59	2.66	2.71	2.76	2.80
	2.62	2.84	2.98	3.08	3.15	3.21	3.25	3.30	3.33
∞	1.96	2.21	2.37	2.47	2.55	2.62	2.67	2.71	2.75
	2.58	2.79	2.92	3.01	3.08	3.14	3.18	3.22	3.25

4.4

4.5 Critical Values of the Duncan Multiple-Range Test

The quantity tabulated was computed from the critical values of the Studentized range (see Section 6.5). The procedure used was to compute $\gamma = (1 - \alpha)^{p-1}$, where $1 - \alpha$ is a chosen significance level. Then the γth critical value from the table of the Studentized range with $n = 2$, call it $R(\gamma, f)$, was used as follows: The critical value for the Duncan multiple-range test, call it $D(p, f, \alpha)$, is obtained as $D(p, f, \alpha) = R(\gamma, f)$ for $p = 2$, and as $D(p, f, \alpha) = R(\gamma, f)$ or $D(p - 1, f, \alpha)$, whichever is the larger, for all values of $p > 2$. The tables are given for $1 - \alpha = 0.90$, 0.95, 0.99, 0.995, and 0.999.

This table is useful in making statements about the difference between two means where p sample means are at hand, all drawn from normal distributions with common variance σ^2. The values $D(p, f, \alpha)$, $D(p - 1, f, \alpha)$, $\ldots$, $D(2, f, \alpha)$ are multiplied by s^2, an estimate of σ^2, the means are ranked, and the means are grouped into like groups by noting all means that differ by less than $s^2 D$. For more details and examples see [56] and [92]. In applying this procedure one must be careful to be sure that the ranges are independent of s^2. The easiest way to make this check is to note what variance is being estimated by the range, and then to check to see if the corresponding mean-square estimate from the analysis of variance is independent of s^2.

4.5

Critical Values of the Duncan Multiple-Range Test [92]

f	p = 2 0.90	0.95	0.99	0.995	0.999	p = 3 0.90	0.95	0.99	0.995	0.999
1	8.929	17.97	90.03	180.1	900.3	8.929	17.97	90.03	180.1	900.3
2	4.130	6.085	14.04	19.93	44.69	4.130	6.085	14.04	19.93	44.69
3	3.328	4.501	8.261	10.55	18.28	3.330	4.516	8.321	10.63	18.45
4	3.015	3.927	6.512	7.916	12.18	3.074	4.013	6.677	8.126	12.52
5	2.850	3.635	5.702	6.751	9.714	2.934	3.749	5.893	6.980	10.05
6	2.748	3.461	5.243	6.105	8.427	2.846	3.587	5.439	6.334	8.743
7	2.680	3.344	4.949	5.699	7.648	2.785	3.477	5.145	5.922	7.943
8	2.630	3.261	4.746	5.420	7.130	2.742	3.399	4.939	5.638	7.407
9	2.592	3.199	4.596	5.218	6.762	2.708	3.339	4.787	5.430	7.024
10	2.563	3.151	4.482	5.065	6.487	2.682	3.293	4.671	5.273	6.738
11	2.540	3.113	4.392	4.945	6.275	2.660	3.256	4.579	5.149	6.516
12	2.521	3.082	4.320	4.849	6.106	2.643	3.225	4.504	5.048	6.340
13	2.505	3.055	4.260	4.770	5.970	2.628	3.200	4.442	4.966	6.195
14	2.491	3.033	4.210	4.704	5.856	2.616	3.178	4.391	4.897	6.075
15	2.479	3.014	4.168	4.647	5.760	2.605	3.160	4.347	4.838	5.974
16	2.469	2.998	4.131	4.599	5.678	2.596	3.144	4.309	4.787	5.888
17	2.460	2.984	4.099	4.557	5.608	2.588	3.130	4.275	4.744	5.813
18	2.452	2.971	4.071	4.521	5.546	2.580	3.118	4.246	4.705	5.748
19	2.445	2.960	4.046	4.488	5.492	2.574	3.107	4.220	4.671	5.691
20	2.439	2.950	4.024	4.460	5.444	2.568	3.097	4.197	4.641	5.640
24	2.420	2.919	3.956	4.371	5.297	2.550	3.066	4.126	4.547	5.484
30	2.400	2.888	3.889	4.285	5.156	2.532	3.035	4.056	4.456	5.335
40	2.381	2.858	3.825	4.202	5.022	2.514	3.006	3.988	4.369	5.191
60	2.363	2.829	3.762	4.122	4.894	2.497	2.976	3.922	4.284	5.055
120	2.344	2.800	3.702	4.045	4.771	2.479	2.947	3.858	4.201	4.924
∞	2.326	2.772	3.643	3.970	4.654	2.462	2.918	3.796	4.121	4.798

f	p = 5 0.90	0.95	0.99	0.995	0.999	p = 10 0.90	0.95	0.99	0.995	0.999
1	8.929	17.97	90.03	180.1	900.3	8.929	17.97	90.03	180.1	900.3
2	4.130	6.085	14.04	19.93	44.69	4.130	6.085	14.04	19.93	44.69
3	3.330	4.516	8.321	10.63	18.45	3.330	4.516	8.321	10.63	18.45
4	3.081	4.033	6.756	8.238	12.73	3.081	4.033	6.756	8.238	12.75
5	2.970	3.814	6.040	7.167	10.35	2.970	3.814	6.074	7.228	10.49
6	2.908	3.680	5.614	6.547	9.055	2.911	3.697	5.703	6.679	9.294
7	2.864	3.588	5.334	6.145	8.252	2.878	3.626	5.464	6.320	8.500
8	2.832	3.521	5.135	5.864	7.708	2.858	3.579	5.291	6.064	8.004
9	2.808	3.470	4.986	5.657	7.316	2.847	3.547	5.160	5.871	7.619
10	2.788	3.430	4.871	5.498	7.021	2.839	3.522	5.058	5.722	7.327
11	2.772	3.397	4.780	5.372	6.791	2.835	3.501	4.975	5.603	7.097
12	2.759	3.370	4.706	5.270	6.607	2.832	3.484	4.907	5.505	6.911
13	2.748	3.348	4.644	5.186	6.457	2.829	3.470	4.850	5.424	6.759
14	2.739	3.329	4.591	5.116	6.332	2.827	3.457	4.802	5.355	6.631
15	2.731	3.312	4.547	5.055	6.225	2.825	3.446	4.760	5.297	6.522
16	2.723	3.298	4.509	5.003	6.135	2.824	3.437	4.724	5.245	6.429
17	2.717	3.285	4.475	4.958	6.056	2.822	3.429	4.693	5.201	6.348
18	2.712	3.274	4.445	4.918	5.988	2.821	3.421	4.664	5.162	6.277
19	2.707	3.264	4.419	4.883	5.927	2.820	3.415	4.639	5.127	6.214
20	2.702	3.255	4.395	4.851	5.873	2.819	3.409	4.617	5.095	6.158
24	2.688	3.226	4.322	4.753	5.708	2.816	3.390	4.546	4.997	5.984
30	2.674	3.199	4.250	4.658	5.549	2.813	3.371	4.477	4.901	5.817
40	2.660	3.171	4.180	4.566	5.396	2.810	3.352	4.408	4.806	5.654
60	2.646	3.143	4.111	4.476	5.249	2.807	3.333	4.340	4.713	5.498
120	2.632	3.116	4.044	4.388	5.109	2.804	3.314	4.272	4.622	5.346
∞	2.619	3.089	3.978	4.303	4.974	2.801	3.294	4.205	4.532	5.199

Critical Values of the Duncan Multiple-Range Test (*cont.*)

f	p = 15 0.90	0.95	0.99	0.995	0.999	p = 20 0.90	0.95	0.99	0.995	0.999
1	8.929	17.97	90.03	180.1	900.3	8.929	17.97	90.03	180.1	900.3
2	4.130	6.085	14.04	19.93	44.69	4.130	6.085	14.04	19.93	44.69
3	3.330	4.516	8.321	10.63	18.45	3.330	4.516	8.321	10.63	18.45
4	3.081	4.033	6.756	8.238	12.75	3.081	4.033	6.756	8.238	12.75
5	2.970	3.814	6.074	7.228	10.49	2.970	3.814	6.074	7.228	10.49
6	2.911	3.697	5.703	6.682	9.329	2.911	3.697	5.703	6.682	9.329
7	2.878	3.626	5.472	6.345	8.609	2.878	3.626	5.472	6.345	8.627
8	2.858	3.579	5.317	6.113	8.108	2.858	3.579	5.317	6.119	8.149
9	2.847	3.547	5.203	5.938	7.739	2.847	3.547	5.206	5.956	7.794
10	2.839	3.526	5.112	5.800	7.456	2.839	3.526	5.124	5.829	7.522
11	2.835	3.510	5.039	5.690	7.231	2.835	3.510	5.059	5.727	7.304
12	2.833	3.499	4.978	5.599	7.050	2.833	3.499	5.006	5.642	7.128
13	2.832	3.490	4.928	5.523	6.900	2.832	3.490	4.960	5.571	6.982
14	2.833	3.484	4.884	5.458	6.774	2.833	3.485	4.921	5.511	6.858
15	2.834	3.478	4.846	5.402	6.666	2.834	3.481	4.887	5.459	6.753
16	2.836	3.473	4.813	5.354	6.574	2.836	3.478	4.858	5.413	6.661
17	2.838	3.469	4.785	5.311	6.493	2.838	3.476	4.832	5.373	6.582
18	2.840	3.465	4.759	5.274	6.422	2.840	3.474	4.808	5.338	6.512
19	2.842	3.462	4.736	5.240	6.359	2.843	3.474	4.788	5.306	6.450
20	2.845	3.459	4.716	5.210	6.303	2.845	3.473	4.769	5.277	6.394
24	2.851	3.449	4.651	5.116	6.129	2.857	3.471	4.710	5.187	6.221
30	2.859	3.439	4.586	5.022	5.958	2.873	3.470	4.650	5.098	6.051
40	2.866	3.429	4.521	4.930	5.793	2.890	3.469	4.591	5.008	5.885
60	2.874	3.419	4.456	4.838	5.632	2.908	3.467	4.530	4.919	5.723
120	2.883	3.409	4.392	4.747	5.476	2.928	3.466	4.469	4.830	5.565
∞	2.892	3.399	4.327	4.657	5.324	2.949	3.466	4.408	4.740	5.409

f	p = 50 0.90	0.95	0.99	0.995	0.999	p = 100 0.90	0.95	0.99	0.995	0.999
1	8.929	17.97	90.03	180.1	900.3	8.929	17.97	90.03	180.1	900.3
2	4.130	6.085	14.04	19.93	44.69	4.130	6.085	14.04	19.93	44.69
3	3.330	4.516	8.321	10.63	18.45	3.330	4.516	8.321	10.63	18.45
4	3.081	4.033	6.756	8.238	12.75	3.081	4.033	6.756	8.238	12.75
5	2.970	3.814	6.074	7.228	10.49	2.970	3.814	6.074	7.228	10.49
6	2.911	3.697	5.703	6.682	9.329	2.911	3.697	5.703	6.682	9.329
7	2.878	3.626	5.472	6.345	8.627	2.878	3.626	5.472	6.345	8.627
8	2.858	3.579	5.317	6.119	8.161	2.858	3.579	5.317	6.119	8.161
9	2.847	3.547	5.206	5.957	7.832	2.847	3.547	5.206	5.957	7.832
10	2.839	3.526	5.124	5.836	7.588	2.839	3.526	5.124	5.836	7.588
11	2.835	3.510	5.061	5.744	7.400	2.835	3.510	5.061	5.744	7.400
12	2.833	3.499	5.011	5.670	7.251	2.833	3.499	5.011	5.670	7.251
13	2.832	3.490	4.972	5.611	7.126	2.832	3.490	4.972	5.611	7.132
14	2.833	3.485	4.940	5.563	7.019	2.833	3.485	4.940	5.563	7.034
15	2.834	3.481	4.914	5.523	6.927	2.834	3.481	4.914	5.523	6.951
16	2.836	3.478	4.892	5.489	6.848	2.836	3.478	4.892	5.489	6.881
17	2.838	3.476	4.874	5.461	6.777	2.838	3.476	4.874	5.461	6.821
18	2.840	3.474	4.858	5.436	6.715	2.840	3.474	4.858	5.436	6.770
19	2.843	3.474	4.845	5.414	6.660	2.843	3.474	4.845	5.415	6.723
20	2.845	3.474	4.833	5.394	6.610	2.845	3.474	4.833	5.397	6.681
24	2.857	3.477	4.802	5.329	6.451	2.857	3.477	4.802	5.343	6.547
30	2.873	3.486	4.772	5.264	6.294	2.873	3.486	4.777	5.298	6.412
40	2.898	3.504	4.740	5.197	6.137	2.898	3.504	4.764	5.261	6.274
60	2.936	3.537	4.707	5.128	5.980	2.936	3.537	4.765	5.223	6.134
120	3.001	3.585	4.673	5.056	5.822	3.001	3.601	4.770	5.182	5.988
∞	3.091	3.640	4.635	4.981	5.663	3.163	3.735	4.776	5.136	5.837

5. NONCENTRAL *t* AND TOLERANCE LIMITS

5.1 Factors for Computing Critical Values of the Noncentral *t*-Distribution

The cumulative distribution function of noncentral t with f degrees of freedom and noncentrality parameter δ is given by

$$\Pr\{T_f \leq t\} = \frac{\sqrt{2\pi}}{\Gamma(f/2)2^{(f-2)/2}} \int_0^\infty P\left(\frac{tx}{\sqrt{f}} - \delta\right) x^{f-1} Z(x)\, dx,$$

where

$$P(x) = \frac{1}{\sqrt{2\pi}} \int_{-\infty}^x \exp(-t^2/2)\, dt \quad \text{and} \quad Z(x) = \frac{1}{\sqrt{2\pi}} \exp(-x^2/2).$$

In Section 2.2 the noncentral t-distribution was defined in terms of a sample from a normal distribution. The two definitions are equivalent. By repeated integration by parts of the above expression, one can obtain (see [150] or [161]) for f an odd integer

$$\Pr\{T_f \leq t\} = P\left(\frac{-\delta\sqrt{f}}{\sqrt{f+t^2}}\right) + 2T\left(\frac{\delta\sqrt{f}}{\sqrt{f+t^2}}, \frac{t}{\sqrt{f}}\right)$$

$$+ 2\left[M_1 + \frac{1}{3} M_3 + \frac{1}{3 \cdot 5} M_5 + \cdots + \frac{1}{3 \cdot 5 \cdot 7 \dots (f-2)} M_{f-2}\right],$$

where the function $T(h, a)$ is defined in Section 8.5, and for f an even integer

$$\Pr\{T_f \leq t\} = P(-\delta) + \sqrt{2\pi}$$

$$\times \left[M_0 + \frac{1}{1! \cdot 2} M_2 + \frac{1}{2! \cdot 2^2} M_4 + \cdots + \frac{1}{\left(\dfrac{f-2}{2}\right)! 2^{(f-2)/2}} M_{f-2}\right],$$

where

$$M_{-1} = 0,$$

$$M_0 = \frac{t}{\sqrt{f+t^2}} Z\left(\frac{\sqrt{f}\delta}{\sqrt{f+t^2}}\right) P\left(\frac{\delta t}{\sqrt{f+t^2}}\right),$$

$$M_1 = \frac{\delta t\sqrt{f}}{f+t^2} M_0 + \frac{t\sqrt{f}}{f+t^2} \cdot \frac{1}{\sqrt{2\pi}} Z(\delta),$$

$$\vdots$$

$$M_k = \frac{\delta t\sqrt{f}}{f+t^2} M_{k-1} + \frac{(k-1)f}{f+t^2} M_{k-2},$$

$$\vdots$$

Note that
$$\Pr\{T_f \leq 0\} = P(-\delta)$$
and
$$\Pr\{T_f < t|\delta\} = 1 - \Pr\{T_f < -t| - \delta\}.$$

Also if $\delta = 0$, the noncentral t-distribution reduces to Student's t-distribution; in fact, the above formulas were used to compute Student's t-distribution here (see Section 2.1).

If δ and f are given, the tables given here may be used to compute t_0 in
$$\Pr\{T_f \leq t_0|\delta, f\} = 0.90, 0.95, \quad \text{or} \quad 0.99.$$

One first computes
$$\eta = \frac{\delta}{\sqrt{2f}}\left(1 + \frac{\delta^2}{2f}\right)^{-1/2}$$

and then enters the table with η and f, and interpolates for a value λ. Interpolation with respect to f may be done linearly with respect to $144/f$. After obtaining λ, t_0 is obtained by the formula

$$t_0 = \frac{\delta + \lambda\left(1 + \frac{\delta^2}{2f} - \frac{\lambda^2}{2f}\right)^{1/2}}{1 - (\lambda^2/2f)}.$$

This involves a great deal of work to obtain t_0, but actually this table with the accompanying calculations contains a tremendous amount of information in a very compact form. Section 5.3 contains tables which were, for the most part, computed from this table for a specific application.

Factors for Computing Critical Values of the Noncentral t-Distribution

$\Pr\{(\text{noncentral } t \text{ with } f \text{ degrees of freedom}) \leq t_0\} = 0.90$

η \ f	4	5	6	7	8	9	16	36	144	∞
1.0	1.3699	1.3677	1.3645	1.3613	1.3582	1.3554	1.3412	1.3238	1.3038	1.2816
0.9	1.370	1.367	1.363	1.360	1.357	1.3540	1.3397	1.3224	1.3028	1.2816
0.8	1.369	1.366	1.362	1.359	1.356	1.3526	1.3380	1.3206	1.3015	1.2816
0.7	1.369	1.365	1.361	1.358	1.354	1.3507	1.3357	1.3184	1.3001	1.2816
0.6	1.368	1.364	1.360	1.355	1.352	1.3484	1.3329	1.3158	1.2983	1.2816
0.5	1.367	1.362	1.357	1.353	1.349	1.3455	1.3294	1.3128	1.2964	1.2816
0.4	1.366	1.360	1.354	1.350	1.345	1.3413	1.3256	1.3093	1.2943	1.2816
0.3	1.364	1.357	1.351	1.345	1.341	1.3368	1.3207	1.3052	1.2919	1.2816
0.2	1.360	1.352	1.346	1.339	1.335	1.3309	1.3149	1.3007	1.2893	1.2816
0.1	1.355	1.346	1.338	1.332	1.328	1.3236	1.3083	1.2957	1.2866	1.2816
0.0	1.3479	1.3374	1.3295	1.3234	1.3187	1.3149	1.3010	1.2903	1.2838	1.2816
-0.1	1.337	1.326	1.318	1.312	1.308	1.3047	1.2926	1.2846	1.2809	1.2816
-0.2	1.323	1.312	1.305	1.299	1.296	1.2931	1.2836	1.2784	1.2778	1.2816
-0.3	1.306	1.297	1.290	1.286	1.283	1.2801	1.2738	1.2720	1.2748	1.2816
-0.4	1.285	1.277	1.272	1.269	1.267	1.2657	1.2634	1.2656	1.2718	1.2816
-0.5	1.259	1.254	1.252	1.251	1.250	1.2503	1.2527	1.2591	1.2688	1.2816
-0.6	1.231	1.230	1.231	1.231	1.233	1.2341	1.2418	1.2526	1.2661	1.2816
-0.7	1.200	1.204	1.208	1.212	1.215	1.2179	1.2311	1.2466	1.2636	1.2816
-0.8	1.169	1.179	1.187	1.193	1.198	1.2024	1.2209	1.2409	1.2612	1.2816
-0.9	1.139	1.155	1.166	1.175	1.182	1.1880	1.2121	1.2359	1.2591	1.2816
-1.0	1.1160	1.1357	1.1499	1.1608	1.1694	1.1765	1.2049	1.2319	1.2575	1.2816

$$\eta = \frac{\delta}{\sqrt{2f}}\left(1 + \frac{\delta^2}{2f}\right)^{-\frac{1}{2}}$$

$$t_0 = \frac{\delta + \lambda\left(1 + \frac{\delta^2}{2f} - \frac{\lambda^2}{2f}\right)^{\frac{1}{2}}}{\left(1 - \frac{\lambda^2}{2f}\right)}$$

Computed from Table IV in Ref. 101.

5.1

Factors for Computing Critical Values of the Noncentral *t*-Distribution (*cont.*)

Pr{noncentral *t* with *f* degrees of freedom $\leq t_0$} = 0.95

η \ f	4	5	6	7	8	9	16	36	144	∞
1.0	1.6362	1.6487	1.6556	1.6597	1.6622	1.6638	1.6665	1.6635	1.6560	1.6449
0.9	1.643	1.655	1.662	1.666	1.668	1.6695	1.6711	1.6667	1.6576	1.6449
0.8	1.650	1.662	1.668	1.672	1.674	1.6747	1.6751	1.6691	1.6586	1.6449
0.7	1.657	1.668	1.674	1.677	1.679	1.6796	1.6782	1.6707	1.6589	1.6449
0.6	1.664	1.675	1.680	1.682	1.684	1.6838	1.6804	1.6714	1.6587	1.6449
0.5	1.671	1.681	1.686	1.687	1.687	1.6871	1.6817	1.6709	1.6580	1.6449
0.4	1.679	1.687	1.690	1.691	1.691	1.6896	1.6816	1.6698	1.6568	1.6449
0.3	1.687	1.693	1.694	1.693	1.692	1.6902	1.6804	1.6677	1.6550	1.6449
0.2	1.693	1.697	1.696	1.694	1.692	1.6898	1.6779	1.6646	1.6529	1.6449
0.1	1.698	1.699	1.697	1.693	1.690	1.6874	1.6738	1.6606	1.6504	1.6449
0.0	1.7024	1.6993	1.6948	1.6903	1.6862	1.6827	1.6683	1.6558	1.6477	1.6449
-0.1	1.702	1.695	1.689	1.684	1.679	1.6756	1.6611	1.6503	1.6447	1.6449
-0.2	1.698	1.688	1.680	1.674	1.669	1.6657	1.6525	1.6442	1.6417	1.6449
-0.3	1.687	1.676	1.667	1.661	1.657	1.6535	1.6427	1.6378	1.6388	1.6449
-0.4	1.670	1.658	1.650	1.645	1.642	1.6391	1.6322	1.6314	1.6359	1.6449
-0.5	1.646	1.636	1.630	1.627	1.624	1.6231	1.6213	1.6252	1.6334	1.6449
-0.6	1.615	1.610	1.607	1.606	1.606	1.6066	1.6108	1.6195	1.6313	1.6449
-0.7	1.582	1.583	1.585	1.587	1.589	1.5911	1.6019	1.6150	1.6299	1.6449
-0.8	1.551	1.559	1.565	1.571	1.575	1.5792	1.5954	1.6122	1.6291	1.6449
-0.9	1.531	1.544	1.553	1.561	1.567	1.5722	1.5925	1.6116	1.6292	1.6449
-1.0	1.5277	1.5431	1.5542	1.5625	1.5691	1.5744	1.5952	1.6141	1.6307	1.6449

$$\eta = \frac{\delta}{\sqrt{2f}}\left(1 + \frac{\delta^2}{2f}\right)^{-\frac{1}{2}}$$

$$t_0 = \frac{\delta + \lambda\left(1 + \frac{\delta^2}{2f} - \frac{\lambda^2}{2f}\right)^{\frac{1}{2}}}{\left(1 - \frac{\lambda^2}{2f}\right)}$$

Taken from Table V in Ref. 101 except $\eta = 1.0$, 0.0, and -1.0, for which the values were computed from the appropriate chi-square and *t* statistics.

Factors for Computing Critical Values of the Noncentral t-Distribution (cont.)

$\Pr\{(\text{noncentral } t \text{ with } f \text{ degrees of freedom}) \leq t_0\} = 0.99$

η \ f	4	5	6	7	8	9	16	36	144	∞
1.0	2.0576	2.1094	2.1434	2.1675	2.1853	2.1992	2.2474	2.2832	2.3089	2.3263
0.9	2.08	2.13	2.16	2.19	2.20	2.216	2.264	2.296	2.316	2.3263
0.8	2.09	2.14	2.18	2.20	2.22	2.233	2.279	2.308	2.323	2.3263
0.7	2.10	2.15	2.19	2.22	2.24	2.249	2.293	2.318	2.328	2.3263
0.6	2.11	2.17	2.21	2.23	2.25	2.266	2.306	2.327	2.331	2.3263
0.5	2.13	2.19	2.23	2.25	2.27	2.282	2.318	2.334	2.334	2.3263
0.4	2.15	2.21	2.25	2.27	2.29	2.298	2.329	2.339	2.335	2.3263
0.3	2.17	2.23	2.27	2.29	2.31	2.314	2.337	2.342	2.335	2.3263
0.2	2.20	2.25	2.29	2.31	2.32	2.328	2.344	2.343	2.334	2.3263
0.1	2.23	2.28	2.31	2.32	2.33	2.339	2.349	2.342	2.333	2.3263
0.0	2.2575	2.3044	2.3276	2.3396	2.3460	2.3493	2.3500	2.3401	2.3302	2.3263
-0.1	2.29	2.33	2.34	2.35	2.35	2.354	2.348	2.336	2.327	2.3263
-0.2	2.32	2.35	2.36	2.36	2.36	2.355	2.343	2.330	2.324	2.3263
-0.3	2.35	2.36	2.36	2.36	2.35	2.350	2.335	2.324	2.322	2.3263
-0.4	2.36	2.36	2.36	2.35	2.35	2.339	2.324	2.317	2.319	2.3263
-0.5	2.36	2.35	2.34	2.33	2.33	2.323	2.313	2.311	2.317	2.3263
-0.6	2.34	2.33	2.31	2.31	2.30	2.304	2.302	2.307	2.317	2.3263
-0.7	2.30	2.29	2.29	2.29	2.29	2.288	2.295	2.306	2.318	2.3263
-0.8	2.26	2.26	2.27	2.28	2.28	2.282	2.296	2.310	2.321	2.3263
-0.9	2.26	2.27	2.28	2.28	2.30	2.295	2.311	2.322	2.327	2.3263
-1.0	2.3246	2.3307	2.3345	2.3370	2.3388	2.3401	2.3431	2.3424	2.3371	2.3263

$$\eta = \frac{\delta}{\sqrt{2f}}\left(1 + \frac{\delta^2}{2f}\right)^{-\frac{1}{2}}$$

$$t_0 = \frac{\delta + \lambda\left(1 + \dfrac{\delta^2}{2f} - \dfrac{\lambda^2}{2f}\right)^{\frac{1}{2}}}{\left(1 - \dfrac{\lambda^2}{2f}\right)}$$

Computed from Table IV in Ref. 101.

5.2 Factors for Computing the Noncentrality Parameter of the Noncentral *t*-Distribution

If t_0 and f are given, the tables here may be used to compute δ in

$$\Pr\{T_f(\delta) \le t_0|t_0, f\} = 0.90, 0.95, \quad \text{or} \quad 0.99.$$

One first computes

$$y = \left(1 + \frac{t_0^2}{2f}\right)^{-1/2} \quad \text{and} \quad y' = \frac{t_0}{\sqrt{2f}}\left(1 + \frac{t_0^2}{2f}\right)^{-1/2}.$$

Then with y and y' one enters the table to get λ, from which δ is computed as

$$\delta = t_0 - \lambda\left(1 + \frac{t_0^2}{2f}\right)^{1/2}.$$

Again a tremendous amount of information has been stored in the table and the accompanying calculations in a very compact form. See [180] and [101] for applications and additional tables. See [62] for another application.

Factors for Computing the Noncentrality Parameter
of the Noncentral *t*-Distribution [101]

Pr{(noncentral *t* with *f* degrees of freedom) $\leq t_0$} = 0.90

y'	y	4	5	6	7	8	9	16	36	144	∞
-1.0	0.0	1.116	1.136	1.150	1.161	1.169	1.1765	1.2049	1.2319	1.2575	1.2816
	0.1	1.116	1.136	1.150	1.161	1.170	1.1768	1.2051	1.2321	1.2576	1.2816
	0.2	1.118	1.137	1.151	1.162	1.171	1.1777	1.2057	1.2325	1.2578	1.2816
	0.3	1.121	1.140	1.154	1.164	1.172	1.1793	1.2069	1.2332	1.2581	1.2816
	0.4	1.125	1.143	1.157	1.167	1.175	1.1819	1.2087	1.2343	1.2586	1.2816
	0.5	1.131	1.149	1.162	1.171	1.179	1.1856	1.2114	1.2360	1.2594	1.2816
	0.6	1.140	1.157	1.169	1.178	1.185	1.1912	1.2153	1.2385	1.2606	1.2816
	0.7	1.153	1.168	1.179	1.187	1.194	1.1992	1.2210	1.2421	1.2623	1.2816
-0.6	0.8	1.173	1.185	1.194	1.201	1.206	1.2110	1.2295	1.2475	1.2649	1.2816
-0.5		1.191	1.201	1.208	1.214	1.218	1.2222	1.2376	1.2527	1.2673	1.2816
-0.4		1.209	1.217	1.223	1.227	1.231	1.2338	1.2461	1.2582	1.2700	1.2816
-0.3		1.228	1.233	1.238	1.241	1.244	1.2458	1.2548	1.2639	1.2728	1.2816
-0.2		1.246	1.250	1.253	1.255	1.256	1.2578	1.2638	1.2697	1.2757	1.2816
-0.1		1.264	1.266	1.267	1.268	1.269	1.2698	1.2727	1.2756	1.2786	1.2816
0.0	1.0	1.282	1.282	1.282	1.282	1.282	1.2816	1.2816	1.2816	1.2816	1.2816
0.1		1.298	1.297	1.295	1.294	1.294	1.2929	1.2902	1.2874	1.2845	1.2816
0.2		1.313	1.310	1.308	1.306	1.305	1.3038	1.2985	1.2930	1.2873	1.2816
0.3		1.327	1.323	1.320	1.318	1.316	1.3140	1.3064	1.2984	1.2901	1.2816
0.4		1.340	1.335	1.331	1.328	1.326	1.3233	1.3137	1.3035	1.2927	1.2816
0.5		1.350	1.345	1.341	1.337	1.334	1.3316	1.3204	1.3082	1.2952	1.2816
0.6	0.8	1.358	1.353	1.349	1.345	1.342	1.3387	1.3263	1.3124	1.2974	1.2816
	0.7	1.365	1.360	1.355	1.352	1.348	1.3453	1.3320	1.3166	1.2997	1.2816
	0.6	1.367	1.363	1.359	1.355	1.352	1.3492	1.3354	1.3193	1.3012	1.2816
	0.5	1.368	1.365	1.361	1.358	1.354	1.3516	1.3377	1.3210	1.3021	1.2816
	0.4	1.369	1.366	1.362	1.359	1.356	1.3531	1.3392	1.3222	1.3028	1.2816
	0.3	1.369	1.367	1.363	1.360	1.357	1.3541	1.3401	1.3229	1.3032	1.2816
	0.2	1.370	1.367	1.364	1.361	1.358	1.3548	1.3408	1.3234	1.3035	1.2816
	0.1	1.370	1.367	1.364	1.361	1.358	1.3552	1.3411	1.3237	1.3037	1.2816
1.0	0.0	1.370	1.368	1.364	1.361	1.358	1.3554	1.3413	1.3238	1.3038	1.2816

$$y = \left(1 + \frac{t_0^2}{2f}\right)^{-1/2},$$

$$y' = \frac{t_0}{\sqrt{2f}}\left(1 + \frac{t_0^2}{2f}\right)^{-1/2},$$

$$\delta = t_0 - \lambda\left(1 + \frac{t_0^2}{2f}\right)^{1/2},$$

where λ is read from the table.

5.2

Factors for Computing the Noncentrality Parameter
of the Noncentral *t*-Distribution (*cont.*)

Pr{noncentral *t* with *f* degrees of freedom $\leq t_0$} = 0.95

y'	y	4	5	6	7	8	9	16	36	144	∞
-1.0	0.0	1.528	1.543	1.554	1.563	1.569	1.5744	1.5952	1.6141	1.6307	1.6449
	0.1	1.527	1.543	1.554	1.562	1.569	1.5742	1.5950	1.6139	1.6306	1.6449
	0.2	1.527	1.542	1.553	1.562	1.568	1.5736	1.5945	1.6135	1.6303	1.6449
	0.3	1.526	1.542	1.553	1.561	1.567	1.5728	1.5937	1.6129	1.6300	1.6449
	0.4	1.526	1.541	1.552	1.560	1.567	1.5720	1.5930	1.6122	1.6295	1.6449
	0.5	1.526	1.541	1.552	1.560	1.566	1.5717	1.5924	1.6116	1.6291	1.6449
	0.6	1.529	1.543	1.553	1.561	1.567	1.5724	1.5926	1.6115	1.6289	1.6449
	0.7	1.534	1.548	1.557	1.565	1.570	1.5751	1.5942	1.6123	1.6292	1.6449
-0.6	0.8	1.546	1.557	1.566	1.572	1.577	1.5816	1.5986	1.6149	1.6303	1.6449
-0.5		1.559	1.569	1.576	1.581	1.586	1.5895	1.6041	1.6183	1.6319	1.6449
-0.4		1.575	1.582	1.588	1.593	1.596	1.5990	1.6110	1.6226	1.6339	1.6449
-0.3		1.592	1.597	1.602	1.605	1.608	1.6097	1.6187	1.6276	1.6363	1.6449
-0.2		1.609	1.613	1.616	1.618	1.620	1.6212	1.6272	1.6331	1.6390	1.6449
-0.1		1.627	1.629	1.630	1.632	1.632	1.6332	1.6360	1.6390	1.6419	1.6449
0.0	1.0	1.645	1.645	1.645	1.645	1.645	1.6449	1.6449	1.6449	1.6449	1.6449
0.1		1.661	1.660	1.658	1.658	1.657	1.6561	1.6534	1.6506	1.6478	1.6449
0.2		1.676	1.673	1.671	1.669	1.668	1.6665	1.6614	1.6561	1.6506	1.6449
0.3		1.688	1.684	1.681	1.679	1.677	1.6756	1.6686	1.6610	1.6531	1.6449
0.4		1.697	1.693	1.690	1.687	1.685	1.6830	1.6745	1.6652	1.6553	1.6449
0.5		1.702	1.698	1.695	1.692	1.690	1.6881	1.6789	1.6685	1.6571	1.6449
0.6	0.8	1.703	1.700	1.697	1.695	1.693	1.6906	1.6815	1.6707	1.6584	1.6449
	0.7	1.696	1.695	1.694	1.692	1.691	1.6895	1.6817	1.6714	1.6590	1.6449
	0.6	1.685	1.687	1.687	1.687	1.686	1.6855	1.6797	1.6706	1.6588	1.6449
	0.5	1.673	1.677	1.680	1.680	1.680	1.6803	1.6767	1.6691	1.6583	1.6449
	0.4	1.661	1.668	1.672	1.674	1.675	1.6750	1.6735	1.6674	1.6576	1.6449
	0.3	1.651	1.660	1.665	1.668	1.670	1.6704	1.6706	1.6658	1.6569	1.6449
	0.2	1.643	1.654	1.660	1.663	1.666	1.6669	1.6684	1.6645	1.6564	1.6449
	0.1	1.639	1.650	1.657	1.661	1.663	1.6646	1.6670	1.6637	1.6560	1.6449
1.0	0.0	1.636	1.648	1.655	1.660	1.662	1.6638	1.6665	1.6634	1.6559	1.6449

$$y = \left(1 + \frac{t_0^2}{2f}\right)^{-1/2},$$

$$y' = \frac{t_0}{\sqrt{2f}}\left(1 + \frac{t_0^2}{2f}\right)^{-1/2},$$

$$\delta = t_0 - \lambda\left(1 + \frac{t_0^2}{2f}\right)^{1/2},$$

where λ is read from the table.

5.2

Factors for Computing the Noncentrality Parameter
of the Noncentral *t*-Distribution (cont.)

Pr{noncentral *t* with *f* degrees of freedom $\leq t_0$} = 0.99

y'	y	4	5	6	7	8	9	16	36	144	∞
-1.0	0.0	2.32	2.33	2.33	2.34	2.34	2.340	2.343	2.342	2.337	2.326
	0.1	2.32	2.33	2.33	2.34	2.34	2.339	2.342	2.342	2.337	2.326
	0.2	2.32	2.32	2.33	2.33	2.33	2.335	2.339	2.339	2.335	2.326
	0.3	2.31	2.32	2.32	2.32	2.33	2.328	2.334	2.335	2.333	2.326
	0.4	2.30	2.31	2.31	2.32	2.32	2.320	2.327	2.330	2.330	2.326
	0.5	2.29	2.30	2.30	2.30	2.31	2.310	2.318	2.324	2.327	2.326
	0.6	2.27	2.28	2.29	2.29	2.30	2.299	2.310	2.318	2.323	2.326
	0.7	2.26	2.27	2.28	2.28	2.29	2.289	2.301	2.311	2.320	2.326
-0.6	0.8	2.25	2.26	2.27	2.28	2.28	2.282	2.295	2.307	2.317	2.326
-0.5		2.26	2.26	2.27	2.28	2.28	2.282	2.294	2.306	2.317	2.326
-0.4		2.26	2.27	2.28	2.28	2.28	2.286	2.297	2.307	2.317	2.326
-0.3		2.28	2.28	2.29	2.29	2.29	2.293	2.302	2.310	2.319	2.326
-0.2		2.29	2.30	2.30	2.30	2.30	2.303	2.309	2.315	2.321	2.326
-0.1		2.31	2.31	2.31	2.31	2.31	2.315	2.318	2.320	2.323	2.326
0.0	1.0	2.33	2.33	2.33	2.33	2.33	2.326	2.326	2.326	2.326	2.326
0.1		2.34	2.34	2.34	2.34	2.34	2.337	2.335	2.332	2.329	2.326
0.2		2.35	2.35	2.35	2.35	2.35	2.347	2.342	2.337	2.332	2.326
0.3		2.36	2.36	2.36	2.36	2.35	2.353	2.347	2.341	2.334	2.326
0.4		2.36	2.36	2.36	2.36	2.36	2.356	2.350	2.343	2.335	2.326
0.5		2.36	2.36	2.36	2.36	2.35	2.353	2.349	2.343	2.335	2.326
0.6	0.8	2.34	2.34	2.34	2.34	2.34	2.344	2.343	2.340	2.334	2.326
	0.7	2.30	2.31	2.32	2.32	2.32	2.324	2.329	2.332	2.330	2.326
	0.6	2.26	2.27	2.28	2.29	2.30	2.299	2.313	2.322	2.326	2.326
	0.5	2.21	2.23	2.25	2.26	2.27	2.274	2.296	2.312	2.322	2.326
	0.4	2.16	2.19	2.21	2.23	2.24	2.250	2.280	2.302	2.317	2.326
	0.3	2.12	2.16	2.19	2.20	2.22	2.229	2.267	2.294	2.314	2.326
	0.2	2.09	2.13	2.16	2.19	2.20	2.213	2.256	2.288	2.311	2.326
	0.1	2.07	2.12	2.15	2.17	2.19	2.203	2.250	2.285	2.309	2.326
1.0	0.0	2.06	2.11	2.15	2.17	2.19	2.199	2.247	2.283	2.309	2.326

$$y = \left(1 + \frac{t_0^2}{2f}\right)^{-1/2},$$

$$y' = \frac{t_0}{\sqrt{2f}}\left(1 + \frac{t_0^2}{2f}\right)^{-1/2},$$

$$\delta = t_0 - \lambda\left(1 + \frac{t_0^2}{2f}\right)^{1/2},$$

where λ is read from the table.

5.3 One-Sided Tolerance Limit Factors for a Normal Distribution

At hand are estimates $\bar{x}$ and s of the mean and standard deviation, based on n observations and f degrees of freedom, respectively, of a normal distribution. Required is a value of k for a tolerance limit of the form $\bar{x} + ks$ so that a statement can be made of the form, "At least a proportion, P, of the normal population is less than $\bar{x} + ks$ with confidence γ." The value $\bar{x} + ks$ is called an upper tolerance limit. For a lower tolerance limit $\bar{x} - ks$ is used, and the statement is, "At least a proportion, P, of the population is greater than $\bar{x} - ks$ with confidence γ." When a statement based on a sample is said to be true with confidence γ, the meaning is that the probability is γ that the statement is correct if the assumptions about the population and sample are correct.

The quantity tabulated is k as a function of P, γ, f, and n. Mathematically, k is determined by

$$\Pr\{(\text{noncentral } t \text{ with } \delta = K_p\sqrt{n}) \leq k\sqrt{n}\} = \gamma,$$

where the noncentral t has f degrees of freedom and K_p is defined by

$$\frac{1}{\sqrt{2\pi}} \int_{-\infty}^{K_p} \exp\left(-x^2/2\right) dx = P.$$

The tables given here were computed from the Johnson and Welch tables [101], except that for $f = 1$, 2, and 3, the exact formulas given in Section 5.1 were used to evaluate the probability integral, and k was determined by trial and error. The values of k can also be used in sampling inspection plans. See [161] and [180] for examples of applications. Since many applications arise where $f = n - 1$, one of the tables has been prepared for this case.

One-Sided Tolerance Limit Factors for a Normal Distribution

Values of k for $\gamma = 0.90$ and $n = 1$

f	0.900	0.950	0.975	0.990	0.999	f	0.900	00.950	0.975	0.990	0.999
1	10.532	13.220	15.641	18.513	24.574	46	2.624	3.003	3.334	3.719	4.530
2	4.800	5.769	6.640	7.681	9.911	47	2.622	3.001	3.331	3.717	4.526
3	3.817	4.515	5.140	5.885	7.487	48	2.621	3.000	3.330	3.715	4.523
4	3.428	4.021	4.551	5.182	6.537	49	2.620	2.998	3.328	3.712	4.520
5	3.223	3.761	4.239	4.809	6.030	50	2.619	2.997	3.326	3.710	4.517
6	3.095	3.599	4.047	4.578	5.715	51	2.617	2.995	3.324	3.708	4.514
7	3.010	3.491	3.917	4.422	5.502	52	2.616	2.994	3.323	3.706	4.511
8	2.948	3.412	3.822	4.309	5.347	53	2.615	2.993	3.321	3.704	4.508
9	2.900	3.352	3.751	4.224	5.230	54	2.614	2.991	3.320	3.703	4.506
10	2.863	3.305	3.695	4.156	5.138	55	2.613	2.990	3.318	3.701	4.503
11	2.833	3.268	3.651	4.102	5.064	56	2.613	2.989	3.317	3.699	4.501
12	2.809	3.237	3.614	4.058	5.003	57	2.612	2.988	3.315	3.697	4.499
13	2.789	3.212	3.584	4.021	4.952	58	2.611	2.987	3.314	3.696	4.496
14	2.772	3.190	3.558	3.990	4.908	59	2.610	2.986	3.313	3.694	4.494
15	2.757	3.172	3.536	3.964	4.871	60	2.609	2.985	3.312	3.693	4.492
16	2.744	3.156	3.517	3.941	4.839	61	2.608	2.984	3.310	3.691	4.490
17	2.733	3.141	3.499	3.920	4.810	62	2.608	2.983	3.309	3.690	4.488
18	2.723	3.129	3.484	3.901	4.785	63	2.607	2.982	3.308	3.689	4.486
19	2.714	3.117	3.471	3.885	4.762	64	2.606	2.981	3.307	3.687	4.485
20	2.706	3.107	3.459	3.871	4.742	65	2.606	2.980	3.306	3.686	4.483
21	2.699	3.098	3.448	3.858	4.724	66	2.605	2.979	3.305	3.685	4.481
22	2.692	3.090	3.438	3.846	4.707	67	2.604	2.978	3.304	3.684	4.479
23	2.687	3.083	3.429	3.835	4.692	68	2.604	2.978	3.303	3.683	4.478
24	2.681	3.076	3.421	3.825	4.678	69	2.603	2.977	3.302	3.682	4.476
25	2.676	3.070	3.414	3.816	4.666	70	2.602	2.976	3.301	3.681	4.475
26	2.672	3.064	3.407	3.808	4.654	71	2.602	2.976	3.301	3.680	4.473
27	2.668	3.059	3.400	3.801	4.644	72	2.601	2.975	3.300	3.679	4.472
28	2.664	3.054	3.395	3.794	4.634	73	2.601	2.974	3.299	3.678	4.471
29	2.660	3.050	3.389	3.787	4.625	74	2.600	2.974	3.298	3.677	4.469
30	2.657	3.045	3.384	3.781	4.616	75	2.600	2.973	3.297	3.676	4.468
31	2.654	3.041	3.380	3.775	4.608	80	2.598	2.970	3.294	3.671	4.462
32	2.651	3.038	3.375	3.770	4.601	85	2.595	2.967	3.291	3.668	4.457
33	2.648	3.034	3.371	3.765	4.594	90	2.594	2.965	3.288	3.664	4.452
34	2.646	3.031	3.367	3.760	4.587	95	2.592	2.963	3.286	3.661	4.448
35	2.643	3.028	3.364	3.756	4.581	100	2.591	2.961	3.283	3.659	4.444
36	2.641	3.025	3.360	3.752	4.575	110	2.588	2.958	3.280	3.654	4.437
37	2.639	3.022	3.357	3.748	4.569	120	2.586	2.955	3.276	3.650	4.432
38	2.637	3.020	3.354	3.744	4.564	130	2.584	2.953	3.274	3.647	4.427
39	2.635	3.017	3.351	3.740	4.559	140	2.583	2.951	3.271	3.644	4.423
40	2.633	3.015	3.348	3.737	4.554	150	2.581	2.950	3.269	3.642	4.420
41	2.631	3.013	3.345	3.733	4.549	200	2.577	2.944	3.262	3.633	4.407
42	2.630	3.011	3.343	3.730	4.545	300	2.572	2.938	3.255	3.624	4.395
43	2.628	3.009	3.340	3.727	4.541	500	2.568	2.933	3.249	3.618	4.385
44	2.626	3.007	3.338	3.725	4.537	1000	2.566	2.930	3.245	3.613	4.379
45	2.625	3.005	3.336	3.722	4.533						

One-Sided Tolerance Limit Factors for a Normal Distribution (cont.)

Values of k for $\Upsilon = 0.90$ and n = 2

f	0.900	0.950	p 0.975	0.990	0.999	f	0.900	0.950	p 0.975	0.990	0.999
1	10.253	13.090	15.586	18.500	24.582	46	2.248	2.630	2.964	3.354	4.174
2	4.405	5.431	6.345	7.427	9.716	47	2.246	2.628	2.961	3.351	4.170
3	3.426	4.161	4.817	5.596	7.253	48	2.245	2.627	2.959	3.348	4.167
4	3.042	3.664	4.220	4.878	6.282	49	2.244	2.625	2.957	3.346	4.163
5	2.838	3.400	3.900	4.494	5.760	50	2.243	2.623	2.956	3.344	4.160
6	2.712	3.237	3.703	4.255	5.433	51	2.242	2.622	2.954	3.342	4.157
7	2.628	3.127	3.569	4.094	5.212	52	2.240	2.621	2.952	3.339	4.153
8	2.566	3.047	3.472	3.976	5.050	53	2.239	2.619	2.950	3.337	4.150
9	2.520	2.986	3.399	3.887	4.927	54	2.238	2.618	2.949	3.335	4.148
10	2.483	2.939	3.342	3.818	4.830	55	2.238	2.617	2.947	3.333	4.145
11	2.454	2.901	3.295	3.761	4.752	56	2.237	2.616	2.946	3.332	4.142
12	2.430	2.869	3.257	3.715	4.687	57	2.236	2.614	2.944	3.330	4.140
13	2.410	2.843	3.225	3.676	4.633	58	2.235	2.613	2.943	3.328	4.137
14	2.394	2.821	3.198	3.643	4.586	59	2.234	2.612	2.942	3.327	4.135
15	2.379	2.803	3.175	3.614	4.546	60	2.233	2.611	2.940	3.325	4.132
16	2.367	2.786	3.155	3.589	4.511	61	2.233	2.610	2.939	3.323	4.130
17	2.356	2.772	3.137	3.568	4.481	62	2.232	2.609	2.938	3.322	4.128
18	2.346	2.759	3.121	3.548	4.453	63	2.231	2.608	2.937	3.320	4.126
19	2.337	2.747	3.107	3.531	4.429	64	2.230	2.607	2.936	3.319	4.124
20	2.329	2.737	3.095	3.516	4.407	65	2.230	2.606	2.935	3.318	4.122
21	2.322	2.728	3.084	3.502	4.387	66	2.229	2.606	2.934	3.316	4.120
22	2.316	2.719	3.073	3.489	4.370	67	2.228	2.605	2.933	3.315	4.118
23	2.310	2.712	3.064	3.478	4.353	68	2.228	2.604	2.932	3.314	4.116
24	2.304	2.705	3.055	3.467	4.338	69	2.227	2.603	2.931	3.313	4.115
25	2.300	2.698	3.048	3.458	4.324	70	2.227	2.602	2.930	3.312	4.113
26	2.295	2.693	3.041	3.449	4.312	71	2.226	2.602	2.929	3.310	4.111
27	2.291	2.687	3.034	3.441	4.300	72	2.226	2.601	2.928	3.309	4.110
28	2.287	2.682	3.028	3.433	4.289	73	2.225	2.600	2.927	3.308	4.108
29	2.284	2.678	3.022	3.426	4.279	74	2.225	2.600	2.926	3.307	4.107
30	2.281	2.673	3.017	3.420	4.270	75	2.224	2.599	2.925	3.306	4.105
31	2.278	2.669	3.012	3.414	4.261	80	2.222	2.596	2.922	3.302	4.098
32	2.275	2.666	3.007	3.408	4.253	85	2.220	2.593	2.918	3.298	4.092
33	2.272	2.662	3.003	3.403	4.245	90	2.218	2.591	2.915	3.294	4.087
34	2.270	2.659	2.999	3.397	4.238	95	2.216	2.589	2.913	3.291	4.082
35	2.267	2.656	2.995	3.393	4.231	100	2.215	2.587	2.911	3.288	4.078
36	2.265	2.653	2.992	3.388	4.224	110	2.212	2.584	2.907	3.283	4.071
37	2.263	2.650	2.988	3.384	4.218	120	2.210	2.581	2.903	3.279	4.065
38	2.261	2.647	2.985	3.380	4.212	130	2.209	2.579	2.900	3.275	4.060
39	2.259	2.645	2.982	3.376	4.206	140	2.207	2.577	2.898	3.272	4.055
40	2.257	2.642	2.979	3.372	4.201	150	2.206	2.575	2.896	3.269	4.051
41	2.255	2.640	2.976	3.369	4.196	200	2.201	2.569	2.888	3.260	4.037
42	2.253	2.638	2.973	3.365	4.191	300	2.196	2.563	2.880	3.250	4.023
43	2.252	2.636	2.971	3.362	4.187	500	2.193	2.558	2.875	3.243	4.012
44	2.250	2.634	2.968	3.359	4.182	1000	2.190	2.554	2.870	3.238	4.004
45	2.249	2.632	2.966	3.356	4.178						

One-Sided Tolerance Limit Factors for a Normal Distribution (cont.)

Values of k for $\Upsilon = 0.90$ and n = 3

f	0.900	0.950	0.975	0.990	0.999	f	0.900	0.950	0.975	0.990	0.999
1	10.204	13.080	15.587	18.504	24.585	46	2.082	2.467	2.803	3.196	4.024
2	4.258	5.311	6.244	7.340	9.651	47	2.081	2.465	2.801	3.193	4.020
3	3.271	4.027	4.699	5.492	7.171	48	2.080	2.463	2.798	3.190	4.016
4	2.885	3.525	4.093	4.764	6.190	49	2.079	2.462	2.796	3.188	4.012
5	2.680	3.256	3.768	4.374	5.661	50	2.077	2.460	2.794	3.185	4.008
6	2.553	3.090	3.567	4.130	5.329	51	2.076	2.459	2.793	3.183	4.005
7	2.468	2.977	3.430	3.965	5.103	52	2.075	2.457	2.791	3.181	4.002
8	2.405	2.896	3.330	3.844	4.937	53	2.074	2.456	2.789	3.179	3.998
9	2.359	2.834	3.255	3.753	4.811	54	2.073	2.455	2.787	3.176	3.995
10	2.322	2.786	3.196	3.681	4.711	55	2.072	2.453	2.786	3.174	3.992
11	2.292	2.747	3.149	3.623	4.630	56	2.071	2.452	2.784	3.173	3.989
12	2.268	2.715	3.109	3.575	4.563	57	2.070	2.451	2.783	3.171	3.987
13	2.248	2.688	3.076	3.534	4.506	58	2.070	2.450	2.781	3.169	3.984
14	2.231	2.665	3.048	3.500	4.458	59	2.069	2.449	2.780	3.167	3.981
15	2.216	2.646	3.024	3.470	4.417	60	2.068	2.447	2.778	3.165	3.979
16	2.204	2.629	3.003	3.444	4.380	61	2.067	2.446	2.777	3.164	3.976
17	2.192	2.614	2.985	3.421	4.348	62	2.066	2.445	2.776	3.162	3.974
18	2.182	2.600	2.968	3.401	4.319	63	2.066	2.444	2.775	3.161	3.972
19	2.173	2.588	2.954	3.383	4.294	64	2.065	2.443	2.774	3.159	3.970
20	2.165	2.578	2.940	3.367	4.271	65	2.064	2.443	2.772	3.158	3.967
21	2.158	2.568	2.929	3.353	4.250	66	2.064	2.442	2.771	3.156	3.965
22	2.152	2.560	2.918	3.339	4.232	67	2.063	2.441	2.770	3.155	3.963
23	2.146	2.552	2.908	3.327	4.214	68	2.062	2.440	2.769	3.154	3.961
24	2.140	2.545	2.899	3.316	4.199	69	2.062	2.439	2.768	3.152	3.959
25	2.136	2.538	2.891	3.306	4.184	70	2.061	2.438	2.767	3.151	3.958
26	2.131	2.532	2.884	3.297	4.171	71	2.061	2.438	2.766	3.150	3.956
27	2.127	2.526	2.877	3.288	4.158	72	2.060	2.437	2.765	3.149	3.954
28	2.123	2.521	2.870	3.280	4.147	73	2.060	2.436	2.764	3.148	3.952
29	2.119	2.517	2.865	3.273	4.136	74	2.059	2.435	2.763	3.147	3.951
30	2.116	2.512	2.859	3.266	4.126	75	2.059	2.435	2.763	3.146	3.949
31	2.113	2.508	2.854	3.260	4.116	80	2.056	2.432	2.759	3.141	3.942
32	2.110	2.504	2.849	3.253	4.107	85	2.054	2.429	2.755	3.136	3.935
33	2.107	2.500	2.844	3.248	4.099	90	2.052	2.426	2.752	3.132	3.930
34	2.105	2.497	2.840	3.242	4.091	95	2.051	2.424	2.749	3.129	3.924
35	2.102	2.494	2.836	3.237	4.084	100	2.049	2.422	2.747	3.126	3.920
36	2.100	2.491	2.832	3.233	4.077	110	2.047	2.419	2.743	3.120	3.912
37	2.098	2.488	2.829	3.228	4.070	120	2.045	2.416	2.739	3.116	3.905
38	2.096	2.485	2.825	3.224	4.064	130	2.043	2.414	2.736	3.112	3.899
39	2.094	2.482	2.822	3.220	4.058	140	2.041	2.412	2.734	3.109	3.895
40	2.092	2.480	2.819	3.216	4.053	150	2.040	2.410	2.731	3.106	3.890
41	2.090	2.477	2.816	3.212	4.047	200	2.035	2.403	2.723	3.096	3.875
42	2.088	2.475	2.813	3.209	4.042	300	2.030	2.397	2.715	3.086	3.860
43	2.087	2.473	2.810	3.205	4.037	500	2.027	2.392	2.709	3.078	3.848
44	2.085	2.471	2.808	3.202	4.033	1000	2.024	2.388	2.704	3.072	3.839
45	2.084	2.469	2.805	3.199	4.028						

One-Sided Tolerance Limit Factors for a Normal Distribution (*cont.*)

Values of k for Υ = 0.90 and n = 4

f	p 0.900	0.950	0.975	0.990	0.999	f	p 0.900	0.950	0.975	0.990	0.999
1	10.193	13.081	15.589	18.506	24.587	46	1.985	2.371	2.709	3.104	3.938
2	4.182	5.251	6.193	7.297	9.619	47	1.984	2.369	2.707	3.101	3.933
3	3.188	3.957	4.637	5.438	7.129	48	1.982	2.368	2.704	3.099	3.929
4	2.799	3.449	4.025	4.705	6.143	49	1.981	2.366	2.702	3.096	3.925
5	2.591	3.177	3.697	4.310	5.609	50	1.980	2.364	2.700	3.093	3.922
6	2.463	3.009	3.492	4.063	5.274	51	1.979	2.363	2.698	3.091	3.918
7	2.376	2.895	3.354	3.896	5.046	52	1.977	2.361	2.696	3.088	3.914
8	2.314	2.811	3.252	3.772	4.877	53	1.976	2.360	2.694	3.086	3.911
9	2.266	2.749	3.175	3.679	4.749	54	1.975	2.358	2.693	3.084	3.908
10	2.229	2.699	3.115	3.606	4.647	55	1.974	2.357	2.691	3.082	3.905
11	2.199	2.659	3.066	3.546	4.564	56	1.973	2.356	2.689	3.080	3.901
12	2.174	2.626	3.026	3.497	4.496	57	1.973	2.354	2.688	3.078	3.899
13	2.154	2.599	2.992	3.455	4.438	58	1.972	2.353	2.686	3.076	3.896
14	2.136	2.576	2.963	3.420	4.388	59	1.971	2.352	2.685	3.074	3.893
15	2.121	2.555	2.938	3.389	4.345	60	1.970	2.351	2.683	3.072	3.890
16	2.109	2.538	2.916	3.362	4.308	61	1.969	2.350	2.682	3.070	3.888
17	2.097	2.523	2.897	3.339	4.275	62	1.968	2.349	2.681	3.069	3.885
18	2.087	2.509	2.881	3.318	4.245	63	1.968	2.348	2.679	3.067	3.883
19	2.078	2.497	2.866	3.300	4.219	64	1.967	2.347	2.678	3.066	3.880
20	2.069	2.486	2.852	3.283	4.196	65	1.966	2.346	2.677	3.064	3.878
21	2.062	2.476	2.840	3.268	4.174	66	1.966	2.345	2.676	3.063	3.876
22	2.056	2.467	2.829	3.254	4.154	67	1.965	2.344	2.675	3.061	3.874
23	2.050	2.459	2.819	3.242	4.137	68	1.964	2.343	2.674	3.060	3.872
24	2.044	2.452	2.810	3.230	4.120	69	1.964	2.342	2.673	3.059	3.870
25	2.039	2.445	2.801	3.220	4.105	70	1.963	2.342	2.672	3.057	3.868
26	2.035	2.439	2.793	3.210	4.091	71	1.963	2.341	2.671	3.056	3.866
27	2.030	2.433	2.786	3.201	4.078	72	1.962	2.340	2.670	3.055	3.864
28	2.026	2.427	2.779	3.193	4.066	73	1.961	2.339	2.669	3.054	3.862
29	2.023	2.423	2.773	3.185	4.055	74	1.961	2.338	2.668	3.052	3.861
30	2.019	2.418	2.767	3.178	4.044	75	1.960	2.338	2.667	3.051	3.859
31	2.016	2.414	2.762	3.171	4.035	80	1.958	2.335	2.663	3.046	3.851
32	2.013	2.410	2.757	3.165	4.025	85	1.956	2.332	2.659	3.041	3.844
33	2.010	2.406	2.752	3.159	4.017	90	1.954	2.329	2.656	3.037	3.838
34	2.008	2.402	2.748	3.153	4.009	95	1.952	2.327	2.653	3.034	3.832
35	2.005	2.399	2.744	3.148	4.001	100	1.951	2.325	2.650	3.030	3.827
36	2.003	2.396	2.740	3.143	3.993	110	1.948	2.321	2.646	3.025	3.819
37	2.001	2.393	2.736	3.138	3.987	120	1.946	2.318	2.642	3.020	3.812
38	1.999	2.390	2.732	3.133	3.980	130	1.944	2.316	2.639	3.016	3.806
39	1.997	2.387	2.729	3.129	3.974	140	1.943	2.314	2.636	3.013	3.800
40	1.995	2.384	2.725	3.125	3.968	150	1.941	2.312	2.634	3.009	3.796
41	1.993	2.382	2.722	3.121	3.962	200	1.936	2.305	2.625	2.998	3.779
42	1.991	2.380	2.719	3.118	3.957	300	1.932	2.298	2.617	2.988	3.763
43	1.989	2.377	2.717	3.114	3.952	500	1.928	2.293	2.610	2.979	3.750
44	1.988	2.375	2.714	3.111	3.947	1000	1.925	2.289	2.605	2.973	3.740
45	1.986	2.373	2.711	3.107	3.942						

One-Sided Tolerance Limit Factors for a Normal Distribution (cont.)

Values of k for $\gamma = 0.95$ and n = 1

f	0.900	0.950	0.975	0.990	0.999	f	0.900	0.950	0.975	0.990	0.999
1	21.171	26.546	31.391	37.140	49.275	46	3.021	3.407	3.743	4.137	4.964
2	7.006	8.378	9.616	11.096	14.275	47	3.019	3.404	3.740	4.133	4.959
3	5.074	5.957	6.750	7.699	9.743	48	3.017	3.402	3.737	4.130	4.954
4	4.369	5.079	5.718	6.480	8.119	49	3.015	3.399	3.735	4.126	4.950
5	4.007	4.629	5.186	5.849	7.274	50	3.013	3.397	3.732	4.123	4.945
6	3.789	4.360	4.869	5.472	6.769	51	3.011	3.395	3.729	4.120	4.941
7	3.644	4.180	4.655	5.219	6.431	52	3.010	3.393	3.727	4.117	4.937
8	3.541	4.052	4.504	5.040	6.193	53	3.008	3.391	3.724	4.114	4.933
9	3.463	3.955	4.391	4.906	6.011	54	3.006	3.389	3.722	4.112	4.929
10	3.403	3.880	4.302	4.800	5.867	55	3.005	3.387	3.720	4.109	4.926
11	3.354	3.820	4.231	4.717	5.754	56	3.003	3.385	3.718	4.106	4.922
12	3.315	3.771	4.174	4.649	5.662	57	3.002	3.383	3.716	4.104	4.919
13	3.283	3.731	4.126	4.593	5.586	58	3.001	3.382	3.714	4.102	4.916
14	3.255	3.697	4.086	4.545	5.521	59	2.999	3.380	3.712	4.099	4.913
15	3.232	3.668	4.052	4.504	5.467	60	2.998	3.379	3.710	4.097	4.910
16	3.212	3.643	4.022	4.469	5.419	61	2.997	3.377	3.708	4.095	4.907
17	3.194	3.620	3.996	4.438	5.377	62	2.996	3.376	3.707	4.093	4.904
18	3.178	3.601	3.973	4.410	5.339	63	2.995	3.374	3.705	4.091	4.901
19	3.164	3.583	3.952	4.385	5.305	64	2.994	3.373	3.703	4.089	4.899
20	3.151	3.568	3.934	4.363	5.276	65	2.993	3.372	3.702	4.087	4.896
21	3.140	3.554	3.917	4.344	5.248	66	2.992	3.370	3.700	4.086	4.894
22	3.129	3.541	3.902	4.326	5.224	67	2.991	3.369	3.699	4.084	4.891
23	3.120	3.530	3.888	4.310	5.202	68	2.990	3.368	3.698	4.082	4.889
24	3.112	3.519	3.876	4.295	5.182	69	2.989	3.367	3.696	4.081	4.887
25	3.104	3.509	3.865	4.282	5.163	70	2.988	3.366	3.695	4.079	4.884
26	3.097	3.501	3.854	4.269	5.146	71	2.987	3.365	3.694	4.077	4.882
27	3.090	3.493	3.845	4.258	5.130	72	2.986	3.364	3.692	4.076	4.880
28	3.084	3.485	3.836	4.247	5.116	73	2.985	3.363	3.691	4.074	4.878
29	3.078	3.478	3.828	4.237	5.102	74	2.984	3.362	3.690	4.073	4.876
30	3.073	3.472	3.820	4.228	5.090	75	2.984	3.361	3.689	4.072	4.874
31	3.068	3.466	3.813	4.220	5.078	80	2.980	3.356	3.683	4.065	4.866
32	3.064	3.460	3.806	4.212	5.067	85	2.977	3.352	3.679	4.060	4.858
33	3.059	3.455	3.800	4.204	5.057	90	2.974	3.349	3.675	4.055	4.851
34	3.055	3.450	3.794	4.197	5.048	95	2.971	3.346	3.671	4.050	4.845
35	3.052	3.445	3.789	4.191	5.038	100	2.969	3.343	3.668	4.046	4.839
36	3.048	3.441	3.783	4.185	5.030	110	2.965	3.338	3.662	4.039	4.830
37	3.045	3.436	3.778	4.179	5.022	120	2.962	3.334	3.657	4.034	4.822
38	3.041	3.432	3.774	4.173	5.014	130	2.959	3.331	3.653	4.029	4.815
39	3.038	3.429	3.769	4.167	5.007	140	2.957	3.328	3.650	4.025	4.810
40	3.035	3.425	3.765	4.162	5.000	150	2.955	3.325	3.647	4.021	4.805
41	3.033	3.421	3.761	4.158	4.993	200	2.948	3.316	3.636	4.008	4.787
42	3.030	3.418	3.757	4.153	4.987	300	2.940	3.307	3.625	3.996	4.769
43	3.028	3.415	3.753	4.149	4.981	500	2.935	3.300	3.617	3.986	4.755
44	3.025	3.412	3.750	4.144	4.975	1000	2.930	3.295	3.611	3.978	4.745
45	3.023	3.409	3.746	4.140	4.969						

One-Sided Tolerance Limit Factors for a Normal Distribution (cont.)

Values of k for $\Upsilon = 0.95$ and n = 2

f	p 0.900	0.950	0.975	0.990	0.999	f	p 0.900	0.950	0.975	0.990	0.999
1	20.581	26.260	31.257	37.094	49.276	46	2.535	2.925	3.265	3.664	4.505
2	6.386	7.845	9.148	10.691	13.962	47	2.533	2.922	3.262	3.660	4.499
3	4.508	5.443	6.280	7.275	9.397	48	2.531	2.920	3.259	3.657	4.494
4	3.830	4.581	5.253	6.050	7.754	49	2.530	2.918	3.256	3.653	4.489
5	3.481	4.136	4.719	5.413	6.901	50	2.528	2.915	3.254	3.650	4.484
6	3.273	3.869	4.400	5.032	6.385	51	2.526	2.913	3.251	3.647	4.480
7	3.133	3.691	4.187	4.777	6.041	52	2.524	2.911	3.249	3.644	4.475
8	3.035	3.564	4.036	4.596	5.793	53	2.523	2.909	3.246	3.641	4.471
9	2.960	3.469	3.922	4.458	5.606	54	2.521	2.907	3.244	3.638	4.467
10	2.901	3.394	3.831	4.350	5.459	55	2.520	2.905	3.242	3.635	4.463
11	2.855	3.335	3.760	4.264	5.341	56	2.519	2.904	3.239	3.632	4.459
12	2.817	3.287	3.702	4.194	5.245	57	2.517	2.902	3.237	3.630	4.456
13	2.786	3.247	3.654	4.136	5.165	58	2.516	2.900	3.235	3.627	4.452
14	2.760	3.214	3.614	4.088	5.097	59	2.515	2.899	3.233	3.625	4.449
15	2.738	3.185	3.580	4.046	5.040	60	2.514	2.897	3.232	3.623	4.446
16	2.718	3.160	3.550	4.010	4.990	61	2.512	2.896	3.230	3.621	4.442
17	2.701	3.138	3.523	3.978	4.946	62	2.511	2.894	3.228	3.618	4.439
18	2.686	3.118	3.499	3.950	4.906	63	2.510	2.893	3.226	3.616	4.436
19	2.672	3.101	3.478	3.924	4.871	64	2.509	2.891	3.225	3.614	4.433
20	2.660	3.085	3.460	3.901	4.840	65	2.508	2.890	3.223	3.612	4.431
21	2.649	3.071	3.443	3.881	4.811	66	2.507	2.889	3.222	3.610	4.428
22	2.639	3.059	3.428	3.862	4.785	67	2.506	2.888	3.220	3.609	4.425
23	2.630	3.047	3.414	3.845	4.762	68	2.505	2.886	3.219	3.607	4.423
24	2.622	3.037	3.401	3.830	4.740	69	2.504	2.885	3.217	3.605	4.420
25	2.615	3.027	3.390	3.816	4.720	70	2.504	2.884	3.216	3.603	4.418
26	2.608	3.019	3.379	3.803	4.702	71	2.503	2.883	3.214	3.602	4.416
27	2.602	3.011	3.369	3.791	4.685	72	2.502	2.882	3.213	3.600	4.413
28	2.596	3.003	3.360	3.780	4.669	73	2.501	2.881	3.212	3.599	4.411
29	2.591	2.996	3.352	3.770	4.655	74	2.500	2.880	3.211	3.597	4.409
30	2.586	2.990	3.344	3.760	4.641	75	2.500	2.879	3.210	3.596	4.407
31	2.581	2.984	3.337	3.751	4.628	80	2.496	2.874	3.204	3.589	4.397
32	2.577	2.978	3.330	3.743	4.616	85	2.493	2.871	3.199	3.583	4.389
33	2.572	2.973	3.324	3.735	4.605	90	2.490	2.867	3.195	3.578	4.381
34	2.569	2.968	3.318	3.728	4.595	95	2.488	2.864	3.191	3.573	4.375
35	2.565	2.963	3.312	3.721	4.585	100	2.486	2.861	3.188	3.569	4.369
36	2.562	2.959	3.307	3.714	4.576	110	2.482	2.856	3.182	3.562	4.358
37	2.558	2.955	3.301	3.708	4.567	120	2.479	2.852	3.177	3.556	4.350
38	2.555	2.951	3.297	3.702	4.558	130	2.476	2.849	3.173	3.551	4.342
39	2.552	2.947	3.292	3.696	4.551	140	2.474	2.846	3.169	3.546	4.336
40	2.549	2.943	3.288	3.691	4.543	150	2.472	2.843	3.166	3.543	4.330
41	2.547	2.940	3.283	3.686	4.536	200	2.465	2.834	3.155	3.529	4.311
42	2.544	2.936	3.279	3.681	4.529	300	2.458	2.825	3.144	3.515	4.291
43	2.542	2.933	3.276	3.677	4.523	500	2.453	2.818	3.136	3.505	4.276
44	2.540	2.930	3.272	3.672	4.516	1000	2.449	2.813	3.129	3.497	4.264
45	2.537	2.928	3.269	3.668	4.510						

5.3

One-Sided Tolerance Limit Factors for a Normal Distribution (*cont.*)

Values of k for $\Upsilon = 0.95$ and n = 3

f	p 0.900	0.950	0.975	0.990	0.999	f	p 0.900	0.950	0.975	0.990	0.999
1	20.472	26.230	31.251	37.094	49.277	46	2.322	2.715	3.058	3.460	4.310
2	6.155	7.656	8.986	10.553	13.857	47	2.320	2.712	3.055	3.456	4.305
3	4.284	5.248	6.106	7.122	9.276	48	2.318	2.709	3.052	3.453	4.299
4	3.612	4.385	5.073	5.888	7.620	49	2.316	2.707	3.049	3.449	4.294
5	3.265	3.937	4.536	5.248	6.762	50	2.315	2.705	3.046	3.445	4.289
6	3.057	3.669	4.214	4.861	6.242	51	2.313	2.702	3.043	3.442	4.284
7	2.918	3.489	3.999	4.603	5.893	52	2.311	2.700	3.040	3.439	4.279
8	2.819	3.363	3.846	4.418	5.641	53	2.310	2.698	3.038	3.436	4.275
9	2.745	3.267	3.730	4.279	5.450	54	2.308	2.696	3.036	3.433	4.270
10	2.687	3.191	3.638	4.168	5.300	55	2.307	2.694	3.033	3.430	4.266
11	2.641	3.131	3.565	4.081	5.180	56	2.305	2.693	3.031	3.427	4.262
12	2.604	3.082	3.506	4.009	5.081	57	2.304	2.691	3.029	3.424	4.258
13	2.573	3.042	3.458	3.949	4.999	58	2.303	2.689	3.027	3.422	4.254
14	2.547	3.008	3.416	3.899	4.929	59	2.302	2.688	3.025	3.419	4.251
15	2.524	2.979	3.381	3.857	4.869	60	2.300	2.686	3.023	3.417	4.247
16	2.505	2.954	3.351	3.819	4.817	61	2.299	2.684	3.021	3.415	4.244
17	2.487	2.932	3.324	3.787	4.771	62	2.298	2.683	3.019	3.412	4.241
18	2.472	2.912	3.300	3.757	4.731	63	2.297	2.682	3.017	3.410	4.237
19	2.459	2.894	3.278	3.731	4.694	64	2.296	2.680	3.016	3.408	4.234
20	2.447	2.878	3.259	3.708	4.662	65	2.295	2.679	3.014	3.406	4.231
21	2.436	2.864	3.242	3.687	4.632	66	2.294	2.678	3.012	3.404	4.229
22	2.426	2.851	3.226	3.668	4.605	67	2.293	2.676	3.011	3.402	4.226
23	2.417	2.840	3.212	3.650	4.581	68	2.292	2.675	3.009	3.400	4.223
24	2.409	2.829	3.199	3.634	4.558	69	2.291	2.674	3.008	3.398	4.220
25	2.402	2.819	3.187	3.620	4.538	70	2.290	2.673	3.006	3.397	4.218
26	2.395	2.810	3.176	3.606	4.518	71	2.289	2.672	3.005	3.395	4.215
27	2.389	2.802	3.165	3.593	4.501	72	2.289	2.671	3.004	3.393	4.213
28	2.383	2.794	3.156	3.582	4.484	73	2.288	2.669	3.002	3.392	4.210
29	2.377	2.787	3.147	3.571	4.469	74	2.287	2.668	3.001	3.390	4.208
30	2.372	2.781	3.139	3.561	4.454	75	2.286	2.667	3.000	3.389	4.206
31	2.368	2.775	3.132	3.552	4.441	80	2.283	2.663	2.994	3.382	4.196
32	2.363	2.769	3.125	3.543	4.428	85	2.280	2.659	2.989	3.375	4.187
33	2.359	2.763	3.118	3.535	4.417	90	2.277	2.655	2.985	3.370	4.178
34	2.355	2.758	3.112	3.527	4.405	95	2.275	2.652	2.981	3.365	4.171
35	2.352	2.754	3.106	3.520	4.395	100	2.272	2.649	2.977	3.360	4.165
36	2.348	2.749	3.100	3.513	4.385	110	2.269	2.644	2.971	3.353	4.154
37	2.345	2.745	3.095	3.506	4.376	120	2.266	2.640	2.966	3.346	4.144
38	2.342	2.741	3.090	3.500	4.367	130	2.263	2.637	2.962	3.341	4.136
39	2.339	2.737	3.085	3.494	4.359	140	2.261	2.634	2.958	3.336	4.130
40	2.336	2.733	3.081	3.489	4.351	150	2.259	2.631	2.955	3.332	4.123
41	2.334	2.730	3.077	3.483	4.343	200	2.252	2.621	2.943	3.318	4.102
42	2.331	2.726	3.072	3.478	4.336	300	2.245	2.612	2.932	3.304	4.081
43	2.329	2.723	3.069	3.474	4.329	500	2.239	2.605	2.923	3.292	4.064
44	2.326	2.720	3.065	3.469	4.323	1000	2.235	2.600	2.916	3.284	4.052
45	2.324	2.717	3.061	3.465	4.316						

One-Sided Tolerance Limit Factors for a Normal Distribution (cont.)

Values of k for Υ = 0.95 and n = 4

f	0.900	0.950	0.975	0.990	0.999	f	0.900	0.950	0.975	0.990	0.999
1	20.444	26.227	31.252	37.095	49.278	46	2.196	2.591	2.937	3.342	4.199
2	6.035	7.559	8.904	10.483	13.804	47	2.194	2.588	2.933	3.338	4.193
3	4.162	5.144	6.015	7.042	9.214	48	2.192	2.586	2.930	3.334	4.187
4	3.491	4.278	4.977	5.802	7.551	49	2.190	2.583	2.927	3.330	4.182
5	3.143	3.828	4.438	5.159	6.689	50	2.188	2.581	2.924	3.327	4.176
6	2.934	3.558	4.113	4.769	6.166	51	2.187	2.578	2.921	3.323	4.171
7	2.795	3.377	3.895	4.509	5.814	52	2.185	2.576	2.918	3.320	4.166
8	2.696	3.250	3.740	4.322	5.559	53	2.184	2.574	2.916	3.316	4.162
9	2.622	3.152	3.623	4.180	5.366	54	2.182	2.572	2.913	3.313	4.157
10	2.564	3.076	3.530	4.068	5.214	55	2.181	2.570	2.911	3.310	4.153
11	2.517	3.015	3.456	3.979	5.093	56	2.179	2.568	2.909	3.307	4.149
12	2.480	2.965	3.396	3.906	4.992	57	2.178	2.567	2.906	3.305	4.145
13	2.449	2.925	3.346	3.846	4.908	58	2.177	2.565	2.904	3.302	4.141
14	2.422	2.890	3.304	3.794	4.837	59	2.175	2.563	2.902	3.299	4.137
15	2.400	2.861	3.268	3.750	4.775	60	2.174	2.562	2.900	3.297	4.133
16	2.381	2.835	3.237	3.712	4.722	61	2.173	2.560	2.898	3.294	4.129
17	2.363	2.813	3.210	3.678	4.675	62	2.172	2.558	2.896	3.292	4.126
18	2.348	2.793	3.185	3.649	4.633	63	2.171	2.557	2.894	3.290	4.123
19	2.334	2.775	3.163	3.622	4.596	64	2.170	2.556	2.893	3.287	4.119
20	2.322	2.759	3.144	3.598	4.562	65	2.169	2.554	2.891	3.285	4.116
21	2.311	2.744	3.126	3.576	4.532	66	2.168	2.553	2.889	3.283	4.113
22	2.301	2.731	3.110	3.557	4.504	67	2.167	2.552	2.888	3.281	4.110
23	2.292	2.719	3.095	3.539	4.479	68	2.166	2.550	2.886	3.279	4.107
24	2.284	2.708	3.082	3.522	4.456	69	2.165	2.549	2.885	3.277	4.105
25	2.276	2.698	3.070	3.507	4.434	70	2.164	2.548	2.883	3.276	4.102
26	2.270	2.689	3.058	3.493	4.415	71	2.163	2.547	2.882	3.274	4.099
27	2.263	2.680	3.048	3.480	4.396	72	2.162	2.546	2.880	3.272	4.097
28	2.257	2.673	3.038	3.468	4.379	73	2.161	2.545	2.879	3.270	4.094
29	2.252	2.665	3.029	3.457	4.364	74	2.161	2.543	2.878	3.269	4.092
30	2.247	2.659	3.021	3.447	4.349	75	2.160	2.542	2.876	3.267	4.089
31	2.242	2.652	3.013	3.437	4.335	80	2.156	2.538	2.871	3.260	4.079
32	2.238	2.646	3.005	3.428	4.322	85	2.153	2.534	2.865	3.253	4.069
33	2.234	2.641	2.999	3.419	4.310	90	2.151	2.530	2.861	3.247	4.060
34	2.230	2.636	2.992	3.411	4.298	95	2.148	2.527	2.857	3.242	4.053
35	2.226	2.631	2.986	3.404	4.287	100	2.146	2.524	2.853	3.238	4.046
36	2.223	2.626	2.980	3.396	4.277	110	2.142	2.519	2.847	3.230	4.034
37	2.219	2.622	2.975	3.390	4.267	120	2.139	2.514	2.841	3.223	4.024
38	2.216	2.618	2.970	3.383	4.258	130	2.136	2.511	2.837	3.217	4.016
39	2.213	2.614	2.965	3.377	4.249	140	2.134	2.508	2.833	3.212	4.008
40	2.210	2.610	2.960	3.371	4.241	150	2.132	2.505	2.829	3.208	4.002
41	2.208	2.606	2.956	3.366	4.233	200	2.125	2.495	2.817	3.193	3.979
42	2.205	2.603	2.952	3.361	4.226	300	2.118	2.486	2.805	3.178	3.957
43	2.203	2.600	2.948	3.356	4.219	500	2.112	2.478	2.796	3.166	3.939
44	2.200	2.597	2.944	3.351	4.212	1000	2.108	2.473	2.789	3.157	3.926
45	2.198	2.594	2.940	3.346	4.205						

5.3

One-Sided Tolerance Limit Factors for a Normal Distribution (cont.)

	Values of k for γ = 0.90 and n = f + 1						Values of k for γ = 0.95 and n = f + 1				
n	0.900	0.950	0.975	0.990	0.999	n	0.900	0.950	0.975	0.990	0.999
2	10.253	13.090	15.586	18.500	24.582	2	20.581	26.260	31.257	37.094	49.276
3	4.258	5.311	6.244	7.340	9.651	3	6.155	7.656	8.986	10.553	13.857
4	3.188	3.957	4.637	5.438	7.129	4	4.162	5.144	6.015	7.042	9.214
5	2.744	3.401	3.983	4.668	6.113	5	3.413	4.210	4.916	5.749	7.509
6	2.494	3.093	3.621	4.243	5.556	6	3.008	3.711	4.332	5.065	6.614
7	2.333	2.893	3.389	3.972	5.201	7	2.756	3.401	3.971	4.643	6.064
8	2.219	2.754	3.227	3.783	4.955	8	2.582	3.188	3.724	4.355	5.689
9	2.133	2.650	3.106	3.641	4.771	9	2.454	3.032	3.543	4.144	5.414
10	2.066	2.568	3.011	3.532	4.628	10	2.355	2.911	3.403	3.981	5.204
11	2.012	2.503	2.936	3.444	4.515	11	2.275	2.815	3.291	3.852	5.036
12	1.966	2.448	2.872	3.371	4.420	12	2.210	2.736	3.201	3.747	4.900
13	1.928	2.403	2.820	3.310	4.341	13	2.155	2.670	3.125	3.659	4.787
14	1.895	2.363	2.774	3.257	4.274	14	2.108	2.614	3.060	3.585	4.690
15	1.866	2.329	2.735	3.212	4.215	15	2.068	2.566	3.005	3.520	4.607
16	1.842	2.299	2.700	3.172	4.164	16	2.032	2.523	2.956	3.463	4.534
17	1.819	2.272	2.670	3.137	4.118	17	2.002	2.486	2.913	3.414	4.471
18	1.800	2.249	2.643	3.106	4.078	18	1.974	2.453	2.875	3.370	4.415
19	1.781	2.228	2.618	3.078	4.041	19	1.949	2.423	2.840	3.331	4.364
20	1.765	2.208	2.597	3.052	4.009	20	1.926	2.396	2.809	3.295	4.319
21	1.750	2.190	2.575	3.028	3.979	21	1.905	2.371	2.781	3.262	4.276
22	1.736	2.174	2.557	3.007	3.952	22	1.887	2.350	2.756	3.233	4.238
23	1.724	2.159	2.540	2.987	3.927	23	1.869	2.329	2.732	3.206	4.204
24	1.712	2.145	2.525	2.969	3.904	24	1.853	2.309	2.711	3.181	4.171
25	1.702	2.132	2.510	2.952	3.882	25	1.838	2.292	2.691	3.158	4.143
30	1.657	2.080	2.450	2.884	3.794	30	1.778	2.220	2.608	3.064	4.022
35	1.623	2.041	2.406	2.833	3.730	35	1.732	2.166	2.548	2.994	3.934
40	1.598	2.010	2.371	2.793	3.679	40	1.697	2.126	2.501	2.941	3.866
45	1.577	1.986	2.344	2.762	3.638	45	1.669	2.092	2.463	2.897	3.811
50	1.560	1.965	2.320	2.735	3.604	50	1.646	2.065	2.432	2.863	3.766
60	1.532	1.933	2.284	2.694	3.552	60	1.609	2.022	2.384	2.807	3.695
70	1.511	1.909	2.257	2.663	3.513	70	1.581	1.990	2.348	2.766	3.643
80	1.495	1.890	2.235	2.638	3.482	80	1.560	1.965	2.319	2.733	3.601
90	1.481	1.874	2.217	2.618	3.456	90	1.542	1.944	2.295	2.706	3.567
100	1.470	1.861	2.203	2.601	3.435	100	1.527	1.927	2.276	2.684	3.539
120	1.452	1.841	2.179	2.574	3.402	120	1.503	1.899	2.245	2.649	3.495
145	1.436	1.821	2.158	2.550	3.371	145	1.481	1.874	2.217	2.617	3.455
300	1.386	1.765	2.094	2.477	3.280	300	1.417	1.800	2.133	2.522	3.335
500	1.362	1.736	2.062	2.442	3.235	500	1.385	1.763	2.092	2.475	3.277
∞	1.282	1.645	1.960	2.326	3.090	∞	1.282	1.645	1.960	2.326	3.090

5.3

5.4 Two-Sided Tolerance Limit Factors for a Normal Distribution

At hand are estimates $\bar{x}$ and s of the mean and standard deviation, based on n observations and f degrees of freedom, respectively, of a normal distribution. Required is a value of k for tolerance limits of the form $\bar{x} \pm ks$ so that a statement can be made of the form, "At least a proportion, P, of the normal population is between $\bar{x} - ks$ and $\bar{x} + ks$ with confidence γ."

Wald and Wolfowitz [233] showed that k can be approximated by $k \cong ru$, where r is a function of n and P and is determined from the normal distribution function

$$\frac{1}{\sqrt{2\pi}} \int_{(1/\sqrt{n})-r}^{(1/\sqrt{n})+r} \exp\left(-t^2/2\right) dt = P,$$

and u is a function of f and γ and is defined in terms of the $(1 - \gamma)$th critical value of the chi-square distribution as

$$u = \sqrt{f/X_{1-\gamma,f}^2} \, .$$

Wald and Wolfowitz went through the derivation with $f = n - 1$, but Wallis [236] showed that there need be no connection between f and n. The tables given here give r and u for many different values of P, n, γ, and f. Weissberg and Beatty [243], who computed these tables, give examples of their use. Bowker wrote a chapter in [62] giving examples and a table of k with $f = n - 1$.

Two-Sided Tolerance Limit Factors for a Normal Distribution [243]

Table of $r(n, P)$

n	.50	.75	.90	.95	.99	.999
1	1.0505	1.6859	2.2844	2.6463	3.3266	4.0903
2	0.8557	1.4333	2.0078	2.3624	3.0368	3.7983
3	0.7929	1.3412	1.8979	2.2457	2.9128	3.6708
4	0.7622	1.2940	1.8388	2.1815	2.8422	3.5965
5	0.7442	1.2654	1.8019	2.1408	2.7963	3.5472
6	0.7322	1.2463	1.7768	2.1127	2.7640	3.5119
7	0.7237	1.2326	1.7587	2.0922	2.7399	3.4853
8	0.7175	1.2224	1.7448	2.0765	2.7211	3.4644
9	0.7127	1.2144	1.7340	2.0641	2.7066	3.4476
10	0.7088	1.2080	1.7253	2.0541	2.6945	3.4338
11	0.7056	1.2027	1.7182	2.0459	2.6845	3.4223
12	0.7030	1.1984	1.7122	2.0390	2.6760	3.4125
13	0.7008	1.1947	1.7071	2.0331	2.6688	3.4040
14	0.6989	1.1915	1.7027	2.0280	2.6625	3.3967
15	0.6973	1.1887	1.6990	2.0236	2.6571	3.3902
16	0.6958	1.1863	1.6956	2.0197	2.6523	3.3845
17	0.6945	1.1842	1.6926	2.0163	2.6480	3.3794
18	0.6934	1.1823	1.6901	2.0132	2.6441	3.3748
19	0.6924	1.1807	1.6877	2.0105	2.6407	3.3707
20	0.6915	1.1792	1.6855	2.0080	2.6376	3.3670
21	0.6907	1.1778	1.6837	2.0058	2.6348	3.3636
22	0.6900	1.1765	1.6819	2.0037	2.6322	3.3605
23	0.6893	1.1754	1.6803	2.0018	2.6298	3.3576
24	0.6887	1.1743	1.6788	2.0001	2.6276	3.3550
25	0.6881	1.1734	1.6775	1.9985	2.6256	3.3526
26	0.6875	1.1725	1.6762	1.9971	2.6238	3.3503
27	0.6870	1.1717	1.6750	1.9957	2.6221	3.3482
28	0.6866	1.1709	1.6740	1.9945	2.6205	3.3462
29	0.6862	1.1702	1.6730	1.9933	2.6190	3.3444
30	0.6858	1.1695	1.6721	1.9922	2.6176	3.3427
31	0.6854	1.1689	1.6712	1.9912	2.6163	3.3411
32	0.6851	1.1683	1.6704	1.9902	2.6150	3.3396
33	0.6848	1.1678	1.6696	1.9893	2.6138	3.3382
34	0.6845	1.1673	1.6689	1.9885	2.6128	3.3368
35	0.6842	1.1668	1.6682	1.9877	2.6118	3.3356
36	0.6839	1.1663	1.6676	1.9869	2.6108	3.3344
37	0.6836	1.1659	1.6670	1.9862	2.6098	3.3333
38	0.6834	1.1655	1.6664	1.9855	2.6090	3.3322
39	0.6832	1.1651	1.6658	1.9848	2.6082	3.3311
40	0.6830	1.1647	1.6653	1.9842	2.6074	3.3301
41	0.6828	1.1643	1.6648	1.9836	2.6067	3.3292
42	0.6826	1.1640	1.6643	1.9831	2.6059	3.3283
43	0.6824	1.1637	1.6639	1.9825	2.6052	3.3275
44	0.6822	1.1634	1.6635	1.9820	2.6045	3.3267
45	0.6820	1.1632	1.6631	1.9816	2.6039	3.3259
46	0.6818	1.1629	1.6627	1.9811	2.6033	3.3251
47	0.6817	1.1626	1.6623	1.9806	2.6027	3.3244
48	0.6815	1.1623	1.6619	1.9802	2.6022	3.3237
49	0.6814	1.1620	1.6616	1.9798	2.6017	3.3231
50	0.6813	1.1618	1.6612	1.9794	2.6012	3.3225

5.4

Two-Sided Tolerance Limit Factors for a Normal Distribution (*cont.*)

Table of $r(n, P)$

n	.50	.75	.90	.95	.99	.999
51	0.6811	1.1616	1.6609	1.9790	2.6007	3.3219
52	0.6810	1.1614	1.6606	1.9787	2.6002	3.3213
53	0.6808	1.1612	1.6603	1.9783	2.5997	3.3207
54	0.6807	1.1610	1.6600	1.9780	2.5993	3.3202
55	0.6806	1.1608	1.6597	1.9777	2.5989	3.3197
56	0.6805	1.1606	1.6595	1.9773	2.5985	3.3192
57	0.6804	1.1604	1.6592	1.9770	2.5981	3.3187
58	0.6803	1.1602	1.6590	1.9767	2.5977	3.3182
59	0.6802	1.1601	1.6587	1.9765	2.5973	3.3177
60	0.6801	1.1600	1.6585	1.9762	2.5970	3.3173
61	0.6800	1.1598	1.6583	1.9759	2.5966	3.3169
62	0.6799	1.1597	1.6581	1.9757	2.5963	3.3164
63	0.6799	1.1595	1.6579	1.9754	2.5960	3.3160
64	0.6798	1.1594	1.6577	1.9752	2.5957	3.3156
65	0.6797	1.1592	1.6575	1.9750	2.5954	3.3152
66	0.6796	1.1591	1.6573	1.9747	2.5951	3.3149
67	0.6796	1.1590	1.6571	1.9745	2.5948	3.3145
68	0.6795	1.1588	1.6569	1.9743	2.5945	3.3142
69	0.6794	1.1587	1.6567	1.9741	2.5943	3.3139
70	0.6793	1.1586	1.6566	1.9739	2.5940	3.3135
71	0.6793	1.1585	1.6564	1.9737	2.5937	3.3132
72	0.6792	1.1583	1.6562	1.9735	2.5935	3.3129
73	0.6791	1.1582	1.6561	1.9733	2.5932	3.3126
74	0.6791	1.1581	1.6559	1.9731	2.5930	3.3123
75	0.6790	1.1580	1.6558	1.9730	2.5928	3.3120
76	0.6789	1.1579	1.6557	1.9728	2.5926	3.3118
77	0.6789	1.1578	1.6555	1.9726	2.5924	3.3115
78	0.6788	1.1577	1.6554	1.9725	2.5921	3.3112
79	0.6788	1.1576	1.6552	1.9723	2.5919	3.3110
80	0.6787	1.1575	1.6551	1.9722	2.5917	3.3107
81	0.6787	1.1575	1.6550	1.9720	2.5916	3.3105
82	0.6786	1.1574	1.6548	1.9719	2.5914	3.3102
83	0.6786	1.1573	1.6547	1.9717	2.5912	3.3100
84	0.6785	1.1572	1.6546	1.9716	2.5910	3.3098
85	0.6785	1.1571	1.6545	1.9714	2.5908	3.3095
86	0.6784	1.1571	1.6544	1.9713	2.5906	3.3093
87	0.6784	1.1570	1.6543	1.9712	2.5905	3.3091
88	0.6783	1.1569	1.6542	1.9711	2.5903	3.3089
89	0.6783	1.1568	1.6541	1.9709	2.5901	3.3087
90	0.6782	1.1568	1.6540	1.9708	2.5900	3.3085
91	0.6782	1.1567	1.6539	1.9707	2.5898	3.3083
92	0.6782	1.1566	1.6538	1.9706	2.5897	3.3081
93	0.6781	1.1565	1.6537	1.9705	2.5896	3.3079
94	0.6781	1.1565	1.6536	1.9703	2.5894	3.3077
95	0.6780	1.1564	1.6535	1.9702	2.5893	3.3076
96	0.6780	1.1564	1.6534	1.9701	2.5891	3.3074
97	0.6780	1.1563	1.6533	1.9700	2.5890	3.3072
98	0.6779	1.1562	1.6532	1.9699	2.5889	3.3070
99	0.6779	1.1562	1.6531	1.9698	2.5887	3.3069
100	0.6779	1.1561	1.6531	1.9697	2.5886	3.3067

5.4

Two-Sided Tolerance Limit Factors for a Normal Distribution (*cont.*)

Table of r(n, P)

n	.50	.75	.90	.95	.99	.999
102	0.6778	1.1560	1.6529	1.9695	2.5884	3.3065
104	0.6777	1.1559	1.6527	1.9694	2.5881	3.3061
106	0.6777	1.1558	1.6526	1.9692	2.5879	3.3058
108	0.6776	1.1557	1.6525	1.9690	2.5877	3.3055
110	0.6776	1.1556	1.6523	1.9689	2.5874	3.3053
112	0.6775	1.1555	1.6522	1.9687	2.5873	3.3050
114	0.6775	1.1554	1.6521	1.9685	2.5870	3.3048
116	0.6774	1.1553	1.6519	1.9684	2.5869	3.3045
118	0.6774	1.1552	1.6518	1.9682	2.5867	3.3043
120	0.6773	1.1551	1.6517	1.9681	2.5865	3.3041
122	0.6773	1.1551	1.6516	1.9680	2.5863	3.3039
124	0.6772	1.1550	1.6515	1.9679	2.5861	3.3036
126	0.6772	1.1549	1.6514	1.9677	2.5860	3.3034
128	0.6771	1.1548	1.6513	1.9676	2.5858	3.3032
130	0.6771	1.1548	1.6512	1.9675	2.5857	3.3030
132	0.6771	1.1547	1.6511	1.9674	2.5855	3.3029
134	0.6770	1.1546	1.6510	1.9673	2.5854	3.3027
136	0.6770	1.1546	1.6509	1.9672	2.5852	3.3025
138	0.6769	1.1545	1.6508	1.9671	2.5851	3.3023
140	0.6769	1.1545	1.6507	1.9670	2.5850	3.3022
142	0.6769	1.1544	1.6506	1.9669	2.5848	3.3020
144	0.6768	1.1544	1.6506	1.9668	2.5847	3.3018
146	0.6768	1.1543	1.6505	1.9667	2.5846	3.3017
148	0.6768	1.1542	1.6504	1.9666	2.5845	3.3015
150	0.6767	1.1542	1.6503	1.9665	2.5844	3.3014
152	0.6767	1.1541	1.6503	1.9664	2.5843	3.3013
154	0.6767	1.1541	1.6502	1.9663	2.5841	3.3011
156	0.6767	1.1540	1.6501	1.9662	2.5840	3.3010
158	0.6766	1.1540	1.6501	1.9662	2.5839	3.3008
160	0.6766	1.1539	1.6500	1.9661	2.5838	3.3007
162	0.6766	1.1539	1.6499	1.9660	2.5837	3.3006
164	0.6765	1.1539	1.6499	1.9659	2.5837	3.3005
166	0.6765	1.1538	1.6498	1.9659	2.5835	3.3003
168	0.6765	1.1538	1.6497	1.9658	2.5835	3.3002
170	0.6765	1.1537	1.6497	1.9657	2.5834	3.3001
172	0.6765	1.1537	1.6496	1.9657	2.5833	3.3000
174	0.6764	1.1537	1.6496	1.9656	2.5832	3.2999
176	0.6764	1.1536	1.6495	1.9655	2.5831	3.2998
178	0.6764	1.1536	1.6495	1.9655	2.5830	3.2997
180	0.6764	1.1536	1.6494	1.9654	2.5829	3.2996
182	0.6763	1.1535	1.6494	1.9653	2.5829	3.2995
184	0.6763	1.1535	1.6493	1.9653	2.5828	3.2994
186	0.6763	1.1534	1.6493	1.9652	2.5827	3.2993
188	0.6763	1.1534	1.6492	1.9652	2.5826	3.2992
190	0.6763	1.1534	1.6492	1.9651	2.5826	3.2991
192	0.6762	1.1533	1.6491	1.9651	2.5825	3.2990
194	0.6762	1.1533	1.6491	1.9650	2.5824	3.2989
196	0.6762	1.1533	1.6490	1.9650	2.5824	3.2988
198	0.6762	1.1533	1.6490	1.9649	2.5823	3.2988
200	0.6762	1.1532	1.6490	1.9649	2.5822	3.2987

Two-Sided Tolerance Limit Factors for a Normal Distribution (cont.)

Table of r(n, P)

n	P .50	.75	.90	.95	.99	.999
205	0.6761	1.1532	1.6489	1.9647	2.5821	3.2985
210	0.6761	1.1531	1.6488	1.9646	2.5819	3.2983
215	0.6761	1.1530	1.6487	1.9645	2.5818	3.2981
220	0.6760	1.1530	1.6486	1.9644	2.5817	3.2980
225	0.6760	1.1529	1.6485	1.9643	2.5815	3.2978
230	0.6760	1.1529	1.6484	1.9642	2.5814	3.2976
235	0.6759	1.1528	1.6484	1.9641	2.5813	3.2975
240	0.6759	1.1527	1.6483	1.9640	2.5812	3.2973
245	0.6759	1.1527	1.6482	1.9640	2.5811	3.2972
250	0.6758	1.1527	1.6481	1.9639	2.5810	3.2971
260	0.6758	1.1526	1.6480	1.9637	2.5808	3.2968
270	0.6757	1.1525	1.6479	1.9636	2.5806	3.2966
280	0.6757	1.1524	1.6478	1.9635	2.5804	3.2964
290	0.6757	1.1523	1.6477	1.9633	2.5803	3.2962
300	0.6756	1.1523	1.6476	1.9632	2.5801	3.2960
310	0.6756	1.1522	1.6475	1.9631	2.5800	3.2958
320	0.6755	1.1522	1.6474	1.9630	2.5798	3.2956
330	0.6755	1.1521	1.6473	1.9629	2.5797	3.2955
340	0.6755	1.1520	1.6473	1.9628	2.5796	3.2953
350	0.6755	1.1520	1.6472	1.9628	2.5795	3.2952
360	0.6754	1.1519	1.6471	1.9627	2.5794	3.2951
370	0.6754	1.1519	1.6471	1.9626	2.5793	3.2950
380	0.6754	1.1519	1.6470	1.9625	2.5792	3.2948
390	0.6754	1.1518	1.6470	1.9625	2.5791	3.2947
400	0.6753	1.1518	1.6469	1.9624	2.5790	3.2946
410	0.6753	1.1518	1.6469	1.9624	2.5790	3.2945
420	0.6753	1.1517	1.6468	1.9623	2.5789	3.2944
430	0.6753	1.1517	1.6468	1.9622	2.5788	3.2943
440	0.6753	1.1517	1.6467	1.9622	2.5788	3.2943
450	0.6752	1.1516	1.6467	1.9621	2.5787	3.2942
460	0.6752	1.1516	1.6466	1.9621	2.5786	3.2941
470	0.6752	1.1516	1.6466	1.9621	2.5786	3.2940
480	0.6752	1.1515	1.6466	1.9620	2.5785	3.2940
490	0.6752	1.1515	1.6465	1.9620	2.5785	3.2939
500	0.6752	1.1515	1.6465	1.9619	2.5784	3.2938
550	0.6751	1.1514	1.6464	1.9618	2.5782	3.2935
600	0.6751	1.1513	1.6462	1.9616	2.5780	3.2933
650	0.6750	1.1512	1.6461	1.9615	2.5778	3.2930
700	0.6750	1.1512	1.6460	1.9614	2.5777	3.2929
750	0.6749	1.1511	1.6459	1.9613	2.5775	3.2927
800	0.6749	1.1511	1.6459	1.9612	2.5774	3.2926
850	0.6749	1.1510	1.6458	1.9611	2.5773	3.2925
900	0.6749	1.1510	1.6458	1.9611	2.5773	3.2923
950	0.6748	1.1509	1.6457	1.9610	2.5772	3.2923
1000	0.6748	1.1509	1.6457	1.9609	2.5771	3.2922
2000	0.6747	1.1506	1.6453	1.9605	2.5765	3.2914
3000	0.6746	1.1505	1.6451	1.9603	2.5763	3.2911
5000	0.6746	1.1505	1.6450	1.9602	2.5761	3.2909
10000	0.6745	1.1504	1.6449	1.9601	2.5760	3.2907
∞	0.6745	1.1504	1.6449	1.9600	2.5758	3.2905

5.4

Two-Sided Tolerance Limit Factors for a Normal Distribution (cont.)

Table of $u(f, \gamma)$

f	γ					
	.50	.75	.90	.95	.99	.999
1	1.4826	3.1383	7.9579	15.9472	79.7863	798.0867
2	1.2011	1.8644	3.0808	4.4154	9.9749	31.6228
3	1.1261	1.5729	2.2658	2.9200	5.1113	11.1111
4	1.0916	1.4424	1.9393	2.3724	3.6692	6.6372
5	1.0719	1.3673	1.7621	2.0893	3.0034	4.8795
6	1.0592	1.3179	1.6499	1.9154	2.6230	3.9684
7	1.0503	1.2827	1.5719	1.7972	2.3769	3.4214
8	1.0437	1.2561	1.5141	1.7110	2.2043	3.0553
9	1.0387	1.2352	1.4694	1.6452	2.0762	2.7939
10	1.0346	1.2183	1.4337	1.5931	1.9771	2.6002
11	1.0314	1.2043	1.4043	1.5506	1.8980	2.4490
12	1.0287	1.1925	1.3797	1.5153	1.8332	2.3281
13	1.0264	1.1824	1.3587	1.4854	1.7792	2.2288
14	1.0245	1.1735	1.3406	1.4597	1.7332	2.1456
15	1.0228	1.1658	1.3248	1.4373	1.6936	2.0752
16	1.0213	1.1590	1.3108	1.4176	1.6592	2.0147
17	1.0200	1.1528	1.2983	1.4001	1.6288	1.9620
18	1.0189	1.1473	1.2871	1.3845	1.6019	1.9156
19	1.0179	1.1423	1.2770	1.3704	1.5778	1.8746
20	1.0170	1.1377	1.2678	1.3576	1.5560	1.8379
21	1.0162	1.1335	1.2594	1.3460	1.5363	1.8048
22	1.0154	1.1296	1.2517	1.3353	1.5184	1.7750
23	1.0147	1.1261	1.2446	1.3255	1.5020	1.7478
24	1.0141	1.1228	1.2380	1.3165	1.4868	1.7229
25	1.0136	1.1197	1.2319	1.3081	1.4729	1.7001
26	1.0130	1.1169	1.2262	1.3002	1.4600	1.6791
27	1.0125	1.1142	1.2209	1.2929	1.4479	1.6596
28	1.0121	1.1117	1.2159	1.2861	1.4367	1.6415
29	1.0116	1.1093	1.2112	1.2797	1.4263	1.6247
30	1.0112	1.1071	1.2068	1.2737	1.4164	1.6090
31	1.0109	1.1049	1.2026	1.2680	1.4072	1.5943
32	1.0105	1.1030	1.1987	1.2627	1.3985	1.5805
33	1.0102	1.1011	1.1950	1.2575	1.3903	1.5675
34	1.0099	1.0993	1.1914	1.2528	1.3825	1.5552
35	1.0096	1.0976	1.1881	1.2482	1.3751	1.5437
36	1.0094	1.0959	1.1849	1.2438	1.3681	1.5327
37	1.0091	1.0944	1.1818	1.2397	1.3615	1.5224
38	1.0089	1.0929	1.1789	1.2358	1.3552	1.5125
39	1.0086	1.0915	1.1761	1.2320	1.3491	1.5031
40	1.0084	1.0901	1.1734	1.2284	1.3434	1.4942
41	1.0082	1.0888	1.1709	1.2249	1.3379	1.4857
42	1.0080	1.0876	1.1684	1.2216	1.3326	1.4776
43	1.0078	1.0863	1.1661	1.2184	1.3276	1.4698
44	1.0076	1.0852	1.1638	1.2154	1.3227	1.4623
45	1.0075	1.0841	1.1616	1.2124	1.3181	1.4552
46	1.0073	1.0830	1.1595	1.2096	1.3136	1.4483
47	1.0072	1.0819	1.1575	1.2069	1.3093	1.4418
48	1.0070	1.0810	1.1555	1.2042	1.3052	1.4354
49	1.0069	1.0800	1.1536	1.2017	1.3012	1.4294
50	1.0067	1.0791	1.1518	1.1993	1.2973	1.4235

5.4

Two-Sided Tolerance Limit Factors for a Normal Distribution (*cont.*)

Table of $u(f, \gamma)$

f	.50	.75	.90	.95	.99	.999
51	1.0066	1.0781	1.1500	1.1969	1.2936	1.4179
52	1.0065	1.0773	1.1483	1.1946	1.2900	1.4124
53	1.0063	1.0764	1.1467	1.1924	1.2866	1.4072
54	1.0062	1.0756	1.1451	1.1903	1.2832	1.4021
55	1.0061	1.0748	1.1435	1.1882	1.2800	1.3972
56	1.0060	1.0740	1.1420	1.1862	1.2768	1.3925
57	1.0059	1.0733	1.1406	1.1842	1.2738	1.3879
58	1.0058	1.0726	1.1392	1.1823	1.2708	1.3834
59	1.0057	1.0718	1.1378	1.1805	1.2680	1.3791
60	1.0056	1.0712	1.1364	1.1787	1.2651	1.3749
61	1.0055	1.0705	1.1351	1.1769	1.2625	1.3709
62	1.0054	1.0698	1.1338	1.1752	1.2598	1.3669
63	1.0053	1.0692	1.1326	1.1736	1.2573	1.3631
64	1.0052	1.0686	1.1314	1.1720	1.2548	1.3594
65	1.0051	1.0679	1.1302	1.1704	1.2524	1.3558
66	1.0051	1.0674	1.1291	1.1689	1.2500	1.3523
67	1.0050	1.0668	1.1280	1.1674	1.2477	1.3489
68	1.0049	1.0663	1.1269	1.1660	1.2455	1.3455
69	1.0048	1.0657	1.1258	1.1646	1.2433	1.3423
70	1.0048	1.0652	1.1248	1.1631	1.2411	1.3391
71	1.0047	1.0646	1.1238	1.1618	1.2391	1.3360
72	1.0046	1.0641	1.1228	1.1605	1.2371	1.3330
73	1.0046	1.0636	1.1218	1.1592	1.2350	1.3301
74	1.0045	1.0631	1.1209	1.1579	1.2331	1.3272
75	1.0045	1.0626	1.1200	1.1567	1.2312	1.3244
76	1.0044	1.0622	1.1191	1.1555	1.2294	1.3217
77	1.0043	1.0617	1.1182	1.1543	1.2276	1.3190
78	1.0043	1.0613	1.1173	1.1532	1.2258	1.3164
79	1.0042	1.0608	1.1164	1.1520	1.2241	1.3138
80	1.0042	1.0604	1.1156	1.1510	1.2224	1.3114
81	1.0041	1.0600	1.1148	1.1499	1.2207	1.3089
82	1.0041	1.0596	1.1140	1.1488	1.2191	1.3066
83	1.0040	1.0592	1.1132	1.1478	1.2175	1.3042
84	1.0040	1.0588	1.1125	1.1467	1.2159	1.3019
85	1.0039	1.0584	1.1117	1.1458	1.2144	1.2997
86	1.0039	1.0580	1.1109	1.1448	1.2129	1.2975
87	1.0038	1.0576	1.1102	1.1438	1.2114	1.2953
88	1.0038	1.0573	1.1095	1.1429	1.2100	1.2933
89	1.0037	1.0569	1.1088	1.1419	1.2086	1.2912
90	1.0037	1.0566	1.1082	1.1410	1.2072	1.2891
91	1.0037	1.0562	1.1075	1.1401	1.2059	1.2872
92	1.0036	1.0558	1.1068	1.1393	1.2045	1.2852
93	1.0036	1.0555	1.1062	1.1384	1.2032	1.2833
94	1.0035	1.0552	1.1055	1.1376	1.2019	1.2814
95	1.0035	1.0548	1.1049	1.1367	1.2007	1.2796
96	1.0035	1.0546	1.1043	1.1359	1.1994	1.2778
97	1.0034	1.0542	1.1037	1.1351	1.1982	1.2760
98	1.0034	1.0539	1.1031	1.1343	1.1970	1.2742
99	1.0034	1.0536	1.1025	1.1335	1.1958	1.2725
100	1.0033	1.0533	1.1019	1.1328	1.1947	1.2708

Two-Sided Tolerance Limit Factors for a Normal Distribution (*cont.*)

Table of $u(f, \gamma)$

f	.50	.75	.90	.95	.99	.999
101	1.0033	1.0530	1.1013	1.1320	1.1936	1.2693
102	1.0033	1.0527	1.1008	1.1313	1.1924	1.2677
103	1.0032	1.0524	1.1002	1.1306	1.1913	1.2661
104	1.0032	1.0522	1.0997	1.1299	1.1903	1.2645
105	1.0032	1.0519	1.0992	1.1292	1.1892	1.2629
106	1.0032	1.0516	1.0986	1.1285	1.1881	1.2614
107	1.0031	1.0513	1.0981	1.1278	1.1871	1.2599
108	1.0031	1.0511	1.0976	1.1271	1.1861	1.2584
109	1.0031	1.0508	1.0971	1.1264	1.1851	1.2570
110	1.0030	1.0506	1.0966	1.1258	1.1841	1.2555
111	1.0030	1.0503	1.0961	1.1252	1.1831	1.2541
112	1.0030	1.0501	1.0956	1.1245	1.1822	1.2527
113	1.0030	1.0498	1.0952	1.1239	1.1812	1.2514
114	1.0029	1.0496	1.0947	1.1233	1.1803	1.2500
115	1.0029	1.0493	1.0943	1.1227	1.1794	1.2487
116	1.0029	1.0491	1.0938	1.1221	1.1785	1.2474
117	1.0029	1.0489	1.0934	1.1215	1.1776	1.2461
118	1.0028	1.0486	1.0929	1.1209	1.1767	1.2449
119	1.0028	1.0484	1.0925	1.1203	1.1758	1.2436
120	1.0028	1.0482	1.0920	1.1198	1.1750	1.2424
121	1.0028	1.0480	1.0916	1.1192	1.1741	1.2412
122	1.0027	1.0478	1.0912	1.1187	1.1733	1.2400
123	1.0027	1.0475	1.0908	1.1181	1.1725	1.2388
124	1.0027	1.0473	1.0904	1.1176	1.1717	1.2376
125	1.0027	1.0471	1.0900	1.1170	1.1709	1.2365
126	1.0027	1.0469	1.0896	1.1165	1.1701	1.2353
127	1.0026	1.0467	1.0892	1.1160	1.1693	1.2342
128	1.0026	1.0465	1.0888	1.1155	1.1685	1.2331
129	1.0026	1.0463	1.0884	1.1150	1.1678	1.2320
130	1.0026	1.0461	1.0880	1.1145	1.1670	1.2309
131	1.0026	1.0459	1.0877	1.1140	1.1663	1.2299
132	1.0025	1.0457	1.0873	1.1135	1.1656	1.2288
133	1.0025	1.0455	1.0869	1.1130	1.1649	1.2278
134	1.0025	1.0454	1.0866	1.1126	1.1641	1.2268
135	1.0025	1.0452	1.0862	1.1121	1.1634	1.2258
136	1.0025	1.0450	1.0859	1.1116	1.1628	1.2248
137	1.0024	1.0448	1.0855	1.1112	1.1621	1.2238
138	1.0024	1.0446	1.0852	1.1107	1.1614	1.2228
139	1.0024	1.0444	1.0849	1.1103	1.1607	1.2219
140	1.0024	1.0443	1.0845	1.1098	1.1601	1.2209
141	1.0024	1.0441	1.0842	1.1094	1.1594	1.2200
142	1.0024	1.0439	1.0839	1.1090	1.1588	1.2191
143	1.0023	1.0438	1.0835	1.1086	1.1581	1.2181
144	1.0023	1.0436	1.0832	1.1081	1.1575	1.2172
145	1.0023	1.0434	1.0829	1.1077	1.1569	1.2164
146	1.0023	1.0433	1.0826	1.1073	1.1563	1.2155
147	1.0023	1.0431	1.0823	1.1069	1.1556	1.2146
148	1.0023	1.0429	1.0820	1.1065	1.1550	1.2137
149	1.0022	1.0428	1.0817	1.1061	1.1544	1.2129
150	1.0022	1.0426	1.0814	1.1057	1.1539	1.2120

5.4

Two-Sided Tolerance Limit Factors for a Normal Distribution (cont.)

Table of $u(f, \gamma)$

f	.50	.75	.90	.95	.99	.999
152	1.0022	1.0423	1.0808	1.1049	1.1527	1.2104
154	1.0022	1.0420	1.0802	1.1042	1.1516	1.2088
156	1.0021	1.0417	1.0796	1.1034	1.1504	1.2072
158	1.0021	1.0414	1.0791	1.1027	1.1494	1.2056
160	1.0021	1.0412	1.0785	1.1020	1.1483	1.2041
162	1.0021	1.0409	1.0780	1.1013	1.1472	1.2026
164	1.0020	1.0406	1.0775	1.1006	1.1462	1.2012
166	1.0020	1.0403	1.0770	1.0999	1.1452	1.1997
168	1.0020	1.0401	1.0765	1.0993	1.1442	1.1983
170	1.0020	1.0398	1.0760	1.0986	1.1433	1.1970
172	1.0019	1.0396	1.0755	1.0980	1.1423	1.1956
174	1.0019	1.0393	1.0750	1.0974	1.1414	1.1943
176	1.0019	1.0391	1.0746	1.0968	1.1405	1.1930
178	1.0019	1.0388	1.0741	1.0962	1.1396	1.1917
180	1.0019	1.0386	1.0736	1.0956	1.1387	1.1905
182	1.0018	1.0384	1.0732	1.0950	1.1378	1.1893
184	1.0018	1.0382	1.0728	1.0944	1.1370	1.1881
186	1.0018	1.0379	1.0723	1.0939	1.1362	1.1869
188	1.0018	1.0377	1.0719	1.0933	1.1353	1.1857
190	1.0018	1.0375	1.0715	1.0928	1.1345	1.1846
192	1.0017	1.0373	1.0711	1.0922	1.1338	1.1835
194	1.0017	1.0371	1.0707	1.0917	1.1330	1.1824
196	1.0017	1.0369	1.0703	1.0912	1.1322	1.1813
198	1.0017	1.0367	1.0699	1.0907	1.1315	1.1802
200	1.0017	1.0365	1.0695	1.0902	1.1307	1.1792
202	1.0017	1.0363	1.0692	1.0897	1.1300	1.1781
204	1.0016	1.0361	1.0688	1.0892	1.1293	1.1771
206	1.0016	1.0359	1.0684	1.0887	1.1286	1.1761
208	1.0016	1.0357	1.0681	1.0883	1.1279	1.1752
210	1.0016	1.0355	1.0677	1.0878	1.1272	1.1742
212	1.0016	1.0353	1.0674	1.0874	1.1265	1.1732
214	1.0016	1.0352	1.0670	1.0869	1.1259	1.1723
216	1.0015	1.0350	1.0667	1.0865	1.1252	1.1714
218	1.0015	1.0348	1.0664	1.0860	1.1246	1.1705
220	1.0015	1.0346	1.0661	1.0856	1.1239	1.1696
222	1.0015	1.0345	1.0657	1.0852	1.1233	1.1687
224	1.0015	1.0343	1.0654	1.0848	1.1227	1.1678
226	1.0015	1.0342	1.0651	1.0844	1.1221	1.1670
228	1.0015	1.0340	1.0648	1.0840	1.1215	1.1661
230	1.0015	1.0338	1.0645	1.0836	1.1209	1.1653
232	1.0014	1.0337	1.0642	1.0832	1.1203	1.1645
234	1.0014	1.0335	1.0639	1.0828	1.1197	1.1637
236	1.0014	1.0334	1.0636	1.0824	1.1192	1.1629
238	1.0014	1.0332	1.0633	1.0820	1.1186	1.1621
240	1.0014	1.0331	1.0630	1.0816	1.1181	1.1613
242	1.0014	1.0329	1.0627	1.0813	1.1175	1.1606
244	1.0014	1.0328	1.0625	1.0809	1.1170	1.1598
246	1.0014	1.0326	1.0622	1.0806	1.1165	1.1591
248	1.0013	1.0325	1.0619	1.0802	1.1159	1.1584
250	1.0013	1.0324	1.0617	1.0799	1.1154	1.1576

Two-Sided Tolerance Limit Factors for a Normal Distribution (*cont.*)

Table of $u(f, \gamma)$

f	.50	.75	.90	.95	.99	.999
255	1.0013	1.0320	1.0610	1.0790	1.1142	1.1559
260	1.0013	1.0317	1.0604	1.0782	1.1129	1.1542
265	1.0013	1.0314	1.0598	1.0774	1.1118	1.1525
270	1.0012	1.0310	1.0592	1.0766	1.1106	1.1509
275	1.0012	1.0307	1.0586	1.0758	1.1095	1.1493
280	1.0012	1.0305	1.0580	1.0751	1.1084	1.1478
285	1.0012	1.0302	1.0575	1.0744	1.1074	1.1463
290	1.0012	1.0299	1.0569	1.0737	1.1063	1.1449
295	1.0011	1.0296	1.0564	1.0730	1.1053	1.1435
300	1.0011	1.0294	1.0559	1.0724	1.1044	1.1422
305	1.0011	1.0291	1.0554	1.0717	1.1034	1.1409
310	1.0011	1.0288	1.0549	1.0711	1.1025	1.1396
315	1.0011	1.0286	1.0545	1.0705	1.1016	1.1383
320	1.0010	1.0284	1.0540	1.0699	1.1007	1.1371
325	1.0010	1.0281	1.0536	1.0693	1.0999	1.1359
330	1.0010	1.0279	1.0531	1.0687	1.0991	1.1348
335	1.0010	1.0277	1.0527	1.0682	1.0983	1.1336
340	1.0010	1.0275	1.0523	1.0677	1.0975	1.1325
345	1.0010	1.0273	1.0519	1.0671	1.0967	1.1315
350	1.0010	1.0270	1.0515	1.0666	1.0959	1.1304
355	1.0009	1.0268	1.0511	1.0661	1.0952	1.1294
360	1.0009	1.0266	1.0507	1.0656	1.0945	1.1284
365	1.0009	1.0265	1.0504	1.0651	1.0938	1.1274
370	1.0009	1.0263	1.0500	1.0647	1.0931	1.1264
375	1.0009	1.0261	1.0497	1.0642	1.0924	1.1255
380	1.0009	1.0259	1.0493	1.0637	1.0917	1.1246
385	1.0009	1.0257	1.0490	1.0633	1.0911	1.1237
390	1.0009	1.0255	1.0486	1.0629	1.0905	1.1228
395	1.0008	1.0254	1.0483	1.0624	1.0898	1.1219
400	1.0008	1.0252	1.0480	1.0620	1.0892	1.1211
405	1.0008	1.0250	1.0477	1.0616	1.0886	1.1203
410	1.0008	1.0249	1.0474	1.0612	1.0880	1.1194
415	1.0008	1.0247	1.0471	1.0608	1.0875	1.1186
420	1.0008	1.0246	1.0468	1.0604	1.0869	1.1179
425	1.0008	1.0244	1.0465	1.0601	1.0863	1.1171
430	1.0008	1.0243	1.0462	1.0597	1.0858	1.1163
435	1.0008	1.0241	1.0459	1.0593	1.0853	1.1156
440	1.0008	1.0240	1.0456	1.0590	1.0847	1.1149
445	1.0007	1.0238	1.0454	1.0586	1.0842	1.1142
450	1.0007	1.0237	1.0451	1.0583	1.0837	1.1135
455	1.0007	1.0235	1.0448	1.0579	1.0832	1.1128
460	1.0007	1.0234	1.0446	1.0576	1.0827	1.1121
465	1.0007	1.0233	1.0443	1.0573	1.0822	1.1114
470	1.0007	1.0231	1.0441	1.0569	1.0818	1.1108
475	1.0007	1.0230	1.0438	1.0566	1.0813	1.1101
480	1.0007	1.0229	1.0436	1.0563	1.0809	1.1095
485	1.0007	1.0228	1.0433	1.0560	1.0804	1.1089
490	1.0007	1.0226	1.0431	1.0557	1.0800	1.1083
495	1.0007	1.0225	1.0429	1.0554	1.0795	1.1077
500	1.0007	1.0224	1.0427	1.0551	1.0791	1.1071

Two-Sided Tolerance Limit Factors for a Normal Distribution (cont.)

Table of $u(f, \gamma)$

f	.50	.75	.90	.95	.99	.999
510	1.0007	1.0222	1.0422	1.0545	1.0783	1.1059
520	1.0006	1.0220	1.0418	1.0540	1.0774	1.1048
530	1.0006	1.0217	1.0414	1.0534	1.0767	1.1037
540	1.0006	1.0215	1.0410	1.0529	1.0759	1.1027
550	1.0006	1.0213	1.0406	1.0524	1.0752	1.1017
560	1.0006	1.0211	1.0402	1.0519	1.0744	1.1007
570	1.0006	1.0209	1.0398	1.0514	1.0737	1.0997
580	1.0006	1.0207	1.0395	1.0509	1.0730	1.0988
590	1.0006	1.0205	1.0391	1.0505	1.0724	1.0978
600	1.0006	1.0204	1.0388	1.0500	1.0717	1.0970
610	1.0005	1.0202	1.0384	1.0496	1.0711	1.0961
620	1.0005	1.0200	1.0381	1.0492	1.0705	1.0952
630	1.0005	1.0199	1.0378	1.0488	1.0699	1.0944
640	1.0005	1.0197	1.0375	1.0484	1.0693	1.0936
650	1.0005	1.0195	1.0372	1.0480	1.0687	1.0928
660	1.0005	1.0194	1.0369	1.0476	1.0682	1.0921
670	1.0005	1.0192	1.0366	1.0472	1.0676	1.0913
680	1.0005	1.0191	1.0363	1.0468	1.0671	1.0906
690	1.0005	1.0189	1.0360	1.0465	1.0666	1.0899
700	1.0005	1.0188	1.0358	1.0461	1.0661	1.0892
710	1.0005	1.0187	1.0355	1.0458	1.0656	1.0885
720	1.0005	1.0185	1.0352	1.0455	1.0651	1.0878
730	1.0005	1.0184	1.0350	1.0451	1.0646	1.0872
740	1.0005	1.0183	1.0347	1.0448	1.0642	1.0866
750	1.0004	1.0181	1.0345	1.0445	1.0637	1.0859
760	1.0004	1.0180	1.0343	1.0442	1.0633	1.0853
770	1.0004	1.0179	1.0340	1.0439	1.0628	1.0847
780	1.0004	1.0178	1.0338	1.0436	1.0624	1.0841
790	1.0004	1.0176	1.0336	1.0433	1.0620	1.0836
800	1.0004	1.0175	1.0334	1.0430	1.0616	1.0830
820	1.0004	1.0173	1.0329	1.0425	1.0608	1.0819
840	1.0004	1.0171	1.0325	1.0419	1.0600	1.0809
860	1.0004	1.0169	1.0321	1.0414	1.0593	1.0799
880	1.0004	1.0167	1.0317	1.0409	1.0585	1.0789
900	1.0004	1.0165	1.0314	1.0405	1.0579	1.0779
920	1.0004	1.0163	1.0310	1.0400	1.0572	1.0770
940	1.0004	1.0161	1.0307	1.0395	1.0565	1.0761
960	1.0003	1.0160	1.0303	1.0391	1.0559	1.0753
980	1.0003	1.0158	1.0300	1.0387	1.0553	1.0745
1000	1.0003	1.0156	1.0297	1.0383	1.0547	1.0737
2000	1.0002	1.0109	1.0208	1.0268	1.0381	1.0511
3000	1.0001	1.0089	1.0169	1.0217	1.0309	1.0414
4000	1.0001	1.0077	1.0146	1.0188	1.0267	1.0356
5000	1.0001	1.0068	1.0130	1.0168	1.0238	1.0318
6000	1.0001	1.0062	1.0119	1.0153	1.0217	1.0290
7000	1.0000	1.0058	1.0110	1.0141	1.0200	1.0267
8000	1.0000	1.0054	1.0103	1.0132	1.0187	1.0250
9000	1.0000	1.0051	1.0097	1.0124	1.0176	1.0235
10000	1.0000	1.0048	1.0092	1.0118	1.0167	1.0223
∞	1.0000	1.0000	1.0000	1.0000	1.0000	1.0000

6. RANGE, STUDENTIZED RANGE, AND MEAN SQUARE SUCCESSIVE DIFFERENCE

6.1 Critical Values of the Sample Range from a Normal Distribution

Let $x_1, x_2 \ldots, x_n$ denote n independent observations from a population with cumulative distribution function $P(x)$. Let $x_{(1)}, x_{(2)}, \ldots, x_{(n)}$ denote the same observations in ascending order of magnitude. The sample range is defined as $W = x_{(n)} - x_{(1)}$, and its cumulative distribution function is given by

$$\text{Pr } \{\text{range} \leq w\} = \int_{-\infty}^{+\infty} n[P(x + w) - P(x)]^{n-1} \, dP(x).$$

If the population is normally distributed, then $P(x)$ is defined as in Section 1.1. For the tables here, a value of w/σ is given in the table such that $\text{Pr } \{\text{range} \leq w/\sigma\} = $ probability level, where σ is the standard deviation of X. Harter [91] lists some applications of the range.

Reference [150] gives formulas for the distribution of the range in samples of Size 2 or 3. For samples of Size 2 from a normal population, $\text{Pr } \{\text{range} \leq w\} = \frac{1}{2}[1 + P(w/\sqrt{2})]$, where P may be read from Table 1.1. For Size 3 from a normal population, $\text{Pr } \{\text{range} \leq w\} = 1 - 12T(w/\sqrt{2}, 1/\sqrt{3})$, where the T-function is given in Section 8.5. McKay and Pearson [137] consider the distribution of the range for any sample size.

Critical Values of the Sample Range from a Normal Distribution [92]

n	Probability Level									
	0.005	0.01	0.025	0.05	0.10	0.90	0.95	0.975	0.99	0.995
2	0.009	0.018	0.044	0.089	0.178	2.326	2.772	3.170	3.643	3.970
3	0.135	0.191	0.303	0.431	0.618	2.902	3.314	3.682	4.120	4.424
4	0.343	0.434	0.595	0.760	0.979	3.240	3.633	3.984	4.403	4.694
5	0.555	0.665	0.850	1.030	1.261	3.478	3.858	4.197	4.603	4.886
6	0.749	0.870	1.066	1.253	1.488	3.661	4.030	4.361	4.757	5.033
7	0.922	1.048	1.251	1.440	1.676	3.808	4.170	4.494	4.882	5.154
8	1.075	1.205	1.410	1.600	1.835	3.931	4.286	4.605	4.987	5.255
9	1.212	1.343	1.550	1.740	1.973	4.037	4.387	4.700	5.078	5.341
10	1.335	1.467	1.674	1.863	2.094	4.129	4.474	4.784	5.157	5.418
11	1.446	1.578	1.784	1.973	2.202	4.211	4.552	4.858	5.227	5.485
12	1.547	1.679	1.884	2.071	2.299	4.285	4.622	4.925	5.290	5.546
13	1.639	1.771	1.976	2.161	2.387	4.351	4.685	4.985	5.348	5.602
14	1.724	1.856	2.059	2.243	2.467	4.412	4.743	5.041	5.400	5.652
15	1.803	1.934	2.136	2.319	2.541	4.468	4.796	5.092	5.448	5.699
16	1.876	2.007	2.207	2.389	2.609	4.519	4.845	5.139	5.493	5.742
17	1.944	2.074	2.274	2.454	2.673	4.568	4.891	5.183	5.535	5.783
18	2.008	2.137	2.336	2.515	2.732	4.612	4.934	5.224	5.574	5.820
19	2.068	2.197	2.394	2.572	2.787	4.654	4.974	5.262	5.611	5.856
20	2.125	2.253	2.449	2.626	2.840	4.694	5.012	5.299	5.645	5.889
22	2.229	2.356	2.549	2.724	2.935	4.767	5.081	5.365	5.709	5.951
24	2.323	2.448	2.640	2.813	3.021	4.832	5.144	5.425	5.766	6.006
26	2.408	2.532	2.722	2.893	3.100	4.892	5.201	5.480	5.818	6.057
28	2.487	2.610	2.798	2.967	3.171	4.947	5.253	5.530	5.866	6.103
30	2.559	2.681	2.867	3.034	3.237	4.997	5.301	5.577	5.911	6.146
32	2.625	2.746	2.931	3.097	3.298	5.044	5.346	5.620	5.952	6.186
34	2.688	2.807	2.991	3.155	3.354	5.087	5.388	5.660	5.990	6.223
36	2.746	2.864	3.046	3.210	3.407	5.128	5.427	5.698	6.026	6.258
38	2.800	2.918	3.098	3.261	3.456	5.166	5.463	5.733	6.060	6.291
40	2.851	2.969	3.148	3.309	3.503	5.202	5.498	5.766	6.092	6.322
50	3.070	3.183	3.357	3.513	3.702	5.357	5.646	5.909	6.228	6.454
60	3.243	3.354	3.523	3.675	3.859	5.480	5.764	6.023	6.338	6.561
70	3.385	3.494	3.660	3.809	3.989	5.582	5.863	6.118	6.429	6.649
80	3.506	3.613	3.776	3.922	4.099	5.669	5.947	6.199	6.507	6.725
90	3.611	3.716	3.876	4.021	4.195	5.745	6.020	6.270	6.575	6.792
100	3.703	3.807	3.965	4.107	4.279	5.812	6.085	6.333	6.636	6.850

6.2 Moments of the Range of a Normal Distribution

The range is defined as in Section 6.1 above. The expected value of W^k is defined as

$$E(W^k) = \int_0^\infty w^k n(n-1) \int_{-\infty}^{+\infty} [P(x+w) - P(x)]^{n-2} Z(x) Z(x+w) \, dx \, dw,$$

where $Z(x) = dP(x)/dx$, and for the normal distribution it is defined as in Section 1.1.

The quantities tabulated are $E(W)$, $\sigma^2(W)$,

$$\alpha_3(W) = \frac{E\{[W - E(W)]^3\}}{\sigma^3(W)},$$

and

$$\alpha_4(W) = \frac{E\{[W - E(W)]^4\}}{\sigma^4(W)},$$

for the range from a standardized normal distribution. If σ is the standard deviation of any normal distribution, then the values in the table for $E(W)$ and $\sigma^2(W)$ need to be multiplied by σ and σ^2, respectively, to get the corresponding mean range and variance of the range for any normal distribution. The range is used to estimate σ in a great deal of quality control work. If a single sample is used, then the range of the sample is divided by the tabulated value $E(W)$ to obtain an estimate of σ for the population. Sometimes several ranges are averaged and then divided by $E(W)$. Standard deviations and approximate percentage points of these estimates are given by Grubbs and Weaver [80].

Moments of the Range of a Normal Distribution [92]

n	E(W)	$\sigma^2(W)$	$\alpha_3(W)$	$\alpha_4(W)$	n	E(W)	$\sigma^2(W)$	$\alpha_3(W)$	$\alpha_4(W)$
2	1.128	0.727	0.995	3.869	20	3.735	0.531	0.403	3.257
3	1.693	0.789	0.646	3.286	22	3.819	0.518	0.406	3.265
4	2.059	0.774	0.523	3.188	24	3.895	0.507	0.409	3.272
5	2.326	0.747	0.466	3.169	26	3.964	0.497	0.412	3.279
6	2.534	0.719	0.435	3.170	28	4.027	0.488	0.415	3.285
7	2.704	0.694	0.418	3.176	30	4.086	0.480	0.417	3.291
8	2.847	0.672	0.407	3.184	32	4.139	0.472	0.420	3.297
9	2.970	0.653	0.401	3.192	34	4.189	0.465	0.423	3.302
10	3.078	0.635	0.398	3.200	36	4.236	0.459	0.425	3.307
11	3.173	0.620	0.396	3.207	38	4.280	0.453	0.428	3.311
12	3.258	0.606	0.395	3.214	40	4.322	0.448	0.430	3.315
13	3.336	0.594	0.395	3.221	50	4.498	0.425	0.440	3.334
14	3.407	0.582	0.395	3.227	60	4.639	0.408	0.449	3.349
15	3.472	0.572	0.396	3.233	70	4.755	0.395	0.456	3.361
16	3.532	0.562	0.397	3.238	80	4.854	0.384	0.462	3.372
17	3.588	0.554	0.398	3.243	90	4.939	0.374	0.467	3.381
18	3.640	0.546	0.400	3.248	100	5.015	0.366	0.472	3.390
19	3.689	0.538	0.401	3.253					

6.2

6.3 Critical Values for the G-Test for Testing the Deviation of the Sample Mean from a Preassigned Value Using the Sample Range

The quantities tabulated are the critical values of the ratio $(\bar{x} - \mu_0)/w$, where $\bar{x}$ and w are the sample mean and the sample range respectively for a sample of size n from a normal population, and μ_0 is a hypothesized value of the population mean. For a given γ the value is that one exceeded with probability less than α, where $\alpha = 1 - \gamma$ is the significance level of the test. The statistic is symmetric. If a two-tailed test is needed, the hypothesis that the population mean is μ_0 is rejected if the test statistic exceeds the tabulated value or is smaller than minus the tabulated value. The significance level of the test is then $2(1 - \gamma)$.

In other words, critical values of a statistic are given for testing the hypothesis that the mean of a normal distribution is a given value. Here the sample range is substituted for the sample standard deviation in the usual t-test (Section 2.2).

Daly [37] showed that the power of this procedure is approximately the same as for the usual Student's t-test (Section 2.2) for $n \leq 10$. Lord [125] examined the power of the test (normal deviate)/(independent range or mean-range estimate of standard error) and concluded that there was very little difference in power between the G-test and Student's t-test.

If there is more than one subgroup of observations from which a range may be computed, the reader is referred to some tables by Jackson and Ross [98] which give critical values of the G-test in this case. The tables given here apply only if there are no subgroups, i.e., there is a single sample of n observations.

Critical Values for the G-Test for Testing the Deviation of the Sample Mean from a Preassigned Value Using the Sample Range [124]
(Normal Population)

n	0.95	0.975	Critical Value 0.99	0.995	0.999	0.9995
2	3.157	6.353	15.910	31.828	159.16	318.31
3	0.885−	1.304	2.111	3.008	6.77	9.58
4	0.529	0.717	1.023	1.316	2.29	2.85+
5	0.388	0.507	0.685+	0.843	1.32	1.58
6	0.312	0.399	0.523	0.628	0.92	1.07
7	0.263	0.333	0.429	0.507	0.71	0.82
8	0.230	0.288	0.366	0.429	0.59	0.67
9	0.205−	0.255+	0.322	0.374	0.50	0.57
10	0.186	0.230	0.288	0.333	0.44	0.50
11	0.170	0.210	0.262	0.302	0.40	0.44
12	0.158	0.194	0.241	0.277	0.36	0.40
13	0.147	0.181	0.224	0.256	0.33	0.37
14	0.138	0.170	0.209	0.239	0.31	0.34
15	0.131	0.160	0.197	0.224	0.29	0.32
16	0.124	0.151	0.186	0.212	0.27	0.30
17	0.118	0.144	0.177	0.201	0.26	0.28
18	0.113	0.137	0.168	0.191	0.24	0.26
19	0.108	0.131	0.161	0.182	0.23	0.25+
20	0.104	0.126	0.154	0.175−	0.22	0.24

6.3

6.4 Critical Values for the G-Test for Testing the Significance of the Difference Between the Means of Two Samples of Equal Size

The quantities tabulated are the critical values of the ratio

$$\frac{|\bar{x}_1 - \bar{x}_2|}{(w_1 + w_2)/2},$$

where $\bar{x}_1$ and $\bar{x}_2$ respectively are the means of two samples (each of size n), and w_1 and w_2 are the sample ranges of the two samples. When the observations are from normal distributions, the statistic exceeds the value tabulated with probability $1 - \gamma$. As in Section 6.3, the statistic is symmetric, and two-tailed tests may be performed. The statements on power given in Section 6.3 also apply to this test.

If a sample from which $\bar{x}_1$ is obtained is made up of m_1 subgroups of n each, and the sample from which $\bar{x}_2$ was obtained is made up of m_2 subgroups of n each, the reader is referred to a paper by Jackson and Ross [98] which gives critical values for the statistic. Here, the tables apply only if $m_1 = m_2 = 1$.

For a further extension of these test procedures, the reader is referred to an article by Žaludová [251].

Critical Values for the G-Test for Testing the Significance of the Difference between the Means of Two Samples of Equal Size [124]
(Normal Population)

n	Critical Value					
	0.95	0.975	0.99	0.995	0.999	0.9995
2	2.322	3.427	5.553	7.916	17.81	25.23
3	0.974	1.272	1.715-	2.093	3.27	4.18
4	0.644	0.813	1.047	1.237	1.74	1.99
5	0.493	0.613	0.772	0.896	1.21	1.35+
6	0.405+	0.499	0.621	0.714	0.94	1.03
7	0.347	0.426	0.525+	0.600	0.77	0.85-
8	0.306	0.373	0.459	0.521	0.67	0.73
9	0.275-	0.334	0.409	0.464	0.59	0.64
10	0.250	0.304	0.371	0.419	0.53	0.58
11	0.233	0.280	0.340	0.384	0.48	0.52
12	0.214	0.260	0.315+	0.355+	0.44	0.48
13	0.201	0.243	0.294	0.331	0.41	0.45-
14	0.189	0.228	0.276	0.311	0.39	0.42
15	0.179	0.216	0.261	0.293	0.36	0.39
16	0.170	0.205-	0.247	0.278	0.34	0.37
17	0.162	0.195+	0.236	0.264	0.33	0.35+
18	0.155+	0.187	0.225+	0.252	0.31	0.34
19	0.149	0.179	0.216	0.242	0.30	0.32
20	0.143	0.172	0.207	0.232	0.29	0.31

6.5 Critical Values of the Studentized Range from a Normal Distribution

A sample of n observations is taken from a normal population, and the difference between the largest and smallest values in the sample is designated the sample range W. The sample standard deviation s is computed from another sample from the same population as in Section 2.2, or if there are observations from different normal populations with a common standard deviation, this standard deviation may be estimated from an analysis of variance. The quantities given in the tables are the critical values of $q = W/s$, where W is the range from a sample of size n, and s is independent of W and has f degrees of freedom, i.e., the quantity q is given which satisfies the equation

$$\Pr\left\{\frac{W}{s} \leq q\right\}$$
$$= \int_0^\infty \left[\Gamma\left(\frac{f}{2}\right)\right]^{-1} 2^{-(f/2)+1} f^{(f/2)} x^{f-1} \exp\left(-fx^2/2\right) w(qx)\, dx = \gamma,$$

where $w(qx)$ is the probability integral of the range for samples of size n (Section 6.1), and $\gamma = 0.005, 0.01, 0.025, 0.05, 0.10, 0.90, 0.95, 0.975, 0.99,$ and 0.995.

Some additional values of the Studentized range may be obtained from tables of the critical values of the Duncan multiple-range test (Section 4.5). Applications include short-cut tests in the analysis of variance. Note that W and s must be independent in order to obtain the Studentized range. Harter [91] gives a more extensive table of the Studentized range than the one given here.

The problem is different if the ratio of range to standard deviation is taken from the same sample of size n. David, Hartley, and Pearson [47] give a table of critical values for a single sample from a normal distribution. Thomson [223] gives bounds on W/s (single sample of size n) as follows:

$$\text{Upper bound of } W/s: \sqrt{2(n-1)},$$

$$\text{Lower bound of } W/s: \begin{cases} 2\sqrt{(n-1)/n} & \text{for } n \text{ even} \\ 2\sqrt{n/(n+1)} & \text{for } n \text{ odd.} \end{cases}$$

These bounds are distribution-free. Thomson also gives a formula for the critical values of W/s from a single sample from a normal distribution when $n = 3$. In this case the critical values are given by $2\cos[30°(1-\gamma)]$.

Note that the Studentized range tabulated here is for independent estimates of W and s, while the discussion in the preceding paragraph applies to the ratio of W/s from a single sample of size n.

Critical Values of the Studentized Range from a Normal Distribution [92]

f = 1

n	.005	.01	.025	.05	.10	.90	.95	.975	.99	.995
2	.0111	.0223	.0556	.1113	.2240	8.929	17.97	35.99	90.03	180.1
3	.1351	.1919	.3070	.4428	.6526	13.44	26.98	54.00	135.0	270.1
4	.2975	.3797	.5313	.6973	.9446	16.36	32.82	65.69	164.3	328.5
5	.4363	.5308	.7002	.8828	1.152	18.49	37.08	74.22	185.6	371.2
6	.5482	.6498	.8301	1.024	1.309	20.15	40.41	80.87	202.2	404.4
7	.6391	.7455	.9339	1.136	1.435	21.51	43.12	86.29	215.8	431.6
8	.7145	.8245	1.019	1.228	1.539	22.64	45.40	90.85	227.2	454.4
9	.7782	.8912	1.091	1.307	1.627	23.62	47.36	94.77	237.0	474.0
10	.8331	.9486	1.153	1.374	1.704	24.48	49.07	98.20	245.6	491.1
11	.8810	.9988	1.208	1.434	1.771	25.24	50.59	101.3	253.2	506.3
12	.9234	1.042	1.256	1.486	1.831	25.92	51.96	104.0	260.0	520.0
13	.9613	1.082	1.299	1.534	1.884	26.54	53.20	106.5	266.2	532.4
14	.9955	1.119	1.338	1.577	1.933	27.10	54.33	108.8	271.8	543.6
15	1.026	1.151	1.374	1.616	1.978	27.62	55.36	110.8	277.0	554.0
16	1.054	1.181	1.407	1.651	2.018	28.10	56.32	112.7	281.8	563.6
17	1.081	1.209	1.437	1.685	2.057	28.54	57.22	114.5	286.3	572.5
18	1.105	1.234	1.465	1.716	2.092	28.96	58.04	116.2	290.4	580.9
19	1.127	1.258	1.491	1.744	2.125	29.35	58.83	117.7	294.3	588.7
20	1.149	1.280	1.515	1.771	2.156	29.71	59.56	119.2	298.0	596.0
24	1.221	1.357	1.600	1.865	2.263	30.99	62.12	124.3	310.8	621.7
30	1.305	1.446	1.698	1.974	2.389	32.50	65.15	130.4	326.0	652.0
40	1.407	1.554	1.818	2.107	2.544	34.38	68.92	137.9	344.8	689.6
60	1.540	1.696	1.976	2.284	2.749	36.91	73.97	148.1	370.1	740.2
100	1.693	1.860	2.160	2.490	2.990	39.91	79.98	160.0	400.1	800.3

f = 3

n	.005	.01	.025	.05	.10	.90	.95	.975	.99	.995
2	.0096	.0193	.0481	.0963	.1932	3.328	4.501	5.907	8.261	10.55
3	.1349	.1913	.3044	.4351	.6294	4.467	5.910	7.661	10.62	13.50
4	.3217	.4084	.5644	.7285	.9564	5.199	6.825	8.808	12.17	15.45
5	.4955	.5976	.7737	.9531	1.197	5.738	7.502	9.660	13.33	16.91
6	.6427	.7532	.9404	1.128	1.383	6.162	8.037	10.34	14.24	18.06
7	.7660	.8816	1.076	1.270	1.532	6.511	8.478	10.89	15.00	19.01
8	.8701	.9892	1.189	1.388	1.656	6.806	8.853	11.37	15.64	19.83
9	.9592	1.081	1.284	1.487	1.761	7.062	9.177	11.78	16.20	20.53
10	1.036	1.160	1.367	1.574	1.852	7.287	9.462	12.14	16.69	21.15
11	1.104	1.229	1.439	1.649	1.933	7.487	9.717	12.46	17.13	21.70
12	1.164	1.291	1.504	1.716	2.004	7.667	9.946	12.75	17.53	22.20
13	1.218	1.347	1.562	1.777	2.068	7.832	10.15	13.01	17.89	22.66
14	1.267	1.397	1.614	1.831	2.126	7.982	10.35	13.26	18.22	23.08
15	1.311	1.442	1.662	1.881	2.179	8.120	10.53	13.48	18.52	23.46
16	1.352	1.484	1.706	1.927	2.228	8.249	10.69	13.69	18.81	23.82
17	1.390	1.523	1.746	1.970	2.273	8.368	10.84	13.88	19.07	24.15
18	1.424	1.559	1.784	2.009	2.315	8.479	10.98	14.06	19.32	24.46
19	1.456	1.592	1.818	2.045	2.354	8.584	11.11	14.23	19.55	24.76
20	1.487	1.623	1.851	2.080	2.391	8.683	11.24	14.39	19.77	25.03
24	1.590	1.730	1.963	2.198	2.518	9.029	11.68	14.95	20.53	26.00
30	1.710	1.853	2.094	2.336	2.667	9.440	12.21	15.62	21.44	27.15
40	1.854	2.003	2.253	2.505	2.849	9.954	12.87	16.46	22.59	28.60
60	2.042	2.198	2.462	2.727	3.090	10.65	13.76	17.59	24.13	30.55
100	2.257	2.423	2.702	2.985	3.372	11.48	14.82	18.95	25.99	32.90

6.5

Critical Values of the Studentized Range
from a Normal Distribution (*cont.*)

f = 5

n	.005	.01	.025	.05	.10	.90	.95	.975	.99	.995
2	.0093	.0187	.0466	.0933	.1870	2.850	3.635	4.474	5.702	6.751
3	.1349	.1911	.3038	.4336	.6249	3.717	4.602	5.558	6.976	8.196
4	.3290	.4172	.5748	.7389	.9635	4.264	5.218	6.257	7.804	9.141
5	.5149	.6196	.7984	.9778	1.217	4.664	5.673	6.775	8.421	9.847
6	.6758	.7894	.9795	1.167	1.414	4.979	6.033	7.186	8.913	10.41
7	.8126	.9315	1.128	1.321	1.574	5.238	6.330	7.527	9.321	10.88
8	.9293	1.051	1.253	1.449	1.707	5.458	6.582	7.816	9.669	11.28
9	1.029	1.154	1.359	1.558	1.820	5.648	6.802	8.068	9.972	11.63
10	1.118	1.244	1.451	1.654	1.918	5.816	6.995	8.291	10.24	11.93
11	1.195	1.323	1.533	1.737	2.005	5.966	7.168	8.490	10.48	12.21
12	1.263	1.393	1.605	1.811	2.082	6.101	7.324	8.670	10.70	12.46
13	1.326	1.456	1.670	1.878	2.151	6.223	7.466	8.834	10.89	12.69
14	1.382	1.513	1.729	1.938	2.214	6.336	7.596	8.984	11.08	12.90
15	1.433	1.565	1.782	1.994	2.271	6.440	7.717	9.124	11.24	13.09
16	1.479	1.613	1.831	2.044	2.324	6.536	7.828	9.253	11.40	13.27
17	1.523	1.657	1.877	2.091	2.373	6.626	7.932	9.374	11.55	13.44
18	1.563	1.698	1.919	2.134	2.419	6.710	8.030	9.486	11.68	13.60
19	1.600	1.736	1.959	2.175	2.461	6.789	8.122	9.593	11.81	13.75
20	1.635	1.772	1.995	2.213	2.501	6.863	8.208	9.693	11.93	13.89
24	1.755	1.893	2.122	2.344	2.638	7.123	8.512	10.04	12.36	14.38
30	1.893	2.035	2.269	2.497	2.799	7.435	8.875	10.47	12.87	14.96
40	2.060	2.207	2.448	2.684	2.996	7.825	9.330	11.00	13.52	15.71
60	2.277	2.430	2.682	2.929	3.255	8.353	9.949	11.72	14.39	16.72
100	2.525	2.686	2.952	3.213	3.558	8.988	10.69	12.59	15.45	17.94

f = 10

n	.005	.01	.025	.05	.10	.90	.95	.975	.99	.995
2	.0091	.0182	.0455	.0909	.1823	2.563	3.151	3.725	4.482	5.065
3	.1348	.1910	.3034	.4325	.6216	3.270	3.877	4.474	5.270	5.888
4	.3353	.4248	.5840	.7484	.9705	3.704	4.327	4.943	5.769	6.412
5	.5328	.6399	.8213	1.001	1.236	4.018	4.654	5.287	6.136	6.800
6	.7075	.8242	1.017	1.204	1.446	4.264	4.912	5.558	6.428	7.109
7	.8587	.9809	1.180	1.371	1.617	4.465	5.124	5.782	6.669	7.365
8	.9895	1.114	1.318	1.512	1.760	4.636	5.305	5.972	6.875	7.584
9	1.103	1.230	1.437	1.633	1.882	4.783	5.461	6.138	7.055	7.775
10	1.203	1.332	1.540	1.738	1.989	4.913	5.599	6.285	7.213	7.944
11	1.293	1.423	1.632	1.830	2.082	5.029	5.722	6.416	7.356	8.096
12	1.372	1.503	1.714	1.913	2.167	5.134	5.833	6.534	7.485	8.234
13	1.444	1.576	1.787	1.988	2.242	5.229	5.935	6.643	7.603	8.360
14	1.510	1.642	1.854	2.055	2.311	5.317	6.028	6.742	7.712	8.476
15	1.569	1.702	1.915	2.117	2.374	5.397	6.114	6.834	7.812	8.583
16	1.624	1.758	1.971	2.174	2.431	5.472	6.194	6.920	7.906	8.683
17	1.675	1.809	2.023	2.226	2.485	5.542	6.269	7.000	7.993	8.777
18	1.722	1.856	2.071	2.275	2.535	5.607	6.339	7.075	8.076	8.865
19	1.766	1.900	2.116	2.321	2.582	5.668	6.405	7.146	8.153	8.947
20	1.807	1.942	2.159	2.364	2.625	5.726	6.467	7.212	8.226	9.026
24	1.948	2.085	2.304	2.511	2.776	5.930	6.686	7.447	8.483	9.302
30	2.112	2.251	2.473	2.683	2.952	6.173	6.948	7.729	8.794	9.635
40	2.310	2.452	2.678	2.894	3.168	6.479	7.279	8.086	9.187	10.06
60	2.567	2.713	2.947	3.169	3.453	6.895	7.730	8.574	9.726	10.64
100	2.861	3.013	3.257	3.488	3.785	7.396	8.276	9.167	10.39	11.35

Critical Values of the Studentized Range
from a Normal Distribution (cont.)

f = 15

n	.005	.01	.025	.05	.10	.90	.95	.975	.99	.995
2	.0090	.0180	.0451	.0902	.1808	2.479	3.014	3.522	4.168	4.647
3	.1348	.1910	.3033	.4321	.6205	3.140	3.674	4.182	4.836	5.325
4	.3376	.4276	.5873	.7519	.9732	3.540	4.076	4.589	5.252	5.750
5	.5396	.6476	.8300	1.010	1.244	3.828	4.367	4.885	5.556	6.061
6	.7201	.8379	1.031	1.218	1.458	4.052	4.595	5.118	5.796	6.308
7	.8774	1.001	1.201	1.392	1.634	4.235	4.782	5.309	5.994	6.511
8	1.014	1.141	1.345	1.538	1.782	4.390	4.940	5.471	6.162	6.685
9	1.134	1.263	1.469	1.663	1.908	4.524	5.077	5.612	6.309	6.837
10	1.240	1.371	1.578	1.773	2.019	4.641	5.198	5.737	6.439	6.971
11	1.335	1.466	1.674	1.870	2.116	4.746	5.306	5.848	6.555	7.091
12	1.419	1.551	1.761	1.957	2.203	4.841	5.404	5.949	6.660	7.200
13	1.497	1.628	1.838	2.035	2.282	4.927	5.493	6.041	6.757	7.300
14	1.567	1.699	1.909	2.106	2.353	5.006	5.574	6.125	6.845	7.392
15	1.631	1.764	1.974	2.171	2.419	5.079	5.649	6.203	6.927	7.477
16	1.690	1.823	2.034	2.231	2.479	5.147	5.720	6.276	7.003	7.556
17	1.744	1.878	2.089	2.287	2.535	5.209	5.785	6.344	7.074	7.630
18	1.795	1.929	2.140	2.339	2.587	5.269	5.846	6.407	7.142	7.699
19	1.842	1.977	2.188	2.387	2.635	5.324	5.904	6.467	7.204	7.765
20	1.887	2.021	2.233	2.432	2.681	5.376	5.958	6.523	7.264	7.827
24	2.040	2.175	2.388	2.588	2.839	5.560	6.149	6.723	7.474	8.046
30	2.218	2.354	2.569	2.770	3.024	5.780	6.379	6.962	7.728	8.311
40	2.434	2.571	2.789	2.993	3.250	6.057	6.669	7.265	8.049	8.647
60	2.714	2.854	3.077	3.286	3.549	6.433	7.065	7.682	8.492	9.111
100	3.034	3.179	3.409	3.625	3.896	6.888	7.546	8.189	9.035	9.680

f = 20

n	.005	.01	.025	.05	.10	.90	.95	.975	.99	.995
2	.0090	.0180	.0449	.0898	.1800	2.439	2.950	3.427	4.024	4.460
3	.1348	.1910	.3032	.4320	.6200	3.078	3.578	4.047	4.639	5.074
4	.3389	.4291	.5891	.7537	.9747	3.462	3.958	4.426	5.018	5.455
5	.5432	.6517	.8347	1.015	1.248	3.736	4.232	4.700	5.294	5.732
6	.7267	.8452	1.039	1.227	1.465	3.950	4.445	4.914	5.510	5.951
7	.8875	1.011	1.212	1.403	1.644	4.124	4.620	5.089	5.688	6.131
8	1.028	1.155	1.359	1.552	1.794	4.271	4.768	5.238	5.839	6.285
9	1.152	1.281	1.487	1.680	1.923	4.398	4.896	5.368	5.970	6.418
10	1.261	1.392	1.599	1.793	2.036	4.510	5.008	5.481	6.087	6.537
11	1.359	1.490	1.698	1.893	2.135	4.609	5.108	5.583	6.191	6.642
12	1.447	1.579	1.787	1.982	2.224	4.699	5.199	5.675	6.285	6.738
13	1.527	1.659	1.868	2.062	2.304	4.780	5.282	5.759	6.371	6.826
14	1.600	1.732	1.941	2.135	2.378	4.855	5.357	5.836	6.450	6.907
15	1.666	1.799	2.008	2.202	2.445	4.924	5.427	5.907	6.523	6.981
16	1.728	1.861	2.070	2.264	2.506	4.987	5.493	5.974	6.591	7.051
17	1.785	1.918	2.127	2.322	2.564	5.047	5.553	6.036	6.654	7.116
18	1.838	1.971	2.181	2.375	2.617	5.103	5.610	6.093	6.714	7.177
19	1.888	2.021	2.230	2.425	2.667	5.155	5.663	6.148	6.771	7.235
20	1.934	2.067	2.277	2.471	2.714	5.205	5.714	6.200	6.823	7.289
24	2.095	2.228	2.438	2.633	2.876	5.378	5.891	6.381	7.011	7.481
30	2.282	2.416	2.626	2.822	3.066	5.586	6.104	6.600	7.237	7.713
40	2.509	2.644	2.856	3.053	3.299	5.847	6.373	6.876	7.523	8.008
60	2.805	2.941	3.157	3.357	3.606	6.203	6.740	7.255	7.919	8.416
100	3.143	3.283	3.503	3.709	3.965	6.633	7.187	7.718	8.404	8.917

6.5

Critical Values of the Studentized Range
from a Normal Distribution (cont.)

| f = 60 | | | | | | | | | |
n	.005	.01	.025	.05	.10	.90	.95	.975	.99	.995
2	.0089	.0178	.0445	.0891	.1785	2.363	2.829	3.251	3.762	4.122
3	.1348	.1910	.3031	.4316	.6189	2.959	3.399	3.798	4.282	4.625
4	.3414	.4321	.5927	.7575	.9777	3.312	3.737	4.124	4.595	4.928
5	.5508	.6604	.8445	1.024	1.257	3.562	3.977	4.356	4.818	5.146
6	.7412	.8610	1.057	1.244	1.480	3.755	4.163	4.536	4.991	5.316
7	.9096	1.035	1.237	1.427	1.665	3.911	4.314	4.682	5.133	5.454
8	1.058	1.187	1.392	1.583	1.821	4.042	4.441	4.806	5.253	5.571
9	1.190	1.320	1.527	1.718	1.955	4.155	4.550	4.912	5.356	5.673
10	1.308	1.439	1.646	1.837	2.073	4.254	4.646	5.006	5.447	5.762
11	1.413	1.545	1.753	1.943	2.178	4.342	4.732	5.089	5.528	5.841
12	1.509	1.642	1.848	2.038	2.272	4.421	4.808	5.164	5.601	5.913
13	1.597	1.729	1.935	2.124	2.356	4.493	4.878	5.232	5.667	5.979
14	1.677	1.809	2.015	2.203	2.434	4.558	4.942	5.295	5.728	6.039
15	1.751	1.883	2.088	2.275	2.505	4.619	5.001	5.352	5.785	6.094
16	1.820	1.951	2.155	2.342	2.571	4.675	5.056	5.406	5.837	6.146
17	1.883	2.014	2.218	2.404	2.632	4.727	5.107	5.456	5.886	6.194
18	1.943	2.073	2.276	2.462	2.689	4.775	5.154	5.503	5.931	6.239
19	1.998	2.128	2.331	2.516	2.742	4.821	5.199	5.546	5.974	6.281
20	2.051	2.181	2.382	2.566	2.792	4.864	5.241	5.588	6.015	6.321
24	2.232	2.361	2.561	2.743	2.965	5.015	5.389	5.733	6.158	6.462
30	2.446	2.574	2.771	2.950	3.170	5.196	5.566	5.908	6.330	6.632
40	2.708	2.834	3.028	3.205	3.421	5.422	5.789	6.127	6.546	6.846
60	3.053	3.177	3.368	3.542	3.755	5.730	6.093	6.429	6.843	7.143
100	3.450	3.572	3.762	3.934	4.146	6.102	6.462	6.795	7.207	7.504

| f = ∞ | | | | | | | | | |
n										
2	.0089	.0177	.0443	.0887	.1777	2.326	2.772	3.170	3.643	3.970
3	.1348	.1909	.3031	.4314	.6184	2.902	3.314	3.682	4.120	4.424
4	.3427	.4337	.5946	.7595	.9794	3.240	3.633	3.984	4.403	4.694
5	.5549	.6650	.8497	1.030	1.261	3.478	3.858	4.197	4.603	4.886
6	.7490	.8695	1.066	1.253	1.488	3.661	4.030	4.361	4.757	5.033
7	.9218	1.048	1.251	1.440	1.676	3.808	4.170	4.494	4.882	5.154
8	1.075	1.205	1.410	1.600	1.835	3.931	4.286	4.605	4.987	5.255
9	1.212	1.343	1.550	1.740	1.973	4.037	4.387	4.700	5.078	5.341
10	1.335	1.467	1.674	1.863	2.094	4.129	4.474	4.784	5.157	5.418
11	1.446	1.578	1.784	1.973	2.202	4.211	4.552	4.858	5.227	5.485
12	1.547	1.679	1.884	2.071	2.299	4.285	4.622	4.925	5.290	5.546
13	1.639	1.771	1.976	2.161	2.387	4.351	4.685	4.985	5.348	5.602
14	1.724	1.856	2.059	2.243	2.467	4.412	4.743	5.041	5.400	5.652
15	1.803	1.934	2.136	2.319	2.541	4.468	4.796	5.092	5.448	5.699
16	1.876	2.007	2.207	2.389	2.609	4.519	4.845	5.139	5.493	5.742
17	1.944	2.074	2.274	2.454	2.673	4.568	4.891	5.183	5.535	5.783
18	2.008	2.137	2.336	2.515	2.732	4.612	4.934	5.224	5.574	5.820
19	2.068	2.197	2.394	2.572	2.787	4.654	4.974	5.262	5.611	5.856
20	2.125	2.253	2.449	2.626	2.840	4.694	5.012	5.299	5.645	5.889
24	2.323	2.448	2.640	2.813	3.021	4.832	5.144	5.425	5.766	6.006
30	2.559	2.681	2.867	3.034	3.237	4.997	5.301	5.577	5.911	6.146
40	2.851	2.969	3.148	3.309	3.503	5.202	5.498	5.766	6.092	6.322
60	3.243	3.354	3.523	3.675	3.859	5.480	5.764	6.023	6.338	6.561
100	3.703	3.807	3.965	4.107	4.279	5.812	6.085	6.333	6.636	6.850

6.6 Critical Values of the Ratio of the Mean Square Successive Difference to the Sample Variance

Let X be a random variable which is normally distributed with mean μ and standard deviation σ. A sample of size n is randomly selected from this distribution, and the sample mean and the sample variance are calculated as in Section 2.2 above, that is, s^2 is computed with a divisor of $n - 1$. This is emphasized because there are several tables of the statistic to be considered here which have assumed a divisor of n for s^2, notably [87] and [88].

The mean square successive difference is defined by

$$\Delta^2 = \frac{1}{n-1} \sum_{i=1}^{n-1} (x_{i+1} - x_i)^2.$$

The quantity tabulated is that value of k which solves the equation

$$\Pr\left\{\frac{\Delta^2}{s^2} \le k\right\} = \gamma.$$

Only small values of γ are given, since most applications involve the lower tail of the distribution. Hart [88] gives values of k for $\gamma = 0.95$, 0.99, and 0.999 also, but with s^2 defined with a divisor of n instead of $n - 1$. The distribution of Δ^2/s^2 was derived by von Neumann [232].

Critical Values of the Ratio of the Mean
Square Square Successive Difference to the Sample Variance

f	0.001	0.01	0.05	f	0.001	0.01	0.05
4	0.5898	0.6256	0.7805	36	1.0416	1.2581	1.4656
5	0.4161	0.5379	0.8204	37	1.0529	1.2673	1.4726
				38	1.0639	1.2763	1.4793
6	0.3634	0.5615	0.8902	39	1.0746	1.2850	1.4858
7	0.3695	0.6140	0.9359	40	1.0850	1.2934	1.4921
8	0.4036	0.6628	0.9825				
9	0.4420	0.7088	1.0244	41	1.0950	1.3017	1.4982
10	0.4816	0.7518	1.0623	42	1.1048	1.3096	1.5041
				43	1.1142	1.3172	1.5098
11	0.5197	0.7915	1.0965	44	1.1233	1.3246	1.5154
12	0.5557	0.8280	1.1276	45	1.1320	1.3317	1.5206
13	0.5898	0.8618	1.1558				
14	0.6223	0.8931	1.1816	46	1.1404	1.3387	1.5257
15	0.6532	0.9221	1.2053	47	1.1484	1.3453	1.5305
				48	1.1561	1.3515	1.5351
16	0.6826	0.9491	1.2272	49	1.1635	1.3573	1.5395
17	0.7104	0.9743	1.2473	50	1.1705	1.3629	1.5437
18	0.7368	0.9979	1.2660				
19	0.7617	1.0199	1.2834	51	1.1774	1.3683	1.5477
20	0.7852	1.0406	1.2996	52	1.1843	1.3738	1.5518
				53	1.1910	1.3792	1.5557
21	0.8073	1.0601	1.3148	54	1.1976	1.3846	1.5596
22	0.8283	1.0785	1.3290	55	1.2041	1.3899	1.5634
23	0.8481	1.0958	1.3425				
24	0.8668	1.1122	1.3552	56	1.2104	1.3949	1.5670
25	0.8846	1.1278	1.3671	57	1.2166	1.3999	1.5707
				58	1.2227	1.4048	1.5743
26	0.9017	1.1426	1.3785	59	1.2288	1.4096	1.5779
27	0.9182	1.1567	1.3892	60	1.2349	1.4144	1.5814
28	0.9341	1.1702	1.3994				
29	0.9496	1.1830	1.4091				
30	0.9645	1.1951	1.4183				
31	0.9789	1.2067	1.4270				
32	0.9925	1.2177	1.4354				
33	1.0055	1.2283	1.4434				
34	1.0180	1.2386	1.4511				
35	1.0300	1.2485	1.4585				

6.6

7. ORDER STATISTICS FROM THE NORMAL DISTRIBUTION

7.1 Expected Values of Order Statistics from a Normal Distribution

The quantity tabulated here is defined by

$$E(X_{(k)}) = \int_{-\infty}^{+\infty} \frac{n!}{(k-1)!(n-k)!} x[P(x)]^{n-k}[Q(x)]^{k-1}Z(x)\,dx,$$

where $P(x)$, $Q(x)$, and $Z(x)$ are as defined in Section 1.1. If a sample of size n is drawn from a normal distribution with mean zero and standard deviation one, and is then ordered from largest to smallest, the expected value of the kth ordered sample value is given by $E(X_{(k)})$. Note that these values are symmetric about zero, and in fact if n is odd and $k = (n+1)/2$, then $E(X_{(k)}) = 0$. In the table, values are consistently given down to the middle order statistic, and if there is room without making the table larger, values at the middle and beyond are given. Missing values may be obtained by noting that $E(X_{(k)}) = -E(X_{(n-k+1)})$, and that the middle value is zero when n is odd, as noted above.

One use often made of these tables is to take observations which are ranks and replace them by the expected values of the corresponding normal order statistics. In this case, the next step often involves an analysis of variance of the normal order statistics, and it is convenient to have the total sum of squares of the rank order statistics for each n. A table of the total sum of squares is given after the expected values of the order statistics. Ruben [188] gives a formula for this total sum of squares which does not require knowledge of the individual expected values.

Teichroew [220] gives a table of these expected values to ten decimal places up through $n = 20$. Harter [89] gives a table of these expected values to five decimal places for $n = 2(1)100$ and for values of n, none of whose prime factors exceeds seven, up through $n = 400$.

Expected Values of Order Statistics from a
Normal Distribution [89]

Rank	2	3	4	5	6	7	8
				Sample Size			
1	0.5642	0.8463	1.0294	1.1630	1.2672	1.3522	1.4236
2	-0.5642	0.0000	0.2970	0.4950	0.6418	0.7574	0.8522
3		-0.8463	-0.2970	0.0000	0.2015	0.3527	0.4728
4			-1.0294	-0.4950	-0.2015	0.0000	0.1525

Rank	9	10	11	12	13	14	15
1	1.4850	1.5388	1.5864	1.6292	1.6680	1.7034	1.7359
2	0.9323	1.0014	1.0619	1.1157	1.1641	1.2079	1.2479
3	0.5720	0.6561	0.7288	0.7928	0.8498	0.9011	0.9477
4	0.2745	0.3758	0.4620	0.5368	0.6028	0.6618	0.7149
5	0.0000	0.1227	0.2249	0.3122	0.3883	0.4556	0.5157
6	-0.2745	-0.1227	0.0000	0.1026	0.1905	0.2673	0.3353
7	-0.5720	-0.3758	-0.2249	-0.1026	0.0000	0.0882	0.1653

Rank	16	17	18	19	20	21	22
1	1.7660	1.7939	1.8200	1.8445	1.8675	1.8892	1.9097
2	1.2847	1.3188	1.3504	1.3799	1.4076	1.4336	1.4582
3	0.9903	1.0295	1.0657	1.0995	1.1309	1.1605	1.1882
4	0.7632	0.8074	0.8481	0.8859	0.9210	0.9538	0.9846
5	0.5700	0.6195	0.6648	0.7066	0.7454	0.7815	0.8153
6	0.3962	0.4513	0.5016	0.5477	0.5903	0.6298	0.6667
7	0.2338	0.2952	0.3508	0.4016	0.4483	0.4915	0.5316
8	0.0773	0.1460	0.2077	0.2637	0.3149	0.3620	0.4056
9	-0.0773	0.0000	0.0688	0.1307	0.1870	0.2384	0.2858
10	-0.2338	-0.1460	-0.0688	0.0000	0.0620	0.1184	0.1700
11	-0.3962	-0.2952	-0.2077	-0.1307	-0.0620	0.0000	0.0564

Rank	23	24	25	26	27	28	29
1	1.9292	1.9477	1.9653	1.9822	1.9983	2.0137	2.0285
2	1.4814	1.5034	1.5243	1.5442	1.5633	1.5815	1.5989
3	1.2144	1.2392	1.2628	1.2851	1.3064	1.3267	1.3462
4	1.0136	1.0409	1.0668	1.0914	1.1147	1.1370	1.1582
5	0.8470	0.8768	0.9050	0.9317	0.9570	0.9812	1.0041
6	0.7012	0.7335	0.7641	0.7929	0.8202	0.8461	0.8708
7	0.5690	0.6040	0.6369	0.6679	0.6973	0.7251	0.7515
8	0.4461	0.4839	0.5193	0.5527	0.5841	0.6138	0.6420
9	0.3297	0.3705	0.4086	0.4444	0.4780	0.5098	0.5398
10	0.2175	0.2616	0.3027	0.3410	0.3771	0.4110	0.4430
11	0.1081	0.1558	0.2001	0.2413	0.2798	0.3160	0.3501
12	0.0000	0.0518	0.0995	0.1439	0.1852	0.2239	0.2602
13	-0.1081	-0.0518	0.0000	0.0478	0.0922	0.1336	0.1724
14	-0.2175	-0.1558	-0.0995	-0.0478	0.0000	0.0444	0.0859

Expected Values of Order Statistics from a
Normal Distribution (cont.)

			Sample Size				
Rank	30	31	32	33	34	35	36
1	2.0428	2.0565	2.0697	2.0824	2.0947	2.1066	2.1181
2	1.6156	1.6317	1.6471	1.6620	1.6764	1.6902	1.7036
3	1.3648	1.3827	1.3999	1.4164	1.4323	1.4476	1.4624
4	1.1786	1.1980	1.2167	1.2347	1.2520	1.2686	1.2847
5	1.0261	1.0471	1.0672	1.0865	1.1051	1.1229	1.1402
6	0.8944	0.9169	0.9384	0.9590	0.9789	0.9979	1.0162
7	0.7767	0.8007	0.8236	0.8455	0.8666	0.8868	0.9062
8	0.6688	0.6944	0.7187	0.7420	0.7643	0.7857	0.8063
9	0.5683	0.5955	0.6213	0.6460	0.6695	0.6921	0.7138
10	0.4733	0.5021	0.5294	0.5555	0.5804	0.6043	0.6271
11	0.3824	0.4129	0.4418	0.4694	0.4957	0.5208	0.5449
12	0.2945	0.3269	0.3575	0.3867	0.4144	0.4409	0.4662
13	0.2088	0.2432	0.2757	0.3065	0.3358	0.3637	0.3903
14	0.1247	0.1613	0.1957	0.2283	0.2592	0.2886	0.3166
15	0.0415	0.0804	0.1169	0.1515	0.1842	0.2152	0.2446
16	-0.0415	0.0000	0.0389	0.0755	0.1101	0.1428	0.1739
17	-0.1247	-0.0804	-0.0389	0.0000	0.0366	0.0712	0.1040
18	-0.2088	-0.1613	-0.1169	-0.0755	-0.0366	0.0000	0.0346

Rank	37	38	39	40	41	42	43
1	2.1293	2.1401	2.1506	2.1608	2.1707	2.1803	2.1897
2	1.7166	1.7291	1.7413	1.7531	1.7646	1.7757	1.7865
3	1.4768	1.4906	1.5040	1.5170	1.5296	1.5419	1.5538
4	1.3002	1.3151	1.3296	1.3437	1.3573	1.3705	1.3833
5	1.1568	1.1728	1.1883	1.2033	1.2178	1.2319	1.2456
6	1.0339	1.0509	1.0674	1.0833	1.0987	1.1136	1.1281
7	0.9250	0.9430	0.9604	0.9772	0.9935	1.0092	1.0245
8	0.8260	0.8451	0.8634	0.8811	0.8983	0.9148	0.9308
9	0.7346	0.7547	0.7740	0.7926	0.8106	0.8279	0.8447
10	0.6490	0.6701	0.6904	0.7099	0.7287	0.7469	0.7645
11	0.5679	0.5900	0.6113	0.6318	0.6515	0.6705	0.6889
12	0.4904	0.5136	0.5359	0.5574	0.5780	0.5979	0.6171
13	0.4158	0.4401	0.4635	0.4859	0.5075	0.5283	0.5483
14	0.3434	0.3689	0.3934	0.4169	0.4394	0.4611	0.4820
15	0.2727	0.2995	0.3252	0.3498	0.3734	0.3960	0.4178
16	0.2034	0.2316	0.2585	0.2842	0.3089	0.3326	0.3553
17	0.1351	0.1647	0.1929	0.2199	0.2457	0.2704	0.2942
18	0.0674	0.0985	0.1282	0.1564	0.1835	0.2093	0.2341
19	0.0000	0.0328	0.0640	0.0936	0.1219	0.1490	0.1749
20	-0.0674	-0.0328	0.0000	0.0312	0.0608	0.0892	0.1163
21	-0.1351	-0.0985	-0.0640	-0.0312	0.0000	0.0297	0.0580

7.1

Expected Values of Order Statistics from a
Normal Distribution (cont.)

Rank	44	45	46	47	48	49	50
1	2.1988	2.2077	2.2164	2.2249	2.2331	2.2412	2.2491
2	1.7971	1.8073	1.8173	1.8271	1.8366	1.8458	1.8549
3	1.5653	1.5766	1.5875	1.5982	1.6086	1.6187	1.6286
4	1.3957	1.4078	1.4196	1.4311	1.4422	1.4531	1.4637
5	1.2588	1.2717	1.2842	1.2964	1.3083	1.3198	1.3311
6	1.1421	1.1558	1.1690	1.1819	1.1944	1.2066	1.2185
7	1.0392	1.0536	1.0675	1.0810	1.0942	1.1070	1.1195
8	0.9463	0.9614	0.9760	0.9902	1.0040	1.0174	1.0304
9	0.8610	0.8767	0.8920	0.9068	0.9212	0.9353	0.9489
10	0.7815	0.7979	0.8139	0.8294	0.8444	0.8590	0.8732
11	0.7067	0.7238	0.7405	0.7566	0.7723	0.7875	0.8022
12	0.6356	0.6535	0.6709	0.6877	0.7040	0.7198	0.7351
13	0.5676	0.5863	0.6044	0.6219	0.6388	0.6552	0.6712
14	0.5022	0.5217	0.5405	0.5586	0.5763	0.5933	0.6099
15	0.4389	0.4591	0.4787	0.4976	0.5159	0.5336	0.5508
16	0.3772	0.3983	0.4187	0.4383	0.4573	0.4757	0.4935
17	0.3170	0.3390	0.3602	0.3806	0.4003	0.4194	0.4379
18	0.2579	0.2808	0.3029	0.3241	0.3446	0.3644	0.3836
19	0.1997	0.2236	0.2465	0.2686	0.2899	0.3105	0.3304
20	0.1422	0.1671	0.1910	0.2140	0.2361	0.2575	0.2781
21	0.0851	0.1111	0.1360	0.1599	0.1830	0.2051	0.2265
22	0.0283	0.0555	0.0814	0.1064	0.1303	0.1534	0.1756
23	-0.0283	0.0000	0.0271	0.0531	0.0781	0.1020	0.1251
24	-0.0851	-0.0555	-0.0271	0.0000	0.0260	0.0509	0.0749
25	-0.1422	-0.1111	-0.0814	-0.0531	-0.0260	0.0000	0.0250

Sum of Squares of Mean Deviation Tabulated

N		N		N		N	
2	0.63664328	14	11.79470862	26	23.59923910	38	35.49198824
3	1.43244738	15	12.77103438	27	24.58820060	39	36.48560998
4	2.29574672	16	13.74978118	28	25.57763100	40	37.47917202
5	3.19518800	17	14.72997328	29	26.56681700	41	38.47307888
6	4.11661066	18	15.71093046	30	27.55833734	42	39.46603722
7	5.05299378	19	16.69436982	31	28.54967814	43	40.46052292
8	5.99935578	20	17.67818594	32	29.53958358	44	41.45346200
9	6.95388508	21	18.66327990	33	30.53077890	45	42.44788234
10	7.91491108	22	19.64926646	34	31.52318272	46	43.44266176
11	8.87894004	23	20.63612304	35	32.51405038	47	44.43796372
12	9.84752162	24	21.62254738	36	33.50676302	48	45.43212870
13	10.81989566	25	22.61066016	37	34.50062866	49	46.42638220
						50	47.42212550

7.2 Estimates of the Mean and Standard Deviation in Censored Samples from a Normal Distribution

A sample of n observations from a normal distribution has been taken. The observations are ordered from largest to smallest $X_{(1)}, X_{(2)}, \ldots, X_{(n)}$. The r_1 largest observations are deleted, and the r_2 smallest observations are deleted. Using just the remaining $n - r_1 - r_2$ observations, $X_{(r_1+1)}, \ldots, X_{(n-r_2)}$, estimates of the mean and standard deviation are required. The quantities tabulated give the most efficient unbiased linear estimates of the mean and standard deviation in samples of sizes ≤ 10 from a normal population. Also given in the right-hand column is the variance of the estimate given on each line. Sarhan and Greenberg [191] give eight decimal places of accuracy for the constants, which have been rounded to four decimal places in the table given here. In [191] coefficients to four decimal places with $11 \leq n \leq 15$ are given. These authors, Sarhan and Greenberg, indicate that they have eight-decimal-place tables up through $n = 20$.

A simplified estimate of the mean has been proposed by Winsor to Dixon [53]. This Winsorized mean is obtained by taking $i = $ maximum (r_1, r_2) and then computing the mean as

$$[(i + 1)X_{(i+1)} + X_{(i+2)} + \cdots + X_{(n-i-1)} + (i + 1)X_{(n-i)}]/n.$$

The variances of this estimate may be obtained in the obvious manner from the tables given in Section 7.3. They have been computed for a few values of n as follows:

VARIANCES OF THE WINSORIZED MEAN FOR A CENSORED
SAMPLE FROM A NORMAL DISTRIBUTION

n	i	Variance
3	1	0.4487
4	1	0.2982
5	1	0.2258
	2	0.2868
6	1	0.1826
	2	0.2147
7	1	0.1535
	2	0.1732
	3	0.2104
8	1	0.1326
	2	0.1457
	3	0.1682
9	1	0.1168
	2	0.1261
	3	0.1410
	4	0.1661

Estimates of the Mean (First Line) and
Standard Deviation (Second Line)
in Censored Samples from a Normal Distribution [191]

n	r_1	r_2	Estimate	Variance
2	0	0	$0.5000(X_1 + X_2)$	0.5000
			$0.8862(X_1 - X_2)$	0.5708
3	0	0	$0.3333(X_1 + X_2 + X_3)$	0.3333
			$0.5908(X_1 - X_3)$	0.2755
	0	1	X_1	0.4487
			$1.1816(X_1 - X_2)$	0.6378
4	0	0	$0.2500(X_1 + X_2 + X_3 + X_4)$	0.2500
			$0.4539(X_1 - X_4) + 0.1102(X_2 - X_3)$	0.1801
	0	1	$0.6431X_1 + 0.2408X_2 + 0.1161X_3$	0.2870
			$0.8239X_1 - 0.1268X_2 - 0.6971X_3$	0.3021
	0	2	$0.4056(X_1 - X_2) + X_1$	0.5130
			$1.3654(X_1 - X_2)$	0.6730
	1	1	$0.5000(X_2 + X_3)$	0.2982
			$1.6834(X_2 - X_3)$	0.7057
5	0	0	$0.2000(X_1 + X_2 + X_3 + X_4 + X_5)$	0.2000
			$0.3724(X_1 - X_5) + 0.1352(X_2 - X_4)$	0.1333
	0	1	$0.4771X_1 + 0.2147X_2 + 0.1830X_3 + 0.1252X_4$	0.2177
			$0.6511X_1 + 0.0274X_2 - 0.1668X_3 - 0.5117X_4$	0.1948
	0	2	$0.9139X_1 + 0.1498X_2 - 0.0638X_3$	0.2839
			$0.9817X_1 - 0.2121X_2 - 0.7696X_3$	0.3181
	0	3	$0.7411(X_1 - X_2) + X_1$	0.6112
			$1.4971(X_1 - X_2)$	0.6957
	1	1	$0.3893(X_2 + X_4) + 0.2214X_3$	0.2258
			$1.0101(X_2 + X_4)$	0.3297
	1	2	X_2	0.2868
			$2.0201(X_2 - X_3)$	0.7406
6	0	0	$0.1667(X_1 + X_2 + X_3 + X_4 + X_5 + X_6)$	0.1667
			$0.3175(X_1 - X_6) + 0.1386(X_2 - X_5) + 0.0432(X_3 - X_4)$	0.1057
	0	1	$0.3799X_1 + 0.1828X_2 + 0.1680X_3 + 0.1510X_4 + 0.1183X_5$	0.1769
			$0.5448X_1 + 0.0740X_2 - 0.0406X_3 - 0.1685X_4 - 0.4097X_5$	0.1428

Estimates of the Mean (First Line) and
Standard Deviation (Second Line)
in Censored Samples from a Normal Distribution (*cont.*)

n	r_1	r_2	Estimate	Variance
6	0	2	$0.6828X_1 + 0.1761X_2 + 0.1226X_3 + 0.0185X_4$	0.2068
			$0.7909X_1 - 0.0290X_2 - 0.2091X_3 - 0.5528X_4$	0.2044
	0	3	$1.1511X_1 + 0.0649X_2 - 0.2159X_3$	0.2999
			$1.1004X_1 - 0.2760X_2 - 0.8244X_3$	0.3292
	0	4	$1.0261(X_1 - X_2) + X_1$	0.7186
			$1.5988(X_1 - X_2)$	0.7119
	1	1	$0.3198(X_2 + X_5) + 0.1802(X_3 + X_4)$	0.1825
			$0.7531(X_2 - X_5) + 0.0829(X_3 - X_4)$	0.2102
	1	2	$0.6680X_2 + 0.1781X_3 + 0.1539X_4$	0.2070
			$1.2317X_2 - 0.0878X_3 - 1.1438X_4$	0.3460
	1	3	$0.4578(X_2 - X_3) + X_2$	0.3296
			$2.2717(X_2 - X_3)$	0.7628
	2	2	$0.5000(X_3 + X_4)$	0.2147
			$2.4808(X_3 - X_4)$	0.7747
7	0	0	$0.1429(X_1 + X_2 + X_3 + X_4 + X_5 + X_6 + X_7)$	0.1429
			$0.2778(X_1 - X_7) + 0.1351(X_2 - X_6) + 0.0625(X_3 - X_5)$	0.0875
	0	1	$0.3159X_1 + 0.1571X_2 + 0.1487X_3 + 0.1400X_4 + 0.1295X_5 + 0.1088X_6$	0.1494
			$0.4716X_1 + 0.0901X_2 + 0.0114X_3 - 0.0681X_4 - 0.1610X_5 - 0.3440X_6$	0.1123
	0	2	$0.5462X_1 + 0.1626X_2 + 0.1375X_3 + 0.1072X_4 + 0.0465X_5$	0.1660
			$0.6709X_1 + 0.0321X_2 - 0.0718X_3 - 0.1943X_4 - 0.4370X_5$	0.1493
	0	3	$0.8686X_1 + 0.1375X_2 + 0.0677X_3 - 0.0738X_4$	0.2071
			$0.8994X_1 - 0.0717X_2 - 0.2428X_3 - 0.5848X_4$	0.2114
	0	4	$1.3609X_1 - 0.0135X_2 - 0.3474X_3$	0.3248
			$1.1951X_1 - 0.3269X_2 - 0.8682X_3$	0.3375
	0	5	$1.2733(X_1 - X_2) + X_1$	0.8264
			$1.6812(X_1 - X_2)$	0.7243
	1	1	$0.2718(X_2 + X_6) + 0.1520(X_3 + X_5) + 0.1524X_4$	0.1535
			$0.6108(X_2 - X_6) + 0.1061(X_3 - X_5)$	0.1527
	1	2	$0.5186X_2 + 0.1634X_3 + 0.1432X_4 + 0.1748X_5$	0.1668
			$0.9298X_2 + 0.0248X_3 - 0.1258X_4 - 0.8288X_5$	0.2201

Estimates of the Mean (First Line) and
Standard Deviation (Second Line)
in Censored Samples from a Normal Distribution (*cont.*)

n	r_1	r_2	Estimate	Variance
7	1	3	$0.9321X_2 + 0.1270X_3 - 0.0592X_4$	0.2095
			$1.4030X_2 - 0.1548X_3 - 1.2483X_4$	0.3572
	1	4	$0.8716(X_2 - X_3) + X_2$	0.3954
			$2.4712\,(X_2 - X_3)$	0.7785
	2	2	$0.4157(X_3 + X_5) + 0.1686X_4$	0.1731
			$1.4176(X_3 - X_5)$	0.3622
	2	3	X_3	0.2104
			$2.8352(X_3 - X_4)$	0.7962
8	0	0	$0.1250(X_1 + X_2 + X_3 + X_4 + X_5 + X_6 + X_7 + X_8)$	0.1250
			$0.2476(X_1 - X_8) + 0.1294(X_2 - X_7) + 0.0713(X_3 - X_6) + 0.0230(X_4 - X_5)$	0.0746
	0	1	$0.2704X_1 + 0.1370X_2 + 0.1318X_3 + 0.1265X_4 + 0.1208X_5$ $+ 0.1139X_6 + 0.0997X_7$	0.1295
			$0.4175X_1 + 0.0951X_2 + 0.0364X_3 - 0.0200X_4 - 0.0796X_5$ $-0.1515X_6 - 0.2978X_7$	0.0924
	0	2	$0.4555X_1 + 0.1451X_2 + 0.1309X_3 + 0.1153X_4 + 0.0962X_5 + 0.0569X_6$	0.1399
			$0.5868X_1 + 0.0570X_2 - 0.0132X_3 - 0.0881X_4 - 0.1788X_5 - 0.3638X_6$	0.1171
	0	3	$0.6993X_1 + 0.1413X_2 + 0.1084X_3 + 0.0677X_4 - 0.0167X_5$	0.1623
			$0.7709X_1 + 0.0002X_2 - 0.0970X_3 - 0.2156X_4 - 0.4586X_5$	0.1542
	0	4	$1.0372X_1 + 0.1001X_2 + 0.0176X_3 - 0.1549X_4$	0.2138
			$0.9878X_1 - 0.1061X_2 - 0.2707X_3 - 0.6110X_4$	0.2168
	0	5	$1.5487X_1 - 0.0855X_2 - 0.4632X_3$	0.3541
			$1.2735X_1 - 0.3690X_2 - 0.9045X_3$	0.3441
	0	6	$1.4915(X_1 - X_2) + X_1$	0.9310
			$1.7502(X_1 - X_2)$	0.7342
	1	1	$0.2367(X_2 + X_7) + 0.1315(X_3 + X_6) + 0.1319(X_4 + X_5)$	0.1326
			$0.5184(X_2 - X_7) + 0.1115(X_3 - X_6) + 0.0361(X_4 - X_5)$	0.1193
	1	2	$0.4282X_2 + 0.1442X_3 + 0.1338X_4 + 0.1222X_5 + 0.1716X_6$	0.1409
			$0.7615X_2 + 0.0630X_3 - 0.0318X_4 - 0.1319X_5 - 0.6608X_6$	0.1594
	1	3	$0.7102X_2 + 0.1406X_3 + 0.1061X_4 + 0.0431X_5$	0.1623
			$1.0696X_2 - 0.0197X_3 - 0.1605X_4 - 0.8894X_5$	0.2272

7.2

Estimates of the Mean (First Line) and
Standard Deviation (Second Line)
in Censored Samples from a Normal Distribution (*cont.*)

	r_1	r_2	Estimate	Variance
8	1	4	$1.1778X_2 + 0.0741X_3 - 0.2519X_4$	0.2233
			$1.5423X_2 - 0.2086X_3 - 1.3337X_4$	0.3655
	1	5	$1.2462(X_2 - X_3) + X_2$	0.4711
			$2.6357(X_2 - X_3)$	0.7904
	2	2	$0.3569(X_3 + X_6) + 0.1431(X_4 + X_5)$	0.1457
			$1.0357(X_3 - X_6) + 0.0674(X_4 - X_5)$	0.2300
	2	3	$0.6829X_3 + 0.1429X_4 + 0.1742X_5$	0.1627
			$1.6338X_3 - 0.0678X_4 - 1.5661X_5$	0.3732
	2	4	$0.4761(X_3 - X_4) + X_3$	0.2392
			$3.1220(X_3 - X_4)$	0.8113
	3	3	$0.5000(X_4 + X_5)$	0.1682
			$3.2784(X_4 - X_5)$	0.8171
9	0	0	$0.1111(X_1 + X_2 + X_3 + X_4 + X_5 + X_6 + X_7 + X_8 + X_9)$	0.1111
			$0.2237(X_1 - X_9) + 0.1233(X_2 - X_8) + 0.0751(X_3 - X_7) + 0.0360(X_4 - X_6)$	0.0650
	0	1	$0.2365X_1 + 0.1212X_2 + 0.1177X_3 + 0.1142X_4 + 0.1106X_5$ $+ 0.1067X_6 + 0.1018X_7 + 0.0915X_8$	0.1144
			$0.3757X_1 + 0.0954X_2 + 0.0492X_3 + 0.0062X_4 - 0.0370X_5$ $- 0.0841X_6 - 0.1421X_7 - 0.2633X_8$	0.0784
	0	2	$0.3909X_1 + 0.1294X_2 + 0.1204X_3 + 0.1110X_4 + 0.1006X_5$ $+ 0.0876X_6 + 0.0602X_7$	0.1214
			$0.5239X_1 + 0.0678X_2 + 0.0160X_3 - 0.0364X_4 - 0.0938X_5$ $- 0.1647X_6 - 0.3129X_7$	0.0960
	0	3	$0.5860X_1 + 0.1320X_2 + 0.1133X_3 + 0.0923X_4 + 0.0660X_5 + 0.0104X_6$	0.1352
			$0.6797X_1 + 0.0317X_2 - 0.0333X_3 - 0.1048X_4 - 0.1936X_5 - 0.3797X_6$	0.1207
	0	4	$0.8408X_1 + 0.1199X_2 + 0.0809X_3 + 0.0316X_4 - 0.07311X_5$	0.1629
			$0.8537X_1 - 0.0256X_2 - 0.1181X_3 - 0.2335X_4 - 0.4766X_5$	0.1581
	0	5	$1.1912X_1 + 0.0644X_2 - 0.0284X_3 - 0.2272X_4$	0.2241
			$1.0622X_1 - 0.1348X_2 - 0.2944X_3 - 0.6330X_4$	0.2212
	0	6	$1.7185X_1 - 0.1521X_2 - 0.5664X_3$	0.3854
			$1.3402X_1 - 0.4047X_2 - 0.9355X_3$	0.3494

7.2

Estimates of the Mean (First Line) and
Standard Deviation (Second Line)
in Censored Samples from a Normal Distribution (cont.)

n	r_1	r_2	Estimate	Variance
9	0	7	$1.6868(X_1 - X_2) + X_1$	1.0313
			$1.8092(X_1 - X_2)$	0.7423
	1	1	$0.2097(X_2 + X_8) + 0.1159(X_3 + X_7) + 0.1162(X_4 + X_6) + 0.1163X_5$	0.1167
			$0.4527(X_2 - X_8) + 0.1107(X_3 - X_7) + 0.0532(X_4 - X_6)$	0.0976
	1	2	$0.3663X_2 + 0.1275X_3 + 0.1214X_4 + 0.1148X_5 + 0.1074X_6 + 0.1626X_7$	0.1224
			$0.6514X_2 + 0.0775X_3 + 0.0109X_4 - 0.0563X_5 - 0.1291X_6 - 0.5544X_7$	0.1242
	1	3	$0.5804X_2 + 0.1321X_3 + 0.1140X_4 + 0.0936X_5 + 0.0799X_6$	0.1352
			$0.8828X_2 + 0.0299X_3 - 0.0578X_4 - 0.1535X_5 - 0.7015X_6$	0.1645
	1	4	$0.8916X_2 + 0.1153X_3 + 0.0699X_4 - 0.0768X_5$	0.1647
			$1.1852X_2 - 0.0558X_3 - 0.1896X_4 - 0.9399X_5$	0.2327
	1	5	$1.4054X_2 + 0.0218X_3 - 0.4272X_4$	0.2435
			$1.6591X_2 - 0.2534X_3 - 1.4057X_4$	0.3720
	1	6	$1.5874(X_2 - X_3) + X_2$	0.5505
			$2.7753(X_2 - X_3)$	0.7998
	2	2	$0.3134(X_3 + X_7) + 0.1243(X_4 + X_6) + 0.1246X_5$	0.1261
			$0.8317(X_3 - X_7) + 0.0885(X_4 - X_6)$	0.1662
	2	3	$0.5440X_3 + 0.1330X_4 + 0.1191X_5 + 0.2040X_6$	0.1361
			$1.2022X_3 + 0.0223X_4 - 0.1023X_5 - 1.1222X_6$	0.2371
	2	4	$0.9429X_3 + 0.1098X_4 - 0.0527X_5$	0.1657
			$1.8122X_3 - 0.1227X_4 - 1.6894X_5$	0.3814
	2	5	$0.9229(X_3 - X_4) + X_3$	0.2851
			$3.3620(X_3 - X_4)$	0.8227
	3	3	$0.4315(X_4 + X_6) + 0.1370X_5$	0.1410
			$1.8213(X_4 - X_6)$	0.3841
	3	4	X_4	0.1661
			$3.6426(X_4 - X_5)$	0.8317
10	0	0	$0.1000(X_1 + X_2 + X_3 + X_4 + X_5 + X_6 + X_7 + X_8 + X_9 + X_{10})$	0.1000
			$0.2044(X_1 - X_{10}) + 0.1172(X_2 - X_9) + 0.0763(X_3 - X_8)$	0.0576
			$\quad + 0.0436(X_4 - X_7) + 0.0142(X_5 - X_6)$	

Estimates of the Mean (First Line) and
Standard Deviation (Second Line)
in Censored Samples from a Normal Distribution (*cont.*)

n	r_1	r_2	Estimate	Variance
10	0	1	$0.2101X_1 + 0.1085X_2 + 0.1060X_3 + 0.1036X_4 + 0.1011X_5$ $+ 0.0986X_6 + 0.0957X_7 + 0.0921X_8 + 0.0843X_9$	0.1025
			$0.3423X_1 + 0.0937X_2 + 0.0559X_3 + 0.0215X_4 - 0.0119X_5$ $- 0.0465X_6 - 0.0851X_7 - 0.1334X_8 - 0.2364X_9$	0.0681
	0	2	$0.3424X_1 + 0.1161X_2 + 0.1099X_3 + 0.1037X_4 + 0.0972X_5$ $+ 0.0898X_6 + 0.0804X_7 + 0.0605X_8$	0.1075
			$0.4746X_1 + 0.0722X_2 + 0.0319X_3 - 0.0077X_4 - 0.0488X_5$ $- 0.0947X_6 - 0.1523X_7 - 0.2753X_8$	0.0813
	0	3	$0.5045X_1 + 0.1207X_2 + 0.1089X_3 + 0.0962X_4 + 0.0818X_5$ $+ 0.0636X_6 + 0.0244X_7$	0.1167
			$0.6107X_1 + 0.0469X_2 - 0.0006X_3 - 0.0502X_4 - 0.1058X_5$ $- 0.1758X_6 - 0.3252X_7$	0.0989
	0	4	$0.7078X_1 + 0.1185X_2 + 0.0962X_3 + 0.0707X_4 + 0.0383X_5 - 0.0316X_6$	0.1336
			$0.7576X_1 + 0.0111X_2 - 0.0501X_3 - 0.1192X_4 - 0.2063X_5 - 0.3930X_6$	0.1237
	0	5	$0.9718X_1 + 0.0990X_2 + 0.0549X_3 - 0.0016X_4 - 0.1240X_5$	0.1664
			$0.9243X_1 - 0.0472X_2 - 0.1362X_3 - 0.2491X_4 - 0.4919X_5$	0.1613
	0	6	$1.3327X_1 + 0.0305X_2 - 0.0709X_3 - 0.2923X_4$	0.2366
			$1.1263X_1 - 0.1593X_2 - 0.3150X_3 - 0.6520X_4$	0.2248
	0	7	$1.8734X_1 - 0.2138X_2 - 0.6596X_3$	0.4174
			$1.3981X_1 - 0.4357X_2 - 0.9625X_3$	0.3539
	0	8	$1.8634(X_1 - X_2) + X_1$	1.1269
			$1.8608(X_1 - X_2)$	0.7491
	1	1	$0.1884(X_2 + X_9) + 0.1036(X_3 + X_8) + 0.1040(X_4 + X_7) + 0.1041(X_5 + X_6)$	0.1043
			$0.4034(X_2 - X_9) + 0.1074(X_3 - X_8) + 0.0616(X_4 - X_7) + 0.0201(X_5 - X_6)$	0.0824
	1	2	$0.3209X_2 + 0.1138X_3 + 0.1098X_4 + 0.1057X_5 + 0.1013X_6$ $+ 0.0961X_7 + 0.1525X_8$	0.1085
			$0.5726X_2 + 0.0827X_3 + 0.0325X_4 - 0.0166X_5 - 0.0674X_6$ $- 0.1235X_7 - 0.4803X_8$	0.1014
	1	3	$0.4933X_2 + 0.1204X_3 + 0.1095X_4 + 0.0979X_5 + 0.0846X_6 + 0.0942X_7$	0.1168
			$0.7599X_2 + 0.0514X_3 - 0.0097X_4 - 0.0734X_5 - 0.1440X_6 - 0.5842X_7$	0.1280
	1	4	$0.7261X_2 + 0.1179X_3 + 0.0938X_4 + 0.0665X_5 - 0.0043X_6$	0.1339
			$0.9844X_2 + 0.0031X_3 - 0.0797X_4 - 0.1719X_5 - 0.7359X_6$	0.1685

Estimates of the Mean (First Line) and
Standard Deviation (Second Line)
in Censored Samples from a Normal Distribution (*cont.*)

n	r_1	r_2	Estimate	Variance
10	1	5	$1.0623X_2 + 0.0892X_3 + 0.0351X_4 - 0.1866X_5$	0.1712
			$1.2835X_2 - 0.0859X_3 - 0.2145X_4 - 0.9831X_5$	0.2371
	1	6	$1.6166X_2 - 0.0289X_3 - 0.5877X_4$	0.2672
			$1.7595X_2 - 0.2918X_3 - 1.4678X_4$	0.3773
	1	7	$1.9000(X_2 - X_3) + X_2$	0.6304
			$2.8960(X_2 - X_3)$	0.8075
	2	2	$0.2798(X_3 + X_8) + 0.1099(X_4 + X_7) + 0.1103(X_5 + X_6)$	0.1113
			$0.7021(X_3 - X_8) + 0.0947(X_4 - X_7) + 0.0310(X_5 - X_6)$	0.1292
	2	3	$0.4592X_3 + 0.1198X_4 + 0.1122X_5 + 0.1038X_6 + 0.2050X_7$	0.1180
			$0.9711X_3 + 0.0549X_4 - 0.0262X_5 - 0.1101X_6 - 0.8898X_7$	0.1713
	2	4	$0.7281X_3 + 0.1178X_4 + 0.0935X_5 + 0.0606X_6$	0.1339
			$1.3415X_3 - 0.0144X_4 - 0.1318X_5 - 1.1952X_6$	0.2426
	2	5	$1.1914X_3 + 0.0735X_4 - 0.2648X_5$	0.1767
			$1.9635X_3 - 0.1688X_4 - 1.7947X_5$	0.3877
	2	6	$1.3406(X_3 - X_4) + X_3$	0.3401
			$3.5677(X_3 - X_4)$	0.8316
	3	3	$0.3807(X_4 + X_7) + 0.1193(X_5 + X_6)$	0.1218
			$1.2832(X_4 - X_7) + 0.0559(X_5 - X_6)$	0.2442
	3	4	$0.6930X_4 + 0.1198X_5 + 0.1871X_6$	0.1343
			$2.0344X_4 - 0.0553X_5 - 1.9791X_6$	0.3921
	3	5	$0.4847(X_4 - X_5) + X_4$	0.1866
			$3.9511(X_4 - X_5)$	0.8426
	4	4	$0.5000(X_5 + X_6)$	0.1383
			$4.0761(X_5 - X_6)$	0.8458

7.2

7.3 Variances and Covariances of Order Statistics in Samples up to 20 from a Normal Population

A sample of size n is taken from a normal distribution with standard deviation equal to one. The sample values are arranged in decreasing order of magnitude as in Sections 7.1 and 7.2, giving $X_{(1)}, X_{(2)}, \ldots, X_{(n)}$. The quantity tabulated is

$$\text{cov}\,(X_{(i)}X_{(j)}) = E(X_{(i)}X_{(j)}) - E(X_{(i)})E(X_{(j)})$$

where $E(X_{(i)})$ has been defined in Section 7.1, and

$$E(X_{(i)}X_{(j)}) = \frac{n!}{(i-1)!(j-i-1)!(n-j)!} \int_{-\infty}^{+\infty} \int_{-\infty}^{y} xyZ(x)Z(y)$$
$$\times [P(x)]^{i-1}[Q(y)]^{n-j}[P(y) - P(x)]^{j-i-1}\, dx\, dy,$$

where Z, P, and Q are defined as in Section 1.1.

Note that $\text{cov}\,(X_{(i)}X_{(j)}) = \text{cov}\,(X_{(n-i+1)}X_{(n-j+1)})$, and if $i = j$, the quantity given is the variance of the ith-order statistic. Teichroew [220] gives a ten-decimal-place table of $E(X_{(i)}X_{(j)})$, and Sarhan and Greenberg [191] give the variances and covariances to ten decimal places for $n \leq 20$.

Variances and Covariances of Order Statistics in Samples up to 20 from a Normal Population [191]

n	i	j	Value
2	1	1	0.6817
		2	0.3183
	2	2	0.6817
3	1	1	0.5595
		2	0.2757
		3	0.1649
	2	2	0.4487
4	1	1	0.4917
		2	0.2456
		3	0.1580
		4	0.1047
	2	2	0.3605
		3	0.2359
5	1	1	0.4475
		2	0.2243
		3	0.1481
		4	0.1058
		5	0.0742
	2	2	0.3115
		3	0.2084
		4	0.1499
	3	3	0.2868
6	1	1	0.4159
		2	0.2085
		3	0.1394
		4	0.1024
		5	0.0774
		6	0.0563
	2	2	0.2796
		3	0.1890
		4	0.1397
		5	0.1059
	3	3	0.2462
		4	0.1833
7	1	1	0.3919
		2	0.1962
		3	0.1321
		4	0.0985
		5	0.0766
		6	0.0599
		7	0.0448
	2	2	0.2567
		3	0.1745
		4	0.1307
		5	0.1020
		6	0.0800

n	i	j	Value
7	3	3	0.2197
		4	0.1656
		5	0.1296
	4	4	0.2104
8	1	1	0.3729
		2	0.1863
		3	0.1260
		4	0.0947
		5	0.0748
		6	0.0602
		7	0.0483
		8	0.0368
	2	2	0.2394
		3	0.1632
		4	0.1233
		5	0.0976
		6	0.0787
		7	0.0632
	3	3	0.2008
		4	0.1524
		5	0.1210
		6	0.0978
	4	4	0.1872
		5	0.1492
9	1	1	0.3574
		2	0.1781
		3	0.1207
		4	0.0913
		5	0.0727
		6	0.0595
		7	0.0491
		8	0.0401
		9	0.0311
	2	2	0.2257
		3	0.1541
		4	0.1170
		5	0.0934
		6	0.0765
		7	0.0632
		8	0.0517
	3	3	0.1864
		4	0.1421
		5	0.1138
		6	0.0934
		7	0.0772
	4	4	0.1706

n	i	j	Value
9	4	5	0.1370
		6	0.1127
	5	5	0.1661
10	1	1	0.3443
		2	0.1713
		3	0.1163
		4	0.0882
		5	0.0707
		6	0.0584
		7	0.0489
		8	0.0411
		9	0.0340
		10	0.0267
	2	2	0.2145
		3	0.1466
		4	0.1117
		5	0.0897
		6	0.0742
		7	0.0622
		8	0.0523
		9	0.0434
	3	3	0.1750
		4	0.1338
		5	0.1077
		6	0.0892
		7	0.0749
		8	0.0630
	4	4	0.1579
		5	0.1275
		6	0.1058
		7	0.0889
	5	5	0.1511
		6	0.1256
11	1	1	0.3332
		2	0.1654
		3	0.1124
		4	0.0855
		5	0.0688
		6	0.0572
		7	0.0484
		8	0.0412
		9	0.0351
		10	0.0294
		11	0.0233
	2	2	0.2052
		3	0.1403

7.3

Variances and Covariances of Order Statistics in Samples
up to 20 from a Normal Population (*cont.*)

n	i	j	Value	n	i	j	Value	n	i	j	Value
11	2	4	0.1071	12	3	4	0.1212	13	3	6	0.0793
		5	0.0864			5	0.0983			7	0.0679
		6	0.0719			6	0.0822			8	0.0589
		7	0.0609			7	0.0701			9	0.0514
		8	0.0520			8	0.0604			10	0.0450
		9	0.0443			9	0.0523			11	0.0391
		10	0.0371			10	0.0450		4	4	0.1330
	3	3	0.1657		4	4	0.1398			5	0.1083
		4	0.1270			5	0.1136			6	0.0910
		5	0.1026			6	0.0952			7	0.0780
		6	0.0855			7	0.0812			8	0.0677
		7	0.0725			8	0.0701			9	0.0592
		8	0.0619			9	0.0607			10	0.0517
		9	0.0528		5	5	0.1306		5	5	0.1233
	4	4	0.1480			6	0.1096			6	0.1037
		5	0.1199			7	0.0937			7	0.0890
		6	0.1000			8	0.0809			8	0.0774
		7	0.0849		6	6	0.1266			9	0.0676
		8	0.0725			7	0.1084		6	6	0.1183
	5	5	0.1396	13	1	1	0.3152			7	0.1017
		6	0.1167			2	0.1557			8	0.0884
		7	0.0992			3	0.1059		7	7	0.1168
	6	6	0.1372			4	0.0809	14	1	1	0.3077
12	1	1	0.3236			5	0.0655			2	0.1517
		2	0.1602			6	0.0548			3	0.1032
		3	0.1089			7	0.0469			4	0.0789
		4	0.0831			8	0.0406			5	0.0640
		5	0.0671			9	0.0354			6	0.0537
		6	0.0560			10	0.0309			7	0.0461
		7	0.0477			11	0.0269			8	0.0401
		8	0.0410			12	0.0229			9	0.0352
		9	0.0354			13	0.0184			10	0.0310
		10	0.0305		2	2	0.1904			11	0.0273
		11	0.0258			3	0.1302			12	0.0239
		12	0.0206			4	0.0997			13	0.0205
	2	2	0.1973			5	0.0809			14	0.0166
		3	0.1349			6	0.0678		2	2	0.1844
		4	0.1032			7	0.0580			3	0.1261
		5	0.0835			8	0.0503			4	0.0967
		6	0.0698			9	0.0439			5	0.0785
		7	0.0595			10	0.0384			6	0.0660
		8	0.0512			11	0.0333			7	0.0567
		9	0.0443			12	0.0284			8	0.0494
		10	0.0381		3	3	0.1514			9	0.0434
		11	0.0323			4	0.1163			10	0.0382
	3	3	0.1580			5	0.0945			11	0.0337

Variances and Covariances of Order Statistics in Samples
up to 20 from a Normal Population (cont.)

n	i	j	Value	n	i	j	Value	n	i	j	Value
14	2	12	0.0295	15	1	15	0.0151	15	7	7	0.1027
		13	0.0253		2	2	0.1791			8	0.0900
	3	3	0.1457			3	0.1224			9	0.0797
		4	0.1120			4	0.0939		8	8	0.1017
		5	0.0911			5	0.0764	16	1	1	0.2950
		6	0.0767			6	0.0643			2	0.1449
		7	0.0659			7	0.0554			3	0.0985
		8	0.0574			8	0.0484			4	0.0754
		9	0.0505			9	0.0427			5	0.0613
		10	0.0445			10	0.0379			6	0.0517
		11	0.0392			11	0.0337			7	0.0446
		12	0.0343			12	0.0299			8	0.0390
	4	4	0.1272			13	0.0263			9	0.0345
		5	0.1037			14	0.0227			10	0.0308
		6	0.0874		3	3	0.1407			11	0.0275
		7	0.0752			4	0.1082			12	0.0246
		8	0.0655			5	0.0882			13	0.0220
		9	0.0576			6	0.0743			14	0.0195
		10	0.0508			7	0.0641			15	0.0169
		11	0.0448			8	0.0560			16	0.0138
	5	5	0.1171			9	0.0494		2	2	0.1744
		6	0.0988			10	0.0439			3	0.1191
		7	0.0851			11	0.0390			4	0.0914
		8	0.0742			12	0.0347			5	0.0745
		9	0.0653			13	0.0305			6	0.0628
		10	0.0576		4	4	0.1222			7	0.0542
	6	6	0.1115			5	0.0997			8	0.0475
		7	0.0961			6	0.0842			9	0.0421
		8	0.0840			7	0.0726			10	0.0375
		9	0.0739			8	0.0635			11	0.0336
	7	7	0.1090			9	0.0561			12	0.0300
		8	0.0953			10	0.0498			13	0.0268
15	1	1	0.3010			11	0.0443			14	0.0237
		2	0.1481			12	0.0394			15	0.0206
		3	0.1007		5	5	0.1119		3	3	0.1363
		4	0.0771			6	0.0945			4	0.1049
		5	0.0626			7	0.0816			5	0.0855
		6	0.0527			8	0.0714			6	0.0722
		7	0.0453			9	0.0631			7	0.0624
		8	0.0396			10	0.0561			8	0.0547
		9	0.0349			11	0.0499			9	0.0484
		10	0.0310		6	6	0.1059			10	0.0432
		11	0.0275			7	0.0915			11	0.0387
		12	0.0244			8	0.0801			12	0.0346
		13	0.0215			9	0.0709			13	0.0309
		14	0.0185			10	0.0630			14	0.0274

Variances and Covariances of Order Statistics in Samples up to 20 from a Normal Population (*cont.*)

n	i	j	Value	n	i	j	Value	n	i	j	Value
16	4	4	0.1179	17	1	17	0.0127	17	5	11	0.0478
		5	0.0963		2	2	0.1701			12	0.0431
		6	0.0813			3	0.1162			13	0.0388
		7	0.0703			4	0.0892		6	6	0.0969
		8	0.0617			5	0.0727			7	0.0840
		9	0.0547			6	0.0614			8	0.0739
		10	0.0488			7	0.0531			9	0.0657
		11	0.0437			8	0.0466			10	0.0589
		12	0.0391			9	0.0414			11	0.0530
		13	0.0349			10	0.0370			12	0.0478
	5	5	0.1074			11	0.0333		7	7	0.0929
		6	0.0908			12	0.0300			8	0.0818
		7	0.0785			13	0.0270			9	0.0728
		8	0.0689			14	0.0242			10	0.0653
		9	0.0611			15	0.0215			11	0.0588
		10	0.0546			16	0.0188		8	8	0.0907
		11	0.0489		3	3	0.1324			9	0.0808
		12	0.0438			4	0.1019			10	0.0725
	6	6	0.1010			5	0.0831		9	9	0.0900
		7	0.0875			6	0.0703	18	1	1	0.2845
		8	0.0768			7	0.0608			2	0.1393
		9	0.0682			8	0.0534			3	0.0946
		10	0.0609			9	0.0475			4	0.0725
		11	0.0545			10	0.0425			5	0.0590
	7	7	0.0974			11	0.0382			6	0.0499
		8	0.0856			12	0.0344			7	0.0431
		9	0.0760			13	0.0310			8	0.0379
		10	0.0679			14	0.0278			9	0.0337
	8	8	0.0957			15	0.0247			10	0.0303
		9	0.0850		4	4	0.1140			11	0.0273
17	1	1	0.2895			5	0.0932			12	0.0247
		2	0.1419			6	0.0788			13	0.0224
		3	0.0965			7	0.0682			14	0.0203
		4	0.0739			8	0.0600			15	0.0182
		5	0.0601			9	0.0533			16	0.0163
		6	0.0507			10	0.0477			17	0.0142
		7	0.0438			11	0.0429			18	0.0118
		8	0.0385			12	0.0387		2	2	0.1663
		9	0.0341			13	0.0349			3	0.1135
		10	0.0305			14	0.0313			4	0.0872
		11	0.0274		5	5	0.1034			5	0.0711
		12	0.0247			6	0.0876			6	0.0601
		13	0.0223			7	0.0759			7	0.0520
		14	0.0200			8	0.0667			8	0.0458
		15	0.0177			9	0.0593			9	0.0407
		16	0.0155			10	0.0531			10	0.0365

Variances and Covariances of Order Statistics in Samples up to 20 from a Normal Population (cont.)

n	i	j	Value	n	i	j	Value	n	i	j	Value
18	2	11	0.0330	18	6	9	0.0636	19	2	12	0.0296
		12	0.0298			10	0.0571			13	0.0270
		13	0.0270			11	0.0516			14	0.0246
		14	0.0245			12	0.0467			15	0.0223
		15	0.0221			13	0.0424			16	0.0202
		16	0.0197		7	7	0.0890			17	0.0181
		17	0.0172			8	0.0785			18	0.0159
	3	3	0.1289			9	0.0700		3	3	0.1257
		4	0.0992			10	0.0629			4	0.0967
		5	0.0810			11	0.0569			5	0.0790
		6	0.0685			12	0.0515			6	0.0669
		7	0.0594		8	8	0.0865			7	0.0580
		8	0.0522			9	0.0772			8	0.0512
		9	0.0465			10	0.0694			9	0.0456
		10	0.0417			11	0.0627			10	0.0410
		11	0.0377		9	9	0.0853			11	0.0371
		12	0.0341			10	0.0767			12	0.0337
		13	0.0309	19	1	1	0.2799			13	0.0307
		14	0.0280			2	0.1368			14	0.0280
		15	0.0252			3	0.0929			15	0.0254
		16	0.0225			4	0.0712			16	0.0230
	4	4	0.1106			5	0.0580			17	0.0206
		5	0.0904			6	0.0490		4	4	0.1075
		6	0.0766			7	0.0425			5	0.0879
		7	0.0664			8	0.0374			6	0.0745
		8	0.0584			9	0.0333			7	0.0646
		9	0.0520			10	0.0300			8	0.0570
		10	0.0467			11	0.0271			9	0.0509
		11	0.0422			12	0.0246			10	0.0458
		12	0.0382			13	0.0224			11	0.0414
		13	0.0346			14	0.0204			12	0.0376
		14	0.0313			15	0.0185			13	0.0343
		15	0.0283			16	0.0168			14	0.0312
	5	5	0.0999			17	0.0150			15	0.0284
		6	0.0847			18	0.0132			16	0.0257
		7	0.0734			19	0.0109		5	5	0.0968
		8	0.0647		2	2	0.1628			6	0.0821
		9	0.0577			3	0.1111			7	0.0713
		10	0.0518			4	0.0853			8	0.0629
		11	0.0467			5	0.0696			9	0.0561
		12	0.0423			6	0.0589			10	0.0505
		13	0.0384			7	0.0510			11	0.0457
		14	0.0348			8	0.0450			12	0.0416
	6	6	0.0932			9	0.0401			13	0.0379
		7	0.0809			10	0.0360			14	0.0345
		8	0.0713			11	0.0326			15	0.0314

Variances and Covariances of Order Statistics in Samples up to 20 from a Normal Population (cont.)

n	i	j	Value	n	i	j	Value	n	i	j	Value
19	6	6	0.0900	20	2	3	0.1088	20	4	17	0.0235
		7	0.0782			4	0.0836		5	5	0.0940
		8	0.0690			5	0.0682			6	0.0798
		9	0.0616			6	0.0578			7	0.0693
		10	0.0555			7	0.0501			8	0.0612
		11	0.0502			8	0.0442			9	0.0547
		12	0.0457			9	0.0395			10	0.0493
		13	0.0416			10	0.0356			11	0.0448
		14	0.0379			11	0.0322			12	0.0408
	7	7	0.0856			12	0.0294			13	0.0373
		8	0.0756			13	0.0268			14	0.0341
		9	0.0675			14	0.0245			15	0.0312
		10	0.0608			15	0.0225			16	0.0285
		11	0.0551			16	0.0205		6	6	0.0872
		12	0.0501			17	0.0186			7	0.0758
		13	0.0457			18	0.0167			8	0.0670
	8	8	0.0828			19	0.0147			9	0.0599
		9	0.0740		3	3	0.1228			10	0.0540
		10	0.0667			4	0.0945			11	0.0490
		11	0.0604			5	0.0772			12	0.0447
		12	0.0550			6	0.0655			13	0.0408
	9	9	0.0813			7	0.0568			14	0.0374
		10	0.0733			8	0.0501			15	0.0342
		11	0.0664			9	0.0448		7	7	0.0826
	10	10	0.0808			10	0.0403			8	0.0730
20	1	1	0.2757			11	0.0366			9	0.0653
		2	0.1345			12	0.0333			10	0.0589
		3	0.0913			13	0.0305			11	0.0535
		4	0.0700			14	0.0279			12	0.0488
		5	0.0571			15	0.0255			13	0.0446
		6	0.0483			16	0.0233			14	0.0408
		7	0.0418			17	0.0211		8	8	0.0796
		8	0.0369			18	0.0190			9	0.0713
		9	0.0329		4	4	0.1047			10	0.0643
		10	0.0297			5	0.0856			11	0.0584
		11	0.0269			6	0.0726			12	0.0533
		12	0.0245			7	0.0631			13	0.0487
		13	0.0224			8	0.0557		9	9	0.0778
		14	0.0205			9	0.0498			10	0.0703
		15	0.0187			10	0.0448			11	0.0638
		16	0.0171			11	0.0407			12	0.0582
		17	0.0155			12	0.0371		10	10	0.0769
		18	0.0139			13	0.0339			11	0.0699
		19	0.0123			14	0.0310				
		20	0.0102			15	0.0284				
	2	2	0.1596			16	0.0259				

8. MULTIVARIATE NORMAL AND t-DISTRIBUTIONS

8.1 Critical Values for the Circular Normal Distribution

The quantity tabulated is that value of B for which

$$P = \frac{1}{2\pi\sqrt{1-\rho^2}} \iint\limits_{U^2 \leq B^2} \exp\left(-U^2/2\right) \, dx \, dy,$$

where

$$U^2 = \frac{1}{1-\rho^2}\left\{\left(\frac{x-\mu_x}{\sigma_x}\right)^2 - 2\rho\left(\frac{x-\mu_x}{\sigma_x}\right)\left(\frac{y-\mu_y}{\sigma_y}\right) + \left(\frac{y-\mu_y}{\sigma_y}\right)^2\right\}.$$

This may be rewritten as

$$P = 1 - \exp\left(-B^2/2\right),$$

or

$$B = \sqrt{-2\log_e(1-P)}.$$

When $U^2 = B^2$ is a circle, i.e., when $\rho = 0$ and $\sigma_x = \sigma_y$, the distribution is called a circular normal distribution. The table derives its name from the fact that the majority of applications are to the circular normal case.

Critical Values for the Circular Normal Distribution

P	B	P	B	P	B
0.01	0.1418	0.46	1.1101	0.91	2.1945
0.02	0.2010	0.47	1.1268	0.92	2.2475
0.03	0.2468	0.48	1.1436	0.93	2.3062
0.04	0.2857	0.49	1.1605	0.94	2.3721
0.05	0.3203	0.50	1.1774	0.95	2.4477
0.06	0.3518	0.51	1.1944	0.96	2.5373
0.07	0.3810	0.52	1.2116	0.97	2.6482
0.08	0.4084	0.53	1.2288	0.98	2.7971
0.09	0.4343	0.54	1.2462	0.99	3.0349
0.10	0.4590	0.55	1.2637	0.991	3.0694
0.11	0.4828	0.56	1.2814	0.992	3.1075
0.12	0.5056	0.57	1.2992	0.993	3.1502
0.13	0.5278	0.58	1.3172	0.994	3.1987
0.14	0.5492	0.59	1.3354	0.995	3.2552
0.15	0.5701	0.60	1.3537	0.996	3.3231
0.16	0.5905	0.61	1.3723	0.997	3.4086
0.17	0.6105	0.62	1.3911	0.998	3.5255
0.18	0.6300	0.63	1.4101	0.999	3.7169
0.19	0.6492	0.64	1.4294	0.9991	3.7452
0.20	0.6680	0.65	1.4490	0.9992	3.7765
0.21	0.6866	0.66	1.4689	0.9993	3.8117
0.22	0.7049	0.67	1.4891	0.9994	3.8519
0.23	0.7230	0.68	1.5096	0.9995	3.8989
0.24	0.7409	0.69	1.5305	0.9996	3.9558
0.25	0.7585	0.70	1.5518	0.9997	4.0278
0.26	0.7760	0.71	1.5735	0.9998	4.1273
0.27	0.7934	0.72	1.5956	0.9999	4.2919
0.28	0.8106	0.73	1.6182	0.99995	4.4505
0.29	0.8276	0.74	1.6414	0.99999	4.7985
0.30	0.8446	0.75	1.6651	0.999995	4.9409
0.31	0.8615	0.76	1.6894	0.999999	5.2565
0.32	0.8783	0.77	1.7145	0.9999995	5.3868
0.33	0.8950	0.78	1.7402	0.9999999	5.6777
0.34	0.9116	0.79	1.7667	0.99999995	5.7985
0.35	0.9282	0.80	1.7941	0.99999999	6.0697
0.36	0.9448	0.81	1.8225	0.999999995	6.1829
0.37	0.9613	0.82	1.8519	0.999999999	6.4379
0.38	0.9778	0.83	1.8825		
0.39	0.9943	0.84	1.9145		
0.40	1.0108	0.85	1.9479		
0.41	1.0273	0.86	1.9830		
0.42	1.0438	0.87	2.0200		
0.43	1.0603	0.88	2.0593		
0.44	1.0769	0.89	2.1011		
0.45	1.0935	0.90	2.1460		

8.1

8.2 Offset Circle Probabilities for the Circular Normal Distribution

A circular normal distribution is defined as a bivariate normal distribution (see Section 8.5) with correlation zero and the two standard deviations equal to σ. The distribution will be centered at the origin, i.e., both means will be taken to be equal to zero. The probability of a random point falling outside an offset circle of radius r_d with center at $(D, 0)$ may be read from the tables. This is precisely the same as the probability of a random circle of radius r_d missing a point located at $(D, 0)$. Mathematically the quantity tabulated may be defined by

$$q\left(\frac{r_d}{\sigma}, \frac{D}{\sigma}\right) = 1 - p\left(\frac{r_d}{\sigma}, \frac{D}{\sigma}\right),$$

where

$$p\left(\frac{r_d}{\sigma}, \frac{D}{\sigma}\right) = \frac{1}{2\pi\sigma^2} \iint\limits_{(x-D)^2+y^2 \leq r_d^2} \exp\left[-\tfrac{1}{2}(x^2 + y^2)/\sigma^2\right] dx\, dy.$$

The quantity $p(r_d/\sigma, D)$ may be used to obtain the cumulative distribution function of the noncentral chi-square (see Section 3.4) with two degrees of freedom [206]. If λ is the noncentrality parameter for a random variable Z with the noncentral chi-square distribution with two degrees of freedom, then $\Pr\{Z \leq t\} = p(t, \sqrt{\lambda})$.

The quantity $p(r_d/\sigma, D/\sigma)$ is very often referred to as the circular coverage function. It or $q(r_d/\sigma, D/\sigma)$ has been tabulated extensively by Bell Aircraft Corporation [16], Marcum [132], Lowe [126], and others. It is considered implicitly by Oberg [154], Moranda [146], Chasen [31], and many others. A great deal of related work has been done, e.g., Gurland [81] and Daniels [39]. Ruben [187] has a series of papers along these lines.

The circular coverage function is related to the distribution of a quadratic form in two dimensions (see Section 8.3). Using the notation above and the notation of Section 8.3, let u_1, u_2 have a circular normal distribution with standard deviations equal to one; then

$$\Pr\{a_1 u_1^2 + a_2 u_2^2 \leq t\} = q(B, A) - q(A, B),$$

where

$$A = \tfrac{1}{2}[\sqrt{t/a_1} + \sqrt{t/a_2}] \quad \text{and} \quad B = \tfrac{1}{2}|\sqrt{t/a_1} - \sqrt{t/a_2}|,$$

and where the vertical bars on the formula for B indicate that the absolute value should be taken. For example, if $a_1 = 0.1$, $a_2 = 0.9$, and $t = 0.9$, then $A = 2$ and $B = 1$, or

$$\begin{aligned}
\Pr\{0.1 u_1^2 + 0.9 u_2^2 \leq 0.9\} &= q(1, 2) - q(2, 1) \\
&= 0.918 - 0.269 \\
&= 0.649,
\end{aligned}$$

which agrees with the result in Table 8.3.

Offset Circle Probabilities for the Circular Normal Distribution [178]

$(r_d - D)/\sigma$

D/σ	-2.0	-2.1	-2.2	-2.3	-2.4	-2.5	-2.6	-2.7	-2.8	-2.9	-3.0	-3.1	-3.2	-3.3	-3.4	-3.5	-3.6	-3.7	-3.8	-3.9
.0																				
.1																				
.2																				
.3																				
.4																				
.5																				
.6																				
.7																				
.8																				
.9																				
1.0																				
1.1																				
1.2																				
1.3																				
1.4																				
1.5																				
1.6																				
1.7																				
1.8																				
1.9																				
2.0	1.000																			
2.1	.999	1.000																		
2.2	.998	1.000	1.000																	
2.3	.997	.999	1.000	1.000																
2.4	.995	.997	.999	1.000	1.000															
2.5	.994	.996	.998	.999	1.000	1.000														
2.6	.993	.995	.997	.998	.999	1.000	1.000													
2.7	.992	.994	.996	.998	.999	.999	1.000	1.000												
2.8	.991	.993	.995	.997	.998	.999	.999	1.000	1.000											
2.9	.990	.993	.995	.997	.998	.999	.999	1.000	1.000	1.000										
3.0	.989	.992	.994	.996	.997	.998	.999	.999	1.000	1.000	1.000									
3.1	.989	.992	.994	.996	.997	.998	.999	.999	.999	1.000	1.000	1.000								
3.2	.988	.991	.993	.995	.997	.998	.999	.999	.999	1.000	1.000	1.000	1.000							
3.3	.988	.991	.993	.995	.996	.998	.998	.999	.999	1.000	1.000	1.000	1.000	1.000						
3.4	.987	.990	.993	.995	.996	.997	.998	.999	.999	.999	1.000	1.000	1.000	1.000	1.000					
3.5	.987	.990	.993	.995	.996	.997	.998	.999	.999	.999	1.000	1.000	1.000	1.000	1.000	1.000				
3.6	.986	.990	.992	.994	.996	.997	.998	.998	.999	.999	1.000	1.000	1.000	1.000	1.000	1.000	1.000			
3.7	.986	.989	.992	.994	.996	.997	.998	.998	.999	.999	1.000	1.000	1.000	1.000	1.000	1.000	1.000	1.000		
3.8	.986	.989	.992	.994	.996	.997	.998	.998	.999	.999	.999	1.000	1.000	1.000	1.000	1.000	1.000	1.000	1.000	
3.9	.986	.989	.992	.994	.995	.997	.998	.998	.999	.999	.999	1.000	1.000	1.000	1.000	1.000	1.000	1.000	1.000	1.000

8.2

Offset Circle Probabilities for the Circular Normal Distribution (*cont.*)

$(r_d - D)/\sigma$

D/σ	0	-.1	-.2	-.3	-.4	-.5	-.6	-.7	-.8	-.9	-1.0	-1.1	-1.2	-1.3	-1.4	-1.5	-1.6	-1.7	-1.8	-1.9
.0	1.000																			
.1	.995	1.000																		
.2	.981	.995	1.000																	
.3	.958	.981	.995	1.000																
.4	.929	.959	.982	.995	1.000															
.5	.896	.932	.961	.983	.996	1.000														
.6	.860	.901	.935	.963	.983	.996	1.000													
.7	.825	.868	.907	.939	.965	.984	.996	1.000												
.8	.791	.836	.877	.913	.943	.968	.986	.997	1.000											
.9	.760	.806	.848	.886	.920	.948	.970	.987	.997	1.000										
1.0	.733	.778	.821	.860	.902	.927	.952	.973	.988	.997	1.000									
1.1	.709	.754	.797	.836	.873	.905	.933	.957	.976	.989	.997	1.000								
1.2	.688	.733	.775	.815	.852	.885	.915	.940	.962	.978	.990	.998	1.000							
1.3	.671	.715	.756	.796	.833	.867	.897	.924	.947	.966	.981	.991	.998	1.000						
1.4	.656	.699	.741	.780	.816	.850	.881	.909	.933	.953	.970	.983	.992	.998	1.000					
1.5	.644	.686	.727	.766	.802	.836	.867	.895	.920	.941	.959	.974	.985	.993	.998	1.000				
1.6	.633	.675	.716	.754	.790	.824	.855	.883	.908	.930	.949	.965	.978	.987	.994	.999	1.000			
1.7	.624	.666	.706	.744	.780	.814	.845	.873	.898	.920	.940	.956	.970	.981	.989	.995	.999	1.000		
1.8	.616	.658	.697	.736	.771	.805	.836	.864	.889	.912	.931	.948	.963	.974	.984	.991	.996	.999	1.000	
1.9	.610	.651	.690	.728	.764	.797	.828	.856	.882	.904	.924	.941	.956	.968	.978	.986	.992	.997	.999	1.000
2.0	.604	.644	.684	.722	.757	.791	.822	.850	.875	.898	.918	.936	.950	.963	.974	.982	.989	.994	.997	.999
2.1	.598	.639	.678	.716	.752	.785	.816	.844	.870	.893	.913	.930	.946	.959	.969	.978	.985	.991	.995	.998
2.2	.593	.634	.673	.711	.747	.780	.811	.839	.865	.888	.908	.926	.941	.955	.966	.975	.982	.988	.992	.996
2.3	.589	.630	.669	.706	.742	.776	.807	.835	.861	.884	.904	.922	.938	.951	.962	.972	.979	.985	.990	.994
2.4	.585	.626	.665	.702	.738	.771	.803	.831	.857	.880	.901	.919	.935	.948	.960	.969	.977	.983	.988	.992
2.5	.582	.622	.661	.699	.734	.768	.799	.828	.854	.877	.898	.916	.932	.946	.957	.967	.975	.981	.986	.991
2.6	.578	.619	.658	.695	.731	.765	.796	.825	.851	.874	.895	.914	.930	.943	.955	.965	.973	.980	.985	.989
2.7	.575	.615	.655	.692	.728	.762	.793	.822	.848	.872	.893	.911	.928	.941	.953	.963	.971	.978	.984	.988
2.8	.572	.613	.652	.689	.725	.759	.790	.819	.846	.869	.891	.909	.926	.940	.952	.962	.970	.977	.983	.987
2.9	.570	.610	.649	.687	.722	.756	.788	.817	.843	.867	.889	.907	.924	.938	.950	.960	.969	.976	.982	.986
3.0	.567	.608	.647	.684	.720	.754	.785	.815	.841	.865	.887	.906	.922	.937	.949	.959	.968	.975	.981	.985
3.1	.565	.605	.644	.682	.718	.752	.783	.813	.839	.863	.885	.904	.921	.935	.948	.958	.967	.974	.980	.985
3.2	.563	.603	.642	.680	.716	.750	.781	.811	.837	.862	.883	.903	.920	.934	.947	.957	.966	.973	.979	.984
3.3	.561	.601	.640	.678	.714	.748	.780	.809	.836	.860	.882	.901	.918	.933	.946	.956	.965	.973	.979	.984
3.4	.559	.599	.638	.676	.712	.746	.778	.807	.834	.859	.881	.900	.917	.932	.945	.955	.964	.972	.978	.983
3.5	.558	.598	.637	.674	.710	.744	.776	.806	.833	.857	.879	.899	.916	.931	.944	.955	.964	.971	.978	.983
3.6	.556	.596	.635	.673	.709	.743	.775	.804	.831	.856	.878	.898	.915	.930	.943	.954	.963	.971	.977	.982
3.7	.554	.594	.633	.671	.707	.741	.773	.803	.830	.855	.877	.897	.914	.929	.942	.953	.963	.970	.977	.982
3.8	.553	.593	.632	.670	.706	.740	.772	.802	.829	.854	.876	.896	.913	.928	.941	.953	.962	.970	.976	.982
3.9	.552	.591	.631	.668	.704	.739	.771	.800	.828	.853	.875	.895	.912	.928	.941	.952	.962	.969	.976	.981

8.2

Offset Circle Probabilities for the Circular Normal Distribution (cont.)

$(r_d - D)/\sigma$

b/D	2.0	1.9	1.8	1.7	1.6	1.5	1.4	1.3	1.2	1.1	1.0	.9	.8	.7	.6	.5	.4	.3	.2	.1
.0	.135	.164	.198	.236	.278	.325	.375	.430	.487	.546	.607	.667	.726	.783	.835	.882	.923	.956	.980	.995
.1	.111	.137	.166	.200	.237	.280	.326	.377	.431	.489	.548	.608	.668	.727	.784	.836	.883	.923	.956	.980
.2	.111	.115	.141	.170	.204	.243	.285	.332	.383	.437	.494	.553	.613	.672	.731	.787	.838	.885	.925	.957
.3	.093	.099	.121	.148	.178	.212	.251	.294	.341	.392	.446	.502	.561	.620	.679	.736	.791	.842	.887	.926
.4	.069	.086	.106	.130	.157	.188	.223	.263	.306	.353	.404	.458	.514	.572	.630	.688	.744	.798	.847	.891
.5	.062	.077	.095	.116	.141	.169	.201	.237	.278	.322	.369	.420	.473	.529	.586	.643	.699	.754	.805	.853
.6	.056	.070	.086	.106	.128	.154	.184	.217	.255	.296	.340	.388	.439	.492	.546	.602	.658	.712	.765	.815
.7	.052	.064	.080	.098	.119	.143	.170	.201	.236	.274	.316	.361	.409	.460	.512	.566	.620	.674	.727	.778
.8	.048	.060	.075	.091	.111	.134	.160	.189	.221	.258	.297	.340	.385	.434	.484	.536	.588	.641	.693	.743
.9	.046	.057	.071	.087	.105	.127	.151	.179	.210	.244	.282	.322	.366	.412	.460	.510	.560	.612	.663	.712
1.0	.044	.055	.067	.083	.100	.121	.144	.171	.200	.233	.269	.308	.350	.394	.440	.488	.537	.587	.636	.685
1.1	.042	.052	.065	.079	.096	.116	.139	.164	.193	.224	.258	.296	.336	.379	.424	.470	.518	.566	.614	.663
1.2	.041	.051	.063	.077	.093	.112	.134	.159	.186	.217	.250	.287	.326	.367	.410	.455	.502	.549	.596	.642
1.3	.039	.049	.061	.075	.091	.109	.130	.154	.181	.211	.243	.279	.316	.357	.399	.443	.488	.534	.580	.626
1.4	.038	.048	.059	.073	.088	.106	.127	.150	.176	.205	.237	.272	.309	.348	.390	.433	.477	.522	.567	.612
1.5	.037	.047	.058	.071	.086	.104	.124	.147	.173	.201	.232	.266	.302	.341	.381	.424	.467	.511	.556	.600
1.6	.037	.046	.057	.069	.084	.102	.122	.144	.169	.197	.228	.261	.297	.335	.375	.416	.459	.502	.546	.590
1.7	.036	.045	.055	.068	.083	.100	.119	.141	.166	.194	.224	.256	.292	.329	.369	.410	.452	.495	.538	.581
1.8	.035	.043	.055	.067	.081	.098	.117	.139	.163	.191	.221	.253	.287	.324	.363	.404	.446	.488	.531	.574
1.9	.035	.043	.054	.066	.080	.097	.116	.137	.161	.188	.218	.249	.283	.319	.359	.399	.440	.482	.525	.567
2.0	.034	.043	.053	.065	.079	.095	.114	.135	.159	.185	.214	.246	.280	.316	.354	.394	.435	.477	.519	.562
2.1	.034	.042	.052	.064	.078	.094	.112	.133	.157	.183	.212	.243	.277	.313	.351	.390	.431	.472	.514	.557
2.2	.033	.041	.051	.063	.077	.093	.111	.132	.155	.181	.210	.241	.274	.310	.347	.386	.427	.468	.510	.552
2.3	.033	.041	.051	.062	.076	.092	.110	.130	.154	.179	.207	.238	.271	.307	.344	.383	.423	.464	.506	.548
2.4	.032	.040	.050	.062	.075	.091	.109	.129	.152	.177	.205	.236	.269	.304	.341	.380	.420	.461	.502	.544
2.5	.032	.040	.050	.061	.075	.090	.108	.128	.151	.176	.204	.234	.267	.302	.338	.377	.417	.458	.499	.540
2.6	.032	.040	.049	.061	.074	.089	.107	.127	.149	.174	.202	.232	.265	.299	.336	.374	.414	.455	.496	.537
2.7	.031	.039	.049	.060	.073	.088	.105	.126	.148	.173	.201	.230	.263	.297	.334	.372	.412	.452	.493	.534
2.8	.031	.039	.048	.060	.073	.088	.105	.125	.148	.172	.199	.229	.261	.295	.332	.370	.409	.450	.490	.532
2.9	.031	.039	.048	.059	.072	.087	.104	.124	.146	.171	.198	.227	.259	.294	.330	.368	.407	.447	.488	.529
3.0	.031	.038	.048	.059	.071	.086	.104	.123	.145	.170	.197	.226	.258	.292	.328	.366	.405	.445	.486	.527
3.1	.030	.038	.047	.058	.071	.086	.103	.122	.144	.168	.195	.225	.256	.290	.326	.364	.403	.443	.484	.525
3.2	.030	.038	.047	.058	.070	.085	.102	.121	.143	.168	.194	.223	.255	.289	.325	.362	.401	.441	.482	.522
3.3	.030	.038	.047	.057	.070	.085	.102	.121	.142	.167	.193	.222	.254	.287	.323	.361	.399	.439	.480	.521
3.4	.030	.037	.046	.057	.070	.084	.101	.120	.142	.166	.192	.221	.253	.286	.322	.359	.398	.438	.478	.519
3.5	.030	.037	.046	.057	.069	.084	.101	.120	.141	.165	.191	.220	.251	.285	.320	.358	.396	.436	.476	.517
3.6	.029	.037	.046	.056	.069	.083	.100	.119	.140	.164	.190	.219	.250	.284	.319	.356	.395	.434	.475	.515
3.7	.029	.037	.046	.056	.069	.083	.100	.118	.140	.163	.190	.218	.249	.283	.318	.355	.393	.433	.473	.514
3.8	.029	.037	.045	.056	.068	.083	.099	.118	.139	.163	.189	.217	.248	.282	.317	.354	.392	.432	.472	.513
3.9	.029	.036	.045	.056	.068	.082	.099	.117	.138	.162	.188	.217	.248	.281	.316	.353	.391	.430	.471	.511

8.2

Offset Circle Probabilities for the Circular Normal Distribution (cont.)

Column headers are D/σ (0.0 – 3.9); row labels are $(r_d - D)/\sigma$ (2.1 – 4.0).

$(r_d-D)/\sigma$ \ D/σ	0.0	0.1	0.2	0.3	0.4	0.5	0.6	0.7	0.8	0.9	1.0	1.1	1.2	1.3	1.4	1.5	1.6	1.7	1.8	1.9	2.0	2.1	2.2	2.3	2.4	2.5	2.6	2.7	2.8	2.9	3.0	3.1	3.2	3.3	3.4	3.5	3.6	3.7	3.8	3.9
2.1	.110	.090	.075	.063	.055	.049	.044	.041	.038	.036	.035	.033	.032	.031	.030	.030	.029	.028	.028	.027	.027	.027	.026	.026	.026	.025	.025	.025	.025	.024	.024	.024	.024	.024	.024	.023	.023	.023	.023	.023
2.2	.089	.072	.059	.050	.044	.039	.035	.032	.030	.029	.027	.026	.025	.025	.024	.023	.023	.022	.022	.022	.021	.021	.021	.020	.020	.020	.020	.020	.019	.019	.019	.019	.019	.019	.019	.018	.018	.018	.018	.018
2.3	.071	.057	.047	.039	.034	.030	.027	.025	.024	.022	.021	.020	.020	.019	.019	.018	.018	.017	.017	.017	.017	.016	.016	.016	.016	.015	.015	.015	.015	.015	.015	.015	.015	.014	.014	.014	.014	.014	.014	.014
2.4	.056	.045	.036	.030	.026	.023	.021	.019	.018	.017	.016	.016	.015	.015	.014	.014	.013	.013	.013	.012	.012	.012	.012	.012	.012	.011	.011	.011	.011	.011	.011	.011	.011	.011	.011	.011	.011	.011	.011	.011
2.5	.044	.035	.028	.023	.020	.018	.016	.015	.014	.013	.013	.012	.012	.011	.011	.010	.010	.010	.009	.009	.009	.009	.009	.009	.009	.009	.009	.009	.009	.008	.008	.008	.008	.008	.008	.008	.008	.008	.008	.008
2.6	.034	.027	.021	.018	.015	.014	.012	.011	.011	.010	.010	.009	.009	.009	.008	.008	.008	.008	.008	.008	.007	.007	.007	.007	.007	.007	.007	.007	.007	.006	.006	.006	.006	.006	.006	.006	.006	.006	.006	.006
2.7	.026	.020	.016	.013	.012	.010	.009	.009	.008	.008	.007	.007	.007	.006	.006	.006	.006	.006	.006	.006	.005	.005	.005	.005	.005	.005	.005	.005	.005	.005	.005	.005	.005	.005	.005	.005	.005	.005	.005	.005
2.8	.020	.015	.012	.010	.009	.008	.007	.006	.006	.006	.005	.005	.005	.005	.005	.005	.004	.004	.004	.004	.004	.004	.004	.004	.004	.004	.004	.004	.004	.004	.004	.004	.004	.004	.004	.004	.004	.003	.003	.003
2.9	.015	.011	.009	.007	.006	.006	.005	.005	.004	.004	.004	.004	.004	.004	.003	.003	.003	.003	.003	.003	.003	.003	.003	.003	.003	.003	.003	.003	.003	.003	.003	.003	.003	.003	.003	.003	.003	.003	.003	.003
3.0	.011	.008	.007	.005	.005	.004	.004	.003	.003	.003	.003	.003	.003	.003	.003	.002	.002	.002	.002	.002	.002	.002	.002	.002	.002	.002	.002	.002	.002	.002	.002	.002	.002	.002	.002	.002	.002	.002	.002	.002
3.1	.008	.006	.005	.004	.003	.003	.003	.002	.002	.002	.002	.002	.002	.002	.002	.002	.002	.002	.002	.002	.002	.002	.002	.001	.001	.001	.001	.001	.001	.001	.001	.001	.001	.001	.001	.001	.001	.001	.001	.001
3.2	.006	.004	.003	.003	.002	.002	.002	.002	.002	.002	.001	.001	.001	.001	.001	.001	.001	.001	.001	.001	.001	.001	.001	.001	.001	.001	.001	.001	.001	.001	.001	.001	.001	.001	.001	.001	.001	.001	.001	.001
3.3	.004	.003	.002	.002	.002	.002	.001	.001	.001	.001	.001	.001	.001	.001	.001	.001	.001	.001	.001	.001	.001	.001	.001	.001	.001	.001	.001	.001	.001	.001	.001	.001	.001	.001	.001	.001	.001	.001	.001	.001
3.4	.003	.002	.002	.001	.001	.001	.001	.001	.001	.001	.001	.001	.001	.001	.001	.001	.001	.001	.001	.001	.001	.001	.001	.001	.001	.001	.001	.001	.001	.001	.001	.001	.001	.001	.001	.001	.001	.001	.001	.001
3.5	.002	.002	.001	.001	.001	.001	.001	.001	.001	.001	.000	.000	.000	.000	.000	.000	.000	.000	.000	.000	.000	.000	.000	.000	.000	.000	.000	.000	.000	.000	.000	.000	.000	.000	.000	.000	.000	.000	.000	.000
3.6	.002	.001	.001	.001	.001	.001	.000	.000	.000	.000	.000	.000	.000	.000	.000	.000	.000	.000	.000	.000	.000	.000	.000	.000	.000	.000	.000	.000	.000	.000	.000	.000	.000	.000	.000	.000	.000	.000	.000	.000
3.7	.001	.001	.001	.000	.000	.000	.000	.000	.000	.000	.000	.000	.000	.000	.000	.000	.000	.000	.000	.000	.000	.000	.000	.000	.000	.000	.000	.000	.000	.000	.000	.000	.000	.000	.000	.000	.000	.000	.000	.000
3.8	.001	.001	.000	.000	.000	.000	.000	.000	.000	.000	.000	.000	.000	.000	.000	.000	.000	.000	.000	.000	.000	.000	.000	.000	.000	.000	.000	.000	.000	.000	.000	.000	.000	.000	.000	.000	.000	.000	.000	.000
3.9	.000	.000	.000	.000	.000	.000	.000	.000	.000	.000	.000	.000	.000	.000	.000	.000	.000	.000	.000	.000	.000	.000	.000	.000	.000	.000	.000	.000	.000	.000	.000	.000	.000	.000	.000	.000	.000	.000	.000	.000
4.0	.000	.000	.000	.000	.000	.000	.000	.000	.000	.000	.000	.000	.000	.000	.000	.000	.000	.000	.000	.000	.000	.000	.000	.000	.000	.000	.000	.000	.000	.000	.000	.000	.000	.000	.000	.000	.000	.000	.000	.000

8.2

Offset Circle Probabilities for the Circular Normal Distribution (cont.)

d/σ	-2.0	-2.1	-2.2	-2.3	-2.4	-2.5	-2.6	-2.7	-2.8	2.9	-3.0	-3.1	-3.2	-3.3	-3.4	-3.5	-3.6	-3.7	-3.8	-3.9
4.0	.985	.989	.991	.994	.995	.997	.998	.998	.999	.999	.999	1.000	1.000	1.000	1.000	1.000	1.000	1.000	1.000	1.000
4.1	.985	.989	.991	.993	.995	.996	.997	.998	.999	.999	.999	1.000	1.000	1.000	1.000	1.000	1.000	1.000	1.000	1.000
4.2	.985	.988	.991	.993	.995	.996	.997	.998	.999	.999	.999	1.000	1.000	1.000	1.000	1.000	1.000	1.000	1.000	1.000
4.3	.985	.988	.991	.993	.995	.996	.997	.998	.999	.999	.999	1.000	1.000	1.000	1.000	1.000	1.000	1.000	1.000	1.000
4.4	.984	.988	.991	.993	.995	.996	.997	.998	.999	.999	.999	1.000	1.000	1.000	1.000	1.000	1.000	1.000	1.000	1.000
4.5	.984	.988	.991	.993	.995	.996	.997	.998	.999	.999	.999	.999	1.000	1.000	1.000	1.000	1.000	1.000	1.000	1.000
4.6	.984	.988	.991	.993	.995	.996	.997	.998	.999	.999	.999	.999	1.000	1.000	1.000	1.000	1.000	1.000	1.000	1.000
4.7	.984	.988	.990	.993	.995	.996	.997	.998	.998	.999	.999	.999	1.000	1.000	1.000	1.000	1.000	1.000	1.000	1.000
4.8	.984	.987	.990	.993	.995	.996	.997	.998	.998	.999	.999	.999	1.000	1.000	1.000	1.000	1.000	1.000	1.000	1.000
4.9	.984	.987	.990	.993	.994	.996	.997	.998	.998	.999	.999	.999	1.000	1.000	1.000	1.000	1.000	1.000	1.000	1.000
5.0	.983	.987	.990	.992	.994	.996	.997	.998	.998	.999	.999	.999	1.000	1.000	1.000	1.000	1.000	1.000	1.000	1.000
5.1	.983	.987	.990	.992	.994	.996	.997	.998	.998	.999	.999	.999	1.000	1.000	1.000	1.000	1.000	1.000	1.000	1.000
5.2	.983	.987	.990	.992	.994	.996	.997	.997	.998	.999	.999	.999	.999	1.000	1.000	1.000	1.000	1.000	1.000	1.000
5.3	.983	.987	.990	.992	.994	.996	.997	.997	.998	.999	.999	.999	.999	1.000	1.000	1.000	1.000	1.000	1.000	1.000
5.4	.983	.987	.989	.992	.994	.995	.997	.997	.998	.999	.999	.999	.999	1.000	1.000	1.000	1.000	1.000	1.000	1.000
5.5	.983	.987	.990	.992	.994	.996	.997	.998	.998	.999	.999	.999	.999	1.000	1.000	1.000	1.000	1.000	1.000	1.000
5.6	.983	.986	.990	.992	.994	.996	.997	.998	.998	.999	.999	.999	.999	1.000	1.000	1.000	1.000	1.000	1.000	1.000
5.7	.983	.986	.990	.992	.994	.996	.997	.998	.998	.999	.999	.999	.999	1.000	1.000	1.000	1.000	1.000	1.000	1.000
5.8	.982	.986	.990	.992	.994	.996	.997	.998	.998	.999	.999	.999	.999	1.000	1.000	1.000	1.000	1.000	1.000	1.000
5.9	.982	.986	.989	.992	.994	.995	.996	.997	.998	.998	.999	.999	.999	1.000	1.000	1.000	1.000	1.000	1.000	1.000
6.0	.982	.986	.989	.992	.994	.996	.997	.997	.998	.999	.999	.999	.999	1.000	1.000	1.000	1.000	1.000	1.000	1.000
6.5	.982	.986	.989	.991	.994	.996	.996	.997	.998	.998	.999	.999	.999	.999	1.000	1.000	1.000	1.000	1.000	1.000
7.0	.981	.985	.989	.991	.993	.995	.996	.997	.998	.998	.999	.999	.999	.999	1.000	1.000	1.000	1.000	1.000	1.000
7.5	.981	.985	.989	.991	.993	.995	.996	.997	.998	.998	.999	.999	.999	.999	1.000	1.000	1.000	1.000	1.000	1.000
8.0	.981	.985	.988	.991	.993	.995	.996	.997	.998	.998	.999	.999	.999	.999	1.000	1.000	1.000	1.000	1.000	1.000
8.5	.981	.985	.988	.991	.993	.995	.996	.997	.998	.998	.999	.999	.999	.999	1.000	1.000	1.000	1.000	1.000	1.000
9.0	.980	.984	.988	.990	.992	.994	.996	.997	.998	.998	.999	.999	.999	.999	1.000	1.000	1.000	1.000	1.000	1.000
9.5	.980	.984	.987	.990	.992	.994	.996	.997	.998	.998	.999	.999	.999	.999	1.000	1.000	1.000	1.000	1.000	1.000
10.0	.980	.984	.987	.990	.992	.994	.996	.997	.998	.998	.999	.999	.999	.999	1.000	1.000	1.000	1.000	1.000	1.000
11.0	.980	.984	.987	.990	.992	.994	.996	.997	.998	.998	.999	.999	.999	.999	1.000	1.000	1.000	1.000	1.000	1.000
12.0	.980	.984	.988	.990	.992	.994	.996	.997	.998	.998	.999	.999	.999	.999	1.000	1.000	1.000	1.000	1.000	1.000
13.0	.979	.984	.987	.990	.992	.994	.996	.997	.998	.998	.999	.999	.999	.999	1.000	1.000	1.000	1.000	1.000	1.000
14.0	.979	.983	.987	.990	.992	.994	.996	.997	.998	.998	.999	.999	.999	.999	1.000	1.000	1.000	1.000	1.000	1.000
15.0	.979	.983	.987	.990	.992	.994	.996	.997	.998	.998	.999	.999	.999	.999	1.000	1.000	1.000	1.000	1.000	1.000
16.0	.979	.983	.987	.990	.992	.994	.996	.997	.998	.998	.999	.999	.999	.999	1.000	1.000	1.000	1.000	1.000	1.000
17.0	.979	.983	.987	.990	.992	.994	.996	.997	.998	.998	.999	.999	.999	.999	1.000	1.000	1.000	1.000	1.000	1.000
18.0	.979	.983	.987	.990	.992	.994	.996	.997	.998	.998	.999	.999	.999	.999	1.000	1.000	1.000	1.000	1.000	1.000
19.0	.979	.983	.987	.990	.992	.994	.996	.997	.998	.998	.999	.999	.999	.999	1.000	1.000	1.000	1.000	1.000	1.000
20.0	.979	.982	.987	.990	.992	.994	.996	.997	.998	.998	.999	.999	.999	.999	1.000	1.000	1.000	1.000	1.000	1.000
∞	.977	.982	.986	.989	.992	.994	.995	.997	.997	.998	.999	.999	.999	1.000	1.000	1.000	1.000	1.000	1.000	1.000

8.2

Offset Circle Probabilities for the Circular Normal Distribution (*cont.*)

$(r_d - D)/\sigma$

D/σ	0	-.1	-.2	-.3	-.4	-.5	-.6	-.7	-.8	-.9	-1.0	-1.1	-1.2	-1.3	-1.4	-1.5	-1.6	-1.7	-1.8	-1.9
4.0	.550	.590	.629	.667	.703	.737	.769	.799	.827	.852	.874	.894	.912	.927	.940	.952	.961	.969	.976	.981
4.1	.549	.589	.628	.666	.702	.736	.768	.798	.826	.851	.873	.893	.911	.926	.940	.951	.961	.969	.975	.981
4.2	.548	.588	.627	.665	.701	.735	.767	.797	.825	.850	.872	.893	.910	.926	.939	.950	.960	.968	.975	.980
4.3	.547	.587	.626	.663	.700	.734	.766	.796	.824	.849	.872	.892	.910	.925	.939	.950	.960	.968	.975	.980
4.4	.546	.586	.625	.662	.699	.733	.765	.795	.823	.848	.871	.891	.909	.925	.938	.950	.959	.968	.974	.980
4.5	.545	.584	.623	.661	.698	.732	.764	.794	.822	.847	.870	.890	.908	.924	.938	.949	.959	.967	.974	.980
4.6	.544	.583	.623	.660	.697	.731	.763	.794	.821	.847	.869	.890	.908	.924	.937	.949	.958	.967	.974	.979
4.7	.543	.583	.622	.659	.696	.730	.763	.793	.821	.846	.869	.889	.907	.923	.937	.948	.958	.967	.974	.979
4.8	.542	.582	.621	.659	.695	.729	.762	.792	.820	.845	.868	.889	.907	.923	.936	.948	.958	.966	.973	.979
4.9	.541	.581	.620	.658	.694	.729	.761	.791	.819	.845	.868	.888	.906	.922	.936	.948	.958	.966	.973	.977
5.0	.540	.580	.619	.657	.693	.728	.760	.791	.819	.844	.867	.888	.906	.922	.936	.947	.957	.966	.973	.979
5.1	.539	.579	.618	.656	.692	.727	.760	.790	.818	.843	.867	.887	.905	.921	.935	.947	.957	.966	.973	.979
5.2	.539	.578	.617	.655	.691	.726	.759	.789	.817	.843	.866	.887	.905	.921	.935	.947	.957	.965	.973	.978
5.3	.538	.578	.617	.655	.691	.726	.758	.789	.817	.842	.865	.886	.905	.921	.935	.947	.957	.965	.972	.978
5.4	.537	.577	.616	.654	.690	.725	.758	.788	.816	.842	.865	.886	.904	.920	.934	.946	.956	.965	.972	.977
5.5	.536	.576	.615	.653	.690	.724	.757	.788	.816	.841	.865	.885	.904	.920	.934	.946	.956	.965	.972	.978
5.6	.536	.576	.615	.653	.689	.724	.756	.787	.815	.841	.864	.885	.903	.920	.934	.946	.956	.965	.972	.978
5.7	.535	.575	.614	.652	.688	.723	.756	.786	.815	.840	.864	.885	.903	.919	.933	.945	.956	.964	.972	.978
5.8	.535	.574	.613	.651	.688	.723	.755	.786	.814	.840	.863	.884	.903	.919	.933	.945	.956	.964	.972	.978
5.9	.534	.574	.613	.651	.687	.722	.755	.785	.814	.840	.863	.884	.902	.919	.933	.945	.955	.964	.971	.977
6.0	.533	.573	.612	.650	.687	.722	.754	.785	.813	.839	.863	.883	.902	.918	.933	.945	.955	.964	.971	.977
6.5	.531	.571	.610	.648	.684	.719	.752	.783	.811	.837	.861	.882	.901	.917	.932	.944	.954	.963	.971	.977
7.0	.529	.568	.607	.646	.682	.717	.750	.781	.810	.836	.859	.881	.899	.916	.931	.943	.954	.963	.970	.976
7.5	.527	.566	.606	.644	.680	.715	.748	.779	.808	.834	.858	.879	.898	.915	.930	.942	.953	.962	.970	.976
8.0	.525	.565	.604	.642	.679	.714	.747	.778	.807	.833	.857	.878	.898	.914	.929	.942	.953	.961	.969	.976
8.5	.524	.563	.602	.641	.677	.713	.746	.777	.806	.832	.856	.878	.897	.914	.928	.941	.952	.961	.969	.975
9.0	.522	.562	.601	.639	.676	.711	.744	.776	.805	.831	.855	.877	.896	.913	.928	.941	.952	.961	.969	.975
9.5	.521	.561	.600	.638	.675	.710	.744	.775	.804	.830	.854	.876	.896	.913	.927	.940	.951	.961	.968	.975
10.0	.520	.560	.599	.637	.674	.709	.743	.774	.803	.830	.854	.876	.895	.912	.927	.940	.951	.960	.968	.975
11.0	.518	.558	.597	.635	.672	.708	.741	.772	.802	.828	.853	.875	.894	.911	.926	.939	.950	.960	.968	.974
12.0	.517	.556	.596	.634	.671	.706	.740	.771	.800	.827	.852	.874	.893	.911	.926	.939	.950	.960	.967	.974
13.0	.515	.555	.594	.633	.670	.705	.739	.770	.799	.826	.851	.873	.893	.910	.925	.938	.950	.959	.967	.974
14.0	.514	.554	.593	.632	.669	.704	.738	.769	.799	.826	.850	.872	.892	.909	.925	.938	.949	.959	.967	.974
15.0	.513	.553	.592	.631	.668	.703	.737	.769	.798	.825	.850	.872	.892	.909	.924	.938	.949	.959	.967	.974
16.0	.512	.552	.592	.630	.667	.703	.736	.768	.797	.824	.849	.871	.891	.909	.924	.937	.949	.958	.967	.973
17.0	.512	.552	.591	.629	.666	.702	.736	.767	.797	.824	.849	.871	.891	.908	.924	.937	.949	.958	.966	.973
18.0	.511	.551	.590	.629	.666	.701	.735	.767	.796	.823	.848	.870	.890	.908	.923	.937	.948	.958	.966	.973
19.0	.511	.550	.590	.628	.665	.701	.735	.766	.796	.823	.848	.870	.890	.908	.923	.937	.948	.958	.966	.973
20.0	.510	.550	.589	.627	.665	.700	.734	.766	.795	.823	.847	.870	.890	.908	.923	.936	.948	.958	.966	.973
∞	.500	.540	.579	.618	.655	.691	.726	.758	.788	.816	.841	.864	.885	.903	.919	.933	.945	.955	.964	.971

D/σ

Offset Circle Probabilities for the Circular Normal Distribution (*cont.*)

	.1	.2	.3	.4	.5	.6	.7	.8	.9	1.0	1.1	1.2	1.3	1.4	1.5	1.6	1.7	1.8	1.9	2.0
4.0	.510	.469	.429	.390	.352	.315	.280	.247	.216	.187	.161	.138	.117	.098	.082	.068	.055	.045	.036	.029
4.1	.509	.468	.428	.389	.351	.314	.279	.246	.215	.187	.161	.137	.116	.098	.081	.067	.055	.045	.036	.029
4.2	.507	.467	.427	.388	.350	.313	.278	.245	.214	.186	.160	.137	.116	.097	.081	.067	.055	.045	.036	.029
4.3	.506	.466	.426	.387	.349	.312	.277	.244	.214	.185	.160	.136	.116	.097	.081	.067	.054	.044	.036	.028
4.4	.505	.465	.425	.386	.348	.311	.276	.244	.213	.185	.159	.136	.115	.097	.081	.066	.054	.044	.036	.028
4.5	.504	.464	.424	.385	.347	.310	.276	.243	.212	.184	.159	.135	.115	.096	.080	.066	.054	.044	.035	.028
4.6	.503	.463	.423	.384	.346	.310	.275	.242	.212	.184	.158	.135	.114	.096	.080	.066	.054	.044	.035	.028
4.7	.502	.462	.422	.383	.345	.309	.274	.242	.211	.183	.158	.135	.114	.096	.080	.066	.054	.044	.035	.028
4.8	.502	.461	.421	.382	.344	.308	.274	.241	.211	.183	.157	.134	.114	.095	.079	.065	.053	.043	.035	.028
4.9	.501	.460	.421	.382	.344	.307	.273	.240	.210	.182	.157	.134	.113	.095	.079	.065	.053	.043	.035	.028
5.0	.500	.460	.420	.381	.343	.307	.272	.240	.210	.182	.156	.134	.113	.095	.079	.065	.053	.043	.035	.028
5.1	.499	.459	.419	.380	.342	.306	.272	.239	.209	.181	.156	.133	.113	.095	.079	.065	.053	.043	.035	.028
5.2	.498	.458	.418	.379	.342	.306	.271	.239	.209	.181	.156	.133	.112	.094	.079	.065	.052	.043	.035	.027
5.3	.498	.457	.417	.379	.341	.305	.270	.238	.208	.181	.155	.133	.112	.094	.078	.064	.052	.043	.034	.027
5.4	.497	.457	.417	.378	.341	.304	.270	.238	.208	.180	.155	.132	.112	.094	.078	.064	.052	.043	.034	.027
5.5	.496	.456	.416	.378	.340	.304	.270	.237	.207	.180	.155	.132	.112	.094	.078	.064	.052	.043	.034	.027
5.6	.496	.455	.416	.377	.339	.303	.269	.237	.207	.179	.154	.132	.111	.093	.078	.064	.052	.043	.034	.027
5.7	.495	.455	.415	.376	.339	.303	.269	.237	.207	.179	.154	.131	.111	.093	.078	.064	.052	.042	.034	.027
5.8	.494	.454	.414	.376	.338	.302	.268	.236	.206	.179	.154	.131	.111	.093	.077	.064	.051	.042	.034	.027
5.9	.494	.454	.414	.375	.338	.302	.268	.236	.206	.178	.153	.131	.111	.093	.077	.064	.052	.042	.034	.027
6.0	.493	.453	.414	.375	.337	.301	.267	.235	.206	.178	.153	.132	.110	.093	.077	.064	.052	.043	.034	.027
6.5	.491	.451	.411	.373	.335	.299	.265	.234	.204	.177	.152	.129	.109	.092	.076	.063	.051	.042	.033	.027
7.0	.488	.449	.409	.371	.333	.296	.264	.232	.203	.175	.151	.128	.109	.091	.076	.062	.051	.041	.033	.026
7.5	.487	.447	.407	.369	.332	.296	.262	.231	.201	.174	.150	.128	.108	.090	.075	.062	.050	.041	.032	.026
8.0	.485	.445	.406	.367	.330	.295	.261	.230	.200	.173	.149	.127	.107	.090	.075	.061	.050	.041	.032	.026
8.5	.483	.444	.404	.366	.329	.294	.260	.229	.199	.173	.148	.126	.107	.089	.074	.061	.050	.040	.032	.026
9.0	.482	.442	.403	.365	.328	.292	.259	.228	.199	.172	.147	.126	.106	.089	.074	.061	.050	.040	.031	.026
9.5	.481	.441	.402	.364	.327	.292	.258	.227	.198	.171	.147	.125	.106	.088	.073	.060	.049	.040	.031	.025
10.0	.480	.440	.401	.363	.326	.291	.257	.226	.197	.170	.146	.125	.105	.088	.073	.060	.049	.040	.032	.025
11.0	.478	.438	.399	.361	.324	.289	.256	.225	.196	.169	.145	.124	.104	.087	.073	.060	.049	.039	.032	.025
12.0	.477	.437	.398	.360	.323	.288	.255	.224	.195	.168	.145	.123	.104	.087	.072	.059	.048	.039	.031	.025
13.0	.475	.436	.396	.360	.322	.287	.254	.223	.194	.167	.144	.122	.103	.086	.072	.059	.048	.039	.031	.025
14.0	.474	.435	.396	.358	.321	.286	.253	.222	.193	.167	.143	.122	.103	.086	.071	.059	.048	.039	.031	.025
15.0	.473	.434	.395	.357	.320	.285	.252	.221	.193	.167	.143	.121	.102	.086	.071	.058	.048	.038	.031	.024
16.0	.473	.433	.394	.356	.319	.285	.252	.221	.192	.166	.142	.121	.102	.085	.071	.058	.047	.038	.031	.024
17.0	.472	.432	.393	.355	.319	.284	.251	.220	.192	.165	.142	.121	.102	.085	.071	.058	.047	.038	.030	.024
18.0	.471	.432	.393	.355	.318	.283	.251	.220	.191	.165	.142	.120	.101	.085	.070	.058	.047	.038	.030	.024
19.0	.471	.431	.392	.354	.318	.283	.250	.219	.191	.165	.141	.120	.101	.085	.070	.058	.047	.038	.031	.024
20.0	.470	.430	.392	.354	.317	.283	.250	.219	.191	.165	.141	.120	.101	.084	.070	.058	.047	.038	.030	.024
∞	.460	.421	.382	.345	.309	.274	.242	.212	.184	.159	.136	.115	.097	.081	.067	.055	.045	.036	.029	.023

Offset Circle Probabilities for the Circular Normal Distribution (*cont.*)

$(r_d - D)/\sigma$

D/σ	4.0	3.9	3.8	3.7	3.6	3.5	3.4	3.3	3.2	3.1	3.0	2.9	2.8	2.7	2.6	2.5	2.4	2.3	2.2	2.1
4.0	.000	.000	.000	.000	.000	.000	.000	.001	.001	.001	.002	.003	.003	.005	.006	.008	.011	.014	.018	.023
4.1	.000	.000	.000	.000	.000	.000	.000	.001	.001	.001	.002	.002	.003	.005	.006	.008	.011	.014	.018	.023
4.2	.000	.000	.000	.000	.000	.000	.000	.001	.001	.001	.002	.002	.003	.005	.006	.008	.011	.014	.018	.023
4.3	.000	.000	.000	.000	.000	.000	.000	.001	.001	.001	.002	.002	.003	.005	.006	.008	.011	.014	.018	.022
4.4	.000	.000	.000	.000	.000	.000	.000	.001	.001	.001	.002	.002	.003	.005	.006	.008	.010	.014	.018	.022
4.5	.000	.000	.000	.000	.000	.000	.000	.001	.001	.001	.002	.002	.003	.004	.006	.008	.010	.014	.017	.022
4.6	.000	.000	.000	.000	.000	.000	.000	.001	.001	.001	.002	.002	.003	.004	.006	.008	.010	.014	.017	.022
4.7	.000	.000	.000	.000	.000	.000	.000	.001	.001	.001	.002	.002	.003	.004	.006	.008	.010	.013	.017	.022
4.8	.000	.000	.000	.000	.000	.000	.000	.001	.001	.001	.002	.002	.003	.004	.006	.008	.010	.013	.017	.022
4.9	.000	.000	.000	.000	.000	.000	.000	.001	.001	.001	.002	.002	.003	.004	.006	.008	.010	.013	.017	.022
5.0	.000	.000	.000	.000	.000	.000	.000	.001	.001	.001	.002	.002	.003	.004	.006	.008	.010	.013	.017	.022
5.1	.000	.000	.000	.000	.000	.000	.000	.001	.001	.001	.002	.002	.003	.004	.006	.008	.010	.013	.017	.022
5.2	.000	.000	.000	.000	.000	.000	.000	.001	.001	.001	.002	.002	.003	.004	.006	.008	.010	.013	.017	.022
5.3	.000	.000	.000	.000	.000	.000	.000	.001	.001	.001	.002	.002	.003	.004	.006	.008	.010	.013	.017	.022
5.4	.000	.000	.000	.000	.000	.000	.000	.001	.001	.001	.002	.002	.003	.004	.006	.008	.010	.013	.017	.022
5.5	.000	.000	.000	.000	.000	.000	.000	.001	.001	.001	.002	.002	.003	.004	.006	.008	.010	.013	.017	.022
5.6	.000	.000	.000	.000	.000	.000	.000	.001	.001	.001	.002	.002	.003	.004	.006	.008	.010	.013	.017	.021
5.7	.000	.000	.000	.000	.000	.000	.000	.001	.001	.001	.002	.002	.003	.004	.006	.008	.010	.013	.017	.021
5.8	.000	.000	.000	.000	.000	.000	.000	.001	.001	.001	.002	.002	.003	.004	.006	.008	.010	.013	.017	.021
5.9	.000	.000	.000	.000	.000	.000	.000	.001	.001	.001	.002	.002	.003	.004	.006	.008	.010	.012	.017	.021
6.0	.000	.000	.000	.000	.000	.000	.000	.001	.001	.001	.002	.002	.003	.004	.006	.008	.010	.013	.017	.022
6.5	.000	.000	.000	.000	.000	.000	.000	.001	.001	.001	.002	.002	.003	.004	.006	.008	.010	.013	.016	.021
7.0	.000	.000	.000	.000	.000	.000	.000	.001	.001	.001	.002	.002	.003	.004	.006	.007	.010	.013	.016	.021
7.5	.000	.000	.000	.000	.000	.000	.000	.001	.001	.001	.002	.002	.003	.004	.006	.007	.009	.012	.016	.021
8.0	.000	.000	.000	.000	.000	.000	.000	.001	.001	.001	.002	.002	.003	.004	.005	.007	.010	.012	.016	.020
8.5	.000	.000	.000	.000	.000	.000	.000	.001	.001	.001	.002	.002	.003	.004	.005	.007	.009	.012	.016	.020
9.0	.000	.000	.000	.000	.000	.000	.000	.001	.001	.001	.002	.002	.003	.004	.005	.007	.009	.012	.016	.020
9.5	.000	.000	.000	.000	.000	.000	.000	.001	.001	.001	.002	.002	.003	.004	.005	.007	.009	.012	.016	.020
10.0	.000	.000	.000	.000	.000	.000	.000	.001	.001	.001	.002	.002	.003	.004	.005	.007	.009	.012	.016	.020
11.0	.000	.000	.000	.000	.000	.000	.000	.001	.001	.001	.001	.002	.003	.004	.005	.007	.009	.012	.015	.020
12.0	.000	.000	.000	.000	.000	.000	.000	.001	.001	.001	.001	.002	.003	.004	.005	.007	.009	.012	.015	.020
13.0	.000	.000	.000	.000	.000	.000	.000	.001	.001	.001	.001	.002	.003	.004	.005	.007	.009	.011	.015	.019
14.0	.000	.000	.000	.000	.000	.000	.000	.001	.001	.001	.001	.002	.003	.004	.005	.007	.009	.011	.015	.019
15.0	.000	.000	.000	.000	.000	.000	.000	.001	.001	.001	.001	.002	.003	.004	.005	.007	.009	.012	.015	.019
16.0	.000	.000	.000	.000	.000	.000	.000	.001	.001	.001	.001	.002	.003	.004	.005	.007	.009	.012	.015	.019
17.0	.000	.000	.000	.000	.000	.000	.000	.001	.001	.001	.001	.002	.003	.004	.005	.007	.009	.012	.015	.019
18.0	.000	.000	.000	.000	.000	.000	.000	.001	.001	.001	.001	.002	.003	.004	.005	.007	.009	.011	.015	.019
19.0	.000	.000	.000	.000	.000	.000	.000	.001	.001	.001	.001	.002	.003	.004	.005	.007	.009	.011	.015	.019
20.0	.000	.000	.000	.000	.000	.000	.000	.001	.001	.001	.001	.002	.003	.004	.005	.007	.009	.011	.015	.019
∞	.000	.000	.000	.000	.000	.000	.000	.000	.001	.001	.001	.002	.003	.003	.005	.006	.008	.011	.014	.018

8.3 Distribution of a Quadratic Form in Two Dimensions

Let X_1, X_2 be independently distributed according to normal distributions with means equal to zero and standard deviations equal to σ_1 and σ_2, respectively. Required is the probability that $b_1 X_1^2 + b_2 X_2^2$ is less than or equal to r. Define

$$c = \frac{b_1}{\sigma_1^2} + \frac{b_2}{\sigma_2^2}, \qquad a_1 = \frac{b_1}{c\sigma_1^2},$$

$$a_2 = \frac{b_2}{c\sigma_2^2}, \qquad t = \frac{r}{c}.$$

Then

$$\Pr\{b_1 X_1^2 + b_2 X_2^2 \le r\} = P_2(a_1, a_2; t),$$

where $P_2(a_1, a_2; t)$ is the quantity given in the table. See Section 8.2 for the relationship of this distribution to the circular coverage function. The quantity $P_2(a_1, a_2; t)$ gives the probability of falling inside an ellipse centered at the origin when the underlying distribution is bivariate normal with zero means. If there is correlation between X and Y, the table may still be used, but a circularizing transformation must first be applied; e.g., the transformation

$$u = \frac{1}{\sqrt{1 - \rho^2}}\left(\frac{x_1}{\sigma_1} - \frac{\rho x_2}{\sigma_2}\right), \qquad v = \frac{x_1}{\sigma_1},$$

will yield a circular normal distribution and will take the original ellipse into another ellipse still centered at the origin. The probability of a random point falling within an offset ellipse, i.e., an ellipse with a center different from the center of the distribution, cannot be obtained from this table. However, DiDonato and Jarnigan [51] give a table from which this probability may be obtained. Solomon [205] has given a more extensive table of the probabilities given here. Harter [90], Grad and Solomon [76], and Weingarten and DiDonato [241] also give tables of this type. Van Brocklin and Murray [229] give a graphical procedure for finding bivariate probabilities over any type of area.

Distribution of a Quadratic Form in Two Dimensions [205]

a_2, a_1	t				
	0.1	0.2	0.3	0.4	0.5
.5 , .5	0.09516	0.18127	0.25918	0.32968	0.39347
.6 , .4	0.09693	0.18429	0.26304	0.33405	0.39809
2/3, 1/3	0.10033	0.19005	0.27033	0.34222	0.40664
.7 , .3	0.10288	0.19432	0.27568	0.34815	0.41278
.75 , .25	0.10814	0.20299	0.28637	0.35982	0.42468
.8 , .2	0.11581	0.21529	0.30112	0.37550	0.44023
.875, .125	0.13546	0.24481	0.33434	0.40866	0.47117
.9 , .1	0.14608	0.25941	0.34945	0.42257	0.48315
.95 , .05	0.18130	0.30018	0.38581	0.45206	0.50596
.99 , .01	0.23588	0.33838	0.41150	0.46966	0.51820

a_2, a_1	0.6	0.7	0.8	0.9	1.0
.5 , .5	0.45119	0.50341	0.55067	0.59343	0.63212
.6 , .4	0.45585	0.50797	0.55500	0.59746	0.63579
2/3, 1/3	0.46441	0.51625	0.56279	0.60462	0.64223
.7 , .3	0.47048	0.52205	0.56819	0.60952	0.64658
.75 , .25	0.48206	0.53294	0.57814	0.61839	0.65429
.8 , .2	0.49678	0.54640	0.59009	0.62872	0.66297
.875, .125	0.52435	0.57011	0.60985	0.64467	0.67540
.9 , .1	0.53423	0.57795	0.61587	0.64910	0.67848
.95 , .05	0.55133	0.59040	0.62460	0.65488	0.68192
.99 , .01	0.55982	0.59615	0.62827	0.65692	0.68266

a_2, a_1	1.5	2.0	3.0	4.0	5.0
.5 , .5	0.77687	0.86466	0.95021	0.98168	0.99326
.6 , .4	0.77849	0.86461	0.94871	0.98023	0.99227
2/3, 1/3	0.78108	0.86424	0.94600	0.97773	0.99057
.7 , .3	0.78262	0.86379	0.94412	0.97608	0.98946
.75 , .25	0.78491	0.86255	0.94066	0.97316	0.98752
.8 , .2	0.78664	0.86036	0.93653	0.96984	0.98531
.875, .125	0.78670	0.85500	0.92944	0.96436	0.98160
.9 , .1	0.78581	0.85274	0.92695	0.96244	0.98028
.95 , .05	0.78296	0.84784	0.92187	0.95851	0.97753
.99 , .01	0.78009	0.84374	0.91776	0.95531	

8.4 Inverse of the Distribution of a Quadratic Form in Two Dimensions

The quantity tabulated here is the value of t that makes $P_2(a_1, a_2; t) = 0.05(0.05)0.30(0.10)0.70(0.05)0.95$ for various values of a_1 and a_2 where $P_2(a_1, a_2; t)$ is defined as in Section 8.3. Solomon [205] and Marsaglia [133] give more extensive tables of this type. Harter [90] also has a table of this kind.

Inverse of the Distribution of a Quadratic Form in Two Dimensions [205]

a_2, a_1	0.05	0.10	0.15	0.20	0.25
.5 , .5	0.05129	0.10536	0.16252	0.22314	0.28768
.6 , .4	0.05028	0.10334	0.15950	0.21914	0.28271
2/3, 1/3	0.04843	0.09965	0.15398	0.21181	0.27361
.7 , .3	0.04712	0.09703	0.15006	0.20661	0.26716
.75 , .25	0.04460	0.09199	0.14254	0.19664	0.25480
.8 , .2	0.04130	0.08541	0.13271	0.18363	0.23870
.875, .125	0.03438	0.07162	0.11215	0.15650	0.20530
.9 , .1	0.03131	0.06551	0.10308	0.14458	0.19073
.95 , .05	0.02313	0.04928	0.07910	0.11342	0.15324
.99 , .01	0.01138	0.02648	0.04698	0.07474	0.11126

a_2, a_1	0.30	0.40	0.50	0.60	0.70
.5 , .5	0.35667	0.51083	0.69315	0.91629	1.20397
.6 , .4	0.35076	0.50315	0.68403	0.90632	1.19442
2/3, 1/3	0.33995	0.48917	0.66749	0.88841	1.17762
.7 , .3	0.33229	0.47930	0.65586	0.87598	1.16628
.75 , .25	0.31763	0.46048	0.63392	0.85288	1.14603
.8 , .2	0.29859	0.43625	0.60610	0.82451	1.12301
.875, .125	0.25934	0.38738	0.55228	0.77393	1.08956
.9 , .1	0.24239	0.36699	0.53123	0.75648	1.08136
.95 , .05	0.19982	0.31955	0.48800	0.72681	1.07335
.99 , .01	0.15746	0.28250	0.46056	0.71137	1.07355

a_2, a_1	0.75	0.80	0.85	0.90	0.95
.5 , .5	1.38629	1.60944	1.89712	2.30259	2.99573
.6 , .4	1.37788	1.60335	1.89552	2.31015	3.02651
2/3, 1/3	1.36346	1.59358	1.89452	2.32662	3.08552
.7 , .3	1.35404	1.58778	1.89536	2.34024	3.12873
.75 , .25	1.33805	1.57944	1.90046	2.37008	3.21192
.8 , .2	1.32168	1.57416	1.91341	2.41396	3.31578
.875, .125	1.30467	1.58112	1.95486	2.50704	3.49933
.9 , .1	1.30358	1.58912	1.97473	2.54369	3.56514
.95 , .05	1.30969	1.61255	2.02073	2.62218	3.70114
.99 , .01	1.32016	1.63604	2.06160	2.68856	3.81311

8.4

8.5 A Function for Computing Bivariate Normal Probabilities

The quantity tabulated is defined as

$$T(h, a) = \frac{1}{2\pi} \int_0^a \frac{\exp\left[-h^2(1 + x^2)/2\right]}{1 + x^2} \, dx.$$

The T-function is tabulated only for $0 \leq a \leq 1$ and ∞, but it is possible to obtain other values for $1 < a < \infty$ by use of the formula

$$T(h, a) = \tfrac{1}{2}P(h) + \tfrac{1}{2}P(ah) - P(h)P(ah) - T(ah, 1/a),$$

where $P(h)$ is the normal integral defined in Section 1.1.

Values for negative a and/or h may be obtained by using $T(h, -a) = -T(h, a)$ and $T(-h, a) = T(h, a)$. For additional properties of the T-function and a description of how the table was computed, the reader is referred to [162]. Formulas for the noncentral t-distribution involving the T-function were given in Section 5.1.

Let

$$B(h, k; \rho) = \frac{1}{2\pi\sqrt{1 - \rho^2}} \int_{-\infty}^h \int_{-\infty}^k \exp\left[-\frac{1}{2} \frac{x^2 - 2\rho xy + y^2}{1 - \rho^2}\right] dx \, dy,$$

which is equal to $\Pr\{X \leq h, Y \leq k; \rho\}$ where X and Y have a joint bivariate normal distribution with means zero, variances one, and correlation equal to ρ. This probability may be expressed in terms of the T-function as follows:

$$B(h, k; \rho) = \tfrac{1}{2}P(h) + \tfrac{1}{2}P(k) - T(h, a_h) - T(k, a_k) - \{^0_{1/2},$$

where the upper choice is made if $hk > 0$ and if $hk = 0$ but $h + k \geq 0$, and the lower choice is made otherwise, and where

$$a_h = \frac{k}{h\sqrt{1 - \rho^2}} - \frac{\rho}{\sqrt{1 - \rho^2}} \quad \text{and} \quad a_k = \frac{h}{k\sqrt{1 - \rho^2}} - \frac{\rho}{\sqrt{1 - \rho^2}}.$$

Indeed, the T-function can be used to evaluate the probability that any two normally distributed random variables (correlated or not) will fall in any region bounded by a polygon [162].

Table A has a coarse interval in the parameter a and an interval fine enough for ordinary linear interpolation in the parameter h. Table B has intervals in parameter a fine enough for ordinary linear interpolation and has parameter h at a coarse interval. Ordinary linear interpolation may be used throughout Table C. Tables A and B were designed for interpolation as follows. To interpolate for a value $T(h_2, a_2)$, say, consecutive values a_1 and a_3 should be picked from Table A so that $a_1 \leq a_2 < a_3$, and consecutive values h_1 and h_3 should be picked from Table B so that

$h_1 \leq h_2 < h_3$. Then the interpolated value of $T(h_2, a_2)$ is obtained from

$$T(h_2, a_2) = \sum_{i=1}^{3} \sum_{j=1}^{3} w_{ij} T(h_i, a_j),$$

where the weights w_{ij} are given by

$$w_{ij} = \begin{pmatrix} -(1-b)(1-c) & 1-c & -b(1-c) \\ (1-b) & 0 & b \\ -(1-b)c & c & -bc \end{pmatrix},$$

where

$$b = \frac{a_2 - a_1}{a_3 - a_1} \quad \text{and} \quad c = \frac{h_2 - h_1}{h_3 - h_1}.$$

The weights were obtained by considering the result of ordinary linear interpolating, say, $T(h_2, a_1) - T(h_1, a_1)$ and $T(h_2, a_3) - T(h_1, a_3)$. These numbers are interpolated with respect to a to obtain $T(h_2, a_2) - T(h_1, a_2)$, and then $T(h_1, a_2)$ is added. This process may also be followed with (h_3, a_1), (h_3, a_3), and (h_3, a_2). If the two estimates of $T(h_2, a_2)$ are then combined as in linear interpolation with respect to h, that is, $(1 - c)$ times the first estimate plus c times the second, then the above weights w_{ij} follow. The interpolation on the differences could also have been first with respect to h to obtain the two estimates, and then with respect to a between these two. The same weights w_{ij} are obtained by doing this.

This method of interpolation has resulted in a reduction of approximately 90 percent from the size table which would be needed for linear interpolation. Quadratic interpolation using Bessel's formula would give comparable results to the new method with an additional reduction of approximately 80 percent in the number of entries, but the additional work involved more than outweighs this reduction in the number of entries. The procedure given here may be termed a compromise between linear and quadratic interpolation.

EXAMPLE. Find $T(0.15, 0.625)$. From the tables, the following entries are extracted:

	a		
h	.50	.625	.75
0	.073792	.088903	.102416
.15	.072902		.101082
.25	.071347	.085848	.098755

The weights to be applied are

	a		
h	.50	.625	.75
0	$-.2$	.4	$-.2$
.15	.5		.5
.25	$-.3$	.6	$-.3$

The result is $T(0.15, 0.625) = 0.0877898$. Empirical examination of the errors in interpolation by this scheme shows that the maximum error that would occur anywhere in the region of Tables A and B is seven in the sixth decimal place. For applications of the bivariate normal distribution, see [150]. Severo and Zelen [197] give graphs from which bivariate normal probabilities may be read. Weiler [240] gives charts from which the means and standard deviations of truncated bivariate normal distributions may be obtained.

A Function for Computing Bivariate Normal Probabilities [162]

Table A of $T(h, a)$

h \ a	0.25	0.50	0.75	1.00
0.00	0.038990	0.073792	0.102416	0.125000
0.01	0.038988	0.073788	0.102410	0.124992
0.02	0.038982	0.073776	0.102393	0.124968
0.03	0.038972	0.073756	0.102363	0.124928
0.04	0.038958	0.073728	0.102321	0.124873
0.05	0.038940	0.073692	0.102267	0.124801
0.06	0.038918	0.073649	0.102202	0.124714
0.07	0.038892	0.073597	0.102124	0.124611
0.08	0.038862	0.073538	0.102035	0.124492
0.09	0.038829	0.073470	0.101934	0.124357
0.10	0.038791	0.073395	0.101821	0.124207
0.11	0.038750	0.073312	0.101697	0.124041
0.12	0.038704	0.073221	0.101561	0.123860
0.13	0.038655	0.073122	0.101413	0.123663
0.14	0.038602	0.073016	0.101253	0.123450
0.15	0.038545	0.072902	0.101082	0.123223
0.16	0.038484	0.072780	0.100900	0.122980
0.17	0.038419	0.072651	0.100706	0.122722
0.18	0.038350	0.072514	0.100501	0.122449
0.19	0.038278	0.072369	0.100285	0.122162
0.20	0.038202	0.072217	0.100057	0.121859
0.21	0.038122	0.072058	0.099819	0.121542
0.22	0.038038	0.071891	0.099569	0.121210
0.23	0.037951	0.071717	0.099308	0.120864
0.24	0.037860	0.071535	0.099037	0.120503
0.25	0.037766	0.071347	0.098755	0.120129
0.26	0.037668	0.071151	0.098462	0.119740
0.27	0.037566	0.070948	0.098158	0.119337
0.28	0.037461	0.070738	0.097844	0.118921
0.29	0.037352	0.070521	0.097520	0.118492
0.30	0.037240	0.070297	0.097186	0.118048
0.31	0.037124	0.070066	0.096841	0.117592
0.32	0.037005	0.069828	0.096487	0.117123
0.33	0.036882	0.069584	0.096122	0.116641
0.34	0.036756	0.069333	0.095748	0.116146
0.35	0.036627	0.069076	0.095365	0.115639
0.36	0.036495	0.068812	0.094971	0.115119
0.37	0.036359	0.068542	0.094569	0.114587
0.38	0.036220	0.068265	0.094157	0.114044
0.39	0.036078	0.067983	0.093736	0.113489
0.40	0.035933	0.067694	0.093306	0.112922
0.41	0.035785	0.067399	0.092868	0.112344
0.42	0.035634	0.067098	0.092421	0.111755
0.43	0.035479	0.066791	0.091965	0.111155
0.44	0.035322	0.066479	0.091501	0.110545

A Function for Computing Bivariate Normal Probabilities (*cont.*)

Table A of $T(h, a)$

h \ a	0.25	0.50	0.75	1.00
0.45	0.035162	0.066161	0.091028	0.109924
0.46	0.034999	0.065837	0.090548	0.109293
0.47	0.034834	0.065508	0.090060	0.108652
0.48	0.034665	0.065173	0.089564	0.108001
0.49	0.034494	0.064834	0.089060	0.107341
0.50	0.034320	0.064489	0.088549	0.106671
0.51	0.034144	0.064139	0.088031	0.105993
0.52	0.033965	0.063784	0.087506	0.105305
0.53	0.033783	0.063424	0.086974	0.104609
0.54	0.033599	0.063059	0.086435	0.103905
0.55	0.033413	0.062690	0.085889	0.103193
0.56	0.033224	0.062316	0.085337	0.102473
0.57	0.033033	0.061938	0.084779	0.101745
0.58	0.032840	0.061555	0.084215	0.101010
0.59	0.032645	0.061168	0.083645	0.100268
0.60	0.032447	0.060778	0.083069	0.099519
0.61	0.032247	0.060383	0.082487	0.098764
0.62	0.032046	0.059984	0.081901	0.098002
0.63	0.031842	0.059581	0.081309	0.097234
0.64	0.031636	0.059175	0.080712	0.096460
0.65	0.031429	0.058765	0.080110	0.095681
0.66	0.031219	0.058352	0.079504	0.094896
0.67	0.031008	0.057936	0.078893	0.094106
0.68	0.030795	0.057516	0.078278	0.093312
0.69	0.030581	0.057093	0.077658	0.092512
0.70	0.030365	0.056667	0.077035	0.091709
0.71	0.030147	0.056239	0.076408	0.090901
0.72	0.029928	0.055807	0.075777	0.090089
0.73	0.029707	0.055373	0.075143	0.089274
0.74	0.029485	0.054937	0.074506	0.088455
0.75	0.029262	0.054498	0.073866	0.087634
0.76	0.029038	0.054056	0.073223	0.086809
0.77	0.028812	0.053613	0.072577	0.085982
0.78	0.028585	0.053167	0.071928	0.085152
0.79	0.028357	0.052720	0.071278	0.084320
0.80	0.028128	0.052270	0.070625	0.083486
0.81	0.027898	0.051819	0.069970	0.082651
0.82	0.027667	0.051367	0.069313	0.081814
0.83	0.027435	0.050912	0.068655	0.080975
0.84	0.027202	0.050457	0.067995	0.080136
0.85	0.026968	0.050000	0.067333	0.079296
0.86	0.026734	0.049542	0.066671	0.078455
0.87	0.026499	0.049083	0.066007	0.077614
0.88	0.026264	0.048622	0.065343	0.076773
0.89	0.026027	0.048161	0.064678	0.075932

8.5

A Function for Computing Bivariate Normal Probabilities (cont.)

Table A of $T(h, a)$

h \ a	0.25	0.50	0.75	1.00
0.90	0.025791	0.047700	0.064013	0.075091
0.91	0.025554	0.047237	0.063347	0.074251
0.92	0.025316	0.046775	0.062681	0.073411
0.93	0.025079	0.046311	0.062015	0.072572
0.94	0.024840	0.045848	0.061349	0.071734
0.95	0.024602	0.045384	0.060684	0.070898
0.96	0.024363	0.044920	0.060018	0.070063
0.97	0.024125	0.044456	0.059354	0.069230
0.98	0.023886	0.043992	0.058690	0.068398
0.99	0.023647	0.043528	0.058027	0.067569
1.00	0.023408	0.043065	0.057365	0.066742
1.01	0.023169	0.042602	0.056704	0.065917
1.02	0.022931	0.042139	0.056044	0.065095
1.03	0.022692	0.041677	0.055386	0.064276
1.04	0.022454	0.041216	0.054729	0.063459
1.05	0.022216	0.040755	0.054075	0.062646
1.06	0.021978	0.040295	0.053421	0.061836
1.07	0.021740	0.039836	0.052770	0.061029
1.08	0.021503	0.039378	0.052121	0.060226
1.09	0.021266	0.038922	0.051474	0.059426
1.10	0.021030	0.038466	0.050830	0.058630
1.11	0.020794	0.038012	0.050188	0.057839
1.12	0.020559	0.037559	0.049548	0.057051
1.13	0.020325	0.037107	0.048911	0.056268
1.14	0.020091	0.036657	0.048277	0.055489
1.15	0.019857	0.036209	0.047646	0.054714
1.16	0.019625	0.035762	0.047018	0.053945
1.17	0.019393	0.035317	0.046393	0.053180
1.18	0.019162	0.034874	0.045771	0.052420
1.19	0.018931	0.034432	0.045152	0.051664
1.20	0.018702	0.033993	0.044537	0.050914
1.21	0.018473	0.033556	0.043925	0.050169
1.22	0.018246	0.033120	0.043317	0.049430
1.23	0.018019	0.032687	0.042712	0.048696
1.24	0.017794	0.032256	0.042112	0.047967
1.25	0.017569	0.031828	0.041515	0.047244
1.26	0.017345	0.031402	0.040922	0.046527
1.27	0.017123	0.030978	0.040333	0.045815
1.28	0.016902	0.030556	0.039748	0.045109
1.29	0.016682	0.030138	0.039167	0.044409
1.30	0.016463	0.029721	0.038590	0.043715
1.31	0.016245	0.029308	0.038018	0.043027
1.32	0.016028	0.028897	0.037450	0.042345
1.33	0.015813	0.028488	0.036886	0.041670
1.34	0.015599	0.028083	0.036327	0.041000

8.5

A Function for Computing Bivariate Normal Probabilities (*cont.*)

Table A of $T(h, a)$

h \ a	0.25	0.50	0.75	1.00
1.35	0.015387	0.027680	0.035773	0.040337
1.36	0.015176	0.027281	0.035223	0.039680
1.37	0.014966	0.026884	0.034678	0.039030
1.38	0.014757	0.026490	0.034137	0.038386
1.39	0.014550	0.026099	0.033601	0.037749
1.40	0.014345	0.025711	0.033070	0.037118
1.41	0.014140	0.025326	0.032543	0.036493
1.42	0.013938	0.024944	0.032022	0.035875
1.43	0.013737	0.024566	0.031505	0.035264
1.44	0.013537	0.024190	0.030994	0.034659
1.45	0.013339	0.023818	0.030487	0.034061
1.46	0.013142	0.023449	0.029985	0.033470
1.47	0.012947	0.023084	0.029489	0.032885
1.48	0.012754	0.022721	0.028997	0.032308
1.49	0.012562	0.022362	0.028511	0.031736
1.50	0.012372	0.022006	0.028029	0.031172
1.51	0.012184	0.021654	0.027553	0.030614
1.52	0.011997	0.021305	0.027082	0.030063
1.53	0.011812	0.020959	0.026616	0.029519
1.54	0.011628	0.020617	0.026155	0.028982
1.55	0.011446	0.020279	0.025700	0.028451
1.56	0.011266	0.019943	0.025249	0.027927
1.57	0.011088	0.019611	0.024804	0.027410
1.58	0.010911	0.019283	0.024364	0.026899
1.59	0.010736	0.018958	0.023929	0.026395
1.60	0.010563	0.018637	0.023500	0.025898
1.61	0.010391	0.018319	0.023075	0.025408
1.62	0.010221	0.018005	0.022656	0.024924
1.63	0.010053	0.017694	0.022242	0.024447
1.64	0.009887	0.017387	0.021833	0.023976
1.65	0.009723	0.017083	0.021430	0.023512
1.66	0.009560	0.016783	0.021032	0.023055
1.67	0.009399	0.016486	0.020638	0.022604
1.68	0.009240	0.016193	0.020250	0.022159
1.69	0.009082	0.015903	0.019868	0.021721
1.70	0.008927	0.015617	0.019490	0.021290
1.71	0.008773	0.015334	0.019117	0.020865
1.72	0.008621	0.015055	0.018750	0.020446
1.73	0.008470	0.014780	0.018388	0.020033
1.74	0.008322	0.014508	0.018030	0.019627
1.75	0.008175	0.014239	0.017678	0.019227
1.76	0.008030	0.013974	0.017331	0.018833
1.77	0.007887	0.013713	0.016989	0.018446
1.78	0.007745	0.013454	0.016651	0.018064
1.79	0.007605	0.013200	0.016319	0.017689

A Function for Computing Bivariate Normal Probabilities (cont.)

Table A of $T(h, a)$

h \ a	0.25	0.50	0.75	1.00
1.80	0.007467	0.012949	0.015992	0.017320
1.81	0.007331	0.012701	0.015669	0.016956
1.82	0.007197	0.012457	0.015352	0.016599
1.83	0.007064	0.012216	0.015039	0.016247
1.84	0.006933	0.011978	0.014731	0.015901
1.85	0.006804	0.011744	0.014428	0.015561
1.86	0.006676	0.011514	0.014130	0.015227
1.87	0.006550	0.011286	0.013836	0.014898
1.88	0.006426	0.011062	0.013547	0.014575
1.89	0.006304	0.010841	0.013263	0.014258
1.90	0.006183	0.010624	0.012983	0.013946
1.91	0.006064	0.010410	0.012708	0.013639
1.92	0.005947	0.010199	0.012437	0.013338
1.93	0.005831	0.009991	0.012171	0.013042
1.94	0.005717	0.009786	0.011909	0.012752
1.95	0.005605	0.009585	0.011652	0.012467
1.96	0.005495	0.009387	0.011399	0.012187
1.97	0.005386	0.009192	0.011150	0.011911
1.98	0.005278	0.009000	0.010905	0.011641
1.99	0.005172	0.008811	0.010665	0.011376
2.00	0.005068	0.008625	0.010429	0.011116
2.01	0.004966	0.008442	0.010197	0.010861
2.02	0.004865	0.008263	0.009970	0.010611
2.03	0.004765	0.008086	0.009746	0.010365
2.04	0.004667	0.007912	0.009527	0.010124
2.05	0.004571	0.007741	0.009311	0.009887
2.06	0.004476	0.007573	0.009099	0.009656
2.07	0.004383	0.007408	0.008891	0.009428
2.08	0.004291	0.007245	0.008687	0.009205
2.09	0.004201	0.007086	0.008487	0.008987
2.10	0.004112	0.006929	0.008291	0.008773
2.11	0.004025	0.006775	0.008098	0.008563
2.12	0.003939	0.006624	0.007909	0.008357
2.13	0.003854	0.006476	0.007724	0.008155
2.14	0.003771	0.006330	0.007542	0.007958
2.15	0.003690	0.006187	0.007363	0.007764
2.16	0.003610	0.006046	0.007188	0.007575
2.17	0.003531	0.005908	0.007017	0.007389
2.18	0.003453	0.005772	0.006849	0.007207
2.19	0.003377	0.005639	0.006684	0.007029
2.20	0.003303	0.005509	0.006523	0.006855
2.21	0.003229	0.005381	0.006364	0.006684
2.22	0.003157	0.005255	0.006209	0.006517
2.23	0.003086	0.005132	0.006058	0.006354
2.24	0.003017	0.005011	0.005909	0.006194

8.5

A Function for Computing Bivariate Normal Probabilities (cont.)

Table A of $T(h, a)$

h \ a	0.25	0.50	0.75	1.00
2.25	0.002948	0.004893	0.005763	0.006038
2.26	0.002881	0.004777	0.005620	0.005884
2.27	0.002816	0.004663	0.005481	0.005735
2.28	0.002751	0.004551	0.005344	0.005588
2.29	0.002688	0.004442	0.005210	0.005445
2.30	0.002625	0.004334	0.005079	0.005305
2.31	0.002565	0.004229	0.004951	0.005167
2.32	0.002505	0.004126	0.004825	0.005034
2.33	0.002446	0.004025	0.004702	0.004903
2.34	0.002388	0.003926	0.004582	0.004774
2.35	0.002332	0.003829	0.004465	0.004649
2.36	0.002277	0.003735	0.004350	0.004527
2.37	0.002222	0.003642	0.004237	0.004407
2.38	0.002169	0.003551	0.004127	0.004291
2.39	0.002117	0.003462	0.004020	0.004177
2.40	0.002066	0.003375	0.003915	0.004065
2.41	0.002016	0.003289	0.003812	0.003956
2.42	0.001967	0.003206	0.003711	0.003850
2.43	0.001919	0.003124	0.003613	0.003746
2.44	0.001872	0.003044	0.003517	0.003645
2.45	0.001826	0.002966	0.003424	0.003546
2.46	0.001781	0.002890	0.003332	0.003449
2.47	0.001737	0.002815	0.003243	0.003355
2.48	0.001693	0.002742	0.003155	0.003263
2.49	0.001651	0.002670	0.003070	0.003173
2.50	0.001609	0.002600	0.002987	0.003086
2.51	0.001569	0.002532	0.002905	0.003000
2.52	0.001529	0.002465	0.002826	0.002917
2.53	0.001490	0.002400	0.002748	0.002835
2.54	0.001452	0.002336	0.002673	0.002756
2.55	0.001415	0.002274	0.002599	0.002679
2.56	0.001379	0.002213	0.002527	0.002603
2.57	0.001343	0.002153	0.002457	0.002530
2.58	0.001308	0.002095	0.002388	0.002458
2.59	0.001274	0.002039	0.002321	0.002388
2.60	0.001241	0.001983	0.002256	0.002320
2.61	0.001209	0.001929	0.002192	0.002253
2.62	0.001177	0.001876	0.002130	0.002189
2.63	0.001146	0.001825	0.002070	0.002126
2.64	0.001115	0.001774	0.002011	0.002064
2.65	0.001086	0.001725	0.001953	0.002004
2.66	0.001057	0.001677	0.001897	0.001946
2.67	0.001028	0.001630	0.001843	0.001889
2.68	0.001001	0.001585	0.001789	0.001834
2.69	0.000974	0.001540	0.001737	0.001780

A Function for Computing Bivariate Normal Probabilities (cont.)

Table A of $T(h, a)$

h \ a	0.25	0.50	0.75	1.00
2.70	0.000947	0.001497	0.001687	0.001727
2.71	0.000922	0.001454	0.001638	0.001676
2.72	0.000896	0.001413	0.001590	0.001627
2.73	0.000872	0.001373	0.001543	0.001578
2.74	0.000848	0.001334	0.001498	0.001531
2.75	0.000824	0.001295	0.001453	0.001485
2.76	0.000802	0.001258	0.001410	0.001441
2.77	0.000779	0.001222	0.001368	0.001397
2.78	0.000758	0.001186	0.001327	0.001355
2.79	0.000736	0.001152	0.001288	0.001314
2.80	0.000716	0.001118	0.001249	0.001274
2.81	0.000696	0.001085	0.001211	0.001235
2.82	0.000676	0.001054	0.001175	0.001198
2.83	0.000657	0.001022	0.001139	0.001161
2.84	0.000638	0.000992	0.001104	0.001125
2.85	0.000620	0.000963	0.001071	0.001091
2.86	0.000602	0.000934	0.001038	0.001057
2.87	0.000585	0.000906	0.001006	0.001024
2.88	0.000568	0.000879	0.000975	0.000992
2.89	0.000551	0.000853	0.000945	0.000961
2.90	0.000535	0.000827	0.000916	0.000931
2.91	0.000520	0.000802	0.000887	0.000902
2.92	0.000504	0.000777	0.000859	0.000874
2.93	0.000490	0.000754	0.000833	0.000846
2.94	0.000475	0.000731	0.000806	0.000819
2.95	0.000461	0.000708	0.000781	0.000793
2.96	0.000448	0.000686	0.000756	0.000768
2.97	0.000434	0.000665	0.000732	0.000743
2.98	0.000421	0.000645	0.000709	0.000720
2.99	0.000409	0.000625	0.000687	0.000696
3.00	0.000396	0.000605	0.000665	0.000674
3.01	0.000384	0.000586	0.000643	0.000652
3.02	0.000373	0.000568	0.000623	0.000631
3.03	0.000361	0.000550	0.000603	0.000611
3.04	0.000350	0.000533	0.000583	0.000591
3.05	0.000340	0.000516	0.000564	0.000571
3.06	0.000329	0.000499	0.000546	0.000553
3.07	0.000319	0.000483	0.000528	0.000535
3.08	0.000309	0.000468	0.000511	0.000517
3.09	0.000300	0.000453	0.000494	0.000500
3.10	0.000290	0.000438	0.000478	0.000483
3.11	0.000281	0.000424	0.000462	0.000467
3.12	0.000273	0.000410	0.000447	0.000452
3.13	0.000264	0.000397	0.000432	0.000437
3.14	0.000256	0.000384	0.000417	0.000422

A Function for Computing Bivariate Normal Probabilities (cont.)

Table B of $T(h, a)$

h \ a	0.00	0.01	0.02	0.03	0.04
0.00	0.000000	0.001591	0.003183	0.004773	0.006363
0.25	0.000000	0.001543	0.003085	0.004626	0.006167
0.50	0.000000	0.001404	0.002809	0.004212	0.005615
0.75	0.000000	0.001201	0.002402	0.003603	0.004802
1.00	0.000000	0.000965	0.001930	0.002895	0.003858
1.25	0.000000	0.000729	0.001457	0.002185	0.002912
1.50	0.000000	0.000517	0.001033	0.001549	0.002064
1.75	0.000000	0.000344	0.000688	0.001032	0.001375
2.00	0.000000	0.000215	0.000431	0.000646	0.000860
2.25	0.000000	0.000127	0.000253	0.000379	0.000506
2.50	0.000000	0.000070	0.000140	0.000210	0.000279
2.75	0.000000	0.000036	0.000073	0.000109	0.000145
3.00	0.000000	0.000018	0.000035	0.000053	0.000071
3.25	0.000000	0.000008	0.000016	0.000024	0.000032

h \ a	0.05	0.06	0.07	0.08	0.09
0.00	0.007951	0.009538	0.011123	0.012705	0.014285
0.25	0.007706	0.009244	0.010780	0.012314	0.013845
0.50	0.007016	0.008416	0.009814	0.011209	0.012603
0.75	0.006000	0.007197	0.008392	0.009585	0.010775
1.00	0.004821	0.005782	0.006741	0.007698	0.008653
1.25	0.003638	0.004363	0.005086	0.005807	0.006527
1.50	0.002579	0.003092	0.003604	0.004115	0.004624
1.75	0.001717	0.002059	0.002399	0.002739	0.003077
2.00	0.001074	0.001288	0.001500	0.001712	0.001923
2.25	0.000631	0.000757	0.000881	0.001005	0.001129
2.50	0.000348	0.000417	0.000486	0.000555	0.000622
2.75	0.000181	0.000216	0.000252	0.000287	0.000322
3.00	0.000088	0.000105	0.000123	0.000140	0.000157
3.25	0.000040	0.000048	0.000056	0.000064	0.000072

h \ a	0.10	0.11	0.12	0.13	0.14
0.00	0.015863	0.017437	0.019008	0.020575	0.022138
0.25	0.015373	0.016898	0.018420	0.019938	0.021452
0.50	0.013993	0.015380	0.016764	0.018144	0.019521
0.75	0.011963	0.013147	0.014328	0.015506	0.016680
1.00	0.009605	0.010555	0.011501	0.012444	0.013384
1.25	0.007244	0.007958	0.008670	0.009379	0.010084
1.50	0.005131	0.005635	0.006138	0.006638	0.007135
1.75	0.003413	0.003748	0.004081	0.004412	0.004740
2.00	0.002133	0.002341	0.002548	0.002754	0.002958
2.25	0.001251	0.001373	0.001494	0.001614	0.001733
2.50	0.000690	0.000757	0.000823	0.000888	0.000953
2.75	0.000357	0.000391	0.000426	0.000459	0.000492
3.00	0.000174	0.000190	0.000207	0.000223	0.000239
3.25	0.000079	0.000087	0.000094	0.000102	0.000109

A Function for Computing Bivariate Normal Probabilities (*cont.*)
Table B of $T(h, a)$

h \ a	0.15	0.16	0.17	0.18	0.19
0.00	0.023697	0.025251	0.026800	0.028344	0.029883
0.25	0.022962	0.024467	0.025968	0.027463	0.028953
0.50	0.020893	0.022260	0.023623	0.024980	0.026333
0.75	0.017850	0.019015	0.020176	0.021331	0.022482
1.00	0.014319	0.015251	0.016178	0.017100	0.018018
1.25	0.010786	0.011485	0.012179	0.012869	0.013555
1.50	0.007629	0.008120	0.008608	0.009092	0.009573
1.75	0.005067	0.005391	0.005712	0.006031	0.006347
2.00	0.003160	0.003360	0.003559	0.003755	0.003950
2.25	0.001850	0.001967	0.002082	0.002195	0.002308
2.50	0.001017	0.001081	0.001143	0.001205	0.001266
2.75	0.000525	0.000558	0.000590	0.000621	0.000652
3.00	0.000255	0.000270	0.000285	0.000300	0.000315
3.25	0.000116	0.000123	0.000130	0.000136	0.000143

h \ a	0.20	0.21	0.22	0.23	0.24
0.00	0.031416	0.032944	0.034465	0.035980	0.037488
0.25	0.030437	0.031916	0.033388	0.034854	0.036313
0.50	0.027679	0.029020	0.030355	0.031683	0.033005
0.75	0.023627	0.024766	0.025899	0.027027	0.028148
1.00	0.018930	0.019837	0.020739	0.021635	0.022525
1.25	0.014237	0.014913	0.015585	0.016252	0.016913
1.50	0.010050	0.010523	0.010992	0.011456	0.011917
1.75	0.006659	0.006969	0.007276	0.007579	0.007879
2.00	0.004142	0.004332	0.004520	0.004705	0.004888
2.25	0.002418	0.002528	0.002635	0.002741	0.002846
2.50	0.001325	0.001384	0.001442	0.001499	0.001555
2.75	0.000682	0.000712	0.000741	0.000769	0.000797
3.00	0.000329	0.000343	0.000357	0.000371	0.000384
3.25	0.000149	0.000156	0.000162	0.000167	0.000173

h \ a	0.25	0.26	0.27	0.28	0.29
0.00	0.038990	0.040484	0.041971	0.043451	0.044923
0.25	0.037766	0.039211	0.040649	0.042080	0.043503
0.50	0.034320	0.035628	0.036929	0.038223	0.039509
0.75	0.029262	0.030370	0.031470	0.032564	0.033650
1.00	0.023408	0.024286	0.025156	0.026021	0.026878
1.25	0.017569	0.018219	0.018864	0.019502	0.020135
1.50	0.012372	0.012823	0.013269	0.013710	0.014147
1.75	0.008175	0.008467	0.008756	0.009041	0.009322
2.00	0.005068	0.005246	0.005421	0.005593	0.005762
2.25	0.002948	0.003049	0.003148	0.003245	0.003341
2.50	0.001609	0.001663	0.001716	0.001767	0.001817
2.75	0.000824	0.000851	0.000877	0.000902	0.000927
3.00	0.000396	0.000409	0.000421	0.000432	0.000444
3.25	0.000179	0.000184	0.000189	0.000194	0.000199

A Function for Computing Bivariate Normal Probabilities (*cont.*)

Table B of $T(h, a)$

h \ a	0.30	0.31	0.32	0.33	0.34
0.00	0.046387	0.047843	0.049291	0.050730	0.052161
0.25	0.044918	0.046326	0.047725	0.049115	0.050497
0.50	0.040787	0.042057	0.043319	0.044573	0.045818
0.75	0.034728	0.035799	0.036862	0.037916	0.038963
1.00	0.027728	0.028571	0.029407	0.030235	0.031056
1.25	0.020761	0.021381	0.021994	0.022601	0.023201
1.50	0.014578	0.015003	0.015424	0.015839	0.016248
1.75	0.009599	0.009873	0.010142	0.010406	0.010667
2.00	0.005929	0.006092	0.006253	0.006411	0.006565
2.25	0.003434	0.003526	0.003615	0.003703	0.003789
2.50	0.001866	0.001914	0.001961	0.002006	0.002050
2.75	0.000951	0.000974	0.000997	0.001019	0.001040
3.00	0.000455	0.000465	0.000476	0.000486	0.000495
3.25	0.000204	0.000209	0.000213	0.000217	0.000221

h \ a	0.35	0.36	0.37	0.38	0.39
0.00	0.053583	0.054997	0.056401	0.057797	0.059183
0.25	0.051871	0.053235	0.054591	0.055937	0.057275
0.50	0.047054	0.048282	0.049501	0.050711	0.051912
0.75	0.040001	0.041031	0.042052	0.043065	0.044068
1.00	0.031868	0.032673	0.033470	0.034259	0.035040
1.25	0.023795	0.024381	0.024961	0.025533	0.026098
1.50	0.016652	0.017050	0.017443	0.017829	0.018210
1.75	0.010923	0.011175	0.011423	0.011666	0.011905
2.00	0.006717	0.006866	0.007011	0.007154	0.007293
2.25	0.003872	0.003954	0.004034	0.004112	0.004188
2.50	0.002093	0.002135	0.002176	0.002215	0.002254
2.75	0.001061	0.001081	0.001101	0.001119	0.001137
3.00	0.000505	0.000513	0.000522	0.000530	0.000538
3.25	0.000225	0.000229	0.000232	0.000236	0.000239

h \ a	0.40	0.41	0.42	0.43	0.44
0.00	0.060559	0.061927	0.063284	0.064633	0.065971
0.25	0.058602	0.059921	0.061230	0.062529	0.063818
0.50	0.053103	0.054285	0.055458	0.056621	0.057775
0.75	0.045063	0.046048	0.047025	0.047992	0.048950
1.00	0.035812	0.036576	0.037332	0.038079	0.038817
1.25	0.026656	0.027207	0.027750	0.028286	0.028815
1.50	0.018585	0.018954	0.019318	0.019675	0.020026
1.75	0.012140	0.012370	0.012595	0.012816	0.013033
2.00	0.007430	0.007563	0.007693	0.007820	0.007944
2.25	0.004261	0.004333	0.004403	0.004471	0.004537
2.50	0.002291	0.002327	0.002362	0.002395	0.002428
2.75	0.001155	0.001171	0.001188	0.001203	0.001218
3.00	0.000546	0.000553	0.000560	0.000567	0.000573
3.25	0.000242	0.000245	0.000248	0.000250	0.000253

8.5

A Function for Computing Bivariate Normal Probabilities (*cont.*)

Table B of $T(h, a)$

h \ a	0.45	0.46	0.47	0.48	0.49
0.00	0.067299	0.068618	0.069926	0.071225	0.072513
0.25	0.065098	0.066368	0.067628	0.068877	0.070117
0.50	0.058918	0.060052	0.061176	0.062290	0.063395
0.75	0.049898	0.050837	0.051767	0.052687	0.053597
1.00	0.039547	0.040268	0.040980	0.041684	0.042379
1.25	0.029336	0.029849	0.030355	0.030854	0.031345
1.50	0.020371	0.020710	0.021043	0.021370	0.021691
1.75	0.013245	0.013453	0.013656	0.013855	0.014049
2.00	0.008065	0.008183	0.008298	0.008410	0.008519
2.25	0.004601	0.004663	0.004723	0.004782	0.004838
2.50	0.002459	0.002490	0.002519	0.002547	0.002574
2.75	0.001232	0.001246	0.001259	0.001272	0.001284
3.00	0.000579	0.000585	0.000590	0.000595	0.000600
3.25	0.000255	0.000257	0.000259	0.000262	0.000263

h \ a	0.50	0.51	0.52	0.53	0.54
0.00	0.073792	0.075060	0.076318	0.077566	0.078803
0.25	0.071347	0.072566	0.073775	0.074974	0.076163
0.50	0.064489	0.065573	0.066647	0.067710	0.068764
0.75	0.054498	0.055389	0.056270	0.057141	0.058003
1.00	0.043065	0.043742	0.044410	0.045069	0.045720
1.25	0.031828	0.032304	0.032772	0.033232	0.033685
1.50	0.022006	0.022315	0.022619	0.022916	0.023207
1.75	0.014239	0.014425	0.014606	0.014783	0.014956
2.00	0.008625	0.008728	0.008828	0.008926	0.009020
2.25	0.004893	0.004946	0.004997	0.005046	0.005094
2.50	0.002600	0.002626	0.002650	0.002673	0.002695
2.75	0.001295	0.001306	0.001317	0.001327	0.001337
3.00	0.000605	0.000610	0.000614	0.000618	0.000622
3.25	0.000265	0.000267	0.000268	0.000270	0.000271

h \ a	0.55	0.56	0.57	0.58	0.59
0.00	0.080030	0.081247	0.082453	0.083649	0.084835
0.25	0.077341	0.078509	0.079667	0.080814	0.081951
0.50	0.069807	0.070841	0.071864	0.072876	0.073879
0.75	0.058855	0.059697	0.060530	0.061353	0.062165
1.00	0.046361	0.046994	0.047618	0.048233	0.048839
1.25	0.034131	0.034569	0.034999	0.035422	0.035838
1.50	0.023492	0.023771	0.024045	0.024312	0.024574
1.75	0.015124	0.015288	0.015448	0.015604	0.015756
2.00	0.009112	0.009201	0.009287	0.009370	0.009451
2.25	0.005140	0.005184	0.005227	0.005268	0.005308
2.50	0.002716	0.002737	0.002756	0.002775	0.002793
2.75	0.001346	0.001354	0.001363	0.001370	0.001378
3.00	0.000625	0.000629	0.000632	0.000635	0.000638
3.25	0.000273	0.000274	0.000275	0.000276	0.000277

A Function for Computing Bivariate Normal Probabilities (cont.)

Table B of T(h, a)

h \ a	0.60	0.61	0.62	0.63	0.64
0.00	0.086010	0.087176	0.088330	0.089475	0.090609
0.25	0.083078	0.084194	0.085300	0.086396	0.087482
0.50	0.074871	0.075854	0.076826	0.077788	0.078739
0.75	0.062969	0.063762	0.064546	0.065320	0.066084
1.00	0.049436	0.050024	0.050604	0.051175	0.051738
1.25	0.036246	0.036646	0.037040	0.037426	0.037805
1.50	0.024831	0.025081	0.025326	0.025566	0.025800
1.75	0.015904	0.016048	0.016188	0.016324	0.016456
2.00	0.009530	0.009606	0.009679	0.009750	0.009818
2.25	0.005346	0.005383	0.005418	0.005452	0.005485
2.50	0.002810	0.002826	0.002842	0.002857	0.002871
2.75	0.001385	0.001391	0.001398	0.001404	0.001409
3.00	0.000640	0.000643	0.000645	0.000647	0.000649
3.25	0.000278	0.000279	0.000280	0.000280	0.000281

h \ a	0.65	0.66	0.67	0.68	0.69
0.00	0.091733	0.092847	0.093950	0.095044	0.096127
0.25	0.088557	0.089622	0.090677	0.091722	0.092756
0.50	0.079681	0.080612	0.081534	0.082445	0.083347
0.75	0.066839	0.067584	0.068320	0.069046	0.069762
1.00	0.052291	0.052836	0.053373	0.053901	0.054421
1.25	0.038177	0.038541	0.038899	0.039250	0.039594
1.50	0.026028	0.026251	0.026469	0.026682	0.026889
1.75	0.016585	0.016709	0.016831	0.016948	0.017063
2.00	0.009885	0.009949	0.010010	0.010070	0.010127
2.25	0.005516	0.005546	0.005574	0.005602	0.005628
2.50	0.002884	0.002897	0.002909	0.002921	0.002932
2.75	0.001415	0.001420	0.001424	0.001429	0.001433
3.00	0.000651	0.000653	0.000655	0.000656	0.000658
3.25	0.000282	0.000282	0.000283	0.000283	0.000284

h \ a	0.70	0.71	0.72	0.73	0.74
0.00	0.097200	0.098263	0.099316	0.100360	0.101393
0.25	0.093781	0.094796	0.095800	0.096795	0.097780
0.50	0.084239	0.085120	0.085992	0.086854	0.087707
0.75	0.070469	0.071167	0.071856	0.072535	0.073205
1.00	0.054932	0.055435	0.055929	0.056416	0.056894
1.25	0.039930	0.040261	0.040584	0.040901	0.041211
1.50	0.027091	0.027289	0.027481	0.027669	0.027851
1.75	0.017173	0.017281	0.017385	0.017486	0.017583
2.00	0.010182	0.010236	0.010287	0.010336	0.010384
2.25	0.005653	0.005677	0.005700	0.005722	0.005743
2.50	0.002942	0.002952	0.002961	0.002970	0.002979
2.75	0.001437	0.001441	0.001444	0.001447	0.001450
3.00	0.000659	0.000660	0.000662	0.000663	0.000664
3.25	0.000284	0.000285	0.000285	0.000285	0.000286

8.5

A Function for Computing Bivariate Normal Probabilities (cont.)

Table B of $T(h, a)$

h \ a	0.75	0.76	0.77	0.78	0.79
0.00	0.102416	0.103430	0.104434	0.105428	0.106413
0.25	0.098755	0.099720	0.100675	0.101621	0.102557
0.50	0.088549	0.089382	0.090206	0.091020	0.091824
0.75	0.073866	0.074518	0.075161	0.075794	0.076420
1.00	0.057365	0.057827	0.058282	0.058728	0.059167
1.25	0.041515	0.041812	0.042103	0.042388	0.042666
1.50	0.028029	0.028203	0.028371	0.028536	0.028695
1.75	0.017678	0.017770	0.017858	0.017944	0.018027
2.00	0.010429	0.010473	0.010515	0.010556	0.010595
2.25	0.005763	0.005782	0.005800	0.005818	0.005834
2.50	0.002987	0.002994	0.003001	0.003008	0.003014
2.75	0.001453	0.001456	0.001458	0.001461	0.001463
3.00	0.000665	0.000665	0.000666	0.000667	0.000668
3.25	0.000286	0.000286	0.000286	0.000287	0.000287

h \ a	0.80	0.81	0.82	0.83	0.84
0.00	0.107388	0.108354	0.109310	0.110257	0.111195
0.25	0.103484	0.104401	0.105309	0.106208	0.107097
0.50	0.092620	0.093406	0.094182	0.094950	0.095708
0.75	0.077036	0.077643	0.078242	0.078832	0.079414
1.00	0.059598	0.060022	0.060438	0.060847	0.061248
1.25	0.042939	0.043205	0.043466	0.043721	0.043970
1.50	0.028851	0.029002	0.029149	0.029292	0.029431
1.75	0.018107	0.018184	0.018259	0.018331	0.018401
2.00	0.010632	0.010668	0.010702	0.010735	0.010766
2.25	0.005850	0.005865	0.005879	0.005892	0.005905
2.50	0.003020	0.003026	0.003031	0.003036	0.003041
2.75	0.001465	0.001467	0.001469	0.001470	0.001472
3.00	0.000668	0.000669	0.000669	0.000670	0.000670
3.25	0.000287	0.000287	0.000287	0.000287	0.000287

h \ a	0.85	0.86	0.87	0.88	0.89
0.00	0.112124	0.113043	0.113954	0.114855	0.115747
0.25	0.107977	0.108848	0.109710	0.110563	0.111407
0.50	0.096458	0.097198	0.097930	0.098653	0.099367
0.75	0.079988	0.080553	0.081109	0.081658	0.082199
1.00	0.061642	0.062029	0.062409	0.062782	0.063148
1.25	0.044213	0.044451	0.044683	0.044910	0.045132
1.50	0.029566	0.029697	0.029825	0.029948	0.030068
1.75	0.018469	0.018533	0.018596	0.018656	0.018715
2.00	0.010796	0.010825	0.010853	0.010879	0.010905
2.25	0.005917	0.005929	0.005940	0.005950	0.005960
2.50	0.003045	0.003049	0.003053	0.003057	0.003060
2.75	0.001473	0.001475	0.001476	0.001477	0.001478
3.00	0.000671	0.000671	0.000672	0.000672	0.000672
3.25	0.000288	0.000288	0.000288	0.000288	0.000288

A Function for Computing Bivariate Normal Probabilities (cont.)

Table B of $T(h, a)$

h \ a	0.90	0.91	0.92	0.93	0.94
0.00	0.116631	0.117506	0.118372	0.119230	0.120079
0.25	0.112243	0.113069	0.113887	0.114696	0.115497
0.50	0.100073	0.100770	0.101458	0.102138	0.102810
0.75	0.082731	0.083256	0.083772	0.084281	0.084783
1.00	0.063507	0.063859	0.064205	0.064544	0.064877
1.25	0.045348	0.045559	0.045766	0.045967	0.046163
1.50	0.030185	0.030298	0.030408	0.030514	0.030617
1.75	0.018771	0.018825	0.018877	0.018927	0.018975
2.00	0.010929	0.010952	0.010974	0.010995	0.011015
2.25	0.005969	0.005978	0.005986	0.005994	0.006001
2.50	0.003063	0.003066	0.003069	0.003072	0.003074
2.75	0.001479	0.001480	0.001481	0.001482	0.001482
3.00	0.000672	0.000673	0.000673	0.000673	0.000673
3.25	0.000288	0.000288	0.000288	0.000288	0.000288

h \ a	0.95	0.96	0.97	0.98	0.99
0.00	0.120920	0.121752	0.122576	0.123392	0.124200
0.25	0.116290	0.117074	0.117850	0.118617	0.119377
0.50	0.103474	0.104129	0.104777	0.105416	0.106047
0.75	0.085276	0.085762	0.086241	0.086713	0.087177
1.00	0.065203	0.065523	0.065837	0.066145	0.066446
1.25	0.046355	0.046542	0.046724	0.046902	0.047075
1.50	0.030717	0.030814	0.030908	0.030999	0.031087
1.75	0.019021	0.019066	0.019109	0.019150	0.019189
2.00	0.011034	0.011052	0.011069	0.011086	0.011101
2.25	0.006008	0.006015	0.006021	0.006027	0.006032
2.50	0.003076	0.003078	0.003080	0.003082	0.003084
2.75	0.001483	0.001483	0.001484	0.001485	0.001485
3.00	0.000673	0.000674	0.000674	0.000674	0.000674
3.25	0.000288	0.000288	0.000288	0.000288	0.000288

h \ a	1.00	1.25	1.50	2.00	∞
0.00	0.125000	0.142612	0.156416	0.176208	0.250000
0.25	0.120129	0.136540	0.149156	0.166613	0.200647
0.50	0.106671	0.119952	0.129584	0.141581	0.154269
0.75	0.087634	0.096973	0.103119	0.109570	0.113314
1.00	0.066742	0.072452	0.075735	0.078468	0.079328
1.25	0.047244	0.050283	0.051753	0.052673	0.052825
1.50	0.031172	0.032582	0.033134	0.033383	0.033404
1.75	0.019227	0.019798	0.019973	0.020028	0.020030
2.00	0.011116	0.011318	0.011365	0.011375	0.011375
2.25	0.006038	0.006100	0.006111	0.006112	0.006112
2.50	0.003086	0.003103	0.003105	0.003105	0.003105
2.75	0.001485	0.001490	0.001490	0.001490	0.001490
3.00	0.000674	0.000675	0.000675	0.000675	0.000675
3.25	0.000288	0.000289	0.000289	0.000289	0.000289

A Function for Computing Bivariate Normal Probabilities (cont.)

Table C of $T(h, a)$

h \ a	0.10	0.20	0.25	0.30	0.35	0.40	0.45
3.00	0.000174	0.000329	0.000396	0.000455	0.000505	0.000546	0.000579
3.05	0.000149	0.000283	0.000340	0.000389	0.000431	0.000466	0.000494
3.10	0.000128	0.000242	0.000290	0.000333	0.000368	0.000397	0.000420
3.15	0.000109	0.000206	0.000248	0.000283	0.000313	0.000338	0.000357
3.20	0.000093	0.000176	0.000211	0.000241	0.000266	0.000286	0.000302
3.25	0.000079	0.000149	0.000179	0.000204	0.000225	0.000242	0.000255
3.30	0.000067	0.000127	0.000151	0.000172	0.000190	0.000204	0.000215
3.35	0.000057	0.000107	0.000128	0.000145	0.000160	0.000172	0.000181
3.40	0.000048	0.000090	0.000108	0.000122	0.000134	0.000144	0.000151
3.45	0.000040	0.000076	0.000090	0.000103	0.000113	0.000120	0.000126
3.50	0.000034	0.000064	0.000076	0.000086	0.000094	0.000101	0.000105
3.60	0.000024	0.000044	0.000053	0.000060	0.000065	0.000070	0.000073
3.70	0.000017	0.000031	0.000036	0.000041	0.000045	0.000048	0.000050
3.80	0.000011	0.000021	0.000025	0.000028	0.000030	0.000032	0.000034
3.90	0.000008	0.000014	0.000017	0.000019	0.000020	0.000022	0.000023
4.00	0.000005	0.000010	0.000011	0.000013	0.000014	0.000014	0.000015
4.20	0.000002	0.000004	0.000005	0.000005	0.000006	0.000006	0.000006
4.40	0.000001	0.000002	0.000002	0.000002	0.000002	0.000003	0.000003
4.60	0.000000	0.000001	0.000001	0.000001	0.000001	0.000001	0.000001
4.76	0.000000	0.000000	0.000000	0.000000	0.000000	0.000000	0.000000

h \ a	0.45	0.50	0.60	0.70	0.80	1.00	∞
3.00	0.000579	0.000605	0.000640	0.000659	0.000668	0.000674	0.000675
3.05	0.000494	0.000516	0.000545	0.000560	0.000567	0.000571	0.000572
3.10	0.000420	0.000438	0.000462	0.000474	0.000480	0.000483	0.000484
3.15	0.000357	0.000372	0.000391	0.000401	0.000405	0.000408	0.000408
3.20	0.000302	0.000314	0.000330	0.000338	0.000341	0.000343	0.000344
3.25	0.000255	0.000265	0.000278	0.000284	0.000287	0.000288	0.000289
3.30	0.000215	0.000223	0.000233	0.000238	0.000241	0.000242	0.000242
3.35	0.000181	0.000187	0.000196	0.000199	0.000201	0.000202	0.000202
3.40	0.000151	0.000157	0.000163	0.000167	0.000168	0.000168	0.000168
3.45	0.000126	0.000131	0.000136	0.000139	0.000140	0.000140	0.000140
3.50	0.000105	0.000109	0.000113	0.000115	0.000116	0.000116	0.000116
3.60	0.000073	0.000075	0.000078	0.000079	0.000079	0.000080	0.000080
3.70	0.000050	0.000051	0.000053	0.000054	0.000054	0.000054	0.000054
3.80	0.000034	0.000035	0.000036	0.000036	0.000036	0.000036	0.000036
3.90	0.000023	0.000023	0.000024	0.000024	0.000024	0.000024	0.000024
4.00	0.000015	0.000015	0.000016	0.000016	0.000016	0.000016	0.000016
4.20	0.000006	0.000006	0.000007	0.000007	0.000007	0.000007	0.000007
4.40	0.000003	0.000003	0.000003	0.000003	0.000003	0.000003	0.000003
4.60	0.000001	0.000001	0.000001	0.000001	0.000001	0.000001	0.000001
4.76	0.000000	0.000000	0.000000	0.000000	0.000000	0.000000	0.000000

8.6 Critical Values for the Spherical Normal Distribution

The quantity tabulated is that value of B for which

$$P = \left(\frac{1}{2\pi}\right)^{3/2} \frac{1}{\sigma_x \sigma_y \sigma_z} \iiint_{U^2 \leq B^2} \exp\left(-U^2/2\right) dx\, dy\, dz,$$

where

$$U^2 = \left(\frac{x - \mu_x}{\sigma_x}\right)^2 + \left(\frac{y - \mu_y}{\sigma_y}\right)^2 + \left(\frac{z - \mu_z}{\sigma_z}\right)^2.$$

This may be rewritten as

$$P = \left(\frac{1}{2\pi}\right)^{3/2} \int_0^{2\pi} \int_0^{\pi} \int_0^{B} r^2 \sin\phi \exp\left(-r^2/2\right) dr\, d\phi\, d\theta$$

$$= 2P(B) - 2BZ(B) - 1,$$

where $P(B)$ and $Z(B)$ are the univariate normal integral and density as defined in Section 1.1. When $U^2 = B^2$ is a sphere, i.e., when $\sigma_x = \sigma_y = \sigma_z$, the distribution is called the spherical normal distribution. The table derives its name from the fact that the majority of applications are to the spherical normal case.

Critical Values for the Spherical Normal Distribution

P	B	P	B	P	B
0.01	0.3389	0.41	1.3842	0.81	2.1824
0.02	0.4299	0.42	1.4013	0.82	2.2114
0.03	0.4951	0.43	1.4183	0.83	2.2416
0.04	0.5479	0.44	1.4354	0.84	2.2730
0.05	0.5932	0.45	1.4524	0.85	2.3059
0.06	0.6334	0.46	1.4695	0.86	2.3404
0.07	0.6699	0.47	1.4866	0.87	2.3767
0.08	0.7035	0.48	1.5037	0.88	2.4153
0.09	0.7349	0.49	1.5209	0.89	2.4563
0.10	0.7644	0.50	1.5382	0.90	2.5003
0.11	0.7924	0.51	1.5555	0.91	2.5478
0.12	0.8192	0.52	1.5729	0.92	2.5997
0.13	0.8447	0.53	1.5904	0.93	2.6571
0.14	0.8694	0.54	1.6080	0.94	2.7216
0.15	0.8932	0.55	1.6257	0.95	2.7955
0.16	0.9162	0.56	1.6436	0.96	2.8829
0.17	0.9386	0.57	1.6616	0.97	2.9912
0.18	0.9605	0.58	1.6797	0.98	3.1365
0.19	0.9818	0.59	1.6980	0.99	3.3682
0.20	1.0026	0.60	1.7164	0.991	3.4019
0.21	1.0230	0.61	1.7351	0.992	3.4390
0.22	1.0430	0.62	1.7540	0.993	3.4806
0.23	1.0627	0.63	1.7730	0.994	3.5280
0.24	1.0821	0.64	1.7924	0.995	3.5830
0.25	1.1012	0.65	1.8119	0.996	3.6492
0.26	1.1200	0.66	1.8318	0.997	3.7325
0.27	1.1386	0.67	1.8519	0.998	3.8465
0.28	1.1570	0.68	1.8724	0.999	4.0331
0.29	1.1751	0.69	1.8932	0.9991	4.0607
0.30	1.1932	0.70	1.9144	0.9992	4.0912
0.31	1.2110	0.71	1.9360	0.9993	4.1256
0.32	1.2288	0.72	1.9580	0.9994	4.1648
0.33	1.2464	0.73	1.9804	0.9995	4.2107
0.34	1.2638	0.74	2.0034	0.9996	4.2661
0.35	1.2812	0.75	2.0269	0.9997	4.3365
0.36	1.2985	0.76	2.0510	0.9998	4.4335
0.37	1.3158	0.77	2.0757	0.9999	4.5943
0.38	1.3330	0.78	2.1012	0.99999	5.0894
0.39	1.3501	0.79	2.1274	0.999999	5.5376
0.40	1.3672	0.80	2.1544	0.9999999	5.9503

8.7 Distribution of a Quadratic Form in Three Dimensions

Let u_1, u_2, u_3 be normally distributed independent random variables with means zero and standard deviations equal to one. Required is the probability

$$\Pr \{a_1 u_1^2 + a_2 u_2^2 + a_3 u_3^2 \leq t\} = P_3(a_1, a_2, a_3; t),$$

where $P(a_1, a_2, a_3; t)$ is given in the tables. If the u's are not independent, or if the means are not zero, a transformation of the variables must first be applied to reduce the probability distribution to a spherical normal distribution, i.e., to a trivariate normal distribution with correlations zero, means zero, and standard deviations equal to one. If the resulting ellipsoid into which a random point is to fall is still centered at the origin, then these tables apply. See Section 8.3 for a more complete discussion of this type of problem. The procedures given there are easily extended to the three-dimensional case considered here. Solomon [205] has given a more extensive table of these probabilities than has been given here.

Distribution of a Quadratic Form in Three Dimensions [205]

a_3, a_2, a_1	t				
	0.1	0.2	0.3	0.4	0.5
1/3, 1/3, 1/3	0.03997	0.10357	0.17457	0.24699	0.31773
.4, .3, .3	0.04048	0.10472	0.17628	0.24910	0.32007
.4, .4, .2	0.04259	0.10942	0.18300	0.25711	0.32868
.5, .3, .2	0.04385	0.11229	0.18727	0.26241	0.33462
.6, .2, .2	0.04840	0.12248	0.20204	0.28027	0.35413
.5, .4, .1	0.05169	0.12818	0.20810	0.28517	0.35699
.6, .3, .1	0.05421	0.13380	0.21625	0.29505	0.36786
.7, .2, .1	0.06062	0.14765	0.23570	0.31793	0.39225
.8, .1, .1	0.07663	0.17931	0.27644	0.36190	0.43528
.9, .05, .05	0.12136	0.24910	0.34889	0.42624	0.48795

a_3, a_2, a_1	t				
	0.6	0.7	0.8	0.9	1.0
1/3, 1/3, 1/3	0.38506	0.44809	0.50636	0.55977	0.60837
.4, .3, .3	0.38749	0.45048	0.50863	0.56184	0.61020
.4, .4, .2	0.39612	0.45868	0.51607	0.56832	0.61560
.5, .3, .2	0.40235	0.46489	0.52204	0.57386	0.62059
.6, .2, .2	0.42229	0.48428	0.54016	0.59021	0.63486
.5, .4, .1	0.42278	0.48247	0.53633	0.58476	0.62822
.6, .3, .1	0.43400	0.49354	0.54687	0.59449	0.63696
.7, .2, .1	0.45839	0.51682	0.56827	0.61354	0.65340
.8, .1, .1	0.49789	0.55137	0.59729	0.63698	0.67154
.9, .05, .05	0.53875	0.58169	0.61869	0.65104	0.67962

a_3, a_2, a_1	t				
	1.5	2.0	3.0	4.0	5.0
1/3, 1/3, 1/3	0.78771	0.88839	0.97071	0.99262	0.99818
.4, .3, .3	0.78815	0.88786	0.96977	0.99203	0.99791
.4, .4, .2	0.78840	0.88529	0.96684	0.99048	0.99727
.5, .3, .2	0.79008	0.88443	0.96445	0.98871	0.99631
.6, .2, .2	0.79348	0.88075	0.95762	0.98399	0.99372
.5, .4, .1	0.78625	0.87695	0.95895	0.98613	0.99528
.6, .3, .1	0.78940	0.87588	0.95494	0.98291	0.99338
.7, .2, .1	0.79332	0.87202	0.94726	0.97703	0.98965
.8, .1, .1	0.79248	0.86317	0.93650	0.96904	0.98447
.9, .05, .05	0.78410	0.84944	0.92277	0.95889	0.97767

8.8 Inverse of the Distribution of a Quadratic Form in Three Dimensions

The quantity tabulated here is the value of t that makes $P_3(a_1, a_2; t) = 0.05(0.05)0.30(0.10)0.70(0.05)0.95$, where $P_3(a_1, a_2; t)$ is defined as in Section 8.7. Solomon [205] and Marsaglia [133] give more extensive tables of this type.

Inverse of the Distribution of a Quadratic Form in Three Dimensions [205]

a_3, a_2, a_1	P				
	0.05	0.10	0.15	0.20	0.25
1/3,1/3,1/3	0.11728	0.19479	0.26593	0.33506	0.40418
.4, .3, .3	0.11625	0.19316	0.26380	0.33250	0.40125
.4, .4, .2	0.11216	0.18678	0.25560	0.32281	0.39030
.5, .3, .2	0.10987	0.18308	0.25070	0.31680	0.38328
.6, .2, .2	0.10238	0.17104	0.23479	0.29744	0.36079
.5, .4, .1	0.09760	0.16439	0.22726	0.28978	0.35364
.6, .3, .1	0.09424	0.15876	0.21956	0.28009	0.34203
.7, .2, .1	0.08676	0.14632	0.20263	0.25892	0.31679
.8, .1, .1	0.07254	0.12306	0.17144	0.22048	0.27166
.9,.05,.05	0.04892	0.08481	0.12076	0.15894	0.20079

a_3, a_2, a_1	0.30	0.40	0.50	0.60	0.70
1/3, 1/3,1/3	0.47455	0.62306	0.78866	0.98206	1.22163
.4, .3, .3	0.47129	0.61928	0.78461	0.97807	1.21833
.4, .4, .2	0.45932	0.60597	0.77106	0.96586	1.20999
.5, .3, .2	0.45138	0.59641	0.76030	0.95463	1.19972
.6, .2, .2	0.42604	0.56630	0.72707	0.92096	1.17086
.5, .4, .1	0.42001	0.56429	0.73141	0.93385	1.19378
.6, .3, .1	0.40653	0.54733	0.71153	0.91234	1.17351
.7, .2, .1	0.37740	0.51111	0.66990	0.86874	1.13540
.8, .1, .1	0.32617	0.44995	0.60367	0.80640	1.09354
.9,.05,.05	0.24771	0.36331	0.52213	0.74773	1.07910

a_3, a_2, a_1	0.75	0.80	0.85	0.90	0.95
1/3,1/3,1/3	1.36945	1.54721	1.77235	2.08380	2.60492
.4, .3, .3	1.36691	1.54593	1.77322	2.08866	2.61919
.4, .4, .2	1.36210	1.54641	1.78193	2.11122	2.67018
.5, .3, .2	1.35337	1.54058	1.78149	2.12162	2.70823
.6, .2, .2	1.33067	1.52864	1.78857	2.16491	2.83545
.5, .4, .1	1.35845	1.56011	1.82047	2.18826	2.81991
.6, .3, .1	1.34096	1.54819	1.81920	2.20868	2.89436
.7, .2, .1	1.31108	1.53323	1.83076	2.26967	3.06160
.8, .1, .1	1.28969	1.54273	1.88657	2.39803	3.32698
.9,.05,.05	1.30761	1.60311	2.00537	2.60393	3.68536

8.9 A Function for Computing Trivariate Normal Probabilities

The quantity tabulated here is defined by

$$S(h, a, b) = \int_{-\infty}^{h} T(ax, b)Z(x)\, dx,$$

where $T(h, a)$ is defined in Section 8.5, and $Z(x)$ is the normal probability density defined in Section 1.1. This function is used to evaluate

$$C(h, k, m; \rho_{12}, \rho_{13}, \rho_{23}) = \Pr\{X_1 \leq h, X_2 \leq k, X_3 \leq m\},$$

where X_1, X_2, X_3 have a joint trivariate normal distribution with zero means and unit variances, and such that the correlation between X_i and X_j is ρ_{ij}, $i \neq j$. If $h = k = m = 0$, then

$$C(0, 0, 0; \rho_{12}, \rho_{13}, \rho_{23}) = \frac{1}{4\pi}(2\pi - \arccos \rho_{12} - \arccos \rho_{13} - \arccos \rho_{23}).$$

The formulas connecting $C(h, k, m; \rho_{12}, \rho_{13}, \rho_{23})$ and $S(h, a, b)$ are:

Case i: $h \geq 0, k \geq 0, m \geq 0$ or $h \leq 0, k \leq 0, m \leq 0$,

$$\begin{aligned}
C(h, k, m; \rho_{12}, \rho_{13}, \rho_{23}) = {}& \tfrac{1}{2}[(1 - \delta_{a_1 c_1})P(h) + (1 - \delta_{a_2 c_2})P(k) \\
& + (1 - \delta_{a_3 c_3})P(m)] - \tfrac{1}{2}[T(h, a_1) + T(h, c_1) + T(k, a_2) + T(k, c_2) \\
& + T(m, a_3) + T(m, c_3)] - [S(h, a_1, b_1) + S(h, c_1, d_1) \\
& + S(k, a_2, b_2) + S(k, c_2, d_2) + S(m, a_3, b_3) + S(m, c_3, d_3)].
\end{aligned}$$

Case ii: $h \geq 0, k \geq 0, m < 0$ or $h \leq 0, k \leq 0, m > 0$,

$$\begin{aligned}
C(h, k, m; \rho_{12}, \rho_{13}, \rho_{23}) = {}& \tfrac{1}{2}[P(h) + P(k) - \delta_{hk}] - T(h, a_1) - T(k, c_2) \\
& - C(h, k, -m; \rho_{12}, -\rho_{13}, -\rho_{23}),
\end{aligned}$$

where

$$a_1 = \frac{k - h\rho_{12}}{h(1 - \rho_{12}^2)^{1/2}}, \quad a_2 = \frac{m - k\rho_{23}}{k(1 - \rho_{23}^2)^{1/2}}, \quad a_3 = \frac{h - m\rho_{13}}{m(1 - \rho_{13}^2)^{1/2}},$$

$$c_1 = \frac{m - h\rho_{13}}{h(1 - \rho_{13}^2)^{1/2}}, \quad c_2 = \frac{h - k\rho_{12}}{k(1 - \rho_{12}^2)^{1/2}}, \quad c_3 = \frac{k - m\rho_{23}}{m(1 - \rho_{23}^2)^{1/2}},$$

$$b_1 = \frac{(1 - \rho_{12}^2)(m - h\rho_{13}) - (\rho_{23} - \rho_{12}\rho_{13})(k - h\rho_{12})}{(k - h\rho_{12})\,\Delta^{1/2}},$$

$$d_1 = \frac{(1 - \rho_{13}^2)(k - h\rho_{12}) - (\rho_{23} - \rho_{12}\rho_{13})(m - h\rho_{13})}{(m - h\rho_{13})\,\Delta^{1/2}},$$

$$b_2 = \frac{(1 - \rho_{23}^2)(h - k\rho_{12}) - (\rho_{13} - \rho_{12}\rho_{23})(m - k\rho_{23})}{(m - k\rho_{23}) \Delta^{1/2}},$$

$$d_2 = \frac{(1 - \rho_{12}^2)(m - k\rho_{23}) - (\rho_{13} - \rho_{12}\rho_{23})(h - k\rho_{12})}{(h - k\rho_{12}) \Delta^{1/2}},$$

$$b_3 = \frac{(1 - \rho_{13}^2)(k - m\rho_{23}) - (\rho_{12} - \rho_{13}\rho_{23})(h - m\rho_{13})}{(h - m\rho_{13}) \Delta^{1/2}},$$

$$d_3 = \frac{(1 - \rho_{23}^2)(h - m\rho_{13}) - (\rho_{12} - \rho_{13}\rho_{23})(k - m\rho_{23})}{(k - m\rho_{23}) \Delta^{1/2}},$$

$$\Delta = 1 - \rho_{12}^2 - \rho_{13}^2 - \rho_{23}^2 + 2\rho_{12}\rho_{13}\rho_{23},$$

$$\delta_{xy} = \begin{cases} 0 \text{ if } (\operatorname{sgn} x)(\operatorname{sgn} y) = 1, \\ +1 \text{ otherwise,} \end{cases}$$

and

$$\operatorname{sgn} x = \begin{cases} 1 \text{ if } x \geq 0, \\ -1 \text{ if } x < 0. \end{cases}$$

The S-function is tabulated for $0 < b \leq 1$, but it is possible to obtain values for $1 < b < \infty$ by use of one of the following formulas, $a > 0$, $b > 0$:

$$S(h, a, b) = [P(h) - \tfrac{1}{2}]T(ah, b) - [P(hab) - \tfrac{1}{2}]T(ah, 1/a)$$
$$+ S(hab, 1/b, 1/a),$$

$$S(h, a, b) = (\tfrac{1}{4})P(h) + [P(hab) - \tfrac{1}{2}]T(h, a) - S(hab, 1/ab, a)$$
$$-S(h, ab, 1/b).$$

If $a > 1, b > 1$, then the first formula should be used, and if $0 < a \leq 1$, $b > 1$, then the last formula should be used. Values for negative h, a, or b may be obtained by using

$$S(-h, a, b) = S(\infty, a, b) - S(h, a, b),$$
$$S(h, -a, b) = S(h, a, b),$$
$$S(h, a, -b) = -S(h, a, b).$$

The reader is referred to Steck's paper [207] for any further details and for a worked example. McFadden [136] considers a special case of the quadrivariate normal integral.

A Function for Computing Trivariate Normal Probabilities [207]

a = 0

h\b	0.1	0.2	0.3	0.4	0.5	0.6	0.7	0.8	0.9	1.0
0.0	.0079314	.0157082	.0231934	.0302797	.0368959	.0430052	.0486000	.0536942	.0583156	.0625000
0.1	.0085632	.0169595-	.0250409	.0326917	.0398349	.0464308	.0524713	.0579712	.0629607	.0674785-
0.2	.0091887	.0181983	.0268700	.0350797	.0427446	.0498224	.0563041	.0622057	.0675597	.0724075-
0.3	.0098018	.0194126	.0286629	.0374204	.0455968	.0531468	.0600610	.0663565	.0720677	.0772389
0.4	.0103968	.0205910	.0304029	.0396920	.0483648	.0563731	.0637070	.0703847	.0764426	.0819277
0.5	.0109685+	.0217233	.0320747	.0418746	.0510243	.0594730	.0672102	.0742550+	.0806461	.0864328
0.6	.0115123	.0228004	.0336651	.0439508	.0535542	.0624218	.0705426	.0779368	.0846447	.0907184
0.7	.0120245+	.0238148	.0351629	.0459063	.0559369	.0651990	.0736812	.0814043	.0884106	.0947545+
0.8	.0125021	.0247607	.0365595-	.0477296	.0581586	.0677886	.0766077	.0846375+	.0919222	.0985181
0.9	.0129431	.0256340	.0378488	.0494129	.0602097	.0701793	.0793094	.0876224	.0951640	.1019925-
1.0	.0133460	.0264321	.0390273	.0509514	.0620843	.0723644	.0817788	.0903506	.0981270	.1051681
1.1	.0137107	.0271543	.0400937	.0523436	.0637808	.0743417	.0840133	.0928194	.1008083	.1080417
1.2	.0140374	.0278014	.0410491	.0535909	.0653006	.0761132	.0860153	.0950312	.1032104	.1106163
1.3	.0143272	.0283754	.0418965+	.0546973	.0666487	.0776846	.0877911	.0969931	.1053412	.1129000
1.4	.0145817	.0288794	.0426408	.0556689	.0678326	.0790645+	.0893505+	.0987160	.1072124	.1149054
1.5	.0148030	.0293176	.0432878	.0565137	.0688620	.0802643	.0907064	.1002141	.1088394	.1166491
∞	.0158628	.0314165-	.0463868	.0605595-	.0737918	.0860104	.0972001	.1073884	.1166311	.1250000

a = 0.1

h\b	0.1	0.2	0.3	0.4	0.5	0.6	0.7	0.8	0.9	1.0
0.0	.0078919	.0156293	.0230749	.0301218	.0366986	.0427685-	.0483239	.0533787	.0579608	.0621060
0.1	.0085237	.0168805-	.0249224	.0325337	.0396375-	.0461940	.0521951	.0576557	.0626059	.0670844
0.2	.0091491	.0181192	.0267513	.0349214	.0425469	.0495851	.0560274	.0618896	.0672042	.0720127
0.3	.0097620	.0193331	.0285436	.0372614	.0453981	.0529084	.0597830	.0660388	.0717105	.0768422
0.4	.0103567	.0205108	.0302825+	.0395315+	.0481642	.0561325+	.0634264	.0700641	.0760821	.0815273
0.5	.0109278	.0216419	.0319526	.0417118	.0508208	.0592289	.0669255-	.0739298	.0802803	.0860266
0.6	.0114708	.0227173	.0335405-	.0437847	.0533466	.0621727	.0702522	.0776049	.0842715-	.0903039
0.7	.0119819	.0237296	.0350350+	.0457358	.0557238	.0649435-	.0733331	.0810637	.0880277	.0943292
0.8	.0124582	.0246728	.0364276	.0475538	.0579388	.0675250+	.0763002	.0842862	.0915271	.0980793
0.9	.0128975-	.0255428	.0377121	.0492307	.0599819	.0699061	.0789907	.0872584	.0947546	.1015378
1.0	.0132987	.0263373	.0388851	.0507619	.0618475+	.0720803	.0814474	.0899720	.0977012	.1046952
1.1	.0136613	.0270555+	.0399455+	.0521461	.0635339	.0740456	.0836679	.0924247	.1003644	.1075488
1.2	.0139859	.0276983	.0408944	.0533848	.0650430	.0758041	.0855547	.0946193	.1027472	.1101018
1.3	.0142734	.0282677	.0417351	.0544821	.0663798	.0773619	.0874147	.0965631	.1048576	.1123629
1.4	.0145256	.0287671	.0424724	.0554444	.0675521	.0787280	.0889580	.0982676	.1067081	.1143452
1.5	.0147446	.0292007	.0431125+	.0562799	.0685699	.0799139	.0902977	.0997470	.1083142	.1160658
∞	.0157838	.0312585+	.0461499	.0602437	.0733971	.0855369	.0966478	.1067575-	.1159217	.1242121

A Function for Computing Trivariate Normal Probabilities (cont.)

a = 0.2

h\b	0.1	0.2	0.3	0.4	0.5	0.6	0.7	0.8	0.9	1.0
0.0	.0077769	.0153993	.0227302	.0296626	.0361251	.0420812	.0475234	.0524654	.0569355-	.0609693
0.1	.0084086	.0166505-	.0245775+	.0320743	.0390638	.0455066	.0513943	.0567421	.0615802	.0659473
0.2	.0090338	.0178887	.0264058	.0344611	.0419721	.0488964	.0552251	.0609743	.0661766	.0708734
0.3	.0096462	.0191014	.0281964	.0367988	.0448204	.0522162	.0589766	.0651189	.0706776	.0756971
0.4	.0102397	.0202769	.0299320	.0390645-	.0475810	.0554336	.0626123	.0691353	.0750393	.0803712
0.5	.0108091	.0214046	.0315968	.0412378	.0502289	.0585196	.0660992	.0729871	.0792218	.0848531
0.6	.0113496	.0224751	.0331773	.0433009	.0527424	.0614486	.0694086	.0766425-	.0831908	.0891057
0.7	.0118575+	.0234808	.0346621	.0452390	.0551034	.0641999	.0725169	.0800754	.0869179	.0930987
0.8	.0123297	.0244160	.0360426	.0470409	.0572984	.0667574	.0754059	.0832658	.0903831	.0968087
0.9	.0127643	.0252766	.0373130	.0486988	.0593178	.0691100	.0780633	.0862001	.0935661	.1002199
1.0	.0131601	.0260602	.0384697	.0502084	.0611563	.0712518	.0804821	.0888706	.0964642	.1033234
1.1	.0135168	.0267665+	.0395122	.0515688	.0628129	.0731814	.0826610	.0912757	.0990740	.1061177
1.2	.0138349	.0273965+	.0404420	.0527819	.0642901	.0749017	.0846032	.0934193	.1013995-	.1086071
1.3	.0141158	.0279526	.0412627	.0538526	.0655936	.0764195+	.0863166	.0953100	.1034502	.1108019
1.4	.0143612	.0284384	.0419795+	.0547877	.0667319	.0777448	.0878124	.0969602	.1052396	.1127166
1.5	.0145733	.0288584	.0425992	.0555960	.0677157	.0788899	.0891045+	.0983855-	.1067848	.1143696
∞	.0155537	.0307986	.0454604	.0593251	.0722502	.0841624	.0950467	.1049309	.1138709	.1219386

a = 0.3

h\b	0.1	0.2	0.3	0.4	0.5	0.6	0.7	0.8	0.9	1.0
0.0	.0075958	.0150376	.0221884	.0289417	.0352265-	.0410064	.0462742	.0510441	.0553443	.0592109
0.1	.0082275+	.0162886	.0240356	.0313533	.0381650-	.0444315-	.0501448	.0553204	.0599886	.0641885-
0.2	.0088524	.0175261	.0258628	.0337387	.0410715-	.0478191	.0539730	.0595497	.0645817	.0691109
0.3	.0094637	.0187369	.0276505-	.0360724	.0439149	.0511330	.0577177	.0636865-	.0690740	.0739249
0.4	.0100555-	.0199088	.0293806	.0383806	.0466664	.0543395+	.0613407	.0676883	.0734192	.0785807
0.5	.0106220	.0210306	.0310367	.0404926	.0492998	.0574081	.0648073	.0715169	.0775758	.0830337
0.6	.0111584	.0220930	.0326049	.0425393	.0517928	.0603127	.0680881	.0751397	.0815081	.0872456
0.7	.0116609	.0230880	.0340737	.0444560	.0541271	.0630319	.0711590	.0785299	.0851871	.0911853
0.8	.0121266	.0240100	.0354344	.0462315-	.0562891	.0655498	.0740019	.0816676	.0885913	.0948296
0.9	.0125533	.0248549	.0366813	.0478582	.0582695+	.0678558	.0766049	.0845398	.0917063	.0981633
1.0	.0129402	.0256209	.0378116	.0493325-	.0600639	.0699446	.0789620	.0871399	.0945254	.1011792
1.1	.0132872	.0263078	.0388249	.0506540	.0616721	.0718161	.0810732	.0894679	.0970485-	.1038774
1.2	.0135950+	.0269170	.0397236	.0518258	.0630976	.0734745-	.0829434	.0915293	.0992818	.1062646
1.3	.0138651	.0274516	.0405120	.0528534	.0643474	.0749280	.0845819	.0933346	.1012367	.1083533
1.4	.0140095+	.0279155-	.0411960	.0537449	.0654312	.0761880	.0860018	.0948982	.1029291	.1101606
1.5	.0143008	.0283137	.0417832	.0545098	.0663609	.0772684	.0872186	.0962377	.1043781	.1117072
∞	.0151917	.0300752	.0443769	.0578835-	.0704530	.0820128	.0925485-	.1020882	.1106887	.1184219

8.9

A Function for Computing Trivariate Normal Probabilities (cont.)

a = 0.4

h\b	0.1	0.2	0.3	0.4	0.5	0.6	0.7	0.8	0.9	1.0
0.0	.0073624	.0145715-	.0214912	.0280157	.0340745-	.0396321	.0446818	.0492383	.0533303	.0569943
0.1	.0079940	.0158224	.0233382	.0304269	.0370126	.0430567	.0485519	.0535140	.0579740	.0619711
0.2	.0086184	.0170589	.0251638	.0328102	.0399165+	.0464412	.0523765-	.0577392	.0625624	.0668884
0.3	.0092284	.0182670	.0269474	.0351386	.0427532	.0497471	.0561117	.0618651	.0670425+	.0716889
0.4	.0098175+	.0194337	.0286699	.0373868	.0454919	.0529383	.0597168	.0658465+	.0713648	.0763193
0.5	.0103800	.0205475+	.0303140	.0395324	.0481053	.0559828	.0631554	.0696431	.0754853	.0807322
0.6	.0109108	.0215985-	.0318652	.0415565-	.0505699	.0588534	.0663966	.0732206	.0793668	.0848877
0.7	.0114059	.0225788	.0333117	.0434436	.0528673	.0615283	.0694159	.0765520	.0829797	.0887540
0.8	.0118624	.0234825+	.0346452	.0451828	.0549839	.0639918	.0721954	.0796174	.0863027	.0923083
0.9	.0122785+	.0243061	.0358601	.0467669	.0569111	.0662340	.0747241	.0824049	.0893228	.0955368
1.0	.0126534	.0250480	.0369542	.0481930	.0586455-	.0682510	.0769976	.0849097	.0920349	.0984343
1.1	.0129872	.0257085+	.0379282	.0494621	.0601882	.0700441	.0790177	.0871339	.0944417	.1010038
1.2	.0132810	.0262899	.0387851	.0505783	.0615444	.0716196	.0807915-	.0890856	.0965521	.1032552
1.3	.0135367	.0267957	.0395304	.0515486	.0627227	.0729877	.0823308	.0907780	.0983807	.1052044
1.4	.0137566	.0272306	.0401710	.0523823	.0637346	.0741618	.0836508	.0922282	.0999464	.1068719
1.5	.0139436	.0276002	.0407153	.0530904	.0645935+	.0751576	.0847695+	.0934563	.1012710	.1082813
8	.0147248	.0291430	.0429825-	.0560313	.0681490	.0792642	.0893636	.0984766	.1066607	.1139887

a = 0.5

h\b	0.1	0.2	0.3	0.4	0.5	0.6	0.7	0.8	0.9	1.0
0.0	.0070917	.0140314	.0206845-	.0269462	.0327475-	.0380537	.0428591	.0471792	.0510432	.0544882
0.1	.0077232	.0152821	.0225312	.0293571	.0356851	.0414777	.0467285+	.0514541	.0556860	.0594641
0.2	.0083469	.0165173	.0243548	.0317378	.0385857	.0448583	.0505485+	.0556740	.0602686	.0643748
0.3	.0089552	.0177219	.0261332	.0340591	.0414137	.0481538	.0542716	.0597861	.0647331	.0691579
0.4	.0095411	.0188821	.0278459	.0362943	.0441361	.0513254	.0578539	.0637415-	.0690261	.0737558
0.5	.0100984	.0199857	.0294746	.0384195-	.0467239	.0543392	.0612567	.0674972	.0731007	.0781178
0.6	.0106220	.0210222	.0310042	.0404147	.0491526	.0571667	.0644477	.0710174	.0769178	.0822020
0.7	.0111077	.0219838	.0324227	.0422646	.0514034	.0597858	.0674020	.0742746	.0804475+	.0859761
0.8	.0115528	.0228647	.0337219	.0439580	.0534630	.0621811	.0701021	.0772496	.0836691	.0894181
0.9	.0119556	.0236616	.0348968	.0454890	.0553239	.0643439	.0725385+	.0799320	.0865714	.0925164
1.0	.0123155-	.0243736	.0359462	.0468556	.0569841	.0662721	.0747089	.0823194	.0891522	.0952688
1.1	.0126331	.0250018	.0368717	.0480603	.0584466	.0679694	.0766177	.0844171	.0914176	.0976822
1.2	.0129099	.0255492	.0376778	.0491089	.0597186	.0694444	.0782749	.0862365+	.0933802	.0997708
1.3	.0131482	.0260202	.0383711	.0500102	.0608111	.0707101	.0796955-	.0877943	.0950587	.1015548
1.4	.0133508	.0264205	.0389600	.0507752	.0617376	.0717823	.0808976	.0891110	.0964757	.1030589
1.5	.0135208	.0267565-	.0394539	.0514163	.0625134	.0726792	.0819020	.0902097	.0975565-	.1043106
8	.0141834	.0280628	.0413690	.0538924	.0654949	.0761074	.0857182	.0943583	.1020864	.1089764

A Function for Computing Trivariate Normal Probabilities (cont.)

a = 0.6

h\b	0.1	0.2	0.3	0.4	0.5	0.6	0.7	0.8	0.9	1.0
0.0	.0067981	.0134463	.0198118	.0257918	.0313188	.0363597	.0409097	.0449854	.0486166	.0518406
0.1	.0074295+	.0146968	.0216582	.0282023	.0345559	.0397830	.0447783	.0492594	.0532583	.0568153
0.2	.0080524	.0159303	.0234794	.0305797	.0371525+	.0431588	.0485928	.0534729	.0578337	.0617181
0.3	.0086586	.0171307	.0252515-	.0328926	.0399699	.0464415+	.0523010	.0575681	.0622792	.0664801
0.4	.0092405-	.0182830	.0269522	.0351119	.0426725+	.0495894	.0558556	.0614918	.0665366	.0710386
0.5	.0097916	.0193741	.0285623	.0372123	.0452293	.0525661	.0592152	.0651982	.0705558	.0753391
0.6	.0103065+	.0203934	.0300659	.0391730	.0476149	.0553419	.0623460	.0686498	.0742959	.0793379
0.7	.0107811	.0213326	.0314510	.0409782	.0498100	.0578943	.0652227	.0718186	.0777266	.0830024
0.8	.0112126	.0221863	.0327094	.0426175+	.0518021	.0602089	.0678290	.0746868	.0808206	.0863123
0.9	.0115996	.0229518	.0338374	.0440859	.0535851	.0622786	.0701572	.0772463	.0835934	.0892588
1.0	.0119420	.0236289	.0348345+	.0453832	.0551589	.0641037	.0722080	.0794979	.0860227	.0918443
1.1	.0122409	.0242198	.0357041	.0465136	.0565290	.0656908	.0739892	.0814509	.0881268	.0940803
1.2	.0124983	.0247283	.0364522	.0474851	.0577053	.0670517	.0755145-	.0831210	.0899233	.0959866
1.3	.0127170	.0251601	.0370869	.0483087	.0587013	.0682026	.0768025+	.0845291	.0914355-	.0975884
1.4	.0129002	.0255218	.0376181	.0489974	.0595332	.0691624	.0778750-	.0856996	.0926903	.0989153
1.5	.0130516	.0258207	.0380567	.0495653	.0602183	.0699517	.0787555-	.0866589	.0937169	.0999988
∞	.0135962	.0268926	.0396236	.0515836	.0626377	.0727194	.0818195-	.0899707	.0972331	.1036813

a = 0.7

h\b	0.1	0.2	0.3	0.4	0.5	0.6	0.7	0.8	0.9	1.0
0.0	.0064941	.0128409	.0189104	.0246019	.0298500	.0346233	.0389184	.0427525+	.0461562	.0491670
0.1	.0071254	.0140912	.0207563	.0270118	.0327864	.0380458	.0427860	.0470254	.0507967	.0541403
0.2	.0077473	.0153228	.0225747	.0293855-	.0356783	.0414160	.0465938	.0512314	.0553636	.0590336
0.3	.0083510	.0165182	.0243393	.0316884	.0384833	.0446838	.0502847	.0553067	.0597867	.0637708
0.4	.0089282	.0176612	.0260261	.0338891	.0411627	.0478038	.0538069	.0591934	.0640026	.0682832
0.5	.0094721	.0187379	.0276145+	.0359606	.0436834	.0507373	.0571161	.0628424	.0679574	.0725124
0.6	.0099770	.0197370	.0290880	.0378811	.0460189	.0534531	.0601772	.0662146	.0716085-	.0764126
0.7	.0104387	.0206504	.0304344	.0396350+	.0481500-	.0559290	.0629649	.0692822	.0749259	.0799520
0.8	.0108546	.0214731	.0316465-	.0412126	.0500652	.0581517	.0654646	.0720292	.0778924	.0831125-
0.9	.0112238	.0222031	.0327212	.0426104	.0517603	.0601165+	.0676713	.0744508	.0805035-	.0858897
1.0	.0115467	.0228412	.0336601	.0438302	.0533378	.0618269	.0695893	.0765522	.0827654	.0882914
1.1	.0118249	.0233907	.0344680	.0448787	.0545063	.0632931	.0712308	.0783473	.0846941	.0903353
1.2	.0120611	.0238565	.0351528	.0457665+	.0555588	.0645307	.0726139	.0798571	.0863129	.0920473
1.3	.0122586	.0242466	.0357246	.0465069	.0564719	.0655595-	.0737614	.0811070	.0876504	.0934587
1.4	.0124213	.0245675-	.0361950-	.0471152	.0572043	.0664016	.0746987	.0821259	.0887381	.0946040
1.5	.0125534	.0248277	.0365762	.0476073	.0577959	.0670804	.0754527	.0829435-	.0896090	.0955188
∞	.0129882	.0256819	.0378208	.0492038	.0597001	.0692466	.0778367	.0855050+	.0923124	.0983340

8.9

A Function for Computing Trivariate Normal Probabilities (cont.)

a = 0.8

h\b	0.1	0.2	0.3	0.4	0.5	0.6	0.7	0.8	0.9	1.0
0.0	.0061894	.0122347	.0180090	.0234144	.0283879	.0328998	.0369480	.0405506	.0437383	.0465488
0.1	.0068205-	.0134846	.0198545-	.0258237	.0313235+	.0363214	.0408145+	.0448222	.0483774	.0515206
0.2	.0074413	.0147141	.0216696	.0281930	.0342100	.0396350-	.0446147	.0490195+	.0529346	.0564030
0.3	.0080421	.0159038	.0234256	.0304845+	.0370007	.0429356	.0482856	.0530720	.0573320	.0611118
0.4	.0086141	.0170361	.0250965-	.0326640	.0396535+	.0460239	.0517708	.0569165-	.0615005+	.0655716
0.5	.0091497	.0180963	.0266602	.0347027	.0421332	.0489083	.0550229	.0605004	.0653823	.0697199
0.6	.0096432	.0190727	.0280997	.0365779	.0444123	.0515566	.0580055-	.0637832	.0689334	.0735097
0.7	.0100904	.0199573	.0294029	.0382744	.0464719	.0539471	.0606941	.0667382	.0721249	.0769102
0.8	.0104892	.0207456	.0305635+	.0397837	.0483021	.0560683	.0630762	.0693520	.0749428	.0799072
0.9	.0108389	.0214367	.0315801	.0411042	.0499012	.0579189	.0651507	.0716239	.0773874	.0825017
1.0	.0111406	.0220326	.0324559	.0422404	.0512751	.0595059	.0669264	.0735646	.0794710	.0847082
1.1	.0113967	.0225380	.0331980	.0432018	.0524357	.0608441	.0684204	.0751937	.0812161	.0865518
1.2	.0116105+	.0229597	.0338164	.0440020	.0533998	.0619533	.0696561	.0765379	.0826522	.0880652
1.3	.0117862	.0233059	.0343234	.0446568	.0541873	.0628574	.0706606	.0776278	.0838137	.0892858
1.4	.0119281	.0235853	.0347322	.0451839	.0548197	.0635817	.0714634	.0784965-	.0847368	.0902534
1.5	.0120409	.0238072	.0350564	.0456011	.0553193	.0641523	.0720941	.0791770	.0854580	.0910071
∞	.0123787	.0244694	.0360180	.0468289	.0567759	.0657996	.0738960	.0811011	.0874767	.0930977

a = 0.9

h\b	0.1	0.2	0.3	0.4	0.5	0.6	0.7	0.8	0.9	1.0
0.0	.0058910	.0116416	.0171284	.0222566	.0269655+	.0312275-	.0350415+	.0384264	.0414131	.0440387
0.1	.0065219	.0128912	.0189733	.0246651	.0299002	.0346479	.0389068	.0426966	.0460505+	.0490086
0.2	.0071415+	.0141182	.0207848	.0270296	.0327806	.0380042	.0426984	.0468841	.0505966	.0538788
0.3	.0077391	.0153014	.0225311	.0293082	.0355551	.0412355+	.0463468	.0509109	.0549652	.0585556
0.4	.0083051	.0164219	.0241841	.0314638	.0381783	.0442882	.0497905-	.0547081	.0590807	.0629566
0.5	.0088316	.0174637	.0257204	.0334659	.0406123	.0471180	.0529790	.0582196	.0628814	.0670153
0.6	.0093125-	.0184150+	.0271222	.0352912	.0428291	.0496919	.0558752	.0614043	.0663227	.0706839
0.7	.0097439	.0192680	.0283782	.0369248	.0448106	.0519891	.0584558	.0642367	.0693775-	.0739339
0.8	.0101240	.0200191	.0294832	.0383603	.0465491	.0540011	.0607115-	.0667074	.0720363	.0767562
0.9	.0104528	.0206685+	.0304376	.0395984	.0480460	.0557301	.0626458	.0688212	.0743054	.0791588
1.0	.0107323	.0212199	.0312470	.0406468	.0493112	.0571883	.0642732	.0705949	.0762044	.0811641
1.1	.0109654	.0216797	.0319210	.0415183	.0503607	.0583950-	.0656163	.0720549	.0777631	.0828053
1.2	.0111565-	.0220561	.0324721	.0422296	.0512152	.0593742	.0667041	.0732337	.0790177	.0841223
1.3	.0113102	.0223588	.0329145-	.0427993	.0518981	.0601559	.0675683	.0741674	.0800084	.0851591
1.4	.0114318	.0225977	.0332632	.0432475-	.0524337	.0607667	.0682421	.0748930	.0807757	.0859595+
1.5	.0115261	.0227830	.0335331	.0435935-	.0528462	.0612355+	.0687576	.0754461	.0813588	.0865658
∞	.0117819	.0232833	.0342569	.0445132	.0539311	.0624549	.0700830	.0768528	.0828261	.0880774

A Function for Computing Trivariate Normal Probabilities (cont.)

a = 1.0

h\b	0.1	0.2	0.3	0.4	0.5	0.6	0.7	0.8	0.9	1.0
0.0	.0056037	.0110711	.0162824	.0211461	.0256041	.0296305+	.0332256	.0364084	.0392099	.0416667
0.1	.0062344	.0123202	.0181267	.0235538	.0285378	.0330498	.0370895-	.0406770	.0438456	.0466346
0.2	.0068526	.0135445+	.0199340	.0259127	.0314113	.0363978	.0408715-	.0448536	.0483793	.0514912
0.3	.0074466	.0147206	.0216696	.0281770	.0341679	.0396077	.0444949	.0488518	.0527159	.0561324
0.4	.0080060	.0158278	.0233028	.0303064	.0367583	.0426211	.0478928	.0525969	.0567729	.0604687
0.5	.0085224	.0168495+	.0248089	.0322683	.0391423	.0453911	.0510119	.0560294	.0604852	.0644297
0.6	.0089897	.0177735+	.0261700	.0340393	.0412916	.0478843	.0538145+	.0591079	.0638079	.0679676
0.7	.0094041	.0185896	.0273752	.0356056	.0431893	.0500817	.0562796	.0618095+	.0667171	.0710577
0.8	.0097644	.0193042	.0284212	.0369628	.0448307	.0519783	.0584021	.0641299	.0692090	.0736974
0.9	.0100714	.0199101	.0293106	.0381150-	.0462212	.0535811	.0601912	.0660802	.0712975-	.0759031
1.0	.0103278	.0204157	.0300518	.0390733	.0473751	.0549077	.0616675+	.0676847	.0730101	.0777061
1.1	.0105378	.0208293	.0306571	.0398543	.0483130	.0559828	.0628603	.0689767	.0743846	.0791482
1.2	.0107063	.0211608	.0311415+	.0404478	.0490598	.0568362	.0638039	.0699951	.0754642	.0802770
1.3	.0108388	.0214213	.0315214	.0409656	.0496423	.0574995+	.0645347	.0707811	.0762943	.0811419
1.4	.0109410	.0216219	.0318134	.0413395-	.0500873	.0580045+	.0650891	.0713750-	.0769192	.0817907
1.5	.0110183	.0217733	.0320333	.0416202	.0504203	.0583811	.0655008	.0718143	.0773798	.0822672
∞	.0112074	.0221422	.0325647	.0422921	.0512082	.0592610	.0664511	.0728168	.0784198	.0833333

a = 1.1

h\b	0.1	0.2	0.3	0.4	0.5	0.6	0.7	0.8	0.9	1.0
0.0	.0053304	.0105287	.0154790	.0200932	.0243158	.0281225-	.0315115+	.0345114	.0371435+	.0394469
0.1	.0059609	.0117774	.0173227	.0225001	.0272484	.0315404	.0353769	.0387782	.0417772	.0444127
0.2	.0065776	.0129987	.0191255+	.0248530	.0301143	.0348794	.0391483	.0429427	.0462974	.0492541
0.3	.0071677	.0141669	.0208493	.0271015+	.0328513	.0380658	.0427443	.0469097	.0505989	.0538565-
0.4	.0077199	.0152597	.0224610	.0292022	.0354059	.0410363	.0460925-	.0505981	.0545923	.0581224
0.5	.0082254	.0162596	.0239345-	.0311208	.0377359	.0437417	.0491366	.0539454	.0582094	.0619783
0.6	.0086780	.0171544	.0252517	.0328337	.0398129	.0461488	.0518394	.0569106	.0614059	.0653776
0.7	.0090744	.0179375+	.0264033	.0343288	.0416222	.0482410	.0541829	.0594750+	.0641626	.0683006
0.8	.0094140	.0186079	.0273877	.0356045-	.0431627	.0500178	.0561675+	.0616400	.0664827	.0707528
0.9	.0096985+	.0191690	.0282105-	.0366686	.0444445-	.0514920	.0578089	.0634247	.0683887	.0727603
1.0	.0099318	.0196285-	.0288830	.0375364	.0454868	.0526870	.0591349	.0648613	.0699172	.0743643
1.1	.0101188	.0199964	.0294205+	.0382282	.0463152	.0536335+	.0601813	.0659906	.0711141	.0756155+
1.2	.0102654	.0202846	.0298406	.0387674	.0469588	.0543661	.0609880	.0668576	.0720293	.0765686
1.3	.0103779	.0205053	.0301617	.0391783	.0474474	.0549201	.0615955+	.0675078	.0727129	.0772777
1.4	.0104623	.0206706	.0304016	.0394843	.0478101	.0553295+	.0620426	.0679842	.0732117	.0777931
1.5	.0105242	.0207918	.0305770	.0397073	.0480731	.0556253	.0623640	.0683253	.0735673	.0781592
∞	.0106608	.0210574	.0309581	.0401864	.0486316	.0562450-	.0630291	.0690227	.0742870	.0788938

A Function for Computing Trivariate Normal Probabilities (cont.)

a = 1.2

h\b	0.1	0.2	0.3	0.4	0.5	0.6	0.7	0.8	0.9	1.0
0.0	.0050726	.0100174	.0147226	.0191032	.0231063	.0267093	.0299142	.0327405+	.0352184	.0373829
0.1	.0057028	.0112656	.0165655+	.0215091	.0260377	.0301258	.0337748	.0370054	.0399499	.0423462
0.2	.0063179	.0124836	.0183634	.0238554	.0288953	.0334549	.0375348	.0411567	.0443353	.0471713
0.3	.0069037	.0136432	.0200743	.0260868	.0316111	.0366157	.0411010	.0450898	.0486188	.0517314
0.4	.0074481	.0147206	.0216627	.0281566	.0341270	.0395401	.0443955-	.0487171	.0525437	.0559217
0.5	.0079419	.0156972	.0231013	.0300287	.0363993	.0421765-	.0473596	.0519736	.0560594	.0596659
0.6	.0083790	.0165610	.0243723	.0316802	.0383999	.0444926	.0499572	.0548199	.0591235+	.0629198
0.7	.0087566	.0173066	.0254678	.0331011	.0401172	.0464755+	.0521747	.0572421	.0617227	.0656707
0.8	.0090749	.0179345-	.0263889	.0342932	.0415543	.0481299	.0540187	.0592492	.0638686	.0679335+
0.9	.0093368	.0184504	.0271445+	.0352686	.0427268	.0494751	.0555126	.0608690	.0655936	.0697452
1.0	.0095470	.0188642	.0277491	.0360471	.0436594	.0505411	.0566917	.0621422	.0669438	.0711575-
1.1	.0097117	.0191879	.0282211	.0366529	.0443826	.0513646	.0575986	.0631171	.0679731	.0722296
1.2	.0098377	.0194350-	.0285805+	.0371129	.0449295+	.0519845-	.0582783	.0638445+	.0687376	.0730225+
1.3	.0099317	.0196191	.0288476	.0374534	.0453327	.0524395+	.0587748	.0643733	.0692910	.0735940
1.4	.0100001	.0197529	.0290411	.0376992	.0456226	.0527651	.0591283	.0647481	.0696813	.0739956
1.5	.0100487	.0198478	.0291780	.0378724	.0458258	.0529922	.0593737	.0650069	.0699498	.0742707
∞	.0101452	.0200349	.0294451	.0382063	.0462126	.0534185+	.0598284	.0654811	.0704368	.0747658

a = 1.3

h\b	0.1	0.2	0.3	0.4	0.5	0.6	0.7	0.8	0.9	1.0
0.0	.0048308	.0095382	.0140142	.0181773	.0219768	.0253916	.0284245+	.0310950+	.0334325+	.0354713
0.1	.0054608	.0107859	.0158564	.0205821	.0249068	.0288066	.0322834	.0353578	.0380617	.0404320
0.2	.0060741	.0120003	.0176489	.0229212	.0277556	.0321249	.0360308	.0394949	.0425511	.0452393
0.3	.0066553	.0131507	.0193460	.0251343	.0304483	.0352582	.0395650+	.0433914	.0467735+	.0497541
0.4	.0071914	.0142114	.0209095+	.0271709	.0329230	.0381332	.0428021	.0469535-	.0506256	.0538638
0.5	.0076728	.0151633	.0223111	.0289939	.0351341	.0406967	.0456818	.0501142	.0540344	.0574904
0.6	.0080937	.0159947	.0235337	.0305812	.0370551	.0429181	.0481699	.0528367	.0569611	.0605938
0.7	.0084518	.0167015+	.0245714	.0319256	.0386777	.0447887	.0502581	.0551135+	.0593996	.0631695+
0.8	.0087485-	.0172864	.0254284	.0330330	.0400104	.0463197	.0519608	.0569625-	.0613715+	.0652439
0.9	.0089877	.0177573	.0261171	.0339280+	.0410746	.0475376	.0533095+	.0584206	.0629198	.0668653
1.0	.0091755+	.0181265+	.0266557	.0346123	.0419011	.0484793	.0543477	.0595378	.0641004	.0680960
1.1	.0093190	.0184082	.0270655-	.0351369	.0425252	.0491872	.0551242	.0603693	.0649749	.0690035-
1.2	.0094258	.0186174	.0273689	.0355238	.0429835-	.0497045+	.0556888	.0609707	.0656043	.0696537
1.3	.0095031	.0187685+	.0275875+	.0358015-	.0433108	.0500720	.0560878	.0613936	.0660448	.0701067
1.4	.0095576	.0188749	.0277408	.0359953	.0435381	.0503259	.0563620	.0616826	.0663444	.0704137
∞	.0096616	.0190765-	.0280285-	.0363545-	.0439535+	.0507832	.0568491	.0621900	.0668650+	.0709426

A Function for Computing Trivariate Normal Probabilities (cont.)

a = 1.4

h\b	0.1	0.2	0.3	0.4	0.5	0.6	0.7	0.8	0.9	1.0
0.0	.0046050-	.0090908	.0133534	.0173144	.0209255+	.0241670	.0270421	.0295701	.0317800	.0337049
0.1	.0052347	.0103379	.0151947	.0197181	.0238542	.0275802	.0308989	.0338307	.0364066	.0386628
0.2	.0058460	.0115485-	.0169814	.0220495+	.0266933	.0308871	.0346329	.0379524	.0408788	.0434509
0.3	.0064223	.0126890	.0186637	.0242429	.0293614	.0339909	.0381329	.0418099	.0450575-	.0479173
0.4	.0069495+	.0137320	.0202008	.0262444	.0317923	.0368136	.0413092	.0453029	.0488323	.0519418
0.5	.0074179	.0146579	.0215636	.0280158	.0339393	.0393007	.0441004	.0483634	.0521295+	.0554459
0.6	.0078219	.0154557	.0227359	.0295366	.0357778	.0414240	.0464755+	.0509585+	.0549150+	.0583949
0.7	.0081602	.0161229	.0237146	.0308029	.0373041	.0431806	.0484329	.0530884	.0571915+	.0607947
0.8	.0084352	.0166646	.0245074	.0318258	.0385326	.0445888	.0499952	.0547808	.0589920	.0626837
0.9	.0086522	.0170914	.0251306	.0326272	.0394913	.0456829	.0512033	.0560830	.0603703	.0641230
1.0	.0088185-	.0174179	.0256060	.0332363	.0402167	.0465068	.0521084	.0570534	.0613923	.0651848
1.1	.0089422	.0176603	.0259578	.0336853	.0407490	.0471082	.0527654	.0577540	.0621263	.0659437
1.2	.0090315-	.0178350-	.0262105+	.0340065-	.0411278	.0475338	.0532278	.0582443	.0626372	.0664695-
1.3	.0090941	.0179572	.0263867	.0342292	.0413892	.0478258	.0535431	.0585769	.0629820	.0668227
1.4	.0091367	.0180401	.0265058	.0343792	.0415641	.0480200	.0537517	.0587956	.0632077	.0670530
∞	.0092099	.0181816	.0267068	.0346288	.0418510	.0483340	.0540842	.0591403	.0635600	.0674097

a = 1.5

h\b	0.1	0.2	0.3	0.4	0.5	0.6	0.7	0.8	0.9	1.0
0.0	.0043945-	.0086741	.0127383	.0165120	.0199490	.0230309	.0257612	.0281591	.0302527	.0320743
0.1	.0050239	.0099206	.0145787	.0189145+	.0228762	.0264423	.0296159	.0324172	.0348766	.0370291
0.2	.0055332	.0111270	.0163593	.0212377	.0257050+	.0297368	.0333355-	.0365225-	.0393303	.0417969
0.3	.0062042	.0122570	.0180258	.0234101	.0283470	.0328094	.0367991	.0403386	.0434626	.0462118
0.4	.0067221	.0132814	.0195350+	.0253745+	.0307317	.0355769	.0399115-	.0437589	.0471563	.0501470
0.5	.0071769	.0141802	.0208572	.0270922	.0328120	.0379845-	.0426108	.0467155+	.0503380	.0535243
0.6	.0075636	.0149434	.0219780	.0285447	.0345659	.0400075-	.0448704	.0491806	.0529797	.0563165+
0.7	.0078817	.0155706	.0228971	.0297324	.0359951	.0416494	.0466964	.0511636	.0550946	.0585413
0.8	.0081352	.0160694	.0236263	.0306716	.0371208	.0429368	.0481212	.0527029	.0567279	.0602506
0.9	.0083306	.0164535-	.0241861	.0313899	.0379779	.0439121	.0491947	.0538564	.0579452	.0615178
1.0	.0084765+	.0167396	.0246018	.0319211	.0386087	.0446260	.0499761	.0546971	.0588211	.0624248
1.1	.0085820	.0169459	.0249005+	.0323012	.0390575-	.0451215+	.0505255-	.0552745+	.0594299	.0630521
1.2	.0086557	.0170898	.0251082	.0325641	.0393662	.0454763	.0508988	.0556686	.0598388	.0634713
1.3	.0087057	.0171871	.0252479	.0327400	.0395716	.0457044	.0511439	.0559258	.0601044	.0637424
∞	.0087890	.0173481	.0254767	.0330241	.0398981	.0460617	.0515223	.0563181	.0605053	.0641485+

8.9

A Function for Computing Trivariate Normal Probabilities (cont.)

a = 1.6

h\b	0.1	0.2	0.3	0.4	0.5	0.6	0.7	0.8	0.9	1.0
0.0	.0041986	.0082864	.0121665+	.0157667	.0190429	.0219777	.0245751	.0268539	.0288415+	.0305692
0.1	.0048277	.0095322	.0140059	.0181679	.0219684	.0253872	.0284275+	.0311094	.0334625+	.0355208
0.2	.0054348	.0107342	.0157799	.0204824	.0247863	.0286685+	.0321319	.0351973	.0378967	.0402669
0.3	.0060002	.0118531	.0174298	.0226326	.0274007	.0317081	.0355570	.0389696	.0419799	.0446276
0.4	.0065084	.0128580	.0189098	.0245581	.0297370	.0344179	.0386025+	.0423141	.0455890	.0484696
0.5	.0069491	.0137287	.0201900	.0262202	.0317483	.0367434	.0412070	.0451636	.0486518	.0517168
0.6	.0073180	.0144566	.0212581	.0276031	.0334161	.0386644	.0433495-	.0474972	.0511484	.0543511
0.7	.0076160	.0150437	.0221176	.0287121	.0347485+	.0401922	.0450451	.0493345+	.0531037	.0564035-
0.8	.0078484	.0155005+	.0227845-	.0295696	.0357739	.0413621	.0463364	.0507259	.0545761	.0579403
0.9	.0080231	.0158435+	.0232836	.0302086	.0365343	.0422248	.0472830	.0517397	.0556425-	.0590472
1.0	.0081500-	.0160920	.0236439	.0306677	.0370076	.0428374	.0479510	.0524506	.0563859	.0598145+
1.1	.0082389	.0162657	.0238947	.0309856	.0374517	.0432565-	.0484050-	.0529307	.0568850-	.0603270
1.2	.0082990	.0163828	.0240631	.0311980	.0376999	.0435327	.0487022	.0532431	.0572078	.0606568
1.3	.0083382	.0164589	.0241721	.0313346	.0378586	.0437082	.0488897	.0534389	.0574091	.0608617
∞	.0083972	.0165727	.0243330	.0315334	.0380858	.0439554	.0491502	.0537078	.0576831	.0611384

a = 1.7

h\b	0.1	0.2	0.3	0.4	0.5	0.6	0.7	0.8	0.9	1.0
0.0	.0040164	.0079259	.0116351	.0150746	.0182022	.0210015+	.0234768	.0256465-	.0275373	.0291794
0.1	.0046452	.0091710	.0134735+	.0174744	.0211260	.0244089	.0273268	.0298993	.0321551	.0341276
0.2	.0052499	.0103684	.0152405+	.0197796	.0239323	.0276764	.0310150-	.0339686	.0365686	.0388506
0.3	.0058095-	.0114756	.0168729	.0219065+	.0265176	.0306811	.0343996	.0376949	.0406003	.0431544
0.4	.0063074	.0124601	.0183224	.0237916	.0288036	.0333309	.0373756	.0409606	.0441215+	.0468998
0.5	.0067337	.0133019	.0195594	.0253964	.0307439	.0355721	.0398830	.0437006	.0470630	.0500144
0.6	.0070846	.0139940	.0205743	.0267089	.0323249	.0373904	.0419076	.0459021	.0494141	.0524908
0.7	.0073626	.0145412	.0213745-	.0277400	.0335614	.0388055-	.0434748	.0475965-	.0512133	.0543751
0.8	.0075743	.0149572	.0219809	.0285183	.0344900	.0398622	.0446380	.0488463	.0525322	.0557482
0.9	.0077295-	.0152614	.0224227	.0290825+	.0351595+	.0406194	.0454661	.0497303	.0534592	.0567075-
1.0	.0078389	.0154753	.0227321	.0294756	.0356230	.0411401	.0460317	.0503300	.0540841	.0573505-
1.1	.0079130	.0156198	.0229403	.0297386	.0359312	.0414839	.0464025-	.0507205+	.0544885+	.0577644
1.2	.0079613	.0157138	.0230750+	.0299078	.0361281	.0417019	.0466359	.0509647	.0547399	.0580205-
∞	.0080328	.0158517	.0232703	.0301493	.0364044	.0420030	.0469536	.0512930	.0550745+	.0583588

8.9

A Function for Computing Trivariate Normal Probabilities (cont.)

a = 1.8

h\b	0.1	0.2	0.3	0.4	0.5	0.6	0.7	0.8	0.9	1.0
0.0	.0038469	.0075907	.0111413	.0144318	.0174220	.0200963	.0224591	.0245287	.0263308	.0278948
0.1	.0044753	.0088351	.0129786	.0168302	.0203439	.0235015−	.0263066	.0287785+	.0309454	.0328393
0.2	.0050776	.0100276	.0147382	.0191255+	.0231380	.0267543	.0299777	.0328284	.0353369	.0375381
0.3	.0056310	.0111225−	.0163522	.0212280	.0256928	.0297225+	.0333200	.0365066	.0393148	.0417824
0.4	.0061184	.0120858	.0177700	.0230710	.0279266	.0323102	.0362240	.0396908	.0427454	.0454282
0.5	.0065298	.0128980	.0189980	.0246174	.0297945+	.0344655−	.0386324	.0423194	.0455635−	.0484083
0.6	.0068627	.0135541	.0199242	.0258592	.0312883	.0361809	.0405393	.0443892	.0477700	.0507283
0.7	.0071208	.0140620	.0206660	.0268137	.0324308	.0374857	.0419811	.0459444	.0494176	.0524499
0.8	.0073128	.0144388	.0212144	.0275160	.0332668	.0384344	.0430225+	.0470602	.0505919	.0536692
0.9	.0074495+	.0147066	.0216026	.0280105+	.0338518	.0390939	.0437414	.0478250+	.0513914	.0544941
1.0	.0075430	.0148890	.0218658	.0283439	.0342436	.0395324	.0442158	.0483261	.0519117	.0550279
1.1	.0076041	.0150080	.0220368	.0285591	.0344947	.0398112	.0445151	.0486401	.0522357	.0553585+
1.2	.0076425−	.0150825−	.0221431	.0286921	.0346486	.0399808	.0446959	.0488285−	.0524289	.0555548
∞	.0076939	.0151813	.0222826	.0288637	.0348637	.0401925+	.0449183	.0490574	.0526616	.0557896

a = 1.9

h\b	0.1	0.2	0.3	0.4	0.5	0.6	0.7	0.8	0.9	1.0
0.0	.0036892	.0072788	.0106820	.0138344	.0166973	.0192561	.0215154	.0234928	.0252135+	.0267059
0.1	.0043172	.0085225−	.0125181	.0162312	.0196173	.0226590	.0253601	.0277396	.0298247	.0316466
0.2	.0049169	.0097098	.0142700	.0185162	.0223985−	.0258964	.0290132	.0317690	.0341932	.0363199
0.3	.0054639	.0107918	.0158643	.0205931	.0249215−	.0288266	.0323114	.0353969	.0381150−	.0405024
0.4	.0059403	.0117333	.0172500−	.0223929	.0271015−	.0313502	.0351414	.0384974	.0414524	.0440460
0.5	.0063366	.0125153	.0183979	.0238798	.0288958	.0334183	.0374495+	.0410133	.0441461	.0468906
0.6	.0066514	.0131354	.0193056	.0250511	.0303028	.0350313	.0392395+	.0429527	.0462098	.0490564
0.7	.0068902	.0136049	.0199905−	.0259308	.0313538	.0362290	.0405599	.0443736	.0477115+	.0506220
0.8	.0070632	.0139442	.0204835−	.0265608	.0321019	.0370757	.0414867	.0453637	.0487506	.0516981
0.9	.0071829	.0141782	.0208221	.0269911	.0326093	.0376458	.0421059	.0460203	.0494348	.0524022
1.0	.0072620	.0143324	.0210441	.0272713	.0329374	.0380115−	.0425000−	.0464350+	.0498640	.0528412
1.1	.0073119	.0144294	.0211829	.0274454	.0331396	.0382350+	.0427389	.0466846	.0501207	.0531024
∞	.0073784	.0145576	.0213640	.0276688	.0333946	.0385122	.0430307	.0469856	.0504271	.0534118

A Function for Computing Trivariate Normal Probabilities (cont.)

h\b	0.1	0.2	0.3	0.4	0.5	0.6	0.7	0.8	0.9	1.0
a = 2.0										
0.0	.0035423	.0069884	.0102545+	.0132786	.0160236	.0184755-	.0206391	.0225316	.0241775-	.0256041
0.1	.0041699	.0082312	.0120894	.0156738	.0189416	.0218759	.0244810	.0267751	.0287849	.0305407
0.2	.0047669	.0094131	.0138332	.0179480	.0217092	.0250972	.0281153	.0307831	.0331294	.0351874
0.3	.0053072	.0104818	.0154080	.0199984	.0241991	.0279879	.0313676	.0343589	.0369930	.0393057
0.4	.0057724	.0114008	.0167596	.0217536	.0263239	.0304456	.0341216	.0373736	.0402351	.0427449
0.5	.0061533	.0121523	.0178620	.0231803	.0280439	.0324258	.0363287	.0397761	.0428039	.0454538
0.6	.0064501	.0127366	.0187165+	.0242816	.0293648	.0339377	.0380035-	.0415872	.0447273	.0474686
0.7	.0066701	.0131687	.0193460	.0250889	.0303273	.0350321	.0392071	.0428794	.0460898	.0488858
0.8	.0068251	.0134725+	.0197868	.0256509	.0309929	.0357833	.0400269	.0437526	.0470036	.0498298
0.9	.0069292	.0136757	.0200800	.0260225+	.0314297	.0362724	.0405563	.0443121	.0475848	.0504262
1.0	.0069955+	.0138049	.0202655+	.0262559	.0317019	.0365745-	.0408806	.0446521	.0479356	.0507841
1.1	.0070358	.0138830	.0203770	.0263951	.0319791	.0367516	.0410691	.0448483	.0481368	.0509882
∞	.0070846	.0139768	.0205091	.0265573	.0320471	.0369569	.0412781	.0450632	.0483549	.0512082
a = 2.2										
0.0	.0032775+	.0064651	.0094846	.0122783	.0148118	.0170727	.0190656	.0208071	.0223201	.0236303
0.1	.0039042	.0077062	.0113169	.0146700	.0177255-	.0204679	.0229015-	.0250437	.0269197	.0285583
0.2	.0044955-	.0088765+	.0130433	.0169211	.0204643	.0236546	.0264956	.0290059	.0312129	.0331481
0.3	.0050217	.0099171	.0145760	.0189155-	.0228845+	.0264621	.0296514	.0324723	.0349543	.0371318
0.4	.0054634	.0107895-	.0158580	.0205785+	.0248951	.0287842	.0322489	.0353104	.0380007	.0403572
0.5	.0058134	.0114792	.0168685+	.0218840	.0264654	.0305876	.0342537	.0374865-	.0403207	.0427965+
0.6	.0060748	.0119934	.0176190	.0228486	.0276188	.0319031	.0357053	.0390501	.0419749	.0445227
0.7	.0062592	.0123548	.0181442	.0235197	.0284155+	.0328047	.0366920	.0401042	.0430809	.0456680
0.8	.0063817	.0125944	.0184905-	.0239592	.0289332	.0333856	.0373221	.0407714	.0437753	.0463818
0.9	.0064587	.0127442	.0187057	.0242303	.0292498	.0337375-	.0377003	.0411684	.0441854	.0468005-
1.0	.0065042	.0128324	.0188317	.0243878	.0294319	.0339380	.0379139	.0413908	.0444134	.0470320
∞	.0065550+	.0129302	.0189693	.0245567	.0296237	.0341454	.0381313	.0416142	.0446402	.0472607

A Function for Computing Trivariate Normal Probabilities (cont.)

a = 2.4

h\b	0.1	0.2	0.3	0.4	0.5	0.6	0.7	0.8	0.9	1.0
0.0	.0030462	.0060082	.0088128	.0114061	.0137561	.0158517	.0176973	.0193088	.0207077	.0219183
0.1	.0036720	.0072474	.0106422	.0137939	.0166650+	.0192411	.0215265-	.0235377	.0252988	.0268367
0.2	.0042569	.0084052	.0123498	.0160201	.0193727	.0223905+	.0250772	.0274505-	.0295366	.0313653
0.3	.0047681	.0094158	.0138377	.0179549	.0217189	.0251099	.0281309	.0308011	.0331490	.0352072
0.4	.0051857	.0102400	.0150478	.0195228	.0236116	.0272922	.0305676	.0334583	.0359954	.0382146
0.5	.0055046	.0108679	.0159665+	.0207074	.0250332	.0289205-	.0323725-	.0354116	.0380015-	.0403909
0.6	.0057323	.0113150+	.0166176	.0215419	.0260277	.0300504	.0336144	.0367440	.0394754	.0418503
0.7	.0058842	.0116124	.0170484	.0220902	.0266757	.0307802	.0344089	.0375884	.0403572	.0427595-
0.8	.0059790	.0117971	.0173144	.0224262	.0270692	.0312189	.0348819	.0380863	.0408727	.0432869
0.9	.0060342	.0119044	.0174679	.0226183	.0272919	.0314646	.0351442	.0383599	.0411536	.0435725-
∞	.0060925-	.0120164	.0176256	.0228121	.0275123	.0317033	.0353946	.0386176	.0414155-	.0433366

a = 2.6

h\b	0.1	0.2	0.3	0.4	0.5	0.6	0.7	0.8	0.9	1.0
0.0	.0028431	.0056070	.0082232	.0106411	.0128309	.0147823	.0164999	.0179985+	.0192987	.0204231
0.1	.0034678	.0068442	.0100495+	.0130248	.0157346	.0181656	.0203218	.0222192	.0238805-	.0253312
0.2	.0040460	.0079885-	.0117370	.0152241	.0184089	.0212750+	.0238260	.0260791	.0280590	.0297943
0.3	.0045414	.0089676	.0131777	.0170964	.0206774	.0239017	.0267727	.0293086	.0315367	.0334883
0.4	.0049343	.0097424	.0143143	.0185671	.0224500+	.0259420	.0290463	.0317828	.0341814	.0362766
0.5	.0052226	.0103097	.0151428	.0196332	.0237262	.0273996	.0306571	.0335206	.0360226	.0382008
0.6	.0054185-	.0106938	.0157010	.0203464	.0245731	.0283580	.0317060	.0346412	.0371986	.0394187
0.7	.0055416	.0109343	.0160484	.0207869	.0250911	.0289333	.0323345+	.0353057	.0378894	.0401279
0.8	.0056133	.0110737	.0162483	.0210379	.0253833	.0292621	.0326814	.0356688	.0382634	.0405090
0.9	.0056519	.0111485-	.0163546	.0211701	.0255354	.0294287	.0328580	.0358519	.0384505+	.0406985-
∞	.0056862	.0112140	.0164464	.0212821	.0256618	.0295646	.0329997	.0359970	.0385974	.0408463

a = 2.8

h\b	0.1	0.2	0.3	0.4	0.5	0.6	0.7	0.8	0.9	1.0
0.0	.0026637	.0052528	.0077028	.0099662	.0120152	.0138400	.0154454	.0168454	.0180593	.0191087
0.1	.0032873	.0064877	.0095258	.0123455+	.0149133	.0172167	.0192596	.0210572	.0226311	.0240057
0.2	.0038584	.0076177	.0111918	.0145163	.0175520	.0202836	.0227144	.0248608	.0267468	.0283993
0.3	.0043373	.0085639	.0125834	.0163234	.0197396	.0228141	.0255499	.0279648	.0300850-	.0319406
0.4	.0047050+	.0092889	.0136458	.0176962	.0213914	.0247116	.0276601	.0302562	.0325288	.0345113
0.5	.0049637	.0097972	.0143870	.0186478	.0225276	.0260054	.0290853	.0317887	.0341474	.0361975+
0.6	.0051302	.0101233	.0148597	.0192499	.0232397	.0268080	.0299600	.0327192	.0351199	.0372010
0.7	.0052285-	.0103148	.0151352	.0195977	.0236467	.0272615+	.0304486	.0332332	.0356517	.0377449
0.8	.0052815+	.0104177	.0152821	.0197811	.0238589	.0274951	.0306972	.0334921	.0359172	.0380144
∞	.0053274	.0105056	.0154057	.0199325-	.0240304	.0276801	.0308908	.0336907	.0361186	.0382174

A Function for Computing Trivariate Normal Probabilities (cont.)

h\b	0.1	0.2	0.3	0.4	0.5	0.6	0.7	0.8	0.9	1.0
a = 3.0										
0.0	.0025044	.0049384	.0072410	.0093675+	.0112918	.0130049	.0145112	.0158243	.0169624	.0179458
0.1	.0031268	.0051709	.0090604	.0117420	.0141340	.0163744	.0183171	.0200266	.0215235+	.0228310
0.2	.0036903	.0072857	.0107037	.0138327	.0167851	.0193963	.0217197	.0237709	.0255728	.0271514
0.3	.0041521	.0081979	.0120445-	.0156225-	.0188892	.0218277	.0244409	.0267459	.0287680	.0305364
0.4	.0044948	.0088729	.0130326	.0168974	.0204206	.0235834	.0263890	.0288566	.0310139	.0328934
0.5	.0047250+	.0093248	.0136904	.0177399	.0214237	.0247221	.0276393	.0301965-	.0324244	.0343583
0.6	.0048650-	.0095985-	.0140860	.0182421	.0220153	.0253860	.0283596	.0309595-	.0332188	.0351750-
0.7	.0049421	.0097484	.0143009	.0185121	.0223297	.0257343	.0287329	.0313503	.0336214	.0355853
0.8	.0049805-	.0098227	.0144065-	.0186432	.0224803	.0258990	.0289072	.0315308	.0338056	.0357718
∞	.0050088	.0098767	.0144820	.0187350+	.0225836	.0260098	.0290225-	.0316486	.0339248	.0358916
a = 3.2										
0.0	.0023622	.0046577	.0068289	.0088334	.0106468	.0122605+	.0136789	.0149149	.0159858	.0169109
0.1	.0028833	.0058876	.0086444	.0112029	.0135326	.0156224	.0174759	.0191071	.0205356	.0217835-
0.2	.0035388	.0069865+	.0102639	.0133118	.0160942	.0185971	.0208238	.0227893	.0245154	.0260273
0.3	.0039831	.0078637	.0115525+	.0149825-	.0181123	.0209270	.0234281	.0256326	.0275651	.0292534
0.4	.0043009	.0084893	.0124672	.0161608	.0195255+	.0225432	.0252174	.0275666	.0296180	.0314029
0.5	.0045042	.0088880	.0130463	.0169008	.0204039	.0235370	.0263049	.0287281	.0308367	.0326648
0.6	.0046205+	.0091149	.0133735-	.0173146	.0208894	.0240794	.0268908	.0293461	.0314776	.0333215-
0.7	.0046800	.0092304	.0135384	.0175208	.0211281	.0243425+	.0271712	.0296382	.0317773	.0336260
∞	.0047243	.0093153	.0136577	.0176669	.0212936	.0245210	.0273579	.0298298	.0319717	.0338217
a = 3.4										
0.0	.0022346	.0044059	.0064592	.0083546	.0100686	.0115935-	.0129334	.0141006	.0151117	.0159847
0.1	.0028544	.0056331	.0082708	.0107186	.0129477	.0149473	.0167210	.0182821	.0196494	.0208440
0.2	.0034015-	.0067154	.0098653	.0127943	.0154680	.0178728	.0200117	.0218994	.0235568	.0250080
0.3	.0038279	.0075569	.0111007	.0143947	.0173996	.0200995+	.0224975-	.0246095+	.0264594	.0280740
0.4	.0041212	.0081339	.0119433	.0154784	.0186963	.0215797	.0241324	.0263723	.0283260	.0300239
0.5	.0042994	.0084828	.0124491	.0161231	.0194592	.0224400	.0250705-	.0273708	.0293703	.0311019
0.6	.0043949	.0086688	.0127165+	.0164600	.0198528	.0228778	.0255412	.0278652	.0298811	.0316237
0.7	.0044401	.0087563	.0128410	.0166149	.0200311	.0230731	.0257483	.0280801	.0301007	.0318461
∞	.0044691	.0088117	.0129184	.0167092	.0201372	.0231870	.0258669	.0282013	.0302233	.0319694

A Function for Computing Trivariate Normal Probabilities (cont.)

$a = 3.6$

h\b	0.1	0.2	0.3	0.4	0.5	0.6	0.7	0.8	0.9	1.0
0.0	.0021195+	.0041789	.0061261	.0079231	.0095478	.0109929	.0122623	.0133678	.0143251	.0151516
0.1	.0027379	.0054033	.0079334	.0102815-	.0124199	.0143382	.0160400	.0175380	.0188502	.0199969
0.2	.0032763	.0064682	.0095019	.0123227	.0148972	.0172124	.0192713	.0210879	.0226824	.0240781
0.3	.0036846	.0072735+	.0106834	.0138519	.0167408	.0193351	.0216376	.0236641	.0254374	.0269839
0.4	.0039541	.0078032	.0114559	.0148437	.0179252	.0206839	.0231238	.0252625+	.0271259	.0287434
0.5	.0041090	.0081062	.0118943	.0154009	.0185824	.0214225+	.0239264	.0261138	.0280133	.0296569
0.6	.0041866	.0082570	.0121103	.0156720	.0188977	.0217716	.0243000	.0265047	.0284157	.0300667
∞	.0042390	.0083578	.0122522	.0158462	.0190957	.0219858	.0245246	.0267356	.0286503	.0303033

$a = 3.8$

h\b	0.1	0.2	0.3	0.4	0.5	0.6	0.7	0.8	0.9	1.0
0.0	.0020154	.0039734	.0058245+	.0075326	.0090766	.0104495+	.0116553	.0127052	.0136141	.0143987
0.1	.0026322	.0051948	.0076273	.0098850+	.0119412	.0137859	.0154226	.0168635-	.0181259	.0192291
0.2	.0031616	.0062416	.0091689	.0118904	.0143739	.0166070	.0185924	.0203437	.0218805+	.0232251
0.3	.0035516	.0070105+	.0102961	.0133479	.0161292	.0186253	.0208391	.0227860	.0244882	.0259713
0.4	.0037981	.0074945+	.0110010	.0142514	.0172057	.0199484	.0221834	.0242281	.0260078	.0275511
0.5	.0039318	.0077557	.0113780	.0147291	.0177674	.0204774	.0228644	.0249480	.0267558	.0283190
0.6	.0039940	.0078764	.0115505-	.0149447	.0180170	.0207524	.0231575+	.0252534	.0270692	.0286373
∞	.0040307	.0079468	.0116491	.0150652	.0181532	.0208991	.0233107	.0254104	.0272283	.0287974

$a = 4.0$

h\b	0.1	0.2	0.3	0.4	0.5	0.6	0.7	0.8	0.9	1.0
0.0	.0019206	.0037865+	.0055504	.0071777	.0086484	.0099559	.0111040	.0121035-	.0129686	.0137152
0.1	.0025359	.0050048	.0073485-	.0095238	.0115051	.0132829	.0148604	.0162493	.0174663	.0185302
0.2	.0030560	.0060330	.0088622	.0114922	.0138920	.0160493	.0179669	.0196578	.0211412	.0224385+
0.3	.0034276	.0067654	.0099350+	.0128781	.0155589	.0179633	.0200944	.0219670	.0236029	.0250269
0.4	.0036520	.0072056	.0105752	.0136971	.0165326	.0190670	.0213043	.0232616	.0249636	.0264381
0.5	.0037665-	.0074289	.0108969	.0141035+	.0170083	.0195983	.0218775+	.0238655-	.0255892	.0270786
∞	.0038413	.0075731	.0111008	.0143554	.0172968	.0199118	.0222081	.0242069	.0259372	.0274304

$a = 4.2$

h\b	0.1	0.2	0.3	0.4	0.5	0.6	0.7	0.8	0.9	1.0
0.0	.0018342	.0036160	.0053002	.0068539	.0082578	.0095057	.0106013	.0115548	.0123801	.0130922
0.1	.0024478	.0048310	.0070934	.0091934	.0111063	.0128228	.0143462	.0156876	.0168632	.0178910
0.2	.0029533	.0058400	.0085784	.0111238	.0134459	.0155330	.0173877	.0190227	.0204564	.0217097
0.3	.0033116	.0065359	.0095971	.0124383	.0150250+	.0173436	.0193972	.0212003	.0227741	.0241428
0.4	.0035149	.0069345	.0101758	.0131772	.0159015+	.0183346	.0204807	.0223567	.0239865-	.0253973
0.5	.0036122	.0071240	.0104482	.0135203	.0163022	.0187800	.0209595-	.0228593	.0245056	.0259275+
∞	.0036684	.0072320	.0106005-	.0137077	.0165155+	.0190113	.0212025+	.0231096	.0247602	.0261844

8.9

A Function for Computing Trivariate Normal Probabilities (cont.)

a	h\b	0.1	0.2	0.3	0.4	0.5	0.6	0.7	0.8	0.9	1.0
a = 4.4	0.0	.0017550	.0034598	.0050711	.0065573	.0079001	.0090934	.0101410	.0110527	.0118415+	.0125222
	0.1	.0023669	.0046714	.0068591	.0088900	.0107400	.0124004	.0138740	.0151719	.0163095-	.0173041
	0.2	.0028675+	.0056607	.0083148	.0107814	.0130313	.0150530	.0168491	.0184318	.0198192	.0210314
	0.3	.0032026	.0063204	.0092797	.0120252	.0145235+	.0167616	.0187423	.0204801	.0219956	.0233125+
	0.4	.0033860	.0066796	.0098004	.0126888	.0153088	.0176471	.0197080	.0215080	.0230707	.0244224
	0.5	.0034681	.0068393	.0100294	.0129762	.0156432	.0180175-	.0201047	.0219231	.0234982	.0248581
	∞	.0035100	.0069196	.0101422	.0131146	.0158001	.0181869	.0202821	.0221053	.0236831	.0250444
a = 4.6	0.0	.0016822	.0033162	.0048605+	.0062847	.0075714	.0087148	.0097183	.0105915-	.0113470	.0119988
	0.1	.0022923	.0045242	.0066432	.0086103	.0104025-	.0120110	.0134389	.0146966	.0157991	.0167631
	0.2	.0027829	.0054934	.0080688	.0104619	.0126444	.0146049	.0163462	.0178800	.0192239	.0203976
	0.3	.0030999	.0061174	.0089806	.0116360	.0140511	.0162132	.0181254	.0198018	.0212625+	.0225308
	0.4	.0032646	.0064396	.0094471	.0122292	.0147513	.0170007	.0189819	.0207111	.0222112	.0235081
	0.5	.0033334	.0065732	.0096380	.0124681	.0150283	.0173064	.0193081	.0210514	.0225607	.0238634
	∞	.0033644	.0066325-	.0097211	.0125695+	.0151428	.0174295+	.0194366	.0211829	.0226940	.0239976
a = 4.8	0.0	.0016151	.0031838	.0046664	.0060335+	.0072685-	.0083658	.0093287	.0101665+	.0108914	.0115166
	0.1	.0022234	.0043881	.0064435-	.0083517	.0100903	.0116510	.0130365-	.0142570	.0153270	.0162628
	0.2	.0027036	.0053368	.0078385-	.0101627	.0122819	.0141851	.0158749	.0173628	.0186658	.0198033
	0.3	.0030029	.0059256	.0086981	.0112684	.0136048	.0156952	.0175428	.0191613	.0205704	.0217929
	0.4	.0031502	.0062134	.0091141	.0117962	.0142263	.0163924	.0182989	.0199619	.0214038	.0226496
	∞	.0032301	.0063677	.0093328	.0120670	.0145369	.0167315+	.0186575-	.0203331	.0217828	.0230332
a = 5.0	0.0	.0015530	.0030614	.0044869	.0058012	.0069884	.0080431	.0089687	.0097738	.0104703	.0110711
	0.1	.0021594	.0042619	.0062582	.0081117	.0098007	.0113169	.0126631	.0138491	.0148890	.0157985
	0.2	.0026291	.0051897	.0076220	.0098815+	.0119412	.0137905-	.0154317	.0168763	.0181408	.0192439
	0.3	.0029111	.0057440	.0084307	.0109203	.0131824	.0152050+	.0169915-	.0185552	.0199158	.0210952
	0.4	.0030422	.0060000	.0087999	.0113878	.0137315-	.0158193	.0176559	.0192569	.0206444	.0218427
	∞	.0031060	.0061229	.0089737	.0116024	.0139768	.0160863	.0179373	.0195476	.0209407	.0221422
a = 5.5	0.0	.0014165+	.0027923	.0040923	.0052907	.0063730	.0073344	.0081778	.0089113	.0095458	.0100929
	0.1	.0020178	.0039826	.0058483	.0075809	.0091599	.0105778	.0118369	.0129465-	.0139195-	.0147706
	0.2	.0024608	.0048571	.0071327	.0092455+	.0111704	.0128971	.0144282	.0157743	.0169511	.0179763
	0.3	.0027013	.0053292	.0078197	.0101254	.0122128	.0140860	.0157335-	.0171732	.0184237	.0195060
	0.4	.0027975-	.0055164	.0080886	.0104639	.0126128	.0145248	.0162049	.0176679	.0189345+	.0200276
	∞	.0028331	.0055847	.0081845+	.0105815-	.0127460	.0146687	.0163555+	.0178226	.0190915+	.0201858

8.9

A Function for Computing Trivariate Normal Probabilities (cont.)

h\b	0.1	0.2	0.3	0.4	0.5	0.6	0.7	0.8	0.9	1.0
a = 6.0										
0.0	.0013018	.0025661	.0037606	.0048617	.0058559	.0067389	.0075135-	.0081870	.0087694	.0092717
0.1	.0018976	.0037454	.0055002	.0071300	.0086156	.0099498	.011347	.0121791	.0130949	.0138961
0.2	.0023133	.0045655-	.0067035-	.0086876	.0104938	.0121128	.0135468	.0148060	.0159053	.0168616
0.3	.0025156	.0049621	.0072792	.0094225-	.0113652	.0130977	.0146233	.0159546	.0171094	.0181076
∞	.0026036	.0051323	.0075212	.0097235-	.0117119	.0134778	.0150269	.0163740	.0175389	.0185433
a = 6.5										
0.0	.0012041	.0023734	.0034781	.0044963	.0054156	.0062319	.0069479	.0075704	.0081087	.0085728
0.1	.0017940	.0035410	.0052002	.0067413	.0081462	.0094080	.0105288	.0115166	.0123829	.0131407
0.2	.0021821	.0043063	.0063219	.0081914	.0098920	.0114148	.0127622	.0139438	.0149741	.0158691
0.3	.0023502	.0046351	.0067979	.0087969	.0106070	.0122194	.0136377	.0148739	.0159451	.0168700
∞	.0024081	.0047468	.0069562	.0089927	.0108312	.0124639	.0138958	.0151409	.0162174	.0171456
a = 7.0										
0.0	.0011198	.0022074	.0032347	.0041815+	.0050363	.0057952	.0064608	.0070395-	.0075398	.0079711
0.1	.0017035+	.0033625-	.0049381	.0064018	.0077361	.0089346	.0099991	.0109373	.0117599	.0124793
0.2	.0020643	.0040733	.0059789	.0077453	.0093508	.0107871	.0120565+	.0131685-	.0141367	.0149767
0.3	.0022021	.0043424	.0063674	.0082376	.0099298	.0114357	.0127591	.0139116	.0149094	.0157704
∞	.0022397	.0044147	.0064694	.0083631	.0100726	.0115905-	.0129216	.0140789	.0150795+	.0159421
a = 7.5										
0.0	.0010465+	.0020628	.0030228	.0039076	.0047062	.0054153	.0060370	.0065776	.0070449	.0074477
0.1	.0016237	.0032049	.0047067	.0061018	.0073737	.0085160	.0095306	.0104246	.0112084	.0118936
0.2	.0019575-	.0038621	.0056679	.0073408	.0088601	.0102180	.0114168	.0124657	.0133778	.0141682
0.3	.0020690	.0040796	.0059810	.0077361	.0093229	.0107341	.0119733	.0130518	.0139850+	.0147899
∞	.0020931	.0041257	.0060457	.0078152	.0094124	.0108305+	.0120741	.0131551	.0140897	.0148954
a = 8.0										
0.0	.0009822	.0019359	.0028368	.0036671	.0044164	.0050817	.0056651	.0061722	.0066105+	.0069884
0.1	.0015525-	.0030643	.0045003	.0058342	.0070502	.0081422	.0091120	.0099664	.0107152	.0113696
0.2	.0018599	.0036693	.0053841	.0069716	.0084123	.0096987	.0108332	.0118248	.0126862	.0134317
0.3	.0019492	.0038429	.0056333	.0072851	.0087777	.0101044	.0112687	.0122816	.0131577	.0139130
∞	.0019643	.0038719	.0056737	.0073341	.0088329	.0101634	.0113301	.0123443	.0132211	.0139768

8.10 The Maximum of a p-Dimensional Normal Distribution with All Correlations Equal to 0, $\frac{1}{4}$, or $\frac{1}{2}$

Given is a p-dimensional normal distribution with the correlation between each pair of variables always equal to $\rho \geq 0$, and with means zero and variances all equal to one. Required is the probability that all p of the random variables are less than h, that is, the cumulative distribution function of the maximum of the p-variates. It can be shown [58] or [211] that this probability is given by

$$I = \int_{-\infty}^{+\infty} Z(x) \left[P\left(\frac{x\sqrt{\rho} + h}{\sqrt{1-\rho}}\right) \right]^p dx,$$

where Z and P are defined as in Section 1.1. This quantity is tabulated for $p = 2(1)8$ and $\rho = 0$, $\frac{1}{4}$, or $\frac{1}{2}$. It was obtained by a Hermite-Gauss quadrature formula. Integration by parts and changing variables yields

$$I = 1 - \frac{p}{\sqrt{\pi}} \int_{-\infty}^{+\infty} P\left(\frac{u\sqrt{2-2\rho} - h}{\sqrt{\rho}}\right) [P(\sqrt{2}\,u)]^{p-1} \exp(-u^2)\, du.$$

This second form was also integrated by means of the Hermite-Gauss procedure. The quantities in the table are the result of rounding off the answers from the two integrations until they agreed everywhere, i.e., until a uniform number of significant figures was obtained for each value of p. Some tables prepared by Teichroew [221] are similar to those given here. Das [43] also considers the class of integrals of this section.

The Maximum of a p-Dimensional Normal Distribution with All Correlations Equal to 0 (first line), $\frac{1}{4}$ (second line), or $\frac{1}{2}$ (third line)

h	2	3	4	5	6	7	8
-2.50	0.000	0.000	0.000	0.000	0.000	0.000	0.000
	0.000	0.000	0.000	0.000	0.000	0.000	0.000
	0.001	0.000	0.000	0.000	0.000	0.000	0.000
-2.40	0.000	0.000	0.000	0.000	0.000	0.000	0.000
	0.000	0.000	0.000	0.000	0.000	0.000	0.000
	0.001	0.000	0.000	0.000	0.000	0.000	0.000
-2.30	0.000	0.000	0.000	0.000	0.000	0.000	0.000
	0.000	0.000	0.000	0.000	0.000	0.000	0.000
	0.001	0.000	0.000	0.000	0.000	0.000	0.000
-2.20	0.000	0.000	0.000	0.000	0.000	0.000	0.000
	0.001	0.000	0.000	0.000	0.000	0.000	0.000
	0.002	0.001	0.000	0.000	0.000	0.000	0.000
-2.10	0.000	0.000	0.000	0.000	0.000	0.000	0.000
	0.001	0.000	0.000	0.000	0.000	0.000	0.000
	0.003	0.001	0.000	0.000	0.000	0.000	0.000
-2.00	0.001	0.000	0.000	0.000	0.000	0.000	0.000
	0.002	0.000	0.000	0.000	0.000	0.000	0.000
	0.004	0.001	0.001	0.000	0.000	0.000	0.000
-1.90	0.001	0.000	0.000	0.000	0.000	0.000	0.000
	0.002	0.000	0.000	0.000	0.000	0.000	0.000
	0.006	0.002	0.001	0.001	0.000	0.000	0.000
-1.80	0.001	0.000	0.000	0.000	0.000	0.000	0.000
	0.004	0.001	0.000	0.000	0.000	0.000	0.000
	0.008	0.003	0.001	0.001	0.001	0.000	0.000
-1.70	0.002	0.000	0.000	0.000	0.000	0.000	0.000
	0.005	0.001	0.000	0.000	0.000	0.000	0.000
	0.010	0.004	0.002	0.001	0.001	0.001	0.000
-1.60	0.003	0.000	0.000	0.000	0.000	0.000	0.000
	0.007	0.002	0.000	0.000	0.000	0.000	0.000
	0.014	0.006	0.003	0.002	0.001	0.001	0.001
-1.50	0.004	0.000	0.000	0.000	0.000	0.000	0.000
	0.010	0.002	0.001	0.000	0.000	0.000	0.000
	0.018	0.008	0.004	0.003	0.002	0.001	0.001
-1.40	0.007	0.001	0.000	0.000	0.000	0.000	0.000
	0.014	0.003	0.001	0.000	0.000	0.000	0.000
	0.024	0.011	0.006	0.004	0.003	0.002	0.001
-1.30	0.009	0.001	0.000	0.000	0.000	0.000	0.000
	0.018	0.005	0.002	0.001	0.000	0.000	0.000
	0.031	0.015	0.009	0.006	0.004	0.003	0.002
-1.20	0.013	0.002	0.000	0.000	0.000	0.000	0.000
	0.024	0.007	0.003	0.001	0.001	0.000	0.000
	0.040	0.020	0.012	0.008	0.006	0.004	0.003

The Maximum of a p-Dimensional Normal Distribution with All Correlations Equal to 0 (first line), $\frac{1}{4}$ (second line), or $\frac{1}{2}$ (third line) (cont.)

h	2	3	4	5	6	7	8
-1.10	0.018	0.002	0.000	0.000	0.000	0.000	0.000
	0.032	0.010	0.004	0.002	0.001	0.001	0.000
	0.050	0.026	0.016	0.011	0.008	0.006	0.005
-1.00	0.025	0.004	0.001	0.000	0.000	0.000	0.000
	0.042	0.015	0.006	0.003	0.002	0.001	0.001
	0.063	0.034	0.021	0.015	0.011	0.009	0.007
-0.90	0.034	0.006	0.001	0.000	0.000	0.000	0.000
	0.053	0.020	0.009	0.005	0.003	0.002	0.001
	0.077	0.043	0.028	0.020	0.015	0.012	0.010
-0.80	0.045	0.010	0.002	0.000	0.000	0.000	0.000
	0.068	0.028	0.013	0.007	0.004	0.003	0.002
	0.095	0.055	0.037	0.027	0.021	0.016	0.013
-0.70	0.059	0.014	0.003	0.001	0.000	0.000	0.000
	0.085	0.037	0.018	0.010	0.006	0.004	0.003
	0.115	0.069	0.048	0.035	0.027	0.022	0.018
-0.60	0.075	0.021	0.006	0.002	0.000	0.000	0.000
	0.104	0.048	0.026	0.015	0.009	0.006	0.004
	0.138	0.086	0.061	0.046	0.036	0.030	0.025
-0.50	0.095	0.029	0.009	0.003	0.001	0.000	0.000
	0.127	0.063	0.035	0.021	0.014	0.009	0.006
	0.163	0.106	0.076	0.059	0.047	0.039	0.033
-0.40	0.119	0.041	0.014	0.005	0.002	0.001	0.000
	0.154	0.080	0.046	0.029	0.019	0.014	0.010
	0.192	0.128	0.095	0.074	0.060	0.050	0.043
-0.30	0.146	0.056	0.021	0.008	0.003	0.001	0.000
	0.183	0.101	0.061	0.040	0.027	0.020	0.014
	0.223	0.154	0.116	0.092	0.076	0.065	0.056
-0.20	0.177	0.074	0.031	0.013	0.006	0.002	0.001
	0.216	0.125	0.079	0.053	0.038	0.028	0.021
	0.258	0.183	0.141	0.114	0.095	0.081	0.071
-0.10	0.212	0.097	0.045	0.021	0.009	0.004	0.002
	0.252	0.153	0.101	0.070	0.051	0.038	0.029
	0.294	0.215	0.169	0.139	0.117	0.102	0.089
0.00	0.250	0.125	0.063	0.031	0.016	0.008	0.004
	0.290	0.185	0.127	0.091	0.068	0.052	0.041
	0.333	0.250	0.200	0.167	0.143	0.125	0.111
0.10	0.291	0.157	0.085	0.046	0.025	0.013	0.007
	0.331	0.221	0.156	0.115	0.088	0.069	0.055
	0.374	0.288	0.234	0.198	0.172	0.152	0.136
0.20	0.336	0.194	0.113	0.065	0.038	0.022	0.013
	0.374	0.260	0.190	0.144	0.113	0.090	0.073
	0.416	0.328	0.272	0.233	0.204	0.182	0.165

The Maximum of a *p*-Dimensional Normal Distribution with All Correlations Equal to 0 (first line), $\frac{1}{4}$ (second line), or $\frac{1}{2}$ (third line) (*cont.*)

h	2	3	4	5	6	7	8
0.30	0.382	0.236	0.146	0.090	0.056	0.034	0.021
	0.419	0.302	0.228	0.178	0.142	0.116	0.096
	0.459	0.370	0.312	0.271	0.240	0.216	0.197
0.40	0.430	0.282	0.185	0.121	0.079	0.052	0.034
	0.464	0.347	0.269	0.215	0.176	0.146	0.123
	0.503	0.414	0.355	0.312	0.279	0.254	0.233
0.50	0.478	0.331	0.229	0.158	0.109	0.076	0.052
	0.510	0.394	0.314	0.257	0.214	0.181	0.155
	0.546	0.459	0.399	0.355	0.321	0.294	0.272
0.60	0.527	0.382	0.277	0.201	0.146	0.106	0.077
	0.556	0.442	0.361	0.302	0.256	0.221	0.192
	0.589	0.504	0.444	0.400	0.365	0.337	0.314
0.70	0.575	0.436	0.330	0.250	0.190	0.144	0.109
	0.601	0.491	0.411	0.350	0.302	0.265	0.234
	0.631	0.549	0.490	0.446	0.411	0.382	0.358
0.80	0.621	0.490	0.386	0.304	0.240	0.189	0.149
	0.644	0.540	0.461	0.400	0.352	0.312	0.280
	0.671	0.593	0.537	0.493	0.458	0.429	0.404
0.90	0.666	0.543	0.443	0.362	0.295	0.241	0.196
	0.685	0.588	0.512	0.452	0.404	0.363	0.330
	0.709	0.636	0.582	0.540	0.505	0.477	0.452
1.00	0.708	0.596	0.501	0.422	0.355	0.298	0.251
	0.724	0.634	0.563	0.505	0.457	0.417	0.382
	0.745	0.678	0.627	0.586	0.553	0.524	0.500
1.10	0.747	0.646	0.558	0.482	0.417	0.360	0.311
	0.761	0.679	0.612	0.557	0.511	0.471	0.436
	0.779	0.717	0.669	0.631	0.599	0.572	0.548
1.20	0.783	0.693	0.613	0.543	0.480	0.425	0.376
	0.794	0.721	0.660	0.608	0.564	0.525	0.492
	0.809	0.754	0.710	0.674	0.644	0.618	0.596
1.30	0.816	0.737	0.665	0.601	0.543	0.490	0.443
	0.825	0.759	0.704	0.657	0.615	0.579	0.547
	0.837	0.788	0.748	0.715	0.687	0.663	0.642
1.40	0.845	0.777	0.714	0.656	0.603	0.555	0.510
	0.852	0.795	0.746	0.703	0.665	0.631	0.600
	0.862	0.819	0.783	0.753	0.728	0.705	0.685
1.50	0.871	0.813	0.758	0.708	0.660	0.616	0.575
	0.876	0.827	0.784	0.745	0.711	0.680	0.652
	0.885	0.847	0.815	0.788	0.765	0.745	0.727
1.60	0.893	0.844	0.798	0.754	0.713	0.674	0.637
	0.898	0.856	0.818	0.784	0.754	0.726	0.700
	0.904	0.871	0.844	0.820	0.800	0.781	0.765

The Maximum of a p-Dimensional Normal Distribution with All Correlations Equal to 0 (first line), $\frac{1}{4}$ (second line), or $\frac{1}{2}$ (third line) (cont.)

h	2	3	4	5	6	7	8
1.70	0.913	0.872	0.833	0.796	0.761	0.727	0.694
	0.916	0.881	0.849	0.819	0.793	0.768	0.745
	0.921	0.893	0.870	0.849	0.831	0.815	0.800
1.80	0.929	0.896	0.864	0.833	0.803	0.774	0.746
	0.932	0.902	0.875	0.850	0.827	0.806	0.786
	0.936	0.912	0.892	0.874	0.859	0.844	0.831
1.90	0.943	0.916	0.890	0.864	0.840	0.815	0.792
	0.945	0.921	0.898	0.878	0.858	0.840	0.823
	0.948	0.929	0.912	0.897	0.883	0.871	0.860
2.00	0.955	0.933	0.912	0.891	0.871	0.851	0.832
	0.956	0.937	0.918	0.901	0.885	0.869	0.855
	0.959	0.943	0.928	0.916	0.904	0.894	0.884
2.10	0.965	0.947	0.930	0.914	0.897	0.881	0.866
	0.965	0.950	0.935	0.921	0.907	0.895	0.882
	0.967	0.954	0.943	0.932	0.923	0.914	0.906
2.20	0.972	0.959	0.946	0.932	0.919	0.907	0.894
	0.973	0.960	0.949	0.937	0.926	0.916	0.906
	0.974	0.964	0.954	0.946	0.938	0.931	0.924
2.30	0.979	0.968	0.958	0.948	0.937	0.927	0.917
	0.979	0.969	0.960	0.951	0.942	0.934	0.926
	0.980	0.972	0.964	0.957	0.951	0.945	0.939
2.40	0.984	0.976	0.968	0.960	0.952	0.944	0.936
	0.984	0.976	0.969	0.962	0.955	0.948	0.942
	0.985	0.978	0.972	0.967	0.962	0.957	0.952
2.50	0.988	0.981	0.975	0.969	0.963	0.957	0.951
	0.988	0.982	0.976	0.971	0.965	0.960	0.955
	0.988	0.983	0.979	0.974	0.970	0.966	0.963
2.60	0.991	0.986	0.981	0.977	0.972	0.968	0.963
	0.991	0.986	0.982	0.978	0.974	0.970	0.966
	0.991	0.987	0.984	0.980	0.977	0.974	0.971
2.70	0.993	0.990	0.986	0.983	0.979	0.976	0.973
	0.993	0.990	0.987	0.983	0.980	0.977	0.974
	0.993	0.990	0.988	0.985	0.983	0.980	0.978
2.80	0.995	0.992	0.990	0.987	0.985	0.982	0.980
	0.995	0.992	0.990	0.988	0.985	0.983	0.981
	0.995	0.993	0.991	0.989	0.987	0.985	0.983
2.90	0.996	0.994	0.993	0.991	0.989	0.987	0.985
	0.996	0.994	0.993	0.991	0.989	0.987	0.986
	0.996	0.995	0.993	0.992	0.990	0.989	0.988
3.00	0.997	0.996	0.995	0.993	0.992	0.991	0.989
	0.997	0.996	0.995	0.993	0.992	0.991	0.990
	0.997	0.996	0.995	0.994	0.993	0.992	0.991

8.10

8.11 The Maximum of a p-Dimensional Normal Distribution with All Correlations Equal to $1/[1 + \sqrt{p}]$

The quantity tabulated here is defined as in Section 8.10 with $\rho = 1/[1 + \sqrt{p}]$ where, as before, p is the number of dimensions of the normal distribution. That is, the quantity tabulated is the cumulative distribution function for the maximum of p normally distributed variables, all with the same correlation, $\rho = 1/[1 + \sqrt{p}]$, with means equal to zero, and with standard deviations equal to one. The same computation and check procedures were used as in Section 8.10.

The Maximum of a p-Dimensional Normal Distribution with All Correlations Equal to $1/(1 + \sqrt{p})$

h	2	3	4	5	6	7	8
-3.00	0.00005	0.00000	0.00000	0.00000	0.00001	0.00001	0.00000
-2.90	0.00008	0.00001	0.00000	0.00000	0.00001	0.00001	0.00000
-2.80	0.00013	0.00001	0.00000	0.00000	0.00001	0.00001	0.00000
-2.70	0.00020	0.00002	0.00000	0.00000	0.00001	0.00001	0.00000
-2.60	0.00030	0.00003	0.00000	0.00001	0.00001	0.00001	0.00000
-2.50	0.00046	0.00005	0.00001	0.00001	0.00001	0.00001	0.00000
-2.40	0.00069	0.00009	0.00002	0.00001	0.00001	0.00001	0.00000
-2.30	0.00102	0.00015	0.00003	0.00001	0.00001	0.00001	0.00000
-2.20	0.00149	0.00024	0.00005	0.00002	0.00002	0.00001	0.00000
-2.10	0.00215	0.00038	0.00008	0.00002	0.00002	0.00001	0.00000
-2.00	0.00307	0.00059	0.00014	0.00004	0.00002	0.00001	0.00000
-1.90	0.00432	0.00090	0.00023	0.00007	0.00003	0.00001	0.00000
-1.80	0.00601	0.00137	0.00037	0.00012	0.00005	0.00002	0.00000
-1.70	0.00826	0.00204	0.00059	0.00020	0.00008	0.00003	0.00000
-1.60	0.01121	0.00300	0.00093	0.00033	0.00013	0.00005	0.00000
-1.50	0.01504	0.00435	0.00145	0.00053	0.00022	0.00009	0.00000
-1.40	0.01994	0.00621	0.00220	0.00086	0.00037	0.00016	0.00003
-1.30	0.02612	0.00874	0.00330	0.00136	0.00060	0.00027	0.00008
-1.20	0.03383	0.01213	0.00486	0.00211	0.00097	0.00046	0.00018
-1.10	0.04329	0.01659	0.00705	0.00321	0.00155	0.00077	0.00035
-1.00	0.05478	0.02238	0.01005	0.00481	0.00243	0.00126	0.00064
-0.90	0.06853	0.02977	0.01410	0.00709	0.00373	0.00203	0.00110
-0.80	0.08479	0.03905	0.01948	0.01026	0.00564	0.00320	0.00183
-0.70	0.10374	0.05055	0.02649	0.01459	0.00836	0.00493	0.00294
-0.60	0.12557	0.06456	0.03546	0.02039	0.01215	0.00745	0.00463
-0.50	0.15038	0.08138	0.04676	0.02802	0.01735	0.01101	0.00709
-0.40	0.17822	0.10127	0.06075	0.03786	0.02430	0.01595	0.01062
-0.30	0.20905	0.12443	0.07778	0.05031	0.03342	0.02265	0.01554
-0.20	0.24276	0.15100	0.09813	0.06578	0.04514	0.03153	0.02228
-0.10	0.27917	0.18103	0.12207	0.08462	0.05989	0.04305	0.03127

The Maximum of a p-Dimensional Normal Distribution with All Correlations Equal to $1/(1 + \sqrt{p})$ (cont.)

h	2	3	4	5	6	7	8
0.00	0.31797	0.21446	0.14975	0.10716	0.07810	0.05769	0.04302
0.10	0.35882	0.25114	0.18123	0.13363	0.10013	0.07591	0.05806
0.20	0.40128	0.29078	0.21644	0.16417	0.12627	0.09814	0.07689
0.30	0.44487	0.33302	0.25518	0.19877	0.15672	0.12471	0.09997
0.40	0.48906	0.37737	0.29712	0.23728	0.19150	0.15582	0.12766
0.50	0.53330	0.42327	0.34180	0.27941	0.23050	0.19154	0.16016
0.60	0.57706	0.47010	0.38866	0.32469	0.27341	0.23171	0.19748
0.70	0.61982	0.51722	0.43702	0.37254	0.31975	0.27599	0.23941
0.80	0.66107	0.56397	0.48617	0.42225	0.36888	0.32383	0.28552
0.90	0.70041	0.60970	0.53534	0.47301	0.42000	0.37450	0.33516
1.00	0.73747	0.65382	0.58380	0.52399	0.47226	0.42713	0.38751
1.10	0.77196	0.69583	0.63084	0.57436	0.52472	0.48076	0.44160
1.20	0.80369	0.73527	0.67581	0.62330	0.57647	0.53441	0.49642
1.30	0.83252	0.77182	0.71819	0.67012	0.62666	0.58711	0.55092
1.40	0.85843	0.80524	0.75753	0.71419	0.67451	0.63796	0.60413
1.50	0.88143	0.83540	0.79355	0.75505	0.71939	0.68619	0.65513
1.60	0.90161	0.86227	0.82605	0.79235	0.76081	0.73115	0.70315
1.70	0.91913	0.88591	0.85497	0.82590	0.79844	0.77238	0.74758
1.80	0.93415	0.90643	0.88036	0.85564	0.83209	0.80957	0.78798
1.90	0.94688	0.92404	0.90235	0.88162	0.86172	0.84257	0.82409
2.00	0.95756	0.93895	0.92114	0.90399	0.88742	0.87138	0.85583
2.10	0.96642	0.95143	0.93698	0.92299	0.90939	0.89616	0.88326
2.20	0.97368	0.96175	0.95017	0.93890	0.92790	0.91714	0.90661
2.30	0.97957	0.97018	0.96102	0.95206	0.94327	0.93464	0.92617
2.40	0.98429	0.97698	0.96982	0.96278	0.95586	0.94904	0.94231
2.50	0.98804	0.98241	0.97688	0.97142	0.96604	0.96071	0.95545
2.60	0.99098	0.98670	0.98247	0.97829	0.97415	0.97005	0.96599
2.70	0.99326	0.99004	0.98684	0.98368	0.98054	0.97742	0.97433
2.80	0.99502	0.99261	0.99023	0.98786	0.98551	0.98316	0.98084
2.90	0.99635	0.99458	0.99282	0.99106	0.98932	0.98758	0.98585
3.00	0.99735	0.99606	0.99477	0.99349	0.99221	0.99094	0.98967

8.12 Means and Standard Deviations for the Maximum of a p-Dimensional Normal Distribution with Correlations Equal to 0, $\frac{1}{4}$, $\frac{1}{2}$, or $1/[1 + \sqrt{\rho}]$

The mean of the maximum of p normally distributed variables with common correlation equal to ρ, means all zero, and all standard deviations equal to one is given by

$$E(h) = p(p - 1)\sqrt{1 - \rho} \int_{-\infty}^{+\infty} [P(x)]^{p-2}[Z(x)]^2 \, dx.$$

Similarly, the expected value of the maximum squared is given by

$$E(h^2) = 1 + \frac{p(p - 1)(p - 2)(1 - \rho)}{2} \int_{-\infty}^{+\infty} [P(x)]^{p-3}[Z(x)]^3 \, dx.$$

These quantities are widely tabulated for $\rho = 0$ (see Section 7 above, for example, or see Ruben [186]). Since ρ enters only as a multiplicative factor, the means and variances for any ρ are readily computed from those with $\rho = 0$, as was done here. Some special cases of particular interest are:

when $p = 2$, $\quad E(h) = \sqrt{\dfrac{1 - \rho}{\pi}}$, $\quad E(h^2) = 1$, and

when $p = 3$, $\quad E(h) = \dfrac{3}{2}\sqrt{\dfrac{1 - \rho}{\pi}}$, $\quad E(h^2) = 1 + \dfrac{\sqrt{3}\,(1 - \rho)}{2\pi}$, and

when $p = 4$, $\quad E(h) = 3\sqrt{\dfrac{1 - \rho}{\pi}}\left[1 - \dfrac{1}{\pi} \arccos \dfrac{1}{3}\right]$,

$$E(h^2) = 1 + \frac{\sqrt{3}\,(1 - \rho)}{\pi}.$$

Means and Standard Deviations for the Maximum of a p-Dimensional Normal Distribution with Correlations
Equal to 0, $\frac{1}{4}$, $\frac{1}{2}$, or $1/(1 + \sqrt{p})$

p	$Ep(h)$	$Ep(h^2)$	$\sigma p(h)$
		$\rho = 0$	
2	0.56419	1.00000	0.82565
3	0.84628	1.27566	0.74798
4	1.02938	1.55133	0.70122
5	1.16296	1.80002	0.66898
6	1.26721	2.02174	0.64492
7	1.35218	2.22030	0.62603
8	1.42360	2.39953	0.61065
		$\rho = 1/4$	
2	0.48860	1.00000	0.87251
3	0.73290	1.20675	0.81829
4	0.89147	1.41350	0.78663
5	1.00716	1.60002	0.76528
6	1.09743	1.76630	0.74963
7	1.17102	1.91523	0.73752
8	1.23287	2.04965	0.72779
		$\rho = 1/2$	
2	0.39894	1.00000	0.91698
3	0.59841	1.13783	0.88303
4	0.72788	1.27566	0.86363
5	0.82234	1.40001	0.85074
6	0.89605	1.51087	0.84141
7	0.95613	1.61015	0.83424
8	1.00664	1.69977	0.82852
		$\rho = 1/(1 + \sqrt{p})$	
2	0.43181	1.00000	0.90196
3	0.67383	1.17476	0.84895
4	0.84048	1.36755	0.81311
5	0.96672	1.55280	0.78629
6	1.06784	1.72554	0.76502
7	1.15190	1.88558	0.74747
8	1.22363	2.03397	0.73260

8.13 Critical Values for Testing the General Linear Hypothesis

Suppose $\mathbf{x}_1, \mathbf{x}_2, \ldots, \mathbf{x}_N$ are a set of N observations, $\mathbf{x}_\alpha$ being drawn from a normal distribution with mean $\beta \mathbf{z}_\alpha$ and variance covariance matrix $\boldsymbol{\Sigma}$. The vectors $\mathbf{z}_\alpha$ (with q components) are assumed known, and the $(p \times p)$-matrix $\boldsymbol{\Sigma}$ and the $(p \times q)$-matrix β are unknown.

Anderson [3] derives the likelihood ratio criterion for testing the hypothesis $H \colon \beta_1 = \beta_1^*$, where β_1^* is a given matrix and β_1 is a partition of $\beta = (\beta_1 \beta_2)$ such that β_1 has q_1 columns and β_2 has q_2 columns.

Assume that $N \geq p + q$ and define $n = N - q_1 - q_2 = N - q$, $m = n + \frac{1}{2}(q_1 - p - 1)$, $A = (a_{ij})$, $A_{ij} = $ cofactor of a_{ij} in A, and

$$U = \lambda^{2/N} = \frac{|N\hat{\boldsymbol{\Sigma}}_\Omega|}{|N\hat{\boldsymbol{\Sigma}}_\Omega + (\beta_{1\Omega} - \beta_1^*)A_{11.2}(\hat{\beta}_{1\Omega} - \beta_1^*)'|},$$

where

$$A_{11.2} = A_{11} - A_{12}A_{22}^{-1}A_{21},$$

and where

$$a_{ij} = \sum_{\alpha=1}^{N} z_{i\alpha}z_{j\alpha}.$$

The quantity tabulated at the top of the page for Table 8.13 is that value of z that makes $\Pr\{-m \log U_{p,q_1,n} \leq z\} = 1 - \gamma$, where $\gamma = 0.95$ and 0.99. At the bottom of the page, $p = q_1 = 3$, and that value of u is given such that $\Pr\{U \leq u\} = 1 - \gamma$ for $\gamma = 0.95$ and 0.99. Anderson [3] gives some cases where special functions of U lead to the F-distribution. The reader is referred to Chapter 8 of Anderson's book for more details. Pillai [175] gives some tables along the lines of the tables given here.

Critical Values for Testing the General Linear Hypothesis

$$\Pr\{-m \log U_{p,q_1,n} \leq z\} = 1 - \gamma, \text{ where } m = n + \tfrac{1}{2}(q_1 - p - 1)$$

p	q_1*	n	γ 0.95	0.99
3	3	8	17.4	22.3
3	3	9	17.3	22.2
3	3	10	17.2	22.1
3	3	11	17.2	22.0
3	3	12-14	17.1	21.9
3	3	15-21	17.0	21.8
3	3	22-28	17.0	21.7
3	3	29-∞	16.9	21.7
1	1	10	3.83	6.61
1	2	10	5.99	9.21
2	2	10	9.52	13.35
1	3	10	7.85	11.42
2	3	10	12.71	16.99
3	3	10	17.19	22.07
1	4	10	9.59	13.46
2	4	10	15.75	20.48
3	4	10	21.51	26.89
4	4	10	27.17	33.19
1	5	10	11.27	15.41
2	5	10	18.71	23.81
3	5	10	25.73	31.59
4	5	10	32.66	39.21
5	5	10	39.72	47.03

* Values for $p = q_1 = 3$ were taken from p. 209 of Ref. 3 .

$$\Pr\{U_{3, 3, n} \leq u\} = 1 - \gamma$$

p	q_1**	n	γ 0.95	0.99
3	3	3	8.59×10^{-5}	4.09×10^{-6}
3	3	4	3.30×10^{-3}	6.6×10^{-4}
3	3	5	0.0183	0.00626
3	3	6	0.0447	
3	3	7	0.0794	
3	3	8	0.105	
3	3	9	0.131	
3	3	10	0.162	0.0979

** From p. 199 of Ref. 3. The numbers are not accurately computed (perhaps to two significant figures only).

8.14 Graphs of Some Upper Percentage Points of the Distribution of the Largest Characteristic Root

The quantity which may be read from these graphs is that value of X_α such that

$$\Pr\{\theta_s \leq X_\alpha(s, m, n)\} = 1 - \alpha,$$

where θ_s is the largest of the s nonzero roots of the $(p \times p)$-matrix $S_{12}S_{22}^{-1}S_{12}'S_{11}^{-1}$, and

$$S = \begin{bmatrix} S_{11} & S_{12} \\ S_{12}' & S_{22} \end{bmatrix}$$

is the sample covariance matrix from a $(p + q)$-variate normal population based on $N - 1$ degrees of freedom. The parameters are defined by $s = \min(p, q)$, $m = (|p - q| - 1)/2$, and $n = (N - p - q - 2)/2$. With these definitions the critical values of θ_s are useful in testing the independence between a set of p correlated variates and a set of q correlated variates in a $(p + q)$-variate normal population. They are also useful in testing the general linear hypothesis (see Section 8.13 above). Heck [95] summarizes these procedures and gives many references to their derivations and related work. He also points out that upper percentage points of the generalized beta distribution [71], [69], and [70] correspond to values which may be read from these graphs for $\alpha = 0.01$ and 0.05.

On each page, the graphs appear for a particular $s[=2(1)5]$ and $\alpha[=0.01,$ 0.025, and 0.05] for $m = -\frac{1}{2}$, 0(1)10, and n from 5 to 1000. The curves corresponding to the twelve values of m on each page are in two sections, the lower section being the continuation of the upper section, with an overlap occurring from $X_\alpha = 0.50$ to 0.55. Of the two scales for X_α at the bottom of the page, the upper scale corresponds to the upper set of curves and the lower scale to the lower set. The lowest curve in each case (with the exception of the third chart) corresponds to $m = -\frac{1}{2}$, the next lowest to $m = 0$, etc., to the uppermost curve, which corresponds to $m = 10$. The scale for n is on the left margin of the page and is logarithmic. The values of $X_\alpha(s, m, n)$ may be read from the charts correct to two decimal places.

238

Graphs of Some Upper Percentage Points of the Distribution of the Largest Characteristic Root [95]

$$\Pr\{\theta_s \leq X_\alpha(s, m, n)\} = 1 - \alpha$$

CHART I

$$s = 2, \quad \alpha = 0.01$$

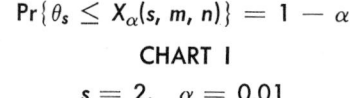

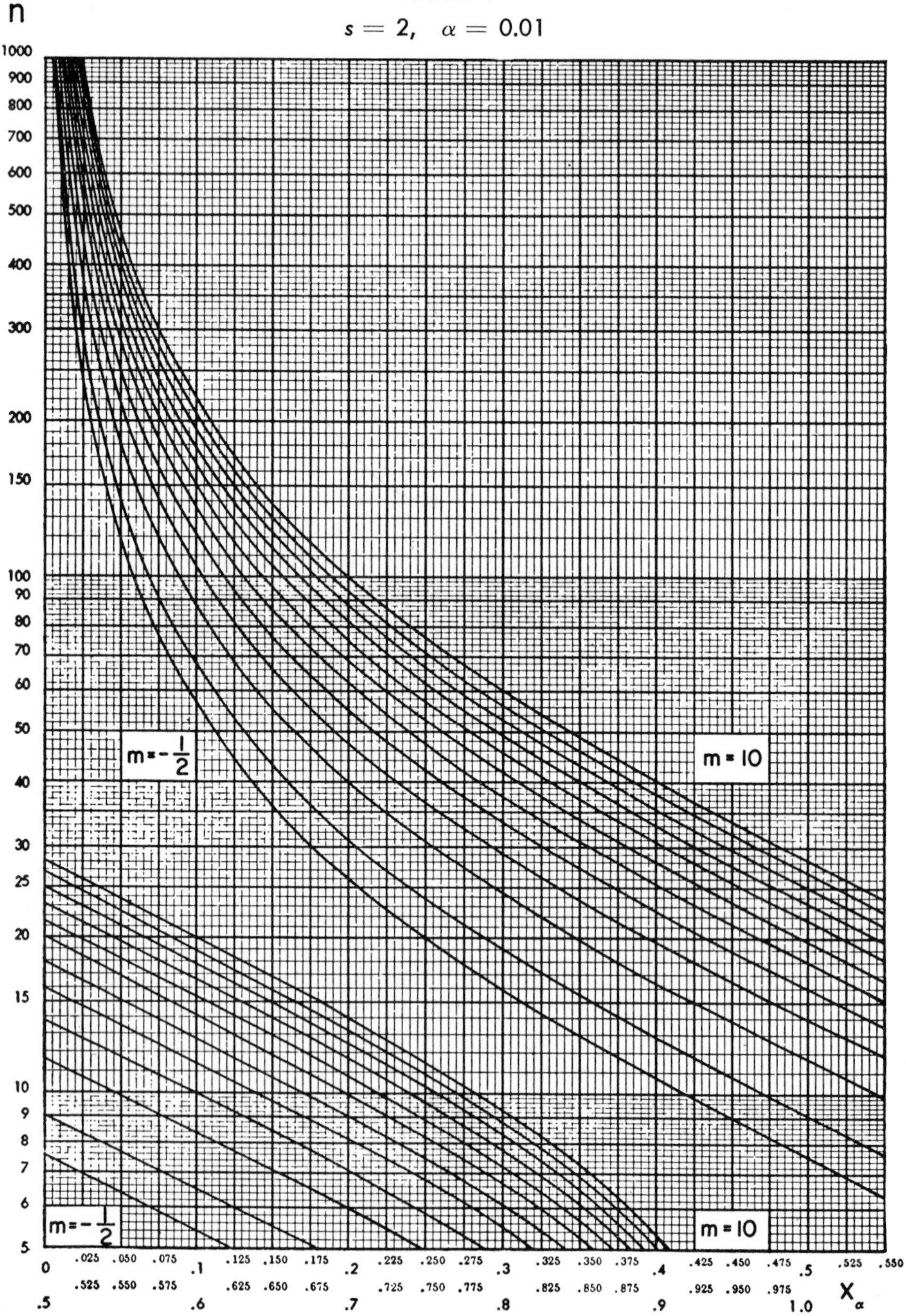

n

1000
900
800
700
600
500
400

300

200

150

100
90
80
70
60

50
40

30
25

20

15

10
9
8
7

6

5

$m = -\frac{1}{2}$　　　　　　　　　　$m = 10$

$m = -\frac{1}{2}$　　　　　　　　　　$m = 10$

0　.025　.050　.075　.1　.125　.150　.175　.2　.225　.250　.275　.3　.325　.350　.375　.4　.425　.450　.475　.5　.525　.550

.5　.525　.550　.575　.6　.625　.650　.675　.7　.725　.750　.775　.8　.825　.850　.875　.9　.925　.950　.975　1.0　X_α

8.14

Graphs of Some Upper Percentage Points of the Distribution of the Largest Characteristic Root (cont.)

$$\Pr\{\theta_s \le X_\alpha(s, m, n)\} = 1 - \alpha$$

CHART II

$$s = 2, \quad \alpha = 0.025$$

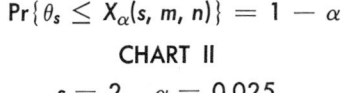

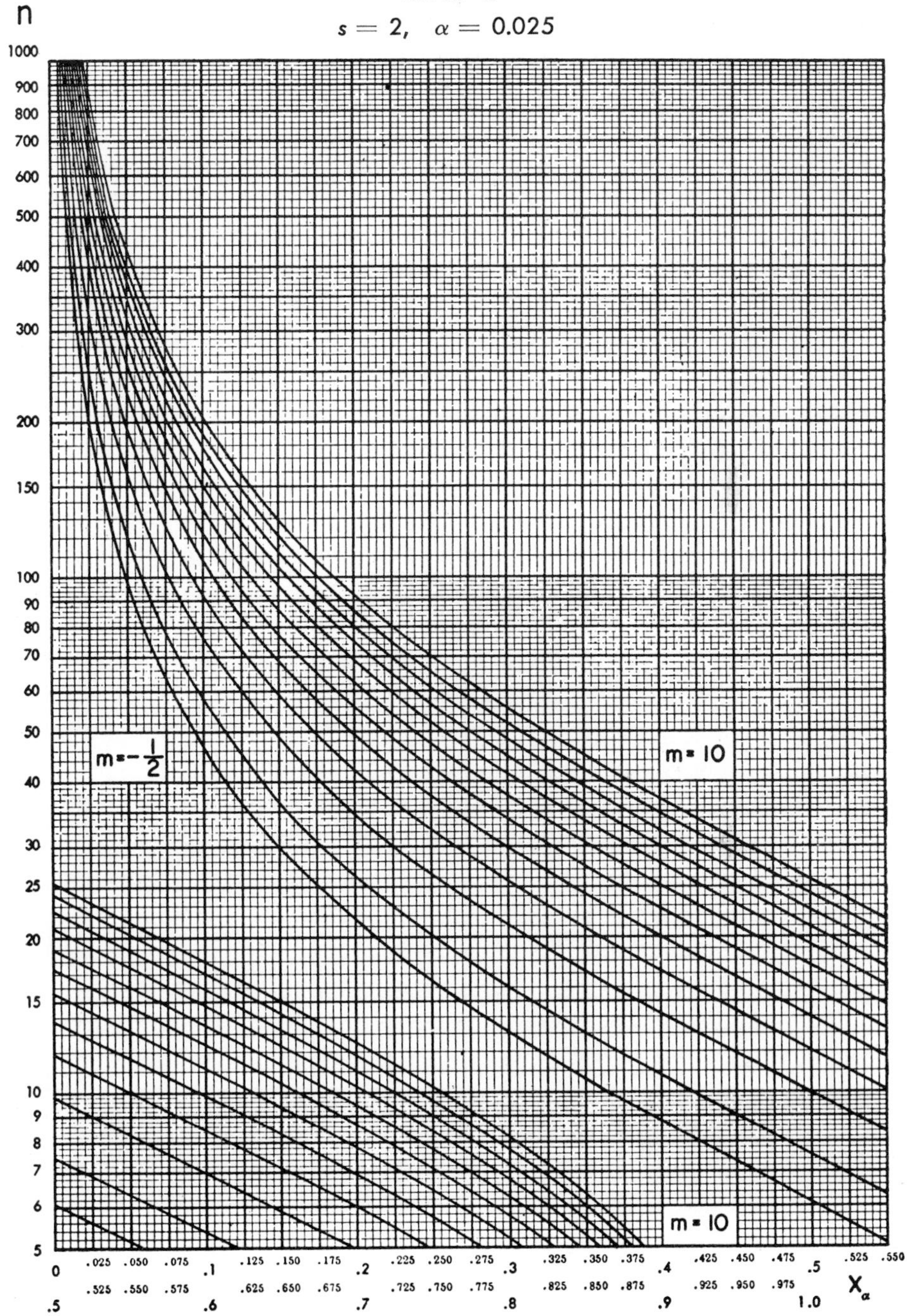

n

$m = -\frac{1}{2}$		$m = 10$	

$m = 10$

X$_\alpha$

240

$$\Pr\{\theta_s \leq X_\alpha(s, m, n)\} = 1 - \alpha$$

CHART III

$$s = 2, \quad \alpha = 0.05$$

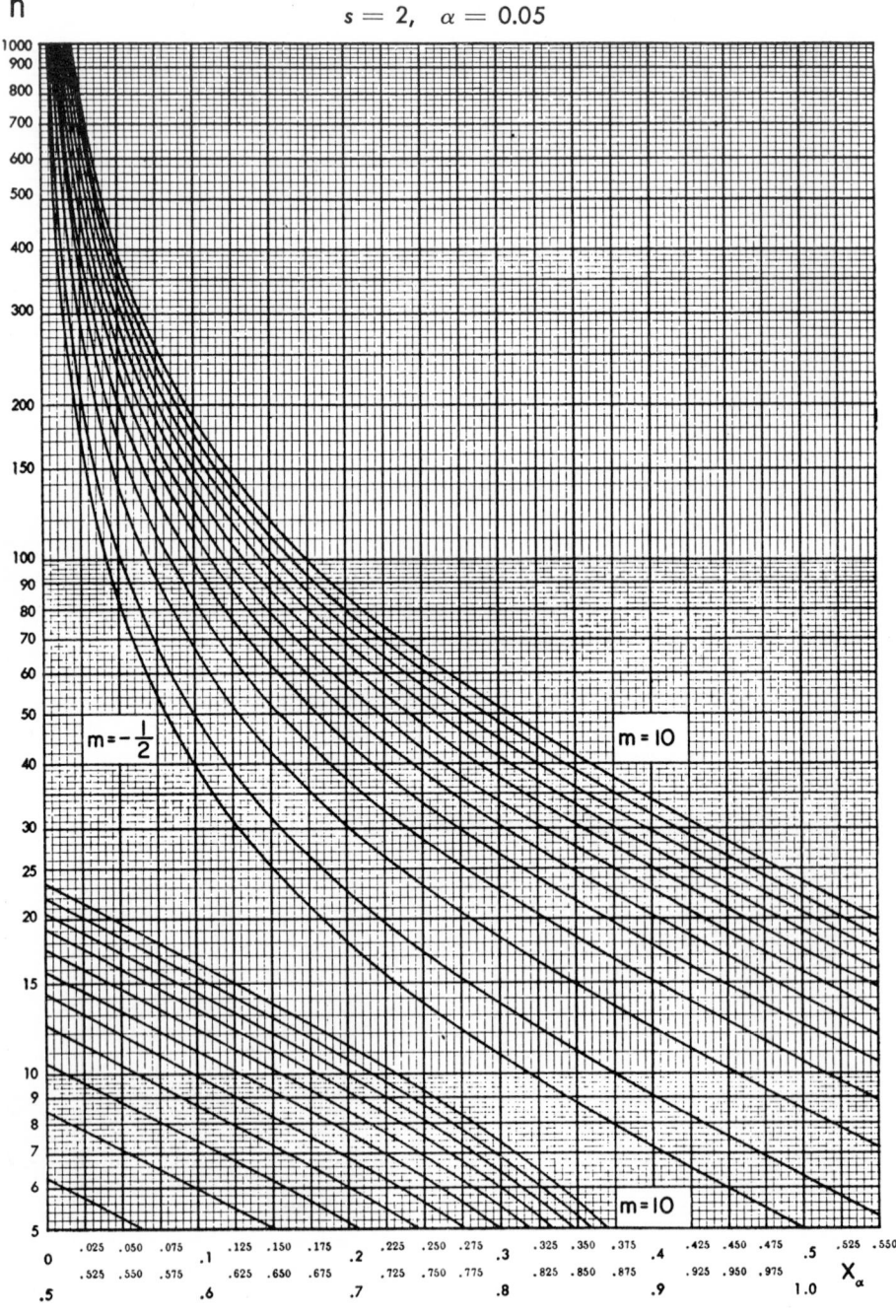

Graphs of Some Upper Percentage Points of the Distribution of the Largest Characteristic Root (cont.)

$$\Pr\{\theta_s \le X_\alpha(s, m, n)\} = 1 - \alpha$$

CHART IV

$$s = 3, \quad \alpha = 0.01$$

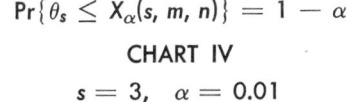

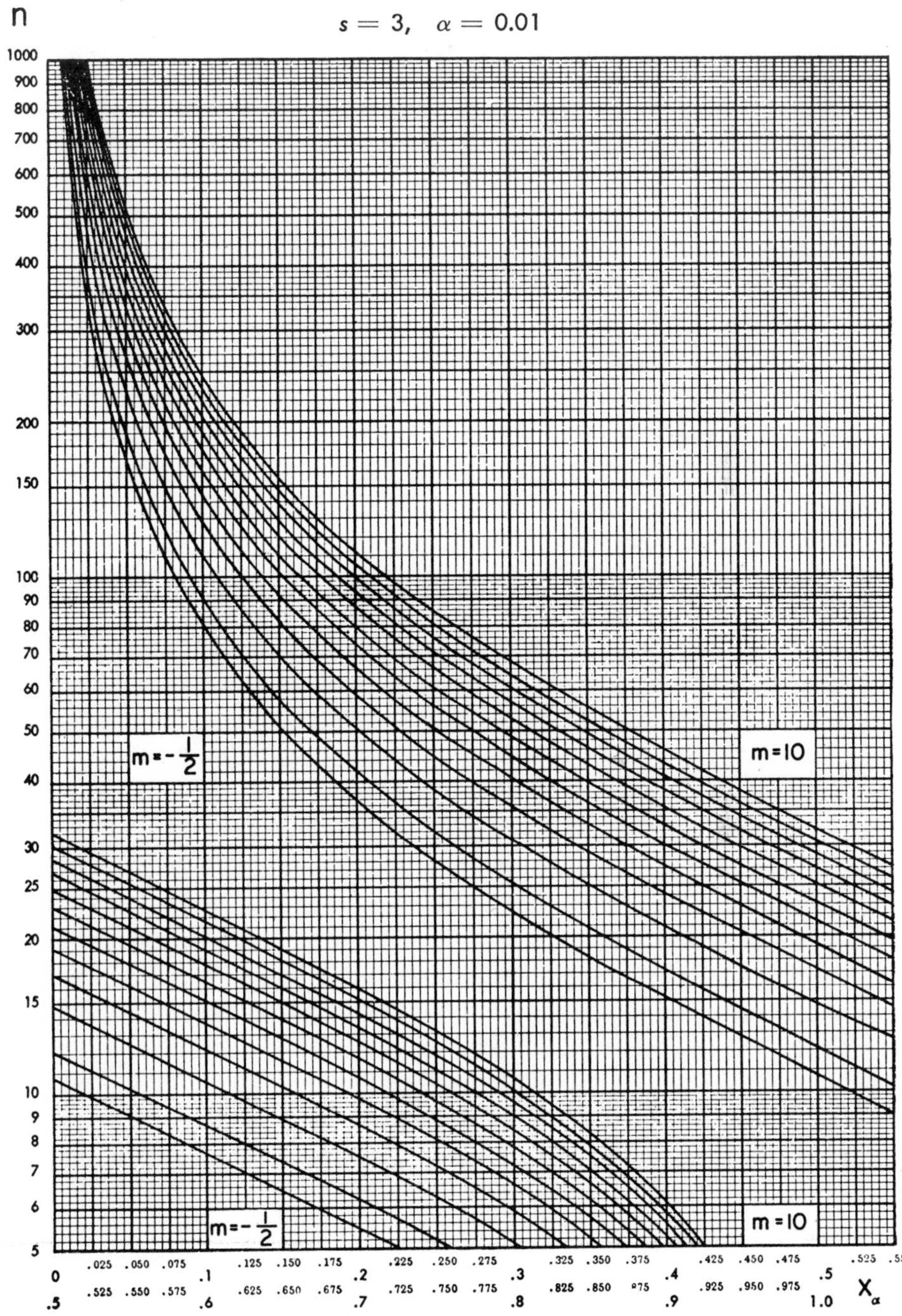

n

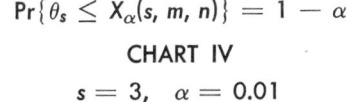

X_α

Graphs of Some Upper Percentage Points of the Distribution
of the Largest Characteristic Root (cont.)

$$\Pr\{\theta_s \le X_\alpha(s, m, n)\} = 1 - \alpha$$

CHART V

$$s = 3, \quad \alpha = 0.025$$

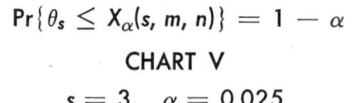

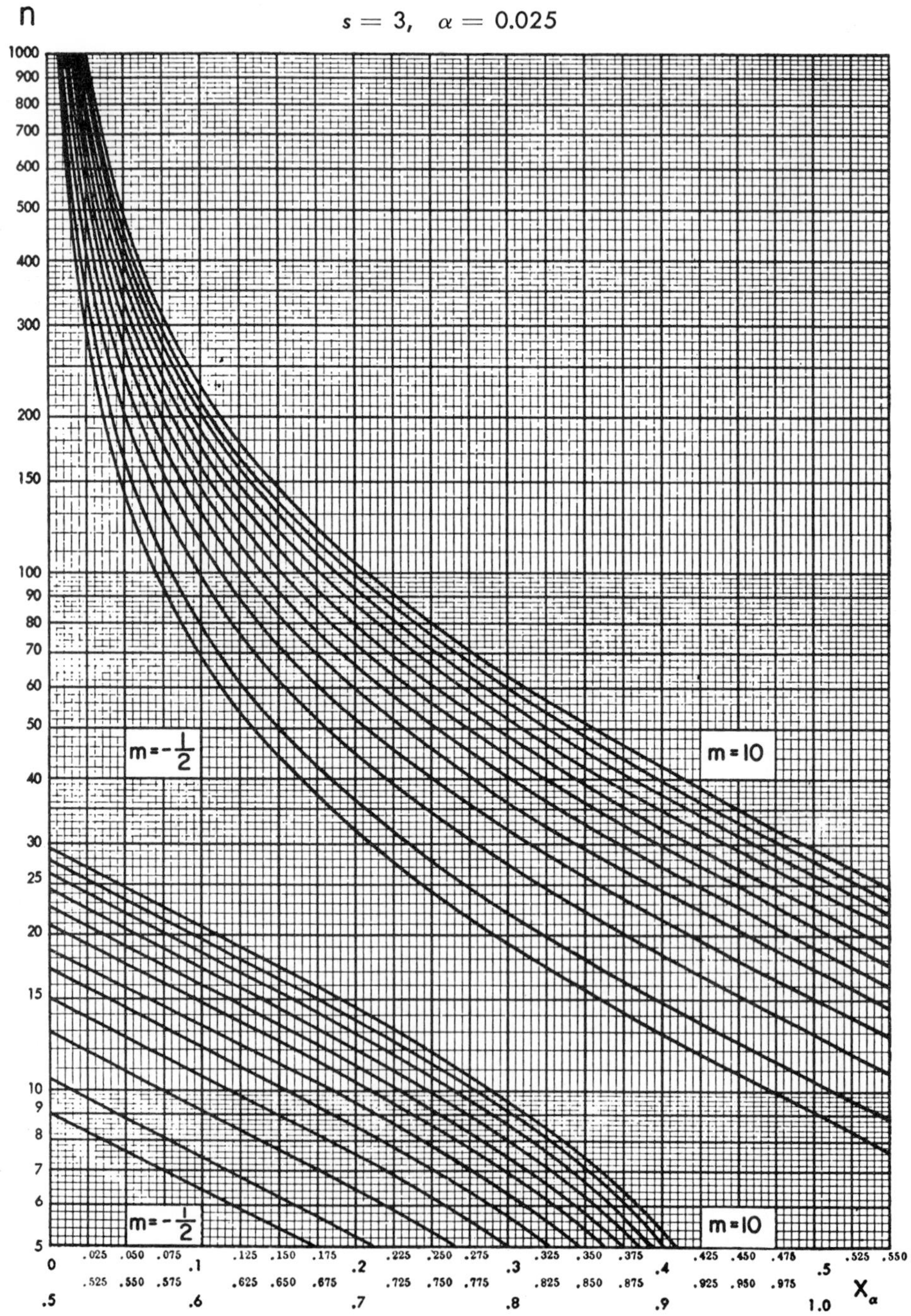

n

$m = -\frac{1}{2}$

$m = 10$

$m = -\frac{1}{2}$

$m = 10$

X_α

Graphs of Some Upper Percentage Points of the Distribution of the Largest Characteristic Root (cont.)

$$\Pr\{\theta_s \le X_\alpha(s, m, n)\} = 1 - \alpha$$

CHART VI

$$s = 3, \quad \alpha = 0.05$$

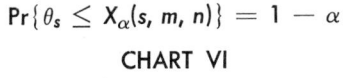

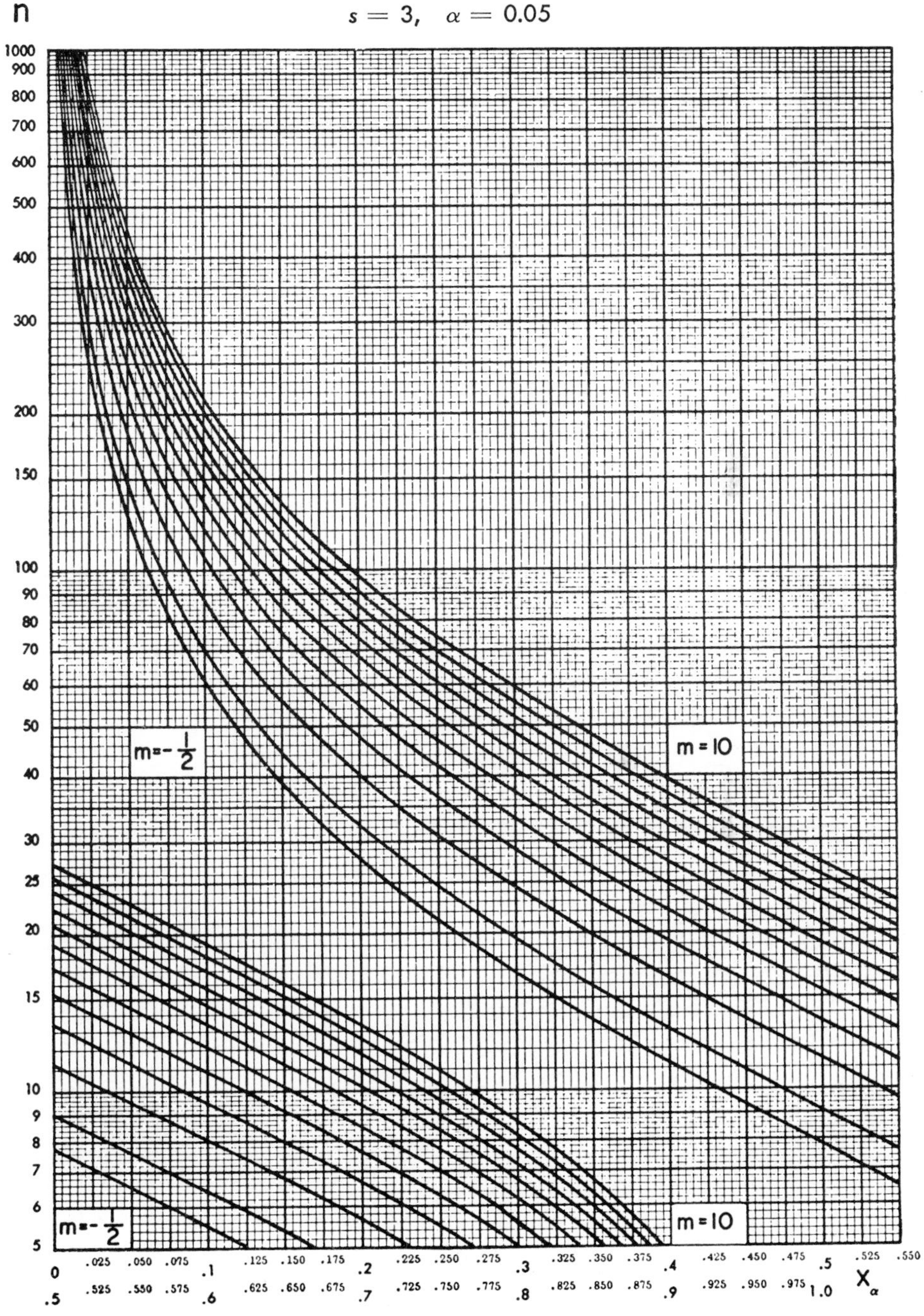

n

$m = -\frac{1}{2}$

$m = 10$

$m = -\frac{1}{2}$

$m = 10$

X_α

8.14

Graphs of Some Upper Percentage Points of the Distribution
of the Largest Characteristic Root (cont.)

$$\Pr\{\theta_s \le X_\alpha(s, m, n)\} = 1 - \alpha$$

CHART VII

n

$$s = 4, \quad \alpha = 0.01$$

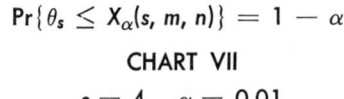

X_α

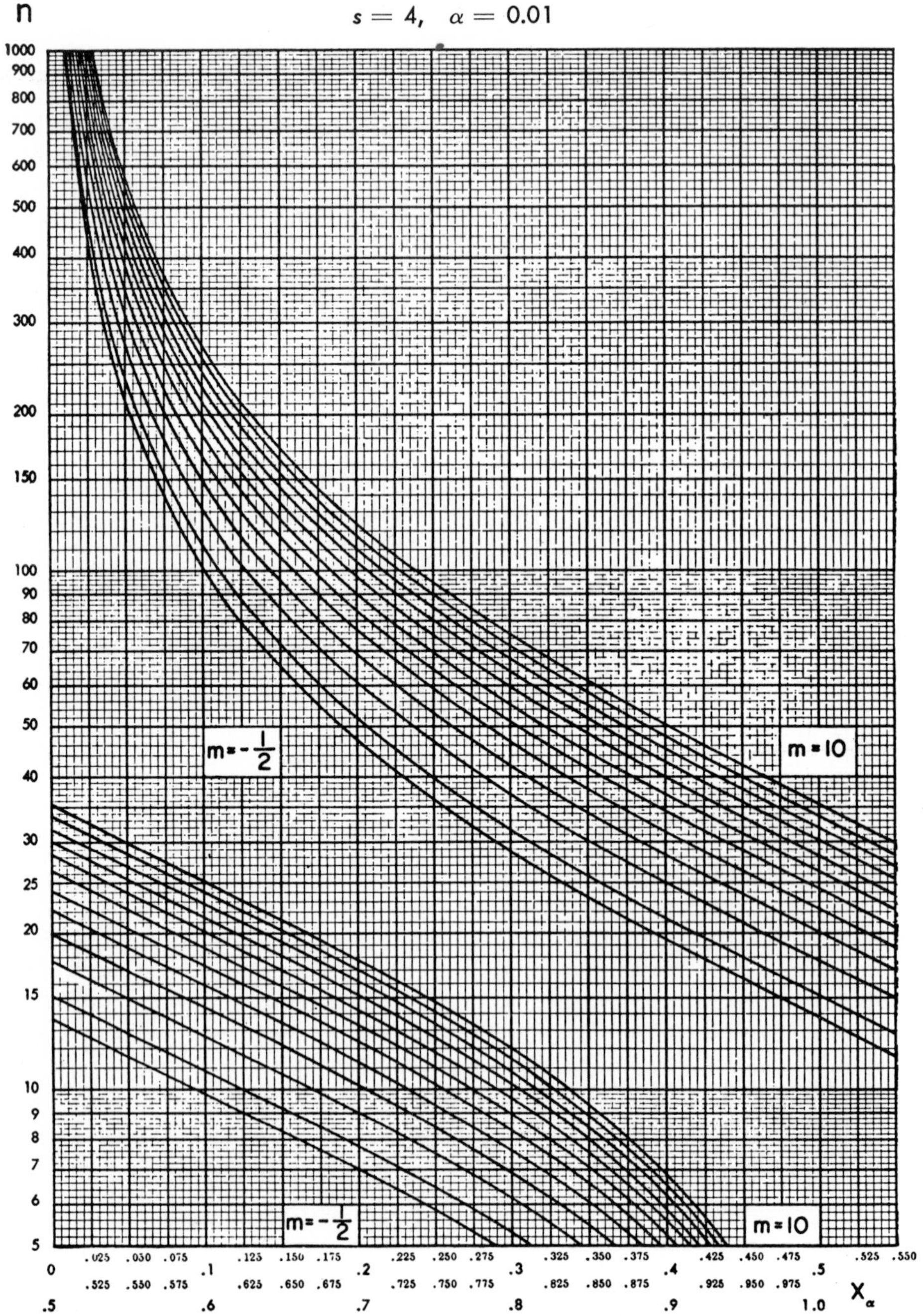

Graphs of Some Upper Percentage Points of the Distribution of the Largest Characteristic Root (cont.)

$$Pr\{\theta_s \leq X_\alpha(s, m, n)\} = 1 - \alpha$$

CHART VIII

n

$$s = 4, \quad \alpha = 0.025$$

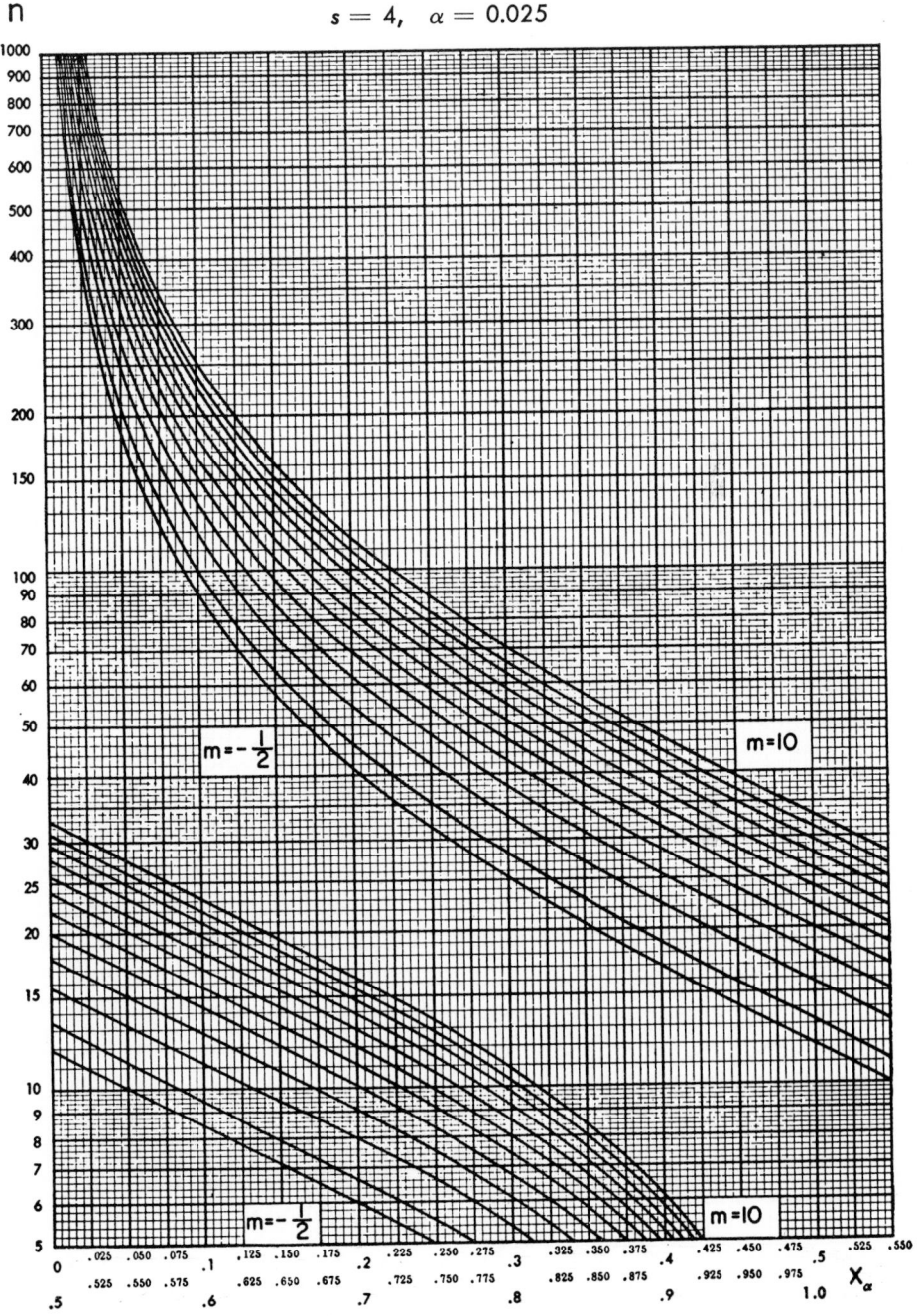

X_α

246

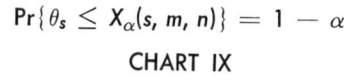

Graphs of Some Upper Percentage Points of the Distribution
of the Largest Characteristic Root (*cont.*)

$$\Pr\{\theta_s \le X_\alpha(s, m, n)\} = 1 - \alpha$$

CHART IX

$s = 4, \quad \alpha = 0.05$

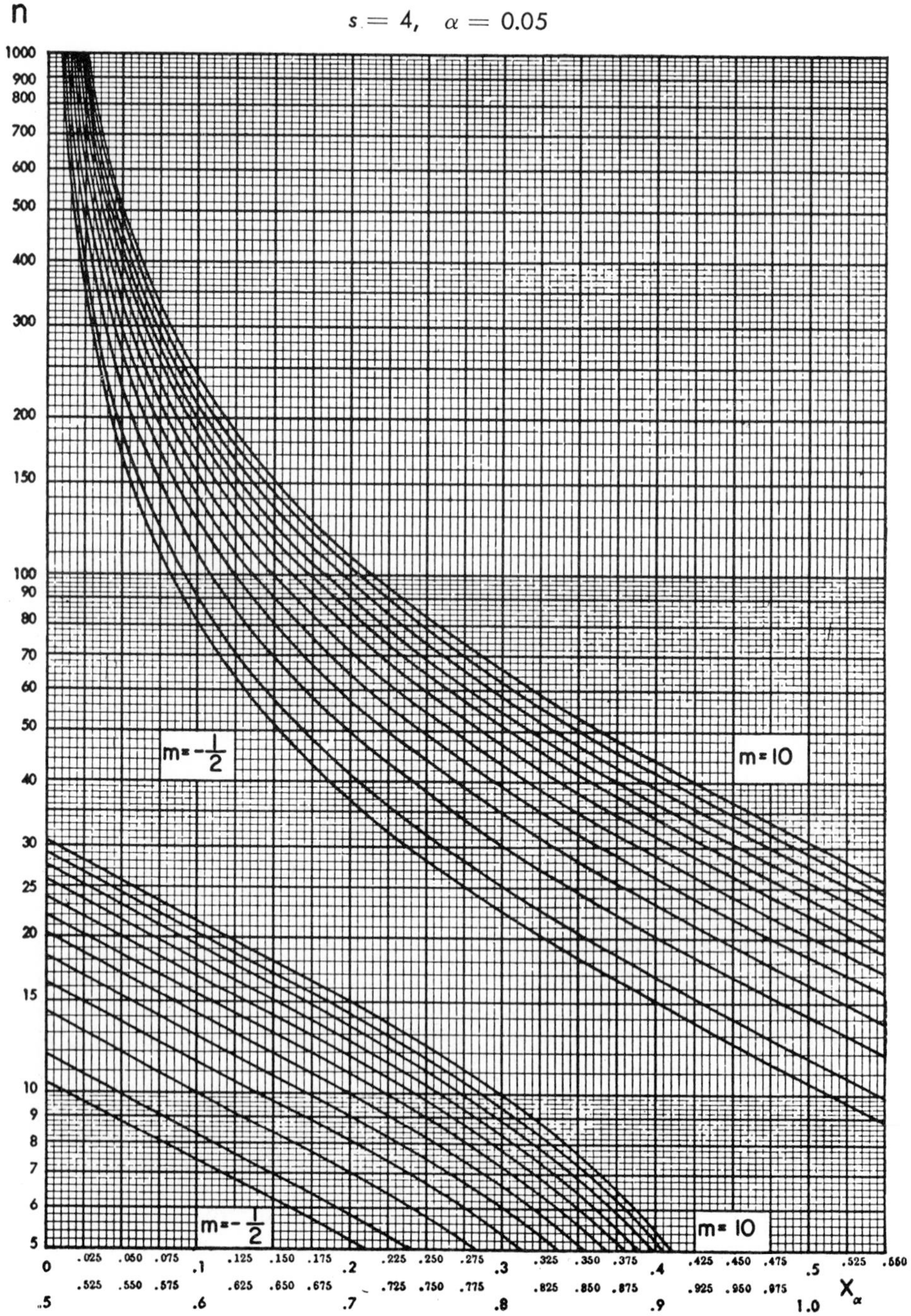

n

1000
900
800
700
600
500
400
300
200
150
100
90
80
70
60
50
40
30
25
20
15
10
9
8
7
6
5

$m = -\frac{1}{2}$

$m = 10$

$m = -\frac{1}{2}$

$m = 10$

.025 .050 .075   .125 .150 .175   .225 .250 .275   .325 .350 .375   .425 .450 .475   .525 .550

0   .1   .2   .3   .4   .5

.525 .550 .575   .625 .650 .675   .725 .750 .775   .825 .850 .875   .925 .950 .975

.5   .6   .7   .8   .9   1.0

X_α

8.14

Graphs of Some Upper Percentage Points of the Distribution of the Largest Characteristic Root (cont.)

$$\Pr\{\theta_s \le X_\alpha(s, m, n)\} = 1 - \alpha$$

CHART X

$$s = 5, \quad \alpha = 0.01$$

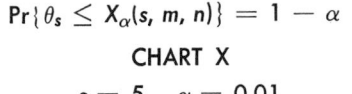

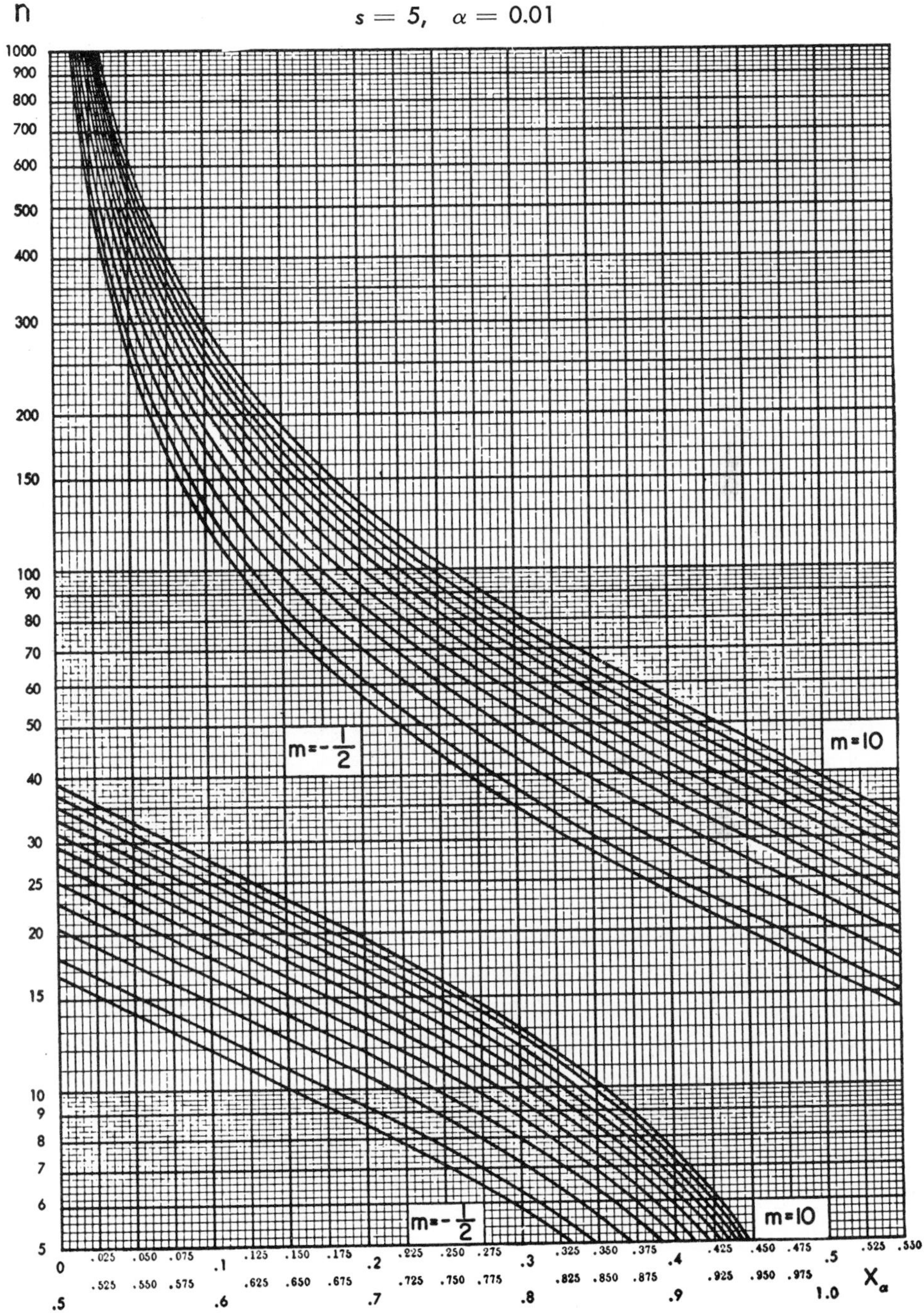

n

$m = -\tfrac{1}{2}$

$m = 10$

$m = -\tfrac{1}{2}$

$m = 10$

X_α

8.14

Graphs of Some Upper Percentage Points of the Distribution of the Largest Characteristic Root (cont.)

$$\Pr\{\theta_s \le X_\alpha(s, m, n)\} = 1 - \alpha$$

CHART XI

$$s = 5, \quad \alpha = 0.025$$

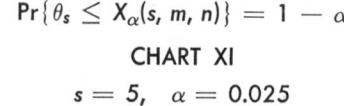

n

$m = -\frac{1}{2}$

$m = 10$

$m = -\frac{1}{2}$

$m = 10$

X_α

8.14

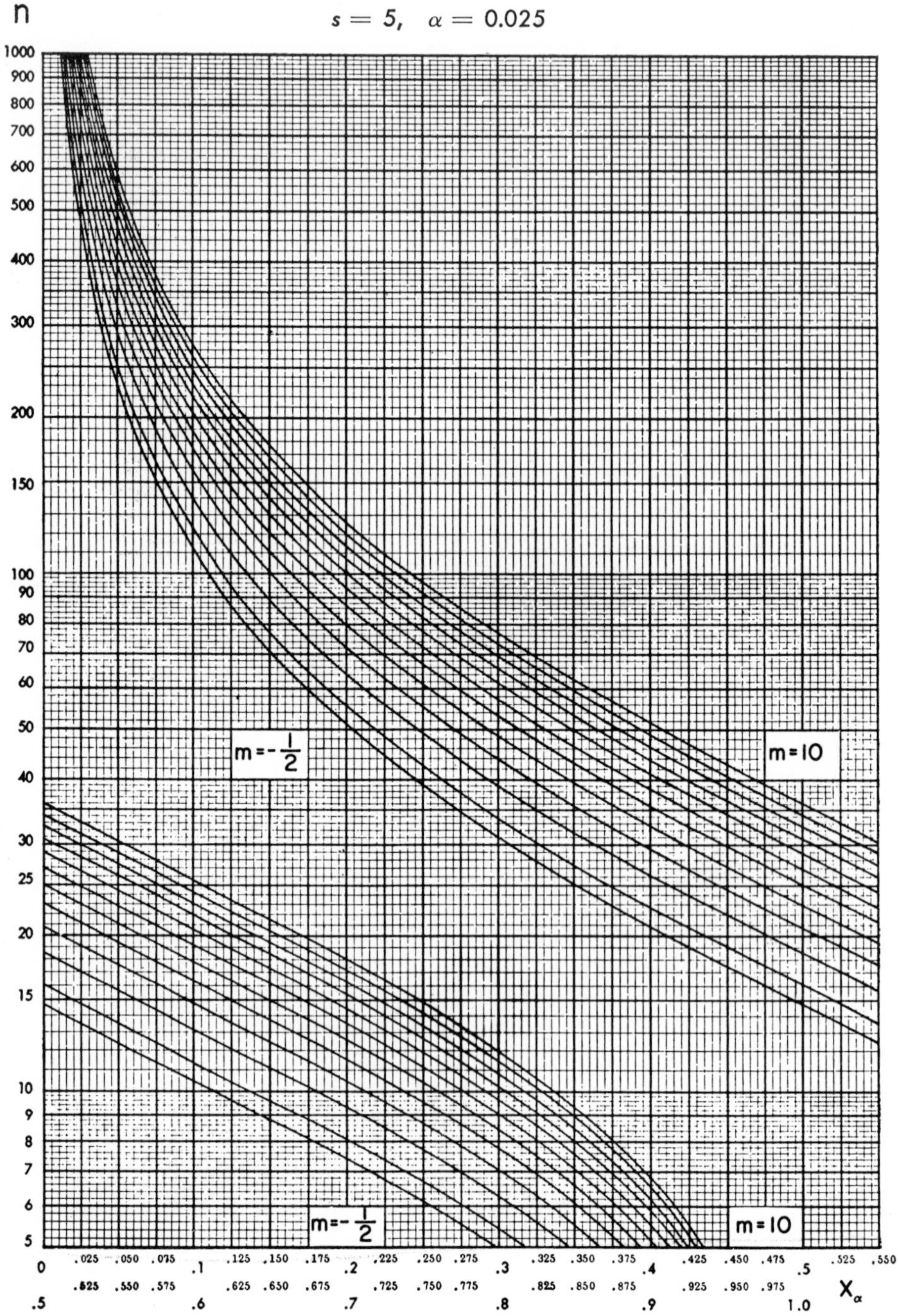

Graphs of Some Upper Percentage Points of the Distribution of the Largest Characteristic Root (cont.)

$$\Pr\{\theta_s \leq X_\alpha(s, m, n)\} = 1 - \alpha$$

CHART XII

$$s = 5, \quad \alpha = 0.05$$

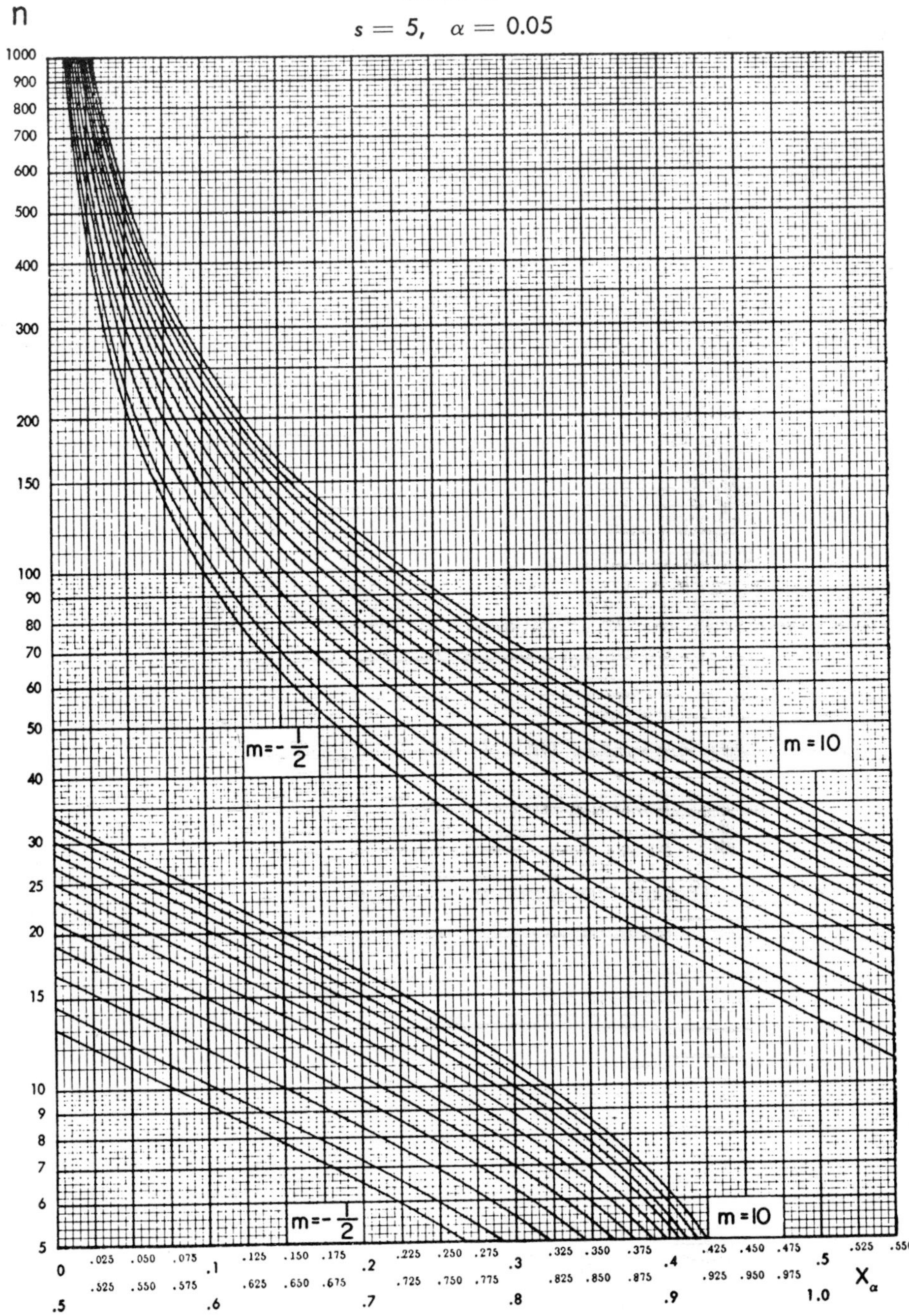

n

$m = -\frac{1}{2}$

$m = 10$

X_α

8.14

8.15 Critical Values of a Bivariate t-Distribution with $\rho = \pm 0.5$

The quantity tabulated is that value of t which satisfies the following equation:

$$\frac{1}{\pi\sqrt{3}} \int_{-\infty}^{t} \int_{-\infty}^{t} \left[1 + \frac{4(x^2 \pm xy + y^2)}{3f}\right]^{-(f+2)/2} dx\, dy = \gamma,$$

where $\gamma = 0.50, 0.75, 0.90, 0.95$, and 0.99, and where for plus-or-minus, the minus sign is taken for the $\rho = +0.5$ table, and the plus sign is taken for the $\rho = -0.5$ table.

This table is useful in certain multiple-decision problems. For example, see [169] and [14]. See Section 4.4 above for a p-variate extension, i.e., in Section 4.4, $p = 2$ corresponds to the values with $\rho = \frac{1}{2}$ given here.

Critical Values of a Bivariate t-Distribution [59]

$$\rho = +0.5$$

f	0.50	0.75	0.90	0.95	0.99
1	0.500	1.708	4.696	9.511	47.733
2	0.446	1.291	2.539	3.805	8.879
3	0.428	1.186	2.130	2.939	5.483
4	0.420	1.138	1.963	2.611	4.408
5	0.414	1.111	1.874	2.441	3.900
6	0.411	1.094	1.817	2.337	3.608
7	0.409	1.082	1.779	2.268	3.419
8	0.407	1.073	1.751	2.218	3.287
9	0.405	1.066	1.730	2.180	3.190
10	0.404	1.061	1.714	2.151	3.115
11	0.403	1.056	1.701	2.128	3.056
12	0.402	1.053	1.690	2.109	3.009
13	0.402	1.050	1.680	2.093	2.969
14	0.401	1.047	1.673	2.079	2.936
15	0.401	1.045	1.666	2.067	2.908
16	0.400	1.043	1.660	2.057	2.884
17	0.400	1.041	1.655	2.049	2.863
18	0.400	1.040	1.651	2.041	2.844
19	0.399	1.038	1.647	2.034	2.828
20	0.399	1.037	1.643	2.028	2.813
21	0.399	1.036	1.640	2.022	2.800
22	0.399	1.035	1.637	2.017	2.788
23	0.398	1.034	1.634	2.013	2.778
24	0.398	1.033	1.632	2.009	2.768
25	0.398	1.033	1.629	2.005	2.759
26	0.398	1.032	1.627	2.001	2.751
27	0.398	1.031	1.626	1.998	2.743
28	0.398	1.031	1.624	1.995	2.736
29	0.397	1.030	1.622	1.992	2.730
30	0.397	1.029	1.621	1.990	2.724
33	0.397	1.028	1.617	1.983	2.708
36	0.397	1.027	1.613	1.977	2.695
39	0.397	1.026	1.610	1.972	2.684
42	0.396	1.025	1.608	1.968	2.674
45	0.396	1.024	1.606	1.965	2.666

Critical Values of a Bivariate *t*-Distribution (*cont.*)

$$\rho = +0.5$$

f	0.50	0.75	0.90	0.95	0.99
48	0.396	1.024	1.604	1.962	2.659
51	0.396	1.023	1.603	1.959	2.653
54	0.396	1.023	1.601	1.957	2.648
57	0.396	1.022	1.600	1.954	2.643
60	0.396	1.022	1.599	1.953	2.639
75	0.395	1.020	1.594	1.945	2.622
90	0.395	1.019	1.592	1.941	2.611
105	0.395	1.019	1.590	1.937	2.604
120	0.395	1.018	1.588	1.935	2.598
150	0.395	1.017	1.586	1.931	2.590
300	0.394	1.016	1.582	1.924	2.574
600	0.394	1.015	1.580	1.920	2.566
∞	0.39351	1.01391	1.57700	1.91634	2.55781

$$\rho = -0.5$$

f	0.50	0.75	0.90	0.95	0.99
1	0.867	2.225	5.881	11.850	59.385
2	0.744	1.553	2.864	4.231	9.777
3	0.708	1.395	2.333	3.161	5.812
4	0.691	1.325	2.121	2.767	4.595
5	0.681	1.286	2.008	2.566	4.028
6	0.674	1.261	1.938	2.444	3.706
7	0.670	1.243	1.891	2.363	3.499
8	0.666	1.231	1.857	2.305	3.355
9	0.664	1.221	1.831	2.261	3.250
10	0.662	1.213	1.811	2.228	3.169
11	0.660	1.207	1.794	2.201	3.106
12	0.658	1.202	1.781	2.179	3.055
13	0.657	1.197	1.770	2.160	3.012
14	0.656	1.193	1.760	2.145	2.977
15	0.655	1.190	1.752	2.131	2.947
16	0.654	1.187	1.745	2.120	2.921
17	0.654	1.185	1.739	2.110	2.898
18	0.653	1.183	1.733	2.101	2.879
19	0.653	1.181	1.729	2.093	2.861
20	0.652	1.179	1.724	2.086	2.846

Critical Values of a Bivariate *t*-Distribution (*cont.*)

$$\rho = -0.5$$

f	0.50	0.75	0.90	0.95	0.99
21	0.652	1.178	1.720	2.080	2.832
22	0.651	1.176	1.717	2.074	2.819
23	0.651	1.175	1.714	2.069	2.808
24	0.651	1.174	1.711	2.064	2.797
25	0.650	1.173	1.708	2.060	2.788
26	0.650	1.172	1.705	2.056	2.779
27	0.650	1.171	1.703	2.052	2.771
28	0.649	1.170	1.701	2.049	2.764
29	0.649	1.169	1.699	2.046	2.757
30	0.649	1.168	1.697	2.043	2.750
33	0.648	1.166	1.692	2.035	2.734
36	0.648	1.165	1.688	2.028	2.720
39	0.648	1.163	1.685	2.023	2.708
42	0.647	1.162	1.682	2.018	2.698
45	0.647	1.161	1.679	2.014	2.690
48	0.647	1.160	1.677	2.011	2.683
51	0.646	1.159	1.675	2.008	2.676
54	0.646	1.159	1.674	2.005	2.670
57	0.646	1.158	1.672	2.003	2.665
60	0.646	1.157	1.671	2.001	2.661
75	0.645	1.155	1.666	1.993	2.643
90	0.645	1.154	1.662	1.987	2.632
105	0.645	1.153	1.660	1.983	2.624
120	0.644	1.152	1.658	1.980	2.618
150	0.644	1.151	1.655	1.976	2.609
300	0.643	1.149	1.650	1.968	2.593
600	0.643	1.148	1.648	1.964	2.584
∞	0.64235	1.14630	1.64457	1.95993	2.57568

8.15

9. LOGISTIC, POISSON, AND BINOMIAL DISTRIBUTIONS

9.1 The Logistic Probability Distribution

The probability density for the logistic probability distribution is given by

$$f(X) = \frac{\pi \exp\left[-\dfrac{\pi}{\sqrt{3}}\left(\dfrac{X - \mu}{\sigma}\right)\right]}{\sigma\sqrt{3}\left\{1 + \exp\left[-\dfrac{\pi}{\sqrt{3}}\left(\dfrac{X - \mu}{\sigma}\right)\right]\right\}^2}, \quad -\infty \leq X \leq +\infty,$$

where μ is the expected value of X and σ is the standard deviation of X. If we let $t = (X - \mu)/\sigma$, then the standardized form of the density becomes

$$g(t) = -\frac{\pi \exp\left(-\dfrac{\pi}{\sqrt{3}}\,t\right)}{\sqrt{3}\left[1 + \exp\left(-\dfrac{\pi}{\sqrt{3}}\,t\right)\right]^2}, \quad -\infty \leq t \leq +\infty.$$

The cumulative probability distribution for the standardized form is given by

$$G(t) = \int_{-\infty}^{t} g(x)\, dx = \frac{1}{1 + \exp\left(-\dfrac{\pi}{3}\,t\right)}, \quad -\infty \leq t \leq +\infty.$$

The quantities given in the table are $g(t)$ and $G(t)$ as defined above.

This distribution is of interest because it has a shape very much like the normal distribution of Section 1.1. Its main application has been to "logit analysis," although in a slightly altered form from the above. See Ref. [18] for an example.

The Logistic Probability Distribution

t	G(t)	g(t)	t	G(t)	g(t)
0.00	0.5000	0.4534	0.35	0.6536	0.4107
0.01	0.5045	0.4534	0.36	0.6577	0.4084
0.02	0.5091	0.4533	0.37	0.6618	0.4060
0.03	0.5136	0.4531	0.38	0.6658	0.4036
0.04	0.5181	0.4529	0.39	0.6698	0.4011
0.05	0.5227	0.4525	0.40	0.6738	0.3986
0.06	0.5272	0.4521	0.41	0.6778	0.3961
0.07	0.5317	0.4516	0.42	0.6817	0.3935
0.08	0.5362	0.4511	0.43	0.6857	0.3909
0.09	0.5407	0.4504	0.44	0.6896	0.3883
0.10	0.5452	0.4497	0.45	0.6934	0.3856
0.11	0.5497	0.4490	0.46	0.6973	0.3829
0.12	0.5542	0.4481	0.47	0.7011	0.3801
0.13	0.5587	0.4472	0.48	0.7049	0.3773
0.14	0.5631	0.4462	0.49	0.7086	0.3745
0.15	0.5676	0.4452	0.50	0.7124	0.3716
0.16	0.5720	0.4440	0.51	0.7161	0.3688
0.17	0.5765	0.4428	0.52	0.7197	0.3659
0.18	0.5809	0.4416	0.53	0.7234	0.3629
0.19	0.5853	0.4402	0.54	0.7270	0.3600
0.20	0.5897	0.4389	0.55	0.7306	0.3570
0.21	0.5941	0.4374	0.56	0.7341	0.3540
0.22	0.5985	0.4359	0.57	0.7377	0.3510
0.23	0.6028	0.4343	0.58	0.7412	0.3480
0.24	0.6071	0.4326	0.59	0.7446	0.3449
0.25	0.6115	0.4309	0.60	0.7481	0.3418
0.26	0.6158	0.4291	0.61	0.7515	0.3388
0.27	0.6200	0.4273	0.62	0.7548	0.3357
0.28	0.6243	0.4254	0.63	0.7582	0.3326
0.29	0.6286	0.4235	0.64	0.7615	0.3294
0.30	0.6328	0.4215	0.65	0.7648	0.3263
0.31	0.6370	0.4194	0.66	0.7680	0.3232
0.32	0.6412	0.4173	0.67	0.7712	0.3200
0.33	0.6453	0.4151	0.68	0.7744	0.3169
0.34	0.6495	0.4129	0.69	0.7776	0.3137

9.1

The Logistic Probability Distribution (cont.)

t	G(t)	g(t)	t	G(t)	g(t)
0.70	0.7807	0.3106	1.25	0.9061	0.1543
0.71	0.7838	0.3074	1.30	0.9136	0.1432
0.72	0.7868	0.3042	1.35	0.9205	0.1328
0.73	0.7899	0.3011	1.40	0.9269	0.1230
0.74	0.7929	0.2979	1.45	0.9328	0.1137
0.75	0.7958	0.2947	1.50	0.9382	0.1051
0.76	0.7987	0.2916	1.55	0.9433	0.0970
0.77	0.8016	0.2884	1.60	0.9479	0.0895
0.78	0.8045	0.2853	1.65	0.9522	0.0825
0.79	0.8074	0.2821	1.70	0.9562	0.0760
0.80	0.8102	0.2790	1.75	0.9598	0.0699
0.81	0.8129	0.2758	1.80	0.9632	0.0643
0.82	0.8157	0.2727	1.85	0.9663	0.0591
0.83	0.8184	0.2696	1.90	0.9691	0.0543
0.84	0.8211	0.2665	1.95	0.9717	0.0498
0.85	0.8237	0.2634	2.00	0.9741	0.0457
0.86	0.8263	0.2603	2.05	0.9763	0.0420
0.87	0.8289	0.2572	2.10	0.9783	0.0385
0.88	0.8315	0.2542	2.15	0.9802	0.0353
0.89	0.8340	0.2511	2.20	0.9818	0.0323
0.90	0.8365	0.2481	2.25	0.9834	0.0296
0.91	0.8390	0.2450	2.30	0.9848	0.0271
0.92	0.8414	0.2420	2.35	0.9861	0.0248
0.93	0.8438	0.2391	2.40	0.9873	0.0227
0.94	0.8462	0.2361	2.45	0.9884	0.0208
0.95	0.8485	0.2331	2.50	0.9894	0.0191
0.96	0.8508	0.2302	2.55	0.9903	0.0174
0.97	0.8531	0.2273	2.60	0.9911	0.0160
0.98	0.8554	0.2244	2.65	0.9919	0.0146
0.99	0.8576	0.2215	2.70	0.9926	0.0133
1.00	0.8598	0.2186	2.75	0.9932	0.0122
1.05	0.8704	0.2046	2.80	0.9938	0.0112
1.10	0.8803	0.1911	2.85	0.9943	0.0102
1.15	0.8895	0.1782	2.90	0.9948	0.0093
1.20	0.8981	0.1660	2.95	0.9953	0.0085
			3.00	0.9957	0.0078

9.2 Inverse of the Logistic Probability Distribution

The quantities given in this table are defined by

$$p = \int_{-\infty}^{t} g(x) \, dx = G(t),$$

where $g(t)$ and $G(t)$ are defined as in Section 9.1. That is, the value of t is given which makes the cumulative probability equal to p. Then $g(t)$ is computed.

Inverse of the Logistic Probability Distribution

p	t	g(t)	p	t	g(t)
0.50	0.0000	0.4534	0.925	1.3851	0.1258
0.51	0.0221	0.4533	0.930	1.4261	0.1181
0.52	0.0441	0.4527	0.935	1.4699	0.1102
0.53	0.0662	0.4518	0.940	1.5170	0.1023
0.54	0.0884	0.4505	0.945	1.5679	0.0943
0.55	0.1106	0.4489	0.950	1.6234	0.0862
0.56	0.1330	0.4469	0.955	1.6843	0.0779
0.57	0.1554	0.4446	0.960	1.7522	0.0696
0.58	0.1780	0.4418	0.965	1.8286	0.0613
0.59	0.2007	0.4388	0.970	1.9165	0.0528
0.60	0.2235	0.4353	0.975	2.0198	0.0442
0.61	0.2466	0.4315	0.980	2.1457	0.0356
0.62	0.2699	0.4273	0.985	2.3071	0.0268
0.63	0.2934	0.4228	0.990	2.5334	0.0180
0.64	0.3172	0.4179			
0.65	0.3413	0.4126	0.991	2.5921	0.0162
0.66	0.3657	0.4070	0.992	2.6576	0.0144
0.67	0.3904	0.4010	0.993	2.7317	0.0126
0.68	0.4156	0.3947	0.994	2.8173	0.0108
0.69	0.4411	0.3880	0.995	2.9184	0.0090
0.70	0.4671	0.3809	0.996	3.0419	0.0072
0.71	0.4937	0.3735	0.997	3.2011	0.0054
0.72	0.5207	0.3657	0.998	3.4252	0.0036
0.73	0.5484	0.3575	0.999	3.8079	0.0018
0.74	0.5767	0.3490			
0.75	0.6057	0.3401	0.9991	3.8660	0.0016
0.76	0.6355	0.3308	0.9992	3.9310	0.0014
0.77	0.6662	0.3212	0.9993	4.0047	0.0013
0.78	0.6978	0.3112	0.9994	4.0897	0.0011
0.79	0.7305	0.3009	0.9995	4.1903	0.0009
0.80	0.7643	0.2902	0.9996	4.3134	0.0007
0.81	0.7994	0.2791	0.9997	4.4721	0.0005
0.82	0.8360	0.2677	0.9998	4.6957	0.0004
0.83	0.8742	0.2559	0.9999	5.0779	0.0002
0.84	0.9142	0.2438			
0.85	0.9563	0.2313	0.9999 5	5.4601	0.0000 9
0.86	1.0008	0.2184	0.9999 9	6.3474	0.0000 2
0.87	1.0481	0.2051	0.9999 95	6.7296	0.0000 09
0.88	1.0985	0.1915	0.9999 99	7.6169	0.0000 02
0.89	1.1527	0.1776	0.9999 995	7.9990	0.0000 009
0.900	1.2114	0.1632	0.9999 999	8.8864	0.0000 002
0.905	1.2427	0.1559	0.9999 9995	9.2685	0.0000 0009
0.910	1.2756	0.1486	0.9999 9999	10.1559	0.0000 0002
0.915	1.3101	0.1411	0.9999 9999 5	10.5380	0.0000 0000 9
0.920	1.3465	0.1335	0.9999 9999 9	11.4253	0.0000 0000 2

9.3 The Cumulative Poisson Distribution

The quantity tabulated is the cumulative Poisson distribution and is given by

$$\sum_{j=0}^{X} \exp{(-\lambda)}\, \frac{\lambda^{j}}{j!}, \quad \text{where } \lambda > 0.$$

Only a short table (two pages) is given here, but more extensive tables of the individual terms in this sum have been given by Kitagawa [108] and Molina [141], and of the upper tail of this sum by Molina [141]. Molina tabulates through $\lambda = 100$. The Sextons [198] give some corrections to Kitagawa's tables. The cumulative Poisson distribution and the cumulative chi-square distribution are related as follows:

$$\sum_{j=0}^{a-1} \frac{\exp{(-\lambda)}\lambda^{j}}{j!} = \frac{1}{2^{f/2}(f/2)} \int_{u}^{\infty} x^{(f-2)/2} \exp{(-x/2)}\, dx,$$

where $f = 2a$ and $u = 2\lambda$. This is proved by repeated integration by parts [192].

The Cumulative Poisson Distribution

λ

X	0.001	0.005	0.010	0.015	0.020	0.025
0	0.9990 0050	0.9950 1248	0.9900 4983	0.9851 1194	0.9801 9867	0.9753 099
1	0.9999 9950	0.9999 8754	0.9999 5033	0.9998 8862	0.9998 0264	0.9996 927
2	1.0000 0000	0.9999 9998	0.9999 9983	0.9999 9945	0.9999 9868	0.9999 974
3	-	1.0000 0000	1.0000 0000	1.0000 0000	0.9999 9999	1.0000 000
4	-	-	-	-	1.0000 0000	1.0000 000

λ

X	0.030	0.035	0.040	0.045	0.050	0.055
0	0.970 446	0.965 605	0.960 789	0.955 997	0.951 229	0.946 485
1	0.999 559	0.999 402	0.999 221	0.999 017	0.998 791	0.998 542
2	0.999 996	0.999 993	0.999 990	0.999 985	0.999 980	0.999 973
3	1.000 000	1.000 000	1.000 000	1.000 000	1.000 000	1.000 000

λ

X	0.060	0.065	0.070	0.075	0.080	0.085
0	0.941 765	0.937 067	0.932 394	0.927 743	0.923 116	0.918 512
1	0.998 270	0.997 977	0.997 661	0.997 324	0.996 966	0.996 586
2	0.999 966	0.999 956	0.999 946	0.999 934	0.999 920	0.999 904
3	0.999 999	0.999 999	0.999 999	0.999 999	0.999 998	0.999 998
4	1.000 000	1.000 000	1.000 000	1.000 000	1.000 000	1.000 000

λ

X	0.090	0.095	0.100	0.200	0.300	0.400
0	0.913 931	0.909 373	0.904 837	0.818 731	0.740 818	0.670 320
1	0.996 185	0.995 763	0.995 321	0.982 477	0.963 064	0.938 448
2	0.999 886	0.999 867	0.999 845	0.998 852	0.996 401	0.992 074
3	0.999 997	0.999 997	0.999 996	0.999 943	0.999 734	0.999 224
4	1.000 000	1.000 000	1.000 000	0.999 998	0.999 984	0.999 939
5				1.000 000	0.999 999	0.999 996
6					1.000 000	1.000 000

λ

X	0.500	0.600	0.700	0.800	0.900	1.000
0	0.606 531	0.548 812	0.496 585	0.449 329	0.406 570	0.367 879
1	0.909 796	0.878 099	0.844 195	0.808 792	0.772 482	0.735 759
2	0.985 612	0.976 885	0.965 858	0.952 577	0.937 143	0.919 699
3	0.998 248	0.996 642	0.994 247	0.990 920	0.986 541	0.981 012
4	0.999 828	0.999 606	0.999 214	0.998 589	0.997 656	0.996 340
5	0.999 986	0.999 961	0.999 910	0.999 816	0.999 657	0.999 406
6	0.999 999	0.999 997	0.999 991	0.999 979	0.999 957	0.999 917
7	1.000 000	1.000 000	0.999 999	0.999 998	0.999 995	0.999 990
8			1.000 000	1.000 000	1.000 000	0.999 999
9						1.000 000

The Cumulative Poisson Distribution (cont.)

X	1.20	1.40	1.60	1.80	λ 2.00	2.50	3.00	3.50
0	0.3012	0.2466	0.2019	0.1653	0.1353	0.0821	0.0498	0.0302
1	0.6626	0.5918	0.5249	0.4628	0.4060	0.2873	0.1991	0.1359
2	0.8795	0.8335	0.7834	0.7306	0.6767	0.5438	0.4232	0.3208
3	0.9662	0.9463	0.9212	0.8913	0.8571	0.7576	0.6472	0.5366
4	0.9923	0.9857	0.9763	0.9636	0.9473	0.8912	0.8153	0.7254
5	0.9985	0.9968	0.9940	0.9896	0.9834	0.9580	0.9161	0.8576
6	0.9997	0.9994	0.9987	0.9974	0.9955	0.9858	0.9665	0.9347
7	1.0000	0.9999	0.9997	0.9994	0.9989	0.9958	0.9881	0.9733
8		1.0000	1.0000	0.9999	0.9998	0.9989	0.9962	0.9901
9				1.0000	1.0000	0.9997	0.9989	0.9967
10						0.9999	0.9997	0.9990
11						1.0000	0.9999	0.9997
12							1.0000	0.9999
13								1.0000

X	4.00	4.50	5.00	6.00	λ 7.00	8.00	9.00	10.00
0	0.0183	0.0111	0.0067	0.0025	0.0009	0.0003	0.0001	0.0000
1	0.0916	0.0611	0.0404	0.0174	0.0073	0.0030	0.0012	0.0005
2	0.2381	0.1736	0.1247	0.0620	0.0296	0.0138	0.0062	0.0028
3	0.4335	0.3423	0.2650	0.1512	0.0818	0.0424	0.0212	0.0103
4	0.6288	0.5321	0.4405	0.2851	0.1730	0.0996	0.0550	0.0293
5	0.7851	0.7029	0.6160	0.4457	0.3007	0.1912	0.1157	0.0671
6	0.8893	0.8311	0.7622	0.6063	0.4497	0.3134	0.2068	0.1301
7	0.9489	0.9134	0.8666	0.7440	0.5987	0.4530	0.3239	0.2202
8	0.9786	0.9597	0.9319	0.8472	0.7291	0.5925	0.4577	0.3328
9	0.9919	0.9829	0.9682	0.9161	0.8305	0.7166	0.5874	0.4579
10	0.9972	0.9933	0.9863	0.9574	0.9015	0.8159	0.7060	0.5830
11	0.9991	0.9976	0.9945	0.9799	0.9467	0.8881	0.8030	0.6968
12	0.9997	0.9992	0.9980	0.9912	0.9730	0.9362	0.8758	0.7916
13	0.9999	0.9997	0.9993	0.9964	0.9872	0.9658	0.9261	0.8645
14	1.0000	0.9999	0.9998	0.9986	0.9943	0.9827	0.9585	0.9165
15		1.0000	0.9999	0.9995	0.9976	0.9918	0.9780	0.9513
16			1.0000	0.9998	0.9990	0.9963	0.9889	0.9730
17				0.9999	0.9996	0.9984	0.9947	0.9857
18				1.0000	0.9999	0.9993	0.9976	0.9928
19						0.9997	0.9989	0.9965
20					1.0000	0.9999	0.9996	0.9984
21						1.0000	0.9998	0.9993
22							0.9999	0.9997
23							1.0000	0.9999
24								1.0000

9.3

9.4 Upper Confidence Limits for the Expectation λ of a Poisson Variable with Small Observed Frequency

The quantity tabulated is that value of λ which makes

$$\sum_{j=0}^{c} \exp(-\lambda) \frac{\lambda^j}{j!} \le 1 - \gamma.$$

Among other things, this table is useful for setting confidence limits on a proportion p when the results are available of sampling from a binomial distribution where the sample size n is large and p is small (see Sections 9.5 and 9.6). For example, if a sample of 1000 items drawn at random from an infinite population yielded four defective items, then a 99.5 percent upper confidence limit on p is found by putting $\gamma = 0.995$ and $c = 4$ in the table, and reading $\lambda = np = 12.595$; or $p = 0.012595$ is a 99.5 percent upper confidence limit on p based on this sample. The confidence limit so obtained is an upper bound on the one defined by the Clopper-Pearson system (see Section 9.6).

Upper Confidence Limits for the Expectation λ
of a Poisson Variable with Small Observed Frequency

γ	0	1	2	3	4
0.500	0.694	1.679	2.675	3.673	4.671
0.600	0.917	2.023	3.106	4.176	5.237
0.700	1.204	2.440	3.616	4.763	5.891
0.750	1.387	2.693	3.921	5.110	6.275
0.800	1.610	2.995	4.280	5.516	6.721
0.850	1.898	3.373	4.724	6.014	7.267
0.900	2.303	3.890	5.323	6.681	7.994
0.910	2.408	4.022	5.474	6.849	8.176
0.920	2.526	4.169	5.642	7.035	8.377
0.930	2.660	4.334	5.830	7.242	8.602
0.940	2.814	4.523	6.045	7.479	8.857
0.950	2.996	4.744	6.296	7.754	9.154
0.960	3.219	5.013	6.599	8.086	9.511
0.970	3.507	5.356	6.984	8.506	9.961
0.975	3.689	5.572	7.225	8.768	10.242
0.980	3.913	5.834	7.517	9.085	10.581
0.985	4.200	6.170	7.889	9.487	11.011
0.990	4.606	6.639	8.406	10.046	11.605
0.991	4.711	6.760	8.540	10.189	11.758
0.992	4.829	6.895	8.688	10.349	11.927
0.993	4.962	7.048	8.855	10.529	12.118
0.994	5.116	7.223	9.048	10.735	12.337
0.995	5.299	7.431	9.274	10.978	12.595
0.996	5.522	7.683	9.550	11.273	12.907
0.997	5.810	8.008	9.903	11.650	13.306
0.998	6.215	8.462	10.396	12.177	13.861
0.999	6.908	9.234	11.229	13.063	14.795
0.9991	7.014	9.351	11.355	13.196	14.935
0.9992	7.131	9.481	11.495	13.345	15.091
0.9993	7.265	9.628	11.654	13.513	15.268
0.9994	7.419	9.798	11.836	13.706	15.471
0.9995	7.601	9.999	12.052	13.935	15.710
0.9996	7.825	10.244	12.315	14.212	16.002
0.9997	8.112	10.560	12.652	14.569	16.376
0.9998	8.518	11.003	13.125	15.068	16.898
0.9999	9.211	11.757	13.929	15.914	17.783
0.99991	9.316	11.871	14.050	16.042	17.916
0.99992	9.434	11.999	14.186	16.185	18.065
0.99993	9.568	12.143	14.339	16.346	18.233
0.99994	9.722	12.310	14.516	16.532	18.427
0.99995	9.904	12.507	14.725	16.751	18.656
0.99996	10.127	12.748	14.981	17.019	18.935
0.99997	10.415	13.058	15.309	17.363	19.293
0.99998	10.820	13.494	15.770	17.846	19.796
0.99999	11.513	14.237	16.554	18.666	20.649
0.999995	12.207	14.978	17.334	19.481	21.494

9.5 The Cumulative Binomial Distribution

The quantity tabulated is

$$B(n, A, p) = \sum_{j=0}^{A} \frac{n!}{j!(n-j)!} \, p^j(1-p)^{n-j},$$

where $0 \leq A \leq n$, which is the cumulative binomial distribution. In an n-fold independent repetition of a simple alternative with probability p of success and $1 - p$ of failure, the probability of A or fewer successes is given in the table. More extensive tables of this function have been given by Harvard University [94], the Ordnance Corps [228], the National Bureau of Standards [148], Romig [182], Robertson [181], and probably many others.

Since the tabulation is for $p = \frac{1}{16}(\frac{1}{16})\frac{1}{2}$, it is necessary to use the relationship

$$B(n, A, p) = 1 - B(n, n - A + 1, 1 - p) \quad \text{for } p > \tfrac{1}{2}.$$

These tables may also be used to read off the cumulative distribution function for the negative binomial (Pascal) probability distribution. Consider a simple alternative, with probability of success p and probability of failure $1 - p$. Then the probability that it takes $X + n$ independent repetitions, or less, of the simple alternative to achieve n successes is given by

$$p^n \sum_{j=0}^{X} \binom{n+j-1}{n-1} (1-p)^j = 1 - B(X + n, n - 1, p).$$

Wise [249] and Patil [167] give proofs of the equivalence of these two sums.

The cumulative binomial may also be expressed in terms of the incomplete beta integral as follows:

$$B(n, A, p) = 1 - I_p(A + 1, n - A),$$

where

$$I_x(p, q) = \frac{(p + q - 1)!}{(p - 1)!(q - 1)!} \int_0^x t^{p-1}(1 - t)^{q-1} \, dt.$$

Pearson [174] tabulated the incomplete beta function. Bahadur [11] gives some approximations to the binomial distribution function. Smith [203] and Raff [177] have computed the errors committed by using various approximations to the binomial distribution function.

The Cumulative Binomial Distribution

p

n	A	1/16	2/16	3/16	4/16	5/16	6/16	7/16	8/16
2	0	0.8789	0.7656	0.6602	0.5625	0.4727	0.3906	0.3164	0.2500
	1	0.9961	0.9844	0.9648	0.9375	0.9023	0.8594	0.8086	0.7500
	2	1.0000	1.0000	1.0000	1.0000	1.0000	1.0000	1.0000	1.0000
3	0	0.8240	0.6699	0.5364	0.4219	0.3250	0.2441	0.1780	0.1250
	1	0.9888	0.9570	0.9077	0.8437	0.7681	0.6836	0.5933	0.5000
	2	0.9998	0.9980	0.9934	0.9844	0.9695	0.9473	0.9163	0.8750
	3	1.0000	1.0000	1.0000	1.0000	1.0000	1.0000	1.0000	1.0000
4	0	0.7725	0.5862	0.4358	0.3164	0.2234	0.1526	0.1001	0.0625
	1	0.9785	0.9211	0.8381	0.7383	0.6296	0.5188	0.4116	0.3125
	2	0.9991	0.9929	0.9773	0.9492	0.9065	0.8484	0.7749	0.6875
	3	1.0000	0.9998	0.9988	0.9961	0.9905	0.9802	0.9634	0.9375
	4	1.0000	1.0000	1.0000	1.0000	1.0000	1.0000	1.0000	1.0000
5	0	0.7242	0.5129	0.3541	0.2373	0.1536	0.0954	0.0563	0.0312
	1	0.9656	0.8793	0.7627	0.6328	0.5027	0.3815	0.2753	0.1875
	2	0.9978	0.9839	0.9512	0.8965	0.8200	0.7248	0.6160	0.5000
	3	0.9999	0.9989	0.9947	0.9844	0.9642	0.9308	0.8809	0.8125
	4	1.0000	1.0000	0.9998	0.9990	0.9970	0.9926	0.9840	0.9687
	5	1.0000	1.0000	1.0000	1.0000	1.0000	1.0000	1.0000	1.0000
6	0	0.6789	0.4488	0.2877	0.1780	0.1056	0.0596	0.0317	0.0156
	1	0.9505	0.8335	0.6861	0.5339	0.3936	0.2742	0.1795	0.1094
	2	0.9958	0.9709	0.9159	0.8306	0.7208	0.5960	0.4669	0.3437
	3	0.9998	0.9970	0.9866	0.9624	0.9192	0.8535	0.7650	0.6562
	4	1.0000	0.9998	0.9988	0.9954	0.9868	0.9694	0.9389	0.8906
	5	1.0000	1.0000	1.0000	0.9998	0.9991	0.9972	0.9930	0.9844
	6	1.0000	1.0000	1.0000	1.0000	1.0000	1.0000	1.0000	1.0000
7	0	0.6365	0.3927	0.2338	0.1335	0.0726	0.0373	0.0178	0.0078
	1	0.9335	0.7854	0.6114	0.4449	0.3036	0.1937	0.1148	0.0625
	2	0.9929	0.9537	0.8728	0.7564	0.6186	0.4753	0.3412	0.2266
	3	0.9995	0.9938	0.9733	0.9294	0.8572	0.7570	0.6346	0.5000
	4	1.0000	0.9995	0.9965	0.9871	0.9656	0.9260	0.8628	0.7734
	5	1.0000	1.0000	0.9997	0.9987	0.9952	0.9868	0.9693	0.9375
	6	1.0000	1.0000	1.0000	0.9999	0.9997	0.9990	0.9969	0.9922
	7	1.0000	1.0000	1.0000	1.0000	1.0000	1.0000	1.0000	1.0000
8	0	0.5967	0.3436	0.1899	0.1001	0.0499	0.0233	0.0100	0.0039
	1	0.9150	0.7363	0.5406	0.3671	0.2314	0.1350	0.0724	0.0352
	2	0.9892	0.9327	0.8238	0.6785	0.5201	0.3697	0.2422	0.1445
	3	0.9991	0.9888	0.9545	0.8862	0.7826	0.6514	0.5062	0.3633
	4	1.0000	0.9988	0.9922	0.9727	0.9318	0.8626	0.7630	0.6367
	5	1.0000	0.9999	0.9991	0.9958	0.9860	0.9640	0.9227	0.8555
	6	1.0000	1.0000	0.9999	0.9996	0.9983	0.9944	0.9849	0.9648
	7	1.0000	1.0000	1.0000	1.0000	0.9999	0.9996	0.9987	0.9961
	8	1.0000	1.0000	1.0000	1.0000	1.0000	1.0000	1.0000	1.0000

The Cumulative Binomial Distribution (cont.)

n	A	1/16	2/16	3/16	p 4/16	5/16	6/16	7/16	8/16
9	0	0.5594	0.3007	0.1543	0.0751	0.0343	0.0146	0.0056	0.0020
	1	0.8951	0.6872	0.4748	0.3003	0.1747	0.0931	0.0451	0.0195
	2	0.9846	0.9081	0.7707	0.6007	0.4299	0.2817	0.1679	0.0898
	3	0.9985	0.9817	0.9300	0.8343	0.7006	0.5458	0.3907	0.2539
	4	0.9999	0.9975	0.9851	0.9511	0.8851	0.7834	0.6506	0.5000
	5	1.0000	0.9998	0.9978	0.9900	0.9690	0.9260	0.8528	0.7461
	6	1.0000	1.0000	0.9998	0.9987	0.9945	0.9830	0.9577	0.9102
	7	1.0000	1.0000	1.0000	0.9999	0.9994	0.9977	0.9926	0.9805
	8	1.0000	1.0000	1.0000	1.0000	1.0000	0.9999	0.9994	0.9980
	9	1.0000	1.0000	1.0000	1.0000	1.0000	1.0000	1.0000	1.0000
10	0	0.5245	0.2631	0.1254	0.0563	0.0236	0.0091	0.0032	0.0010
	1	0.8741	0.6389	0.4147	0.2440	0.1308	0.0637	0.0278	0.0107
	2	0.9790	0.8805	0.7152	0.5256	0.3501	0.2110	0.1142	0.0547
	3	0.9976	0.9725	0.9001	0.7759	0.6160	0.4467	0.2932	0.1719
	4	0.9998	0.9955	0.9748	0.9219	0.8275	0.6943	0.5369	0.3770
	5	1.0000	0.9995	0.9955	0.9803	0.9428	0.8725	0.7644	0.6230
	6	1.0000	1.0000	0.9994	0.9965	0.9865	0.9616	0.9118	0.8281
	7	1.0000	1.0000	1.0000	0.9996	0.9979	0.9922	0.9773	0.9453
	8	1.0000	1.0000	1.0000	1.0000	0.9998	0.9990	0.9964	0.9893
	9	1.0000	1.0000	1.0000	1.0000	1.0000	0.9999	0.9997	0.9990
	10	1.0000	1.0000	1.0000	1.0000	1.0000	1.0000	1.0000	1.0000
11	0	0.4917	0.2302	0.1019	0.0422	0.0162	0.0057	0.0018	0.0005
	1	0.8522	0.5919	0.3605	0.1971	0.0973	0.0432	0.0170	0.0059
	2	0.9724	0.8503	0.6589	0.4552	0.2816	0.1558	0.0764	0.0327
	3	0.9965	0.9610	0.8654	0.7133	0.5329	0.3583	0.2149	0.1133
	4	0.9997	0.9927	0.9608	0.8854	0.7614	0.6014	0.4303	0.2744
	5	1.0000	0.9990	0.9916	0.9657	0.9068	0.8057	0.6649	0.5000
	6	1.0000	0.9999	0.9987	0.9924	0.9729	0.9282	0.8473	0.7256
	7	1.0000	1.0000	0.9999	0.9988	0.9943	0.9807	0.9487	0.8867
	8	1.0000	1.0000	1.0000	0.9999	0.9992	0.9965	0.9881	0.9673
	9	1.0000	1.0000	1.0000	1.0000	0.9999	0.9996	0.9983	0.9941
	10	1.0000	1.0000	1.0000	1.0000	1.0000	1.0000	0.9999	0.9995
	11	1.0000	1.0000	1.0000	1.0000	1.0000	1.0000	1.0000	1.0000
12	0	0.4610	0.2014	0.0828	0.0317	0.0111	0.0036	0.0010	0.0002
	1	0.8297	0.5467	0.3120	0.1584	0.0720	0.0291	0.0104	0.0032
	2	0.9649	0.8180	0.6029	0.3907	0.2240	0.1135	0.0504	0.0193
	3	0.9950	0.9472	0.8267	0.6488	0.4544	0.2824	0.1543	0.0730
	4	0.9995	0.9887	0.9429	0.8424	0.6900	0.5103	0.3361	0.1938
	5	1.0000	0.9982	0.9858	0.9456	0.8613	0.7291	0.5622	0.3872
	6	1.0000	0.9998	0.9973	0.9857	0.9522	0.8822	0.7675	0.6128
	7	1.0000	1.0000	0.9996	0.9972	0.9876	0.9610	0.9043	0.8062
	8	1.0000	1.0000	1.0000	0.9996	0.9977	0.9905	0.9708	0.9270
	9	1.0000	1.0000	1.0000	1.0000	0.9997	0.9984	0.9938	0.9807
	10	1.0000	1.0000	1.0000	1.0000	1.0000	0.9998	0.9992	0.9968
	11	1.0000	1.0000	1.0000	1.0000	1.0000	1.0000	1.0000	0.9998
	12	1.0000	1.0000	1.0000	1.0000	1.0000	1.0000	1.0000	1.0000

The Cumulative Binomial Distribution (*cont.*)

p

n	A	1/16	2/16	3/16	4/16	5/16	6/16	7/16	8/16
13	0	0.4321	0.1762	0.0673	0.0238	0.0077	0.0022	0.0006	0.0001
	1	0.8067	0.5035	0.2690	0.1267	0.0530	0.0195	0.0063	0.0017
	2	0.9565	0.7841	0.5484	0.3326	0.1765	0.0819	0.0329	0.0112
	3	0.9931	0.9310	0.7847	0.5843	0.3824	0.2191	0.1089	0.0461
	4	0.9992	0.9835	0.9211	0.7940	0.6164	0.4248	0.2565	0.1334
	5	0.9999	0.9970	0.9778	0.9198	0.8078	0.6470	0.4633	0.2905
	6	1.0000	0.9996	0.9952	0.9757	0.9238	0.8248	0.6777	0.5000
	7	1.0000	1.0000	0.9992	0.9944	0.9765	0.9315	0.8445	0.7095
	8	1.0000	1.0000	0.9999	0.9990	0.9945	0.9795	0.9417	0.8666
	9	1.0000	1.0000	1.0000	0.9999	0.9991	0.9955	0.9838	0.9539
	10	1.0000	1.0000	1.0000	1.0000	0.9999	0.9993	0.9968	0.9888
	11	1.0000	1.0000	1.0000	1.0000	1.0000	0.9999	0.9996	0.9983
	12	1.0000	1.0000	1.0000	1.0000	1.0000	1.0000	1.0000	0.9999
	13	1.0000	1.0000	1.0000	1.0000	1.0000	1.0000	1.0000	1.0000
14	0	0.4051	0.1542	0.0546	0.0178	0.0053	0.0014	0.0003	0.0001
	1	0.7833	0.4626	0.2312	0.1010	0.0388	0.0130	0.0038	0.0009
	2	0.9471	0.7490	0.4960	0.2811	0.1379	0.0585	0.0213	0.0065
	3	0.9908	0.9127	0.7404	0.5213	0.3181	0.1676	0.0756	0.0287
	4	0.9988	0.9770	0.8955	0.7415	0.5432	0.3477	0.1919	0.0898
	5	0.9999	0.9953	0.9671	0.8883	0.7480	0.5637	0.3728	0.2120
	6	1.0000	0.9993	0.9919	0.9617	0.8876	0.7581	0.5839	0.3953
	7	1.0000	0.9999	0.9985	0.9897	0.9601	0.8915	0.7715	0.6047
	8	1.0000	1.0000	0.9998	0.9978	0.9889	0.9615	0.8992	0.7880
	9	1.0000	1.0000	1.0000	0.9997	0.9976	0.9895	0.9654	0.9102
	10	1.0000	1.0000	1.0000	1.0000	0.9996	0.9979	0.9911	0.9713
	11	1.0000	1.0000	1.0000	1.0000	1.0000	0.9997	0.9984	0.9935
	12	1.0000	1.0000	1.0000	1.0000	1.0000	1.0000	0.9998	0.9991
	13	1.0000	1.0000	1.0000	1.0000	1.0000	1.0000	1.0000	0.9999
	14	1.0000	1.0000	1.0000	1.0000	1.0000	1.0000	1.0000	1.0000
15	0	0.3798	0.1349	0.0444	0.0134	0.0036	0.0009	0.0002	0.0000
	1	0.7596	0.4241	0.1981	0.0802	0.0283	0.0087	0.0023	0.0005
	2	0.9369	0.7132	0.4463	0.2361	0.1069	0.0415	0.0136	0.0037
	3	0.9881	0.8922	0.6946	0.4613	0.2618	0.1267	0.0518	0.0176
	4	0.9983	0.9689	0.8665	0.6865	0.4729	0.2801	0.1410	0.0592
	5	0.9998	0.9930	0.9537	0.8516	0.6840	0.4827	0.2937	0.1509
	6	1.0000	0.9988	0.9873	0.9434	0.8439	0.6852	0.4916	0.3036
	7	1.0000	0.9998	0.9972	0.9827	0.9374	0.8415	0.6894	0.5000
	8	1.0000	1.0000	0.9995	0.9958	0.9799	0.9352	0.8433	0.6964
	9	1.0000	1.0000	0.9999	0.9992	0.9949	0.9790	0.9364	0.8491
	10	1.0000	1.0000	1.0000	0.9999	0.9990	0.9947	0.9799	0.9408
	11	1.0000	1.0000	1.0000	1.0000	0.9999	0.9990	0.9952	0.9824
	12	1.0000	1.0000	1.0000	1.0000	1.0000	0.9999	0.9992	0.9963
	13	1.0000	1.0000	1.0000	1.0000	1.0000	1.0000	0.9999	0.9995
	14	1.0000	1.0000	1.0000	1.0000	1.0000	1.0000	1.0000	1.0000
	15	1.0000	1.0000	1.0000	1.0000	1.0000	1.0000	1.0000	1.0000

The Cumulative Binomial Distribution (cont.)

p

n	A	1/16	2/16	3/16	4/16	5/16	6/16	7/16	8/16
16	0	0.3561	0.1181	0.0361	0.0100	0.0025	0.0005	0.0001	0.0000
	1	0.7359	0.3879	0.1693	0.0635	0.0206	0.0057	0.0014	0.0003
	2	0.9258	0.6771	0.3998	0.1971	0.0824	0.0292	0.0086	0.0021
	3	0.9849	0.8698	0.6480	0.4050	0.2134	0.0947	0.0351	0.0106
	4	0.9977	0.9593	0.8342	0.6302	0.4069	0.2226	0.1020	0.0384
	5	0.9997	0.9900	0.9373	0.8103	0.6180	0.4067	0.2269	0.1051
	6	1.0000	0.9981	0.9810	0.9204	0.7940	0.6093	0.4050	0.2272
	7	1.0000	0.9997	0.9954	0.9729	0.9082	0.7829	0.6029	0.4018
	8	1.0000	1.0000	0.9991	0.9925	0.9666	0.9001	0.7760	0.5982
	9	1.0000	1.0000	0.9999	0.9984	0.9902	0.9626	0.8957	0.7728
	10	1.0000	1.0000	1.0000	0.9997	0.9977	0.9888	0.9609	0.8949
	11	1.0000	1.0000	1.0000	1.0000	0.9996	0.9974	0.9885	0.9616
	12	1.0000	1.0000	1.0000	1.0000	0.9999	0.9995	0.9975	0.9894
	13	1.0000	1.0000	1.0000	1.0000	1.0000	0.9999	0.9996	0.9979
	14	1.0000	1.0000	1.0000	1.0000	1.0000	1.0000	1.0000	0.9997
	15	1.0000	1.0000	1.0000	1.0000	1.0000	1.0000	1.0000	1.0000
	16	1.0000	1.0000	1.0000	1.0000	1.0000	1.0000	1.0000	1.0000
17	0	0.3338	0.1033	0.0293	0.0075	0.0017	0.0003	0.0001	0.0000
	1	0.7121	0.3542	0.1443	0.0501	0.0149	0.0038	0.0008	0.0001
	2	0.9139	0.6409	0.3566	0.1637	0.0631	0.0204	0.0055	0.0012
	3	0.9812	0.8457	0.6015	0.3530	0.1724	0.0701	0.0235	0.0064
	4	0.9969	0.9482	0.7993	0.5739	0.3464	0.1747	0.0727	0.0245
	5	0.9996	0.9862	0.9180	0.7653	0.5520	0.3377	0.1723	0.0717
	6	1.0000	0.9971	0.9728	0.8929	0.7390	0.5333	0.3271	0.1662
	7	1.0000	0.9995	0.9927	0.9598	0.8725	0.7178	0.5163	0.3145
	8	1.0000	0.9999	0.9984	0.9876	0.9484	0.8561	0.7002	0.5000
	9	1.0000	1.0000	0.9997	0.9969	0.9828	0.9391	0.8433	0.6855
	10	1.0000	1.0000	1.0000	0.9994	0.9954	0.9790	0.9323	0.8338
	11	1.0000	1.0000	1.0000	0.9999	0.9990	0.9942	0.9764	0.9283
	12	1.0000	1.0000	1.0000	1.0000	0.9998	0.9987	0.9935	0.9755
	13	1.0000	1.0000	1.0000	1.0000	1.0000	0.9998	0.9987	0.9936
	14	1.0000	1.0000	1.0000	1.0000	1.0000	1.0000	0.9998	0.9988
	15	1.0000	1.0000	1.0000	1.0000	1.0000	1.0000	1.0000	0.9999
	16	1.0000	1.0000	1.0000	1.0000	1.0000	1.0000	1.0000	1.0000
18	0	0.3130	0.0904	0.0238	0.0056	0.0012	0.0002	0.0000	0.0000
	1	0.6885	0.3228	0.1227	0.0395	0.0108	0.0025	0.0005	0.0001
	2	0.9013	0.6051	0.3168	0.1353	0.0480	0.0142	0.0034	0.0007
	3	0.9770	0.8201	0.5556	0.3057	0.1383	0.0515	0.0156	0.0038
	4	0.9959	0.9354	0.7622	0.5187	0.2920	0.1355	0.0512	0.0154
	5	0.9994	0.9814	0.8958	0.7175	0.4878	0.2765	0.1287	0.0481
	6	0.9999	0.9957	0.9625	0.8610	0.6806	0.4600	0.2593	0.1189
	7	1.0000	0.9992	0.9889	0.9431	0.8308	0.6486	0.4335	0.2403
	8	1.0000	0.9999	0.9973	0.9807	0.9247	0.8042	0.6198	0.4073
	9	1.0000	1.0000	0.9995	0.9946	0.9721	0.9080	0.7807	0.5927

The Cumulative Binomial Distribution (*cont.*)

n	A	1/16	2/16	3/16	4/16	5/16	6/16	7/16	8/16
						p			
18	10	1.0000	1.0000	0.9999	0.9988	0.9915	0.9640	0.8934	0.7597
	11	1.0000	1.0000	1.0000	0.9998	0.9979	0.9885	0.9571	0.8811
	12	1.0000	1.0000	1.0000	1.0000	0.9996	0.9970	0.9860	0.9519
	13	1.0000	1.0000	1.0000	1.0000	0.9999	0.9994	0.9964	0.9846
	14	1.0000	1.0000	1.0000	1.0000	1.0000	0.9999	0.9993	0.9962
	15	1.0000	1.0000	1.0000	1.0000	1.0000	1.0000	0.9999	0.9993
	16	1.0000	1.0000	1.0000	1.0000	1.0000	1.0000	1.0000	0.9999
	17	1.0000	1.0000	1.0000	1.0000	1.0000	1.0000	1.0000	1.0000
19	0	0.2934	0.0791	0.0193	0.0042	0.0008	0.0001	0.0000	0.0000
	1	0.6650	0.2938	0.1042	0.0310	0.0078	0.0016	0.0003	0.0000
	2	0.8880	0.5698	0.2804	0.1113	0.0364	0.0098	0.0021	0.0004
	3	0.9722	0.7933	0.5108	0.2631	0.1101	0.0375	0.0103	0.0022
	4	0.9947	0.9209	0.7235	0.4654	0.2440	0.1040	0.0356	0.0096
	5	0.9992	0.9757	0.8707	0.6678	0.4266	0.2236	0.0948	0.0318
	6	0.9999	0.9939	0.9500	0.8251	0.6203	0.3912	0.2022	0.0835
	7	1.0000	0.9988	0.9840	0.9225	0.7838	0.5779	0.3573	0.1796
	8	1.0000	0.9998	0.9957	0.9713	0.8953	0.7459	0.5383	0.3238
	9	1.0000	1.0000	0.9991	0.9911	0.9573	0.8691	0.7103	0.5000
	10	1.0000	1.0000	0.9998	0.9977	0.9854	0.9430	0.8441	0.6762
	11	1.0000	1.0000	1.0000	0.9995	0.9959	0.9793	0.9292	0.8204
	12	1.0000	1.0000	1.0000	0.9999	0.9990	0.9938	0.9734	0.9165
	13	1.0000	1.0000	1.0000	1.0000	0.9998	0.9985	0.9919	0.9682
	14	1.0000	1.0000	1.0000	1.0000	1.0000	0.9997	0.9980	0.9904
	15	1.0000	1.0000	1.0000	1.0000	1.0000	1.0000	0.9996	0.9978
	16	1.0000	1.0000	1.0000	1.0000	1.0000	1.0000	1.0000	0.9996
	17	1.0000	1.0000	1.0000	1.0000	1.0000	1.0000	1.0000	1.0000
	18	1.0000	1.0000	1.0000	1.0000	1.0000	1.0000	1.0000	1.0000
20	0	0.2751	0.0692	0.0157	0.0032	0.0006	0.0001	0.0000	0.0000
	1	0.6418	0.2669	0.0883	0.0243	0.0056	0.0011	0.0002	0.0000
	2	0.8741	0.5353	0.2473	0.0913	0.0275	0.0067	0.0013	0.0002
	3	0.9670	0.7653	0.4676	0.2252	0.0870	0.0271	0.0067	0.0013
	4	0.9933	0.9050	0.6836	0.4148	0.2021	0.0790	0.0245	0.0059
	5	0.9989	0.9688	0.8431	0.6172	0.3695	0.1788	0.0689	0.0207
	6	0.9999	0.9916	0.9351	0.7858	0.5598	0.3284	0.1552	0.0577
	7	1.0000	0.9981	0.9776	0.8982	0.7327	0.5079	0.2894	0.1316
	8	1.0000	0.9997	0.9935	0.9591	0.8605	0.6829	0.4591	0.2517
	9	1.0000	0.9999	0.9984	0.9861	0.9379	0.8229	0.6350	0.4119
	10	1.0000	1.0000	0.9997	0.9961	0.9766	0.9153	0.7856	0.5881
	11	1.0000	1.0000	0.9999	0.9991	0.9926	0.9657	0.8920	0.7483
	12	1.0000	1.0000	1.0000	0.9998	0.9981	0.9884	0.9541	0.8684
	13	1.0000	1.0000	1.0000	1.0000	0.9996	0.9968	0.9838	0.9423
	14	1.0000	1.0000	1.0000	1.0000	0.9999	0.9993	0.9953	0.9793
	15	1.0000	1.0000	1.0000	1.0000	1.0000	0.9999	0.9989	0.9941
	16	1.0000	1.0000	1.0000	1.0000	1.0000	1.0000	0.9998	0.9987
	17	1.0000	1.0000	1.0000	1.0000	1.0000	1.0000	1.0000	0.9998
	18	1.0000	1.0000	1.0000	1.0000	1.0000	1.0000	1.0000	1.0000
	19	1.0000	1.0000	1.0000	1.0000	1.0000	1.0000	1.0000	1.0000

The Cumulative Binomial Distribution (cont.)

n	A	1/16	2/16	3/16	4/16	p 5/16	6/16	7/16	8/16
21	0	0.2579	0.0606	0.0128	0.0024	0.0004	0.0001	0.0000	0.0000
	1	0.6189	0.2422	0.0747	0.0190	0.0040	0.0007	0.0001	0.0000
	2	0.8596	0.5018	0.2175	0.0745	0.0206	0.0046	0.0008	0.0001
	3	0.9612	0.7366	0.4263	0.1917	0.0684	0.0195	0.0044	0.0007
	4	0.9917	0.8875	0.6431	0.3674	0.1662	0.0596	0.0167	0.0036
	5	0.9986	0.9609	0.8132	0.5666	0.3172	0.1414	0.0495	0.0133
	6	0.9998	0.9888	0.9179	0.7436	0.5003	0.2723	0.1175	0.0392
	7	1.0000	0.9973	0.9696	0.8701	0.6787	0.4405	0.2307	0.0946
	8	1.0000	0.9995	0.9906	0.9439	0.8206	0.6172	0.3849	0.1917
	9	1.0000	0.9999	0.9975	0.9794	0.9137	0.7704	0.5581	0.3318
	10	1.0000	1.0000	0.9995	0.9936	0.9645	0.8806	0.7197	0.5000
	11	1.0000	1.0000	0.9999	0.9983	0.9876	0.9468	0.8454	0.6682
	12	1.0000	1.0000	1.0000	0.9996	0.9964	0.9799(	0.9269	0.8083
	13	1.0000	1.0000	1.0000	0.9999	0.9991	0.9936	0.9708	0.9054
	14	1.0000	1.0000	1.0000	1.0000	0.9998	0.9983	0.9903	0.9608
	15	1.0000	1.0000	1.0000	1.0000	1.0000	0.9996	0.9974	0.9867
	16	1.0000	1.0000	1.0000	1.0000	1.0000	0.9999	0.9994	0.9964
	17	1.0000	1.0000	1.0000	1.0000	1.0000	1.0000	0.9999	0.9993
	18	1.0000	1.0000	1.0000	1.0000	1.0000	1.0000	1.0000	0.9999
	19	1.0000	1.0000	1.0000	1.0000	1.0000	1.0000	1.0000	1.0000
	20	1.0000	1.0000	1.0000	1.0000	1.0000	1.0000	1.0000	1.0000
22	0	0.2418	0.0530	0.0104	0.0018	0.0003	0.0000	0.0000	0.0000
	1	0.5963	0.2195	0.0631	0.0149	0.0029	0.0005	0.0001	0.0000
	2	0.8445	0.4693	0.1907	0.0606	0.0154	0.0031	0.0005	0.0001
	3	0.9548	0.7072	0.3871	0.1624	0.0535	0.0139	0.0028	0.0004
	4	0.9898	0.8687	0.6024	0.3235	0.1356	0.0445	0.0113	0.0022
	5	0.9981	0.9517	0.7813	0.5168	0.2700	0.1107	0.0352	0.0085
	6	0.9997	0.9853	0.8983	0.6994	0.4431	0.2232	0.0877	0.0262
	7	1.0000	0.9963	0.9599	0.8385	0.6230	0.3774	0.1812	0.0669
	8	1.0000	0.9992	0.9866	0.9254	0.7762	0.5510	0.3174	0.1431
	9	1.0000	0.9999	0.9962	0.9705	0.8846	0.7130	0.4823	0.2617
	10	1.0000	1.0000	0.9991	0.9900	0.9486	0.8393	0.6490	0.4159
	11	1.0000	1.0000	0.9998	0.9971	0.9804	0.9220	0.7904	0.5841
	12	1.0000	1.0000	1.0000	0.9993	0.9936	0.9675	0.8913	0.7383
	13	1.0000	1.0000	1.0000	0.9999	0.9982	0.9885	0.9516	0.8569
	14	1.0000	1.0000	1.0000	1.0000	0.9996	0.9966	0.9818	0.9331
	15	1.0000	1.0000	1.0000	1.0000	0.9999	0.9991	0.9943	0.9738
	16	1.0000	1.0000	1.0000	1.0000	1.0000	0.9998	0.9985	0.9915
	17	1.0000	1.0000	1.0000	1.0000	1.0000	1.0000	0.9997	0.9978
	18	1.0000	1.0000	1.0000	1.0000	1.0000	1.0000	1.0000	0.9996
	19	1.0000	1.0000	1.0000	1.0000	1.0000	1.0000	1.0000	0.9999
	20	1.0000	1.0000	1.0000	1.0000	1.0000	1.0000	1.0000	1.0000
23	0	0.2266	0.0464	0.0084	0.0013	0.0002	0.0000	0.0000	0.0000
	1	0.5742	0.1987	0.0532	0.0116	0.0021	0.0003	0.0000	0.0000
	2	0.8290	0.4381	0.1668	0.0492	0.0115	0.0021	0.0003	0.0000
	3	0.9479	0.6775	0.3503	0.1370	0.0416	0.0099	0.0018	0.0002
	4	0.9876	0.8485	0.5621	0.2832	0.1100	0.0330	0.0076	0.0013

The Cumulative Binomial Distribution (cont.)

n	A	1/16	2/16	3/16	4/16	5/16	6/16	7/16	8/16
					p				
23	5	0.9976	0.9413	0.7478	0.4685	0.2280	0.0859	0.0247	0.0053
	6	0.9996	0.9811	0.8763	0.6537	0.3890	0.1810	0.0647	0.0173
	7	1.0000	0.9949	0.9484	0.8037	0.5668	0.3196	0.1403	0.0466
	8	1.0000	0.9988	0.9816	0.9037	0.7283	0.4859	0.2578	0.1050
	9	1.0000	0.9998	0.9944	0.9592	0.8507	0.6522	0.4102	0.2024
	10	1.0000	1.0000	0.9986	0.9851	0.9286	0.7919	0.5761	0.3388
	11	1.0000	1.0000	0.9997	0.9954	0.9705	0.8910	0.7285	0.5000
	12	1.0000	1.0000	0.9999	0.9988	0.9895	0.9504	0.8471	0.6612
	13	1.0000	1.0000	1.0000	0.9997	0.9968	0.9806	0.9252	0.7976
	14	1.0000	1.0000	1.0000	0.9999	0.9992	0.9935	0.9686	0.8950
	15	1.0000	1.0000	1.0000	1.0000	0.9998	0.9982	0.9888	0.9534
	16	1.0000	1.0000	1.0000	1.0000	1.0000	0.9996	0.9967	0.9827
	17	1.0000	1.0000	1.0000	1.0000	1.0000	0.9999	0.9992	0.9947
	18	1.0000	1.0000	1.0000	1.0000	1.0000	1.0000	0.9998	0.9987
	19	1.0000	1.0000	1.0000	1.0000	1.0000	1.0000	1.0000	0.9998
	20	1.0000	1.0000	1.0000	1.0000	1.0000	1.0000	1.0000	1.0000
	21	1.0000	1.0000	1.0000	1.0000	1.0000	1.0000	1.0000	1.0000
24	0	0.2125	0.0406	0.0069	0.0010	0.0001	0.0000	0.0000	0.0000
	1	0.5524	0.1797	0.0448	0.0090	0.0015	0.0002	0.0000	0.0000
	2	0.8131	0.4082	0.1455	0.0398	0.0086	0.0014	0.0002	0.0000
	3	0.9405	0.6476	0.3159	0.1150	0.0322	0.0070	0.0011	0.0001
	4	0.9851	0.8271	0.5224	0.2466	0.0886	0.0243	0.0051	0.0008
	5	0.9970	0.9297	0.7130	0.4222	0.1911	0.0661	0.0172	0.0033
	6	0.9995	0.9761	0.8522	0.6074	0.3387	0.1453	0.0472	0.0113
	7	0.9999	0.9932	0.9349	0.7662	0.5112	0.2676	0.1072	0.0320
	8	1.0000	0.9983	0.9754	0.8787	0.6778	0.4235	0.2064	0.0758
	9	1.0000	0.9997	0.9920	0.9453	0.8125	0.5898	0.3435	0.1537
	10	1.0000	0.9999	0.9978	0.9787	0.9043	0.7395	0.5035	0.2706
	11	1.0000	1.0000	0.9995	0.9928	0.9574	0.8538	0.6618	0.4194
	12	1.0000	1.0000	0.9999	0.9979	0.9835	0.9281	0.7953	0.5806
	13	1.0000	1.0000	1.0000	0.9995	0.9945	0.9693	0.8911	0.7294
	14	1.0000	1.0000	1.0000	0.9999	0.9984	0.9887	0.9496	0.8463
	15	1.0000	1.0000	1.0000	1.0000	0.9996	0.9964	0.9799	0.9242
	16	1.0000	1.0000	1.0000	1.0000	0.9999	0.9990	0.9932	0.9680
	17	1.0000	1.0000	1.0000	1.0000	1.0000	0.9998	0.9981	0.9887
	18	1.0000	1.0000	1.0000	1.0000	1.0000	1.0000	0.9996	0.9967
	19	1.0000	1.0000	1.0000	1.0000	1.0000	1.0000	0.9999	0.9992
	20	1.0000	1.0000	1.0000	1.0000	1.0000	1.0000	1.0000	0.9999
	21	1.0000	1.0000	1.0000	1.0000	1.0000	1.0000	1.0000	1.0000
	22	1.0000	1.0000	1.0000	1.0000	1.0000	1.0000	1.0000	1.0000
25	0	0.1992	0.0355	0.0056	0.0008	0.0001	0.0000	0.0000	0.0000
	1	0.5312	0.1623	0.0377	0.0070	0.0011	0.0001	0.0000	0.0000
	2	0.7968	0.3796	0.1266	0.0321	0.0064	0.0010	0.0001	0.0000
	3	0.9325	0.6176	0.2840	0.0962	0.0248	0.0049	0.0007	0.0001
	4	0.9823	0.8047	0.4837	0.2137	0.0710	0.0178	0.0033	0.0005

The Cumulative Binomial Distribution (cont.)

p

n	A	1/16	2/16	3/16	4/16	5/16	6/16	7/16	8/16
25	5	0.9962	0.9169	0.6772	0.3783	0.1591	0.0504	0.0119	0.0020
	6	0.9993	0.9703	0.8261	0.5611	0.2926	0.1156	0.0341	0.0073
	7	0.9999	0.9910	0.9194	0.7265	0.4573	0.2218	0.0810	0.0216
	8	1.0000	0.9977	0.9678	0.8506	0.6258	0.3651	0.1630	0.0539
	9	1.0000	0.9995	0.9889	0.9287	0.7704	0.5275	0.2835	0.1148
	10	1.0000	0.9999	0.9967	0.9703	0.8756	0.6834	0.4335	0.2122
	11	1.0000	1.0000	0.9992	0.9893	0.9408	0.8110	0.5926	0.3450
	12	1.0000	1.0000	0.9998	0.9966	0.9754	0.9003	0.7369	0.5000
	13	1.0000	1.0000	1.0000	0.9991	0.9911	0.9538	0.8491	0.6550
	14	1.0000	1.0000	1.0000	0.9998	0.9972	0.9814	0.9240	0.7878
	15	1.0000	1.0000	1.0000	1.0000	0.9992	0.9935	0.9667	0.8852
	16	1.0000	1.0000	1.0000	1.0000	0.9998	0.9981	0.9874	0.9461
	17	1.0000	1.0000	1.0000	1.0000	1.0000	0.9995	0.9960	0.9784
	18	1.0000	1.0000	1.0000	1.0000	1.0000	0.9999	0.9989	0.9927
	19	1.0000	1.0000	1.0000	1.0000	1.0000	1.0000	0.9998	0.9980
	20	1.0000	1.0000	1.0000	1.0000	1.0000	1.0000	1.0000	0.9995
	21	1.0000	1.0000	1.0000	1.0000	1.0000	1.0000	1.0000	0.9999
	22	1.0000	1.0000	1.0000	1.0000	1.0000	1.0000	1.0000	1.0000

9.6 Confidence Limits on a Proportion

The quantity tabulated is that value of p such that (upper limit)

$$\sum_{j=0}^{X} \frac{n!}{j!(n-j)!} p^j (1-p)^{n-j} = 1 - \gamma$$

when $\gamma > \frac{1}{2}$. Or it is that value of p such that (lower limit)

$$\sum_{j=X}^{n} \frac{n!}{j!(n-j)!} p^j (1-p)^{n-j} = \gamma$$

when $\gamma < \frac{1}{2}$. If $X = 0$, the lower limit is taken to be zero, and if $X = n$, the upper limit is taken to be one. This is the Clopper-Pearson [33] system of confidence limits on the binomial parameter p. Another system has been tabulated by Crow [35] which gives a shorter two-sided confidence interval than the Clopper-Pearson system.

The tables were computed by using the well-known relationship between the F-distribution and the binomial distribution. For the lower confidence limit this is

$$p_L(n, X) = \frac{X}{X + (n - X + 1)F_{\gamma, 2n-2X+2, 2X}},$$

and for the upper limit it is

$$p_U(n, X) = 1 - p_L(n, n - X),$$

where F_{γ, n_1, n_2} is the γth critical value of the F-distribution (Section 4.1) with n_1 degrees of freedom for the numerator and n_2 degrees of freedom for the denominator. A great many independent tabulations of these functions have been made. To mention a few, Clopper and Pearson [33] made a graph of the limits. Thompson [222] made tabulations which were extended by Clark [32] and Pachares [166]. Leone et al. [117] also prepared an eight-decimal-place table of p up through $n = 100$. Grubbs [79] gives some values of p that apply specifically to sampling plans. Mainland [128] and Mainland et al. [129] have at least two such tables. Hald [85] also tables p.

Confidence Limits on a Proportion

n	γ	1-α	0	1	2	3	4	γ
	.005	.990	.0000	.0025	.0414	.1109	.1851	.005
	.995		.9950	.9975	.9983	.9987	.9990	.995
	.010	.980	.0000	.0050	.0589	.1409	.2221	.010
	.990		.9900	.9950	.9967	.9975	.9980	.990
	.025	.950	.0000	.0126	.0943	.1941	.2836	.025
1	.975		.9750	.9874	.9916	.9937	.9949	.975
	.050	.900	.0000	.0253	.1353	.2486	.3426	.050
	.950		.9500	.9747	.9830	.9873	.9898	.950
	.100	.800	.0000	.0513	.1958	.3205	.4161	.100
	.900		.9000	.9487	.9655	.9740	.9791	.900
	.250	.500	.0000	.1340	.3263	.4563	.5458	.250
	.750		.7500	.8660	.9086	.9306	.9441	.750
	.005	.990	.0000	.0017	.0294	.0828	.1436	.005
	.995		.9293	.9586	.9706	.9771	.9813	.995
	.010	.980	.0000	.0033	.0420	.1056	.1731	.010
	.990		.9000	.9411	.9580	.9673	.9732	.990
	.025	.950	.0000	.0084	.0676	.1466	.2228	.025
2	.975		.8419	.9057	.9324	.9473	.9567	.975
	.050	.900	.0000	.0170	.0976	.1893	.2713	.050
	.950		.7764	.8647	.9024	.9236	.9372	.950
	.100	.800	.0000	.0345	.1426	.2466	.3332	.100
	.900		.6838	.8042	.8574	.8878	.9074	.900
	.250	.500	.0000	.0914	.2430	.3594	.4468	.250
	.750		.5000	.6737	.7570	.8062	.8388	.750
	.005	.990	.0000	.0013	.0229	.0663	.1177	.005
	.995		.8290	.8891	.9172	.9337	.9447	.995
	.010	.980	.0000	.0025	.0327	.0847	.1423	.010
	.990		.7846	.8591	.8944	.9153	.9292	.990
	.025	.950	.0000	.0063	.0527	.1181	.1841	.025
3	.975		.7076	.8059	.8534	.8819	.9010	.975
	.050	.900	.0000	.0127	.0764	.1532	.2253	.050
	.950		.6316	.7514	.8107	.8468	.8712	.950
	.100	.800	.0000	.0260	.1122	.2009	.2786	.100
	.900		.5358	.6795	.7534	.7991	.8304	.900
	.250	.500	.0000	.0694	.1938	.2969	.3788	.250
	.750		.3700	.5437	.6406	.7031	.7469	.750

Confidence Limits on a Proportion (*cont.*)

n − x	γ	1−α	x = 5	6	7	8	9	γ	n − x
	.005	.990	.2540	.3151	.3685	.4150	.4557	.005	
	.995		.9992	.9993	.9994	.9994	.9995	.995	
	.010	.980	.2943	.3566	.4101	.4560	.4956	.010	
	.990		.9983	.9986	.9987	.9989	.9990	.990	
	.025	.950	.3588	.4213	.4735	.5175	.5550	.025	
1	.975		.9958	.9964	.9968	.9972	.9975	.975	1
	.050	.900	.4182	.4793	.5293	.5709	.6058	.050	
	.950		.9915	.9927	.9936	.9943	.9949	.950	
	.100	.800	.4897	.5474	.5938	.6316	.6632	.100	
	.900		.9826	.9851	.9869	.9884	.9895	.900	
	.250	.500	.6105	.6593	.6973	.7277	.7526	.250	
	.750		.9532	.9597	.9647	.9685	.9716	.750	
	.005	.990	.2030	.2578	.3074	.3518	.3915	.005	
	.995		.9842	.9863	.9879	.9891	.9902	.995	
	.010	.980	.2363	.2932	.3437	.3883	.4277	.010	
	.990		.9773	.9803	.9826	.9845	.9859	.990	
	.025	.950	.2904	.3491	.3999	.4439	.4822	.025	
2	.975		.9633	.9681	.9719	.9748	.9772	.975	2
	.050	.900	.3413	.4003	.4504	.4931	.5299	.050	
	.950		.9466	.9536	.9590	.9632	.9667	.950	
	.100	.800	.4038	.4618	.5099	.5504	.5848	.100	
	.900		.9212	.9314	.9392	.9455	.9505	.900	
	.250	.500	.5139	.5668	.6095	.6446	.6739	.250	
	.750		.8620	.8794	.8928	.9036	.9124	.750	
	.005	.990	.1697	.2191	.2649	.3067	.3448	.005	
	.995		.9525	.9584	.9630	.9667	.9697	.995	
	.010	.980	.1982	.2500	.2971	.3396	.3778	.010	
	.990		.9392	.9466	.9525	.9572	.9610	.990	
	.025	.950	.2449	.2993	.3475	.3903	.4281	.025	
3	.975		.9148	.9251	.9333	.9398	.9451	.975	3
	.050	.900	.2892	.3449	.3934	.4356	.4727	.050	
	.950		.8889	.9022	.9127	.9212	.9281	.950	
	.100	.800	.3446	.4006	.4483	.4892	.5247	.100	
	.900		.8531	.8705	.8842	.8952	.9043	.900	
	.250	.500	.4445	.4980	.5423	.5795	.6112	.250	
	.750		.7794	.8045	.8244	.8407	.8541	.750	

Confidence Limits on a Proportion (cont.)

x

γ	1-α	0	1	2	3	4	γ
.005	.990	.0000	.0010	.0187	.0553	.0999	.005
.995		.7341	.8149	.8564	.8823	.9001	.995
.010	.980	.0000	.0020	.0268	.0708	.1210	.010
.990		.6838	.7779	.8269	.8577	.8791	.990
.025	.950	.0000	.0051	.0433	.0990	.1570	.025
.975		.6024	.7164	.7772	.8159	.8430	.975
.050	.900	.0000	.0102	.0629	.1288	.1929	.050
.950		.5271	.6574	.7287	.7747	.8071	.950
.100	.800	.0000	.0209	.0926	.1696	.2397	.100
.900		.4377	.5839	.6668	.7214	.7603	.900
.250	.500	.0000	.0559	.1612	.2531	.3291	.250
.750		.2929	.4542	.5532	.6212	.6709	.750
.005	.990	.0000	.0008	.0158	.0475	.0868	.005
.995		.6534	.7460	.7970	.8303	.8539	.995
.010	.980	.0000	.0017	.0227	.0608	.1053	.010
.990		.6019	.7057	.7637	.8018	.8290	.990
.025	.950	.0000	.0042	.0367	.0852	.1370	.025
.975		.5218	.6412	.7096	.7551	.7880	.975
.050	.900	.0000	.0085	.0534	.1111	.1687	.050
.950		.4507	.5818	.6587	.7108	.7486	.950
.100	.800	.0000	.0174	.0788	.1469	.2104	.100
.900		.3690	.5103	.5962	.6554	.6990	.900
.250	.500	.0000	.0468	.1380	.2206	.2910	.250
.750		.2421	.3895	.4861	.5555	.6080	.750
.005	.990	.0000	.0007	.0137	.0416	.0768	.005
.995		.5865	.6849	.7422	.7809	.8091	.995
.010	.980	.0000	.0014	.0197	.0534	.0932	.010
.990		.5358	.6434	.7068	.7500	.7817	.990
.025	.950	.0000	.0036	.0319	.0749	.1216	.025
.975		.4593	.5787	.6509	.7007	.7376	.975
.050	.900	.0000	.0073	.0464	.0978	.1500	.050
.950		.3930	.5207	.5997	.6551	.6965	.950
.100	.800	.0000	.0149	.0686	.1295	.1876	.100
.900		.3187	.4526	.5382	.5994	.6458	.900
.250	.500	.0000	.0403	.1206	.1955	.2609	.250
.750		.2063	.3407	.4332	.5020	.5555	.750

n = 4 (first block), n = 5 (second block), n = 6 (third block)

Confidence Limits on a Proportion (cont.)

x

Υ	1-α	5	6	7	8	9	Υ	
.005	.990	.1461	.1909	.2332	.2725	.3087	.005	
.995		.9132	.9232	.9312	.9376	.9429	.995	
.010	.980	.1710	.2183	.2622	.3024	.3391	.010	
.990		.8947	.9068	.9163	.9241	.9305	.990	
.025	.950	.2120	.2624	.3079	.3489	.3857	.025	
.975		.8630	.8784	.8907	.9007	.9091	.975	4
.050	.900	.2514	.3035	.3498	.3909	.4274	.050	
.950		.8313	.8500	.8649	.8771	.8873	.950	
.100	.800	.3010	.3542	.4005	.4410	.4766	.100	
.900		.7896	.8124	.8308	.8458	.8584	.900	
.250	.500	.3920	.4445	.4889	.5269	.5597	.250	
.750		.7090	.7391	.7636	.7838	.8009	.750	
.005	.990	.1283	.1693	.2085	.2454	.2799	.005	
.995		.8717	.8855	.8966	.9058	.9134	.995	
.010	.980	.1504	.1940	.2349	.2729	.3080	.010	
.990		.8496	.8656	.8785	.8892	.8981	.990	
.025	.950	.1871	.2338	.2767	.3158	.3514	.025	
.975		.8129	.8325	.8483	.8614	.8724	.975	5
.050	.900	.2224	.2713	.3152	.3548	.3904	.050	
.950		.7776	.8004	.8190	.8343	.8473	.950	
.100	.800	.2673	.3177	.3623	.4018	.4369	.100	
.900		.7327	.7595	.7813	.7995	.8149	.900	
.250	.500	.3507	.4016	.4453	.4833	.5165	.250	
.750		.6493	.6826	.7101	.7332	.7529	.750	
.005	.990	.1145	.1522	.1887	.2235	.2562	.005	
.995		.8307	.8478	.8617	.8733	.8830	.995	
.010	.980	.1344	.1746	.2129	.2488	.2823	.010	
.990		.8060	.8254	.8412	.8543	.8654	.990	
.025	.950	.1675	.2110	.2514	.2886	.3229	.025	
.975		.7662	.7890	.8077	.8234	.8366	.975	6
.050	.900	.1996	.2453	.2871	.3251	.3596	.050	
.950		.7287	.7547	.7760	.7939	.8091	.950	
.100	.800	.2406	.2882	.3309	.3692	.4036	.100	
.900		.6823	.7118	.7363	.7568	.7744	.900	
.250	.500	.3174	.3663	.4090	.4465	.4796	.250	
.750		.5984	.6337	.6632	.6882	.7098	.750	

9.6

Confidence Limits on a Proportion (*cont.*)

	γ	1-α	0	1	2	3	4	γ	
	.005	.990	.0000	.0006	.0121	.0370	.0688	.005	
	.995		.5309	.6315	.6926	.7351	.7668	.995	
	.010	.980	.0000	.0013	.0174	.0475	.0837	.010	
	.990		.4821	.5899	.6563	.7029	.7378	.990	
	.025	.950	.0000	.0032	.0281	.0667	.1093	.025	
7	.975		.4096	.5265	.6001	.6525	.6921	.975	7
	.050	.900	.0000	.0064	.0410	.0873	.1351	.050	
	.950		.3482	.4707	.5496	.6066	.6502	.950	
	.100	.800	.0000	.0131	.0608	.1158	.1692	.100	
	.900		.2803	.4062	.4901	.5517	.5995	.900	
	.250	.500	.0000	.0353	.1072	.1756	.2364	.250	
	.750		.1797	.3027	.3905	.4577	.5111	.750	
	.005	.990	.0000	.0006	.0109	.0333	.0624	.005	
	.995		.4843	.5850	.6482	.6933	.7275	.995	
	.010	.980	.0000	.0011	.0155	.0428	.0759	.010	
	.990		.4377	.5440	.6117	.6604	.6976	.990	
	.025	.950	.0000	.0028	.0252	.0602	.0993	.025	
8	.975		.3694	.4825	.5561	.6097	.6511	.975	8
	.050	.900	.0000	.0057	.0368	.0788	.1229	.050	
	.950		.3123	.4291	.5069	.5644	.6091	.950	
	.100	.800	.0000	.0116	.0545	.1048	.1542	.100	
	.900		.2501	.3684	.4496	.5108	.5590	.900	
	.250	.500	.0000	.0315	.0964	.1593	.2162	.250	
	.750		.1591	.2723	.3554	.4205	.4731	.750	
	.005	.990	.0000	.0005	.0098	.0303	.0571	.005	
	.995		.4450	.5443	.6085	.6552	.6913	.995	
	.010	.980	.0000	.0010	.0141	.0390	.0695	.010	
	.990		.4005	.5044	.5723	.6222	.6609	.990	
	.025	.950	.0000	.0025	.0228	.0549	.0909	.025	
9	.975		.3363	.4450	.5178	.5719	.6143	.975	9
	.050	.900	.0000	.0051	.0333	.0719	.1127	.050	
	.950		.2831	.3942	.4701	.5273	.5726	.950	
	.100	.800	.0000	.0105	.0495	.0957	.1416	.100	
	.900		.2257	.3369	.4152	.4753	.5234	.900	
	.250	.500	.0000	.0284	.0876	.1459	.1991	.250	
	.750		.1428	.2474	.3261	.3888	.4403	.750	

9.6

Confidence Limits on a Proportion (cont.)

x

n	γ	1-α	5	6	7	8	9	γ	n
	.005	.990	.1034	.1383	.1724	.2052	.2363	.005	
	.995		.7915	.8113	.8276	.8412	.8529	.995	
	.010	.980	.1215	.1588	.1947	.2288	.2607	.010	
	.990		.7651	.7871	.8053	.8205	.8335	.990	
	.025	.950	.1517	.1923	.2304	.2659	.2988	.025	
7	.975		.7233	.7486	.7696	.7873	.8025	.975	7
	.050	.900	.1810	.2240	.2636	.3000	.3334	.050	
	.950		.6848	.7129	.7364	.7562	.7733	.950	
	.100	.800	.2187	.2638	.3046	.3416	.3751	.100	
	.900		.6377	.6691	.6954	.7178	.7371	.900	
	.250	.500	.2899	.3368	.3783	.4150	.4478	.250	
	.750		.5547	.5910	.6217	.6481	.6711	.750	
	.005	.990	.0942	.1267	.1588	.1897	.2193	.005	
	.995		.7546	.7765	.7948	.8103	.8236	.995	
	.010	.980	.1108	.1457	.1795	.2118	.2423	.010	
	.990		.7271	.7512	.7712	.7882	.8029	.990	
	.025	.950	.1386	.1766	.2127	.2466	.2782	.025	
8	.975		.6842	.7114	.7341	.7534	.7702	.975	8
	.050	.900	.1657	.2061	.2438	.2786	.3109	.050	
	.950		.6452	.6749	.7000	.7214	.7399	.950	
	.100	.800	.2005	.2432	.2822	.3179	.3505	.100	
	.900		.5982	.6308	.6584	.6821	.7027	.900	
	.250	.500	.2668	.3118	.3519	.3877	.4200	.250	
	.750		.5167	.5535	.5850	.6123	.6362	.750	
	.005	.990	.0866	.1170	.1471	.1764	.2047	.005	
	.995		.7201	.7438	.7637	.7807	.7953	.995	
	.010	.980	.1019	.1346	.1665	.1971	.2263	.010	
	.990		.6920	.7177	.7393	.7577	.7737	.990	
	.025	.950	.1276	.1634	.1975	.2298	.2602	.025	
9	.975		.6486	.6771	.7012	.7218	.7398	.975	9
	.050	.900	.1527	.1909	.2267	.2601	.2912	.050	
	.950		.6096	.6404	.6666	.6891	.7088	.950	
	.100	.800	.1851	.2256	.2629	.2973	.3289	.100	
	.900		.5631	.5964	.6249	.6495	.6711	.900	
	.250	.500	.2471	.2902	.3289	.3638	.3954	.250	
	.750		.4835	.5204	.5522	.5800	.6046	.750	

x = n − x

9.6

Confidence Limits on a Proportion (cont.)

γ	1-α	0	1	2	3	4	γ	
	.005	.990	.0000	.0005	.0090	.0278	.0526	.005
	.995		.4113	.5086	.5729	.6206	.6579	.995
	.010	.980	.0000	.0009	.0128	.0358	.0640	.010
	.990		.3690	.4698	.5373	.5878	.6274	.990
	.025	.950	.0000	.0023	.0209	.0504	.0839	.025
10	.975		.3085	.4128	.4841	.5381	.5810	.975	10
	.050	.900	.0000	.0047	.0305	.0661	.1041	.050
	.950		.2589	.3644	.4381	.4947	.5400	.950
	.100	.800	.0000	.0095	.0452	.0880	.1309	.100
	.900		.2057	.3102	.3855	.4443	.4920	.900
	.250	.500	.0000	.0258	.0803	.1345	.1846	.250
	.750		.1294	.2266	.3012	.3615	.4117	.750
	.005	.990	.0000	.0004	.0083	.0257	.0488	.005
	.995		.3822	.4770	.5410	.5892	.6273	.995
	.010	.980	.0000	.0008	.0118	.0331	.0594	.010
	.990		.3421	.4395	.5062	.5567	.5969	.990
	.025	.950	.0000	.0021	.0192	.0466	.0779	.025
11	.975		.2849	.3848	.4545	.5080	.5510	.975	11
	.050	.900	.0000	.0043	.0281	.0611	.0967	.050
	.950		.2384	.3387	.4101	.4657	.5108	.950
	.100	.800	.0000	.0087	.0417	.0815	.1218	.100
	.900		.1889	.2875	.3598	.4170	.4640	.900
	.250	.500	.0000	.0237	.0741	.1248	.1720	.250
	.750		.1184	.2091	.2798	.3377	.3865	.750
	.005	.990	.0000	.0004	.0076	.0239	.0455	.005
	.995		.3569	.4490	.5123	.5605	.5991	.995
	.010	.980	.0000	.0008	.0110	.0307	.0554	.010
	.990		.3187	.4128	.4783	.5285	.5690	.990
	.025	.950	.0000	.0019	.0178	.0433	.0727	.025
12	.975		.2646	.3603	.4281	.4809	.5238	.975	12
	.050	.900	.0000	.0039	.0260	.0568	.0903	.050
	.950		.2209	.3163	.3854	.4398	.4844	.950
	.100	.800	.0000	.0081	.0387	.0759	.1138	.100
	.900		.1746	.2678	.3372	.3928	.4389	.900
	.250	.500	.0000	.0219	.0688	.1163	.1611	.250
	.750		.1091	.1941	.2612	.3169	.3642	.750

Confidence Limits on a Proportion (cont.)

x

n	γ	1-α	5	6	7	8	9	γ	n
	.005	.990	.0801	.1086	.1371	.1650	.1919	.005	
	.995		.6882	.7132	.7344	.7526	.7684	.995	
	.010	.980	.0944	.1251	.1552	.1844	.2124	.010	
	.990		.6597	.6865	.7093	.7289	.7460	.990	
	.025	.950	.1182	.1520	.1844	.2153	.2445	.025	
10	.975		.6162	.6456	.6707	.6924	.7114	.975	10
	.050	.900	.1417	.1778	.2119	.2440	.2740	.050	
	.950		.5774	.6089	.6359	.6593	.6799	.950	
	.100	.800	.1720	.2104	.2461	.2792	.3099	.100	
	.900		.5317	.5654	.5944	.6197	.6421	.900	
	.250	.500	.2302	.2714	.3088	.3427	.3736	.250	
	.750		.4543	.4909	.5228	.5509	.5759	.750	
	.005	.990	.0745	.1014	.1284	.1549	.1806	.005	
	.995		.6585	.6845	.7068	.7259	.7428	.995	
	.010	.980	.0878	.1168	.1454	.1733	.2001	.010	
	.990		.6299	.6577	.6814	.7019	.7199	.990	
	.025	.950	.1102	.1421	.1730	.2025	.2306	.025	
11	.975		.5866	.6167	.6425	.6649	.6847	.975	11
	.050	.900	.1321	.1664	.1990	.2297	.2586	.050	
	.950		.5483	.5802	.6078	.6318	.6531	.950	
	.100	.800	.1606	.1972	.2314	.2633	.2929	.100	
	.900		.5035	.5373	.5667	.5924	.6153	.900	
	.250	.500	.2154	.2549	.2910	.3239	.3541	.250	
	.750		.4283	.4646	.4964	.5246	.5498	.750	
	.005	.990	.0697	.0951	.1207	.1460	.1707	.005	
	.995		.6310	.6578	.6808	.7008	.7185	.995	
	.010	.980	.0822	.1096	.1368	.1634	.1891	.010	
	.990		.6025	.6308	.6553	.6765	.6953	.990	
	.025	.950	.1031	.1334	.1629	.1912	.2182	.025	
12	.975		.5596	.5900	.6164	.6394	.6598	.975	12
	.050	.900	.1238	.1564	.1875	.2171	.2450	.050	
	.950		.5219	.5540	.5819	.6063	.6281	.950	
	.100	.800	.1506	.1855	.2183	.2491	.2778	.100	
	.900		.4781	.5118	.5413	.5673	.5905	.900	
	.250	.500	.2024	.2404	.2752	.3072	.3366	.250	
	.750		.4051	.4409	.4724	.5005	.5258	.750	

9.6

Confidence Limits on a Proportion (cont.)

	γ	1-α	0	1	2	3	4	γ	
	.005	.990	.0000	.0003	.0063	.0197	.0378	.005	
	.995		.2976	.3814	.4413	.4884	.5271	.995	
	.010	.980	.0000	.0006	.0090	.0254	.0461	.010	
	.990	.	.2644	.3488	.4099	.4583	.4983	.990	
	.025	.950	.0000	.0016	.0146	.0358	.0605	.025	
15	.975		.2180	.3023	.3644	.4142	.4557	.975	15
	.050	.900	.0000	.0032	.0213	.0470	.0753	.050	
	.950		.1810	.2640	.3262	.3767	.4191	.950	
	.100	.800	.0000	.0066	.0317	.0629	.0951	.100	
	.900		.1423	.2222	.2837	.3344	.3775	.900	
	.250	.500	.0000	.0178	.0566	.0968	.1353	.250	
	.750		.0883	.1596	.2178	.2674	.3105	.750	
	.005	.990	.0000	.0002	.0048	.0153	.0295	.005	
	.995		.2327	.3043	.3577	.4012	.4379	.995	
	.010	.980	.0000	.0005	.0069	.0196	.0360	.010	
	.990		.2057	.2768	.3305	.3745	.4118	.990	
	.025	.950	.0000	.0012	.0112	.0278	.0474	.025	
20	.975		.1684	.2382	.2916	.3359	.3738	.975	20
	.050	.900	.0000	.0024	.0164	.0365	.0590	.050	
	.950		.1391	.2067	.2595	.3036	.3418	.950	
	.100	.800	.0000	.0050	.0244	.0489	.0747	.100	
	.900		.1087	.1729	.2242	.2678	.3059	.900	
	.250	.500	.0000	.0136	.0437	.0756	.1068	.250	
	.750		.0670	.1232	.1705	.2120	.2491	.750	
	.005	.990	.0000	.0002	.0039	.0124	.0242	.005	
	.995		.1910	.2530	.3005	.3401	.3742	.995	
	.010	.980	.0000	.0004	.0056	.0160	.0295	.010	
	.990		.1682	.2294	.2767	.3163	.3506	.990	
	.025	.950	.0000	.0010	.0091	.0227	.0389	.025	
25	.975		.1372	.1964	.2429	.2823	.3167	.975	25
	.050	.900	.0000	.0020	.0133	.0298	.0485	.050	
	.950		.1129	.1699	.2153	.2542	.2884	.950	
	.100	.800	.0000	.0040	.0199	.0400	.0615	.100	
	.900		.0880	.1415	.1853	.2233	.2570	.900	
	.250	.500	.0000	.0110	.0356	.0620	.0882	.250	
	.750		.0539	.1002	.1401	.1757	.2079	.750	

9.6

Confidence Limits on a Proportion (cont.)

x

γ	1-α	5	6	7	8	9	γ	
	.005	.990	.0583	.0801	.1024	.1246	.1465	.005
	.995		.5598	.5878	.6122	.6337	.6530	.995
	.010	.980	.0688	.0925	.1162	.1397	.1626	.010
	.990		.5321	.5612	.5868	.6093	.6295	.990
15	.025	.950	.0866	.1128	.1387	.1638	.1880	.025	15
	.975		.4910	.5217	.5487	.5726	.5941	.975
	.050	.900	.1041	.1325	.1599	.1864	.2116	.050
	.950		.4556	.4873	.5154	.5404	.5629	.950
	.100	.800	.1269	.1576	.1867	.2144	.2406	.100
	.900		.4149	.4477	.4768	.5028	.5264	.900
	.250	.500	.1714	.2052	.2366	.2658	.2931	.250
	.750		.3484	.3822	.4126	.4400	.4649	.750
	.005	.990	.0459	.0635	.0817	.1002	.1186	.005
	.995		.4698	.4976	.5225	.5448	.5651	.995
	.010	.980	.0542	.0734	.0929	.1125	.1318	.010
	.990		.4443	.4728	.4983	.5213	.5422	.990
20	.025	.950	.0683	.0897	.1112	.1322	.1529	.025	20
	.975		.4070	.4364	.4628	.4865	.5083	.975
	.050	.900	.0823	.1056	.1285	.1509	.1725	.050
	.950		.3754	.4053	.4322	.4566	.4790	.950
	.100	.800	.1006	.1260	.1505	.1741	.1968	.100
	.900		.3397	.3699	.3973	.4223	.4452	.900
	.250	.500	.1366	.1650	.1918	.2172	.2412	.250
	.750		.2824	.3127	.3404	.3659	.3895	.750
	.005	.990	.0378	.0526	.0680	.0838	.0996	.005
	.995		.4042	.4309	.4550	.4769	.4972	.995
	.010	.980	.0447	.0609	.0774	.0942	.1109	.010
	.990		.3809	.4080	.4325	.4548	.4755	.990
25	.025	.950	.0564	.0745	.0928	.1109	.1288	.025	25
	.975		.3473	.3747	.3997	.4225	.4437	.975
	.050	.900	.0681	.0878	.1075	.1268	.1456	.050
	.950		.3190	.3466	.3718	.3950	.4165	.950
	.100	.800	.0834	.1050	.1261	.1466	.1665	.100
	.900		.2874	.3150	.3403	.3637	.3855	.900
	.250	.500	.1136	.1380	.1613	.1837	.2050	.250
	.750		.2374	.2645	.2897	.3131	.3350	.750

9.6

Confidence Limits on a Proportion (cont.)

	Υ	1-α	0	1	2	3	4	Υ	
	.005	.990	.0000	.0001	.0020	.0065	.0127	.005	
	.995		.1005	.1369	.1664	.1922	.2154	.995	
	.010	.980	.0000	.0002	.0029	.0084	.0156	.010	
	.990		.0880	.1232	.1520	.1774	.2003	.990	
	.025	.950	.0000	.0005	.0047	.0118	.0206	.025	
50	.975		.0711	.1045	.1321	.1567	.1790	.975	50
	.050	.900	.0000	.0010	.0069	.0156	.0257	.050	
	.950		.0582	.0897	.1162	.1399	.1616	.950	
	.100	.800	.0000	.0021	.0103	.0210	.0327	.100	
	.900		.0450	.0741	.0991	.1217	.1426	.900	
	.250	.500	.0000	.0056	.0185	.0327	.0472	.250	
	.750		.0273	.0519	.0740	.0945	.1137	.750	
	.005	.990	.0000	.0001	.0010	.0033	.0065	.005	
	.995		.0516	.0713	.0878	.1026	.1162	.995	
	.010	.980	.0000	.0001	.0015	.0043	.0080	.010	
	.990		.0450	.0639	.0799	.0943	.1076	.990	
	.025	.950	.0000	.0003	.0024	.0060	.0106	.025	
100	.975		.0362	.0539	.0691	.0828	.0956	.975	100
	.050	.900	.0000	.0005	.0035	.0080	.0132	.050	
	.950		.0295	.0461	.0604	.0736	.0859	.950	
	.100	.800	.0000	.0010	.0052	.0107	.0169	.100	
	.900		.0228	.0380	.0513	.0637	.0754	.900	
	.250	.500	.0000	.0028	.0094	.0168	.0244	.250	
	.750		.0138	.0264	.0381	.0491	.0597	.750	
	.005	.990	.0000	.0000	.0002	.0007	.0013	.005	
	.995		.0105	.0147	.0183	.0217	.0248	.995	
	.010	.980	.0000	.0000	.0003	.0009	.0016	.010	
	.990		.0092	.0132	.0166	.0198	.0229	.990	
	.025	.950	.0000	.0001	.0005	.0012	.0022	.025	
500	.975		.0074	.0111	.0143	.0173	.0202	.975	500
	.050	.900	.0000	.0001	.0007	.0016	.0027	.050	
	.950		.0060	.0094	.0125	.0153	.0181	.950	
	.100	.800	.0000	.0002	.0011	.0022	.0035	.100	
	.900		.0046	.0077	.0106	.0132	.0158	.900	
	.250	.500	.0000	.0006	.0019	.0034	.0050	.250	
	.750		.0028	.0054	.0078	.0101	.0124	.750	

9.6

Confidence Limits on a Proportion (*cont.*)

n	γ	1-α	5	6	7	8	9	γ	n
	.005	.990	.0201	.0283	.0371	.0461	.0554	.005	
	.995		.2367	.2563	.2746	.2918	.3082	.995	
	.010	.980	.0239	.0328	.0423	.0520	.0619	.010	
	.990		.2213	.2408	.2590	.2761	.2925	.990	
	.025	.950	.0302	.0403	.0508	.0615	.0722	.025	
50	.975		.1996	.2187	.2367	.2537	.2699	.975	50
	.050	.900	.0365	.0477	.0591	.0705	.0820	.050	
	.950		.1817	.2005	.2183	.2350	.2511	.950	
	.100	.800	.0449	.0573	.0697	.0820	.0942	.100	
	.900		.1621	.1804	.1978	.2143	.2301	.900	
	.250	.500	.0616	.0759	.0899	.1037	.1171	.250	
	.750		.1320	.1493	.1658	.1816	.1969	.750	
	.005	.990	.0104	.0147	.0194	.0243	.0294	.005	
	.995		.1291	.1411	.1527	.1637	.1744	.995	
	.010	.980	.0123	.0171	.0222	.0274	.0329	.010	
	.990		.1201	.1320	.1433	.1541	.1647	.990	
	.025	.950	.0156	.0211	.0267	.0325	.0385	.025	
100	.975		.1077	.1191	.1301	.1407	.1510	.975	100
	.050	.900	.0189	.0249	.0311	.0374	.0438	.050	
	.950		.0975	.1086	.1193	.1296	.1397	.950	
	.100	.800	.0233	.0300	.0368	.0436	.0505	.100	
	.900		.0865	.0972	.1075	.1175	.1272	.900	
	.250	.500	.0322	.0400	.0477	.0554	.0631	.250	
	.750		.0699	.0797	.0893	.0987	.1078	.750	
	.005	.990	.0021	.0030	.0040	.0051	.0062	.005	
	.995		.0278	.0306	.0334	.0362	.0389	.995	
	.010	.980	.0025	.0035	.0046	.0057	.0069	.010	
	.990		.0258	.0285	.0313	.0339	.0366	.990	
	.025	.950	.0032	.0044	.0056	.0068	.0081	.025	
500	.975		.0230	.0256	.0282	.0308	.0333	.975	500
	.050	.900	.0039	.0052	.0065	.0079	.0093	.050	
	.950		.0207	.0233	.0258	.0282	.0307	.950	
	.100	.800	.0048	.0062	.0077	.0092	.0107	.100	
	.900		.0183	.0207	.0231	.0254	.0278	.900	
	.250	.500	.0067	.0083	.0100	.0117	.0135	.250	
	.750		.0147	.0169	.0190	.0212	.0233	.750	

$x = n - x$

$p = \dfrac{x}{n}$

9.7 Confidence Limits on Functions of Binomial Parameters

Steck [208] describes how a system of upper confidence limits for a function of binomial parameters may be computed from observations of the individual binomial populations (assumed independent). This procedure is applicable to finding upper confidence limits for the failure rate of a complex assembly, given data on the failure rates of its constituents. The general problem is too complicated to discuss here, and in fact, it is still not satisfactorily solved [122], [127], [49], [21] Buehler [28] discusses one particular case for which the charts given here provide an answer. If two dissimilar components A and B are in parallel, the system will fail only if both A and B fail. If q_A is the probability that A fails, and q_B is the probability that B fails, an upper confidence limit on the product $q_A q_B$ is required. Suppose n observations on A and n observations on B are available. Figures 1, 2, and 3 give 90 percent, 95 percent, and 99 percent upper confidence limits on the product $q_A q_B$, given n observations where both A and B have no failures $(0, 0)$, or where A has 1 and B has none $(1, 0)$, or where A has none and B has 1 $(0, 1)$.

Figures 4, 5, and 6 apply to a series parallel circuit of two dissimilar components, i.e., the two components A and B are connected as follows:

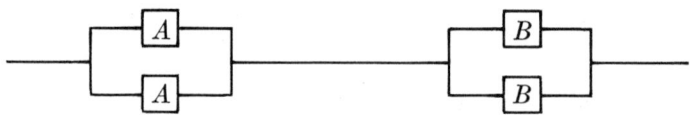

In this case the function for which an upper confidence limit is wanted is $1 - (1 - q_A^2)(1 - q_B^2)$. Figures 4, 5, and 6 provide the necessary upper confidence limit. These results are derived by assuming an ordering on the observations. In Figures 1, 2, and 3 this ordering makes a difference, while in Figures 4, 5, and 6 it makes no difference. Consult Steck's [208] paper for more details. Lipow and Riley [123] give some extensive tables for series (one, two, and three components) circuits.

Confidence Limits on Functions of Binomial Parameters [208]

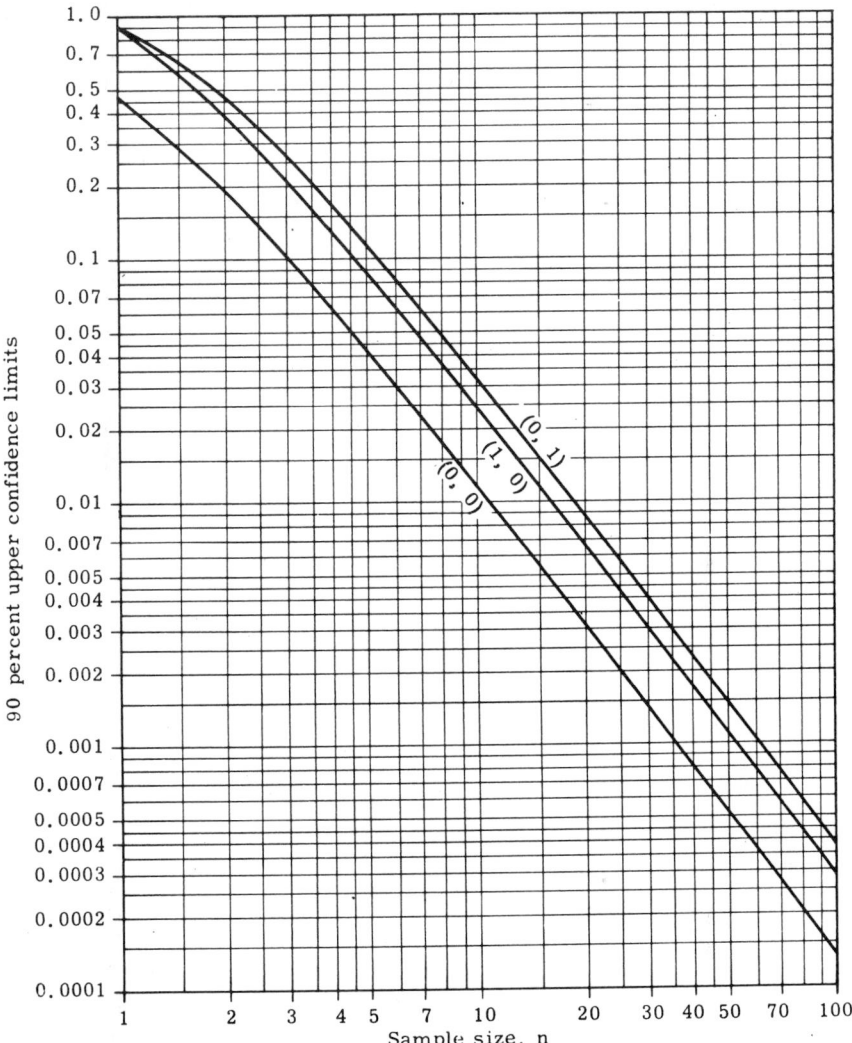

Fig. 1. 90% upper confidence limits for the failure probability of a parallel circuit of A and B components as a function of sample size n and observed failures (x, y) [(x, y) denotes an observation consisting of x failures of A and y failures of B].

Confidence Limits on Functions of Binomial Parameters (cont.)

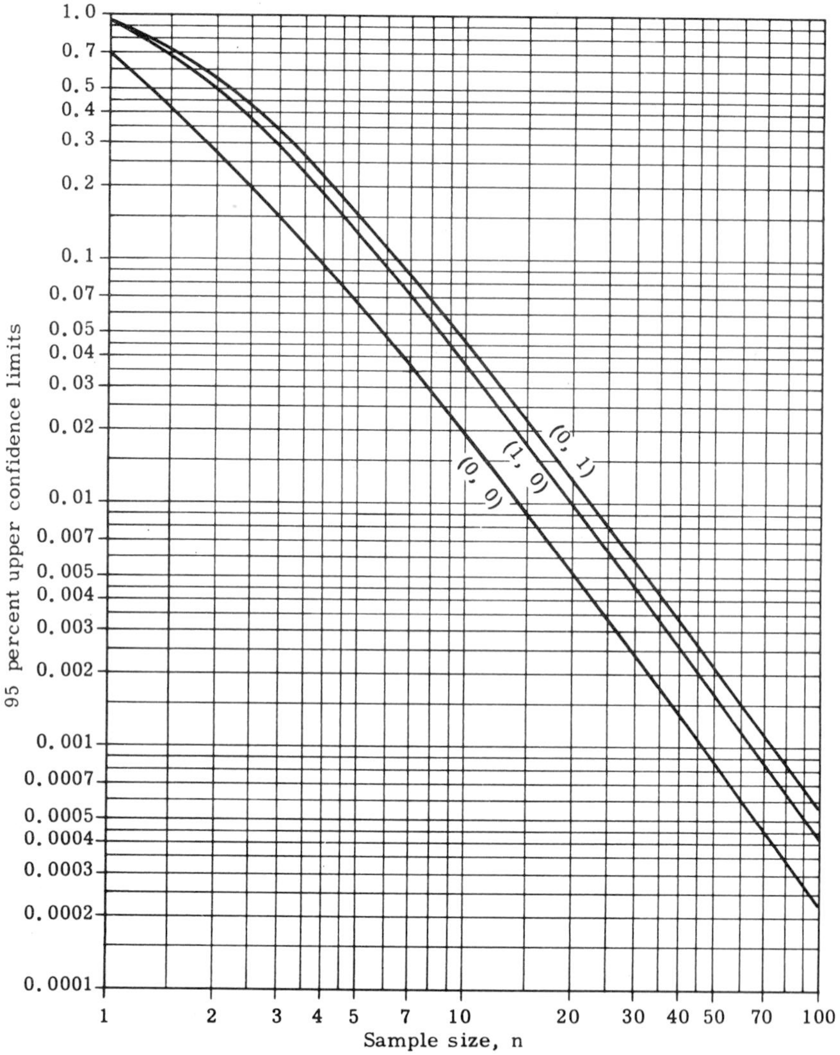

Fig. 2. 95% upper confidence limits for the failure probability of a parallel circuit of A and B components as a function of sample size n and observed failures (x, y) [(x, y) denotes an observation consisting of x failures of A and y failures of B].

Confidence Limits on Functions of Binomial Parameters (*cont.*)

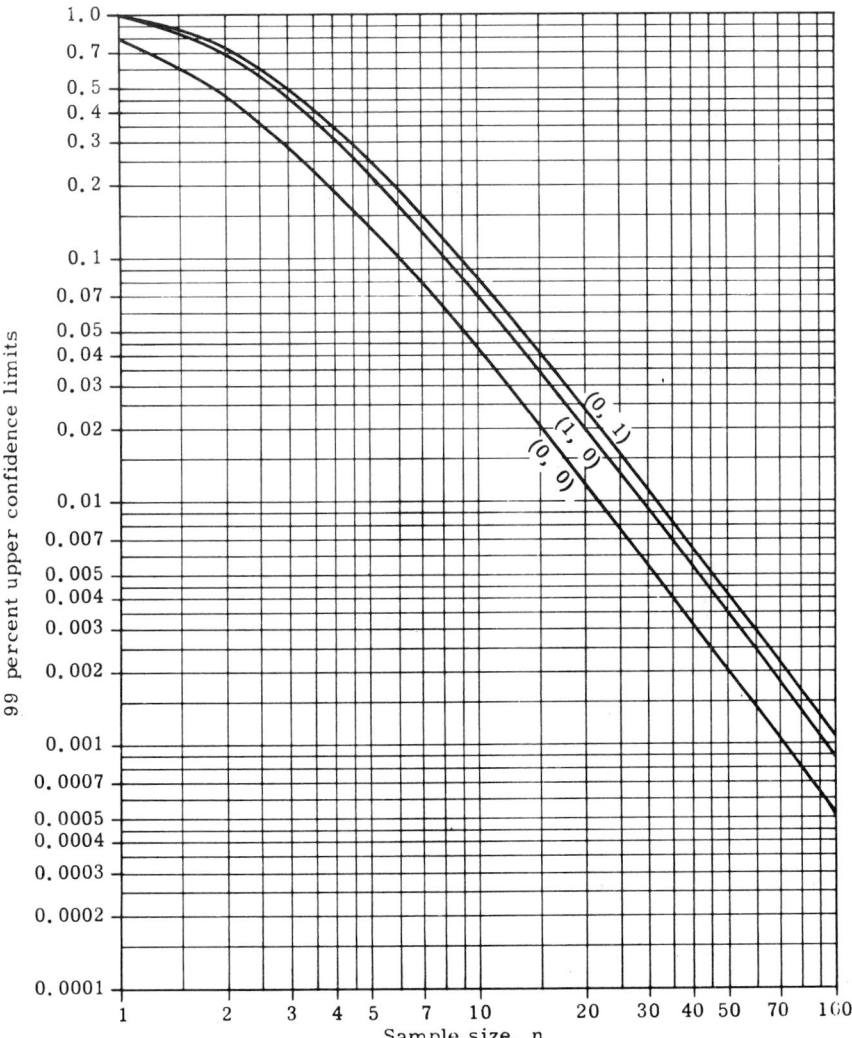

Fig. 3. 99% upper confidence limits for the failure probability of a parallel circuit of *A* and *B* components as a function of sample size *n* and observed failures (*x, y*) [(*x, y*) denotes an observation consisting of *x* failures of *A* and *y* failures of *B*].

9.7

Confidence Limits on Functions of Binomial Parameters (*cont.*)

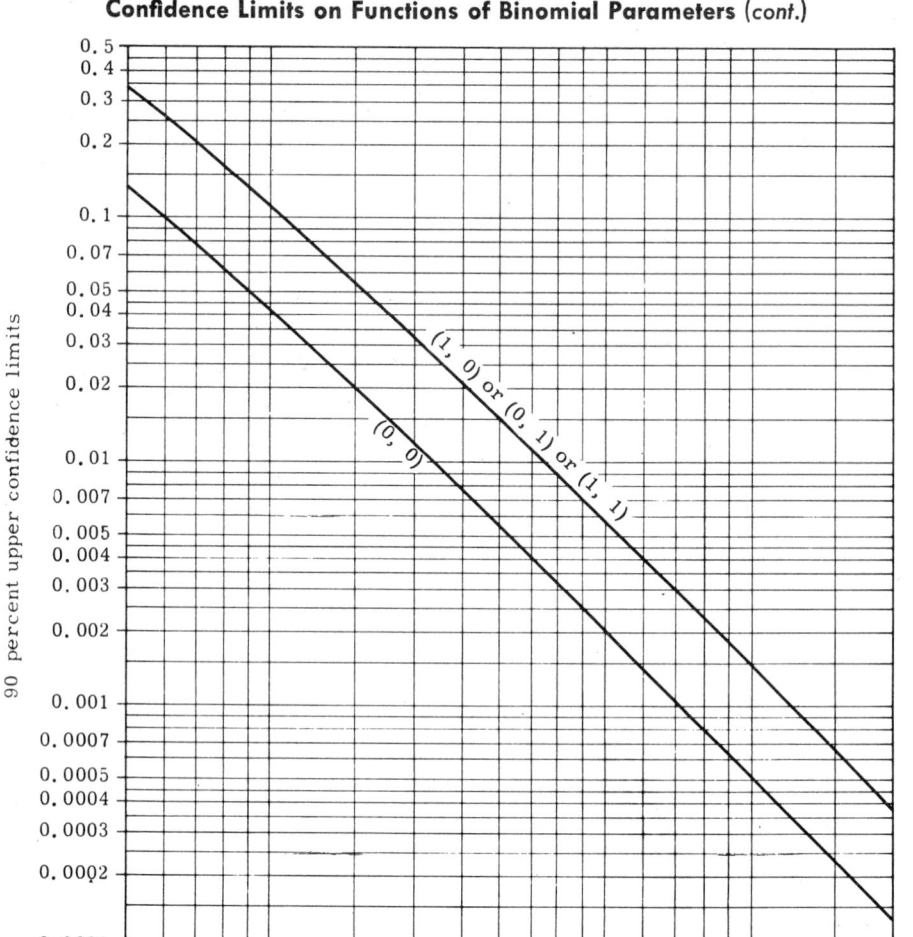

Fig. 4. 90% upper confidence limits for the failure probability of a series-parallel circuit of *A* and *B* components as a function of sample size *n* and observed failures (*x, y*) [(*x, y*) denotes an observation consisting of *x* failures of *A* and *y* failures of *B*].

9.7

Confidence Limits on Functions of Binomial Parameters (cont.)

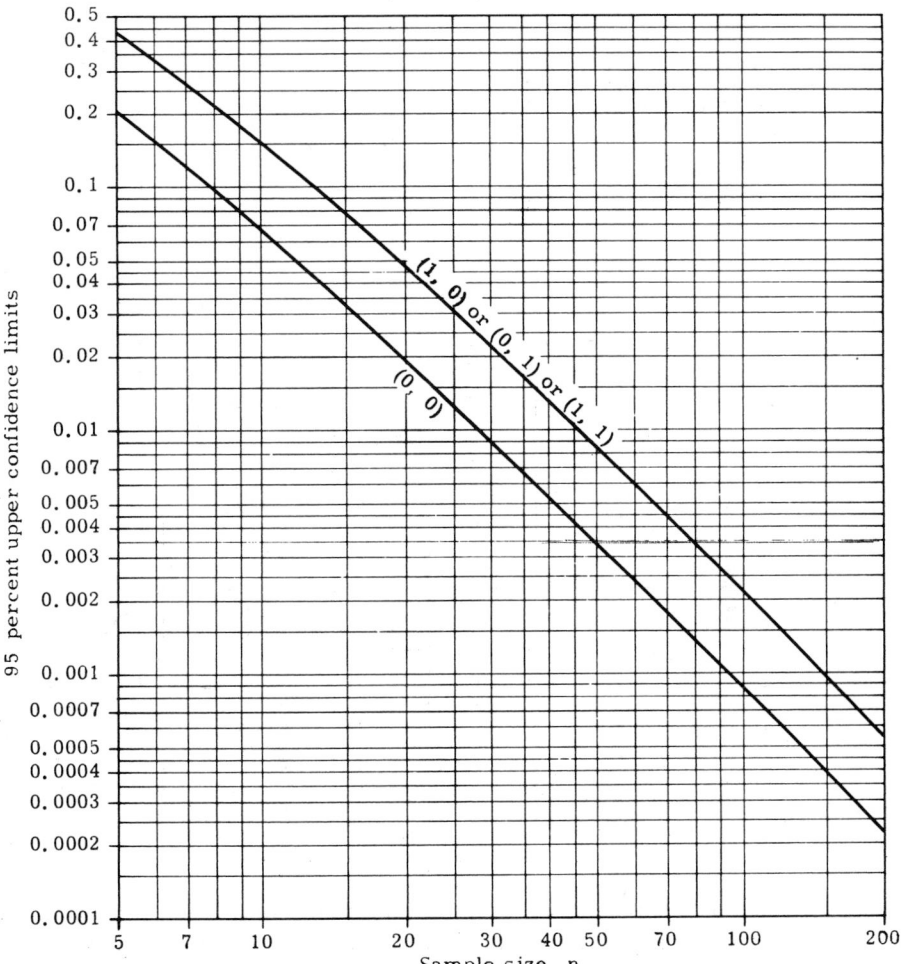

Fig. 5. 95% upper confidence limits for the failure probability of a series-parallel circuit of A and B components as a function of sample size n and observed failures (x, y) [(x, y) denotes an observation consisting of x failures of A and y failures of B].

Confidence Limits on Functions of Binomial Parameters (*cont.*)

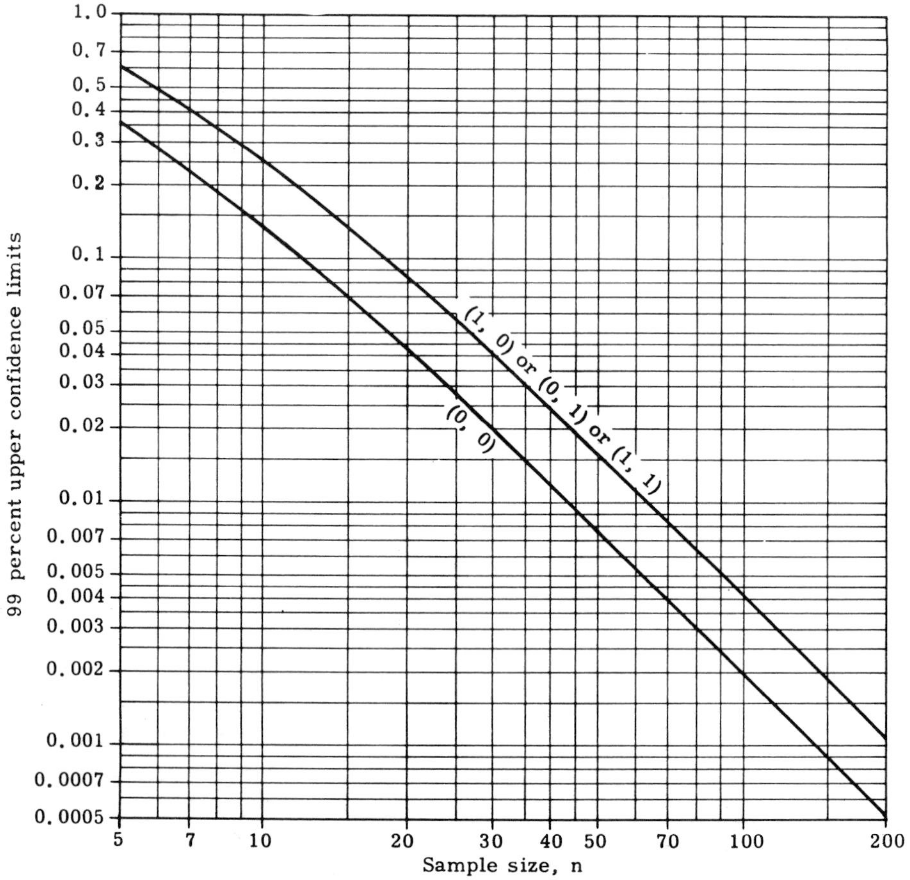

Fig. 6. 99% upper confidence limits for the failure probability of a series-parallel circuit of A and B components as a function of sample size n and observed failures (x, y) [(x, y) denotes an observation consisting of x failures of A and y failures of B].

9.8 Arcsine Transformation of 0 or 1 Observed Values

Let p be the proportion of items that possess a particular characteristic in a sample of n from an infinite population where the population has a proportion θ possessing that particular characteristic. Then the mean of p is θ, and the variance of p is $\theta(1 - \theta)/n$. If the transformation

$$\phi = 2 \arcsin \sqrt{p}$$

is applied to p, then ϕ has a variance which is approximately equal to $1/n$ and which is independent of the unknown parameter θ.

If p is equal to zero or one, instead of the above transformation, the following transformations are recommended:

$$\phi_0 = 2 \arcsin \sqrt{1/(4n)} \quad \text{for } p = 0,$$

and

$$\phi_1 = \pi - \phi_0 \quad \text{for } p = 1.$$

The tables given here are for ϕ_0 and ϕ_1. See Chapter 16 of [62] for a fuller discussion of these transformations.

Arcsine Transformation of 0 or 1 Observed Values

N	ϕ_0	ϕ_1	N	ϕ_0	ϕ_1
5	0.4510	2.6906	50	0.1415	3.0001
6	0.4111	2.7305	51	0.1401	3.0015
7	0.3803	2.7613	52	0.1388	3.0028
8	0.3554	2.7862	53	0.1375	3.0041
9	0.3349	2.8067	54	0.1362	3.0054
10	0.3176	2.8240	55	0.1349	3.0067
11	0.3027	2.8389	56	0.1337	3.0079
12	0.2897	2.8519	57	0.1326	3.0090
13	0.2782	2.8633	58	0.1314	3.0102
14	0.2681	2.8735	59	0.1303	3.0113
15	0.2589	2.8827	60	0.1292	3.0124
16	0.2507	2.8909	61	0.1281	3.0135
17	0.2431	2.8985	62	0.1271	3.0145
18	0.2363	2.9053	63	0.1261	3.0155
19	0.2299	2.9117	64	0.1251	3.0165
20	0.2241	2.9175	65	0.1241	3.0175
21	0.2187	2.9229	66	0.1232	3.0184
22	0.2136	2.9280	67	0.1222	3.0193
23	0.2089	2.9327	68	0.1213	3.0203
24	0.2045	2.9371	69	0.1205	3.0211
25	0.2003	2.9413	70	0.1196	3.0220
26	0.1964	2.9452	71	0.1187	3.0228
27	0.1927	2.9488	72	0.1179	3.0237
28	0.1893	2.9523	73	0.1171	3.0245
29	0.1860	2.9556	74	0.1163	3.0253
30	0.1828	2.9588	75	0.1155	3.0261
31	0.1798	2.9617	76	0.1148	3.0268
32	0.1770	2.9646	77	0.1140	3.0276
33	0.1743	2.9673	78	0.1133	3.0283
34	0.1717	2.9699	79	0.1126	3.0290
35	0.1692	2.9724	80	0.1119	3.0297
36	0.1669	2.9747	81	0.1112	3.0304
37	0.1646	2.9770	82	0.1105	3.0311
38	0.1624	2.9792	83	0.1098	3.0318
39	0.1603	2.9813	84	0.1092	3.0324
40	0.1583	2.9833	85	0.1085	3.0331
41	0.1563	2.9853	86	0.1079	3.0337
42	0.1545	2.9871	87	0.1073	3.0343
43	0.1526	2.9889	88	0.1067	3.0349
44	0.1509	2.9907	89	0.1060	3.0355
45	0.1492	2.9924	90	0.1055	3.0361
46	0.1476	2.9940	91	0.1049	3.0367
47	0.1460	2.9956	92	0.1043	3.0373
48	0.1445	2.9971	93	0.1037	3.0379
49	0.1430	2.9986	94	0.1032	3.0384

Arcsine Transformation of 0 or 1 Observed Values (cont.)

N	ϕ_0	ϕ_1	N	ϕ_0	ϕ_1
95	0.1026	3.0389	500	0.0447	3.0969
96	0.1021	3.0395	510	0.0443	3.0973
97	0.1016	3.0400	520	0.0439	3.0977
98	0.1011	3.0405	530	0.0434	3.0982
99	0.1005	3.0410	540	0.0430	3.0986
100	0.1000	3.0416	550	0.0426	3.0989
110	0.0954	3.0462	560	0.0423	3.0993
120	0.0913	3.0503	570	0.0419	3.0997
130	0.0877	3.0539	580	0.0415	3.1001
140	0.0845	3.0571	590	0.0412	3.1004
150	0.0817	3.0599	600	0.0408	3.1008
160	0.0791	3.0625	610	0.0405	3.1011
170	0.0767	3.0649	620	0.0402	3.1014
180	0.0746	3.0670	630	0.0398	3.1017
190	0.0726	3.0690	640	0.0395	3.1021
200	0.0707	3.0709	650	0.0392	3.1024
210	0.0690	3.0726	660	0.0389	3.1027
220	0.0674	3.0742	670	0.0386	3.1030
230	0.0659	3.0756	680	0.0384	3.1032
240	0.0646	3.0770	690	0.0381	3.1035
250	0.0633	3.0783	700	0.0378	3.1038
260	0.0620	3.0796	710	0.0375	3.1041
270	0.0609	3.0807	720	0.0373	3.1043
280	0.0598	3.0818	730	0.0370	3.1046
290	0.0587	3.0829	740	0.0368	3.1048
300	0.0577	3.0838	750	0.0365	3.1051
310	0.0568	3.0848	760	0.0363	3.1053
320	0.0559	3.0857	770	0.0360	3.1056
330	0.0551	3.0865	780	0.0358	3.1058
340	0.0542	3.0874	790	0.0356	3.1060
350	0.0535	3.0881	800	0.0354	3.1062
360	0.0527	3.0889	810	0.0351	3.1065
370	0.0520	3.0896	820	0.0349	3.1067
380	0.0513	3.0903	830	0.0347	3.1069
390	0.0506	3.0910	840	0.0345	3.1071
400	0.0500	3.0916	850	0.0343	3.1073
410	0.0494	3.0922	860	0.0341	3.1075
420	0.0488	3.0928	880	0.0337	3.1079
430	0.0482	3.0934	900	0.0333	3.1083
440	0.0477	3.0939	920	0.0330	3.1086
450	0.0471	3.0944	940	0.0326	3.1090
460	0.0466	3.0950	960	0.0323	3.1093
470	0.0461	3.0955	980	0.0319	3.1096
480	0.0456	3.0959			
490	0.0452	3.0964	1000	0.0316	3.1100

9.9 Transformation of a Proportion p to $\phi = 2\ \text{arcsin}\ \sqrt{p}$

See Section 9.8 for an explanation of this table.

Transformation of a Proportion p to $\phi = 2\ \text{arcsin}\ \sqrt{p}$

p	ϕ	p	ϕ	p	ϕ
0.0001	0.0200	0.005	0.1415	0.050	0.4510
0.0002	0.0283	0.006	0.1551	0.051	0.4556
0.0003	0.0346	0.007	0.1675	0.052	0.4601
0.0004	0.0400	0.008	0.1791	0.053	0.4646
0.0005	0.0447	0.009	0.1900	0.054	0.4690
0.0006	0.0490	0.010	0.2003	0.055	0.4735
0.0007	0.0529	0.011	0.2101	0.056	0.4778
0.0008	0.0566	0.012	0.2195	0.057	0.4821
0.0009	0.0600	0.013	0.2285	0.058	0.4864
0.0010	0.0633	0.014	0.2372	0.059	0.4907
0.0011	0.0663	0.015	0.2456	0.060	0.4949
0.0012	0.0693	0.016	0.2537	0.061	0.4991
0.0013	0.0721	0.017	0.2615	0.062	0.5033
0.0014	0.0749	0.018	0.2691	0.063	0.5074
0.0015	0.0775	0.019	0.2766	0.064	0.5115
0.0016	0.0800	0.020	0.2838	0.065	0.5156
0.0017	0.0825	0.021	0.2909	0.066	0.5196
0.0018	0.0849	0.022	0.2977	0.067	0.5236
0.0019	0.0872	0.023	0.3045	0.068	0.5276
0.0020	0.0895	0.024	0.3111	0.069	0.5316
0.0021	0.0917	0.025	0.3176	0.070	0.5355
0.0022	0.0938	0.026	0.3239	0.071	0.5394
0.0023	0.0960	0.027	0.3301	0.072	0.5433
0.0024	0.0980	0.028	0.3362	0.073	0.5472
0.0025	0.1000	0.029	0.3423	0.074	0.5510
0.0026	0.1020	0.030	0.3482	0.075	0.5548
0.0027	0.1040	0.031	0.3540	0.076	0.5586
0.0028	0.1059	0.032	0.3597	0.077	0.5624
0.0029	0.1078	0.033	0.3653	0.078	0.5661
0.0030	0.1096	0.034	0.3709	0.079	0.5698
0.0031	0.1114	0.035	0.3764	0.080	0.5735
0.0032	0.1132	0.036	0.3818	0.081	0.5772
0.0033	0.1150	0.037	0.3871	0.082	0.5808
0.0034	0.1167	0.038	0.3924	0.083	0.5845
0.0035	0.1184	0.039	0.3976	0.084	0.5881
0.0036	0.1201	0.040	0.4027	0.085	0.5917
0.0037	0.1217	0.041	0.4078	0.086	0.5953
0.0038	0.1234	0.042	0.4128	0.087	0.5988
0.0039	0.1250	0.043	0.4178	0.088	0.6024
0.0040	0.1266	0.044	0.4227	0.089	0.6059
0.0041	0.1282	0.045	0.4275	0.090	0.6094
0.0042	0.1297	0.046	0.4323	0.091	0.6129
0.0043	0.1312	0.047	0.4371	0.092	0.6163
0.0044	0.1328	0.048	0.4418	0.093	0.6198
0.0045	0.1343	0.049	0.4464	0.094	0.6232

Transformation of a Proportion p to $\phi = 2$ arcsin $\sqrt{p}$ (cont.)

p	ϕ	p	ϕ	p	ϕ
0.095	0.6266	0.140	0.7670	0.185	0.8892
0.096	0.6300	0.141	0.7699	0.186	0.8918
0.097	0.6334	0.142	0.7727	0.187	0.8944
0.098	0.6368	0.143	0.7756	0.188	0.8969
0.099	0.6402	0.144	0.7785	0.189	0.8995
0.100	0.6435	0.145	0.7813	0.190	0.9021
0.101	0.6468	0.146	0.7841	0.191	0.9046
0.102	0.6501	0.147	0.7870	0.192	0.9071
0.103	0.6534	0.148	0.7898	0.193	0.9097
0.104	0.6567	0.149	0.7926	0.194	0.9122
0.105	0.6600	0.150	0.7954	0.195	0.9147
0.106	0.6632	0.151	0.7982	0.196	0.9173
0.107	0.6665	0.152	0.8010	0.197	0.9198
0.108	0.6697	0.153	0.8038	0.198	0.9223
0.109	0.6729	0.154	0.8065	0.199	0.9248
0.110	0.6761	0.155	0.8093	0.200	0.9273
0.111	0.6793	0.156	0.8121	0.201	0.9298
0.112	0.6825	0.157	0.8148	0.202	0.9323
0.113	0.6857	0.158	0.8176	0.203	0.9348
0.114	0.6888	0.159	0.8203	0.204	0.9373
0.115	0.6920	0.160	0.8230	0.205	0.9397
0.116	0.6951	0.161	0.8258	0.206	0.9422
0.117	0.6982	0.162	0.8285	0.207	0.9447
0.118	0.7013	0.163	0.8312	0.208	0.9471
0.119	0.7044	0.164	0.8339	0.209	0.9496
0.120	0.7075	0.165	0.8366	0.210	0.9521
0.121	0.7106	0.166	0.8393	0.211	0.9545
0.122	0.7136	0.167	0.8420	0.212	0.9570
0.123	0.7167	0.168	0.8446	0.213	0.9594
0.124	0.7197	0.169	0.8473	0.214	0.9619
0.125	0.7227	0.170	0.8500	0.215	0.9643
0.126	0.7258	0.171	0.8526	0.216	0.9667
0.127	0.7288	0.172	0.8553	0.217	0.9692
0.128	0.7318	0.173	0.8579	0.218	0.9716
0.129	0.7347	0.174	0.8606	0.219	0.9740
0.130	0.7377	0.175	0.8632	0.220	0.9764
0.131	0.7407	0.176	0.8658	0.221	0.9788
0.132	0.7437	0.177	0.8685	0.222	0.9812
0.133	0.7466	0.178	0.8711	0.223	0.9836
0.134	0.7495	0.179	0.8737	0.224	0.9860
0.135	0.7525	0.180	0.8763	0.225	0.9884
0.136	0.7554	0.181	0.8789	0.226	0.9908
0.137	0.7583	0.182	0.8815	0.227	0.9932
0.138	0.7612	0.183	0.8841	0.228	0.9956
0.139	0.7641	0.184	0.8867	0.229	0.9980

Transformation of a Proportion p to $\phi = 2$ arcsin $\sqrt{p}$ (cont.)

p	ϕ	p	ϕ	p	ϕ
0.230	1.0004	0.275	1.1040	0.320	1.2025
0.231	1.0027	0.276	1.1063	0.321	1.2047
0.232	1.0051	0.277	1.1085	0.322	1.2068
0.233	1.0075	0.278	1.1107	0.323	1.2090
0.234	1.0098	0.279	1.1130	0.324	1.2111
0.235	1.0122	0.280	1.1152	0.325	1.2132
0.236	1.0146	0.281	1.1174	0.326	1.2154
0.237	1.0169	0.282	1.1196	0.327	1.2175
0.238	1.0193	0.283	1.1219	0.328	1.2196
0.239	1.0216	0.284	1.1241	0.329	1.2218
0.240	1.0239	0.285	1.1263	0.330	1.2239
0.241	1.0263	0.286	1.1285	0.331	1.2260
0.242	1.0286	0.287	1.1307	0.332	1.2281
0.243	1.0310	0.288	1.1329	0.333	1.2303
0.244	1.0333	0.289	1.1351	0.334	1.2324
0.245	1.0356	0.290	1.1374	0.335	1.2345
0.246	1.0379	0.291	1.1396	0.336	1.2366
0.247	1.0403	0.292	1.1418	0.337	1.2387
0.248	1.0426	0.293	1.1440	0.338	1.2408
0.249	1.0449	0.294	1.1461	0.339	1.2430
0.250	1.0472	0.295	1.1483	0.340	1.2451
0.251	1.0495	0.296	1.1505	0.341	1.2472
0.252	1.0518	0.297	1.1527	0.342	1.2493
0.253	1.0541	0.298	1.1549	0.343	1.2514
0.254	1.0564	0.299	1.1571	0.344	1.2535
0.255	1.0587	0.300	1.1593	0.345	1.2556
0.256	1.0610	0.301	1.1615	0.346	1.2577
0.257	1.0633	0.302	1.1636	0.347	1.2598
0.258	1.0656	0.303	1.1658	0.348	1.2619
0.259	1.0679	0.304	1.1680	0.349	1.2640
0.260	1.0701	0.305	1.1702	0.350	1.2661
0.261	1.0724	0.306	1.1723	0.351	1.2682
0.262	1.0747	0.307	1.1745	0.352	1.2703
0.263	1.0770	0.308	1.1767	0.353	1.2724
0.264	1.0792	0.309	1.1788	0.354	1.2745
0.265	1.0815	0.310	1.1810	0.355	1.2766
0.266	1.0838	0.311	1.1832	0.356	1.2787
0.267	1.0860	0.312	1.1853	0.357	1.2807
0.268	1.0883	0.313	1.1875	0.358	1.2828
0.269	1.0905	0.314	1.1896	0.359	1.2849
0.270	1.0928	0.315	1.1918	0.360	1.2870
0.271	1.0951	0.316	1.1939	0.361	1.2891
0.272	1.0973	0.317	1.1961	0.362	1.2912
0.273	1.0995	0.318	1.1982	0.363	1.2932
0.274	1.1018	0.319	1.2004	0.364	1.2953

9.9

Transformation of a Proportion p to $\phi = 2$ arcsin $\sqrt{p}$ (cont.)

p	ϕ	p	ϕ	p	ϕ
0.365	1.2974	0.410	1.3898	0.455	1.4807
0.366	1.2995	0.411	1.3918	0.456	1.4827
0.367	1.3016	0.412	1.3939	0.457	1.4847
0.368	1.3036	0.413	1.3959	0.458	1.4867
0.369	1.3057	0.414	1.3979	0.459	1.4887
0.370	1.3078	0.415	1.4000	0.460	1.4907
0.371	1.3098	0.416	1.4020	0.461	1.4927
0.372	1.3119	0.417	1.4040	0.462	1.4947
0.373	1.3140	0.418	1.4061	0.463	1.4967
0.374	1.3160	0.419	1.4081	0.464	1.4987
0.375	1.3181	0.420	1.4101	0.465	1.5007
0.376	1.3202	0.421	1.4121	0.466	1.5027
0.377	1.3222	0.422	1.4142	0.467	1.5047
0.378	1.3243	0.423	1.4162	0.468	1.5068
0.379	1.3264	0.424	1.4182	0.469	1.5088
0.380	1.3284	0.425	1.4202	0.470	1.5108
0.381	1.3305	0.426	1.4223	0.471	1.5128
0.382	1.3325	0.427	1.4243	0.472	1.5148
0.383	1.3346	0.428	1.4263	0.473	1.5168
0.384	1.3367	0.429	1.4283	0.474	1.5188
0.385	1.3387	0.430	1.4303	0.475	1.5208
0.386	1.3408	0.431	1.4324	0.476	1.5228
0.387	1.3428	0.432	1.4344	0.477	1.5248
0.388	1.3449	0.433	1.4364	0.478	1.5268
0.389	1.3469	0.434	1.4384	0.479	1.5288
0.390	1.3490	0.435	1.4404	0.480	1.5308
0.391	1.3510	0.436	1.4424	0.481	1.5328
0.392	1.3531	0.437	1.4445	0.482	1.5348
0.393	1.3551	0.438	1.4465	0.483	1.5368
0.394	1.3572	0.439	1.4485	0.484	1.5388
0.395	1.3592	0.440	1.4505	0.485	1.5408
0.396	1.3613	0.441	1.4525	0.486	1.5428
0.397	1.3633	0.442	1.4545	0.487	1.5448
0.398	1.3654	0.443	1.4565	0.488	1.5468
0.399	1.3674	0.444	1.4586	0.489	1.5488
0.400	1.3694	0.445	1.4606	0.490	1.5508
0.401	1.3715	0.446	1.4626	0.491	1.5528
0.402	1.3735	0.447	1.4646	0.492	1.5548
0.403	1.3756	0.448	1.4666	0.493	1.5568
0.404	1.3776	0.449	1.4686	0.494	1.5588
0.405	1.3796	0.450	1.4706	0.495	1.5608
0.406	1.3817	0.451	1.4726	0.496	1.5628
0.407	1.3837	0.452	1.4746	0.497	1.5648
0.408	1.3857	0.453	1.4767	0.498	1.5668
0.409	1.3878	0.454	1.4787	0.499	1.5688

Transformation of a Proportion p to $\phi = 2$ arcsin $\sqrt{p}$ (cont.)

p	ϕ	p	ϕ	p	ϕ
0.500	1.5708	0.545	1.6609	0.590	1.7518
0.501	1.5728	0.546	1.6629	0.591	1.7538
0.502	1.5748	0.547	1.6649	0.592	1.7559
0.503	1.5768	0.548	1.6669	0.593	1.7579
0.504	1.5788	0.549	1.6690	0.594	1.7599
0.505	1.5808	0.550	1.6710	0.595	1.7620
0.506	1.5828	0.551	1.6730	0.596	1.7640
0.507	1.5848	0.552	1.6750	0.597	1.7660
0.508	1.5868	0.553	1.6770	0.598	1.7681
0.509	1.5888	0.554	1.6790	0.599	1.7701
0.510	1.5908	0.555	1.6810	0.600	1.7722
0.511	1.5928	0.556	1.6830	0.601	1.7742
0.512	1.5948	0.557	1.6850	0.602	1.7762
0.513	1.5968	0.558	1.6871	0.603	1.7783
0.514	1.5988	0.559	1.6891	0.604	1.7803
0.515	1.6008	0.560	1.6911	0.605	1.7824
0.516	1.6028	0.561	1.6931	0.606	1.7844
0.517	1.6048	0.562	1.6951	0.607	1.7865
0.518	1.6068	0.563	1.6971	0.608	1.7885
0.519	1.6088	0.564	1.6991	0.609	1.7906
0.520	1.6108	0.565	1.7012	0.610	1.7926
0.521	1.6128	0.566	1.7032	0.611	1.7947
0.522	1.6148	0.567	1.7052	0.612	1.7967
0.523	1.6168	0.568	1.7072	0.613	1.7988
0.524	1.6188	0.569	1.7092	0.614	1.8008
0.525	1.6208	0.570	1.7113	0.615	1.8029
0.526	1.6228	0.571	1.7133	0.616	1.8049
0.527	1.6248	0.572	1.7153	0.617	1.8070
0.528	1.6268	0.573	1.7173	0.618	1.8090
0.529	1.6288	0.574	1.7193	0.619	1.8111
0.530	1.6308	0.575	1.7214	0.620	1.8132
0.531	1.6328	0.576	1.7234	0.621	1.8152
0.532	1.6348	0.577	1.7254	0.622	1.8173
0.533	1.6368	0.578	1.7274	0.623	1.8193
0.534	1.6388	0.579	1.7295	0.624	1.8214
0.535	1.6409	0.580	1.7315	0.625	1.8235
0.536	1.6429	0.581	1.7335	0.626	1.8255
0.537	1.6449	0.582	1.7355	0.627	1.8276
0.538	1.6469	0.583	1.7376	0.628	1.8297
0.539	1.6489	0.584	1.7396	0.629	1.8317
0.540	1.6509	0.585	1.7416	0.630	1.8338
0.541	1.6529	0.586	1.7437	0.631	1.8359
0.542	1.6549	0.587	1.7457	0.632	1.8380
0.543	1.6569	0.588	1.7477	0.633	1.8400
0.544	1.6589	0.589	1.7497	0.634	1.8421

Transformation of a Proportion p to $\phi = 2$ arcsin $\sqrt{p}$ (cont.)

p	ϕ	p	ϕ	p	ϕ
0.635	1.8442	0.680	1.9391	0.725	2.0376
0.636	1.8463	0.681	1.9412	0.726	2.0398
0.637	1.8483	0.682	1.9434	0.727	2.0420
0.638	1.8504	0.683	1.9455	0.728	2.0443
0.639	1.8525	0.684	1.9477	0.729	2.0465
0.640	1.8546	0.685	1.9498	0.730	2.0488
0.641	1.8567	0.686	1.9520	0.731	2.0510
0.642	1.8588	0.687	1.9541	0.732	2.0533
0.643	1.8608	0.688	1.9563	0.733	2.0556
0.644	1.8629	0.689	1.9584	0.734	2.0578
0.645	1.8650	0.690	1.9606	0.735	2.0601
0.646	1.8671	0.691	1.9628	0.736	2.0624
0.647	1.8692	0.692	1.9649	0.737	2.0646
0.648	1.8713	0.693	1.9671	0.738	2.0669
0.649	1.8734	0.694	1.9693	0.739	2.0692
0.650	1.8755	0.695	1.9714	0.740	2.0715
0.651	1.8776	0.696	1.9736	0.741	2.0737
0.652	1.8797	0.697	1.9758	0.742	2.0760
0.653	1.8818	0.698	1.9780	0.743	2.0783
0.654	1.8839	0.699	1.9801	0.744	2.0806
0.655	1.8860	0.700	1.9823	0.745	2.0829
0.656	1.8881	0.701	1.9845	0.746	2.0852
0.657	1.8902	0.702	1.9867	0.747	2.0875
0.658	1.8923	0.703	1.9889	0.748	2.0898
0.659	1.8944	0.704	1.9911	0.749	2.0921
0.660	1.8965	0.705	1.9933	0.750	2.0944
0.661	1.8986	0.706	1.9954	0.751	2.0967
0.662	1.9008	0.707	1.9976	0.752	2.0990
0.663	1.9029	0.708	1.9998	0.753	2.1013
0.664	1.9050	0.709	2.0020	0.754	2.1037
0.665	1.9071	0.710	2.0042	0.755	2.1060
0.666	1.9092	0.711	2.0064	0.756	2.1083
0.667	1.9113	0.712	2.0087	0.757	2.1106
0.668	1.9135	0.713	2.0109	0.758	2.1130
0.669	1.9156	0.714	2.0131	0.759	2.1153
0.670	1.9177	0.715	2.0153	0.760	2.1176
0.671	1.9198	0.716	2.0175	0.761	2.1200
0.672	1.9220	0.717	2.0197	0.762	2.1223
0.673	1.9241	0.718	2.0219	0.763	2.1247
0.674	1.9262	0.719	2.0242	0.764	2.1270
0.675	1.9284	0.720	2.0264	0.765	2.1294
0.676	1.9305	0.721	2.0286	0.766	2.1318
0.677	1.9326	0.722	2.0309	0.767	2.1341
0.678	1.9348	0.723	2.0331	0.768	2.1365
0.679	1.9369	0.724	2.0353	0.769	2.1389

Transformation of a Proportion p to $\phi = 2$ arcsin $\sqrt{p}$ (cont.)

p	ϕ	p	ϕ	p	ϕ
0.770	2.1412	0.815	2.2523	0.860	2.3746
0.771	2.1436	0.816	2.2549	0.861	2.3775
0.772	2.1460	0.817	2.2575	0.862	2.3804
0.773	2.1484	0.818	2.2601	0.863	2.3833
0.774	2.1508	0.819	2.2627	0.864	2.3862
0.775	2.1532	0.820	2.2653	0.865	2.3891
0.776	2.1556	0.821	2.2679	0.866	2.3920
0.777	2.1580	0.822	2.2705	0.867	2.3950
0.778	2.1604	0.823	2.2731	0.868	2.3979
0.779	2.1628	0.824	2.2758	0.869	2.4009
0.780	2.1652	0.825	2.2784	0.870	2.4039
0.781	2.1676	0.826	2.2810	0.871	2.4068
0.782	2.1700	0.827	2.2837	0.872	2.4098
0.783	2.1724	0.828	2.2863	0.873	2.4128
0.784	2.1749	0.829	2.2890	0.874	2.4158
0.785	2.1773	0.830	2.2916	0.875	2.4189
0.786	2.1797	0.831	2.2943	0.876	2.4219
0.787	2.1822	0.832	2.2970	0.877	2.4249
0.788	2.1846	0.833	2.2996	0.878	2.4280
0.789	2.1871	0.834	2.3023	0.879	2.4310
0.790	2.1895	0.835	2.3050	0.880	2.4341
0.791	2.1920	0.836	2.3077	0.881	2.4372
0.792	2.1944	0.837	2.3104	0.882	2.4403
0.793	2.1969	0.838	2.3131	0.883	2.4434
0.794	2.1994	0.839	2.3158	0.884	2.4465
0.795	2.2019	0.840	2.3186	0.885	2.4496
0.796	2.2043	0.841	2.3213	0.886	2.4528
0.797	2.2068	0.842	2.3240	0.887	2.4559
0.798	2.2093	0.843	2.3268	0.888	2.4591
0.799	2.2118	0.844	2.3295	0.889	2.4623
0.800	2.2143	0.845	2.3323	0.890	2.4655
0.801	2.2168	0.846	2.3351	0.891	2.4687
0.802	2.2193	0.847	2.3378	0.892	2.4719
0.803	2.2218	0.848	2.3406	0.893	2.4751
0.804	2.2243	0.849	2.3434	0.894	2.4784
0.805	2.2269	0.850	2.3462	0.895	2.4816
0.806	2.2294	0.851	2.3490	0.896	2.4849
0.807	2.2319	0.852	2.3518	0.897	2.4882
0.808	2.2345	0.853	2.3546	0.898	2.4915
0.809	2.2370	0.854	2.3575	0.899	2.4948
0.810	2.2395	0.855	2.3603	0.900	2.4981
0.811	2.2421	0.856	2.3631	0.901	2.5014
0.812	2.2446	0.857	2.3660	0.902	2.5048
0.813	2.2472	0.858	2.3689	0.903	2.5082
0.814	2.2498	0.859	2.3717	0.904	2.5115

Transformation of a Proportion p to $\phi = 2$ arcsin $\sqrt{p}$ (cont.)

p	ϕ	p	ϕ	p	ϕ
0.905	2.5149	0.950	2.6906	0.9950	3.0001
0.906	2.5184	0.951	2.6952	0.9955	3.0073
0.907	2.5218	0.952	2.6998	0.9956	3.0088
0.908	2.5253	0.953	2.7045	0.9957	3.0103
0.909	2.5287	0.954	2.7093	0.9958	3.0119
0.910	2.5322	0.955	2.7141	0.9959	3.0134
0.911	2.5357	0.956	2.7189	0.9960	3.0150
0.912	2.5392	0.957	2.7238	0.9961	3.0166
0.913	2.5428	0.958	2.7288	0.9962	3.0182
0.914	2.5463	0.959	2.7338	0.9963	3.0199
0.915	2.5499	0.960	2.7389	0.9964	3.0215
0.916	2.5535	0.961	2.7440	0.9965	3.0232
0.917	2.5571	0.962	2.7492	0.9966	3.0249
0.918	2.5607	0.963	2.7545	0.9967	3.0266
0.919	2.5644	0.964	2.7598	0.9968	3.0284
0.920	2.5681	0.965	2.7652	0.9969	3.0302
0.921	2.5718	0.966	2.7707	0.9970	3.0320
0.922	2.5755	0.967	2.7762	0.9971	3.0338
0.923	2.5792	0.968	2.7819	0.9972	3.0357
0.924	2.5830	0.969	2.7876	0.9973	3.0376
0.925	2.5868	0.970	2.7934	0.9974	3.0396
0.926	2.5906	0.971	2.7993	0.9975	3.0416
0.927	2.5944	0.972	2.8053	0.9976	3.0436
0.928	2.5983	0.973	2.8115	0.9977	3.0456
0.929	2.6022	0.974	2.8177	0.9978	3.0477
0.930	2.6061	0.975	2.8240	0.9979	3.0499
0.931	2.6100	0.976	2.8305	0.9980	3.0521
0.932	2.6140	0.977	2.8371	0.9981	3.0544
0.933	2.6179	0.978	2.8438	0.9982	3.0567
0.934	2.6220	0.979	2.8507	0.9983	3.0591
0.935	2.6260	0.980	2.8578	0.9984	3.0616
0.936	2.6301	0.981	2.8650	0.9985	3.0641
0.937	2.6342	0.982	2.8725	0.9986	3.0667
0.938	2.6383	0.983	2.8801	0.9987	3.0695
0.939	2.6425	0.984	2.8879	0.9988	3.0723
0.940	2.6467	0.985	2.8960	0.9989	3.0752
0.941	2.6509	0.986	2.9044	0.9990	3.0783
0.942	2.6551	0.987	2.9131	0.9991	3.0816
0.943	2.6594	0.988	2.9221	0.9992	3.0850
0.944	2.6638	0.989	2.9314	0.9993	3.0887
0.945	2.6681	0.990	2.9413	0.9994	3.0926
0.946	2.6725	0.991	2.9516	0.9995	3.0969
0.947	2.6770	0.992	2.9625	0.9996	3.1016
0.948	2.6815	0.993	2.9741	0.9997	3.1069
0.949	2.6860	0.994	2.9865	0.9998	3.1133

9.10 Inverse Hyperbolic Sine Transformation

The negative binomial probability distribution was defined in Section 9.5. The cumulative distribution function was described as the probability that $X + n$ independent repetitions, or less, will be needed of the simple alternative, with probability of success p and probability of failure $1 - p$, to achieve n successes. The mean of X is $n(1 - p)/p$, and the variance of X is $n(1 - p)/p^2$.

Beall [13] introduced a transformation which would give a new variable

$$z' = \frac{\text{arcsinh } \sqrt{nx}}{\sqrt{n}}.$$

This was modified by Anscombe [8] to

$$y = 2 \text{ arcsinh } \frac{\sqrt{x + \frac{3}{8}}}{\sqrt{n - \frac{3}{4}}}.$$

If one assumes that $n(1 - p)/p$ is large and $n > 2$, the variance of y is approximately $\psi'(n)$, where $\psi'(n)$ is the second derivative of $\log_e \Gamma(n)$ with respect to n. This is tabulated in Section 9.11. Laubscher [116] considers further modifications.

The quantity tabulated here is $\phi^* = 2 \text{ arcsinh } \sqrt{x}$, from which the above transformations may be computed.

Inverse Hyperbolic Sine Transformation

X	φ*	X	φ*	X	φ*
0.05	0.4436	2.05	2.3126	4.05	2.8984
0.10	0.6224	2.10	2.3324	4.10	2.9094
0.15	0.7564	2.15	2.3518	4.15	2.9203
0.20	0.8670	2.20	2.3709	4.20	2.9310
0.25	0.9624	2.25	2.3895	4.25	2.9417
0.30	1.0470	2.30	2.4078	4.30	2.9522
0.35	1.1232	2.35	2.4258	4.35	2.9626
0.40	1.1929	2.40	2.4435	4.40	2.9729
0.45	1.2572	2.45	2.4608	4.45	2.9831
0.50	1.3170	2.50	2.4779	4.50	2.9932
0.55	1.3729	2.55	2.4946	4.55	3.0032
0.60	1.4254	2.60	2.5111	4.60	3.0131
0.65	1.4750	2.65	2.5273	4.65	3.0229
0.70	1.5221	2.70	2.5433	4.70	3.0326
0.75	1.5668	2.75	2.5590	4.75	3.0422
0.80	1.6094	2.80	2.5744	4.80	3.0518
0.85	1.6502	2.85	2.5896	4.85	3.0612
0.90	1.6892	2.90	2.6046	4.90	3.0705
0.95	1.7267	2.95	2.6194	4.95	3.0798
1.00	1.7627	3.00	2.6339	5.00	3.0890
1.05	1.7975	3.05	2.6482	5.05	3.0981
1.10	1.8309	3.10	2.6624	5.10	3.1071
1.15	1.8633	3.15	2.6763	5.15	3.1160
1.20	1.8946	3.20	2.6900	5.20	3.1248
1.25	1.9248	3.25	2.7036	5.25	3.1336
1.30	1.9542	3.30	2.7169	5.30	3.1423
1.35	1.9827	3.35	2.7301	5.35	3.1509
1.40	2.0104	3.40	2.7431	5.40	3.1594
1.45	2.0373	3.45	2.7560	5.45	3.1679
1.50	2.0634	3.50	2.7687	5.50	3.1763
1.55	2.0889	3.55	2.7812	5.55	3.1846
1.60	2.1137	3.60	2.7935	5.60	3.1929
1.65	2.1380	3.65	2.8058	5.65	3.2011
1.70	2.1616	3.70	2.8178	5.70	3.2092
1.75	2.1846	3.75	2.8297	5.75	3.2173
1.80	2.2072	3.80	2.8415	5.80	3.2253
1.85	2.2292	3.85	2.8532	5.85	3.2332
1.90	2.2507	3.90	2.8647	5.90	3.2411
1.95	2.2718	3.95	2.8760	5.95	3.2489
2.00	2.2924	4.00	2.8873	6.00	3.2566

9.11 Values of ψ' for Use with the Inverse Hyperbolic Sine Transformation

The inverse hyperbolic sine transformation defined in Section 9.10 led to a variance approximately equal to $\psi'(n)$. The quantity $\psi'(n)$ is given by

$$\psi'(n) = \pi^2/6 - (1 + 1/2^2 + 1/3^2 + \cdots + 1/n^2).$$

This is given for $n = 1(1)120$ in the tables.

Values of ψ' for Use with the Inverse Hyperbolic Sine Transformation

n	$\psi'(n)$	n	$\psi'(n)$	n	$\psi'(n)$
1	0.644934	41	0.024095	81	0.012270
2	0.394934	42	0.023528	82	0.012121
3	0.283823	43	0.022987	83	0.011976
4	0.221323	44	0.022471	84	0.011834
5	0.181323	45	0.021977	85	0.011696
6	0.153545	46	0.021505	86	0.011561
7	0.133137	47	0.021052	87	0.011428
8	0.117512	48	0.020618	88	0.011299
9	0.105166	49	0.020201	89	0.011173
10	0.095166	50	0.019801	90	0.011050
11	0.086902	51	0.019417	91	0.010929
12	0.079957	52	0.019047	92	0.010811
13	0.074040	53	0.018691	93	0.010695
14	0.068938	54	0.018348	94	0.010582
15	0.064494	55	0.018018	95	0.010471
16	0.060588	56	0.017699	96	0.010363
17	0.057127	57	0.017391	97	0.010256
18	0.054041	58	0.017094	98	0.010152
19	0.051271	59	0.016806	99	0.010050
20	0.048771	60	0.016529	100	0.009950
21	0.046503	61	0.016260	101	0.009852
22	0.044437	62	0.016000	102	0.009756
23	0.042547	63	0.015748	103	0.009662
24	0.040811	64	0.015504	104	0.009569
25	0.039211	65	0.015267	105	0.009479
26	0.037731	66	0.015037	106	0.009390
27	0.036360	67	0.014815	107	0.009302
28	0.035084	68	0.014598	108	0.009217
29	0.033895	69	0.014388	109	0.009132
30	0.032784	70	0.014184	110	0.009050
31	0.031743	71	0.013986	111	0.008969
32	0.030767	72	0.013793	112	0.008889
33	0.029849	73	0.013605	113	0.008811
34	0.028983	74	0.013423	114	0.008734
35	0.028167	75	0.013245	115	0.008658
36	0.027396	76	0.013072	116	0.008584
37	0.026665	77	0.012903	117	0.008511
38	0.025973	78	0.012739	118	0.008439
39	0.025315	79	0.012578	119	0.008368
40	0.024690	80	0.012422	120	0.008299

9.12 Inverse of the Double Exponential Extreme Value Distribution

The quantity tabulated here is $y = -\log_e(-\log_e p)$. This is the inverse of the cumulative probability distribution function

$$p = \Pr\{Y \leq y\} = \exp(-e^{-y}),$$

where $-\infty < y < \infty$.

Let $f(X)$ be a continuous probability density function, and let $F(x)$ be the corresponding cumulative probability distribution function. Let a large value u of x be defined as the solution of

$$F(u) = 1 - 1/n,$$

where n is a positive integer, and let α be defined by

$$\alpha = nf(u).$$

Now consider the largest value of a sample of n observations, X_n, and assume that n is large and that the random variable X is unlimited in the direction of the largest value. Then the asymptotic cumulative probability distribution of X_n is given by

$$\Pr\{Y \leq y\} = \exp(-e^{-y}),$$

where $y = \alpha(x - u)$. If the original distribution $f(X)$ is known, then α and u are determined from the above equations. If $f(X)$ is unknown, then α and u are estimated from the largest values of N samples of size n. Gumbel [82] outlines the procedure. The National Bureau of Standards has prepared tables [149] similar to those given here and also tables of the cumulative distribution and density of this type of extreme value distribution. See Gumbel [82] for a discussion of other types of asymptotic extreme distributions.

Inverse of the Double Exponential
Extreme Value Distribution

p	x	p	x
0.0001	-2.2203	0.14	-0.6761
0.0002	-2.1421	0.15	-0.6403
0.0003	-2.0933	0.16	-0.6057
0.0004	-2.0572	0.17	-0.5721
0.0005	-2.0283	0.18	-0.5393
0.0006	-2.0040	0.19	-0.5073
0.0007	-1.9830	0.20	-0.4759
0.0008	-1.9644	0.21	-0.4451
0.0009	-1.9478	0.22	-0.4148
0.0010	-1.9326	0.23	-0.3850
0.0020	-1.8269	0.24	-0.3557
0.0030	-1.7594	0.25	-0.3266
0.0040	-1.7086	0.26	-0.2979
0.0050	-1.6674	0.27	-0.2695
0.0060	-1.6324	0.28	-0.2413
0.0070	-1.6018	0.29	-0.2134
0.0080	-1.5745	0.30	-0.1856
0.0090	-1.5498	0.31	-0.1580
0.0100	-1.5272	0.32	-0.1305
0.0150	-1.4350	0.33	-0.1032
0.0200	-1.3641	0.34	-0.0759
0.0250	-1.3053	0.35	-0.0486
0.0300	-1.2546	0.36	-0.0214
0.0350	-1.2097	0.37	0.0058
0.0400	-1.1690	0.38	0.0330
0.0450	-1.1318	0.39	0.0602
0.0500	-1.0972	0.40	0.0874
0.0550	-1.0649	0.41	0.1147
0.0600	-1.0344	0.42	0.1421
0.0650	-1.0055	0.43	0.1696
0.0700	-0.9780	0.44	0.1973
0.0750	-0.9518	0.45	0.2250
0.0800	-0.9265	0.46	0.2529
0.0850	-0.9022	0.47	0.2810
0.0900	-0.8788	0.48	0.3093
0.095	-0.8561	0.49	0.3378
0.100	-0.8340	0.50	0.3665
0.110	-0.7918	0.51	0.3955
0.120	-0.7515	0.52	0.4248
0.130	-0.7131	0.53	0.4543

9.12

Inverse of the Double Exponential
Extreme Value Distribution (cont.)

p	x	p	x
0.54	0.4842	0.920	2.4843
0.55	0.5144	0.925	2.5515
0.56	0.5450	0.930	2.6232
0.57	0.5760	0.935	2.7000
0.58	0.6075	0.940	2.7826
0.59	0.6394	0.945	2.8723
0.60	0.6717	0.950	2.9702
0.61	0.7046	0.955	3.0782
0.62	0.7381	0.960	3.1985
0.63	0.7721	0.965	3.3346
0.64	0.8068	0.970	3.4914
0.65	0.8422	0.975	3.6762
0.66	0.8782	0.980	3.9019
0.67	0.9151	0.985	4.1922
0.68	0.9528	0.990	4.6002
0.69	0.9914	0.9910	4.7060
0.70	1.0309	0.9920	4.8243
0.71	1.0715	0.9930	4.9583
0.72	1.1132	0.9940	5.1130
0.73	1.1561	0.9950	5.2958
0.74	1.2003	0.9960	5.5195
0.75	1.2459	0.9970	5.8076
0.76	1.2930	0.9980	6.2136
0.77	1.3418	0.9990	6.9073
0.78	1.3925	0.9991	7.0127
0.79	1.4451	0.9992	7.1305
0.80	1.4999	0.9993	7.2641
0.81	1.5572	0.9994	7.4183
0.82	1.6172	0.9995	7.6007
0.83	1.6802	0.9996	7.8239
0.84	1.7467	0.9997	8.1116
0.85	1.8170	0.9998	8.5171
0.86	1.8916	0.9999	9.2103
0.87	1.9714	0.99995	9.9035
0.88	2.0570	0.99999	11.5129
0.89	2.1496	0.999995	12.2061
0.90	2.2504	0.999999	13.8155
0.905	2.3044	0.9999995	14.5087
0.910	2.3612	0.9999999	16.1181
0.915	2.4210	0.99999995	16.8112

9.13 The Borel-Tanner Cumulative Distribution

In the theory of queues, the Borel-Tanner cumulative distribution gives the probability that X members, or fewer, of a queue will be served before the queue first vanishes. The queue starts out with r members and has a traffic intensity of α with Poisson arrivals and constant service time. Mathematically, the Borel-Tanner cumulative distribution function is given by

$$\Pr\{X \le x\} = \sum_{i=r}^{x} \frac{r}{(i-r)!} i^{i-r-1} \exp(-\alpha i) \alpha^{i-r},$$

where $(x = r, r+1, \ldots)$, $0 < \alpha < 1$, and $r = 1, 2, \ldots$. The tables given here were computed directly from this sum. Haight and Breuer [84] give a table which covers the cases for $r = 1$ and $\alpha = 0.01(0.01)0.62$. They also include some discussion of the properties of this distribution. The mean of X is $r/(1-\alpha)$, and the variance of X is $(\alpha r)/(1-\alpha)^3$.

The Borel-Tanner Cumulative Distribution

x	r = 1 α = 0.01	x	r = 2 α = 0.01	x	r = 3 α = 0.01	x	r = 4 α = 0.01	x	r = 5 α = 0.01
1	0.99005	2	0.98020	3	0.97045	4	0.96079	5	0.95123
2	0.99985	3	0.99961	4	0.99927	5	0.99884	6	0.99832
						6	0.99997	7	0.99995

x	α = 0.02	x	α = 0.02	x	α = 0.02	x	α = 0.02	x	α = 0.02
1	0.98020	2	0.96079	3	0.94176	4	0.92312	5	0.90484
2	0.99941	3	0.99846	4	0.99715	5	0.99550	6	0.99353
		4	0.99994	5	0.99987	6	0.99976	7	0.99961

x	α = 0.03	x	α = 0.03	x	α = 0.03	x	α = 0.03	x	α = 0.03
1	0.97045	2	0.94176	3	0.91393	4	0.88692	5	0.86071
2	0.99870	3	0.99660	4	0.99375	5	0.99021	6	0.98600
3	0.99993	4	0.99979	5	0.99956	6	0.99923	7	0.99877
								8	0.99990

x	α = 0.04	x	α = 0.04	x	α = 0.04	x	α = 0.04	x	α = 0.04
1	0.96079	2	0.92312	3	0.88692	4	0.85214	5	0.81873
2	0.99771	3	0.99407	4	0.98918	5	0.98314	6	0.97606
3	0.99984	4	0.99952	5	0.99900	6	0.99824	7	0.99722
						7	0.99982	8	0.99970

x	α = 0.05	x	α = 0.05	x	α = 0.05	x	α = 0.05	x	α = 0.05
1	0.95123	2	0.90484	3	0.86071	4	0.81873	5	0.77880
2	0.99647	3	0.99091	4	0.98352	5	0.97449	6	0.96401
3	0.99970	4	0.99910	5	0.99812	6	0.99672	7	0.99484
				6	0.99979	7	0.99959	8	0.99930

x	α = 0.06	x	α = 0.06	x	α = 0.06	x	α = 0.06	x	α = 0.06
1	0.94176	2	0.88692	3	0.83527	4	0.78663	5	0.74082
2	0.99498	3	0.98715	4	0.97686	5	0.96442	6	0.95012
3	0.99949	4	0.99848	5	0.99687	6	0.99456	7	0.99152
		5	0.99981	6	0.99958	7	0.99920	8	0.99864
								9	0.99979

The Borel-Tanner Cumulative Distribution (*cont.*)

r = 1 (cont)		r = 2 (cont)		r = 3 (cont)		r = 4 (cont)		r = 5 (cont)	
x	α = 0.07	x	α = 0.07	x	α = 0.07	x	α = 0.07	x	α = 0.07
1	0.93239	2	0.86936	3	0.81058	4	0.75578	5	0.70469
2	0.99325	3	0.98284	4	0.96930	5	0.95310	6	0.93465
3	0.99921	4	0.99765	5	0.99520	6	0.99173	7	0.98719
		5	0.99967	6	0.99925	7	0.99860	8	0.99764
						8	0.99977	9	0.99958
	α = 0.08		α = 0.08		α = 0.08		α = 0.08		α = 0.08
1	0.92312	2	0.85214	3	0.78663	4	0.72615	5	0.67032
2	0.99129	3	0.97800	4	0.96090	5	0.94065	6	0.91783
3	0.99884	4	0.99659	5	0.99308	6	0.98817	7	0.98181
4	0.99983	5	0.99945	6	0.99878	7	0.99773	8	0.99621
				7	0.99978	8	0.99957	9	0.99924
	α = 0.09		α = 0.09		α = 0.09		α = 0.09		α = 0.09
1	0.91393	2	0.83527	3	0.76338	4	0.69768	5	0.63763
2	0.98911	3	0.97268	4	0.95175	5	0.92722	6	0.89986
3	0.99838	4	0.99528	5	0.99049	6	0.98387	7	0.97536
4	0.99974	5	0.99916	6	0.99813	7	0.99655	8	0.99428
				7	0.99963	8	0.99927	9	0.99872
								10	0.99972
	α = 0.10		α = 0.10		α = 0.10		α = 0.10		α = 0.10
1	0.90484	2	0.81873	3	0.74082	4	0.67032	5	0.60653
2	0.98671	3	0.96689	4	0.94191	5	0.91293	6	0.88094
3	0.99782	4	0.99371	5	0.98740	6	0.97879	7	0.96784
4	0.99961	5	0.99876	6	0.99728	7	0.99501	8	0.99180
		6	0.99975	7	0.99941	8	0.99885	9	0.99798
						9	0.99973	10	0.99951
	α = 0.11		α = 0.11		α = 0.11		α = 0.11		α = 0.11
1	0.89583	2	0.80252	3	0.71892	4	0.64404	5	0.57695
2	0.98411	3	0.96068	4	0.93146	5	0.89789	6	0.86122
3	0.99716	4	0.99185	5	0.98381	6	0.97294	7	0.95926
4	0.99945	5	0.99825	6	0.99620	7	0.99307	8	0.98871
		6	0.99961	7	0.99910	8	0.99825	9	0.99697
						9	0.99956	10	0.99920

The Borel-Tanner Cumulative Distribution (cont.)

r = 1 (cont)		r = 2 (cont)		r = 3 (cont)		r = 4 (cont)		r = 5 (cont)	
x	α = 0.12	x	α = 0.12	x	α = 0.12	x	α = 0.12	x	α = 0.12
1	0.88692	2	0.78663	3	0.69768	4	0.61878	5	0.54881
2	0.98132	3	0.95407	4	0.92044	5	0.88221	6	0.84086
3	0.99639	4	0.98971	5	0.97971	6	0.96632	7	0.94965
4	0.99924	5	0.99761	6	0.99485	7	0.99069	8	0.98494
		6	0.99943	7	0.99869	8	0.99747	9	0.99564
				8	0.99966	9	0.99932	10	0.99876
								11	0.99965
	α = 0.13		α = 0.13		α = 0.13		α = 0.13		α = 0.13
1	0.87810	2	0.77105	3	0.67706	4	0.59452	5	0.52205
2	0.97833	3	0.94709	4	0.90892	5	0.86598	6	0.82001
3	0.99550	4	0.98728	5	0.97509	6	0.95895	7	0.93906
4	0.99898	5	0.99683	6	0.99322	7	0.98784	8	0.98047
5	0.99976	6	0.99919	7	0.99815	8	0.99645	9	0.99393
				8	0.99949	9	0.99897	10	0.99815
						10	0.99970	11	0.99944
	α = 0.14		α = 0.14		α = 0.14		α = 0.14		α = 0.14
1	0.86936	2	0.75578	3	0.65705	4	0.57121	5	0.49659
2	0.97517	3	0.93976	4	0.89695	5	0.84930	6	0.79878
3	0.99449	4	0.98454	5	0.96995	6	0.95084	7	0.92751
4	0.99866	5	0.99589	6	0.99128	7	0.98448	8	0.97526
5	0.99966	6	0.99888	7	0.99746	8	0.99517	9	0.99181
		7	0.99969	8	0.99925	9	0.99851	10	0.99734
						10	0.99954	11	0.99915
	α = 0.15		α = 0.15		α = 0.15		α = 0.15		α = 0.15
1	0.86071	2	0.74082	3	0.63763	4	0.54881	5	0.47237
2	0.97183	3	0.93211	4	0.88459	5	0.83223	6	0.77729
3	0.99335	4	0.98150	5	0.96431	6	0.94201	7	0.91508
4	0.99829	5	0.99479	6	0.98900	7	0.98059	8	0.96930
5	0.99954	6	0.99849	7	0.99660	8	0.99360	9	0.98923
		7	0.99955	8	0.99894	9	0.99790	10	0.99629
				9	0.99967	10	0.99931	11	0.99874
								12	0.99957

The Borel-Tanner Cumulative Distribution (*cont.*)

r = 1 (cont)		r = 2 (cont)		r = 3 (cont)		r = 4 (cont)		r = 5 (cont)	
x	α = 0.16	x	α = 0.16	x	α = 0.16	x	α = 0.16	x	α = 0.16
1	0.85214	2	0.72615	3	0.61878	4	0.52729	5	0.44933
2	0.96833	3	0.92416	4	0.87188	5	0.81486	6	0.75564
3	0.99209	4	0.97815	5	0.95815	6	0.93249	7	0.90182
4	0.99785	5	0.99349	6	0.98638	7	0.97614	8	0.96255
5	0.99938	6	0.99801	7	0.99555	8	0.99169	9	0.98614
		7	0.99938	8	0.99854	9	0.99713	10	0.99496
				9	0.99952	10	0.99901	11	0.99819
								12	0.99935

	α = 0.17		α = 0.17		α = 0.17		α = 0.17		α = 0.17
1	0.84366	2	0.71177	3	0.60050	4	0.50662	5	0.42741
2	0.96467	3	0.91594	4	0.85887	5	0.79726	6	0.73392
3	0.99070	4	0.97450	5	0.95151	6	0.92231	7	0.88778
4	0.99733	5	0.99200	6	0.98340	7	0.97114	8	0.95503
5	0.99919	6	0.99742	7	0.99430	8	0.98943	9	0.98250
		7	0.99915	8	0.99803	9	0.99615	10	0.99331
				9	0.99931	10	0.99860	11	0.99747
						11	0.99949	12	0.99905

	α = 0.18		α = 0.18		α = 0.18		α = 0.18		α = 0.18
1	0.83527	2	0.69768	3	0.58275	4	0.48675	5	0.40657
2	0.96085	3	0.90747	4	0.84559	5	0.77948	6	0.71221
3	0.98917	4	0.97055	5	0.94439	6	0.91152	7	0.87304
4	0.99674	5	0.99031	6	0.98004	7	0.96556	8	0.94673
5	0.99897	6	0.99672	7	0.99281	8	0.98678	9	0.97828
6	0.99966	7	0.99887	8	0.99739	9	0.99496	10	0.99130
		8	0.99960	9	0.99905	10	0.99808	11	0.99655
						11	0.99927	12	0.99864
								13	0.99947

	α = 0.19		α = 0.19		α = 0.19		α = 0.19		α = 0.19
1	0.82696	2	0.68386	3	0.56553	4	0.46767	5	0.38674
2	0.95689	3	0.89876	4	0.83210	5	0.76159	6	0.69057
3	0.98752	4	0.96629	5	0.93681	6	0.90014	7	0.85765
4	0.99607	5	0.98840	6	0.97629	7	0.95939	8	0.93766
5	0.99869	6	0.99590	7	0.99107	8	0.98372	9	0.97346
6	0.99955	7	0.99852	8	0.99661	9	0.99351	10	0.98889
		8	0.99946	9	0.99871	10	0.99742	11	0.99540
				10	0.99950	11	0.99897	12	0.99811
						12	0.99959	13	0.99922

The Borel-Tanner Cumulative Distribution (cont.)

	r = 1 (cont)		r = 2 (cont)		r = 3 (cont)		r = 4 (cont)		r = 5 (cont)
x	$\alpha = 0.20$	x	$\alpha = 0.20$	x	$\alpha = 0.20$	x	$\alpha = 0.20$	x	$\alpha = 0.20$
1	0.81873	2	0.67032	3	0.54881	4	0.44933	5	0.36788
2	0.95279	3	0.88984	4	0.81841	5	0.74363	6	0.66907
3	0.98572	4	0.96174	5	0.92877	6	0.88821	7	0.84169
4	0.99531	5	0.98626	6	0.97214	7	0.95265	8	0.92783
5	0.99837	6	0.99494	7	0.98906	8	0.98022	9	0.96800
6	0.99942	7	0.99809	8	0.99568	9	0.99178	10	0.98605
		8	0.99927	9	0.99828	10	0.99660	11	0.99398
				10	0.99931	11	0.99859	12	0.99742
						12	0.99942	13	0.99890
								14	0.99953
	$\alpha = 0.21$		$\alpha = 0.21$		$\alpha = 0.21$		$\alpha = 0.21$		$\alpha = 0.21$
1	0.81058	2	0.65705	3	0.53259	4	0.43171	5	0.34994
2	0.94856	3	0.88074	4	0.80457	5	0.72566	6	0.64777
3	0.98380	4	0.95689	5	0.92031	6	0.87577	7	0.82522
4	0.99446	5	0.98390	6	0.96760	7	0.94533	8	0.91727
5	0.99800	6	0.99383	7	0.98677	8	0.97626	9	0.96190
6	0.99925	7	0.99758	8	0.99456	9	0.98975	10	0.98273
		8	0.99904	9	0.99775	10	0.99558	11	0.99225
				10	0.99906	11	0.99810	12	0.99655
						12	0.99918	13	0.99847
								14	0.99932
	$\alpha = 0.22$		$\alpha = 0.22$		$\alpha = 0.22$		$\alpha = 0.22$		$\alpha = 0.22$
1	0.80252	2	0.64404	3	0.51685	4	0.41478	5	0.33287
2	0.94421	3	0.87145	4	0.79061	5	0.70771	6	0.62672
3	0.98173	4	0.95175	5	0.91144	6	0.86286	7	0.80830
4	0.99351	5	0.98129	6	0.96264	7	0.93743	8	0.90600
5	0.99757	6	0.99255	7	0.98417	8	0.97182	9	0.95513
6	0.99906	7	0.99698	8	0.99325	9	0.98738	10	0.97892
		8	0.99875	9	0.99710	10	0.99436	11	0.99019
		9	0.99948	10	0.99875	11	0.99748	12	0.99547
				11	0.99946	12	0.99887	13	0.99791
						13	0.99950	14	0.99904

The Borel-Tanner Cumulative Distribution (*cont.*)

r = 1 (cont)		r = 2 (cont)		r = 3 (cont)		r = 4 (cont)		r = 5 (cont)	
x	α = 0.23	x	α = 0.23	x	α = 0.23	x	α = 0.23	x	α = 0.23
1	0.79453	2	0.63128	3	0.50158	4	0.39852	5	0.31664
2	0.93973	3	0.86201	4	0.77655	5	0.68982	6	0.60595
3	0.97953	4	0.94634	5	0.90218	6	0.84953	7	0.79100
4	0.99246	5	0.97844	6	0.95728	7	0.92897	8	0.89406
5	0.99707	6	0.99111	7	0.98126	8	0.96690	9	0.94769
6	0.99882	7	0.99626	8	0.99173	9	0.98466	10	0.97457
7	0.99951	8	0.99840	9	0.99632	10	0.99291	11	0.98776
		9	0.99931	10	0.99836	11	0.99672	12	0.99415
				11	0.99926	12	0.99848	13	0.99721
						13	0.99930	14	0.99867
								15	0.99937

x	α = 0.24	x	α = 0.24	x	α = 0.24	x	α = 0.24	x	α = 0.24
1	0.78663	2	0.61878	3	0.48675	4	0.38289	5	0.30119
2	0.93514	3	0.85242	4	0.76244	5	0.67204	6	0.58551
3	0.97719	4	0.94064	5	0.89255	6	0.83580	7	0.77337
4	0.99131	5	0.97534	6	0.95151	7	0.91997	8	0.88146
5	0.99651	6	0.98949	7	0.97802	8	0.96147	9	0.93957
6	0.99855	7	0.99543	8	0.98997	9	0.98156	10	0.96967
7	0.99938	8	0.99798	9	0.99539	10	0.99119	11	0.98492
		9	0.99909	10	0.99787	11	0.99579	12	0.99255
				11	0.99901	12	0.99799	13	0.99633
						13	0.99904	14	0.99820
								15	0.99912

x	α = 0.25	x	α = 0.25	x	α = 0.25	x	α = 0.25	x	α = 0.25
1	0.77880	2	0.60653	3	0.47237	4	0.36788	5	0.28650
2	0.93043	3	0.84271	4	0.74828	5	0.65438	6	0.56542
3	0.97472	4	0.93468	5	0.88258	6	0.82173	7	0.75548
4	0.99005	5	0.97199	6	0.94533	7	0.91043	8	0.86826
5	0.99588	6	0.98768	7	0.97443	8	0.95554	9	0.93079
6	0.99823	7	0.99447	8	0.98797	9	0.97805	10	0.96419
7	0.99922	8	0.99748	9	0.99430	10	0.98918	11	0.98165
		9	0.99883	10	0.99728	11	0.99467	12	0.99065
		10	0.99945	11	0.99870	12	0.99737	13	0.99525
				12	0.99937	13	0.99870	14	0.99760
						14	0.99936	15	0.99878
								16	0.99938

10. NONPARAMETRIC TOLERANCE LIMITS

10.1 Sample Sizes for One-Sided Nonparametric Tolerance Limits

The quantity tabulated is that value of n such that

$$p^n \leq 1 - \gamma.$$

One finds frequent use for this function when deciding how large a sample is needed to be, say, 100γ percent sure that at least $100p$ percent of any population with a continuous cumulative distribution function lies above the smallest value in a random sample from that population. The quantity n given in the table is the required sample size. A similar statement concerning the largest sample value may also be made. The general procedure for nonparametric tolerance limits was derived by Wilks [246]. Note that in Section 9.6 the values of p which solve the equation $p = (1 - \gamma)^{1/n}$ may be obtained by putting $X = 0$ in the formulas of Section 9.6. In Section 10.2, $1 - (1 - \gamma)^{1/n}$ is tabulated.

Sample Sizes for One-Sided Nonparametric Tolerance Limits

$$p^n \leq 1 - \gamma$$

γ	p 0.500	0.700	0.750	0.800	0.850	0.900	0.950
0.500	1	2	3	4	5	7	14
0.700	2	4	5	6	8	12	24
0.750	3	4	5	7	9	14	28
0.800	3	5	6	8	10	16	32
0.850	3	6	7	9	12	19	37
0.900	4	7	9	11	15	22	45
0.950	5	9	11	14	19	29	59
0.975	6	11	13	17	23	36	72
0.980	6	11	14	18	25	38	77
0.990	7	13	17	21	29	44	90
0.995	8	15	19	24	33	51	104
0.999	10	20	25	31	43	66	135
0.9995	11	22	27	35	47	73	149
0.9999	14	26	33	42	57	88	180

γ	p 0.975	0.980	0.990	0.995	0.999	0.9995	0.9999
0.500	28	35	69	139	693	1386	6932
0.700	48	60	120	241	1204	2408	12040
0.750	55	69	138	277	1386	2772	13863
0.800	64	80	161	322	1609	3219	16094
0.850	75	94	189	379	1897	3794	18971
0.900	91	114	230	460	2302	4605	23025
0.950	119	149	299	598	2995	5990	29956
0.975	146	183	368	736	3688	7376	36887
0.980	155	194	390	781	3911	7823	39119
0.990	182	228	459	919	4603	9209	46050
0.995	210	263	528	1058	5296	10594	52981
0.999	273	342	688	1379	6905	13813	69075
0.9995	301	377	757	1517	7598	15199	76006
0.9999	364	456	917	1838	9206	18417	92099

10.2 Values of $1 - (1 - \gamma)^{1/n}$

The quantity tabulated is $1 - (1 - \gamma)^{1/n}$. This is useful when working with nonparametric tolerance limits (see Section 10.1), and when working with confidence limits on a proportion (see Section 9.6). It is also useful in dealing with the hypergeometric probability distribution (see Section 18.1). In [164] the following inequality is proved:

$$\frac{(N - k)!(N - n)!}{N!(N - k - n)!} \leq \left(1 - \frac{n}{N - \frac{k - 1}{2}}\right)^k.$$

If the quantity on the left is replaced by $1 - \gamma$, and the resulting inequality is solved for n, the result is

$$n \leq [1 - (1 - \gamma)^{1/k}]\left[N - \frac{k - 1}{2}\right].$$

This is a formula for minimum sample size when sampling from a hypergeometric distribution with the requirements that no defectives be found in the sample, and that it be 100γ percent certain that there are no more than k defectives in the lot of N items. Since n and k may be interchanged in the hypergeometric distribution,

$$k \leq [1 - (1 - \gamma)^{1/n}]\left[N - \frac{n - 1}{2}\right]$$

is a 100γ percent upper confidence limit on k, the number of defectives in the lot, if there are no defectives observed in the sample of n from the lot of N items.

Values of $1 - (1 - \gamma)^{1/n}$

n	0.75	0.90	0.95	0.99	n	0.75	0.90	0.95	0.99
1	0.7500	0.9000	0.9500	0.9900	45	0.0303	0.0499	0.0644	0.0973
2	0.5000	0.6838	0.7764	0.9000	50	0.0273	0.0450	0.0582	0.0880
3	0.3700	0.5358	0.6316	0.7846	55	0.0249	0.0410	0.0530	0.0803
4	0.2929	0.4377	0.5271	0.6838	60	0.0228	0.0376	0.0487	0.0739
5	0.2421	0.3690	0.4507	0.6019	65	0.0211	0.0348	0.0450	0.0684
6	0.2063	0.3187	0.3930	0.5358	70	0.0196	0.0324	0.0419	0.0637
7	0.1797	0.2803	0.3482	0.4821	75	0.0183	0.0302	0.0392	0.0596
8	0.1591	0.2501	0.3123	0.4377	80	0.0172	0.0284	0.0368	0.0559
9	0.1428	0.2257	0.2831	0.4005	85	0.0162	0.0267	0.0346	0.0527
10	0.1294	0.2057	0.2589	0.3690	90	0.0153	0.0253	0.0327	0.0499
11	0.1184	0.1889	0.2384	0.3421	95	0.0145	0.0239	0.0310	0.0473
12	0.1091	0.1746	0.2209	0.3187	100	0.0138	0.0228	0.0295	0.0450
13	0.1011	0.1623	0.2058	0.2983	105	0.0131	0.0217	0.0281	0.0429
14	0.0943	0.1517	0.1926	0.2803	110	0.0125	0.0207	0.0269	0.0410
15	0.0883	0.1423	0.1810	0.2644	115	0.0120	0.0198	0.0257	0.0393
16	0.0830	0.1340	0.1707	0.2501	120	0.0115	0.0190	0.0247	0.0376
17	0.0783	0.1267	0.1616	0.2373	125	0.0110	0.0183	0.0237	0.0362
18	0.0741	0.1201	0.1533	0.2257	130	0.0106	0.0176	0.0228	0.0348
19	0.0704	0.1141	0.1459	0.2152	135	0.0102	0.0169	0.0219	0.0335
20	0.0670	0.1087	0.1391	0.2057	140	0.0099	0.0163	0.0212	0.0324
21	0.0639	0.1038	0.1329	0.1969	145	0.0095	0.0158	0.0204	0.0313
22	0.0611	0.0994	0.1273	0.1889	150	0.0092	0.0152	0.0198	0.0302
23	0.0585	0.0953	0.1221	0.1815	155	0.0089	0.0147	0.0191	0.0293
24	0.0561	0.0915	0.1173	0.1746	160	0.0086	0.0143	0.0185	0.0284
25	0.0539	0.0880	0.1129	0.1682	165	0.0084	0.0139	0.0180	0.0275
26	0.0519	0.0848	0.1088	0.1623	170	0.0081	0.0135	0.0175	0.0267
27	0.0500	0.0817	0.1050	0.1568	175	0.0079	0.0131	0.0170	0.0260
28	0.0483	0.0789	0.1015	0.1517	180	0.0077	0.0127	0.0165	0.0253
29	0.0467	0.0763	0.0981	0.1468	185	0.0075	0.0124	0.0161	0.0246
30	0.0452	0.0739	0.0950	0.1423	190	0.0073	0.0120	0.0156	0.0239
31	0.0437	0.0716	0.0921	0.1380	195	0.0071	0.0117	0.0152	0.0233
32	0.0424	0.0694	0.0894	0.1340	200	0.0069	0.0114	0.0149	0.0228
33	0.0411	0.0674	0.0868	0.1303	225	0.0061	0.0102	0.0132	0.0203
34	0.0400	0.0655	0.0843	0.1267	250	0.0055	0.0092	0.0119	0.0183
35	0.0388	0.0637	0.0820	0.1233	275	0.0050	0.0083	0.0108	0.0166
36	0.0378	0.0620	0.0798	0.1201	300	0.0046	0.0076	0.0099	0.0152
37	0.0368	0.0603	0.0778	0.1170	350	0.0040	0.0066	0.0085	0.0131
38	0.0358	0.0588	0.0758	0.1141	400	0.0035	0.0057	0.0075	0.0114
39	0.0349	0.0573	0.0739	0.1114	450	0.0031	0.0051	0.0066	0.0102
40	0.0341	0.0559	0.0722	0.1087	500	0.0028	0.0046	0.0060	0.0092

10.3 Sample Sizes for Two-Sided Nonparametric Tolerance Limits

The quantity tabulated is that value of n which satisfies

$$np^{n-1} - (n-1)p^n \leq 1 - \gamma.$$

This is useful for setting two-sided nonparametric tolerance limits based on the largest and smallest values in the sample. One can be 100γ percent sure that at least $100p$ percent of any population with a continuous cumulative distribution function lies between the extremes of a sample of size n randomly chosen from that population.

Sample Sizes for Two-Sided Nonparametric Tolerance Limits
$$np^{n-1} - (n-1)p^n \leq 1 - \gamma$$

γ	p						
	0.500	0.700	0.750	0.800	0.850	0.900	0.950
0.500	3	6	7	9	11	17	34
0.700	5	8	10	12	16	24	49
0.750	5	9	10	13	18	27	53
0.800	5	9	11	14	19	29	59
0.850	6	10	13	16	22	33	67
0.900	7	12	15	18	25	38	77
0.950	8	14	18	22	30	46	93
0.975	9	17	20	26	35	54	110
0.980	9	17	21	27	37	56	115
0.990	11	20	24	31	42	64	130
0.995	12	22	27	34	47	72	146
0.999	14	27	33	42	58	89	181
0.9995	15	29	36	46	63	96	196
0.9999	18	34	42	54	73	113	230

γ	p						
	0.975	0.980	0.990	0.995	0.999	0.9995	0.9999
0.500	67	84	168	336	1679	3357	16783
0.700	97	122	244	488	2439	4878	24392
0.750	107	134	269	538	2692	5385	26926
0.800	119	149	299	598	2994	5988	29943
0.850	134	168	337	674	3372	6744	33724
0.900	155	194	388	777	3889	7778	38896
0.950	188	236	473	947	4742	9486	47437
0.975	221	277	555	1113	5570	11141	55715
0.980	231	290	581	1165	5832	11666	58337
0.990	263	330	662	1325	6636	13274	66381
0.995	294	369	740	1483	7427	14858	74299
0.999	366	458	920	1843	9230	18463	92330
0.9995	396	496	996	1996	9995	19993	99983
0.9999	465	583	1171	2346	11751	23508	117559

10.4 Values of $\delta(\lambda, \gamma)$ for Determining Sample Sizes for the Birnbaum-McCarty Distribution-Free Upper Confidence Bound for $p = \Pr \{Y < X\}$

Birnbaum and McCarty [24] give a numerical procedure for computing the sample sizes needed for a confidence interval on $p = \Pr \{Y < X\}$ with given width and confidence level where X and Y are independent random variables with continuous cumulative distribution functions.

Let $X_{(1)} \leq X_{(2)} \leq \cdots \leq X_{(n)}$ be an ordered sample of X, and let $Y_{(1)} \leq Y_{(2)} \leq \cdots \leq Y_{(m)}$ be an ordered sample of Y. The Mann-Whitney statistic,

$$U = \text{number of pairs } (X_{(i)}, Y_{(k)}) \text{ such that } Y_{(k)} < X_{(i)}$$

and

$$\hat{p} = \frac{U}{mn},$$

is defined.

It is desired to find the values of m and n that will permit making a statement as follows:

$$\Pr \{p \leq \hat{p} + \epsilon\} \geq \gamma.$$

Actually, values of m and n are found which are upper bounds on the true m and n needed in order to make this probability statement.

To solve this problem, one first arrives at the ratio of m to $m + n$ based on economic considerations. The choice is arbitrary as far as the procedure given here is concerned. If $m = n$, the table in Section 10.5 is more convenient to use. The ratio $\lambda = m/(m + n)$ is computed, and a value of δ is obtained from the table. Then m and n may be computed from $m + n = \delta^2/\epsilon^2$ and λ. This solves the problem.

If the samples are already taken and γ is fixed, and it is desired to find ϵ, then $\epsilon = \delta/\sqrt{m + n}$. If the samples are already taken and ϵ is fixed, and it is desired to find γ, then one must inverse interpolate in the table for γ after entering with $\delta = \epsilon\sqrt{m + n}$ and λ.

**Values* of $\delta(\lambda, \gamma)$ for Determining Sample Sizes
for the Birnbaum-McCarty Distribution-Free
Upper Confidence Bound for $p = \text{Pr}\ \{Y < X\}$**

			λ		
γ	0.1	0.2	0.3	0.4	0.5
0.500	2.5309	2.0272	1.8335	1.7471	1.7218
0.700	3.1463	2.4842	2.2299	2.1166	2.0834
0.750	3.3321	2.6217	2.3486	2.2271	2.1915
0.800	3.5432	2.7778	2.4835	2.3524	2.3140
0.850	3.7947	2.9637	2.6439	2.5014	2.4596
0.900	4.1185	3.2028	2.8501	2.6929	2.6468
0.950	4.6115	3.5667	3.1641	2.9844	2.9317
0.975	5.0499	3.8904	3.4435	3.2440	3.1854
0.980	5.1820	3.9881	3.5278	3.3223	3.2620
0.990	5.5702	4.2749	3.7755	3.5526	3.4871
0.995	5.9301	4.5410	4.0055	3.7665	3.6963
0.999	6.6844	5.0990	4.4884	4.2160	4.1360
0.9995	6.9819	5.3194	4.6792	4.3937	4.3099
0.9999	7.6245	5.7956	5.0919	4.7783	4.6863

*Partially from [24].

10.5 Sample Sizes for the Birnbaum-McCarty Distribution-Free Upper Confidence Bound for $p = \Pr\{Y < X\}$ for Equal Size Samples

Everything is defined as in Section 10.4, except that $m = n$. The table gives an upper bound on the minimum value for n for which the statement

$$\Pr\{p \leq \hat{p} + \epsilon\} \geq \gamma$$

can be made, where $\hat{p}$ is computed from the sample as in Section 10.4, and ϵ and γ are predetermined constants with values strictly between zero and one.

Sample Sizes for the Birnbaum-McCarty Distribution-Free Upper Confidence Bound for $p = \Pr\{Y < X\}$ for Equal Size Samples

γ	0.50	0.30	0.25	0.20	0.15	0.10
0.500	6	17	24	38	66	149
0.700	9	25	35	55	97	218
0.750	10	27	39	61	107	241
0.800	11	30	43	67	119	268
0.850	13	34	49	76	135	303
0.900	15	39	57	88	156	351
0.950	18	48	69	108	191	430
0.975	21	57	82	127	226	508
0.980	22	60	86	134	237	533
0.990	25	68	98	152	271	608
0.995	28	76	110	171	304	684
0.999	35	96	137	214	381	856
0.9995	38	104	149	233	413	929
0.9999	44	123	176	275	489	1099

γ	0.05	0.025	0.02	0.01	0.005
0.500	593	2372	3706	14823	59292
0.700	869	3473	5426	21703	86812
0.750	961	3843	6004	24014	96054
0.800	1071	4284	6694	26773	107092
0.850	1210	4840	7563	30249	120993
0.900	1402	5605	8757	35028	140111
0.950	1719	6876	10744	42975	171898
0.975	2030	8118	12684	50734	202936
0.980	2129	8513	13301	53204	212813
0.990	2432	9728	15200	60800	243198
0.995	2733	10931	17079	68314	273253
0.999	3422	13686	21384	85533	342130
0.9995	3716	14861	23220	92877	371505
0.9999	4393	17570	27452	109808	439229

10.5

11. WILCOXON (MANN-WHITNEY) TESTS

11.1 Cumulative Probabilities for the Wilcoxon Matched Pair Signed Rank Test

Given a set of n pairs of observations, the differences $X_i - Y_i$ are computed. The differences $X_i - Y_i$ are then ranked according to their absolute values. After the ranking is completed, the sign of the difference is attached to the ranks. The sum of the positive ranks, T_n, is computed. Then Pr $\{T_n \leq a\}$ is the quantity given in the table. In this case, the hypothesis tested is that there is no difference between the distributions of X and Y, against the alternative that Pr $\{X > Y\} = b$, where $0 < b < 1$. If a is the value of T_n calculated from the sample, the hypothesis is rejected if Pr $\{T_n \leq a\} \geq 1 - \alpha$, where α is the significance level for the test. Obviously, a two-sided test can also be constructed using these tables.

Another use of the tables is in testing the hypothesis that a distribution is symmetric about a given value M. A random sample of size n is taken from the distribution, and each observation is decreased by M. Disregarding the signs of these differences, rank them from 1 to n. Then assign the sign of the difference to the ranks. The sum of the positive ranks is then treated as in the matched pair signed rank test above.

The cumulative frequencies were computed by the use of the recursion formula:

$$f(n, a) = f(n - 1, a) + f(n - 1, a - n),$$

where $f(n, 0) = 1$; $f(n, -\lambda) = 0$ if $\lambda > 0$; and if $a \geq n(n + 1)/2$, then $f(n, a) = f[n, n(n + 1)/2]$. These cumulative frequencies were then converted to probabilities by computing Pr $\{T_n \leq a\} = f(n, a)/2^n$. The results were rounded to three significant figures. If the fourth figure were a five and the sixth and beyond were zero, then the result was rounded to the nearest even number.

The mean of this distribution is $n(n + 1)/4$, and the variance is $n(2n + 1)(n + 1)/24$. Savage [193] gives a more general form of a nonparametric one-sample test which includes the Wilcoxon signed rank test as a special case.

Cumulative Probabilities for the Wilcoxon Matched Pair Signed Rank Test

$$\Pr\{T_n \le a\} = \text{tabled value}$$

a	n=3	4	5	6	7	8	9	10	11
0	.125	.062	.031	.016	.008	.004	.002$^-$	.001$^-$	.000$^-$
1	.250	.125	.062	.031	.016	.008	.004$^-$	.002$^-$	.001$^-$
2	.375	.188	.094	.047	.023	.012	.006$^-$	.003$^-$	.001$^+$
3	.625	.312	.156	.078	.039	.020	.010$^-$	.005$^-$	.002$^+$
4	.750	.438	.219	.109	.055	.027	.014	.007	.003$^+$
5	.875	.562	.312	.156	.078	.039	.020	.010$^-$	.005$^-$
6	1.000	.688	.406	.219	.109	.055	.027	.014	.007
7		.812	.500	.281	.148	.074	.037	.019	.009
8		.875	.594	.344	.188	.098	.049	.024	.012
9		.938	.688	.422	.234	.125	.064	.032	.016
10		1.000	.781	.500	.289	.156	.082	.042	.021
11			.844	.578	.344	.191	.102	.053	.027
12			.906	.656	.406	.230	.125	.065	.034
13			.938	.719	.469	.273	.150	.080	.042
14			.969	.781	.531	.320	.180	.097	.051
15			1.000	.844	.594	.371	.213	.116	.062
16				.891	.656	.422	.248	.138	.074
17				.922	.711	.473	.285	.161	.087
18				.953	.766	.527	.326	.188	.103
19				.969	.812	.578	.367	.216	.120
20				.984	.852	.629	.410	.246	.139
21				1.000	.891	.680	.455	.278	.160
22					.922	.727	.500	.312	.183
23					.945	.770	.545	.348	.207
24					.961	.809	.590	.385	.232
25					.977	.844	.633	.423	.260
26					.984	.875	.674	.461	.289
27					.992	.902	.715	.500	.319
28					1.000	.926	.752	.539	.350
29						.945	.787	.577	.382
30						.961	.820	.615	.416
31						.973	.850	.652	.449
32						.980	.875	.688	.483
33						.988	.898	.722	.517
34						.992	.918	.754	.551
35						.996	.936	.784	.584
36						1.000	.951	.812	.618
37							.963	.839	.650
38							.973	.862	.681
39							.980	.884	.711
40							.986	.903	.740
41							.990	.920	.768
42							.994	.935	.793
43							.996	.947	.817
44							.998	.958	.840
45							1.000	.968	.861

11.1

Cumulative Probabilities for the Wilcoxon
Matched Pair Signed Rank Test (cont.)

a	12	13	14	15	16	17	18	19	20
0	.000	.000	.000	.000	.000	.000	.000	.000	.000
1	.000	.000	.000	.000	.000	.000	.000	.000	.000
2	$.001^-$	.000	.000	.000	.000	.000	.000	.000	.000
3	$.001^+$	$.001^-$	.000	.000	.000	.000	.000	.000	.000
4	$.002^-$	$.001^-$	.000	.000	.000	.000	.000	.000	.000
5	$.002^+$	$.001^+$	$.001^-$	.000	.000	.000	.000	.000	.000
6	$.003^+$	$.002^-$	$.001^-$	.000	.000	.000	.000	.000	.000
7	$.005^-$	$.002^+$	$.001^+$	$.001^-$	.000	.000	.000	.000	.000
8	.006	$.003^+$	$.002^-$	$.001^-$	.000	.000	.000	.000	.000
9	.008	.004	$.002^+$	$.001^+$	$.001^-$	.000	.000	.000	.000
10	$.010^+$	$.005^+$	.003	$.001^+$	$.001^-$	.000	.000	.000	.000
11	.013	.007	.003	$.002^-$	$.001^-$	.000	.000	.000	.000
12	.017	.009	.004	$.002^+$	$.001^+$	.001	.000	.000	.000
13	.021	.011	$.005^+$	.003	$.001^+$	.001	.000	.000	.000
14	.026	.013	.007	.003	$.002^-$	$.001^-$	.000	.000	.000
15	.032	.016	.008	.004	$.002^+$	$.001^+$	.001	.000	.000
16	.039	.020	$.010^+$	$.005^+$	$.003^-$	$.001^+$	.001	.000	.000
17	.046	.024	.012	.006	$.003^+$	.002	$.001^-$	.000	.000
18	.055	.029	.015	.008	.004	$.002^-$	$.001^-$	.000	.000
19	.065	.034	.018	.009	$.005^-$	$.002^+$	$.001^+$	$.001^-$	.000
20	.076	.040	$.021^-$	.011	$.005^+$	.003	$.001^+$	$.001^-$	.000
21	.088	.047	$.025^-$	.013	.007	.003	$.002^-$	$.001^+$	$.000^-$
22	.102	.055	.029	.015	.008	.004	$.002^+$	$.001^+$	$.001^-$
23	.117	.064	.034	.018	.009	$.005^-$	$.002^+$	$.001^+$	$.001^-$
24	.133	.073	.039	.021	.011	$.005^+$	.003	$.001^+$	$.001^-$
25	.151	.084	.045	.024	.012	.006	.003	.002	$.001^-$
26	.170	.095	.052	.028	.014	.007	.004	$.002^-$	$.001^+$
27	.190	.108	.059	.032	.017	.009	.004	$.002^+$	$.001^+$
28	.212	.122	.068	.036	.019	$.010^+$	$.005^+$	.003	$.001^+$
29	.235	.137	.077	.042	.022	.012	.006	.003	$.002^-$
30	.259	.153	.086	.047	$.025^+$	.013	.007	.004	$.002^-$
31	.285	.170	.097	.053	.029	.015	.008	.004	$.002^+$
32	.311	.188	.108	.060	.033	.017	.009	$.005^-$	$.002^+$
33	.339	.207	.121	.068	.037	.020	$.010^+$	$.005^+$	.003
34	.367	.227	.134	.076	.042	.022	.012	.006	.003
35	.396	.249	.148	.084	.047	$.025^+$	.013	.007	.004
36	.425	.271	.163	.094	.052	.028	.015	.008	.004
37	.455	.294	.179	.104	.058	.032	.017	.009	$.005^-$
38	.485	.318	.195	.115	.065	.036	.019	$.010^+$	$.005^+$
39	.515	.342	.213	.126	.072	.040	.022	.011	.006
40	.545	.368	.232	.138	.080	.044	.024	.013	.007
41	.575	.393	.251	.151	.088	.049	.027	.014	.008
42	.604	.420	.271	.165	.096	.054	.030	.016	.009
43	.633	.446	.292	.180	.106	.060	.033	.018	$.010^-$
44	.661	.473	.313	.195	.116	.066	.037	.020	.011
45	.689	.500	.335	.211	.126	.073	.041	.022	.012

11.1

Cumulative Probabilities for the Wilcoxon
Matched Pair Signed Rank Test (cont.)

a	10	11	12	13	14	15	16	17	18	19	20
46	.976	.880	.715	.527	.357	.227	.137	.080	.045	.025	.013
47	.981	.897	.741	.554	.380	.244	.149	.087	.049	.027	.015
48	.986	.913	.765	.580	.404	.262	.161	.095	.054	.030	.016
49	.990	.926	.788	.607	.428	.281	.174	.103	.059	.033	.018
50	.993	.938	.810	.632	.452	.300	.188	.112	.065	.036	.020
51	.995	.949	.830	.658	.476	.319	.202	.122	.071	.040	.022
52	.997	.958	.849	.682	.500	.339	.217	.132	.077	.044	.024
53	.998	.966	.867	.706	.524	.360	.232	.142	.084	.048	.027
54	.999	.973	.883	.729	.548	.381	.248	.153	.091	.052	.029
55	1.000	.979	.898	.751	.572	.402	.264	.164	.098	.057	.032
56		.984	.912	.773	.596	.423	.281	.176	.106	.062	.035
57		.988	.924	.793	.620	.445	.298	.189	.114	.067	.038
58		.991	.935	.812	.643	.467	.316	.202	.123	.072	.041
59		.993	.945	.830	.665	.489	.334	.215	.132	.078	.045
60		.995	.954	.847	.687	.511	.353	.229	.142	.084	.049
61		.997	.961	.863	.708	.533	.372	.244	.152	.091	.053
62		.998	.968	.878	.729	.555	.391	.259	.162	.098	.057
63		.999	.974	.892	.749	.577	.410	.274	.173	.105	.062
64		.999	.979	.905	.768	.598	.430	.290	.185	.113	.066
65		1.000	.983	.916	.787	.619	.450	.306	.196	.121	.071
66		1.000	.987	.927	.805	.640	.470	.322	.209	.129	.077
67			.990	.936	.821	.661	.490	.339	.221	.138	.082
68			.992	.945	.837	.681	.510	.356	.234	.147	.088
69			.994	.953	.852	.700	.530	.373	.248	.156	.095
70			.995	.960	.866	.719	.550	.391	.261	.166	.101
71			.997	.966	.879	.738	.570	.409	.275	.176	.108
72			.998	.971	.892	.756	.590	.427	.290	.187	.115
73			.998	.976	.903	.773	.609	.445	.305	.198	.123
74			.999	.980	.914	.789	.628	.463	.320	.209	.131
75			.999	.984	.923	.805	.647	.482	.335	.221	.139
76			1.000	.987	.932	.820	.666	.500	.351	.233	.147
77			1.000	.989	.941	.835	.684	.518	.367	.245	.156
78			1.000	.991	.948	.849	.702	.537	.383	.258	.165
79				.993	.955	.862	.719	.555	.399	.271	.174
80				.995	.961	.874	.736	.573	.416	.284	.184
81				.996	.966	.885	.752	.591	.433	.297	.194
82				.997	.971	.896	.768	.609	.449	.311	.205
83				.998	.975	.906	.783	.627	.466	.325	.215
84				.998	.979	.916	.798	.644	.483	.340	.226
85				.999	.982	.924	.812	.661	.500	.354	.237
86				.999	.985	.932	.826	.678	.517	.369	.249
87				.999	.988	.940	.839	.694	.534	.384	.261
88				1.000	.990	.947	.851	.710	.551	.399	.273
89				1.000	.992	.953	.863	.726	.567	.414	.285
90				1.000	.993	.958	.874	.741	.584	.430	.298

11.1

Cumulative Probabilities for the Wilcoxon
Matched Pair Signed Rank Test (cont.)

a	13	14	15	16	17	18	19	20
91	1.000	.995	.964	.884	.756	.601	.445	.311
92		.996	.968	.894	.771	.617	.461	.324
93		.997	.972	.904	.785	.633	.476	.337
94		.997	.976	.912	.798	.649	.492	.351
95		.998	.979	.920	.811	.665	.508	.364
96		.998	.982	.928	.824	.680	.524	.378
97		.999	.985	.935	.836	.695	.539	.392
98		.999	.987	.942	.847	.710	.555	.406
99		.999	.989	.948	.858	.725	.570	.420
100		1.000	.991	.953	.868	.739	.586	.435
101		1.000	.992	.958	.878	.752	.601	.449
102		1.000	.994	.963	.888	.766	.616	.464
103		1.000	.995	.967	.897	.779	.631	.478
104		1.000	.996	.971	.905	.791	.646	.493
105		1.000	.997	.975	.913	.804	.660	.507
106			.997	.978	.920	.815	.675	.522
107			.998	.981	.927	.827	.689	.536
108			.998	.983	.934	.838	.703	.551
109			.999	.986	.940	.848	.716	.565
110			.999	.988	.946	.858	.729	.580
111			.999	.989	.951	.868	.742	.594
112			.999	.991	.956	.877	.755	.608
113			1.000	.992	.960	.886	.767	.622
114			1.000	.993	.964	.894	.779	.636
115			1.000	.995	.968	.902	.791	.649
116			1.000	.995	.972	.909	.802	.663
117			1.000	.996	.975	.916	.813	.676
118			1.000	.997	.978	.923	.824	.689
119			1.000	.997	.980	.929	.834	.702
120			1.000	.998	.983	.935	.844	.715
121				.998	.985	.941	.853	.727
122				.999	.987	.946	.862	.739
123				.999	.988	.951	.871	.751
124				.999	.990	.955	.879	.763
125				.999	.991	.959	.887	.774
126				.999	.993	.963	.895	.785
127				1.000	.994	.967	.902	.795
128				1.000	.995	.970	.909	.806
129				1.000	.995	.973	.916	.816
130				1.000	.996	.976	.922	.826
131				1.000	.997	.978	.928	.835
132				1.000	.997	.981	.933	.844
133				1.000	.998	.983	.938	.853
134				1.000	.998	.985	.943	.861
135				1.000	.998	.987	.948	.869

Cumulative Probabilities for the Wilcoxon
Matched Pair Signed Rank Test (cont.)

a	16	17	n 18	19	20
136	1.000	.999	.988	.952	.877
137		.999	.990	.956	.885
138		.999	.991	.960	.892
139		.999	.992	.964	.899
140		.999	.993	.967	.905
141		1.000	.994	.970	.912
142		1.000	.995	.973	.918
143		1.000	.996	.975	.923
144		1.000	.996	.978	.929
145		1.000	.997	.980	.934
146		1.000	.997	.982	.938
147		1.000	.998	.984	.943
148		1.000	.998	.986	.947
149		1.000	.998	.987	.951
150		1.000	.999	.989	.955
151		1.000	.999	.990	.959
152		1.000	.999	.991	.962
153		1.000	.999	.992	.965
154			.999	.993	.968
155			.999	.994	.971
156			1.000	.995	.973
157			1.000	.995	.976
158			1.000	.996	.978
159			1.000	.996	.980
160			1.000	.997	.982
161			1.000	.997	.984
162			1.000	.998	.985
163			1.000	.998	.987
164			1.000	.998	.988
165			1.000	.999	.989
166			1.000	.999	.990
167			1.000	.999	.991
168			1.000	.999	.992
169			1.000	.999	.993
170			1.000	.999	.994
171			1.000	1.000	.995
172				1.000	.995
173				1.000	.996
174				1.000	.996
175				1.000	.997
176				1.000	.997
177				1.000	.998
178				1.000	.998
179				1.000	.998
180				1.000	.998

11.1

11.2 Exact Cumulative Frequencies for the Wilcoxon (Mann-Whitney) Two-Sample Statistic

Let X and Y be independent random variables with continuous cumulative distribution functions. Let $X_{(1)} \leq X_{(2)} \leq \cdots \leq X_{(n)}$ be an ordered sample of X, and let $Y_{(1)} \leq Y_{(2)} \leq \cdots \leq Y_{(m)}$ be an ordered sample of Y. The Mann-Whitney statistic is defined as

$$U = \text{number of pairs } (X_{(i)}, Y_{(k)}) \text{ such that } Y_{(k)} < X_{(i)}.$$

Let $f(n, m, u)$ be the frequency with which the event $U \leq u$ occurs in samples of sizes m and n when all possible arrangements of the two samples are equally likely. Then it is easy to show from the recurrence relationship given by Mann and Whitney [131] that

$$f(n, m, u) = f(n - 1, m, u - m) + f(n, m - 1, u),$$

where

$$f(n, m, -\xi) = 0 \quad \text{for } \xi > 0,$$

and

$$f(n, m, 0) = 1, \quad f(n, 0, u) = 1, \quad \text{and} \quad f(n, m, u) = f(m, n, u).$$

The table given here was computed by using the recurrence relationship and the boundary conditions given above.

Now U ranges from 0 to nm, and there are $(n + m)!/(n!m!)$ possible ways for nm sample points to be arranged if the X's are not distinguished from one another and if the Y's are not distinguished from one another.

The U-statistic is used to test the hypothesis that the cumulative distribution function of the X's is equal to the cumulative distribution function of the Y's, against the alternative that the cumulative distribution function of the X's is larger than the cumulative distribution function of the Y's. The hypothesis is rejected if the value of U computed from a sample is less than u', where u' is obtained from the table so that

$$\Pr\{U \leq u'\} \leq \alpha.$$

In general, $\Pr\{U \leq u\} = [f(n, m, u)][m!n!]/[(m + n)!]$. The value of $(m + n)!/m!n!$ may be read directly from Table 11.2, since

$$f(n, m, mn) = \frac{(m + n)!}{m!n!}.$$

Wilcoxon [245] introduced the test described above and used the statistic T, which is the sum of the ranks of the Y's when the X's and Y's are ordered together. The relationship between U and T is

$$U = mn + \frac{m(m + 1)}{2} - T.$$

The Mann-Whitney statistic has been generalized by Whitney [244] to a bivariate case. Fix and Hodges [67] give a table of an auxiliary function from which the cumulative probabilities for the Mann-Whitney statistic may be computed, and in some cases to considerably higher values of m and n than are given here. The moments of U have been given by Mann and Whitney [131], and also considered by David [45]. Power of tests of this type have been considered by Tsao [224] and Sundrum [215], who also refer to work of others in this field. Dixon [54] also considers the power of this type of test and gives a bibliography. Birnbaum and Klose [23] give bounds for the variance of U. Kruskal [112] gives the history of the Wilcoxon-Mann-Whitney test. Savage [194] gives a bibliography on non-parametric statistics. Walsh [238] reviews the equivalence (or non-equivalence) of some of Walsh's [239] tests and Wilcoxon's tests. Putter [176] considers the effect of ties on the Wilcoxon two-sample test.

The following corrections to the table given by Auble [10] were made in the tables of Sections 11.4 and 11.5.

m	n	γ	Auble's value	Value here
3	9	0.05	3	4
3	9	0.95	24	23
3	19	0.99	52	53
4	20	0.025	13	14
4	20	0.975	67	66
14	2	0.05	2	3
14	2	0.95	26	25
14	17	0.025	67	69
14	17	0.975	171	169
17	19	0.99	234	235
13	19	0.005	56	57
13	19	0.995	191	190

In addition, the following corrections to the table of Siegel and Tukey [200] were made in the table of Section 11.5.

n_1	n_2	γ	Siegel & Tukey	Value here
1	20	0.95	20	21
6	13	0.999	95	94
10	18	0.95	178	180
13	18	0.001	130	133
20	20	1.00	610	611
15	18	0.05	206	208

Exact Cumulative Frequencies for the Wilcoxon
(Mann-Whitney) Two-Sample Statistic

n=1	
	m
u	1
0	1
1	2

n=2		
	m	
u	1	2
0	1	1
1	2	2
2	3	4
3		5
4	3	6

n=3			
	m		
u	1	2	3
0	1	1	1
1	2	2	2
2	3	4	4
3	4	6	7
4		8	10
5		9	13
6		10	16
7			18
8			19
9	4	10	20

n=4				
	m			
u	1	2	3	4
0	1	1	1	1
1	2	2	2	2
2	3	4	4	4
3	4	6	7	7
4	5	9	11	12
5		11	15	17
6		13	20	24
7		14	24	31
8		15	28	39
9			31	46
10			33	53
11			34	58
12			35	63
13				66
14				68
15				69
16	5	15	35	70

n=5					
	m				
u	1	2	3	4	5
0	1	1	1	1	1
1	2	2	2	2	2
2	3	4	4	4	4
3	4	6	7	7	7
4	5	9	11	12	12
5	6	12	16	18	19
6		15	22	26	28
7		17	28	35	39
8		19	34	46	53
9		20	40	57	69
10		21	45	69	87
11			49	80	106
12			52	91	126
13			54	100	146
14			55	108	165
15			56	114	183
16				119	199
17				122	213
18				124	224
19				125	233
20				126	240
21					245
22					248
23					250
24					251
25	6	21	56	126	252

11.2

Exact Cumulative Frequencies for the Wilcoxon (Mann-Whitney) Two-Sample Statistic (cont.)

n=6

u	m=1	2	3	4	5	6
0	1	1	1	1	1	1
1	2	2	2	2	2	2
2	3	4	4	4	4	4
3	4	6	7	7	7	7
4	5	9	11	12	12	12
5	6	12	16	18	19	19
6	7	16	23	27	29	30
7		19	30	37	41	43
8		22	38	50	57	61
9		24	46	64	76	83
10		26	54	80	99	111
11		27	61	96	124	143
12		28	68	114	153	182
13			73	130	183	224
14			77	146	215	272
15			80	160	247	323
16			82	173	279	378
17			83	183	309	433
18			84	192	338	491
19				198	363	546
20				203	386	601
21				206	405	652
22				208	421	700
23				209	433	742
24				210	443	781
25					450	813
26					455	841
27					458	863
28					460	881
29					461	894
30					462	905
31						912
32						917
33						920
34						922
35						923
36	7	28	84	210	462	924

n=7

u	m=1	2	3	4	5	6	7
0	1	1	1	1	1	1	1
1	2	2	2	2	2	2	2
2	3	4	4	4	4	4	4
3	4	6	7	7	7	7	7
4	5	9	11	12	12	12	12
5	6	12	16	18	19	19	19
6	7	16	23	27	29	30	30
7	8	20	31	38	42	44	45
8		24	40	52	59	63	65
9		27	50	68	80	87	91
10		30	60	87	106	118	125
11		32	70	107	136	155	167
12		34	80	130	171	201	220
13		35	89	153	210	253	283
14		36	97	177	253	314	358
15			104	200	299	382	445
16			109	223	347	458	545
17			113	243	396	539	657
18			116	262	445	627	782
19			118	278	493	717	918
20			119	292	539	811	1064
21			120	303	582	905	1219
22				312	621	999	1381
23				318	656	1089	1547
24				323	686	1177	1716
25				326	712	1258	1885
26				328	733	1334	2051
27				329	750	1402	2213
28				330	763	1463	2368
29					773	1515	2514
30					780	1561	2650
31					785	1598	2775
32					788	1629	2887
33					790	1653	2987
34					791	1672	3074
35					792	1686	3149
36						1697	3212
37						1704	3265
38						1709	3307
39						1712	3341
40						1714	3367
41						1715	3387
42						1716	3402
43							3413
44							3420
45							3425
46							3428
47							3430
48							3431
49	8	36	120	330	792	1716	3432

Exact Cumulative Frequencies for the Wilcoxon (Mann-Whitney) Two-Sample Statistic (cont.)

n=8

u	1	2	3	4	5	6	7	8
0	1	1	1	1	1	1	1	1
1	2	2	2	2	2	2	2	2
2	3	4	4	4	4	4	4	4
3	4	6	7	7	7	7	7	7
4	5	9	11	12	12	12	12	12
5	6	12	16	18	19	19	19	19
6	7	16	23	27	29	30	30	30
7	8	20	31	38	42	44	45	45
8	9	25	41	53	60	64	66	67
9		29	52	70	82	89	93	95
10		33	64	91	110	122	129	133
11		36	76	114	143	162	174	181
12		39	89	141	183	213	232	244
13		41	101	169	228	272	302	321
14		43	113	200	280	343	388	418
15		44	124	231	337	424	489	534
16		45	134	264	400	518	609	675
17			142	295	466	621	746	839
18			149	326	536	737	904	1033
19			154	354	607	860	1080	1254
20			158	381	680	994	1277	1509
21			161	404	751	1133	1491	1793
22			163	425	821	1279	1724	2112
23			164	442	887	1426	1971	2460
24			165	457	950	1577	2234	2843
25				468	1007	1724	2506	3252
26				477	1059	1870	2788	3692
27				483	1104	2009	3073	4153
28				488	1144	2143	3362	4639
29				491	1177	2266	3647	5138
30				493	1205	2382	3929	5653
31				494	1227	2485	4201	6172
32				495	1245	2579	4464	6698
33					1258	2660	4711	7217
34					1268	2731	4944	7732
35					1275	2790	5158	8231
36					1280	2841	5355	8717
37					1283	2881	5531	9178
38					1285	2914	5689	9618
39					1286	2939	5826	10027
40					1287	2959	5946	10410
41						2973	6047	10758
42						2984	6133	11077
43						2991	6203	11361
44						2996	6261	11616
45						2999	6306	11837
46						3001	6342	12031
47						3002	6369	12195
48						3003	6390	12336
49	9	45	165	495	1287	3003	6405	12452

Exact Cumulative Frequencies for the Wilcoxon (Mann-Whitney) Two-Sample Statistic (*cont.*)

n=8 (Cont)

u	1	2	3	4	5	6	7	8
50	9	45	165	495	1287	3003	6416	12549
51							6423	12626
52							6428	12689
53							6431	12737
54							6433	12775
55							6434	12803
56							6435	12825
57								12840
58								12851
59								12858
60								12863
61								12866
62								12868
63								12869
64	9	45	165	495	1287	3003	6435	12870

n=9

u	1	2	3	4	5	6	7	8	9
0	1	1	1	1	1	1	1	1	1
1	2	2	2	2	2	2	2	2	2
2	3	4	4	4	4	4	4	4	4
3	4	6	7	7	7	7	7	7	7
4	5	9	11	12	12	12	12	12	12
5	6	12	16	18	19	19	19	19	19
6	7	16	23	27	29	30	30	30	30
7	8	20	31	38	42	44	45	45	45
8	9	25	41	53	60	64	66	67	67
9	10	30	53	71	83	90	94	96	97
10		35	66	93	112	124	131	135	137
11		39	80	118	147	166	178	185	189
12		43	95	148	190	220	239	251	258
13		46	110	180	240	284	314	333	345
14		49	125	216	298	362	407	437	456
15		51	140	254	364	453	519	564	594
16		53	154	295	438	560	653	720	765
17		54	167	336	519	681	810	905	972
18		55	179	379	607	820	994	1127	1223
19			189	420	700	972	1204	1385	1520
20			197	461	798	1141	1443	1687	1872
21			204	499	899	1323	1711	2032	2283
22			209	535	1001	1519	2008	2426	2759
23			213	567	1103	1724	2333	2867	3304
24			216	597	1204	1941	2687	3362	3926
25			218	622	1302	2162	3066	3905	4625
26			219	644	1395	2389	3469	4502	5407
27			220	662	1483	2616	3893	5147	6274
28				677	1564	2843	4334	5843	7228
29	10	55	220	688	1638	3064	4788	6581	8268

Exact Cumulative Frequencies for the Wilcoxon
(Mann-Whitney) Two-Sample Statistic (*cont.*)

n=9 (Cont)

u	1	2	3	4	5	6	7	8	9
30	10	55	220	697	1704	3281	5252	7364	9396
31				703	1762	3486	5720	8180	10606
32				708	1812	3682	6188	9031	11898
33				711	1855	3864	6652	9904	13266
34				713	1890	4033	7106	10798	14703
35				714	1919	4185	7547	11700	16202
36				715	1942	4324	7971	12610	17757
37					1960	4445	8374	13512	19355
38					1973	4552	8753	14406	20987
39					1983	4643	9107	15279	22643
40					1990	4721	9432	16130	24310
41					1995	4785	9729	16946	25977
42					1998	4839	9997	17729	27633
43					2000	4881	10236	18467	29265
44					2001	4915	10446	19163	30863
45					2002	4941	10630	19808	32418
46						4961	10787	20405	33917
47						4975	10921	20948	35354
48						4986	11033	21443	36722
49						4993	11126	21884	38014
50						4998	11201	22278	39224
51						5001	11262	22623	40352
52						5003	11309	22925	41392
53						5004	11346	23183	42346
54						5005	11374	23405	43213
55							11395	23590	43995
56							11410	23746	44694
57							11421	23873	45316
58							11428	23977	45861
59							11433	24059	46337
60							11436	24125	46748
61							11438	24175	47100
62							11439	24214	47397
63							11440	24243	47648
64								24265	47855
65								24280	48026
66								24291	48164
67								24298	48275
68								24303	48362
69								24306	48431
70								24308	48483
71								24309	48523
72								24310	48553
73									48575
74									48590
75									48601
76									48608
77									48613
78									48616
79									48618
80									48619
81	10	55	220	715	2002	5005	11440	24310	48620

Exact Cumulative Frequencies for the Wilcoxon (Mann-Whitney) Two-Sample Statistic (cont.)

n=10

u	1	2	3	4	5	6	7	8	9	10
0	1	1	1	1	1	1	1	1	1	1
1	2	2	2	2	2	2	2	2	2	2
2	3	4	4	4	4	4	4	4	4	4
3	4	6	7	7	7	7	7	7	7	7
4	5	9	11	12	12	12	12	12	12	12
5	6	12	16	18	19	19	19	19	19	19
6	7	16	23	27	29	30	30	30	30	30
7	8	20	31	38	42	44	45	45	45	45
8	9	25	41	53	60	64	66	67	67	67
9	10	30	53	71	83	90	94	96	97	97
10	11	36	67	94	113	125	132	136	138	139
11		41	82	120	149	168	180	187	191	193
12		46	99	152	194	224	243	255	262	266
13		50	116	187	247	291	321	340	352	359
14		54	134	227	310	374	419	449	468	480
15		57	152	270	382	472	538	583	613	632
16		60	170	318	465	589	683	750	795	825
17		62	187	367	557	723	854	950	1017	1062
18		64	204	420	660	880	1058	1193	1290	1357
19		65	219	473	771	1055	1294	1479	1616	1713
20		66	233	528	892	1254	1568	1819	2008	2146
21			245	581	1019	1472	1879	2212	2470	2661
22			255	634	1153	1713	2232	2669	3014	3276
23			263	683	1290	1971	2624	3188	3644	3996
24			270	731	1431	2251	3061	3781	4375	4843
25			275	774	1572	2544	3538	4443	5208	5821
26			279	814	1713	2854	4058	5185	6157	6952
27			282	849	1850	3173	4616	6001	7224	8241
28			284	881	1984	3503	5214	6901	8421	9711
29			285	907	2111	3835	5843	7875	9747	11363
30			286	930	2232	4173	6506	8932	11215	13223
31				948	2343	4505	7192	10059	12818	15288
32				963	2446	4835	7901	11263	14567	17581
33				974	2538	5154	8623	12528	16454	20098
34				983	2621	5464	9357	13859	18484	22859
35				989	2693	5757	10091	15238	20645	25853
36				994	2756	6037	10825	16668	22942	29099
37				997	2809	6295	11547	18128	25356	32580
38				999	2854	6536	12256	19620	27888	36309
39				1000	2890	6754	12942	21122	30518	40265
40				1001	2920	6953	13605	22636	33242	44457
41					2943	7128	14234	24138	36036	48854
42					2961	7285	14832	25630	38896	53463
43					2974	7419	15390	27090	41793	58247
44					2984	7536	15910	28520	44722	63206
45					2991	7634	16387	29899	47656	68301
46					2996	7717	16824	31230	50585	73527
47					2999	7784	17216	32495	53482	78838
48					3001	7840	17569	33699	56342	84230
49					3002	7883	17880	34826	59136	89654
50	11	66	286	1001	3003	7918	18154	35883	61860	95102

11.2

Exact Cumulative Frequencies for the Wilcoxon
(Mann-Whitney) Two-Sample Statistic (*cont.*)

n=10 (Cont)

u	1	2	3	4	5	6	7	8	9	10
51	11	66	286	1001	3003	7944	18390	36857	64490	100526
52						7964	18594	37757	67022	105918
53						7978	18765	38573	69436	111229
54						7989	18910	39315	71733	116455
55						7996	19029	39977	73894	121550
56						8001	19127	40570	75924	126509
57						8004	19205	41089	77811	131293
58						8006	19268	41546	79560	135902
59						8007	19316	41939	81163	140299
60						8008	19354	42279	82631	144491
61							19382	42565	83957	148447
62							19403	42808	85154	152176
63							19418	43008	86221	155657
64							19429	43175	87170	158903
65							19436	43309	88003	161897
66							19441	43418	88734	164658
67							19444	43503	89364	167175
68							19446	43571	89908	169468
69							19447	43622	90370	171533
70							19448	43662	90762	173393
71								43691	91088	175045
72								43713	91361	176515
73								43728	91583	177804
74								43739	91765	178935
75								43746	91910	179913
76								43751	92026	180760
77								43754	92116	181480
78								43756	92187	182095
79								43757	92240	182610
80								43758	92281	183043
81									92311	183399
82									92333	183694
83									92348	183931
84									92359	184124
85									92366	184276
86									92371	184397
87									92374	184490
88									92376	184563
89									92377	184617
90									92378	184659
91										184689
92										184711
93										184726
94										184737
95										184744
96										184749
97										184752
98										184754
99										184755
100	11	66	286	1001	3003	8008	19448	43758	92378	184756

11.2

11.3 Cumulative Probability Distribution for the Wilcoxon (Mann-Whitney) Two-Sample Rank Test

This table was computed from Table 11.2 as follows:

$$\Pr \{U \leq u\} = f(n, m, u) \frac{m!n!}{(m + n)!},$$

where

$$U = mn + \frac{m(m + 1)}{2} - T,$$

and where T is the Wilcoxon statistic as defined in Section 11.2 and U is the Mann-Whitney statistic as defined also in Section 11.2. Critical values for T are given in Section 11.5.

Cumulative Probability Distribution for the Wilcoxon (Mann-Whitney) Two-Sample Rank Test

$$\Pr\{U \le u\} = \text{tabled value}$$

n = 1

u	m = 1
0	0.500
1	1.000

n = 2

u	1	2
0	0.333	0.167
1	0.667	0.333
2	1.000	0.667
3		0.833
4		1.000

n = 3

u	1	2	3
0	0.250	0.100	0.050
1	0.500	0.200	0.100
2	0.750	0.400	0.200
3	1.000	0.600	0.350
4		0.800	0.500
5		0.900	0.650
6		1.000	0.800
7			0.900
8			0.950
9			1.000

n = 4

u	1	2	3	4
0	0.200	0.067	0.029	0.014
1	0.400	0.133	0.057	0.029
2	0.600	0.267	0.114	0.057
3	0.800	0.400	0.200	0.100
4	1.000	0.600	0.314	0.171
5		0.733	0.429	0.243
6		0.867	0.571	0.343
7		0.933	0.686	0.443
8		1.000	0.800	0.557
9			0.886	0.657
10			0.943	0.757
11			0.971	0.829
12			1.000	0.900
13				0.943
14				0.971
15				0.986
16				1.000

n = 5

u	1	2	3	4	5
0	0.167	0.048	0.018	0.008	0.004
1	0.333	0.095	0.036	0.016	0.008
2	0.500	0.190	0.071	0.032	0.016
3	0.667	0.286	0.125	0.056	0.028
4	0.833	0.429	0.196	0.095	0.048
5	1.000	0.571	0.286	0.143	0.075
6		0.714	0.393	0.206	0.111
7		0.810	0.500	0.278	0.155
8		0.905	0.607	0.365	0.210
9		0.952	0.714	0.452	0.274
10		1.000	0.804	0.548	0.345
11			0.875	0.635	0.421
12			0.929	0.722	0.500
13			0.964	0.794	0.579
14			0.982	0.857	0.655
15			1.000	0.905	0.726
16				0.944	0.790
17				0.968	0.845
18				0.984	0.889
19				0.992	0.925
20				1.000	0.952
21					0.972
22					0.984
23					0.992
24					0.996
25					1.000

Cumulative Probability Distribution for the Wilcoxon (Mann-Whitney) Two-Sample Rank Test (cont.)

n = 6

u	m 1	2	3	4	5	6
0	0.143	0.036	0.012	0.005	0.002	0.001
1	0.286	0.071	0.024	0.010	0.004	0.002
2	0.429	0.143	0.048	0.019	0.009	0.004
3	0.571	0.214	0.083	0.033	0.015	0.008
4	0.714	0.321	0.131	0.057	0.026	0.013
5	0.857	0.429	0.190	0.086	0.041	0.021
6	1.000	0.571	0.274	0.129	0.063	0.032
7		0.679	0.357	0.176	0.089	0.047
8		0.786	0.452	0.238	0.123	0.066
9		0.857	0.548	0.305	0.165	0.090
10		0.929	0.643	0.381	0.214	0.120
11		0.964	0.726	0.457	0.268	0.155
12		1.000	0.810	0.543	0.331	0.197
13			0.869	0.619	0.396	0.242
14			0.917	0.695	0.465	0.294
15			0.952	0.762	0.535	0.350
16			0.976	0.824	0.604	0.409
17			0.988	0.871	0.669	0.469
18			1.000	0.914	0.732	0.531
19				0.943	0.786	0.591
20				0.967	0.835	0.650
21				0.981	0.877	0.706
22				0.990	0.911	0.758
23				0.995	0.937	0.803
24				1.000	0.959	0.845
25					0.974	0.880
26					0.985	0.910
27					0.991	0.934
28					0.996	0.953
29					0.998	0.968
30					1.000	0.979
31						0.987
32						0.992
33						0.996
34						0.998
35						0.999
						1.000

11.3

Cumulative Probability Distribution for the Wilcoxon (Mann-Whitney) Two-Sample Rank Test (cont.)

				n = 7			
				m			
u	1	2	3	4	5	6	7
0	0.125	0.028	0.008	0.003	0.001	0.001	0.000
1	0.250	0.056	0.017	0.006	0.003	0.001	0.001
2	0.375	0.111	0.033	0.012	0.005	0.002	0.001
3	0.500	0.167	0.058	0.021	0.009	0.004	0.002
4	0.625	0.250	0.092	0.036	0.015	0.007	0.003
5	0.750	0.333	0.133	0.055	0.024	0.011	0.006
6	0.875	0.444	0.192	0.082	0.037	0.017	0.009
7	1.000	0.556	0.258	0.115	0.053	0.026	0.013
8		0.667	0.333	0.158	0.074	0.037	0.019
9		0.750	0.417	0.206	0.101	0.051	0.027
10		0.833	0.500	0.264	0.134	0.069	0.036
11		0.889	0.583	0.324	0.172	0.090	0.049
12		0.944	0.667	0.394	0.216	0.117	0.064
13		0.972	0.742	0.464	0.265	0.147	0.082
14		1.000	0.808	0.536	0.319	0.183	0.104
15			0.867	0.606	0.378	0.223	0.130
16			0.908	0.676	0.438	0.267	0.159
17			0.942	0.736	0.500	0.314	0.191
18			0.967	0.794	0.562	0.365	0.228
19			0.983	0.842	0.622	0.418	0.267
20			0.992	0.885	0.681	0.473	0.310
21			1.000	0.918	0.735	0.527	0.355
22				0.945	0.784	0.582	0.402
23				0.964	0.828	0.635	0.451
24				0.979	0.866	0.686	0.500
25				0.988	0.899	0.733	0.549
26				0.994	0.926	0.777	0.598
27				0.997	0.947	0.817	0.645
28				1.000	0.963	0.853	0.690
29					0.976	0.883	0.733
30					0.985	0.910	0.772
31					0.991	0.931	0.809
32					0.995	0.949	0.841
33					0.997	0.963	0.870
34					0.999	0.974	0.896
35					1.000	0.983	0.918
36						0.989	0.936
37						0.993	0.951
38						0.996	0.964
39						0.998	0.973
40						0.999	0.981
41						0.999	0.987
42						1.000	0.991
43							0.994
44							0.997
45							0.998
46							0.999
47							0.999
48							1.000
49							1.000

Cumulative Probability Distribution for the Wilcoxon
(Mann-Whitney) Two-Sample Rank Test (cont.)

n = 8

u	1	2	3	4	5	6	7	8
0	0.111	0.022	0.006	0.002	0.001	0.000	0.000	0.000
1	0.222	0.044	0.012	0.004	0.002	0.001	0.000	0.000
2	0.333	0.089	0.024	0.008	0.003	0.001	0.001	0.000
3	0.444	0.133	0.042	0.014	0.005	0.002	0.001	0.001
4	0.556	0.200	0.067	0.024	0.009	0.004	0.002	0.001
5	0.667	0.267	0.097	0.036	0.015	0.006	0.003	0.001
6	0.778	0.356	0.139	0.055	0.023	0.010	0.005	0.002
7	0.889	0.444	0.188	0.077	0.033	0.015	0.007	0.003
8	1.000	0.556	0.248	0.107	0.047	0.021	0.010	0.005
9		0.644	0.315	0.141	0.064	0.030	0.014	0.007
10		0.733	0.388	0.184	0.085	0.041	0.020	0.010
11		0.800	0.461	0.230	0.111	0.054	0.027	0.014
12		0.867	0.539	0.285	0.142	0.071	0.036	0.019
13		0.911	0.612	0.341	0.177	0.091	0.047	0.025
14		0.956	0.685	0.404	0.218	0.114	0.060	0.032
15		0.978	0.752	0.467	0.262	0.141	0.076	0.041
16		1.000	0.812	0.533	0.311	0.172	0.095	0.052
17			0.861	0.596	0.362	0.207	0.116	0.065
18			0.903	0.659	0.416	0.245	0.140	0.080
19			0.933	0.715	0.472	0.286	0.168	0.097
20			0.958	0.770	0.528	0.331	0.198	0.117
21			0.976	0.816	0.584	0.377	0.232	0.139
22			0.988	0.859	0.638	0.426	0.268	0.164
23			0.994	0.893	0.689	0.475	0.306	0.191
24			1.000	0.923	0.738	0.525	0.347	0.221
25				0.945	0.782	0.574	0.389	0.253
26				0.964	0.823	0.623	0.433	0.287
27				0.976	0.858	0.669	0.478	0.323
28				0.986	0.889	0.714	0.522	0.360
29				0.992	0.915	0.755	0.567	0.399
30				0.996	0.936	0.793	0.611	0.439
31				0.998	0.953	0.828	0.653	0.480
32				1.000	0.967	0.859	0.694	0.520
33					0.977	0.886	0.732	0.561
34					0.985	0.909	0.768	0.601
35					0.991	0.929	0.802	0.640
36					0.995	0.946	0.832	0.677
37					0.997	0.959	0.860	0.713
38					0.998	0.970	0.884	0.747
39					0.999	0.979	0.905	0.779
40					1.000	0.985	0.924	0.809
41						0.990	0.940	0.836
42						0.994	0.953	0.861
43						0.996	0.964	0.883
44						0.998	0.973	0.903
45						0.999	0.980	0.920
46						0.999	0.986	0.935
47						1.000	0.990	0.948
48						1.000	0.993	0.959
49							0.995	0.968

11.3

Cumulative Probability Distribution for the Wilcoxon (Mann-Whitney) Two-Sample Rank Test (cont.)

n = 8 (Cont)

u	1	2	3	4	5	6	7	8
50							0.997	0.975
51							0.998	0.981
52							0.999	0.986
53							0.999	0.990
54							1.000	0.993
55							1.000	0.995
56							1.000	0.997
57								0.998
58								0.999
59								0.999
60								0.999
61								1.000
62								1.000
63								1.000
64								1.000

n = 9

u	1	2	3	4	5	6	7	8	9
0	0.100	0.018	0.005	0.001	0.000	0.000	0.000	0.000	0.000
1	0.200	0.036	0.009	0.003	0.001	0.000	0.000	0.000	0.000
2	0.300	0.073	0.018	0.006	0.002	0.001	0.000	0.000	0.000
3	0.400	0.109	0.032	0.010	0.003	0.001	0.001	0.000	0.000
4	0.500	0.164	0.050	0.017	0.006	0.002	0.001	0.000	0.000
5	0.600	0.218	0.073	0.025	0.009	0.004	0.002	0.001	0.000
6	0.700	0.291	0.105	0.038	0.014	0.006	0.003	0.001	0.001
7	0.800	0.364	0.141	0.053	0.021	0.009	0.004	0.002	0.001
8	0.900	0.455	0.186	0.074	0.030	0.013	0.006	0.003	0.001
9	1.000	0.545	0.241	0.099	0.041	0.018	0.008	0.004	0.002
10		0.636	0.300	0.130	0.056	0.025	0.011	0.006	0.003
11		0.709	0.364	0.165	0.073	0.033	0.016	0.008	0.004
12		0.782	0.432	0.207	0.095	0.044	0.021	0.010	0.005
13		0.836	0.500	0.252	0.120	0.057	0.027	0.014	0.007
14		0.891	0.568	0.302	0.149	0.072	0.036	0.018	0.009
15		0.927	0.636	0.355	0.182	0.091	0.045	0.023	0.012
16		0.964	0.700	0.413	0.219	0.112	0.057	0.030	0.016
17		0.982	0.759	0.470	0.259	0.136	0.071	0.037	0.020
18		1.000	0.814	0.530	0.303	0.164	0.087	0.046	0.025
19			0.859	0.587	0.350	0.194	0.105	0.057	0.031
20			0.895	0.645	0.399	0.228	0.126	0.069	0.039
21			0.927	0.698	0.449	0.264	0.150	0.084	0.047
22			0.950	0.748	0.500	0.303	0.176	0.100	0.057
23			0.968	0.793	0.551	0.344	0.204	0.118	0.068
24			0.982	0.835	0.601	0.388	0.235	0.138	0.081
25			0.991	0.870	0.650	0.432	0.268	0.161	0.095
26			0.995	0.901	0.697	0.477	0.303	0.185	0.111
27			1.000	0.926	0.741	0.523	0.340	0.212	0.129
28				0.947	0.781	0.568	0.379	0.240	0.149
29				0.962	0.818	0.612	0.419	0.271	0.170

11.3

Cumulative Probability Distribution for the Wilcoxon
(Mann-Whitney) Two-Sample Rank Test (cont.)

n = 9 (Cont.)

u	1	2	3	4	5	6	7	8	9
30				0.975	0.851	0.656	0.459	0.303	0.193
31				0.983	0.880	0.697	0.500	0.336	0.218
32				0.990	0.905	0.736	0.541	0.371	0.245
33				0.994	0.927	0.772	0.581	0.407	0.273
34				0.997	0.944	0.806	0.621	0.444	0.302
35				0.999	0.959	0.836	0.660	0.481	0.333
36				1.000	0.970	0.864	0.697	0.519	0.365
37					0.979	0.888	0.732	0.556	0.398
38					0.986	0.909	0.765	0.593	0.432
39					0.991	0.928	0.796	0.629	0.466
40					0.994	0.943	0.824	0.664	0.500
41					0.997	0.956	0.850	0.697	0.534
42					0.998	0.967	0.874	0.729	0.568
43					0.999	0.975	0.895	0.760	0.602
44					1.000	0.982	0.913	0.788	0.635
45					1.000	0.987	0.929	0.815	0.667
46						0.991	0.943	0.839	0.698
47						0.994	0.955	0.862	0.727
48						0.996	0.964	0.882	0.755
49						0.998	0.973	0.900	0.782
50						0.999	0.979	0.916	0.807
51						0.999	0.984	0.931	0.830
52						1.000	0.989	0.943	0.851
53						1.000	0.992	0.954	0.871
54						1.000	0.994	0.963	0.889
55							0.996	0.970	0.905
56							0.997	0.977	0.919
57							0.998	0.982	0.932
58							0.999	0.986	0.943
59							0.999	0.990	0.953
60							1.000	0.992	0.961
61							1.000	0.994	0.969
62							1.000	0.996	0.975
63							1.000	0.997	0.980
64								0.998	0.984
65								0.999	0.988
66								0.999	0.991
67								1.000	0.993
68								1.000	0.995
69								1.000	0.996
70								1.000	0.997
71								1.000	0.998
72								1.000	0.999
73									0.999
74									0.999
75									1.000
76									1.000
77									1.000
78									1.000
79									1.000
80									1.000
81									1.000

Cumulative Probability Distribution for the Wilcoxon (Mann-Whitney) Two-Sample Rank Test (cont.)

n = 10

u	1	2	3	4	5	6	7	8	9	10
0	0.091	0.015	0.003	0.001	0.000	0.000	0.000	0.000	0.000	0.000
1	0.182	0.030	0.007	0.002	0.001	0.000	0.000	0.000	0.000	0.000
2	0.273	0.061	0.014	0.004	0.001	0.000	0.000	0.000	0.000	0.000
3	0.364	0.091	0.024	0.007	0.002	0.001	0.000	0.000	0.000	0.000
4	0.455	0.136	0.038	0.012	0.004	0.001	0.001	0.000	0.000	0.000
5	0.545	0.182	0.056	0.018	0.006	0.002	0.001	0.000	0.000	0.000
6	0.636	0.242	0.080	0.027	0.010	0.004	0.002	0.001	0.000	0.000
7	0.727	0.303	0.108	0.038	0.014	0.005	0.002	0.001	0.000	0.000
8	0.818	0.379	0.143	0.053	0.020	0.008	0.003	0.002	0.001	0.000
9	0.909	0.455	0.185	0.071	0.028	0.011	0.005	0.002	0.001	0.001
10	1.000	0.545	0.234	0.094	0.038	0.016	0.007	0.003	0.001	0.001
11		0.621	0.287	0.120	0.050	0.021	0.009	0.004	0.002	0.001
12		0.697	0.346	0.152	0.065	0.028	0.012	0.006	0.003	0.001
13		0.758	0.406	0.187	0.082	0.036	0.017	0.008	0.004	0.002
14		0.818	0.469	0.227	0.103	0.047	0.022	0.010	0.005	0.003
15		0.864	0.531	0.270	0.127	0.059	0.028	0.013	0.007	0.003
16		0.909	0.594	0.318	0.155	0.074	0.035	0.017	0.009	0.004
17		0.939	0.654	0.367	0.185	0.090	0.044	0.022	0.011	0.006
18		0.970	0.713	0.420	0.220	0.110	0.054	0.027	0.014	0.007
19		0.985	0.766	0.473	0.257	0.132	0.067	0.034	0.017	0.009
20		1.000	0.815	0.527	0.297	0.157	0.081	0.042	0.022	0.012
21			0.857	0.580	0.339	0.184	0.097	0.051	0.027	0.014
22			0.892	0.633	0.384	0.214	0.115	0.061	0.033	0.018
23			0.920	0.682	0.430	0.246	0.135	0.073	0.039	0.022
24			0.944	0.730	0.477	0.281	0.157	0.086	0.047	0.026
25			0.962	0.773	0.523	0.318	0.182	0.102	0.056	0.032
26			0.976	0.813	0.570	0.356	0.209	0.118	0.067	0.038
27			0.986	0.848	0.616	0.396	0.237	0.137	0.078	0.045
28			0.993	0.880	0.661	0.437	0.268	0.158	0.091	0.053
29			0.997	0.906	0.703	0.479	0.300	0.180	0.106	0.062
30			1.000	0.929	0.743	0.521	0.335	0.204	0.121	0.072
31				0.947	0.780	0.563	0.370	0.230	0.139	0.083
32				0.962	0.815	0.604	0.406	0.257	0.158	0.095
33				0.973	0.845	0.644	0.443	0.286	0.178	0.109
34				0.982	0.873	0.682	0.481	0.317	0.200	0.124
35				0.988	0.897	0.719	0.519	0.348	0.223	0.140
36				0.993	0.918	0.754	0.557	0.381	0.248	0.157
37				0.996	0.935	0.786	0.594	0.414	0.274	0.176
38				0.998	0.950	0.816	0.630	0.448	0.302	0.197
39				0.999	0.962	0.843	0.665	0.483	0.330	0.218
40				1.000	0.972	0.868	0.700	0.517	0.360	0.241
41					0.980	0.890	0.732	0.552	0.390	0.264
42					0.986	0.910	0.763	0.586	0.421	0.289
43					0.990	0.926	0.791	0.619	0.452	0.315
44					0.994	0.941	0.818	0.652	0.484	0.342
45					0.996	0.953	0.843	0.683	0.516	0.370
46					0.998	0.964	0.865	0.714	0.548	0.398
47					0.999	0.972	0.885	0.743	0.579	0.427
48					0.999	0.979	0.903	0.770	0.610	0.456
49					1.000	0.984	0.919	0.796	0.640	0.485

11.3

Cumulative Probability Distribution for the Wilcoxon
(Mann-Whitney) Two-Sample Rank Test (cont.)

n = 10 (Cont)

u	1	2	3	4	5	6	7	8	9	10
50					1.000	0.989	0.933	0.820	0.670	0.515
51						0.992	0.946	0.842	0.698	0.544
52						0.995	0.956	0.863	0.726	0.573
53						0.996	0.965	0.882	0.752	0.602
54						0.998	0.972	0.898	0.777	0.630
55						0.999	0.978	0.914	0.800	0.658
56						0.999	0.983	0.927	0.822	0.685
57						1.000	0.988	0.939	0.842	0.711
58						1.000	0.991	0.949	0.861	0.736
59						1.000	0.993	0.958	0.879	0.759
60						1.000	0.995	0.966	0.894	0.782
61							0.997	0.973	0.909	0.803
62							0.998	0.978	0.922	0.824
63							0.998	0.983	0.933	0.843
64							0.999	0.987	0.944	0.860
65							0.999	0.990	0.953	0.876
66							1.000	0.992	0.961	0.891
67							1.000	0.994	0.967	0.905
68							1.000	0.996	0.973	0.917
69							1.000	0.997	0.978	0.928
70							1.000	0.998	0.983	0.938
71								0.998	0.986	0.947
72								0.999	0.989	0.955
73								0.999	0.991	0.962
74								1.000	0.993	0.968
75								1.000	0.995	0.974
76								1.000	0.996	0.978
77								1.000	0.997	0.982
78								1.000	0.998	0.986
79								1.000	0.999	0.988
80								1.000	0.999	0.991
81									0.999	0.993
82									1.000	0.994
83									1.000	0.996
84									1.000	0.997
85									1.000	0.997
86									1.000	0.998
87									1.000	0.999
88									1.000	0.999
89									1.000	0.999
90									1.000	0.999
91										1.000
92										1.000
93										1.000
94										1.000
95										1.000
96										1.000
97										1.000
98										1.000
99										1.000
100										1.000

11.4 Critical Values for the Wilcoxon (Mann-Whitney) Two-Sample Statistic

The quantity in the table is that value of u such that $\Pr\{U \le u\} \le \gamma$ for $\gamma < 0.5$ and $\Pr\{U \ge u\} \le 1 - \gamma$ for $\gamma > 0.5$, where $\gamma = 0.001$, 0.005, 0.01, 0.025, 0.05, 0.10, 0.90, 0.95, 0.975, 0.99, 0.995, and 0.999. The random variable U is defined in Section 11.2. See Section 11.2 for corrections applied to the tables in [10].

Critical Values for the Wilcoxon
(Mann-Whitney) Two-Sample Statistic [10]

n	m	.001	.005	.01	.025	.05	.10	.90	.95	.975	.99	.995	.999
3	2	-	-	-	-	-	0	6	-	-	-	-	-
	3	-	-	-	-	0	1	8	9	-	-	-	-
4	2	-	-	-	-	-	0	8	-	-	-	-	-
	3	-	-	-	-	0	1	11	12	-	-	-	-
	4	-	-	-	0	1	3	13	15	16	-	-	-
5	2	-	-	-	-	0	1	9	10	-	-	-	-
	3	-	-	-	0	1	2	13	14	15	-	-	-
	4	-	-	0	1	2	4	16	18	19	20	-	-
	5	-	0	1	2	4	5	20	21	23	24	25	-
6	2	-	-	-	-	0	1	11	12	-	-	-	-
6	3	-	-	-	1	2	3	15	16	17	-	-	-
	4	-	0	1	2	3	5	19	21	22	23	24	-
	5	-	1	2	3	5	7	23	25	27	28	29	-
	6	-	2	3	5	7	9	27	29	31	33	34	-
7	2	-	-	-	-	0	1	13	14	-	-	-	-
7	3	-	-	0	1	2	4	17	19	20	21	-	-
	4	-	0	1	3	4	6	22	24	25	27	28	-
	5	-	1	3	5	6	8	27	29	30	32	34	-
	6	0	3	4	6	8	11	31	34	36	38	39	42
	7	1	4	6	8	11	13	36	38	41	43	45	48
8	2	-	-	-	0	1	2	14	15	16	-	-	-
	3	-	-	0	2	3	5	19	21	22	24	-	-
	4	-	1	2	4	5	7	25	27	28	30	31	-
	5	0	2	4	6	8	10	30	32	34	36	38	40
	6	1	4	6	8	10	13	35	38	40	42	44	47
8	7	2	6	7	10	13	16	40	43	46	49	50	54
	8	4	7	9	13	15	19	45	49	51	55	57	60
9	1	-	-	-	-	-	0	9	-	-	-	-	-
	2	-	-	-	0	1	2	16	17	18	-	-	-
	3	-	0	1	2	4	5	22	23	25	26	27	-
9	4	-	1	3	4	6	9	27	30	32	33	35	-
	5	1	3	5	7	9	12	33	36	38	40	42	44
	6	2	5	7	10	12	15	39	42	44	47	49	52
	7	3	7	9	12	15	18	45	48	51	54	56	60
	8	5	9	11	15	18	22	50	54	57	61	63	67
9	9	7	11	14	17	21	25	56	60	64	67	70	74
10	1	-	-	-	-	-	0	10	-	-	-	-	-
	2	-	-	-	0	1	3	17	19	20	-	-	-
	3	-	0	1	3	4	6	24	26	27	29	30	-
	4	0	2	3	5	7	10	30	33	35	37	38	40

one-tailed

Critical Values for the Wilcoxon
(Mann-Whitney) Two-Sample Statistic (cont.)

n	m	.001	.005	.01	.025	.05	.10	.90	.95	.975	.99	.995	.999
10	5	1	4	6	8	11	13	37	39	42	44	46	49
	6	3	6	8	11	14	17	43	46	49	52	54	57
	7	5	9	11	14	17	21	49	53	56	59	61	65
	8	6	11	13	17	20	24	56	60	63	67	69	74
	9	8	13	16	20	24	28	62	66	70	74	77	82
10	10	10	16	19	23	27	32	68	73	77	81	84	90
11	1	-	-	-	-	-	0	11	-	-	-	-	-
	2	-	-	-	0	1	3	19	21	22	-	-	-
	3	-	0	1	3	5	7	26	28	30	32	33	-
	4	0	2	4	6	8	11	33	36	38	40	42	44
11	5	2	5	7	9	12	15	40	43	46	48	50	53
	6	4	7	9	13	16	19	47	50	53	57	59	62
	7	6	10	12	16	19	23	54	58	61	65	67	71
	8	8	13	15	19	23	27	61	65	69	73	75	80
	9	10	16	18	23	27	31	68	72	76	81	83	89
11	10	12	18	22	26	31	36	74	79	84	88	92	98
	11	15	21	25	30	34	40	81	87	91	96	100	106
12	1	-	-	-	-	-	0	12	-	-	-	-	-
	2	-	-	-	1	2	4	20	22	23	-	-	-
	3	-	1	2	4	5	8	28	31	32	34	35	-
12	4	0	3	5	7	9	12	36	39	41	43	45	48
	5	2	6	8	11	13	17	43	47	49	52	54	58
	6	4	9	11	14	17	21	51	55	58	61	63	68
	7	7	12	14	18	21	26	58	63	66	70	72	77
	8	9	15	17	22	26	30	66	70	74	79	81	87
12	9	12	18	21	26	30	35	73	78	82	87	90	96
	10	14	21	24	29	34	39	81	86	91	96	99	106
	11	17	24	28	33	38	44	88	94	99	104	108	115
	12	20	27	31	37	42	49	95	102	107	113	117	124
13	1	-	-	-	-	-	0	13	-	-	-	-	-
13	2	-	-	0	1	2	4	22	24	25	26	-	-
	3	-	1	2	4	6	9	30	33	35	37	38	-
	4	1	3	5	8	10	13	39	42	44	47	49	51
	5	3	7	9	12	15	18	47	50	53	56	58	62
	6	5	10	12	16	19	23	55	59	62	66	68	73
13	7	8	13	16	20	24	28	63	67	71	75	78	83
	8	11	17	20	24	28	33	71	76	80	84	87	93
	9	14	20	23	28	33	38	79	84	89	94	97	103
	10	17	24	27	33	37	43	87	93	97	103	106	113
	11	20	27	31	37	42	48	95	101	106	112	116	123

11.4

Critical Values for the Wilcoxon
(Mann-Whitney) Two-Sample Statistic (cont.)

n	m	.001	.005	.01	.025	.05	.10	.90	.95	.975	.99	.995	.999
13	12	23	31	35	41	47	53	103	109	115	121	125	133
	13	26	34	39	45	51	58	111	118	124	130	135	143
14	1	-	-	-	-	-	0	14	-	-	-	-	-
	2	-	-	0	1	3	4	24	25	27	28	-	-
	3	-	1	2	5	7	10	32	35	37	40	41	-
14	4	1	4	6	9	11	15	41	45	47	50	52	55
	5	3	7	10	13	16	20	50	54	57	60	63	67
	6	6	11	13	17	21	25	59	63	67	71	73	78
	7	9	15	17	22	26	31	67	72	76	81	83	89
	8	12	18	22	26	31	36	76	81	86	90	94	100
14	9	15	22	26	31	36	41	85	90	95	100	104	111
	10	19	26	30	36	41	47	93	99	104	110	114	121
	11	22	30	34	40	46	52	102	108	114	120	124	132
	12	25	34	38	45	51	58	110	117	123	130	134	143
	13	29	38	43	50	56	63	119	126	132	139	144	153
14	14	32	42	47	55	61	69	127	135	141	149	154	164
15	1	-	-	-	-	-	0	15	-	-	-	-	-
	2	-	-	0	1	3	5	25	27	29	30	-	-
	3	-	2	3	5	7	10	35	38	40	42	43	-
	4	1	5	7	10	12	16	44	48	50	53	55	59
15	5	4	8	11	14	18	22	53	57	61	64	67	71
	6	7	12	15	19	23	27	63	67	71	75	78	83
	7	10	16	19	24	28	33	72	77	81	86	89	95
	8	14	20	24	29	33	39	81	87	91	96	100	106
	9	17	24	28	34	39	45	90	96	101	107	111	118
15	10	21	29	33	39	44	51	99	106	111	117	121	129
	11	24	33	37	44	50	57	108	115	121	128	132	141
	12	28	37	42	49	55	63	117	125	131	138	143	152
	13	32	42	47	54	61	68	127	134	141	148	153	163
	14	36	46	51	59	66	74	136	144	151	159	164	174
15	15	40	51	56	64	72	80	145	153	161	169	174	185
16	1	-	-	-	-	-	0	16	-	-	-	-	-
	2	-	-	0	1	3	5	27	29	31	32	-	-
	3	-	2	3	6	8	11	37	40	42	45	46	-
	4	2	5	7	11	14	17	47	50	53	57	59	62
16	5	5	9	12	15	19	23	57	61	65	68	71	75
	6	8	13	16	21	25	29	67	71	75	80	83	88
	7	11	18	21	26	30	36	76	82	86	91	94	101
	8	15	22	26	31	36	42	86	92	97	102	106	113
	9	19	27	31	37	42	48	96	102	107	113	117	125

Critical Values for the Wilcoxon
(Mann-Whitney) Two-Sample Statistic (cont.)

n	m	.001	.005	.01	.025	.05	.10	.90	.95	.975	.99	.995	.999
16	10	23	31	36	42	48	54	106	112	118	124	129	137
	11	27	36	41	47	54	61	115	122	129	135	140	149
	12	31	41	46	53	60	67	125	132	139	146	151	161
	13	35	45	51	59	65	74	134	143	149	157	163	173
	14	39	50	56	64	71	80	144	153	160	168	174	185
16	15	43	55	61	70	77	86	154	163	170	179	185	197
	16	48	60	66	75	83	93	163	173	181	190	196	208
17	1	-	-	-	-	-	0	17	-	-	-	-	-
	2	-	-	0	2	3	6	28	31	32	34	-	-
	3	0	2	4	6	9	12	39	42	45	47	49	51
17	4	2	6	8	11	15	18	50	53	57	60	62	66
	5	5	10	13	17	20	25	60	65	68	72	75	80
	6	9	15	18	22	26	31	71	76	80	84	87	93
	7	13	19	23	28	33	38	81	86	91	96	100	106
	8	17	24	28	34	39	45	91	97	102	108	112	119
17	9	21	29	33	39	45	52	101	108	114	120	124	132
	10	25	34	38	45	51	58	112	119	125	132	136	145
	11	29	39	44	51	57	65	122	130	136	143	148	158
	12	34	44	49	57	64	72	132	140	147	155	160	170
	13	38	49	55	63	70	79	142	151	158	166	172	183
17	14	43	54	60	69	77	85	153	161	169	178	184	195
	15	47	60	66	75	83	92	163	172	180	189	195	208
	16	52	65	71	81	89	99	173	183	191	201	207	220
	17	57	70	77	87	96	106	183	193	202	212	219	232
18	1	-	-	-	-	-	0	18	-	-	-	-	-
	2	-	-	0	2	4	6	30	32	34	36	-	-
	3	0	2	4	7	9	13	41	45	47	50	52	54
	4	3	6	9	12	16	20	52	56	60	63	66	69
	5	6	11	14	18	22	27	63	68	72	76	79	84
	6	10	16	19	24	28	34	74	80	84	89	92	98
18	7	14	21	24	30	35	41	85	91	96	102	105	112
	8	18	26	30	36	41	48	96	103	108	114	118	126
	9	23	31	36	42	48	55	107	114	120	126	131	139
	10	27	37	41	48	55	62	118	125	132	139	143	153
	11	32	42	47	55	61	69	129	137	143	151	156	166
18	12	37	47	53	61	68	77	139	148	155	163	169	179
	13	42	53	59	67	75	84	150	159	167	175	181	192
	14	46	58	65	74	82	91	161	170	178	187	194	206
	15	51	64	70	80	88	98	172	182	190	200	206	219
	16	56	70	76	86	95	106	182	193	202	212	218	232

11.4

Critical Values for the Wilcoxon
(Mann-Whitney) Two-Sample Statistic (cont.)

n	m	.001	.005	.01	.025	.05	.10	.90	.95	.975	.99	.995	.999
18	17	61	75	82	93	102	113	193	204	213	224	231	245
	18	66	81	88	99	109	120	204	215	225	236	243	258
19	1	-	-	-	-	0	1	18	19	-	-	-	-
	2	-	0	1	2	4	7	31	34	36	37	38	-
	3	0	3	4	7	10	14	43	47	50	53	54	57
19	4	3	7	9	13	17	21	55	59	63	67	69	73
	5	7	12	15	19	23	28	67	72	76	80	83	88
	6	11	17	20	25	30	36	78	84	89	94	97	103
	7	15	22	26	32	37	43	90	96	101	107	111	118
	8	20	28	32	38	44	51	101	108	114	120	124	132
19	9	25	33	38	45	51	58	113	120	126	133	138	146
	10	29	39	44	52	58	66	124	132	138	146	151	161
	11	34	45	50	58	65	73	136	144	151	159	164	175
	12	40	51	56	65	72	81	147	156	163	172	177	188
	13	45	57	63	72	80	89	158	167	175	184	190	202
19	14	50	63	69	78	87	97	169	179	188	197	203	216
	15	55	69	75	85	94	104	181	191	200	210	216	230
	16	60	74	82	92	101	112	192	203	212	222	230	244
	17	66	81	88	99	109	120	203	214	224	235	242	257
	18	71	87	94	106	116	128	214	226	236	248	255	271
19	19	77	93	101	113	123	135	226	238	248	260	268	284
20	1	-	-	-	-	0	1	19	20	-	-	-	-
	2	-	0	1	2	4	7	33	36	38	39	40	-
	3	0	3	5	8	11	15	45	49	52	55	57	60
	4	3	8	10	14	18	22	58	62	66	70	72	77
20	5	7	13	16	20	25	30	70	75	80	84	87	93
	6	12	18	22	27	32	38	82	88	93	98	102	108
	7	16	24	28	34	39	46	94	101	106	112	116	124
	8	21	30	34	41	47	54	106	113	119	126	130	139
	9	26	36	40	48	54	62	118	126	132	140	144	154
20	10	32	42	47	55	62	70	130	138	145	153	158	168
	11	37	48	53	62	69	78	142	151	158	167	172	183
	12	42	54	60	69	77	86	154	163	171	180	186	198
	13	48	60	67	76	84	94	166	176	184	193	200	212
	14	54	67	73	83	92	102	178	188	197	207	213	226
20	15	59	73	80	90	100	110	190	200	210	220	227	241
	16	65	79	87	98	107	119	201	213	222	233	241	255
	17	70	86	93	105	115	127	213	225	235	247	254	270
	18	76	92	100	112	123	135	225	237	248	260	268	284
	19	82	99	107	119	130	143	237	250	261	273	281	298
	20	88	105	114	127	138	151	249	262	273	286	295	312

11.5 Exact Critical Values for a Nonparametric Sum of Ranks Procedure for Relative Spread in Unpaired Samples (also Wilcoxon's Two-Sample Statistic)

Let X and Y'be independent random variables with continuous cumulative distribution functions. Random samples of n_1 X's and n_2 Y's are available. These two samples are then ordered from smallest to largest in one sequence. Assign Rank 1 to the lowest number in the sequence, Ranks 2 and 3 to the two highest numbers, Ranks 4 and 5 to the next two lowest, etc. (If the total number of observations is odd, the middlemost score is dropped—not assigned a rank—in order that the highest assigned rank will be even.) Next, the total of the ranks R_1 of the smallest group is computed. This statistic may be used to test the null hypothesis that two independent samples come from the same population against the alternative that the samples come from populations differing in variability. Low values of R_1 show greater spread for the first sample. The test has considerable power against the alternative of differing variability, but it is relatively insensitive to differing location.

The quantity tabulated is that value of r_1 such that

$$\Pr\{R_1 \leq r_1\} \leq \gamma \quad \text{for } \gamma < \tfrac{1}{2}$$

and

$$\Pr\{R_1 \geq r_1\} \leq 1 - \gamma \quad \text{for } \gamma > \tfrac{1}{2},$$

where $\gamma = 0$, 0.001, 0.005, 0.01, 0.025, 0.05, 0.10, 0.90, 0.95, 0.975, 0.99 0.995, 0.999, and 1.00.

The quantity tabulated is related to the Mann-Whitney U-statistic in the same way that the Wilcoxon T-statistic is related to U:

$$R = n_1 n_2 + \frac{n_1(n_1 + 1)}{2} - U.$$

In other words, R is exactly equivalent to T (under the null hypothesis), and the tables given here can be used also for finding significance levels of T. See Section 11.2 for corrections applied to the tables in [10] from which the tables in [200] were computed.

Exact Critical Values for a Nonparametric Sum of Ranks Procedure for Relative Spread in Unpaired Samples [200]

(Also Wilcoxon's Two-Sample Statistic)

$$n_1 = 1$$

n_2	0	.001	.005	.01	.025	.05	.10		.90	.95	.975	.99	.995	.999	1.00
≤ 8		(R$_1$	never	reaches	a	one-sided	10%	level	significance	for	$n_2 \leq 8$)				
9	0						1		10						11
10	0						1		11						12
11	0						1		12						13
12	0						1		13						14
13	0						1		14						15
14	0						1		15						16
15	0						1		16						17
16	0						1		17						18
17	0					-	1		18	-					19
18	0					-	1		19	-					20
19	0	-	-	-	-	1	2		19	20	-	-	-	-	21
20	0	-	-	-	-	1	2		20	21	-	-	-	-	22

$$n_1 = 2$$

n_2	0	.001	.005	.01	.025	.05	.10		.90	.95	.975	.99	.995	.999	1.00
2	2						-		-						8
3	2				-		3		9	-					10
4	2				-		3		11	-					12
5	2				3		4		12	13					14
6	2			-	3		4		14	15	-				16
7	2			-	3		4		16	17	-				18
8	2			3	4		5		17	18	19				20
9	2			3	4		5		19	20	21				22
10	2			3	4		6		20	22	23				24
11	2		-	3	4		6		22	24	25	-			26
12	2		-	4	5		7		23	25	26	-			28
13	2		3	4	5		7		25	27	28	29			30
14	2		3	4	6		7		27	28	30	31			32
15	2		3	4	6		8		28	30	32	33			34
16	2		3	4	6		8		30	32	34	35			36
17	2		-	3	5	6	9		31	34	35	37	-		38
18	2	-	-	3	5	7	9		33	35	37	39	-		40
19	2	-	3	4	5	7	10		34	37	39	40	41	-	42
20	2	-	3	4	5	7	10		36	39	41	42	43	-	44

Exact Critical Values for a Nonparametric Sum of Ranks Procedure for Relative Spread in Unpaired Samples (cont.)

$n_1 = 3$

n_2	0	.001	.005	.01	.025	.05	.10	.90	.95	.975	.99	.995	.999	1.00
3	5			-	6	7		14	15	-				16
4	5			-	6	7		17	18	-				19
5	5			-	6	7	8	19	20	21	-			22
6	5			-	7	8	9	21	22	23	-			25
7	5		-	6	7	8	10	23	25	26	27	-		28
8	5		-	6	8	9	11	25	27	28	30	-		31
9	5		6	7	8	10	11	28	29	31	32	33		34
10	5		6	7	9	10	12	30	32	33	35	36		37
11	5		6	7	9	11	13	32	34	36	38	39		40
12	5		7	8	10	11	14	34	37	38	40	41		43
13	5		7	8	10	12	15	36	39	41	43	44		46
14	5		7	8	11	13	16	38	41	43	46	47		49
15	5	-	8	9	11	13	16	41	44	46	48	49	-	52
16	5	-	8	9	12	14	17	43	46	48	51	52	-	55
17	5	6	8	10	12	15	18	45	48	51	53	55	57	58
18	5	6	8	10	13	15	19	47	51	53	56	58	60	61
19	5	6	9	10	13	16	20	49	53	56	59	60	63	64
20	5	6	9	11	14	17	21	51	55	58	61	63	66	67

$n_1 = 4$

n_2	0	.001	.005	.01	.025	.05	.10	.90	.95	.975	.99	.995	.999	1.00
4	9		-	-	10	11	13	23	25	26	-	-		27
5	9		-	10	11	12	14	26	28	29	30	-		31
6	9		10	11	12	13	15	29	31	32	33	34		35
7	9		10	11	13	14	16	32	34	35	37	38		39
8	9	-	11	12	14	15	17	35	37	38	40	41	-	43
9	9	-	11	13	14	16	19	37	40	42	43	45	-	47
10	9	10	12	13	15	17	20	40	43	45	47	48	50	51
11	9	10	12	14	16	18	21	43	46	48	50	52	54	55
12	9	10	13	15	17	19	22	46	49	51	53	55	58	59
13	9	11	13	15	18	20	23	49	52	54	57	59	61	63
14	9	11	14	16	19	21	25	51	55	57	60	62	65	67
15	9	11	15	17	20	22	26	54	58	60	63	65	69	71
16	9	12	15	17	21	24	27	57	60	63	67	69	72	75
17	9	12	16	18	21	25	28	60	63	67	70	72	76	79
18	9	13	16	19	22	26	30	62	66	70	73	76	79	83
19	9	13	17	19	23	27	31	65	69	73	77	79	83	87
20	9	13	18	20	24	28	32	68	72	76	80	82	87	91

11.5

Exact Critical Values for a Nonparametric Sum of Ranks Procedure for Relative Spread in Unpaired Samples (cont.)

$n_1 = 5$

n_2	0	.001	.005	.01	.025	.05	.10		.90	.95	.975	.99	.995	.999	1.00
5	14		15	16	17	19	20		35	36	38	39	40		41
6	14	-	16	17	18	20	22		38	40	42	43	44	-	46
7	14	-	16	18	20	21	23		42	44	45	47	49	-	51
8	14	15	17	19	21	23	25		45	47	49	51	53	55	56
9	14	16	18	20	22	24	27		48	51	53	55	57	59	61
10	14	16	19	21	23	26	28		52	54	57	59	61	64	66
11	14	17	20	22	24	27	30		55	58	61	63	65	68	71
12	14	17	21	23	26	28	32		58	62	64	67	69	73	76
13	14	18	22	24	27	30	33		62	65	68	71	73	77	81
14	14	18	22	25	28	31	35		65	69	72	75	78	82	86
15	14	19	23	26	29	33	37		68	72	76	79	82	86	91
16	14	20	24	27	30	34	38		72	76	80	83	86	90	96
17	14	20	25	28	32	35	40		75	80	83	87	90	95	101
18	14	21	26	29	33	37	42		78	83	87	91	94	99	106
19	14	22	27	30	34	38	43		82	87	91	95	98	103	111
20	14	22	28	31	35	40	45		85	90	95	99	102	108	116

$n_1 = 6$

n_2	0	.001	.005	.01	.025	.05	.10		.90	.95	.975	.99	.995	.999	1.00
6	20	-	23	24	26	28	30		48	50	52	54	55	-	58
7	20	21	24	25	27	29	32		52	55	57	59	60	63	64
8	20	22	25	27	29	31	34		56	59	61	63	65	68	70
9	20	23	26	28	31	33	36		60	63	65	68	70	73	76
10	20	24	27	29	32	35	38		64	67	70	73	75	78	82
11	20	25	28	30	34	37	40		68	71	74	78	80	83	88
12	20	25	30	32	35	38	42		72	76	79	82	84	89	94
13	20	26	31	33	37	40	44		76	80	83	87	89	94	100
14	20	27	32	34	38	42	46		80	84	88	92	94	99	106
15	20	28	33	36	40	44	48		84	88	92	96	99	104	112
16	20	29	34	37	42	46	50		88	92	96	101	104	109	118
17	20	30	36	39	43	47	52		92	97	101	105	108	114	124
18	20	31	37	40	45	49	55		95	101	105	110	113	119	130
19	20	32	38	41	46	51	57		99	105	110	115	118	124	136
20	20	33	39	43	48	53	59		103	109	114	119	123	129	142

11.5

Exact Critical Values for a Nonparametric Sum of Ranks
Procedure for Relative Spread in Unpaired Samples (cont.)

$$n_1 = 7$$

n_2	0	.001	.005	.01	.025	.05	.10		.90	.95	.975	.99	.995	.999	1.00
7	27	29	32	34	36	39	41		64	66	69	71	73	76	78
8	27	30	34	35	38	41	44		68	71	74	77	78	82	85
9	27	31	35	37	40	43	46		73	76	79	82	84	88	92
10	27	33	37	39	42	45	49		77	81	84	87	89	93	99
11	27	34	38	40	44	47	51		82	86	89	93	95	99	106
12	27	35	40	42	46	49	54		86	91	94	98	100	105	113
13	27	36	41	44	48	52	56		91	95	99	103	106	111	120
14	27	37	43	45	50	54	59		95	100	104	109	111	117	127
15	27	38	44	47	52	56	61		100	105	109	114	117	123	134
16	27	39	46	49	54	58	64		104	110	114	119	122	129	141
17	27	41	47	51	56	61	66		109	114	119	124	128	134	148
18	27	42	49	52	58	63	69		113	119	124	130	133	140	155
19	27	43	50	54	60	65	71		118	124	129	135	139	146	162
20	27	44	52	56	62	67	74		122	129	134	140	144	152	169

$$n_1 = 8$$

n_2	0	.001	.005	.01	.025	.05	.10		.90	.95	.975	.99	.995	.999	1.00
8	35	40	43	45	49	51	55		81	85	87	91	93	96	101
9	35	41	45	47	51	54	58		86	90	93	97	99	103	109
10	35	42	47	49	53	56	60		92	96	99	103	105	110	117
11	35	44	49	51	55	59	63		97	101	105	109	111	116	125
12	35	45	51	53	58	62	66		102	106	110	115	117	123	133
13	35	47	53	56	60	64	69		107	112	116	120	123	129	141
14	35	48	54	58	62	67	72		112	117	122	126	130	136	149
15	35	50	56	60	65	69	75		117	123	127	132	136	142	157
16	35	51	58	62	67	72	78		122	128	133	138	142	149	165
17	35	53	60	64	70	75	81		127	133	138	144	148	155	173
18	35	54	62	66	72	77	84		132	139	144	150	154	162	181
19	35	56	64	68	74	80	87		137	144	150	156	160	168	189
20	35	57	66	70	77	83	90		142	149	155	162	166	175	197

11.5

Exact Critical Values for a Nonparametric Sum of Ranks Procedure for Relative Spread in Unpaired Samples (cont.)

$$n_1 = 9$$

n_2	0	.001	.005	.01	.025	.05	.10		.90	.95	.975	.99	.995	.999	1.00
9	44	52	56	59	62	66	70		101	105	109	112	115	119	127
10	44	53	58	61	65	69	73		107	111	115	119	122	127	136
11	44	55	61	63	68	72	76		113	117	121	126	128	134	145
12	44	57	63	66	71	75	80		118	123	127	132	135	141	154
13	44	59	65	68	73	78	83		124	129	134	139	142	148	163
14	44	60	67	71	76	81	86		130	135	140	145	149	156	172
15	44	62	69	73	79	84	90		135	141	146	152	156	163	181
16	44	64	72	76	82	87	93		141	147	152	158	162	170	190
17	44	66	74	78	84	90	97		146	153	159	165	169	177	199
18	44	68	76	81	87	93	100		152	159	165	171	176	184	208
19	44	70	78	83	90	96	103		158	165	171	178	183	191	217
20	44	71	81	85	93	99	107		163	171	177	185	189	199	226

$$n_1 = 10$$

n_2	0	.001	.005	.01	.025	.05	.10		.90	.95	.975	.99	.995	.999	1.00
10	54	65	71	74	78	82	87		123	128	132	136	139	145	156
11	54	67	73	77	81	86	91		129	134	139	143	147	153	166
12	54	69	76	79	84	89	94		136	141	146	151	154	161	176
13	54	72	79	82	88	92	98		142	148	152	158	161	168	186
14	54	74	81	85	91	96	102		148	154	159	165	169	176	196
15	54	76	84	88	94	99	106		154	161	166	172	176	184	206
16	54	78	86	91	97	103	109		161	167	173	179	184	192	216
17	54	80	89	93	100	106	113		167	174	180	187	191	200	226
18	54	82	92	96	103	110	117		173	180	187	194	198	208	236
19	54	84	94	99	107	113	121		179	187	193	201	206	216	246
20	54	87	97	102	110	117	125		185	193	200	208	213	223	256

$$n_1 = 11$$

n_2	0	.001	.005	.01	.025	.05	.10		.90	.95	.975	.99	.995	.999	1.00
11	65	81	87	91	96	100	106		147	153	157	162	166	172	188
12	65	83	90	94	99	104	110		154	160	165	170	174	181	199
13	65	86	93	97	103	108	114		161	167	172	178	182	189	210
14	65	88	96	100	106	112	118		168	174	180	186	190	198	221
15	65	90	99	103	110	116	123		174	181	187	194	198	207	232
16	65	93	102	107	113	120	127		181	188	195	201	206	215	243
17	65	95	105	110	117	123	131		188	196	202	209	214	224	254
18	65	98	108	113	121	127	135		195	203	209	217	222	232	265
19	65	100	111	116	124	131	139		202	210	217	225	230	241	276
20	65	103	114	119	128	135	144		208	217	224	233	238	249	287

11.5

Exact Critical Values for a Nonparametric Sum of Ranks Procedure for Relative Spread in Unpaired Samples (*cont.*)

$$n_1 = 12$$

n_2	0	.001	.005	.01	.025	.05	.10		.90	.95	.975	.99	.995	.999	1.00
12	77	98	105	109	115	120	127		173	180	185	191	195	202	223
13	77	101	109	113	119	125	131		181	187	193	199	203	211	235
14	77	103	112	116	123	129	136		188	195	201	208	212	221	247
15	77	106	115	120	127	133	141		195	203	209	216	221	230	259
16	77	109	119	124	131	138	145		203	210	217	224	229	239	271
17	77	112	122	127	135	142	150		210	218	225	233	238	248	283
18	77	115	125	131	139	146	155		217	226	233	241	247	257	295
19	77	118	129	134	143	150	159		225	234	241	250	255	266	307
20	77	120	132	138	147	155	164		232	241	249	258	264	276	319

$$n_1 = 13$$

n_2	0	.001	.005	.01	.025	.05	.10		.90	.95	.975	.99	.995	.999	1.00
13	90	117	125	130	136	142	149		202	209	215	221	226	234	261
14	90	120	129	134	141	147	154		210	217	223	230	235	244	274
15	90	123	133	138	145	152	159		218	225	232	239	244	254	287
16	90	126	136	142	150	156	165		225	234	240	248	254	264	300
17	90	129	140	146	154	161	170		233	242	249	257	263	274	313
18	90	133	144	150	158	166	175		241	250	258	266	272	283	326
19	90	136	148	154	163	171	180		249	258	266	275	281	293	339
20	90	139	151	158	167	175	185		257	267	275	284	291	303	352

$$n_1 = 14$$

n_2	0	.001	.005	.01	.025	.05	.10		.90	.95	.975	.99	.995	.999	1.00
14	104	137	147	152	160	166	174		232	240	246	254	259	269	302
15	104	141	151	156	164	171	179		241	249	256	264	269	279	316
16	104	144	155	161	169	176	185		249	258	265	273	279	290	330
17	104	148	159	165	174	182	190		258	266	274	283	289	300	344
18	104	151	163	170	179	187	196		266	275	283	292	299	311	358
19	104	155	168	174	183	192	202		274	284	293	302	308	321	372
20	104	159	172	178	188	197	207		283	293	302	312	318	331	386

$$n_1 = 15$$

n_2	0	.001	.005	.01	.025	.05	.10		.90	.95	.975	.99	.995	.999	1.00
15	119	160	171	176	184	192	200		265	273	281	289	294	305	346
16	119	163	175	181	190	197	206		274	283	290	299	305	317	361
17	119	167	180	186	195	203	212		283	292	300	309	315	328	376
18	119	171	184	190	200	208	218		292	302	310	320	326	339	391
19	119	175	189	195	205	214	224		301	311	320	330	336	350	406
20	119	179	193	200	210	220	230		310	320	330	340	347	361	421

Exact Critical Values for a Nonparametric Sum of Ranks
Procedure for Relative Spread in Unpaired Samples (cont.)

$n_1 = 16$

n_2	0	.001	.005	.01	.025	.05	.10		.90	.95	.975	.99	.995	.999	1.00
16	135	184	196	202	211	219	229		299	309	317	326	332	344	393
17	135	188	201	207	217	225	235		309	319	327	337	343	356	409
18	135	192	206	212	222	231	242		318	329	338	348	354	368	425
19	135	196	210	218	228	237	248		328	339	348	358	366	380	441
20	135	201	215	223	234	243	255		337	349	358	369	377	391	457

$n_1 = 17$

n_2	0	.001	.005	.01	.025	.05	.10		.90	.95	.975	.99	.995	.999	1.00
17	152	210	223	230	240	249	259		336	346	355	365	372	385	443
18	152	214	228	235	246	255	266		346	357	366	377	384	398	460
19	152	219	234	241	252	262	273		356	367	377	388	395	410	477
20	152	223	239	246	258	268	280		366	378	388	400	407	423	494

$n_1 = 18$

n_2	0	.001	.005	.01	.025	.05	.10		.90	.95	.975	.99	.995	.999	1.00
18	170	237	252	259	270	280	291		375	386	396	407	414	429	496
19	170	242	258	265	277	287	299		385	397	407	419	426	442	514
20	170	247	263	271	283	294	306		396	408	419	431	439	455	532

$n_1 = 19$

n_2	0	.001	.005	.01	.025	.05	.10		.90	.95	.975	.99	.995	.999	1.00
19	189	267	283	291	303	313	325		416	428	438	450	458	474	552
20	189	272	289	297	309	320	333		427	440	451	463	471	488	571

$n_1 = 20$

n_2	0	.001	.005	.01	.025	.05	.10		.90	.95	.975	.99	.995	.999	1.00
20	209	298	315	324	337	348	361		459	472	483	496	505	522	611

12. SIGN, RUNS, AND QUADRANT TESTS

12.1 Critical Values for the Sign Test and Distribution-Free Confidence Limits on the Median of a Population

The quantity tabulated is that value of A such that

$$B(n, A, \tfrac{1}{2}) = \sum_{j=0}^{A} \frac{n!}{j!(n-j)!2^n} \leq \gamma,$$

where $\gamma = 0.005$, 0.01, 0.025, 0.05, and 0.10. That is, the value of A is given such that a binomial sum (Section 9.5) with $p = \tfrac{1}{2}$ is small.

Let (X, Y) be a pair of random variables, and suppose a sample of size n has been taken from the distribution of these pairs. The differences $X_i - Y_i$ are computed for each of the n pairs, and the statistic S is defined to be the number of negative signs which are observed among the differences. If some of the differences are zero, they are dropped from consideration and the sample size is reduced. The null hypothesis that the distributions of X and Y have the same median against the alternative that the median of X is larger than the median of Y is tested by noting whether the value of S is less than or equal to the value of A given in the table. A two-tailed test may be made by doubling γ and counting the number of times the less frequent sign appears. The above is only one example of the way a sign test may be applied. Dixon and Massey [55], pp. 280–286, give several other examples.

Walsh [237] describes other applications where the tables given here would lead to bounds on the required probability. Cohen [34] considers cases where p is different from one-half. Hodges [97] introduces a bivariate sign test, and Klotz [109] gives the null distribution of this test under conditions more general than Hodges did in the first paper. Hill [96] shows that the null distribution of Hodges' bivariate sign test and the null distribution of a nonparametric test of Daniels [40] are equivalent. Blumen [27] introduces another bivariate sign test. Putter [176] considers the effect of ties on the one-sided sign test.

The values given in the table may also be used to set up a two-sided distribution-free confidence interval on the median of a population based on a sample of n items from a population with a continuous cumulative probability distribution function. Specifically, the table gives values of A such that one can be $(1 - 2\gamma)100$ percent sure that the median of the population is between the Ath largest and the $(n - A + 1)$th largest in the sample.

12.1

Critical Values for the Sign Test and Distribution-Free
Confidence Limits on the Median of a Population

n	0.005	0.01	0.025	0.05	0.10
4	-	-	-	-	0
5	-	-	-	0	0
6	-	-	0	0	0
7	-	0	0	0	1
8	0	0	0	1	1
9	0	0	1	1	2
10	0	0	1	1	2
11	0	1	1	2	2
12	1	1	2	2	3
13	1	1	2	3	3
14	1	2	2	3	4
15	2	2	3	3	4
16	2	2	3	4	4
17	2	3	4	4	5
18	3	3	4	5	5
19	3	4	4	5	6
20	3	4	5	5	6
21	4	4	5	6	7
22	4	5	5	6	7
23	4	5	6	7	7
24	5	5	6	7	8
25	5	6	7	7	8
26	6	6	7	8	9
27	6	7	7	8	9
28	6	7	8	9	10
29	7	7	8	9	10
30	7	8	9	10	10
31	7	8	9	10	11
32	8	8	9	10	11
33	8	9	10	11	12
34	9	9	10	11	12
35	9	10	11	12	13
36	9	10	11	12	13
37	10	10	12	13	14
38	10	11	12	13	14
39	11	11	12	13	15
40	11	12	13	14	15

12.1

Critical Values for the Sign Test and Distribution-Free
Confidence Limits on the Median of a Population (cont.)

n	0.005	0.01	0.025	0.05	0.10
41	11	12	13	14	15
42	12	13	14	15	16
43	12	13	14	15	16
44	13	13	15	16	17
45	13	14	15	16	17
46	13	14	15	16	18
47	14	15	16	17	18
48	14	15	16	17	19
49	15	15	17	18	19
50	15	16	17	18	19
52	16	17	18	19	20
54	17	18	19	20	21
56	17	18	20	21	22
58	18	19	21	22	23
60	19	20	21	23	24
62	20	21	22	24	25
64	21	22	23	24	26
66	22	23	24	25	27
68	22	23	25	26	28
70	23	24	26	27	29
72	24	25	27	28	30
74	25	26	28	29	30
76	26	27	28	30	31
78	27	28	29	31	32
80	28	29	30	32	33
82	28	30	31	33	34
84	29	30	32	33	35
86	30	31	33	34	36
88	31	32	34	35	37
90	32	33	35	36	38
92	33	34	36	37	39
94	34	35	37	38	40
96	34	36	37	39	41
98	35	37	38	40	42
100	36	37	39	41	43

Critical Values for the Sign Test and Distribution-Free
Confidence Limits on the Median of a Population (cont.)

n	0.005	0.01	0.025	0.05	0.10
110	41	42	44	45	47
120	45	46	48	50	52
130	49	51	53	55	57
140	54	55	57	59	61
150	58	60	62	64	66
160	63	64	67	69	71
170	67	69	71	73	76
180	72	73	76	78	80
190	76	78	81	83	85
200	81	83	85	87	90
220	90	92	94	97	99
240	99	101	104	106	109
260	108	110	113	116	119
280	117	120	123	125	128
300	127	129	132	135	138
320	136	138	141	144	148
340	145	148	151	154	157
360	155	157	160	163	167
380	164	166	170	173	177
400	173	176	179	183	186
420	183	185	189	192	196
440	192	195	198	202	206
460	201	204	208	211	215
480	211	214	218	221	225
500	220	223	227	231	235
550	244	247	251	255	259
600	267	271	275	279	283
650	291	294	299	303	308
700	315	318	323	327	332
750	339	342	347	351	356
800	363	366	371	376	381
850	386	390	395	400	405
900	410	414	420	424	430
950	434	438	444	449	454
1000	458	462	468	473	479

12.1

12.2 Power of the Sign Test with a Two-Sided 5-Percent Significance Level

A two-sided sign test (Section 12.1) has been performed at the 5-percent significance level. The probability of rejecting the hypothesis that $p = \frac{1}{2}$, when in fact p is 0.60 or 0.40, p is 0.65 or 0.35, etc., (indicated by $H_1, \ldots, H_8$ in the table), is $P > \beta$.

The smallest number (minimum n) of paired samples that must be employed in order for the two-sided sign test at the 5-percent significance level [$B(n, A, \frac{1}{2}) \leq 0.05$ in Section 12.1] to have power $p > \beta$ is given in the first position in the table. If x of these paired samples give rise to a positive difference, and $n - x$ to a negative difference, and if S is defined to be the smaller of x or $n - x$, then the maximum value that S may attain and still have the results judged significant is given in the second position. Stewart [210] gives an example of the use of this table. Stuart [212] considers the power of a bivariate sign test which is a generalization of a test of serial independence due to Moore and Wallis [143]. Dixon [52] tabulates directly the power of the sign test for the same alternatives as given here for $n = 5(1)20(5)50(10)100$ for significance levels near 5 percent and 1 percent.

Power of the Sign Test with a Two-Sided 5-Percent Significance Level [210]
Minimum n (First) and Maximum Values of Related s (Second)

Power	H_8 0.95	H_7 0.90	H_6 0.85	H_5 0.80	H_4 0.75	H_3 0.70	H_2 0.65	H_1 0.60
$0 < P \leq .05$	-	-	-	-	-	-	7,0	6,0
$P > .05$	-	-	-	-	-	7,0	6,0	9,1
$P > .10$	-	-	-	-	7,0	6,0	9,1	17,4
$P > .15$	-	-	-	8,0	6,0	9,1	12,2	25,7
$P > .20$	-	-	-	7,0	10,1	13,2	17,4	37,12
$P > .25$	-	-	8,0	6,0	14,2	12,2	23,6	44,15
$P > .30$	-	-	7,0	11,1	9,1	18,4	25,7	56,20
$P > .35$	-	-	6,0	10,1	12,2	17,4	30,9	65,24
$P > .40$	-	8,0	-	9,1	16,3	20,5	35,11	74,28
$P > .45$	-	7,0	11,1	-	15,3	26,7	42,14	89,35
$P > .50$		6,0	10,1	13,2	18,4	25,7	44,15	101,40
$P > .55$	-	-	9,1	12,2	17,4	30,9	51,18	112,45
$P > .60$	-	-	14,2	15,3	20,5	36,11	56,20	125,51
$P > .65$	7,0	11,1	13,2	19,4	23,6	35,11	63,23	143,59
$P > .70$	6,0	10,1	12,2	18,4	25,7	40,13	67,25	158,66
$P > .75$	-	9,1	16,3	17,4	28,8	44,15	79,30	175,74
$P > .80$	-	14,2	15,3	20,5	30,9	49,17	90,35	199,85
$P > .85$	11,1	12,2	18,4	25,7	35,11	56,20	101,40	227,98
$P > .90$	9,1	15,3	17,4	28,8	42,14	65,24	114,46	263,115
$P > .95$	12,2	17,4	23,6	35,11	49,17	79,30	143,60	327,145
$P > .99$	15,3	23,6	30,9	44,15	67,25	110,44	199,85	453,205

12.3 Distribution-Free Confidence Limits on the Quartiles of a Population

A continuous cumulative probability distribution function is assumed for a random variable X. A sample of n items is taken from this population and ordered from smallest to largest. A 100γ-percent confidence interval for the first quartile (lowest 25 percent) in the population is found by taking the Ath largest sample value (lower limit) and the Bth largest sample value (upper limit). A 100γ-percent confidence interval for the third quartile (upper 25 percent) in the population is found by taking the Cth largest (lower limit) sample value and the Dth largest sample value (upper limit). For a confidence limit on the median, see Section 12.1.

The values of A and B given in the table were found by solving the equation

$$E(n, A, 0.25) - E(n, B, 0.25) \geq \gamma,$$

where that pair of values (A, B) is taken which minimizes $B - A$, and if there is still a choice, then the pair that yields a probability closest to γ is chosen. The quantity $E(n, r, p)$ is that given by the Harvard Tables [94] and is

$$E(n, r, p) = \sum_{x=r}^{n} \binom{n}{x} (1 - p)^{n-x} p^{x}.$$

The values for C and D were computed from $C = n - B + 1$ and $D = n - A + 1$. Wilks [248] gives a history of this type of confidence limit.

Distribution-Free Confidence Limits on the Quartiles of a Population

$\gamma = 0.99$

n	A	B	C	D	n	A	B	C	D	n	A	B	C	D
2					37	3	17	21	35	94	14	36	59	81
3					38	4	18	21	35	96	14	36	61	83
4	0	4	1	5	39	3	17	23	37	98	14	36	63	85
5	0	5	1	6	40	4	18	23	37	100	15	38	63	86
6	0	5	2	7	41	3	18	24	39	110	17	41	70	94
7	0	6	2	8	42	3	18	25	40	120	19	44	77	102
8	0	6	3	9	43	4	19	25	40	130	21	47	84	110
9	0	6	4	10	44	5	20	25	40	140	23	50	91	118
10	0	7	4	11	45	5	20	26	41	150	25	53	98	126
11	0	7	5	12	46	5	20	27	42	160	25	54	107	136
12	0	8	5	13	47	4	20	28	44	170	29	58	113	142
13	0	8	6	14	48	4	20	29	45	180	31	61	120	150
14	0	9	6	15	49	5	21	29	45	190	32	63	128	159
15	0	9	7	16	50	6	22	29	45	200	34	66	135	167
16	0	9	8	17	52	6	22	31	47	220	40	74	147	181
17	1	11	7	17	54	5	22	33	50	240	44	79	162	197
18	1	11	8	18	56	7	24	33	50	260	48	84	177	213
19	0	10	10	20	58	7	24	35	52	280	53	91	190	228
20	1	11	10	20	60	6	24	37	55	300	57	96	205	244
21	1	11	11	21	62	8	26	37	55	320	61	101	220	260
22	0	11	12	23	64	8	26	39	57	340	66	108	233	275
23	1	12	12	23	66	8	26	41	59	360	68	111	250	293
24	1	12	13	24	68	9	28	41	60	380	75	119	262	306
25	2	14	12	24	70	8	27	44	63	400	79	124	277	322
26	2	14	13	25	72	9	28	45	64	420	82	128	293	339
27	1	13	15	27	74	10	30	45	65	440	88	135	306	353
28	2	14	15	27	76	9	29	48	68	460	91	139	322	370
29	2	14	16	28	78	11	31	48	68	480	97	146	335	384
30	1	14	17	30	80	11	31	50	70	500	100	150	351	401
31	3	16	16	29	82	12	33	50	71	550	113	166	385	438
32	3	16	17	30	84	12	33	52	73	600	122	177	424	479
33	2	15	19	32	86	11	32	55	76	650	134	191	460	517
34	3	16	19	32	88	12	33	56	77	700	146	205	496	555
35	3	16	20	33	90	13	35	56	78	750	159	221	530	592
36	2	16	21	35	92	12	34	59	81	800	167	231	570	634
										850	181	246	605	670
										900	193	260	641	708
										950	205	274	677	746
										1000	214	285	716	787

12.3

Distribution-Free Confidence Limits on the Quartiles of a Population (cont.)

$Y = 0.98$

n	A	B	C	D	n	A	B	C	D	n	A	B	C	D
2					37	3	16	22	35	94	15	35	60	80
3	0	3	1	4	38	3	16	23	36	96	14	34	63	83
4	0	4	1	5	39	4	17	23	36	98	15	35	64	84
5	0	4	2	6	40	4	17	24	37	100	14	35	66	87
6	0	5	2	7	41	5	18	24	37	110	16	38	73	95
7	0	5	3	8	42	5	18	25	38	120	18	41	80	103
8	0	6	3	9	43	4	18	26	40	130	22	45	86	109
9	0	6	4	10	44	4	18	27	41	140	23	47	94	118
10	0	6	5	11	45	5	19	27	41	150	25	50	101	126
11	0	7	5	12	46	6	20	27	41	160	27	53	108	134
12	0	7	6	13	47	6	20	28	42	170	31	58	113	140
13	0	8	6	14	48	6	20	29	43	180	32	59	122	149
14	1	9	6	14	49	6	20	30	44	190	35	63	128	156
15	1	9	7	15	50	5	20	31	46	200	35	64	137	166
16	1	9	8	16	52	7	22	31	46	220	40	70	151	181
17	1	9	9	17	54	7	22	33	48	240	46	78	163	195
18	0	9	10	19	56	7	22	35	50	260	48	81	180	213
19	1	10	10	19	58	8	24	35	51	280	53	87	194	228
20	1	10	11	20	60	7	23	38	54	300	58	93	208	243
21	1	11	11	21	62	8	24	39	55	320	63	99	222	258
22	2	12	11	21	64	7	24	41	58	340	65	103	238	276
23	2	12	12	22	66	8	25	42	59	360	70	109	252	291
24	2	12	13	23	68	10	27	42	59	380	77	117	264	304
25	2	12	14	24	70	10	27	44	61	400	79	120	281	322
26	1	12	15	26	72	10	27	46	63	420	83	125	296	338
27	2	13	15	26	74	11	29	46	64	440	88	131	310	353
28	2	13	16	27	76	10	28	49	67	460	92	136	325	369
29	3	14	16	27	78	11	29	50	68	480	100	145	336	381
30	3	14	17	28	80	12	30	51	69	500	101	147	354	400
31	3	14	18	29	82	11	30	53	72	550	116	164	387	435
32	2	14	19	31	84	13	32	53	72	600	124	174	427	477
33	3	15	19	31	86	12	31	56	75	650	139	191	460	512
34	3	15	20	32	88	13	32	57	76	700	147	201	500	554
35	4	16	20	32	90	12	32	59	79	750	162	218	533	589
36	4	16	21	33	92	13	33	60	80	800	172	229	572	629
										850	183	242	609	668
										900	197	258	643	704
										950	209	272	679	742
										1000	220	284	717	781

12.3

Distribution-Free Confidence Limits on the Quartiles of a Population (cont.)

$\Upsilon = 0.95$

n	A	B	C	D	n	A	B	C	D	n	A	B	C	D
2					37	5	16	22	33	94	15	32	63	80
3	0	3	1	4	38	4	15	24	35	96	17	34	63	80
4	0	4	1	5	39	4	15	25	36	98	16	33	66	83
5	0	4	2	6	40	5	16	25	36	100	17	34	67	84
6	0	4	3	7	41	5	16	26	37	110	19	37	74	92
7	0	5	3	8	42	4	16	27	39	120	22	41	80	99
8	0	5	4	9	43	6	18	26	38	130	22	42	89	109
9	0	5	5	10	44	5	17	28	40	140	24	45	96	117
10	0	6	5	11	45	5	17	29	41	150	27	48	103	124
11	1	7	5	11	46	7	19	28	40	160	29	51	110	132
12	1	7	6	12	47	7	19	29	41	170	30	53	118	141
13	1	7	7	13	48	6	18	31	43	180	34	57	124	147
14	0	7	8	15	49	7	19	31	43	190	35	59	132	156
15	1	8	8	15	50	7	19	32	44	200	37	62	139	164
16	1	8	9	16	52	6	19	34	47	220	41	67	154	180
17	1	8	10	17	54	7	20	35	48	240	46	73	168	195
18	2	10	9	17	56	8	21	36	49	260	53	81	180	208
19	2	10	10	18	58	9	22	37	50	280	55	84	197	226
20	1	9	12	20	60	8	22	39	53	300	59	89	212	242
21	2	10	12	20	62	8	22	41	55	320	64	95	226	257
22	2	10	13	21	64	9	23	42	56	340	68	100	241	273
23	1	10	14	23	66	10	24	43	57	360	73	106	255	288
24	3	12	13	22	68	9	24	45	60	380	77	111	270	304
25	3	12	14	23	70	10	25	46	61	400	83	117	284	318
26	2	11	16	25	72	10	25	48	63	420	89	124	297	332
27	3	12	16	25	74	11	26	49	64	440	92	128	313	349
28	3	12	17	26	76	12	27	50	65	460	96	133	328	365
29	2	12	18	28	78	11	27	52	68	480	100	138	343	381
30	4	14	17	27	80	12	28	53	69	500	106	144	357	395
31	4	14	18	28	82	12	28	55	71	550	117	157	394	434
32	3	13	20	30	84	13	29	56	72	600	131	173	428	470
33	4	14	20	30	86	14	30	57	73	650	143	187	464	508
34	4	14	21	31	88	15	31	58	74	700	153	198	503	548
35	4	14	22	32	90	14	31	60	77	750	163	210	541	588
36	3	14	23	34	92	14	31	62	79	800	174	223	578	627
										850	187	237	614	664
										900	200	251	650	701
										950	210	263	688	741
										1000	225	279	722	776

12.3

Distribution-Free Confidence Limits on the Quartiles of a Population (cont.)

$\gamma = 0.90$

n	A	B	C	D	n	A	B	C	D	n	A	B	C	D
2	0	2	1	3	37	6	15	23	32	94	17	31	64	78
3	0	3	1	4	38	6	15	24	33	96	16	31	66	81
4	0	3	2	5	39	6	15	25	34	98	19	34	65	80
5	0	4	2	6	40	6	15	26	35	100	19	34	67	82
6	0	4	3	7	41	7	17	25	35	110	21	36	75	90
7	0	4	4	8	42	5	15	28	38	120	23	39	82	98
8	0	5	4	9	43	7	17	27	37	130	26	43	88	105
9	1	6	4	9	44	7	17	28	38	140	27	44	97	114
10	0	5	6	11	45	6	16	30	40	150	30	48	103	121
11	1	6	6	11	46	7	17	30	40	160	32	51	110	129
12	1	6	7	12	47	7	17	31	41	170	34	53	118	137
13	0	6	8	14	48	8	18	31	41	180	37	57	124	144
14	1	7	8	14	49	8	18	32	42	190	39	59	132	152
15	2	8	8	14	50	7	18	33	44	200	41	62	139	160
16	2	8	9	15	52	9	20	33	44	220	46	68	153	175
17	2	8	10	16	54	9	20	35	46	240	47	70	171	194
18	2	8	11	17	56	9	20	37	48	260	54	77	184	207
19	1	8	12	19	58	10	21	38	49	280	59	83	198	222
20	2	9	12	19	60	10	21	40	51	300	64	89	212	237
21	3	10	12	19	62	9	21	42	54	320	69	95	226	252
22	3	10	13	20	64	11	23	42	54	340	73	100	241	268
23	3	10	14	21	66	12	24	43	55	360	78	106	255	283
24	3	10	15	22	68	12	24	45	57	380	82	110	271	299
25	2	10	16	24	70	12	24	47	59	400	87	116	285	314
26	2	10	17	25	72	11	24	49	62	420	92	122	299	329
27	4	12	16	24	74	12	25	50	63	440	96	126	315	345
28	4	12	17	25	76	14	27	50	63	460	101	132	329	360
29	3	11	19	27	78	14	27	52	65	480	106	138	343	375
30	4	12	19	27	80	14	27	54	67	500	110	142	359	391
31	4	12	20	28	82	15	28	55	68	550	122	156	395	429
32	3	12	21	30	84	16	30	55	69	600	133	168	433	468
33	5	14	20	29	86	16	30	57	71	650	146	183	468	505
34	4	13	22	31	88	16	30	59	73	700	155	193	508	546
35	4	13	23	32	90	17	31	60	74	750	170	210	541	581
36	5	14	23	32	92	17	31	62	76	800	182	223	578	619
										850	193	235	616	658
										900	205	248	653	696
										950	216	260	691	735
										1000	230	276	725	771

12.3

Distribution-Free Confidence Limits on the Quartiles of a Population (cont.)

$\Upsilon = 0.80$

n	A	B	C	D
2	0	2	1	3
3	0	2	2	4
4	0	3	2	5
5	0	3	3	6
6	0	3	4	7
7	1	5	3	7
8	1	5	4	8
9	0	4	6	10
10	1	5	6	10
11	1	5	7	11
12	1	5	8	12
13	2	7	7	12
14	2	7	8	13
15	1	6	10	15
16	1	6	11	16
17	2	7	11	16
18	3	8	11	16
19	3	8	12	17
20	3	8	13	18
21	2	8	14	20
22	4	10	13	19
23	4	10	14	20
24	4	10	15	21
25	3	9	17	23
26	4	10	17	23
27	4	10	18	24
28	4	10	19	25
29	3	10	20	27
30	5	12	19	26
31	4	11	21	28
32	6	13	20	27
33	6	13	21	28
34	6	13	22	29
35	5	12	24	31
36	6	13	24	31

n	A	B	C	D
37	6	13	25	32
38	7	14	25	32
39	7	14	26	33
40	7	14	27	34
41	8	16	26	34
42	8	16	27	35
43	6	14	30	38
44	8	16	29	37
45	7	15	31	39
46	7	15	32	40
47	9	17	31	39
48	9	17	32	40
49	8	16	34	42
50	9	17	34	42
52	10	19	34	43
54	8	17	38	47
56	11	20	37	46
58	11	20	39	48
60	10	19	42	51
62	12	21	42	51
64	12	21	44	53
66	13	23	44	54
68	11	21	48	58
70	14	24	47	57
72	14	24	49	59
74	15	25	50	60
76	15	25	52	62
78	15	25	54	64
80	15	25	56	66
82	17	28	55	66
84	17	28	57	68
86	15	26	61	72
88	18	29	60	71
90	18	29	62	73
92	17	28	65	76

n	A	B	C	D
94	19	30	65	76
96	19	30	67	78
98	20	32	67	79
100	21	33	68	80
110	23	35	76	88
120	25	38	83	96
130	27	40	91	104
140	30	44	97	111
150	32	46	105	119
160	31	46	115	130
170	34	49	122	137
180	38	53	128	143
190	41	57	134	150
200	43	59	142	158
220	48	65	156	173
240	53	71	170	188
260	57	75	186	204
280	62	81	200	219
300	67	87	214	234
320	71	91	230	250
340	76	97	244	265
360	77	99	262	284
380	83	105	276	298
400	91	114	287	310
420	95	118	303	326
440	100	124	317	341
460	104	128	333	357
480	110	135	346	371
500	114	139	362	387
550	127	154	397	424
600	139	167	434	462
650	146	175	476	505
700	158	188	513	543
750	174	205	546	577
800	182	214	587	619
850	194	227	624	657
900	211	245	656	690
950	223	258	693	728
1000	235	271	730	766

12.3

12.4 Critical Values for the Number-of-Runs Test for Equal-Size Samples

The tables given here have been used in testing data for randomness and for testing whether two samples are from the same population. Consider a sequence of x's and y's, for example, $xxxyyx\ yyyxxx\ldots$, where there are m x's and n y's. Assume $m \leq n$ and define U to be the number of distinct groups of x's (number of runs) in any one arrangement. The quantities tabulated are the largest value of u for which

$$\Pr\{U \leq u\} \leq \gamma \quad \text{for } \gamma = 0.005,\ 0.01,\ 0.025,\ \text{and } 0.05,$$

and the smallest value of u for which

$$\Pr\{U \leq u\} \geq \gamma \quad \text{for } \gamma = 0.95,\ 0.975,\ 0.99,\ \text{and } 0.995.$$

The cumulative probability distribution of U is given by,

$$\Pr\{U \leq u\} = \frac{1}{\dbinom{m+n}{n}} \sum_{j=2}^{u} f_j,$$

where

$$f_j = 2\binom{m-1}{n-1}\binom{n-1}{k-1} \quad \text{when } j = 2k,$$

and

$$f_j = \binom{m-1}{k-1}\binom{n-1}{k-2} + \binom{m-1}{k-2}\binom{n-1}{k-1} \quad \text{when } j = 2k-1.$$

In testing the hypothesis of randomness against an alternative that would tend to yield "too few" runs at level of significance α, the hypothesis of randomness is to be rejected if the value of U computed from the sample is less than or equal to u from the table with $\gamma = \alpha$; otherwise, it is to be accepted.

In testing the hypothesis of randomness against an alternative that would tend to yield "too many" runs at level of significance α, the hypothesis of randomness is to be rejected if the value of U computed from the sample is greater than or equal to $u + 1$ from the table with $\gamma = 1 - \alpha$.

In testing the hypothesis of randomness against an alternative that might yield *either* "too few" runs or "too many" runs at level of significance α, the hypothesis is to be rejected if the value of U computed from the sample is either less than or equal to u from the table with $\gamma = \alpha/2$, or greater than or equal to $u + 1$ from the table with $\gamma = 1 - \alpha/2$.

The tables of this section are for $m = n$. See Section 12.5 for some tables when $m \neq n$. Swed and Eisenhart [216] give examples of the use of the tables and also tabulate the probability distribution. A generalization of this type of runs test may be found in a paper by Barton and David [12].

Critical Values for the Number-of-Runs
Test for Equal-Size Samples [216]

m=n	0.005	0.01	0.025	0.05	0.95	0.975	0.99	0.995
10	5	5	6	6	15	15	16	16
11	5	6	7	7	16	16	17	18
12	6	7	7	8	17	18	18	19
13	7	7	8	9	18	19	20	20
14	7	8	9	10	19	20	21	22
15	8	9	10	11	20	21	22	23
16	9	10	11	11	22	22	23	24
17	10	10	11	12	23	24	25	25
18	10	11	12	13	24	25	26	26
19	11	12	13	14	25	26	27	28
20	12	13	14	15	26	27	28	29
21	13	14	15	16	27	28	29	30
22	14	14	16	17	28	29	31	31
23	14	15	16	17	30	31	32	33
24	15	16	17	18	31	32	33	34
25	16	17	18	19	32	33	34	35
26	17	18	19	20	33	34	35	36
27	18	19	20	21	34	35	36	37
28	18	19	21	22	35	36	38	39
29	19	20	22	23	36	37	39	40
30	20	21	22	24	37	39	40	41
31	21	22	23	25	38	40	41	42
32	22	23	24	25	40	41	42	43
33	23	24	25	26	41	42	43	44
34	23	24	26	27	42	43	45	46
35	24	25	27	28	43	44	46	47
36	25	26	28	29	44	45	47	48
37	26	27	29	30	45	46	48	49
38	27	28	30	31	46	47	49	50
39	28	29	30	32	47	49	50	51
40	29	30	31	33	48	50	51	52
41	29	31	32	34	49	51	52	54
42	30	31	33	35	50	52	54	55
43	31	32	34	35	52	53	55	56
44	32	33	35	36	53	54	56	57
45	33	34	36	37	54	55	57	58
46	34	35	37	38	55	56	58	59
47	35	36	38	39	56	57	59	60
48	35	37	38	40	57	59	60	62
49	36	38	39	41	58	60	61	63

Critical Values for the Number-of-Runs
Test for Equal-Size Samples (*cont.*)

m=n	0.005	0.01	0.025	0.05	0.95	0.975	0.99	0.995
50	37	38	40	42	59	61	63	64
51	38	39	41	43	60	62	64	65
52	39	40	42	44	61	63	65	66
53	40	41	43	45	62	64	66	67
54	41	42	44	45	64	65	67	68
55	42	43	45	46	65	66	68	69
56	42	44	46	47	66	67	69	71
57	43	45	47	48	67	68	70	72
58	44	46	47	49	68	70	71	73
59	45	46	48	50	69	71	73	74
60	46	47	49	51	70	72	74	75
61	47	48	50	52	71	73	75	76
62	48	49	51	53	72	74	76	77
63	49	50	52	54	73	75	77	78
64	49	51	53	55	74	76	78	80
65	50	52	54	56	75	77	79	81
66	51	53	55	57	76	78	80	82
67	52	54	56	58	77	79	81	83
68	53	54	57	58	79	80	83	84
69	54	55	58	59	80	81	84	85
70	55	56	58	60	81	83	85	86
71	56	57	59	61	82	84	86	87
72	57	58	60	62	83	85	87	88
73	57	59	61	63	84	86	88	90
74	58	60	62	64	85	87	89	91
75	59	61	63	65	86	88	90	92
76	60	62	64	66	87	89	91	93
77	61	63	65	67	88	90	92	94
78	62	64	66	68	89	91	93	95
79	63	64	67	69	90	92	95	96
80	64	65	68	70	91	93	96	97
81	65	66	69	71	92	94	97	98
82	66	67	69	71	94	96	98	99
83	66	68	70	72	95	97	99	101
84	67	69	71	73	96	98	100	102
85	68	70	72	74	97	99	101	103
86	69	71	73	75	98	100	102	104
87	70	72	74	76	99	101	103	105
88	71	73	75	77	100	102	104	106
89	72	74	76	78	101	103	105	107

Critical Values for the Number-of-Runs
Test for Equal-Size Samples (cont.)

m=n	0.005	0.01	0.025	0.05	0.95	0.975	0.99	0.995
90	73	74	77	79	102	104	107	108
91	74	75	78	80	103	105	108	109
92	75	76	79	81	104	106	109	110
93	75	77	80	82	105	107	110	112
94	76	78	81	83	106	108	111	113
95	77	79	82	84	107	109	112	114
96	78	80	82	85	108	111	113	115
97	79	81	83	86	109	112	114	116
98	80	82	84	87	110	113	115	117
99	81	83	85	87	112	114	116	118
100	82	84	86	88	113	115	117	119

12.4

12.5 Critical Values for the Number-of-Runs Test

The values tabulated here are defined as in Section 12.4. The difference between the two tables is that here m is not necessarily equal to n.

Critical Values for the Number-of-Runs Test [216]

m	n	0.005	0.01	0.025	0.05	0.95	0.975	0.99	0.995
2	2	-	-	-	-	4	4	4	4
	3	-	-	-	-	5	5	5	5
	4	-	-	-	-	5	5	5	5
	5	-	-	-	-	5	5	5	5
2	6	-	-	-	-	5	5	5	5
	7	-	-	-	-	5	5	5	5
	8	-	-	-	2	5	5	5	5
	9	-	-	-	2	5	5	5	5
	10	-	-	-	2	5	5	5	5
2	11	-	-	-	2	5	5	5	5
	12	-	-	2	2	5	5	5	5
	13	-	-	2	2	5	5	5	5
	14	-	-	2	2	5	5	5	5
	15	-	-	2	2	5	5	5	5
2	16	-	-	2	2	5	5	5	5
	17	-	-	2	2	5	5	5	5
	18	-	-	2	2	5	5	5	5
	19	-	2	2	2	5	5	5	5
	20	-	2	2	2	5	5	5	5
3	3	-	-	-	-	6	6	6	6
	4	-	-	-	-	6	7	7	7
	5	-	-	-	2	7	7	7	7
	6	-	-	2	2	7	7	7	7
	7	-	-	2	2	7	7	7	7
3	8	-	-	2	2	7	7	7	7
	9	-	2	2	2	7	7	7	7
	10	-	2	2	3	7	7	7	7
	11	-	2	2	3	7	7	7	7
	12	2	2	2	3	7	7	7	7
3	13	2	2	2	3	7	7	7	7
	14	2	2	2	3	7	7	7	7
	15	2	2	3	3	7	7	7	7
	16	2	2	3	3	7	7	7	7
	17	2	2	3	3	7	7	7	7
3	18	2	2	3	3	7	7	7	7
	19	2	2	3	3	7	7	7	7
	20	2	2	3	3	7	7	7	7

Critical Values for the Number-of-Runs Test (*cont.*)

m	n	0.005	0.01	0.025	0.05	0.95	0.975	0.99	0.995
4	4	-	-	-	2	7	8	8	8
	5	-	-	2	2	8	8	8	9
	6	-	2	2	3	8	8	9	9
	7	-	2	2	3	8	9	9	9
	8	2	2	3	3	9	9	9	9
4	9	2	2	3	3	9	9	9	9
	10	2	2	3	3	9	9	9	9
	11	2	2	3	3	9	9	9	9
	12	2	3	3	4	9	9	9	9
	13	2	3	3	4	9	9	9	9
	14	2	3	3	4	9	9	9	9
4	15	3	3	3	4	9	9	9	9
	16	3	3	4	4	9	9	9	9
	17	3	3	4	4	9	9	9	9
	18	3	3	4	4	9	9	9	9
	19	3	3	4	4	9	9	9	9
	20	3	3	4	4	9	9	9	9
5	5	-	2	2	3	8	9	9	10
	6	2	2	3	3	9	9	10	10
	7	2	2	3	3	9	10	10	11
	8	2	2	3	3	10	10	11	11
	9	2	3	3	4	10	11	11	11
5	10	3	3	3	4	10	11	11	11
	11	3	3	4	4	11	11	11	11
	12	3	3	4	4	11	11	11	11
	13	3	3	4	4	11	11	11	11
	14	3	3	4	5	11	11	11	11
5	15	3	4	4	5	11	11	11	11
	16	3	4	4	5	11	11	11	11
	17	3	4	4	5	11	11	11	11
	18	4	4	5	5	11	11	11	11
	19	4	4	5	5	11	11	11	11
	20	4	4	5	5	11	11	11	11

Critical Values for the Number-of-Runs Test (cont.)

m	n	0.005	0.01	0.025	0.05	0.95	0.975	0.99	0.995
6	6	2	2	3	3	10	10	11	11
	7	2	3	3	4	10	11	11	12
	8	3	3	3	4	11	11	12	12
	9	3	3	4	4	11	12	12	13
	10	3	3	4	5	11	12	13	13
6	11	3	4	4	5	12	12	13	13
	12	3	4	4	5	12	12	13	13
	13	3	4	5	5	12	13	13	13
	14	4	4	5	5	12	13	13	13
	15	4	4	5	6	13	13	13	13
6	16	4	4	5	6	13	13	13	13
	17	4	5	5	6	13	13	13	13
	18	4	5	5	6	13	13	13	13
	19	4	5	6	6	13	13	13	13
	20	4	5	6	6	13	13	13	13
7	7	3	3	3	4	11	12	12	12
	8	3	3	4	4	12	12	13	13
	9	3	4	4	5	12	13	13	14
	10	3	4	5	5	12	13	14	14
	11	4	4	5	5	13	13	14	14
7	12	4	4	5	6	13	13	14	15
	13	4	5	5	6	13	14	15	15
	14	4	5	5	6	13	14	15	15
	15	4	5	6	6	14	14	15	15
	16	5	5	6	6	14	15	15	15
7	17	5	5	6	7	14	15	15	15
	18	5	5	6	7	14	15	15	15
	19	5	6	6	7	14	15	15	15
	20	5	6	6	7	14	15	15	15
8	8	3	4	4	5	12	13	13	14
	9	3	4	5	5	13	13	14	14
	10	4	4	5	6	13	14	14	15
	11	4	5	5	6	14	14	15	15
	12	4	5	6	6	14	15	15	16

Critical Values for the Number-of-Runs Test (cont.)

m	n	0.005	0.01	0.025	0.05	0.95	0.975	0.99	0.995
8	13	5	5	6	6	14	15	16	16
	14	5	5	6	7	15	15	16	16
	15	5	5	6	7	15	15	16	17
	16	5	6	6	7	15	16	16	17
	17	5	6	7	7	15	16	17	17
8	18	6	6	7	8	15	16	17	17
	19	6	6	7	8	15	16	17	17
	20	6	6	7	8	16	16	17	17
9	9	4	4	5	6	13	14	15	15
	10	4	5	5	6	14	15	15	16
	11	5	5	6	6	14	15	16	16
	12	5	5	6	7	15	15	16	17
	13	5	6	6	7	15	16	17	17
	14	5	6	7	7	16	16	17	17
9	15	6	6	7	8	16	17	17	18
	16	6	6	7	8	16	17	17	18
	17	6	7	7	8	16	17	18	18
	18	6	7	8	8	17	17	18	19
	19	6	7	8	8	17	17	18	19
	20	7	7	8	9	17	17	18	19
10	10	5	5	6	6	15	15	16	16
	11	5	5	6	7	15	16	17	17
	12	5	6	7	7	16	16	17	18
	13	5	6	7	8	16	17	18	18
	14	6	6	7	8	16	17	18	18
10	15	6	7	7	8	17	17	18	19
	16	6	7	8	8	17	18	19	19
	17	7	7	8	9	17	18	19	19
	18	7	7	8	9	18	18	19	20
	19	7	8	8	9	18	19	19	20
	20	7	8	9	9	18	19	19	20
11	11	5	6	7	7	16	16	17	18
	12	6	6	7	8	16	17	18	18
	13	6	6	7	8	17	18	18	19
	14	6	7	8	8	17	18	19	19
	15	7	7	8	9	18	18	19	20

Critical Values for the Number-of-Runs Test (cont.)

m	n	0.005	0.01	0.025	0.05	0.95	0.975	0.99	0.995
11	16	7	7	8	9	18	19	20	20
	17	7	8	9	9	18	19	20	21
	18	7	8	9	10	19	19	20	21
	19	8	8	9	10	19	20	21	21
	20	8	8	9	10	19	20	21	21
12	12	6	7	7	8	17	18	18	19
	13	6	7	8	9	17	18	19	20
	14	7	7	8	9	18	19	20	20
	15	7	8	8	9	18	19	20	21
	16	7	8	9	10	19	20	21	21
12	17	8	8	9	10	19	20	21	21
	18	8	8	9	10	20	20	21	22
	19	8	9	10	10	20	21	22	22
	20	8	9	10	11	20	21	22	22
13	13	7	7	8	9	18	19	20	20
	14	7	8	9	9	19	19	20	21
	15	7	8	9	10	19	20	21	21
	16	8	8	9	10	20	20	21	22
	17	8	9	10	10	20	21	22	22
13	18	8	9	10	11	20	21	22	23
	19	9	9	10	11	21	22	23	23
	20	9	10	10	11	21	22	23	23
14	14	7	8	9	10	19	20	21	22
	15	8	8	9	10	20	21	22	22
	16	8	9	10	11	20	21	22	23
	17	8	9	10	11	21	22	23	23
	18	9	9	10	11	21	22	23	24
14	19	9	10	11	12	22	22	23	24
	20	9	10	11	12	22	23	24	24
15	15	8	9	10	11	20	21	22	23
	16	9	9	10	11	21	22	23	23
	17	9	10	11	11	21	22	23	24
	18	9	10	11	12	22	23	24	24
	19	10	10	11	12	22	23	24	25
	20	10	11	12	12	23	24	25	25

12.5

Critical Values for the Number-of-Runs Test (cont.)

m	n	0.005	0.01	0.025	0.05	0.95	0.975	0.99	0.995
16	16	9	10	11	11	22	22	23	24
	17	9	10	11	12	22	23	24	25
	18	10	10	11	12	23	24	25	25
	19	10	11	12	13	23	24	25	26
	20	10	11	12	13	24	24	25	26
17	17	10	10	11	12	23	24	25	25
	18	10	11	12	13	23	24	25	26
	19	10	11	12	13	24	25	26	26
	20	11	11	13	13	24	25	26	27
18	18	11	11	12	13	24	25	26	26
	19	11	12	13	14	24	25	26	27
	20	11	12	13	14	25	26	27	28
19	19	11	12	13	14	25	26	27	28
	20	12	12	13	14	26	26	28	28
20	20	12	13	14	15	26	27	28	29

12.6 Fraction of Arrangements of *n* Numbers (No Two Alike) with Runs Up or Down of Length *p* or More

Let $a_1, a_2, \ldots, a_n$ be n numbers, no two alike, and let the sequence $S = (h_1, h_2, \ldots, h_n)$ be any permutation of $a_1, a_2, \ldots, a_n$ where S is to be considered a chance variable, and each of the $n!$ permutations of a_1, $a_2, \ldots, a_n$ is assigned the same probability. Consider the derived sequence R whose ith element is the sign (plus-or-minus) of $h_{i+1} - h_i$, ($i = 1$, $2, \ldots, n - 1$). A sequence of p consecutive plus signs immediately preceded by a minus sign is called a run up of length p or more. A sequence of p consecutive minus signs immediately preceded by a plus sign is called a run down of length p or more. When such a run is both immediately preceded and immediately followed by an unlike sign, it is a run of length exactly p. Attention is directed to the distribution of sample arrangements that have at least one run up or down of length p or more.

The quantity tabulated under "Freq" is the frequency with which a run of length p or more (either up or down) occurs, and under "Prob" the quantity tabulated is the probability that a run of length p or more will occur.

Olmstead [157] gives a recurrence formula for the needed frequencies, and this recurrence relationship was used for $n = 2(1)14$ in the tables given here. For $n = 15(5)20(20)100$, 200, 500, 1000, and 5000 and $p \leq 6$, Olmstead extrapolated from smaller values of n. For $p > 6$ and $n \geq 15$, Olmstead used a Poisson exponential as an approximation. Levene and Wolfowitz [118] give the covariance matrix of runs up and down, and Wolfowitz [250] gives the asymptotic distribution.

Fraction of Arrangements of n Numbers (No Two Alike) with Runs Up or Down of Length p or More [157]

	2		3		4		5		6		7	
p	Freq	Prob	Freq	Prob	Freq	Prob	Freq	Prob	Freq	Prob	Freq	Prob
1	2	1.000	6	1.000	24	1.000	120	1.000	720	1.000	5,040	1.00
2		0.000	2	0.333	14	0.583	88	0.733	598	0.831	4,496	0.89
3				0.000	2	0.083	18	0.150	156	0.217	1,388	0.27
4						0.000	2	0.017	22	0.031	224	0.04
5								0.000	2	0.003	26	0.00
6										0.000	2	0.00
7												0.00

	8		9		10		11	
p	Freq	Prob	Freq	Prob	Freq	Prob	Freq	Prob
1	40,320	1.000	362,880	1.000	3,628,800	1.000	39,916,800	1.000
2	37,550	0.931	347,008	0.956	3,527,758	0.972	39,209,216	0.982
3	13,334	0.331	138,422	0.381	1,554,854	0.428	18,835,878	0.472
4	2,352	0.058	26,068	0.072	309,178	0.085	3,926,538	0.098
5	304	0.008	3,600	0.010	44,640	0.012	585,576	0.015
6	30	0.001	396	0.001	5,220	0.001	71,280	0.002
7	2	0.000	34	0.000	500	0.000	7,260	0.000
8		0.000	2	0.000	38	0.000	616	0.000
9				0.000	2	0.000	42	0.000
10						0.000	2	0.000
								0.000

	12		13		14	
p	Freq	Prob	Freq	Prob	Freq	Prob
1	479,001,600	1.000	6,227,020,800	1.000	87,178,291,200	1.000
2	473,596,070	0.989	6,182,284,288	0.993	86,779,569,238	0.995
3	245,249,548	0.512	3,419,024,924	0.549	50,852,433,294	0.583
4	53,333,016	0.111	772,958,890	0.124	11,920,405,298	0.137
5	8,159,498	0.017	120,760,922	0.019	1,895,856,108	0.022
6	1,021,680	0.002	15,442,152	0.002	246,427,634	0.003
7	108,240	0.000	1,681,680	0.000	27,387,360	0.000
8	9,768	0.000	157,872	0.000	2,642,640	0.000
9	744	0.000	12,792	0.000	222,768	0.000
10	46	0.000	884	0.000	16,380	0.000
11	2	0.000	50	0.000	1,036	0.000
12		0.000	2	0.000	54	0.000
13				0.000	2	0.000
14						0.000

12.6

Fraction of Arrangements of *n* Numbers (No Two Alike) with
Runs Up or Down of Length *p* or More (*cont.*)

p	15	20	n 40	60	80
1	1.0000	1.0000	1.0000	1.0000	1.0000
2	0.9971	0.9997	1.0000	1.0000	1.0000
3	0.6150	0.7406	0.9466	0.9890	0.9977
4	0.1492	0.2086	0.4078	0.5568	0.6684
5	0.0241	0.0358	0.0810	0.1241	0.1652
6	0.0032	0.0049	0.0118	0.0187	0.0255
7	0.0004	0.0006	0.0015	0.0023	0.0032
8	0.0000	0.0001	0.0002	0.0003	0.0004
9	0.0000	0.0000	0.0000	0.0000	0.0000
10	0.0000	0.0000	0.0000	0.0000	0.0000
> 10	0.0000	0.0000	0.0000	0.0000	0.0000

p	100	200	n 500	1000	5000
1	1.0000	1.0000	1.0000	1.0000	1.0000
2	1.0000	1.0000	1.0000	1.0000	1.0000
3	0.9995	1.0000	1.0000	1.0000	1.0000
4	0.7518	0.9418	0.9992	1.0000	1.0000
5	0.2044	0.3743	0.6957	0.9085	1.0000
6	0.0322	0.0653	0.1580	0.2925	0.8241
7	0.0041	0.0085	0.0215	0.0428	0.1976
8	0.0005	0.0010	0.0024	0.0049	0.0245
9	0.0000	0.0001	0.0002	0.0005	0.0025
10	0.0000	0.0000	0.0000	0.0000	0.0002
> 10	0.0000	0.0000	0.0000	0.0000	0.0000

12.7 Minimum Sample Sizes n such that the Probability Equals P that the Longest Run on Either Side of the Median Exceeds or Equals s

A sample of n observations of a characteristic X has been obtained, and a particular ordering, $X_1, X_2, \ldots, X_n$, is specified. For example, the quantities may be ordered according to the times of their observation. Assuming a cut at a particular value of X, $(X \neq X_1, X_2, \ldots, X_n)$, such as A, such a series may be divided into groups of consecutive observations that lie, alternately, above and below the cut. The number of observations in each group is called a run of length S.

Olmstead [158] developed methods for computing the probability distribution of S. A probability P is selected and the question is posed, "How large a sample must be taken in order that with probability equal to P at least one run of length s, or longer, will be observed in the sample?" The value of n, the sample size, is given in the tables.

In the table given here the median of the sample is chosen as the cut A (n is even), and the probability of a run of length at least s on either side of the median is considered. That is, the probability is P that a run of length at least s will occur either above the median or below the median if a sample of size n is used.

Minimum Sample Sizes n such that the Probability Equals P that the Longest Run on Either Side of the Median Exceeds or Equals s [158]

Run Length	Probability, P				
s	0.01	0.10	0.50	0.90	0.99
1	2	2	2	2	2
2	4	4	4	8	10
3	6	6	8	16	28
4	8	8	16	36	64
5	10	14	30	76	136
6	12	20	58	152	282
7	16	32	106	296	568
8	22	52	200	580	1150
9	32	86	388	1174	2310
10	42	150	758	2350	4640
11	62	262	1488	4720	9330
12	94	500	2920	9460	18730
13	156	962	5860	10660	37700
14	256	1876	11250	21300	75700
15	418	3670	22600	42600	151600
16	766	7330	45200	85300	303000
17	1472	14090	90100	170500	606000
18	2860	27900	180300	341000	1213000
19	5570	55500	361000	682000	2430000
20	10860	111100	721000	1364000	4850000

12.8 Minimum Sample Sizes *n* such that the Probability Equals *P* that the Longest Run on One Side of the Median Exceeds or Equals *s*

The definitions and comments in the first two paragraphs of Section 12.7 apply.

In the table given here the median of the sample is chosen as the cut A, and the probability of a run of length at least s on one side only (side chosen in advance) of the median is considered. That is, the probability is P that a run of length s will occur on one prechosen side of the median if a sample of size n is used.

Minimum Sample Sizes *n* such that the Probability Equals *P* that the Longest Run on One Side of the Median Exceeds or Equals *s* [158]

Run Length s	Probability, P				
	0.01	0.10	0.50	0.90	0.99
1	2	2	2	2	2
2	4	4	6	8	12
3	6	6	12	22	38
4	8	10	22	54	100
5	10	16	46	116	230
6	14	26	92	260	490
7	18	44	182	530	1044
8	26	78	360	1104	2140
9	38	142	714	2240	4370
10	56	256	1424	4530	8980
11	86	480	2850	9190	18240
12	140	930	5680	18540	37200
13	234	1838	11330	37600	75500
14	410	3630	22700	75700	151700
15	748	7160	45300	151700	303000
16	1446	14190	90600	303000	607000
17	2830	28100	181200	607000	1214000
18	5530	56100	362000	1214000	2430000
19	10860	117300	725000	2430000	4850000
20	21500	235000	1450000	4850000	9710000

12.9 Minimum Sample Sizes n such that the Probability Equals P that the Longest Runs on Each Side of the Median Both Exceed or Equal s

The definitions and comments in the first two paragraphs of Section 12.7 apply.

In the table given here the median of the sample is chosen as the cut A, and the probability P is considered that the shorter of the longest run above and the longest run below the median equals or exceeds s. That is, the probability is P that runs of length at least s must occur on both sides of the median if a sample of size n is used.

Minimum Sample Sizes n such that the Probability Equals P that the Longest Runs on Each Side of the Median Both Exceed or Equal s [158]

Run Length s	Probability, P				
	0.01	0.10	0.50	0.90	0.99
1	2	2	2	2	2
2	4	4	6	10	14
3	6	8	14	26	44
4	8	14	30	68	116
5	12	26	68	152	252
6	20	50	140	322	552
7	34	98	290	676	1164
8	62	194	596	1390	2390
9	116	390	1208	2830	4930
10	216	782	2440	5650	10140
11	446	1182	4910	11750	20700
12	884	2360	9840	23800	42500
13	1762	4720	19890	48600	86700
14	3510	9450	39900	98600	174200
15	6990	18900	80500	197300	348000
16	13930	37800	161300	395000	697000
17	27900	75600	323000	789000	1394000
18	55500	151200	645000	1578000	2790000
19	111000	302000	1290000	3160000	5570000
20	222000	605000	2580000	6310000	11150000

12.10 Minimum Sample Sizes n such that the Probability Equals P that the Longest Runs on Each Side of any Cut Both Exceed or Equal s

The definitions and comments in the first two paragraphs of Section 12.7 apply.

In the table given here the probability is P that the shorter of the longest run above and the longest run below a cut (chosen to maximize the shorter length) is at least of length s if a sample of size n is used.

Minimum Sample Sizes n such that the Probability Equals P that the Longest Runs on Each Side of any Cut Both Exceed or Equal s [158]

Run Length	Probability, P				
s	0.01	0.10	0.50	0.90	0.99
1	2	2	2	2	2
2	4	4	6	8	12
3	6	8	12	22	34
4	8	12	22	48	76
5	12	18	46	96	162
6	16	34	86	192	380
7	24	58	166	382	668
8	38	108	324	760	1342
9	66	204	638	1518	2690
10	118	400	1266	3030	5410
11	228	790	2530	6070	10870
12	444	1568	5050	12130	21500
13	878	3130	10070	24300	43100
14	1750	6220	20100	48500	86200
15	3480	12490	40300	97000	172300
16	6790	25000	80600	194100	345000
17	13860	49900	161100	388000	689000
18	27700	99900	322000	776000	1379000
19	55400	199800	644000	1553000	2760000
20	110800	400000	1289000	3110000	5510000

12.11 Probability of *r* or Fewer Runs of Signs of First Differences in Ordered Series

A series of observations is ordered according to the time the observations were taken. The first differences of this series are calculated. The signs (plus-or-minus) of the differences are noted, and every time a sign differs from the preceding sign a run is counted. The table gives the cumulative probability distribution of the number of runs r for various numbers of observations under the hypothesis that the relative magnitude of an observation in the original series is independent of its position in the series. Edgington [61] gives an example of the use of this table. The mean number of runs is $(2n - 1)/3$, where n is the number of observations in the original series. The number of runs tends to be normally distributed about this mean with a standard deviation of $\sqrt{(16n - 29)/90}$ for large values of n.

Probability of r or Fewer Runs of Signs of First Differences in Ordered Series [61]

r	2	3	4	5	6	7	8	9
1	1.0000	0.3333	0.0833	0.0167	0.0028	0.0004	0.0000	0.0000
2		1.0000	0.5833	0.2500	0.0861	0.0250	0.0063	0.0014
3			1.0000	0.7333	0.4139	0.1909	0.0749	0.0257
4				1.0000	0.8306	0.5583	0.3124	0.1500
5					1.0000	0.8921	0.6750	0.4347
6						1.0000	0.9313	0.7653
7							1.0000	0.9563
8								1.0000

r	10	11	12	13	14	15	16	17
2	0.0003	0.0001	0.0000	0.0000	0.0000	0.0000	0.0000	0.0000
3	0.0079	0.0022	0.0005	0.0001	0.0000	0.0000	0.0000	0.0000
4	0.0633	0.0239	0.0082	0.0026	0.0007	0.0002	0.0001	0.0000
5	0.2427	0.1196	0.0529	0.0213	0.0079	0.0027	0.0009	0.0003
6	0.5476	0.3438	0.1918	0.0964	0.0441	0.0186	0.0072	0.0026
7	0.8329	0.6460	0.4453	0.2749	0.1534	0.0782	0.0367	0.0160
8	0.9722	0.8823	0.7280	0.5413	0.3633	0.2216	0.1238	0.0638
9	1.0000	0.9823	0.9179	0.7942	0.6278	0.4520	0.2975	0.1799
10		1.0000	0.9887	0.9432	0.8464	0.7030	0.5369	0.3770
11			1.0000	0.9928	0.9609	0.8866	0.7665	0.6150
12				1.0000	0.9954	0.9733	0.9172	0.8188
13					1.0000	0.9971	0.9818	0.9400
14						1.0000	0.9981	0.9877
15							1.0000	0.9988
16								1.0000

r	18	19	20	21	22	23	24	25
5	0.0001	0.0000	0.0000	0.0000	0.0000	0.0000	0.0000	0.0000
6	0.0009	0.0003	0.0001	0.0000	0.0000	0.0000	0.0000	0.0000
7	0.0065	0.0025	0.0009	0.0003	0.0001	0.0000	0.0000	0.0000
8	0.0306	0.0137	0.0058	0.0023	0.0009	0.0003	0.0001	0.0000
9	0.1006	0.0523	0.0255	0.0117	0.0050	0.0021	0.0008	0.0003
10	0.2443	0.1467	0.0821	0.0431	0.0213	0.0099	0.0044	0.0018
11	0.4568	0.3144	0.2012	0.1202	0.0674	0.0356	0.0177	0.0084
12	0.6848	0.5337	0.3873	0.2622	0.1661	0.0988	0.0554	0.0294
13	0.8611	0.7454	0.6055	0.4603	0.3276	0.2188	0.1374	0.0815
14	0.9569	0.8945	0.7969	0.6707	0.5312	0.3953	0.2768	0.1827
15	0.9917	0.9692	0.9207	0.8398	0.7286	0.5980	0.4631	0.3384
16	0.9992	0.9944	0.9782	0.9409	0.8749	0.7789	0.6595	0.5292
17	1.0000	0.9995	0.9962	0.9846	0.9563	0.9032	0.8217	0.7148
18		1.0000	0.9997	0.9975	0.9892	0.9679	0.9258	0.8577
19			1.0000	0.9998	0.9983	0.9924	0.9765	0.9436
20				1.0000	0.9999	0.9989	0.9947	0.9830
21					1.0000	0.9999	0.9993	0.9963
22						1.0000	1.0000	0.9995
23							1.0000	1.0000
24								1.0000

12.12 Critical Values for Magnitudes of Quadrant Sums

A set of n pairs of observations is available on the random variables (X, Y), both with continuous cumulative distributions, and a scatter diagram is prepared. The diagram is first divided into two parts by a vertical line, each part containing an equal number of points (a line through the median of the X's). If there is an odd number of points, the line will go through a point and it is discarded. A horizontal line is then constructed in the same manner, dividing the scatter diagram into four quadrants. The quadrants are considered as if the plus sign were attached to the upper right and lower left quadrants, and the minus sign to the upper left and lower right quadrants. Beginning at the right-hand side of the diagram and moving to the left, count (in the order of the abscissas) the observations until forced to cross the horizontal median. Tally the number of observations met before this crossing, attaching the plus sign if they lie in the plus quadrant and the minus sign if they lie in the minus quadrant. Repeat this process moving up from below, moving to the right from the left, and moving down from above. The quadrant sum is the absolute value of the algebraic sum of the four terms thus tallied.

A test of the hypothesis that there is no association between X and Y may be performed by noting whether the quadrant sum exceeds the critical values of the quadrant sum statistic in the table. These critical values were computed under the assumptions that there is no association and that the probability of a tie in x-values or in y-values is zero. Olmstead and Tukey [159] give more details of this computation.

Critical Values for Magnitudes of Quadrant Sums [159]

Significance Level (conservative)	Magnitude of Quadrant Sum*
0.10	9
0.05	11
0.02	13
0.01	14-15
0.005	15-17
0.002	17-19
0.001	18-21

*The smaller magnitude applies for large sample size, the larger magnitude for small sample size. Magnitude equal to or greater than twice the sample size less six should not be used.

12.13 Critical Values for Magnitudes of Octant Sums

This is an obvious extension of the procedure for two variables (X, Y), given in Section 12.12, to three variables (X, Y, Z). The reader is referred to the paper by Olmstead and Tukey [159] for more detail.

Critical Values for Magnitudes of Octant Sums [159]

Significance Level	Magnitude of Octant Sum*
0.10	11
0.05	13
0.02	15
0.01	16
0.005	18
0.002	20
0.001	21

*Computed for large samples only and based on normal approximation.

12.14 Limiting Distribution of a Nonparametric Test of Independence

Let Ω be the class of continuous cumulative distribution functions in two-dimensional Euclidean space, and let ω be the subclass consisting of every member of Ω which is a product of the associated one-dimensional marginal cumulative distribution functions. Let (X_1, Y_1), (X_2, Y_2), $\ldots$, (X_n, Y_n) be independent random pairs with common cumulative distribution function $F(X, Y)$, a member of Ω. The hypothesis to be tested is $H_0: F(X, Y)$ belongs to ω, against the alternative $H_1: F(X, Y)$ belongs to $\Omega - \omega$.

Count the number of points lying in each of the four regions determined by lines through (X_j, Y_j) which are parallel to the axes of the (X, Y) coordinate system; that is, $N_1(j)$ is the number of points in the first quadrant of a coordinate system with axes parallel to the original coordinate system, but with origin at (X_j, Y_j), and $N_2(j)$ is the count for the second quadrant, etc. Then B_n is defined as

$$B_n = n^{-4} \sum_{j=1}^{n} [N_1(j)N_4(j) - N_2(j)N_3(j)]^2.$$

The test procedure is then to reject H_0 and accept H_1 if B_n is too large.

Unfortunately, there are no tables available for finite values of n. The tables given here were obtained by inverting the characteristic function of the limiting distribution of nB_n:

$$E[\exp{(izB)}] = \prod_{j,k=1}^{\infty} \left[1 - \frac{2iz}{\pi^4 j^2 k^2} \right]^{-1/2},$$

where B has the limiting distribution of nB_n. The distribution of $B\pi^4/2$ under H_0 is designated $F(y)$ in the tables, and its inverse is designated $F^{-1}(p)$. Blum, Kiefer, and Rosenblatt [26] have also considered the distribution of this statistic under H_1.

Limiting Distribution of a Nonparametric Test of Independence [26]

$$F(y) = \lim_{n \to \infty} Pr_{H_0}\left\{\tfrac{1}{2}\pi^4 n B_n \le y\right\}$$

y	F(y)	y	F(y)	y	F(y)	y	F(y)
0.30	0.00000	1.65	0.76449	3.00	0.95857	4.35	0.99126
0.35	0.00010	1.70	0.78060	3.05	0.96097	4.40	0.99174
0.40	0.00086	1.75	0.79547	3.10	0.96322	4.45	0.99219
0.45	0.00389	1.80	0.80922	3.15	0.96533	4.50	0.99261
0.50	0.01158	1.85	0.82193	3.20	0.96732	4.55	0.99301
0.55	0.02614	1.90	0.83369	3.25	0.96918	4.60	0.99339
0.60	0.04867	1.95	0.84459	3.30	0.97094	4.65	0.99375
0.65	0.07899	2.00	0.85469	3.35	0.97259	4.70	0.99409
0.70	0.11594	2.05	0.86406	3.40	0.97414	4.75	0.99441
0.75	0.15784	2.10	0.87275	3.45	0.97561	4.80	0.99471
0.80	0.20293	2.15	0.88084	3.50	0.97698	4.85	0.99499
0.85	0.24960	2.20	0.88835	3.55	0.97828	4.90	0.99527
0.90	0.29652	2.25	0.89534	3.60	0.97949	4.95	0.99552
0.95	0.34267	2.30	0.90185	3.65	0.98064	5.00	0.99576
1.00	0.38730	2.35	0.90791	3.70	0.98172	5.50	0.99755
1.05	0.42994	2.40	0.91357	3.75	0.98274	6.00	0.99858
1.10	0.47027	2,45	0.91885	3.80	0.98370	6.50	0.99918
1.15	0.50816	2.50	0.92377	3.85	0.98461	7.00	0.99952
1.20	0.54354	2.55	0.92838	3.90	0.98546	7.50	0.99972
1.25	0.57645	2.60	0.93268	3.95	0.98627	8.00	0.99983
1.30	0.60697	2.65	0.93670	4.00	0.98702	8.50	0.99990
1.35	0.63521	2.70	0.94047	4.05	0.98774	9.00	0.99994
1.40	0.66131	2.75	0.94400	4.10	0.98841	9.50	0.99997
1.45	0.68540	2.80	0.94730	4.15	0.98905	10.00	0.99998
1.50	0.70763	2.85	0.95039	4.20	0.98965	10.50	0.99999
1.55	0.72813	2.90	0.95329	4.25	0.99022	11.00	1.00000
1.60	0.74704	2.95	0.95602	4.30	0.99075		

Critical Values of the Limiting Distribution
of a Nonparametric Test of Independence [26]

p	$F^{-1}(p)$	p	$F^{-1}(p)$
0.9	2.286	0.998	5.68
0.95	2.844	0.999	6.32
0.98	3.622	0.9995	6.96
0.99	4.230	0.9998	7.82
0.995	4.851	0.9999	8.47

13. RANK CORRELATION

13.1 Exact Distribution of Kendall's Rank Correlation Coefficient

The Kendall rank correlation coefficient for two sets of n ranked items (ranked $1, 2, \ldots, n$) may be described as follows: One of the sets is ordered so that the ranks occur in the natural order 1 to n. The pairing of the items of the second set with those of the first and this reordering of the first set induce a new ordering of the ranks on the second set, for example, 3, 8, 5, 4, 6, 1, 7, 2. Starting with Rank 1 in this ordering, count the number of integers to its right and record this score, 2; cross out 1 and count the same way for Rank 2, obtaining the score 0; cross out 2 also and proceed as before. The sum of these scores is a statistic which is denoted by k. In this example $k = 2 + 0 + 5 + 2 + 2 + 1 + 0 = 12$.

Under the assumption that each of the $n(n-1)/2$ possible outcomes for the scores is equally likely, the cumulative probability distribution of k has been computed and is given in the table here: C.P. $= \Pr \{k \leq k'\}$ and c.f. $=$ cumulative frequency of the k's. The reader is referred to Kendall's book [106], p. 68, for a description of the method used to compute these frequencies and distributions. Note the symmetry in the distribution function.

The Kendall rank correlation coefficient is defined as

$$\tau = \frac{4k}{n(n-1)} - 1.$$

This has the property that $-1 \leq \tau \leq 1$. It is not necessary to compute τ in order to use the tables, since they have been prepared using the equivalent variable k. Burr [29] considers the question of tied rankings and gives a table in this case. Sillitto [201] also considers ties. The mean of k is $n(n-1)/4$, and the variance is $n(n-1)(2n+5)/72$.

Exact Distribution of Kendall's Rank Correlation Coefficient

k	c.f.	C.P.	k	c.f.	C.P.	k	c.f.	C.P.
	n = 2			n = 7			n = 8 (cont)	
0	1	0.500	0	1	0.000	24	40209	0.997
1	2	1.000	1	7	0.001	25	40285	0.999
			2	27	0.005	26	40312	1.000
	n = 3		3	76	0.015	27	40319	1.000
0	1	0.167	4	174	0.035	28	40320	1.000
1	3	0.500	5	343	0.068			
2	5	0.833	6	602	0.119		n = 9	
3	6	1.000	7	961	0.191	0	1	0.000
			8	1416	0.281	1	9	0.000
	n = 4		9	1947	0.386	2	44	0.000
0	1	0.042	10	2520	0.500	3	155	0.000
1	4	0.167	11	3093	0.614	4	440	0.001
2	9	0.375	12	3624	0.719	5	1068	0.003
3	15	0.625	13	4079	0.809	6	2298	0.006
4	20	0.833	14	4438	0.881	7	4489	0.012
5	23	0.958	15	4697	0.932	8	8095	0.022
6	24	1.000	16	4866	0.965	9	13640	0.038
			17	4964	0.985	10	21671	0.060
	n = 5		18	5013	0.995	11	32692	0.090
0	1	0.008	19	5033	0.999	12	47087	0.130
1	5	0.042	20	5039	1.000	13	65044	0.179
2	14	0.117	21	5040	1.000	14	86494	0.238
3	29	0.242				15	111078	0.306
4	49	0.408		n = 8		16	138151	0.381
5	71	0.592	0	1	0.000	17	166826	0.460
6	91	0.758	1	8	0.000	18	196054	0.540
7	106	0.883	2	35	0.001	19	224729	0.619
8	115	0.958	3	111	0.003	20	251802	0.694
9	119	0.992	4	285	0.007	21	276386	0.762
10	120	1.000	5	628	0.016	22	297836	0.821
			6	1230	0.031	23	315793	0.870
	n = 6		7	2191	0.054	24	330188	0.910
0	1	0.001	8	3606	0.089	25	341209	0.940
1	6	0.008	9	5546	0.138	26	349240	0.962
2	20	0.028	10	8039	0.199	27	354785	0.978
3	49	0.068	11	11056	0.274	28	358391	0.988
4	98	0.136	12	14506	0.360	29	360582	0.994
5	169	0.235	13	18242	0.452	30	361812	0.997
6	259	0.360	14	22078	0.548	31	362440	0.999
7	360	0.500	15	25814	0.640	32	362725	1.000
8	461	0.640	16	29264	0.726	33	362836	1.000
9	551	0.765	17	32281	0.801	34	362871	1.000
10	622	0.864	18	34774	0.862	35	362879	1.000
11	671	0.932	19	36714	0.911	36	362880	1.000
12	700	0.972	20	38129	0.946			
13	714	0.992	21	39090	0.969			
14	719	0.999	22	39692	0.984			
15	720	1.000	23	40035	0.993			

13.1

Exact Distribution of Kendall's Rank Correlation Coefficient (*cont.*)

k	c.f.	C.P.	k	c.f.	C.P.	k	c.f.	C.P.
n = 10				**n = 10 (cont)**			**n = 11 (cont)**	
0	1	0.000	35	3598561	0.992	20	5647565	0.141
1	10	0.000	36	3612201	0.995	21	7159307	0.179
2	54	0.000	37	3620296	0.998	22	8889115	0.223
3	209	0.000	38	3624785	0.999	23	10822629	0.271
4	649	0.000	39	3627083	1.000	24	12934948	0.324
5	1717	0.000	40	3628151	1.000	25	15191344	0.381
6	4015	0.001	41	3628591	1.000	26	17548819	0.440
7	8504	0.002	42	3628746	1.000	27	19958400	0.500
8	16599	0.005	43	3628790	1.000	28	22367981	0.560
9	30239	0.008	44	3628799	1.000	29	24725456	0.619
10	51909	0.014	45	3628800	1.000	30	26981852	0.676
11	84592	0.023				31	29094171	0.729
12	131635	0.036		**n = 11**		32	31027685	0.777
13	196524	0.054	0	1	0.000	33	32757493	0.821
14	282578	0.078	1	11	0.000	34	34269235	0.859
			2	65	0.000			
15	392588	0.108	3	274	0.000	35	35558953	0.891
16	528441	0.146	4	923	0.000	36	36632180	0.918
17	690778	0.190				37	37502413	0.940
18	878737	0.242	5	2640	0.000	38	38189176	0.957
19	1089826	0.300	6	6655	0.000	39	38715900	0.970
			7	15159	0.000			
20	1319957	0.364	8	31758	0.001	40	39107839	0.980
21	1563651	0.431	9	61997	0.002	41	39390208	0.987
22	1814400	0.500				42	39586678	0.992
23	2065149	0.569	10	113906	0.003	43	39718303	0.995
24	2308843	0.636	11	198497	0.005	44	39802894	0.997
			12	330122	0.008			
25	2538974	0.700	13	526592	0.013	45	39854803	0.998
26	2750063	0.758	14	808961	0.020	46	39885042	0.999
27	2938022	0.810				47	39901641	1.000
28	3100359	0.854	15	1200900	0.030	48	39910145	1.000
29	3236212	0.892	16	1727624	0.043	49	39914160	1.000
			17	2414387	0.060			
30	3346222	0.922	18	3284620	0.082	50	39915877	1.000
31	3432276	0.946	19	4357847	0.109	51	39916526	1.000
32	3497165	0.964				52	39916735	1.000
33	3544208	0.977				53	39916789	1.000
34	3576891	0.986				54	39916799	1.000
						55	39916800	1.000

13.1

Exact Distribution of Kendall's Rank Correlation Coefficient (cont.)

k	c.f.	C.P.	k	c.f.	C.P.
	n = 12			n = 12 (cont)	
0	1	0.000	35	302416337	0.631
1	12	0.000	36	326113569	0.681
2	77	0.000	37	348424638	0.727
3	351	0.000	38	369064995	0.770
4	1274	0.000	39	387822495	0.810
5	3914	0.000	40	404562353	0.845
6	10569	0.000	41	419227105	0.875
7	25728	0.000	42	431831931	0.902
8	57486	0.000	43	442456063	0.924
9	119483	0.000	44	451231272	0.942
10	233389	0.000	45	458328582	0.957
11	431886	0.001	46	463944389	0.969
12	762007	0.002	47	468287077	0.978
13	1288588	0.003	48	471565042	0.984
14	2097484	0.004	49	473976789	0.990
15	3298110	0.007	50	475703490	0.993
16	5024811	0.010	51	476904116	0.996
17	7436568	0.016	52	477713012	0.997
18	10714523	0.022	53	478239593	0.998
19	15057211	0.031	54	478569714	0.999
20	20673018	0.043	55	478768211	1.000
21	27770328	0.058	56	478882117	1.000
22	36545537	0.076	57	478944114	1.000
23	47169669	0.098	58	478975872	1.000
24	59774495	0.125	59	478991031	1.000
25	74439247	0.155	60	478997686	1.000
26	91179105	0.190	61	479000326	1.000
27	109936605	0.230	62	479001249	1.000
28	130576962	0.273	63	479001523	1.000
29	152888031	0.319	64	479001588	1.000
30	176585263	0.369	65	479001599	1.000
31	201321587	0.420	66	479001600	1.000
32	226701707	0.473			
33	252299893	0.527			
34	277680013	0.580			

13.1

13.2 Exact Distribution of Spearman's Rank Correlation Coefficient

Spearman's rank correlation coefficient is defined as

$$\rho = 1 - \frac{6\sum_{i=1}^{n} d_i^2}{n^3 - n},$$

where d_i is the difference between the ranks of the ith pair of the group of n pairs of items, each member of a pair having been ranked among the like members of the other pairs. Let

$$S = \sum d_i^2.$$

Then the probability that the random variable S (under the assumption of no relationship between the two rankings) is less than a fixed value is given in the tables, along with the cumulative frequency of the S's. This table was computed according to the procedure given by Kendall [106], p. 74. See Olds [156] for more information on this method. The entries on pp. 172 and 173 of [106] for $n = 6$, $S = 44$, for $n = 9$, $S = 224$, and for $n = 10$, $S = 272$ and $S = 292$ in the distribution of S were found to be in error and are corrected here. The mean of S is $(n^3 - n)/6$, and the variance is $n^2(n + 1)^2(n - 1)/36$. Olds [156] gives a table of critical values of the distribution of S for $n = 11(1)30$ computed from an approximation.

Exact Distribution of Spearman's Rank Correlation Coefficient

S	cf	CP	S	cf	CP	S	cf	CP
	n = 2			n = 6			n = 7 (Cont)	
0	1	0.500	0	1	$0.0^2 14$	10	86	0.017
2	2	1.000	2	6	$0.0^2 83$	12	121	0.024
			4	12	0.017	14	167	0.033
	n = 3		6	21	0.029	16	222	0.044
			8	37	0.051	18	276	0.055
0	1	0.167						
2	3	0.500	10	49	0.068	20	350	0.069
6	5	0.833	12	63	0.088	22	420	0.083
8	6	1.000	14	87	0.121	24	504	0.100
			16	107	0.149	26	594	0.118
	n = 4		18	128	0.178	28	672	0.133
0	1	0.042	20	151	0.210	30	762	0.151
2	4	0.167	22	179	0.249	32	891	0.177
4	5	0.208	24	203	0.282	34	997	0.198
6	9	0.375	26	237	0.329	36	1120	0.222
8	11	0.458	28	257	0.357	38	1254	0.249
10	13	0.542	30	289	0.401	40	1401	0.278
12	15	0.625	32	331	0.460	42	1499	0.297
14	19	0.792	34	360	0.500	44	1667	0.331
16	20	0.833	36	389	0.540	46	1797	0.357
18	23	0.958	38	431	0.599	48	1972	0.391
20	24	1.000	40	463	0.643	50	2116	0.420
			42	483	0.671	52	2284	0.453
	n = 5		44	517	0.718	54	2428	0.482
			46	541	0.751	56	2612	0.518
0	1	$0.0^2 83$	48	569	0.790	58	2756	0.547
2	5	0.042						
4	8	0.067	50	592	0.822	60	2924	0.580
6	14	0.117	52	613	0.851	62	3068	0.609
8	21	0.175	54	633	0.879	64	3243	0.643
			56	657	0.913	66	3373	0.669
10	27	0.225	58	671	0.932	68	3541	0.703
12	31	0.258						
14	41	0.342	60	683	0.949	70	3639	0.722
16	47	0.392	62	699	0.971	72	3786	0.751
18	57	0.475	64	708	0.983	74	3920	0.778
			66	714	0.992	76	4043	0.802
20	63	0.525	68	719	0.999	78	4149	0.823
22	73	0.608						
24	79	0.658	70	720	1.000	80	4278	0.849
26	89	0.742				82	4368	0.867
28	93	0.775		n = 7		84	4446	0.882
						86	4536	0.900
30	99	0.825	0	1	$0.0^3 20$	88	4620	0.917
32	106	0.883	2	7	$0.0^2 14$			
34	112	0.933	4	17	$0.0^2 34$	90	4690	0.931
36	115	0.958	6	31	$0.0^2 62$	92	4764	0.945
38	119	0.992	8	60	0.012	94	4818	0.956
						96	4873	0.967
40	120	1.000				98	4919	0.976

Exact Distribution of Spearman's Rank Correlation Coefficient (*cont.*)

n = 7 (Cont)

S	cf	CP
100	4954	0.983
102	4980	0.988
104	5009	0.994
106	5023	0.997
108	5033	0.999
110	5039	1.000
112	5040	1.000

n = 8

S	cf	CP
0	1	$0.0^4 25$
2	8	$0.0^3 20$
4	23	$0.0^3 57$
6	45	$0.0^2 11$
8	92	$0.0^2 23$
10	146	$0.0^2 36$
12	216	$0.0^2 54$
14	310	$0.0^2 77$
16	439	0.011
18	563	0.014
20	741	0.018
22	924	0.023
24	1161	0.029
26	1399	0.035
28	1675	0.042
30	1939	0.048
32	2318	0.057
34	2667	0.066
36	3047	0.076
38	3447	0.085
40	3964	0.098
42	4358	0.108
44	4900	0.122
46	5392	0.134
48	6032	0.150
50	6589	0.163
52	7255	0.180
54	7850	0.195
56	8626	0.214
58	9310	0.231
60	10096	0.250
62	10814	0.268
64	11736	0.291
66	12481	0.310
68	13398	0.332

n = 8 (Cont)

S	cf	CP
70	14179	0.352
72	15161	0.376
74	15987	0.397
76	16937	0.420
78	17781	0.441
80	18847	0.467
82	19692	0.488
84	20628	0.512
86	21473	0.533
88	22539	0.559
90	23383	0.580
92	24333	0.603
94	25159	0.624
96	26141	0.648
98	26922	0.668
100	27839	0.690
102	28584	0.709
104	29506	0.732
106	30224	0.750
108	31010	0.769
110	31694	0.786
112	32470	0.805
114	33065	0.820
116	33731	0.837
118	34288	0.850
120	34928	0.866
122	35420	0.878
124	35962	0.892
126	36356	0.902
128	36873	0.915
130	37273	0.924
132	37653	0.934
134	38002	0.943
136	38381	0.952
138	38645	0.958
140	38921	0.965
142	39159	0.971
144	39396	0.977
146	39579	0.982
148	39757	0.986
150	39881	0.989
152	40010	0.992
154	40104	0.995
156	40174	0.996
158	40228	0.998

n = 8 (Cont)

S	cf	CP
160	40275	0.999
162	40297	0.999
164	40312	1.000
166	40319	1.000
168	40320	1.000

n = 9

S	cf	CP
0	1	$0.0^5 28$
2	9	$0.0^4 25$
4	30	$0.0^4 83$
6	64	$0.0^3 18$
8	136	$0.0^3 37$
10	238	$0.0^3 66$
12	368	$0.0^2 10$
14	558	$0.0^2 15$
16	818	$0.0^2 23$
18	1102	$0.0^2 30$
20	1500	$0.0^2 41$
22	1954	$0.0^2 54$
24	2509	$0.0^2 69$
26	3125	$0.0^2 86$
28	3881	0.011
30	4625	0.013
32	5647	0.016
34	6689	0.018
36	7848	0.022
38	9130	0.025
40	10685	0.029
42	12077	0.033
44	13796	0.038
46	15554	0.043
48	17563	0.048
50	19595	0.054
52	21877	0.060
54	24091	0.066
56	26767	0.074
58	29357	0.081
60	32235	0.089
62	35163	0.097
64	38560	0.106
66	41698	0.115
68	45345	0.125
70	48913	0.135
72	52834	0.146
74	56700	0.156

13.2

Exact Distribution of Spearman's Rank Correlation Coefficient (*cont.*)

S	cf	CP	S	cf	CP	S	cf	CP
	n = 9 (Cont)			n = 9 (Cont)			n = 10	
76	61011	0.168	160	297819	0.821	0	1	0.0^628
78	65061	0.179	162	301869	0.832	2	10	0.0^528
			164	306180	0.844	4	38	0.0^410
80	69913	0.193	166	310046	0.854	6	89	0.0^425
82	74405	0.205	168	313967	0.865	8	196	0.0^454
84	79221	0.218						
86	84005	0.231	170	317535	0.875	10	373	0.0^310
88	89510	0.247	172	321182	0.885	12	607	0.0^317
			174	324320	0.894	14	967	0.0^327
90	94464	0.260	176	327717	0.903	16	1465	0.0^340
92	100102	0.276	178	330645	0.911	18	2084	0.0^357
94	105406	0.290						
96	111296	0.307	180	333523	0.919	20	2903	0.0^380
98	116782	0.322	182	336113	0.926	22	3943	0.0^211
			184	338789	0.934	24	5195	0.0^214
100	122970	0.339	186	341003	0.940	26	6723	0.0^219
102	128472	0.354	188	343285	0.946	28	8547	0.0^224
104	134908	0.372						
106	140730	0.388	190	345317	0.952	30	10557	0.0^229
108	146963	0.405	192	347326	0.957	32	13090	0.0^236
			194	349084	0.962	34	15927	0.0^244
110	152987	0.422	196	350803	0.967	36	19107	0.0^253
112	159684	0.440	198	352195	0.971	38	22783	0.0^263
114	165404	0.456						
116	172076	0.474	200	353750	0.975	40	27088	0.0^275
118	178096	0.491	202	355032	0.978	42	31581	0.0^287
			204	356191	0.982	44	36711	0.010
120	184784	0.509	206	357233	0.984	46	42383	0.012
122	190804	0.526	208	358255	0.987	48	48539	0.013
124	197476	0.544						
126	203196	0.560	210	358999	0.989	50	55448	0.015
128	209893	0.578	212	359755	0.991	52	62872	0.017
			214	360371	0.993	54	70702	0.019
130	215917	0.595	216	360926	0.995	56	79475	0.022
132	222150	0.612	218	361380	0.996	58	88867	0.024
134	227972	0.628						
136	234408	0.646	220	361778	0.997	60	98759	0.027
138	239910	0.661	222	362062	0.998	62	109437	0.030
			224	362322	0.998	64	121084	0.033
140	246098	0.678	226	362512	0.999	66	133225	0.037
142	251584	0.693	228	362642	0.999	68	146251	0.040
144	257474	0.710						
146	262778	0.724	230	362744	1.000	70	160169	0.044
148	268416	0.740	232	362816	1.000	72	174688	0.048
			234	362850	1.000	74	190299	0.052
150	273370	0.753	236	362871	1.000	76	206577	0.057
152	278875	0.769	238	362879	1.000	78	223357	0.062
154	283659	0.782						
156	288475	0.795	240	362880	1.000	80	242043	0.067
158	292967	0.807				82	261323	0.072
						84	280909	0.077
						86	301704	0.083
						88	324089	0.089

Exact Distribution of Spearman's Rank Correlation Coefficient (cont.)

S	cf	CP	S	cf	CP	S	cf	CP
n = 10 (Cont)			**n = 10 (Cont)**			**n = 10 (Cont)**		
90	346,985	0.096	180	2,204,455	0.607	270	3,539,933	0.976
92	370,933	0.102	182	2,251,796	0.621	272	3,549,325	0.978
94	395,903	0.109	184	2,298,832	0.633	274	3,558,098	0.981
96	421,915	0.116	186	2,345,722	0.646	276	3,565,928	0.983
98	449,011	0.124	188	2,391,218	0.659	278	3,573,352	0.985
100	477,478	0.132	190	2,437,258	0.672	280	3,580,261	0.987
102	505,905	0.139	192	2,481,842	0.684	282	3,586,417	0.988
104	536,445	0.148	194	2,526,886	0.696	284	3,592,089	0.990
106	567,717	0.156	196	2,569,811	0.708	286	3,597,219	0.991
108	599,491	0.165	198	2,612,235	0.720	288	3,601,712	0.993
110	632,755	0.174	200	2,655,083	0.732	290	3,606,017	0.994
112	667,503	0.184	202	2,697,151	0.743	292	3,609,693	0.995
114	702,002	0.193	204	2,736,537	0.754	294	3,612,873	0.996
116	738,301	0.203	206	2,776,521	0.765	296	3,615,710	0.996
118	774,897	0.214	208	2,815,447	0.776	298	3,618,243	0.997
120	813,353	0.224	210	2,853,903	0.786	300	3,620,253	0.998
122	852,279	0.235	212	2,890,499	0.797	302	3,622,077	0.998
124	892,263	0.246	214	2,926,798	0.807	304	3,623,605	0.999
126	931,649	0.257	216	2,961,297	0.816	306	3,624,857	0.999
128	973,717	0.268	218	2,996,045	0.826	308	3,625,897	0.999
130	1,016,565	0.280	220	3,029,309	0.835	310	3,626,716	0.999
132	1,058,989	0.292	222	3,061,083	0.844	312	3,627,335	1.000
134	1,101,914	0.304	224	3,092,355	0.852	314	3,627,833	1.000
136	1,146,958	0.316	226	3,122,895	0.861	316	3,628,193	1.000
138	1,191,542	0.328	228	3,151,322	0.868	318	3,628,427	1.000
140	1,237,582	0.341	230	3,179,789	0.876	320	3,628,604	1.000
142	1,283,078	0.354	232	3,206,885	0.884	322	3,628,711	1.000
144	1,329,968	0.367	234	3,232,897	0.891	324	3,628,762	1.000
146	1,377,004	0.379	236	3,257,867	0.898	326	3,628,790	1.000
148	1,424,345	0.393	238	3,281,815	0.904	328	3,628,799	1.000
150	1,471,991	0.406	240	3,304,711	0.911	330	3,628,800	1.000
152	1,520,878	0.419	242	3,327,096	0.917			
154	1,569,718	0.433	244	3,347,891	0.923		**n = 11**	
156	1,617,762	0.446	246	3,367,477	0.928			
158	1,666,302	0.459	248	3,386,757	0.933	0	1	$0.0^7 25$
						2	11	$0.0^6 28$
160	1,716,368	0.473	250	3,405,443	0.938	4	47	$0.0^5 12$
162	1,765,338	0.486	252	3,422,223	0.943	6	121	$0.0^5 30$
164	1,814,400	0.500	254	3,438,501	0.948	8	277	$0.0^5 69$
166	1,863,462	0.514	256	3,454,112	0.952			
168	1,912,432	0.527	258	3,468,631	0.956	10	565	$0.0^4 14$
						12	974	$0.0^4 24$
170	1,962,498	0.541	260	3,482,549	0.960	14	1,618	$0.0^4 41$
172	2,011,038	0.554	262	3,495,575	0.963	16	2,548	$0.0^4 64$
174	2,059,082	0.567	264	3,507,716	0.967	18	3,794	$0.0^4 95$
176	2,107,922	0.581	266	3,519,363	0.970			
178	2,156,809	0.594	268	3,530,041	0.973			

13.2

Exact Distribution of Spearman's Rank Correlation Coefficient (cont.)

S	cf	CP	S	cf	CP	S	cf	CP
	n = 11 (Cont)			n = 11 (Cont)			n = 11 (Cont)	
20	5,430	$0.0^3 14$	110	2,429,566	0.061	200	15,894,731	0.398
22	7,668	$0.0^3 19$	112	2,581,919	0.065	202	16,324,563	0.409
24	10,382	$0.0^3 26$	114	2,744,859	0.069	204	16,734,970	0.419
26	13,858	$0.0^3 35$	116	2,908,190	0.073	206	17,170,868	0.430
28	18,056	$0.0^3 45$	118	3,085,090	0.077	208	17,587,363	0.441
30	23,108	$0.0^3 58$	120	3,263,110	0.082	210	18,027,449	0.452
32	29,135	$0.0^3 73$	122	3,453,608	0.087	212	18,444,344	0.462
34	36,441	$0.0^3 91$	124	3,643,760	0.091	214	18,884,724	0.473
36	44,648	$0.0^2 11$	126	3,847,514	0.096	216	19,305,912	0.484
38	54,464	$0.0^2 14$	128	4,052,381	0.102	218	19,748,160	0.495
40	65,848	$0.0^2 16$	130	4,272,633	0.107	220	20,168,640	0.505
42	78,652	$0.0^2 20$	132	4,489,678	0.112	222	20,610,888	0.516
44	92,845	$0.0^2 23$	134	4,722,594	0.118	224	21,032,076	0.527
46	109,597	$0.0^2 27$	136	4,956,028	0.124	226	21,472,456	0.538
48	127,676	$0.0^2 32$	138	5,204,156	0.130	228	21,889,351	0.548
50	148,544	$0.0^2 37$	140	5,449,644	0.137	230	22,329,437	0.559
52	171,124	$0.0^2 43$	142	5,712,530	0.143	232	22,745,932	0.570
54	196,510	$0.0^2 49$	144	5,973,493	0.150	234	23,181,830	0.581
56	223,843	$0.0^2 56$	146	6,250,695	0.157	236	23,592,237	0.591
58	254,955	$0.0^2 64$	148	6,523,539	0.163	238	24,022,069	0.602
60	287,403	$0.0^2 72$	150	6,816,137	0.171	240	24,431,996	0.612
62	323,995	$0.0^2 81$	152	7,104,526	0.178	242	24,857,840	0.623
64	363,135	$0.0^2 91$	154	7,411,262	0.186	244	25,256,759	0.633
66	406,241	0.010	156	7,710,668	0.193	246	25,674,849	0.643
68	451,019	0.011	158	8,030,252	0.201	248	26,071,401	0.653
70	501,547	0.013	160	8,345,178	0.209	250	26,482,487	0.663
72	553,511	0.014	162	8,678,412	0.217	252	26,867,791	0.673
74	610,953	0.015	164	9,002,769	0.226	254	27,269,917	0.683
76	670,301	0.017	166	9,348,585	0.234	256	27,649,244	0.693
78	735,429	0.018	168	9,686,880	0.243	258	28,040,636	0.702
80	803,299	0.020	170	10,046,970	0.252	260	28,410,083	0.712
82	877,897	0.022	172	10,393,880	0.260	262	28,791,745	0.721
84	953,161	0.024	174	10,763,840	0.270	264	29,152,960	0.730
86	1,036,105	0.026	176	11,125,055	0.279	266	29,522,920	0.740
88	1,122,228	0.028	178	11,506,717	0.288	268	29,869,830	0.748
90	1,215,286	0.030	180	11,876,164	0.298	270	30,229,920	0.757
92	1,309,506	0.033	182	12,267,556	0.307	272	30,568,215	0.766
94	1,413,368	0.035	184	12,646,883	0.317	274	30,914,031	0.774
96	1,518,681	0.038	186	13,049,009	0.327	276	31,238,388	0.783
98	1,632,877	0.041	188	13,434,313	0.337	278	31,571,622	0.791
100	1,749,090	0.044	190	13,845,399	0.347	280	31,886,548	0.799
102	1,874,422	0.047	192	14,241,951	0.357	282	32,206,132	0.807
104	2,002,045	0.050	194	14,660,041	0.367	284	32,505,538	0.814
106	2,140,515	0.054	196	15,058,960	0.377	286	32,812,274	0.822
108	2,278,832	0.057	198	15,484,804	0.388	288	33,100,663	0.829

Exact Distribution of Spearman's Rank Correlation Coefficient (cont.)

S	cf	CP	S	cf	CP
n = 11 (Cont)			**n = 11 (Cont)**		
290	33,393,261	0.837	380	39,661,845	0.994
292	33,666,105	0.843	382	39,692,957	0.994
294	33,943,307	0.850	384	39,720,290	0.995
296	34,204,270	0.857	386	39,745,676	0.996
298	34,467,156	0.863	388	39,768,256	0.996
300	34,712,644	0.870	390	39,789,124	0.997
302	34,960,772	0.876	392	39,807,203	0.997
304	35,194,206	0.882	394	39,823,955	0.998
306	35,427,122	0.888	396	39,838,148	0.998
308	35,644,167	0.893	398	39,850,952	0.998
310	35,864,419	0.898	400	39,862,336	0.999
312	36,069,286	0.904	402	39,872,152	0.999
314	36,273,040	0.909	404	39,880,359	0.999
316	36,463,192	0.913	406	39,887,665	0.999
318	36,653,690	0.918	408	39,893,692	0.999
320	36,831,710	0.923	410	39,898,744	1.000
322	37,008,610	0.927	412	39,902,942	1.000
324	37,171,941	0.931	414	39,906,418	1.000
326	37,334,881	0.935	416	39,909,132	1.000
328	37,487,234	0.939	418	39,911,370	1.000
330	37,637,968	0.943	420	39,913,006	1.000
332	37,776,285	0.946	422	39,914,252	1.000
334	37,914,755	0.950	424	39,915,182	1.000
336	38,042,378	0.953	426	39,915,826	1.000
338	38,167,710	0.956	428	39,916,235	1.000
340	38,283,923	0.959	430	39,916,523	1.000
342	38,398,119	0.962	432	39,916,679	1.000
344	38,503,432	0.965	434	39,916,753	1.000
346	38,607,294	0.967	436	39,916,789	1.000
348	38,701,514	0.970	438	39,916,799	1.000
350	38,794,572	0.972	440	39,916,800	1.000
352	38,880,695	0.974			
354	38,963,639	0.976			
356	39,038,903	0.978			
358	39,113,501	0.980			
360	39,181,371	0.982			
362	39,246,499	0.983			
364	39,305,847	0.985			
366	39,363,289	0.986			
368	39,415,253	0.987			
370	39,465,781	0.989			
372	39,510,559	0.990			
374	39,553,665	0.991			
376	39,592,805	0.992			
378	39,629,397	0.993			

14. NONPARAMETRIC ANALYSIS OF VARIANCE

14.1 Exact Distribution of Friedman's Chi-Square Statistic

Friedman [73] introduced the X_r^2 statistic defined as

$$X_r^2 = \frac{12}{np(p+1)} \sum_{j=1}^{p} \left(\sum_{i=1}^{n} r_{ij} \right)^2 - 3n(p+1),$$

where data in each of n rows of an $n \times p$ two-way table have been ranked (separately), and r_{ij} is the rank of the quantity in the ith row and the jth column. The ranks r_{ij} then take on values from 1 to p in n different rows. The quantities given in the table are: $\text{Pr} = \text{Pr}\{X_r^2 \geq x^2\}$, Freq = frequency with which X_r^2 takes on the value x^2, and Total = frequency with which X_r^2 takes on the value x^2 or a larger value. All these quantities are computed under the assumption that there is no relationship between the n rows. A test of the hypothesis that the n rows are independent can be made at the α-significance level by rejecting this hypothesis if $X_r^2 \geq x^2$ where $\text{Pr}\{X_r^2 \geq x^2\} \leq \alpha$. The tables enable one to carry out this test for $p = 3$ or $p = 4$ columns of data. Friedman [73] shows that as n approaches infinity, X_r^2 approaches the chi-square distribution (Section 3.1). The asymptotic efficiency of X_r^2 is considered by van Elteren and Noether [231].

14.1

Exact Distribution of Friedman's Chi-Square Statistic

$$\text{Pr} = \text{Pr}\{\text{Friedman's chi-square} \geq \chi^2\}$$

$$p = 3$$

n = 2

χ^2	Freq	Total	Pr
0	1	6	1.000
1	2	5	0.833
3	2	3	0.500
4	1	1	0.167

n = 3

χ^2	Freq	Total	Pr
0.000	2	36	1.000
0.667	15	34	0.944
2.000	6	19	0.528
2.667	6	13	0.361
4.667	6	7	0.194
6.000	1	1	0.028

n = 4

χ^2	Freq	Total	Pr
0.0	15	216	1.000
0.5	60	201	0.931
1.5	48	141	0.653
2.0	34	93	0.431
3.5	32	59	0.273
4.5	12	27	0.125
6.0	6	15	0.069
6.5	8	9	0.042
8.0	1	1	$0.0^2 46$

n = 5

χ^2	Freq	Total	Pr
0.0	60	1,296	1.000
0.4	340	1,236	0.954
1.2	220	896	0.691
1.6	200	676	0.522
2.8	240	476	0.367
3.6	75	236	0.182
4.8	40	161	0.124
5.2	70	121	0.093
6.4	20	51	0.039
7.6	20	31	0.024
8.4	10	11	$0.0^2 85$
10.0	1	1	$0.0^3 77$

n = 6

χ^2	Freq	Total	Pr
0.00	340	7,776	1.000
0.33	1,680	7,436	0.956
1.00	1,320	5,756	0.740
1.33	1,095	4,436	0.570
2.33	1,380	3,341	0.430
3.00	530	1,961	0.252
4.00	330	1,431	0.184
4.33	540	1,101	0.142
5.33	156	561	0.072
6.33	180	405	0.052
7.00	132	225	0.029
8.33	30	93	0.012
9.00	20	63	$0.0^2 81$
9.33	30	43	$0.0^2 55$
10.33	12	13	$0.0^2 17$
12.00	1	1	$0.0^3 13$

n = 7

χ^2	Freq	Total	Pr
0.000	1,680	46,656	1.000
0.286	9,135	44,976	0.964
0.857	6,930	35,841	0.768
1.143	6,230	28,911	0.620
2.000	8,470	22,681	0.486
2.571	3,171	14,211	0.305
3.429	2,100	11,040	0.237
3.714	3,724	8,940	0.192
4.571	1,232	5,216	0.112
5.429	1,582	3,984	0.085
6.000	1,134	2,402	0.051
7.143	301	1,268	0.027
7.714	210	967	0.021
8.000	364	757	0.016
8.857	224	393	$0.0^2 84$
10.286	42	169	$0.0^2 36$
10.571	70	127	$0.0^2 27$
11.143	42	57	$0.0^2 12$
12.286	14	15	$0.0^3 32$
14.000	1	1	$0.0^4 21$

14.1

Exact Distribution of Friedman's Chi-Square Statistic (cont.)

$$Pr = Pr\{\text{Friedman's chi-square} \geq \chi^2\}$$

$$p = 3$$

n = 8

χ^2	Freq	Total	Pr
0.00	9,135	279,936	1.000
0.25	48,440	270,801	0.967
0.75	39,200	222,361	0.794
1.00	34,636	183,161	0.654
1.75	49,056	148,525	0.531
2.25	19,656	99,469	0.355
3.00	13,776	79,813	0.285
3.25	24,192	66,037	0.236
4.00	8,330	41,845	0.149
4.75	11,424	33,515	0.120
5.25	8,960	22,091	0.079
6.25	2,632	13,131	0.047
6.75	2,016	10,499	0.038
7.00	3,472	8,483	0.030
7.75	2,240	5,011	0.018
9.00	540	2,771	$0.0^2 99$
9.25	896	2,231	$0.0^2 80$
9.75	672	1,335	$0.0^2 48$
10.75	352	663	$0.0^2 24$
12.00	70	311	$0.0^2 11$
12.25	168	241	$0.0^3 86$
13.00	56	73	$0.0^3 26$
14.25	16	17	$0.0^4 61$
16.00	1	1	$0.0^5 36$

n = 9

χ^2	Freq	Total	Pr
0.000	48,440	1,679,616	1.000
0.222	264,726	1,631,176	0.971
0.667	215,208	1,366,450	0.814
0.889	195,552	1,151,242	0.685
1.556	287,784	955,690	0.569
2.000	116,214	667,906	0.398
2.667	84,672	551,692	0.328
2.889	152,964	467,020	0.278
3.556	55,440	314,056	0.187
4.222	79,632	258,616	0.154

n = 9 (Cont)

χ^2	Freq	Total	Pr
4.667	63,252	178,984	0.107
5.556	20,070	115,732	0.069
6.000	15,792	95,662	0.057
6.222	28,224	79,870	0.048
6.889	19,800	51,646	0.031
8.000	5,392	31,846	0.019
8.222	9,212	26,454	0.016
8.667	7,016	17,242	0.010
9.556	4,400	10,226	$0.0^2 61$
10.667	896	5,826	$0.0^2 35$
10.889	2,673	4,930	$0.0^2 29$
11.556	1,040	2,257	$0.0^2 13$
12.667	746	1,217	$0.0^3 72$
13.556	140	471	$0.0^3 28$
14.000	56	331	$0.0^3 20$
14.222	184	275	$0.0^3 16$
14.889	72	91	$0.0^4 54$
16.222	18	19	$0.0^4 11$
18.000	1	1	$0.0^6 60$

n = 10

χ^2	Freq	Total	Pr
0.0	264,726	10,077,696	1.000
0.2	1,446,060	9,812,970	0.974
0.6	1,208,340	8,366,910	0.830
0.8	1,099,140	7,158,570	0.710
1.4	1,664,040	6,059,430	0.601
1.8	691,740	4,395,390	0.436
2.4	520,380	3,703,650	0.368
2.6	943,320	3,183,270	0.316
3.2	352,500	2,239,950	0.222
3.8	525,000	1,887,450	0.187
4.2	431,640	1,362,450	0.135
5.0	143,884	930,810	0.092
5.4	117,068	786,926	0.078
5.6	210,496	669,858	0.066
6.2	153,816	459,362	0.046

14.1

Exact Distribution of Friedman's Chi-Square Statistic (cont.)

$$Pr = Pr\{\text{Friedman's chi-square} \geq \chi^2\}$$

$$p = 3$$

n = 10 (Cont)

χ^2	Freq	Total	Pr
7.2	46,943	305,546	0.030
7.4	77,828	258,603	0.026
7.8	62,676	180,775	0.018
8.6	44,732	118,099	0.012
9.6	9,352	73,367	$0.0^2 73$
9.8	29,978	64,015	$0.0^2 64$
10.4	12,290	34,037	$0.0^2 34$
11.4	11,244	21,747	$0.0^2 22$
12.2	1,988	10,503	$0.0^2 10$
12.6	1,252	8,515	$0.0^3 84$
12.8	3,438	7,263	$0.0^3 72$
13.4	1,860	3,825	$0.0^3 38$
14.6	1,188	1,965	$0.0^3 19$
15.0	140	777	$0.0^4 77$
15.2	196	637	$0.0^4 63$
15.8	128	441	$0.0^4 44$
16.2	202	313	$0.0^4 31$
16.8	90	111	$0.0^4 11$
18.2	20	21	$0.0^5 21$
20.0	1	1	$0.0^7 99$

n = 11

χ^2	Freq	Total	Pr
0.000	1,446,060	60,466,176	1.000
0.182	7,996,296	59,020,116	0.976
0.545	6,754,440	51,023,820	0.844
0.727	6,218,520	44,269,380	0.732
1.273	9,646,560	38,050,860	0.629
1.636	4,059,000	28,404,300	0.470
2.182	3,132,360	24,345,300	0.403
2.364	5,749,920	21,212,940	0.351
2.909	2,210,584	15,463,020	0.256
3.455	3,385,352	13,252,436	0.219
3.818	2,825,400	9,867,084	0.163
4.545	984,899	7,041,684	0.116
4.909	813,324	6,056,785	0.100
5.091	1,485,096	5,243,461	0.087
5.636	1,131,198	3,758,365	0.062

n = 11 (Cont)

χ^2	Freq	Total	Pr
6.545	372,410	2,627,167	0.043
6.727	603,840	2,254,757	0.037
7.091	499,162	1,650,917	0.027
7.818	393,868	1,151,755	0.019
8.727	79,816	757,887	0.013
8.909	281,095	678,071	0.011
9.455	121,764	396,976	$0.0^2 66$
10.364	126,902	275,212	$0.0^2 46$
11.091	22,420	148,310	$0.0^2 25$
11.455	16,462	125,890	$0.0^2 21$
11.636	42,612	109,428	$0.0^2 18$
12.182	26,192	66,816	$0.0^2 11$
13.273	20,494	40,624	$0.0^3 67$
13.636	2,184	20,130	$0.0^3 33$
13.818	3,648	17,946	$0.0^3 30$
14.364	3,398	14,298	$0.0^3 24$
14.727	4,647	10,900	$0.0^3 18$
15.273	3,196	6,253	$0.0^3 10$
16.545	2,160	3,057	$0.0^4 51$
16.909	324	897	$0.0^4 15$
17.636	218	573	$0.0^5 95$
18.182	222	355	$0.0^5 59$
18.727	110	133	$0.0^5 22$
20.182	22	23	$0.0^6 38$
22.000	1	1	$0.0^7 17$

n = 12

χ^2	Freq	Total	Pr
0.000	7,996,296	362,797,056	1.000
0.167	44,396,352	354,800,760	0.978
0.500	38,076,192	310,404,408	0.856
0.667	35,210,736	272,328,216	0.751
1.167	55,725,120	237,117,480	0.654
1.500	23,825,584	181,392,360	0.500
2.000	18,781,832	157,566,776	0.434
2.167	34,661,200	138,784,944	0.383
2.667	13,619,219	104,123,744	0.287
3.167	21,337,136	90,504,525	0.249

Exact Distribution of Friedman's Chi-Square Statistic (cont.)

$$Pr = Pr\{Friedman's\ chi\text{-}square \geq \chi^2\}$$

$$p = 3$$

n = 12 (Cont)				n = 13			
χ^2	Freq	Total	Pr	χ^2	Freq	Total	Pr
3.500	18,142,532	69,167,389	0.191	0.000	44,396,352	2,176,782,336	1.000
4.167	6,539,592	51,024,857	0.141	0.154	248,133,600	2,132,385,984	0.980
4.500	5,474,288	44,485,265	0.123	0.462	214,939,296	1,884,252,384	0.866
4.667	10,071,600	39,010,977	0.108	0.615	200,099,440	1,669,313,088	0.767
5.167	7,918,144	28,939,377	0.080	1.077	322,175,008	1,469,213,648	0.675
6.000	2,791,060	21,021,233	0.058	1.385	139,216,275	1,147,038,640	0.527
6.167	4,374,378	18,230,173	0.050	1.846	111,723,456	1,007,822,365	0.463
6.500	3,735,766	13,855,795	0.038	2.000	207,658,058	896,098,909	0.412
7.167	3,186,036	10,120,029	0.028	2.462	83,168,908	688,440,851	0.316
8.000	626,260	6,933,993	0.019	2.923	132,724,708	605,271,943	0.278
8.167	2,359,072	6,307,733	0.017	3.231	114,305,702	472,547,235	0.217
8.667	1,062,586	3,948,661	0.011	3.846	42,470,955	358,241,533	0.165
9.500	1,209,732	2,886,075	0.0^280	4.154	35,783,114	315,770,578	0.145
10.167	206,530	1,676,343	0.0^246	4.308	66,456,532	279,987,464	0.129
10.500	177,422	1,469,813	0.0^241	4.769	53,797,238	213,530,932	0.098
10.667	433,138	1,292,391	0.0^236	5.538	20,002,844	159,733,694	0.073
11.167	292,216	859,253	0.0^224	5.692	30,382,840	139,730,850	0.064
12.167	252,968	567,037	0.0^216	6.000	26,612,744	109,348,010	0.050
12.500	26,068	314,069	0.0^387	6.615	24,226,492	82,735,266	0.038
12.667	46,972	288,001	0.0^379	7.385	4,580,908	58,508,774	0.027
13.167	50,040	241,029	0.0^366	7.538	18,429,168	53,927,866	0.025
13.500	65,488	190,989	0.0^353	8.000	8,601,172	35,498,698	0.016
14.000	52,572	125,501	0.0^335	8.769	10,378,226	26,897,526	0.012
15.167	41,900	72,929	0.0^320	9.385	1,735,580	16,519,300	0.0^276
15.500	7,264	31,029	0.0^486	9.692	1,658,344	14,783,720	0.0^268
16.167	7,028	23,765	0.0^466	9.846	3,887,260	13,125,376	0.0^260
16.667	6,830	16,737	0.0^446	10.308	2,805,320	9,238,116	0.0^242
17.167	5,596	9,907	0.0^427	11.231	2,593,672	6,432,796	0.0^230
18.167	324	4,311	0.0^412	11.538	253,502	3,839,124	0.0^218
18.500	2,716	3,987	0.0^411	11.692	493,392	3,585,622	0.0^216
18.667	542	1,271	0.0^535	12.154	583,474	3,092,230	0.0^214
19.500	328	729	0.0^520	12.462	734,836	2,508,756	0.0^212
20.167	244	401	0.0^511	12.923	649,748	1,773,920	0.0^381
20.667	132	157	0.0^643	14.000	565,184	1,124,172	0.0^352
22.167	24	25	0.0^769	14.308	104,906	558,988	0.0^326
24.000	1	1	0.0^828	14.923	116,342	454,082	0.0^321
				15.385	110,348	337,740	0.0^316
				15.846	104,676	227,392	0.0^310
				16.615	324	122,716	0.0^456
				16.769	7,806	122,392	0.0^456

Exact Distribution of Friedman's Chi-Square Statistic (*cont.*)
$$\text{Pr} = \text{Pr}\{\text{Friedman's chi-square} \geq \chi^2\}$$
$$p = 3$$

	n = 13 (Cont)				n = 14 (Cont)		
χ^2	Freq	Total	Pr	χ^2	Freq	Total	Pr
17.077	61,800	114,586	$0.0^4 53$	9.143	32,135,902	120,614,792	$0.0^2 92$
17.231	14,944	52,786	$0.0^4 24$	9.571	24,464,636	88,478,890	$0.0^2 68$
18.000	13,298	37,842	$0.0^4 17$	10.429	23,642,670	64,014,254	$0.0^2 49$
18.615	9,571	24,544	$0.0^4 11$	10.714	2,228,972	40,371,584	$0.0^2 31$
19.077	8,664	14,973	$0.0^5 69$	10.857	4,589,308	38,142,612	$0.0^2 29$
19.538	324	6,309	$0.0^5 29$	11.286	5,828,052	33,553,304	$0.0^2 26$
19.846	866	5,985	$0.0^5 27$	11.571	7,156,464	27,725,252	$0.0^2 21$
20.462	4,208	5,119	$0.0^5 24$	12.000	6,768,668	20,568,788	$0.0^2 16$
21.385	460	911	$0.0^6 42$	13.000	6,214,020	13,800,120	$0.0^2 11$
22.154	268	451	$0.0^6 21$	13.286	1,215,958	7,586,100	$0.0^3 58$
22.615	156	183	$0.0^7 84$	13.857	1,471,046	6,370,142	$0.0^3 49$
24.154	26	27	$0.0^7 12$	14.286	1,371,391	4,899,096	$0.0^3 38$
26.000	1	1	$0.0^9 46$	14.714	1,415,036	3,527,705	$0.0^3 27$
				15.429	8,130	2,112,669	$0.0^3 16$
				15.571	121,688	2,104,539	$0.0^3 16$
	n = 14			15.857	922,570	1,982,851	$0.0^3 15$
0.000	248,133,600	13,060,694,016	1.000	16.000	243,218	1,060,281	$0.0^4 81$
0.143	1,392,623,344	12,812,560,416	0.981	16.714	245,086	817,063	$0.0^4 63$
0.429	1,218,641,088	11,419,937,072	0.874	17.286	176,624	571,977	$0.0^4 44$
0.571	1,139,403,475	10,201,295,984	0.781	17.714	184,598	395,353	$0.0^4 30$
1.000	1,861,790,000	9,061,892,509	0.694				
				18.143	9,644	210,755	$0.0^4 16$
1.286	813,101,414	7,200,102,509	0.551	18.429	23,074	201,111	$0.0^4 15$
1.714	662,557,774	6,387,001,095	0.489	19.000	119,892	178,037	$0.0^4 14$
1.857	1,237,422,696	5,724,443,321	0.438	19.857	22,118	58,145	$0.0^5 45$
2.286	503,650,990	4,487,020,625	0.344	20.571	13,806	36,027	$0.0^5 28$
2.714	816,158,140	3,983,369,635	0.305				
				21.000	13,682	22,221	$0.0^5 17$
3.000	711,916,262	3,167,211,495	0.242	21.143	1,190	8,539	$0.0^6 65$
3.571	271,274,692	2,455,295,233	0.188	21.571	866	7,349	$0.0^6 56$
3.857	229,564,080	2,184,020,541	0.167	22.286	460	6,483	$0.0^6 50$
4.000	429,389,460	1,954,456,461	0.150	22.429	4,902	6,023	$0.0^6 46$
4.429	356,549,068	1,525,067,001	0.117				
				23.286	616	1,121	$0.0^7 86$
5.143	138,923,853	1,168,517,933	0.089	24.143	294	505	$0.0^7 39$
5.286	204,180,160	1,029,594,080	0.079	24.571	182	211	$0.0^7 16$
5.571	183,464,274	825,413,920	0.063	26.143	28	29	$0.0^8 22$
6.143	176,253,404	641,949,646	0.049	28.000	1	1	$0.0^{10} 77$
6.857	32,118,420	465,696,242	0.036				
7.000	136,647,318	433,577,822	0.033				
7.429	65,681,126	296,930,504	0.023				
8.143	82,859,512	231,249,378	0.018				
8.714	13,556,136	148,389,866	0.011				
9.000	14,218,938	134,833,730	0.010				

Exact Distribution of Friedman's Chi-Square Statistic (cont.)

$$\text{Pr} = \text{Pr}\{\text{Friedman's chi-square} \geq \chi^2\}$$

$$p = 3$$

χ^2	Freq	Total	Pr	χ^2	Freq	Total	Pr
	n = 15				n = 15 (Cont)		
0.000	1,392,623,344	78,364,164,096	1.000	14.800	10,909,684	26,618,661	$0.0^3 34$
0.133	7,850,733,939	76,971,540,752	0.982	14.933	3,196,744	15,708,977	$0.0^3 20$
0.400	6,925,843,638	69,120,806,813	0.882	15.600	3,455,908	12,512,233	$0.0^3 16$
0.533	6,504,796,934	62,194,963,175	0.794	16.133	2,307,767	9,056,325	$0.0^3 12$
0.933	10,766,620,198	55,690,166,241	0.711	16.533	2,618,492	6,748,558	$0.0^4 86$
1.200	4,742,267,161	44,923,546,043	0.573	16.933	171,856	4,130,066	$0.0^4 53$
1.600	3,915,370,836	40,181,278,882	0.513	17.200	496,498	3,958,210	$0.0^4 51$
1.733	7,348,484,758	36,265,908,046	0.463	17.733	2,041,434	3,461,712	$0.0^4 44$
2.133	3,033,715,064	28,917,423,288	0.369	18.533	564,334	1,420,278	$0.0^4 18$
2.533	4,979,130,266	25,883,708,224	0.330	19.200	181,820	855,944	$0.0^4 11$
2.800	4,389,370,728	20,904,577,958	0.267	19.600	223,250	674,124	$0.0^5 86$
3.333	1,711,040,173	16,515,207,230	0.211	19.733	33,584	450,874	$0.0^5 58$
3.600	1,449,727,760	14,804,167,057	0.189	20.133	144,616	417,290	$0.0^5 53$
3.733	2,731,396,064	13,354,439,297	0.170	20.800	143,492	272,674	$0.0^5 35$
4.133	2,321,420,490	10,623,043,233	0.136	20.933	42,092	129,182	$0.0^5 16$
4.800	804,077,164	8,301,622,743	0.106	21.733	36,442	87,090	$0.0^6 11$
4.933	1,477,046,212	7,497,545,579	0.096	22.533	19,927	50,648	$0.0^6 65$
5.200	1,368,700,536	6,020,499,367	0.077	22.800	2,056	30,721	$0.0^6 39$
5.733	966,401,686	4,651,798,831	0.059	22.933	19,228	28,665	$0.0^6 37$
6.400	354,383,614	3,685,397,145	0.047	23.333	1,326	9,437	$0.0^6 12$
6.533	975,510,145	3,331,013,531	0.043	24.133	1,076	8,111	$0.0^6 10$
6.933	617,908,082	2,355,503,386	0.030	24.400	5,674	7,035	$0.0^7 90$
7.600	354,313,640	1,737,595,304	0.022	25.200	798	1,361	$0.0^7 17$
8.133	237,706,484	1,383,281,664	0.018	26.133	322	563	$0.0^8 72$
8.400	250,766,576	1,145,575,180	0.015	26.533	210	241	$0.0^8 31$
8.533	113,658,646	894,808,604	0.011	28.133	30	31	$0.0^9 40$
8.933	198,998,966	781,149,958	0.010	30.000	1	1	$0.0^{10} 13$
9.733	198,891,568	582,150,992	$0.0^2 74$				
10.000	18,145,444	383,259,424	$0.0^2 49$				
10.133	39,277,028	365,113,980	$0.0^2 47$				
10.533	52,728,554	325,836,952	$0.0^2 42$				
10.800	63,363,983	273,108,398	$0.0^2 35$				
11.200	63,035,460	209,744,415	$0.0^2 27$				
12.133	60,205,812	146,708,955	$0.0^2 19$				
12.400	12,253,312	86,503,143	$0.0^2 11$				
12.933	15,716,018	74,249,831	$0.0^3 95$				
13.333	14,469,678	58,533,813	$0.0^3 75$				
13.733	15,805,988	44,064,135	$0.0^3 56$				
14.400	131,332	28,258,147	$0.0^3 36$				
14.533	1,508,154	28,126,815	$0.0^3 36$				

14.1

Exact Distribution of Friedman's Chi-Square Statistic (cont.)

$$Pr = Pr\{\text{Friedman's chi-square} \geq \chi^2\}$$

$$p = 4$$

n = 2

χ^2	Freq	Total	Pr
0.0	1	24	1.000
0.6	3	23	0.958
1.2	1	20	0.833
1.8	4	19	0.792
2.4	2	15	0.625
3.0	2	13	0.542
3.6	2	11	0.458
4.2	4	9	0.375
4.8	1	5	0.208
5.4	3	4	0.167
6.0	1	1	0.042

n = 3

χ^2	Freq	Total	Pr
0.2	24	576	1.000
0.6	28	552	0.958
1.0	105	524	0.910
1.8	65	419	0.727
2.2	52	354	0.615
2.6	45	302	0.524
3.4	68	257	0.446
3.8	20	189	0.328
4.2	50	169	0.293
5.0	14	119	0.207
5.4	12	105	0.182
5.8	50	93	0.161
6.6	12	43	0.075
7.0	16	31	0.054
7.4	5	15	0.026
8.2	9	10	0.017
9.0	1	1	$0.0^2 17$

n = 4

χ^2	Freq	Total	Pr
0.0	105	13,824	1.000
0.3	858	13,719	0.992
0.6	444	12,861	0.930
0.9	1,434	12,417	0.898
1.2	568	10,983	0.794
1.5	1,015	10,415	0.753
1.8	400	9,400	0.680
2.1	1,702	9,000	0.651
2.4	205	7,298	0.528
2.7	1,126	7,093	0.513
3.0	569	5,967	0.432
3.3	532	5,398	0.390
3.6	434	4,866	0.352
3.9	1,151	4,432	0.321
4.5	530	3,281	0.237
4.8	146	2,751	0.199
5.1	411	2,605	0.188
5.4	238	2,194	0.159
5.7	490	1,956	0.141
6.0	175	1,466	0.106
6.3	224	1,291	0.093
6.6	112	1,067	0.077
6.9	154	955	0.069
7.2	50	801	0.058
7.5	249	751	0.054
7.8	23	502	0.036
8.1	200	479	0.035
8.4	94	279	0.020
8.7	30	185	0.013
9.3	78	155	0.011
9.6	5	77	$0.0^2 56$
9.9	44	72	$0.0^2 52$
10.2	6	28	$0.0^2 20$
10.8	9	22	$0.0^2 16$
11.1	12	13	$0.0^3 94$
12.0	1	1	$0.0^4 72$

14.1

Exact Distribution of Friedman's Chi-Square Statistic (cont.)

$$\text{Pr} = \text{Pr}\{\text{Friedman's chi-square} \geq \chi^2\}$$
$$p = 4$$

n = 5

χ^2	Freq	Total	Pr
0.12	8,511	331,776	1.000
0.36	10,032	323,265	0.974
0.60	28,927	313,233	0.944
1.08	29,154	284,306	0.857
1.32	19,599	255,152	0.769
1.56	19,212	235,553	0.710
2.04	29,513	216,341	0.652
2.28	14,345	186,828	0.563
2.52	25,567	172,483	0.520
3.00	12,380	146,916	0.443
3.24	12,474	134,536	0.406
3.48	22,289	122,062	0.368
3.96	11,379	99,773	0.301
4.20	11,540	88,394	0.266
4.44	6,346	76,854	0.232
4.92	16,837	70,508	0.213
5.16	3,601	53,671	0.162
5.40	10,706	50,070	0.151
5.88	5,636	39,364	0.119
6.12	4,221	33,728	0.102
6.36	5,806	29,507	0.089
6.84	1,584	23,701	0.071
7.08	3,080	22,117	0.067
7.32	2,759	19,037	0.057
7.80	5,305	16,278	0.049
8.04	198	10,973	0.033
8.28	2,942	10,775	0.032
8.76	850	7,833	0.024
9.00	1,956	6,983	0.021
9.24	1,340	5,027	0.015
9.72	622	3,687	0.011
9.96	522	3,065	$0.0^{2}92$
10.20	629	2,543	$0.0^{2}77$
10.68	975	1,914	$0.0^{2}58$
10.92	182	939	$0.0^{2}28$
11.16	198	757	$0.0^{2}23$
11.64	92	559	$0.0^{2}17$
11.88	102	467	$0.0^{2}14$
12.12	232	365	$0.0^{2}11$
12.60	12	133	$0.0^{3}40$

n = 5 (Cont)

χ^2	Freq	Total	Pr
12.84	68	121	$0.0^{3}36$
13.08	7	53	$0.0^{3}16$
13.56	30	46	$0.0^{3}14$
14.04	15	16	$0.0^{4}48$
15.00	1	1	$0.0^{5}30$

n = 6

χ^2	Freq	Total	Pr
0.0	28,927	7,962,624	1.000
0.2	356,043	7,933,697	0.996
0.4	111,696	7,577,654	0.952
0.6	474,091	7,465,958	0.938
0.8	275,974	6,991,867	0.878
1.0	370,022	6,715,893	0.843
1.2	144,134	6,345,871	0.797
1.4	822,076	6,201,737	0.779
1.6	80,052	5,379,661	0.676
1.8	454,868	5,299,609	0.666
2.0	340,664	4,844,741	0.608
2.2	197,670	4,504,077	0.566
2.4	189,730	4,306,407	0.541
2.6	713,312	4,116,677	0.517
3.0	338,401	3,403,365	0.427
3.2	86,339	3,064,964	0.385
3.4	292,282	2,978,625	0.374
3.6	130,408	2,686,343	0.337
3.8	374,809	2,555,935	0.321
4.0	120,696	2,181,126	0.274
4.2	212,401	2,060,430	0.259
4.4	92,048	1,848,029	0.232
4.6	222,868	1,755,981	0.221
4.8	22,289	1,533,113	0.193
5.0	218,273	1,510,824	0.190
5.2	62,471	1,292,551	0.162
5.4	216,763	1,230,080	0.154
5.6	111,363	1,013,317	0.127
5.8	33,019	901,954	0.113
6.2	170,584	868,935	0.109

Exact Distribution of Friedman's Chi-Square Statistic (cont.)

$$\text{Pr} = \text{Pr}\{\text{Friedman's chi-square} \geq \chi^2\}$$
$$p = 4$$

n = 6 (Cont)   n = 6 (Cont)

χ^2	Freq	Total	Pr	χ^2	Freq	Total	Pr
6.4	9,288	698,351	0.088	15.4	26	226	$0.0^4 28$
6.6	104,719	689,063	0.087	15.8	98	200	$0.0^4 25$
6.8	53,013	584,344	0.073	16.0	8	102	$0.0^4 13$
7.0	31,133	531,331	0.067	16.2	30	94	$0.0^4 12$
7.2	37,155	500,198	0.063	16.4	45	64	$0.0^5 80$
7.4	122,234	463,043	0.058	17.0	18	19	$0.0^5 24$
7.6	12,780	340,809	0.043	18.0	1	1	$0.0^6 13$
7.8	37,555	328,029	0.041				
8.0	24,635	290,474	0.036				
8.2	17,175	265,839	0.033			n = 7	
8.4	32,361	248,664	0.031	0.086	3,029,022	191,102,976	1.000
8.6	48,260	216,303	0.027	0.257	3,934,474	188,073,954	0.984
8.8	975	168,043	0.021	0.429	11,097,158	184,139,480	0.964
9.0	32,973	167,068	0.021	0.771	11,350,228	173,042,322	0.905
9.4	14,654	134,095	0.017	0.943	9,684,569	161,692,094	0.846
9.6	1,770	119,441	0.015	1.114	7,856,343	152,007,525	0.795
9.8	29,997	117,671	0.015	1.457	14,678,336	144,151,182	0.754
10.0	10,623	87,674	0.011	1.629	4,863,084	129,472,846	0.678
10.2	7,144	77,051	$0.0^2 97$	1.800	10,738,918	124,609,762	0.652
10.4	7,073	69,907	$0.0^2 88$	2.143	6,089,869	113,870,844	0.596
10.6	12,751	62,834	$0.0^2 79$	2.314	5,923,034	107,780,975	0.564
10.8	4,528	50,083	$0.0^2 63$	2.486	13,886,926	101,857,941	0.533
11.0	13,001	45,555	$0.0^2 57$	2.829	7,755,274	87,971,015	0.460
11.4	6,474	32,554	$0.0^2 41$	3.000	7,968,798	80,215,741	0.420
11.6	2,904	26,080	$0.0^2 33$	3.171	3,742,788	72,246,943	0.378
11.8	6,829	23,176	$0.0^2 29$	3.514	9,992,213	68,504,155	0.358
12.0	2,372	16,347	$0.0^2 21$	3.686	1,200,143	58,511,942	0.306
12.2	2,870	13,975	$0.0^2 18$	3.857	6,918,642	57,311,799	0.300
12.6	3,075	11,105	$0.0^2 14$	4.200	4,641,720	50,393,157	0.264
12.8	644	8,030	$0.0^2 10$	4.371	4,554,630	45,751,437	0.239
13.0	1,003	7,386	$0.0^3 93$	4.543	5,331,129	41,196,807	0.216
13.2	1,267	6,383	$0.0^3 80$	4.886	1,159,400	35,865,678	0.188
13.4	2,445	5,116	$0.0^3 64$	5.057	3,478,987	34,706,278	0.182
13.6	122	2,671	$0.0^3 34$	5.229	2,646,474	31,227,291	0.163
13.8	678	2,549	$0.0^3 32$	5.571	5,248,038	28,580,817	0.150
14.0	462	1,871	$0.0^3 23$	5.743	749,926	23,332,779	0.122
14.6	720	1,409	$0.0^3 18$	5.914	3,345,214	22,582,853	0.118
14.8	19	689	$0.0^4 87$	6.257	1,460,157	19,237,639	0.101
15.0	432	670	$0.0^4 84$	6.429	2,293,072	17,777,482	0.093
15.2	12	238	$0.0^4 30$	6.600	1,554,351	15,484,410	0.081

14.1

Exact Distribution of Friedman's Chi-Square Statistic (cont.)

$$\text{Pr} = \Pr\{\text{Friedman's chi-square} \geq \chi^2\}$$
$$p = 4$$

n = 7 (Cont)   n = 7 (Cont)

χ^2	Freq	Total	Pr	χ^2	Freq	Total	Pr
6.943	1,998,115	13,930,059	0.073	16.029	26	12,189	$0.0^4 64$
7.114	805,829	11,931,944	0.062	16.200	4,841	12,163	$0.0^4 64$
7.286	1,313,531	11,126,115	0.058	16.543	887	7,322	$0.0^4 38$
7.629	2,081,634	9,812,584	0.051	16.714	2,674	6,435	$0.0^4 34$
7.800	648,275	7,730,950	0.040	16.886	951	3,761	$0.0^4 20$
7.971	627,134	7,082,675	0.037	17.229	178	2,810	$0.0^4 15$
8.314	299,266	6,455,541	0.034	17.400	588	2,632	$0.0^4 14$
8.486	476,364	6,156,275	0.032	17.571	897	2,044	$0.0^4 11$
8.657	1,117,673	5,679,911	0.030	17.914	772	1,147	$0.0^5 60$
9.000	520,825	4,562,238	0.024	18.257	42	375	$0.0^5 20$
9.171	522,740	4,041,413	0.021	18.771	134	333	$0.0^5 17$
9.343	451,797	3,518,673	0.018	18.943	114	199	$0.0^5 10$
9.686	476,630	3,066,876	0.016	19.286	63	85	$0.0^6 44$
9.857	135,183	2,590,246	0.014	19.971	21	22	$0.0^6 12$
10.029	718,409	2,455,063	0.013	21.000	1	1	$0.0^8 52$
10.371	181,652	1,736,654	$0.0^2 91$				
10.543	30,185	1,555,002	$0.0^2 81$				
10.714	220,107	1,524,817	$0.0^2 80$		**n = 8**		
11.057	253,014	1,304,710	$0.0^2 68$				
11.229	300,293	1,051,696	$0.0^2 55$	0.00	11,097,158	4,586,471,424	1.000
				0.15	141,640,799	4,575,374,266	0.998
11.400	6,447	751,403	$0.0^2 39$	0.30	45,747,925	4,433,733,467	0.967
11.743	108,987	744,956	$0.0^2 39$	0.45	196,500,372	4,387,985,542	0.957
11.914	44,964	635,969	$0.0^2 33$	0.60	111,218,439	4,191,485,170	0.914
12.086	38,364	591,005	$0.0^2 31$				
12.429	126,780	552,641	$0.0^2 29$	0.75	167,821,700	4,080,266,731	0.890
				0.90	48,645,920	3,912,445,031	0.853
12.600	49,245	425,861	$0.0^2 22$	1.05	358,814,110	3,863,799,111	0.842
12.771	113,046	376,616	$0.0^2 20$	1.20	47,322,133	3,504,985,001	0.764
13.114	47,157	263,570	$0.0^2 14$	1.35	207,857,961	3,457,662,868	0.754
13.286	6,721	216,413	$0.0^2 11$				
13.457	50,053	209,692	$0.0^2 11$	1.50	146,704,063	3,249,804,907	0.709
				1.65	78,095,732	3,103,100,844	0.677
13.800	47,017	159,639	$0.0^3 84$	1.80	105,175,216	3,025,005,112	0.660
13.971	10,925	112,622	$0.0^3 59$	1.95	367,363,399	2,919,829,896	0.637
14.143	24,994	101,697	$0.0^3 53$	2.25	216,052,959	2,552,466,497	0.557
14.486	9,696	76,703	$0.0^3 40$				
14.657	21,666	67,007	$0.0^3 35$	2.40	42,047,303	2,336,413,538	0.509
				2.55	136,264,571	2,294,366,235	0.500
14.829	14,185	45,341	$0.0^3 24$	2.70	81,441,193	2,158,101,664	0.471
15.171	38	31,156	$0.0^3 16$	2.85	223,161,388	2,076,660,471	0.453
15.343	3,679	31,118	$0.0^3 16$	3.00	65,998,841	1,853,499,083	0.404
15.514	6,927	27,439	$0.0^3 14$				
15.857	8,323	20,512	$0.0^3 11$				

Exact Distribution of Friedman's Chi-Square Statistic (*cont.*)

$$\text{Pr} = \text{Pr}\{\text{Friedman's chi-square} \geq \chi^2\}$$

$$p = 4$$

n = 8 (Cont)   n = 8 (Cont)

χ^2	Freq	Total	Pr	χ^2	Freq	Total	Pr
3.15	115,828,189	1,787,500,242	0.390	10.05	8,228,906	58,789,892	0.013
3.30	75,397,453	1,671,672,053	0.364	10.20	4,835,702	50,560,986	0.011
3.45	104,263,765	1,596,274,600	0.348	10.35	3,420,386	45,725,284	0.010
3.75	130,233,912	1,492,010,835	0.325	10.50	3,326,337	42,304,898	$0.0^2 92$
3.90	64,952,316	1,361,776,923	0.297	10.65	148,351	38,978,561	$0.0^2 85$
4.05	163,182,433	1,296,824,607	0.283	10.80	6,447	38,830,210	$0.0^2 85$
4.20	76,261,402	1,133,642,174	0.247	10.95	7,303,999	38,823,763	$0.0^2 85$
4.35	61,183,577	1,057,380,772	0.231	11.10	1,019,893	31,519,764	$0.0^2 69$
4.65	149,280,845	996,197,195	0.217	11.25	5,012,086	30,499,871	$0.0^2 66$
4.80	12,419,131	846,916,350	0.185	11.40	1,611,994	25,487,785	$0.0^2 56$
4.95	92,138,550	834,497,219	0.182	11.55	3,453,018	23,875,791	$0.0^2 52$
5.10	31,039,556	742,358,669	0.162	11.85	2,902,643	20,422,773	$0.0^2 45$
5.25	11,462,064	711,319,113	0.155	12.00	1,500,895	17,520,130	$0.0^2 38$
5.40	39,659,420	699,857,049	0.153	12.15	1,508,191	16,019,235	$0.0^2 35$
5.55	102,327,988	660,197,629	0.144	12.30	1,861,187	14,511,044	$0.0^2 32$
5.70	9,664,817	557,869,641	0.122	12.45	1,126,534	12,649,857	$0.0^2 28$
5.85	35,546,567	548,204,824	0.120	12.60	787,888	11,523,323	$0.0^2 25$
6.00	24,244,461	512,658,257	0.112	12.75	2,580,161	10,735,435	$0.0^2 23$
6.15	37,889,943	488,413,796	0.106	12.90	6,447	8,155,274	$0.0^2 18$
6.30	32,785,653	450,523,853	0.098	13.05	1,255,251	8,148,827	$0.0^2 18$
6.45	64,316,001	417,738,200	0.091	13.20	52,549	6,893,576	$0.0^2 15$
6.75	45,529,193	353,422,199	0.077	13.35	472,768	6,841,027	$0.0^2 15$
7.05	24,199,169	307,893,006	0.067	13.50	524,812	6,368,259	$0.0^2 14$
7.20	2,187,932	283,693,837	0.062	13.65	1,130,653	5,843,447	$0.0^2 13$
7.35	42,339,887	281,505,905	0.061	13.80	575,289	4,712,794	$0.0^2 10$
7.50	13,403,955	239,166,018	0.052	13.95	1,008,927	4,137,505	$0.0^3 90$
7.65	13,595,779	225,762,063	0.049	14.25	50,523	3,128,578	$0.0^3 68$
7.80	16,024,551	212,166,284	0.046	14.55	873,967	3,078,055	$0.0^3 67$
7.95	20,859,253	196,141,733	0.043	14.70	16,086	2,204,088	$0.0^3 48$
8.10	6,559,932	175,282,480	0.038	14.85	123,780	2,188,002	$0.0^3 48$
8.25	26,453,317	168,722,548	0.037	15.00	207,613	2,064,222	$0.0^3 45$
8.55	14,812,491	142,269,231	0.031	15.15	332,591	1,856,609	$0.0^3 40$
8.70	7,900,435	127,456,740	0.028	15.30	29,877	1,524,018	$0.0^3 33$
8.85	15,652,422	119,556,305	0.026	15.45	451,484	1,494,141	$0.0^3 33$
9.00	7,471,236	103,903,883	0.023	15.60	201,710	1,042,657	$0.0^3 23$
9.15	7,041,690	96,432,647	0.021	15.75	25,997	840,947	$0.0^3 18$
9.45	18,376,470	89,390,957	0.019	15.90	156,226	814,950	$0.0^3 18$
9.60	2,569,244	71,014,487	0.015	16.05	14,222	658,724	$0.0^3 14$
9.75	7,303,017	68,445,243	0.015	16.20	62,456	644,502	$0.0^3 14$
9.90	2,352,334	61,142,226	0.013	16.35	106,511	582,046	$0.0^3 13$

Exact Distribution of Friedman's Chi-Square Statistic (cont.)

$$Pr = Pr\{\text{Friedman's chi-square} \geq \chi^2\}$$
$$p = 4$$

n = 8 (Cont)

χ^2	Freq	Total	Pr
16.65	210,537	475,535	$0.0^3 10$
16.80	5,792	264,998	$0.0^4 58$
16.95	49,697	259,206	$0.0^4 57$
17.25	22,678	209,509	$0.0^4 46$
17.40	18,345	186,831	$0.0^4 41$
17.55	63,514	168,486	$0.0^4 37$
17.70	24,129	104,972	$0.0^4 23$
17.85	306	80,843	$0.0^4 18$
18.15	12,383	80,537	$0.0^4 18$
18.30	8,344	68,154	$0.0^4 15$
18.45	13,276	59,810	$0.0^4 13$
18.60	5,739	46,534	$0.0^4 10$
18.75	13,599	40,795	$0.0^5 89$
19.05	12,029	27,196	$0.0^5 59$
19.35	178	15,167	$0.0^5 33$
19.50	2,025	14,989	$0.0^5 33$
19.65	5,416	12,964	$0.0^5 28$
19.80	1,945	7,548	$0.0^5 16$
19.95	934	5,603	$0.0^5 12$
20.25	1,402	4,669	$0.0^5 10$
20.40	156	3,267	$0.0^6 71$
20.55	1,166	3,111	$0.0^6 68$
20.70	42	1,945	$0.0^6 42$
20.85	1,170	1,903	$0.0^6 41$
21.15	270	733	$0.0^6 16$
21.75	239	463	$0.0^6 10$
21.90	115	224	$0.0^7 49$
22.20	84	109	$0.0^7 24$
22.95	24	25	$0.0^8 55$
24.00	1	1	$0.0^9 22$

14.2 Kruskal-Wallis Distribution (Ranks in One Criterion Variance Analysis) for Three Samples, Each of Size Five or Less, in the Neighborhood of the 10-, 5-, 1-Percent Points

Given three samples of size n_i each, $i = 1, 2, 3$, the rank test considered here requires that all the observations be ranked together and that the sum of the ranks be obtained for each of the three samples. The test statistic (assuming no ties) is then

$$H = \frac{12}{N(N + 1)} \sum_{i=1}^{3} \frac{R_i^2}{n_i} - 3(N + 1),$$

where $N = \sum_{i=1}^{3} n_i$, and $R =$ the sum of the ranks of the ith sample. Large values of H lead to rejection of the null hypothesis that there is no difference in the three samples. If the samples come from identical populations and the n_i are not too small, then H is approximately distributed as chi-square (Section 3.1) with two degrees of freedom. With just two samples, the general procedure reduces to the Wilcoxon two-sample test (Sections 11.2 through 11.5). If there are more than three samples, the reader is referred to the Kruskal-Wallis paper [113]. The tables given here list the probabilities (correct to three decimal places) associated with certain values of H with various combinations of n_1, n_2, and n_3 computed under the assumption that all possible combinations of ranks are equally likely. Wallace [234] gives approximations to the distribution of H. The asymptotic relative efficiency of H with respect to the classical F test is discussed by Andrews [5].

Kruskal-Wallis Distribution (Ranks in One Criterion Variance Analysis) for Three Samples, Each of Size Five or Less, in the Neighborhood of the 10-, 5-, and 1-Percent Points [113]

n_1	n_2	n_3	H	Probability	n_1	n_2	n_3	H	Probability
2	1	1	2.7000	0.500	4	3	1	5.8333	0.021
								5.2083	0.050
2	2	1	3.6000	0.200				5.0000	0.057
								4.0556	0.093
2	2	2	4.5714	0.067				3.8889	0.129
			3.7143	0.200					
					4	3	2	6.4444	0.008
3	1	1	3.2000	0.300				6.3000	0.010
								5.4444	0.046
3	2	1	4.2857	0.100				5.4000	0.051
			3.8571	0.133				4.5111	0.098
								4.4444	0.102
3	2	2	5.3572	0.029					
			4.7143	0.048	4	3	3	6.7455	0.010
			4.5000	0.067				6.7091	0.013
			4.4643	0.105				5.7909	0.046
								5.7203	0.050
3	3	1	5.1429	0.043				4.7091	0.092
			4.5714	0.100				4.7000	0.101
			4.0000	0.129					
					4	4	1	6.6667	0.010
3	3	2	6.2500	0.011				6.1667	0.022
			5.3611	0.032				4.9667	0.048
			5.1389	0.061				4.8667	0.054
			4.5556	0.100				4.1667	0.082
			4.2500	0.121				4.0667	0.102
3	3	3	7.2000	0.004	4	4	2	7.0364	0.006
			6.4889	0.011				6.8727	0.011
			5.6889	0.029				5.4545	0.046
			5.6000	0.050				5.2364	0.052
			5.0667	0.086				4.5545	0.098
			4.6222	0.100				4.4455	0.103
4	1	1	3.5714	0.200	4	4	3	7.1439	0.010
								7.1364	0.011
4	2	1	4.8214	0.057				5.5985	0.049
			4.5000	0.076				5.5758	0.051
			4.0179	0.114				4.5455	0.099
								4.4773	0.102
4	2	2	6.0000	0.014					
			5.3333	0.033	4	4	4	7.6538	0.008
			5.1250	0.052				7.5385	0.011
			4.4583	0.100				5.6923	0.049
			4.1667	0.105				5.6538	0.054
								4.6539	0.097
								4.5001	0.104

Kruskal-Wallis Distribution (Ranks in One Criterion Variance Analysis) for Three Samples, Each of Size Five or Less, in the Neighborhood of the 10-, 5-, and 1-Percent Points (cont.)

n_1	n_2	n_3	H	Probability	n_1	n_2	n_3	H	Probability
5	1	1	3.8571	0.143	5	4	3	7.4449	0.010
								7.3949	0.011
5	2	1	5.2500	0.036				5.6564	0.049
			5.0000	0.048				5.6308	0.050
			4.4500	0.071				4.5487	0.099
			4.200	0.095				4.5231	0.103
			4.0500	0.119					
					5	4	4	7.7604	0.009
5	2	2	6.5333	0.008				7.7440	0.011
			6.1333	0.013				5.6571	0.049
			5.1600	0.034				5.6176	0.050
			5.0400	0.056				4.6187	0.100
			4.3733	0.090				4.5527	0.102
			4.2933	0.122					
					5	5	1	7.3091	0.009
5	3	1	6.4000	0.012				6.8364	0.011
			4.9600	0.048				5.1273	0.046
			4.8711	0.052				4.9091	0.053
			4.0178	0.095				4.1091	0.086
			3.8400	0.123				4.0364	0.105
5	3	2	6.9091	0.009	5	5	2	7.3385	0.010
			6.8218	0.010				7.2692	0.010
			5.2509	0.049				5.3385	0.047
			5.1055	0.052				5.2462	0.051
			4.6509	0.091				4.6231	0.097
			4.4945	0.101				4.5077	0.100
5	3	3	7.0788	0.009	5	5	3	7.5780	0.010
			6.9818	0.011				7.5429	0.010
			5.6485	0.049				5.7055	0.046
			5.5152	0.051				5.6264	0.051
			4.5333	0.097				4.5451	0.100
			4.4121	0.109				4.5363	0.102
5	4	1	6.9545	0.008	5	5	4	7.8229	0.010
			6.8400	0.011				7.7914	0.010
			4.9855	0.044				5.6627	0.049
			4.8600	0.056				5.6429	0.050
			3.9873	0.098				4.5229	0.099
			3.9600	0.102				4.5200	0.101
					5	5	5	8.0000	0.009
5	4	2	7.2045	0.009				7.9800	0.010
			7.1182	0.010				5.7800	0.049
			5.2727	0.049				5.6600	0.051
			5.2682	0.050				4.5600	0.100
			4.5409	0.098				4.5000	0.102
			4.5182	0.101					

15. KOLMOGOROV-SMIRNOV STATISTICS

15.1 Critical Values for the Kolmogorov-Smirnov One-Sample Statistic

Let $F(x)$ be the continuous cumulative distribution function of a random variable X, and let $F_n(x)$ be the empirical distribution function determined by a sample $X_1, X_2, \ldots, X_n$, that is,

$$F_n(x) = \begin{cases} 0 & \text{for } x < X_{(1)}, \\ i/n & \text{for } X_{(i)} \leq x < X_{(i+1)}, \\ 1 & \text{for } x \geq X_{(n)}, \end{cases}$$

where $X_{(1)}, X_{(2)}, \ldots, X_{(n)}$ are the sample values ordered from smallest to largest. The probability $P_n(\epsilon)$ that $F(x)$ is everywhere majorized by $F_n(x) + \epsilon$ is independent of $F(x)$. Define the function

$$D^+(n) = \text{supremum over all } x \text{ of } \{F_n(x) - F(x)\}.$$

The table gives values of ϵ which satisfy

$$\Pr \{D^+(n) \geq \epsilon\} = \frac{1-p}{2},$$

or equivalently,

$$\frac{1-p}{2} = \epsilon \sum_{j=0}^{[n-n\epsilon]} \frac{n!}{j!(n-j)!} \left(1 - \epsilon - \frac{j}{n}\right)^{n-j} \left(\epsilon + \frac{j}{n}\right)^{j-1},$$

where $[n - n\epsilon]$ is the largest integer contained in $n(1 - \epsilon)$. The asymptotic formula for ϵ is

$$\bar{\epsilon} = \sqrt{(-\log_e \alpha)/2n}.$$

In addition to some of the values given here, Birnbaum and Tingey [25] give some values for $(1 - p)/2 = 0.001$.

Miller [140] shows that if

$$D(n) = \text{supremum over all } x \text{ of } |F_n(x) - F(x)|,$$

then

$$\Pr \{D(n) \geq \epsilon\} \cong 1 - p,$$

and hence the tables given here may be used for the two-sided case as well as the one-sided case. Birnbaum [20] tabulates some values of ϵ in his Table 2 for this two-sided case.

Dempster [50] and Dwass [60] give generalizations of the Kolmogorov-Smirnov statistics. Kiefer [107] considers k-sample analogues of the Kolmogorov-Smirnov statistics. Darling [41] gives a history of the Kolmogorov-Smirnov statistics and an extensive bibliography.

Critical Values for the Kolmogorov-Smirnov One-Sample Statistic [140]

$\Pr\{D^+(n) \geq \text{tabled value}\} = (1 - p)/2 \; ; \; \Pr\{D(n) \geq \text{tabled value}\} \cong 1 - p$

n	p = .80	p = .90	p = .95	p = .98	p = .99
1	.90000	.95000	.97500	.99000	.99500
2	.68377	.77639	.84189	.90000	.92929
3	.56481	.63604	.70760	.78456	.82900
4	.49265	.56522	.62394	.68887	.73424
5	.44698	.50945	.56328	.62718	.66853
6	.41037	.46799	.51926	.57741	.61661
7	.38148	.43607	.48342	.53844	.57581
8	.35831	.40962	.45427	.50654	.54179
9	.33910	.38746	.43001	.47960	.51332
10	.32260	.36866	.40925	.45662	.48893
11	.30829	.35242	.39122	.43670	.46770
12	.29577	.33815	.37543	.41918	.44905
13	.28470	.32549	.36143	.40362	.43247
14	.27481	.31417	.34890	.38970	.41762
15	.26588	.30397	.33760	.37713	.40420
16	.25778	.29472	.32733	.36571	.39201
17	.25039	.28627	.31796	.35528	.38086
18	.24360	.27851	.30936	.34569	.37062
19	.23735	.27136	.30143	.33685	.36117
20	.23156	.26473	.29408	.32866	.35241
21	.22617	.25858	.28724	.32104	.34427
22	.22115	.25283	.28087	.31394	.33666
23	.21645	.24746	.27490	.30728	.32954
24	.21205	.24242	.26931	.30104	.32286
25	.20790	.23768	.26404	.29516	.31657
26	.20399	.23320	.25907	.28962	.31064
27	.20030	.22898	.25438	.28438	.30502
28	.19680	.22497	.24993	.27942	.29971
29	.19348	.22117	.24571	.27471	.29466
30	.19032	.21756	.24170	.27023	.28987
31	.18732	.21412	.23788	.26596	.28530
32	.18445	.21085	.23424	.26189	.28094
33	.18171	.20771	.23076	.25801	.27677
34	.17909	.20472	.22743	.25429	.27279
35	.17659	.20185	.22425	.25073	.26897
36	.17418	.19910	.22119	.24732	.26532
37	.17188	.19646	.21826	.24404	.26180
38	.16966	.19392	.21544	.24089	.25843
39	.16753	.19148	.21273	.23786	.25518
40	.16547	.18913	.21012	.23494	.25205
41	.16349	.18687	.20760	.23213	.24904
42	.16158	.18468	.20517	.22941	.24613
43	.15974	.18257	.20283	.22679	.24332
44	.15796	.18053	.20056	.22426	.24060
45	.15623	.17856	.19837	.22181	.23798
46	.15457	.17665	.19625	.21944	.23544
47	.15295	.17481	.19420	.21715	.23298
48	.15139	.17302	.19221	.21493	.23059
49	.14987	.17128	.19028	.21277	.22828
50	.14840	.16959	.18841	.21068	.22604

15.1

Critical Values for the Kolmogorov- Smirnov One-Sample Statistic (*cont.*)

n	p = .80	p = .90	p = .95	p = .98	p = .99
51	.14697	.16796	.18659	.20864	.22386
52	.14558	.16637	.18482	.20667	.22174
53	.14423	.16483	.18311	.20475	.21968
54	.14292	.16332	.18144	.20289	.21768
55	.14164	.16186	.17981	.20107	.21574
56	.14040	.16044	.17823	.19930	.21384
57	.13919	.15906	.17669	.19758	.21199
58	.13801	.15771	.17519	.19590	.21019
59	.13686	.15639	.17373	.19427	.20844
60	.13573	.15511	.17231	.19267	.20673
61	.13464	.15385	.17091	.19112	.20506
62	.13357	.15263	.16956	.18960	.20343
63	.13253	.15144	.16823	.18812	.20184
64	.13151	.15027	.16693	.18667	.20029
65	.13052	.14913	.16567	.18525	.19877
66	.12954	.14802	.16443	.18387	.19729
67	.12859	.14693	.16322	.18252	.19584
68	.12766	.14587	.16204	.18119	.19442
69	.12675	.14483	.16088	.17990	.19303
70	.12586	.14381	.15975	.17863	.19167
71	.12499	.14281	.15864	.17739	.19034
72	.12413	.14183	.15755	.17618	.18903
73	.12329	.14087	.15649	.17498	.18776
74	.12247	.13993	.15544	.17382	.18650
75	.12167	.13901	.15442	.17268	.18528
76	.12088	.13811	.15342	.17155	.18408
77	.12011	.13723	.15244	.17045	.18290
78	.11935	.13636	.15147	.16938	.18174
79	.11860	.13551	.15052	.16832	.18060
80	.11787	.13467	.14960	.16728	.17949
81	.11716	.13385	.14868	.16626	.17840
82	.11645	.13305	.14779	.16526	.17732
83	.11576	.13226	.14691	.16428	.17627
84	.11508	.13148	.14605	.16331	.17523
85	.11442	.13072	.14520	.16236	.17421
86	.11376	.12997	.14437	.16143	.17321
87	.11311	.12923	.14355	.16051	.17223
88	.11248	.12850	.14274	.15961	.17126
89	.11186	.12779	.14195	.15873	.17031
90	.11125	.12709	.14117	.15786	.16938
91	.11064	.12640	.14040	.15700	.16846
92	.11005	.12572	.13965	.15616	.16755
93	.10947	.12506	.13891	.15533	.16666
94	.10889	.12440	.13818	.15451	.16579
95	.10833	.12375	.13746	.15371	.16493
96	.10777	.12312	.13675	.15291	.16408
97	.10722	.12249	.13606	.15214	.16324
98	.10668	.12187	.13537	.15137	.16242
99	.10615	.12126	.13469	.15061	.16161
100	.10563	.12067	.13403	.14987	.16081

15.1

15.2 Probability Distribution of the Kolmogorov-Smirnov One-Sample Statistic

The quantity tabulated here is the probability distribution of

$$\Pr \{D(n) \leq c/n\},$$

where

$$D(n) = \text{supremum over all } x \text{ of } |F_n(x) - F(x)|,$$

where $F_n(x)$ and $F(x)$ are defined as in Section 15.1. The formula for this computation is

$$\Pr \{D(n) < c/n\} = \frac{n!}{n^n} \exp (n) R_{0,n}(c),$$

where $R_{i,k}(c)$ is defined for all integers i and all non-negative integers k, and $c = 1, 2, \ldots, n$, and

$$R_{0,0}(c) = 1,$$
$$R_{i,0}(c) = 0 \quad \text{for } i \neq 0,$$
$$R_{i,k}(c) = 0 \quad \text{for } |i| \geq c,$$

and

$$R_{i,k+1}(c) = \exp (-1) \sum_{S=0}^{2r-1} \frac{R_{i+1-S,k}(c)}{S!}.$$

Probability Distribution of the Kolmogorov-Smirnov One-Sample Statistic [20]

$$\Pr\{D(n) \le c/n\} = \text{tabled value}$$

				n				
c	1	2	3	4	5	6	7	8
1	1.00000	.50000	.22222	.09375	.03840	.01543	.00612	.00240
2		1.00000	.92593	.81250	.69120	.57656	.47446	.38659
3			1.00000	.99219	.96992	.93441	.88937	.83842
4				1.00000	.99936	.99623	.98911	.97741
5					1.00000	.99996	.99960	.99849
6						1.00000	1.00000	.99996
7								1.00000

				n				
c	9	10	11	12	13	14	15	16
1	.00094	.00036	.00014	.00005	.00002	.00001	.00000	.00000
2	.31261	.25128	.20100	.16014	.12715	.10066	.07950	.06265
3	.78442	.72946	.67502	.62209	.57136	.52323	.47795	.43564
4	.96121	.94101	.91747	.89126	.86304	.83337	.80275	.77158
5	.99615	.99222	.98648	.97885	.96935	.95807	.94517	.93081
6	.99982	.99943	.99865	.99732	.99530	.99250	.98882	.98425
7	1.00000	.99998	.99993	.99979	.99953	.99908	.99837	.99736
8		1.00000	1.00000	.99999	.99997	.99993	.99984	.99968
9				1.00000	1.00000	1.00000	.99999	.99997
10							1.00000	1.00000

				n				
c	17	18	19	20	21	22	23	24
1	.00000	.00000	.00000	.00000	.00000	.00000	.00000	.00000
2	.04927	.03869	.03033	.02374	.01857	.01450	.01132	.00882
3	.39630	.35991	.32636	.29553	.26729	.24147	.21793	.19650
4	.74019	.70887	.67784	.64728	.61733	.58811	.55970	.53216
5	.91517	.89844	.88079	.86237	.84335	.82386	.80401	.78392
6	.97875	.97235	.96506	.95693	.94802	.93837	.92805	.91712
7	.99598	.99419	.99195	.98924	.98605	.98236	.97817	.97349
8	.99944	.99907	.99856	.99788	.99700	.99590	.99456	.99296
9	.99994	.99989	.99980	.99968	.99949	.99924	.99890	.99846
10	1.00000	.99999	.99998	.99996	.99993	.99989	.99982	.99973
11		1.00000	1.00000	1.00000	.99999	.99999	.99998	.99996
12					1.00000	1.00000	1.00000	1.00000

Probability Distribution of the Kolmogorov-Smirnov One-Sample Statistic (*cont.*)

c	25	26	27	28	29	30	31	32
1	.00000	.00000	.00000	.00000	.00000	.00000	.00000	.00000
2	.00687	.00535	.00416	.00323	.00251	.00195	.00151	.00117
3	.17702	.15935	.14334	.12885	.11575	.10392	.09325	.08363
4	.50554	.47987	.45517	.43145	.40870	.38693	.36612	.34624
5	.76368	.74338	.72309	.70288	.68280	.66290	.64323	.62382
6	.90565	.89368	.88128	.86851	.85541	.84203	.82843	.81463
7	.96832	.96269	.95661	.95010	.94318	.93588	.92822	.92022
8	.99110	.98895	.98651	.98378	.98076	.97745	.97384	.96995
9	.99792	.99725	.99645	.99551	.99441	.99315	.99172	.99012
10	.99960	.99943	.99921	.99894	.99861	.99821	.99773	.99717
11	.99994	.99990	.99985	.99979	.99971	.99960	.99946	.99930
12	.99999	.99999	.99998	.99997	.99995	.99992	.99989	.99985
13	1.00000	1.00000	1.00000	1.00000	.99999	.99999	.99998	.99997
14					1.00000	1.00000	1.00000	1.00000

c	33	34	35	36	37	38	39	40
1	.00000	.00000	.00000	.00000	.00000	.00000	.00000	.00000
2	.00091	.00070	.00054	.00042	.00033	.00025	.00020	.00015
3	.07497	.06717	.06016	.05386	.04820	.04312	.03856	.03448
4	.32729	.30923	.29205	.27570	.26018	.24544	.23145	.21819
5	.60470	.58590	.56744	.54934	.53161	.51427	.49733	.48078
6	.80069	.78663	.77250	.75831	.74410	.72990	.71572	.70159
7	.91192	.90332	.89447	.88538	.87608	.86658	.85690	.84707
8	.96578	.96134	.95664	.95168	.94648	.94104	.93539	.92952
9	.98834	.98638	.98423	.98191	.97939	.97670	.97382	.97077
10	.99652	.99578	.99494	.99399	.99294	.99178	.99050	.98910
11	.99910	.99886	.99857	.99824	.99785	.99741	.99692	.99636
12	.99980	.99973	.99965	.99954	.99942	.99928	.99911	.99891
13	.99996	.99994	.99992	.99990	.99986	.99982	.99977	.99971
14	1.00000	.99999	.99999	.99998	.99997	.99996	.99995	.99993
15		1.00000	1.00000	1.00000	.99999	.99999	.99999	.99999

c	41	42	43	44	45	46	47	48
1	.00000	.00000	.00000	.00000	.00000	.00000	.00000	.00000
2	.00012	.00009	.00007	.00005	.00004	.00003	.00002	.00002
3	.03081	.02753	.02459	.02196	.01960	.01750	.01561	.01393
4	.20562	.19373	.18247	.17181	.16174	.15222	.14323	.13474
5	.46464	.44891	.43359	.41868	.40418	.39008	.37639	.36310
6	.68752	.67354	.65965	.64588	.63223	.61872	.60536	.59215
7	.83711	.82702	.81684	.80657	.79623	.78583	.77539	.76492
8	.92345	.91719	.91075	.90415	.89739	.89048	.88344	.87628
9	.96754	.96413	.96056	.95682	.95293	.94888	.94467	.94033
10	.98759	.98596	.98421	.98233	.98033	.97822	.97598	.97363
11	.99573	.99504	.99428	.99344	.99253	.99154	.99047	.98933
12	.99868	.99842	.99813	.99779	.99742	.99701	.99655	.99605
13	.99963	.99955	.99945	.99933	.99919	.99904	.99886	.99866
14	.99991	.99988	.99985	.99982	.99977	.99972	.99966	.99959
15	.99998	.99997	.99996	.99995	.99994	.99993	.99991	.99988

Probability Distribution of the Kolmogorov-Smirnov One-Sample Statistic (*cont.*)

c	n 49	50	51	52	53	54	55	56
1	.00000	.00000	.00000	.00000	.00000	.00000	.00000	.00000
2	.00001	.00001	.00001	.00001	.00001	.00000	.00000	.00000
3	.01242	.01108	.00988	.00880	.00785	.00699	.00623	.00555
4	.12672	.11916	.11203	.10530	.09896	.09298	.08735	.08205
5	.35020	.33769	.32556	.31381	.30242	.29140	.28073	.27041
6	.57911	.56623	.55353	.54101	.52868	.51654	.50459	.49283
7	.75442	.74392	.73342	.72294	.71247	.70203	.69162	.68126
8	.86899	.86160	.85412	.84654	.83889	.83116	.82337	.81552
9	.93584	.93122	.92648	.92161	.91662	.91152	.90632	.90102
10	.97115	.96856	.96586	.96304	.96011	.95708	.95393	.95069
11	.98810	.98679	.98540	.98392	.98237	.98073	.97900	.97720
12	.99550	.99490	.99425	.99356	.99280	.99200	.99113	.99022
13	.99844	.99820	.99792	.99762	.99729	.99693	.99654	.99611
14	.99951	.99941	.99931	.99919	.99906	.99891	.99875	.99857
15	.99986	.99983	.99979	.99975	.99970	.99964	.99958	.99951

c	n 57	58	59	60	61	62	63	64
1	.00000	.00000	.00000	.00000	.00000	.00000	.00000	.00000
2	.00000	.00000	.00000	.00000	.00000	.00000	.00000	.00000
3	.00494	.00440	.00392	.00349	.00310	.00276	.00246	.00219
4	.07706	.07236	.06793	.06377	.05986	.05617	.05271	.04946
5	.26042	.25077	.24144	.23242	.22371	.21529	.20717	.19933
6	.48128	.46992	.45876	.44780	.43705	.42649	.41614	.40599
7	.67094	.66068	.65049	.64035	.63029	.62030	.61040	.60057
8	.80762	.79968	.79171	.78370	.77567	.76761	.75955	.75148
9	.89562	.89013	.88455	.87889	.87316	.86736	.86150	.85557
10	.94734	.94390	.94036	.93674	.93302	.92921	.92533	.92136
11	.97531	.97334	.97129	.96916	.96695	.96466	.96230	.95986
12	.98924	.98821	.98712	.98598	.98477	.98351	.98218	.98080
13	.99565	.99515	.99462	.99406	.99345	.99281	.99212	.99140
14	.99837	.99815	.99791	.99765	.99737	.99707	.99674	.99639
15	.99943	.99934	.99925	.99914	.99902	.99889	.99874	.99858

c	n 65	66	67	68	69	70	71	72
1	.00000	.00000	.00000	.00000	.00000	.00000	.00000	.00000
2	.00000	.00000	.00000	.00000	.00000	.00000	.00000	.00000
3	.00195	.00173	.00154	.00137	.00122	.00108	.00096	.00086
4	.04640	.04352	.04082	.03828	.03589	.03365	.03155	.02958
5	.19176	.18445	.17741	.17061	.16406	.15774	.15165	.14578
6	.39603	.38628	.37672	.36736	.35819	.34921	.34043	.33183
7	.59083	.58119	.57163	.56217	.55280	.54354	.53437	.52531
8	.74340	.73533	.72726	.71919	.71115	.70311	.69510	.68712
9	.84958	.84355	.83746	.83133	.82516	.81895	.81271	.80644
10	.91731	.91320	.90901	.90475	.90042	.89604	.89159	.88709
11	.95735	.95476	.95211	.94938	.94659	.94373	.94080	.93781
12	.97936	.97786	.97630	.97469	.97301	.97128	.96950	.96765
13	.99063	.98983	.98898	.98809	.98716	.98619	.98518	.98412
14	.99602	.99562	.99519	.99474	.99425	.99374	.99321	.99264
15	.99841	.99823	.99803	.99781	.99758	.99733	.99707	.99678

Probability Distribution of the Kolmogorov-Smirnov One-Sample Statistic (cont.)

	n							
c	73	74	75	76	77	78	79	80
1	.00000	.00000	.00000	.00000	.00000	.00000	.00000	.00000
2	.00000	.00000	.00000	.00000	.00000	.00000	.00000	.00000
3	.00076	.00068	.00060	.00053	.00047	.00042	.00037	.00033
4	.02772	.02598	.02435	.02282	.02138	.02003	.01877	.01758
5	.14013	.13468	.12943	.12438	.11951	.11482	.11031	.10597
6	.32342	.31519	.30714	.29928	.29159	.28407	.27672	.26955
7	.51635	.50750	.49875	.49011	.48158	.47316	.46485	.45664
8	.67916	.67123	.66333	.65546	.64764	.63985	.63211	.62441
9	.80014	.79382	.78748	.78112	.77475	.76836	.76197	.75557
10	.88253	.87792	.87326	.86856	.86381	.85902	.85419	.84932
11	.93476	.93165	.92848	.92525	.92197	.91864	.91525	.91182
12	.96576	.96380	.96180	.95974	.95762	.95546	.95324	.95098
13	.98302	.98187	.98069	.97946	.97819	.97687	.97552	.97412
14	.99204	.99142	.99076	.99008	.98936	.98861	.98783	.98702
15	.99648	.99616	.99582	.99546	.99508	.99468	.99426	.99382

	n							
c	81	82	83	84	85	86	87	88
1	.00000	.00000	.00000	.00000	.00000	.00000	.00000	.00000
2	.00000	.00000	.00000	.00000	.00000	.00000	.00000	.00000
3	.00030	.00026	.00023	.00021	.00018	.00016	.00015	.00013
4	.01647	.01542	.01444	.01353	.01267	.01186	.01110	.01040
5	.10178	.09776	.09389	.09017	.08659	.08314	.07983	.07664
6	.26253	.25569	.24900	.24247	.23609	.22986	.22379	.21786
7	.44855	.44056	.43269	.42493	.41727	.40973	.40229	.39497
8	.61675	.60914	.60159	.59408	.58662	.57922	.57188	.56459
9	.74917	.74276	.73636	.72996	.72356	.71717	.71079	.70442
10	.84442	.83949	.83452	.82953	.82451	.81947	.81440	.80932
11	.90833	.90480	.90123	.89761	.89395	.89025	.88651	.88273
12	.94867	.94630	.94390	.94144	.93894	.93640	.93381	.93118
13	.97268	.97119	.96967	.96811	.96650	.96486	.96317	.96145
14	.98618	.98531	.98440	.98346	.98249	.98149	.98046	.97939
15	.99336	.99287	.99237	.99184	.99129	.99071	.99011	.98949

	n							
c	89	90	91	92	94	96	98	100
1	.00000	.00000	.00000	.00000	.00000	.00000	.00000	.00000
2	.00000	.00000	.00000	.00000	.00000	.00000	.00000	.00000
3	.00011	.00010	.00009	.00008	.00006	.00005	.00004	.00003
4	.00973	.00911	.00853	.00798	.00699	.00612	.00536	.00469
5	.07357	.07063	.06779	.06507	.05994	.05520	.05082	.04678
6	.21207	.20643	.20092	.19555	.18520	.17536	.16600	.15712
7	.38775	.38064	.37364	.36674	.35327	.34021	.32757	.31533
8	.55735	.55018	.54306	.53600	.52207	.50839	.49496	.48178
9	.69806	.69172	.68539	.67908	.66651	.65403	.64165	.62937
10	.80421	.79909	.79395	.78880	.77847	.76810	.75771	.74731
11	.87892	.87507	.87119	.86728	.85937	.85136	.84324	.83504
12	.92851	.92580	.92305	.92026	.91457	.90874	.90278	.89670
13	.95969	.95789	.95605	.95418	.95032	.94632	.94218	.93791
14	.97830	.97717	.97601	.97482	.97234	.96974	.96702	.96417
15	.98884	.98818	.98748	.98677	.98526	.98366	.98196	.98016

15.3 Probability Distribution of the Kolmogorov-Smirnov One-Sided Two-Sample Statistic

Let $F_n(x)$ and $G_n(y)$ be the empirical distribution functions determined by a sample of n X's and a sample of n Y's, respectively, where both X and Y have continuous cumulative distribution functions and are independent of each other. The quantity tabulated is

$$\Pr\{D^+(n, n) \le r\},$$

where

$$D^+(n, n) = \text{supremum over all } x \text{ of } \{F_n(x) - G_n(x)\}.$$

See Birnbaum and Hall's paper [22] for the computation formulas.

Probability Distribution of the Kolmogorov-Smirnov One-Sided Two-Sample Statistic [22]
$\Pr\{D^+(n, n) \le r\}$ = tabled value

nr	1	2	3	4	5	6
0	0.500000	0.333333	0.250000	0.200000	0.166666	0.142857
1	1.000000	0.833333	0.700000	0.600000	0.523809	0.464285
2		1.000000	0.950000	0.885714	0.821428	0.761904
3			1.000000	0.985714	0.960317	0.928571
4				1.000000	0.996031	0.987012
5					1.000000	0.998917
6						1.000000

nr	7	8	9	10	11	12
0	0.125000	0.111111	0.100000	0.090909	0.083333	0.076923
1	0.416666	0.377777	0.345454	0.318181	0.294871	0.274725
2	0.708333	0.660606	0.618181	0.580419	0.546703	0.516483
3	0.893939	0.858585	0.823776	0.790209	0.758241	0.728021
4	0.973484	0.956487	0.937062	0.916083	0.894230	0.872010
5	0.995920	0.990675	0.983216	0.973776	0.962669	0.950226
6	0.999708	0.998756	0.996853	0.993829	0.989630	0.984281
7	1.000000	0.999922	0.999629	0.998971	0.997816	0.996070
8		1.000000	0.999979	0.999891	0.999672	0.999251
9			1.000000	0.999994	0.999968	0.999897
10				1.000000	0.999998	0.999991
11					1.000000	0.999999
12						1.000000

Probability Distribution of the Kolmogorov-Smirnov One-Sided Two-Sample Statistic (cont.)

nr	13	14	15	16	17	18
0	0.071428	0.066666	0.062500	0.058823	0.055555	0.052631
1	0.257142	0.241666	0.227941	0.215686	0.204678	0.194736
2	0.489285	0.464705	0.442401	0.422084	0.403508	0.386466
3	0.699579	0.672875	0.647832	0.624354	0.602339	0.581681
4	0.849789	0.827829	0.806308	0.785345	0.765018	0.745371
5	0.936753	0.922523	0.907765	0.892672	0.877401	0.862076
6	0.977863	0.970485	0.962267	0.953336	0.943808	0.933796
7	0.993675	0.990608	0.986875	0.982500	0.977523	0.971990
8	0.998562	0.997550	0.996172	0.994400	0.992219	0.989626
9	0.999750	0.999489	0.999081	0.998492	0.997694	0.996665
10	0.999968	0.999918	0.999823	0.999664	0.999423	0.999080
11	0.999997	0.999990	0.999973	0.999940	0.999880	0.999785
12	0.999999	0.999999	0.999997	0.999991	0.999980	0.999958
13	1.000000	1.000000	0.999999	0.999999	0.999997	0.999993
14		1.000000	1.000000	1.000000	0.999999	0.999999
15			1.000000	1.000000	1.000000	0.999999
16				1.000000	1.000000	1.000000
17					1.000000	1.000000
18						1.000000

nr	19	20	21	22	23	24
0	0.050000	0.047619	0.045454	0.043478	0.041666	0.040000
1	0.185714	0.177489	0.169960	0.163043	0.156666	0.150769
2	0.370779	0.356295	0.342885	0.330434	0.318846	0.308034
3	0.562281	0.544042	0.526877	0.510702	0.495441	0.481025
4	0.726425	0.708187	0.690650	0.673801	0.657621	0.642086
5	0.846798	0.831646	0.816681	0.801950	0.787488	0.773321
6	0.923399	0.912705	0.901793	0.890731	0.879577	0.868380
7	0.965955	0.959470	0.952590	0.945365	0.937846	0.930077
8	0.986625	0.983229	0.979455	0.975326	0.970865	0.966097
9	0.995388	0.993850	0.992047	0.989976	0.987639	0.985043
10	0.998616	0.998016	0.997266	0.996355	0.995274	0.994017
11	0.999642	0.999442	0.999171	0.998820	0.998379	0.997839
12	0.999921	0.999864	0.999780	0.999663	0.999504	0.999299
13	0.999985	0.999972	0.999949	0.999915	0.999866	0.999797
14	0.999997	0.999995	0.999990	0.999981	0.999968	0.999948
15	0.999999	0.999999	0.999998	0.999996	0.999993	0.999988
16	1.000000	0.999999	0.999999	0.999999	0.999998	0.999997
17	1.000000	1.000000	1.000000	1.000000	0.999999	0.999999
18	1.000000	1.000000	1.000000	1.000000	1.000000	1.000000
19	1.000000	1.000000	1.000000	1.000000	1.000000	1.000000
20		1.000000	1.000000	1.000000	1.000000	1.000000

15.3

Probability Distribution of the Kolmogorov-Smirnov One-Sided Two-Sample Statistic (*cont.*)

nr	25	26	27	28	29	30
0	0.038461	0.037037	0.035714	0.034482	0.033333	0.032258
1	0.145299	0.140211	0.135467	0.131034	0.126881	0.122983
2	0.297924	0.288451	0.279556	0.271190	0.263306	0.255865
3	0.467390	0.454479	0.442237	0.430617	0.419574	0.409069
4	0.627173	0.612856	0.599108	0.585903	0.573216	0.561022
5	0.759466	0.745936	0.732738	0.719875	0.707348	0.695154
6	0.857183	0.846022	0.834926	0.823922	0.813028	0.802262
7	0.922100	0.913953	0.905672	0.897287	0.888827	0.880316
8	0.961050	0.955747	0.950216	0.944479	0.938562	0.932486
9	0.982194	0.979103	0.975780	0.972239	0.968493	0.964555
10	0.992581	0.990963	0.989165	0.987187	0.985034	0.982709
11	0.997192	0.996432	0.995554	0.994554	0.993429	0.992178
12	0.999039	0.998719	0.998333	0.997875	0.997340	0.996725
13	0.999704	0.999583	0.999430	0.999241	0.999010	0.998734
14	0.999918	0.999878	0.999823	0.999752	0.999662	0.999550
15	0.999980	0.999968	0.999950	0.999926	0.999895	0.999853
16	0.999995	0.999992	0.999987	0.999980	0.999970	0.999956
17	0.999999	0.999998	0.999997	0.999995	0.999992	0.999988
18	0.999999	0.999999	0.999999	0.999998	0.999998	0.999997
19	1.000000	1.000000	0.999999	0.999999	0.999999	0.999999
20	1.000000	1.000000	0.999999	0.999999	0.999999	0.999999

nr	31	32	34	36	38	40
0	0.031250	0.030303	0.028571	0.027027	0.025641	0.024390
1	0.119318	0.115864	0.109523	0.103840	0.098717	0.094076
2	0.248830	0.242169	0.229858	0.218732	0.208630	0.199416
3	0.399064	0.389525	0.371726	0.355454	0.340525	0.326782
4	0.549298	0.538019	0.516712	0.496940	0.478554	0.461425
5	0.683290	0.671750	0.649616	0.628693	0.608916	0.590215
6	0.791638	0.781167	0.760713	0.740949	0.721895	0.703559
7	0.871777	0.863229	0.846173	0.829262	0.812582	0.796197
8	0.926272	0.919939	0.906988	0.893763	0.880371	0.866904
9	0.960438	0.956157	0.947152	0.937643	0.927724	0.917480
10	0.980219	0.977568	0.971814	0.965504	0.958699	0.951459
11	0.990799	0.989294	0.985907	0.982033	0.977697	0.972929
12	0.996027	0.995241	0.993403	0.991200	0.988630	0.985698
13	0.998410	0.998034	0.997113	0.995952	0.994533	0.992849
14	0.999412	0.999247	0.998821	0.998253	0.997524	0.996619
15	0.999800	0.999733	0.999552	0.999294	0.998945	0.998490
16	0.999937	0.999912	0.999841	0.999733	0.999578	0.999364
17	0.999982	0.999973	0.999948	0.999906	0.999841	0.999748
18	0.999995	0.999992	0.999984	0.999969	0.999944	0.999905
19	0.999998	0.999998	0.999995	0.999990	0.999981	0.999967
20	0.999999	0.999999	0.999998	0.999997	0.999994	0.999989

15.4 Probability Distribution of the Kolmogorov-Smirnov Two-Sample Statistic

Let $F_n(x)$ and $G_n(y)$ be defined as in Section 15.3. The quantity tabulated is

$$\Pr\{D(n, n) \le r\},$$

where

$$D(n, n) = \text{supremum over all } x \text{ of } |F_n(x) - G_n(x)|.$$

The table given here is an extension of a table due to Massey [135] and was taken from Birnbaum and Hall [22].

Probability Distribution of the Kolmogorov-Smirnov Two-Sample Statistic [22]

$\Pr\{D(n, n) \le r\}$ = tabled value

			n			
nr	1	2	3	4	5	6
1	1.000000	0.666666	0.400000	0.228571	0.126984	0.069264
2		1.000000	0.900000	0.771428	0.642857	0.525974
3			1.000000	0.971428	0.920634	0.857142
4				1.000000	0.992063	0.974025
5					1.000000	0.997835
6						1.000000

			n			
nr	7	8	9	10	11	12
1	0.037296	0.019891	0.010530	0.005542	0.002903	0.001514
2	0.424825	0.339860	0.269888	0.213070	0.167412	0.131018
3	0.787878	0.717327	0.648292	0.582476	0.520849	0.463902
4	0.946969	0.912975	0.874125	0.832178	0.788523	0.744224
5	0.991841	0.981351	0.966433	0.947552	0.925339	0.900453
6	0.999417	0.997513	0.993706	0.987659	0.979260	0.968563
7	1.000000	0.999844	0.999259	0.997943	0.995633	0.992140
8		1.000000	0.999958	0.999783	0.999345	0.998503
9			1.000000	0.999989	0.999937	0.999795
10				1.000000	0.999997	0.999982
11					1.000000	0.999999
12						1.000000

Probability Distribution of the Kolmogorov-
Smirnov Two-Sample Statistic (cont.)

nr	n 13	14	15	16	17	18
1	0.000787	0.000408	0.000211	0.000109	0.000056	0.000028
2	0.102194	0.079484	0.061668	0.047743	0.036892	0.028460
3	0.411803	0.364515	0.321861	0.283588	0.249392	0.218952
4	0.700079	0.656679	0.614453	0.573706	0.534647	0.497409
5	0.873512	0.845065	0.815583	0.785465	0.755040	0.724581
6	0.955727	0.940970	0.924535	0.906673	0.887622	0.867606
7	0.987350	0.981217	0.973751	0.965002	0.955047	0.943981
8	0.997125	0.995100	0.992344	0.988800	0.984439	0.979252
9	0.999500	0.998979	0.998162	0.996984	0.995389	0.993331
10	0.999937	0.999836	0.999646	0.999329	0.998847	0.998160
11	0.999995	0.999981	0.999947	0.999880	0.999761	0.999570
12	0.999999	0.999998	0.999994	0.999983	0.999960	0.999916
13	1.000000	1.000000	0.999999	0.999998	0.999994	0.999987
14		1.000000	1.000000	0.999999	0.999999	0.999998
15			1.000000	1.000000	1.000000	0.999999
16				1.000000	1.000000	1.000000
17					1.000000	1.000000
18						1.000000

nr	n 19	20	21	22	23	24
1	0.000014	0.000007	0.000003	0.000001	0.000001	0.000000
2	0.021922	0.016863	0.012955	0.009942	0.007622	0.005838
3	0.191938	0.168030	0.146921	0.128321	0.111963	0.097599
4	0.462071	0.428664	0.397187	0.367613	0.339899	0.313982
5	0.694310	0.664409	0.635020	0.606260	0.578218	0.550963
6	0.846826	0.825466	0.803687	0.781631	0.759421	0.737166
7	0.931910	0.918942	0.905183	0.890738	0.875705	0.860177
8	0.973250	0.966458	0.958911	0.950653	0.941731	0.932196
9	0.990776	0.987701	0.984094	0.979952	0.975279	0.970086
10	0.997232	0.996032	0.994532	0.992710	0.990548	0.988034
11	0.999285	0.998884	0.998343	0.997641	0.996759	0.995679
12	0.999843	0.999729	0.999561	0.999326	0.999009	0.998598
13	0.999971	0.999944	0.999899	0.999831	0.999732	0.999594
14	0.999995	0.999990	0.999980	0.999963	0.999936	0.999895
15	0.999999	0.999998	0.999996	0.999993	0.999986	0.999976
16	0.999999	0.999999	0.999999	0.999998	0.999997	0.999995
17	1.000000	1.000000	1.000000	0.999999	0.999999	0.999999
18	1.000000	1.000000	1.000000	1.000000	1.000000	0.999999
19	1.000000	1.000000	1.000000	1.000000	1.000000	1.000000
20		1.000000	1.000000	1.000000	1.000000	1.000000

Probability Distribution of the Kolmogorov-Smirnov Two-Sample Statistic (cont.)

nr	n 25	26	27	28	29	30
1	0.000000	0.000000	0.000000	0.000000	0.000000	0.000000
2	0.004468	0.003417	0.002611	0.001993	0.001521	0.001160
3	0.085006	0.073980	0.064337	0.055914	0.048563	0.042153
4	0.289796	0.267262	0.246302	0.226833	0.208772	0.192036
5	0.524546	0.499004	0.474362	0.450633	0.427822	0.405929
6	0.714957	0.692876	0.670992	0.649361	0.628035	0.607054
7	0.844239	0.827971	0.811443	0.794721	0.777865	0.760926
8	0.922101	0.911498	0.900437	0.888969	0.877140	0.864996
9	0.964388	0.958206	0.951561	0.944480	0.936988	0.929112
10	0.985162	0.981927	0.978330	0.974375	0.970069	0.965419
11	0.994385	0.992865	0.991109	0.989109	0.986859	0.984356
12	0.998079	0.997439	0.996666	0.995750	0.994681	0.993451
13	0.999409	0.999167	0.998861	0.998482	0.998020	0.997469
14	0.999837	0.999756	0.999647	0.999505	0.999325	0.999100
15	0.999960	0.999936	0.999901	0.999853	0.999790	0.999706
16	0.999991	0.999985	0.999975	0.999961	0.999940	0.999912
17	0.999998	0.999996	0.999994	0.999999	0.999984	0.999976
18	0.999999	0.999999	0.999998	0.999998	0.999999	0.999994
19	0.999999	0.999999	0.999999	0.999999	0.999999	0.999998
20	1.000000	1.000000	0.999999	0.999999	0.999999	0.999999

nr	n 31	32	34	36	38	40
1	0.000000	0.000000	0.000000	0.000000	0.000000	0.000000
2	0.000884	0.000674	0.000390	0.000226	0.000130	0.000075
3	0.036570	0.031710	0.023808	0.017844	0.013354	0.009980
4	0.176546	0.162222	0.136773	0.115119	0.096746	0.081194
5	0.384946	0.364860	0.327315	0.293133	0.262120	0.234068
6	0.586454	0.566263	0.527197	0.489989	0.454713	0.421399
7	0.743954	0.726991	0.693241	0.659934	0.627272	0.595412
8	0.852579	0.839930	0.814080	0.787713	0.761059	0.734312
9	0.920879	0.912317	0.894313	0.875305	0.855485	0.835027
10	0.960438	0.955137	0.943629	0.931011	0.917402	0.902925
11	0.981599	0.978588	0.971814	0.964067	0.955395	0.945858
12	0.992054	0.990483	0.986806	0.982400	0.977260	0.971396
13	0.996821	0.996069	0.994228	0.991904	0.989067	0.985698
14	0.998825	0.998494	0.997644	0.996507	0.995049	0.993239
15	0.999600	0.999466	0.999104	0.998589	0.997891	0.996981
16	0.999875	0.999825	0.999683	0.999467	0.999156	0.998729
17	0.999964	0.999947	0.999896	0.999812	0.999683	0.999496
18	0.999990	0.999985	0.999968	0.999938	0.999888	0.999812
19	0.999997	0.999996	0.999991	0.999981	0.999963	0.999934
20	0.999999	0.999999	0.999997	0.999994	0.999988	0.999978

15.5 Probability Distribution of the Kolmogorov-Smirnov Three-Sample Statistic

Let $F_n^{(1)}(x)$, $F_n^{(2)}(y)$, and $F_n^{(3)}(z)$ be the empirical distribution functions determined by a sample of n X's, a sample of n Y's, and a sample of n Z's, respectively, where X, Y, and Z all have continuous cumulative distribution functions and are independent of each other. The quantity tabulated is

$$\Pr\{D(n, n, n) \le r\},$$

where

$$D(n, n, n) = \text{supremum over all } i, j, \text{ and } x \text{ of } |F_n^{(i)}(x) - F_n^{(j)}(x)|,$$

where $i, j = 1, 2,$ or 3.

Probability Distribution of the Kolmogorov-Smirnov Three-Sample Statistic [22]

$\Pr\{D(n, n, n) \le r\} =$ tabled value

nr	1	2	3	4	5	6
1	1.000000	0.400000	0.128571	0.037402	0.010275	0.002719
2		1.000000	0.771428	0.539220	0.355929	0.226374
3			1.000000	0.926406	0.811093	0.684084
4				1.000000	0.978188	0.932164
5					1.000000	0.993829
6						1.000000

nr	7	8	9	10	11	12
1	0.000701	0.000177	0.000044	0.000010	0.000002	0.000000
2	0.140271	0.085256	0.051053	0.030213	0.017709	0.010297
3	0.562086	0.453012	0.359715	0.282279	0.219397	0.169169
4	0.868227	0.793917	0.715417	0.637148	0.562027	0.491832
5	0.977501	0.950288	0.913501	0.869301	0.819975	0.767590
6	0.998303	0.992915	0.982475	0.966446	0.944960	0.918575
7	1.000000	0.999541	0.997847	0.994114	0.987711	0.978261
8		1.000000	0.999877	0.999362	0.998093	0.995691
9			1.000000	0.999967	0.999815	0.999399
10				1.000000	0.999991	0.999947
11					1.000000	0.999997
12						1.000000

Probability Distribution of the Kolmogorov-Smirnov Three-Sample Statistic (cont.)

nr	13	14	15	16	17	18
1	0.000000					
2	0.005948					
3	0.129569					
4	0.427525					
5	0.713862					
6	0.888073	0.854312	0.818130	0.780302	0.741507	0.702328
7	0.965629	0.949882	0.931228	0.909969	0.886458	0.861064
8	0.991826	0.986249	0.978802	0.969415	0.958096	0.944916
9	0.998539	0.997044	0.994729	0.991436	0.987039	0.981452
10	0.999814	0.999518	0.998964	0.998049	0.996668	0.994723
11	0.999985	0.999943	0.999844	0.999646	0.999298	0.998744
12	0.999999	0.999995	0.999983	0.999950	0.999881	0.999754
13	1.000000	0.999999	0.999998	0.999994	0.999984	0.999961
14		1.000000	0.999999	0.999999	0.999998	0.999995
15			1.000000	0.999999	0.999999	0.999999

nr	19	20	22	24	26	28
6	0.663250	0.624670				
7	0.834155	0.806081				
8	0.929988	0.913459	0.876276	0.834896	0.790312	0.744128
9	0.974624	0.966539	0.946679	0.922382	0.893835	0.862177
10	0.992126	0.988805	0.979784	0.967557	0.951678	0.932761
11	0.997922	0.996773	0.993268	0.987984	0.980202	0.970227
12	0.999539	0.999205	0.998039	0.996114	0.992702	0.988029
13	0.999915	0.999834	0.999504	0.998965	0.997584	0.995632
14	0.999987	0.999971	0.999892	0.999844	0.999284	0.998556
15	0.999998	0.999996	0.999980	0.999928	0.999811	0.999569

nr	30	32	34	36	38	40
8	0.697257					
9	0.828007	0.792099	0.754883	0.717132	0.679257	0.641658
10	0.910963	0.886657	0.860253	0.832162	0.802779	0.772473
11	0.957886	0.943250	0.926465	0.907727	0.887261	0.865309
12	0.981779	0.973852	0.964215	0.952885	0.939929	0.925445
13	0.992789	0.988907	0.983879	0.977629	0.970120	0.961345
14	0.997392	0.995668	0.993276	0.990117	0.986113	0.981208
15	0.999139	0.998444	0.997404	0.995937	0.993968	0.991430
16	0.999741	0.999486	0.999073	0.998447	0.997552	0.996333

15.6 Limiting Distribution of the Kolmogorov-Smirnov $D(n)$ Statistic

The quantity tabulated is

$$L(Z) = 1 - 2 \sum_{j=1}^{\infty} (-1)^{j-1} \exp(-j^2 Z^2)$$

$$= \frac{\sqrt{2\pi}}{Z} \sum_{j=1}^{\infty} \exp[-(2j-1)^2 \pi^2 / 8Z^2].$$

Let $D(n)$ be defined as in Section 15.1, i.e.,

$$D(n) = \text{supremum over all } x \text{ of } |F_n(x) - F(x)|.$$

Then $\lim_{n \to \infty} \Pr \{\sqrt{n}\, D(n) \le Z\} = L(Z)$.

Suppose that it is desired to use a Kolmogorov-Smirnov test of size α to test the hypothesis $F = F_0$ against the alternative $F = F_1$ such that the probability of rejecting $F = F_0$ is to exceed a given number β, $0 < \beta < 1$, when $F = F_1$ where

$$\text{supremum over all } x \text{ of } |F_1(x) - F_0(x)| \ge l > 0.$$

Assuming that the test used is of the form, "Reject $F = F_0$ if and only if $\sqrt{n}\, D(n) > h_{1,\alpha}$ where $L(h_{1,\alpha}) = 1 - \alpha$," then a simple choice of sample size is given by

$$n = \left[\left(\frac{\sqrt{-\{\log_e (1 - \beta)\}/2} + h_{1,\alpha}}{l} \right)^2 + 1 \right],$$

where the square bracket $[a]$ denotes the integral part of a.

This formula is based on a result of Okamoto [155] and is given by Rosenblatt [185]. Rosenblatt [185] also has formulas which are more complicated and give considerable reduction in sample size.

Limiting Distribution of the Kolmogorov-Smirnov
$D(n)$ Statistic [202]
$$\text{Lim}_{n\to\infty} \; \text{Pr}\{\sqrt{n}\, D(n) \le Z\} = L(Z)$$

Z	L(Z)	Z	L(Z)	Z	L(Z)	Z	L(Z)
0.28	0.000001	0.73	0.339113	1.18	0.876548	1.76	0.995922
0.29	0.000004	0.74	0.355981	1.19	0.882258	1.78	0.996460
0.30	0.000009	0.75	0.372833	1.20	0.887750	1.80	0.996932
0.31	0.000021	0.76	0.389640	1.21	0.893030	1.82	0.997346
0.32	0.000046	0.77	0.406372	1.22	0.898104	1.84	0.997707
0.33	0.000091	0.78	0.423002	1.23	0.902972	1.86	0.998023
0.34	0.000171	0.79	0.439505	1.24	0.907648	1.88	0.998297
0.35	0.000303	0.80	0.455857	1.25	0.912132	1.90	0.998536
0.36	0.000511	0.81	0.472041	1.26	0.916432	1.92	0.998744
0.37	0.000826	0.82	0.488030	1.27	0.920556	1.94	0.998924
0.38	0.001285	0.83	0.503808	1.28	0.924505	1.96	0.999079
0.39	0.001929	0.84	0.519366	1.29	0.928288	1.98	0.999213
0.40	0.002808	0.85	0.534682	1.30	0.931908	2.00	0.999329
0.41	0.003972	0.86	0.549744	1.31	0.935370	2.02	0.999428
0.42	0.005476	0.87	0.564546	1.32	0.938682	2.04	0.999516
0.43	0.007377	0.88	0.579070	1.33	0.941848	2.06	0.999588
0.44	0.009730	0.89	0.593316	1.34	0.944872	2.08	0.999650
0.45	0.012590	0.90	0.607270	1.35	0.947756	2.10	0.999705
0.46	0.016005	0.91	0.620928	1.36	0.950512	2.12	0.999750
0.47	0.020022	0.92	0.634286	1.37	0.953142	2.14	0.999790
0.48	0.024682	0.93	0.647338	1.38	0.955650	2.16	0.999822
0.49	0.030017	0.94	0.660082	1.39	0.958040	2.18	0.999852
0.50	0.036055	0.95	0.672516	1.40	0.960318	2.20	0.999874
0.51	0.042814	0.96	0.684636	1.41	0.962486	2.22	0.999896
0.52	0.050306	0.97	0.696444	1.42	0.964552	2.24	0.999912
0.53	0.058534	0.98	0.707940	1.43	0.966516	2.26	0.999926
0.54	0.067497	0.99	0.719126	1.44	0.968382	2.28	0.999940
0.55	0.077183	1.00	0.730000	1.45	0.970158	2.30	0.999949
0.56	0.087577	1.01	0.740566	1.46	0.971846	2.32	0.999958
0.57	0.098656	1.02	0.750826	1.47	0.973448	2.34	0.999965
0.58	0.110395	1.03	0.760780	1.48	0.974970	2.36	0.999970
0.59	0.122760	1.04	0.770434	1.49	0.976412	2.38	0.999976
0.60	0.135718	1.05	0.779794	1.50	0.977782	2.40	0.999980
0.61	0.149229	1.06	0.788860	1.52	0.980310	2.42	0.999984
0.62	0.163225	1.07	0.797636	1.54	0.982578	2.44	0.999987
0.63	0.177753	1.08	0.806128	1.56	0.984610	2.46	0.999989
0.64	0.192677	1.09	0.814342	1.58	0.986426	2.48	0.999991
0.65	0.207987	1.10	0.822282	1.60	0.988048	2.50	0.999 9925
0.66	0.223637	1.11	0.829950	1.62	0.989492	2.55	0.999 9956
0.67	0.239582	1.12	0.837356	1.64	0.990777	2.60	0.999 9974
0.68	0.255780	1.13	0.844502	1.66	0.991917	2.65	0.999 9984
0.69	0.272189	1.14	0.851394	1.68	0.992928	2.70	0.999 9990
0.70	0.288765	1.15	0.858038	1.70	0.993823	2.80	0.999 9997
0.71	0.305471	1.16	0.864442	1.72	0.994612	2.90	0.999 99990
0.72	0.322265	1.17	0.870612	1.74	0.995309	3.00	0.999 99997

15.7 Limiting Distribution of the Statistic $\sqrt{n}\,[D^+(n) + D^-(n)]$

Let $D^+(n)$ be defined as in Section 15.1, i.e.,

$$D^+(n) = \text{supremum over all } x \text{ of } \{F_n(x) - F(x)\}$$
$$= \text{maximum over } i = 1, 2, \ldots, n \text{ of } \{(i/n) - F(x_{(i)})\},$$

and let

$$D^-(n) = \text{supremum over all } x \text{ of } \{F(x) - F_n(x)\}$$
$$= \text{maximum over } i = 1, 2, \ldots, n \text{ of } \{F(x_{(i)}) - [(i - 1)/n]\}.$$

Thus

$$D^+(n) + D^-(n) \equiv \text{supremum over } I, \text{ an interval, of } |P_F(I) - P_{F_n}(I)|,$$

where Rosenblatt [185] shows that

$$\liminf_{n \to \infty} \Pr\{\sqrt{n}\,[D^+(n) + D^-(n)] \le Z\} = P(Z),$$

where

$$P(Z) = 1 + \sum_{j=1}^{\infty} [2 - 8j^2 Z^2] \exp(-2j^2 Z^2).$$

The quantity tabulated is $P = P(Z)$.

Let $P(h_{2,\alpha}) = 1 - \alpha$. Then asymptotically for all intervals I,

$$P_{F_n}(I) - \frac{h_{2,\alpha}}{\sqrt{n}} \le P_F(I) \le P_{F_n}(I) + \frac{h_{2,\alpha}}{\sqrt{n}},$$

where if $I = (a, b]$, $P_{F_n}(I) = F_n(b) - F_n(a)$, and $P_F(I) = F(b) - F(a)$. It is believed that the asymptotic results are conservative for finite sample sizes. Thus, for example, if X_i can take on values $\lambda_1, \lambda_2, \ldots$ with probabilities $P_1, P_2, \ldots$, then this permits one to obtain simultaneous $1 - \alpha$ confidence intervals for the parameters $P_1, P_2, \ldots$.

Limiting Distribution of the Statistic $\sqrt{n}\,[D^+(n) + D^-(n)]$

Z	P	Z	P	Z	P	Z	P
0.50	0.000001	1.05	0.243174	1.50	0.822255	1.95	0.985848
0.52	0.000003	1.06	0.257083	1.51	0.830121	1.96	0.986769
0.54	0.000007	1.07	0.271223	1.52	0.837724	1.97	0.987635
0.56	0.000021	1.08	0.285570	1.53	0.845067	1.98	0.988450
0.58	0.000054	1.09	0.300099	1.54	0.852155	1.99	0.989216
0.60	0.000128	1.10	0.314786	1.55	0.858991	2.00	0.989936
0.62	0.000276	1.11	0.329607	1.56	0.865580	2.01	0.990612
0.64	0.000553	1.12	0.344538	1.57	0.871927	2.02	0.991247
0.66	0.001035	1.13	0.359554	1.58	0.878036	2.03	0.991843
0.68	0.001824	1.14	0.374632	1.59	0.883913	2.04	0.992402
0.70	0.003050	1.15	0.389749	1.60	0.889563	2.05	0.992925
0.71	0.003874	1.16	0.404883	1.61	0.894991	2.06	0.993416
0.72	0.004867	1.17	0.420012	1.62	0.900203	2.07	0.993875
0.73	0.006050	1.18	0.435114	1.63	0.905203	2.08	0.994305
0.74	0.007447	1.19	0.450170	1.64	0.909998	2.09	0.994707
0.75	0.009082	1.20	0.465160	1.65	0.914593	2.10	0.995083
0.76	0.010978	1.21	0.480064	1.66	0.918994	2.12	0.995762
0.77	0.013159	1.22	0.494865	1.67	0.923206	2.14	0.996355
0.78	0.015650	1.23	0.509546	1.68	0.927235	2.16	0.996870
0.79	0.018472	1.24	0.524090	1.69	0.931087	2.18	0.997317
0.80	0.021649	1.25	0.538483	1.70	0.934766	2.20	0.997704
0.81	0.025202	1.26	0.552710	1.71	0.938280	2.22	0.998039
0.82	0.029149	1.27	0.566758	1.72	0.941633	2.24	0.998328
0.83	0.033510	1.28	0.580614	1.73	0.944830	2.26	0.998577
0.84	0.038300	1.29	0.594266	1.74	0.947878	2.28	0.998791
0.85	0.043534	1.30	0.607703	1.75	0.950781	2.30	0.998975
0.86	0.049223	1.31	0.620917	1.76	0.953546	2.32	0.999132
0.87	0.055378	1.32	0.633898	1.77	0.956175	2.34	0.999267
0.88	0.062006	1.33	0.646638	1.78	0.958676	2.36	0.999382
0.89	0.069112	1.34	0.659129	1.79	0.961053	2.40	0.999562
0.90	0.076699	1.35	0.671366	1.80	0.963311	2.44	0.999692
0.91	0.084767	1.36	0.683343	1.81	0.965455	2.48	0.999785
0.92	0.093313	1.37	0.695055	1.82	0.967488	2.52	0.999851
0.93	0.102333	1.38	0.706498	1.83	0.969417	2.56	0.999898
0.94	0.111821	1.39	0.717669	1.84	0.971245	2.60	0.999930
0.95	0.121767	1.40	0.728565	1.85	0.972976	2.64	0.999953
0.96	0.132161	1.41	0.739183	1.86	0.974615	2.68	0.999968
0.97	0.142989	1.42	0.749524	1.87	0.976166	2.72	0.999979
0.98	0.154236	1.43	0.759585	1.88	0.977633	2.76	0.999986
0.99	0.165887	1.44	0.769367	1.89	0.979020	2.80	0.999991
1.00	0.177924	1.45	0.778871	1.90	0.980329	2.84	0.999994
1.01	0.190326	1.46	0.788097	1.91	0.981566	2.88	0.999996
1.02	0.203075	1.47	0.797046	1.92	0.982733	2.92	0.999997
1.03	0.216147	1.48	0.805720	1.93	0.983833	2.96	0.999998
1.04	0.229521	1.49	0.814122	1.94	0.984871	3.04	1.000000

15.7

16. CRAMÉR-VON MISES, AND RANDOM DIVISION OF AN INTERVAL DISTRIBUTION

16.1 Limiting Distribution of the Cramér-von Mises $n\omega^2$ Statistic

Let $F_n(x)$ and $F(x)$ be defined as in Section 15.1. The Cramér-von Mises statistic ω^2 is defined as

$$\omega^2 = n \int_{-\infty}^{+\infty} [F_n(x) - F(x)]^2 \, dF(x).$$

The quantity tabulated here is

$$\lim_{n \to \infty} \text{Pr} \{n\omega^2 \le z\} = a(z).$$

See Anderson and Darling's paper [4] for the computing formula for $a(z)$. Kiefer [107] gives a k-sample analogue of the Cramér-von Mises statistic. Darling [41] gives a history of the Cramér-von Mises statistics and an extensive bibliography.

Limiting Distribution of the Cramér-
von Mises $n\omega^2$ Statistic [4]

$$\text{Lim}_{n \to \infty} [\Pr\{n\omega^2 \leq z\}] = a(z)$$

z	a(z)	z	a(z)	z	a(z)
0.02480	0.01	0.08562	0.34	0.17159	0.67
0.02878	0.02	0.08744	0.35	0.17568	0.68
0.03177	0.03	0.08928	0.36	0.17992	0.69
0.03430	0.04	0.09115	0.37	0.18433	0.70
0.03656	0.05	0.09306	0.38	0.18892	0.71
0.03865	0.06	0.09499	0.39	0.19371	0.72
0.04061	0.07	0.09696	0.40	0.19870	0.73
0.04247	0.08	0.09896	0.41	0.20392	0.74
0.04427	0.09	0.10100	0.42	0.20939	0.75
0.04601	0.10	0.10308	0.43	0.21512	0.76
0.04772	0.11	0.10520	0.44	0.22114	0.77
0.04939	0.12	0.10736	0.45	0.22748	0.78
0.05103	0.13	0.10956	0.46	0.23417	0.79
0.05265	0.14	0.11182	0.47	0.24124	0.80
0.05426	0.15	0.11412	0.48	0.24874	0.81
0.05586	0.16	0.11647	0.49	0.25670	0.82
0.05746	0.17	0.11888	0.50	0.26520	0.83
0.05904	0.18	0.12134	0.51	0.27429	0.84
0.06063	0.19	0.12387	0.52	0.28406	0.85
0.06222	0.20	0.12646	0.53	0.29460	0.86
0.06381	0.21	0.12911	0.54	0.30603	0.87
0.06541	0.22	0.13183	0.55	0.31849	0.88
0.06702	0.23	0.13463	0.56	0.33217	0.89
0.06863	0.24	0.13751	0.57	0.34730	0.90
0.07025	0.25	0.14046	0.58	0.36421	0.91
0.07189	0.26	0.14350	0.59	0.38331	0.92
0.07354	0.27	0.14663	0.60	0.40520	0.93
0.07521	0.28	0.14986	0.61	0.43077	0.94
0.07690	0.29	0.15319	0.62	0.46136	0.95
0.07860	0.30	0.15663	0.63	0.49929	0.96
0.08032	0.31	0.16018	0.64	0.54885	0.97
0.08206	0.32	0.16385	0.65	0.61981	0.98
0.08383	0.33	0.16765	0.66	0.74346	0.99
				1.16786	0.999

16.2 Sample Sizes Needed with a 5-Percent One-Sample Test Using $D^+(n)$, $\omega^2(n)$, $\omega'(n)$, and $\pi_1(2n)$ to Obtain a Power of 0.95

Chapman [30] studies the power of several one-sided goodness-of-fit tests. He considers $D^+(n)$, which is defined as in Section 15.1, $\omega^2(n) = \omega^2$, which is defined as in Section 16.1, $\omega'(n)$, defined as

$$\omega'(n) = n \int_{-\infty}^{+\infty} [F_n(x) - F(x)]\, dF(x),$$

where $F_n(x)$ and $F(x)$ are defined as in Section 16.1 and $\pi_1(2n)$, defined as follows: Let $U_1, U_2, \ldots, U_n$ be a random sample of n observations from the uniform probability distribution on the interval 0 to 1. Then

$$\pi_1(2n) = -2 \sum_{j=1}^{n} \log_e U_j.$$

It can be shown that $\pi_1(2n)$ has the chi-square distribution (Section 3.1) with $2n$ degrees of freedom.

A minimum power alternative is one where the cumulative distribution function of the alternative coincides with the distribution function $F(x)$ being tested, except that at one point it jumps by δ above $F(x)$ and then remains constant until it intersects $F(x)$ again, from which point it again coincides with $F(x)$.

A maximum power alternative is one where the alternative cumulative distribution function $G(x)$ is δ above $F(x)$ wherever possible; that is, $G(x) = F(x) + \delta$ for $0 \leq F(x) \leq F[k(\delta, x)]$ where $k(\delta, x)$ is the minimum value of x for which $G(x) = 1$.

Sample sizes needed for various δ's to attain a power of 0.95 with a 0.05 significance level test are given in the table.

Massey [134] gives a formula for a lower bound on the power of the $D(n)$ test and of the $D(n, n)$ test as n approaches infinity. Birnbaum [19] gives upper and lower bounds for the power of the $D^+(n)$ test. Kac, Kiefer, and Wolfowitz [103] compare the powers of the chi-square, Kolmogorov-Smirnov, and Cramér-von Mises tests asymptotically. See Section 15.6 for another determination of sample size to attain a given power.

Sample Sizes Needed with a 5-Percent One-Sample Test Using $D^+(n)$, $\omega^2(n)$, $\omega'(n)$, and $\pi_1(2n)$ to Obtain a Power of 0.95 [30]

For Minimum Power Alternatives (δ)

Test	0.05	0.1	0.2	0.3	0.4	0.5
$D^+(n)$	1,675	419	105	47	27	17
$\omega^2(n)$	14,038	2,290	406	153	78	45
$\omega'(n)$	569,067	34,233	1,867	304	77	25
$\pi_1(2n)$	1,677,025	102,081	23,903	4,463	1,325	511

For Maximum Power Alternatives (δ)

Test	0.01	0.02	0.03	0.04	0.05	0.06	0.07	0.08	0.09	0.10
$D^+(n)$	29,679	7,420	3,298	6,855	1,188	825	606	464	367	297
$\omega^2(n)$	4,761	1,057	540	302	204	160	104	80	65	53
$\omega'(n)$	9,108	2,296	1,027	583	375	261	193	148	117	95
$\pi_1(2n)$	3,067	936	471	291	200	148	115	92	77	65

16.3 Critical Values of Sherman's Statistic for the Random Division of an Interval

If n points are selected independently from a uniform distribution on a unit interval ($x = 0$ to $x = 1$), there arise $n + 1$ subintervals, each of expected length $1/(n + 1)$. If L_j is the length of the jth interval from the left, then W is defined as

$$W = \frac{1}{2} \sum_{j=1}^{n+1} \left| L_j - \frac{1}{n+1} \right|.$$

The cumulative distribution function of W, $F(w)$ is 0 for $w < 0$, and 1 for $w > n/(n + 1)$. For $0 \leq w \leq n/(n + 1)$, the distribution of W is

$$F(w) = b_n w^n + b_{n-1} w^{n-1} + \cdots + b_1 w + b_0 + 1,$$

where

$$b_k = \sum_{i=0}^{r} (-1)^{i+j+1} \binom{n+1}{i+1} \binom{i+j}{i} \binom{n}{j} \left(\frac{n-i}{n+1} \right)^{n-j},$$

and r is determined by

$$\frac{n-r-1}{n+1} \leq w < \frac{n-r}{n+1}.$$

The values of w' such that

$$\Pr\{W \leq w'\} = \gamma,$$

where $\gamma = 0.90, 0.95$, and 0.99, are given in the tables.

The mean of W is

$$\left(\frac{n}{n+1} \right)^{n+1},$$

and the variance of W is

$$\frac{2n^{n+2} + n(n-1)^{n+2}}{(n+2)(n+1)^{n+2}} - \left(\frac{n}{n+1} \right)^{2n+2}.$$

Moran [144] and [145] defines a statistic $S = \sum_{j=1}^{n} L_j^2$ and shows that the distribution approaches normality. This statistic is in a certain sense a companion statistic of W. Darling [42] gives a general discussion of the problem of a random division of an interval. The limiting joint distribution of the largest and smallest sample spacings is given by Weiss [242].

Critical Values of Sherman's Statistic for
the Random Division of an Interval [199]

$$\Pr\{W \le \text{tabled value}\} = \gamma$$

n	0.90	0.95	0.99
1	0.45000	0.47500	0.49500
2	0.48410	0.53757	0.60893
3	0.46673	0.51792	0.61428
4	0.46850	0.50955	0.58870
5	0.46195	0.50181	0.57442
6	0.45847	0.49398	0.56263
7	0.45434	0.48801	0.55128
8	0.45100	0.48243	0.54241
9	0.44786	0.47772	0.53435
10	0.44510	0.47346	0.52743
11	0.44257	0.46970	0.52126
12	0.44029	0.46630	0.51577
13	0.43820	0.46323	0.51082
14	0.43628	0.46043	0.50634
15	0.43452	0.45786	0.50225
16	0.43288	0.45550	0.49851
17	0.43137	0.45332	0.49506
18	0.42995	0.45130	0.49188
19	0.42863	0.44942	0.48892
20	0.42739	0.44766	0.48617

17. MATCHING AND MULTINOMIAL DISTRIBUTIONS

17.1 Probability of h or More Matches

The model being considered here is best described in terms of playing cards, although it obviously applies to much more general situations. Two identical decks of cards, each having s suits of c cards per suit, are available. One deck, the target deck, has some fixed but arbitrary arrangement, and the second deck, the call deck, is arranged at random. Cards from the two decks are compared, and if cards at the same point in the arrangements of the two decks agree as to suit, a match has occurred. The quantity tabulated is

$m(s, c; h) = \Pr \{h$ or more matches in two decks of cards having s suits of c cards per suit$\}$

$$= \frac{1}{n!} \sum_{i=h}^{n} (-1)^{i-h} \binom{i}{h} (n - i)! H_i,$$

where H_i is the coefficient of x^i in the expansion of

$$\left(\sum_{j=0}^{c} \frac{c!c!x^j}{j!(c - j)!(c - j)!} \right)^s.$$

The table is arranged first by groups in order of increasing c, then within groups in order of increasing s. It will be noticed that within each group the distributions seem to approach a limiting distribution— the Poisson (Section 9.3)—but the approach is slower for groups with larger c. The mean of the matching distribution is c, and the variance is $c(n - c)/(n - 1)$. The reader is referred to Gilbert's paper [74] for a fuller discussion of approximations to the distribution.

Probability of *h* or More Matches [74]

$m(s, c; h) = \Pr\{h$ or more matches in two decks

having s suits of c cards per suit$\} = $ tabled value

h	m(2, 1; h)	m(2, 2; h)	m(2, 3; h)	m(2, 4; h)	m(2, 5; h)	m(2, 6; h)
0	1.00000	1.00000	1.00000	1.00000	1.00000	1.00000
1	0.50000	0.83333	0.95000	0.98571	0.99603	0.99892
2	0.50000	0.83333	0.95000	0.98571	0.99603	0.99892
3		0.16667	0.50000	0.75714	0.89682	0.95996
4		0.16667	0.50000	0.75714	0.89682	0.95996
5			0.05000	0.24286	0.50000	0.71645
6			0.05000	0.24286	0.50000	0.71645
7				0.01428	0.10397	0.28355
8				0.01428	0.10397	0.28355
9					0.00397	0.04004
10					0.00397	0.04004
11						0.00108
12						0.00108

h	m(2, 7; h)	m(2, 8; h)	m(2, 9; h)	m(2,10; h)	m(2,11; h)	m(2,12; h)
0	1.00000	1.00000	1.00000	1.00000	1.00000	1.00000
1	0.99971	0.99992	0.99998	0.99999	1.00000	1.00000
2	0.99971	0.99992	0.99998	0.99999	1.00000	1.00000
3	0.98543	0.99495	0.99831	0.99945	0.99983	0.99995
4	0.98543	0.99495	0.99831	0.99945	0.99983	0.99995
5	0.85693	0.93403	0.97166	0.98849	0.99554	0.99834
6	0.85693	0.93403	0.97166	0.98849	0.99554	0.99834
7	0.50000	0.69036	0.82653	0.91055	0.95694	0.98044
8	0.50000	0.69036	0.82653	0.91055	0.95694	0.98044
9	0.14306	0.30964	0.50000	0.67186	0.80257	0.88983
10	0.14306	0.30964	0.50000	0.67186	0.80257	0.88983
11	0.01457	0.06597	0.17347	0.32814	0.50000	0.65786
12	0.01457	0.06597	0.17347	0.32814	0.50000	0.65786
13	0.00029	0.00505	0.02834	0.08945	0.19743	0.34214
14	0.00029	0.00505	0.02834	0.08945	0.19743	0.34214
15		0.00008	0.00169	0.01151	0.04305	0.11017
16		0.00008	0.00169	0.01151	0.04305	0.11017
17			0.00002	0.00055	0.00446	0.01956
18			0.00002	0.00055	0.00446	0.01956

17.1

Probability of h or More Matches (cont.)

h	$m(3, 1; h)$	$m(3, 2; h)$	$m(3, 3; h)$	$m(3, 4; h)$	$m(3, 5; h)$	$m(3, 6; h)$
0	1.00000	1.00000	1.00000	1.00000	1.00000	1.00000
1	0.66667	0.88889	0.96667	0.99001	0.99702	0.99911
2	0.16667	0.62222	0.83810	0.93737	0.97700	0.99186
3	0.16667	0.32222	0.61310	0.80646	0.91278	0.96331
4		0.14444	0.35417	0.60052	0.78150	0.89136
5		0.01111	0.16131	0.37117	0.59102	0.76155
6		0.01111	0.04881	0.18831	0.38388	0.58399
7			0.01667	0.07472	0.21077	0.39331
8			0.00060	0.02485	0.09571	0.22923
9			0.00060	0.00511	0.03624	0.11416
10				0.00141	0.01074	0.04838
11				0.00003	0.00281	0.01709
12				0.00003	0.00043	0.00513
13					0.00010	0.00120
14					0.00000	0.00026
15						0.00003
16						0.00001

h	$m(3, 7; h)$	$m(4, 1; h)$	$m(4, 2; h)$	$m(4, 3; h)$	$m(4, 4; h)$	$m(4, 5; h)$
0	1.00000	1.00000	1.00000	1.00000	1.00000	1.00000
1	0.99974	0.62500	0.88214	0.96258	0.98813	0.99624
2	0.99720	0.29167	0.61548	0.82875	0.93005	0.97286
3	0.98532	0.04167	0.32341	0.60010	0.79355	0.90271
4	0.94969	0.04167	0.13294	0.35404	0.58930	0.76776
5	0.87266		0.03532	0.16724	0.37156	0.58113
6	0.74532		0.00992	0.06322	0.19645	0.38408
7	0.57839		0.00040	0.01864	0.08658	0.21933
8	0.40070		0.00040	0.00461	0.03174	0.10764
9	0.24472			0.00073	0.00962	0.04528
10	0.13051			0.00015	0.00242	0.01630
11	0.06040			0.00000	0.00049	0.00500
12	0.02404			0.00000	0.00009	0.00131
13	0.00823				0.00001	0.00029
14	0.00237					0.00005
15	0.00059					0.00001
16	0.00011					
17	0.00002					

Probability of *h* or More Matches (*cont.*)

h	m(5, 1; h)	m(5, 2; h)	m(5, 3; h)	m(5, 4; h)	m(5, 5; h)	m(6, 1; h)
0	1.00000	1.00000	1.00000	1.00000	1.00000	1.00000
1	0.63333	0.87870	0.96016	0.98693	0.99571	0.63194
2	0.25833	0.60991	0.82266	0.92558	0.97026	0.26528
3	0.09167	0.32451	0.59456	0.78646	0.89690	0.07778
4	0.00833	0.13262	0.35335	0.58385	0.76033	0.02222
5	0.00833	0.04179	0.17154	0.37138	0.57600	0.00139
6		0.01033	0.06808	0.20090	0.38406	0.00139
7		0.00177	0.02215	0.09232	0.22380	
8		0.00036	0.00592	0.03609	0.11374	
9		0.00001	0.00130	0.01202	0.05043	
10		0.00001	0.00023	0.00342	0.01953	
11			0.00004	0.00083	0.00662	
12			0.00000	0.00017	0.00196	
13				0.00003	0.00051	
14					0.00012	
15					0.00002	

h	m(6, 2; h)	m(6, 3; h)	m(7, 1; h)	m(7, 2; h)	m(7, 3; h)	m(8, 1; h)
0	1.00000	1.00000	1.00000	1.00000	1.00000	1.00000
1	0.87632	0.95852	0.63214	0.87462	0.95734	0.63212
2	0.60689	0.81875	0.26409	0.60483	0.81603	0.26426
3	0.32406	0.59113	0.08075	0.32383	0.58882	0.08023
4	0.13450	0.35313	0.01825	0.13580	0.35301	0.01912
5	0.04396	0.17407	0.00436	0.04538	0.17578	0.00350
6	0.01144	0.07113	0.00020	0.01226	0.07319	0.00072
7	0.00237	0.02425	0.00020	0.00270	0.02569	0.00002
8	0.00041	0.00694		0.00049	0.00766	0.00002
9	0.00005	0.00167		0.00007	0.00195	
10	0.00001	0.00034		0.00001	0.00043	
11		0.00006			0.00008	
12		0.00001			0.00001	
13						
14						

Probability of *h* or More Matches (*cont.*)

h	m(8, 2; h)	m(8, 3; h)	m(9, 1; h)	m(9, 2; h)
0	1.00000	1.00000	1.00000	1.00000
1	0.87335	0.95645	0.63212	0.87237
2	0.60334	0.81402	0.26424	0.60220
3	0.32369	0.58715	0.08031	0.32360
4	0.13676	0.35295	0.01897	0.13749
5	0.04640	0.17702	0.00369	0.04716
6	0.01285	0.07467	0.00056	0.01330
7	0.00295	0.02674	0.00010	0.00313
8	0.00056	0.00820	0.00000	0.00062
9	0.00009	0.00217		0.00010
10	0.00001	0.00050		0.00002
11		0.00010		
12		0.00002		

h	m(10,1;h)	m(10,2; h)	m(11, 1;h)	m(11,2; h)
0	1.00000	1.00000	1.00000	1.00000
1	0.63212	0.87158	0.63212	0.87094
2	0.26424	0.60131	0.26424	0.60060
3	0.08030	0.32354	0.08030	0.32350
4	0.01899	0.13806	0.01899	0.13853
5	0.00366	0.04776	0.00365	0.04824
6	0.00060	0.01365	0.00059	0.01394
7	0.00008	0.00328	0.00008	0.00340
8	0.00001	0.00067	0.00001	0.00071
9		0.00012		0.00013
10		0.00002		0.00002

17.1

17.2 Critical Points for the Number of Occupied Cells in the Multinomial Distribution with Equally Probable Cells

The occupancy probability distribution function $H(x, k, N)$ is considered where

$$H(x, k, N) = \sum_{i=1}^{x} \binom{k}{i} \sum_{j=0}^{i} (-1)^j \binom{i}{j} \left(\frac{i-j}{k}\right)^N,$$

which is the probability of having x or less cells occupied when N balls are randomly and independently distributed among k equally probable cells.

The tables give the minimum values of N which satisfy

$$H(x, k, N) \leq \gamma,$$

where $\gamma = 0.01, 0.025, 0.05,$ and 0.10 for lower tail probabilities. This tail is used to test the null hypothesis that all cells are equally likely against the alternative of unequal cell probabilities.

The tables also give the maximum values of N which satisfy

$$H(x - 1, k, N) \geq \gamma$$

for $\gamma = 0.90, 0.95, 0.975,$ and 0.99 for upper tail probabilities. This tail is used to test the null hypothesis that all cells are equally likely against the alternative of a nonrandom but nearly even allocation among the cells. Dash marks indicate the nonexistence of entries.

Johnson [100] gives an approximation to the multinomial distribution function. Johnson and Young [102] give some applications of the multinomial distribution. Kozelka [110] approximates the distribution of the maximum of k cells and gives a short table.

Critical Points for the Number of Occupied Cells in the Multinomial Distribution with Equally Probable Cells [152]

Minimum N such that $H(x, k, N) \leq \gamma$ (first position)
Maximum N such that $H(x - 1, k, N) \geq \gamma$ (second position)

k	x	.01,.99	.05,.95	.10,.90
2	1	8, -	6, -	5, -
3	1	6, -	4, -	4, -
	2	15, -	11, -	9, -
4	1	5, -	4, -	3, -
	2	10, -	7, -	6, -
	3	21, -	16, -	13, -
	4	-, -	-, -	-, 4
5	1	4, -	3, -	3, -
	2	8, -	6, -	5, -
	3	14, -	11, -	9, -
	4	28, -	21, -	18, -
	5	-, -	-, 5	-, 5
6	1	4, -	3, -	3, -
	2	7, -	6, -	5, -
	3	11, -	9, -	8, -
	4	18, -	14, -	13, -
	5	>30, -	27, -	23, 5
	6	-, -	-, 6	-, 7
7	1	4, -	3, -	3, -
	2	7, -	5, -	5, -
	3	10, -	8, -	7, -
	4	15, -	12, -	11, -
	5	23, -	18, -	16, -
	6	>30, -	>30, 6	28, 6
	7	-, 7	-, 8	-, 9
8	1	4, -	3, -	3, -
	2	6, -	5, -	4, -
	3	9, -	7, -	7, -
	4	13, -	11, -	10, -
	5	19, -	15, -	13, -
	6	28, -	22, -	20, 6
	7	-, -	-, 7	-, 8
	8	-, 8	-, 10	-, 12
9	1	4, -	3, -	3, -
	2	6, -	5, -	4, -
	3	9, -	7, -	6, -
	4	12, -	10, -	9, -
	5	16, -	13, -	12, -
	6	23, -	18, -	16, -
	7	>30, -	26, 7	23, 7
	8	-, 8	-, 9	-, 10
	9	-, 10	-, 12	-, 14
10	1	3, -	3, -	2, -
	2	6, -	5, -	4, -
	3	8, -	7, -	6, -
	4	11, -	9, -	8, -
	5	15, -	12, -	11, -
	6	20, -	16, -	15, -
	7	27, -	22, -	20, 7
	8	>30, -	>30, 8	27, 9
	9	-, 9	-, 11	-, 12
	10	-, 12	-, 15	-, 16
11	1	3, -	3, -	2, -
	2	6, -	5, -	4, -
	3	8, -	7, -	6, -
	4	11, -	9, -	8, -
	5	14, -	12, -	11, -
	6	18, -	15, -	14, -
	7	23, -	19, -	17, 7
	8	>30, -	25, 8	23, 8
	9	-, 9	-, 10	-, 11
	10	-, 11	-, 13	-, 14
	11	-, 14	-, 17	-, 19
12	1	3, -	3, -	2, -
	2	5, -	4, -	4, -
	3	8, -	6, -	6, -
	4	10, -	9, -	8, -
	5	13, -	11, -	10, -

Critical Points for the Number of Occupied Cells in the Multinomial Distribution with Equally Probable Cells (cont.)

k	x	.01,.99	.05,.95	.10,.90
12	6	17, -	14, -	13, -
	7	21, -	18, -	16, -
	8	27, -	22, 8	20, 8
	9	>30, -	29, 9	26, 10
	10	-, 10	-, 12	-, 13
	11	-, 12	-, 15	-, 16
	12	-, 16	-, 19	-, 22
13	1	3, -	3, -	2, -
	2	5, -	4, -	4, -
	3	7, -	6, -	6, -
	4	10, -	8, -	8, -
	5	12, -	11, -	10, -
	6	16, -	13, -	12, -
	7	19, -	16, -	15, -
	8	24, -	20, -	19, 8
	9	30, -	25, 9	23, 10
	10	>30, 10	>30, 11	29, 12
	11	-, 12	-, 13	-, 14
	12	-, 14	-, 17	-, 18
	13	-, 18	-, 22	-, 24
14	1	3, -	3, -	2, -
	2	5, -	4, -	4, -
	3	7, -	6, -	6, -
	4	9, -	8, -	7, -
	5	12, -	10, -	9, -
	6	15, -	13, -	12, -
	7	18, -	16, -	14, -
	8	22, -	19, -	17, 8
	9	27, -	23, 9	21, 9
	10	>30, -	29, 10	26, 11
	11	-, 11	-, 13	-, 14
	12	-, 13	-, 15	-, 16
	13	-, 16	-, 19	-, 20
	14	-, 20	-, 24	-, 27
15	1	3, -	3, -	2, -
	2	5, -	4, -	4, -
	3	7, -	6, -	5, -
	4	9, -	8, -	7, -
	5	12, -	10, -	9, -
	6	14, -	12, -	11, -
	7	17, -	15, -	14, -
	8	21, -	18, -	17, -
	9	25, -	22, 9	20, 9
	10	>30, -	26, 10	24, 11
	11	>30, 11	>30, 12	29, 13
	12	-, 13	-, 14	-, 15
	13	-, 15	-, 17	-, 18
	14	-, 18	-, 21	-, 23
	15	-, 23	-, 27	-, 30
16	1	3, -	3, -	2, -
	2	5, -	4, -	4, -
	3	7, -	6, -	5, -
	4	9, -	8, -	7, -
	5	11, -	10, -	9, -
	6	14, -	12, -	11, -
	7	17, -	14, -	13, -
	8	20, -	17, -	16, -
	9	24, -	20, -	19, 9
	10	28, -	24, 10	22, 10
	11	>30, 11	29, 12	27, 12
	12	-, 12	-, 14	-, 15
	13	-, 14	-, 16	-, 17
	14	-, 17	-, 19	-, 21
	15	-, 20	-, 23	-, 25
	16	-, 25	-, 30	-,>30
17	1	3, -	3, -	2, -
	2	5, -	4, -	4, -
	3	7, -	6, -	5, -
	4	9, -	8, -	7, -
	5	11, -	9, -	9, -

17.2

Critical Points for the Number of Occupied Cells in the Multinomial Distribution with Equally Probable Cells (cont.)

k	x	.01,.99	.05,.95	.10,.90
17	6	13, -	12, -	11, -
	7	16, -	14, -	13, -
	8	19, -	17, -	15, -
	9	23, -	19, -	18, 9
	10	27, -	23, 10	21, 10
	11	>30, -	27, 11	25, 12
	12	>30, 12	>30, 13	30, 14
	13	-, 14	-, 15	-, 16
	14	-, 16	-, 18	-, 19
	15	-, 18	-, 21	-, 23
	16	-, 22	-, 25	-, 28
	17	-, 27	-, 30	-, 30
18	1	3, -	3, -	2, -
	2	5, -	4, -	4, -
	3	7, -	6, -	5, -
	4	9, -	7, -	7, -
	5	11, -	9, -	9, -
	6	13, -	11, -	10, -
	7	16, -	14, -	13, -
	8	18, -	16, -	15, -
	9	22, -	19, -	17, 9
	10	25, -	22, 10	20, 10
	11	30, -	26, 11	24, 12
	12	>30, 12	30, 13	28, 14
	13	-, 13	-, 15	-, 16
	14	-, 15	-, 17	-, 18
	15	-, 17	-, 20	-, 21
	16	-, 20	-, 23	-, 25
	17	-, 24	-, 28	-, 30
	18	-, 30	-,>30	-,>30
19	1	3, -	3, -	2, -
	2	5, -	4, -	4, -
	3	7, -	6, -	5, -
	4	8, -	7, -	7, -
	5	11, -	9, -	8, -

k	x	.01,.99	.05,.95	.10,.90
19	6	13, -	11, -	10, -
	7	15, -	13, -	12, -
	8	18, -	16, -	14, -
	9	21, -	18, -	17, -
	10	24, -	21, -	19, 10
	11	28, -	24, 11	23, 11
	12	>30, -	28, 13	26, 13
	13	>30, 13	>30, 14	30, 15
	14	-, 15	-, 16	-, 17
	15	-, 17	-, 19	-, 20
	16	-, 19	-, 22	-, 23
	17	-, 22	-, 25	-, 27
	18	-, 26	-, 30	-,>30
	19	-, 30	-, -	-, -
20	1	3, -	2, -	2, -
	2	5, -	4, -	4, -
	3	6, -	6, -	5, -
	4	8, -	7, -	7, -
	5	10, -	9, -	8, -
	6	12, -	11, -	10, -
	7	15, -	13, -	12, -
	8	17, -	15, -	14, -
	9	20, -	18, -	16, -
	10	23, -	20, -	19, 10
	11	27, -	23, 11	22, 11
	12	>30, -	27, 12	25, 13
	13	>30, 13	>30, 14	29, 15
	14	-, 14	-, 16	-, 17
	15	-, 16	-, 18	-, 19
	16	-, 18	-, 21	-, 22
	17	-, 21	-, 24	-, 25
	18	-, 24	-, 27	-, 30
	19	-, 28	-,>30	-,>30
	20	-, 30	-, -	-, -

17.2

18. HYPERGEOMETRIC DISTRIBUTION

18.1 The Hypergeometric Probability Distribution

The terminology of sampling inspection will be used to define the parameters needed in the table. Let

$$N = \text{the number of items in a lot,}$$
$$n = \text{the number of items in a sample taken from the lot,}$$
$$k = \text{the number of defective items in the lot,}$$
$$x = \text{the number of defective items observed in the sample.}$$

Then the probability
Pr {exactly x defectives are found in the sample}

$$\equiv p(x) \equiv p(N, n, k, x)$$

$$\equiv \frac{k!n!}{(k-x)!(n-x)!x!} \frac{(N-k)!(N-n)!}{N!(N-k-n+x)!},$$

where x is an integer such that max $[0, n+k-N] \leq x \leq$ min $[n, k]$, and
Pr {x defectives or fewer are found in the sample}

$$\equiv P(x) \equiv P(N, n, k, x)$$

$$\equiv \sum_{i=\max[0,n+k-N]}^{x} \frac{k!n!}{(k-i)!(n-i)!i!} \frac{(N-k)!(N-n)!}{N!(N-k-n+i)!}.$$

There are several symmetries in the hypergeometric probability distribution. These are expressed in terms of the following identities for point probabilities:

$$p(N, n, k, x) \equiv p(N, k, n, x)$$
$$\equiv p(N, n, N-k, n-x)$$
$$\equiv p(N, N-n, k, k-x)$$
$$\equiv p(N, N-n, N-k, N-n-k+x),$$

and for cumulative probabilities:

$$P(N, n, k, x) \equiv P(N, k, n, x)$$
$$\equiv P(N, N-n, N-k, N-n-k+x)$$
$$\equiv 1 - P(N, n, N-k, n-x-1)$$
$$\equiv 1 - P(N, N-n, k, k-x-1),$$

18.1

where the value of $P(N, n, k, x)$ is 1 if either $n - x - 1$ or $k - x - 1$ becomes negative. The above identities may be applied more than once if desired. For example, suppose $P(16, 12, 10, 6)$ is needed. This is equal to $P(16, 4, 6, 0)$ by the second identity, and this in turn is equal to $P(16, 6, 4, 0)$ by the first one. Investigation of these identities shows that every hypergeometric probability can be expressed directly in terms of a hypergeometric probability with $0 \leq x \leq k \leq n \leq \frac{1}{2}N$ by the use of these identities.

All hypergeometric point and cumulative probabilities with $N \leq 20$ are given in the table. More extensive tables have been given by Lieberman and Owen [120], along with a summary of several applications. One important application is to exceedance theory. Two interesting relationships are given by

Pr $\{x$ or more among m future trials will exceed the rth largest among n observations$\} = P(m + n, n, x + r - 1, r - 1)$ for $0 \leq x \leq m$ and $1 \leq r \leq n$

and

Pr $\{x$ or more among m future trials will lie between the largest and smallest values in a sample of $n\}$
$$= 1 - P(m + n, n, m - x + 2, 1) \quad \text{for } 0 \leq x \leq m.$$

The Hypergeometric Probability Distribution

N	n	k	x	PX	px	N	n	k	x	PX	px
2	1	1	0	0.500000	0.500000	7	3	2	2	1.000000	0.142857
2	1	1	1	1.000000	0.500000	7	3	3	0	0.114286	0.114286
3	1	1	0	0.666667	0.666667	7	3	3	1	0.628571	0.514286
3	1	1	1	1.000000	0.333333	7	3	3	2	0.971429	0.342857
4	1	1	0	0.750000	0.750000	7	3	3	3	1.000000	0.028571
4	1	1	1	1.000000	0.250000	8	1	1	0	0.875000	0.875000
4	2	1	0	0.500000	0.500000	8	1	1	1	1.000000	0.125000
4	2	1	1	1.000000	0.500000	8	2	1	0	0.750000	0.750000
4	2	2	0	0.166667	0.166667	8	2	1	1	1.000000	0.250000
4	2	2	1	0.833333	0.666667	8	2	2	0	0.535714	0.535714
4	2	2	2	1.000000	0.166667	8	2	2	1	0.964286	0.428571
5	1	1	0	0.800000	0.800000	8	2	2	2	1.000000	0.035714
5	1	1	1	1.000000	0.200000	8	3	1	0	0.625000	0.625000
5	2	1	0	0.600000	0.600000	8	3	1	1	1.000000	0.375000
5	2	1	1	1.000000	0.400000	8	3	2	0	0.357143	0.357143
5	2	2	0	0.300000	0.300000	8	3	2	1	0.892857	0.535714
5	2	2	1	0.900000	0.600000	8	3	2	2	1.000000	0.107143
5	2	2	2	1.000000	0.100000	8	3	3	0	0.178571	0.178571
6	1	1	0	0.833333	0.833333	8	3	3	1	0.714286	0.535714
6	1	1	1	1.000000	0.166667	8	3	3	2	0.982143	0.267857
6	2	1	0	0.666667	0.666667	8	3	3	3	1.000000	0.017857
6	2	1	1	1.000000	0.333333	8	4	1	0	0.500000	0.500000
6	2	2	0	0.400000	0.400000	8	4	1	1	1.000000	0.500000
6	2	2	1	0.933333	0.533333	8	4	2	0	0.214286	0.214286
6	2	2	2	1.000000	0.066667	8	4	2	1	0.785714	0.571428
6	3	1	0	0.500000	0.500000	8	4	2	2	1.000000	0.214286
6	3	1	1	1.000000	0.500000	8	4	3	0	0.071429	0.071429
6	3	2	0	0.200000	0.200000	8	4	3	1	0.500000	0.428571
6	3	2	1	0.800000	0.600000	8	4	3	2	0.928571	0.428571
6	3	2	2	1.000000	0.200000	8	4	3	3	1.000000	0.071429
6	3	3	0	0.050000	0.050000	8	4	4	0	0.014286	0.014286
6	3	3	1	0.500000	0.450000	8	4	4	1	0.242857	0.228571
6	3	3	2	0.950000	0.450000	8	4	4	2	0.757143	0.514286
6	3	3	3	1.000000	0.050000	8	4	4	3	0.985714	0.228571
7	1	1	0	0.857143	0.857143	8	4	4	4	1.000000	0.014286
7	1	1	1	1.000000	0.142857	9	1	1	0	0.888889	0.888889
7	2	1	0	0.714286	0.714286	9	1	1	1	1.000000	0.111111
7	2	1	1	1.000000	0.285714	9	2	1	0	0.777778	0.777778
7	2	2	0	0.476190	0.476190	9	2	1	1	1.000000	0.222222
7	2	2	1	0.952381	0.476190	9	2	2	0	0.583333	0.583333
7	2	2	2	1.000000	0.047619	9	2	2	1	0.972222	0.388889
7	3	1	0	0.571429	0.571429	9	2	2	2	1.000000	0.027778
7	3	1	1	1.000000	0.428571	9	3	1	0	0.666667	0.666667
7	3	2	0	0.285714	0.285714	9	3	1	1	1.000000	0.333333
7	3	2	1	0.857143	0.571429	9	3	2	0	0.416667	0.416667

The Hypergeometric Probability Distribution (*cont.*)

N	n	k	x	PX	px	N	n	k	x	PX	px
9	3	2	1	0.916667	0.500000	10	4	4	0	0.071429	0.071429
9	3	2	2	1.000000	0.083333	10	4	4	1	0.452381	0.380952
9	3	3	0	0.238095	0.238095	10	4	4	2	0.880952	0.428571
9	3	3	1	0.773810	0.535714	10	4	4	3	0.995238	0.114286
9	3	3	2	0.988095	0.214286	10	4	4	4	1.000000	0.004762
9	3	3	3	1.000000	0.011905	10	5	1	0	0.500000	0.500000
9	4	1	0	0.555556	0.555556	10	5	1	1	1.000000	0.500000
9	4	1	1	1.000000	0.444444	10	5	2	0	0.222222	0.222222
9	4	2	0	0.277778	0.277778	10	5	2	1	0.777778	0.555556
9	4	2	1	0.833333	0.555556	10	5	2	2	1.000000	0.222222
9	4	2	2	1.000000	0.166667	10	5	3	0	0.083333	0.083333
9	4	3	0	0.119048	0.119048	10	5	3	1	0.500000	0.416667
9	4	3	1	0.595238	0.476190	10	5	3	2	0.916667	0.416667
9	4	3	2	0.952381	0.357143	10	5	3	3	1.000000	0.083333
9	4	3	3	1.000000	0.047619	10	5	4	0	0.023810	0.023810
9	4	4	0	0.039683	0.039683	10	5	4	1	0.261905	0.238095
9	4	4	1	0.357143	0.317460	10	5	4	2	0.738095	0.476190
9	4	4	2	0.833333	0.476190	10	5	4	3	0.976190	0.238095
9	4	4	3	0.992063	0.158730	10	5	4	4	1.000000	0.023810
9	4	4	4	1.000000	0.007936	10	5	5	0	0.003968	0.003968
10	1	1	0	0.900000	0.900000	10	5	5	1	0.103175	0.099206
10	1	1	1	1.000000	0.100000	10	5	5	2	0.500000	0.396825
10	2	1	0	0.800000	0.800000	10	5	5	3	0.896825	0.396825
10	2	1	1	1.000000	0.200000	10	5	5	4	0.996032	0.099206
10	2	2	0	0.622222	0.622222	10	5	5	5	1.000000	0.003968
10	2	2	1	0.977778	0.355556	11	1	1	0	0.909091	0.909091
10	2	2	2	1.000000	0.022222	11	1	1	1	1.000000	0.090909
10	3	1	0	0.700000	0.700000	11	2	1	0	0.818182	0.818182
10	3	1	1	1.000000	0.300000	11	2	1	1	1.000000	0.181818
10	3	2	0	0.466667	0.466667	11	2	2	0	0.654545	0.654545
10	3	2	1	0.933333	0.466667	11	2	2	1	0.981818	0.327273
10	3	2	2	1.000000	0.066667	11	2	2	2	1.000000	0.018182
10	3	3	0	0.291667	0.291667	11	3	1	0	0.727273	0.727273
10	3	3	1	0.816667	0.525000	11	3	1	1	1.000000	0.272727
10	3	3	2	0.991667	0.175000	11	3	2	0	0.509091	0.509091
10	3	3	3	1.000000	0.008333	11	3	2	1	0.945455	0.436364
10	4	1	0	0.600000	0.600000	11	3	2	2	1.000000	0.054545
10	4	1	1	1.000000	0.400000	11	3	3	0	0.339394	0.339394
10	4	2	0	0.333333	0.333333	11	3	3	1	0.848485	0.509091
10	4	2	1	0.866667	0.533333	11	3	3	2	0.993939	0.145455
10	4	2	2	1.000000	0.133333	11	3	3	3	1.000000	0.006061
10	4	3	0	0.166667	0.166667	11	4	1	0	0.636364	0.636364
10	4	3	1	0.666667	0.500000	11	4	1	1	1.000000	0.363636
10	4	3	2	0.966667	0.300000	11	4	2	0	0.381818	0.381818
10	4	3	3	1.000000	0.033333	11	4	2	1	0.890909	0.509091

The Hypergeometric Probability Distribution (*cont.*)

N	n	k	x	PX	px	N	n	k	x	PX	px
11	4	2	2	1.000000	0.109091	12	3	3	3	1.000000	0.004545
11	4	3	0	0.212121	0.212121	12	4	1	0	0.666667	0.666667
11	4	3	1	0.721212	0.509091	12	4	1	1	1.000000	0.333333
11	4	3	2	0.975757	0.254545	12	4	2	0	0.424242	0.424242
11	4	3	3	1.000000	0.024242	12	4	2	1	0.909091	0.484848
11	4	4	0	0.106061	0.106061	12	4	2	2	1.000000	0.090909
11	4	4	1	0.530303	0.424242	12	4	3	0	0.254545	0.254545
11	4	4	2	0.912121	0.381818	12	4	3	1	0.763636	0.509091
11	4	4	3	0.996970	0.084848	12	4	3	2	0.981818	0.218182
11	4	4	4	1.000000	0.003030	12	4	3	3	1.000000	0.018182
11	5	1	0	0.545455	0.545455	12	4	4	0	0.141414	0.141414
11	5	1	1	1.000000	0.454545	12	4	4	1	0.593939	0.452525
11	5	2	0	0.272727	0.272727	12	4	4	2	0.933333	0.339394
11	5	2	1	0.818182	0.545455	12	4	4	3	0.997980	0.064646
11	5	2	2	1.000000	0.181818	12	4	4	4	1.000000	0.002020
11	5	3	0	0.121212	0.121212	12	5	1	0	0.583333	0.583333
11	5	3	1	0.575758	0.454546	12	5	1	1	1.000000	0.416667
11	5	3	2	0.939394	0.363636	12	5	2	0	0.318182	0.318182
11	5	3	3	1.000000	0.060606	12	5	2	1	0.848485	0.530303
11	5	4	0	0.045455	0.045455	12	5	2	2	1.000000	0.151515
11	5	4	1	0.348485	0.303030	12	5	3	0	0.159091	0.159091
11	5	4	2	0.803030	0.454545	12	5	3	1	0.636364	0.477273
11	5	4	3	0.984848	0.181818	12	5	3	2	0.954546	0.318182
11	5	4	4	1.000000	0.015152	12	5	3	3	1.000000	0.045455
11	5	5	0	0.012987	0.012987	12	5	4	0	0.070707	0.070707
11	5	5	1	0.175325	0.162338	12	5	4	1	0.424242	0.353535
11	5	5	2	0.608225	0.432900	12	5	4	2	0.848485	0.424242
11	5	5	3	0.932900	0.324675	12	5	4	3	0.989899	0.141414
11	5	5	4	0.997835	0.064935	12	5	4	4	1.000000	0.010101
11	5	5	5	1.000000	0.002164	12	5	5	0	0.026515	0.026515
12	1	1	0	0.916667	0.916667	12	5	5	1	0.247475	0.220960
12	1	1	1	1.000000	0.083333	12	5	5	2	0.689394	0.441919
12	2	1	0	0.833333	0.833333	12	5	5	3	0.954545	0.265151
12	2	1	1	1.000000	0.166667	12	5	5	4	0.998737	0.044192
12	2	2	0	0.681818	0.681818	12	5	5	5	1.000000	0.001263
12	2	2	1	0.984848	0.303030	12	6	1	0	0.500000	0.500000
12	2	2	2	1.000000	0.015152	12	6	1	1	1.000000	0.500000
12	3	1	0	0.750000	0.750000	12	6	2	0	0.227273	0.227273
12	3	1	1	1.000000	0.250000	12	6	2	1	0.772727	0.545455
12	3	2	0	0.545455	0.545455	12	6	2	2	1.000000	0.227273
12	3	2	1	0.954545	0.409091	12	6	3	0	0.090909	0.090909
12	3	2	2	1.000000	0.045455	12	6	3	1	0.500000	0.409091
12	3	3	0	0.381818	0.381818	12	6	3	2	0.909091	0.409091
12	3	3	1	0.872727	0.490909	12	6	3	3	1.000000	0.090909
12	3	3	2	0.995455	0.122727	12	6	4	0	0.030303	0.030303

The Hypergeometric Probability Distribution (cont.)

N	n	k	x	PX	px	N	n	k	x	PX	px
12	6	4	1	0.272727	0.242424	13	4	4	3	0.998601	0.050350
12	6	4	2	0.727273	0.454546	13	4	4	4	1.000000	0.001399
12	6	4	3	0.969697	0.242424	13	5	1	0	0.615385	0.615385
12	6	4	4	1.000000	0.030303	13	5	1	1	1.000000	0.384615
12	6	5	0	0.007576	0.007576	13	5	2	0	0.358974	0.358974
12	6	5	1	0.121212	0.113636	13	5	2	1	0.871795	0.512821
12	6	5	2	0.500000	0.378788	13	5	2	2	1.000000	0.128205
12	6	5	3	0.878788	0.378788	13	5	3	0	0.195804	0.195804
12	6	5	4	0.992424	0.113636	13	5	3	1	0.685315	0.489511
12	6	5	5	1.000000	0.007576	13	5	3	2	0.965035	0.279720
12	6	6	0	0.001082	0.001082	13	5	3	3	1.000000	0.034965
12	6	6	1	0.040043	0.038961	13	5	4	0	0.097902	0.097902
12	6	6	2	0.283550	0.243507	13	5	4	1	0.489510	0.391608
12	6	6	3	0.716450	0.432900	13	5	4	2	0.881119	0.391608
12	6	6	4	0.959957	0.243507	13	5	4	3	0.993007	0.111888
12	6	6	5	0.998918	0.038961	13	5	4	4	1.000000	0.006993
12	6	6	6	1.000000	0.001082	13	5	5	0	0.043512	0.043512
13	1	1	0	0.923077	0.923077	13	5	5	1	0.315462	0.271950
13	1	1	1	1.000000	0.076923	13	5	5	2	0.750583	0.435120
13	2	1	0	0.846154	0.846154	13	5	5	3	0.968143	0.217560
13	2	1	1	1.000000	0.153846	13	5	5	4	0.999223	0.031080
13	2	2	0	0.705128	0.705128	13	5	5	5	1.000000	0.000777
13	2	2	1	0.987179	0.282051	13	6	1	0	0.538461	0.538461
13	2	2	2	1.000000	0.012821	13	6	1	1	1.000000	0.461538
13	3	1	0	0.769231	0.769231	13	6	2	0	0.269231	0.269231
13	3	1	1	1.000000	0.230769	13	6	2	1	0.807692	0.538461
13	3	2	0	0.576923	0.576923	13	6	2	2	1.000000	0.192308
13	3	2	1	0.961538	0.384615	13	6	3	0	0.122378	0.122378
13	3	2	2	1.000000	0.038462	13	6	3	1	0.562937	0.440559
13	3	3	0	0.419580	0.419580	13	6	3	2	0.930070	0.367133
13	3	3	1	0.891608	0.472028	13	6	3	3	1.000000	0.069930
13	3	3	2	0.996504	0.104895	13	6	4	0	0.048951	0.048951
13	3	3	3	1.000000	0.003496	13	6	4	1	0.342657	0.293706
13	4	1	0	0.692308	0.692308	13	6	4	2	0.783217	0.440559
13	4	1	1	1.000000	0.307692	13	6	4	3	0.979021	0.195804
13	4	2	0	0.461538	0.461538	13	6	4	4	1.000000	0.020979
13	4	2	1	0.923077	0.461538	13	6	5	0	0.016317	0.016317
13	4	2	2	1.000000	0.076923	13	6	5	1	0.179487	0.163170
13	4	3	0	0.293706	0.293706	13	6	5	2	0.587413	0.407925
13	4	3	1	0.797203	0.503497	13	6	5	3	0.913753	0.326340
13	4	3	2	0.986014	0.188811	13	6	5	4	0.995338	0.081585
13	4	3	3	1.000000	0.013986	13	6	5	5	1.000000	0.004662
13	4	4	0	0.176224	0.176224	13	6	6	0	0.004079	0.004079
13	4	4	1	0.646154	0.469930	13	6	6	1	0.077506	0.073427
13	4	4	2	0.948252	0.302098	13	6	6	2	0.383450	0.305944

The Hypergeometric Probability Distribution (*cont.*)

N	n	k	x	PX	px	N	n	k	x	PX	px
13	6	6	3	0.791375	0.407925	14	5	4	2	0.905095	0.359640
13	6	6	4	0.974942	0.183566	14	5	4	3	0.995005	0.089910
13	6	6	5	0.999417	0.024476	14	5	4	4	1.000000	0.004995
13	6	6	6	1.000000	0.000583	14	5	5	0	0.062937	0.062937
14	1	1	0	0.928571	0.928571	14	5	5	1	0.377622	0.314685
14	1	1	1	1.000000	0.071429	14	5	5	2	0.797203	0.419580
14	2	1	0	0.857143	0.857143	14	5	5	3	0.977023	0.179820
14	2	1	1	1.000000	0.142857	14	5	5	4	0.999500	0.022478
14	2	2	0	0.725275	0.725275	14	5	5	5	1.000000	0.000499
14	2	2	1	0.989011	0.263736	14	6	1	0	0.571429	0.571429
14	2	2	2	1.000000	0.010989	14	6	1	1	1.000000	0.428571
14	3	1	0	0.785714	0.785714	14	6	2	0	0.307692	0.307692
14	3	1	1	1.000000	0.214286	14	6	2	1	0.835165	0.527472
14	3	2	0	0.604396	0.604396	14	6	2	2	1.000000	0.164835
14	3	2	1	0.967033	0.362637	14	6	3	0	0.153846	0.153846
14	3	2	2	1.000000	0.032967	14	6	3	1	0.615385	0.461538
14	3	3	0	0.453297	0.453297	14	6	3	2	0.945055	0.329670
14	3	3	1	0.906593	0.453297	14	6	3	3	1.000000	0.054945
14	3	3	2	0.997253	0.090659	14	6	4	0	0.069930	0.069930
14	3	3	3	1.000000	0.002747	14	6	4	1	0.405594	0.335664
14	4	1	0	0.714286	0.714286	14	6	4	2	0.825175	0.419580
14	4	1	1	1.000000	0.285714	14	6	4	3	0.985015	0.159840
14	4	2	0	0.494505	0.494505	14	6	4	4	1.000000	0.014985
14	4	2	1	0.934066	0.439560	14	6	5	0	0.027972	0.027972
14	4	2	2	1.000000	0.065934	14	6	5	1	0.237762	0.209790
14	4	3	0	0.329670	0.329670	14	6	5	2	0.657343	0.419580
14	4	3	1	0.824176	0.494505	14	6	5	3	0.937063	0.279720
14	4	3	2	0.989011	0.164835	14	6	5	4	0.997003	0.059940
14	4	3	3	1.000000	0.010989	14	6	5	5	1.000000	0.002997
14	4	4	0	0.209790	0.209790	14	6	6	0	0.009324	0.009324
14	4	4	1	0.689311	0.479520	14	6	6	1	0.121212	0.111888
14	4	4	2	0.959041	0.269730	14	6	6	2	0.470862	0.349650
14	4	4	3	0.999001	0.039960	14	6	6	3	0.843823	0.372960
14	4	4	4	1.000000	0.000999	14	6	6	4	0.983683	0.139860
14	5	1	0	0.642857	0.642857	14	6	6	5	0.999667	0.015984
14	5	1	1	1.000000	0.357143	14	6	6	6	1.000000	0.000333
14	5	2	0	0.395604	0.395604	14	7	1	0	0.500000	0.500000
14	5	2	1	0.890110	0.494505	14	7	1	1	1.000000	0.500000
14	5	2	2	1.000000	0.109890	14	7	2	0	0.230769	0.230769
14	5	3	0	0.230769	0.230769	14	7	2	1	0.769231	0.538461
14	5	3	1	0.725275	0.494506	14	7	2	2	1.000000	0.230769
14	5	3	2	0.972528	0.247253	14	7	3	0	0.096154	0.096154
14	5	3	3	1.000000	0.027473	14	7	3	1	0.500000	0.403846
14	5	4	0	0.125874	0.125874	14	7	3	2	0.903846	0.403846
14	5	4	1	0.545455	0.419580	14	7	3	3	1.000000	0.096154

The Hypergeometric Probability Distribution (*cont.*)

N	n	k	x	PX	px	N	n	k	x	PX	px
14	7	4	0	0.034965	0.034965	15	4	2	1	0.942857	0.419048
14	7	4	1	0.279720	0.244755	15	4	2	2	1.000000	0.057143
14	7	4	2	0.720280	0.440559	15	4	3	0	0.362637	0.362637
14	7	4	3	0.965035	0.244755	15	4	3	1	0.846154	0.483516
14	7	4	4	1.000000	0.034965	15	4	3	2	0.991209	0.145055
14	7	5	0	0.010490	0.010490	15	4	3	3	1.000000	0.008791
14	7	5	1	0.132867	0.122378	15	4	4	0	0.241758	0.241758
14	7	5	2	0.500000	0.367133	15	4	4	1	0.725275	0.483516
14	7	5	3	0.867133	0.367133	15	4	4	2	0.967033	0.241758
14	7	5	4	0.989510	0.122378	15	4	4	3	0.999267	0.032234
14	7	5	5	1.000000	0.010490	15	4	4	4	1.000000	0.000733
14	7	6	0	0.002331	0.002331	15	5	1	0	0.666667	0.666667
14	7	6	1	0.051282	0.048951	15	5	1	1	1.000000	0.333333
14	7	6	2	0.296037	0.244755	15	5	2	0	0.428571	0.428571
14	7	6	3	0.703963	0.407925	15	5	2	1	0.904762	0.476190
14	7	6	4	0.948718	0.244755	15	5	2	2	1.000000	0.095238
14	7	6	5	0.997669	0.048951	15	5	3	0	0.263736	0.263736
14	7	6	6	1.000000	0.002331	15	5	3	1	0.758242	0.494506
14	7	7	0	0.000291	0.000291	15	5	3	2	0.978022	0.219780
14	7	7	1	0.014569	0.014277	15	5	3	3	1.000000	0.021978
14	7	7	2	0.143065	0.128496	15	5	4	0	0.153846	0.153846
14	7	7	3	0.500000	0.356935	15	5	4	1	0.593407	0.439560
14	7	7	4	0.856935	0.356935	15	5	4	2	0.923077	0.329670
14	7	7	5	0.985431	0.128496	15	5	4	3	0.996337	0.073260
14	7	7	6	0.999708	0.014277	15	5	4	4	1.000000	0.003663
14	7	7	7	1.000000	0.000291	15	5	5	0	0.083916	0.083916
15	1	1	0	0.933333	0.933333	15	5	5	1	0.433566	0.349650
15	1	1	1	1.000000	0.066667	15	5	5	2	0.833167	0.399600
15	2	1	0	0.866667	0.866667	15	5	5	3	0.983017	0.149850
15	2	1	1	1.000000	0.133333	15	5	5	4	0.999667	0.016650
15	2	2	0	0.742857	0.742857	15	5	5	5	1.000000	0.000333
15	2	2	1	0.990476	0.247619	15	6	1	0	0.600000	0.600000
15	2	2	2	1.000000	0.009524	15	6	1	1	1.000000	0.400000
15	3	1	0	0.800000	0.800000	15	6	2	0	0.342857	0.342857
15	3	1	1	1.000000	0.200000	15	6	2	1	0.857143	0.514286
15	3	2	0	0.628571	0.628571	15	6	2	2	1.000000	0.142857
15	3	2	1	0.971429	0.342857	15	6	3	0	0.184615	0.184615
15	3	2	2	1.000000	0.028571	15	6	3	1	0.659341	0.474725
15	3	3	0	0.483516	0.483516	15	6	3	2	0.956044	0.296703
15	3	3	1	0.918681	0.435165	15	6	3	3	1.000000	0.043956
15	3	3	2	0.997802	0.079121	15	6	4	0	0.092308	0.092308
15	3	3	3	1.000000	0.002198	15	6	4	1	0.461538	0.369231
15	4	1	0	0.733333	0.733333	15	6	4	2	0.857143	0.395604
15	4	1	1	1.000000	0.266667	15	6	4	3	0.989011	0.131868
15	4	2	0	0.523810	0.523810	15	6	4	4	1.000000	0.010989

The Hypergeometric Probability Distribution (*cont.*)

N	n	k	x	PX	px	N	n	k	x	PX	px
15	6	5	0	0.041958	0.041958	15	7	7	5	0.991142	0.091375
15	6	5	1	0.293706	0.251748	15	7	7	6	0.999845	0.008702
15	6	5	2	0.713287	0.419580	15	7	7	7	1.000000	0.000155
15	6	5	3	0.953047	0.239760	16	1	1	0	0.937500	0.937500
15	6	5	4	0.998002	0.044955	16	1	1	1	1.000000	0.062500
15	6	5	5	1.000000	0.001998	16	2	1	0	0.875000	0.875000
15	6	6	0	0.016783	0.016783	16	2	1	1	1.000000	0.125000
15	6	6	1	0.167832	0.151049	16	2	2	0	0.758333	0.758333
15	6	6	2	0.545455	0.377622	16	2	2	1	0.991667	0.233333
15	6	6	3	0.881119	0.335664	16	2	2	2	1.000000	0.008333
15	6	6	4	0.989011	0.107892	16	3	1	0	0.812500	0.812500
15	6	6	5	0.999800	0.010789	16	3	1	1	1.000000	0.187500
15	6	6	6	1.000000	0.000200	16	3	2	0	0.650000	0.650000
15	7	1	0	0.533333	0.533333	16	3	2	1	0.975000	0.325000
15	7	1	1	1.000000	0.466667	16	3	2	2	1.000000	0.025000
15	7	2	0	0.266667	0.266667	16	3	3	0	0.510714	0.510714
15	7	2	1	0.800000	0.533333	16	3	3	1	0.928571	0.417857
15	7	2	2	1.000000	0.200000	16	3	3	2	0.998214	0.069643
15	7	3	0	0.123077	0.123077	16	3	3	3	1.000000	0.001786
15	7	3	1	0.553846	0.430769	16	4	1	0	0.750000	0.750000
15	7	3	2	0.923077	0.369231	16	4	1	1	1.000000	0.250000
15	7	3	3	1.000000	0.076923	16	4	2	0	0.550000	0.550000
15	7	4	0	0.051282	0.051282	16	4	2	1	0.950000	0.400000
15	7	4	1	0.338461	0.287179	16	4	2	2	1.000000	0.050000
15	7	4	2	0.769231	0.430769	16	4	3	0	0.392857	0.392857
15	7	4	3	0.974359	0.205128	16	4	3	1	0.864286	0.471429
15	7	4	4	1.000000	0.025641	16	4	3	2	0.992857	0.128571
15	7	5	0	0.018648	0.018648	16	4	3	3	1.000000	0.007143
15	7	5	1	0.181818	0.163170	16	4	4	0	0.271978	0.271978
15	7	5	2	0.573427	0.391608	16	4	4	1	0.755494	0.483516
15	7	5	3	0.899767	0.326340	16	4	4	2	0.973077	0.217582
15	7	5	4	0.993007	0.093240	16	4	4	3	0.999450	0.026374
15	7	5	5	1.000000	0.006993	16	4	4	4	1.000000	0.000549
15	7	6	0	0.005594	0.005594	16	5	1	0	0.687500	0.687500
15	7	6	1	0.083916	0.078322	16	5	1	1	1.000000	0.312500
15	7	6	2	0.377622	0.293706	16	5	2	0	0.458333	0.458333
15	7	6	3	0.769231	0.391608	16	5	2	1	0.916667	0.458333
15	7	6	4	0.965035	0.195804	16	5	2	2	1.000000	0.083333
15	7	6	5	0.998601	0.033566	16	5	3	0	0.294643	0.294643
15	7	6	6	1.000000	0.001399	16	5	3	1	0.785714	0.491071
15	7	7	0	0.001243	0.001243	16	5	3	2	0.982143	0.196429
15	7	7	1	0.031702	0.030458	16	5	3	3	1.000000	0.017857
15	7	7	2	0.214452	0.182751	16	5	4	0	0.181319	0.181319
15	7	7	3	0.595183	0.380730	16	5	4	1	0.634615	0.453297
15	7	7	4	0.899767	0.304584	16	5	4	2	0.936813	0.302198

The Hypergeometric Probability Distribution (cont.)

N	n	k	x	PX	px	N	n	k	x	PX	px
16	5	4	3	0.997253	0.060440	16	7	4	1	0.392308	0.323077
16	5	4	4	1.000000	0.002747	16	7	4	2	0.807692	0.415385
16	5	5	0	0.105769	0.105769	16	7	4	3	0.980769	0.173077
16	5	5	1	0.483517	0.377747	16	7	4	4	1.000000	0.019231
16	5	5	2	0.861264	0.377747	16	7	5	0	0.028846	0.028846
16	5	5	3	0.987179	0.125916	16	7	5	1	0.230769	0.201923
16	5	5	4	0.999771	0.012592	16	7	5	2	0.634615	0.403846
16	5	5	5	1.000000	0.000229	16	7	5	3	0.923077	0.288462
16	6	1	0	0.625000	0.625000	16	7	5	4	0.995192	0.072115
16	6	1	1	1.000000	0.375000	16	7	5	5	1.000000	0.004808
16	6	2	0	0.375000	0.375000	16	7	6	0	0.010490	0.010490
16	6	2	1	0.875000	0.500000	16	7	6	1	0.120629	0.110140
16	6	2	2	1.000000	0.125000	16	7	6	2	0.451049	0.330420
16	6	3	0	0.214286	0.214286	16	7	6	3	0.818182	0.367133
16	6	3	1	0.696429	0.482143	16	7	6	4	0.975524	0.157343
16	6	3	2	0.964286	0.267857	16	7	6	5	0.999126	0.023601
16	6	3	3	1.000000	0.035714	16	7	6	6	1.000000	0.000874
16	6	4	0	0.115385	0.115385	16	7	7	0	0.003147	0.003147
16	6	4	1	0.510989	0.395604	16	7	7	1	0.054545	0.051399
16	6	4	2	0.881868	0.370879	16	7	7	2	0.285839	0.231294
16	6	4	3	0.991758	0.109890	16	7	7	3	0.671329	0.385490
16	6	4	4	1.000000	0.008242	16	7	7	4	0.928322	0.256993
16	6	5	0	0.057692	0.057692	16	7	7	5	0.994405	0.066084
16	6	5	1	0.346154	0.288462	16	7	7	6	0.999912	0.005507
16	6	5	2	0.758242	0.412088	16	7	7	7	1.000000	0.000087
16	6	5	3	0.964286	0.206044	16	8	1	0	0.500000	0.500000
16	6	5	4	0.998626	0.034341	16	8	1	1	1.000000	0.500000
16	6	5	5	1.000000	0.001374	16	8	2	0	0.233333	0.233333
16	6	6	0	0.026224	0.026224	16	8	2	1	0.766667	0.533333
16	6	6	1	0.215035	0.188811	16	8	2	2	1.000000	0.233333
16	6	6	2	0.608392	0.393357	16	8	3	0	0.100000	0.100000
16	6	6	3	0.908092	0.299700	16	8	3	1	0.500000	0.400000
16	6	6	4	0.992383	0.084291	16	8	3	2	0.900000	0.400000
16	6	6	5	0.999875	0.007492	16	8	3	3	1.000000	0.100000
16	6	6	6	1.000000	0.000125	16	8	4	0	0.038462	0.038462
16	7	1	0	0.562500	0.562500	16	8	4	1	0.284615	0.246154
16	7	1	1	1.000000	0.437500	16	8	4	2	0.715385	0.430769
16	7	2	0	0.300000	0.300000	16	8	4	3	0.961538	0.246154
16	7	2	1	0.825000	0.525000	16	8	4	4	1.000000	0.038462
16	7	2	2	1.000000	0.175000	16	8	5	0	0.012821	0.012821
16	7	3	0	0.150000	0.150000	16	8	5	1	0.141026	0.128205
16	7	3	1	0.600000	0.450000	16	8	5	2	0.500000	0.358974
16	7	3	2	0.937500	0.337500	16	8	5	3	0.858974	0.358974
16	7	3	3	1.000000	0.062500	16	8	5	4	0.987179	0.128205
16	7	4	0	0.069231	0.069231	16	8	5	5	1.000000	0.012821

The Hypergeometric Probability Distribution (*cont.*)

N	n	k	x	PX	px	N	n	k	x	PX	px
16	8	6	0	0.003496	0.003496	17	4	3	0	0.420588	0.420588
16	8	6	1	0.059441	0.055944	17	4	3	1	0.879412	0.458823
16	8	6	2	0.304196	0.244755	17	4	3	2	0.994118	0.114706
16	8	6	3	0.695804	0.391608	17	4	3	3	1.000000	0.005882
16	8	6	4	0.940560	0.244755	17	4	4	0	0.300420	0.300420
16	8	6	5	0.996504	0.055944	17	4	4	1	0.781092	0.480672
16	8	6	6	1.000000	0.003496	17	4	4	2	0.977731	0.196639
16	8	7	0	0.000699	0.000699	17	4	4	3	0.999580	0.021849
16	8	7	1	0.020280	0.019580	17	4	4	4	1.000000	0.000420
16	8	7	2	0.157343	0.137063	17	5	1	0	0.705882	0.705882
16	8	7	3	0.500000	0.342657	17	5	1	1	1.000000	0.294118
16	8	7	4	0.842657	0.342657	17	5	2	0	0.485294	0.485294
16	8	7	5	0.979720	0.137063	17	5	2	1	0.926470	0.441176
16	8	7	6	0.999301	0.019580	17	5	2	2	1.000000	0.073529
16	8	7	7	1.000000	0.000699	17	5	3	0	0.323529	0.323529
16	8	8	0	0.000078	0.000078	17	5	3	1	0.808823	0.485294
16	8	8	1	0.005051	0.004973	17	5	3	2	0.985294	0.176471
16	8	8	2	0.065967	0.060917	17	5	3	3	1.000000	0.014706
16	8	8	3	0.309635	0.243668	17	5	4	0	0.207983	0.207983
16	8	8	4	0.690366	0.380731	17	5	4	1	0.670168	0.462185
16	8	8	5	0.934033	0.243668	17	5	4	2	0.947479	0.277311
16	8	8	6	0.994950	0.060917	17	5	4	3	0.997899	0.050420
16	8	8	7	0.999923	0.004973	17	5	4	4	1.000000	0.002101
16	8	8	8	1.000000	0.000078	17	5	5	0	0.127990	0.127990
17	1	1	0	0.941176	0.941176	17	5	5	1	0.527957	0.399968
17	1	1	1	1.000000	0.058824	17	5	5	2	0.883484	0.355527
17	2	1	0	0.882353	0.882353	17	5	5	3	0.990142	0.106658
17	2	1	1	1.000000	0.117647	17	5	5	4	0.999838	0.009696
17	2	2	0	0.772059	0.772059	17	5	5	5	1.000000	0.000162
17	2	2	1	0.992647	0.220588	17	6	1	0	0.647059	0.647059
17	2	2	2	1.000000	0.007353	17	6	1	1	1.000000	0.352941
17	3	1	0	0.823529	0.823529	17	6	2	0	0.404412	0.404412
17	3	1	1	1.000000	0.176471	17	6	2	1	0.889706	0.485294
17	3	2	0	0.669118	0.669118	17	6	2	2	1.000000	0.110294
17	3	2	1	0.977941	0.308824	17	6	3	0	0.242647	0.242647
17	3	2	2	1.000000	0.022059	17	6	3	1	0.727941	0.485294
17	3	3	0	0.535294	0.535294	17	6	3	2	0.970588	0.242647
17	3	3	1	0.936765	0.401471	17	6	3	3	1.000000	0.029412
17	3	3	2	0.998529	0.061765	17	6	4	0	0.138655	0.138655
17	3	3	3	1.000000	0.001471	17	6	4	1	0.554622	0.415966
17	4	1	0	0.764706	0.764706	17	6	4	2	0.901260	0.346639
17	4	1	1	1.000000	0.235294	17	6	4	3	0.993697	0.092437
17	4	2	0	0.573529	0.573529	17	6	4	4	1.000000	0.006303
17	4	2	1	0.955882	0.382353	17	6	5	0	0.074661	0.074661
17	4	2	2	1.000000	0.044118	17	6	5	1	0.394635	0.319974

The Hypergeometric Probability Distribution (*cont.*)

N	n	k	x	PX	px	N	n	k	x	PX	px
17	6	5	2	0.794602	0.399968	17	7	7	7	1.000000	0.000051
17	6	5	3	0.972366	0.177763	17	8	1	0	0.529412	0.529412
17	6	5	4	0.999030	0.026665	17	8	1	1	1.000000	0.470588
17	6	5	5	1.000000	0.000970	17	8	2	0	0.264706	0.264706
17	6	6	0	0.037330	0.037330	17	8	2	1	0.794118	0.529412
17	6	6	1	0.261312	0.223982	17	8	2	2	1.000000	0.205882
17	6	6	2	0.661280	0.399968	17	8	3	0	0.123529	0.123529
17	6	6	3	0.927925	0.266645	17	8	3	1	0.547059	0.423529
17	6	6	4	0.994586	0.066661	17	8	3	2	0.917647	0.370588
17	6	6	5	0.999919	0.005333	17	8	3	3	1.000000	0.082353
17	6	6	6	1.000000	0.000081	17	8	4	0	0.052941	0.052941
17	7	1	0	0.588235	0.588235	17	8	4	1	0.335294	0.282353
17	7	1	1	1.000000	0.411765	17	8	4	2	0.758823	0.423529
17	7	2	0	0.330882	0.330882	17	8	4	3	0.970588	0.211765
17	7	2	1	0.845588	0.514706	17	8	4	4	1.000000	0.029412
17	7	2	2	1.000000	0.154412	17	8	5	0	0.020362	0.020362
17	7	3	0	0.176471	0.176471	17	8	5	1	0.183258	0.162896
17	7	3	1	0.639706	0.463235	17	8	5	2	0.563348	0.380090
17	7	3	2	0.948529	0.308824	17	8	5	3	0.889140	0.325792
17	7	3	3	1.000000	0.051471	17	8	5	4	0.990950	0.101810
17	7	4	0	0.088235	0.088235	17	8	5	5	1.000000	0.009050
17	7	4	1	0.441176	0.352941	17	8	6	0	0.006787	0.006787
17	7	4	2	0.838235	0.397059	17	8	6	1	0.088235	0.081448
17	7	4	3	0.985294	0.147059	17	8	6	2	0.373303	0.285068
17	7	4	4	1.000000	0.014706	17	8	6	3	0.753394	0.380090
17	7	5	0	0.040724	0.040724	17	8	6	4	0.957014	0.203620
17	7	5	1	0.278281	0.237557	17	8	6	5	0.997738	0.040724
17	7	5	2	0.685520	0.407240	17	8	6	6	1.000000	0.002262
17	7	5	3	0.940045	0.254525	17	8	7	0	0.001851	0.001851
17	7	5	4	0.996606	0.056561	17	8	7	1	0.036405	0.034554
17	7	5	5	1.000000	0.003394	17	8	7	2	0.217812	0.181407
17	7	6	0	0.016968	0.016968	17	8	7	3	0.580625	0.362814
17	7	6	1	0.159502	0.142534	17	8	7	4	0.882970	0.302345
17	7	6	2	0.515837	0.356335	17	8	7	5	0.986631	0.103661
17	7	6	3	0.855204	0.339367	17	8	7	6	0.999589	0.012958
17	7	6	4	0.982466	0.127262	17	8	7	7	1.000000	0.000411
17	7	6	5	0.999434	0.016968	17	8	8	0	0.000370	0.000370
17	7	6	6	1.000000	0.000566	17	8	8	1	0.012217	0.011847
17	7	7	0	0.006170	0.006170	17	8	8	2	0.108968	0.096750
17	7	7	1	0.081756	0.075586	17	8	8	3	0.399218	0.290251
17	7	7	2	0.353867	0.272110	17	8	8	4	0.762032	0.362814
17	7	7	3	0.731798	0.377931	17	8	8	5	0.955533	0.193501
17	7	7	4	0.947758	0.215960	17	8	8	6	0.996997	0.041464
17	7	7	5	0.996349	0.048591	17	8	8	7	0.999959	0.002962
17	7	7	6	0.999948	0.003599	17	8	8	8	1.000000	0.000041

The Hypergeometric Probability Distribution (cont.)

N	n	k	x	PX	px	N	n	k	x	PX	px
18	1	1	0	0.944444	0.944444	18	5	5	1	0.567460	0.417250
18	1	1	1	1.000000	0.055556	18	5	5	2	0.901260	0.333800
18	2	1	0	0.888889	0.888889	18	5	5	3	0.992297	0.091036
18	2	1	1	1.000000	0.111111	18	5	5	4	0.999883	0.007586
18	2	2	0	0.784314	0.784314	18	5	5	5	1.000000	0.000117
18	2	2	1	0.993464	0.209150	18	6	1	0	0.666667	0.666667
18	2	2	2	1.000000	0.006536	18	6	1	1	1.000000	0.333333
18	3	1	0	0.833333	0.833333	18	6	2	0	0.431373	0.431373
18	3	1	1	1.000000	0.166667	18	6	2	1	0.901961	0.470588
18	3	2	0	0.686274	0.686274	18	6	2	2	1.000000	0.098039
18	3	2	1	0.980392	0.294118	18	6	3	0	0.269608	0.269608
18	3	2	2	1.000000	0.019608	18	6	3	1	0.754902	0.485294
18	3	3	0	0.557598	0.557598	18	6	3	2	0.975490	0.220588
18	3	3	1	0.943627	0.386029	18	6	3	3	1.000000	0.024510
18	3	3	2	0.998774	0.055147	18	6	4	0	0.161765	0.161765
18	3	3	3	1.000000	0.001225	18	6	4	1	0.593137	0.431372
18	4	1	0	0.777778	0.777778	18	6	4	2	0.916667	0.323529
18	4	1	1	1.000000	0.222222	18	6	4	3	0.995098	0.078431
18	4	2	0	0.594771	0.594771	18	6	4	4	1.000000	0.004902
18	4	2	1	0.960784	0.366013	18	6	5	0	0.092437	0.092437
18	4	2	2	1.000000	0.039216	18	6	5	1	0.439076	0.346639
18	4	3	0	0.446078	0.446078	18	6	5	2	0.824230	0.385154
18	4	3	1	0.892157	0.446078	18	6	5	3	0.978291	0.154062
18	4	3	2	0.995098	0.102941	18	6	5	4	0.999300	0.021008
18	4	3	3	1.000000	0.004902	18	6	5	5	1.000000	0.000700
18	4	4	0	0.327124	0.327124	18	6	6	0	0.049774	0.049774
18	4	4	1	0.802941	0.475817	18	6	6	1	0.305753	0.255979
18	4	4	2	0.981372	0.178431	18	6	6	2	0.705721	0.399968
18	4	4	3	0.999673	0.018301	18	6	6	3	0.942739	0.237018
18	4	4	4	1.000000	0.000327	18	6	6	4	0.996068	0.053329
18	5	1	0	0.722222	0.722222	18	6	6	5	0.999946	0.003878
18	5	1	1	1.000000	0.277778	18	6	6	6	1.000000	0.000054
18	5	2	0	0.509804	0.509804	18	7	1	0	0.611111	0.611111
18	5	2	1	0.934640	0.424837	18	7	1	1	1.000000	0.388889
18	5	2	2	1.000000	0.065359	18	7	2	0	0.359477	0.359477
18	5	3	0	0.350490	0.350490	18	7	2	1	0.862745	0.503268
18	5	3	1	0.828431	0.477941	18	7	2	2	1.000000	0.137255
18	5	3	2	0.987745	0.159314	18	7	3	0	0.202206	0.202206
18	5	3	3	1.000000	0.012255	18	7	3	1	0.674020	0.471814
18	5	4	0	0.233660	0.233660	18	7	3	2	0.957108	0.283088
18	5	4	1	0.700980	0.467320	18	7	3	3	1.000000	0.042892
18	5	4	2	0.955882	0.254902	18	7	4	0	0.107843	0.107843
18	5	4	3	0.998366	0.042484	18	7	4	1	0.485294	0.377451
18	5	4	4	1.000000	0.001634	18	7	4	2	0.862745	0.377451
18	5	5	0	0.150210	0.150210	18	7	4	3	0.988562	0.125817

The Hypergeometric Probability Distribution (*cont.*)

N	n	k	x	PX	px	N	n	k	x	PX	px
18	7	4	4	1.000000	0.011438	18	8	6	3	0.798642	0.361991
18	7	5	0	0.053922	0.053922	18	8	6	4	0.968326	0.169683
18	7	5	1	0.323529	0.269608	18	8	6	5	0.998492	0.030166
18	7	5	2	0.727941	0.404412	18	8	6	6	1.000000	0.001508
18	7	5	3	0.952614	0.224673	18	8	7	0	0.003771	0.003771
18	7	5	4	0.997549	0.044935	18	8	7	1	0.056561	0.052790
18	7	5	5	1.000000	0.002451	18	8	7	2	0.278281	0.221720
18	7	6	0	0.024887	0.024887	18	8	7	3	0.647813	0.369532
18	7	6	1	0.199095	0.174208	18	8	7	4	0.911765	0.263952
18	7	6	2	0.572398	0.373303	18	8	7	5	0.990950	0.079186
18	7	6	3	0.883484	0.311086	18	8	7	6	0.999749	0.008798
18	7	6	4	0.987179	0.103695	18	8	7	7	1.000000	0.000251
18	7	6	5	0.999623	0.012443	18	8	8	0	0.001028	0.001028
18	7	6	6	1.000000	0.000377	18	8	8	1	0.022967	0.021939
18	7	7	0	0.010370	0.010370	18	8	8	2	0.157343	0.134375
18	7	7	1	0.111991	0.101621	18	8	8	3	0.479844	0.322501
18	7	7	2	0.416855	0.304864	18	8	8	4	0.815783	0.335939
18	7	7	3	0.779789	0.362934	18	8	8	5	0.969354	0.153572
18	7	7	4	0.961256	0.181467	18	8	8	6	0.998149	0.028795
18	7	7	5	0.997549	0.036293	18	8	8	7	0.999977	0.001828
18	7	7	6	0.999969	0.002420	18	8	8	8	1.000000	0.000023
18	7	7	7	1.000000	0.000031	18	9	1	0	0.500000	0.500000
18	8	1	0	0.555556	0.555556	18	9	1	1	1.000000	0.500000
18	8	1	1	1.000000	0.444444	18	9	2	0	0.235294	0.235294
18	8	2	0	0.294118	0.294118	18	9	2	1	0.764706	0.529412
18	8	2	1	0.816993	0.522876	18	9	2	2	1.000000	0.235294
18	8	2	2	1.000000	0.183007	18	9	3	0	0.102941	0.102941
18	8	3	0	0.147059	0.147059	18	9	3	1	0.500000	0.397059
18	8	3	1	0.588235	0.441176	18	9	3	2	0.897059	0.397059
18	8	3	2	0.931373	0.343137	18	9	3	3	1.000000	0.102941
18	8	3	3	1.000000	0.068627	18	9	4	0	0.041176	0.041176
18	8	4	0	0.068627	0.068627	18	9	4	1	0.288235	0.247059
18	8	4	1	0.382353	0.313726	18	9	4	2	0.711765	0.423529
18	8	4	2	0.794118	0.411765	18	9	4	3	0.958823	0.247059
18	8	4	3	0.977124	0.183006	18	9	4	4	1.000000	0.041176
18	8	4	4	1.000000	0.022876	18	9	5	0	0.014706	0.014706
18	8	5	0	0.029412	0.029412	18	9	5	1	0.147059	0.132353
18	8	5	1	0.225490	0.196078	18	9	5	2	0.500000	0.352941
18	8	5	2	0.617647	0.392157	18	9	5	3	0.852941	0.352941
18	8	5	3	0.911765	0.294118	18	9	5	4	0.985294	0.132353
18	8	5	4	0.993464	0.081699	18	9	5	5	1.000000	0.014706
18	8	5	5	1.000000	0.006536	18	9	6	0	0.004525	0.004525
18	8	6	0	0.011312	0.011312	18	9	6	1	0.065611	0.061086
18	8	6	1	0.119909	0.108597	18	9	6	2	0.309955	0.244344
18	8	6	2	0.436652	0.316742	18	9	6	3	0.690045	0.380090

The Hypergeometric Probability Distribution (cont.)

N	n	k	x	PX	px	N	n	k	x	PX	px
18	9	6	4	0.934389	0.244344	19	3	3	3	1.000000	0.001032
18	9	6	5	0.995475	0.061086	19	4	1	0	0.789474	0.789474
18	9	6	6	1.000000	0.004525	19	4	1	1	1.000000	0.210526
18	9	7	0	0.001131	0.001131	19	4	2	0	0.614035	0.614035
18	9	7	1	0.024887	0.023756	19	4	2	1	0.964912	0.350877
18	9	7	2	0.167421	0.142534	19	4	2	2	1.000000	0.035088
18	9	7	3	0.500000	0.332579	19	4	3	0	0.469556	0.469556
18	9	7	4	0.832579	0.332579	19	4	3	1	0.902993	0.433437
18	9	7	5	0.975113	0.142534	19	4	3	2	0.995872	0.092879
18	9	7	6	0.998869	0.023756	19	4	3	3	1.000000	0.004128
18	9	7	7	1.000000	0.001131	19	4	4	0	0.352167	0.352167
18	9	8	0	0.000206	0.000206	19	4	4	1	0.821723	0.469556
18	9	8	1	0.007610	0.007404	19	4	4	2	0.984262	0.162539
18	9	8	2	0.076717	0.069107	19	4	4	3	0.999742	0.015480
18	9	8	3	0.318593	0.241876	19	4	4	4	1.000000	0.000258
18	9	8	4	0.681407	0.362814	19	5	1	0	0.736842	0.736842
18	9	8	5	0.923283	0.241876	19	5	1	1	1.000000	0.263158
18	9	8	6	0.992390	0.069107	19	5	2	0	0.532164	0.532164
18	9	8	7	0.999794	0.007404	19	5	2	1	0.941520	0.409357
18	9	8	8	1.000000	0.000206	19	5	2	2	1.000000	0.058480
18	9	9	0	0.000021	0.000021	19	5	3	0	0.375645	0.375645
18	9	9	1	0.001687	0.001666	19	5	3	1	0.845201	0.469556
18	9	9	2	0.028342	0.026656	19	5	3	2	0.989680	0.144479
18	9	9	3	0.173468	0.145125	19	5	3	3	1.000000	0.010320
18	9	9	4	0.500000	0.326532	19	5	4	0	0.258256	0.258256
18	9	9	5	0.826532	0.326532	19	5	4	1	0.727812	0.469556
18	9	9	6	0.971658	0.145125	19	5	4	2	0.962590	0.234778
18	9	9	7	0.998313	0.026656	19	5	4	3	0.998710	0.036120
18	9	9	8	0.999979	0.001666	19	5	4	4	1.000000	0.001290
18	9	9	9	1.000000	0.000021	19	5	5	0	0.172171	0.172171
19	1	1	0	0.947368	0.947368	19	5	5	1	0.602597	0.430427
19	1	1	1	1.000000	0.052632	19	5	5	2	0.915635	0.313037
19	2	1	0	0.894737	0.894737	19	5	5	3	0.993894	0.078259
19	2	1	1	1.000000	0.105263	19	5	5	4	0.999914	0.006020
19	2	2	0	0.795322	0.795322	19	5	5	5	1.000000	0.000086
19	2	2	1	0.994152	0.198830	19	6	1	0	0.684211	0.684211
19	2	2	2	1.000000	0.005848	19	6	1	1	1.000000	0.315789
19	3	1	0	0.842105	0.842105	19	6	2	0	0.456140	0.456140
19	3	1	1	1.000000	0.157895	19	6	2	1	0.912281	0.456140
19	3	2	0	0.701754	0.701754	19	6	2	2	1.000000	0.087719
19	3	2	1	0.982456	0.280702	19	6	3	0	0.295150	0.295150
19	3	2	2	1.000000	0.017544	19	6	3	1	0.778122	0.482972
19	3	3	0	0.577915	0.577915	19	6	3	2	0.979360	0.201238
19	3	3	1	0.949432	0.371517	19	6	3	3	1.000000	0.020640
19	3	3	2	0.998968	0.049536	19	6	4	0	0.184469	0.184469

The Hypergeometric Probability Distribution (cont.)

N	n	k	x	PX	px	N	n	k	x	PX	px
19	6	4	1	0.627193	0.442724	19	7	7	1	0.144082	0.128364
19	6	4	2	0.929050	0.301858	19	7	7	2	0.474160	0.330079
19	6	4	3	0.996130	0.067079	19	7	7	3	0.817992	0.343832
19	6	4	4	1.000000	0.003870	19	7	7	4	0.970806	0.152814
19	6	5	0	0.110681	0.110681	19	7	7	5	0.998313	0.027507
19	6	5	1	0.479618	0.368937	19	7	7	6	0.999980	0.001667
19	6	5	2	0.848555	0.368937	19	7	7	7	1.000000	0.000020
19	6	5	3	0.982714	0.134159	19	8	1	0	0.578947	0.578947
19	6	5	4	0.999484	0.016770	19	8	1	1	1.000000	0.421053
19	6	5	5	1.000000	0.000516	19	8	2	0	0.321637	0.321637
19	6	6	0	0.063246	0.063246	19	8	2	1	0.836257	0.514620
19	6	6	1	0.347855	0.284609	19	8	2	2	1.000000	0.163743
19	6	6	2	0.743145	0.395290	19	8	3	0	0.170279	0.170279
19	6	6	3	0.953966	0.210821	19	8	3	1	0.624355	0.454076
19	6	6	4	0.997088	0.043123	19	8	3	2	0.942208	0.317853
19	6	6	5	0.999963	0.002875	19	8	3	3	1.000000	0.057792
19	6	6	6	1.000000	0.000037	19	8	4	0	0.085139	0.085139
19	7	1	0	0.631579	0.631579	19	8	4	1	0.425697	0.340557
19	7	1	1	1.000000	0.368421	19	8	4	2	0.823013	0.397317
19	7	2	0	0.385965	0.385965	19	8	4	3	0.981940	0.158927
19	7	2	1	0.877193	0.491228	19	8	4	4	1.000000	0.018060
19	7	2	2	1.000000	0.122807	19	8	5	0	0.039732	0.039732
19	7	3	0	0.227038	0.227038	19	8	5	1	0.266770	0.227038
19	7	3	1	0.703818	0.476780	19	8	5	2	0.664087	0.397317
19	7	3	2	0.963880	0.260062	19	8	5	3	0.928965	0.264878
19	7	3	3	1.000000	0.036120	19	8	5	4	0.995184	0.066219
19	7	4	0	0.127709	0.127709	19	8	5	5	1.000000	0.004816
19	7	4	1	0.525026	0.397317	19	8	6	0	0.017028	0.017028
19	7	4	2	0.882611	0.357585	19	8	6	1	0.153251	0.136223
19	7	4	3	0.990970	0.108359	19	8	6	2	0.493808	0.340557
19	7	4	4	1.000000	0.009030	19	8	6	3	0.834365	0.340557
19	7	5	0	0.068111	0.068111	19	8	6	4	0.976264	0.141899
19	7	5	1	0.366099	0.297988	19	8	6	5	0.998968	0.022704
19	7	5	2	0.763416	0.397317	19	8	6	6	1.000000	0.001032
19	7	5	3	0.962074	0.198658	19	8	7	0	0.006549	0.006549
19	7	5	4	0.998194	0.036120	19	8	7	1	0.079900	0.073351
19	7	5	5	1.000000	0.001806	19	8	7	2	0.336628	0.256728
19	7	6	0	0.034056	0.034056	19	8	7	3	0.703382	0.366754
19	7	6	1	0.238390	0.204334	19	8	7	4	0.932603	0.229221
19	7	6	2	0.621517	0.383127	19	8	7	5	0.993729	0.061126
19	7	6	3	0.905315	0.283798	19	8	7	6	0.999841	0.006113
19	7	6	4	0.990454	0.085139	19	8	7	7	1.000000	0.000159
19	7	6	5	0.999742	0.009288	19	8	8	0	0.002183	0.002183
19	7	6	6	1.000000	0.000258	19	8	8	1	0.037112	0.034929
19	7	7	0	0.015718	0.015718	19	8	8	2	0.208264	0.171152

The Hypergeometric Probability Distribution (cont.)

N	n	k	x	PX	px	N	n	k	x	PX	px
19	8	8	3	0.550568	0.342304	19	9	8	4	0.745058	0.350083
19	8	8	4	0.856196	0.305628	19	9	8	5	0.945106	0.200048
19	8	8	5	0.978447	0.122251	19	9	8	6	0.995118	0.050012
19	8	8	6	0.998823	0.020375	19	9	8	7	0.999881	0.004763
19	8	8	7	0.999987	0.001164	19	9	8	8	1.000000	0.000119
19	8	8	8	1.000000	0.000013	19	9	9	0	0.000108	0.000108
19	9	1	0	0.526316	0.526316	19	9	9	1	0.004492	0.004384
19	9	1	1	1.000000	0.473684	19	9	9	2	0.051257	0.046764
19	9	2	0	0.263158	0.263158	19	9	9	3	0.242211	0.190954
19	9	2	1	0.789474	0.526316	19	9	9	4	0.585929	0.343718
19	9	2	2	1.000000	0.210526	19	9	9	5	0.872361	0.286432
19	9	3	0	0.123839	0.123839	19	9	9	6	0.981478	0.109117
19	9	3	1	0.541796	0.417957	19	9	9	7	0.999015	0.017537
19	9	3	2	0.913313	0.371517	19	9	9	8	0.999989	0.000974
19	9	3	3	1.000000	0.086687	19	9	9	9	1.000000	0.000011
19	9	4	0	0.054180	0.054180	20	1	1	0	0.950000	0.950000
19	9	4	1	0.332817	0.278638	20	1	1	1	1.000000	0.050000
19	9	4	2	0.750774	0.417957	20	2	1	0	0.900000	0.900000
19	9	4	3	0.967492	0.216718	20	2	1	1	1.000000	0.100000
19	9	4	4	1.000000	0.032508	20	2	2	0	0.805263	0.805263
19	9	5	0	0.021672	0.021672	20	2	2	1	0.994737	0.189474
19	9	5	1	0.184210	0.162539	20	2	2	2	1.000000	0.005263
19	9	5	2	0.555727	0.371517	20	3	1	0	0.850000	0.850000
19	9	5	3	0.880805	0.325077	20	3	1	1	1.000000	0.150000
19	9	5	4	0.989164	0.108359	20	3	2	0	0.715789	0.715789
19	9	5	5	1.000000	0.010836	20	3	2	1	0.984211	0.268421
19	9	6	0	0.007740	0.007740	20	3	2	2	1.000000	0.015789
19	9	6	1	0.091331	0.083591	20	3	3	0	0.596491	0.596491
19	9	6	2	0.369969	0.278638	20	3	3	1	0.954386	0.357895
19	9	6	3	0.741486	0.371517	20	3	3	2	0.999123	0.044737
19	9	6	4	0.950464	0.208978	20	3	3	3	1.000000	0.000877
19	9	6	5	0.996904	0.046440	20	4	1	0	0.800000	0.800000
19	9	6	6	1.000000	0.003096	20	4	1	1	1.000000	0.200000
19	9	7	0	0.002382	0.002382	20	4	2	0	0.631579	0.631579
19	9	7	1	0.039890	0.037509	20	4	2	1	0.968421	0.336842
19	9	7	2	0.219933	0.180043	20	4	2	2	1.000000	0.031579
19	9	7	3	0.570017	0.350083	20	4	3	0	0.491228	0.491228
19	9	7	4	0.870088	0.300071	20	4	3	1	0.912281	0.421053
19	9	7	5	0.982615	0.112527	20	4	3	2	0.996491	0.084211
19	9	7	6	0.999285	0.016671	20	4	3	3	1.000000	0.003509
19	9	7	7	1.000000	0.000714	20	4	4	0	0.375645	0.375645
19	9	8	0	0.000595	0.000595	20	4	4	1	0.837977	0.462332
19	9	8	1	0.014884	0.014289	20	4	4	2	0.986584	0.148607
19	9	8	2	0.114908	0.100024	20	4	4	3	0.999793	0.013209
19	9	8	3	0.394975	0.280067	20	4	4	4	1.000000	0.000206

The Hypergeometric Probability Distribution (*cont.*)

N	n	k	x	PX	px	N	n	k	x	PX	px
20	5	1	0	0.750000	0.750000	20	6	6	5	0.999974	0.002167
20	5	1	1	1.000000	0.250000	20	6	6	6	1.000000	0.000026
20	5	2	0	0.552632	0.552632	20	7	1	0	0.650000	0.650000
20	5	2	1	0.947368	0.394737	20	7	1	1	1.000000	0.350000
20	5	2	2	1.000000	0.052632	20	7	2	0	0.410526	0.410526
20	5	3	0	0.399123	0.399123	20	7	2	1	0.889474	0.478947
20	5	3	1	0.859649	0.460526	20	7	2	2	1.000000	0.110526
20	5	3	2	0.991228	0.131579	20	7	3	0	0.250877	0.250877
20	5	3	3	1.000000	0.008772	20	7	3	1	0.729825	0.478947
20	5	4	0	0.281734	0.281734	20	7	3	2	0.969298	0.239474
20	5	4	1	0.751290	0.469556	20	7	3	3	1.000000	0.030702
20	5	4	2	0.968008	0.216718	20	7	4	0	0.147575	0.147575
20	5	4	3	0.998968	0.030960	20	7	4	1	0.560784	0.413209
20	5	4	4	1.000000	0.001032	20	7	4	2	0.898865	0.338080
20	5	5	0	0.193692	0.193692	20	7	4	3	0.992776	0.093911
20	5	5	1	0.633901	0.440209	20	7	4	4	1.000000	0.007224
20	5	5	2	0.927374	0.293473	20	7	5	0	0.083011	0.083011
20	5	5	3	0.995098	0.067724	20	7	5	1	0.405831	0.322820
20	5	5	4	0.999935	0.004837	20	7	5	2	0.793215	0.387384
20	5	5	5	1.000000	0.000064	20	7	5	3	0.969298	0.176084
20	6	1	0	0.700000	0.700000	20	7	5	4	0.998645	0.029347
20	6	1	1	1.000000	0.300000	20	7	5	5	1.000000	0.001354
20	6	2	0	0.478947	0.478947	20	7	6	0	0.044272	0.044272
20	6	2	1	0.921053	0.442105	20	7	6	1	0.276703	0.232430
20	6	2	2	1.000000	0.078947	20	7	6	2	0.664087	0.387384
20	6	3	0	0.319298	0.319298	20	7	6	3	0.922343	0.258256
20	6	3	1	0.798246	0.478947	20	7	6	4	0.992776	0.070433
20	6	3	2	0.982456	0.184211	20	7	6	5	0.999819	0.007043
20	6	3	3	1.000000	0.017544	20	7	6	6	1.000000	0.000181
20	6	4	0	0.206605	0.206605	20	7	7	0	0.022136	0.022136
20	6	4	1	0.657379	0.450774	20	7	7	1	0.177090	0.154954
20	6	4	2	0.939112	0.281734	20	7	7	2	0.525735	0.348645
20	6	4	3	0.996904	0.057792	20	7	7	3	0.848555	0.322820
20	6	4	4	1.000000	0.003096	20	7	7	4	0.977683	0.129128
20	6	5	0	0.129128	0.129128	20	7	7	5	0.998813	0.021130
20	6	5	1	0.516512	0.387384	20	7	7	6	0.999987	0.001174
20	6	5	2	0.868679	0.352167	20	7	7	7	1.000000	0.000013
20	6	5	3	0.986068	0.117389	20	8	1	0	0.600000	0.600000
20	6	5	4	0.999613	0.013545	20	8	1	1	1.000000	0.400000
20	6	5	5	1.000000	0.000387	20	8	2	0	0.347368	0.347368
20	6	6	0	0.077477	0.077477	20	8	2	1	0.852632	0.505263
20	6	6	1	0.387384	0.309907	20	8	2	2	1.000000	0.147368
20	6	6	2	0.774768	0.387384	20	8	3	0	0.192982	0.192982
20	6	6	3	0.962590	0.187822	20	8	3	1	0.656140	0.463158
20	6	6	4	0.997807	0.035217	20	8	3	2	0.950877	0.294737

The Hypergeometric Probability Distribution (*cont.*)

N	n	k	x	PX	px	N	n	k	x	PX	px
20	8	3	3	1.000000	0.049123	20	9	4	0	0.068111	0.068111
20	8	4	0	0.102167	0.102167	20	9	4	1	0.374613	0.306502
20	8	4	1	0.465428	0.363261	20	9	4	2	0.783282	0.408669
20	8	4	2	0.846852	0.381424	20	9	4	3	0.973994	0.190712
20	8	4	3	0.985552	0.138700	20	9	4	4	1.000000	0.026006
20	8	4	4	1.000000	0.014448	20	9	5	0	0.029799	0.029799
20	8	5	0	0.051084	0.051084	20	9	5	1	0.221362	0.191563
20	8	5	1	0.306502	0.255418	20	9	5	2	0.604489	0.383127
20	8	5	2	0.703818	0.397317	20	9	5	3	0.902477	0.297988
20	8	5	3	0.942208	0.238390	20	9	5	4	0.991873	0.089396
20	8	5	4	0.996388	0.054180	20	9	5	5	1.000000	0.008127
20	8	5	5	1.000000	0.003612	20	9	6	0	0.011919	0.011919
20	8	6	0	0.023839	0.023839	20	9	6	1	0.119195	0.107276
20	8	6	1	0.187307	0.163468	20	9	6	2	0.425697	0.306502
20	8	6	2	0.544892	0.357585	20	9	6	3	0.783282	0.357585
20	8	6	3	0.862745	0.317853	20	9	6	4	0.962074	0.178793
20	8	6	4	0.981940	0.119195	20	9	6	5	0.997833	0.035759
20	8	6	5	0.999278	0.017337	20	9	6	6	1.000000	0.002167
20	8	6	6	1.000000	0.000722	20	9	7	0	0.004257	0.004257
20	8	7	0	0.010217	0.010217	20	9	7	1	0.057895	0.053638
20	8	7	1	0.105573	0.095356	20	9	7	2	0.272446	0.214551
20	8	7	2	0.391641	0.286068	20	9	7	3	0.630031	0.357585
20	8	7	3	0.749226	0.357585	20	9	7	4	0.898220	0.268189
20	8	7	4	0.947885	0.198658	20	9	7	5	0.987616	0.089396
20	8	7	5	0.995563	0.047678	20	9	7	6	0.999536	0.011919
20	8	7	6	0.999897	0.004334	20	9	7	7	1.000000	0.000464
20	8	7	7	1.000000	0.000103	20	9	8	0	0.001310	0.001310
20	8	8	0	0.003930	0.003930	20	9	8	1	0.024887	0.023577
20	8	8	1	0.054227	0.050298	20	9	8	2	0.156918	0.132031
20	8	8	2	0.259610	0.205382	20	9	8	3	0.464992	0.308073
20	8	8	3	0.611694	0.352084	20	9	8	4	0.795071	0.330079
20	8	8	4	0.886759	0.275066	20	9	8	5	0.960110	0.165039
20	8	8	5	0.984560	0.097801	20	9	8	6	0.996785	0.036675
20	8	8	6	0.999231	0.014670	20	9	8	7	0.999929	0.003144
20	8	8	7	0.999993	0.000762	20	9	8	8	1.000000	0.000071
20	8	8	8	1.000001	0.000008	20	9	9	0	0.000327	0.000327
20	9	1	0	0.550000	0.550000	20	9	9	1	0.009169	0.008841
20	9	1	1	1.000000	0.450000	20	9	9	2	0.079900	0.070731
20	9	2	0	0.289474	0.289474	20	9	9	3	0.310955	0.231055
20	9	2	1	0.810526	0.521053	20	9	9	4	0.657538	0.346583
20	9	2	2	1.000000	0.189474	20	9	9	5	0.905097	0.247559
20	9	3	0	0.144737	0.144737	20	9	9	6	0.987616	0.082520
20	9	3	1	0.578947	0.434211	20	9	9	7	0.999405	0.011789
20	9	3	2	0.926316	0.347368	20	9	9	8	0.999994	0.000589
20	9	3	3	1.000000	0.073684	20	9	9	9	1.000000	0.000006

The Hypergeometric Probability Distribution (*cont.*)

N	n	k	x	PX	px	N	n	k	x	PX	px
20	10	1	0	0.500000	0.500000	20	10	9	1	0.002739	0.002679
20	10	1	1	1.000000	0.500000	20	10	9	2	0.034889	0.032150
20	10	2	0	0.236842	0.236842	20	10	9	3	0.184925	0.150036
20	10	2	1	0.763158	0.526316	20	10	9	4	0.500000	0.315075
20	10	2	2	1.000000	0.236842	20	10	9	5	0.815075	0.315075
20	10	3	0	0.105263	0.105263	20	10	9	6	0.965111	0.150036
20	10	3	1	0.500000	0.394737	20	10	9	7	0.997261	0.032150
20	10	3	2	0.894737	0.394737	20	10	9	8	0.999940	0.002679
20	10	3	3	1.000000	0.105263	20	10	9	9	1.000000	0.000060
20	10	4	0	0.043344	0.043344	20	10	10	0	0.000005	0.000005
20	10	4	1	0.291022	0.247678	20	10	10	1	0.000547	0.000541
20	10	4	2	0.708978	0.417957	20	10	10	2	0.011507	0.010960
20	10	4	3	0.956656	0.247678	20	10	10	3	0.089448	0.077941
20	10	4	4	1.000000	0.043344	20	10	10	4	0.328141	0.238693
20	10	5	0	0.016254	0.016254	20	10	10	5	0.671859	0.343718
20	10	5	1	0.151703	0.135449	20	10	10	6	0.910552	0.238693
20	10	5	2	0.500000	0.348297	20	10	10	7	0.988493	0.077941
20	10	5	3	0.848297	0.348297	20	10	10	8	0.999453	0.010960
20	10	5	4	0.983746	0.135449	20	10	10	9	0.999995	0.000541
20	10	5	5	1.000000	0.016254	20	10	10	10	1.000000	0.000005
20	10	6	0	0.005418	0.005418	21	1	1	0	0.952381	0.952381
20	10	6	1	0.070433	0.065015	21	1	1	1	1.000000	0.047619
20	10	6	2	0.314242	0.243808	21	2	1	0	0.904762	0.904762
20	10	6	3	0.685759	0.371517	21	2	1	1	1.000000	0.095238
20	10	6	4	0.929567	0.243808	21	2	2	0	0.814286	0.814286
20	10	6	5	0.994582	0.065015	21	2	2	1	0.995238	0.180952
20	10	6	6	1.000000	0.005418	21	2	2	2	1.000000	0.004762
20	10	7	0	0.001548	0.001548	21	3	1	0	0.857143	0.857143
20	10	7	1	0.028638	0.027090	21	3	1	1	1.000000	0.142857
20	10	7	2	0.174923	0.146285	21	3	2	0	0.728571	0.728571
20	10	7	3	0.500000	0.325077	21	3	2	1	0.985714	0.257143
20	10	7	4	0.825077	0.325077	21	3	2	2	1.000000	0.014286
20	10	7	5	0.971362	0.146285	21	3	3	0	0.613534	0.613534
20	10	7	6	0.998452	0.027090	21	3	3	1	0.958647	0.345113
20	10	7	7	1.000000	0.001548	21	3	3	2	0.999248	0.040601
20	10	8	0	0.000357	0.000357	21	3	3	3	1.000000	0.000752
20	10	8	1	0.009883	0.009526	21	4	1	0	0.809524	0.809524
20	10	8	2	0.084901	0.075018	21	4	1	1	1.000000	0.190476
20	10	8	3	0.324958	0.240057	21	4	2	0	0.647619	0.647619
20	10	8	4	0.675042	0.350083	21	4	2	1	0.971429	0.323809
20	10	8	5	0.915099	0.240057	21	4	2	2	1.000000	0.028571
20	10	8	6	0.990117	0.075018	21	4	3	0	0.511278	0.511278
20	10	8	7	0.999643	0.009526	21	4	3	1	0.920301	0.409023
20	10	8	8	1.000000	0.000357	21	4	3	2	0.996992	0.076692
20	10	9	0	0.000060	0.000060	21	4	3	3	1.000000	0.003008

The Hypergeometric Probability Distribution (cont.)

N	n	k	x	PX	px	N	n	k	x	PX	px
21	4	4	0	0.397661	0.397661	21	6	6	0	0.092234	0.092234
21	4	4	1	0.852130	0.454469	21	6	6	1	0.424278	0.332043
21	4	4	2	0.988471	0.136341	21	6	6	2	0.801600	0.377322
21	4	4	3	0.999833	0.011362	21	6	6	3	0.969298	0.167699
21	4	4	4	1.000000	0.000167	21	6	6	4	0.998323	0.029025
21	5	1	0	0.761905	0.761905	21	6	6	5	0.999982	0.001659
21	5	1	1	1.000000	0.238095	21	6	6	6	1.000000	0.000018
21	5	2	0	0.571429	0.571429	21	7	1	0	0.666667	0.666667
21	5	2	1	0.952381	0.380952	21	7	1	1	1.000000	0.333333
21	5	2	2	1.000000	0.047619	21	7	2	0	0.433333	0.433333
21	5	3	0	0.421053	0.421053	21	7	2	1	0.900000	0.466667
21	5	3	1	0.872180	0.451128	21	7	2	2	1.000000	0.100000
21	5	3	2	0.992481	0.120301	21	7	3	0	0.273684	0.273684
21	5	3	3	1.000000	0.007519	21	7	3	1	0.752632	0.478947
21	5	4	0	0.304094	0.304094	21	7	3	2	0.973684	0.221053
21	5	4	1	0.771930	0.467836	21	7	3	3	1.000000	0.026316
21	5	4	2	0.972431	0.200501	21	7	4	0	0.167251	0.167251
21	5	4	3	0.999164	0.026733	21	7	4	1	0.592982	0.425731
21	5	4	4	1.000000	0.000835	21	7	4	2	0.912281	0.319298
21	5	5	0	0.214654	0.214654	21	7	4	3	0.994152	0.081871
21	5	5	1	0.661851	0.447196	21	7	4	4	1.000000	0.005848
21	5	5	2	0.937049	0.275198	21	7	5	0	0.098383	0.098383
21	5	5	3	0.996019	0.058971	21	7	5	1	0.442724	0.344341
21	5	5	4	0.999951	0.003931	21	7	5	2	0.818369	0.375645
21	5	5	5	1.000000	0.000049	21	7	5	3	0.974888	0.156519
21	6	1	0	0.714286	0.714286	21	7	5	4	0.998968	0.024080
21	6	1	1	1.000000	0.285714	21	7	5	5	1.000000	0.001032
21	6	2	0	0.500000	0.500000	21	7	6	0	0.055341	0.055341
21	6	2	1	0.928571	0.428571	21	7	6	1	0.313596	0.258256
21	6	2	2	1.000000	0.071429	21	7	6	2	0.700980	0.387384
21	6	3	0	0.342105	0.342105	21	7	6	3	0.935758	0.234778
21	6	3	1	0.815790	0.473684	21	7	6	4	0.994453	0.058695
21	6	3	2	0.984962	0.169173	21	7	6	5	0.999871	0.005418
21	6	3	3	1.000000	0.015038	21	7	6	6	1.000000	0.000129
21	6	4	0	0.228070	0.228070	21	7	7	0	0.029515	0.029515
21	6	4	1	0.684210	0.456140	21	7	7	1	0.210294	0.180779
21	6	4	2	0.947368	0.263158	21	7	7	2	0.571852	0.361558
21	6	4	3	0.997494	0.050125	21	7	7	3	0.873151	0.301299
21	6	4	4	1.000000	0.002506	21	7	7	4	0.982714	0.109563
21	6	5	0	0.147575	0.147575	21	7	7	5	0.999149	0.016434
21	6	5	1	0.550052	0.402477	21	7	7	6	0.999991	0.000843
21	6	5	2	0.885449	0.335397	21	7	7	7	1.000000	0.000009
21	6	5	3	0.988648	0.103199	21	8	1	0	0.619048	0.619048
21	6	5	4	0.999705	0.011057	21	8	1	1	1.000000	0.380952
21	6	5	5	1.000000	0.000295	21	8	2	0	0.371429	0.371429

18.2 Critical Values for Testing Two-by-Two Tables

The quantities tabulated here are critical values for another special case of the hypergeometric probability distribution, i.e., maximum values of N' such that for all $N \leq N'$,

$$P(N, n, k, x) \leq 0.05, 0.025, 0.01, \text{ or } 0.005,$$

for $x = 0(1)7$. There is some overlap between these tables and the tables in Sections 18.4 and 18.5.

These tables were designed to test two-by-two contingency tables, which may be represented as follows:

Characteristic II	Characteristic I		Totals
	Has	Does not have	
Has	x	$k - x$	k
Does not have	$n - x$	$N - n - k + x$	$N - k$
Totals	n	$N - n$	N

When it is desired to test the equality of two proportions, the available data may be displayed in this manner. For example, suppose a sample of 20 is taken from the product of the manufacturer presently employed, and 4 defective items are found. A new manufacturer's product is sampled and found to have only 3 defective items out of 25 sampled. On the basis of these samples, is the new manufacturer's product significantly better than the present manufacturer's? In two-by-two table form this is:

Product	Manufacturer		Totals
	Present	New	
Defective	4	3	7
Nondefective	16	22	38
Totals	20	25	45

A preliminary test must be made to be sure that the sample proportion nondefective of the new manufacturer is better than the proportion nondefective for the present manufacturer. Here $\frac{22}{25} > \frac{16}{20}$, and hence, the new manufacturer is better in this sample. However, is this significantly better statistically (at the 5-percent level, say)? That is, is the hypothesis accepted or rejected that the proportions of nondefective items produced by the two manufacturers are the same? Let x = smallest value in the two-by-two table = 3, and $k - x$ = next smallest value lined up with x properly = 4; then the other values are determined. Hence, $x = 3$, $k = 7$, $n = 25$, and $N = 45$. Enter the 5-percent table $P(N, n, k, 3) \leq 0.05$, with $n = 25$ and $k = 7$. The value of N read from the table of critical values is 33. Since this value is less than the 45 total showing in the two-by-two table, the hypothesis that there is no difference between the manufacturers is accepted. The hypothesis is rejected only if the N from the table of critical values equals or exceeds the N from the two-by-two table. For a two-sided test, no preliminary consideration of the proportions is necessary, and the significance level is double that recorded. Other tables giving significance values for two-by-two tables have been given by Finney [64], Latscha [114], Armsen [9], Mainland and Murray [130], and many others. Bennett and Hsu [17] and Pearson and Merrington [173] consider the power of the above test. Section 18.3 gives sample sizes to attain certain power values.

Critical Values for Testing Two-by-Two Tables
Values of N' such that for N's Less than or Equal to N'

$$P(N,n,k,0) \le 0.05$$

n	1	2	3	4	5	6	7	8	9	10	11
1											
2											
3			6								
4			7	9							
5		7	9	11	13						
6		8	10	13	15	18					
7		9	12	14	17	20	23				
8		10	13	16	19	23	26	29			
9		12	15	18	22	25	29	32	36		
10		13	16	20	24	28	31	35	39	43	
11		14	18	22	26	30	34	38	43	47	51
12		16	20	24	28	33	37	42	46	51	54
13		17	21	26	30	35	40	45	50	54	59
14		18	23	28	33	38	43	48	53	58	
15		19	24	30	35	40	46	51	57		
16		21	26	31	37	43	49	54			
17		22	27	33	39	45	51	58			
18		23	29	35	42	48	54				
19	20	25	31	37	44	50	57				
20	21	26	32	39	46	53					

$$P(N,n,k,1) \le 0.05$$

n	3	4	5	6	7	8	9	10	11	12	13
1											
2											
3											
4											
5			9								
6		9	10	12							
7		10	12	13	15						
8		11	13	15	17	19					
9		12	15	17	19	21	24				
10	12	14	16	19	21	23	26	28			
11	13	15	18	20	23	26	28	31	34		
12	14	16	19	22	25	28	31	33	36	39	
13	15	18	21	24	27	30	33	36	39	42	45
14	16	19	22	25	29	32	35	38	42	45	48
15	17	20	24	27	30	34	37	41	45	48	
16	18	22	25	29	32	36	40	44	47		
17	20	23	27	30	34	38	42	46			
18	21	24	28	32	36	40	44	49			
19	22	26	30	34	38	42	47				
20	23	27	31	36	40	45	49				

18.2

Critical Values for Testing Two-by-Two Tables
Values of N' such that for N's Less than or Equal to N' (cont.)

$$P(N, n, k, 2) \leq 0.05$$

n	4	5	6	7	8	9	10	11	12	13	14
6											
7			11	12							
8			12	13	15						
9		12	13	15	17	18					
10		13	15	16	18	20	22				
11		14	16	18	20	22	24	26			
12		15	17	19	22	24	26	28	31		
13		16	19	21	23	26	28	30	33	35	
14	16	18	20	22	25	27	30	32	35	38	40
15	17	19	21	24	27	29	32	35	37	40	43
16	18	20	23	25	28	31	34	37	40	42	45
17	19	21	24	27	30	33	36	39	42	45	48
18	20	23	25	28	32	35	38	41	44	47	
19	21	24	27	30	33	36	40	43	46		
20	22	25	28	31	35	38	42	45	49		
21	23	26	30	33	36	40	44	47			
22	24	27	31	34	38	42	46	49			
23	25	29	32	36	40	44	48				
24	27	30	34	38	41	45					
25	28	31	35	39	43	47					

$$P(N, n, k, 3) \leq 0.05$$

n	5	6	7	8	9	10	11	12	13	14	15
6											
7											
8				13							
9			13	14	15						
10			14	15	17	18					
11			15	17	18	20	22				
12		15	16	18	20	22	24	25			
13		16	18	19	21	23	25	27	29		
14		17	19	21	23	25	27	29	31	33	
15		18	20	22	24	27	29	31	33	35	38
16		19	21	24	26	28	30	33	35	38	40
17		20	23	25	27	30	32	35	37	40	42
18		22	24	26	29	31	34	37	39	42	44
19	21	23	25	28	30	33	36	38	41	44	47
20	22	24	27	29	32	35	38	40	43	46	49
21	23	25	28	31	33	36	39	42	45	48	
22	24	26	29	32	35	38	41	44	47		
23	25	27	30	33	36	40	43	46	49		
24	26	29	32	35	38	41	45	48			
25	27	30	33	36	40	43	46				

Critical Values for Testing Two-by-Two Tables
Values of N' such that for N's Less than or Equal to N' (cont.)

$P(N,n,k,4) \le 0.05$

n	6	7	8	9	10	11	12	13	14	15	16
6											
7											
8											
9											
10				15	16						
11				16	17	19					
12			16	17	19	20	22				
13			17	19	20	22	24	25			
14			18	20	22	23	25	27	29		
15		18	19	21	23	25	27	29	31	32	
16		19	21	22	24	26	28	30	32	34	36
17		20	22	24	26	28	30	32	34	36	38
18		21	23	25	27	29	32	34	36	38	40
19		22	24	26	29	31	33	36	38	40	42
20		23	25	28	30	32	35	37	40	42	45
21		24	27	29	31	34	36	39	41	44	47
22		26	28	30	33	35	38	41	43	46	49
23	25	27	29	32	34	37	40	42	45	48	
24	26	28	30	33	36	39	41	44	47		
25	27	29	32	34	37	40	43	46	49		

$P(N,n,k,5) \le 0.05$

n	7	8	9	10	11	12	13	14	15	16	17
11					17						
12				17	18	19					
13				18	19	21	22				
14			18	19	21	22	24	25			
15			19	20	22	24	25	27	29		
16			20	22	23	25	27	29	30	32	
17		20	21	23	25	27	28	30	32	34	36
18		21	22	24	26	28	30	32	34	36	38
19		22	24	25	27	29	31	33	35	38	40
20		23	25	27	29	31	33	35	37	39	41
21		24	26	28	30	32	34	37	39	41	43
22		25	27	29	31	34	36	38	41	43	45
23		26	28	31	33	35	38	40	42	45	47
24		27	30	32	34	37	39	42	44	47	49
25		28	31	33	36	38	41	43	46	48	
26		30	32	34	37	40	42	45	47		
27		31	33	36	38	41	44	46	49		
28	30	32	34	37	40	42	45	48			
29	31	33	36	38	41	44	47				
30	32	34	37	40	42	45	48				

Critical Values for Testing Two-by-Two Tables
Values of N' such that for N's Less than or Equal to N' (cont.)

$$P(N,n,k,6) \leq 0.05$$

n	9	10	11	12	13	14	15	16	17	18	19
11											
12				18							
13				19	20						
14			19	20	21	23					
15			20	21	23	24	26				
16		20	21	23	24	26	27	29			
17		21	23	24	26	27	29	31	32		
18		22	24	25	27	29	30	32	34	36	
19		23	25	27	28	30	32	34	36	37	39
20	23	24	26	28	30	32	33	35	37	39	41
21	24	25	27	29	31	33	35	37	39	41	43
22	25	27	28	30	32	34	37	39	41	43	45
23	26	28	30	32	34	36	38	40	42	45	47
24	27	29	31	33	35	37	40	42	44	46	49
25	28	30	32	34	37	39	41	43	46	48	
26	29	31	33	36	38	40	43	45	47		
27	30	32	35	37	39	42	44	47	49		
28	31	34	36	38	41	43	46	48			
29	32	35	37	40	42	45	47				
30	34	36	38	41	44	46	49				

$$P(N,n,k,7) \leq 0.05$$

n	10	11	12	13	14	15	16	17	18	19	20
11											
12											
13											
14				20	21						
15				21	22	24					
16			21	22	23	25	26				
17			22	23	25	26	28	29			
18		22	23	25	26	28	29	31	32		
19		23	24	26	27	29	31	32	34	35	
20		24	25	27	29	30	32	34	36	37	39
21		25	27	28	30	32	34	35	37	39	41
22		26	28	30	31	33	35	37	39	41	43
23	26	27	29	31	33	35	37	39	41	42	44
24	27	28	30	32	34	36	38	40	42	44	46
25	28	30	31	33	35	38	40	42	44	46	48
26	29	31	33	35	37	39	41	43	45	48	
27	30	32	34	36	38	40	43	45	47	49	
28	31	33	35	37	40	42	44	46	49		
29	32	34	36	39	41	43	46	48			
30	33	35	38	40	42	45	47	49			

18.2

Critical Values for Testing Two-by-Two Tables
Values of N' such that for N's Less than or Equal to N' (cont.)

$P(N,n,k,0) \leq 0.025$

n	1	2	3	4	5	6	7	8	9	10	11
1											
2											
3											
4				8							
5			8	10	11						
6			9	11	13	15					
7			11	13	15	18	20				
8		10	12	14	17	20	22	25			
9		11	13	16	19	22	25	28	31		
10		12	15	18	21	24	27	30	34	37	
11		13	16	19	23	26	30	33	36	40	43
12		14	18	21	25	28	32	36	39	43	47
13		16	19	23	27	30	34	38	42	46	
14		17	20	24	28	33	37	41	45		
15		18	22	26	30	35	39	44	48		
16		19	23	28	32	37	42	46			
17		20	25	29	34	39	44	49			
18		21	26	31	36	41	47				
19		23	27	33	38	43	49				
20		24	29	34	40	46					

$P(N,n,k,1) \leq 0.025$

n	3	4	5	6	7	8	9	10	11	12	13
6			10	11							
7			11	12	14						
8		11	12	14	16	18					
9		12	14	16	18	20	22				
10		13	15	17	19	21	24	26			
11		14	16	19	21	23	26	28	30		
12		15	18	20	23	25	28	30	33	35	
13		17	19	22	24	27	30	32	35	38	41
14	16	18	20	23	26	29	32	35	38	40	43
15	17	19	22	25	28	31	34	37	40	43	46
16	18	20	23	26	29	33	36	39	42	46	49
17	19	22	25	28	31	35	38	41	45	48	
18	20	23	26	29	33	36	40	44	47		
19	21	24	27	31	35	38	42	46			
20	22	25	29	33	36	40	44	48			
21	23	27	30	34	38	42	46				
22	24	28	32	36	40	44	48				
23	25	29	33	37	42	46					
24	27	30	34	39	43	48					
25	28	31	36	40	45						

Critical Values for Testing Two-by-Two Tables
Values of N' such that for N's Less than or Equal to N' (cont.)

$$P(N, n, k, 2) \leq 0.025$$

n	4	5	6	7	8	9	10	11	12	13	14
6											
7											
8				13	14						
9			13	14	16	17					
10			14	16	17	19	21				
11			15	17	19	21	22	24			
12		15	16	18	20	22	24	26	28		
13		16	18	20	22	24	26	28	30	32	
14		17	19	21	23	25	28	30	32	34	37
15		18	20	22	25	27	29	32	34	37	39
16		19	21	24	26	29	31	34	36	39	41
17		20	23	25	28	30	33	36	38	41	44
18		22	24	27	29	32	35	38	40	43	46
19		23	25	28	31	34	37	40	42	45	48
20		24	27	29	32	35	38	41	45	48	
21	23	25	28	31	34	37	40	43	47		
22	24	26	29	32	35	39	42	45	49		
23	25	27	30	34	37	40	44	47			
24	26	29	32	35	38	42	46	49			
25	27	30	33	36	40	44	47				

$$P(N, n, k, 3) \leq 0.025$$

n	6	7	8	9	10	11	12	13	14	15	16
6											
7											
8											
9				15							
10			15	16	18						
11			16	18	19	21					
12		16	17	19	21	22	24				
13		17	19	20	22	24	26	27			
14		18	20	22	24	25	27	29	31		
15	18	19	21	23	25	27	29	31	33	35	
16	19	20	22	24	27	29	31	33	35	37	39
17	20	22	24	26	28	30	32	35	37	39	41
18	21	23	25	27	30	32	34	37	39	41	44
19	22	24	26	29	31	34	36	38	41	43	46
20	23	25	28	30	33	35	38	40	43	45	48
21	24	27	29	32	34	37	39	42	45	47	
22	25	28	30	33	36	38	41	44	47	49	
23	27	29	32	34	37	40	43	46	49		
24	28	30	33	36	39	42	45	48			
25	29	31	34	37	40	43	46	49			

Critical Values for Testing Two-by-Two Tables
Values of N' such that for N's Less than or Equal to N' (cont.)

$$P(N,n,k,4) \leq 0.025$$

n	7	8	9	10	11	12	13	14	15	16	17
11				17	18						
12			17	18	20	21					
13			18	19	21	22	24				
14		18	19	21	22	24	26	27			
15		19	20	22	24	25	27	29	31		
16		20	22	23	25	27	29	31	32	34	
17		21	23	25	27	28	30	32	34	36	38
18		22	24	26	28	30	32	34	36	38	40
19	22	23	25	27	29	31	34	36	38	40	42
20	23	25	27	29	31	33	35	37	40	42	44
21	24	26	28	30	32	35	37	39	41	44	46
22	25	27	29	31	34	36	38	41	43	46	48
23	26	28	30	33	35	38	40	42	45	47	
24	27	29	32	34	37	39	42	44	47	49	
25	28	30	33	35	38	41	43	46	49		
26	29	32	34	37	39	42	45	48			
27	30	33	35	38	41	44	46	49			
28	31	34	37	39	42	45	48				
29	33	35	38	41	44	47					
30	34	36	39	42	45	48					

$$P(N,n,k,5) \leq 0.025$$

n	8	9	10	11	12	13	14	15	16	17	18
11											
12				18	19						
13				19	20	22					
14			19	20	21	23	24				
15			20	21	23	24	26	27			
16			21	23	24	26	27	29	31		
17		21	22	24	25	27	29	31	32	34	
18		22	23	25	27	29	30	32	34	36	38
19		23	25	26	28	30	32	34	36	38	39
20		24	26	28	30	31	33	35	37	39	41
21		25	27	29	31	33	35	37	39	41	43
22	25	26	28	30	32	34	36	39	41	43	45
23	26	27	29	32	34	36	38	40	42	45	47
24	27	29	31	33	35	37	39	42	44	46	49
25	28	30	32	34	36	39	41	43	46	48	
26	29	31	33	35	38	40	43	45	47		
27	30	32	34	37	39	42	44	47	49		
28	31	33	36	38	41	43	46	48			
29	32	34	37	39	42	44	47				
30	33	36	38	41	43	46	49				

Critical Values for Testing Two-by-Two Tables
Values of N' such that for N's Less than or Equal to N' (cont.)

$$P(N,n,k,6) \le 0.025$$

n	9	10	11	12	13	14	15	16	17	18	19
11											
12											
13					20						
14				20	21	22					
15				21	22	24	25				
16			21	22	23	25	26	28			
17			22	23	25	26	28	29	31		
18			23	24	26	28	29	31	32	34	
19		23	24	26	27	29	31	32	34	36	37
20		24	25	27	29	30	32	34	36	37	39
21		25	26	28	30	32	34	35	37	39	41
22		26	28	29	31	33	35	37	39	41	43
23		27	29	31	33	35	36	38	40	42	44
24		28	30	32	34	36	38	40	42	44	46
25		29	31	33	35	37	39	41	44	46	48
26	29	30	32	34	37	39	41	43	45	47	
27	30	32	34	36	38	40	42	45	47	49	
28	31	33	35	37	39	41	44	46	48		
29	32	34	36	38	41	43	45	48			
30	33	35	37	39	42	44	47	49			

$$P(N,n,k,7) \le 0.025$$

n	10	11	12	13	14	15	16	17	18	19	20
11											
12											
13											
14											
15					22	23					
16				22	23	24	26				
17				23	24	26	27	28			
18			23	24	25	27	28	30	31		
19			24	25	27	28	30	31	33	34	
20			25	26	28	29	31	33	34	36	38
21			26	28	29	31	32	34	36	38	39
22		26	27	29	30	32	34	36	37	39	41
23		27	28	30	32	34	35	37	39	41	43
24		28	29	31	33	35	37	39	40	42	44
25		29	31	32	34	36	38	40	42	44	46
26		30	32	34	36	38	39	41	43	46	48
27		31	33	35	37	39	41	43	45	47	49
28		32	34	36	38	40	42	44	47	49	
29	32	33	35	37	39	42	44	46	48		
30	33	34	36	39	41	43	45	47			

18.2

Critical Values for Testing Two-by-Two Tables
Values of N' such that for N's Less than or Equal to N' (cont.)

$$P(N,n,k,0) \leq 0.01$$

n	2	3	4	5	6	7	8	9	10	11	12
1											
2											
3											
4											
5			9	10							
6			10	12	14						
7		10	11	13	15	17					
8		11	13	15	17	19	22				
9		12	14	17	19	21	24	26			
10		13	16	18	21	24	26	29	31		
11		15	17	20	23	26	28	31	34	37	
12		16	19	22	25	28	31	34	37	40	43
13	15	17	20	23	26	30	33	36	40	43	46
14	16	18	22	25	28	32	35	39	42	46	49
15	17	20	23	27	30	34	37	41	45	49	
16	18	21	25	28	32	36	40	44	48		
17	19	22	26	30	34	38	42	46			
18	20	24	27	32	36	40	44	49			
19	21	25	29	33	38	42	47				
20	22	26	30	35	39	44	49				

$$P(N,n,k,1) \leq 0.01$$

n	3	4	5	6	7	8	9	10	11	12	13
6											
7				12	13						
8				13	15	16					
9			13	14	16	18	20				
10			14	16	18	20	21	23			
11			15	17	19	21	23	25	27		
12		15	17	19	21	23	25	27	29	32	
13		16	18	20	22	25	27	29	32	34	36
14		17	19	21	24	26	29	31	34	36	39
15		18	20	23	25	28	30	33	36	38	41
16		19	22	24	27	30	32	35	38	41	43
17		20	23	26	28	31	34	37	40	43	46
18		22	24	27	30	33	36	39	42	45	48
19		23	25	28	31	35	38	41	44	47	
20		24	27	30	33	36	40	43	46		
21		25	28	31	35	38	41	45	48		
22		26	29	33	36	40	43	47			
23	25	27	31	34	38	41	45	49			
24	26	28	32	35	39	43	47				
25	27	30	33	37	41	45	49				

Critical Values for Testing Two-by-Two Tables
Values of N' such that for N's Less than or Equal to N' (cont.)

$$P(N,n,k,2) \leq 0.01$$

n	5	6	7	8	9	10	11	12	13	14	15
6											
7											
8				14							
9				15	16						
10			15	16	18	19					
11			16	18	19	21	23				
12		16	17	19	21	22	24	26			
13		17	19	20	22	24	26	28	30		
14		18	20	22	24	26	28	30	32	34	
15		19	21	23	25	27	29	32	34	36	38
16		20	22	25	27	29	31	33	36	38	40
17	20	22	24	26	28	31	33	35	38	40	42
18	21	23	25	27	30	32	35	37	40	42	45
19	22	24	26	29	31	34	36	39	41	44	47
20	23	25	28	30	33	35	38	41	43	46	49
21	24	26	29	32	34	37	40	43	45	48	
22	25	28	30	33	36	39	41	44	47		
23	26	29	31	34	37	40	43	46	49		
24	27	30	33	36	39	42	45	48			
25	28	31	34	37	40	43	47				

$$P(N,n,k,3) \leq 0.01$$

n	6	7	8	9	10	11	12	13	14	15	16
6											
7											
8											
9											
10					17						
11				17	18	20					
12			17	18	20	21	23				
13			18	19	21	22	24	26			
14			19	21	22	24	26	27	29		
15		19	20	22	24	25	27	29	31	33	
16		20	21	23	25	27	29	31	33	35	36
17		21	23	25	26	28	30	32	34	36	38
18		22	24	26	28	30	32	34	36	38	40
19		23	25	27	29	31	34	36	38	40	42
20		24	26	28	31	33	35	37	40	42	44
21	24	25	28	30	32	34	37	39	41	44	46
22	25	27	29	31	33	36	38	41	43	46	48
23	26	28	30	32	35	37	40	42	45	48	
24	27	29	31	34	36	39	41	44	47	49	
25	28	30	33	35	38	40	43	46	49		

18.2

Critical Values for Testing Two-by-Two Tables
Values of N' such that for N's Less than or Equal to N' (cont.)

$$P(N,n,k,4) \leq 0.01$$

n	7	8	9	10	11	12	13	14	15	16	17
11											
12					19	20					
13				19	20	21	23				
14				20	21	23	24	26			
15			20	21	23	24	26	27	29		
16			21	22	24	26	27	29	31	32	
17			22	24	25	27	29	31	32	34	36
18		22	23	25	27	28	30	32	34	36	38
19		23	24	26	28	30	32	34	36	37	39
20		24	26	27	29	31	33	35	37	39	41
21		25	27	29	31	33	35	37	39	41	43
22		26	28	30	32	34	36	38	40	43	45
23		27	29	31	33	35	38	40	42	44	47
24		28	30	32	35	37	39	41	44	46	48
25		29	31	34	36	38	41	43	45	48	
26	29	31	33	35	37	40	42	45	47		
27	30	32	34	36	39	41	44	46	49		
28	31	33	35	38	40	43	45	48			
29	32	34	36	39	41	44	47	49			
30	33	35	37	40	43	45	48				

$$P(N,n,k,5) \leq 0.01$$

n	9	10	11	12	13	14	15	16	17	18	19
11											
12											
13					21						
14				21	22	23					
15			21	22	23	25	26				
16			22	23	25	26	28	29			
17		22	23	25	26	28	29	31	32		
18		23	24	26	27	29	31	32	34	36	
19		24	25	27	29	30	32	34	36	37	39
20		25	27	28	30	32	34	35	37	39	41
21	25	26	28	30	31	33	35	37	39	41	43
22	26	27	29	31	33	35	37	39	40	42	44
23	27	28	30	32	34	36	38	40	42	44	46
24	28	30	32	33	35	38	40	42	44	46	48
25	29	31	33	35	37	39	41	43	45	48	
26	30	32	34	36	38	40	43	45	47	49	
27	31	33	35	37	40	42	44	46	49		
28	32	34	36	39	41	43	46	48			
29	33	35	38	40	42	45	47	49			
30	34	37	39	41	44	46	49				

Critical Values for Testing Two-by-Two Tables
Values of N' such that for N's Less than or Equal to N' (cont.)

$P(N,n,k,6) \leq 0.01$

n	10	11	12	13	14	15	16	17	18	19	20
11											
12											
13											
14					22						
15					23	24					
16				23	24	25	27				
17		23		24	25	27	28	30			
18			24	25	27	28	30	31	33		
19			25	26	28	29	31	33	34	36	
20		25	26	28	29	31	32	34	36	37	39
21		26	27	29	31	32	34	36	37	39	41
22		27	28	30	32	34	35	37	39	41	42
23		28	30	31	33	35	37	39	40	42	44
24		29	31	33	34	36	38	40	42	44	46
25	29	30	32	34	36	38	40	41	43	45	47
26	30	31	33	35	37	39	41	43	45	47	49
27	31	33	34	36	38	40	42	44	47	49	
28	32	34	36	38	40	42	44	46	48		
29	33	35	37	39	41	43	45	47			
30	34	36	38	40	42	45	47	49			

$P(N,n,k,7) \leq 0.01$

n	11	12	13	14	15	16	17	18	19	20	21
16					24	25					
17				24	25	26	27				
18				25	26	27	29	30			
19			25	26	27	29	30	32	33		
20				26	27	29	30	32	33	35	36
21			27	28	30	31	33	34	36	38	39
22		27	28	30	31	33	34	36	37	39	41
23		28	29	31	32	34	36	37	39	41	42
24		29	30	32	34	35	37	39	40	42	44
25		30	31	32	35	37	38	40	42	44	46
26		31	33	34	36	38	40	42	43	45	47
27		32	34	36	37	39	41	43	45	47	49
28	32	33	35	37	39	41	43	44	46	48	
29	33	34	36	38	40	42	44	46	48		
30	34	35	37	39	41	43	45	47	49		
31	35	37	39	41	43	45	47	49			
32	36	38	40	42	44	46	48				
33	37	39	41	43	45	47					
34	38	40	42	44	46	49					
35	39	41	43	45	48						

18.2

Critical Values for Testing Two-by-Two Tables
Values of N' such that for N's Less than or Equal to N' (cont.)

$$P(N,n,k,0) \le 0.005$$

n	2	3	4	5	6	7	8	9	10	11	12
1											
2											
3											
4											
5				10							
6		10	11	13							
7		11	13	14	16						
8		12	14	16	18	20					
9		12	14	16	18	20	22	24			
10		13	15	17	19	22	24	26	29		
11		14	16	19	21	24	26	29	31	34	
12		15	18	20	23	25	28	31	34	36	39
13		16	19	22	24	27	30	33	36	39	42
14		18	20	23	26	29	32	35	38	41	45
15		19	22	25	28	31	34	37	41	44	47
16		20	23	26	29	33	36	40	43	47	
17		21	24	28	31	35	38	42	46	49	
18		22	26	29	33	37	40	44	48		
19	21	24	27	31	35	38	42	46			
20	22	25	28	32	36	40	44	49			

$$P(N,n,k,1) \le 0.005$$

n	4	5	6	7	8	9	10	11	12	13	14
6											
7				13							
8			13	14	15						
9			14	15	17	19					
10		14	15	17	19	20	22				
11		15	16	18	20	22	24	26			
12		16	18	20	22	24	26	28	30		
13		17	19	21	23	25	27	30	32	34	
14		18	20	23	25	27	29	32	34	36	38
15	18	20	22	24	26	29	31	33	36	38	41
16	19	21	23	25	28	30	33	35	38	40	43
17	20	22	24	27	29	32	35	37	40	43	45
18	21	23	26	28	31	34	36	39	42	45	48
19	22	24	27	30	33	35	38	41	44	47	
20	23	26	28	31	34	37	40	43	46	49	
21	24	27	30	33	36	39	42	45	48		
22	25	28	31	34	37	40	44	47			
23	26	29	32	36	39	42	46	49			
24	28	30	34	37	40	44	47				
25	29	32	35	38	42	46	49				

18.2

Critical Values for Testing Two-by-Two Tables
Values of N' such that for N's Less than or Equal to N' (cont.)

$$P(N,n,k,2) \leq 0.005$$

n	5	6	7	8	9	10	11	12	13	14	15
6											
7											
8											
9					16						
10				16	17	19					
11			16	17	19	20	22				
12			17	18	20	22	23	25			
13			18	20	21	23	25	27	28		
14		18	19	21	23	25	26	28	30	32	
15		19	20	22	24	26	28	30	32	34	36
16		20	22	24	26	28	30	32	34	36	38
17		21	23	25	27	29	31	33	36	38	40
18		22	24	26	28	31	33	35	37	40	42
19		23	25	28	30	32	34	37	39	42	44
20		24	27	29	31	34	36	39	41	44	46
21	24	26	28	30	33	35	38	40	43	45	48
22	25	27	29	32	34	37	39	42	45	47	
23	26	28	30	33	36	38	41	44	47	49	
24	27	29	32	34	37	40	43	45	48		
25	28	30	33	36	38	41	44	47			

$$P(N,n,k,3) \leq 0.005$$

n	6	7	8	9	10	11	12	13	14	15	16
11					18	19					
12				18	19	20	22				
13				19	20	22	23	25			
14			19	20	22	23	25	26	28		
15			20	21	23	25	26	28	30	31	
16			21	23	24	26	28	29	31	33	35
17			22	24	26	27	29	31	33	35	37
18		22	23	25	27	29	31	33	35	37	39
19		23	24	26	28	30	32	34	36	38	40
20		24	26	28	30	32	34	36	38	40	42
21		25	27	29	31	33	35	37	40	42	44
22		26	28	30	32	34	37	39	41	44	46
23		27	29	31	34	36	38	41	43	45	48
24		28	30	33	35	37	40	42	45	47	
25		29	32	34	36	39	41	44	46	49	
26			30	33	35	38	40	43	45	48	
27	30	32	34	36	39	42	44	47			
28	31	33	35	38	40	43	46	49			
29	32	34	36	39	42	44	47				
30	33	35	38	40	43	46	49				

Critical Values for Testing Two-by-Two Tables
Values of N' such that for N's Less than or Equal to N' (cont.)

$$P(N, n, k, 4) \leq 0.005$$

n	8	9	10	11	12	13	14	15	16	17	18
11											
12					20						
13				20	21	22					
14				21	22	24	25				
15			21	22	24	25	27	28			
16			22	23	25	26	28	30	31		
17		22	23	25	26	28	29	31	33	35	
18		23	24	26	28	29	31	33	34	36	38
19		24	25	27	29	31	32	34	36	38	40
20		25	27	28	30	32	34	36	38	40	42
21		26	28	30	32	33	35	37	39	41	43
22	26	27	29	31	33	35	37	39	41	43	45
23	27	28	30	32	34	36	38	41	43	45	47
24	28	30	32	34	36	38	40	42	44	46	49
25	29	31	33	35	37	39	41	44	46	48	
26	30	32	34	36	38	41	43	45	48		
27	31	33	35	37	40	42	44	47	49		
28	32	34	36	39	41	43	46	48			
29	33	35	38	40	42	45	47				
30	34	37	39	41	44	46	49				

$$P(N, n, k, 5) \leq 0.005$$

n	9	10	11	12	13	14	15	16	17	18	19
11											
12											
13											
14					22	23					
15				22	23	24	26				
16				23	24	26	27	28			
17			23	24	25	27	28	30	31		
18			24	25	27	28	30	31	33	35	
19			25	26	28	30	31	33	34	36	38
20		25	26	28	29	31	33	34	36	38	39
21		26	27	29	31	32	34	36	38	39	41
22		27	28	30	32	34	35	37	39	41	43
23		28	30	31	33	35	37	39	41	43	44
24		29	31	33	34	36	38	40	42	44	46
25		30	32	34	36	38	40	42	44	46	48
26	30	31	33	35	37	39	41	43	45	47	
27	31	32	34	36	38	40	43	45	47	49	
28	32	34	36	38	40	42	44	46	48		
29	33	35	37	39	41	43	45	48			
30	34	36	38	40	42	45	47	49			

Critical Values for Testing Two-by-Two Tables
Values of N' such that for N's Less than or Equal to N' (cont.)

$$P(N, n, k, 6) \leq 0.005$$

n	10	11	12	13	14	15	16	17	18	19	20
11											
12											
13											
14											
15						24					
16					24	25	26				
17				24	25	26	28	29			
18				25	26	27	29	30	32		
19				26	27	29	30	32	33	35	
20			26	27	29	30	32	33	35	36	38
21			27	28	30	31	33	35	36	38	39
22			28	29	31	33	34	36	38	39	41
23		28	29	31	32	34	36	37	39	41	43
24		29	30	32	34	35	37	39	41	42	44
25		30	31	33	35	37	38	40	42	44	46
26		31	33	34	36	38	40	42	44	46	47
27		32	34	36	37	39	41	43	45	47	49
28		33	35	37	39	41	43	45	47	49	
29		34	36	38	40	42	44	46	48		
30	34	35	37	39	41	43	45	47			

$$P(N, n, k, 7) \leq 0.005$$

n	11	12	13	14	15	16	17	18	19	20	21
16											
17							26	27			
18						26	27	28	30		
19						27	28	30	31	32	
20					27	28	29	31	32	34	35
21					28	29	31	32	34	35	37	38
22				28	29	30	32	33	35	37	38	40
23				29	30	32	33	35	36	38	40	41
24				30	31	33	34	36	38	39	41	43
25				31	33	34	36	37	39	41	43	44
26		31	32	34	35	37	39	41	42	44	46
27		32	33	35	37	38	40	42	44	46	47
28		33	34	36	38	40	41	43	45	47	49
29		34	36	37	39	41	43	45	47	49	
30		35	37	38	40	42	44	46	48		
31		36	38	40	42	43	45	47	49		
32		37	39	41	43	45	47	49			
33	37	38	40	42	44	46	48				
34	38	39	41	43	45	47	49				
35	39	40	42	44	47	49					

18.3 Number of Cases Required for Comparing Two Proportions

Let P_1 be the proportion of successes in population one, and let P_2 be the proportion of successes in population two. Suppose samples are taken from the two populations in order to perform the one-sided test outlined in Section 18.2 for the equality of two proportions at the $\alpha = 0.05$ or $\alpha = 0.01$ significance levels. Also, suppose that values of P_1 and P_2 are given such that if these are the true values of the P's, the equality hypothesis is accepted with probability less than or equal to $\beta = 0.05, 0.01,$ or 0.10. The table gives the number of trials required for *each* of the two populations used in the experiment.

The values of n in the table were computed from the formula given by Paulson and Wallis in [62], p. 259:

$$n = \frac{1}{2}\left(\frac{K_\alpha + K_\beta}{\arcsin \sqrt{P_1} - \arcsin \sqrt{P_2}}\right)^2,$$

where K_ϵ is defined by

$$\frac{1}{\sqrt{2\pi}}\int_{K_\epsilon}^{\infty} \exp\left(-x^2/2\right) dx = \epsilon,$$

and the angles are measured in radians.

Number of Cases Required for Comparing Two Proportions

α = 0.05

P_2	β	P_1 0.001	0.01	0.05	0.10	0.15	0.20	0.25	0.30	0.40	0.50	β
0.001			1152	144	65	41	29	23	19	13	10	0.05
0.01	0.10	912		345	111	62	41	31	24	16	12	
0.05		114	273		585	183	96	61	44	26	18	
0.10		51	88	463		939	269	133	82	42	26	
0.15		32	49	145	743		1245	342	164	66	36	
0.20		23	33	76	213	985		1506	403	111	53	
0.25		18	24	49	106	271	1192		1723	209	79	
0.30		15	19	35	65	130	319	1364		491	128	
0.40		11	13	21	33	52	88	165	388		534	0.05
0.50	0.10	8	10	14	20	29	42	63	102	423		

α = 0.01

P_2	β	P_1 0.001	0.01	0.05	0.10	0.15	0.20	0.25	0.30	0.40	0.50	β
0.001			2305	288	129	81	58	45	37	26	20	0.01
0.01	0.05	1679		689	221	123	82	61	48	32	24	
0.05		210	502		1169	366	191	122	87	52	35	
0.10		94	161	852		1877	538	266	163	83	51	
0.15		59	90	266	1368		2489	683	327	132	73	
0.20		43	60	140	392	1814		3012	805	223	105	
0.25		33	44	89	194	498	2194		3447	417	158	
0.30		27	35	63	119	239	587	2511		981	256	
0.40		19	24	38	60	96	162	304	715		1068	0.01
0.50	0.05	14	17	26	37	53	77	116	187	778		

18.3

18.4 Critical Values for a Nonparametric Test of Location

The quantities tabulated here are critical values for a special case of the hypergeometric probability distribution, i.e., minimum values of s_0 such that for all $s \geq s_0$,

$$P(m + n, n, s, 0) \leq 0.05 \text{ or } 0.01$$

for m, $n = 1(1)50$. If two independent random samples of n points and m points are drawn from two populations respectively, with continuous cumulative distribution functions, a test of the hypothesis that the medians of the two populations are equal, given that the dispersions are the same, is afforded by counting the number of points in one sample which are larger than the largest in the other sample. The hypothesis is rejected if this number equals or exceeds the value tabulated. These tables are also useful in setting tolerance limits on a second sample, given a first sample [247], [163]. For large and approximately equal sample sizes, the critical values of s turn out to be 5 for the 5-percent values and 7 for the 1-percent values. Sukhatme [213] also gives a test of location.

Critical Values for a Nonparametric Test of Location [184]

5% values of *s*

n	1	2	3	4	5	6	7	8	9	10	11	12	13	14	15	16	17	18	19	20	21	22	23	24	25
1	-	-	-	-	-	-	-	-	-	-	-	-	-	-	-	-	-	-	-	20	21	22	23	24	25
2	-	-	-	-	5	6	7	8	9	9	10	11	12	13	13	14	15	16	16	17	18	19	20	20	21
3	-	-	-	4	5	5	6	7	7	8	9	9	10	11	11	12	12	13	14	14	15	16	16	17	18
4	-	-	3	4	4	5	5	6	6	7	8	8	9	9	10	10	11	11	12	12	13	13	14	14	15
5	-	2	3	3	4	4	5	5	6	6	7	7	8	8	9	9	9	10	10	11	11	12	12	13	13
6	-	2	3	3	4	4	4	5	5	6	6	6	7	7	8	8	8	9	9	10	10	10	11	11	12
7	-	2	3	3	3	4	4	5	5	5	6	6	6	7	7	7	8	8	8	9	9	9	10	10	11
8	-	2	3	3	3	4	4	4	5	5	5	6	6	6	6	7	7	7	8	8	8	9	9	9	10
9	-	2	3	3	3	4	4	4	4	4	5	5	5	6	6	6	7	7	7	7	8	8	8	9	9
10	-	2	2	3	3	3	4	4	4	4	5	5	5	5	6	6	6	6	7	7	7	8	8	8	8
11	-	2	2	3	3	3	3	4	4	4	4	5	5	5	5	6	6	6	6	7	7	7	7	8	8
12	-	2	2	3	3	3	3	3	4	4	4	4	5	5	5	5	6	6	6	6	6	7	7	7	7
13	-	2	2	2	3	3	3	3	4	4	4	4	4	5	5	5	5	6	6	6	6	6	7	7	7
14	-	2	2	2	3	3	3	3	3	4	4	4	4	4	5	5	5	5	6	6	6	6	6	6	7
15	-	2	2	2	3	3	3	3	3	4	4	4	4	4	4	5	5	5	5	5	6	6	6	6	6
16	-	2	2	2	2	3	3	3	3	3	4	4	4	4	4	5	5	5	5	5	5	6	6	6	6
17	-	2	2	2	2	3	3	3	3	3	4	4	4	4	4	4	5	5	5	5	5	5	6	6	6
18	-	2	2	2	2	3	3	3	3	3	3	4	4	4	4	4	4	5	5	5	5	5	5	5	6
19	-	2	2	2	2	3	3	3	3	3	3	3	4	4	4	4	4	4	5	5	5	5	5	5	5
20	1	2	2	2	2	2	3	3	3	3	3	3	4	4	4	4	4	4	4	5	5	5	5	5	5
21	1	2	2	2	2	2	3	3	3	3	3	3	3	4	4	4	4	4	4	4	5	5	5	5	5
22	1	2	2	2	2	2	3	3	3	3	3	3	3	4	4	4	4	4	4	4	4	5	5	5	5
23	1	2	2	2	2	2	2	3	3	3	3	3	3	3	4	4	4	4	4	4	4	4	5	5	5
24	1	2	2	2	2	2	2	3	3	3	3	3	3	3	3	4	4	4	4	4	4	4	4	5	5
25	1	2	2	2	2	2	2	3	3	3	3	3	3	3	3	4	4	4	4	4	4	4	4	5	5
26	1	2	2	2	2	2	2	2	3	3	3	3	3	3	3	3	4	4	4	4	4	4	4	4	5
27	1	2	2	2	2	2	2	2	3	3	3	3	3	3	3	3	4	4	4	4	4	4	4	4	4
28	1	2	2	2	2	2	2	2	3	3	3	3	3	3	3	3	3	4	4	4	4	4	4	4	4
29	1	2	2	2	2	2	2	2	3	3	3	3	3	3	3	3	3	4	4	4	4	4	4	4	4
30	1	2	2	2	2	2	2	2	2	3	3	3	3	3	3	3	3	3	4	4	4	4	4	4	4
31	1	2	2	2	2	2	2	2	2	3	3	3	3	3	3	3	3	3	3	4	4	4	4	4	4
32	1	2	2	2	2	2	2	2	2	3	3	3	3	3	3	3	3	3	3	4	4	4	4	4	4
33	1	2	2	2	2	2	2	2	2	2	3	3	3	3	3	3	3	3	3	3	4	4	4	4	4
34	1	2	2	2	2	2	2	2	2	2	3	3	3	3	3	3	3	3	3	3	4	4	4	4	4
35	1	2	2	2	2	2	2	2	2	2	3	3	3	3	3	3	3	3	3	3	3	4	4	4	4
36	1	2	2	2	2	2	2	2	2	2	3	3	3	3	3	3	3	3	3	3	3	3	4	4	4
37	1	2	2	2	2	2	2	2	2	2	2	3	3	3	3	3	3	3	3	3	3	3	4	4	4
38	1	2	2	2	2	2	2	2	2	2	2	3	3	3	3	3	3	3	3	3	3	3	3	4	4
39	1	1	2	2	2	2	2	2	2	2	2	3	3	3	3	3	3	3	3	3	3	3	3	4	4
40	1	1	2	2	2	2	2	2	2	2	2	2	3	3	3	3	3	3	3	3	3	3	3	3	4
41	1	1	2	2	2	2	2	2	2	2	2	2	3	3	3	3	3	3	3	3	3	3	3	3	4
42	1	1	2	2	2	2	2	2	2	2	2	2	3	3	3	3	3	3	3	3	3	3	3	3	3
43	1	1	2	2	2	2	2	2	2	2	2	2	3	3	3	3	3	3	3	3	3	3	3	3	3
44	1	1	2	2	2	2	2	2	2	2	2	2	2	3	3	3	3	3	3	3	3	3	3	3	3
45	1	1	2	2	2	2	2	2	2	2	2	2	2	3	3	3	3	3	3	3	3	3	3	3	3
46	1	1	2	2	2	2	2	2	2	2	2	2	2	3	3	3	3	3	3	3	3	3	3	3	3
47	1	1	2	2	2	2	2	2	2	2	2	2	2	2	3	3	3	3	3	3	3	3	3	3	3
48	1	1	2	2	2	2	2	2	2	2	2	2	2	2	3	3	3	3	3	3	3	3	3	3	3
49	1	1	2	2	2	2	2	2	2	2	2	2	2	2	3	3	3	3	3	3	3	3	3	3	3
50	1	1	2	2	2	2	2	2	2	2	2	2	2	2	3	3	3	3	3	3	3	3	3	3	3

18.4

Critical Values for a Nonparametric Test of Location (cont.)

5% values of s

n	26	27	28	29	30	31	32	33	34	35	36	37	38	39	40	41	42	43	44	45	46	47	48	49	50
1	26	27	28	29	30	31	32	33	34	35	36	37	38	39	39	40	41	42	43	44	45	46	47	48	49
2	22	23	23	24	25	26	26	27	28	29	30	30	31	32	33	33	34	35	36	37	37	38	39	40	40
3	18	19	19	20	21	21	22	23	23	24	24	25	26	26	27	28	28	29	30	30	31	31	32	33	33
4	15	16	17	17	18	18	19	19	20	20	21	21	22	22	23	23	24	24	25	26	26	27	27	28	28
5	14	14	14	15	15	16	16	17	17	18	18	18	19	19	20	20	21	21	22	22	23	23	23	24	24
6	12	12	13	13	14	14	14	15	15	16	16	16	17	17	18	18	18	19	19	20	20	20	21	21	21
7	11	11	12	12	12	13	13	13	14	14	14	15	15	15	16	16	16	17	17	18	18	18	19	19	19
8	10	10	11	11	11	12	12	12	12	13	13	13	14	14	14	15	15	15	16	16	16	17	17	17	17
9	9	9	10	10	10	11	11	11	11	12	12	12	13	13	13	13	14	14	14	15	15	15	15	16	16
10	9	9	9	9	10	10	10	10	11	11	11	11	12	12	12	12	13	13	13	14	14	14	14	15	15
11	8	8	9	9	9	9	9	10	10	10	10	11	11	11	11	12	12	12	12	13	13	13	13	14	14
12	8	8	8	8	8	9	9	9	9	10	10	10	10	10	11	11	11	11	12	12	12	12	12	13	13
13	7	7	8	8	8	8	8	9	9	9	9	9	10	10	10	10	11	11	11	11	11	11	11	12	12
14	7	7	7	7	8	8	8	8	8	9	9	9	9	9	10	10	10	10	10	10	11	11	11	11	11
15	7	7	7	7	7	7	8	8	8	8	8	9	9	9	9	9	9	10	10	10	10	10	11	11	11
16	6	6	7	7	7	7	7	7	8	8	8	8	8	9	9	9	9	9	9	10	10	10	10	10	10
17	6	6	6	7	7	7	7	7	7	8	8	8	8	8	8	8	9	9	9	9	9	9	10	10	10
18	6	6	6	6	6	7	7	7	7	7	7	8	8	8	8	8	8	8	9	9	9	9	9	9	9
19	6	6	6	6	6	6	7	7	7	7	7	7	7	8	8	8	8	8	8	8	8	9	9	9	9
20	5	6	6	6	6	6	6	6	7	7	7	7	7	7	7	8	8	8	8	8	8	8	8	9	9
21	5	5	6	6	6	6	6	6	6	6	7	7	7	7	7	7	7	8	8	8	8	8	8	8	9
22	5	5	5	6	6	6	6	6	6	6	6	7	7	7	7	7	7	7	7	8	8	8	8	8	8
23	5	5	5	6	6	6	6	6	6	6	6	6	7	7	7	7	7	7	7	7	7	7	7	8	8
24	5	5	5	5	5	5	6	6	6	6	6	6	6	6	7	7	7	7	7	7	7	7	7	7	8
25	5	5	5	5	5	5	5	6	6	6	6	6	6	6	6	6	7	7	7	7	7	7	7	7	7
26	5	5	5	5	5	5	5	5	6	6	6	6	6	6	6	6	6	7	7	7	7	7	7	7	7
27	5	5	5	5	5	5	5	5	5	6	6	6	6	6	6	6	6	6	6	6	7	7	7	7	7
28	4	5	5	5	5	5	5	5	5	5	5	6	6	6	6	6	6	6	6	6	6	6	7	7	7
29	4	4	5	5	5	5	5	5	5	5	5	5	6	6	6	6	6	6	6	6	6	6	6	7	7
30	4	4	4	5	5	5	5	5	5	5	5	5	5	6	6	6	6	6	6	6	6	6	6	7	7
31	4	4	4	4	5	5	5	5	5	5	5	5	5	5	6	6	6	6	6	6	6	6	6	6	6
32	4	4	4	4	4	5	5	5	5	5	5	5	5	5	5	5	6	6	6	6	6	6	6	6	6
33	4	4	4	4	4	4	5	5	5	5	5	5	5	5	5	5	5	6	6	6	6	6	6	6	6
34	4	4	4	4	4	4	4	5	5	5	5	5	5	5	5	5	5	5	6	6	6	6	6	6	6
35	4	4	4	4	4	4	4	5	5	5	5	5	5	5	5	5	5	5	5	6	6	6	6	6	6
36	4	4	4	4	4	4	4	4	5	5	5	5	5	5	5	5	5	5	5	5	6	6	6	6	6
37	4	4	4	4	4	4	4	4	4	5	5	5	5	5	5	5	5	5	5	5	5	5	6	6	6
38	4	4	4	4	4	4	4	4	4	4	5	5	5	5	5	5	5	5	5	5	5	5	5	5	6
39	4	4	4	4	4	4	4	4	4	4	4	5	5	5	5	5	5	5	5	5	5	5	5	5	5
40	4	4	4	4	4	4	4	4	4	4	4	4	5	5	5	5	5	5	5	5	5	5	5	5	5
41	4	4	4	4	4	4	4	4	4	4	4	4	4	5	5	5	5	5	5	5	5	5	5	5	5
42	4	4	4	4	4	4	4	4	4	4	4	4	4	4	5	5	5	5	5	5	5	5	5	5	5
43	3	4	4	4	4	4	4	4	4	4	4	4	4	4	4	5	5	5	5	5	5	5	5	5	5
44	3	4	4	4	4	4	4	4	4	4	4	4	4	4	4	5	5	5	5	5	5	5	5	5	5
45	3	3	4	4	4	4	4	4	4	4	4	4	4	4	4	4	5	5	5	5	5	5	5	5	5
46	3	3	4	4	4	4	4	4	4	4	4	4	4	4	4	4	4	4	5	5	5	5	5	5	5
47	3	3	3	4	4	4	4	4	4	4	4	4	4	4	4	4	4	4	4	5	5	5	5	5	5
48	3	3	3	3	4	4	4	4	4	4	4	4	4	4	4	4	4	4	4	4	5	5	5	5	5
49	3	3	3	3	4	4	4	4	4	4	4	4	4	4	4	4	4	4	4	4	4	5	5	5	5
50	3	3	3	3	3	4	4	4	4	4	4	4	4	4	4	4	4	4	4	4	4	5	5	5	5

Critical Values for a Nonparametric Test of Location (cont.)

1% values of s

n	1	2	3	4	5	6	7	8	9	10	11	12	13	14	15	16	17	18	19	20	21	22	23	24	25
1	-	-	-	-	-	-	-	-	-	-	-	-	-	-	-	-	-	-	-	-	-	-	-	-	-
2	-	-	-	-	-	-	-	-	-	-	-	-	13	14	15	16	17	18	19	20	21	22	23	23	24
3	-	-	-	-	-	-	7	8	9	10	11	11	12	13	14	15	15	16	17	18	18	19	20	21	22
4	-	-	-	-	5	6	7	8	8	9	10	10	11	12	12	13	14	14	15	16	16	17	18	19	19
5	-	-	-	4	5	6	6	7	8	8	9	9	10	11	11	12	12	13	14	14	15	15	16	17	17
6	-	-	-	4	5	5	6	6	7	8	8	9	9	10	10	11	11	12	12	13	14	14	15	15	16
7	-	-	3	4	5	5	6	6	7	7	8	8	9	9	9	10	10	11	11	12	12	13	13	14	14
8	-	-	3	4	4	5	5	6	6	7	7	8	8	8	9	9	10	10	11	11	12	12	12	13	13
9	-	-	3	4	4	5	5	5	6	6	7	7	8	8	8	9	9	10	10	10	11	11	12	12	12
10	-	-	3	4	4	4	5	5	6	6	6	7	7	7	8	8	9	9	9	10	10	11	11	11	12
11	-	-	3	3	4	4	5	5	5	6	6	6	7	7	7	8	8	9	9	9	10	10	10	11	11
12	-	-	3	3	4	4	4	5	5	5	6	6	6	7	7	7	8	8	8	9	9	9	10	10	10
13	-	2	3	3	4	4	4	5	5	5	6	6	6	7	7	7	7	8	8	8	9	9	9	10	10
14	-	2	3	3	4	4	4	4	5	5	5	6	6	6	7	7	7	7	8	8	8	9	9	9	9
15	-	2	3	3	3	4	4	4	5	5	5	5	6	6	6	7	7	7	7	8	8	8	9	9	9
16	-	2	3	3	3	4	4	4	4	5	5	5	6	6	6	6	7	7	7	7	8	8	8	8	9
17	-	2	3	3	3	4	4	4	4	5	5	5	5	6	6	6	6	7	7	7	7	8	8	8	8
18	-	2	3	3	3	3	4	4	4	5	5	5	5	5	6	6	6	6	7	7	7	7	8	8	8
19	-	2	3	3	3	3	4	4	4	4	5	5	5	5	6	6	6	6	6	7	7	7	7	8	8
20	-	2	3	3	3	3	4	4	4	4	5	5	5	5	5	6	6	6	6	7	7	7	7	7	8
21	-	2	3	3	3	3	4	4	4	4	4	5	5	5	5	6	6	6	6	6	7	7	7	7	7
22	-	2	3	3	3	3	3	4	4	4	4	5	5	5	5	5	6	6	6	6	6	7	7	7	7
23	-	2	2	3	3	3	3	4	4	4	4	4	5	5	5	5	5	6	6	6	6	6	7	7	7
24	-	2	2	3	3	3	3	4	4	4	4	4	5	5	5	5	5	6	6	6	6	6	6	7	7
25	-	2	2	3	3	3	3	4	4	4	4	4	4	5	5	5	5	5	6	6	6	6	6	6	7
26	-	2	2	3	3	3	3	3	4	4	4	4	4	5	5	5	5	5	5	6	6	6	6	6	6
27	-	2	2	3	3	3	3	3	4	4	4	4	4	4	5	5	5	5	5	6	6	6	6	6	6
28	-	2	2	3	3	3	3	3	4	4	4	4	4	4	5	5	5	5	5	5	6	6	6	6	6
29	-	2	2	3	3	3	3	3	3	4	4	4	4	4	5	5	5	5	5	5	6	6	6	6	6
30	-	2	2	3	3	3	3	3	3	4	4	4	4	4	4	5	5	5	5	5	5	6	6	6	6
31	-	2	2	3	3	3	3	3	3	4	4	4	4	4	4	5	5	5	5	5	5	5	6	6	6
32	-	2	2	2	3	3	3	3	3	4	4	4	4	4	4	4	5	5	5	5	5	5	5	6	6
33	-	2	2	2	3	3	3	3	3	3	4	4	4	4	4	4	5	5	5	5	5	5	5	6	6
34	-	2	2	2	3	3	3	3	3	3	4	4	4	4	4	4	4	5	5	5	5	5	5	5	6
35	-	2	2	2	3	3	3	3	3	3	4	4	4	4	4	4	4	5	5	5	5	5	5	5	5
36	-	2	2	2	3	3	3	3	3	3	4	4	4	4	4	4	4	4	5	5	5	5	5	5	5
37	-	2	2	2	3	3	3	3	3	3	3	4	4	4	4	4	4	4	5	5	5	5	5	5	5
38	-	2	2	2	3	3	3	3	3	3	3	4	4	4	4	4	4	4	4	5	5	5	5	5	5
39	-	2	2	2	3	3	3	3	3	3	3	4	4	4	4	4	4	4	4	5	5	5	5	5	5
40	-	2	2	2	3	3	3	3	3	3	3	3	4	4	4	4	4	4	4	4	5	5	5	5	5
41	-	2	2	2	2	3	3	3	3	3	3	3	4	4	4	4	4	4	4	4	5	5	5	5	5
42	-	2	2	2	2	3	3	3	3	3	3	3	4	4	4	4	4	4	4	4	5	5	5	5	5
43	-	2	2	2	2	3	3	3	3	3	3	3	4	4	4	4	4	4	4	4	4	5	5	5	5
44	-	2	2	2	2	3	3	3	3	3	3	3	3	4	4	4	4	4	4	4	4	5	5	5	5
45	-	2	2	2	2	3	3	3	3	3	3	3	3	4	4	4	4	4	4	4	4	4	5	5	5
46	-	2	2	2	2	3	3	3	3	3	3	3	3	4	4	4	4	4	4	4	4	4	5	5	5
47	-	2	2	2	2	3	3	3	3	3	3	3	3	4	4	4	4	4	4	4	4	4	4	5	5
48	-	2	2	2	2	3	3	3	3	3	3	3	3	3	4	4	4	4	4	4	4	4	4	5	5
49	-	2	2	2	2	3	3	3	3	3	3	3	3	3	4	4	4	4	4	4	4	4	4	4	5
50	-	2	2	2	2	2	3	3	3	3	3	3	3	3	4	4	4	4	4	4	4	4	4	4	5

18.4

Critical Values for a Nonparametric Test of Location (cont.)

1% values of s

n	26	27	28	29	30	31	32	33	34	35	36	37	38	39	40	41	42	43	44	45	46	47	48	49	50
1	-	-	-	-	-	-	-	-	-	-	-	-	-	-	-	-	-	-	-	-	-	-	-	-	-
2	25	26	27	28	29	30	31	32	32	33	34	35	36	37	38	39	40	41	41	42	43	44	45	46	47
3	22	23	24	25	26	26	27	28	29	29	30	31	32	33	33	34	35	36	37	37	38	39	40	40	41
4	20	21	21	22	23	23	24	25	25	26	27	27	28	29	30	30	31	32	32	33	34	34	35	36	36
5	18	18	19	20	20	21	22	22	23	23	24	25	25	26	26	27	28	28	29	29	30	31	31	32	32
6	16	17	17	18	18	19	19	20	21	21	22	22	23	23	24	24	25	25	26	26	27	28	28	29	29
7	15	15	16	16	17	17	18	18	19	19	20	20	21	21	22	22	23	23	24	24	25	25	26	26	26
8	14	14	15	15	16	16	16	17	17	18	18	19	19	19	20	20	21	21	22	22	23	23	23	24	24
9	13	13	14	14	14	15	15	16	16	16	17	17	18	18	18	19	19	20	20	20	21	21	22	22	22
10	12	12	13	13	13	14	14	15	15	15	16	16	16	17	17	18	18	18	19	19	19	20	20	21	21
11	11	12	12	12	13	13	13	14	14	14	15	15	15	16	16	16	17	17	18	18	18	19	19	19	20
12	11	11	11	12	12	12	13	13	13	14	14	14	15	15	15	16	16	16	17	17	17	17	18	18	18
13	10	10	11	11	11	12	12	12	13	13	13	14	14	14	14	15	15	15	16	16	16	17	17	17	17
14	10	10	10	11	11	11	11	12	12	12	13	13	13	13	14	14	14	15	15	15	15	16	16	16	17
15	9	10	10	10	10	11	11	11	11	12	12	12	13	13	13	13	14	14	14	14	15	15	15	15	16
16	9	9	9	10	10	10	10	11	11	11	11	12	12	12	13	13	13	13	14	14	14	14	15	15	15
17	9	9	9	9	10	10	10	10	11	11	11	11	12	12	12	12	12	13	13	13	13	14	14	14	14
18	8	9	9	9	9	9	10	10	10	10	11	11	11	11	12	12	12	12	12	13	13	13	13	14	14
19	8	8	8	9	9	9	9	10	10	10	10	10	11	11	11	11	12	12	12	12	12	13	13	13	13
20	8	8	8	8	9	9	9	9	9	10	10	10	10	11	11	11	11	11	12	12	12	12	12	13	13
21	8	8	8	8	8	9	9	9	9	9	10	10	10	10	10	11	11	11	11	11	12	12	12	12	12
22	7	8	8	8	8	8	9	9	9	9	9	10	10	10	10	10	10	11	11	11	11	11	12	12	12
23	7	7	8	8	8	8	8	8	9	9	9	9	9	10	10	10	10	10	11	11	11	11	11	11	12
24	7	7	7	7	8	8	8	8	8	9	9	9	9	9	9	10	10	10	10	10	11	11	11	11	11
25	7	7	7	7	8	8	8	8	8	8	9	9	9	9	9	9	10	10	10	10	10	10	11	11	11
26	7	7	7	7	7	7	8	8	8	8	8	8	9	9	9	9	9	9	10	10	10	10	10	10	11
27	7	7	7	7	7	7	7	8	8	8	8	8	8	9	9	9	9	9	9	10	10	10	10	10	10
28	6	7	7	7	7	7	7	7	8	8	8	8	8	8	9	9	9	9	9	9	9	10	10	10	10
29	6	6	7	7	7	7	7	7	7	8	8	8	8	8	8	9	9	9	9	9	9	9	10	10	10
30	6	6	6	7	7	7	7	7	7	7	8	8	8	8	8	8	8	9	9	9	9	9	9	9	10
31	6	6	6	6	7	7	7	7	7	7	7	8	8	8	8	8	8	8	9	9	9	9	9	9	9
32	6	6	6	6	6	7	7	7	7	7	7	7	7	8	8	8	8	8	8	9	9	9	9	9	9
33	6	6	6	6	6	6	7	7	7	7	7	7	7	8	8	8	8	8	8	8	9	9	9	9	9
34	6	6	6	6	6	6	6	7	7	7	7	7	7	7	8	8	8	8	8	8	8	8	9	9	9
35	6	6	6	6	6	6	6	7	7	7	7	7	7	7	7	8	8	8	8	8	8	8	8	9	9
36	6	6	6	6	6	6	6	6	7	7	7	7	7	7	7	7	8	8	8	8	8	8	8	8	9
37	5	6	6	6	6	6	6	6	6	7	7	7	7	7	7	7	7	8	8	8	8	8	8	8	8
38	5	5	6	6	6	6	6	6	6	6	7	7	7	7	7	7	7	7	8	8	8	8	8	8	8
39	5	5	6	6	6	6	6	6	6	6	6	7	7	7	7	7	7	7	7	8	8	8	8	8	8
40	5	5	5	6	6	6	6	6	6	6	6	6	7	7	7	7	7	7	7	7	7	8	8	8	8
41	5	5	5	5	6	6	6	6	6	6	6	6	6	7	7	7	7	7	7	7	7	7	8	8	8
42	5	5	5	5	6	6	6	6	6	6	6	6	6	7	7	7	7	7	7	7	7	7	7	8	8
43	5	5	5	5	5	6	6	6	6	6	6	6	6	6	7	7	7	7	7	7	7	7	7	7	8
44	5	5	5	5	5	5	6	6	6	6	6	6	6	6	6	7	7	7	7	7	7	7	7	7	7
45	5	5	5	5	5	5	6	6	6	6	6	6	6	6	6	6	7	7	7	7	7	7	7	7	7
46	5	5	5	5	5	5	5	6	6	6	6	6	6	6	6	6	6	7	7	7	7	7	7	7	7
47	5	5	5	5	5	5	5	5	6	6	6	6	6	6	6	6	6	6	7	7	7	7	7	7	7
48	5	5	5	5	5	5	5	5	6	6	6	6	6	6	6	6	6	6	6	7	7	7	7	7	7
49	5	5	5	5	5	5	5	5	5	6	6	6	6	6	6	6	6	6	6	6	7	7	7	7	7
50	5	5	5	5	5	5	5	5	5	5	6	6	6	6	6	6	6	6	6	6	7	7	7	7	7

18.4

18.5 Critical Values for a Nonparametric Test of Dispersion

The quantities tabulated here are critical values for another special case of the hypergeometric probability distribution, i.e., minimum values of r_0 such that for all $r \geq r_0$,

$$P(m + n, n, r + 1, 1) \leq 0.05 \quad \text{or} \quad 0.01$$

for $m, n = 1(1)50$. If two independent random samples of n points and m points are drawn from two populations respectively, with continuous cumulative distribution functions, a test of the hypothesis that the dispersions of the two populations are equal, given that the medians are the same, is afforded by counting the number of points in one sample which are outside the extremes in the other sample. The hypothesis is rejected if this number equals or exceeds the value tabulated. For large and approximately equal sample sizes, the critical values of r turn out to be 7 for the 5-percent values and 10 for the 1-percent values.

These tables are also useful in setting tolerance limits on a second sample, given a first sample [247], [163]. Sukhatme [214] considers the power of the above test of dispersion. Ansari and Bradley [6] discuss another test of dispersion. Sukhatme [213] has proposed two other rank order dispersion tests.

Critical Values for a Nonparametric Test of Dispersion [183]

5% values of r

n	2	3	4	5	6	7	8	9	10	11	12	13	14	15	16	17	18	19	20	21	22	23	24	25
2	-	-	-	-	-	-	-	-	-	-	-	-	-	-	-	-	-	-	-	-	-	-	-	-
3	-	-	-	-	-	-	-	9	10	11	12	13	14	15	16	16	17	18	19	20	21	22	22	23
4	-	-	-	5	6	7	8	9	9	10	11	12	12	13	14	15	15	16	17	18	18	19	20	21
5	-	-	4	5	6	6	7	8	8	9	10	10	11	12	12	13	14	14	15	16	16	17	18	18
6	-	3	4	5	5	6	7	7	8	8	9	9	10	11	11	12	12	13	14	14	15	15	16	17
7	-	3	4	4	5	6	6	7	7	8	8	9	9	10	10	11	11	12	12	13	13	14	15	15
8	-	3	4	4	5	5	6	6	7	7	8	8	9	9	10	10	10	11	11	12	12	13	13	14
9	-	3	4	4	4	5	5	6	6	7	7	8	8	8	9	9	10	10	11	11	11	12	12	13
10	2	3	3	4	4	5	5	5	6	6	7	7	8	8	8	9	9	10	10	10	11	11	11	12
11	2	3	3	4	4	4	5	5	6	6	6	7	7	7	8	8	9	9	9	10	10	10	11	11
12	2	3	3	4	4	4	5	5	5	6	6	6	7	7	7	8	8	8	9	9	10	10	10	11
13	2	3	3	3	4	4	4	5	5	5	6	6	6	7	7	7	8	8	8	9	9	9	10	10
14	2	3	3	3	4	4	4	5	5	5	6	6	6	6	7	7	7	8	8	8	9	9	9	10
15	2	3	3	3	4	4	4	4	5	5	5	6	6	6	7	7	7	7	8	8	8	9	9	9
16	2	3	3	3	3	4	4	4	5	5	5	5	6	6	6	7	7	7	7	8	8	8	8	9
17	2	2	3	3	3	4	4	4	4	5	5	5	6	6	6	6	7	7	7	7	8	8	8	8
18	2	2	3	3	3	4	4	4	4	5	5	5	5	6	6	6	6	7	7	7	7	7	8	8
19	2	2	3	3	3	3	4	4	4	4	5	5	5	5	6	6	6	6	7	7	7	7	8	8
20	2	2	3	3	3	3	4	4	4	4	5	5	5	5	5	6	6	6	6	7	7	7	7	7
21	2	2	3	3	3	3	4	4	4	4	4	5	5	5	5	6	6	6	6	6	7	7	7	7
22	2	2	3	3	3	3	3	4	4	4	4	5	5	5	5	5	6	6	6	6	6	7	7	7
23	2	2	2	3	3	3	3	4	4	4	4	4	5	5	5	5	5	6	6	6	6	6	7	7
24	2	2	2	3	3	3	3	4	4	4	4	4	5	5	5	5	5	6	6	6	6	6	6	7
25	2	2	2	3	3	3	3	3	4	4	4	4	4	5	5	5	5	5	6	6	6	6	6	6
26	2	2	2	3	3	3	3	3	4	4	4	4	4	5	5	5	5	5	5	6	6	6	6	6
27	2	2	2	3	3	3	3	3	4	4	4	4	4	4	5	5	5	5	5	5	6	6	6	6
28	2	2	2	3	3	3	3	3	3	4	4	4	4	4	5	5	5	5	5	5	6	6	6	6
29	2	2	2	3	3	3	3	3	3	4	4	4	4	4	4	5	5	5	5	5	5	6	6	6
30	2	2	2	2	3	3	3	3	3	4	4	4	4	4	4	5	5	5	5	5	5	5	6	6
31	2	2	2	2	3	3	3	3	3	3	4	4	4	4	4	4	5	5	5	5	5	5	6	6
32	2	2	2	2	3	3	3	3	3	3	4	4	4	4	4	4	5	5	5	5	5	5	5	6
33	2	2	2	2	3	3	3	3	3	3	4	4	4	4	4	4	4	5	5	5	5	5	5	5
34	2	2	2	2	3	3	3	3	3	3	3	4	4	4	4	4	4	5	5	5	5	5	5	5
35	2	2	2	2	3	3	3	3	3	3	3	4	4	4	4	4	4	5	5	5	5	5	5	5
36	2	2	2	2	2	3	3	3	3	3	3	4	4	4	4	4	4	4	4	5	5	5	5	5
37	2	2	2	2	2	3	3	3	3	3	3	3	4	4	4	4	4	4	4	5	5	5	5	5
38	2	2	2	2	2	3	3	3	3	3	3	3	4	4	4	4	4	4	4	4	5	5	5	5
39	2	2	2	2	2	3	3	3	3	3	3	3	4	4	4	4	4	4	4	4	5	5	5	5
40	2	2	2	2	2	3	3	3	3	3	3	3	3	4	4	4	4	4	4	4	4	5	5	5
41	2	2	2	2	2	3	3	3	3	3	3	3	3	4	4	4	4	4	4	4	4	5	5	5
42	2	2	2	2	2	2	3	3	3	3	3	3	3	4	4	4	4	4	4	4	4	4	5	5
43	2	2	2	2	2	2	3	3	3	3	3	3	3	3	4	4	4	4	4	4	4	4	5	5
44	2	2	2	2	2	2	3	3	3	3	3	3	3	3	4	4	4	4	4	4	4	4	5	5
45	2	2	2	2	2	2	3	3	3	3	3	3	3	3	4	4	4	4	4	4	4	4	4	5
46	2	2	2	2	2	2	3	3	3	3	3	3	3	3	3	4	4	4	4	4	4	4	4	4
47	2	2	2	2	2	2	3	3	3	3	3	3	3	3	3	4	4	4	4	4	4	4	4	4
48	2	2	2	2	2	2	3	3	3	3	3	3	3	3	3	4	4	4	4	4	4	4	4	4
49	2	2	2	2	2	2	2	3	3	3	3	3	3	3	3	3	4	4	4	4	4	4	4	4
50	2	2	2	2	2	2	2	3	3	3	3	3	3	3	3	3	4	4	4	4	4	4	4	4

18.5

Critical Values for a Nonparametric Test of Dispersion (cont.)

5% Values of r

n	26	27	28	29	30	31	32	33	34	35	36	37	38	39	40	41	42	43	44	45	46	47	48	49	50
2	-	-	-	-	-	-	-	-	-	-	-	-	-	39	40	41	42	43	44	45	46	47	48	49	50
3	24	25	26	27	28	29	29	30	31	32	33	34	35	35	36	37	38	39	40	41	41	42	43	44	45
4	21	22	23	24	24	25	26	27	27	28	29	30	30	31	32	33	33	34	35	36	36	37	38	39	39
5	19	20	20	21	22	22	23	24	24	25	26	26	27	28	28	29	30	30	31	32	32	33	33	34	35
6	17	18	18	19	19	20	21	21	22	22	23	24	24	25	25	26	26	27	28	28	29	29	30	31	31
7	16	16	17	17	18	18	19	19	20	20	21	21	22	22	23	23	24	24	25	25	26	27	27	28	28
8	14	15	15	16	16	17	17	18	18	19	19	19	20	20	21	21	22	22	23	23	24	24	25	25	26
9	13	14	14	15	15	15	16	16	17	17	18	18	18	19	19	20	20	21	21	21	22	22	23	23	24
10	12	13	13	14	14	14	15	15	15	16	16	17	17	17	18	18	19	19	19	20	20	21	21	21	22
11	12	12	12	13	13	13	14	14	14	15	15	16	16	16	17	17	17	18	18	19	19	19	20	20	20
12	11	11	12	12	12	13	13	13	14	14	14	15	15	15	16	16	16	17	17	17	18	18	18	19	19
13	10	11	11	11	12	12	12	13	13	13	14	14	14	14	15	15	15	16	16	16	17	17	17	18	18
14	10	10	10	11	11	11	12	12	12	13	13	13	13	14	14	14	15	15	15	15	16	16	16	17	17
15	9	10	10	10	10	11	11	11	12	12	12	12	13	13	13	14	14	14	14	15	15	15	16	16	16
16	9	9	9	10	10	10	11	11	11	11	12	12	12	12	13	13	13	13	14	14	14	15	15	15	15
17	9	9	9	9	10	10	10	10	11	11	11	11	12	12	12	12	13	13	13	13	14	14	14	14	15
18	8	9	9	9	9	9	10	10	10	10	11	11	11	11	12	12	12	12	13	13	13	13	14	14	14
19	8	8	8	9	9	9	9	10	10	10	10	11	11	11	11	11	12	12	12	12	13	13	13	14	14
20	8	8	8	8	9	9	9	9	9	10	10	10	10	11	11	11	11	11	12	12	12	12	13	13	13
21	7	8	8	8	8	9	9	9	9	9	10	10	10	10	10	11	11	11	11	11	12	12	12	12	12
22	7	7	8	8	8	8	8	9	9	9	9	9	10	10	10	10	10	11	11	11	11	11	12	12	12
23	7	7	7	8	8	8	8	8	9	9	9	9	9	10	10	10	10	10	11	11	11	11	11	11	12
24	7	7	7	7	8	8	8	8	8	9	9	9	9	9	9	10	10	10	10	10	11	11	11	11	11
25	7	7	7	7	7	8	8	8	8	8	8	9	9	9	9	9	10	10	10	10	10	10	11	11	11
26	7	7	7	7	7	7	8	8	8	8	8	8	9	9	9	9	9	9	10	10	10	10	10	10	11
27	6	7	7	7	7	7	7	8	8	8	8	8	8	8	9	9	9	9	9	9	10	10	10	10	10
28	6	6	7	7	7	7	7	7	7	8	8	8	8	8	8	9	9	9	9	9	9	10	10	10	10
29	6	6	6	7	7	7	7	7	7	7	8	8	8	8	8	8	9	9	9	9	9	9	10	10	10
30	6	6	6	6	7	7	7	7	7	7	7	8	8	8	8	8	8	9	9	9	9	9	9	9	10
31	6	6	6	6	6	7	7	7	7	7	7	7	8	8	8	8	8	8	8	9	9	9	9	9	9
32	6	6	6	6	6	6	7	7	7	7	7	7	7	8	8	8	8	8	8	8	9	9	9	9	9
33	6	6	6	6	6	6	6	7	7	7	7	7	7	7	8	8	8	8	8	8	8	9	9	9	9
34	5	6	6	6	6	6	6	6	7	7	7	7	7	7	7	8	8	8	8	8	8	8	8	9	9
35	5	6	6	6	6	6	6	6	6	7	7	7	7	7	7	7	8	8	8	8	8	8	8	8	9
36	5	5	6	6	6	6	6	6	6	6	7	7	7	7	7	7	7	8	8	8	8	8	8	8	8
37	5	5	5	6	6	6	6	6	6	6	6	7	7	7	7	7	7	7	7	8	8	8	8	8	8
38	5	5	5	5	6	6	6	6	6	6	6	6	7	7	7	7	7	7	7	7	8	8	8	8	8
39	5	5	5	5	6	6	6	6	6	6	6	6	6	7	7	7	7	7	7	7	7	8	8	8	8
40	5	5	5	5	5	6	6	6	6	6	6	6	6	7	7	7	7	7	7	7	7	7	8	8	8
41	5	5	5	5	5	5	6	6	6	6	6	6	6	6	7	7	7	7	7	7	7	7	7	8	8
42	5	5	5	5	5	5	6	6	6	6	6	6	6	6	6	7	7	7	7	7	7	7	7	7	8
43	5	5	5	5	5	5	5	6	6	6	6	6	6	6	6	6	7	7	7	7	7	7	7	7	7
44	5	5	5	5	5	5	5	5	6	6	6	6	6	6	6	6	6	7	7	7	7	7	7	7	7
45	5	5	5	5	5	5	5	5	5	6	6	6	6	6	6	6	6	6	7	7	7	7	7	7	7
46	5	5	5	5	5	5	5	5	5	6	6	6	6	6	6	6	6	6	6	6	7	7	7	7	7
47	5	5	5	5	5	5	5	5	5	5	6	6	6	6	6	6	6	6	6	6	7	7	7	7	7
48	4	5	5	5	5	5	5	5	5	5	5	6	6	6	6	6	6	6	6	6	6	7	7	7	7
49	4	5	5	5	5	5	5	5	5	5	5	6	6	6	6	6	6	6	6	6	6	6	7	7	7
50	4	4	5	5	5	5	5	5	5	5	5	5	6	6	6	6	6	6	6	6	6	6	6	7	7

Critical Values for a Nonparametric Test of Dispersion (*cont.*)

1% values of *r*

n	2	3	4	5	6	7	8	9	10	11	12	13	14	15	16	17	18	19	20	21	22	23	24	25
2	-	-	-	-	-	-	-	-	-	-	-	-	-	-	-	-	-	-	-	-	-	-	-	-
3	-	-	-	-	-	-	-	-	-	-	-	-	-	-	-	-	-	-	-	-	-	23	24	25
4	-	-	-	-	-	-	-	-	-	11	12	13	14	15	16	17	17	18	19	20	21	22	23	24
5	-	-	-	-	-	-	8	9	10	11	11	12	13	14	15	15	16	17	18	19	19	20	21	22
6	-	-	-	-	6	7	8	9	9	10	11	11	12	13	14	14	15	15	16	17	18	19	19	20
7	-	-	-	5	6	7	7	8	9	9	10	11	11	12	13	13	14	15	15	16	17	17	18	19
8	-	-	-	5	6	6	7	8	8	9	9	10	11	11	12	12	13	14	14	15	15	16	17	17
9	-	-	4	5	6	6	7	7	8	8	9	10	10	11	11	12	12	13	13	14	15	15	16	16
10	-	-	4	5	5	6	6	7	7	8	9	9	10	10	11	11	12	12	13	13	14	14	15	15
11	-	-	4	5	5	6	6	7	7	8	8	9	9	10	10	11	11	12	12	12	13	13	14	14
12	-	3	4	4	5	5	6	6	7	7	8	8	9	9	10	10	11	11	11	12	12	13	13	14
13	-	3	4	4	5	5	6	6	7	7	7	8	8	9	9	10	10	10	11	11	12	12	13	13
14	-	3	4	4	5	5	6	6	6	7	7	8	8	8	9	9	9	10	10	11	11	12	12	12
15	-	3	4	4	5	5	5	6	6	7	7	7	8	8	9	9	9	10	10	10	11	11	12	12
16	-	3	4	4	4	5	5	6	6	6	7	7	7	8	8	9	9	9	10	10	10	11	11	11
17	-	3	4	4	4	5	5	5	6	6	7	7	7	8	8	8	9	9	9	10	10	10	11	11
18	-	3	3	4	4	5	5	5	6	6	6	7	7	7	8	8	8	9	9	9	10	10	10	11
19	-	3	3	4	4	5	5	5	6	6	6	7	7	7	7	8	8	8	9	9	9	10	10	10
20	-	3	3	4	4	4	5	5	5	6	6	6	7	7	7	8	8	8	8	9	9	9	10	10
21	-	3	3	4	4	4	5	5	5	6	6	6	6	7	7	7	8	8	8	9	9	9	9	10
22	-	3	3	4	4	4	5	5	5	5	6	6	6	7	7	7	7	8	8	8	9	9	9	9
23	-	3	3	4	4	4	4	5	5	5	6	6	6	6	7	7	7	8	8	8	8	9	9	9
24	2	3	3	4	4	4	4	5	5	5	6	6	6	6	7	7	7	7	8	8	8	8	9	9
25	2	3	3	3	4	4	4	5	5	5	5	6	6	6	6	7	7	7	7	8	8	8	8	9
26	2	3	3	3	4	4	4	5	5	5	5	6	6	6	6	7	7	7	7	8	8	8	8	8
27	2	3	3	3	4	4	4	4	5	5	5	5	6	6	6	6	7	7	7	7	8	8	8	8
28	2	3	3	3	4	4	4	4	5	5	5	5	6	6	6	6	7	7	7	7	7	8	8	8
29	2	3	3	3	4	4	4	4	5	5	5	5	6	6	6	6	6	7	7	7	7	8	8	8
30	2	3	3	3	4	4	4	4	4	5	5	5	5	6	6	6	6	7	7	7	7	7	8	8
31	2	3	3	3	3	4	4	4	4	5	5	5	5	6	6	6	6	6	7	7	7	7	7	8
32	2	3	3	3	3	4	4	4	4	5	5	5	5	5	6	6	6	6	6	7	7	7	7	7
33	2	3	3	3	3	4	4	4	4	5	5	5	5	5	6	6	6	6	6	7	7	7	7	7
34	2	3	3	3	3	4	4	4	4	4	5	5	5	5	5	6	6	6	6	6	7	7	7	7
35	2	3	3	3	3	4	4	4	4	4	5	5	5	5	5	6	6	6	6	6	7	7	7	7
36	2	3	3	3	3	4	4	4	4	4	5	5	5	5	5	6	6	6	6	6	6	7	7	7
37	2	3	3	3	3	3	4	4	4	4	5	5	5	5	5	5	6	6	6	6	6	7	7	7
38	2	3	3	3	3	3	4	4	4	4	4	5	5	5	5	5	6	6	6	6	6	6	7	7
39	2	3	3	3	3	3	4	4	4	4	4	5	5	5	5	5	5	6	6	6	6	6	7	7
40	2	2	3	3	3	3	4	4	4	4	4	5	5	5	5	5	5	6	6	6	6	6	6	7
41	2	2	3	3	3	3	4	4	4	4	4	4	5	5	5	5	5	6	6	6	6	6	6	6
42	2	2	3	3	3	3	4	4	4	4	4	4	5	5	5	5	5	5	6	6	6	6	6	6
43	2	2	3	3	3	3	3	4	4	4	4	4	5	5	5	5	5	5	6	6	6	6	6	6
44	2	2	3	3	3	3	3	4	4	4	4	4	5	5	5	5	5	5	5	6	6	6	6	6
45	2	2	3	3	3	3	3	4	4	4	4	4	4	5	5	5	5	5	5	6	6	6	6	6
46	2	2	3	3	3	3	3	4	4	4	4	4	4	5	5	5	5	5	5	5	6	6	6	6
47	2	2	3	3	3	3	3	4	4	4	4	4	4	5	5	5	5	5	5	5	6	6	6	6
48	2	2	3	3	3	3	3	3	4	4	4	4	4	4	5	5	5	5	5	5	6	6	6	6
49	2	2	3	3	3	3	3	3	4	4	4	4	4	4	5	5	5	5	5	5	5	6	6	6
50	2	2	3	3	3	3	3	3	4	4	4	4	4	4	5	5	5	5	5	5	5	6	6	6

18.5

Critical Values for a Nonparametric Test of Dispersion (*cont.*)

1% values of r

n	26	27	28	29	30	31	32	33	34	35	36	37	38	39	40	41	42	43	44	45	46	47	48	49	50
2	-	-	-	-	-	-	-	-	-	-	-	-	-	-	-	-	-	-	-	-	-	-	-	-	-
3	26	27	28	29	30	31	32	33	34	35	36	37	38	39	39	40	41	42	43	44	45	46	47	48	49
4	24	25	26	27	28	29	30	30	31	32	33	34	35	36	36	37	38	39	40	41	42	42	43	44	45
5	22	23	24	25	26	26	27	28	29	29	30	31	32	33	33	34	35	36	37	37	38	39	40	40	41
6	21	21	22	23	24.	24	25	26	26	27	28	29	29	30	31	31	32	33	33	34	35	36	36	37	38
7	19	20	20	21	22	22	23	24	24	25	26	26	27	28	28	29	30	30	31	31	32	33	33	34	35
8	18	18	19	20	20	21	21	22	23	23	24	24	25	26	26	27	27	28	29	29	30	30	31	31	32
9	17	17	18	18	19	19	20	21	21	22	22	23	23	24	24	25	25	26	27	27	28	28	29	29	30
10	16	16	17	17	18	18	19	19	20	20	21	21	22	22	23	23	24	24	25	25	26	26	27	27	28
11	15	15	16	16	17	17	18	18	19	19	20	20	21	21	21	22	22	23	23	24	24	25	25	26	26
12	14	15	15	15	16	16	17	17	18	18	19	19	19	20	20	21	21	22	22	23	23	23	24	24	25
13	13	14	14	15	15	16	16	16	17	17	18	18	18	19	19	20	20	21	21	21	22	22	23	23	23
14	13	13	14	14	14	15	15	16	16	16	17	17	18	18	18	19	19	20	20	20	21	21	21	22	22
15	12	13	13	13	14	14	15	15	15	16	16	16	17	17	18	18	18	19	19	19	20	20	20	21	21
16	12	12	13	13	13	14	14	14	15	15	15	16	16	16	17	17	17	18	18	19	19	19	20	20	20
17	11	12	12	12	13	13	13	14	14	14	15	15	15	16	16	16	17	17	17	18	18	18	19	19	19
18	11	11	12	12	12	13	13	13	14	14	14	15	15	15	15	16	16	16	17	17	17	18	18	18	19
19	11	11	11	12	12	12	12	13	13	13	14	14	14	15	15	15	16	16	16	16	17	17	17	18	18
20	10	11	11	11	11	12	12	12	13	13	13	14	14	14	14	15	15	15	16	16	16	16	17	17	17
21	10	10	11	11	11	11	12	12	12	13	13	13	13	14	14	14	14	15	15	15	16	16	16	16	17
22	10	10	10	10	11	11	11	12	12	12	12	13	13	13	13	14	14	14	15	15	15	15	16	16	16
23	9	10	10	10	10	11	11	11	12	12	12	12	13	13	13	13	14	14	14	14	15	15	15	15	16
24	9	9	10	10	10	10	11	11	11	11	12	12	12	12	13	13	13	14	14	14	14	14	15	15	15
25	9	9	9	10	10	10	10	11	11	11	11	12	12	12	12	13	13	13	13	14	14	14	14	15	15
26	9	9	9	9	10	10	10	10	11	11	11	11	12	12	12	12	12	13	13	13	13	14	14	14	14
27	9	9	9	9	9	10	10	10	10	11	11	11	11	11	12	12	12	12	13	13	13	13	14	14	14
28	8	9	9	9	9	9	10	10	10	10	11	11	11	11	11	12	12	12	13	13	13	13	13	13	14
29	8	8	9	9	9	9	9	10	10	10	10	11	11	11	11	11	12	12	12	12	13	13	13	13	13
30	8	8	8	9	9	9	9	9	10	10	10	10	11	11	11	11	11	12	12	12	12	12	13	13	13
31	8	8	8	8	9	9	9	9	9	10	10	10	10	10	11	11	11	11	11	12	12	12	12	12	13
32	8	8	8	8	8	9	9	9	9	9	10	10	10	10	10	11	11	11	11	11	12	12	12	12	12
33	8	8	8	8	8	9	9	9	9	9	9	10	10	10	10	10	11	11	11	11	11	12	12	12	12
34	7	8	8	8	8	8	9	9	9	9	9	9	10	10	10	10	10	11	11	11	11	11	12	12	12
35	7	7	8	8	8	8	8	9	9	9	9	9	9	10	10	10	10	10	11	11	11	11	11	11	12
36	7	7	8	8	8	8	8	8	9	9	9	9	9	9	10	10	10	10	10	11	11	11	11	11	11
37	7	7	7	8	8	8	8	8	8	9	9	9	9	9	9	10	10	10	10	10	11	11	11	11	11
38	7	7	7	7	8	8	8	8	8	8	9	9	9	9	9	10	10	10	10	10	10	11	11	11	11
39	7	7	7	7	8	8	8	8	8	8	9	9	9	9	9	9	10	10	10	10	10	10	10	11	11
40	7	7	7	7	7	8	8	8	8	8	8	9	9	9	9	9	9	10	10	10	10	10	10	10	11
41	7	7	7	7	7	7	8	8	8	8	8	8	9	9	9	9	9	9	10	10	10	10	10	10	10
42	7	7	7	7	7	7	8	8	8	8	8	8	8	9	9	9	9	9	9	10	10	10	10	10	10
43	6	7	7	7	7	7	7	8	8	8	8	8	8	8	9	9	9	9	9	9	10	10	10	11	11
44	6	7	7	7	7	7	7	7	8	8	8	8	8	8	8	9	9	9	9	9	9	10	10	10	10
45	6	6	7	7	7	7	7	7	7	8	8	8	8	8	8	9	9	9	9	9	9	9	10	10	10
46	6	6	7	7	7	7	7	7	7	8	8	8	8	8	8	8	9	9	9	9	9	9	9	10	10
47	6	6	6	7	7	7	7	7	7	7	8	8	8	8	8	8	9	9	9	9	9	9	9	9	9
48	6	6	6	7	7	7	7	7	7	7	7	8	8	8	8	8	8	8	9	9	9	9	9	9	9
49	6	6	6	6	7	7	7	7	7	7	7	8	8	8	8	8	8	8	8	9	9	9	9	9	9
50	6	6	6	6	6	7	7	7	7	7	7	7	8	8	8	8	8	8	8	8	9	9	9	9	9

19. PRODUCT MOMENT CORRELATION COEFFICIENT

19.1 Critical Values for the Product Moment Correlation Coefficient when $\rho = 0$

When the population product moment correlation coefficient ρ is zero, the sample product moment correlation coefficient r based on n pairs of observations has a distribution which is related to Student's t-distribution with $n - 2$ degrees of freedom (Section 2.1) as follows:

$$t = r\sqrt{(n - 2)/(1 - r^2)}.$$

The critical values for Student's t-distribution were transformed to give the values in the table here. Given a sample of size n, the value r' is given in the table such that

$$\Pr\{r \le r' | \rho = 0\} = \gamma,$$

where $\gamma = 0.75, 0.90, 0.95, 0.975, 0.99,$ and 0.995.

Critical Values for the Product Moment
Correlation Coefficient when $\rho = 0$
$$\Pr\{r \le \text{tabled value} \,|\, \rho = 0\} = \gamma$$

n	0.75	0.90	0.95	0.975	0.99	0.995
3	0.7071	0.9511	0.9877	0.9969	0.9995	0.9999
4	0.5000	0.8000	0.9000	0.9500	0.9800	0.9900
5	0.4040	0.6870	0.8054	0.8783	0.9343	0.9587
6	0.3473	0.6084	0.7293	0.8114	0.8822	0.9172
7	0.3091	0.5509	0.6694	0.7545	0.8329	0.8745
8	0.2811	0.5067	0.6215	0.7067	0.7887	0.8343
9	0.2596	0.4716	0.5822	0.6664	0.7498	0.7977
10	0.2423	0.4428	0.5493	0.6319	0.7155	0.7646
11	0.2281	0.4187	0.5214	0.6021	0.6851	0.7348
12	0.2161	0.3981	0.4973	0.5760	0.6581	0.7079
13	0.2058	0.3802	0.4762	0.5529	0.6339	0.6835
14	0.1968	0.3646	0.4575	0.5324	0.6120	0.6614
15	0.1890	0.3507	0.4409	0.5140	0.5923	0.6411
16	0.1820	0.3383	0.4259	0.4973	0.5742	0.6226
17	0.1757	0.3271	0.4124	0.4822	0.5577	0.6055
18	0.1700	0.3170	0.4000	0.4683	0.5426	0.5897
19	0.1649	0.3077	0.3887	0.4555	0.5285	0.5751
20	0.1602	0.2992	0.3783	0.4438	0.5155	0.5614
21	0.1558	0.2914	0.3687	0.4329	0.5034	0.5487
22	0.1518	0.2841	0.3598	0.4227	0.4921	0.5368
23	0.1481	0.2774	0.3515	0.4132	0.4815	0.5256
24	0.1447	0.2711	0.3438	0.4044	0.4716	0.5151
25	0.1415	0.2653	0.3365	0.3961	0.4622	0.5052
30	0.1281	0.2407	0.3061	0.3610	0.4226	0.4629
35	0.1179	0.2220	0.2826	0.3338	0.3916	0.4296
40	0.1098	0.2070	0.2638	0.3120	0.3665	0.4026
45	0.1032	0.1947	0.2483	0.2940	0.3457	0.3801
50	0.0976	0.1843	0.2353	0.2787	0.3281	0.3610
60	0.0888	0.1678	0.2144	0.2542	0.2997	0.3301
70	0.0820	0.1550	0.1982	0.2352	0.2776	0.3060
80	0.0765	0.1448	0.1852	0.2199	0.2597	0.2864
90	0.0720	0.1364	0.1745	0.2072	0.2449	0.2702
100	0.0682	0.1292	0.1654	0.1966	0.2324	0.2565

19.2 The Transformation $z = \tanh^{-1} r$ for the Correlation Coefficient

The mean and variance of the sample product moment correlation coefficient r depend in a complicated way on ρ, the population product moment correlation coefficient, and on n, the sample size. When n is large and the absolute value of ρ is considerably less than one, the mean of r is approximately ρ, and the variance of r is approximately $(1 - \rho^2)^2/n$. If one takes

$$z = \frac{1}{2} \log_e \frac{1 + r}{1 - r} = \tanh^{-1} r,$$

then z is approximately normally distributed with the variance of z approximately equal to $1/(n - 3)$ which does not depend on ρ. The mean of z is approximately $\tanh^{-1} \rho$. This type of transformation is known as a variance stabilizing transformation and is used wherever it is necessary to assume that the variance is constant over many values of ρ, for example, in the analysis of variance.

The distribution of r for various values of ρ and n has been tabulated by David [44].

The Transformation $z = \tanh^{-1} r$
for the Correlation Coefficient

r	z	r	z	r	z
0.00	0.0000	0.45	0.4847	0.90	1.4722
0.01	0.0100	0.46	0.4973	0.91	1.5275
0.02	0.0200	0.47	0.5101	0.92	1.5890
0.03	0.0300	0.48	0.5230	0.93	1.6584
0.04	0.0400	0.49	0.5361	0.94	1.7380
0.05	0.0500	0.50	0.5493	0.95	1.8318
0.06	0.0601	0.51	0.5627	0.96	1.9459
0.07	0.0701	0.52	0.5763	0.961	1.9588
0.08	0.0802	0.53	0.5901	0.962	1.9721
0.09	0.0902	0.54	0.6042	0.963	1.9857
0.10	0.1003	0.55	0.6184	0.964	1.9996
0.11	0.1104	0.56	0.6328	0.965	2.0139
0.12	0.1206	0.57	0.6475	0.966	2.0287
0.13	0.1307	0.58	0.6625	0.967	2.0439
0.14	0.1409	0.59	0.6777	0.968	2.0595
0.15	0.1511	0.60	0.6931	0.969	2.0756
0.16	0.1614	0.61	0.7089	0.970	2.0923
0.17	0.1717	0.62	0.7250	0.971	2.1095
0.18	0.1820	0.63	0.7414	0.972	2.1273
0.19	0.1923	0.64	0.7582	0.973	2.1457
0.20	0.2027	0.65	0.7753	0.974	2.1649
0.21	0.2132	0.66	0.7928	0.975	2.1847
0.22	0.2237	0.67	0.8107	0.976	2.2054
0.23	0.2342	0.68	0.8291	0.977	2.2269
0.24	0.2448	0.69	0.8480	0.978	2.2494
0.25	0.2554	0.70	0.8673	0.979	2.2729
0.26	0.2661	0.71	0.8872	0.980	2.2976
0.27	0.2769	0.72	0.9076	0.981	2.3235
0.28	0.2877	0.73	0.9287	0.982	2.3507
0.29	0.2986	0.74	0.9505	0.983	2.3796
0.30	0.3095	0.75	0.9730	0.984	2.4101
0.31	0.3205	0.76	0.9962	0.985	2.4427
0.32	0.3316	0.77	1.0203	0.986	2.4774
0.33	0.3428	0.78	1.0454	0.987	2.5147
0.34	0.3541	0.79	1.0714	0.988	2.5550
0.35	0.3654	0.80	1.0986	0.989	2.5987
0.36	0.3769	0.81	1.1270	0.990	2.6467
0.37	0.3884	0.82	1.1568	0.991	2.6996
0.38	0.4001	0.83	1.1881	0.992	2.7587
0.39	0.4118	0.84	1.2212	0.993	2.8257
0.40	0.4236	0.85	1.2562	0.994	2.9031
0.41	0.4356	0.86	1.2933	0.995	2.9945
0.42	0.4477	0.87	1.3331	0.996	3.1063
0.43	0.4599	0.88	1.3758	0.997	3.2504
0.44	0.4722	0.89	1.4219	0.998	3.4534

19.2

19.3 Critical Values of the Multiple Correlation Coefficient

Let $X_1, X_2, \ldots, X_k$ have the k-variate normal distribution, and let the regression of X_1 on the other $k - 1$ variates be Z. The product moment correlation coefficient between X_1 and Z is called the multiple correlation coefficient of X_1 on Z, and is denoted by $R_{1 \cdot 23 \ldots k}$. When $R_{1 \cdot 23 \ldots k}$ is zero, then the αth critical value of the distribution of its estimate $\hat{R}(\alpha)_{1 \cdot 23 \ldots k}$, obtained from a sample of n observations in the usual way, is related to the αth critical value of the F-distribution as follows:

$$\hat{R}(\alpha)_{1 \cdot 23 \ldots k} = \sqrt{\frac{(k - 1)F(\alpha)}{(n - k) + (k - 1)F(\alpha)}},$$

where $F(\alpha)$ is the αth critical value of the F-distribution with $(k - 1)$ degrees of freedom for the numerator and $(n - k)$ degrees of freedom for the denominator.

The tables given here were computed from the tables of the F-distribution (Section 4.1) using this formula. The degrees of freedom f in the table are computed from $f = n - k$, where n is the sample size and k is the number of variates.

Critical Values of the Multiple Correlation Coefficient

(0.95 values on first line and 0.99 values on second line)

$Pr\{R \le \text{tabled value}\} = 0.95$ or 0.99

f	Number of Variables 3	4	5	6	f	Number of Variables 3	4	5	6
1	0.999	0.999	0.999	1.000	18	0.532	0.587	0.628	0.660
	1.000	1.000	1.000	1.000		0.633	0.678	0.710	0.736
2	0.975	0.983	0.987	0.990	19	0.520	0.575	0.615	0.647
	0.995	0.997	0.997	0.998		0.620	0.665	0.697	0.723
3	0.930	0.950	0.961	0.968	20	0.509	0.563	0.604	0.636
	0.977	0.983	0.987	0.990		0.607	0.652	0.685	0.712
4	0.881	0.912	0.930	0.942	21	0.498	0.552	0.593	0.624
	0.949	0.962	0.970	0.975		0.596	0.641	0.674	0.700
5	0.836	0.874	0.898	0.914	22	0.488	0.542	0.582	0.614
	0.917	0.937	0.949	0.957		0.585	0.630	0.663	0.690
6	0.795	0.839	0.867	0.886	23	0.479	0.532	0.572	0.604
	0.886	0.911	0.927	0.938		0.574	0.619	0.653	0.679
7	0.758	0.807	0.838	0.860	24	0.470	0.523	0.562	0.594
	0.855	0.885	0.904	0.918		0.565	0.609	0.643	0.669
8	0.726	0.777	0.811	0.835	25	0.462	0.514	0.553	0.585
	0.827	0.860	0.882	0.898		0.555	0.600	0.633	0.660
9	0.697	0.750	0.786	0.812	26	0.454	0.506	0.545	0.576
	0.800	0.837	0.861	0.878		0.546	0.590	0.624	0.651
10	0.671	0.726	0.763	0.790	27	0.446	0.498	0.536	0.568
	0.776	0.814	0.840	0.859		0.538	0.582	0.615	0.642
11	0.648	0.703	0.741	0.770	28	0.439	0.490	0.529	0.560
	0.753	0.793	0.821	0.841		0.529	0.573	0.607	0.633
12	0.627	0.683	0.722	0.751	29	0.432	0.483	0.521	0.552
	0.732	0.773	0.802	0.824		0.522	0.565	0.598	0.625
13	0.608	0.664	0.703	0.733	30	0.425	0.476	0.514	0.545
	0.712	0.755	0.785	0.807		0.514	0.557	0.591	0.618
14	0.590	0.646	0.686	0.717	40	0.373	0.419	0.455	0.484
	0.694	0.737	0.768	0.791		0.454	0.494	0.526	0.552
15	0.574	0.630	0.670	0.701	60	0.308	0.348	0.380	0.406
	0.677	0.721	0.752	0.776		0.377	0.414	0.442	0.467
16	0.559	0.615	0.655	0.687	120	0.221	0.251	0.275	0.295
	0.662	0.706	0.738	0.762		0.272	0.300	0.322	0.342
17	0.545	0.601	0.641	0.673					
	0.647	0.691	0.724	0.749					

19.3

20. ORTHOGONAL POLYNOMIALS, RANDOM NUMBERS, AND CONSTANTS

20.1 Orthogonal Polynomials

A sample of n pairs of observations (x, y) is available, and the values of x are equally spaced. Suppose that a regression curve of y on x is to be obtained. The ith degree orthogonal polynomial tabulated here is indicated in the table by ξ_i for $i = 1, 2, 3$. The first step in obtaining the regression function is to decide on the degree of the polynomial to be fitted. Suppose this degree is I, where $I = 1, 2, 3$. Then for each i between 1 and I, the n observed x values are replaced by the numbers from the table listed under n and ξ_i. Next, each y is multiplied by the corresponding tabulated ξ_i value, and the sum $\sum \xi_i y$ over all n entries is formed. A separate sum is made for each orthogonal polynomial of degree i for $1 \leq i \leq I$.

The number immediately under the line at the foot of ξ_i in the table is $\sum \xi^2$, where the sum is over the n tabulated entries for ξ_i. The regression coefficient of y on ξ_i is given by $b_i = \sum \xi_i y / \sum \xi^2$, and the regression polynomial of degree I of y on x is $\bar{y} + b_1 \xi_1 + \cdots + b_I \xi_I$, $1 \leq I \leq 3$, where ξ_i is the polynomial in x of degree i given under the heading for the appropriate value of n, and $\bar{y}$ is the mean of the y's. Anderson and Houseman [2] give extensive tables of orthogonal polynomials through the fifth degree and $n = 104$.

Orthogonal Polynomials

$n = 3(1)12$, first, second, and third order

ξ_1	ξ_2		ξ_1	ξ_2	ξ_3		ξ_1	ξ_2	ξ_3		ξ_1	ξ_2	ξ_3		ξ_1	ξ_2	ξ_3
	n = 3			**n = 4**				**n = 5**				**n = 6**				**n = 7**	
-1	+1		-3	+1	-1		-2	+2	-1		-5	+5	-5		-3	+5	-1
0	-2		-1	-1	+3		-1	-1	+2		-3	-1	+7		-2	0	+1
+1	+1		+1	-1	-3		0	-2	0		-1	-4	+4		-1	-3	+1
			+3	+1	+1		+1	-1	-2		+1	-4	-4		0	-4	0
							+2	+2	+1		+3	-1	-7		+1	-3	-1
											+5	+5	+5		+2	0	-1
															+3	+5	+1

| 2 | 6 | | 20 | 4 | 20 | | 10 | 14 | 10 | | 70 | 84 | 180 | | 28 | 84 | 6 |

$n=3$: $x-2$; $3x^2-12x+10$; ----

$n=4$: $2x-5$; x^2-5x+5; $\frac{1}{3}(10x^3-75x^2+167x-105)$

$n=5$: $x-3$; x^2-6x+7; $\frac{1}{6}(5x^3-45x^2+118x-84)$

$n=6$: $2x-7$; $\frac{1}{2}(3x^2-21x+28)$; $\frac{1}{6}(10x^3-105x^2+317x-252)$

$n=7$: $x-4$; $x^2-8x+12$; $\frac{1}{6}(x^3-12x^2+41x-36)$

ξ_1	ξ_2	ξ_3		ξ_1	ξ_2	ξ_3		ξ_1	ξ_2	ξ_3		ξ_1	ξ_2	ξ_3		ξ_1	ξ_2	ξ_3
	n = 8				**n = 9**				**n = 10**				**n = 11**				**n = 12**
-7	+7	-7		-4	+28	-14		-9	+6	-42		-5	+15	-30		-11	+55	-33
-5	+1	+5		-3	+7	+7		-7	+2	+14		-4	+6	+6		-9	+25	+3
-3	-3	+7		-2	-8	+13		-5	-1	+35		-3	-1	+22		-7	+1	+21
-1	-5	+3		-1	-17	+9		-3	-3	+31		-2	-6	+23		-5	-17	+25
+1	-5	-3		0	-20	0		-1	-4	+12		-1	-9	+14		-3	-29	+19
+3	-3	-7		+1	-17	-9		+1	-4	-12		0	-10	0		-1	-35	+7
+5	+1	-5		+2	-8	-13		+3	-3	-31		+1	-9	-14		+1	-35	-7
+7	+7	+7		+3	+7	-7		+5	-1	-35		+2	-6	-23		+3	-29	-19
				+4	+28	+14		+7	+2	-14		+3	-1	-22		+5	-17	-25
								+9	+6	+42		+4	+6	-6		+7	+1	-21
												+5	+15	+30		+9	+25	-3
																+11	+55	+33

| 168 | 168 | 264 | | 60 | 2772 | 990 | | 330 | 132 | 8580 | | 110 | 858 | 4290 | | 572 | 12012 | 5148 |

$n=8$: $2x-9$; $x^2-9x+15$; $\frac{1}{3}(2x^3-27x^2+103x-99)$

$n=9$: $x-5$; $3x^2-30x+55$; $\frac{1}{6}(5x^3-75x^2+316x-330)$

$n=10$: $2x-11$; $\frac{1}{2}(x^2-11x+22)$; $\frac{1}{6}(10x^3-165x^2+761x-858)$

$n=11$: $x-6$; $x^2-12x+26$; $\frac{1}{6}(5x^3-90x^2+451x-546)$

$n=12$: $2x-13$; $3x^2-39x+91$; $\frac{1}{3}(2x^3-39x^2+211x-273)$

20.2 Random Numbers

The random numbers given here were generated within a computing machine by using various octal starters (see Table A below) and multiplying by the octal number 2000005. This result modulo 2^{35} was then used as the starter for the second random number. Each random number was obtained by taking the seven bits (seven binary digits) immediately preceding the right-hand 18 bits of the 35 binary digits plus sign which were kept as the new starter. These seven bits were then converted to decimal digits, and if the result was between 00 and 99, the answer was kept; otherwise, the answer was deleted and another random number generated. The numbers were printed in groups of four, which will be called quartets. Morrison [147] discusses the above procedure for generating random numbers.

Each set of 4000 random digits so obtained (two pages) was summarized together, and various statistics were computed for each set. The values of the starters and chi-square goodness-of-fit statistics are summarized below in Table A.

The poker test consisted of noting the number of quartets of numbers with no like digits (expected value 504), the number with one pair (expected value 432), the number with two pairs (expected value 27), and the number with three of a kind or four of a kind (expected value 37). The usual chi-square goodness-of-fit statistic was then computed for each set of 4000 digits, that is,

$$\chi^2 = \sum_{i=1}^{4} \frac{(\text{observed}_i - \text{expected}_i)^2}{\text{expected}_i}.$$

The values of this statistic are given in Table A below.

For the frequency distribution of digits, the number of times each digit appeared among the 4000 was found. This number was compared with its expected value of 400 in the usual chi-square goodness-of-fit statistic.

For the frequency distribution of pairs of digits, the first two digits were examined, and a score was placed for the number between 00 and 99 that corresponded to the two digits; then the next two digits were examined, etc. Note that pairs made up of the second and third digits were not examined. If they had been examined, a serial test due to Good [75] would have been applied. In the case here, however, each of the frequencies of the pairs of digits was compared with 20, the expected value, and the chi-square goodness-of-fit test was applied yielding the chi-square values noted in Table A.

For the distance-between-zeros frequency, the number of digits between consecutive zeros was counted. This time the expected value was computed as outlined by Bell [15] as follows: The number of different runs was noted from the frequency distribution of digits (equals the number of zeros minus one), and the expected value for i digits between zeros was computed as: $(0.9)^i (0.1)$ (number of zeros minus one). The values of the usual chi-square goodness-of-fit statistic are listed in Table A.

The data on the ten sets were combined according to the method outlined by Snedecor [204] to give the sum of ten chi-squares, pooled chi-square, and heterogeneity chi-square tests. The values for these chi-squares are given in Table A.

Ten sets of 4000 digits each (20 pages) are given. All the sets passed all four of the tests (significance level 10 percent for each tail) applied to them. When any one set failed one of the tests, that set was deleted and a new set computed. This was considered proper here since the number of random digits (40,000) is relatively small, and this table would usually be used only for relatively short sets of random numbers. If a long sequence of random digits is needed, one would expect to obtain a proportion of rejections close to the chosen significance level. Since this need not be true for short sequences of random digits, care must be exercised in using short sequences of random digits extracted from long sequences. The reader is referred to the RAND [179] set of random digits if he has need of several thousand of them. For short sets of random digits, the set given here should be sufficient.

TABLE A

SUMMARY OF STARTERS AND VALUES OF CHI-SQUARE
FOR TABLE OF RANDOM NUMBERS

Pages	Starter	Poker	Frequency of digits	Frequency of pairs	Distance between zeros
519–520	41, 210, 542, 351	1.8	7.9	89.1	16.8
521–522	120, 063, 150, 215	1.9	5.9	99.9	16.7
523–524	43, 641, 255, 041	0.7	10.3	108.3	16.9
525–526	73, 306, 514, 235	6.0	10.8	94.2	23.3
527–528	270, 056, 656, 171	1.3	4.1	91.1	27.0
529–530	315, 705, 200, 725	2.0	6.0	77.3	17.4
531–532	204, 434, 411, 105	0.9	8.2	90.5	16.4
533–534	173, 067, 740, 575	0.7	6.8	100.7	19.8
535–536	307, 232, 176, 555	1.0	6.9	89.3	17.0
537–538	237, 644, 544, 405	3.9	11.7	92.7	20.6
Sum of ten chi-squares		20.2	78.6	933.1	191.9
Pooled chi-square		3.8	11.1	102.5	55.7
Heterogeneity chi-square		16.4	67.5	830.6	136.2

Random Numbers

1368	9621	9151	2066	1208	2664	9822	6599	6911	5112
5953	5936	2541	4011	0408	3593	3679	1378	5936	2651
7226	9466	9553	7671	8599	2119	5337	5953	6355	6889
8883	3454	6773	8207	5576	6386	7487	0190	0867	1298
7022	5281	1168	4099	8069	8721	8353	9952	8006	9045
4576	1853	7884	2451	3488	1286	4842	7719	5795	3953
8715	1416	7028	4616	3470	9938	5703	0196	3465	0034
4011	0408	2224	7626	0643	1149	8834	6429	8691	0143
1400	3694	4482	3608	1238	8221	5129	6105	5314	8385
6370	1884	0820	4854	9161	6509	7123	4070	6759	6113
4522	5749	8084	3932	7678	3549	0051	6761	6952	7041
7195	6234	6426	7148	9945	0358	3242	0519	6550	1327
0054	0810	2937	2040	2299	4198	0846	3937	3986	1019
5166	5433	0381	9686	5670	5129	2103	1125	3404	8785
1247	3793	7415	7819	1783	0506	4878	7673	9840	6629
8529	7842	7203	1844	8619	7404	4215	9969	6948	5643
8973	3440	4366	9242	2151	0244	0922	5887	4883	1177
9307	2959	5904	9012	4951	3695	4529	7197	7179	3239
2923	4276	9467	9868	2257	1925	3382	7244	1781	8037
6372	2808	1238	8098	5509	4617	4099	6705	2386	2830
6922	1807	4900	5306	0411	1828	8634	2331	7247	3230
9862	8336	6453	0545	6127	2741	5967	8447	3017	5709
3371	1530	5104	3076	5506	3101	4143	5845	2095	6127
6712	9402	9588	7019	9248	9192	4223	6555	7947	2474
3071	8782	7157	5941	8830	8563	2252	8109	5880	9912
4022	9734	7852	9096	0051	7387	7056	9331	1317	7833
9682	8892	3577	0326	5306	0050	8517	4376	0788	5443
6705	2175	9904	3743	1902	5393	3032	8432	0612	7972
1872	8292	2366	8603	4288	6809	4357	1072	6822	5611
2559	7534	2281	7351	2064	0611	9613	2000	0327	6145
4399	3751	9783	5399	5175	8894	0296	9483	0400	2272
6074	8827	2195	2532	7680	4288	6807	3101	6850	6410
5155	7186	4722	6721	0838	3632	5355	9369	2006	7681
3193	2800	6184	7891	9838	6123	9397	4019	8389	9508
8610	1880	7423	3384	4625	6653	2900	6290	9286	2396
4778	8818	2992	6300	4239	9595	4384	0611	7687	2088
3987	1619	4164	2542	4042	7799	9084	0278	8422	4330
2977	0248	2793	3351	4922	8878	5703	7421	2054	4391
1312	2919	8220	7285	5902	7882	1403	5354	9913	7109
3890	7193	7799	9190	3275	7840	1872	6232	5295	3148
0793	3468	8762	2492	5854	8430	8472	2264	9279	2128
2139	4552	3444	6462	2524	8601	3372	1848	1472	9667
8277	9153	2880	9053	6880	4284	5044	8931	0861	1517
2236	4778	6639	0862	9509	2141	0208	1450	1222	5281
8837	7686	1771	3374	2894	7314	6856	0440	3766	6047
6605	6380	4599	3333	0713	8401	7146	8940	2629	2006
8399	8175	3525	1646	4019	8390	4344	8975	4489	3423
8053	3046	9102	4515	2944	9763	3003	3408	1199	2791
9837	9378	3237	7016	7593	5958	0068	3114	0456	6840
2557	6395	9496	1884	0612	8102	4402	5498	0422	3335

Random Numbers (cont.)

2671	4690	1550	2262	2597	8034	0785	2978	4409	0237
9111	0250	3275	7519	9740	4577	2064	0286	3398	1348
0391	6035	9230	4999	3332	0608	6113	0391	5789	9926
2475	2144	1886	2079	3004	9686	5669	4367	9306	2595
5336	5845	2095	6446	5694	3641	1085	8705	5416	9066
6808	0423	0155	1652	7897	4335	3567	7109	9690	3739
8525	0577	8940	9451	6726	0876	3818	7607	8854	3566
0398	0741	8787	3043	5063	0617	1770	5048	7721	7032
3623	9636	3638	1406	5731	3978	8068	7238	9715	3363
0739	2644	4917	8866	3632	5399	5175	7422	2476	2607
6713	3041	8133	8749	8835	6745	3597	3476	3816	3455
7775	9315	0432	8327	0861	1515	2297	3375	3713	9174
8599	2122	6842	9202	0810	2936	1514	2090	3067	3574
7955	3759	5254	1126	5553	4713	9605	7909	1658	5490
4766	0070	7260	6033	7997	0109	5993	7592	5436	1727
5165	1670	2534	8811	8231	3721	7947	5719	2640	1394
9111	0513	2751	8256	2931	7783	1281	6531	7259	6993
1667	1084	7889	8963	7018	8617	6381	0723	4926	4551
2145	4587	8585	2412	5431	4667	1942	7238	9613	2212
2739	5528	1481	7528	9368	1823	6979	2547	7268	2467
8769	5480	9160	5354	9700	1362	2774	7980	9157	8788
6531	9435	3422	2474	1475	0159	3414	5224	8399	5820
2937	4134	7120	2206	5084	9473	3958	7320	9878	8609
1581	3285	3727	8924	6204	0797	0882	5945	9375	9153
6268	1045	7076	1436	4165	0143	0293	4190	7171	7932
4293	0523	8625	1961	1039	2856	4889	4358	1492	3804
6936	4213	3212	7229	1230	0019	5998	9206	6753	3762
5334	7641	3258	3769	1362	2771	6124	9813	7915	8960
9373	1158	4418	8826	5665	5896	0358	4717	8232	4859
6968	9428	8950	5346	1741	2348	8143	5377	7695	0685
4229	0587	8794	4009	9691	4579	3302	7673	9629	5246
3807	7785	7097	5701	6639	0723	4819	0900	2713	7650
4891	8829	1642	2155	0796	0466	2946	2970	9143	6590
1055	2968	7911	7479	8199	9735	8271	5339	7058	2964
2983	2345	0568	4125	0894	8302	0506	6761	7706	4310
4026	3129	2968	8053	2797	4022	9838	9611	0975	2437
4075	0260	4256	0337	2355	9371	2954	6021	5783	2827
8488	5450	1327	7358	2034	8060	1788	6913	6123	9405
1976	1749	5742	4098	5887	4567	6064	2777	7830	5668
2793	4701	9466	9554	8294	2160	7486	1557	4769	2781
0916	6272	6825	7188	9611	1181	2301	5516	5451	6832
5961	1149	7946	1950	2010	0600	5655	0796	0569	4365
3222	4189	1891	8172	8731	4769	2782	1325	4238	9279
1176	7834	4600	9992	9449	5824	5344	1008	6678	1921
2369	8971	2314	4806	5071	8908	8274	4936	3357	4441
0041	4329	9265	0352	4764	9070	7527	7791	1094	2008
0803	8302	6814	2422	6351	0637	0514	0246	1845	8594
9965	7804	3930	8803	0268	1426	3130	3613	3947	8086
0011	2387	3148	7559	4216	2946	2865	6333	1916	2259
1767	9871	3914	5790	5287	7915	8959	1346	5482	9251

Random Numbers (cont.)

```
2604   3074   0504   3828   7881   0797   1094   4098   4940   7067
6930   4180   3074   0060   0909   3187   8991   0682   2385   2307
6160   9899   9084   5704   5666   3051   0325   4733   5905   9226
4884   1857   2847   2581   4870   1782   2980   0587   8797   5545
7294   2009   9020   0006   4309   3941   5645   6238   5052   4150

3478   4973   1056   3687   3145   5988   4214   5543   9185   9375
1764   7860   4150   2881   9895   2531   7363   8756   3724   9359
3025   0890   6436   3461   1411   0303   7422   2684   6256   3495
1771   3056   6630   4982   2386   2517   4747   5505   8785   8708
0254   1892   9066   4890   8716   2258   2452   3913   6790   6331

8537   9966   8224   9151   1855   8911   4422   1913   2000   1482
1475   0261   4465   4803   8231   6469   9935   4256   0648   7768
5209   5569   8410   3041   4325   7290   3381   5209   5571   9458
5456   5944   6038   3210   7165   0723   4820   1846   0005   3865
5043   6694   4853   8425   5871   1322   1052   1452   2486   1669

1719   0148   6977   1244   6443   5955   7945   1218   9391   6485
7432   2955   3933   8110   8585   1893   9218   7153   7566   6040
4926   4761   7812   7439   6436   3145   5934   7852   9095   9497
0769   0683   3768   1048   8519   2987   0124   3064   1881   3177
0805   3139   8514   5014   3274   6395   0549   3858   0820   6406

0204   7273   4964   5475   2648   6977   1371   6971   4850   6873
0092   1733   2349   2648   6609   5676   6445   3271   8867   3469
3139   4867   3666   9783   5088   4852   4143   7923   3858   0504
2033   7430   4389   7121   9982   0651   9110   9731   6421   4731
3921   0530   3605   8455   4205   7363   3081   3931   9331   1313

4111   9244   8135   9877   9529   9160   4407   9077   5306   0054
6573   1570   6654   3616   2049   7001   5185   7108   9270   6550
8515   8029   6880   4329   9367   1087   9549   1684   4838   5686
3590   2106   3245   1989   3529   3828   8091   6054   5656   3035
7212   9909   5005   7660   2620   6406   0690   4240   4070   6549

6701   0154   8806   1716   7029   6776   9465   8818   2886   3547
3777   9532   1333   8131   2929   6987   2408   0487   9172   6177
2495   3054   1692   0089   4090   2983   2136   8947   4625   7177
2073   8878   9742   3012   0042   3996   9930   1651   4982   9645
2252   8004   7840   2105   3033   8749   9153   2872   5100   8674

2104   2224   4052   2273   4753   4505   7156   5417   9725   7599
2371   0005   3844   6654   3246   4853   4301   8886   5217   1153
3270   1214   9649   1872   6930   9791   0248   2687   8126   1501
6209   7237   1966   5541   4224   7080   7630   6422   1160   5675
1309   9126   2920   4359   1726   0562   9654   4182   4097   7493

2406   8013   3634   6428   8091   5925   3923   1686   6097   9670
7365   9859   9378   7084   9402   9201   1815   7064   4324   7081
2889   4738   9929   1476   0785   3832   1281   5821   3690   9185
7951   3781   4755   6986   1659   5727   8108   9816   5759   4188
4548   6778   7672   9101   3911   8127   1918   8512   4197   6402

5701   8342   2852   4278   3343   9830   1756   0546   6717   3114
2187   7266   1210   3797   1636   7917   9933   3518   6923   6349
9360   6640   1315   6284   8265   7232   0291   3467   1088   7834
7850   7626   0745   1992   4998   7349   6451   6186   8916   4292
6186   9233   6571   0925   1748   5490   5264   3820   9829   1335
```

Random Numbers (cont.)

6063	2353	8531	8892	4109	5782	2283	1385	0699	5927
6305	1326	4551	2815	8937	2908	0698	5509	4303	9911
0143	0187	8127	2026	8313	8341	2479	4722	6602	2236
1031	0754	7989	4948	1804	3025	0997	9562	3674	7876
2022	3227	2147	5613	2857	8859	4941	7274	9412	0620
9149	0806	9751	8870	9677	9676	1854	8094	7658	7012
5863	0513	1402	3866	8696	9142	6063	2252	7818	2477
8724	0806	9644	8284	7010	0868	9076	4915	5751	9214
6783	4207	2958	5295	3175	3396	8117	5918	1037	4319
0862	1620	4690	0036	9654	4078	1918	8721	8454	7671
9394	2466	6427	5395	9393	0520	7074	0634	5578	4023
3220	3058	7787	7706	4094	5603	3303	8300	6185	8705
1491	3503	0584	7221	6176	0116	0309	1975	0910	3535
4368	5705	8579	5790	7244	6547	8495	7973	1805	7251
2325	4026	2919	8327	0267	2616	6572	8620	8245	6257
0591	1775	5134	8709	7373	3332	0507	5525	7640	2840
3471	1461	1149	6798	6070	9930	1862	3672	6718	3849
2600	9885	6219	3668	1005	5418	5832	0416	4220	4692
9572	7874	6034	4514	2628	1693	0628	2200	9006	3795
0822	2790	9386	5783	2689	2565	1565	0349	3410	5216
4329	3028	2549	2529	9434	3083	6800	8569	9290	8298
9289	5212	2355	9367	1297	1638	9282	3720	7178	2695
3932	9960	3399	1700	8253	1375	4594	6024	1223	5383
2282	0648	7561	7528	5870	7907	0713	8608	9682	8576
9933	3416	5957	2574	5553	5534	4707	3206	0963	2459
9015	6416	6603	2967	7591	5013	2878	8424	5452	4659
1539	0719	2637	9969	8450	4489	3528	3364	1459	9708
6849	5595	7969	2582	5627	1920	9772	8560	0892	6500
2523	7769	3536	9611	1079	1694	1254	4195	5799	5928
0701	7355	0587	8878	3446	1137	7690	0647	1407	6362
2163	8543	4594	6022	0496	8648	2999	1262	6702	0811
0327	5727	1070	5996	8660	9024	2135	9799	8414	9136
2169	3160	8707	6361	6339	4054	3251	7397	3480	5805
8393	8147	5360	4150	2990	3380	1789	7436	4781	0337
9726	9151	2064	0609	5878	9095	9737	2897	6510	8891
0515	2296	2636	9756	5313	7754	0916	6066	3905	1298
0649	8398	5614	0140	3155	2211	4988	3674	7663	0620
0026	9426	8005	8579	5774	7962	5092	5856	1626	0980
3422	0092	1626	1298	2475	1997	9796	7076	1541	1731
8191	1983	9164	1885	5468	8216	4327	8109	5880	9804
7408	0486	7654	4829	2711	6592	4785	5901	7147	9314
8261	9440	8118	6338	8157	9052	9093	8449	4066	4894
9274	8838	8342	3114	0455	6212	8862	6701	0099	0501
2699	0383	1400	3484	1492	4683	5369	3851	5870	0903
8740	0349	3502	3971	9960	6325	6727	4715	2945	9938
0247	2372	0424	0578	0036	1619	4479	7108	8520	1487
5136	9444	8343	1152	3615	1420	8923	7307	3978	5724
4844	8931	0964	2878	8212	9328	2656	1965	4805	0634
0205	8457	4333	2555	5353	9201	1606	2715	4014	1877
2517	5061	7642	3891	7713	7066	5435	1200	7455	5562

Random Numbers (cont.)

8529	7631	7050	2275	4383	0162	1937	0302	7109	9024
4272	3581	6632	5942	9513	6119	7721	7033	4632	6904
6009	1247	3898	2058	6466	8697	9562	3254	9644	8076
8714	0867	1189	9909	5113	7899	7558	2765	5076	2377
5862	5635	9795	6127	2872	5351	3380	2010	2836	4794
2834	0662	4423	2226	8886	4902	6038	3214	9241	1735
4537	0620	3480	6208	6784	4835	4567	5961	1202	8426
4090	3275	7424	3820	0108	5045	9145	7824	8365	5893
0827	6802	9469	4171	7282	4667	1838	5054	5145	5126
9104	5561	0764	6940	6960	2201	9636	0020	1845	1992
6395	0676	0014	3881	1247	3897	1951	2503	2864	6120
5860	4900	5410	2079	3125	7185	3593	3680	1846	9771
4869	7923	3859	1031	4559	2451	3592	3470	9728	3145
9482	9765	1065	6314	9731	7905	8245	6366	6283	7678
5106	6509	7110	1452	2693	2047	9311	9242	3977	5411
4932	9177	1521	8351	9323	6138	0147	6597	2757	2492
6979	7002	5668	8975	4593	5470	3210	7432	9644	8830
6392	0329	6775	9257	5190	0858	9602	5415	7922	3333
8115	4891	9133	8740	0349	3183	3662	0602	9763	6661
3962	2652	9426	8003	7631	7262	8127	1919	9353	9323
6760	6323	5492	6287	9442	4659	1136	7479	7883	1716
6216	2155	0832	7787	8022	2445	7512	2459	5158	6907
9684	9605	6838	9176	0684	3202	5595	8180	5352	9092
4656	5208	5255	1654	0591	2192	0875	3609	7364	7593
5664	6896	1992	4789	8101	8005	8682	6839	9601	5515
3987	2522	7665	1561	8164	2106	3559	9274	8626	2168
4786	1354	7318	0697	1381	6380	9580	7420	1848	1367
2430	6737	8440	8489	5691	9136	4691	0560	8603	4510
8616	5854	9854	0481	5877	8567	8239	8512	4199	7558
6225	3511	5336	8899	6965	8279	0529	9118	8078	4301
6654	3405	9538	4950	3170	5234	4458	2951	2062	4167
5303	4532	7187	8899	6975	0474	2187	7372	4547	9630
7486	2727	9740	2195	2112	8781	2406	8221	7598	7981
4999	3648	8313	8612	0078	1904	6313	9176	0997	9562
0680	1020	8141	3907	2033	7323	7096	7287	3041	4010
7401	8220	4851	3593	3678	1271	2563	4197	6717	3325
0066	2090	2961	0765	7437	5197	7929	9274	1368	9618
1882	4099	9294	4850	7082	8577	4762	8229	2863	5313
8231	3741	4893	9976	6201	2429	6105	5312	7335	4463
9402	9619	1779	3147	7140	1983	9160	0027	1270	1678
1637	8438	7649	1448	0273	5717	1825	7941	8345	2317
2103	2096	9248	9294	4958	3694	0085	6993	9408	3834
4465	4803	8562	8795	4919	9770	6864	8402	8091	5789
3852	2250	6978	6770	9076	4797	8036	1515	2497	1095
0793	5024	0470	8933	1793	2906	8995	0565	7505	7778
7311	5316	9218	3850	5241	4709	4709	4254	7349	6769
1779	2728	7148	9941	8777	0434	9693	5512	2251	7733
6105	5105	3599	7389	0183	2034	7642	3995	9766	4578
8698	2587	2087	7638	1872	0418	6340	9451	6937	4530
3937	3988	2038	1144	2640	1631	4008	1921	4546	9104

Random Numbers (cont.)

2271	2572	8665	3272	9033	8256	2822	3646	7599	0270
3025	0788	5311	7792	1837	4739	4552	3234	5572	9885
3382	6151	1011	3778	9951	7709	8060	2258	8536	2290
7870	5799	6032	9043	4526	8100	1957	9539	5370	0046
1697	0002	2340	6959	1915	1626	1297	1533	6572	3835
3395	3381	1862	3250	8614	5683	6757	5628	2551	6971
6081	6526	3028	2338	5702	8819	3679	4829	9909	4712
3470	9879	2935	1141	6398	6387	5634	9589	3212	7963
0432	8641	5020	6612	1038	1547	0948	4278	0020	6509
4995	5596	8286	8377	8567	8237	3520	8244	5694	3326
8246	6718	3851	5870	1216	2107	1387	1621	5509	5772
7825	8727	2849	3501	3551	1001	0123	7873	5926	6078
6258	2450	2962	1183	3666	4156	4454	8239	4551	2920
3235	5783	2701	2378	7460	3398	1223	4688	3674	7872
2525	9008	5997	0885	1053	2340	7066	5328	6412	5054
5852	9739	1457	8999	2789	9068	9829	1336	3148	7875
0440	3769	7864	4029	4494	9829	1339	4910	1303	9161
0820	4641	2375	2542	4093	5364	1145	2848	2792	0431
7114	2842	8554	6881	6377	9427	8216	1193	8042	8449
6558	9301	9096	0577	8520	5923	4717	0188	8545	8745
0345	9937	5569	0279	8951	6183	7787	7808	5149	2185
7430	2074	9427	8422	4082	5629	2971	9456	0649	7981
8030	7345	3389	4739	5911	1022	9189	2565	1982	8577
6272	6718	3849	4715	3156	2823	4174	8733	5600	7702
4894	9847	5611	4763	8755	3388	5114	3274	6681	3657
2676	5984	6806	2692	4012	0934	2436	0869	9557	2490
9305	2074	9378	7670	8284	7431	7361	2912	2251	7395
5138	2461	7213	1905	7775	9881	8782	6272	0632	4418
2452	4200	8674	9202	0812	3986	1143	7343	2264	9072
8882	3033	8746	7390	8609	1144	2531	6944	8869	1570
1087	9336	8020	9166	4472	8293	2904	7949	3165	7400
5666	2841	8134	9588	2915	4116	2802	6917	3993	8764
9790	2228	9702	1690	7170	7511	1937	0723	4505	7155
3250	8860	3294	2684	6572	3415	5750	8726	2647	6596
5450	3922	0950	0890	6434	2306	2781	1066	3681	2404
5765	0765	7311	5270	5910	7009	0240	7435	4568	6484
8408	1939	0599	5347	2160	7376	4696	6969	0787	3838
8460	7658	6906	9177	1492	4680	3719	3456	8681	6736
4198	7244	3849	4819	1008	6781	3388	5253	7041	6712
9872	4441	6712	9614	2736	5533	9062	2534	0855	7946
6485	0487	0004	5563	1481	1546	8245	6116	6920	0990
2064	0512	9509	0341	8131	7778	8609	9417	1216	4189
9927	8987	5321	3125	9992	9449	5951	5872	2057	5731
4918	9690	6121	8770	6053	6931	7252	5409	1869	4229
8099	5821	3899	2685	6781	3178	0096	2986	8878	8991
1901	4974	1262	6810	4673	8772	6616	2632	7891	9970
8273	6675	4925	3924	2274	3860	1662	7480	8674	4503
2878	8213	3170	5126	0434	9481	7029	8688	4027	3340
6088	1182	3242	0835	1765	8819	3462	9820	5759	4189
5773	6600	5306	0354	8295	0148	6608	9064	3421	8570

2742	6731	3741	4890	8818	3208	3171	5755	2301	5517
9112	8964	7544	8932	1281	2355	5563	1638	7331	2387
0462	1288	6055	6983	0294	5271	4846	1094	4234	5361
4616	3678	1168	1044	6235	6534	5263	9716	3890	6999
4976	3383	9718	1256	9764	0393	7132	6904	2607	4733
9852	1453	9473	2914	4262	7582	9644	7969	3711	8334
7535	0446	3178	0206	5295	2991	5923	3215	8824	9362
7469	6789	4044	7141	1840	6288	7101	0746	2695	7019
1886	1976	1856	9117	7133	7428	9700	0223	3753	0230
6268	0733	1136	7479	7881	0953	5499	1158	4729	1442
2097	9561	2830	0500	3695	4707	4083	8432	0611	7583
3735	1763	8090	1457	8894	0426	0433	9165	4050	1432
9296	5868	7340	8139	7202	0465	9028	7987	3800	4555
8527	5288	8545	9063	3106	4875	5945	3058	7682	5313
7866	9022	0844	5307	0612	8102	8529	7529	6106	5733
9954	5248	6636	4988	3463	2461	5451	4552	3026	1554
2613	8184	5800	6939	5684	7008	0950	0891	6856	0228
2668	4852	8006	8893	6596	9808	3623	9518	3102	6927
3002	2998	5357	6634	7099	2299	0198	4755	0795	3344
8422	4435	0134	4587	4886	2413	2774	6136	8993	2721
3690	2492	7171	7720	6509	7549	2330	5733	4730	1759
0813	6790	6858	1489	2669	3743	1901	4971	8280	1127
6477	5289	4092	4223	6454	7632	7577	2816	9202	0811
0772	2160	7236	0812	4195	5589	0830	8261	9232	5944
5692	9870	3583	8997	1533	6466	8830	7271	3809	3291
2080	3828	7880	0586	8482	7811	6807	3309	2729	8636
1039	3382	7600	1077	4455	8806	1822	1669	7501	5622
7227	0104	4141	1521	9104	5563	1392	8238	4882	0861
8506	6348	4612	8252	1062	1757	0964	2983	2244	0253
5086	0303	7423	3298	3979	2831	2257	1508	7642	3891
0092	1629	0377	3590	2209	4839	6332	1490	3092	2590
0935	5565	2315	8030	7651	5189	0075	9353	1921	9572
2605	3973	8204	4143	2677	0034	8601	3340	8383	2818
7277	9889	0390	5579	4620	5650	0310	2082	4664	0494
5484	3900	3485	0741	9069	5920	4326	7704	6525	2503
6905	7127	5933	1137	7583	6450	5658	7678	3444	5163
8387	5323	3753	1859	6043	0294	5110	6340	9137	6137
4094	4957	0163	9717	4118	4276	9465	8820	4127	2954
4951	3781	5101	1815	7068	6379	7252	1086	8919	5677
9047	0199	5068	7447	1664	9278	1708	3625	2864	1351
7274	9512	0074	6677	8676	0222	3335	1976	1645	3914
9192	4011	0255	5458	6942	8043	6201	1587	0972	3391
0554	1690	6333	1931	9433	2661	8690	2313	6999	3436
9231	5627	1815	7171	8036	1832	2031	6298	6073	7121
3995	9677	7765	3194	3222	4191	2734	4469	8617	6694
2402	6250	9362	7373	4757	1716	1942	0417	5921	7456
5295	7385	5474	2123	7035	9983	5192	1840	6176	3818
5177	1191	2106	3351	5057	0967	4538	1246	3374	3286
7315	3365	7203	1231	0546	6612	1038	1425	2709	5780
5775	7517	8974	3961	2183	5295	3096	8536	9442	3139

Random Numbers (cont.)

```
5500  2276  6307  2346  1285  7000  5306  0414  3383  2137
3251  8902  8843  2112  8567  8131  8116  5270  5994  7445
4675  1435  2192  0874  2897  0262  5092  5541  4014  2086
3543  6130  4247  4859  2660  7852  9096  0578  0097  4746
3521  8772  6612  0721  3899  2999  1263  7017  8057  4983

5573  9396  3464  1702  9204  3389  5678  2589  0288  4633
7478  7569  7551  3380  2152  5411  2647  7242  2800  6183
3339  2854  9691  9562  3252  9848  6030  8472  2266  1270
5505  8474  3167  8552  5409  1556  4247  4652  2953  5394
6381  2086  5457  7703  2758  2963  8167  6712  9820  5654

6975  5239  0762  5846  2431  0543  4956  8787  9651  2605
7185  4019  7332  2820  4853  8636  9505  6575  0365  6648
4510  1658  5615  2194  1901  4975  1895  4383  0415  3771
7752  0105  4769  2994  7445  0781  4960  4253  9451  6518
4834  4043  6591  3646  8918  4603  1970  9145  7615  3905

8866  6036  9755  4508  9061  2080  3406  9856  1298  6281
6622  4612  2030  7299  8414  8822  5176  9443  6054  6462
9094  8973  3335  2183  5192  1630  0959  8143  9182  8012
5618  6445  2983  0375  2540  2735  4901  5515  4787  7058
2705  2693  1944  8074  2015  3261  5529  7193  5401  9531

1797  4334  3293  2632  3770  1675  9363  7795  3331  8995
9448  5174  5869  0448  8613  4400  6938  5161  8691  2838
3461  1304  9682  8577  4449  1896  8328  1698  7138  1141
7092  5007  5596  8522  2580  4495  4728  8948  4434  2438
5533  4294  0939  4050  1225  6414  5895  0148  7053  5935

7852  8988  5951  4919  7404  2426  4450  2358  3082  4561
8313  8456  9892  0981  6736  8021  6226  5573  1664  9489
1158  2241  9861  7588  2669  5480  9160  4267  1690  7278
9338  7226  0025  8844  8181  5565  2418  9394  0837  3106
7711  1336  3251  8902  8425  5766  3262  5848  3545  7073

2656  1863  3884  6516  6922  1808  1896  8853  0964  3089
7980  9370  2850  3818  7281  8352  9637  0618  2430  6525
1409  7865  5908  4296  1888  2792  4014  1667  1295  0814
7657  6630  5000  1493  5459  5869  0315  8134  9587  2184
2863  5450  1329  8787  8795  4604  2615  0075  1433  7707

3988  2042  2906  8995  0818  9288  1650  0803  8319  2533
4551  2815  8941  4893  8612  4844  0042  3890  7069  8512
5772  4732  2829  3931  9540  6256  5420  2179  9448  5489
9150  1435  3817  8975  4276  9569  0175  6663  0045  5549
5764  7914  8280  1337  3779  8197  9105  5985  1054  2866

5895  0044  5021  3846  7599  0398  5212  9509  0134  4656
6857  1174  8085  6503  5355  3027  1708  3626  7059  0167
2538  2669  3746  3270  1214  9983  8434  1344  1160  3292
9983  1387  1410  8891  2523  8705  9190  2986  7654  5142
5061  9529  2922  2199  8310  6954  8090  5371  0672  6281

9999  4226  2815  8817  5606  5190  0495  7867  9968  5951
9078  5936  2393  7875  6871  3163  9203  2863  5693  9973
4823  2291  8925  6306  1717  0320  2549  3107  5488  0303
1232  1384  5698  9313  3501  3238  7227  0220  6118  7655
7694  6484  0279  8528  7214  1750  0577  8418  0698  5403
```

Random Numbers (cont.)

```
9207  6903  9703  2028  3460  0778  3795  0698  3974  8522
1886  2080  3719  3602  3896  1214  9862  1969  6782  9327
6963  4197  6405  8683  7573  0842  9306  2596  7404  9999
1797  2315  5434  0787  3809  9129  4511  0708  2181  9119
6534  5578  4158  6256  3721  7515  3905  1905  7153  3552

2325  4238  8861  6098  8837  7690  0497  8848  6601  1553
6598  4628  1023  9747  4860  3437  7414  7609  9938  8335
4592  5016  4434  7133  7218  4602  1690  7914  8819  3600
1765  8822  5278  2324  3715  0431  7780  4955  9683  8998
6139  3275  7731  3351  5306  0323  5387  3901  4151  2922

3911  8334  5465  6647  8773  7456  9954  5141  3573  5570
6840  0366  6962  3462  1724  6661  7221  6074  9262  3461
5572  8838  8132  9398  0737  7125  7388  7686  9814  1760
2337  5303  3720  3917  7238  9925  7940  7818  1676  9780
3138  6014  4909  1143  7551  3380  2713  7649  2784  0175

1921  9046  6300  7460  8271  5547  6701  0098  8559  0490
6735  5991  6857  0756  1943  7657  6399  1052  1816  7694
6089  1958  8748  8310  6953  7775  9274  1579  2548  7028
1767  9764  0628  5037  1549  9048  0644  3850  5555  6104
1748  3753  1385  0381  9998  4075  7729  2301  5831  3510

7589  4195  5691  2192  0770  0900  2608  5048  5751  9322
9717  9635  7972  1198  6177  0745  2199  8205  4559  9159
9063  3318  6412  4632  6904  2713  7858  3089  7970  4058
0915  5751  9112  1040  0561  9128  4285  5149  3002  2868
6456  8457  3348  4322  6493  8656  7532  1384  6198  1236

8700  0874  3291  7324  4471  5375  6769  2113  0950  0682
8050  3921  0741  8814  4262  7477  7042  7027  4275  2143
6663  2373  0845  8119  6862  7477  7148  9840  7154  4495
3648  5449  3166  7921  3125  9884  5739  1775  4927  5394
4238  9071  4578  2589  0076  6636  7915  8739  4907  6195

6015  5642  4642  2904  7841  4004  7299  8310  6953  7986
1088  7727  1060  9589  3315  9763  6349  5029  6314  9714
2027  6143  5814  9032  9856  1146  5864  6943  8234  0896
1929  8697  3478  5184  6468  9513  6333  1699  7348  6139
7651  4561  1036  9359  6992  8957  0203  8199  9733  7220

1629  0688  9118  7121  7870  5877  2438  1767  9065  4264
5650  0473  0543  5273  5716  1335  0448  8490  6438  4090
0604  0231  1836  4004  5457  8963  7017  8226  9427  8318
0602  9868  2575  8785  8517  8975  4276  9677  2064  0599
5913  4536  4377  5975  3607  6362  6467  5009  1142  7238

9111  0238  9718  4707  3767  0311  2967  1839  5788  9242
7787  7707  4838  5910  3042  4640  2299  4400  4446  0423
5731  3738  3526  2380  8557  8789  9577  1122  8310  7057
4827  9203  2758  2946  5915  0771  1426  2919  8014  4156
1653  8923  5386  3684  7891  5200  9884  5545  2742  7205

3561  7178  2486  1353  6928  9463  7229  1545  7616  4224
8301  8225  7398  4084  8697  9670  7404  9893  1467  3681
5658  7221  6074  8944  6446  7141  2731  6380  4621  2703
4819  1007  6258  4628  0705  0757  4546  8906  7679  4180
9239  0523  3369  6234  6115  1524  8575  3502  3971  9376
```

Random Numbers (*cont.*)

```
0366   6390   2107   3875   4488   2911   1727   8108   3484   6370
3686   8812   8754   2758   3079   2994   3642   1580   1475   0366
4195   4602   1481   7324   8570   6913   6228   1934   6165   0554
8180   5460   0134   4469   8619   7723   8084   3293   1895   4886
1498   7883   5280   0692   7202   1273   3334   1554   3303   8569

9428   8633   9606   7679   4182   4035   6849   5593   6712   9822
9630   5879   9342   9618   8513   4399   9734   7744   4600   0224
1086   8918   7713   5909   2620   6612   0616   1298   2476   2386
2478   3551   1247   8004   0301   6672   6176   0682   2493   6381
2808   1133   5853   8737   9804   2404   7400   5904   8803   0377

8934   2047   4963   4531   6391   9064   3526   2482   9328   5556
1156   1191   1182   3032   8640   4681   3932   6975   4926   4870
5677   7494   0987   8870   4837   5267   4119   4163   1953   3553
3719   3586   5775   7309   5111   0919   7721   7032   1164   2105
6556   8472   1848   1056   3670   7509   0854   7210   9336   8127

1246   3476   4027   3654   2444   9040   5331   2363   4738   9822
6591   3387   4109   7956   5837   6914   6435   2624   8610   4005
8197   9026   4868   6372   2695   7143   2783   1925   3383   9060
5035   4569   7158   8531   8891   0975   6329   1329   8746   0989
1563   9650   2139   7696   7511   1725   7292   0664   8440   8593

6034   4512   1505   3857   0290   3270   8389   9612   1892   8707
2435   0238   6478   5727   0862   1621   5228   5038   2000   0433
9418   4486   5992   7172   8353   6516   6605   6387   8126   1603
3116   1295   0563   6475   4382   9902   6621   9209   8060   1787
5426   5517   5603   3722   4965   5892   8135   5214   9877   6429

2494   6696   5881   1198   2055   4624   4592   4788   7477   7149
1362   2650   8867   6503   5250   7622   5989   5909   2623   7875
5622   8415   9553   7882   1402   4723   7101   1917   8305   0440
6687   5386   9837   9111   8123   3859   1134   6321   4756   1325
0045   5546   2340   7068   6692   3802   8740   0563   8253   1589

3441   4562   1126   6427   7674   6564   1996   9167   4995   6200
9354   3914   6037   7309   5111   3080   3616   2152   2426   4450
8655   6422   1264   7859   3622   8979   7253   4257   5523   4808
0143   0292   0220   2205   4773   4964   5055   5460   0240   7505
5860   4714   6437   3670   5881   1131   7609   9690   3736   7266

8400   6939   5684   7116   3472   4006   1069   5272   5209   8271
3262   4214   5901   1064   7064   4286   1038   1178   3658   4628
2220   1426   2920   8956   8142   4642   3008   9816   5548   7753
9734   7954   9700   1489   3213   8400   7043   7552   4019   9938
3178   1061   8942   8397   4898   3793   6603   2864   6014   5225

4189   6015   5328   8242   0427   1270   1992   4789   8075   7632
4774   5282   1202   5496   8949   8940   9032   6872   3581   6631
9541   6606   6881   4916   5257   3207   9530   4546   9880   0479
4560   8877   8779   1690   6959   1916   2049   7214   0761   5111
2719   2098   7631   2574   5660   8600   2922   1570   6442   8082

7081   8366   4236   6582   9193   4328   8842   1588   1391   7714
2300   5410   2186   6846   4440   6180   6021   5258   3080   3723
4090   3091   2193   1295   0563   6579   6249   9151   1959   8949
2656   1861   2833   0067   2726   3697   5862   6058   8434   1240
9465   8924   6068   1461   0656   2718   1468   5401   9638   0931
```

Random Numbers (cont.)

```
0430  2613  7878  5595  8076  3068  4113  7962  4989  3987
6095  8618  7024  5831  8995  0902  3972  4894  2153  5764
6720  4690  2123  7101  1166  0087  3042  4745  4690  3173
8948  4609  9126  2814  8383  2951  1958  8212  4131  5313
3268  0189  9175  0473  4295  2993  7027  4153  3864  7542

5473  1540  5681  3933  7826  3823  9933  3101  6742  2364
2951  2169  3096  8663  8147  5255  1756  0650  8493  7024
1031  4981  9118  7969  2688  8229  2863  5320  6124  9920
6010  3219  2640  2737  6055  7298  7628  8430  8159  8506
7534  1369  9935  4358  1490  3193  2906  8893  6850  0891

1529  4760  9897  8352  9742  3222  4402  5286  7490  8293
8640  4369  2154  0167  8358  4086  2082  4454  8300  6078
4802  5490  5581  5666  2838  6789  4990  4780  8211  9244
5575  7527  5181  5048  6590  2984  3675  3713  9279  2444
8567  8238  4885  2201  9949  6557  9036  0762  5741  0075

3274  7170  8828  3802  8740  0349  3301  0854  6672  7755
7241  5444  3332  9411  0974  9305  1968  6590  2879  8846
9775  0637  0620  3371  1320  2326  5367  2505  7106  8327
5967  8343  1255  6275  8485  2979  4725  8253  1482  7908
7751  6866  9343  2573  9731  6516  8446  2564  4320  5098

5351  8360  4701  0334  6325  6623  5137  9967  3771  2139
9489  7125  7285  6006  9644  8078  4301  8991  7505  7908
4123  5242  6491  7400  5045  7933  0171  4898  3955  2712
6300  7627  8988  6159  9272  7495  1516  3011  4975  1997
8692  3259  4187  0708  1821  5341  9440  0223  3858  0821

3971  0814  5119  6038  1296  2652  0170  3593  1459  0425
1458  9604  6418  7922  3438  3212  8105  6187  9651  2711
1532  5944  6461  2186  6531  9642  7027  4512  1871  1547
4358  4732  2836  7479  7775  9372  5429  3719  3704  0959
4771  3705  1207  6469  3964  3735  6951  6726  1822  6737

8320  3056  6632  6155  3391  6854  2468  7444  0255  3133
0780  1789  7331  2176  2761  8899  6595  9499  3543  5813
4070  5232  3454  6773  8100  2066  1208  3083  6906  8123
5346  1848  1476  0788  5314  8818  2993  6710  8478  8989
9998  3687  9759  6679  2548  1029  3827  7357  1508  7640

3645  8649  3296  0892  7380  0197  4126  0455  6421  0426
2557  6761  7808  5045  9141  5541  4223  6136  9505  4995
1087  9755  4751  5061  2832  4231  1508  7534  0844  5725
6355  5538  2461  5869  0447  6704  1861  2725  8901  8212
8426  6186  9022  1265  8066  7173  8981  0181  0794  0397

3513  0498  9207  7115  3367  8342  0415  4787  7058  6874
8415  9346  4334  2976  3382  5732  4626  8733  5606  0797
5604  4248  5282  1402  4514  2419  9922  0440  3763  4844
3293  0554  1972  9984  1488  1936  0002  4826  8885  4399
0482  6386  7228  6668  5710  7267  1942  7027  4138  9070

4496  8432  0507  5735  8649  3503  4284  4731  2598  8563
9909  4716  7697  8245  5921  3583  7679  4077  1490  4665
8029  7193  5378  7464  5161  8795  4537  2816  8367  6919
8435  7008  0739  8069  8406  0862  1831  1584  5723  8733
4520  9775  0803  8260  7956  4495  6670  6761  6847  4544
```

Random Numbers (*cont.*)

1306	1189	5731	3968	5606	5084	8947	3897	1636	7810
0422	2431	0649	8085	5053	4722	6598	5044	9040	5121
6597	2022	6168	5060	8656	6733	6364	7649	1871	4328
7965	6541	5645	6243	7658	6903	9911	5740	7824	8520
7695	6937	0406	8894	0441	8135	9797	7285	5905	9539
5160	7851	8464	6789	3938	4197	6511	0407	9329	2232
2961	0551	0539	8288	7478	7565	5581	5771	5442	8761
1428	4183	4312	5445	4854	9157	9158	5218	1464	3634
3666	5642	4539	1561	7849	7520	2547	0756	1206	2033
6543	6799	7454	9052	6689	1946	2574	9386	0304	7945
9975	6080	7423	3175	9377	6951	6519	8287	8994	5532
4866	0956	7545	7723	8085	4948	2228	9583	4415	7065
8239	7068	6694	5168	3117	1586	0237	6160	9585	1133
8722	9191	3386	3443	0434	4586	4150	1224	6204	0937
1330	9120	8785	8382	2929	7089	3109	6742	2468	7025
2296	2952	4764	9070	6356	9192	4012	0618	2219	1109
3582	7052	3132	4519	9250	2486	0830	8472	2160	7046
5872	9207	7222	6494	8973	3545	6967	8490	5264	9821
1134	6324	6201	3792	5651	0538	4676	2064	0584	7996
1403	4497	7390	8503	8239	4236	8022	2914	4368	4529
3393	7025	3381	3553	2128	1021	8353	6413	5161	8583
1137	7896	3602	0060	7850	7626	0854	6565	4260	6220
7437	5198	8772	6927	8527	6851	2709	5992	7383	1071
8414	8820	3917	7238	9821	6073	6658	1280	9643	7761
8398	5224	2749	7311	5740	9771	7826	9533	3800	4553
0995	8935	2939	3092	2496	0359	0318	4697	7181	4035
6657	0755	9685	4017	6581	7292	5643	5064	1142	1297
8875	8369	7868	0190	9278	1709	4253	9346	4335	3769
8399	6702	0586	6428	7985	2979	4513	1970	1989	3105
6703	1024	2064	0393	6815	8502	1375	4171	6970	1201
4730	1653	9032	9855	0957	7366	0325	5178	7959	5371
8400	6834	3187	8688	1079	1480	6776	9888	7585	9998
3647	8002	6726	0877	4552	3238	7542	7804	3933	9475
6789	5197	8037	2354	9262	5497	0005	3986	1767	7981
2630	2721	2810	2185	6323	5679	4931	8336	6662	3566
1374	8625	1644	3342	1587	0762	6057	8011	2666	3759
1572	7625	9110	4409	0239	7059	3415	5537	2250	7292
9678	2877	7579	4935	0449	8119	6969	5383	1717	6719
0882	6781	3538	4090	3092	2365	6001	3446	9985	6007
0006	4205	2389	4365	1981	8158	7784	6256	3842	5603
4611	9861	7916	9305	2074	9462	0254	4827	9198	3974
1093	3784	4190	6332	1175	8599	9735	8584	6581	7194
3374	3545	6865	8819	3342	1676	2264	6014	5012	2458
3650	9676	1436	4374	4716	5548	8276	6235	6742	2154
7292	5749	7977	7602	9205	3599	3880	9537	4423	2330
2353	8319	2850	4026	3027	1708	3518	7034	7132	6903
1094	2009	8919	5676	7283	4982	9642	7235	8167	3366
0568	4002	0587	7165	1094	2006	7471	0940	4366	9554
5606	4070	5233	4339	6543	6695	5799	5821	3953	9458
8285	7537	1181	2300	5294	6892	1627	3372	1952	3028

Random Numbers (*cont.*)

2444	9039	4803	8568	1590	2420	2547	2470	8179	4617
5748	7767	2800	6289	2814	8381	1549	9519	3341	1192
7761	8583	0852	5619	6864	8506	9643	7763	9611	1289
6838	9280	2654	0812	3988	2146	5095	0150	8043	9079
6440	2631	3033	9167	4998	7036	0133	7428	9702	1376
8829	0094	2887	3802	5497	0318	5168	6377	9216	2802
9845	4796	2951	4449	1999	2691	5328	7674	7004	6212
5072	9000	3887	5739	7920	6074	4715	3681	2721	2701
9035	0553	1272	2600	3828	8197	8852	9092	8027	6144
5562	1080	2222	0336	1411	0303	7424	3713	9278	1918
2757	2650	8727	3953	9579	2442	8041	9869	2887	3933
6397	1848	1476	0787	4990	4666	1208	2769	3922	1158
9208	7641	3575	4279	1282	1840	5999	1806	7809	5885
2418	9289	6120	8141	3908	5577	3590	2317	8975	4593
7300	9006	5659	8258	3662	0332	5369	3640	0563	7939
6870	2535	8916	3245	2256	4350	6064	2438	2002	1272
2914	7309	4045	7513	3195	4166	0878	5184	6680	2655
0868	8657	8118	6340	9452	7460	3291	5778	1167	0312
7994	6579	6461	2292	9554	8309	5036	0974	9517	8293
8587	0764	6687	9150	1642	2050	4934	0027	1376	5040
8016	8345	2257	5084	8004	7949	3205	3972	7640	3478
5581	5775	7517	9076	4699	8313	8401	7147	9416	7184
2015	3364	6688	2631	2152	2220	1637	8333	4838	5699
7327	8987	5741	0102	1173	7350	7080	7420	1847	0741
3589	1991	1764	8355	9684	9423	7101	1063	4151	4875
2188	6454	7319	1215	0473	6589	2355	9579	7004	6209
2924	0472	9878	7966	2491	5662	5635	2789	2564	1249
1961	1669	2219	1113	9175	0260	4046	8142	4432	2664
2393	9637	0410	7536	0972	5153	0708	1935	1143	1704
7585	4424	2648	6728	2233	3518	7267	1732	1926	3833
0197	4021	9207	7327	9212	7017	8060	6216	1942	6817
9719	5336	5532	8537	2980	8252	4971	0110	6209	1556
8866	4785	6007	8006	9043	4109	5570	9249	9905	2152
5744	3957	8786	9023	1472	7275	1014	1104	0832	7680
7149	5721	1389	6581	7196	7072	6360	3084	7009	0239
7710	8479	9345	7773	9086	1202	8845	3163	7937	6163
5246	5651	0432	8644	6341	9661	2361	8377	8673	6098
3576	0013	7381	0124	8559	9813	9080	6984	0926	2169
3026	1464	2671	4691	0353	5289	8754	2442	7799	8983
6591	4365	8717	2365	5686	8377	8675	9798	7745	6360
0402	3257	0480	5038	1998	2935	1306	1190	2406	2596
7105	7654	4745	4482	8471	1424	2031	7803	4367	6816
7181	4140	1046	0885	1264	7755	1653	8924	5822	4401
3655	3282	2178	8134	3291	7262	8229	2866	7065	4806
5121	6717	3117	1901	5184	6467	8954	3884	0279	8635
3618	3098	9208	7429	1578	1917	7927	2696	3704	0833
0166	3638	4947	1414	4799	9189	2459	5056	5982	6154
6187	9653	3658	4730	1652	8096	8288	9368	5531	7788
1234	1448	0276	7290	1667	2823	3755	5642	4854	8844
8949	8731	4875	5724	2962	1182	2930	7539	4526	7252

Random Numbers (*cont.*)

4357	4146	8353	9952	8004	7945	1530	5207	4730	1967
5339	7325	6862	7584	8634	3485	2278	5832	0612	8118
6583	8433	0717	0606	9284	2719	1888	2889	0285	2765
6564	3526	2171	3809	3428	5523	9078	0648	7768	3326
4811	1933	3763	6265	8931	0649	8085	6177	4450	2139
6931	7236	1230	0441	4013	1352	6563	1499	7332	3068
8755	3390	6120	7825	9005	7012	1643	9934	4044	7022
6742	2260	3443	0190	9278	1816	7697	7933	0067	2906
6655	3930	9014	6032	7574	1685	5258	3100	5358	1929
8514	4806	4124	9286	0449	5051	4772	4651	0038	1580
8135	5004	7299	8981	4689	1950	2271	2201	8344	3852
4414	6855	0127	5489	5157	6386	7492	3736	7164	0498
3727	7959	5056	5983	8021	0204	7616	4325	7454	5039
5434	7342	0314	7252	0067	2800	6292	4706	3454	6881
7195	8828	9869	2785	3186	8375	7414	7232	0401	2483
2705	8245	6251	9611	1077	0641	0195	7024	6202	3899
1547	8981	4972	1280	4286	5678	0338	8096	8284	7010
3424	1435	1354	7631	7260	7361	0151	8903	9056	8684
8969	7551	3695	4915	7921	2913	3840	9031	9747	9735
5225	8720	8898	2478	3342	9200	8836	7269	2992	6284
6432	9861	1516	2849	2539	2208	4595	8616	6170	5865
3085	5903	8319	2744	0814	7318	8619	7614	3265	5999
0264	1246	3687	9759	6995	6565	3949	1012	0179	0059
8710	2419	6065	0036	9650	2027	6042	5467	1839	5577
5736	9001	3132	4521	9973	5070	8078	4150	2276	5059
7529	1339	4802	5751	3785	7125	4922	8877	9530	6499
5133	7995	8030	7408	2186	0725	5554	5664	6791	9677
3170	9915	6960	2621	6718	4059	9919	1007	6469	5410
3024	0680	1127	8088	0200	5868	0084	6362	6808	3727
4398	3121	7749	8191	2087	8270	5233	3980	6774	8522
0082	5419	7659	2061	2506	7573	1157	3979	2309	0811
4351	6516	6814	5898	3973	8103	3616	2049	7843	0568
3268	0086	7580	1337	3884	5679	4830	4509	9587	2184
4391	8487	4884	1488	2249	6661	5774	7205	2717	0730
7328	0705	0652	9424	7082	8579	5647	5571	9667	5855
3835	2938	2671	4691	0559	8382	2825	4928	5379	8635
8731	4980	8674	4506	7262	8127	2022	2178	7463	4842
2995	7868	0683	3768	0625	9887	7060	0514	0034	8600
5597	9028	5660	5006	8325	9677	2169	3196	0357	7811
3081	5876	8150	1360	1868	9265	3277	8465	7502	6458
7406	4439	5683	6877	2920	9588	3002	2869	3746	3690
5969	9442	7696	7510	1620	4973	1911	1288	6160	9797
4765	9647	4364	1037	4975	1998	1359	1346	6125	5078
3219	2532	7577	2815	8696	9248	9410	9282	6572	3940
6906	8859	5044	8826	6218	3206	9034	0843	9832	2703
7993	3141	0103	4528	7988	4635	8478	9094	9077	5306
2549	3737	7686	0723	4505	6841	1379	6460	1869	5700
3672	7033	4844	0149	7412	6370	1884	0717	5740	8477
2217	0293	3978	5933	1032	5192	1732	2137	9357	5941
3162	9968	6369	1258	0416	4326	7840	6525	2608	5255

20.2

Random Numbers (*cont.*)

1758	1489	2774	6033	9813	1052	1816	7484	1699	7350
6430	8803	0478	4157	5626	1603	1339	4666	1207	2135
4893	8857	1717	1533	6572	8408	2173	4754	0272	1305
1516	2733	7326	8674	9233	1799	5281	0797	0885	0947
4950	3171	5756	3036	9047	8719	8498	1312	7124	4787
0549	6775	9360	6639	0990	0037	7309	4702	0812	4195
1018	7027	7569	7549	2539	2315	8030	7663	3881	8264
2241	9965	9729	7092	4891	9239	0738	1804	3025	1030
1602	0708	2201	9848	6241	1084	8142	8555	7291	5016
5840	8381	1549	9902	6935	3681	6420	0214	8489	5911
1676	0367	7484	1595	5693	3008	9816	7311	6162	1024
6048	4175	8940	9029	8306	8892	4127	1709	4043	6591
5549	9621	2563	0515	0560	9021	0632	4309	4044	7010
5317	4584	9418	4600	0640	9668	6379	6515	6310	7916
2532	7784	6469	4793	5957	4123	6555	3237	6915	6960
2300	5412	3106	4877	6936	4109	8060	1896	6881	7028
1499	8699	4534	5367	7557	2701	2587	2521	2159	6991
6201	3791	2946	2863	5684	5517	7448	2227	8991	7505
6839	9736	8312	8068	7339	5395	9559	3416	6169	5484
0092	5537	1933	3186	8482	6680	2656	1864	4535	2193
1862	3253	6515	6299	2929	2219	9145	7511	2146	4962
9886	6744	3097	8894	0446	3494	8211	1723	6138	3181
5289	9071	1231	0651	9109	7448	2228	9700	0224	4595
2685	7104	7193	5506	2993	7028	4830	3866	8698	0277
6055	7092	4786	6847	4543	7448	2017	4114	8385	3625
4092	4995	0280	9371	3375	3503	4496	8642	5388	1831
5951	4937	3670	5797	5030	6524	2265	7748	7875	6976
7687	3849	4821	2373	1157	4208	3623	9399	7349	6663
8665	3463	2055	4872	2702	1807	9056	8576	4237	8757
3193	3011	8899	6721	0086	2623	7977	7578	4024	1997
9181	7365	9135	1669	2007	7784	6363	6913	6017	6588
9459	2175	5728	4933	0111	6703	1234	2410	1620	4859
9874	5278	2849	3163	6372	2600	9887	7060	3919	1111
7729	2099	7513	2774	6030	8260	9023	1368	9513	6122
4699	8102	3001	7947	1659	6571	1969	7152	7356	1062
1872	7244	3954	7422	2688	8649	0156	1965	5012	2461
9636	0123	2438	1757	4204	1650	2486	0002	4724	7412
6403	9054	7632	7469	8973	3332	0294	5062	0303	7315
4433	3293	2314	7431	2389	4094	5062	0118	0046	6070
2361	3933	8026	0431	8012	3214	8927	7355	0585	7638
4077	8463	6580	6983	0181	3327	6812	1755	3387	4569
6678	0006	3686	8478	9187	2291	9032	9852	1450	7940
6499	2582	5207	4627	0456	4245	3583	8996	1006	5839
6663	9021	0319	7908	1241	9977	7042	6923	2539	2103
9999	4503	6105	5525	1068	6272	7036	0200	6291	2841
9048	6982	3845	6865	9029	8700	0349	3416	8236	1129
5136	9653	3654	2863	5565	8923	5596	8389	9927	9092
9906	1070	5693	3012	1218	7309	4361	3041	4327	8423
4198	7035	8182	6270	6461	2079	2998	5507	9605	6734
2030	5878	8989	6789	4359	1820	5063	9199	7751	6337

Random Numbers (*cont.*)

6977	6081	6733	6363	7124	2985	3434	8499	1989	3109
8377	8357	3350	4595	6235	6532	6556	8575	3370	1992
3034	9586	1765	8717	2363	4741	8509	4710	4886	2410
9903	9539	5787	8692	3367	8343	0942	5605	4772	4438
6955	8569	2111	7416	8660	9795	6551	2171	4123	5869
5483	0587	8690	2422	7334	3626	6218	3210	6876	2500
5733	4729	1443	6895	7864	3421	3390	6435	2518	5483
0126	9533	3548	2999	0951	1381	6696	6250	9404	3552
4329	9158	9291	2629	1976	5815	9556	9016	6604	5456
3776	8729	0478	4410	0551	0223	4173	8312	7975	6768
1539	0850	5347	2268	5847	3227	0650	8474	5658	7783
3390	5370	0046	5861	5215	0102	1071	6404	9787	8271
1562	6106	5840	8594	8217	5062	0410	7008	1476	0788
9408	3412	3881	4737	9370	1603	0916	6167	4329	9370
2306	4439	5476	3383	8966	8757	0861	1202	8422	4241
8196	8288	9236	8022	1886	1765	8925	6413	5370	0463
8489	5702	8822	5071	8599	2016	3681	2403	6983	0307
7652	6009	5347	2476	2345	9456	0441	4013	1246	3582
2450	3068	3892	7924	4594	5814	9135	1562	9506	7492
1464	2104	2222	4195	5376	7292	0876	3923	1368	9830
9256	5105	3984	1032	5298	4652	2534	8515	7818	1676
2337	5302	3016	7027	4269	7610	0337	7981	9892	0878
6127	2754	9052	6676	7836	5739	7486	2727	9952	7943
7703	5246	5965	7505	7656	0439	3194	3642	1598	6388
2380	8220	0781	5001	5831	0052	9742	3222	4256	5206
4934	0027	0957	8223	8835	6847	4963	4948	2015	3262
5658	7890	9610	4052	2378	7462	4422	2014	2629	2152
6628	4078	1603	1126	4666	1626	1835	0553	1377	5172
4022	8875	8190	1670	2429	6103	4391	8594	8410	2939
6969	0067	2907	9407	8325	9885	6218	2993	6816	1394
1936	8890	0633	4732	3074	0701	7147	9311	9060	5571
7533	7325	5710	6848	5280	0586	8167	3573	6810	4675
8545	7774	9637	6347	3831	7486	1553	2762	0008	7850
9191	3756	1190	2500	1048	9191	3495	2218	0800	0224
9651	2710	6095	8724	9870	3558	7113	2313	6895	1360
9210	8794	4376	0999	2186	0242	0341	8131	8013	3842
6579	6563	3003	3722	5070	8389	9928	9598	0942	5397
4706	3243	1047	7912	7290	2963	1499	6809	3941	5642
9916	7802	3249	6768	1470	4810	5634	9691	4261	6742
1766	8626	5498	5400	6187	9337	8545	9589	3318	6202
7033	9265	0140	1512	7125	5604	4247	4757	1612	9822
7608	9274	8733	5800	6832	2033	7325	8045	1446	5874
7860	3940	5331	2152	2743	0397	0002	2234	3623	9424
2108	3520	7825	8851	8164	2000	0431	7804	6695	5481
8131	8119	6655	4141	1524	8368	7519	0684	3119	5906
1646	4333	2559	7642	3995	9567	7486	2410	1202	8424
8135	9798	7880	7593	0972	3726	9904	9474	4503	5809
4504	6317	6686	9799	8522	0263	0513	1232	3876	4689
6992	8960	1661	6955	8806	1820	1094	4449	2647	7032
7980	9474	4505	6737	8649	0260	4149	9547	5404	8054

Random Numbers (cont.)

9320	4692	0980	6212	8754	2656	2176	3618	2889	5056
4095	6550	1222	5071	8535	8915	0627	1278	9953	8740
1748	5279	5238	8754	2758	3071	4537	0408	3172	5864
9499	3649	8940	9451	6729	0584	7325	8256	3036	0813
4032	5945	8642	5506	4231	1404	5878	8886	4903	6983
0556	2822	3230	8247	7350	7186	5982	6155	3284	3129
2098	7991	3518	7761	8583	8441	8702	2517	4957	5450
7478	7461	3680	6107	6363	7017	8183	5191	1208	2977
7569	7655	5563	1499	7333	3311	3568	5062	0407	9708
0982	6840	4171	7387	7059	8947	3896	1428	4075	0262
6588	2958	6768	1709	0240	7609	9906	1174	7980	9157
3541	4892	9553	7565	5788	9109	7127	6145	7074	0802
3978	0755	1561	7850	8043	9185	9273	8103	3513	0738
6807	3074	0441	6711	9357	5627	1918	8617	6695	5377
4465	4907	5278	3479	5519	9740	4684	5860	6711	9120
6086	4619	5233	3980	6986	1871	4643	3638	1176	2387
3874	3751	2274	5384	2555	5351	8463	6268	0628	3250
0342	8660	9586	1765	8822	5069	7550	3275	7727	1272
4767	0418	6234	6324	5946	3686	9023	1787	6578	0545
8624	1120	4126	3277	8568	8975	4278	9870	3475	5242
1622	5612	0780	2711	6806	2492	5541	3906	4173	0951
8911	4110	8482	5838	7227	0222	0199	5175	8999	2583
1459	9816	7206	3453	5933	1031	4664	0494	7658	7008
1000	0465	2736	5739	7487	3146	6717	3114	0036	9442
3392	6604	5774	7099	3018	6235	6848	5173	9732	6907
0497	8904	4390	8068	7813	0390	5580	5250	7625	0327
0874	2929	2301	5618	6445	3090	1666	0457	7468	5742
2299	4202	9583	4311	5312	7982	9366	0117	1149	8733
4416	7488	3569	5167	2614	5529	2092	7068	6381	4797
4264	8400	7041	6713	3819	3073	8349	7980	9266	0563
5281	0828	5537	6161	3739	8713	0496	8653	5528	1586
7100	0641	4474	0478	6780	4497	9996	3459	8261	5321
7804	7032	6243	2113	0422	1780	4360	8180	5355	3028
5981	5104	3494	8037	7981	9896	2846	1741	2824	4696
1294	5844	1885	1451	1853	7985	2872	1388	2389	3986
4749	9640	1313	5475	2959	9821	8455	5580	5353	9208
3290	3608	6890	7752	0099	9386	0513	1807	5952	5723
2232	2816	9869	2785	3080	5250	7939	7072	9992	9660
1796	1888	2800	6833	2664	3503	4498	9353	9975	5835
1024	1013	0502	4407	0747	3017	5603	3302	8093	6712
7597	4956	9892	0983	7470	5569	8620	7828	7462	4426
1667	1399	2687	8019	6567	5020	6301	8216	1294	0082
1620	4690	0037	7308	4399	3543	6024	1015	1521	9420
2147	5719	2534	8509	4901	5936	2664	2775	6873	4189
7033	2977	3589	1894	9727	0458	5480	9265	3067	3785
7949	3159	4296	2094	5605	4561	2611	9372	0216	9201
5408	1029	3929	8691	0353	5290	9595	6774	8520	4537
7082	2284	1678	7460	3292	8516	8446	2694	6893	2257
9564	4284	9054	7319	1319	0788	5310	7058	7585	7851
7866	7259	6678	1814	6540	5222	7347	5401	6436	0971

Random Numbers (cont.)

6089	1628	2233	3415	5747	6929	9579	7109	9021	0531
0351	4447	0844	7293	6274	7666	2477	3846	4103	1129
6948	7614	3481	5984	2001	0442	4850	6873	3939	2418
4776	6516	6709	8165	2628	1690	8620	7825	9005	9952
0287	1412	0935	4932	2404	7195	6340	9452	7042	6817
3830	5838	7436	4987	3359	0278	8424	5030	6629	4599
4030	4873	3332	0506	4874	5595	8077	3590	2003	1127
3849	9514	6749	9881	8909	3185	7957	8231	4008	2178
8398	4005	0438	2777	7702	4513	2313	7184	3100	5482
5202	7105	6737	8543	9724	4471	3632	1927	4154	4287
8995	0813	6897	2703	4667	1945	8497	0778	8988	5848
8094	7445	0673	6491	7711	3101	7476	6411	4216	8231
0150	7937	6160	9795	6128	3303	8571	3056	6733	6362
7949	2749	7415	7816	0522	8004	2663	9372	0317	9935
4490	3631	4982	9645	8644	1008	6781	3493	7809	6324
9781	4352	7149	7947	2266	9306	2695	0805	8368	7307
8855	0945	1322	1159	5046	9981	0124	8293	2723	2435
2705	8772	6823	6135	4829	2923	3963	2958	7399	4204
6070	0151	8464	6792	0102	2621	7033	5263	9718	4561
6388	5844	1467	5144	5885	2978	4031	5312	7122	0162
0995	8616	6064	2983	1509	8272	5863	6161	4052	2381
5839	8068	7925	1749	5960	4033	6361	6199	5225	9113
1581	3178	0479	3258	1929	5145	5126	0535	9798	8005
4082	8011	2647	7139	1771	3060	8918	7712	5199	9191
0789	5560	6218	2994	7234	7641	3153	1586	2291	9238
5830	7614	3516	7027	4408	0004	3074	1975	0909	1141
0521	7633	0069	3852	6436	0658	3664	7066	5436	1515
5592	6605	6398	0741	9072	7745	6001	2010	9651	2606
3269	0678	1272	2911	2886	0725	5975	3504	4632	8640
8252	0640	8837	7898	4439	5683	6750	2346	9877	6322
9804	4036	2904	8158	7996	2442	7806	3913	5474	2123
2701	2849	2751	8150	4068	5707	5743	3327	6931	7482
2550	5256	1525	3380	2503	2653	0705	0440	3636	4005
7073	0254	9157	9038	2000	0536	0812	3881	0284	2346
1037	4422	2014	2735	5214	9354	1725	7572	1096	5234
5257	2710	7268	2469	7969	3816	2826	5306	0371	3809
8939	8717	2365	5892	8150	0628	1686	0409	4723	7204
9102	4514	2526	0641	0311	2651	9110	9945	0465	2628
5775	7310	5214	2938	2671	4796	2745	1530	5102	2128
9509	0237	6267	0311	2663	2567	2551	4555	4599	1572
4036	8230	3606	0164	2985	6712	9610	0446	4092	5855
5313	7961	4777	4142	2469	7656	5981	2923	0050	5510
0781	5104	3283	2660	0665	5998	1301	3129	2969	8303
1759	5258	3071	5483	0163	9719	5023	9304	1441	5747
4468	7802	3260	7969	4029	4393	9200	8309	6638	0075
0153	5822	4192	3365	7311	5238	1144	2220	1844	8026
0407	9528	9677	5410	2082	4772	4544	8287	8795	4813
1928	4721	5968	8657	8118	6337	7585	1506	6628	3972
8359	4188	3416	6066	3770	8288	9379	4077	1554	1418
0894	8038	8460	7867	5315	8950	9571	5481	9789	0252

Random Numbers (cont.)

6589	3105	4773	4754	0478	4303	9913	6789	5911	3359
3899	2916	8552	5830	7828	8312	2925	0577	8414	8923
3101	7266	1315	6404	6420	0002	2339	6543	6696	6006
2355	9579	7109	8915	0745	2094	5812	8213	1562	9049
5105	3598	0663	4948	2120	5545	0054	0916	5855	2903
5198	8456	1521	9313	9925	8043	9393	0625	9990	8714
1344	0777	1216	8552	5408	1137	7962	0007	7008	0423
4927	5184	6468	9622	4196	5997	8777	4660	7107	8641
0156	1965	4911	2042	2800	5870	1004	4998	3226	2872
5484	3294	0707	4523	1240	9449	5699	9839	4240	9843
8842	1582	7811	6913	6015	5539	3195	3954	7631	6945
6370	1887	2397	5586	9626	3840	7445	9143	6896	3546
1961	3115	0770	0803	2041	5155	1460	5145	5233	4294
7106	7469	8341	5475	5707	9501	4867	2721	2808	1344
6224	9258	5613	1353	6920	5440	7610	4470	1621	5212
5643	5272	5214	6945	9081	7719	5991	6037	8990	7115
1079	1799	3650	9678	2486	0301	6671	5338	6476	5052
6888	6608	2202	6939	5682	6193	3574	9201	9570	1620
6365	8382	2491	5117	5063	0616	1298	2267	3561	8730
8915	0851	5306	0171	6127	3833	6477	5307	0506	5189
7832	3665	7799	9399	7769	3743	2112	9700	0640	1976
2315	7923	3965	4368	6831	1613	9928	9644	1678	8083
5223	7876	7291	0350	3922	0947	4999	0197	4336	3926
2744	0254	9913	6897	2684	1490	3088	0513	2333	6474
8739	2856	4512	5575	0909	1354	7633	8265	7293	5140
1484	8959	1238	8086	8495	0149	7307	4190	8301	6217
5146	6825	7186	6443	9289	4571	7723	7873	5824	5343
5038	8126	1366	4683	5296	3704	1076	4028	4075	0470
1505	6298	6494	9183	8538	3213	8713	0651	3379	9658
5989	7335	4570	7300	9005	9954	5039	2419	0050	5382
1811	5074	2919	9766	5433	0280	9367	1192	3472	5046
1593	3995	9668	8167	8083	1820	0990	2087	4991	5330
2799	5173	9735	8268	3993	8345	2321	8667	4537	0410
1965	4907	0171	4899	4434	1052	1545	7509	0825	5872
4246	4230	0823	3220	9484	1031	4874	5593	7028	5040
4852	7901	6545	5234	4472	8733	5726	8003	7422	2478
8612	6663	2523	9412	5693	8602	5659	8278	1165	7735
6038	3632	5484	4527	4303	2259	9273	7920	4019	8599
4068	5429	9160	4724	7727	1271	2570	7617	4852	8002
0806	9960	3186	8062	0868	8866	5265	3502	4307	9393
9756	5312	7230	1965	4804	3955	7736	9545	3969	6341
8334	5572	8627	2696	3597	3165	0134	4710	4568	6591
1363	2905	1087	8988	8232	4521	9464	8463	0619	2847
0953	5181	4940	6752	7792	1521	9417	1004	5009	9799
1193	7834	4719	9250	0764	1039	1911	1079	1483	8220
7600	1005	9904	9894	2006	7364	9173	0628	3985	0382
0490	5475	2648	7019	1781	6272	6614	2090	0035	9337
3188	9019	0366	7064	4393	7024	3066	3157	3349	4172
4280	5961	1163	4634	8058	7311	5270	3690	4660	7238
6919	0150	7941	8344	1782	0045	6049	2648	6978	1920

20.2

Random Numbers (cont.)

0173	5717	1901	4974	1263	7229	1337	3989	2355	9472
5755	5773	6697	2561	2833	0067	2905	8366	4358	4733
1927	4148	1474	4806	0861	1412	0934	2857	9177	1528
0052	0108	9581	8158	7994	7199	5329	8844	2321	2056
7737	7731	3347	3229	4909	1155	0692	9548	1053	2337
1077	3897	0319	7196	6758	5609	8077	3787	8018	4385
4172	7494	9158	9425	7941	8342	0835	1977	2064	0599
5132	5490	5369	3369	1150	9468	6622	9836	8899	6596
5139	8069	8723	9556	9892	0875	3711	8546	2596	7618
0939	3841	9976	6203	0482	6385	6890	8068	8171	3802
5275	8576	5659	8519	9917	8045	4014	1878	6690	2212
1094	4009	9977	2066	1627	4506	7472	0426	1485	1451
1255	5119	5797	4969	1739	9386	5780	1129	5690	1353
1726	7900	6186	8919	3614	4368	8803	0479	4830	3761
9718	4603	2088	5199	9391	1085	7848	6978	1708	3415
4682	4878	7359	2977	3911	6161	9965	8713	0392	6291
7373	4756	1069	0677	0431	7905	9768	2365	5999	1805
4899	4198	6494	9185	9272	7626	9530	9895	2426	4658
4141	1733	2454	5250	7937	6159	9272	7496	3491	0560
7292	1088	9860	7097	9589	3424	1120	3809	3395	0150
1436	3432	9030	3864	7856	1861	2831	2573	9628	5039
1925	3484	2170	6757	4983	9856	1188	7625	0220	2566
4869	8762	1129	0391	1981	8260	8814	9985	9273	7910
3755	5121	6928	8737	4762	8334	5466	6962	3252	9428
3764	5476	3485	1266	8591	6753	8086	7446	0988	1079
2677	1643	7714	8931	0966	3758	2347	1703	2386	9693
0550	4490	3737	7897	4228	5763	9219	8749	8942	9320
9247	8773	7454	9052	6291	1635	5780	1339	4657	9957
8852	5358	3780	9805	2721	2807	0504	3930	9223	6080
1629	0482	6487	5530	7528	1725	7464	3302	1376	4808
8626	2486	1666	0769	0434	4713	6015	5540	3801	8317
0568	1532	6257	4310	4569	6801	1586	0030	2508	9482
7848	7001	5622	8207	5599	5820	3478	5182	5206	4205
2057	5941	8812	3212	7898	4859	2662	8898	6070	9673
2838	6476	4687	3250	8601	2220	1531	5731	4088	3568
3235	5888	5197	8035	1273	9734	7640	3050	4595	6339
1016	6920	0990	2422	7648	0503	3406	9751	1199	6844
2018	4811	5845	2199	8204	4036	3114	0350	3923	1369
6869	7443	8515	5541	4224	6765	0351	4450	2498	9149
0626	3931	9328	4923	3370	5830	8876	8901	8005	8787
9869	3101	3908	6995	6670	6758	5615	2297	3477	4762
3632	2240	7469	6581	7524	1432	7399	4321	5967	8343
2478	3235	6137	3777	9531	4063	1624	0263	5699	0506
8207	5620	4793	1399	2793	4189	3835	2727	9848	6241
7389	8092	2615	8604	5000	1129	4908	0698	5350	2857
3687	9339	9386	5675	2778	9951	7717	1424	1998	8303
8335	5989	5700	4563	6871	3164	2814	8383	2708	0384
7639	3091	2194	1661	7605	7527	8104	9474	4714	0974
4463	4197	6718	3640	0562	7205	2721	2806	0301	9634
9564	4655	8780	5353	9207	4838	6016	5855	0130	6087

20.3 Special Constants

This table is self-explanatory. Note that when a minus sign precedes a logarithm, the entire logarithm is negative, including the mantissa.

Special Constants

Constant	Value			Logarithm to Base 10		
π	3.14159	26535	89793	0.49714	98726	94134
$1/\pi$	0.31830	98861	83790	-0.49714	98726	94134
$\sqrt{\pi}$	1.77245	38509	05516	0.24857	49363	47067
$1/\sqrt{\pi}$	0.56418	95835	47756	-0.24857	49363	47067
$\sqrt{2\pi}$	2.50662	82746	31000	0.39908	99341	79058
$1/\sqrt{2\pi}$	0.39894	22804	01432	-0.39908	99341	79058
π^2	9.86960	44010	89359	0.99429	97453	88268
$\pi/180$	0.01745	32925	19943	-1.75812	26324	09172
$180/\pi$	57.29577	95130	82321	1.75812	26324	09172
$\pi/2$	1.57079	63267	94897	0.19611	98770	30153
$\sqrt{e}$	1.64872	12707	00128	0.21714	72409	51626
e	2.71828	18284	59045	0.43429	44819	03252
e^2	7.38905	60989	30650	0.86858	89638	06504
e^3	20.08553	69231	87668	1.30288	34457	09755
e^4	54.59815	00331	44239	1.73717	79276	13007
$\sqrt{2}$	1.41421	35623	73095	0.15051	49978	31991
$\sqrt{3}$	1.73205	08075	68877	0.23856	06273	59831
$\sqrt{5}$	2.23606	79774	99790	0.34948	50021	68009
$\sqrt{7}$	2.64575	13110	64591	0.42254	90200	07128
$\sqrt{10}$	3.16227	76601	68379	0.50000	00000	00000
$1/\sqrt{3}$	0.57735	02691	89626	-0.23856	06273	59831
$1/\sqrt{2}$	0.70710	67811	86548	-0.15051	49978	31991
$\sqrt{2/3}$	0.81649	65809	27726	-0.08804	56295	27841
$\sqrt{3}/2$	0.86602	54037	84438	-0.06246	93683	04150
$2/\sqrt{3}$	1.15470	05383	79251	0.06246	93683	04150
Euler's γ	0.57721	56649	01533	-0.23866	18912	16832

(cont.)

20.3

Special Constants (*cont.*)

Degrees	Radians	Sin A	Cos A	Tan A	Cot A	Sec A	Cosec A
0	0	0	1	0	∞	1	∞
30	π/6	1/2	√3/2	1/√3	√3	2/√3	2
45	π/4	1/√2	1/√2	1	1	√2	√2
60	π/3	√3/2	1/2	√3	1/√3	2	2/√3
90	π/2	1	0	∞	0	∞	1
120	2π/3	√3/2	-1/2	-√3	-1/√3	-2	2/√3
135	3π/4	1/√2	-1/√2	-1	-1	-√2	√2
150	5π/6	1/2	-√3/2	-1/√3	-√3	-2/√3	2
180	π	0	-1	0	-∞	-1	∞
210	7π/6	-1/2	-√3/2	1/√3	√3	-2/√3	-2
225	5π/4	-1/√2	-1/√2	1	1	-√2	-√2
240	4π/3	-√3/2	-1/2	√3	1/√3	-2	-2/√3
270	3π/2	-1	0	∞	0	-∞	-1
300	5π/3	-√3/2	1/2	-√3	-1/√3	2	-2/√3
315	7π/4	-1/√2	1/√2	-1	-1	√2	-√2
330	11π/6	-1/2	√3/2	-1/√3	-√3	2/√3	-2
360	2π	0	1	0	-∞	1	-∞

In each case where the value is ∞ or -∞, the value given is obtained by approaching A through increasing values of A; if the approach is made through decreasing values of A, the sign is changed.

20.3

BIBLIOGRAPHY

✓ [1] ABDEL-ATY, S. H., "Approximate formulae for the percentage points and the probability integral of the non-central X^2 distribution," *Biometrika*, **41** (1954), 538–540.

[2] ANDERSON, R. L., and E. E. HOUSEMAN, *Tables of Orthogonal Polynomial Values Extended to N = 104*, Research Bulletin No. 297, Ames, Iowa: Iowa Agricultural Experiment Station, 1942.

[3] ANDERSON, T. W., *An Introduction to Multivariate Statistical Analysis*, New York: John Wiley and Sons, Inc., 1958.

[4] ANDERSON, T. W., and D. A. DARLING, "Asymptotic theory of certain 'goodness of fit' criteria based on stochastic processes," *Annals of Mathematical Statistics*, **23** (1952), 193–212.

[5] ANDREWS, F. C., "Asymptotic behavior of some rank tests for analysis of variance," *Annals of Mathematical Statistics*, **25** (1954), 724–736.

[6] ANSARI, A. R., and R. A. BRADLEY, "Rank-sum tests for dispersions," *Annals of Mathematical Statistics*, **31** (1960), 1174–1189.

[7] ANSCOMBE, F. J., "Rejection of outliers," *Technometrics*, **2** (1960), 123–147.

[8] ANSCOMBE, F. J., "The transformation of Poisson, binomial, and negative-binomial data," *Biometrika*, **35** (1948), 246–254.

[9] ARMSEN, P., "Tables for significance tests of 2 × 2 contingency tables," *Biometrika*, **42** (1955), 494–511.

[10] AUBLE, D., *Extended Tables for the Mann-Whitney Statistic*, Institute of Educational Research Bulletin, Vol. 1, No. 2, Indiana University, 1953.

[11] BAHADUR, R. R., "Some approximations to the binomial distribution function," *Annals of Mathematical Statistics*, **31** (1960), 43–54.

[12] BARTON, D. E., and F. N. DAVID, "Multiple runs," *Biometrika*, **44** (1957), 168–178 and 534.

[13] BEALL, G., "The transformation of data from entomological field experiments so that the analysis of variance becomes applicable," *Biometrika*, **32** (1942), 243–262.

[14] BECHHOFER, R. E., C. W. DUNNETT, and M. SOBEL, "A two-sample multiple decision procedure for ranking means of normal populations with a common unknown variance," *Biometrika*, **41** (1954), 170–176.

[15] BELL, S., "A simple asymptotically chi-square statistic for distributions of runs," submitted to the *Annals of Mathematical Statistics*, November 1960.

[16] Bell Aircraft Corporation, *Table of Circular Normal Probabilities*, Report No. 02-949-106, June 1956. See *Mathematical Tables and Other Aids to Computations*, **11** (1957), Review No. 86.

[17] BENNETT, B. M., and P. HSU, "On the power function of the exact test for the 2 × 2 contingency table," *Biometrika*, **47** (1960), 393–398.

[18] BERKSON, J., "A statistically precise and relatively simple method of estimating the bio-assay with quantal response, based on the logistic function," *Journal of the American Statistical Association*, **48** (1953), 565–599.

[19] BIRNBAUM, Z. W., "On the power of a one-sided test of fit for continuous probability functions," *Annals of Mathematical Statistics*, **24** (1953), 484–489.

[20] BIRNBAUM, Z. W., "Numerical tabulation of the distribution of Kolmogorov's statistic for finite sample size," *Journal of the American Statistical Association*, **47** (1952), 425–441.

[21] BIRNBAUM, Z. W., J. D. ESARY, and S. C. SAUNDERS, "Multi-component systems and structures and their reliability," *Technometrics*, **3** (1961), 55–77.

[22] BIRNBAUM, Z. W., and R. A. HALL, "Small sample distributions for multi-sample statistics of the Smirnov type," *Annals of Mathematical Statistics*, **31** (1960), 710–720.

[23] BIRNBAUM, Z. W., and O. M. KLOSE, "Bounds for the variance of the Mann-Whitney statistic," *Annals of Mathematical Statistics*, **28** (1957), 933–945.

[24] BIRNBAUM, Z. W., and R. C. McCARTY, "A distribution-free upper confidence bound for $\Pr\{Y < X\}$, based on independent samples of X and Y," *Annals of Mathematical Statistics*, **29** (1958), 558–562.

[25] BIRNBAUM, Z. W., and F. H. TINGEY, "One-sided confidence contours for probability distribution functions," *Annals of Mathematical Statistics*, **22** (1951), 592–596.

[26] BLUM, J. R., J. KIEFER, and M. ROSENBLATT, "Distribution free tests of independence based on the sample distribution function," *Annals of Mathematical Statistics*, **32** (1961), 485–498.

[27] BLUMEN, I., "A new bivariate sign test," *Journal of the American Statistical Association*, **53** (1958), 448–456.

[28] BUEHLER, R. J., "Confidence intervals for the product of two binomial parameters," *Journal of the American Statistical Association*, **52** (1957), 482–493.

[29] BURR, E. J., "The distribution of Kendall's score S for a pair of tied rankings," *Biometrika*, **47** (1960), 151–171.

[30] CHAPMAN, D. G., "A comparative study of several one-sided goodness-of-fit tests," *Annals of Mathematical Statistics*, **29** (1958), 655–674.

[31] CHASEN, S. H., *Percentages of a Bivariate Normal Distribution Within Circles of Various Radii (Elliptical Case)*, Report No. NATC-AD-154381, U. S. Naval Air Test Center, Patuxent River, Maryland, February 1958.

[32] CLARK, R. E., "Percentage points of the incomplete beta function," *Journal of the American Statistical Association*, **48** (1953), 831–843.

[33] CLOPPER, C. J., and E. S. PEARSON, "The use of confidence or fiducial limits illustrated in the case of the binomial," *Biometrika*, **26** (1934), 404–413.

[34] COHEN, A., "Tables for the sign test when observations are estimates of binomial parameters," *Journal of the American Statistical Association*, **54** (1959), 784–793.

[35] CROW, E. L., "Confidence intervals for a proportion," *Biometrika*, **43** (1956), 423–435.

[36] CROW, E. L., F. A. DAVIS, and M. W. MAXFIELD, *Statistics Manual*, China Lake, California: U. S. Naval Ordnance Test Station, 1955.

[37] DALY, J. F., "The use of the sample range in an analogue of Student's t-test," *Annals of Mathematical Statistics*, **17** (1946), 71–74.

[38] DANIEL, C., "Locating outliers in factorial experiments," *Technometrics*, **2** (1960), 149–156.

[39] DANIELS, H. E., "The covering circle of a sample from a circular normal distribution," *Biometrika*, **39** (1952), 137–143.

[40] DANIELS, H. E., "A distribution-free test for regression parameters," *Annals of Mathematical Statistics*, **25** (1954), 499–513.

[41] DARLING, D. A., "The Kolmogorov-Smirnov, Cramér-von Mises Tests," *Annals of Mathematical Statistics*, **28** (1957), 823–838.

[42] DARLING, D. A., "On a class of problems related to the random division of an interval," *Annals of Mathematical Statistics*, **24** (1953), 239–253.

[43] DAS, S. C., "The numerical evaluation of a class of integrals. II," *Proceedings of the Cambridge Philosophical Society*, **52** (1956), 442–448.

[44] DAVID, F. N., *Tables of the Correlation Coefficient*, Cambridge, England: The University Press, 1938.

[45] DAVID, F. N., "A note on Wilcoxon's and allied tests," *Biometrika*, **43** (1956), 485–488.

[46] DAVID, H. A., "Upper 5 and 1% points of the maximum F-ratio," *Biometrika*, **39** (1952), 422–424.

[47] DAVID, H. A., H. O. HARTLEY, and E. S. PEARSON, "The distribution of the ratio, in a single normal sample, of range to standard deviation," *Biometrika*, **41** (1954), 482–493.

[48] DAVIES, O. L., *The Design and Analysis of Industrial Experiments*, London: Oliver and Boyd, 1954.

[49] DE CICCA, H., *The Reliability of Weapon Systems Estimated from Component Test Data Alone*, Technical Note No. 1, Reliability Branch-ORDSW-DR, December 1959.

[50] DEMPSTER, A. P., "Generalized D_n^+ statistics," *Annals of Mathematical Statistics*, **30** (1959), 593–597.

[51] DiDONATO, A. R., and M. P. JARNIGAN, *Integration of the General Bivariate Gaussian Distribution Over an Offset Ellipse*, Report No. 1710, U. S. Naval Weapons Laboratory, Dahlgren, Virginia, 1960.

[52] DIXON, W. J., "Power functions of the sign test and power efficiency for normal alternatives," *Annals of Mathematical Statistics*, **24** (1953), 467–473.

[53] DIXON, W. J., "Simplified estimation from censored normal samples," *Annals of Mathematical Statistics*, **31** (1960), 385–391.

[54] DIXON, W. J., "Power under normality of several nonparametric tests," *Annals of Mathematical Statistics*, **25** (1954), 610–614.

[55] DIXON, W. J., and F. J. MASSEY, JR., *Introduction to Statistical Analysis*, Second Edition, New York: McGraw-Hill Book Co., Inc., 1957.

[56] DUNCAN, D. B., "Multiple range and multiple F tests," *Biometrics*, **11** (1955), 1–42.

[57] DUNNETT, C. W., "A multiple comparison procedure for comparing several treatments with a control," *Journal of the American Statistical Association*, **50** (1955), 1096–1121.

[58] DUNNETT, C. W., and M. SOBEL, "Approximations to the probability integral and certain percentage points of a multivariate analogue of Student's t-distribution," *Biometrika*, **42** (1955), 258–260.

[59] DUNNETT, C. W., and M. SOBEL, "A bivariate generalization of Student's t-distribution, with tables for certain special cases," *Biometrika*, **41** (1954), 153–169.

[60] DWASS, M., "The distribution of a generalized D_n^+ statistic," *Annals of Mathematical Statistics*, **30** (1959), 1024–1028.

[61] EDGINGTON, E. S., "Probability table for number of runs of signs of first differences in ordered series," *Journal of the American Statistical Association*, **56** (1961), 156–159.

[62] EISENHART, C., M. W. HASTAY, and W. A. WALLIS, *Selected Techniques of Statistical Analysis*, New York: McGraw-Hill Book Company, Inc., 1947.

[63] FEDERIGHI, E. T., "Extended tables of the percentage points of Student's *t*-distribution," *Journal of the American Statistical Association*, **54** (1959), 683–688.

[64] FINNEY, D. J., "The Fisher-Yates test of significance in 2×2 contingency tables," *Biometrika*, **35** (1948), 145–156. These tables are reproduced in *Biometrika Tables for Statisticians*, Vol. 1, by Hartley and Pearson, Cambridge University Press, 1954, 188–193.

[65] FISHER, R. A., and E. A. CORNISH, "The percentile points of distributions having known cumulants," *Technometrics*, **2** (1960), 209–225.

[66] FIX, E., "Tables of noncentral χ^2," *University of California Publications in Statistics*, Vol. 1, No. 2 (1949), 15–19.

[67] FIX, E., and J. L. HODGES, JR., "Significance probabilities of the Wilcoxon test," *Annals of Mathematical Statistics*, **26** (1955), 301–312.

[68] FIX, E., J. L. HODGES, JR., and E. L. LEHMANN, "The restricted chi-square test," *Probability and Statistics: The Harald Cramér Volume* (Edited by Ulf Grenander), Stockholm: Almquist and Wiksell; New York: John Wiley and Sons, Inc., 1959, 92–107.

[69] FOSTER, F. G., "Upper percentage points of the generalized beta distribution. II," *Biometrika*, **44** (1957), 441–453.

[70] FOSTER, F. G., "Upper percentage points of the generalized beta distribution. III," *Biometrika*, **45** (1958), 492–503.

[71] FOSTER, F. G., and D. H. REES, "Upper percentage points of the generalized beta distribution. I," *Biometrika*, **44** (1957), 237–247.

[72] FOX, M., "Charts of the power of the F-test," *Annals of Mathematical Statistics*, **27** (1956), 484–497.

[73] FRIEDMAN, M., "The use of ranks to avoid the assumption of normality in the analysis of variance," *Journal of the American Statistical Association*, **32** (1937), 675–701.

[74] GILBERT, E. J., "The matching problem," *Psychometrika*, **21** (1956), 253–266.

[75] GOOD, I. J., "The serial test for sampling numbers and other tests for randomness," *Proceedings of the Cambridge Philosophical Society*, **49** (1953), 276–284.

[76] GRAD, A., and H. SOLOMON, "Distribution of quadratic forms and some applications," *Annals of Mathematical Statistics*, **26** (1955), 464–477.

[77] GRAYBILL, F. A., and R. D. MORRISON, "Sample size for a specified width confidence interval on the variance of a normal distribution," *Biometrics*, **16** (1960), 636–641.

[78] GREENWOOD, J. A., and M. M. SANDOMIRE, "Sample size required for estimating the standard deviation as a percent of its true value," *Journal of the American Statistical Association*, **45** (1950), 257–260.

[79] GRUBBS, F. E., "On designing single sampling inspection plans," *Annals of Mathematical Statistics*, **20** (1949), 242–256.

[80] GRUBBS, F. E., and C. L. WEAVER, "The best unbiased estimate of population standard deviation based on group ranges," *Journal of the American Statistical Association*, **42** (1947), 224–241.

[81] GURLAND, J., "Distribution of definite and of indefinite quadratic forms," *Annals of Mathematical Statistics*, **26** (1955), 122–127.

[82] GUMBEL, E. J., *Statistics of Extremes*, New York: Columbia University Press, 1958.

[83] HAIGHT, F. A., "Index to the distributions of mathematical statistics," *Journal of Research of the National Bureau of Standards*, **65B** (1961), 23–60.

[84] HAIGHT, F. A., and M. A. BREUER, "The Borel-Tanner distribution," *Biometrika*, **47** (1960), 143–150.

[85] HALD, A., *Statistical Tables and Formulas*, New York: John Wiley and Sons, Inc., 1952.

[86] HARRIS, M., D. G. HORVITZ, and A. M. MOOD, "On the determination of sample sizes in designing experiments," *Journal of the American Statistical Association*, **43** (1948), 391–402.

[87] HART, B. I., "Tabulation of the probabilities for the' ratio of the mean square successive difference to the variance," *Annals of Mathematical Statistics*, **13** (1942), 207–214.

[88] HART, B. I., "Significance levels for the ratio of the mean square successive difference to the variance," *Annals of Mathematical Statistics*, **13** (1942), 445–447.

[89] HARTER, H. L., *Expected Values of Normal Order Statistics*, Technical Report 60–292, Aeronautical Research Laboratories, Wright-Patterson Air Force Base, June 1960.

[90] HARTER, H. L., "Circular error probabilities," *Journal of the American Statistical Association*, **55** (1960), 723–731.

[91] HARTER, H. L., "Tables of range and studentized range," *Annals of Mathematical Statistics*, **31** (1960), 1122–1147.

[92] HARTER, H. L., D. S. CLEMM, and E. H. GUTHRIE, *The Probability Integrals of the Range and of the Studentized Range*, Vols. I and II, Wright Air Development Center Technical Report 58–484, 1959.

[93] HARTLEY, H. O., and E. S. PEARSON, "Table of the probability integral of the *t*-distribution," *Biometrika*, **37** (1950), 168–172.

[94] Harvard University Computation Laboratory, *Tables of the Cumulative Binomial Probability Distribution*, Cambridge, Massachusetts: Harvard University Press, 1955.

[95] HECK, D. L., "Charts of some upper percentage points of the distribution of the largest characteristic root," *Annals of Mathematical Statistics*, **31** (1960), 625–642.

[96] HILL, B. M., "A relationship between Hodges' bivariate sign test and a non-parametric test of Daniels," *Annals of Mathematical Statistics*, **31** (1960), 1190–1192.

[97] HODGES, J. L., JR., "A bivariate sign test," *Annals of Mathematical Statistics*, **26** (1955), 523–527.

[98] JACKSON, J. E., and E. L. Ross, "Extended tables for use with the "*G*" test for means," *Journal of the American Statistical Association*, **50** (1955), 416–433 and 1332.

[99] JOHNSON, N. L., "On an extension of the connexion between Poisson and chi-square distributions," *Biometrika*, **46** (1959), 352–363.

[100] JOHNSON, N. L., "An approximation to the multinomial distribution: some properties and applications," *Biometrika*, **47** (1960), 93–102.

[101] JOHNSON, N. L., and B. L. WELCH, "Applications of the non-central *t*-distribution," *Biometrika*, **31** (1940), 362–389.

[102] JOHNSON, N. L., and D. H. YOUNG, "Some applications of two approximations to the multinomial distribution," *Biometrika*, **47** (1960), 463–469.

[103] KAC, M., J. KIEFER, and J. WOLFOWITZ, "On tests of normality and other tests of goodness of fit based on distance methods," *Annals of Mathematical Statistics*, **26** (1955), 189–211.

[104] KENDALL, M. G., *The Advanced Theory of Statistics*, Vol. I, London: Charles Griffin and Company, Ltd., 1948.

[105] KENDALL, M. G., *The Advanced Theory of Statistics*, Vol. II, London: Charles Griffin and Company, Ltd., 1948.

[106] KENDALL, M. G., *Rank Correlation Methods*, London: Charles Griffin and Company, Ltd., Second Edition, 1955.

[107] KIEFER, J., "*K*-sample analogues of the Kolmogorov-Smirnov and Cramér-von Mises tests," *Annals of Mathematical Statistics*, **30** (1959), 420–447.

[108] KITAGAWA, T., *Tables of Poisson Distribution*, Tokyo: Baifukan, 1952.

[109] KLOTZ, J., "Null distribution of the Hodges bivariate sign test," *Annals of Mathematical Statistics*, **30** (1959), 1029–1033.

[110] KOZELKA, R. M., "Approximate upper percentage points for extreme values in multinomial sampling," *Annals of Mathematical Statistics*, **27** (1956), 507–512.

[111] KRUSKAL, W. H., "Some remarks on wild observations," *Technometrics*, **2** (1960), 1–3.

[112] KRUSKAL, W. H., "Historical notes on the Wilcoxon unpaired two-sample test," *Journal of the American Statistical Association*, **52** (1957), 356–360.

[113] KRUSKAL, W. H., and W. A. WALLIS, "Use of ranks in one-criterion variance analysis," *Journal of the American Statistical Association*, **47** (1952), 583–621, and **48** (1953), 907–911.

[114] LATSCHA, R., "Tests of significance in a 2×2 contingency table: Extension of Finney's tables," *Biometrika*, **40** (1953), 74–86.

[115] LAUBSCHER, N. F., "Normalizing the noncentral *t* and *F* distributions," *Annals of Mathematical Statistics*, **31** (1960), 1105–1112.

[116] LAUBSCHER, N. F., "On stabilizing the binomial and negative binomial variances," *Journal of the American Statistical Association*, **56** (1961), 143–150.

[117] LEONE, F. C., G. E. HAYNAM, J. T. CHU, and C. W. TOPP, *Percentiles of the Binomial Distribution*, AFOSR Report No. TN-60-620, Cleveland 6, Ohio: Case Institute of Technology, Statistical Laboratory, June 1960.

[118] LEVENE, H., and J. WOLFOWITZ, "The covariance matrix of runs up and down," *Annals of Mathematical Statistics*, **15** (1944), 58–69.

[119] LEWIS, T., "99.9 and 0.1% points of the χ^2 distribution," *Biometrika*, **40** (1953), 421–426.

[120] LIEBERMAN, G. J., and D. B. OWEN, *Tables of the Hypergeometric Probability Distribution*, Stanford, California: Stanford University Press, 1961.

[121] LINDLEY, D. V., D. A. EAST, and P. A. HAMILTON, "Tables for making inferences about the variance of a normal distribution," *Biometrika*, **47** (1960), 433–437.

[122] LIPOW, M., *Measurement of Over-All Reliability Utilizing Results of Independent Subsystem Tests*, Report No. GM-TR-0165-00506, Los Angeles 45, California: Space Technology Laboratories, Inc., P. O. Box 95001, October 1958.

[123] LIPOW, M., and J. RILEY, *Tables of Upper Confidence Limits on Failure Probability of 1, 2, and 3 Component Serial Systems*, Report No. TR-59-0000-00756, Los Angeles 45, California: Space Technology Laboratories, P. O. Box 95001, July 1959.

[124] LORD, E., "The use of range in place of standard deviation in the t-test," *Biometrika*, **34** (1947), 41–67.

[125] LORD, E., "Power of the modified t-test (u-test) based on range," *Biometrika*, **37** (1950), 64–77.

[126] LOWE, J. R., "A table of the integral of the bivariate normal distribution over an offset circle," *Journal of the Royal Statistical Society*, **22** (1960), Series B, 177–187.

[127] MADANSKY, A. *Approximate Confidence Limits for the Reliability of Series and Parallel Systems*, Report No. RM-2552, Santa Monica, California: The RAND Corporation, April 1960.

[128] MAINLAND, D., "Statistical methods in medical research," *Canadian Journal of Research*, **26** (1948), Section E, 1–166.

[129] MAINLAND, D., L. HERRERA, and M. I. SUTCLIFFE, *Tables for Use with Binomial Samples*, New York 16, New York: Department of Medical Statistics, New York University College of Medicine, 1956.

[130] MAINLAND, D., and I. M. MURRAY, "Tables for use in fourfold contingency tests," *Science*, **116** (1952), 591–594.

[131] MANN, H. B., and D. R. WHITNEY, "On a test of whether one of two random variables is stochastically larger than the other," *Annals of Mathematical Statistics*, **18** (1947), 50–60.

[132] MARCUM, J. I., *Table of Q Functions*, Report No. RM-339, Santa Monica, California: The RAND Corporation, January 1, 1950.

[133] MARSAGLIA, G., *Tables of the Distribution of Quadratic Forms of Ranks Two and Three*, Report No. DI-82-0015-1, Math. Note No. 213, Seattle, Washington: Boeing Scientific Research Laboratories, August 1960.

[134] MASSEY, F. J., JR., "A note on the power of a nonparametric test," *Annals of Mathematical Statistics*, **21** (1950), 440–443, and **23** (1952), 637–638.

[135] MASSEY, F. J., JR., "The distribution of the maximum deviation between two sample cumulative step functions," *Annals of Mathematical Statistics*, **22** (1951), 125–128.

[136] McFADDEN, J. A., "Two expansions for the quadrivariate normal integral," *Biometrika*, **47** (1960), 325–333.

[137] McKay, A. T., and E. S. Pearson, "A note on the distribution of range in samples of n," *Biometrika*, **25** (1933), 415–420.

[138] Merrington, M., and E. S. Pearson, "An approximation to the distribution of non-central t," *Biometrika*, **45** (1958), 484–491.

[139] Merrington, M., and C. M. Thompson, "Tables of percentage points of the inverted beta (F) distribution," *Biometrika*, **33** (1943), 73–88.

[140] Miller, L. H., "Table of percentage points of Kolmogorov statistics," *Journal of the American Statistical Association*, **51** (1956), 111–121.

[141] Molina, E. C., *Poisson's Exponential Binomial Limit*, New York: D. Van Nostrand Company, Inc., 1942.

[142] Mood, A. M., "Erratum: On the determination of sample sizes in designing experiments," *Journal of the American Statistical Association*, **46** (1951), 515.

[143] Moore, G. H., and W. A. Wallis, "Time series significance tests based on signs of differences," *Journal of the American Statistical Association*, **38** (1943), 153–164.

[144] Moran, P. A. P., "The random division of an interval," *Supplement to the Journal of the Royal Statistical Society*, **9** (1947), 92–98.

[145] Moran, P. A. P., "The random division of an interval. III," *Journal of the Royal Statistical Society*, Series B, **15** (1953), 77–80.

[146] Moranda, P. B., "Comparison of estimates of circular probable error," *Journal of the American Statistical Association*, **54** (1959), 794–800.

[147] Morrison, D. R., "Geometric progressions modulo n as random number generators," Sandia Corporation Reprint SCR-22, June 1958. (Available from the Office of Technical Services, Department of Commerce, Washington 25, D. C.) Paper presented at the Organizational Meeting of the Southwestern Section, Association for Computing Machinery, October 1957.

[148] National Bureau of Standards, *Tables of the Binomial Probability Distribution*, Applied Mathematics, Series 6, Washington 25, D. C.: U. S. Government Printing Office, Superintendent of Documents, 1950.

[149] National Bureau of Standards, *Probability Tables for the Analysis of Extreme-Value Data*, Applied Mathematics Series 22, Washington 25, D. C.: U. S. Government Printing Office, Superintendent of Documents, 1953.

[150] National Bureau of Standards, *Tables of the Bivariate Normal Distribution Function and Related Functions*, Applied Mathematics, Series 50, Washington 25, D. C.: U. S. Government Printing Office, Superintendent of Documents, 1959.

[151] Neyman, J., and B. Tokarska, "Errors of the second kind in testing 'Student's' hypothesis," *Journal of the American Statistical Association*, **31** (1936), 318–326.

[152] Nicholson, W. L., "Occupancy probability distribution critical points," *Biometrika*, **48** (1961), 175–180.

[153] Norton, H. W., *Mathematical Tables and Other Aids to Computation*, Review No. 199, **6** (1952), 35–38.

[154] Oberg, E. N., "Approximate formulas for the radii of circles which include a specified fraction of a normal bivariate distribution," *Annals of Mathematical Statistics*, **18** (1947), 442–447.

[155] OKAMOTO, M., "Some inequalities relating to the partial sum of binomial probabilities," *Annals of the Institute of Statistical Mathematics*, **10** (1958), 29–35.

[156] OLDS, E. G., "Distributions of sums of squares of rank differences for small numbers of individuals," *Annals of Mathematical Statistics*, **9** (1938), 133–148.

[157] OLMSTEAD, P. S., "Distribution of sample arrangements for runs up and down," *Annals of Mathematical Statistics*, **17** (1946), 24–33.

[158] OLMSTEAD, P. S., "Runs determined in a sample by an arbitrary cut," *Bell System Technical Journal*, **37** (1958), 55–82.

[159] OLMSTEAD, P. S., and J. W. TUKEY, "A corner test for association," *Annals of Mathematical Statistics*, **18** (1947), 495–513.

[160] OSTLE, B., *Statistics in Research*, Ames, Iowa: Iowa State College Press, 1954.

[161] OWEN, D. B., *Table of Factors for One-Sided Tolerance Limits for a Normal Distribution*, Sandia Corporation Monograph SCR-13, April 1958. (Available from the Office of Technical Services, Department of Commerce, Washington, D. C.)

[162] OWEN, D. B., "Tables for computing bivariate normal probabilities," *Annals of Mathematical Statistics*, **27** (1956), 1075–1090.

[163] OWEN, D. B., "Distribution free tolerance limits for an additional finite sample as obtained from the hypergeometric distribution," *Proceedings of the Western Region ASQC Conference*, Milwaukee: American Society for Quality Control, 1961, pp. S-1–S-12.

[164] OWEN, D. B., E. J. GILBERT, G. P. STECK, and D. A. YOUNG, *A Formula for Determining Sample Size in Hypergeometric Sampling When Zero Defectives are Observed in the Sample*, Sandia Corporation Technical Memorandum SCTM-178-59(51), June 1959. (Available from the Office of Technical Services, Department of Commerce, Washington, D. C.)

[165] PACHARES, J., "Tables for unbiased tests on the variance of a normal population, "*Annals of Mathematical Statistics*, **32** (1961), 84–87.

[166] PACHARES, J., "Tables of confidence limits for the binomial distribution," *Journal of the American Statistical Association*, **55** (1960), 521–533.

[167] PATIL, G. P., "On the evaluation of the negative binomial distribution with examples," *Technometrics*, **2** (1960), 501–505.

[168] PATNAIK, P. B., "The non-central chi-square and *F*-distributions and their applications," *Biometrika*, **36** (1949), 202–232.

[169] PAULSON, E., "On the comparison of several experimental categories with a control," *Annals of Mathematical Statistics*, **23** (1952), 239–246.

[170] PEARSON, E. S., "Note on an approximation to the distribution of non-central chi-square," *Biometrika*, **46** (1959), 364.

[171] PEARSON, E. S., Editor, "The normal probability function: Tables of certain area-ordinate ratios and of their reciprocals," *Biometrika*, **42** (1955), 217–222.

[172] PEARSON, E. S., and H. O. HARTLEY, *Biometrika Tables for Statisticians*, Vol. I, Cambridge, England: The University Press, 1954.

[173] PEARSON, E. S., and M. MERRINGTON, "2 × 2 tables; the power function of the test on a randomized experiment," *Biometrika*, **35** (1948), 331–345.

[174] PEARSON, K., *Tables of the Incomplete Beta-Function*, Cambridge, England: The University Press, 1934.

[175] PILLAI, K. C. S., *Concise Tables for Statisticians*, Manila: The Statistical Center, University of the Philippines, 1957.

[176] PUTTER, J., "The treatment of ties in some nonparametric tests," *Annals of Mathematical Statistics*, **26** (1955), 368–386.

[177] RAFF, M. S., "On approximating the point binomial," *Journal of the American Statistical Association*, **51** (1956), 293–303.

[178] RAND Report, R-234, *Offset Circle Probabilities*, Santa Monica, California: The RAND Corporation, March 14, 1952.

[179] RAND Corp., *A Million Random Digits with* 100,000 *Normal Deviates*, Glencoe, Illinois: Free Press, 1955.

[180] RESNIKOFF, G. J., and G. J. LIEBERMAN, *Tables of the Non-Central t-Distribution*, Stanford, California: Stanford University Press, 1957.

[181] ROBERTSON, W. H., *Tables of the Binomial Distribution Function for Small Values of p*, Sandia Corporation Monograph SCR-143, January 1960. (Available from the Office of Technical Services, Department of Commerce, Washington, D. C.)

[182] ROMIG, H. G., *50–100 Binomial Tables*, New York: John Wiley and Sons, Inc., 1953.

[183] ROSENBAUM, S., "Tables for a nonparametric test of dispersion," *Annals of Mathematical Statistics*, **24** (1953), 663–668.

[184] ROSENBAUM, S., "Tables for a nonparametric test of location," *Annals of Mathematical Statistics*, **25** (1954), 146–150.

[185] ROSENBLATT, J. I., "Some modified Kolmogorov-Smirnov tests of approximate hypotheses and their properties," *Annals of Mathematical Statistics*, June 1962. See also "Tests and Confidence Intervals Based on the Metric $d_2 = D^+ + D^-$," submitted to *Annals of Mathematical Statistics*, February 1962.

[186] RUBEN, H., "On the moments of order statistics in samples from normal populations," *Biometrika*, **41** (1954), 200–227.

[187] RUBEN, H., "Probability content of regions under spherical normal distributions, I," *Annals of Mathematical Statistics*, **31** (1960), 598–618.

[188] RUBEN, H., "On the sum of squares of normal scores," *Biometrika*, **43** (1956), 456–458.

[189] SANKARAN, M., "On the non-central chi-square distribution," *Biometrika*, **46** (1959), 235–237.

[190] SARHAN, A. E., "Estimation of the mean and standard deviation by order statistics," *Annals of Mathematical Statistics*, **25** (1954), 317–328, and **26** (1955), 505–511 and 576–592.

[191] SARHAN, A. E., and B. G. GREENBERG, "Estimation of location and scale parameters by order statistics from singly and doubly censored samples," *Annals of Mathematical Statistics*, **27** (1956), 427–451.

[192] SATTERTHWAITE, F. E., "Binomial and Poisson confidence limits," *Industrial Quality Control*, Vol. 13, No. 11 (May 1957), 56–59.

[193] SAVAGE, I. R., "Contributions to the theory of rank order statistics— the one-sample case," *Annals of Mathematical Statistics*, **30** (1959), 1018–1023.

[194] SAVAGE, I. R., "Bibliography of nonparametric statistics and related topics," *Journal of the American Statistical Association*, **48** (1953), 844–906.

[195] Scheffé, H., "A method for judging all contrasts in the analysis of variance," *Biometrika*, **40** (1953), 87–104.

[196] Severo, N. C., and M. Zelen, "Normal approximation to the chi-square and noncentral F probability functions," *Biometrika*, **47** (1960), 411–416.

[197] Severo, N. C., and M. Zelen, "Graphs for bivariate normal probabilities," *Annals of Mathematical Statistics*, **31** (1960), 619–624.

[198] Sexton, C. R., C. A. Sexton, and J. A. Sexton, "Table errata No. 270 (on reference [108] above)," *Mathematical Tables and Other Aids to Computation*, **13** (1959), 141–142.

[199] Sherman, B., "Percentiles of the ω_n statistic," *Annals of Mathematical Statistics*, **28** (1957), 259–261.

[200] Siegel, S., and J. W. Tukey, "A nonparametric sum of ranks procedure for relative spread in unpaired samples," *Journal of the American Statistical Association*, **55** (1960), 429–445.

[201] Sillitto, G. P., "The distribution of Kendall's τ coefficient of rank correlation in rankings containing ties," *Biometrika*, **34** (1947), 36–40.

[202] Smirnov, N., "Table for estimating the goodness of fit of empirical distributions," *Annals of Mathematical Statistics*, **19** (1948), 279–281.

[203] Smith, E. S., *Binomial, Normal and Poisson Probabilities*, Box 224C, RD 2, Bel Air, Maryland: 1953 and 1954. See review in *Journal of the American Statistical Association*, **52** (1957), 106–107.

[204] Snedecor, G. W., *Statistical Methods*, Ames, Iowa: Iowa State College Press, 1956, 212–215.

[205] Solomon, H., *Distribution of Quadratic Forms—Tables and Applications*, Technical Report No. 45, Applied Mathematics and Statistics Laboratories, Stanford University, 1960.

[206] Steck, G. P., *Uses of the Table of the Circular Coverage Function*, Sandia Corporation Technical Memorandum SCTM-214-58(51), July 22, 1958. (Available from the Office of Technical Services, Department of Commerce, Washington, D. C.)

[207] Steck, G. P., "A table for computing trivariate normal probabilities," *Annals of Mathematical Statistics*, **29** (1958), 780–800.

[208] Steck, G. P., *Upper Confidence Limits for the Failure Probability of Complex Networks*, Sandia Corporation Research Report No. SC-4133(TR), December 1957. (Available from the Office of Technical Services, Department of Commerce, Washington, D. C.)

[209] Steck, G. P., D. B. Owen, and J. M. Wiesen, *Confidence Intervals for the Standard Deviation of a Normal Population*, Sandia Corporation Technical Memorandum SCTM-241-56(51), January 15, 1957. (Available from the Office of Technical Services, Department of Commerce, Washington, D. C.)

[210] Stewart, W. M., "A note on the power of the sign test," *Annals of Mathematical Statistics*, **12** (1941), 236–239.

[211] Stuart, A., "Equally correlated variates and the multinormal integral," *Journal of the Royal Statistical Society*, Series B, **20** (1958), 373–378.

[212] Stuart, A., "The power of two difference-sign tests," *Journal of the American Statistical Association*, **47** (1952), 416–424.

[213] Sukhatme, B. V., "Testing the hypothesis that two populations differ only in location," *Annals of Mathematical Statistics*, **29** (1958), 60–78.

[214] Sukhatme, B. V., "Power of some two-sample non-parametric tests," *Biometrika*, **47** (1960), 355–362.

[215] Sundrum, R. M., "The power of Wilcoxon's 2-sample test," *Journal of the Royal Statistical Society*, Series B, **15** (1953), 246–252.

[216] Swed, F. S., and C. Eisenhart, "Tables for testing the randomness of grouping in a sequence of alternatives," *Annals of Mathematical Statistics*, **14** (1943), 66–87.

[217] Tang, P. C., "The power function of the analysis of variance tests with tables and illustrations of their use," *Statistical Research Memoirs*, **2** (1938), 126–149.

[218] Tate, R. F., "The theory of correlation between two continuous variables when one is dichotomized," *Biometrika*, **42** (1955), 205–216.

[219] Teichroew, D., "Empirical power functions for nonparametric two-sample tests for small samples," *Annals of Mathematical Statistics*, **26** (1955), 340–344.

[220] Teichroew, D., "Tables of expected values of order statistics and products of order statistics for samples of size twenty and less from the normal distribution," *Annals of Mathematical Statistics*, **27** (1956), 410–426.

[221] Teichroew, D., *Probabilities Associated with Order Statistics in Samples from Two Normal Populations with Equal Variance*, Maryland: Chemical Corps Engineering Agency, Army Chemical Center, ENASR No. ES-3, December 7, 1955.

[222] Thompson, C. M., "Tables of percentage points of the incomplete beta-function," *Biometrika*, **32** (1941), 151–181.

[223] Thomson, G. W., "Bounds for the ratio of range to standard deviation," *Biometrika*, **42** (1955), 268–269.

[224] Tsao, C. K., "Approximations to the power of rank tests," *Annals of Mathematical Statistics*, **28** (1957), 159–172.

[225] Tukey, J. W., "The problem of multiple comparisons," unpublished notes in private circulation, Princeton University, 1953, 396 pages.

[226] Tukey, J. W., "Comparing individual means in the analysis of variance," *Biometrics*, **5** (1949), 99–114.

[227] Tukey, J. W., "Quick and dirty methods in statistics, Part II, Simple analyses for standard designs," *Proceedings Fifth Annual Convention, American Society for Quality Control*, 1951, 189–197.

[228] U. S. Army, Ordnance Corps, *Tables of Cumulative Binomial Probabilities*, Ordnance Corps Pamphlet ORDP20-1, Washington, D. C., September 1952.

[229] Van Brocklin, G. R., Jr., and P. G. Murray, "A polar-planimeter method for determining the probability of hitting a target," *Operations Research*, **4** (1956), 87–91.

[230] Van Eeden, C., *Some Approximations to the Percentage Points of the Noncentral t-Distribution*, Mathematisch Centrum Report No. S242, Amsterdam, 1959.

[231] Van Elteren, Ph., and G. E. Noether, "The asymptotic efficiency of the χ_r^2-test for a balanced incomplete block design," *Biometrika*, **46** (1959), 475–477.

[232] von Neumann, J., "Distribution of the ratio of the mean square successive difference to the variance," *Annals of Mathematical Statistics*, **12** (1941), 367–395.

[233] Wald, A., and J. Wolfowitz, "Tolerance limits for a normal distribution," *Annals of Mathematical Statistics*, **17** (1946), 208–215.

[234] Wallace, D. L., "Simplified beta-approximations to the Kruskal-Wallis *H* test," *Journal of the American Statistical Association*, **54** (1959), 225–230.

[235] Wallace, D. L., "Bounds on normal approximations to Student's and the chi-square distributions," *Annals of Mathematical Statistics*, **30** (1959), 1121–1130.

[236] Wallis, W. A., "Tolerance intervals for linear regressions," *Second Berkeley Symposium on Mathematical Statistics and Probability*, edited by J. Neyman, Berkeley: University of California Press, 1951, 43–51.

[237] Walsh, J. E., "Some bounded significance level properties of the equal-tail sign test," *Annals of Mathematical Statistics*, **22** (1951), 408–417.

[238] Walsh, J. E., "Comments on 'the simplest signed-rank tests,'" *Journal of the American Statistical Association*, **54** (1959), 213–224.

[239] Walsh, J. E., "Some nonparametric tests of whether the largest observations of a set are too large or too small," *Annals of Mathematical Statistics*, **21** (1950), 583–592, and **24** (1953), 134–135.

[240] Weiler, H., "Means and standard deviations of a truncated normal bivariate distribution," *Australian Journal of Statistics*, **1** (1959), 73–81.

[241] Weingarten, H., and A. R. DiDonato, "A table of generalized circular error," *Mathematics of Computation*, **15** (1961), 169–173.

[242] Weiss, L., "The limiting joint distribution of the largest and smallest sample spacings," *Annals of Mathematical Statistics*, **30** (1959), 590–593.

[243] Weissberg, A., and G. H. Beatty, *Tables of Tolerance-Limit Factors for Normal Distributions*, Columbus, Ohio: Battelle Memorial Institute, December 1959.

[244] Whitney, D. R., "A bivariate extension of the *U* statistic," *Annals of Mathematical Statistics*, **22** (1951), 274–282.

[245] Wilcoxon, F., "Individual comparisons by ranking methods," *Biometrics Bulletin*, **1** (1945), 80–83.

[246] Wilks, S. S., "Determination of sample sizes for setting tolerance limits," *Annals of Mathematical Statistics*, **12** (1941), 91–96.

[247] Wilks, S. S., "Statistical prediction with special reference to the problem of tolerance limits," *Annals of Mathematical Statistics*, **13** (1942), 400–409.

[248] Wilks, S. S., "Nonparametric statistical inference," *Probability and Statistics: The Harald Cramér Volume* (Edited by Ulf Grenander), Stockholm: Almquist and Wiksell; New York: John Wiley and Sons, Inc., 1959, 331–354.

[249] Wise, M. E., "The incomplete beta function as a contour integral and a quickly converging series for its inverse," *Biometrika*, **37** (1950), 208–218.

[250] Wolfowitz, J., "Asymptotic distribution of runs up and down," *Annals of Mathematical Statistics*, **15** (1944), 163–172.

[251] Žaludová, A. H., "The non-central *t*-test (*q*-test) based on range in place of standard deviation," *Acta Technica* (1960), 143–185.

INDEX

Note: Numbers within parentheses refer to tables.

ABCDE698765432